THE
CHALLENGE
OF
DEMOCRACY

Kenneth Janda
Northwestern University

Jeffrey M. Berry
Tufts University

Jerry Goldman
Northwestern University

THE CHALLENGE OF DEMOCRACY

Government in America

Second Edition

Houghton Mifflin Company   Boston   Dallas   Geneva, Illinois   Palo Alto   Princeton, New Jersey

Printed in the U.S.A.

Library of Congress Catalog Card Number: 88-81336

ISBN: 0-395-43292-8

ABCDEFGHIJ-VH-943210-898

Illustration Credits

Illustrations by Boston Graphics, Inc.
Cover photo: Ralph Mercer Photography
Frontispiece: Robert Llewellyn
Preface photo: Paul Conklin

Chapter 1: **Page 2 (Opener):** Robert Llewellyn; **5:** By
permission of the Houghton Library, Harvard University;
6: Sygma; **8:** © George Gerster/Photo Researchers, Inc.; **9:**
Wide World Photos; **12–13:** National Archives; **15:** J. P.
Laffont/Sygma; **16:** © Daemmrich/Uniphoto; **18**(left):
Claus Meyer/Black Star; **18**(right): Ferdinando Scianna/
Magnum; **19:** Andrew Popper/The Picture Group; **29:**
Copyright, 1987, G. B. Trudeau. Reprinted with permis-
sion of Universal Press Syndicate. All rights reserved.
    Chapter 2: **Page 32 (Opener):** Bob Daemmrich/The Im-
age Works; **34:** Wide World Photos; **39:** Jim Wilson/*The
Boston Globe*; **41:** Bruce Flynn/Stock, Boston; **42:** Michael
Coers. Copyright © 1975 *The Louisville Times*. Reprinted
with permission. **45:** Kenneth Martin; **48:** Terry Ashe/
Time Magazine; **50:** Paul Conklin; **51**(left): © Ken Gallard/
Uniphoto; **51**(right): © Jon Zolner/Uniphoto.
    Essay A: **Page 59**(top): Reprinted with permission of
Ford Motor Company; **59**(bottom left): State Historical Society of Wisconsin; **59**(bottom right): Library of Congress;
61(top): Alan Mercer/Stock, Boston; **61**(middle): Courtesy
of International Business Machines Corporation;
61(bottom): Pamela Price/The Picture Group.
    Chapter 3: **Page 64 (Opener):** Paul Conklin/Uniphoto;
66: UPI/Bettman Newsphotos; **67:** J. P. Laffont/Sygma; **68:**
National Archives; **72:** Courtesy of the John Carter Brown
Library at Brown University; **75:** John Trumbull, *The Declaration of Independence.* Copyright Yale University Art
Gallery; **78:** The Granger Collection; **81:** The Thomas Gil-
crease Institute of American History and Art, Tulsa, Oklahoma; **83:** *Doonesbury* © 1987 G. B. Trudeau. Reprinted
with permission of Universal Press Syndicate. All rights
reserved; **90–91:** Paul Hosefros/*The New York Times*; **97:**
Courtesy of the New York Historical Society, New York
City; **99:** National Archives.

Copyright page continues on page A-84.

For our children
Susan and Katy
Rachel and Jessica
John, Matt, and Josh

Brief Contents

Essays and Selected Features

ESSAYS

COMPARED WITH WHAT?

POLITICS IN THE INFORMATION AGE

Contents

Contents

Preface

We wanted to write an American government textbook that students would like and would credit for shaping their thinking about politics. The response to the first edition of *The Challenge of Democracy* was gratifying. Now, with the second edition, we believe more than ever that students will like *The Challenge of Democracy* and that they will use its framework to analyze politics long after their studies end.

We have tried to discuss a complex subject, politics, in a captivating and understandable way. American politics isn't dull, and its textbooks needn't be either. Although working on this revision was more work than any of us originally imagined, we also have had more fun along the way than we ever thought possible.

We think that an introductory American government text can go beyond simply offering students basic information about the political process. A text can also teach students how political scientists think about politics. In our profession, we try to organize, analyze, and interpret political events, trends, and problems. We want to encourage students to organize, analyze, and interpret American politics and government, too.

THEMATIC FRAMEWORK

It is easy for students to become frustrated with the sheer amount of information assigned each week in an introductory American government course. Our framework provides a way for them to put this information into a broader perspective. Most important, our framework enables students to recognize and think critically about the difficult choices we face as citizens and voters.

Two themes run through our book. In Chapter 1, we suggest that American politics often reflects conflicts between the values of *freedom* and *order* and between the values of *freedom* and *equality*. These value conflicts are prominent in contemporary American society, and they help to explain political controversy and consensus in earlier eras.

In Chapter 3, for example, we argue that the Constitution was designed to promote order and virtually ignored issues of political and social equality. However, equality was later served by several amendments to the Constitution. In Chapter 17, "Order and Civil Liberties," and in Chapter 18, "Equality and Civil Rights," we demonstrate how many of this nation's most controversial issues are conflicts among individuals holding differing values concerning freedom, order, and equality. Views on issues such as school prayer are not just political opinions, but rather choices about a philosophy that citizens want government to follow. Yet these choices are difficult, sometimes excruciatingly so.

The second theme, introduced in Chapter 2, asks students to consider two competing models of government. One way that government can make decisions is by means of *majoritarian* principles, that is, by taking the actions desired by a majority of citizens. Majoritarianism is a focus of discussion, for example, in Chapter 8, "Political Parties, Campaigns, and Elections," where we treat the real and the ideal roles of political parties. A contrasting model of government, *pluralism*, is built around the interaction of government decision makers with groups concerned about issues that directly affect them. Pluralism is a focus in Chapter 14, "The Washington Community," where we discuss issue networks in the nation's capital.

These models are not mere abstractions; we use them to illustrate the dynamics of the American political system. In Chapter 6, "The Mass Media," we discuss the media's role in the reporting of public opinion, which advances the cause of majoritarianism. Chapter 10, "Congress," begins with a discussion of the confrontation between the public's wish for a new, simplified tax law and the interest-group defense of the old, benefit-bestowing tax law. The tension between majoritarianism and pluralism is common in our political system, and we have tried to help students understand the advantages and disadvantages of each model.

As appropriate in each chapter, we use the themes to discuss relevant issues. All Americans profess a commitment to equality, but "equality" means different things to different people. In Chapter 18, we follow a detailed presentation of the development of affirmative action policy with a discussion of different conceptions of equality, invoking the related concepts introduced in Chapter 1.

Throughout the book we stress that it is the *students* who must choose among the competing values and models of government. Although the three of us have strong opinions about which choices are best, we do not believe it is our role to tell college students our answers to the broad questions we pose. We hope that students will recognize that maintaining a democracy requires difficult choices; this is why we have titled our book *The Challenge of Democracy.*

FEATURES OF THE BOOK

In many ways, the most important features of the book are the two themes just described, for they provide a consistent thread that underlies the presentation of factual material. We also use some other strategies to help students understand what they read.

Each chapter begins with a vignette that draws the student into the chapter and suggests the major themes of the book. It is followed by a few focus questions that alert the student to the central ideas addressed in the chapter.

We believe that students can better evaluate how our political system works when they compare it with politics in other countries. Each chapter has at least one boxed feature—called "Compared With What?"—that treats its topic in a comparative perspective. How much importance do citizens throughout the world place on the value of *order*? How much do Americans participate in politics compared with citizens elsewhere? How much does the United States spend on social insurance and defense compared with other countries? These and other questions are addressed by the "Compared With What?" boxes.

The second edition contains a new set of boxed features entitled "Politics in the Information Age." Each box provides a clear example of how media and modern technology are changing American politics. For example, in Chapter 2, we contemplate the effects of allowing citizens to vote on issues by means of computer terminals in their homes.

Additional boxed features discuss topics in more detail or explain them through illustration. For example, in Chapter 8, we discuss *The Wizard of Oz* as a political fable written about the Progressive party around the turn of the century. In Chapter 15, "The Economics of Public Policy," we illustrate the lack of consensus among economists on key principles of economic theory.

Another feature of *The Challenge of Democracy* is the set of four "Essays," linked by a common theme—transformations in American politics. They appear between the major parts of the book. The essays discuss transformations in American society, in political art, in party politics, and in public policy. Each essay illustrates and describes important subjects discussed in the chapters.

Each chapter concludes with lists of key terms and suggested readings. The book itself concludes with an Epilogue that examines Gorbachev's problems in reforming the Soviet system and assesses whether government in America does what the people want. Finally, the appendix contains *Federalist Papers* Nos. 10 and 51, other basic documents of American government (including an annotated, accessible Constitution), and a glossary of terms.

THE TEACHING PACKAGE

When we began writing *The Challenge of Democracy*, we viewed the book as part of a tightly integrated set of instructional materials. We have worked closely with some very talented political scientists and with educational specialists at Houghton Mifflin to produce what we think is a superior set of ancillary materials to help both students and instructors throughout the course.

The primary purpose of the *Instructor's Manual*, written by the authors (and ably updated by Ethan Cosgriff), is to provide teachers with classroom material that relates directly to the thematic framework and organization of the book. It includes learning objectives, chapter synopses, lecture outlines, and suggested classroom and individual activities. The accompanying *Test Item Bank*, prepared by Nicholas Strinkowski of Hartwick College, provides over 1,500 test items—identification, multiple-choice, and essay. The *Study Guide*, written by Melissa Butler of Wabash College, is keyed closely to the book. It contains an overview of each chapter, exercises on reading tables and graphs, suggested topics for student research, and multiple-choice questions for practice. The transparency package, containing thirty-six full-color overhead transparencies, is available to adopters of the book. Adopters may also receive a videotape that highlights key political events and personalities discussed in the text.

Computer software ancillaries available to adopters include *LectureBank*, an inventory of detailed ideas for lecture topics; *Microtest*, a test generation program containing all the items in the printed *Test Item Bank*; and *GPA: Grade Performance Analyzer*, which enables instructors to create rosters for each course section and to monitor and analyze student performance throughout the term. Other software ancillaries are designed to improve students' understanding: *Microstudy Plus*, a computerized study guide, and *IDEAlog*, an interactive exercise introducing students to the value conflicts theme in the book. For instructors who want to introduce students to data analysis there are a disk and workbook called *Crosstabs*, which allows students to do creative research using survey data on the presidential election and data on voting in Congress. The *Crosstabs* materials were prepared in collaboration with Philip Schrodt of the University of Kansas.

ACKNOWLEDGMENTS

Our first thanks again must go to Melissa Butler of Wabash College, who wrote Chapter 4, "Federalism," and Chapter 19, "Foreign and Defense Policy." We could not have worked with a colleague more adept at incorporating the book's themes and special features into these chapters. We are also grateful to our friends at Northwestern and Tufts—particularly Timothy Breen, Jay Casper, Richard Eichenberg, Paul Friesema, Reid Hastie, Herbert Jacob, Don Klein, Ben Page, Kent Portney, Karl de Schweinitz, Ed Sidlow, Wesley Skogan, Donald Strickland, Tom Tyler, and Garry Wills—for their advice and assistance at many points in the preparation of the manuscript. We also wish to thank Alan D. Monroe for commenting on our Epilogue; and we are grateful for the contributions of Ethan Cosgriff and Michael Reynolds at vital stages in our schedule. We extend our special thanks to Philip Schrodt of the University of Kansas for writing the data analysis computer program used in *Crosstabs*. We also wish to thank Robert Baumgartner and Natalie Pelster of the Northwestern University Library, Leslie Bailey and Richard Johnson of Northwestern's Language Laboratory, and Ellen Pool on the staff of the Northwestern political science department, for their assistance in completing this project.

The authors (left to right):
Ken Janda, Jerry Goldman,
Jeff Berry

We have been fortunate to obtain the help of many outstanding political scientists across the country who reviewed drafts of our chapters for the first and the second editions. They made many suggestions for improvement. We found their comments enormously helpful, and we thank them for taking valuable time away from their own teaching and research to write their detailed reports. More specifically, our thanks go to

David Ahern, University of Dayton

James Anderson, Texas A & M University

Theodore Arrington, University of North Carolina, Charlotte

Denise Baer, Northeastern University

Thad Beyle, University of North Carolina, Chapel Hill

Michael Binford, Georgia State University

Bonnie Browne, Texas A & M University

J. Vincent Buck, California State University, Fullerton

Gregory A. Caldeira, University of Iowa

Robert Casier, Santa Barbara City College

John Chubb, Stanford University

Allan Cigler, University of Kansas

Stanley Clark, California State University, Bakersfield
Ronald Claunch, Stephen F. Austin State University
Gary Copeland, University of Oklahoma
Cornelius P. Cotter, University of Wisconsin, Milwaukee
Victor D'Lugin, University of Hartford
Henry Fearnley, College of Marin
Elizabeth Flores, Del Mar College
Patricia S. Florestano, University of Maryland
Steve Frank, St. Cloud State University
Mitchel Gerber, Hofstra University
Dorith Grant-Wisdom, Howard University
Kenneth Hayes, University of Maine
Ronald Hedlund, University of Wisconsin, Milwaukee
Roberta Herzberg, Indiana University
Peter Howse, American River College
Scott Keeter, Virginia Commonwealth University
Sarah W. Keidan, Oakland Community College (Mich.)
Beat Kernen, Southwest Missouri State University
Vance Krites, Indiana University (Penn.)
Clyde Kuhn, California State University, Sacramento
Wayne McIntosh, University of Maryland
Michael Maggiotto, University of South Carolina
Steve J. Mazurana, University of Northern Colorado
Jim Morrow, Tulsa Junior College
William Mugleston, Mountain View College
Bruce Odom, Trinity Valley Community College
Bruce Oppenheimer, University of Houston
Richard Pacelle, Indiana University
Robert Pecorella, St. John's University
James Perkins, San Antonio College
Denny E. Pilant, Southwest Missouri State University
Gilbert K. St. Clair, University of New Mexico
Barbara Salmore, Drew University
William A. Schultze, San Diego State University
Thomas Sevener, Santa Rosa Junior College
Kenneth S. Sherrill, Hunter College
Sanford R. Silverburg, Catawba College
Mark Silverstein, Boston University
Charles Sohner, El Camino College
Robert J. Spitzer, State University of New York, Cortland

Dale Story, University of Texas, Arlington

Nicholas Strinkowski, Hartwick College

Gary D. Wekkin, University of Central Arkansas

Jonathan West, University of Miami

John Winkle, University of Mississippi

Clifford Wirth, University of New Hampshire

Ann Wynia, North Hennepin Community College

Jerry L. Yeric, University of North Texas

Finally, we want to acknowledge again our debt to the superb staff at Houghton Mifflin, who worked as hard as we did at making this book a reality while tolerating our shenanigans. Once again, they deserve combat pay and Purple Hearts for their efforts.

K.J., J.B., J.G.

PART I

DILEMMAS OF DEMOCRACY

1

Freedom, Order, or Equality?

Which is better: to live under a government that allows individuals complete freedom to do whatever they please or under one that enforces strict law and order? Which is better: to allow businesses and private clubs to discriminate in choosing their customers and members or to pass laws that enforce equality among races and sexes?

For many people, none of these alternatives is satisfactory. All of them pose difficult dilemmas of choice. These dilemmas are tied to opposing philosophies that place different values on freedom, order, and equality.

This book explains American government and politics in light of these dilemmas. It does more than explain the workings of our government; it encourages you to think about what government should—and should not—do. And it judges the American government against democratic ideals, encouraging you to think about how government should make its decisions. As its title implies, *The Challenge of Democracy* argues that good government often involves tough choices.

College students frequently say that American government and politics are hard to understand. In fact, many people voice the same complaint. Nearly three-quarters of a national sample interviewed after the 1984 presidential election agreed with the statement "Politics and government seem so complicated that a person like me can't understand what's going on."[1] With this book, we hope to improve your understanding of "what's going on" by analyzing and evaluating the norms or values that people use to judge political events. Our purpose is not to preach what people ought to favor in making policy decisions; it is to teach what values they have favored.

Teaching without preaching is not easy; no one can exclude personal values completely from political analysis. But our approach minimizes this problem by concentrating on the dilemmas that confront governments when they are forced to choose between policies that threaten equally cherished values. An example: People value both freedom and human life. Studies clearly show that seat belts save lives. Does this mean a government should force its citizens to wear seat belts? Or should it allow citizens the freedom *not* to wear seat belts—sacrificing lives in the process.

Every government policy reflects a choice between conflicting values. We want you to understand this concept, to understand that all government policies reinforce certain values (norms) at the expense of others. We want you to interpret policy issues (for example, should buckling up be mandatory?) with an understanding of the fundamental values in question (individual freedom versus safety and order) and the broader political overtones (conservative or liberal politics).

By looking beyond specifics to underlying normative principles, you should be able to make more sense out of politics. Our framework for analysis does not encompass all the complexities of American government, but it should help your knowledge grow by improving your digestion of political information. We begin by considering the basic purposes of government. In short, why do we need it?

THE PURPOSES OF GOVERNMENT

Most people do not like being told what to do. Fewer still like being coerced into acting a certain way. Yet every day, millions of American motorists dutifully drive on the right-hand side of the street and obediently stop at red lights. Every year, millions of U.S. citizens struggle to complete their income tax forms before midnight, April 15. In both of these examples, the coercive power of government is at work. If people do not like being coerced, why do they submit to it? In other words, why do we have government?

Government can be defined as the legitimate use of force—including imprisonment and execution—to control human behavior within territorial boundaries. All governments require citizens to surrender some freedom in the process of being governed. Although some governments minimize their infringement on personal freedom, no government has as a goal the maximization of personal freedom. Governments exist to control; *to govern* means "to control." Why do people surrender their freedom to this control? To obtain the benefits of government. Throughout history, government seems to have served three major purposes: maintaining order (preserving life and protecting property), providing public goods, and promoting equality.

Maintaining Order

Maintaining order is the oldest objective of government. **Order** in this context is rich with meaning. Let's start with "law and order."

Leviathan, Hobbes's All-Powerful Sovereign
This engraving is from the 1651 edition of Leviathan, *by Thomas Hobbes. It shows Hobbes's sovereign brandishing a sword in one hand and the scepter of justice in the other. He watches over an orderly town, made peaceful by his absolute authority. But note that the sovereign's body is composed of tiny images of his subjects. He exists only through them. Hobbes explains that such governmental power can be created only if men "confer all their power and strength upon one man, or upon one assembly of men, that may reduce all their wills, by plurality of voices, unto one will."*

Maintaining order here means establishing the rule of law to preserve life and to protect property. For the seventeenth-century philosopher Thomas Hobbes (1588–1679), preserving life was the most important function of government. In his classic philosophical treatise, *Leviathan* (1651), Hobbes described life without government as life in a "state of nature." Without rules, people would live like animals, stealing and killing for personal benefit. In Hobbes's classic phrase, life in a state of nature would be "solitary, poor, nasty, brutish, and short." He believed that a single ruler, or *sovereign,* must possess unquestioned authority to guarantee the safety of the weak against attacks of the strong. Hobbes characterized his all-powerful government as Leviathan, a biblical sea monster. He believed that complete obedience to Leviathan's strict laws was a small price to pay for the security of living in a civil society.

Most of us can only imagine what a state of nature would be like. We might think of the Old West in the days before the Lone Ranger (or John Wayne) rode into town and established law and order. But in some parts of the world today, people actually are living in a state of lawlessness. For more than a decade, the Lebanese have lived under a central government that is not strong enough to control warring religious factions. Films of the street fighting in the strife-torn city of Beirut, shown with regularity on the six o'clock news, give us a good picture of what a state of nature might be like.

In his focus on life in the cruel state of nature, Hobbes saw government primarily as a means for survival. Other theorists, taking survival for granted, believed that government protected order by preserving pri-

Life in a Twentieth-Century "State of Nature" Seventeenth-century philosopher Thomas Hobbes characterized life without government as life in a state of nature—it would be "solitary, poor, nasty, brutish, and short." Some three hundred years later, we get a picture of life in a state of nature in Beirut, Lebanon, where the central government has collapsed and citizens try to survive amidst the gunfire and bombings of warring religious factions.

vate property (goods and land owned by individuals). Foremost among them was John Locke (1632–1704), an English philosopher. In *Two Treatises on Government* (1690), he wrote that the protection of life, liberty, and property was the basic objective of government. His thinking strongly influenced the Declaration of Independence. The declaration's famous phrase that identifies "Life, Liberty, and the pursuit of Happiness" as "unalienable Rights" of citizens under government reflects that influence.

Not everyone believes that the protection of private property is a valid objective of government. The German philosopher Karl Marx (1818–1883) rejected the private ownership of property that is used in the production of goods or services. Marx's ideas form the basis of **communism,** a complex theory that gives ownership of all land and productive facilities to the people—that is, the government. In line with communist theory, the Soviet Union operates under a constitution that sets forth the following principles of government ownership:

> State property, i.e., the common property of the Soviet people, is the principal form of socialist property.
>
> The land, its minerals, waters, and forests are the exclusive property of the state. The state owns the basic means of production in industry, construction, and agriculture; means of transport and communication; the banks; the property of state-run trade organizations and public utilities, and other state-run undertakings; most urban housing; and other property necessary for state purposes.[2]

Outside communist societies, the extent to which government must protect property or can take it away is a political issue that forms the basis of much ideological thinking across the world. As you will see, Americans hold very strong views on the sanctity of private property.

Providing Public Goods

After governments have established basic order, they can pursue other ends. Using their coercive powers, they can tax citizens to raise funds to spend on **public goods**—such as education, sanitation, and parks. These services benefit all citizens but are not likely to be produced by the voluntary acts of individuals. The government of ancient Rome, for example, built aqueducts to carry fresh water from the mountains to the city. Road building was another public good provided by the Roman government.

Government action to provide public goods can be controversial. During President James Monroe's administration (1817–1825), many people thought that building the Cumberland Road (between Cumberland, Maryland, and Wheeling, West Virginia) was not a proper function of the national government, the Romans notwithstanding. Over time, the scope of government functions in the United States has expanded. During President Dwight Eisenhower's administration in the 1950s, the national government outdid the Romans' noble road building. Despite his basic conservatism, Eisenhower launched the massive Interstate Highway System at a cost of $27 billion (in 1950s' dollars). Yet some government

A Concrete Example of a Public Good
Governments use tax money to undertake projects that benefit virtually all citizens but that are not likely to be undertaken by any group of individuals. Expressways are one example of a public good (except when you are stuck in one at rush hour).

enterprises that are common in other countries—running railroads, operating coal mines, generating electric power—are politically controversial or even unacceptable in the United States. People disagree on how far the government ought to go in using its power to tax in providing public goods and services and how much should be handled by private business for profit.

Promoting Equality

The promotion of equality has not always been a major objective of government. It has gained prominence only in this century, in the aftermath of industrialization and urbanization. Confronted by the contrast of poverty amidst plenty, some political leaders in European nations pioneered extensive government programs to improve life for the lower classes. Under the emerging concept of the **welfare state,** government's role expanded to provide individuals with medical care, education, and a guaranteed income, "from the cradle to the grave." Sweden, Britain, and other nations adopted welfare programs aimed at reducing social inequalities. This relatively new purpose of government has been by far the most controversial. Taxation for public goods (building roads and schools, for example) is often opposed because of its cost alone. Taxation for government programs to promote economic and social equality is opposed more strongly on principle.

The key issue here is the government's role in redistributing income—taking from the wealthy to give to the poor. Charity (voluntary giving to the poor) has a strong basis in Western religious traditions; using the power of the state to support the poor does not. (In Charles

Rosa Parks: She Sat for Equality
Rosa Parks had just finished a day's work as a seamstress and was sitting in the front of a bus in Montgomery, Alabama, going home. A white man claimed her seat, which he could do according to the law in December 1955. When she refused to move and was arrested, angry blacks, led by Dr. Martin Luther King, Jr., began a boycott of the Montgomery bus company.

Dickens's nineteenth-century novels, the power of the state was used to imprison the poor, not to support them.) Using the state to redistribute income was originally a radical idea, set forth by Marx as the ultimate principle of developed communism: "from each according to his ability, to each according to his needs."[3] This extreme has never operated in any government, not even in communist states. But over time, taking from the rich to help the needy has become a legitimate function of most governments.

That legitimacy is not without controversy, however. Especially since the Great Depression of the 1930s, the government's role in redistributing income to promote economic equality has been a major source of policy debate in the United States. Food stamps and Aid to Families with Dependent Children (AFDC) are typical examples of government programs that tend to redistribute income—and generate controversy.

Government can also promote social equality through policies that do not redistribute income. For example, it can regulate social behavior to enforce equality—as it did when the Supreme Court ruled in 1987 that Rotary Clubs must admit women members. Policies that regulate social behavior, like those that redistribute income, inevitably clash with the value of personal freedom.

A CONCEPTUAL FRAMEWORK FOR ANALYZING GOVERNMENT

Citizens have very different views on how vigorously they want government to maintain order, provide public goods, and promote equality. Of the three objectives, providing for public goods usually is less controversial than maintaining order or promoting equality. After all, government spending for highways, schools, and parks carries benefits for nearly every citizen. Moreover, these services merely cost money. The cost of maintaining order and promoting equality is greater than money; it usually means a trade-off of basic values.

To understand government and the political process, you must be able to recognize these trade-offs and identify the basic values involved in them. Just as people sit back from a wide-screen motion picture to gain perspective, to understand American government you need to take a broad view, a much broader view than that offered by examining specific political events. You need to employ political concepts.

A *concept* is a generalized idea. It groups various events, objects, or qualities under a common classification or label. The conceptual framework that guides this book consists of five concepts that figure prominently in political analysis. We regard these five concepts as especially important to a broad understanding of American politics, and we use them repeatedly throughout the book. This framework will help you evaluate political happenings long after you have read this text.

The five concepts that we emphasize deal with the fundamental issues of *what* government tries to do and *how* it decides to do it. The concepts that relate to what government tries to do are *order, freedom,* and *equality.* All governments by definition value order; maintaining order is part of the meaning of government. Most governments at least claim to preserve individual freedom while they maintain order, although they vary widely in the extent to which they succeed. Very few governments even profess to guarantee equality, and governments differ greatly in policies that pit equality against freedom. Our conceptual framework should help you evaluate the extent to which the United States pursues—and achieves—all three values through its government.

How government chooses the proper mix of order, freedom, and equality in its policymaking has to do with the *process* of choice rather than the outcome. We evaluate the American governmental process using two models of democratic government: the *majoritarian* and the *pluralist.* Most governments profess to be democracies. Whether they are or not depends on their (and our) meaning of the term. Even countries that Americans agree are democracies—for example, the United States and Britain—differ substantially in the type of democracy they practice. We use our conceptual models of democratic government both to classify the type of democracy practiced in the United States and to evaluate the government's success in fulfilling that model.

We can organize these five concepts into two groups.

- Concepts that identify the *values* pursued by government:
  Freedom
  Order
  Equality
- Concepts that describe *models* of democratic government:
  Majoritarian democracy
  Pluralist democracy

The rest of this chapter examines freedom, order, and equality as conflicting values pursued by government. In Chapter 2, we discuss majoritarian democracy and pluralist democracy as alternative institutional models for implementing democratic government.

THE CONCEPTS OF FREEDOM, ORDER, AND EQUALITY

These three terms—*freedom, order,* and *equality*—have different connotations in American politics. Both *freedom* and *equality* are positive terms that politicians have learned to use to their own advantage. Consequently, *freedom* and *equality* mean different things to different people at different times—depending on the political context in which they are used. *Order,* on the other hand, has negative connotations. For most people, it symbolizes government intrusion in private lives. Except during periods of social strife, few politicians call openly for more order. Because all governments infringe on freedom, we examine that concept first.

Freedom

Freedom can be used in two major senses: *freedom to* and *freedom from.* Franklin Delano Roosevelt used the word in both senses in a speech he made shortly after the Unites States entered World War II. He described four freedoms—freedom of religion, freedom of speech, freedom from fear, and freedom from want. The noted illustrator Norman Rockwell gave Americans a vision of these freedoms in a classic set of paintings published in the *Saturday Evening Post* (see Feature 1.1).

Freedom to is the absence of constraints on behavior. In this sense, freedom is synonymous with *liberty.* Two of Rockwell's paintings—*Freedom of Worship* and *Freedom of Speech*—exemplify this type of freedom.

Freedom from underlies the message of the other paintings, *Freedom from Fear* and *Freedom from Want.* Here *freedom* suggests immunity from fear and want. In the modern political context, *freedom from* often symbolizes the fight against exploitation and oppression. The cry "Freedom Now!" of the civil rights movement in the 1960s conveyed this meaning. If you recognize that freedom in this sense means immunity from discrimination, you can see that it comes close to the concept of equality.[4] We avoid using *freedom* to mean "freedom from"; for this sense of the word, we simply use *equality.*

Order

When order is viewed in the narrow sense of preserving life and protecting property, most citizens would concede the importance of maintaining order, and thereby grant the need for government. However, when it is viewed in the broader sense of preserving the social order, people are more likely to argue that this is not a legitimate function of

The Four Freedoms

Norman Rockwell became famous in the 1940s for the humorous, home-spun covers he painted for the *Saturday Evening Post*, a weekly magazine. Inspired by an address to Congress in which President Roo-sevelt outlined his goals for world civilization, Rockwell painted "The Four Freedoms." The paintings were first reproduced in the *Saturday Evening Post*. Their immense popularity led the government

Freedom of Speech

Freedom of Worship

government (see Compared With What? 1.1). *Social order* refers to established patterns of authority in society and to traditional modes of behavior. It is the accepted way of doing things. The prevailing social order prescribes behavior in many different areas: how students should dress in school (neatly, no purple hair) and behave toward their teachers (respectfully); under what conditions people should have sexual relations (married and of different sexes); what the press should not publish (sexually explicit photographs); and what the proper attitude toward religion and country should be (reverential). It is important to remember that social order can change. Today, perfectly respectable men and women wear bathing suits that would have caused a scandal at the turn of the century.

to print posters of the illustrations for the treasury Department's war bond drive. The Office of War Information also reproduced "The Four Freedoms" and circulated the posters in schools, club houses, railroad stations, post offices, and other public buildings. Officials even had copies dropped into the European front to remind soldiers of the liberties for which they were fighting. It is said that no other paintings in the world have ever been reproduced or circulated in such vast numbers as "The Four Freedoms."

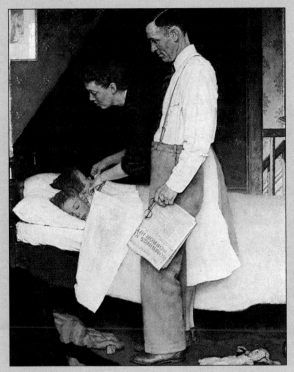

Freedom from Fear

Freedom from Want

A government can protect the established order under its **police power**—its authority to safeguard citizens' health, morals, safety, and welfare. The extent to which government should use this authority is a topic of ongoing debate in the United States and is constantly being redefined by our courts. There are those who fear the evolution of a *police state*—government that uses its power to regulate nearly all aspects of behavior. For example, South Africa has laws governing intermarriage between blacks and whites, laws prescribing where married people of mixed race can live. It is no accident that the chief law enforcement officer in South Africa is the minister of law and order.

Most governments are inherently conservative; they tend to resist social change. But some governments have as a primary objective the

COMPARED WITH WHAT? 1.1

The Importance of Order as a Political Value

Compared with citizens in other nations, Americans simply do not think maintaining order is very important. Surveys in the United States and twelve European countries asked respondents to select which of the following four national goals was the "most important in the long run":

- Maintaining order in the nation
- Giving the people more say in important government decisions
- Fighting rising prices
- Protecting freedom of speech

Just 29 percent of those surveyed in the United States chose "maintaining order." Only respondents in Belgium, who were more concerned about "fighting rising prices" than were people in any other nation, attached less importance to maintaining order. Compared with citizens in most other Western countries, Americans seem to want less government control of social behavior.

Source: Jacques–René Rabier, Helene Riffault, and Ronald Inglehart, *Euro-Barometer 24: Entry of Spain and Portugal, October, 1985* (Ann Arbor, Mich.: Inter-University Consortium for Political and Social Research, Study 8513, 1986), p. 12.

restructuring of the social order. Social change is most dramatic when an established government is overthrown through force and replaced by a revolutionary government. Governments can work at changing social patterns more gradually through the legal process. Our use of the term *order* in this book includes all three aspects of the term: preserving life, protecting property, and maintaining traditional patterns of social relationships.

Equality

Like *freedom* and *order, equality* is used in different senses, to support different causes.

Political equality is easy to define: Each citizen has one and only one vote. This basic concept is central to democratic theory—a subject we explore at length in Chapter 2. But when some people advocate political equality, they mean more than "one person, one vote." These people contend that an urban ghetto dweller and the chairman of the board of General Motors are not politically equal despite the fact that each has one vote. Through occupation or wealth, some citizens are more able than others to influence political decisions. For example, wealthy citizens can exert influence by advertising in the mass media or by contacting friends in high places. Lacking great wealth and political connections, most citizens do not have this kind of influence. Thus, some analysts argue that equality in wealth, education, and status—that is, **social equality**—is necessary for true political equality. There are two routes to achieving social equality: providing equal opportunities and ensuring equal outcomes.

Equality of opportunity means that each person has the same chance to succeed in life. This idea is deeply ingrained in American culture. We do not have titles of nobility, owning property is not a requirement for holding public office, public schools and libraries are free to all. To many people, the concept of social equality is satisfied just by offering oppor-

Are Poor People Really Free?
Some critics argue that people are not politically free unless they are socially equal. Those who hold this view believe that government should redistribute income to produce equality of outcome, *not just equality of* opportunity. *The conception of equality that you choose affects your position on the modern dilemma of government.*

tunities for people to advance themselves. It is not essential that people end up being equal after using those opportunities.

For others, true social equality means nothing less than **equality of outcome.**[5] They believe that society must see to it that people *are* equal. It is not enough for governments to provide people with equal opportunities; they must also design policies to redistribute wealth and status so that economic and social equality are actually achieved. In education, equality of outcome has led to federal laws that require comparable funding for men's and women's college sports. In business, equality of outcome has led to affirmative action programs to increase minority hiring, to the active recruitment of women, blacks, and Hispanics to fill jobs. Equality of outcome here also has produced federal laws that require employers to pay men and women equally for equal work.

Some link equality of outcome with the concept of governmental **rights**—the idea that every citizen is entitled to certain benefits of government, that government should guarantee its citizens adequate (if not equal) housing, employment, medical care, and income as a matter of right. If citizens are entitled to government benefits as a matter of right, then government efforts to promote equality of outcome become legitimized.

Clearly, the concept of equality of outcome is very different from that of equality of opportunity, and it requires a much greater degree of government activity. It is also the concept of equality that clashes most directly with the concept of freedom. By taking from one to give to another—which is necessary for the redistribution of income and sta-

Drive Toward Equality
The tremendous growth in women's sports on college campuses today is largely a result of a national law that promoted sexual equality in education. Under Title IX, *part of a 1972 law dealing with educational policy, Congress prohibited sex discrimination in schools and colleges that receive federal funds. Enforced by the Department of Education's Office for Civil Rights,* Title IX *required schools and colleges to provide "reasonably comparable" activities to students of both sexes. Colleges responded by expanding their competitive sports programs for women, including awarding a comparable number of athletic scholarships.*

tus—the government clearly creates winners and losers. The winners may believe that justice has been served by the redistribution. The losers often feel strongly that their freedom to enjoy their income and status has suffered.

TWO DILEMMAS OF GOVERNMENT

The two major dilemmas facing American government in the 1980s stem from the oldest and the newest objectives of government. The oldest is maintaining order; the newest, promoting equality. Both order and equality are important social values, but government cannot pursue either without sacrificing a third important value: individual freedom. The clash between freedom and order forms the *original* dilemma of government; the clash between freedom and equality, the *modern* dilemma of government. Although the dilemmas are very different, each involves trading off some amount of freedom for another value.

The Original Dilemma: Freedom Versus Order

The conflict between freedom and order originates in the very meaning of government as the legitimate use of force to control human behavior. How much freedom must a citizen surrender to government? This dilemma has occupied philosophers for hundreds of years. In the eighteenth century, French philosopher Jean Jacques Rousseau (1712–1778) wrote that the problem of devising a proper government "is to find a form of association which will defend and protect with the whole common force the person and goods of each associate, and in which each, while uniting himself with all, may still obey himself alone, and remain free as before."[6]

The original purpose of government was to protect life and property, to make citizens safe from violence. How well is the American government doing today in guaranteeing the safety of its citizens? Nearly half the respondents in a 1982 national survey said that they were afraid to walk alone at night within a mile of their homes.[7] In our larger urban areas, their fears seem justified. Nearly three out of ten people interviewed in New York City in 1985 reported that they, or a member of their family, had been a victim of crime within the past year.[8] Visitors to New York are well advised to keep out of Central Park after dark. Simply put, Americans do not trust their urban governments to protect them from crime when they go out alone at night.

The climate of fear in urban America stands in stark contrast with the pervasive sense of personal safety in Moscow, Warsaw, Prague, and other communist cities. There it is common to see old and young strolling along late at night on the streets and in the parks. Of course, communist countries give their police greater powers to control guns, monitor citizens' movements, and arrest and imprison suspicious people—which enables them to do a better job of maintaining order. Communist governments have deliberately chosen order over freedom. It is perhaps

Two Trains of Thought
Which scene appeals to you more? The photo on the left shows one of Moscow's handsome subway stations (each station displays a different architectural theme) and its spotless subway cars. The photo on the right shows a subway train in New York City. Soviet visitors to U.S. urban areas are appalled by graffiti-defaced subway cars and buses, which they view as symbols of a breakdown in law and order. For what it's worth, New York City officials report a significant decline in graffiti on public vehicles and buildings in recent years.

not surprising that some Russians who had emigrated to the United States found life here too threatening and returned to the security of the Soviet Union. After living for eight years in New York City, Rebecca Katsap (age sixty-seven) returned to Odessa in 1987, saying, "I was afraid to go out in the street after 4 in the afternoon."[9]

The crisis over Acquired Immune Deficiency Syndrome (AIDS) adds a new twist to the dilemma of freedom versus order. Some health officials believe that AIDS, for which there is no known cure, is the greatest threat in the medical history of the United States. The U.S. Public Health Service estimated that about 1.5 million Americans carried the AIDS virus in their blood in 1987. At the start of 1988, 49,743 cases of the disease had been reported to the Centers for Disease Control, and 27,909 people had died. The Health Service also estimated that 174,000 people will develop AIDS by 1991. The cost of caring for these victims will range between $8 billion and $16 billion.[10]

To combat the spread of the disease in the military, the Department of Defense began testing all applicants for the AIDS virus. Other government agencies have begun testing current employees. And some officials now are calling for widespread mandatory testing within the private sector as well. These programs are strongly opposed by those who believe

***Police Power Versus
Personal Privacy***
Under its police power, government is charged with promoting public health and safety. One way to stop the spread of AIDS involves using blood tests to identify those who carry the deadly disease. But widespread mandatory blood tests infringe on personal privacy and therefore individual freedom. Is such government testing justifiable? It's a dilemma.

they violate individual freedom. Those who are more afraid of AIDS than an infringement on individual rights support aggressive government action to combat the disease.

The value conflict between freedom and order represents the original dilemma of government. In the abstract, people value both freedom and order; but in real life, the two values inherently conflict. Any policy that works toward one of these values by definition takes away from the other. The balance of freedom and order is an issue in major matters (whether or not to allow capital punishment) and in minor ones (how to deal with urban teenagers who spray-paint subway cars). And in a democracy, policy choices hinge on how much citizens value freedom and how much they value order.

The Modern Dilemma: Freedom Versus Equality

Popular opinion has it that freedom and equality go hand in hand. In reality, these two values usually clash when governments enact policies to promote social equality. Because social equality is a relatively recent government objective, deciding between policies that promote equality at the expense of freedom, and vice versa, is the modern dilemma of politics. Consider four examples in recent years.

■ During the 1960s, Congress (through the Equal Pay Act) required employers to pay women and men the same rate for equal work. This means that some employers are forced to pay women more than they would if hiring were based on a free market.

FEATURE 1.2

Promoting Equality by Assessing Comparable Worth

Women's advocates contend that men tend to be paid more than women in part because sex discrimination exists in job classifications and pay rates. They back the idea of pay equity for jobs of comparable worth. If the idea becomes national law, it will involve the government more deeply in promoting social equality. The excerpt below describes one way employers (and government) might determine the comparable worth of two different jobs traditionally held by different sexes.

Should a nurse, usually a woman, be paid as much as a sanitation engineer, often a man? Questions about providing equal pay for jobs of equal value are being raised as interest grows in the relatively new doctrine called "comparable worth." And attempting to answer them is spawning a new career path, mainly in management consulting firms.

Anton Armbruster, an associate of William M. Mercer-Meidinger, an employee benefit and compensation consulting firm, has come up with the following example of how management consultants are providing answers. He uses a point system based on four factors—

know-how, problem-solving requirements, accountability and working conditions.

The nurse probably needs more know-how and more problem-solving ability, but total accountability is about the same because both are important to community health. Working conditions for the engineer, often outdoors in bad weather, are obviously more difficult than those for the typical nurse, so the engineer is credited with a higher number of points in that category.

	Nurse	Sanitary Engineer
Know-how	150	60
Problem solving	75	40
Accountability	175	165
Working conditions	50	185
Total	450	450

Source: Elizabeth M. Fowler, "Comparing the Value of Jobs," *New York Times*, 23 January, 1985. Copyright © 1985 by The New York Times Company. Reprinted by permission.

- During the 1970s, the courts ordered the busing of schoolchildren to achieve equal proportions of blacks and whites in public schools. This action was motivated by concern for educational equality, but it also impaired freedom of choice.

- During the 1980s, some states passed legislation that went beyond the idea of equal pay for equal work to the more radical notion of *pay equity*—equal pay for *comparable* work. Women had to be paid at a rate equal to men's—even if they had different jobs—providing the women's jobs were of "comparable worth." For example, if the skills and responsibilities of a female nurse were found comparable to those of a male sanitation engineer in the same hospital, the woman's salary and the man's salary would have to be the same (see Feature 1.2). Equal pay for equal worth was denounced as "the looniest idea since 'Looney Tunes' came on the screen" by the chairman of President Ronald Reagan's Civil Rights Commission, but it was the law in some states. And in 1986, Congress considered enacting this "looney" idea into law.

- By 1987, government pressure on employers to hire women and minority members resulted in the legalization of *reverse discrimi-*

nation. This means qualified white males are passed over in favor of women or blacks. The Santa Clara County Transportation Agency in California had promoted a white woman to the job of dispatching road crews over a white man who had a slightly higher score in a competitive interviewing process. The man sued, claiming he was a victim of illegal sex discrimination. In a split decision, the Supreme Court ruled that employers sometimes may hire or promote women and minority members over better-qualified men and whites to achieve a work force that reflects the area labor market by sex and race. Opponents of the ruling claim that it restricts employers from hiring and promoting purely on merit (see Chapter 18).

These examples illustrate the problem of using government power to promote equality. The clash between freedom and order is obvious, but that between freedom and equality is more subtle. Often it goes unnoticed by the American people, who think of freedom and equality as complementary rather than conflicting values. When forced to choose between the two, however, Americans tend to choose freedom over equality more often than do people in other countries (see Compared With What? 1.2). The emphasis on equality over freedom is especially strong in the Soviet Union, which guarantees its citizens medical care, inexpensive housing, and other social services. Some Russian émigrés who opted to return to the Soviet Union in 1987 cited the hardships of freedom in the absence of such guarantees. Valeri Klever, an artist who lived for ten years in New York, Maine, and California, returned to Leningrad with this complaint about freedom in the United States: "You have to worry about your life, your apartment, monthly bills, everything. Every month, every day, I was waiting for the next dollar to pay bills. It's not freedom."[11]

The conflicts among freedom, order, and equality explain a great deal of the political conflict in the United States. These conflicts also underlie the ideologies that people use to structure their understanding of politics.

IDEOLOGY AND THE SCOPE OF GOVERNMENT

People hold different opinions about the merits of government policies. Sometimes their views are based on self-interest. For example, senior citizens approve of the social security system more than citizens who do not reap the benefits of the system. Policies also are judged according to individual values and beliefs. Some people hold an assortment of values and beliefs that produce contradictory opinions on government policies. Others organize their opinions into a **political ideology**—a consistent set of values and beliefs about the proper purpose and scope of government.

Political writers often describe the ideologies of politicians and voters as "liberal" or "conservative." In popular usage, liberals favor an active, broad role for government in society; conservatives, a passive,

COMPARED WITH WHAT? 1.2

The Importance of Freedom and Equality as Political Values

Compared with citizens' views of freedom and equality in eleven other nations, Americans value freedom more than others do. Respondents in each country were asked which of the following statements came closer to their own opinion:

- "I find that both freedom and equality are important. But if I were to make up my mind for one or the other, I would consider personal freedom more important, that is, everyone can live in freedom and develop without hindrance."
- "Certainly both freedom and equality are important. But if I were to make up my mind for

one of the two, I would consider equality more important, that is, that nobody is underprivileged and that social class differences are not so strong."

Americans chose freedom by a ratio of nearly 3 to 1, followed closely by the British. No other nations showed such a strong preference for freedom, and citizens in three countries favored equality instead. When we look at this finding together with Americans' disdain for order (see Compared With What? 1.1), the importance of freedom as a political concept in the United States is very clear.

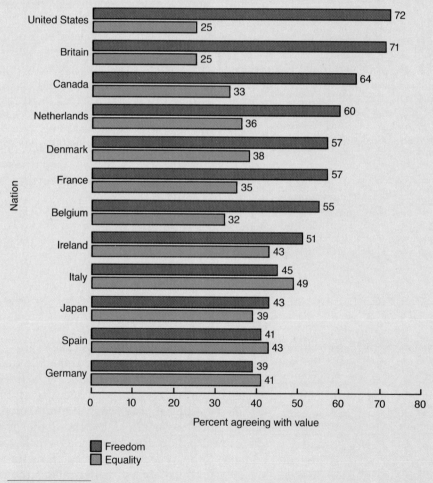

Source: *World Values Survey, 1981–1982.* The tabulation was provided by Professor Ronald F. Inglehart.

narrow role. For example, liberals favored the Social Security Act of 1935 because they wanted the government to help the elderly. Conservatives opposed the act because it committed the federal government to a costly new program. Although relatively few citizens today would advocate scrapping social security, they often divide sharply on ideological grounds over the desirability of other government programs. By carefully analyzing their political ideologies, we can explain their support of and opposition to seemingly diverse government policies.

How far should government go to maintain order, provide public goods, and promote equality? In the United States (as in every other nation), citizens, scholars, and politicians have different answers to this question. We can analyze their positions using normative theories about the proper scope of government—the range of its permissible activities. Imagine a continuum. At one end is the belief that government should do everything; at the other, the belief that government should not exist. These extreme ideologies—from most government to least government—and those that fall between them are shown in Figure 1.1.

Figure 1.1

Ideology and the Scope of Government
We can classify political ideologies according to the scope of action that people are willing to give government in dealing with social and economic problems. In this chart, the three lines map out various philosophical positions along an underlying continuum ranging from "most" to "least" government. Notice that conventional politics in the United States spans only a narrow portion of the theoretical possibilities for government action.

In popular usage, liberals favor a greater scope of government; conservatives, a narrower scope. But over time, this traditional distinction has eroded and now oversimplifies the differences between liberals and conservatives. See Figure 1.2 on page 28 for a more discriminating classification of liberals and conservatives.

Most Government / **Least Government**

Political Theories

Totalitarianism · Libertarianism · Anarchism

Economic Theories

Socialism · Capitalism · Laissez-Faire

Popular Political Labels in America

Liberal · Conservative

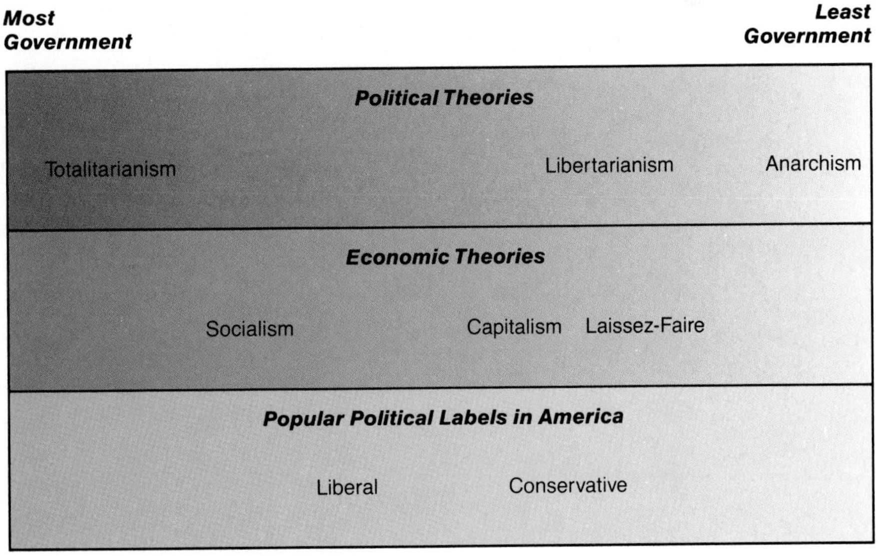

Totalitarianism

Totalitarianism is a belief that government should have unlimited power. A totalitarian government controls all sectors of society: business, labor, education, religion, sports, the arts. A true totalitarian favors a network of laws, rules, and regulations that guides every aspect of individual behavior. The object is to produce a perfect society serving some master plan for "the common good." Totalitarianism has reached its terrifying potential only in literature and films (for example, George Orwell's *1984*), but several real societies have come perilously close to "perfection." One thinks of Hitler's Germany, Stalin's Soviet Union, and perhaps the Ayatollah Khomeini's Iran. Not many people openly profess totalitarianism today, but the concept is useful because it anchors one side of our continuum.

Socialism

Where *totalitarianism* refers to government in general, *socialism* pertains to government's role in the economy. Like communism, socialism is an economic system based on Marxist theory. Under **socialism** (and communism), the scope of government extends to ownership or control of the basic industries that produce goods and services. These include communications, mining, heavy industry, transportation, and power. Although socialism favors a strong role for government in regulating private industry and directing the economy, it allows more room than communism does for private ownership of productive capacity.

Many Americans equate socialism with the communism practiced in the closed societies of the Soviet Union and Eastern Europe. But there is a difference. Although communism in theory was supposed to result in a "withering away" of the state, communist governments in practice tend toward totalitarianism, controlling both political and social life through a dominant party organization. Some socialist governments, however, practice **democratic socialism.** They guarantee civil liberties (such as freedom of speech, freedom of religion) and allow their citizens to determine the extent of government activity through free elections and competitive political parties. Outside the United States, socialism is not an inherently bad thing. In fact, the governments of Britain, Sweden, Germany, and France—among other democracies—have at times since World War II been avowedly "socialist." In the United States, however, socialism has such a bad connotation that Reverend Jesse Jackson initially asked the Democratic Socialists of America, who were preparing to endorse him for the presidency in 1988, *not* to support him. He was afraid that their support would hurt his campaign. Ultimately, the group did endorse Jackson for his position on economic issues, at the same time noting that he was *not* a Socialist.

Capitalism

Capitalism also relates to the government's role in the economy. In contrast to both socialism and communism, **capitalism** supports *free* *enterprise*—private businesses operating without government regulations. Some theorists, most notably economist Milton Friedman, argue that free enterprise is necessary for free politics.[12] This argument, that the economic system of capitalism is essential to democracy, contradicts the tenets of democratic socialism. Whether or not it is valid depends in part on our understanding of democracy—a subject we discuss in Chapter 2.

The United States is decidedly a capitalist country, far more so than Britain or most other Western nations. Despite the U.S. government's enormous budget, it owns or operates relatively few public enterprises. For example, railroads, airlines, and television stations are privately owned in the United States; these businesses are commonly owned by government in other countries. But our government *does* extend its authority into the economic sphere, regulating private businesses and directing the overall economy. American liberals and conservatives both embrace capitalism, but they differ on the nature and amount of government intervention in the economy.

Libertarianism

Libertarianism opposes all government action except that which is necessary to protect life and property. Libertarians grudgingly recognize the necessity of government but believe that government should be as limited as possible. For example, libertarians grant the need for traffic laws to ensure safe and efficient automobile travel. But they oppose laws that set a minimum drinking age as a restriction on individual actions. Libertarians believe that social programs that provide food, clothing, and shelter are outside the proper scope of government. Helping the needy, they insist, should be a matter of individual choice. Libertarians also oppose government ownership of basic industries; in fact, they oppose any government intervention in the economy. This kind of economic policy is called **laissez faire**—a French phrase that means "let (people) do (as they please)."

Libertarians are very vocal advocates of "hands-off" government—in both social and economic spheres. Whereas those who favor a broad scope of government action shun the description "socialist," libertarians make no secret of their identity. The Libertarian party has run candidates in every presidential election from 1976 through 1988. Not one of these candidates, however, has won more than a million votes.

Don't confuse *libertarians* with *liberals*. The words are similar, but their meanings are very different. *Libertarianism* draws on *liberty* as its root and means "absence of governmental constraint." In American political usage, *liberalism* evolved from the root word *liberal*. Over time, it has come to mean something closer to "generous," in the sense that liberals are willing to support government spending on social programs.

Anarchism

Anarchism stands opposite totalitarianism on the political continuum. Anarchists oppose all government, in any form. As a political philosophy, anarchism values freedom above all else. Because all government involves some restriction on personal freedom (for example, forcing people to drive on one side of the road), a pure anarchist would even object to traffic laws. Like totalitarianism, anarchism is not a popular philosophy, but it does have adherents on the political fringes.

On May 4, 1986, an estimated three hundred to five hundred anarchists gathered in Chicago to commemorate the hundredth anniversary of the riot in Haymarket Square, in which an anarchist's bomb killed several policemen. The modern anarchists, who came from all across the nation, ran amok through Chicago's financial district and along the fashionable Michigan Avenue shopping area, defacing property, shouting anticapitalist slogans, and waving black flags (the symbol of anarchism). This unusual gathering was described by one of its planners as "the most significant anarchist event held in America in years"—proof of sorts that anarchism is more bizarre than it is popular.[13] For our purposes, anarchism serves to anchor the right side of the government continuum and to indicate that libertarians are not as extreme in opposing government as is theoretically possible.

Liberals and Conservatives— The Narrow Middle

As shown in Figure 1.1, practical politics in the United States ranges over only the central portion of the continuum. The extreme positions— totalitarianism and anarchism—are rarely argued in public debate. And in this era of distrust of "big government," few American politicians would openly advocate socialism. On the other hand, more than a hundred people ran for Congress in 1984 as candidates of the Libertarian party. Although none won, American libertarians are sufficiently vocal to be heard in the debate over the scope of government.

Still, most of that debate is limited to a narrow range of political thought. On one side are what we commonly call *liberals;* on the other, *conservatives.* In popular usage, liberals favor more government, conservatives less. This distinction is very clear when the issue is government spending to provide public goods. Liberals favor generous government support for education, wildlife protection, public transportation, and a whole range of social programs. Conservatives want smaller government budgets and fewer government programs. They support free enterprise, arguing against government job programs, regulation of business, and legislation of working conditions and wage rates.

But in other areas, liberal and conservative ideologies are less consistent. In theory, liberals favor government activism, yet they oppose government regulation of abortions. In theory, conservatives oppose government activism, yet they support government control over the publication of sexually explicit material. What's going on? Are American political attitudes hopelessly contradictory, or is something missing in our analysis of these ideologies today? Actually, something *is* missing. To understand the liberal and conservative stances on political issues, we have to look not only at the scope of government action but also at the purpose of government action. That is, to understand a political ideology, we have to understand how it incorporates the values of freedom, order, and equality.

AMERICAN POLITICAL IDEOLOGIES AND THE PURPOSE OF GOVERNMENT

Much of American politics revolves around the two dilemmas we described above: freedom versus order and freedom versus equality. These two dilemmas do not account for all political conflict, but they help us gain insight into the workings of politics and organize the seemingly chaotic world of political events, actors, and issues.

Liberals Versus Conservatives: The New Differences

Liberals and conservatives are different, but their differences no longer hinge on the narrow question of the government's role in providing public goods. Liberals still favor more government and conservatives less, but this is no longer the critical difference between them. Today that difference stems from their attitudes toward the purpose of government. Conservatives support the original purpose of government, maintaining social order. They are willing to use the coercive power of the state to force citizens to be orderly. They favor aggressive police action, swift and severe punishment for criminals, and more laws regulating behavior. Conservatives do not stop with defining, preventing, and punishing crime, however. They want to preserve traditional patterns of social relations—the domestic role of women and the importance of religion in school and family life, for example.

Liberals are less likely than conservatives to use government power to maintain order. In general, liberals are more tolerant of deviant lifestyles—for example, homosexual behavior. Liberals do not shy away from using government coercion, but they use it for a different purpose—to promote equality. They support laws ensuring that homosexuals receive equal treatment in employment, housing, and education; that require busing school children to achieve racial equality; that force private businesses to hire and promote women and members of minority groups; that require public carriers to provide equal access to the handicapped; that order cities and states to reapportion election districts so that minority voters can elect minority candidates to public office.

Conservatives do not oppose equality, but they do not value it to the extent of using the government's power to enforce equality. For liberals, the use of that power to guarantee equality is both valid and necessary.

A Two-Dimensional Classification of Ideologies

To classify liberal and conservative ideologies more accurately, we have to incorporate freedom, order, and equality in the classification. We do this using the model in Figure 1.2. It depicts the conflicting values

Ideologies: A Two-Dimensional Framework
*The four ideological types below are defined by the values they favor in re-
solving the two major dilemmas of government: how much freedom should be
sacrificed in pursuit of order and equality? Test yourself by thinking about the
values that are most important to you. Which box in the figure best represents
your combination of values?*

Figure 1.2

along two separate dimensions, each anchored in maximum freedom at
the lower left. One dimension extends horizontally from maximum freedom on the left to maximum order on the right. The other extends
vertically from maximum freedom at the bottom to maximum equality
at the top. Each box represents a different ideological type: libertarians,
liberals, conservatives, and populists.*

Libertarians value freedom more than order or equality. (We will use
this term for people who have libertarian tendencies but who may not
accept the whole philosophy.) In practical terms, libertarians want min-

---

* The ideological groupings we describe here conform to the classification in William S.
Maddox and Stuart A. Lilie, *Beyond Liberal and Conservative: Reassessing the Political
Spectrum* (Washington, D.C.: Cato Institute, 1984), p. 5. However, our formulation—in
terms of the values of freedom, order, and equality—is quite different.

DOONESBURY
Garry Trudeau

Doonesbury "Blow for Individual Freedom"

imal government intervention in both the economic and the social spheres. For example, they oppose food stamp programs and laws against abortion.

Liberals value freedom more than order, but not more than equality. Liberals oppose laws against abortion but support food stamp programs. **Conservatives** value freedom more than equality but would restrict freedom to preserve social order. Conservatives oppose food stamp programs but favor laws against abortion.

Finally, we have the ideological type positioned at the upper right in Figure 1.2. This group values *both* equality and order more than freedom. Its members support both food stamp programs and laws against abortion. We will call this new group **populists.** The term *populist* derives from a rural reform movement that was active in the United States in the late 1800s. Populists thought of government as an instrument to promote the advancement of common people against moneyed or vested interests. They used their voting power both to regulate business and to enforce their moral judgments on minorities whose political and social values differed from the majority's.[14] Today the term aptly describes those who favor government action both to reduce inequalities and to ensure social order.

By analyzing political ideologies on two dimensions rather than one, we can explain why people seem to be liberal on one issue (favoring a broader scope of government action) and conservative on another (favoring less government action). The answer hinges on the action's *purpose:* which value does it promote, order or equality? According to our typology, only libertarians and populists are consistent in their attitudes toward the scope of government activity, whatever its purpose. Libertarians value freedom so highly that they oppose most government efforts to enforce either order or equality. Populists are inclined to trade off freedom for both order and equality. Liberals and conservatives, on the other hand, favor or oppose government activity depending on its purpose. As you will learn in Chapter 5, large groups of Americans fall into each of the four ideological categories. Because Americans choose four different resolutions to the original and modern dilemmas of government, the simple labels *liberal* and *conservative* no longer describe contemporary political ideologies as well as they did in the 1930s, 1940s, and 1950s.

SUMMARY

The challenge of democracy is making difficult choices—choices that inevitably bring important values into conflict. *The Challenge of Democracy* outlines a normative framework for analyzing the policy choices that arise in the pursuit of the purposes of government.

The three major purposes of government are maintaining order, providing public goods, and promoting equality. In pursuing these objectives, every government infringes on individual freedom. But the degree of that infringement depends on the government's (and by extension, its citizens') commitment to order and equality. What we have then are two dilemmas. The first—the original dilemma—centers on the conflict between freedom and order. The second—the modern dilemma—focuses on the conflict between freedom and equality.

Some people have political ideologies that help them resolve the conflicts that arise in political decision making. These ideologies outline the scope and purpose of government. At opposite extremes of the continuum are totalitarianism, which supports government intervention in every aspect of society, and anarchism, which rejects government entirely. An important step back from totalitarianism is socialism. Democratic socialism favors government ownership of basic industries but preserves civil liberties. Capitalism, another economic system, promotes free enterprise. A significant step short of anarchism is libertarianism, which allows government to protect life and property but little else.

In the United States, we use the terms *liberal* and *conservative* to describe a narrow range toward the center of the political continuum. And this is probably accurate if we are just talking about the scope of government action. That is, liberals support a broader role for government than do conservatives. But if we look at both the scope and the purpose of government, a different, sharper distinction emerges.

Conservatives may want less government, but not at the price of maintaining order. In other words, they are willing to use the coercive power of government to impose social order. Liberals too are willing to use the coercive powers of government, but for a different purpose—promoting equality.

It is easier to understand the differences between liberals and conservatives and their views on the scope of government if we incorporate the values of freedom, order, and equality into our description of political ideologies. Libertarians choose freedom over both order and equality. Populists are willing to sacrifice freedom for both order and equality. Liberals value freedom and equality more than order. Conservatives value freedom and order more than equality.

The concepts of government objectives, values, and political ideologies appear repeatedly as we determine who favors what government action and why. So far, we have said little about how government should make its decisions. In Chapter 2, we complete our normative framework for evaluating American politics by examining the nature of democratic theory. There we introduce two key concepts for analyzing how democratic governments make decisions.

Key Terms

government	political ideology
order	totalitarianism
communism	socialism
public goods	democratic socialism
welfare state	capitalism
freedom to	libertarianism
freedom from	laissez faire
police power	anarchism
political equality	libertarians
social equality	liberals
equality of opportunity	conservatives
equality of outcome	populists
rights	

Selected Readings

Corbett, Michael. *Political Tolerance in America: Freedom and Equality in Public Attitudes.* New York: Longman, 1982. Corbett summarizes research on support for civil liberties and civil rights in America. Drawing heavily on public opinion surveys, he shows the generally upward trend in political tolerance and analyzes tolerant attitudes by social groups.

Ebenstein, William, and Edwin Fogelman. *Today's Isms: Communism, Fascism, Capitalism, Socialism.* 9th ed. Englewood Cliffs, N.J.: Prentice-Hall, 1985. This standard source describes the history of each of the four major "isms" and relates each to developments in contemporary politics. It is concise, informative, and readable.

Herson, Lawrence. *The Politics of Ideas: Political Theory and American Public Policy.* Homewood, Ill.: Dorsey Press, 1984. Herson guides a lively journey through American political history, culture, and thought. The book has especially good sections on populism, democracy, and the contemporary nature of liberals and conservatives.

King, Desmond S. *The New Right: Politics, Markets and Citizenship.* Chicago, Ill.: Dorsey Press, 1987. King uses the concepts of freedom, order, and equality to analyze ideological tendencies in Margaret Thatcher's government in Britain and in Reagan's government here. He uses *liberalism* in the European sense, to mean "limiting" state intervention in the economy. In fact, contrary to American practice, this is the way most of the world uses the term.

Maddox, William S., and Stuart A. Lilie. *Beyond Liberal and Conservative: Reassessing the Political Spectrum.* Washington, D.C.: Cato Institute, 1984. Not satisfied with the conventional labels *liberal* and *conservative*, Maddox and Lilie have devised a typology of ideologies based on two dimensions: expansion of personal freedom and government intervention in economic affairs. It is similar to our framework but less theoretical.

McClosky, Herbert, and John Zaller. *The American Ethos: Public Attitudes Toward Capitalism and Democracy.* Cambridge, Mass.: Harvard University Press, 1985. This book analyzes survey data on citizens and opinion leaders. It argues that conflicts between capitalism and democracy have been a feature of American politics. When these conflicts have occurred, they have tended to be resolved in favor of democracy, producing a form of "welfare capitalism."

Medcalf, Linda J., and Kenneth M. Dolbeare. *Neopolitics: American Political Ideas in the 1980s.* Philadelphia: Temple University Press, 1985. This slim volume reviews the history of ideological labels in American politics. It explains the changing meanings of various labels and updates their usage in contemporary politics. It also describes more recent ideological types, among them the "new right."

2

Majoritarian or Pluralist Democracy?

The Theory of Democratic Government

The Meaning and Symbolism of Democracy • The Procedural View of Democracy • A Complication: Direct Versus Indirect Democracy • The Substantive View of Democracy • Procedural Democracy Versus Substantive Democracy

Institutional Models of Democracy

The Majoritarian Model of Democracy • An Alternative Model: Pluralist Democracy • The Majoritarian Model Versus the Pluralist Model • An Undemocratic Model: Elite Theory • Elite Theory Versus Pluralist Theory

Democracies Around the World

Testing for Democratic Government • American Democracy: More Pluralist than Majoritarian

A sniper used a rifle to shoot Martin Luther King, Jr., in Memphis on April 4, 1968. An assassin used a handgun to kill Robert Kennedy in Los Angeles two months later. Despite a police record, King's killer was able to purchase his weapon over the counter. Kennedy's killer bought a cheap "Saturday night special," no questions asked. Both murders vividly recalled President John F. Kennedy's assassination with a mail-order rifle in Dallas in 1963. Now a stunned nation insisted on stricter gun controls. Congress responded quickly by passing the Gun Control Act (1968), which outlawed the interstate sale of handguns and required gun dealers to maintain records of sales. By responding promptly and positively to public opinion, Congress acted as we would expect an elected legislature in a democracy to act.

In 1986, legislation that would weaken the Gun Control Act came before Congress. Under the new law, gun collectors would not have to obtain a license before selling firearms; records of ammunition sales would no longer have to be kept; and federal authorities would be limited to only one unannounced inspection of gun dealers each year.

Public opinion had not changed in the interim. Americans still supported strict controls on handguns. For example, polls consistently showed majorities of nearly three to one in favor of laws requiring a police permit to purchase a gun.[1] The law enforcement community was very vocal in its opposition to the new bill. The executive director of the International Association of Chiefs of Police stated that the new legislation would have "a very detrimental effect on law enforcement and public safety."[2] His judgment was echoed by most of the law and

NRA Aims at State Legislators
Members of the National Rifle Association (NRA) attend a hearing on state legislation for handgun control in Massachusetts. The NRA opposes all aspects of gun control on any level of government, and it carefully keeps track of which legislators are its friends and which are its foes, in anticipation of the next election.

order establishment, including the National Sheriffs Association, the Police Foundation, the Fraternal Order of Police, the National Troopers Coalition, and the American Bar Association (ABA). And scores of police officers came before Congress to argue against relaxing the gun control law.

Despite the combined opposition of the vast majority of the American people and the law enforcement community, the bill was passed. The votes in the Senate and the House weren't even close.* What happened?

What happened was the "gun lobby"—a collection of groups that believe gun controls deprive citizens of their constitutional right to bear arms yet fail to reduce crime. The gun lobby includes the National Rifle Association (NRA), Gun Owners of America, and the Citizens' Committee for the Right to Keep and Bear Arms. Without question, the most important group in the gun lobby is the NRA, whose 3 million members were quick to contact their elected representatives on the gun control issue. In addition to its own advertising against the old law, the NRA contributed $1.5 million in 1985 to sympathetic political committees, capping off a long campaign to relax the 1968 act. On this issue, the gun lobby eventually outweighed both public opinion and the law enforcement community.

The evidence is clear that Congress, in supporting a small constituency—gun owners backed by organized interest groups—voted against what a majority of the people wanted. Was its decision "democratic"? And if it wasn't, can we really say that the United States is a democracy?

In Chapter 1, we discussed three basic values that underlie what government should do. In this chapter, we examine how government should decide what to do. In particular, we set forth criteria for judging whether or not a government's decision-making process is democratic.

THE THEORY OF DEMOCRATIC GOVERNMENT

The origins of democratic theory lie in ancient Greek political thought. Greek philosophers classified governments according to the number of citizens involved in the process. Imagine a continuum running from rule by one person, through rule by a few, to rule by many. The Greeks gave us two different sets of terms to describe each form. One set is based on the root *kratein*, which means "to rule"; the other is based on *archy*, which means "supreme power."

At one extreme is an **autocracy** (or **monarchy**), in which one individual has the power to make all important decisions. The concentration

One	*Few*	*Many*
Autocracy	Aristocracy	Democracy
Monarchy	Oligarchy	Polyarchy

* The key Senate vote to weaken the legislation was 79 to 15; the House vote was 292 to 130.

of power in the hands of one person (usually a king) was a more common form of government in earlier historical periods, although some argue that Hitler ruled Germany autocratically.

Aristocracy literally means "rule by the best"; **oligarchy** puts government power in the hands of "the few." At one time, it was common for the nobility or the major landowners to rule as an aristocracy. Today, *aristocracy* does not properly describe, say, a group of military leaders ruling an underdeveloped country; *oligarchy* is more suitable. There are some who contend that industrialized nations are also oligarchies. They argue that the few individuals who head a nation's key financial, industrial, and communications institutions amount to a **ruling elite,** a small group that governs modern society as surely as the aristocracy governed traditional society.

At the other extreme of the continuum is **democracy,** which means "authority in, or rule by, the people," and a less familiar term, **polyarchy,** which means that "the many" hold the power.[3] Most scholars believe that the United States, Britain, France, and other countries in Western Europe are genuine democracies. Dissenters contend that these countries appear to be democracies because they hold free elections, but that they actually are run by elites for the elites' benefit. Nevertheless, most people today agree that governments *should* be democratic—whatever that means.

The Meaning and Symbolism of Democracy

Americans have a simple answer to the question "Who should govern?" It is "The people." Unfortunately, this answer is too simple. It fails to define who "the people" are. Should we include young children? Recent immigrants? Illegal aliens? This answer also fails to tell us how the people should do the governing. Should they be assembled in a stadium? Vote by mail? Choose others to govern for them? We need to take a closer look at what *government by the people* really means.

The word *democracy* originated in Greek writings around the fifth century B.C. *Demos* referred to the common people, the masses. The ancient Greeks were afraid of democracy—rule by the people. That fear is evident in the term *demagogue.* Applied negatively, it refers to a politician who appeals to and often deceives the masses by manipulating their emotions and prejudices.

Many centuries later, *democracy* still carried the connotation of mob rule. When George Washington was president, opponents of a new political party disparagingly called it a "democratic" party. No one would do that in politics today. In fact, the term has become so popular that the names of more than 20 percent of the world's political parties contain some variation of *democracy.*[4]

In the United States, democracy has become the apple pie and motherhood of political discourse. Like *justice* and *decency, democracy* is used reverently by politicians of all persuasions. Even totalitarian regimes use it. The Soviet Union routinely refers to the communist governments of Eastern Europe as "peoples' democracies." Like other complex concepts, democracy means different things to different people.

There are two major schools of thought about what constitutes democracy. The first believes democracy is a form of government. It emphasizes the *procedures* that enable the people to govern—meeting to discuss issues, voting in elections, running for public office. The second sees democracy in the *substance* of government policies, in freedom of religion and providing for human needs. The *procedural* approach focuses on *how* decisions are made; the *substantive* approach is concerned with *what* government does.[5] Each gives us a set of normative principles that describes how a democracy should function. (Normative principles stress pure ideals and create perfect standards of judgment, which in practice are never fully achieved.)

The Procedural View of Democracy

Procedural democratic theory sets forth principles that describe how government should make decisions. These principles address three distinct questions:

1. *Who* should participate in decision making?
2. *How much* should each participant's vote count?
3. *How many* votes are needed to reach a decision?

According to procedural democratic theory, *everyone* should participate in government decision making. This means everyone within the boundaries of the political community should be allowed to participate in its decision making. And "everyone" really means *everyone*—including the mentally handicapped, convicted felons, recent immigrants, and children. (Some Swedes would even include babies; see Feature 2.1.) If some people are prohibited from participating, they are excluded for practical or political reasons. The theory of democracy itself does not exclude anyone from participation. We refer to this principle as **universal participation.**

How much should each participant's vote count? According to procedural theory, all votes should be counted *equally.* This is the principle of **political equality.**

Notice that universal participation and political equality are two distinct principles. It is not enough for everyone to participate in a decision; all votes must carry equal weight. President Abraham Lincoln reportedly once took a vote among his cabinet members and found that all of them opposed his own position on the issue. He summarized the vote and the decision like this: "The vote is one aye and the rest nay; the aye carries!" Everyone participated, but Lincoln's vote counted more than all the others combined. (No one ever said that presidents have to run their cabinets democratically.)

Finally, how many votes are needed to reach a decision? Procedural theory prescribes that a group should decide to do what the *majority* of its participants (50 percent plus one person more) wants to do. This principle is called **majority rule.** (If participants divide over more than two alternatives and none receives a simple majority, the principle usually defaults to *plurality rule,* in which the group should do what most participants want.)

FEATURE 2.1

Sweden: Cradle of Democracy

According to the principle of universal participation, everyone should be allowed to take part in government decisions. Throughout most of American history, *everyone* meant citizens age twenty-one or older. Now the voting age nationwide is eighteen. But why eighteen? Why not twelve? Why have any age limit at all? A group of physicians in Sweden recently carried the question of age and political rights to its logical conclusion.

STOCKHOLM [Reuters]—Should babies be given the vote?

In Sweden, the issue is no joke. It has been raised by the Swedish Pediatric Association, which proposes that all the country's 1.9 million children get the vote, though it says parents should exercise the vote for children until they are 18.

Worried that society takes insufficient care of families with children, the association has urged the government to examine ways of giving children and parents more political influence.

The pediatric association, representing 800 specialists, called for an official inquiry into the possibilities of changing the electoral system or giving children political representation in some other way.

"One possibility that should be analyzed is that children, represented by their parents, should get the right to vote in general elections," assistant professor Claes Sundelin of Uppsala Hospital, the association's chairman, said in a letter to the Justice Ministry.

Sundelin said the association's members believe children's health and welfare are neglected in comparison with the interests of workers and retirees.

"The most important reason why society pays so little attention to children is quite simply that it is not especially profitable politically," Sundelin said.

The association is eager to dispel any notion that gurgling babies could soon be lining up outside polling booths in their carriages.

"We think the right to take part in the political process begins at birth," Sundelin said. "All children, including the newborn, should have a vote, but this should be exercised by parents until they are old enough to make up their own minds."

When would they be old enough?

"We think the 18-year age limit is reasonable but that parents should listen to their children when voting," he said.

Source: "Should Babies Be Given the Right to Vote?" by Reuters as published in *Chicago Tribune*, 17 October 1985. Reprinted by permission of Reuters.

Majority rule does not necessarily go hand in hand with universal participation and political equality. Group decisions can require an *extraordinary majority*—some stated percentage greater than 50. For example, most bills in the U.S. Senate require just a simple majority to pass, but some issues—the approval of treaties with other nations is one—require a two-thirds majority for passage. Still, majority rule must work in combination with universal participation and political equality to produce truly democratic procedures for decision making.

A Complication: Direct Versus Indirect Democracy

These three principles—universal participation, political equality, and majority rule—are widely recognized as necessary for democratic decision making. In small simple societies, these principles can be met in a **direct democracy,** in which all members of the group meet to make decisions, while observing political equality and majority rule. Something close to direct democracy is practiced in New England villages, where citizens gather in town meetings to make community decisions. Citizens in Derry, New Hampshire, governed themselves in annual town meetings for 158 years. Usually held the second Tuesday in March, the Derry town meeting was an all-day affair that began with the election of officers, then proceeded to decisions on road repairs, building maintenance, and other town issues.

In large complex societies, however, the people cannot assemble in one place to participate directly in government. In Derry, as the population increased, the town meeting was no longer a viable form of government. There was no place to assemble even a fraction of the 25,000 townspeople. In 1985, Derry bowed to growth and switched to a different form of government, an elected town council headed by a mayor.[6] The town still followed democratic principles in voting for members of the town council, but the council decided village policies in place of the people.

Derry changed from direct to **indirect democracy:** Its citizens now participate in government by electing public officials to make government decisions for them. Because their elected officials are expected to represent the voters' views and interests—that is, to serve as the agents of the citizenry—indirect democracy is also known as **representative government.**

Philosopher Jean Jacques Rousseau contended that true democracy is impossible unless all citizens gather together to make their own decisions and to supervise their government.[7] Some theorists today argue

Direct Democracy in a New England Town Meeting
Adults and children alike attend the town meeting in Pittsfield, Vermont. Citizens use the town meeting to govern the activities of their village, which amounts to direct democracy. Town meetings typically run all day. In Pittsfield, baked goods are available at lunch time to give the citizens food for thought during the rest of the meeting.

the same point.[8] They are concerned about democracy in its purest form—direct democracy. Other theorists, among them the nineteenth-century English philosopher John Stuart Mill (1806–1873), accept the necessity of indirect democracy; they believe representative government is the best *possible* form of government.[9]

Adhering to the principles of universal participation, political equality, and majority rule, we can guarantee that the election of representatives is democratic. But what happens after the election? The elected representatives might not make the same decisions the people would have made if they had gathered for the same purpose. To cope with this possibility in representative government, procedural theory gives us a fourth decision-making principle: **responsiveness.** Elected representatives should respond to public opinion; they should do what a majority of the people want, regardless of what it is. That is, elected representatives should do what the people would do if they could assemble to act directly.

Adding responsiveness to deal with the case of indirect democracy, we now have four principles of procedural democracy:

- Universal participation
- Political equality
- Majority rule
- Government responsiveness to public opinion

The Substantive View of Democracy

According to procedural theory, the principle of responsiveness is absolute. The government should do what the majority wants, regardless of what it is. At first this seems a reasonable way to protect the rights of citizens in an indirect democracy. But think for a minute. Christians account for more than 90 percent of the U.S. population. Suppose that the Christian majority backs a constitutional amendment to require Bible reading in public schools, that the amendment is passed by Congress, and that it is ratified by the states. From a strict procedural view, the action would be democratic. But what about freedom of religion? What about the rights of minorities? To limit the government's responsiveness to public opinion, we must look outside procedural democratic theory to substantive democratic theory.

Substantive democratic theory focuses on the substance of government policies, not on the procedures followed in making those policies. It argues that in a democratic government, certain principles must be embodied in government policies. Substantive theorists would reject a law that requires Bible reading in schools because it would violate a substantive principle, the freedom of religion.

In defining the principles that underlie democratic government—and the policies of that government—most substantive theorists agree on a basic criterion: Government policies should guarantee civil liberties (for example, freedom of religion and freedom of expression) and civil rights (for example, protection against discrimination in employment and housing). According to this standard, the claim that the United States is a

. . . *Please Help Me Pass This Test!*
In reality, prayer in school is a serious matter. Surveys regularly show that most Americans believe that schools should be allowed to start each day with a prayer, but the Supreme Court has held that school-organized prayers would violate the Constitution. By making such decisions, the Court is protecting minority rights, but it is denying majority rule.

democracy rests on its record in ensuring its citizens these liberties and rights. (We look at how good this record is in Chapters 17 and 18.)

Agreement among substantive theorists breaks down when discussion moves from civil rights to *social* rights (adequate health care, quality education, decent housing) and *economic* rights (private property, steady employment). They disagree most sharply on whether a government must promote social equality to qualify as a democracy. For example, must a state guarantee unemployment benefits and adequate public housing to be called democratic? Some insist that policies that promote social equality are essential to democratic government.[10] Others limit their requirements to policies that safeguard civil liberties—guaranteed freedoms of action—and civil rights—social treatment to which citizens are entitled.

The political ideology of a theorist tends to explain his or her position on what democracy really requires in substantive policies. Conservative theorists have a narrow view of the scope of democratic government, and a narrow view of the social and economic rights guaranteed by that government. Liberal theorists believe that a democratic government should guarantee its citizens a much broader spectrum of social and economic rights. In Chapters 15 and 16, we review important social and economic policies that our government has actually followed over time. Keep in mind, however, that what the government *has* done is not necessarily a good guide to what a democratic government *should* do.

Procedural Democracy Versus Substantive Democracy

There is a problem with the substantive view of democracy. It does not provide clear, precise criteria that allow us to determine whether a government is or is not democratic. It is, in fact, open to unending arguments over which government policies are truly democratic in the substantive sense. Theorists are free to promote their pet values—separation of church and state, guaranteed employment, equal rights for women, whatever—under the guise of substantive democracy.

There is also a problem with the procedural viewpoint. Although it presents specific criteria for democratic government, those criteria can produce undesirable social policies that prey on minorities. This clashes with **minority rights**—the idea that citizens are entitled to certain things that cannot be denied by majority decisions. There are many different opinions on what those "certain things" are, but freedom of religion is definitely one of them. One way to protect minority rights is to limit the principle of majority rule—to require extraordinary majorities when decisions must be made on certain subjects or to put the issue in the Constitution, beyond the reach of majority rule.

The issue of prayer in school is a good example of the limits on majority rule. No matter how large, majorities in Congress cannot pass a law to allow organized prayer in public schools because the Supreme Court has determined that the Constitution forbids this kind of law. The Constitution could be changed so that it no longer protects religious minorities, but amendment is a cumbersome process that involves ex-

Social Equality in the Classroom
Would our government be democratic if it did not provide for equal educational opportunity through integrated schools? Substantive theorists might argue that democratic government in a multiracial society requires integrated schools. Procedural theorists would leave the issue to be decided by public opinion.

traordinary majorities. When limits like these are put on the principle of majority rule, the minority often rules instead. Those who are committed to majority rule in the procedural conception of democracy have no alternative: They must insist on *unlimited* majority rule, then trust in government by the people.

Clearly, procedural and substantive democracy are not always compatible. In choosing one over the other, we are also choosing to focus on either procedures or policies. As authors of this text, we favor the procedural conception of democracy because it more closely approaches the classical definition of *democracy*—"government by the people." And procedural democracy is founded on clear, well-established rules for decision making. But the theory has a serious drawback: It allows a democratic government to enact policies that can violate the substantive principles of democracy.

Is this a real problem? Or is it simply a question of definition? Because people equate democracy with desirable government, they have trouble accepting undesirable policies in a democratic government. Early political theorists did not attach such overtones to the idea of democracy; they saw it simply as a mechanism for making government decisions. If we do the same, if we realize that democratic government and desirable policies are not necessarily synonymous, then we should be able to live with a political system that sets standards for the decision-making process if not the decisions themselves.

INSTITUTIONAL MODELS OF DEMOCRACY

A small group of people can agree to make democratic decisions directly by using the principles of universal participation, political equality, and majority rule. But even the smallest nations have too many citizens to practice direct democracy. If nations want democracy, they must achieve it through some form of representative government, electing officials to make government decisions. Even then, democratic government is not guaranteed. Governments must have a means for determining what the people want, as well as some means for translating those wants into decisions. In other words, democratic government requires **institutional mechanisms**—established procedures and organizations—to translate public opinion into government policy, to be responsive. Elections, political parties, legislatures, and interest groups (which we discuss in later chapters) are all examples of such institutional mechanisms in politics.

Some democratic theorists favor institutions that tie government decisions closely to the desires of the majority of citizens. If most citizens want laws against the sale of pornography, then the government should outlaw pornography. If citizens want more money spent on defense and less on social welfare (or vice versa), the government should act accordingly. For these theorists, the essence of democratic government is majority rule and responsiveness.

Other theorists place less importance on the principles of majority rule and responsiveness. They do not believe in relying heavily on mass opinion; instead, they favor institutions that allow groups of citizens to defend their interests in government decisions.

Both schools hold a procedural view of democracy but differ in how they interpret *government by the people.* We can summarize these theoretical positions using two alternative models of democracy. As a model, each is a hypothetical plan, a normative blueprint, for achieving democratic government through institutional mechanisms. The *majoritarian model* values participation by the people in general; the *pluralist model* values participation by the people in groups.

The Majoritarian Model of Democracy

The **majoritarian model of democracy** relies on the classical, textbook theory of democracy. It interprets *government by the people* as government by the *majority* of the people. The majoritarian model tries to approximate the people's role in a direct democracy within the limitations of representative government. To force the government to respond to public opinion, the majoritarian model depends on several mechanisms that allow the people to participate directly in the political system.

The popular election of government officials is the primary mechanism for democratic government in the majoritarian model. Citizens are expected to control their representatives' behavior by choosing wisely in the first place and by re-electing or defeating public officials according to their performance. Elections fulfill the first three principles of procedural democratic theory: universal participation, political equality, and majority rule. And the prospect of re-election and the threat of defeat at the polls are expected to motivate public officials to be responsive.

Usually we think of elections only as mechanisms for choosing between candidates for public office. Majoritarian theorists also see them as a means for deciding government policies. An election on a policy issue is called a **referendum.** There are no provisions for referenda at the national level, but they are common at the state level and appeared on the ballot in most states in the 1986 general elections. Citizens in Oregon, for example, had the opportunity to prohibit the use of state money for funding abortions. (Oregonians voted against the prohibition, 55 percent to 45 percent.[11])

In the majoritarian model, citizens are expected to do more than vote. They are expected to learn about the issues, to discuss politics in community meetings, and even to propose legislation through a process called the **initiative.** This process allows citizens who have circulated petitions and gathered a required number of signatures to place issues before the legislature or before the people in referenda. (In fact, the Oregon abortion referendum arose from a citizens' initiative.)

The most fervent advocates of majoritarian democracy would like to see modern technology used to maximize the government's responsiveness to the majority. Some have proposed incorporating public opinion polls, first used regularly in the 1930s, into government decision making. More recently, some have suggested that computers could be used in the referendum process. For instance, citizens could vote on an issue by inserting plastic identification cards into computer terminals installed in all homes.[12] People disagree on the merits of "video voting," but it certainly is technically possible (see Politics in the Information Age 2.1).

Saying No to Nukes
Citizens of Boston, Massachusetts, sign a petition to protest the opening of a nuclear power plant in nearby Seabrook, New Hampshire. Heated controversy over public safety issues has blocked the activation of the $5.4 billion reactor. Massachusetts officials have aided the "stop Seabrook" cause by demanding comprehensive and viable evacuation plans. Signing petitions to request government action is one way that people can involve themselves in politics.

The majoritarian model contends that citizens can control their government if they have adequate mechanisms for popular participation. It also assumes that citizens are knowledgeable about government and politics; that they want to participate in the political process; and that they make rational decisions in voting for their elected representatives.

If these factors are truly necessary to the functioning of majoritarian democracy, then the majoritarian model in the United States is in trouble. Only 26 percent of a national sample of voters interviewed just after the 1984 election said that they "followed what's going on" in government "most of the time." More (37 percent) said that they followed politics "only now and then" or "hardly at all." Further, as we discuss in Chapter 7, voter turnout in presidential elections has fallen to little more than half of the eligible electorate. And those who do vote often choose candidates more from habit (along party lines) than from a close examination of the candidates' positions on the issues.

An Alternative Model: Pluralist Democracy

For years, political scientists struggled valiantly to reconcile the majoritarian model of democracy with polls that showed a widespread ignorance of politics among the American people. One example illustrates the shallowness of public opinion. Throughout President Ronald Reagan's administration, the U.S. government supported the Nicaraguan rebels (the Contras) against the Soviet-backed Sandinista regime. Reagan often described the rebels as "freedom fighters." Still, at the height of congressional debate on a key vote to grant $100 million in aid to the

POLITICS IN THE INFORMATION AGE 2.1

Electronic Democracy

Thanks to computers and telecommunications, we could now involve the masses of citizens directly in government decisions by having them vote on issues using computers in their own homes. Would this be a good idea? A philosopher writing in *PC World*, a computer magazine, sees problems but urges us to trust the people (and the computers).

Imagine a nationwide interactive communications network that connects with every home's personal computer, telephone, and TV set. On this network local, state, and national issues are debated and decided periodically. Each viewpoint is clearly and fairly framed, and unpopular views are defended vigorously by a "public dissenter." Voters, using individual passwords to prevent fraud, cast their ballots at the keyboard. The true voice of the people is regularly and authoritatively expressed. The electronic referendum becomes a part of our lives—as popular as "Monday Night Football," though with much more at stake. . . .

Electronic democracy would profoundly change the way we view "government by the people." Today we popularly elect representatives, who then make policy affecting our lives. Electronic democracy promises speed, accuracy, and convenience without representation. Every issue of local, state, or national importance can be put directly to the voter. Problems of fairness, of course, would have to be solved in the design of such a system. Problems like ensuring universal access and guarding against fraud—which have been with us since the beginning of our republic—would have to be solved. But the key question about electronic democracy is not so much its feasibility as its desirability. . . .

Would "one terminal, one vote" democracy improve the quality of decisions made? Would the First Amendment be defeated if put to a vote of the American people? Would the taking of American hostages by a foreign power

cause a government instantly responsive to the will of its citizens to retaliate by reflex? The masses have commonly been judged as being intemperate in war, shortsighted in peace, and unable to deal with the refinements of economic policy. Recent national polls on political issues tend to support this view.

But if we cannot trust ourselves, who can we trust? If genuine self-government is dangerous, are we not saying that democracy is dangerous—unless restrained by the aristocrat? Is government by the terminal what we really want? Or should we honestly admit that we feel competent to choose our leaders but not to guide them? . . .

If we reject computerized, direct democracy because we fear the outcome, then the whole concept of democracy is in question. Perhaps it is not computers that present the real problem, but placing the ultimate authority in the hands of the governed. And so the answer is at hand: too much democracy—in any form—is dangerous.

I reject this answer because I am a democrat. I realize that people can and sometimes do make terrible mistakes, but I trust them in the long run—certainly more than any elite body. A computerized system of direct participation in public affairs might bring about a better, more robust democracy. . . .

Computers cannot produce a spirit of universal participation, but they can support it. If politics becomes more tangible, more countable, and more keenly sensed and effective because of computers, we may yet revive our flagging democracy. The personal computer, tied to a world of computers, can reinforce the spirit of democracy and endear it to us.

Source: Carl Cohen, *PC World*, July 1984, pp. 21–22. Copyright 1984 PC World Communications. Reprinted by permission.

rebels, only 38 percent of those polled in a national survey realized that the United States and the Contras were on the same side.[13]

Polling did not become an established research tool for studying public opinion until the 1950s. When repeated polls revealed how little the public actually knows about politics, the assumptions of majoritarian democracy came into question. Obviously, the wisdom of government by the people—the very idea of democracy itself—also came into question. If most voters do not know enough to make rational political judgments, why pretend that they should govern at all? In short, why argue for democracy?

In the 1950s, an alternative interpretation of democracy evolved, one tailored to the limited knowledge and participation of the *real* electorate, not the perfection of the ideal one. It was based on the concept of **pluralism**—that modern society consists of innumerable groups of people who share economic, religious, ethnic, or cultural interests. Often people with similar interests organize formal groups: The Future Farmers of America, the Junior Chamber of Commerce, and the Knights of Columbus, for example. Many of these social groups have little contact with government; but occasionally they find themselves backing or opposing government policy. When an organized group seeks to influence government policy, it is called an **interest group.** Many interest groups regularly spend a great deal of time and money trying to influence government policy (see Chapter 9). Among them are the AFL-CIO, the Associated Milk Producers, the National Education Association (NEA), the Moral Majority, Operation PUSH, the National Organization for Women (NOW), and, of course, the NRA.

The **pluralist model of democracy** interprets *government by the people* to mean government by people operating through competing interest groups. According to this model, democracy exists when many (plural) organizations operate separately from the government, press their interests on the government, and even challenge the government.[14] Compared with majoritarian thinking, pluralist theory shifts the focus of democratic government from the mass electorate to organized groups. It changes the criterion for democratic government from responsiveness to mass public opinion to responsiveness to organized groups of citizens.

The two major mechanisms in a pluralist democracy are interest groups and a decentralized structure of government that provides ready access to public officials and that is open to hearing the groups' arguments for or against government policies. In a centralized structure, decisions are made at one point, the top of the hierarchy. The few decision makers at the top are too busy to hear the claims of competing interest groups or to consider those claims in making their decisions. But a decentralized, complex government structure offers the access and openness necessary for pluralist democracy. The ideal is a system that divides government authority among numerous institutions with overlapping authority. Under such a system, competing interest groups have alternative points of access to present and argue their claims.

Our Constitution approaches the pluralist ideal in the way it divides authority among the branches of government. When the National Association for the Advancement of Colored People (NAACP) could not get Congress to outlaw segregated schools in the South, it turned to the federal court system, which did what Congress would not. When Reagan submitted a budget that cut funding for Amtrak trains, train travelers organized and protested to Congress, which restored the funding. According to pluralist democracy, if all opposing interests are allowed to organize, and if the system can be kept open so that all substantial claims have an opportunity to be heard, then the diverse needs of a pluralist society will be served when an issue is decided.

Why They Are Called Lobbyists

At the national level, interest groups are usually represented by highly paid lobbyists. These people are called lobbyists because they often gather in the lobby outside congressional meeting rooms, positioned to contact senators and representatives coming and going. Here, lobbyists are waiting to help members of the House Ways and Means Committee understand the importance of their pet tax loopholes.

Although many scholars have contributed to the model, pluralist democracy is most closely identified with political scientist Robert Dahl. According to Dahl, the fundamental axiom of pluralist democracy is that "instead of a single center of sovereign power there must be multiple centers of power, none of which is or can be wholly sovereign."[15] Some watchwords of pluralist democracy, therefore, are *divided authority, decentralization,* and *open access.*

The Majoritarian Model Versus the Pluralist Model

In majoritarian democracy, individual citizens—not interest groups—control government actions. These citizens must be knowledgeable about government and willing to participate in the electoral process. Majoritarian democracy relies on electoral mechanisms that harness the majority's power to make decisions. Conclusive elections and a centralized structure of government are mechanisms that aid majority rule.

Pluralism does not demand much knowledge from citizens in general. It requires specialized knowledge only from groups of citizens, in particular their leaders. Unlike majoritarian democracy, pluralist democracy seeks to limit majority action so that interest groups can be heard. It relies on strong interest groups and a decentralized government structure—mechanisms that interfere with majority rule, thereby protecting minority interests. We could even say that pluralism allows minorities to rule.

An Undemocratic Model: Elite Theory

If pluralist democracy allows minorities to rule, how does it differ from **elite theory**—the view that a small group of people (a minority) makes most important government decisions? According to elite theory, important government decisions are made by an identifiable and stable minority that shares certain characteristics, usually vast wealth and business connections.* Elitism contends that these few individuals wield power in America because they control its key financial, communications, industrial, and governmental institutions.

According to elite theory, the United States is not a democracy but an oligarchy. Although the voters appear to control government through elections, elite theorists argue that the powerful few in society manage to define the issues and to constrain the possible outcomes of government decisions to suit their own interests. Clearly, elite theory describes a government that operates in an undemocratic fashion.

Elite theory appeals to many people, especially those who believe that wealth dominates politics. The theory also provides plausible explanations for specific political decisions. For example, government spending for new military weapons systems—including enormous overruns in estimated costs—often seems to be controlled by agreements between the military and giant defense contractors.[16] Even President Eisenhower, himself a former five-star general, warned of the influence of the "military-industrial complex" on government policy. (In Chapter 19, we examine that influence in more detail.)

Elite theory breaks down, however, when we try to use it to explain a broader range of political decisions. Dahl suggests that convincing research on the ruling elite model must meet three tests:

1. The hypothetical ruling elite must be a well-defined group.

2. A fair sample of cases involving key political decisions must exist. In those decisions, the preferences of the hypothetical ruling elite must be shown to run counter to the preferences of any other likely group. . . .

3. In such cases, the preferences of the elite must regularly prevail.[17]

Some researchers have attempted the first test, defining the ruling group. One study identified 7,314 "elite positions" in the corporate, public interest, and governmental sectors of society.[18] Although this number represents only a tiny fraction of the nation's population, 7,314 rulers somehow seems many more than "the few."

The second test, identifying a number of government decisions that pit the special interests of the ruling elite against the interests of others, has not been performed in serious research at the national level. This means the third test, determining whether or not elite interests regularly

---

* The classic book on elite theory in American politics is C. Wright Mills, *The Power Elite* (New York: Oxford University Press, 1956). Actually, elite theory argues that elite rule is inevitable in *every* government, indeed in every large organization. See Thomas R. Dye, *Who's Running America? The Conservative Years* (Englewood Cliffs, N.J.: Prentice-Hall, 1986), especially pp. 2-6, for a summary of elite theory.

The Power Elite?
This picture symbolizes the underlying notion of elite theory—that government is driven by wealth. In truth, wealthy people usually have more influence in government than do people of ordinary means. Critics of elite theory point out that it is difficult to demonstrate that an identifiable ruling elite usually sticks together and gets its way in government policy.

prevail in such decisions, also has not been met. Careful studies of decision making in American cities, which should be even more susceptible to elite rule than the nation as a whole, have shown that different groups win on different issues.[19] This also seems to be true in some cases at the national level. For instance, the giant oil, chemical, and steel industries do not always triumph over environmental groups on the issue of air pollution. And what was once the nation's largest corporation, AT&T, was forced to break up its telephone monopoly in suits brought by much smaller communications companies.

The available evidence of government decisions on many different topics does not generally support elite theory—at least in the sense that an identifiable ruling elite usually gets its way in government policy. But elite theory is not dead; it is still forcefully argued by radical critics of American politics.[20] We believe, however, that pluralist theory offers a more satisfactory interpretation of American politics today.

Elite Theory Versus Pluralist Theory

The key difference between elite and pluralist theory lies in the durability of the ruling minority. Unlike elite theory, pluralist theory does not define government conflict in terms of a minority versus *the* majority; instead, it sees many minorities vying with one another in different policy areas. In the management of national forests, for example, many interest groups—logging companies, recreational campers, environmentalists—have joined the political competition. They press their various interests on government through group representatives who are well informed about the issues as they affect group members (see Feature 2.2). According to elite theory, the financial resources of big logging companies ought to win out over the arguments of campers and environmentalists, but this does not always happen.

The pluralist model holds that this type of competition among minority interests also takes place in other policy arenas, including transportation, agriculture, public utilities, and urban housing. Although some groups with "better connections" in government may win more often in individual arenas, no identifiable elite wins consistently across a broad range of issues. The pluralist model, then, rejects the primary implication of elite theory, that a single group dominates government decisions.

Instead, pluralist democracy makes a virtue of the struggle among minority interests. It argues for government that accommodates this struggle and channels the result into government action. According to pluralist democracy, the public is best served if the government structure provides access for different groups to press their claims in competition with one another. Notice that pluralist democracy does not insist that all groups have equal influence on government decisions. In the political

Trees or Lumber?
These photos illustrate the conflict between environmentalists and loggers. Environmentalists envision forests as natural havens from the bustle of modern life; loggers regard them as cash crops for harvesting. Because people cannot build homes or print textbooks without lumber or wood pulp, government must somehow strike a balance between the legitimate interests of these two competing groups.

FEATURE 2.2

Interest Group Conflict over Uses of Forests

According to pluralism, modern society is composed of diverse groups struggling to advance their competing interests. The interplay of interest groups trying to influence government policy is clear in the debate over the use of the national forests. Should they be used primarily for commerce or recreation? Or should they simply be preserved? This news item explains the issues involved.

KALISPELL, Mont., April 12—The future of the country's 120 national forests is being laid out in a process that has attracted criticism both from people who want more economic development of the forests and from those who want less.

In the big Flathead National Forest here in northern Montana, those issues are drawn as clearly as anywhere. People who believe the forests should produce timber and minerals for local jobs are opposing those who want the forest to be managed more like a national park, as a place for recreation and wildlife. . . .

The plans being drawn up are the first long-range, forest-by-forest management blueprints that were required under the National Forest Management Act of 1976. The act requires forest supervisors to look 50 years ahead and draw up detailed plans for each of the 10- to 15-year intervals between now and that "planning horizon." The plans must spell out how much timber cutting will be allowed, where oil and gas drilling may take place, what roads should be built, if any, and what lands should be set aside to remain wild.

Conservationists argue that the act was drawn up to curb policies that resulted in excessive clearcutting of lumber, land erosion, infringement on wildlife habitat and the like. . . .

They say their fears that the timber industry would try to circumvent the act in the new forest plans were confirmed when early draft plans envisaged a massive increase in timber harvesting. Only a public outcry forced the service to retreat, say people like Peter Coppleman, senior counsel at the **Wilderness Society,** a conservation group based in Washington. . . .

Edgar B. Brannon, supervisor of the Flathead National Forest, divides the contending forces in this planning process between "the utilitarians" and the "naturists." To varying degrees, he said, their opposing views are reflected in continuing disagreements about the proper use of the more than 400 million acres of public land in the West and in the rest of the country. . . .

The debate over how national forests should be used is not a new one. Early in the century Gifford Pinchot, the country's first forester and founder of the national forest system, stressed the careful management of woodlands to increase their economic benefit to man. Although he is remembered as a conservationist, he was nonetheless opposed by John Muir, who argued for protecting the bulk of American wild lands from any economic use and went on to found the **Sierra Club,** a conservation lobby. . . .

The timber industry, the dominant but declining source of jobs in the interior Northwest, says the trend toward reduced timber harvests reflects the rise in power of the environmental movement, or the "preservationists," as they are beginning to be called by opponents like John Benneth, director of the **American Forest Institute,** an industry group. . . .

Richard Kuhl, head of the Flathead chapter of the **Montana Wilderness Association,** counters that economics, and not forest policy, is what is hurting the lumber industry. . . .

Of the 32 national forests that have completed their 10- to 15-year plans, 22 have attracted 139 separate appeals, and all but a handful of the appeals are from conservation groups. The 10 remaining forest plans have so far drawn no appeals. . . .

Mr. Brannon's plan for the Flathead National Forest has drawn 39 appeals, 37 of them from environmentalists asking for more wilderness, more wildlife sanctuaries and protection of scenic vistas and the like, and two from industry asking for more timber cutting. . . .

"Because this is the first time around and it is precedent-setting," he said, "we're getting a lot of appeals from groups that want to establish a position, a posture, that they hope will influence later decisions."

struggle, wealthy well-organized groups have an inherent advantage over poorer, inadequately organized groups. In fact, unorganized segments of the population may not even get their concerns placed on the agenda for government consideration, which means that what government does not discuss (its *non*decisions) may be as significant as what it does discuss and decide. Nevertheless, pluralist theory is silent about the proper outcome of the group struggle. As long as all groups are able to participate vigorously in the decision-making process, the process is democratic.

Obviously, pluralist democracy differs from the classic conception based on universal participation, political equality, and majority rule. But the pluralist reliance on access is compatible with contemporary thinking that democratic government should be open to groups that seek redress of grievances. The pluralist concept also fits the facts about the limited political knowledge of most American citizens. Clearly, pluralist democracy is worthy of being embraced as a rival model to majoritarianism, the traditional model of procedural democracy.

DEMOCRACIES AROUND THE WORLD

We have proposed two models of democratic government. The majoritarian model conforms to classical democratic theory for a representative government. According to this model, democracy is a hypothetical form of government that features prompt and complete responsiveness to majority opinion. According to the pluralist model, a government is democratic if it allows minority interests to organize and press their claims freely on government.

No government actually achieves the high degree of responsiveness demanded by the majoritarian model. It is also true that no government offers complete and equal access to the claims of all competing groups, as required by the pluralist model. Still, some nations approach these ideals closely enough to be considered practicing democracies.

Testing for Democratic Government

How do we decide which countries qualify as practicing democracies? We cannot measure a government's degree of responsiveness or access directly, so we must turn to indirect tests of democracy. One test is to look for traits normally associated with democratic government—whether defined from a procedural or from a substantive viewpoint. One scholar, for example, established five criteria for a democracy:[21]

1. *Most adults can participate in the electoral process.* (Embodies the principle of universal participation)
2. *Citizens' votes are secret and are not coerced.* (Embodies the principle of political equality)
3. *Leaders are chosen in free elections, contested by at least two viable political parties.* (Embodies the principle of majority rule)
4. *The government bases its legitimacy on representing the desires of its citizens.* (Embodies the principle of responsiveness)

5. *Citizens, leaders, and party officials enjoy basic freedoms of speech, press, assembly, religion, and organization.* (Substantive policies that create conditions for the practice of the other criteria)

Because the United States fits all these criteria to a fairly high degree, it qualifies as a democracy. How about the other nations of the world? Applying standards similar to these to all nations with a population over 3 million, one writer identified just eighteen nations in addition to the United States as democracies.[22] Like the United States, the following nations have government traditions of widespread participation, political equality, and free elections to choose representatives who pay close attention to public opinion.

Australia	France	New Zealand
Austria	Ireland	Norway
Belgium	Israel	Sweden
Canada	Italy	Switzerland
Denmark	Japan	United Kingdom
Finland	Netherlands	West Germany

Given that more than ninety nations have populations greater than 3 million, nineteen democracies—only about 20 percent of the world's nations—do not seem like very many. By any reckoning, democratic government is relatively rare across the world.

Four of the five criteria above apply to government procedures rather than to the substance of government policy. But all of these criteria apply equally to the majoritarian and pluralist models of democracy. Although the United States clearly qualifies as a democracy according to these criteria, we cannot use them to judge whether it is closer to a majoritarian or to a pluralist democracy.

American Democracy: More Pluralist than Majoritarian

It is not idle speculation to ask what kind of democracy is practiced in the United States. The answer to this question can help us understand why our government can be called *democratic* despite a low level of citizen participation in politics and despite government actions that run contrary to public opinion. The answer may also help us understand why many Americans are not satisfied with the democratic form of government here. As shown in Compared With What? 2.1, only 59 percent of a national sample reported that they were satisfied with the way democracy works in the United States.

Throughout the rest of this book, we probe more deeply to determine how well the United States fits the two alternative models of democracy: majoritarian and pluralist. If our answer is not already apparent, it soon will be. We argue that the political system in the United States rates relatively low according to the majoritarian model of democracy, but that it fulfills the pluralist model very well. It should not be surprising, then, that 80 percent of the wealthiest group of respondents in a national survey were satisfied with the way democracy works in the United States

COMPARED WITH WHAT? 2.1

Satisfaction with Democracy, by Nation

Compared with citizens in twelve other Western countries, Americans are only moderately satisfied with their form of democratic government. When asked in 1985 whether they were "satisfied with the way democracy works" in their country, respondents in five other nations reported higher levels of satisfaction than the 59 percent who were satisfied with "the way democracy is working" in the United States. Of the seven nations whose respondents were less satisfied, three (Spain, Greece, and Portugal) do not have democratic traditions. Spain and Portugal suffered under decades of dictatorship until the late 1970s, and Greece has had a spotty record of free elections since World War II.

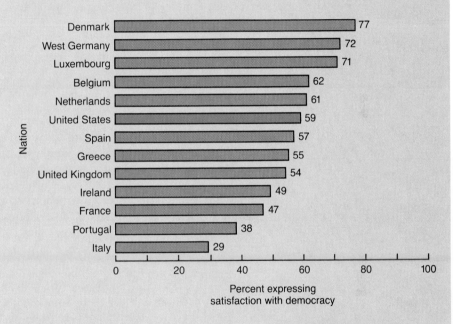

Source: Data for the United States are from *The Gallup Poll, Public Opinion 1985* (Wilmington, Del.: Scholarly Resources, 1986), p. 32; data for the other nations are from Jacques-René Rabier, Helene Riffault, and Ronald Inglehart, *Euro-Barometer 24: Entry of Spain and Portugal, October, 1985* (Ann Arbor, Mich.: Inter-University Consortium for Political and Social Research, Study 8513, 1986), pp. 10–11.

compared with only 43 percent of the poorest group (see Figure 2.1). An advocate of majoritarian democracy once wrote, "The flaw in the pluralist heaven is that the heavenly chorus sings with a strong upper-class accent."[23]

This evaluation of the pluralist nature of American democracy may not mean much to you now. But you will learn that the pluralist model makes the United States look far more democratic than does the majoritarian model. Eventually, it will be up to *you* to decide the answers to

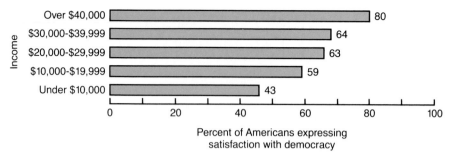

Satisfaction with Democracy in the United States, by Income
As shown in Compared With What? 2.1, Americans surveyed in 1985 were only moderately satisfied with "the way democracy is working" in the United States when compared with citizens in other Western nations. But satisfaction in the United States was closely linked to income. Nearly twice the percentage of the wealthiest respondents were satisfied with the workings of democracy compared with the poorest respondents. There were only slight differences in satisfaction among the vast majority of people in the three middle categories. (Source: The Gallup Poll, Public Opinion 1985 [Wilmington, Del.: Scholarly Resources, 1986], p. 32.)

Figure 2.1

these three questions: Is the pluralist model really an adequate expression of democracy, or is it a perversion of classical ideals designed to portray America as democratic when it really is not? Does the majoritarian model result in a "better" type of democracy? If so, is it possible to devise new mechanisms of government to produce a desirable mix of majority rule and minority rights? These questions should play in the back of your mind as you read more about the workings of American government in meeting the challenge of democracy.

SUMMARY

There are not many democracies in the world. In fact, scholars agree that only about nineteen of the world's larger countries are democratic. Is the United States a democracy? Most scholars believe that it is. But what kind of democracy is it? The answer depends on our definition of *democracy.* Some believe democracy is procedural in nature; they define *democracy* as a form of government in which the people govern through certain institutional mechanisms. Others hold to substantive theory, claiming a government is democratic if its policies promote civil liberties and rights.

In this book, we use the procedural conception of democracy, distinguishing between direct and indirect democracy. In a direct democracy, all citizens gather to govern themselves according to the principles of universal participation, political equality, and majority rule. In an indirect democracy, the citizens

elect representatives to govern for them. If a representative government is elected mostly in accordance with the three principles listed above and is also usually responsive to public opinion, then it qualifies as a democracy.

Procedural democratic theory has produced rival institutional models of democratic government. The classical majoritarian model assumes that people are knowledgeable about government, that they want to participate in the political process, and that they carefully and rationally choose among candidates. But surveys of public opinion and behavior, and voter turnouts, show that this is not the case for most Americans. The pluralist model of democracy was devised to accommodate these findings. It argues that democracy in a complex society requires only that government allow private interests to organize and to press their competing claims openly in the political arena. It differs from elite theory by arguing that different minorities win on different issues. Pluralist democracy works better in a decentralized, organizationally complex government structure than in a centralized, hierarchical one.

In Chapter 1, we talked about three political values—freedom, order, and equality. Here, we've looked at two models of democracy—majoritarian and pluralist. These five concepts are critical to an understanding of American government. The values we described in the last chapter underlie the two questions with which the text began:

■ Which is better: to live under a government that allows individuals complete freedom to do whatever they please or under one that enforces strict law and order?

■ Which is better: to allow businesses and private clubs to discriminate in choosing their customers and members or to pass laws that enforce equality among races and sexes?

The models of democracy we've examined here add another:

■ Which is better: a government that responds immediately to public opinion on all matters or one that responds deliberately to organized groups that argue their cases effectively?

If by the end of this book you understand the issues involved in answering these questions, you will have learned a great deal about American government.

Key Terms

autocracy (monarchy)
aristocracy (oligarchy)
ruling elite
democracy (polyarchy)
procedural democratic theory
universal participation
political equality
majority rule
direct democracy
indirect democracy
representative government
responsiveness
substantive democratic theory
minority rights
institutional mechanisms
majoritarian model of democracy
referendum
initiative
pluralism
interest group
pluralist model of democracy
elite theory

Selected Readings

Barber, Benjamin R. *Strong Democracy: Participatory Politics for a New Age.* Berkeley, Calif.: University of California Press, 1984. Barber favors a "strong democracy," a government that features a high degree of participation by individuals, much as a direct democracy does. He suggests specific institutional reforms to stimulate civic discussion and popular participation in government.

Dahl, Robert A. *Dilemmas of Pluralist Democracy: Autonomy vs. Control.* New Haven, Conn.: Yale University Press, 1982. Dahl is the leading theorist on pluralist democracy. This book clearly explains the pluralist model with reference to governments in other countries as well as that in the United States.

Green, Philip. *Retrieving Democracy: In Search of Civic Equality.* Totowa, N.J.: Rowman and Allanheld, 1985. Green contends that representative government is "pseudodemocracy" because government is not under the direct control of the people. He argues for "egalitarian democracy," a society of truly equal citizens. The book urges fundamental economic reforms to produce a redistribution of wealth, which would facilitate direct democracy.

Mansbridge, Jane. *Beyond Adversary Democracy.* New York: Basic Books, 1982. Mansbridge contrasts "adversary democracy," the kind of open contest that occurs among groups in a large nation, with "unitary democracy," a cooperative form of decision making based on common rather than opposing interests. She illustrates unitary democracy with two case studies of decision making: one in a New England village, the other in an urban crisis center.

Pateman, Carole. *Participation and Democratic Theory.* Cambridge, Eng.: Cambridge University Press, 1970. This work is a highly respected analysis of the importance of individual participation in government to democratic theory. Many later studies draw heavily on this influential study.

Spitz, Elaine. *Majority Rule.* Chatham, N.J.: Chatham House, 1984. Spitz reviews the various meanings of *majority* and *rule* and the place of majority rule in democratic theory, then goes beyond the narrow definition of *majority rule* as a method of deciding between policies. She argues that majoritarianism should be viewed as a "social practice" among people who want to hold their society together when making decisions.

Essay A

Transformations in American Politics: Into the Information Age

The pattern and practice of politics in the United States reflect the nature of our society. Because American society has changed greatly since the Constitution was written and our government formed, politics today is vastly different from politics two hundred years ago. Two changes in particular have had a major impact on American politics: the evolution of the occupational structure and our society's growing technological sophistication.

This country began as an agricultural society; more than 60 percent of the work force were farmers, and the vast majority of people lived in rural areas. Government during this *agricultural age* was minimal. Most politicians were members of the landed gentry; the political process was characterized by the courtesy and deference of its participants. But the industrialization that began after the Civil War affected the composition of the work force. By the 1900s, a plurality of workers had blue-collar jobs, mostly in manufacturing. Huge cities grew to house these workers. Government during the *industrial age* grew to help spur industrial growth and deal with the problems of immigration, urban crowding, and monopolistic business practices. Politics became more oriented to the masses, as candidates courted workers' votes and workers themselves entered the political arena.

The Residence of David Twining, 1787, *by Edward Hicks, 1845–1848. Abby Aldrich Rockefeller Folk Art Center, Williamsburg, Virginia.*

Top: *An assembly line at Ford Motor Company's Highland Park, Michigan, plant, c. 1914.* Bottom left: *An ore breaker, destined for the Utah Copper Company, under construction at the Allis-Chalmers plant in Milwaukee, Wisconsin, c. 1940–1950.* Bottom right: *The shipping department of a salmon canning factory in Astoria, Oregon, 1904.*

Another major change in the work force occurred around 1970. For the first time, white-collar workers, who process and transmit information, outnumbered blue-collar workers, who produce goods. Although some refer to this new era as the "postindustrial society," we prefer to call it the *information age*.

Government in the information age plays an increasingly active role. For example, it tries to stimulate economic growth yet stabilize the economy, protect civil liberties and promote civil rights, and deal with environmental hazards. Politics in the information age relies heavily on social statistics, economic indicators, expert reports, and scientific knowledge in proposing public policy.

We cannot underestimate the importance of technology to politics in the information age. Politicians use information gleaned from poll data and test marketing results to court the support of various groups. As a result, candidates seeking election become more independent of traditional institutions, such as political parties, newspapers, and labor unions. By the same token, the public—often through the media—has greater and faster access to information previously available only to government officials, if available at all. Consequently, more participants in and out of government monitor more actions of government directly. In principle, this greater access to information serves both the majoritarian and pluralist models of democracy; in practice, the particular issue and setting determine which model is better served.

All players in today's political contests depend on the major instruments of the information age: government statistics, scientific findings, public opinion polls, the media, computers, satellites. To examine that debt closely, we have included features called "Politics in the Information Age" throughout this text. The reliance of politics on technology will undoubtedly increase with each advance in collecting, analyzing, transmitting, and consuming information.

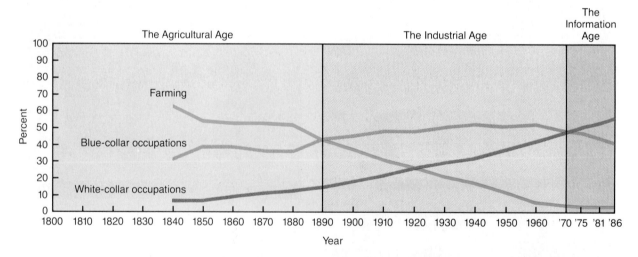

The Transformation of Occupation, 1840–1986

Source: Data for 1840–1890 come from the U.S. Bureau of the Census, Historical Statistics of the United States: Colonial Times to 1970, Bicentennial Edition, Part I, p. 139. Figures for agriculture and fishing are combined for farming percentages. Figures for teaching and trade are combined for white-collar percentages. All other figures are combined for blue-collar percentages. Data for 1900–1950 come from the U.S. Bureau of the Census, Occupation Trends in the United States, 1900 to 1950, p. 7. Figures for manual and service occupations are combined for blue-collar percentages. Data for 1960 come from Historical Statistics of the United States, p. 139. Data for 1970–1981 come from the U.S. Bureau of the Census, Statistical Abstract of the United States, 1982–1983, p. 386. Data for 1986 come from the U.S. Bureau of the Census, Statistical Abstract of the United States, 1987, pp. 376–377.

Top: *Exterior view of a modern office building.* Right: *IBM service coordinators in Atlanta assign repair personnel to on-site jobs through a computer-based system.* Bottom right: *Portable satellite dishes used by television news organizations, at the site of an Amtrak train crash in Maryland, 1987.*

PART II

FOUNDATIONS
OF
AMERICAN
GOVERNMENT

3

The Constitution

T he midnight burglars made a mistake. It led to their capture in the early hours of June 17, 1972, and triggered a constitutional struggle that eventually involved the president of the United States, the Congress, and the Supreme Court. The burglars' mistake seems small: They left a piece of tape over the lock they had tripped to enter the Watergate office and apartment complex in Washington, D.C. But a security guard discovered their tampering and called the police, who surprised the burglars in the offices of the Democratic National Committee at 2:30 A.M. They arrested five men—four Cuban exiles and a former CIA agent. The burglars wore business suits and surgical gloves. They also carried the equipment they needed to photograph the files and bug the offices of the Democratic National Committee.

The arrests took place a month before the 1972 Democratic National Convention. Investigative reporting by the *Washington Post*'s Carl Bernstein and Bob Woodward uncovered a link between the Watergate burglary and the forthcoming election.[1] The burglars were carrying the telephone number of another former CIA agent, now working in the White House. At a news conference on June 22, President Richard Nixon said, "The White House has had no involvement whatsoever in this particular incident."[2] The chairman of his campaign organization, John Mitchell (formerly Nixon's attorney general), ordered an in-house investigation of the incident the same day. Nine days after initiating the investigation, Mitchell resigned from the campaign, citing family problems. Mitchell's investigation exonerated Nixon's re-election committee.

The Unwelcome Wagon Calls

Calls for Richard Nixon's impeachment intensified following the release of taped conversations linking the president to a coverup of the Watergate break-in. On August 8, 1974, a crowd jeering "Jail to the Chief!" stopped traffic along Pennsylvania Avenue in front of the White House. A moving van drove up, as if to hasten the president's departure. The following day, Nixon resigned.

Senators Investigate a President
The Select Committee on Presidential Campaign Activities, shown here, was created by the Senate in 1973 to investigate events surrounding Watergate. Its chairman was Democrat Sam Ervin (seated at the center); its ranking minority member was Republican Howard Baker (to Ervin's right). Baker was prominent during another congressional investigation into possible abuses of executive power, but not as a senator. He was President Ronald Reagan's chief of staff during the Iran-Contra hearings in 1987.

At its convention in July, the Democratic party nominated Senator George McGovern of South Dakota to oppose Nixon in the presidential election. McGovern tried to make the break-in at the Democratic headquarters a campaign issue, but the voters either didn't understand or didn't care. In November 1972, Richard Nixon was re-elected president of the United States, winning forty-nine of fifty states in one of the largest electoral landslides in American history.

The events that followed are described in Feature 3.1. Here we need only note that the Watergate affair posed one of the most serious challenges to the constitutional order of modern American government. The incident ultimately developed into a struggle over the rule of law between the presidency on the one hand and Congress and the courts on the other. President Nixon attempted to use the powers of his office to hide his tampering with the electoral process. In the end, the cover-up was thwarted by the Constitution and by leaders who believed in the Constitution. The constitutional principle of separation of powers among the executive, legislative, and judicial branches prevented the president from controlling the Watergate investigation. The principle of checks and balances allowed Congress to threaten Nixon with impeachment and removal from office. The belief that Nixon had violated the Constitution finally prompted members of his own party to support impeachment.

Nixon resigned the presidency after little more than a year and a half into his second term. In some countries, such an irregular change

FEATURE 3.1

Watergate

The frightening details of the Watergate story did not unfold until after President Nixon's re-election in November 1972. Two months later, in January 1973, seven men went to trial for the break-in itself. They included the five burglars and two men closely connected with the president: E. Howard Hunt (a former CIA agent and White House consultant) and G. Gordon Liddy (counsel to the Committee for the Re-election of the President, or CREEP). The burglars entered guilty pleas. Hunt and Liddy were convicted by a jury. In a letter to the sentencing judge, one of the burglars charged that they had been pressured to plead guilty, that perjury had been committed at the trial, and that others were involved in the break-in. The Senate launched its own investigation of the matter. It set up the Select Committee on Presidential Campaign Activities, chaired by a self-styled constitutional authority, Democratic Senator Sam Ervin from North Carolina.

The testimony before the Ervin committee was shocking. The deputy director of Nixon's re-election committee, Jeb Magruder, confessed to perjury and implicated John Mitchell in planning the burglary. Special Counsel to the President John Dean said that the president had been a party to a cover-up of the crime for eight months. And there were more disclosures, of other political burglaries and of forged State Department cables that were intended to embarrass a possible Democratic candidate, Senator Edward M. Kennedy of Massachusetts.

A stunned nation watching the televised proceedings, learned that the president had secretly tape-recorded all of his conversations in the White House. The Ervin committee asked for the tapes. Nixon refused to produce them, citing the separa-

THE WHITE HOUSE
WASHINGTON

August 9, 1974

Dear Mr. Secretary:

I hereby resign the Office of President of the United States.

Sincerely,

[signature: Richard Nixon]

11.35 AM

The Honorable Henry A. Kissinger
The Secretary of State
Washington, D.C. 20520

tion of powers between the legislative and executive branches and claiming "executive privilege" to withhold information from Congress.

In the midst of all this, Nixon's vice president, Spiro T. Agnew, resigned while under investigation for income tax evasion. The Twenty-fifth Amendment to the Constitution (1967) gave the president

in government leadership means an opportunity for a palace coup, armed revolution, or a military dictatorship. But here the most serious display of public antagonism occurred the night before Nixon resigned: One wag drove up in a moving van, as though to speed the president's departure, while a crowd chanting "Jail to the Chief!" stopped traffic in front of the White House. And, significantly, there was no political violence after Nixon's resignation; in fact, none was expected. Constitutional order in the United States had been put to a test, and it passed with high honors.

In this chapter, we ask some questions about the Constitution. How did it evolve? What form did it take? What values does it reflect? How

the power to choose a new vice president with the consent of Congress. Nixon nominated Gerald Ford, then the Republican leader in the House of Representatives. On December 6, 1973, Ford became the first appointed vice president in the nation's history.

Meanwhile, Nixon was fighting subpoenas demanding the White House tapes. Ordered by a federal court to deliver specific tapes, Nixon proposed a compromise. He would release written summaries of the taped conversations. Archibald Cox, the special prosecutor of the attorney general's office, refused the compromise. Nixon retaliated with the "Saturday Night massacre," in which Attorney General Elliot L. Richardson and his deputy resigned, Cox was fired, and the special prosecutor's office was abolished.

The ensuing furor forced Nixon to appoint another special prosecutor, Leon Jaworski, who eventually brought indictments against Nixon's closest aides. Nixon himself was named as an unindicted co-conspirator. Both the special prosecutor and the defendants wanted the White House tapes, but Nixon continued to resist. Finally, on July 24, 1974, the Supreme Court ruled that the president had to hand over the tapes. At almost the same time, the House Judiciary Committee voted to recommend to the full House that Nixon be impeached for, or charged with, three offenses: impeding and obstructing the investigation of the Watergate break-in; abuse of power and repeated violation of the constitutional rights of citizens; and defiance of House subpoenas.

The Judiciary Committee vote was decisive but far from unanimous. On August 5, however, the committee and the country finally learned the contents of the tapes released under the Supreme Court order. They revealed that Nixon had been aware of a cover-up on June 23, 1972, just six days after the break-in. He had also issued an order to the FBI, saying, "Don't go any further in this case, period!"* Now even the eleven Republican members of the House Judiciary Committee, who had opposed the first vote to impeach, were ready to vote against Nixon.

Faced with the collapse of his support and likely impeachment by the full House, Nixon resigned the presidency on August 8, 1974. Vice President Gerald Ford became the first unelected president of the United States. A month later, acting within his constitutional powers, Ford pardoned private citizen Richard Nixon for all federal crimes that he had committed or may have committed. When questioned by Congress about the circumstances surrounding the pardon, President Ford said, "There was no deal, period." Others were not so fortunate. Three members of the Nixon cabinet (two attorneys general and a secretary of commerce) were convicted and sentenced for their crimes in the Watergate affair. Nixon's White House chief of staff, H. R. Haldeman, and his domestic affairs adviser, John Ehrlichman, were convicted of conspiracy, obstruction of justice, and perjury. And other officials were tried, and most were convicted, on related charges.**

---

* *The Encyclopedia of American Facts and Dates* (New York: Crowell, 1979), p. 946.
** Richard B. Morris, ed., *Encyclopedia of American History* (New York: Harper & Row, 1976), p. 544.

---

is it altered? And which model of democracy—majoritarian or pluralist—does it fit best?

THE REVOLUTIONARY ROOTS OF THE CONSTITUTION

The Constitution itself is just 4,300 words. But those 4,300 words define the basic structure of our national government. It is a comprehensive document, dividing the government into three branches, and describing the powers of those branches, their relationships, and the interaction between government and governed. The Constitution makes itself the supreme law of the land and binds every government official to support it.

Most Americans revere the Constitution as political "scripture." To charge that a political action is unconstitutional is like claiming that it is unholy. And so the Constitution has taken on a symbolism that has strengthened its authority as the basis of American government. Their strong belief in the Constitution has led many politicians to abandon party for principle when constitutional issues are in question. The power and symbolic value of the Constitution were proved once again in the Watergate affair.

The U.S. Constitution is more than two hundred years old. In today's culture, few things that old work very well or are relevant to contemporary life. Yet this document, written in 1787 for an agricultural society huddled along the coast of a wild new land, now guides the political life of a massive urban society in the nuclear age. The stability of the Constitution—and of the political system it created—is all the more remarkable because the Constitution itself was rooted in revolution. In fact, the U.S. Constitution was the first of several national constitutions that stemmed from revolution. Three others—the French constitution of 1791, the Mexican constitution of 1917, and the Russian constitution of 1918—were products of revolutionary movements too.

The noted historian Samuel Eliot Morison observed that "the American Revolution was not fought to *obtain* freedom, but to *preserve* the liberties that Americans already had as colonials."[3] The U.S. Constitution was designed to prevent anarchy by forging a union of states. To understand the values embedded in the Constitution, we must understand its historical roots. They lie in colonial America, in the revolt against British rule, and in the failure of the Articles of Confederation that governed the new nation after the Revolution.

Freedom in Colonial America

Although they were British subjects, the American colonists in the eighteenth century enjoyed a degree of freedom denied to most people in the world. Europeans lived with many reminders of their feudal past, a time when great landowners ruled over unlanded tenants; America had no feudal history. Property inheritance in Europe was fraught with conditions; America imposed few, if any, restrictions. In Europe, established churches required the *tithe* (a compulsory contribution) from parishioners; America had no single established church, and tithing was not an important practice. (Even the Church of England enjoyed little influence in America, although it was established in every southern colony.) In England, subjects could be pressed into service in the Royal Navy; Americans were exempt from such service. European guilds and professional associations restricted access to the trades and professions; American guilds and associations imposed no such restrictions. For the colonists, their relationship with the British Empire was a good one. They maintained the rights of Englishmen and at the same time enjoyed the protection of the English government.

By 1763, Britain and the colonies had reached a compromise between imperial control and colonial self-government. America's foreign affairs and overseas trade were controlled by the king and Parliament, the British legislature; the rest was left to home rule. But the cost of administering the colonies—including the conquest of Spanish Florida and French Canada—was substantial. Because Americans benefited the most, contended their English countrymen, Americans should bear that cost. And the means was to be taxation.

The Road to Revolution

The British believed that taxing the colonies was the obvious way to meet administrative costs; the colonists did not agree. Like most people, they did not want to be taxed. And they especially did not want to be taxed by a distant government in which they had no representation. The Stamp Act of 1765 was the first direct tax on the colonies. Its purpose was to raise revenues for colonial administration and to impose on the colonies a portion of the cost of defense. It was a stern measure. All kinds of documents—complaints, appeals, diplomas, licenses, deeds, newspapers, playing cards—were taxed. And the tax was a nuisance. Documents had to be prepared on specially stamped papers that could be obtained only from official distributors appointed by the Crown.

In the colonies, opposition to the Stamp Act was immediate and widespread. A group of citizens, calling themselves the Sons of Liberty, engaged in acts of resistance. They burned stamped paper and forced official distributors to resign. In October 1765, the Stamp Act Congress convened in New York City—the colonies' first spontaneous act of political union. Delegates from nine colonies restated the colonists' belief "that no taxes should be imposed on them but with their own consent, given personally, or by their representatives."

Opposition to the Stamp Act was so strong that Parliament repealed it in 1766. This was a stunning political victory, a demonstration that, united, the colonists could turn back the world's most powerful nation. But Britain was determined that the colonies would share the cost of their defense. In June and July 1767, Parliament passed the Townshend Acts, which levied duties on paper, glass, paint, and tea entering the colonies. In response, radical colonial leaders organized a boycott of those products and others, to put as much economic pressure on the British as possible.

In 1770 there was hope of reconciliation when Parliament repealed the Townshend Acts except for the duty on tea. Tea consumption dropped sharply, leaving the East India Company (a British trading house) awash in 18 million pounds of unsold tea. In May 1773, Parliament acted to bolster the floundering company. It passed the Tea Act, which reduced the price of tea by letting the East India Company sell tea directly to its colonial agents. These direct sales eliminated both the colonial merchants who purchased their tea from other sources and the colonial

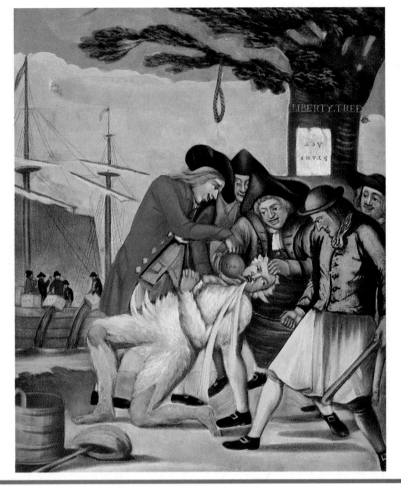

A Uniquely American Protest
Americans protested the Tea Act (1773) by holding the Boston Tea Party (see background, left) and by employing a unique form of punishment—tarring and feathering. An early treatise on the subject offered the following instructions: "First, strip a person naked, then heat the tar until it is thin, and pour upon the naked flesh, or rub it over with a tar brush. After which, sprinkle decently upon the tar, whilst it is yet warm, as many feathers as will stick to it."

smugglers who brought tea in from Holland. But the act retained the hated tax as a test of the king's authority.

The colonists responded by throwing a party, the Boston Tea Party. Disguised as Indians and blacks, a mob boarded three ships and emptied 342 chests of tea into Boston Harbor on the night of December 16, 1773. This act of defiance and destruction could not be ignored. "The die is now cast," wrote George III. "The Colonies must either submit or triumph."[4]

Parliament retaliated by passing the Coercive (or Intolerable) Acts (1774). One of the acts imposed a blockade on Boston until the tea was paid for; another gave royal governors the power to quarter British soldiers in private homes. Now the taxation issue was secondary; more important was the conflict between British demands for order and American demands for liberty. The colonists drew together, sending food and money to surprised Bostonians. The Virginia and Massachusetts assemblies summoned a **continental congress,** an assembly that would speak and act collectively for the people of all the colonies.

The First Continental Congress met in Philadelphia in September 1774. All the colonies except Georgia sent representatives. The objective of the assembly was to restore harmony between Great Britain and the American colonies. In an effort at unity, all colonies were given the same voting power—one vote each. A leader, called the "president," was elected. (The terms *president* and *congress* in American government trace their origins to the First Continental Congress.) In October 1774, the delegates adopted a statement of rights and principles, many of which later found their way into the Declaration of Independence and the Constitution. For example, the congress claimed a right "to life, liberty, and property" and a right "peaceably to assemble, consider of their grievances, and petition the king." Then the congress adjourned, planning to reconvene in May 1775.

Revolutionary Action

By early 1775, however, a movement that the colonists themselves were calling a revolution had already begun. In March 1775, Patrick Henry, in his famous "give me liberty or give me death" speech, predicted the outbreak of fighting in New England. A month later his prediction was reality: The colonists in Massachusetts were fighting the British at Concord and Lexington. Delegates to the Second Continental Congress, meeting in May, faced a dilemma: Should they prepare for war? Or should they try to reconcile with Britain? A military force was organized, and George Washington was appointed commander in chief of the army. Sentiment for independence grew, as the colony-states gradually cut tie after tie with Britain. Still, New York, New Jersey, Pennsylvania, and Maryland resisted self-government. It was not so much that they were afraid of revolution; they were afraid of the type of government that would replace British rule. Tyranny or anarchy was the most likely replacement, and neither was acceptable. Meanwhile, the Second Continental Congress remained in session, to serve as the government of the colony-states.

In 1776, news reached Virginia that the British had hired twelve thousand German mercenaries (known as "Hessians") to end the rebellion. The Virginia delegation called on the Continental Congress to resolve "that these United Colonies are, and of right ought to be, free and Independent States, that they are absolved from all allegiance to the British Crown, and that all political connection between them and the State of Great Britain is, and ought to be, totally dissolved." The decision was made. A committee of five men was appointed to prepare a proclamation expressing the colonies' reasons for declaring independence.

The Declaration of Independence

Thomas Jefferson, a young farmer and lawyer from Virginia, was a member of the committee. Because of his "peculiar felicity of expression," he prepared the draft of the proclamation. The document Jefferson drafted—the **Declaration of Independence**—was substantially unchanged by the committee and the congress. It remains a cherished statement of our heritage, expressing simply, clearly, and rationally the arguments in support of separation from Great Britain.

The principles underlying the declaration were rooted in the writings of the English philosopher John Locke and expressed many times by speakers in congress and in the colonial assemblies. Locke argued that people have God-given, or natural, rights that are inalienable—that is, they cannot be taken away by any government.

For Locke, the most basic of people's natural rights was *property*, a concept that encompassed life and liberty as well as material possessions. In addition, Locke believed that all legitimate political authority exists to preserve these natural rights, and that this authority is based on the consent of those who are governed. The idea of consent is derived from **social contract theory.** This theory states that the people agree to set up rulers for certain purposes and that they have the right to resist or remove rulers who persist in acting against those purposes.[5] In short, government exists, not for the benefit of those who govern, but for the good of its subjects. And, Locke argued, rebellion is the ultimate sanction against the abuse of government power. (In his writings, Locke did not try to justify any particular form of government; nor did he believe in social or political equality.)

Jefferson used similar arguments in the Declaration of Independence. Although he was not an orator, Jefferson was a brilliant wordsmith. His "impassioned simplicity of statement" reverberates to this day with democratic faith:

> We hold these truths to be self-evident, that all men are created equal, that they are endowed by their Creator with certain unalienable Rights, that among these are Life, Liberty and the pursuit of Happiness.

The First Continental Congress had declared in 1774 that the colonists were entitled to "life, liberty, and property." Jefferson reformulated the objectives of government as "Life, Liberty, and the pursuit of Happiness." And he continued:

> That to secure these rights, Governments are instituted among Men, deriving their just powers from the consent of the governed. That whenever any Form of Government becomes destructive of these ends, it is the Right of the People to alter or to abolish it, and to institute new Government, laying its foundation on such Principles and organizing its Powers in such form, as to them shall seem most likely to effect their Safety and Happiness.

He went on to list the many deliberate acts of the king that were working against the legitimate ends of government. Finally, he declared that the colonies were "Free and Independent States," with no political connection to Great Britain.

The major premise of the Declaration of Independence is that the people have a right to revolt when they determine that their government is denying them their legitimate rights. The long list of the king's actions was evidence of that denial. And so the people had the right to rebel, to form a new government.

On July 2, 1776, the Second Continental Congress finally voted for independence. The vote was by state, and the motion carried 11 to 0.

Voting for Independence
The Second Continental Congress voted independence on July 2, 1776. John Adams of Massachusetts viewed the day "as the most memorable epocha [significant event] in the history of America." In this painting by John Trumbull, the drafting committee presents the Declaration of Independence to the patriots who would later sign it. The committee, grouped in front of the desk, consisted of (from left to right): Adams; Roger Sherman (Conn.); Robert Livingston (N.Y.); Thomas Jefferson (Va.); and Benjamin Franklin (Pa.).

(Rhode Island was not present, and the New York delegation, lacking instructions, did not cast its "yea" vote until July 15.) Two days later, the Declaration of Independence was approved with very few changes. Jefferson's original draft had indicted the king for allowing the slave trade to continue. But representatives from Georgia and South Carolina insisted that this phrase be deleted before they would vote for approval. Other representatives removed language they thought would arouse the colonists. But, in the end, Jefferson's compelling words were left almost exactly as he had written them.

The vote for independence came on July 2; the Declaration of Independence was adopted, but not signed, on July 4. By August, fifty-five revolutionaries had signed it, pledging "our Lives, our Fortunes and our sacred Honor" in support of rebellion from the world's most powerful nation. This was no empty pledge: An act of rebellion was treason. If they had lost the revolutionary war, the signers would have faced a gruesome fate. The punishment for treason was hanging, drawing, and quartering—the victim is first hanged until half-dead from strangulation, then disemboweled, and finally cut into four quarters while still alive. We celebrate the Fourth of July with fireworks and flag-waving, parades and picnics. We sometimes forget that the Revolution was a matter of life and death.

The War of Independence lasted far longer than anyone expected. It began in a moment of confusion, when a colonist fired a shot at passing British soldiers on the road to Concord, Massachusetts, on April 19, 1775. It ended with Lord Cornwallis's surrender of his six-thousand-man army at Yorktown, Virginia, on October 19, 1781. It was a costly war: There were more dead and wounded in relation to the population than in any other conflict except the Civil War.[6] With hindsight, of course, we can see that the British were engaged in a hopeless conflict. America was simply too vast to subdue without instituting complete military rule there. Britain also had to transport men and supplies over the enormous distance of the Atlantic Ocean. Finally, although the Americans had neither paid troops nor professional soldiers, they were fighting for a cause—in defense of their liberty. The British never understood the power of this fighting faith.

FROM REVOLUTION TO GOVERNMENT: THE FIRST TRY

By declaring their independence from England, the colonies were leaving themselves without any real central government. So the revolutionaries proclaimed the creation of a *republic*. Strictly speaking, a **republic** is a government without a monarch, but the term had come to mean a government rooted in the consent of the governed, in which power is exercised by representatives who are responsible to the governed. A republic need not be a democracy, and this was fine with the founders; at that time *democracy* was associated with mob rule and instability (see Chapter 2). The revolutionaries were less concerned with who would control their new government than with limiting the powers of that government. They had revolted in the name of liberty, and now they wanted a government with sharply defined powers. To make sure they got one, they meant to define its structure and powers in writing.

The Articles of Confederation

When the Second Continental Congress decided to declare independence from Britain, it also began planning a government for the colonies. Barely a week after the Declaration of Independence was signed, the congress received a committee report on "Articles of Confederation and Perpetual Union." A **confederation** is a loose association of independent states that agree to cooperate on specified matters. In a confederation, the states retain their **sovereignty,** which means that each has supreme power within its borders. The central government is weak; it can only coordinate, not control, the actions of its sovereign states. Consequently, the individual states are strong.

The congress debated the **Articles of Confederation,** the compact among the thirteen original states that established a government of the United States, for more than a year. The Articles were finally adopted on November 15, 1777, but they were greeted by the states with a mixture of apathy and hostility. Most Americans were more interested in local affairs than in national issues, and even the slightest threat to state sovereignty aroused avid republicans. The Articles did not take effect until they had been ratified (approved) by all thirteen states, on March 1, 1781. On March 2, the Continental Congress assumed a new title: "the United States of America in Congress assembled."

The Articles of Confederation jealously guarded state sovereignty;

their provisions clearly reflected the delegates' fears of a strong central government being substituted for British rule. Article II stated:

> Each State retains its sovereignty, freedom, and independence, and every Power, Jurisdiction and right, which is not by this confederation expressly delegated to the United States, in Congress assembled.

Under the Articles, each state, regardless of its size, had one vote in the congress. Votes on financing the war against Britain and other important issues required the consent of at least nine of the thirteen states. The common danger—the war—forced the young republic to function under the Articles, but this first try at a government was inadequate to the task. The delegates had succeeded in crafting a national government that was largely powerless.

The Articles failed for at least four reasons: First, they did not give the national government the power to tax. As a result, the congress had to plead for funds with which to conduct the continuing war with Great Britain and to carry on the affairs of the new nation. Second, except for the appointment of a presiding officer of the congress (the president), the Articles made no provision for an independent leadership position to direct the government. This omission was planned—the colonists feared the re-establishment of a monarchy—but it left the nation without a leader. Third, the Articles did not allow the national government to regulate interstate and foreign commerce. (When John Adams proposed that the confederation enter into a commercial treaty with Britain after the war, he was asked, "Would you like one treaty or thirteen, Mr. Adams?"[7]) Finally, the Articles themselves could not be amended without the unanimous agreement of the congress and the assent of all the state legislatures; thus, each state had the power to veto any changes in the confederation.

The goal of the delegates who drew up the Articles of Confederation was to retain power in the states. This was consistent with republicanism, which viewed the remote power of a national government as a danger to liberty. In this sense alone, the Articles were a grand success. They completely hobbled the infant government.

Disorder Under the Confederation

Once the revolutionary war ended and independence was a reality, it became clear that the national government had neither the economic nor the military power to function. Americans, freed from wartime austerity, rushed to purchase goods from abroad. The national government's efforts to restrict foreign imports were blocked by exporting states, which feared retaliation from their foreign customers. Debt mounted and, for many, bankruptcy followed.

The problem was particularly severe in Massachusetts, where high interest rates and high state taxes were forcing farmers into bankruptcy. In 1786, Daniel Shays, a revolutionary war veteran, marched on a western Massachusetts courthouse with fifteen hundred supporters armed with barrel staves and pitchforks. They wanted to close the courthouse, to prevent the foreclosure of farms by creditors. Later they attacked an

Farmers' Protest Stirs Rebellion
Shays's Rebellion (1786–1787) became a symbol for the urgent need to maintain order. Here, farmers led by Daniel Shays close the courthouse to prevent farm foreclosures by creditors. The uprising demonstrated the military weakness of the confederation: The national government could not muster the funds to fight the insurgents.

arsenal. This revolt against the established order was called **Shays's Rebellion;** it continued into 1787.

Massachusetts appealed to the confederation for help. Horrified by the threat of domestic upheaval, the congress approved a $530,000 requisition for the establishment of a national army. But the plan failed: Every state except Virginia rejected the request for money. Finally the governor of Massachusetts called out the militia and restored order.[8]

The rebellion demonstrated the impotence of the confederation and the urgent need to suppress insurrection and maintain domestic order. It was proof to skeptics that Americans could not govern themselves.

THE CONSTITUTIONAL CONVENTION: THE SECOND TRY

Order, the original purpose of government, was breaking down under the Articles of Confederation. The "league of friendship" envisioned in the Articles was not enough to hold the nation together in peacetime.

Some states had taken halting steps toward a change in government. In 1785, Massachusetts asked the congress to revise the Articles of Confederation, but the congress took no action. In 1786, Virginia invited the states to attend a convention at Annapolis, to explore revisions aimed at improving commercial regulation. The meeting was both a failure and a success. Although only five states sent delegates to Annapolis, the delegates seized the opportunity to call for another meeting, with a far broader mission, in Philadelphia the next year. That convention would be charged with "devis[ing] such further provisions as shall appear . . . necessary to render the constitution of the Federal Government adequate to the exigencies of the Union." The congress later agreed to the convention but limited its mission to "the sole and express purpose of revising the Articles of Confederation."

Shays's Rebellion lent a sense of urgency to the task before the Philadelphia convention. Congress's inability to confront the rebellion was evidence that a stronger national government was necessary to preserve order and property—to protect the states from internal as well as external dangers. "While the Declaration was directed against an excess of authority," remarked Supreme Court Justice Robert H. Jackson some 150 years later, "the Constitution [that followed the Articles of Confederation] was directed against anarchy."[9]

Twelve of the thirteen states named a total of seventy-four delegates to convene in Philadelphia in May 1787. (Rhode Island, derisively renamed "Rogue Island" by a Boston newspaper, was the one exception.) Fifty-five delegates eventually showed up at the State House in Philadelphia, but no more than thirty were present at any one time during that sweltering spring and summer (see Feature 3.2). Although well versed in ideas, they subscribed to the view that "experience must be our guide. Reason may mislead us." The delegates' goal was to fashion a government that would maintain order and preserve liberty.

The Constitutional Convention—at the time, it was called the *Federal Convention*—officially opened on May 25, when representatives of seven states were present to make a quorum. Remember that a year earlier, at Annapolis, five states had called for the convention to draft a new, stronger charter for the national government. The spirit of the Annapolis meeting seems to have pervaded the Constitutional Convention, even though the delegates were authorized only to "revise" the Articles of Confederation. Within the first week of debate, Edmund Randolph of Virginia had presented a long list of changes, suggested by fellow Virginian James Madison, that would replace the weak confederation of states with a powerful national government. The delegates unanimously agreed to debate Randolph's proposal, which was called the *Virginia Plan*. Almost immediately, then, they rejected the idea of amending the Articles of Confederation, working instead to create an entirely new constitution.

The Virginia Plan

The **Virginia Plan** served as the basis of the convention's deliberations for the rest of the summer. It made several important proposals:

80   *Chapter 3 / The Constitution*

FEATURE 3.2

Behind the Scenes in 1787

When the framers of the Constitution convened . . . on May 25, 1787, to try to keep the American Union from falling to pieces, Philadelphia was the foremost city of America.

It was a place of urban culture and accomplishment. Its streets were crowded with people of diverse national origins. Sailors from many countries mixed with leather-clad frontiersmen and with Shawnee and Delaware Indians from the forest.

But the city also reflected the hard life that most Americans lived then. More than half the population existed on the edge of poverty. Prostitution and disease were widespread. Many streets were open sewers. Flies and mosquitoes added their torment to the oppressive heat of that summer, the worst in nearly 40 years. . . .

Court records revealed much child and spouse abuse. Drunkenness was pervasive. Servants of the wealthy, including those of George Washington, spent their evenings in the taverns of a rough waterfront district called Helltown.

Independence Hall, then called the Pennsylvania State House, had seen better days: Its steeple had become shaky and had to be taken down. Across Walnut Street was a four-story stone prison. Prisoners called out for alms and cursed passers-by who failed to oblige.

When George Washington arrived in Philadelphia, he perceived a radical, divisive atmosphere that reflected the country's mood at a time when dissolution of the Union seemed likely and foreign powers waited to pounce. That perception is said to have contributed to a decision to keep the Constitutional Convention's proceedings secret. . . .

There was no press coverage. The public did not learn anything about what had gone on until after the convention adjourned on Sept. 17. Two days later, the *Pennsylvania Packet* published the Constitution, devoting its entire issue to the text. Newspapers everywhere followed suit. No political story had commanded so much space until then.

Sometimes, extraordinary measures were taken to maintain the secrecy. It seemed impossible to keep Benjamin Franklin quiet, wrote Catherine Drinker Bowen in *Miracle at Philadelphia*, a respected history of the convention. As a result, she

reported, "a discreet member" of the convention attended Franklin's convivial dinners to head off the conversation whenever he appeared ready to divulge a secret.

The delegates stayed at private homes and spent many of their evenings talking and plotting strategy at the City Tavern, the Black Horse, the George and the Indian Queen. They drank a lot: The bill for one dinner party of 12 included sixty bottles of wine.

That may be one reason why so many delegates, as historians have noted, were so corpulent. Few stood more than about 5 feet 8 inches tall, but many weighed about 200 pounds or more. The most striking exception was Washington. Every inch the general at 6 feet 2 inches, with wide shoulders and narrow hips, he towered above the convention both literally and figuratively.

The framers were not demi-gods. But many historians believe that their like will not be seen again in one place. Highly educated, they typically were fluent in Latin and Greek. Products of the Enlightenment, they relied on classical Liberalism for the Constitution's philosophical underpinnings.

They were also veterans of the political intrigues of their states and as such were highly practical politicians who knew how to maneuver.

Still, if it were not for Washington, some historians believe, the convention would never have succeeded. His character and authority kept the convention from flying apart.

One facet of his authority is revealed in an anecdote reported by Mrs. Bowen. Gouverneur Morris, a Pennsylvania delegate who drafted the Constitution's final version, accepted a bet proposed by Alexander Hamilton. To win it, Morris had to greet Washington with a slap on the back. That was just not done. "Well, General!" Morris said, and laid his hand on Washington's shoulder. The general said nothing, but Morris later said that Washington's imperious look made him wish . . . that he could sink through the floor.

Source: William K. Stevens, "Behind the Scenes in 1787: Secrecy in the Heat," *New York Times*, 25 May 1987, p. 7. Copyright © 1987 by The New York Times Company. Reprinted by permission.

James Madison, Father of the Constitution
Although he dismissed the accolade, Madison deserved it more than anyone else. Like most fathers, he exercised a powerful influence in debates (and was on the losing side of more than half of his battles).

- That the powers of the government would be divided among three separate branches: a **legislative branch,** for making laws; an **executive branch,** for enforcing laws; and a **judicial branch,** for interpreting laws.

- That the legislature would consist of two houses. The first would be chosen by the people; the second, by the members of the first house, from among persons nominated by the state legislatures.

- That representation in the legislature would be in proportion to taxes paid to the national government, or in proportion to the free population of each state.

- That a one-person executive would be selected by the legislature and would serve for a single term.

- That the executive and a number of federal judges would serve as a council of revision, to approve or veto (disapprove) legislative acts. Their veto could be overridden, however, by a vote of both houses of the legislature.

- That the judiciary would include a supreme court and other lower courts, with judges appointed for life by the legislature.

- That the range of powers of all three branches would be far greater than that assigned the national government by the Articles of Confederation and would include the power of the legislature to override state laws.

By proposing a powerful national legislature that could override state laws, the Virginia Plan clearly advocated a new form of government. It was a compound structure, operating on the states and operating on the people.

Madison was a monumental force in the ensuing debate on the proposals. He kept records of the proceedings that reveal his frequent and brilliant participation and give us insight into his thinking about freedom, order, and equality.

For example, his proposal that senators serve a nine-year term reveals his thinking about equality. Madison foresaw an increase "of those who will labor under all the hardships of life, and secretly sigh for a more equal distribution of its blessings. These may in time outnumber those who are placed above the feelings of indigence."[10] Power, then, could flow into the hands of the numerous poor. The stability of the Senate, however, with its long elective term of nine years and election by the state legislatures, would provide a barrier against the "sighs of the poor" for more equality. Although most of the delegates shared Madison's apprehension of equality, the nine-year term was voted down.

The constitution that emerged from the convention bore only partial resemblance to the document Madison wanted to create. Of the seventy-one specific proposals that Madison endorsed, he ended up on the losing side on forty of them.[11] And the parts of the Virginia Plan that were ultimately adopted in the Constitution were not adopted without challenge. Conflict revolved primarily around the basis of representation in the legislature, the method of choosing legislators, and the structure of the executive branch.

The New Jersey Plan

When it appeared that much of the Virginia Plan would be carried by the large states, the smaller states united in opposition. William Paterson of New Jersey introduced an alternative set of nine resolutions, written to preserve the spirit of the Articles of Confederation by amending rather than replacing them. His **New Jersey Plan** included the following proposals:

- That a single-chamber legislature would have the power to raise revenue and regulate commerce.
- That the states would have equal representation in the legislature and would choose the members of that body.
- That a multiperson executive would be elected by the legislature, with powers similar to those listed in the Virginia Plan but without the right to veto legislation.
- That a supreme judiciary would be created with a very limited jurisdiction. (There was no provision for a system of national courts.)
- That the acts of the legislature would be binding on the states; that is, they would be regarded as the "supreme law of the respective states," and force could be used to compel obedience.

The New Jersey Plan was defeated in the first major convention vote, 7 to 3. However, the small states had enough support to force a compromise on the issue of representation in the legislature. Table 3.1 compares the New Jersey Plan with the Virginia Plan.

The Great Compromise

The Virginia Plan provided for a two-chamber legislature, with representation in both chambers based on population. The idea of having two chambers was never seriously challenged, but the idea of representation according to population stirred up heated and prolonged debate. The smaller states demanded equal representation for all states, but another vote rejected that concept for the House of Representatives. The debate continued. Finally, the Connecticut delegation moved that each

Table 3.1
Major Differences Between the Virginia Plan and the New Jersey Plan

Characteristic	Virginia Plan	New Jersey Plan
Legislature	Two chambers	One chamber
Legislative power	Derived from the people	Derived from the States
Executive	One person	More then one person
Decision rule	Majority	Extraordinary majority
State laws	Legislature can override	Compel obedience
Executive removal	By Congress	By a majority of the states
Courts	National judiciary	No provision
Ratification	By the people	By the states

DOONESBURY

Garry Trudeau

Doonesbury "Equality and the Constitution"

state have an equal vote in the Senate. Still another poll showed that the delegations were equally divided on this proposal.

A committee was created to resolve the deadlock. It consisted of one delegate from each state, chosen by secret ballot. The committee worked through the Independence Day recess, then reported the **Great Compromise** (it is sometimes called the *Connecticut Compromise*): The House of Representatives would initially consist of fifty-six members, apportioned *according to the population of each state.* Revenue-raising acts would originate in the House. Most important, *the states would be represented equally in the Senate,* with two senators each. Senators would be selected by their state legislatures, not directly by the people.

In apportioning representatives in the House, the population of each state was to be determined by adding "the whole Number of free Persons" and "three fifths of all other Persons." The phrase "all other Persons" is, of course, a euphemism for slaves. Nowhere does the Constitution mention slaves or slavery by name, despite the fact that slavery was a major issue in the nation and among the delegates. But by its wording here and in Article IV (which essentially prescribes the return of runaway slaves), the framers were condoning slavery—the most undemocratic of all institutions.

It is doubtful that there would have been a Great Compromise—or even a Constitution—if the delegates had had to resolve the issue of slavery. The southern states would not have ratified a constitution that prohibited slavery. Those who opposed slavery were willing to tolerate it in the interest of the Union, perhaps believing the issue could await another day. But they also expressed some opposition to slavery by permitting the Congress to abolish the slave trade after 1807.

Finally, the delegates accepted the Great Compromise: The smaller states got their equal representation; the larger states, their proportional representation. The small states might dominate the Senate and the large states might control the House, but because all legislation had to be approved by both chambers, neither group would be able to dominate the other.

Compromise on the Presidency

Contention replaced compromise when the delegates turned to the executive branch. They did agree on a one-person executive—a president—but they disagreed on how the executive would be selected and what the term of office would be. Because the delegates distrusted the judgment of the people, they rejected the idea of popular election. At the same time, representatives of the smaller states feared that election by the legislature would allow the larger states to control the executive.

Once again, a committee with one member from each participating state was chosen to effect a compromise. That committee fashioned the cumbersome presidential election system that we know today as the **electoral college.** The college consists of a group of electors who are chosen for the sole purpose of selecting the president and vice president. Each state legislature would choose a number of electors equal to the number of representatives it had in Congress. Each elector would then vote for two people. The person with the most votes would become president, provided that that person had a majority of the votes; the person with the next greatest number of votes would become vice president. (This procedure was changed in 1804 by the Twelfth Amendment, which mandates separate votes for each office.) If no candidate won a majority, then the House of Representatives would choose a president, *with each state having one vote.*

The electoral college compromise removed the fear of a popular vote for president. At the same time, it satisfied the small states. If the electoral college failed to produce a president—which the delegates expected would happen—then an election by the House would give every state the same voice in the selection process.

Finally, the delegates agreed that the president's term of office should be four years and that the president should be eligible for re-election.

The delegates also realized that removing a president from office would be a very serious political matter. For that reason, they involved the other two branches of government in the process. The House alone was empowered to charge a president with "Treason, Bribery, or other high Crimes and Misdemeanors," by a majority vote. The Senate was given the sole power to try the president on the House's charges. It could convict, and thus remove, a president only by a two-thirds vote (an extraordinary majority). And the chief justice of the United States was required to preside over the Senate trial.

THE FINAL PRODUCT

Once the delegates resolved their major disagreements, they dispatched the remaining issues relatively quickly. A committee was then appointed to organize and write up the results of the proceedings. Twenty-three resolutions had been debated and approved by the convention; these were reorganized under seven articles in the draft constitution. The Preamble, which was the last section to be drafted, begins with a phrase that would have been impossible to write when the convention opened. This single sentence contains four elements that would form the foundation of the American political tradition.[12]

- *It creates a people:* "We the People of the United States" was a dramatic departure from a loose confederation of states.

- *It explains the reason for the Constitution:* "in Order to form a more perfect Union" was an indirect way of saying that the first effort, under the Articles of Confederation, had been inadequate.

- *It articulates goals:* "establish Justice, insure domestic Tranquility, provide for the common defence, promote the general Welfare, and secure the Blessings of Liberty to ourselves and our Posterity"; in other words, the government exists to promote order and freedom.

- *It fashions a government:* "do ordain and establish this Constitution for the United States of America."

The Basic Principles

In creating the Constitution, the founders relied on four political principles that together established a revolutionary new political order. These principles were republicanism, federalism, separation of powers, and checks and balances (see Feature 3.3 for a discussion of these principles' philosophical origins).

Republicanism. **Republicanism** is a form of government in which power resides in the people and is exercised by their elected representatives. The framers were determined to avoid aristocracy (rule by a hereditary class), monarchy (rule by one), and direct democracy (rule by the people). A republic was both new and daring: No people had ever been governed by a republic on so vast a scale.

The framers themselves were far from sure that their government could be sustained. They had no model of republican government to follow; moreover, at the time, republican government was thought to be suitable only for small territories, where the interest of the public would be obvious and where government would be within the reach of every citizen. After the convention had ended, Benjamin Franklin was asked what sort of government the new nation would have. "A republic," he replied, "if you can keep it."

Federalism. **Federalism** is the division of power between a central government and regional units. It stands in contrast to **unitary government,** in which all power is vested in a central government. The Articles of Confederation embodied a form of federalism in which political power was divided between the states and the national government, with the states having the greater share. The federalism of the Constitution con-

FEATURE 3.3

The Intellectual Origins of the Constitution

The creation of the U.S. Constitution was a remarkable achievement by a young nation. However, only one of its four basic political principles was "made in America." The other three were inspired by ideas that first grew on foreign soil.

- *Republicanism.* In this form of government, power resides in the people and is exercised by their elected representatives; government is the common business of the citizens, conducted for the common good. The idea of republicanism may be traced to the Greek philosopher Aristotle (384–322 B.C.), who advocated a "mixed" constitution that contained principles of democratic and oligarchic government.

- *Federalism.* The powers of government are shared by a central body and territorial units. Citizens in a federal government are subject to two differentbodies of law. Federalism is the distinctly American idea, created by the Constitutional Convention of 1787.

- *Separation of powers.* The responsibilities of government are divided among separate branches. This idea was formulated in a fragmentary way by John Locke and others, but its fullest exposition came from French philosopher Charles-Louis de Secondat Montesquieu (1689–1755).

- *Checks and balances.* The branches of government scrutinize and restrain each other. This idea was first advanced by two Englishmen, the statesman Henry St. John Bolingbroke (1678–1751) and the jurist William Blackstone (1723–1780).

ferred substantial powers on the national government at the expense of the states.

The constitutional powers vested in the national and state governments are derived from the people, who remain the ultimate sovereign. National and state governments could exercise their powers over persons and property within their own spheres of authority. But, at the same time, the people would restrain both national and state governments to preserve their liberty.

The Constitution listed the powers of the national government and the powers that were denied to the states. All other powers remained with the states. Generally, the states were required to give up only the powers necessary to create an effective national government; the national government was limited to the powers specified in the Constitution. In spite of these specific lists, the Constitution does not clearly describe the spheres of authority within which these powers can be exercised. As we discuss in Chapter 4, limits on the exercise of power by the national government and the states have evolved as a result of political and military conflict; moreover, these limits have changed continually.

Separation of powers. **Separation of powers** is the assignment of the lawmaking, law-enforcing, and law-interpreting functions to independent legislative, executive, and judicial branches of government. Nationally, the lawmaking power resides in Congress; the law-enforcing power resides in the presidency; and the law-interpreting power resides in the courts. Service in one branch prohibits simultaneous service in the others. Separation of powers safeguards liberty by ensuring that all government power does not fall into the hands of a single person or group of people. But the framers' concern with protecting the liberty of the people did not extend to the election process. The Constitution constrained majority rule by limiting the direct influence of the people on that process (see Figure 3.1).

In theory, separation of powers means that one branch cannot exercise the powers of the other branches. In practice, however, the separation is far from complete. One scholar has suggested that what we have instead is "separate institutions *sharing* powers."[13]

Checks and balances. The constitutional system of **checks and balances** is a means of giving each branch of government some scrutiny of and control over the other branches. The framers reasoned that these checks and balances would prevent one branch from ignoring or overpowering the others.

Figure 3.1

The Constitution and the Electoral Process

The framers were afraid of majority rule, and that fear is reflected in the electoral process described in the Constitution. The people, speaking through the voters, had direct input only in the choice of their representatives in the House. The president and senators were elected indirectly, through the electoral college and state legislatures. (The direct election of senators did not become law until 1913, when the Seventeenth Amendment was ratified.) Judicial appointments are, and always have been far removed from representative links to the people. Judges are nominated by the president and approved by the Senate.

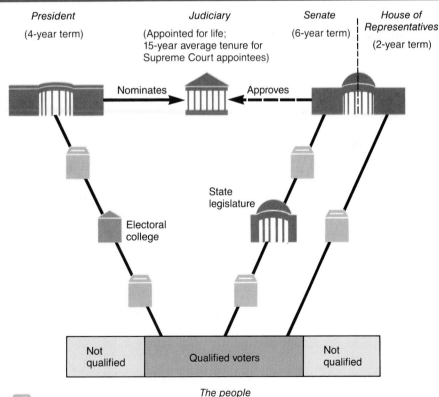

Separation of powers and checks and balances are two distinct principles, but both principles are necessary to ensure that one branch does not dominate the government. Separation of powers divides government responsibilities among the legislative, executive, and judicial branches; checks and balances prevent the exclusive exercise of those powers by any one of the three branches. For example, only the Congress can enact laws. But both the president (through the power of the veto) and the courts (by finding a law in violation of the Constitution) can nullify them. And the process goes on. In a "check on a check," the Congress can override a president's veto by an extraordinary (two-thirds) majority in each chamber; and it is empowered to propose amendments to the Constitution, counteracting the courts' power to find a national law invalid. Figure 3.2 depicts the relationship between separation of powers and checks and balances.

Figure 3.2

Separation of Powers and Checks and Balances

Separation of powers *is the assignment of lawmaking, law-enforcing, and law-interpreting functions to the legislative, executive, and judicial branches. This is illustrated by the diagonal grid in the figure.* Checks and balances *give each branch some power over the other branches. For example, the executive branch possesses some legislative power, and the legislative branch possesses some executive power. These checks and balances are illustrated within the columns and outside the diagonal grid.*

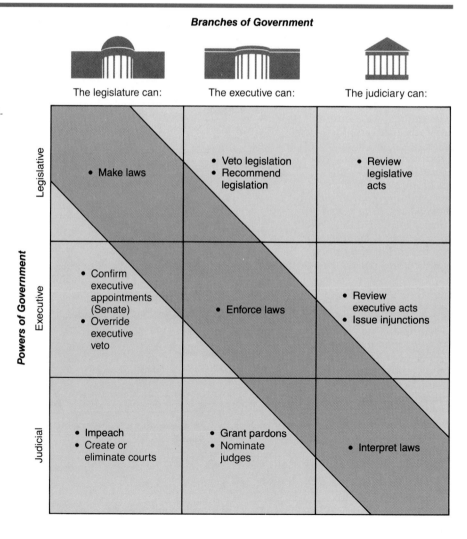

Branches of Government

	The legislature can:	The executive can:	The judiciary can:
Legislative	• Make laws	• Veto legislation • Recommend legislation	• Review legislative acts
Executive	• Confirm executive appointments (Senate) • Override executive veto	• Enforce laws	• Review executive acts • Issue injunctions
Judicial	• Impeach • Create or eliminate courts	• Grant pardons • Nominate judges	• Interpret laws

Powers of Government

The Articles of the Constitution

In addition to the Preamble, the Constitution includes seven articles. The first three establish the internal operation and powers of the separate branches of government. The remaining four define the relationships among the states, explain the process of amendment, declare the supremacy of national law, and explain the procedure for ratifying the Constitution.

Article I: The legislative article. In structuring their new government, the framers began with the legislative branch because they thought lawmaking was the most important function of a republican government. Article I is the most detailed and therefore the longest of all the articles. It defines the **bicameral** (two-chamber) character of the Congress and describes the internal operating procedures of the House of Representatives and the Senate. Section 8 of Article I expresses the principle of **enumerated powers,** which means that Congress can exercise only the powers that the Constitution assigns to Congress. Eighteen powers are enumerated; the first seventeen are specific powers. For example, the third clause of Section 8 gives Congress the power to regulate interstate commerce. (One of the chief problems with the Articles of Confederation was the lack of a means to cope with trade wars between states. The solution was to vest control of interstate commerce in the national government.)

The last clause in Section 8, known as the **necessary and proper clause** (or the **elastic clause**), gives Congress the means to execute the enumerated powers (see the Appendix). This clause is the basis of Congress's **implied powers**—those powers that Congress must have in order to execute its enumerated powers. The power to levy and collect taxes (Clause 1) and the power to coin money and regulate its value (Clause 5), when joined with the necessary and proper clause (Clause 18), *imply* that Congress has the power to charter a bank. Otherwise, the national government would have no means of managing the funds it collects through its power to tax. Implied powers clearly expand the enumerated powers conferred on Congress by the Constitution.

Article II: The executive article. Article II describes the president's term of office, the procedure for electing a president through the electoral college, the qualifications for becoming president, and the president's duties and powers. The last include acting as commander in chief of the military; making treaties (which must be ratified by a two-thirds vote of the Senate); and appointing government officers, diplomats, and judges (again, with the advice and consent of the Senate).

The president also has legislative powers—part of the constitutional system of checks and balances. For example, the Constitution requires that the president periodically inform the Congress of the "State of the Union" and of the policies and programs that the executive branch intends to advocate in the forthcoming year. Today this is done annually, in the president's State of the Union address. Under special circumstances, the president can also convene or adjourn Congress.

History in the Making
A president gives approval to legislation by signing a bill into law. Since the 1960s, the bill-signing ceremony has become an art form, garnering much attention from the media. Here President Ronald Reagan autographs one of the most significant laws of his administration, the Tax Reform Act of 1986 . . .

The duty to "take Care that the Laws be faithfully executed" in Section 3 has provided presidents with a reservoir of power. President Nixon tried to use this power when he refused to turn over the Watergate tapes despite a judicial subpoena in a criminal trial. He claimed executive privilege, an extension of the executive power implied in Article II. But the Supreme Court struck down his claim, arguing that it violated the separation of powers, that the decision to release or withhold information *in a criminal trial* is a judicial, not an executive, function.

Article III: The judicial article. The third article was purposely vague. The Constitution established the Supreme Court as the highest court in the land. But beyond that, the framers were unable to agree on the need for, the size of, or the composition of a national judiciary, or on the procedures it should follow. They left these issues to the Congress, which resolved them by creating the federal court system.

Short of impeachment, federal judges serve for life. They are appointed to indefinite terms on "good Behavior," and their salaries cannot be lowered while they hold office. These stipulations reinforce the separation of powers; they see to it that judges are independent of the other branches, that they do not have to fear retribution in their exercise of judicial power.

The judicial branch can be checked by Congress through its power to create (and eliminate) lower federal courts. Congress can also restrict the power of the lower courts to decide cases. And, as we have noted, the president appoints—with the advice and consent of the Senate—the justices of the Supreme Court and the judges of the lower federal courts.

Article III does not explicitly give the courts the power of **judicial review,** the authority to invalidate congressional or presidential actions.

History for the Taking
. . . and members of Congress appropriate the pens used in the signing ceremony. A presidential aide gathers the remaining souvenirs. These pens serve as mementos of the arduous task of law-making and tokens of appreciation for those who aided in the process.

That power has been inferred from the logic, structure, and theory of the Constitution.

The remaining articles. The remaining four articles of the Constitution cover a lot of ground. Article IV requires that the citizens, judicial acts, and criminal warrants of each state be honored in all other states. This is a provision that promotes equality; it keeps the states from treating outsiders differently from their own citizens. For example, an Illinois court awards Goldman damages against Janda for $10,000. Janda moves to Alaska to avoid payment. Rather than force Goldman to bring a new suit against Janda, the court in Alaska (Judge Berry presiding), under Article IV's full faith and credit clause, honors the Illinois judgment and enforces it as its own. In other words, you can run but you cannot hide. The origin of this clause can be traced to the Articles of Confederation.

Article IV also allows the addition of new states and stipulates that the national government will protect the states against invasion and domestic violence.

Article V specifies the methods for amending (changing) the Constitution. We have more to say about this shortly.

An important component of Article VI is the **supremacy clause,** which asserts that, when they conflict, the Constitution, national laws, and treaties take precedence over state and local laws. This stipulation is vital to the operation of federalism. In keeping with the supremacy clause, Article VI also requires that all national and state officials, elected or appointed, take an oath to support the Constitution. The article also mandates that religion cannot be a qualification for holding government office.

Finally, Article VII describes the ratification process, that approval by conventions in nine states was necessary for the "Establishment" of the Constitution.

The Framers' Motives

Some argue that the Constitution is essentially a conservative document written by wealthy men to advance their own interests. One distinguished historian writing in the early 1900s, Charles A. Beard, maintained that the delegates, who were for the most part wealthy men, had much to gain from a strong national government.[14] Many delegates held government securities that were practically worthless under the Articles of Confederation. A strong national government would protect their property and pay off the nation's debts. Beard claimed that the Constitution was crafted to protect the economic interests of this small group of creditors.

Beard's argument provoked a generation of historians to examine the existing financial records of the convention delegates. Their scholarship has largely discredited his once-popular view.[15] For example, it turns out that seven of the delegates who left the convention or refused to sign the Constitution held public securities worth more than twice the holdings of the thirty-nine delegates who did sign. Moreover, the most influential delegates owned no securities. And only a small number of the delegates appeared to benefit economically from the new government.[16]

What did motivate the framers? Surely economic issues were important, but they were not the major issues. The single most important factor leading to the Constitutional Convention was the inability of the national or state governments to maintain order under the loose structure of the Articles of Confederation. Certainly order involved the protection of property; but the framers had a broader view of property than their portfolios of government securities. They wanted to protect their homes, their families, and their means of livelihood from impending anarchy.

Although they disagreed bitterly on structure, mechanics, and detail, the framers agreed on the most vital issues. For example, three of the most crucial parts of the Constitution—the power to tax, the necessary and proper clause, and the supremacy clause—were approved unanimously without debate. The convention was successful because experience had taught the delegates that a strong national government was essential if the United States was going to survive.

SELLING THE CONSTITUTION

On September 17, 1787, nearly four months after the Constitutional Convention opened, the delegates convened for the last time, to sign the final version of their handiwork. Because several delegates were unwilling to sign the document, the last paragraph was craftily worded to give the impression of unanimity: "Done in Convention by the Unanimous Consent of the *States* present."

Before it could take effect, the Constitution had to be ratified by a minimum of nine state conventions. The support of key states was crucial. In Pennsylvania, the legislature was slow to convene a ratifying convention. Pro-Constitution forces became so frustrated at this dawdling that they broke into a local boardinghouse and hauled two errant legislators through the streets to the state house so the assembly could schedule the convention.

The proponents of the new charter, who wanted a strong national government, called themselves *Federalists*. The opponents of the Constitution were quickly dubbed *Antifederalists*. They claimed, however, that *they* were true federalists because they wanted to protect the states from the tyranny of a strong national government. Elbridge Gerry, a vocal Antifederalist, called his opponents "rats" (because they favored ratification) and maintained that he was an "antirat."[17] Such is the Alice-in-Wonderland character of political discourse. Whatever they were called, the viewpoints of the two groups formed the bases of the first American political parties.

The *Federalist Papers*

Beginning in October 1787, a series of eighty-five newspaper articles appeared under the title *The Federalist: A Commentary on the Constitution of the United States.* The essays were reprinted extensively during the ratification battle. They bore the pen name "Publius" (Latin for "the people") and were written primarily by James Madison and Alexander Hamilton, with some assistance from John Jay. Rationally and quietly, Publius argued in favor of ratification. He was avowedly engaged in an exercise of special pleading. But the articles lacked the thunder that was needed to stir citizens to action; the personal influence of Washington and Franklin probably weighed more heavily than the essays in the ensuing debates. But *The Federalist* (also called the *Federalist Papers*) remains the best single commentary we have on the meaning of the Constitution and the political theory it embodies.

The Antifederalists, not to be outdone, offered their own intellectual basis for rejecting the Constitution. In several essays authored by "Brutus," they attacked the centralization of power in a strong national government, claiming it would obliterate the states and destroy liberty in the process. They defended the status quo, maintaining that the Articles of Confederation established true federal principles.[18]

Of all the *Federalist Papers*, the most magnificent and most frequently cited is "Federalist No. 10," which was written by James Madison (see the Appendix). He argued that the proposed constitution was designed "to break and control the violence of faction": "By a faction, I understand a number of citizens, whether amounting to a majority or minority of the whole, who are united and actuated by some common impulse of passion, or of interest, adverse to the rights of other citizens, or to the permanent and aggregate interests of the community."

Of course, Madison was discussing what we described in Chapter 2 as *pluralism*. What Madison called *factions* today are interest groups or even political parties. According to Madison, "The most common and durable source of factions has been the various and unequal distribution of property." Madison was concerned, not with reducing inequalities of wealth (which he took for granted), but with controlling the seemingly inevitable conflict stemming from them. The Constitution, he argued, was "well-constructed" for this purpose.

Through the mechanism of *representation*, wrote Madison, the Constitution would prevent the tyranny of the majority (mob rule). Government would not be controlled directly by the people, but would be controlled indirectly, by their elected representatives. And those representatives would have the intelligence and the understanding to serve the larger interests of the nation. Moreover, the federal system would require that majorities form first within each state, then organize for effective action at the national level. This and the vastness of the country would make it unlikely that a majority would form "to invade the rights of other citizens."

The purpose of "Federalist No. 10" was to demonstrate that the proposed government was not likely to be ruled by any faction. Contrary to conventional wisdom, Madison argued, the key to controlling the evils of faction is to have a large republic—the larger, the better. The more diverse the society, the less likely it is that an unjust majority can form. Madison certainly had no intention of creating a majoritarian democracy; his view of popular government was much more consistent with the model of pluralist democracy we discussed in Chapter 2.

Madison pressed his argument from a different angle in "Federalist No. 51" (see the Appendix). Asserting that "ambition must be made to counteract ambition," he argued that the separation of powers and checks and balances would control tyranny from any source. If power is distributed equally across the three branches, then each branch has the capacity to counteract the other. In Madison's words, "usurpations are guarded against by a division of the government into distinct and separate departments." Because legislative power tends to predominate in republican governments, legislative authority is divided between the Senate and the House of Representatives, with different methods of selection and terms of office. Additional protection comes through federalism, which divides power "between two distinct governments"—national and state—and subdivides "the portion allotted to each . . . among distinct and separate departments."

The Antifederalists wanted additional separation of powers and additional checks and balances, which, they maintained, would eliminate the threat of tyranny entirely. The Federalists believed that this would make decisive national action virtually impossible. But to ensure ratification, they agreed to a compromise.

A Concession: The Bill of Rights

Despite the eloquence of the *Federalist Papers*, many prominent citizens, including Thomas Jefferson, were unhappy that the Constitution did not list basic civil liberties—the individual freedoms guaranteed to citizens. The omission of a bill of rights was the chief obstacle to the Constitution's adoption by the states. (In fact, seven of the eleven state constitutions that were written in the first five years of independence already included such a list.) The colonists had just rebelled against the British government to preserve their basic freedoms; why didn't the proposed Constitution spell out those freedoms?

The answer was rooted in logic, not politics. Because the national government was limited to those powers that were granted to it and because no power was granted to abridge the people's liberties, then a list of guaranteed freedoms was not necessary. Hamilton, in "Federalist No. 84," went even further, arguing that the addition of a bill of rights would be dangerous. To deny the exercise of a nonexistent power might lead to the exercise of a power that is not specifically denied. Because it is not possible to list all prohibited powers, wrote Hamilton, any attempt to provide a partial list would make the remaining areas vulnerable to government abuse.

But logic was no match for fear. Many states agreed to ratify the Constitution only after Washington suggested that a list of guarantees be added through the amendment process. Well over a hundred amendments were proposed by the states. These were eventually narrowed down to twelve, which were approved by Congress and sent to the states. Ten of them became part of the Constitution in 1791, when Virginia became the eleventh state to approve them.* (Connecticut, Georgia, and Massachusetts finally approved them in 1939, 150 years after they were introduced.) Collectively, these ten amendments are known as the **Bill of Rights.** They restrain the national government from tampering with fundamental rights and civil liberties and emphasize the limited character of national power (see Table 3.2).

Ratification

Delaware was first to ratify the Constitution. (Today, Delaware license plates bear the motto "The First State.") Massachusetts gave its assent after a close contest (187 yeas to 168 nays), but its convention called for the promised bill of rights. New Hampshire, the ninth state to ratify, did so on June 21, 1788. According to Article VII, the Constitution took effect on that date. But this was true only in a technical sense. Two of the remaining states were absolutely critical to the success of the newly formed United States: Virginia and New York together comprised almost 40 percent of its population.

The debate in these states was filled with invective. Virginia ratified by a vote of 89 to 79, but it recommended a declaration of rights and twenty additional amendments to cure other "defects" in the Constitution. The New York convention voted to ratify a week after Virginia did, by a vote of 30 to 27. Had two Federalist delegates switched votes, the Constitution—and in all likelihood, the Union—would have failed. New York, too, recommended the addition of a bill of rights, along with thirty-two other amendments. By August 1788, eleven states had ratified the Constitution.

---

* Vermont joined the Union in March 1791, bringing the number of states to fourteen. Three-fourths of the states were necessary for ratification.

Table 3.2
The Bill of Rights
The first ten amendments to the Constitution are known as the Bill of Rights.
*The following is a list of those amendments grouped conceptually. For the
actual order and wording of the Bill of Rights, see the Appendix.*

Guarantees	*Amendment*
Guarantees for Participation in the Political Process	
No government abridgement of speech of press;	
no government abridgement of peaceable assembly;	
no government abridgement of petitioning government for	
redress.	1
Guarantees Respecting Personal Beliefs	
No government establishment of religion;	
no government prohibition of free religious exercise.	1
Guarantees of Personal Privacy	
Owners' consent necessary to quarter troops in private homes in	
peacetime; quartering during war must be lawful.	3
Government cannot engage in unreasonable searches and	
seizures; warrants to search and seize require probable cause.	4
No compulsion to testify against oneself in criminal cases.	5
Guarantees Against Government Overreaching	
Serious crimes require a grand jury indictment;	
no repeated prosecution for the same offense;	
no loss of life, liberty, of property without due process;	
no government taking of property for public use without just	
compensation.	5
Criminal defendants will have a speedy public trial by impartial	
local jury; defendants informed of accusation; defendants	
confront witnesses against them; defendants use judicial	
process to obtain favorable witnesses; defendants have legal	
assistance for their defense.	6
Civil lawsuits can be tried by juries if controversy exceeds $20;	
in jury trials, factfinding is a jury function.	7
No excessive bail; no excessive fines; no cruel and unusual	
punishment.	8
Other Guarantees	
No government trespass on unspecified fundamental rights.	9
The states of the people reserve the powers no delegated to the	
national government or denied to the states.	10
The people have the right to bear arms.	2

Rhode Island, the only state that did not send a delegate to the
Constitutional Convention was the last state to ratify. When Rhode
Island finally did approve the Constitution on May 29, 1790, it did so by
a vote of only 34 to 32.[19]

The reflection and deliberation that attended the creation and ratification of the Constitution signaled to the world that a new government
could be launched peacefully. The French observer, Alexis de Tocqueville
(1805–1859) later wrote:

> That which is new in the history of societies is to see a great people, warned
> by its lawgivers that the wheels of government are stopping, turn its atten-
> tion on itself without haste or fear, sound the depth of the ill, and then wait

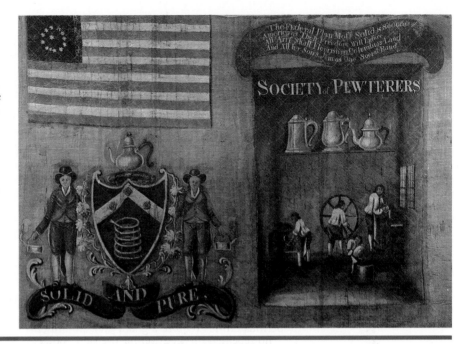

Parading for Principle
New Yorkers held a festive procession on July 23, 1788, three days before their state became the eleventh to ratify the Constitution. Among the five thousand tradespeople who participated were members of the Society of Pewterers, who displayed a silk banner emblazoned with a thirteen-star flag, symbols of their work, and slogans that applauded the "federal plan." The parade was daring for its time: Tailors carried a banner that showed a naked Adam and Eve, which read "And they sewed fig leaves together."

for two years to find the remedy at leisure, and then finally, when the remedy has been indicated, submit to it voluntarily without its costing humanity a single tear or drop of blood.[20]

CONSTITUTIONAL CHANGE

The founders realized that the Constitution would have to be changed from time to time. To this end, they specified a formal amendment process in Article V—a process that was used almost immediately to add the Bill of Rights. With the passage of time, the Constitution also has been altered through judicial interpretation and changes in political practice.

The Formal Amendment Process

There are two stages in the amendment process, **proposal** and **ratification;** both are necessary for an amendment to become part of the Constitution. The Constitution provides two alternative methods for completing each stage (see Figure 3.3). Amendments can be proposed (1) by a two-thirds vote of the House of Representatives and of the Senate or (2) by a national convention, summoned by Congress at the request of two-thirds of the state legislatures. All constitutional amendments to date have been proposed by the first method; the second has never been used.

A proposed amendment can be ratified (1) by a vote of the legislatures of three-fourths of the states, or (2) by a vote of constitutional conven-

Proposal Stage   *Ratification Stage*

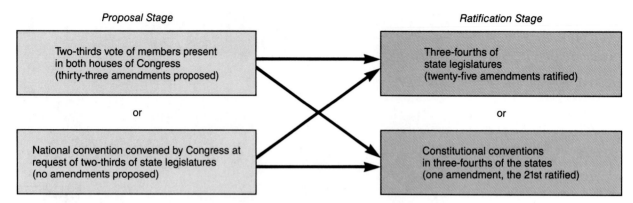

Amending the Constitution
*There are two stages in amending the Constitution: proposal and ratification.
Congress has no control over the proposal stage, but it prescribes the ratification method. Once it has ratified an amendment, a state cannot retract its
action. A state's rejection of an amendment does not bar future reconsideration, however.*

Figure 3.3

tions held in three-fourths of the states. Congress chooses the method
of ratification. It has used the state convention method only once, for
the Twenty-first Amendment, which repealed the Eighteenth (Prohibition).

Notice that the amendment process requires the exercise of **extraordinary majorities.** The framers purposely made it difficult to propose and
ratify amendments (although nowhere near as difficult as the amendment
process under the Articles of Confederation). They wanted only the most
significant issues to lead to constitutional change. Notice, too, that the
president plays no formal role in the process. His approval is not required
to amend the Constitution, although his political influence affects the
success or failure of any amendment effort.

Calling a national convention to propose an amendment has never
been tried. Certainly the method raises several thorny questions. For
example, the Constitution doesn't address the number of delegates who
should attend, the method by which they should be chosen, or the rules
for debating and voting on a proposed amendment. But the major issue
is the limits, if any, on the business of the convention. Remember that
the convention in Philadelphia in 1787 was charged with revising the
Articles of Confederation, yet it drafted an entirely new charter. Would
a national convention, called to consider a particular amendment, be
within its bounds to rewrite the Constitution? No one really knows. But
the question may soon be put to a test. A movement is under way to
convene a constitutional convention to write an amendment that would
require a balanced budget. Thirty-two states have voted to issue a convention call on the budget issue. When thirty-four approve, the Constitution requires that a convention be held.

Most of the Constitution's twenty-six amendments were adopted to
help keep it abreast of changes in political thinking. The first ten amendments (the Bill of Rights) were the price of ratification, but they have

Roll Out the Barrels
The Eighteenth Amendment, which was ratified by the states in 1919, banned the manufacture, sale, or transportation of alcoholic beverages. The amendment was spurred by moral and social reform groups, like the Women's Christian Temperance Union, founded by Evanston, Illinois, resident Frances Willard in 1874. The amendment proved to be an utter failure. People continued to drink, but their alcohol came from illegal sources.

been important to our current system of government. The last sixteen amendments fall into three main categories: They make *public policy;* they correct deficiencies in *government structure;* or they promote *equality* (see Table 3.3). One attempt to make public policy through a constitutional amendment was disastrous. The Eighteenth Amendment (1919) prohibited the manufacture or sale of intoxicating beverages. Prohibition lasted for fourteen years and was an utter failure. Gangsters began bootlegging liquor; people died from drinking home-made booze; and millions regularly broke the law by drinking anyway. Congress had to propose another amendment in 1933 to repeal the Eighteenth. The states ratified this amendment, the Twenty-first, in less than ten months, less time than it took to ratify the Fourteenth Amendment, guaranteeing citizenship, due process, and equal protection.

Since 1787, about ten thousand constitutional amendments have been introduced; only a fraction have passed through the proposal stage. Once an amendment has been voted by the Congress, however, the chances of ratification are very high. Only seven amendments submitted to the states have failed to be ratified. The latest, which called for full congressional representation for Washington, D.C., mustered approval in just sixteen states, twenty-two states short of the required three-fourths.

Interpretation by the Courts

In 1803, in its decision in *Marbury* v. *Madison*, the Supreme Court declared that the courts have the power to nullify government acts when they conflict with the Constitution. (We elaborate on the power of *judicial review* in Chapter 13.) The exercise of judicial review forces the

Table 3.3
Constitutional Amendments: 11 through 26

No.	Proposed	Ratified	Intent	Subject
11	1794	1795	G	Prohibits an individual from suing a state in a federal court without the state's consent.
12	1803	1804	G	Requires the electoral college to vote separately for president and vice president.
13	1865	1865	E	Prohibits slavery.
14	1866	1868	E	Gives citizenship to all persons born or natualized in the United States (former slaves); prevents states from depriving and "person of life, liberty, or property, without due process of law."
15	1869	1870	E	Guarantees that citizens' right to vote cannot be denied "on account of race, color, or previous condition of servitude."
16	1909	1913	E	Gives congress power to collect an income tax.
17	1912	1913	E	Provides for popular election of senators, who were formerly elected by state legislatures.
18	1917	1919	P	Prohibits making and selling intoxicating liquors.
19	1919	1920	E	Gives women the right to vote.
20	1932	1933	G	Changes the presidential inauguration from March 4 to January 20 and sets January 3 for the opening date of Congress.
21	1933	1933	P	Repeals the Eighteenth Amendment.
22	1947	1951	G	Limits a president to two terms.
23	1960	1961	E	Gives citizens of Washington D.C., the right to vote for president.
24	1962	1964	E	Prohibits charging citizens a poll tax to vote.
25	1965	1967	G	Provides for succession in event of death, removal from office, incapacity, or resignation of the president or vice president.
26	1971	1971	E	Lowers the voting age to eighteen.

P Amendments legislating public policy.
G Amendments correcting perceived deficiencies in government structure
E Amendments advancing equality.

courts to interpret the Constitution. In a way, this makes a lot of sense. The judiciary is the law-interpreting branch of the government; the Constitution is the supreme law of the land, fair game then for judicial interpretation. But in interpreting the Constitution, the courts cannot help but give new meaning to its provisions. This is why judicial interpretation is a principal form of constitutional change.

What guidelines should judges use in interpreting the Constitution? For one thing, they must realize that our language—particularly the usage and meaning of many words—has changed over the last two hundred years. They must be careful to think about what the words meant at the time the Constitution was written. Some insist they also must consider the original intent of the framers—not an easy task. Of course, there are records of the Constitutional Convention and the debates surrounding ratification. But there are also many questions about the completeness and accuracy of those records, even Madison's detailed notes. And, at times, the framers chose to be general or vague in writing the document. In part, this may reflect their lack of agreement on or universal understanding of certain provisions in the Constitution.

Political Practice

The Constitution remains silent on many issues. For example, it says nothing about political parties or the president's cabinet, yet both parties and cabinets have exercised considerable influence in American politics. Some constitutional provisions have fallen out of use. The electors in the electoral college, for example, were supposed to exercise their own judgment in voting for president and vice president. Today the electors function simply as a rubber stamp, reflecting the outcome of election contests in their states.

Political practice has altered the distribution of power without changes in the Constitution. The framers intended Congress to be the strongest branch of government. But the president has come to overshadow Congress. Presidents like Lincoln and Franklin Roosevelt used their powers imaginatively to respond to national crises. And their actions served as springboards for future presidents to further enlarge the powers of the office.

The framers could scarcely imagine an urbanized nation of 240 million people stretching across a land mass some 3,000 miles wide. They could never in their wildest nightmares have foreseen the destructiveness of nuclear war or envisioned the influence this would have on the power to declare war. The Constitution gives that power to Congress, to consider and debate this momentous step. But with nuclear annihilation perhaps only minutes away, the legislative power to declare war must give way to the president's power to wage war as the nation's commander in chief. Strict adherence to the Constitution here could destroy the nation's ability to protect itself.

AN EVALUATION OF THE CONSTITUTION

The U.S. Constitution is one of the world's most praised political documents. It is the oldest written national constitution and one of the most widely copied, sometimes word for word (see Compared With What? 3.1). It is also one of the shortest, containing about 4,300 words, not counting the amendments. In fact, the twenty-six amendments (about 3,500 words) are nearly as long as the Constitution itself. The brevity of the Constitution may be one of its greatest strengths. As we noted earlier,

COMPARED WITH WHAT? 3.1

Exporting the Constitution

Entering its third century of existence, the U.S. Constitution is the oldest written national charter still in effect. Its stability and the ideals it expresses have inspired imitations throughout the world.

In overwhelmingly Catholic Ireland, the constitution outlaws abortion and divorce and proclaims the Holy Trinity the source of all political power. Japan's national charter renounces war. Portugal's forbids private ownership of television stations. Peru reprints its charter in the Lima telephone directory, filling pages of fine print. Yet beneath such diversity, each document can trace its rights and freedoms to U.S. soil. Says Joseph Magnet, a law professor at Canada's University of Ottawa: "America has been and remains the great constitutional laboratory for the entire world."

Of the 170 countries that exist today, more than 160 have written charters modeled directly or indirectly on the U.S. version. Those states range from the giant Soviet Union to the tiny Caribbean island country of Grenada. While Poland and France became the first to follow America's lead when they drafted modern constitutions in 1791, the largest impact has been recent. More than three-quarters of today's charters were adopted after World War II. Jawaharlal Nehru, India's first Prime Minister, could have been speaking for the rest of the Third World when he told the U.S. Congress in 1949, "We have been greatly influenced by your own Constitution."

Some charters are roundly ignored. China's declaration of human rights was powerless to stop the abuses of the 1960s Cultural Revolution. In Latin America dictators often simply disregard national charters during times of unrest. Many African leaders have stymied democracy by outlawing opposing political parties and turning their countries into one-party states, often without bothering to amend their charters. Yet so strongly have constitutional ideals taken hold worldwide that few countries dare to abandon them completely.

Indeed, constitutions are living documents that are constantly being created and reshaped. Voters in the Philippines went to the polls in [1987] to approve a new charter, the country's fifth, that prohibits human rights violations and retains Corazon Aquino as President until 1992. In Nicaragua . . ., the Marxist-influenced Sandinista leadership unveiled that country's twelfth constitution in 149 years. . . .

As such figures show, many constitutions have managed to survive only until the next upheaval or military coup. Three-quarters of the world's constitutions have been completely rewritten since they were first adopted, making America's fidelity to a single charter highly unusual. Some experts contend that frequent constitutional changes can be healthy. Says Albert Blaustein, a Rutgers University law professor who has helped draft six foreign charters: "Jefferson concluded that every 20 years the new generation should have its own constitution to meet current needs. That might not be a good idea for the U.S., but it's really not a bad idea for other countries."

the framers simply laid out a structural framework for government; they did not describe relationships and powers in detail. For example, the Constitution gives Congress the power to regulate "Commerce . . . among the several States," but does not define *interstate commerce.* This kind of general wording allows interpretation in keeping with contemporary political, social, and technological developments. Air travel, for instance, was unknown in 1787, but it now falls easily within Congress's power to regulate interstate commerce.

The generality of the U.S. Constitution stands in stark contrast to the specificity of most state constitutions. The constitution of California, for example, provides that "fruit and nut-bearing trees under the age of

Some constitutions are born of disaster. After World War II, Americans played a key role in drafting charters for the defeated nations of Japan and West Germany. The Japanese charter declares that the country will never again make war or maintain an army, navy or air force. As a result, Japan spends only about 1% of its gross national product on defense, freeing the economy for more productive purposes. Ironically, the U.S. is pressing the Japanese to boost defense outlays.

The West German constitution, written under the watchful eye of U.S. occupation leaders, sought to prevent the rise of another Hitler by limiting the executive branch. Recalls Joachim von Elbe, a Bonn legal expert: "We did not want to make the Germans just imitate the American constitutional model but rely on themselves to reform, rebuild and overcome the Nazi period." The framers decreed that the Bundestag, or parliament, could not oust a Chancellor without first choosing a successor. That has helped prevent a return of the political chaos that brought the Nazis to power in the l930s.

Italians, with memories of Mussolini still fresh in their minds, went even further than the Germans in reining in the executive branch. While this has guarded against a new outbreak of tyranny, the inability of any one of Italy's parties to win a majority in parliament has led to frequent political turnover: Italy has had 46 governments since 1945. . . .

Among Third World nations, India has often seemed the most faithful to its U.S.-inspired constitutional ideals. The world's largest democracy included a declaration of "fundamental rights" in its 1949 charter and backed them up by borrowing the U.S. system of judicial review. "Thank God they put in the fundamental rights," says Nani Palkhivala, a constitutional expert who was India's Ambassador to Washington in the late 1970s. He observes, "Since 1947 we have had more harsh and repressive laws than were ever imposed under British rule." Indian courts, however, overturned most of them. . . .

Though many U.S.-inspired constitutions have gone their own ways over the years, the seed planted in Philadelphia in 1789 should continue to flower. "The idea that individuals have rights against government is probably the most profound influence of the U.S. Constitution," says Oscar Schachter, professor emeritus of international law and diplomacy at Columbia University. "The whole notion of human rights as a worldwide movement was grounded in part in the Constitution." Those rights may not always be honored, but they have fired the imaginations of individuals, free and otherwise, around the world. After two centuries, the U.S. Constitution remains the standard against which people of all sorts measure their governments, and some governments even measure themselves.

four years from the time of planting in orchard form and grapevines under the age of three years from the time of planting in vineyard form . . . shall be exempt from taxation" (Article XIII, Section 12). Because they are so specific, most state constitutions are much longer than the U.S. Constitution.

Freedom, Order, and Equality in the Constitution

The revolutionaries' first try at government was embodied in the Articles of Confederation. The result was a weak government that leaned too much toward freedom at the expense of order. Deciding that the confederation was beyond correcting, the revolutionaries chose a new form of government—a *federal* government—and wrote a new constitution. That constitution was aimed at structuring a national government strong enough to maintain order but not so strong that it could dominate the states or infringe on individual freedoms. In short, the Constitution provided a judicious balance between order and freedom. It paid virtually no attention to equality.

Consider social equality. The Constitution never mentioned slavery—a controversial issue even then. In fact, as we discussed earlier, the Constitution implicitly condones slavery in the wording of several articles. Not until the Thirteenth Amendment's ratification in 1865 was slavery prohibited.

The Constitution was designed long before social equality was ever even thought of as an objective of government. In fact, in "Federalist No. 10," Madison held that protection of the "diversities in the faculties of men from which the rights of property originate" is "the first object of government." Over a century later, the Constitution was changed to incorporate a key device for the promotion of social equality—the income tax. The Sixteenth Amendment (1913) gave Congress the power to collect an income tax; it was proposed and ratified to replace a law that had been declared unconstitutional in an 1895 court case. The idea of **progressive taxation** (in which the tax rate increases with income) had long been closely linked to the income tax, and the Sixteenth Amendment gave it a constitutional basis.[21] Progressive taxation later helped promote social equality through the redistribution of income. That is, higher-income people are taxed at higher rates to help fund social programs that benefit low-income people. Social equality itself has never been, and is not now, a prime *constitutional* value. The Constitution has been much more effective in securing order and freedom. A recent poll of Americans reinforces this evaluation (see Figure 3.4).

The Constitution also did not take a stand on political equality. It left voting qualifications to the states, specifying only that people who could vote for "the most numerous Branch of the State Legislature" could also vote for representatives to Congress (Article I, Section 2). In most states at that time, only tax-paying or property-owning white males could vote; blacks and women were universally excluded. These inequalities have been rectified by several amendments (see Table 3.3).

The Constitution did not guarantee blacks citizenship until the Fourteenth Amendment was ratified (1868) and did not give them the right to vote until the Fifteenth Amendment (1870). Women were not guaranteed the right to vote until the Nineteenth Amendment (1920). Finally, the *poll tax* (a tax that people had to pay in order to vote and that tended to disenfranchise blacks) was not eliminated until the Twenty-fourth Amendment (1964). Two other amendments expanded the Constitution's grant of political equality. The Twenty-third Amendment (1961) allowed citizens of Washington, D.C., who are not considered residents of any state, to vote for president. The Twenty-sixth Amendment (1971) extended voting rights to all citizens who are at least eighteen years old.

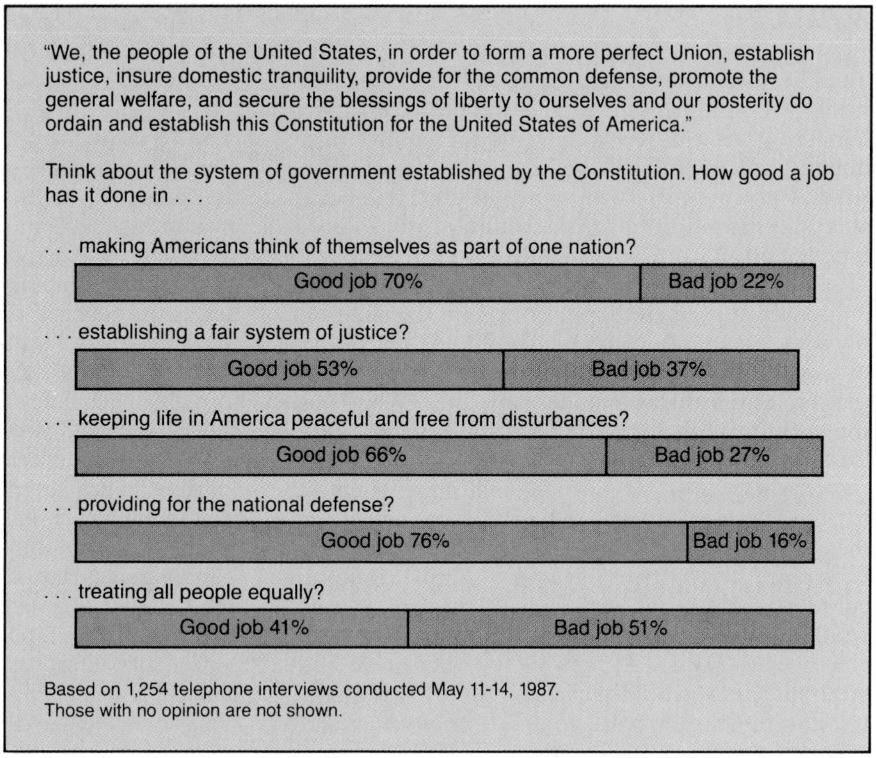

"We the People" Evaluate the Constitution
Two hundred years after the Constitutional Convention, a survey of Americans evaluated the success of the goals articulated in the Constitution's preamble. According to the results, the Constitution has done a good job of forging one nation from separate states and securing an orderly and free society. Though not an explicit goal in the preamble, the Constitution's success in treating all people equally received a relatively poor grade. (Source: New York Times, 26 May 1987, p. 10. Copyright © 1987 by the New York Times Company. Reprinted by permission.)
Figure 3.4

"We, the people of the United States, in order to form a more perfect Union, establish justice, insure domestic tranquility, provide for the common defense, promote the general welfare, and secure the blessings of liberty to ourselves and our posterity do ordain and establish this Constitution for the United States of America."

Think about the system of government established by the Constitution. How good a job has it done in . . .

. . . making Americans think of themselves as part of one nation?

Good job 70%	Bad job 22%

. . . establishing a fair system of justice?

Good job 53%	Bad job 37%

. . . keeping life in America peaceful and free from disturbances?

Good job 66%	Bad job 27%

. . . providing for the national defense?

Good job 76%	Bad job 16%

. . . treating all people equally?

Good job 41%	Bad job 51%

Based on 1,254 telephone interviews conducted May 11-14, 1987.
Those with no opinion are not shown.

The Constitution and Models of Democracy

Think back to our discussion of the models of democracy in Chapter 2. Which model does the Constitution fit: the pluralist or majoritarian? Actually, it is hard to imagine a government framework better suited to the pluralist model of democracy than the Constitution of the United States. It is also hard to imagine a document more at odds with the majoritarian model. Consider Madison's claim, in "Federalist No. 10," that government inevitably involves conflicting factions. This concept fits perfectly with the idea of competing groups in pluralist theory (see Chapter 2). Think about his description in "Federalist No. 51" of the Constitution's ability to guard against the concentration of power in the majority through its separation of powers and checks and balances. This concept—avoiding a single center of government power that might fall under majority control—fits perfectly with pluralist democracy.

The delegates to the Constitutional Convention intended to create a republic, a government based on majority consent; they did not intend to create a democracy, which rests on majority rule. They succeeded admirably in creating that republic. Along the way, they also produced a government that grew into a democracy . . . but a particular type of democracy. The framers neither wanted nor got a democracy that fit the majoritarian model. They perhaps wanted and certainly did get a government that conforms to the pluralist model.

SUMMARY

The U.S. Constitution is more than a historic document, an antique curiosity. Although over two hundred years old, it still governs the politics of a mighty modern nation. It still has the power to force from office a president who won re-election by a landslide and the power to see the country through government crises.

The Constitution was the end product of a revolutionary movement aimed at preserving existing liberties. That movement began with the Declaration of Independence, a proclamation that everyone is entitled to certain rights (among them, life, liberty, and the pursuit of happiness) and that government exists for the good of its citizens. When government denies those rights, the people have the right to rebel.

War with Britain was only part of the process of independence. Some form of government was needed to replace the British monarchy. The Americans chose a republic, and defined the structure of that republic in the Articles of Confederation. The Articles were a failure. Although they guaranteed the states their coveted independence, they left the central government too weak to deal with disorder and insurrection.

The Constitution was the second attempt at government. It created a strong national government, incorporating four political principles: republicanism, federalism, separation of powers, and checks and balances. Republicanism is a form of government in which power resides in the people and is exercised by their elected representatives. Federalism is a division of power between the national government and the states. Separation of powers is a further division of the power of the national government into legislative (lawmaking), executive (law-enforcing), and judiciary (law-interpreting) branches. Finally, the Constitution established a system of checks and balances, giving each branch some scrutiny of and control over the others.

The document written, work began on ratification. A major stumbling block was the Constitution's failure to list the individual liberties the Americans had fought to protect. With the promise of a bill of rights, the Constitution was ratified. These ten amendments guaranteed participation in the political process, personal beliefs, and personal privacy. They also embodied guarantees against government overreaching in criminal prosecutions. Over the years the Constitution has evolved through the formal amendment process, through the exercise of judicial review, and through political practice.

The Constitution was designed to strike a balance between order and freedom. It was not designed to promote equality; in fact, it had to be amended to redress inequality. The framers did not set out to create a democracy. There was little faith in government by the people two centuries ago. Nevertheless, they produced a democratic form of government. That government, with its separation of powers and checks and balances, is remarkably well suited to the pluralist model of democracy. Simple majority rule, which lies at the heart of the majoritarian model, was precisely what the framers wanted to avoid.

The framers also wanted a government that would balance the powers of the national government and the states. The exact balance was a touchy issue, skirted by the delegates at the Constitutional Convention. Some seventy years later, a civil war was fought over that balance of power. That war and countless political battles before and after it have demonstrated that the national government dominates the state governments in our political system. In the next chapter, we look at how a loose confederation of states has evolved into a "more perfect Union."

Key Terms

Continental Congress	federalism
Declaration of Independence	unitary government
social contract theory	separation of powers
republic	checks and balances
confederation	bicameral
sovereignty	enumerated powers
Articles of Confederation	necessary and proper clause
Shays's Rebellion	elastic clause
Virginia Plan	implied powers
legislative branch	judicial review
executive branch	supremacy clause
judicial branch	Bill of Rights
New Jersey Plan	proposal
Great Compromise	ratification
electoral college	extraordinary majorities
republicanism	progressive taxation

Selected Readings

Beard, Charles A. *Economic Interpretation of the Constitution of the United States.* New York: Macmillan, 1913. The classic argument that the framers' economic self-interest was the motivating force behind the Constitution.

Becker, Carl. *The Declaration of Independence: A Study in the History of Political Ideas.* New York: Knopf, 1942. A classic study of the theory and politics of the Declaration of Independence.

Bowen, Catherine Drinker. *Miracle at Philadelphia.* Boston: Atlantic-Little, Brown, 1966. An absorbing, well-written account of the events surrounding the Constitutional Convention.

Kammen, Michael. *A Machine That Would Go of Itself: The Constitution in American Culture.* New York: Knopf, 1986. A remarkable examination of the Constitution's cultural impact. The author argues that Americans' reverence toward the Constitution is inconsistent with their ignorance of its content and meaning.

McDonald, Forrest. *Novus Ordo Seclorum: The Intellectual Origins of the Constitution.* Lawrence, Kan.: University Press of Kansas, 1985. An authoritative examination of the intellectual ferment surrounding the birth of the U.S. Constitution.

Rakove, Jack N. *The Beginnings of National Politics: An Interpretive History of the Continental Congress.* New York: Knopf, 1979. This is a history of the Continental Congress and the difficulties of governing under the Articles of Confederation.

Storing, Herbert J. *What the Anti-Federalists Were For.* Chicago: University of Chicago Press, 1981. An analysis of the arguments against the Constitution.

Wills, Garry. *Explaining America: The Federalist.* Garden City, N.Y.: Doubleday, 1981. This arresting work analyzes the intellectual background of the framers.

Wood, Gordon S. *The Creation of the American Republic, 1776–1787.* Chapel Hill, N.C.: University of North Carolina Press, 1969. A penetrating study of political thought in the early period of the new republic.

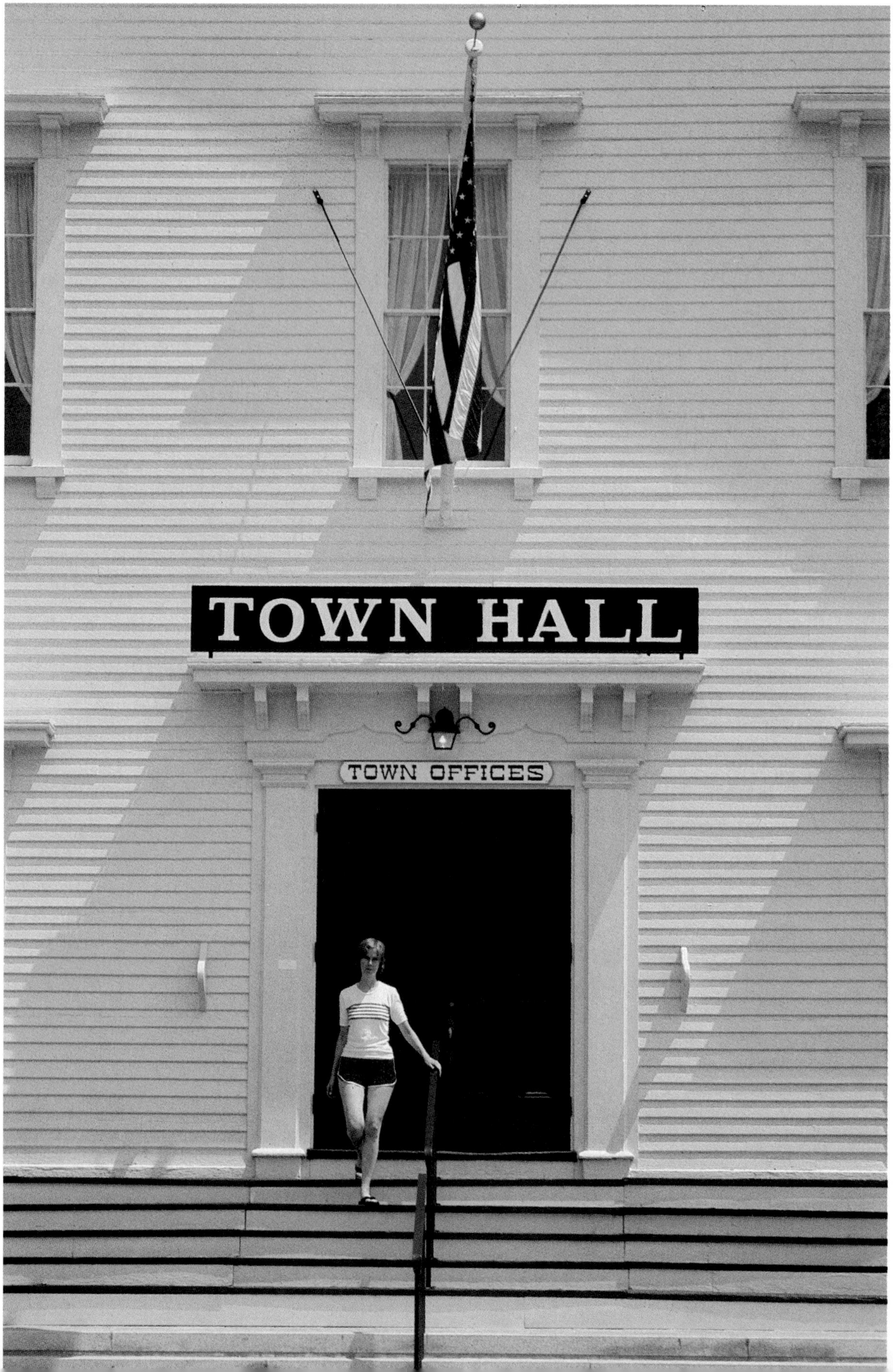
TOWN HALL
TOWN OFFICES

4

Federalism

S teve Oligmueller, age nineteen, Highmore High School class of 1986, had just returned home to South Dakota for the summer. Tonight, he would get together with old friends and swap stories about freshman year at college. They would meet at The Stable, a local bar, to sit, talk, listen to music, and have a couple of beers. In the spring of 1987, South Dakota was one of four states that still allowed people under twenty-one to drink beer. Soon, however, the cost of letting nineteen-year-olds drink beer would go up drastically—not just for Steve and his friends, but for all the taxpayers of South Dakota. The state stood to lose nearly $10 million in federal highway funds unless it raised its minimum drinking age to twenty-one.

Just three years earlier, twenty-nine states and the District of Columbia allowed people under twenty-one to purchase and consume some forms of alcoholic beverages. In 1984, however, an action taken in Washington, D.C., marked the beginning of the end of legalized drinking for those under twenty-one. What happened? Did Congress establish a national minimum drinking age? No, at least not directly. Congress simply added a provision to a highway bill. Under that provision, states would lose 5 percent of their federal highway funds in 1986 and 10 percent in 1987 if they allowed the purchase or consumption of alcohol by those under twenty-one. States themselves would have to change their own laws or risk losing federal funds. But why adopt such a roundabout method to achieve a national objective? If the national government wanted to set twenty-one as a national drinking age, why not act directly and pass legislation to do so?

The simplest answer has to do with the federal system of government. The Constitution divided power between the national and state governments. Regulating liquor sales and setting minimum drinking ages

Unsafe at Any Speed
Mothers Against Drunk Driving (MADD) campaigned hard to get drunken drivers off the road. Their strategies included national advertising—and national legislation. They also took aim at state legislatures, urging tougher sanctions for driving "under the influence." MADD organized this candlelight vigil in memory of victims of drunken drivers.

had always been the responsibilities of state governments. But over the years, the national government has found ways to extend its influence into areas well beyond those originally defined in the Constitution.

How did the national government become concerned about the drinking age? Mothers Against Drunk Driving (MADD) and other interest groups had fought hard to increase public awareness of the dangers of driving drunk, and they argued that a uniform drinking age of twenty-one would reduce highway fatalities. The National Transportation Safety Board estimated that 1,250 lives could be saved each year by raising the drinking age. But campaigning for change on a state-by-state basis would be slow and might even be dangerous. As long as some states allowed teenagers to drink, young people would drive across state lines in order to drink legally. The borders between states would become "blood borders," strewn with the victims of teenage drinking and driving.

Supporters of the legislation believed that the national government's responsibility to maintain order justified intervention here. The lives and safety of people were at stake. Opponents of the plan argued that it constituted age discrimination and infringed on states' rights. They claimed the act was an unwarranted extension of national power, that it limited the freedom of the states and of their citizens.

The bill passed handily and went to President Reagan for signing. Reagan had campaigned on a pledge to reduce the size and scope of the national government, and he strongly opposed replacing state standards with national ones. Where would he come out on this issue, which pitted order against freedom and national standards against state standards? Early on, he opposed the bill; later, he changed his position. At the signing ceremony, he said, "This problem is bigger than the individual states. It's a grave national problem and it touches all our lives. With the problem so clear cut and the proven solution at hand we have no misgiving about this judicious use of federal power. I'm convinced that it will help persuade state legislators to act in the national interest."[1]

Several states took the matter to court, hoping to have the provision declared unconstitutional. In June 1987, the Supreme Court reached its decision in *South Dakota* v. *Dole.*[2] The Court argued that, far from being an infringement on states' rights, the law was a "relatively mild encouragement to the states to enact higher minimum drinking ages than they otherwise would choose." After all, Chief Justice William Rehnquist wrote, the goal of reducing drunk driving was "directly related to one of the main purposes for which highway funds are expended: safe interstate travel."

Rehnquist's words show how much the role of the national government has changed since the Constitution was adopted. In 1985, for example, the national government gave the states close to $15 billion for projects ranging from the research, planning, and construction of roads to state and community safety and outdoor advertising control. Yet, in the early part of the last century, chief executives routinely vetoed bills authorizing roads, canals, and other interstate improvements. The reason? They believed these kinds of projects exceeded the constitutional authority of the national government.

Eventually, of course, the national government did use its authority over interstate commerce and post roads to justify a role in building roads. Witness the 46,000-mile interstate highway system. In the Highway Act of 1984, however, Congress went a step further. Although it recognized the formal power of the states to regulate the minimum drinking age, it used its own powers to tax and spend to encourage the states to implement a national standard. Lawmakers in Washington believed that few states would pass up highway funds to retain power, and they were right.

An important element of federalism was at work here: the dual sovereignty of national and state governments. Congress acknowledged the sovereignty of the states by not legislating a national drinking age. And the states were willing to barter their sovereignty in exchange for needed revenues. As long as this remains true, there are few areas where national power cannot reach.

In this chapter, we examine American federalism in theory and in practice. Is the division of power between nation and states a matter of constitutional principle or practical politics? How does the balance of power between nation and states relate to the conflicts between freedom and order, and between freedom and equality? Does federalism reflect the pluralist or the majoritarian model of democracy?

FEDERALISM AND AMERICAN IDEOLOGY: MYTHS AND METAPHORS

The delegates who met in Philadelphia in 1787 were supposed to repair weaknesses in the Articles of Confederation. Instead, they tackled the problem of making one nation out of thirteen independent states by doing something much more radical. They wrote a new Constitution

Local Cops, National Cops
Local, state, and national governments share certain powers, such as law enforcement. A Los Angeles police officer enforces local criminal laws, against gang activity and drugs, for example (left). The Federal Bureau of Investigation is the principal investigative arm of the national government. Here a FBI SWAT team arrives to quiet a 1988 riot at a federal penitentiary in Atlanta (right).

FEATURE 4.1

Will Massachusetts Invade Central America?

"Will Massachusetts invade Central America?" That's the question peace groups in Massachusetts were asking in 1986. And the answer they got was "No." Governor Michael Dukakis assured the Central America Solidarity Association (CASA) and the Citizens for Political Participation and Action (CPPAX) that he would turn down all invitations to have the Massachusetts National Guard train in Central America. Soon, the governors of Maine, New York, and Vermont announced they too would refuse to send state troops to Central America. And campaigns were launched in Arizona, Arkansas, Iowa, Kentucky, Wisconsin, and other states to convince the governors there to follow suit.

Since the military draft ended in the 1970s, the Defense Department has considered the National Guard forces—the state militias—an integral part of the nation's military strength. President Reagan planned to use these troops to project U.S. power in Central America. In 1986, for example, over five thousand guardsmen from twenty-three states trained in Honduras.

The governors' refusal raised an important question: Who commands the National Guard? The Guard is the state militia, the most powerful tool a governor has to secure order. National Guard troops are often called to quell riots or clean up after floods. But the Guard has ties to the national government as well. In Article I, Section 8, the Constitution provides that Congress may call out or *federalize* the militia "to execute the Laws of the Union, suppress insurrections and repel Invasions." Congress is also empowered to organize, arm, and discipline the militia. The states have reserved to them the authority to appoint officers and to train the militia "according to the discipline prescribed by Congress." Under national law, the governor is commander in chief of the state militia unless the Guard is federalized. But Congress had not federalized the Guard troops before they went to train in Central America. As a result, Dukakis and other like-minded governors stood poised for conflict with the national government.

In the summer of 1986, however, Congress passed a Reagan-backed amendment to a defense appropriations act. This amendment was aimed at preventing governors from blocking the overseas training of National Guard troops. In May 1988 a U.S. District Court judge upheld the constitutionality of the amendment. Nevertheless, some experts believe that the measure does not give the national government the power to override gubernatorial authority; to do that, Congress would have to declare an emergency and federalize the Guard or pass a constitutional amendment limiting the governors' power.

Although the Reagan administration shied away from either of these courses, the intent of its policy was clear. When its professed commitment to returning power to the states ran counter to other policy objectives, the Reagan administration's commitment to states' rights did not stand. Annually, thousands of guardsmen still train in Central America. And one day, Massachusetts militiamen may be called for duty there despite their governor's wishes!

and invented a new political form: federal government. Under this **federalism,** two or more governments would exercise power and authority over the same people and the same territory. Thus, people living in Pennsylvania would be citizens of both the United States and Pennsylvania. Although the governments of the United States and Pennsylvania would share certain powers (the power to tax, for instance), other powers would belong exclusively to one or the other. As Madison wrote in "Federalist No. 10," "The federal Constitution forms a happy combination . . . the great and aggregate interests being referred to the national, and the local and particular to state governments." So the power to coin money belongs to the national government; the power to grant divorces remains a state prerogative. By contrast, authority over the state militia may sometimes belong to the national government and sometimes to the state government (see Feature 4.1). The history of American feder-

COMPARED WITH WHAT? 4.1

Federalism Around the World

Question: What do the following nations have in common: Argentina, Australia, Austria, Brazil, Canada, the Federal Republic of Germany, India, Malaysia, Mexico, Switzerland, the Union of Soviet Socialist Republics, the United States of America, and Yugoslavia?

Answer: Today, these are the only nations in the world with a federal form of government. There are just thirteen of them, a small fraction of the world's countries.

Why would a nation adopt a federal form of government? In theory, a federal system provides a

means of recognizing local diversity while allowing some centralized authority. It also offers a defense against the national government's becoming too powerful. In practice, federalism is often used as a means of governing a large territory or a heterogeneous population (a population with many ethnic, religious, or linguistic groups, for example).

The table below lists some geographic and social characteristics of the world's federal nations, some clues as to why they use the federal form. Several of these nations, though, do not conform to the usual pattern. Why do you think they adopted federalism?

Nation	Population (millions)	Area (million sq. mi.)	Major Racial or Ethnic Groups	Major Languages	Major Religions
Argentina	29.6	1.10	European ancestry (97%)	Spanish	Roman Catholic (92%)
Australia	15.3	7.70	European ancestry (97%)	English	Anglican (36%) Roman Catholic (33%)
Austria	7.6	0.76	Germanic (98%)	German	Roman Catholic (85%)
Brazil	122.0	3.29	Caucasian (60%) Mixed (30%) Black (8%) Indian (2%)	Portuguese	Roman Catholic (93%)
Canada	25.2	9.92	British (45%) French (29%) Other European (23%) Indian, Eskimo (1.5%)	English French	Roman Catholic (45%) United Church (18%) Anglican (12%)
Federal Republic of Germany	59.0	0.25	German	German	Roman Catholic (45%) Protestant (44%)

alism reveals that it has not always been easy to draw a line between what is "great and aggregate" and what is "local and particular."*

Federalism offered a solution to the problem of diversity in America. It also provided a new political model. Although federal systems are fairly rare, as Compared With What? 4.1 shows, a number of other nations have adopted them, often to deal with their own special forms of diversity.

---

* The everyday phrase Americans use to refer to their central government—*federal government*—muddies the waters even more. Technically speaking, we have a *federal system of government* that includes both national and state governments. To avoid confusion from here on, we use the term *national government* rather than *federal government* when we are talking about the central government.

Nation	Population (millions)	Area (million sq. mi.)	Major Racial or Ethnic Groups	Major Languages	Major Religions
India	746.0	3.28	Indo/Aryan (72%) Dravidian (25%) Mongoloid (2%)	Hindu English 14 others	Hindu (83%) Moslem (11%) Sikh Buddhist (2.6%)
Malaysia	14.1	0.33	Malay (50%) Chinese (36%) Indian (10%)	Malay Chinese English Tamil	Muslim Hindu Buddhist Confucian Christian
Mexico	76.0	0.76	Indian-Spanish (55%) American Indian (29%) Caucasian (10%)	Spanish	Christian (97%)
Switzerland	6.5	0.02	Mixed European	German (65%) French (18%) Italian (12%) Romansh (1%)	Roman Catholic (49%) Protestant (48%)
Union of Soviet Socialist Republics	273.8	8.65	Russian (52%) Ukranian (6%) Uzbek (5%) Belorussian (4%)	Russian 18 others	Russian Orthodox Muslim
United States	226.0	3.54	Caucasian (83%) Black (12%) Other (5%)	English	Protestant (65%) Roman Catholic (25%) Jewish (2%)
Yugoslavia	23.1	1.00	Serbian (35%) Croatian (19%) Muslim (8.9%) Slovene (7.8%) Albanian (7.7%) Macedonians (5.9%) Yugoslavs (5.4%) Montenegrins (2.5%)	Serbo-Croatian Slovene Macedonian Albanian Hungarian Italian	Eastern Othodox (41%) Roman Catholic (32%) Muslim (12%)

The Mythology of American Federalism

The founding of America is a comparatively recent, well-documented event; yet, like the founding of Rome and of other ancient states, the beginning of the American republic is shrouded in political mythology. There are truths in these stories, truths that can help us understand people's beliefs and current political practices. The difficulty is in determining just what these truths are.

Federalism in America and the political maneuvering that gave birth to it have given us two very different myths. The first, called **dual federalism,** sees the Constitution as a compact among sovereign states. Of primary importance here are **states' rights,** a concept that reserves to the states all rights not specifically conferred on the national government. According to the myth of dual federalism, a rigid wall separates nation and states. The second myth—**cooperative federalism**—plays down the importance of the states. It describes the Constitution as an agreement made by the people and emphasizes their role as citizens of both nation and state. According to the myth of cooperative federalism, if there is a barrier between federal and state power, it is highly permeable and flexible. Traditionally, dual federalism has been associated with conservatives; cooperative federalism, with liberals. But this distinction may no longer be as sharp as it once was.

A critical difference between dual federalism and cooperative federalism is the way they interpret two sections of the Constitution that set out the terms of the relationship between the national and state governments. Article I, Section 8, lists the enumerated powers of the Congress, then concludes with the **elastic clause,** which gives Congress the power to "make all Laws which shall be necessary and proper for carrying into Execution the foregoing Powers." The Tenth Amendment says that "powers not delegated to the United States by the Constitution, nor prohibited by it to the States, are reserved to the States respectively, or to the people."

Dual, or "Layer Cake," Federalism

In his first inaugural address, President Reagan noted that "the federal government did not create the states; the states created the federal government." In making this statement, Reagan was affirming his belief in dual federalism, in states' rights and sovereignty. Dual federalism portrays the states as powerful components of the federal system—in some ways, the equals of the national government. After all, if the states created the nation, by implication, they can set limits on the activities of the national government. Proponents of states' rights believe that the powers of the national government should be interpreted very narrowly. They insist that, despite the elastic clause, the activities of Congress should be confined to the enumerated powers. And they support their view by quoting the Tenth Amendment.

Political scientists use a metaphor to describe dual federalism. They call it *layer cake federalism.* The powers and functions of national and state governments are distinct and separate—as distinct and separate as the layers of a cake (see Figure 4.1). Each government is supreme in its own "layer," its own sphere of action; the two layers are distinct; and the dimensions of each layer are fixed by the Constitution.

This understanding of federalism has found its way into Supreme Court opinions, particularly in the late nineteenth and early twentieth centuries. For example, in *Hammer* v. *Dagenhart* (1918), which declared that child labor laws were unconstitutional, Justice William Day wrote that "the powers not expressly delegated to the national government are reserved" to the states and to the people.[3] In his wording, Day revised the Constitution slightly and changed the intent of the framers: The Tenth Amendment does not say "expressly." The framers purposely left the word *expressly* out of the amendment because they believed they could not possibly specify every power that might be needed in the future to run the government. Those powers not specifically mentioned, but

The Myth of Dual Federalism:
The Layer Cake Metaphor

Citizens cutting into the
political system will find
clear differences between
state and national powers,
functions, and responsibilities

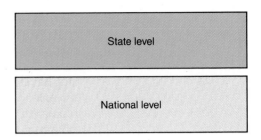

The Myth of Cooperative Federalism:
The Marble Cake Metaphor

**The Myths and
Their Metaphors**
*The two views of federal-
ism can be represented
graphically.*

Figure 4.1

Citizens cutting into the
political system at any point
will find national and state
powers, functions, and
responsibilities mixed and
mingled

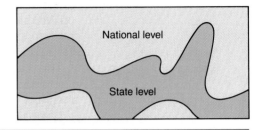

necessary for the implementation of the enumerated powers, are called
the **implied powers.**[4]

Dual federalism—the myth that underlies the layer cake metaphor—
has been challenged on historical and other grounds. Some critics argue
that if the national government is really a creation of the states, it is a
creation of only thirteen states—those that ratified the Constitution.
The other thirty-seven states were admitted after the national government came into being and were created by that government out of land
it had acquired. Another challenge has to do with the ratification process.
Remember, the original thirteen states ratified the Constitution in special conventions, not in state legislatures. Ratification, then, was an act
of the *people*, not the *states*. The question of just where the people fit
into the federal system is not handled very well by dual federalism. The
full text of the Tenth Amendment says that powers not given to the
national government are reserved to the states or *to the people*. These
last four words are very important to critics of the states' rights view.
Why can't the people assign more or less power to the national government? Why shouldn't the people exercise power or seek protection of
their rights through the national government rather than through state
government?

Cooperative, or "Marble Cake," Federalism

The myth of cooperative federalism revolves around the idea that
the people are citizens of both nation and state. The emphasis here is on
the elastic clause, the phrase in Article I, Section 8, that grants the
national government the power to make laws that are *necessary and
proper*, and the role of the national government. Unlike dual federalism,
cooperative federalism blurs the distinction between national and state
powers. The metaphor we use to describe this kind of federalism is a

marble cake. The national and state governments do not act in separate spheres; they are intermingled. Some scholars argue that the layer cake metaphor has never accurately described the American political structure.[5] National and state governments have many common objectives and have often cooperated to achieve them. In the nineteenth century, for example, cooperation—not separation—made it possible to develop transportation systems and to establish land grant colleges. The layer cake might be a good model of what dual federalists *think* the relationship between national and state governments should be, but it does not square with the facts of American history.

Marble cake federalism in not without its critics. They insist that the founders made a distinction between national and state powers, a distinction that marble cake federalism erases.

In fact, at different times in our history, one or the other of these metaphors has been considered an appropriate description of the relationships between levels of government. Conservatives, in their efforts to limit the scope of the national government, have given credence to the layer cake metaphor. At other times, liberals, using the national government to bring about equality, have made the marble cake metaphor more accurate. The truth about federalism in the United States, then, isn't what's written or implied in the Constitution. The Constitution is only the starting point in the debate. The real meaning of American federalism can be found in its implementation.

THE DYNAMICS OF FEDERALISM: LEGAL STICKS AND FINANCIAL CARROTS

Although the Constitution defines a kind of federalism, the actual balance of power between nation and states has always been more a matter of politics than of formal authority. A discussion of federalism, then, must do more than simply list the powers the Constitution assigns the levels of government. The balance of power has shifted substantially since President Madison agonized over the proper role the national government should play in funding roads. Today, that government has assumed functions never dreamed of in the nineteenth century.

Why has power shifted so dramatically from the states to the national government? The answer lies in historical circumstances, not debates over constitutional theory. For example, the greatest test of states' rights came when several Southern states attempted to secede from the Union. The threat of secession challenged the national government's supremacy, a supremacy that Northern armies established militarily on the battlefields of the Civil War. But the Civil War by no means settled all the questions about relations between governments in the United States. Many more remained to be answered, and new issues kept cropping up.

Some changes in the balance of power were the product of constitutional amendments. Several amendments have had an enormous impact, either direct or indirect, on the shape of the federal system. For example, the due process and equal protection clauses of the Fourteenth Amendment (1868) limited states' rights, as did the income tax mandated

Signing Up to Vote
An elderly black woman registers to vote. Compared with actual voting, registering is a time-consuming activity. After this woman's state failed to do the job, the national government stepped in to protect her rights under the Voting Rights Act of 1965.

by the Sixteenth Amendment (1913) and the Seventeenth Amendment's provision for the direct election of senators (1913).*

But most of the national government's power has come to it through legislation, judicial interpretation, and political bartering. There is a saying that there are two ways to get things done, with a stick or a carrot. The national government has used both sticks (legislation, judicial interpretation) and carrots (financial incentives) to expand its power. Here we look at these tools of political change.

Legislation and the Elastic Clause

The elastic clause of the Constitution gives Congress the power to make all laws that are "necessary and proper" to carry out its responsibilities. By using this power in combination with its enumerated powers, Congress has been able to increase the scope of the national government tremendously over the last two centuries. Change has often come in times of crisis and national emergency—during the Civil War, the Great Depression, the world wars. The role of the national government has grown as it has responded to needs and demands that state and local governments were unwilling or unable to meet.

Legislation is one of the sticks the national government has used to achieve goals at the state level, to force the states to comply. The Voting Rights Act of 1965 is a good example. Section 2 of Article I of the Constitution gives the states the power to set voter qualifications. But the Fifteenth Amendment (1870) provides that no person should be denied the right to vote "on account of race, color, or previous condition of servitude." Before the Voting Rights Act, states could not specifically

---

* The Fourteenth Amendment was itself a product of the Civil War.

deny blacks the right to vote, but they could require that voters pass literacy tests or pay poll taxes, requirements that virtually disenfranchised blacks in many states. The Voting Rights Act was designed to correct this political inequality. It gives officials of the national government the power to decide whether individuals are qualified to vote and requires that qualified individuals be allowed to vote in all elections—including primaries and national, state, and local elections. The constitutional authority for the act was found in the elastic clause and in the second section of the Fifteenth Amendment, which gives Congress the power to enforce the amendment through "appropriate legislation."

Judicial Interpretation

The Voting Rights Act was not a unanimous hit. Its critics adopted the language of dual federalism and insisted that the Constitution gives the states the power to determine voter qualifications. Its supporters claimed that the Fifteenth Amendment guarantee of voting rights takes precedence over states' rights and gives the national government new responsibilities. In this instance, the states tried to defend their freedom to set voter qualifications against the national government's effort to promote political equality.

The conflict was ultimately resolved by the Supreme Court, the arbiter of the federal system. The Court settles disputes over the powers of the national and state governments by deciding whether actions of the national or state governments are constitutional (see Chapter 13). In the nineteenth and early twentieth centuries, the Supreme Court often decided in favor of the states; however, since 1937, it has almost always supported the national government in contests involving the balance of power between nation and states.

The growth of national power has been accomplished through a variety of routes. One is the Supreme Court's interpretation of the Constitution's **commerce clause.** The third clause of Article I, Section 8 states that "Congress shall have the power . . . to regulate Commerce . . . among the several States. . . ." In early Court decisions Chief Justice John Marshall (1801–1835) interpreted the word "Commerce" broadly to include virtually every form of commercial activity. The clause's grant of commerce power to the national government substantially withdrew that power from the states. Later decisions by the Court attempted to restrict the national commerce power, but events such as the Great Depression necessitated an enlargement of it. Today, the only limit on the exercise of the commerce power is Congress itself.

During Chief Justice Earl Warren's term (1953–1969), the Court used the Fourteenth Amendment to extend various provisions of the Bill of Rights to the states, shifting power from the states to the national government. Court decisions seriously reduced the states' freedom to decide what constitutes due process of law within their jurisdictions. For example, in one decision, the Court ordered that citizens apprehended by the police must be informed of their constitutional rights and that the arresting officer must preserve those rights.[6] Through the Supreme Court, the national government set minimum standards for due process in criminal cases, standards that the states would have to meet. These standards provide equality before the law for individuals who are suspected of crimes, but critics argue that they hamper state officials in trying to maintain order.

A series of decisions concerning reapportionment—resetting the boundaries of electoral districts—also eroded the power of the states in the early 1960s.[7] Until that time, states had set the boundaries of voting districts, but some had failed to adjust those boundaries to reflect changes in population. As a result, in certain areas, small numbers of rural voters were able to elect as many representatives as were large numbers of urban voters. In deciding cases involving reapportionment, the Court set down a new standard of one person, one vote and forced the states to apply this principle in redrawing their districts and apportioning their legislatures.

In the due process and reapportionment cases, the Supreme Court protected individual rights, in the process championing political equality. But remember, the Supreme Court is part of the national government. When it defends the rights of an individual against a state, it also substitutes a national standard for the state standard governing that relationship.

Grants-in-Aid

In the last three decades, Washington's use of financial "carrots" has rivaled its use of legislation and judicial interpretation as a means of shaping relationships between national and state governments. Since the 1960s, state and local governments have looked to Washington for money more and more often. In 1960, the national government provided 15 percent of the funds spent by state and local governments; by 1980, it was providing 23 percent of those funds. The principal method the national government uses to make money available to the states is through grants-in-aid.

A **grant-in-aid** is money paid by one level of government to another, to be spent for a specific purpose. Most grants-in-aid come with standards or requirements prescribed by Congress. Many are awarded on a matching basis; that is, recipients must make some contribution of their own, which is then matched by the national government. Grants-in-aid take two general forms: categorical grants and block grants.

Categorical grants are targeted for very specific purposes, and restrictions on their use often leave the recipient government relatively little discretion. There are two kinds of categorical grants: formula grants and project grants. **Formula grants,** as their name implies, are distributed according to a particular formula, which specifies who is eligible for the grant and how much each eligible applicant will receive. The formulas used to distribute grant money vary from one grant to another. They may weigh such factors as state per capita income, number of school-age children, urban population, and number of families below the poverty line. In 1987, 134 of the 422 categorical grants offered by the national government were formula grants. The remaining 288 grants were **project grants**—grants awarded on the basis of competitive applications.

Table 4.1
Block and Categorical Grants

Block Grants	Recipient
Urban mass transit	Local government
Community development (two grants)	State and local governments
Elementary, secondary, and vocational education	State government
Job training for disadvantaged adults and youth	State government
Social services	State government
Community services	State government
Preventive health and health services	State government
Alcohol, drug abuse, and mental health services	State government
Alcohol and drug abuse treatment and rehabilitation	State government
Maternal and child health services	State government
Low-income energy assistance	State government
Criminal justice	State government

Examples of Categorical Grants	Recipient
Highway beautification: control of outdoor advertising and junkyards	State government
Vocational education: consumer and homemaking education	State government
Library literacy	State and local governments
Urban park and recreation recovery	Local government

In contrast with categorical grants, **block grants** are awarded for broad, general purposes. They allow recipients considerable freedom in deciding how to allocate money to individual programs. While a categorical grant might be given to promote a very specific activity—say, ethnic heritage studies—a block grant could be offered for elementary, secondary, and vocational education. The state or local government receiving the block grant would then choose the specific educational programs to fund with it. The recipient might use some of the money to support ethnic heritage studies and some to fund consumer education programs. Or the recipient might choose to put all of the money into consumer education programs and spend nothing on ethnic heritage studies. Table 4.1 lists all thirteen block grants and some of the categorical grants made in 1987.

Grants-in-aid are a method of redistributing income. Money is collected by the national government from citizens of all fifty states, then allocated to other citizens, supposedly for worthwhile social purposes. Many grants have worked to remove gross inequalities among states and their citizens. But the formulas used to redistribute this income are not impartial; they are themselves highly political and often subject to debate in Congress.

Whatever its form, grant money comes with strings attached. Many of the strings are there to ensure that the money is used for the purpose for which it was given; other regulations are designed to evaluate how well the grant is working. To this end, the national government may stipulate that recipients follow certain procedures. For example, a recipient may be required to adopt particular accounting procedures or set up special agencies to guarantee that the funds are administered properly.

The national government may also attach other restrictions to the money it grants. Often, these restrictions are designed to achieve some broad national goal, a goal that is not always closely related to the specific purpose of the grant. For example, as we have seen, the Highway Act of 1984 reduced the amount of money available to states that allowed those under age twenty-one to purchase and consume alcoholic beverages. Other grants prohibit discrimination in the activities funded through them. States have been more than willing to accept these limitations. Returning again to the case of the Highway Act. By March 1988, every state in the nation had approved legislation setting twenty-one as the minimum drinking age. The carrot of financial aid has proved to be a powerful incentive for states to relinquish the freedom to set their own standards and to accept those set by the national government.

THE DEVELOPING CONCEPT OF FEDERALISM: FROM LAYER CAKE TO MARBLE CAKE

A student of federalism once remarked that "each generation faced with new problems has had to work out its own version of federalism." Succeeding generations have used sticks and carrots in varying degrees to shift the balance of power back and forth between national and state governments.

McCulloch v. Maryland

Early in the nineteenth century, the nationalist interpretation of federalism triumphed over states' rights. In 1819, under Chief Justice Marshall, the Supreme Court expanded the role of the national government in its decision in *McCulloch* v. *Maryland*.[8] The Court was asked to rule whether Congress had the power to establish a national bank and, if so, whether states had the power to tax that bank. In writing the majority opinion, Marshall supported a broad interpretation of the elastic clause: "Let the end be legitimate, let it be within the scope of the constitution, and all means which are appropriate, which are plainly adapted to that end, which are not prohibited, but consistent with the letter and spirit of the constitution, are constitutional."

The Court clearly agreed that Congress had the power to charter a bank. But did the states—in this case, Maryland—have the power to tax the bank? Arguing that "the power to tax is the power to destroy," Marshall insisted that states could not tax the national government because the powers of the national government came, not from the states, but from the people. Marshall here was embracing cooperative federalism, which sees a direct relationship between the people and the national government, with no need for the states to act as intermediaries. To assume that states had the power to tax the national government would be to give them supremacy over the national government. In that case,

Marshall wrote, "the declaration that the constitution, and the laws made in pursuance thereof, shall be the supreme law of the land is empty and unmeaning declamation." The framers of the Constitution did not intend to create a meaningless document, he reasoned. Therefore, they must have meant to give the national government all the powers necessary to carry out its assigned functions, even if those powers are only implied.

States' Rights and Dual Federalism

Roger B. Taney became Chief Justice in 1836, and during his tenure (1836–1864), the balance of power began to shift back toward the states. The Taney Court recognized firm limits on the powers of the national government. As Taney saw it, the Constitution spoke "not only in the same words but with the same meaning and intent with which it spoke when it came from the framers." In the infamous *Dred Scott* decision (1857), for example, the Court decided that Congress had no power to prohibit slavery in the territories.[9]

Many people assume that the Civil War was fought over slavery. It was not. The real issue was the character of the federal union, of federalism itself. At the time of the Civil War, regional variations between Northern and Southern states were considerable. The Southern economy was based on labor-intensive agriculture, very different from the mechanized manufacturing that was developing in the North. As a result, Southerners wanted cheap manufactured goods and cheap plantation labor. This led them to support both low tariffs on imported goods and slavery. Northerners, to protect their own economy, wanted high tariffs. When they sought national legislation that threatened Southern inter-

Made in the U.S.A.
A young factory worker in the early part of this century. The Supreme Court decided in 1918 that Congress had no power to limit child labor. That power belonged to the states, which resisted imposing limits for fear that such legislation would drive business to other (less restrictive) states.

ests, Southerners demanded states' rights. They even introduced the theory of **nullification**—the idea that a state could declare a particular action of the national government null and void. The Civil War rendered the idea of nullification null and void, but it did not settle the balance between national and state power.

In the decades after the Civil War, the Supreme Court continued to place limits on national power, particularly when the national government attempted to regulate industry. Early in the nineteenth century, the Court decided that the national government had supreme power to regulate interstate commerce.[10] Later on, however, the Court rejected the idea that this power could be used to justify policies not directly related to the smooth functioning of interstate commerce—policies such as setting a national minimum wage or abolishing child labor. In the late nineteenth and early twentieth centuries, the justices were influenced by laissez-faire economic theory, a hands-off approach to business. Time and again the Court ruled that congressional legislation that limited the activities of corporations was unconstitutional because it invaded the domain of the states.

In 1918, for example, when Congress tried to use its power to regulate interstate commerce as the basis for legislation regulating child labor, the Court declared the law unconstitutional. The national government argued that national child labor laws were necessary because individual states would not enact them; to do so would increase the cost of labor in the state, making it less attractive to industry. The Court recognized this argument but was not persuaded, ruling that national legislation regulating child labor ran counter to both the commerce clause (of Article I, Section 8) and the Tenth Amendment. As Justice Day wrote in *Hammer* v. *Dagenhart*:

> The commerce clause was not intended to give Congress a general authority to equalize conditions [of competition between the states]. If Congress can thus regulate matters intrusted to local authority . . . all freedom of commerce will be at an end, and the power of the states over local matters may be eliminated, and thus our system of government practically destroyed.

The New Deal and Its Consequences

It took the Great Depression to test the limits of dual federalism. The problems of the Depression proved too extensive for either state governments or private businesses to handle. So the national government assumed a heavy share of responsibility for providing relief and directing efforts toward economic recovery. Under the "New Deal," President Franklin D. Roosevelt's response to the Depression, Congress enacted various emergency relief programs to restore economic activity and help the unemployed. Many of these measures required the cooperation of national and state governments. For example, the national government offered funds to stimulate state relief efforts. To receive these funds, however, states were usually required to provide administrative supervision or to contribute some money of their own. Relief efforts were removed from the hands of local bodies and centralized. Through the regulations it attached to funds, the national government extended its power and control over the states.[11]

At first, the Supreme Court's view of the Depression was different from that of the other branches of the national government. The justices believed the Depression was an accumulation of local problems, not a national problem demanding national action. In the Court's opinion, the whole structure of federalism was threatened when collections of local troubles were treated as one national problem. Justice Owen Roberts, in the decision in *United States* v. *Butler* (1936), wrote: "It does not help that local conditions throughout the nation have created a situation of national concern; for this is but to say that whenever there is a widespread similarity of local conditions, Congress may ignore constitutional limitations on its own powers and usurp those reserved to the states."[12] In this decision and others, the Court struck down several pieces of regulatory legislation, including the National Industrial Recovery Act, which would have regulated wages, working hours, and business competition.

In 1937, though, with no change in personnel, the Court began to alter its course. It upheld the Social Security Act and the National Labor Relations Act—both New Deal measures. Perhaps the Court had studied the 1936 election returns and was responding to the new nationalist mood in the country. In any event, the Court gave up its effort to set a rigid boundary between national and state power. Only a few years earlier, the Supreme Court had based its thinking about federalism on the Tenth Amendment; but in 1941, Justice Harlan Stone referred to the Tenth Amendment as "a truism that all is retained that has not been surrendered."[13] In short, the Court agreed that the layer cake was stale. From then on, the division of power in the federal system became less relevant, and the relationship between governments became increasingly important.

Some call the New Deal era "revolutionary." There is no doubt that the period was critical in reshaping federalism in the United States. The national and state governments had cooperated before, but the extent of nation-state interaction during Franklin Roosevelt's administration clearly made the marble cake the more accurate metaphor for American federalism. In addition, the size of the national government and its budget increased tremendously. But perhaps the most significant change was in the way Americans thought about both their problems and the role of the national government in solving them. Difficulties that at one time had been seen as personal or local problems now became national problems, requiring national solutions. The *general welfare*, broadly defined, had become a legitimate concern of the national government.

In other respects, however, the New Deal was not very revolutionary. Congress, for example, did not claim that any new powers were needed to deal with the nation's economic problems; it simply used the constitutional powers it had to suit the circumstances. And from the late 1930s on, the Supreme Court upheld Congress's work.

Desegregation and the War on Poverty

During the 1950s and 1960s, the national government assumed the task of promoting social equality by combating racism and poverty. Both of these problems had seemed impossible to solve at the state level.

Matters of race relations had generally been left to the states, which more or less ignored them despite the constitutional amendments passed after the Civil War. Moreover, when the Supreme Court adopted the separate-but-equal doctrine in 1896, states were free to do as much—or as little—as they pleased about racial inequality.[14]

In 1954, however, in *Brown* v. *Board of Education*, the Supreme Court decided that separate was inherently unequal.[15] This put the national government in the position of ordering the integration of public schools. As the civil rights movement focused increasing attention on the problems of discrimination, Congress passed two important pieces of legislation: the Civil Rights Act of 1964 and the Voting Rights Act of 1965. Through these acts, the national government used its legislative stick to outlaw racial discrimination in employment, in public accommodations, and in voter qualifications. The acts themselves sharply limited states' rights where the effect of those rights had been to deny equality.

In the 1960s, President Lyndon Johnson's War on Poverty generated an enormous amount of social legislation and a massive increase in the scope of the national government. In an attempt to provide equality of opportunity and improve the quality of life throughout the United States, the national government used financial carrots—money—to introduce a number of new programs, including vastly increased aid to higher education, aid to elementary and secondary schools, school breakfasts and lunches, food stamps, and a huge array of economic development, public service, and employment-training projects. To administer these programs, government bureaucracies were enlarged, on both national and

Reach Out and Touch Someone
The levels of government in the federal system are now intertwined. Here, in an intergovernmental conference call, New York Senators Daniel Moynihan and Alphonse D'Amato discuss funding projects with New York Governor Mario Cuomo and New York City Mayor Ed Koch.

state levels. In fact, during the 1960s and 1970s, state bureaucracies grew even faster than the national bureaucracy.

Johnson's recipe for marble cake federalism included some new ingredients. Before 1960, nearly all intergovernmental assistance (that is, aid from one level of government to another) had gone from the national government to state governments. But the War on Poverty often gave aid directly to local governments or even to community groups.

As the role of the national government grew larger and was more generally accepted, the focus of the debate over federalism changed. National and state governments were no longer separate, distinct layers; they interacted. But how? The search for answers to this question placed **intergovernmental relations** at center stage. The various levels of American government have become highly interdependent. The study of intergovernmental relations looks at that interdependence and the connections among personnel and policies at different levels of government. It also examines the ways that national, state, and local governments influence one another.

The political dynamics of intergovernmental relations since the 1960s have led to a new metaphor for federalism: **picket fence federalism** (see Figure 4.2). Here, the fence rails are the levels of government—national, state, and local; and the fence slats are the interests of lobbies and groups, both inside and outside of government, and the functions of government. The communities of interest (or functions) represented by each slat make contact at each of the three levels of government. They are able to share information, develop common standards, and exert pressure on each level of government. Government officials themselves may move along the interest slats to influence officials on other rails. On a typical trip to Washington, for instance, the head of a state department of education might have a morning meeting with members of the state's congressional delegation to make them aware of the state's educational needs and priorities; then go on to lunch with lobbyists from the National Education Association (NEA) before testifying in front of a

Figure 4.2

Picket Fence Federalism
The picket fence model shows how functions cross government lines and also connect the officials who work at different levels of government.

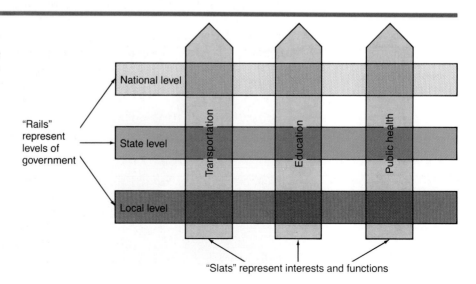

"Rails" represent levels of government

National level

State level

Local level

Transportation

Education

Public health

"Slats" represent interests and functions

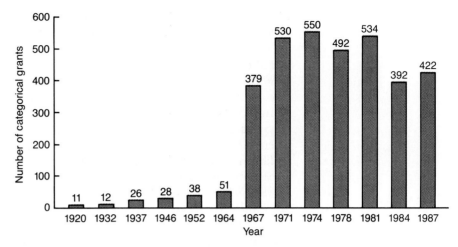

The Growth and Decline of Categorical Grants
National government programs increased as a result of the New Deal and the War on Poverty. Cuts in programs during the Carter and Reagan years brought a temporary halt in the growth of programs, but by the late 1980s, new programs were again being added to meet new needs. (Sources: Advisory Commission on Intergovernmental Relations [ACIR], The Federal Role in the Federal System: The Dynamics of Growth [Washington, D.C., 1980], pp. 120–121; ACIR, Significant Features of Fiscal Federalism [Washington, D.C., 1983], p. 120; and ACIR, A Catalogue of Federal Grant-in-Aid Programs to State and Local Governments; Grants Funded FY 1987 [Washington, D.C., 1987], p. 1.)

Figure 4.3

congressional committee on education and meeting with officials from the U.S. Department of Education. Our tired official might return to the office the next day to find an education chief from a neighboring state on the phone, hoping to find out how the visit went.

Since the 1960s, the national government has provided money for all sorts of local programs—rat control, jellyfish control, crime control, bike path construction, urban gardening, rural fire protection, solid waste disposal, home insulation, library services (see Figure 4.3). Far from being unresponsive, Congress became hyperresponsive. And its willingness to spend national funds increased the importance of existing interest groups and led to the creation of new ones. The result was not just pluralist democracy, but *hyperpluralism*—every conceivable interest had its group. Many smaller (and weaker) state groups united nationally to lobby for national solutions (via national money) to their problems. A number of state and local governments saw a need to lobby for their own interests, perhaps in self-defense.

The growth of government programs, the hyperresponsiveness of Congress, and the pressure of interest groups created a federal system that critics described as "overloaded and out of control." In keeping with the bakery-shop metaphors often used to describe federalism, one writer suggested that layer cake federalism and marble cake federalism had given way to "fruitcake" federalism—a federalism that is formless and indestructible, and offers lots of plums for everyone.[16]

When the Advisory Commission on Intergovernmental Relations (ACIR), a group created by Congress to monitor the federal system, reviewed the operation of that system in 1980, it concluded that fruitcake federalism was dysfunctional, it just did not work. Over the last two decades, the commission said, the system of intergovernmental relations had become "more pervasive, more intrusive, more unmanageable, more ineffective, more costly and more unaccountable."[17]

THE PENDULUM SWINGS BACK . . . MAYBE

Every president since Richard Nixon has expressed disenchantment with the hyperpluralist system of intergovernmental relations. Every president since Nixon has pledged to cut the size of the bureaucracy and return power to the states. Yet reform has been difficult to implement.

Nixon's New Federalism: Revenue Sharing

When Nixon came to office in 1969, he pledged to change a national government he characterized as "overly centralized, overbureaucratized . . . unresponsive as well as inefficient." He dubbed his solution to the problem "new Federalism" and claimed it would channel "power, funds and authority . . . to those governments closest to the people." He expected New Federalism to help restore control of the nation's destiny "by returning a greater share of control to state and local authorities."[18]

The centerpiece of Nixon's New Federalism was *revenue sharing*, in which the national government would turn tax revenues over to the states and localities to spend as they pleased. The plan had two parts: general revenue sharing and special revenue sharing. **General revenue sharing** provided new money to be used as state and local governments saw fit, with very few strings attached. Initially, Congress was quite willing to fund the general revenue sharing program. Because it was a new program, no one was required to give up anything for it. And, when general revenue sharing began in 1972, many states and cities were in the middle of financial crises. The program was very popular with the governments it helped, but over the years members of Congress became less enamored of it. They did not have the same control over revenue sharing funds that they had over the more traditional categorical grants. As a result, Congress did not allow the funding for general revenue sharing to grow as categorical grant funds had. In 1986, general revenue sharing was phased out completely.

The second part of Nixon's New Federalism, **special revenue sharing,** was a plan to consolidate existing categorical grant programs. Money available under several categorical programs in a particular area (for example, health services) would be combined into one large block grant. But Congress was reluctant to lose the political credit and control it had under the existing grant system. In addition, the dynamics of intergovernmental relations worked against the consolidation of programs: Interest groups lobbied hard to keep their pet projects from being consolidated. All of this combined to slow the progress of special revenue sharing during the Nixon years.

Nixon's New Federalism, then, was not very successful in stemming the flow of power from the states to the national government. The dollar

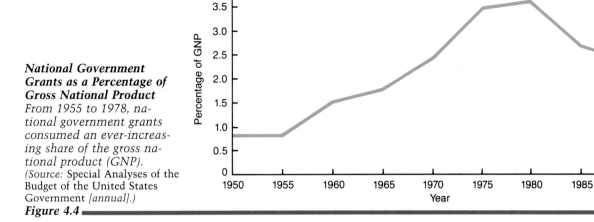

National Government Grants as a Percentage of Gross National Product
From 1955 to 1978, national government grants consumed an ever-increasing share of the gross national product (GNP). *(Source:* Special Analyses of the Budget of the United States Government *[annual].)*
Figure 4.4

amounts of aid continued to grow, and the programs funded continued to increase in number and kind. The national government gave more aid to the states, and that aid carried more and more strings.

The perception that the federal system was bloated and out of control began to take hold. In 1976, Jimmy Carter campaigned for president as an outsider who promised to reduce the size and cost of the national government. And he did have some success. As Figure 4.4 shows, after 1978, federal aid to states and localities actually did begin to drop as a percentage of the gross national product (GNP), the total value of all goods and services produced in the nation in a year.

Reagan's New Federalism: Budget Reductions

Ronald Reagan took office in 1981 promising a "new New Federalism" that would "restore a proper constitutional relationship between the federal, state and local governments." He criticized the contemporary version of federalism, charging that "the federal system had been bent out of shape." The national government had become the senior partner in intergovernmental relations, treating "elected state and local officials as if they were nothing more than administrative agents for federal authority."

Reagan's commitment to reduce taxes as well as government spending meant he could not offer the carrot of new funding to make his New Federalism palatable. He did resurrect an element of Nixon's New Federalism, however—the use of block grants. In the first year of the Reagan administration, Congress agreed to combine seventy-seven categorical grants into nine block grants. To build support for the plan, Reagan emphasized the freedom state officials would have in using their block grant money. He pointed out that the elimination of restrictive categorical programs would reduce administrative burdens, and, as a result, state and local programs could be run at lower cost. State officials were enthusiastic about the prospect of having greater control over grant funds; they were less enthusiastic when they realized that the amounts they

Cities YES! Missiles NO!
*Under the Reagan adminis-
tration's domestic policy,
New Federalism meant cuts
in national government
funds for cities. Reagan's
priorities placed defense
spending ahead of domestic
spending.*

received would be cut by approximately 25 percent. The share of state and local bills footed by the national government began to fall (see Figure 4.5).

In 1982, Reagan proposed a more thorough overhaul of the federal system. This time he offered a *program swap*, in which some forty-four programs previously funded or administered by the national government would be put under state control. At the same time, the national government would take over responsibility for Medicaid, a program of health care for the poor. Initially, Washington would turn back to the states revenues raised through various federal excise and energy taxes, providing them with the money they needed to run the new programs. Eventually, however, the states would be expected to pick up the costs themselves or eliminate the programs.

Reagan's proposed exchange of programs aroused intense opposition. He could not build a winning coalition in support of the plan, and, as a result, his most ambitious effort to remake American federalism failed.

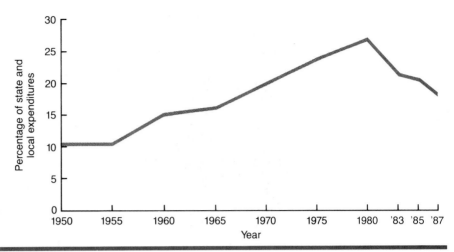

National Government Grants as a Percentage of State and Local Expenditures
States and localities had looked to Washington to provide larger and larger shares of their expenditures. But Reagan's New Federalism and budget cuts forced them to come up with more of their own money.
(Source: Special Analyses of the Budget of the United States Government *[annual].)*
Figure 4.5

Furthermore, after his initial success in 1981, the momentum behind Reagan's efforts to reduce the proliferation of categorical grant programs also slowed considerably. In fact, as Figure 4.3 shows, the number of categorical grants is again on the increase. Many grant programs have been added to respond to new problems and national priorities—for example, halting the spread of AIDS and fighting drug abuse.

If the Reagan administration did not achieve a wholesale reorganization of the federal system, it did prompt a reevaluation of the role of the national government in that system. For example, in the years before Reagan took office, the national government had been used to foster greater economic equality through the redistribution of wealth. The national government played a large part in setting eligibility requirements and benefit levels for food stamps, Aid to Families with Dependent Children (AFDC), and other programs that help the poor. Liberals preferred to use this centralized power to set minimum standards because the national government was willing to do more for the poor than many individual states would have chosen to do had they been left completely to their own devices. But when conservatives, who did not share this commitment to equality, came to power in Washington, these very aid programs proved most vulnerable. Many of Reagan's budget reductions came about by raising eligibility requirements and cutting available benefits of programs designed to assist those living in poverty. As a result, "in the final analysis, Reagan's cuts in federal aid . . . fell disproportionately on one segment of the population: the poor."[19]

OTHER GOVERNMENTS IN THE FEDERAL SYSTEM

We have concentrated in this chapter on the roles the national and state governments play in shaping the federal system. Although the Constitution explicitly recognizes just national and state governments, the American federal system has spawned a multitude of local governments as well. In a recent count, the number exceeded eighty-two thousand!

The Kinds of Local Governments

Americans are citizens of both nation and state; but they also come under the jurisdiction of various local government units. These units include **municipal governments,** the governments of cities and towns. Municipalities, in turn, are located in (or may contain or share boundaries with) counties, which are administered by **county governments.** In addition, most Americans also live in a **school district,** which is responsible for administering local elementary and secondary educational programs. They also may be served by one or more **special districts,** government units created to perform particular functions, often when those functions are best performed across jurisdictional boundaries. Examples of special districts include the Port Authority of New York, the Chicago Sanitary District, and the Southeast Pennsylvania Transit Authority.

These local governments are created by state governments either in their constitutions or through legislation. This means their organization,

Hizzoner, the Mayor.
Her Honor, the Mayor.
A mayor is the elected chief executive and ceremonial officer of a city. In some modest-sized cities, mayors serve part-time. Many big-city mayors rise to national prominence, though no mayor has yet made the leap from city hall to the White House. These mayors are (clockwise, from top left) Henry Cisneros of San Antonio, Texas; Page Worth of Belfast, Maine; Kurt Schmoke of Baltimore, Maryland; and Vernon Squires of Wilmette, Illinois.

powers, responsibilities, and effectiveness vary considerably from state to state. About forty states provide their cities with various forms of **home rule**—the right to enact and enforce legislation in certain administrative areas. By allowing a measure of self-government, home rule gives cities greater freedom of action than they would otherwise have. In contrast, county governments, which are the main units of local government in rural areas, tend to have relatively little legislative power or none at all. Instead, county governments generally serve as administrative units, performing the specific duties assigned to them under state law.

The functions of national, state, city, and county governments and of school and special districts often overlap. In practice, it is now virtually impossible to distinguish among them by using Madison's criteria of great and aggregate interests and local and particular interests. Consider, for example, the case of the rural health officer, or "sanitarian":

> The sanitarian is appointed by the state under merit standards established by the federal government. His base salary comes jointly from state and federal funds, the county provides him with an office and office amenities and pays a portion of his expenses, and the largest city in the county also contributes to his salary by virtue of his appointment as a city plumbing inspector. It is impossible from moment to moment to tell under which governmental hat the sanitarian operates. His work of inspecting the purity of food is carried out under federal standards; but he is enforcing state laws when inspecting commodities that have not been in interstate commerce; and somewhat perversely he also acts under state authority when inspecting milk coming into the county from producing areas across the state border. He is a federal official when impounding impure drugs shipped from a neighboring state; a federal-state officer when distributing typhoid immunization serum; a state officer when enforcing standards of industrial hygiene; a state-local officer when inspecting the city's water supply; and [to complete the circle] a local officer when insisting that the city butchers adopt more hygienic methods of handling their garbage. But he cannot and does not think of himself as acting in these separate capacities. All business in the county that concerns health and sanitation he considers his business.[20]

If a health officer cannot manage to separate the national, state, city, and county functions he performs, how can the ordinary citizen be expected to make sense of this maze of governments? And does the ordinary citizen really benefit from this maze of governments?

So Many Governments: Advantages and Disadvantages

In theory at least, one benefit of breaking down and localizing government is that it brings government closer to the people, it gives them an opportunity to participate in the political process, to have a direct impact on policy. Localized government conjures up visions of informed citizens deciding their own political fate in small communities—the New England town meeting repeated across the nation. From this perspective, overlapping governments appear compatible with a majoritarian view of democracy.

The reality is somewhat different, however. Studies have shown that people are much more likely to vote in national elections than in local elections. Voter turnout in local contests tends to be very low, even though the impact of individual votes is much greater. Furthermore, the fragmentation of powers, functions, and responsibilities among national, state, and local governments makes government as a whole seem very complicated and hence less comprehensible and accessible to ordinary people. In addition, citizens who are busy with the daily matter of making a living have only limited time to devote to public affairs, and involvement in politics can be very time consuming. All these factors tend to keep individual citizens out of politics and to make government more responsive to organized groups, which have the resources—time, money, and know-how—to influence policymaking. Instead of bringing government closer to the people and reinforcing majoritarian democracy, then, the system's enormous complexity tends to encourage pluralism.

Another possible benefit of having many governments is that they enable the country to experiment with new policies on a small scale. New programs or solutions to problems can be tested in one city or state or in a few cities or states. Successful programs can then be adopted by other cities or states or by the nation as a whole. For this reason, states are sometimes called the "laboratories of democracy." For example, when President Reagan asked for a constitutional amendment requiring a balanced national budget—that is, one in which expenditures cannot be greater than income—he had a precedent. Many states have a constitutional provision like this.

Finally, the large number of governments makes it possible for government to respond to the diversity of conditions that prevails in different parts of the country. States and cities differ enormously in population, size, economic resources, climate, and other characteristics—all the diverse elements that French political philosopher Baron de Montesquieu

■ *And Try Not to Breathe*
In 1983, Times Beach, Missouri, was disincorporated and abandoned because of contamination by waste containing dioxin, a highly toxic chemical. Many of the 2,400 residents filed unsuccessful lawsuits against the companies responsible for the improper waste disposal. Disastrous environmental health problems like this are too big to handle on the state or local level and result in calls for assistance from the national government.

FEATURE 4.2

Who Should Make the Rules? Federalism and Public Opinion

In this chapter, we've talked about how the division of responsibilities between national and state governments shifts in ways that usually reflect practical politics rather than constitutional theory. But where do American citizens stand on the question of the distribution of power? What areas do they believe require uniform national standards? A CBS/New York Times poll taken in May 1987 out questions like these to 1,254 people and found some deep divisions on the issues.

Only a few respondents (5 percent) believed that the states have too much power; most (47 percent) thought the balance between states and nation is about right; a sizable minority (39 percent) claimed that the national government has too much power.

When it came down to deciding whether national or state standards are better, here's how opinion divided (respondents with no opinion are not shown):

Should there be one national policy set by the federal government or should the fifty states make their own rules . . .

	Federal	State
. . . in controlling pollution?	49%	46%
. . . in setting penalties for murder?	62	34
. . . on the issue of registration and voting?	64	31
. . . in selecting textbooks in public schools?	35	61
. . . in setting minimum wages?	51	45
. . . in establishing safety standards in factories?	65	31
. . . in setting highway speed limits?	42	56

Source: *New York Times,* 26 May 1987, p. 20.

(1689–1755) argued needed to be taken into account in formulating laws for a society. Smaller political units are better able to respond to particular local conditions and can generally do so quickly. On the other hand, smaller units may not be able to muster the economic resources to meet challenges.

Of course, the United States remains one nation no matter how many local governments there are. The question of how much diversity the nation should tolerate in the way different states treat their citizens is important. Also important is the question of whether the national government (and, indirectly, the citizens of other states) should be called on to foot the bill for the problems that diversity produces. As Feature 4.2 shows, public opinion is split on these issues.

Differences among states have led the national government to play a role in regional development. Throughout American history, the national government has used its funds to equalize disparities in wealth and development among states. The development of the Sunbelt (the southern and southwestern regions of the country) has been, and continues to be, helped considerably by national policies and programs. Tennessee Valley Authority (TVA) electrification and western irrigation projects were funded by the national government; the South, in particular, was helped enormously by national funding formulas designed to aid poorer areas of the country; and California has benefited from national largesse in the form of huge defense contracts. Overall, the Sunbelt states have received more money from the government than they have paid in taxes.

CONTEMPORARY FEDERALISM AND THE DILEMMAS OF DEMOCRACY

When President Reagan came to the White House, conservatives were delighted. They believed his preference for layer cake federalism would mean the dismantling of the liberal welfare state and the end of the national government's efforts to promote social and political equality at the expense of freedom. They argued that different states had different problems and resources, and asserted that, by returning control to state governments, it would be possible to give more play to diversity. States would be free to experiment with alternatives for meeting their problems. States would compete with one another. And people would be free to choose the state government they preferred by simply "voting with their feet"—moving to another state.

In addition, conservative proponents of New Federalism argued that the national government was too remote, too tied to special interests, not responsive to the public at large. The national government overregulated and tried to promote too much uniformity. Moreover, they added, the size and complexity of the federal system led to waste and inefficiency. States, on the other hand, were closer to the people and better able to respond specifically to local needs. If state governments were revitalized, individuals might believe that they could have a greater impact on decision making. The quality of political participation would improve. Furthermore, conservatives believed that shifting power to the states would help them achieve other parts of the political agenda. States, they thought, would work harder to keep taxes down; they would not be willing to spend a lot of money on social welfare programs; and they would be less likely to pass stiff laws regulating businesses. Reagan's New Federalism would bring back the days of laissez faire, when states found it difficult to regulate businesses for fear that industries might move to less restrictive states. Rivalry between states could become a "competition in laxity."

What conservatives hoped for, liberals feared. They remembered that the states' rights model allowed political and social inequalities, that it supported racism. Blacks and city dwellers were often left virtually unrepresented by white state legislators who disproportionately served rural interests. Liberals believed the states were unwilling or unable to protect the rights or provide for the needs of their citizens, whether those citizens were consumers seeking protection from business interests, defendants requiring guarantees of due process of law, or poor people seeking a minimum standard of living.

To what extent were conservative hopes and liberal fears realized as federalism developed in the 1980s? And, how did the development of federalism during this period relate to the dilemmas of democracy?

Federalism and the Values of Freedom, Order, and Equality

Neither the conservatives' hopes nor the liberals' fears were fully realized under Reagan's New Federalism, nor did Reagan himself always embrace the states' rights position. His New Federalism was used mainly as a tool for cutting the national budget by offering less money to the states. Contrary to the expectations of conservatives and liberals alike, however, states themselves proved willing to approve tax increases to pay for social services and education. In an era when Washington was less willing to enforce antitrust legislation, civil rights laws, or affirmative action plans, state governments were more likely to do so. At a time when a conservative national government put little emphasis on the value of equality, state governments did more to embrace it.

Conservatives had thought that the value of freedom would be enhanced if more matters were left to the states. Traditionally, state governments had been relatively small, lacking the wherewithal to limit large corporate interests, for example. But over the past two decades, state governments had changed. Their legislatures had become more professional. They met regularly, for longer periods of time. They maintained larger permanent staffs. Governors showed themselves willing to support major programs to enhance the skills of the work force, to promote research and development, and to subsidize new industries. State governments had become "big governments" themselves. They were better able to tackle problems, and they were not afraid to use their power to promote equality.

To the surprise of liberals, who had looked to the national government to protect individuals by setting reasonable minimum standards for product safety, welfare payments, and employee benefits, states were now willing to set higher standards than the national government. As states took a more active role in setting these standards, they highlighted another challenge for our democracy—the need to maintain order. Where claims of order were raised, the Reagan administration proved quick to back away from its position on states' rights. We saw this in the case of the minimum drinking age and again in the matter of training National Guard troops (see Feature 4.1). Often, for the Reagan administration, maintaining order meant safeguarding corporate interests. For example, in 1986, the administration proposed a new product liability law. It would pre-empt state statutes and reduce the awards plaintiffs could receive from lawsuits against manufacturers of products that harmed them.

In summary, the relationship among the federal system, political ideology, and the values of freedom, order, and equality is no longer as simple as it appeared two decades ago. Then, liberals could look to the national government and cooperative, marble cake federalism to help secure equality. Conservatives could wish for a return to small government, states' rights, and layer cake federalism. In the 1980s, conservatives gave lip service to the ideals of New Federalism but were often reluctant to give up the national power that helped them achieve their vision of order. After all, if they returned power to the states, they might well do more to promote equality than freedom. As one prominent conservative put it, "The Great Society may be over in Washington, but it has just begun in the states."[21]

Federalism and Pluralism

As we discussed in Chapter 2, the system of government in America today supports the pluralist model of democracy. Federalism is an important part of that system. How has it contributed to American pluralism? Do each of the competing views of federalism support pluralism?

Our federal system of government was designed to allay citizens' fears that they might be ruled by majorities of citizens who were residents of distant regions and with whom they did not necessarily agree or share interests. The institutional design, by recognizing the legitimacy of the states as political divisions, also recognized the importance of diversity. The existence and cultivation of diverse interests are hallmarks of pluralism.

Each of the two competing mythologies of federalism supports pluralism but in somewhat different ways. Dual federalism, which has evolved into New Federalism, wants to decentralize government, to shift power to the states. It recognizes the importance of local rather than national standards and applauds the diversity of those standards. This variety allows people, if not a voice in policymaking, the choice of policy under which to live. These factors tend to support pluralist democracy.

In contrast, cooperative federalism is perfectly willing to override local standards for a national standard in the interests of promoting equality. Yet this view of federalism, particularly in its picket fence version, also supports pluralist democracy. It is highly responsive to all manner of group pressures, including pressure at one level from groups unsuccessful at other levels. By blurring the lines of national and state responsibility, this kind of federalism encourages petitioners to try their luck at whichever level of government offers the best chance of success.

SUMMARY

The government framework outlined in the Constitution was the product of political compromise, an acknowledgment of the states' fear of a powerful central government. The division of powers sketched in the Constitution was supposed to turn over great and aggregate matters to the national government, leaving local and particular concerns to the states. Exactly what was great and aggregate and what was local and particular was not fully explained. As a result, two competing myths of federalism emerged. Dual, or layer cake, federalism wanted to retain power in the states and to keep the levels of government separate. Cooperative, or marble cake, federalism emphasized the power of the national government and saw national and state governments working together to solve national problems. In its own way, each view supported the pluralist model of democracy.

Over the years, the national government has used both its enumerated powers and implied powers to become involved in virtually every area of human activity. The tools of political change—the sticks and carrots the national government has used to expand its power—include direct legislation, judicial decisions, and financial incentives in the form of grants.

As its influence grew, so did the government itself. At the same time, intergovernmental relations became more complex. New Federalists, generally conservative, suggested cutting back the size of the national government, reducing federal spending, and turning programs over to the states as a solution to the problem of unwieldy government. Liberals, worried that New Federalists, in their haste to decentralize and cut back, would turn over important responsibilities to states that were unwilling or unable to assume them. Government, rather than being too responsive, would become unresponsive. But neither conservative hopes nor liberal fears were fully realized in the decade of the 1980s. The states proved both willing and able to tackle some major problems. More than this, they were willing to fund many programs that promoted equality.

The debate over federalism will continue in the 1990s, and it may still be couched in terms of the two competing mythologies—dual federalism and cooperative federalism. But, as in the past, the balance of power between the national and state governments will be settled by political means, not theory.

Key Terms

federalism	nullification
dual federalism	intergovernmental
states' rights	relations
cooperative federalism	picket fence federalism
elastic clause	general revenue sharing
implied powers	special revenue sharing
commerce clause	municipal government
grant-in-aid	county government
categorical grant	school district
formula grant	special district
project grant	home rule
block grant	

Selected Readings

Gittell, Marilyn, ed. *State Politics and the New Federalism.* New York: Longmans, 1986. A collection of works on intergovernmental relations that emphasizes the role of the states.

Nathan, Richard P., and Fred C. Doolittle. *Reagan and the States.* Princeton, N.J.: Princeton University Press, 1987. An overview and set of case studies of fiscal federalism as a part of Reagan's New Federalism.

O'Toole, Laurence J., ed. *American Intergovernmental Relations.* Washington, D.C.: Congressional Quarterly, 1985. This general collection of readings includes classics on the subject as well as timely analyses of intergovernmental relations in the Reagan administration.

Reagan, Michael, and John Sanzone. *The New Federalism.* New York: Oxford University Press, 1981. A classic analysis of fiscal federalism with heavy emphasis on grants.

Walker, David B. *Toward a Functioning Federalism.* Cambridge, Mass.: Winthrop, 1981. This work analyzes the overloaded system of intergovernmental relations and offers alternatives to it.

Essay B

The Transformation of Political Art

Throughout our nation's history, political expressions—both positive and negative—have appeared in art. To convey a political message, artists frequently use an icon, or symbol. One of the first and most popular political icons was Liberty. She is by no means uniquely American—her origins lie in ancient Rome, and she has enjoyed great popularity in France. The fierceness of this *Miss Liberty*, created just before the Civil War, suggests that both she and the United States were still poised to defend their freedom.

George Washington may not have been our country's first icon, but he was the first human being to become an American political symbol. He represented military valor, presidential dignity, and paternal wisdom—the personal attributes of a hero. Washington was often paired with Liberty, as the instrument through which her ideals were achieved. In *Liberty and Washington*, she places a laurel wreath—a symbol of honor and glory—on a bust of the deceased president. Gazing toward the sky, she seems to contemplate his place in heaven.

In *Centennial Progress*, painted in 1875, Washington is one of many heroes surrounding Columbia, the female personification of the United States. Along with Thomas Jefferson, Washington occupies a prominent position beside the flag, well above the crowd. Presidents (including Abraham Lincoln and Ulysses S. Grant) and statesmen (such as Benjamin Franklin and Frederick Douglass) gather around the pedestal on which Columbia holds a telegraph wire—a reminder of one of the most important inventions of the century.

By the twentieth century, reverence for Washington still flourished, but at least part of the public had grown sophisticated enough to recognize the humor in Grant Wood's *Parson Weems' Fable*, which pokes fun at America's

affection for the story of young George and the cherry tree. Parson Weems, the creator of the cherry tree fable, draws aside a curtain to reveal the moment of confession. But the center of attention looks odd: Little George has the mature head made famous by Gilbert Stuart's portrait. It is as if Washington sprang to life

Left page: Miss Liberty. *Artist unknown, 1850–1860. Courtesy of the Barenholz Collection. Photo by Schecter Lee, courtesy of the Museum of American Folk Art, New York City.* This page, top left: Liberty and Washington. *Artist unknown, c. 1800–1810. New York State Historical Association, Cooperstown.* Top right: Centennial Progress, *by Montgomery Tiers, 1875. Courtesy William Judson.* Bottom: Parson Weems' Fable, *by Grant Wood, 1939. Courtesy Amon Carter Museum, Fort Worth.*

fully grown, like a mythical god—a characterization suggesting the public's inability to think of him as an ordinary youth.

Not all public figures appearing in American art have been revered as unanimously as George Washington. In fact, some are more martyrs than heroes. Their presence alludes to a darker side of history and a long tradition of public dissent.

For many black Americans, the abolitionist John Brown was a hero. Southern white people generally regarded him as an assassin and possibly a madman. Northern feeling was more ambiguous, but even those who shared Brown's desire to free the slaves questioned the violence of his actions and speculated about his sanity.

Although John Brown is most famous for his 1859 armed raid on Harpers Ferry, Virginia, Brown's hanging was at least as significant for the black artist Horace Pippin. Pippin's grandmother allegedly witnessed the execution and frequently described the event to him. In *John Brown Going to His Hanging*, white people gathered to watch Brown's arrival chat together nonchalantly. But the lone black slave—presumably the artist's grandmother—confronts the viewer with an accusing glare.

Sixty-eight years after John Brown's hanging, another execution shook the country. A court convicted two immigrant anarchists named Nicola Sacco and Bartolomeo Vanzetti of murdering a guard and a paymaster during a Massachusetts robbery. Since there was insuffi-

Top: Bartolomeo Vanzetti and Nicola Sacco, *by Ben Shahn, 1931–1932. Collection, The Museum of Modern Art, New York. Gift of Abby Aldrich Rockefeller.* Bottom: John Brown Going to His Hanging, *by Horace Pippin, 1942. Courtesy of The Pennsylvania Academy of the Fine Arts, Lambert Fund Purchase.*

cient evidence to prove their involvement in the crime, Sacco and Vanzetti's main offenses seem to have been their political convictions and their Italian heritage. The judge openly sided with the prosecution, and the defendants clearly failed to receive as fair a trial as they were constitutionally guaranteed. To those who looked to the United States as a land where freedom of belief is honored, Sacco and Vanzetti's execution was an outrage. Ben Shahn, one of several distressed artists, expressed his anger in a series of paintings called *The Passion of Sacco and Vanzetti*.

Art is sometimes transformed into patriotic propaganda, particularly during times of war. Such was the case with *The Four Freedoms* series Norman Rockwell painted in 1943 (see Chapter 1, pages 12–13). The U.S. government printed and circulated posters of the paintings to remind Americans what they were fighting for. During the Vietnam era, however, art tended to protest rather than support the war. The poster created for the Committee to End the War reinterprets the familiar posters in which Uncle Sam points directly at the viewer and announces, "I want you" (see Chapter 19, page 697, for an example). Here, Uncle Sam is battered and bandaged—ironically recalling Revolutionary War patriots. This weary and disillusioned Uncle Sam has simply had enough.

One of the dominant political themes of the 1980s has been the threat of nuclear war. Contemporary literature, film, video, and drama have reflected this concern, but nowhere has it been more apparent than in the visual arts. Many artists have used frightening images of mushroom clouds or sentimental reminders of the beauty of life to depict this issue. But Mike Glier's painting *Barbara Calling III* is more mysterious and ultimately more disturbing. Behind the back of a jubilantly shouting protester, a menacing figure with blackened face and hands tosses money into the air. His presence might suggest death, the military establishment, or an unspecified evil force. Whatever the interpretation, the figure reminds viewers that, like a shadow, the threat of nuclear war is always with us, just behind our backs.

Top: "I Want Out." *Steve Horn, photographer; Larry Dunst, art director. Poster for the Committee to End the War.* Bottom: Barbara Calling III, *by Mike Glier, 1983. Courtesy Barbara Gladstone Gallery. Photo by eeva-inkeri.*

PART III

LINKING PEOPLE WITH GOVERNMENT

5

Public Opinion and Political Socialization

Fridays are different in Saudi Arabia. After prayers, criminals are paraded in the streets, then punished publicly. Murderers are beheaded, adulterers are flogged, and thieves have their hands chopped off. The Saudi government wants its citizens to get the message: Crime will not be tolerated. Saudi Arabia, which claims the lowest crime rate in the world, is a country that greatly values order.

In contrast, the United States has one of the highest crime rates in the world. Its homicide rate, for example, is three to ten times that of most other Western countries. Although no one is proud of this record, our government would never consider beheading, flogging, or dismembering as a means of lowering the crime rate. First, the Eighth Amendment to the Constitution forbids "cruel and unusual punishment." Second, the public would not tolerate this kind of punishment.

However, the public definitely is not squeamish about the death penalty (capital punishment), at least for certain crimes. The Gallup organization has polled the nation on this issue for fifty years. Except in 1957 and 1966, a clear majority of respondents have consistently supported the death penalty for murder.[1] In fact, public support for capital punishment has increased dramatically since the late 1960s. In 1985, 75 percent of all respondents were in favor of the death penalty for murder, while only 17 percent opposed it. Substantial segments of the public also were in favor of the death penalty for espionage (48 percent), rape (45 percent), and airplane hijacking (45 percent).

Government has been defined as the legitimate use of force to control human behavior. Through most of American history, the execution of people who threaten the social order has been a legal use of government force. In colonial times, capital punishment was imposed, not just for murder, but for antisocial behavior—for denying the "true" God, cursing one's parents, adultery, witchcraft, or being a rebellious child.[2] In the late 1700s, some writers, editors, and clergy argued for abolishing the death sentence. The campaign intensified in the 1840s, and a few states responded by eliminating capital punishment. With the pressures of the Civil War and its aftermath, interest in the cause waned until 1890, when New York State adopted a new technique, electrocution, as the instrument of death. By 1917, twelve states had passed laws against capital punishment. But the outbreak of World War I fed the public's suspicion of foreigners and fear of radicals, leading to renewed support for the death penalty. Reacting to this shift in public opinion, four states restored capital punishment.

The security needs of World War II and postwar fears of Soviet communism fueled continued support for capital punishment. After the Red Scare subsided in the late 1950s, public opposition to the death penalty increased. In 1957, for the first time, polls showed a small majority opposing capital punishment. But public opinion was neither strong enough nor stable enough to force state legislatures to outlaw the death penalty. In keeping with the pluralist model of democracy, abolition efforts shifted from the legislative arena to the courts.

One of the major arguments the abolitionists used was that the death penalty is cruel and unusual punishment, and therefore unconstitutional.

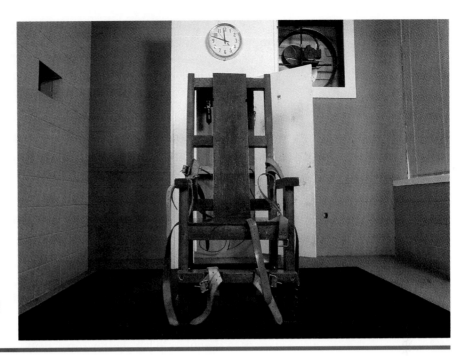

The Death Chamber
*This uncomfortable appara-
tus is the electric chair in a
Louisiana state prison. It
dramatizes the ultimate
power that government has
to control behavior. Capital
crimes may draw capital
punishment.*

Certainly the public did not think capital punishment was either cruel
or unusual in the 1780s. But two hundred years later, its opponents
contended that execution by the state had become cruel and unusual by
contemporary standards. Their argument had some effect on public opinion; in 1966, a bare majority of respondents opposed the death penalty
for only the second time since the Gallup surveys began.

The states responded to this shift in public opinion by reducing the
number of executions each year until, in 1968, they were stopped completely in anticipation of a Supreme Court decision. By then, however,
public opinion had again reversed itself in favor of capital punishment.
Still, in 1972, the Court ruled in a 5-to-4 vote that the death penalty as
imposed by existing state laws was unconstitutional.[3] Its decision was
not well received in many states, and thirty-five state legislatures passed
new laws to get around the Court's ruling. Public approval of the death
penalty jumped almost 10 points and began climbing higher as the nation's homicide rate increased.

In 1976, the Supreme Court changed its position. It ruled that three
of the new state laws—those that provided for consideration of the defendant and the offense before imposing the death sentence—*were* constitutional.[4] And the Court rejected the argument that punishment by
death itself violates the Constitution. In its ruling, the Court also noted
that public opinion favored the death penalty. Now endorsed by the
courts, as well as the public, the death penalty was again available to
the states. Through the end of the 1970s, though, few states applied the
penalty: Only three criminals were executed. Eventually, however, the
states began to heed the clamor, executing about twenty criminals a year
by the mid-1980s.

Does the death penalty deter people from committing murder? Two-thirds of the public think it does.[5] What do people think is the most humane method of execution? Opinion polls tell us that most people favor lethal injection (62 percent) over electrocution (18 percent). The gas chamber has more support (9 percent) than the old-fashioned firing squad (3 percent). But hanging (1 percent) is generally unpopular, and no respondents regard beheading as humane.

The history of public thinking on the death penalty reveals several characteristics of public opinion:

1. *The public's attitudes toward a given government policy can vary over time, often dramatically.* Opinions about capital punishment tend to fluctuate with threats to the social order. The public is more likely to favor capital punishment in times of war and fear of foreign subversion and when crime rates are high.

2. *Public opinion places boundaries on allowable types of public policy.* Chopping off a hand is not acceptable to the public (and surely to courts interpreting the Constitution) as a punishment for theft in the United States, but electrocuting a murderer in private (not in public) is all right.

3. *Citizens are willing to register opinions on matters outside their expertise.* People clearly believe execution by lethal injection is more humane than electrocution, asphyxiation in the gas chamber, or hanging. How can the public know enough about execution to make these judgments?

4. *Governments tend to react to public opinion.* State laws for and against capital punishment have reflected swings in the public mood. Moreover, the Supreme Court's decision in 1972 against capital punishment came when public opinion on the death penalty was sharply divided; the Court's approval of capital punishment in 1976 coincided with a rise in public approval of the death penalty.

5. *The government sometimes does not do what the people want.* Although public opinion overwhelmingly favors the death penalty for murder, few states actually punish murderers with execution. The United States has averaged over twenty thousand homicides annually in the 1980s but has executed fewer than twenty murderers a year.

The last two conclusions bear on our discussion of the majoritarian and pluralist models of democracy in Chapter 2. Here we probe more deeply into the nature, shape, depth, and formation of public opinion in a democratic government. What is the place of public opinion in a democracy? How do people acquire their opinions? What are the major lines of division in public opinion? How do individuals' ideology and knowledge affect their opinions? What is the relationship between public opinion and ideological type?

PUBLIC OPINION AND THE MODELS OF DEMOCRACY

The majoritarian and pluralist models of democracy differ greatly in their assumptions about the role of public opinion in democratic government. According to the classic majoritarian model, the government should do

Stop the Presses! Oops, Too Late . . .
As the 1948 election drew near, few people gave President Harry Truman a chance to defeat his Republican opponent, Thomas E. Dewey. Polling was still new, and virtually all the early polls showed Dewey far ahead. Most organizations simply stopped polling weeks before the election. The Chicago Daily Tribune *believed the polls and proclaimed Dewey's victory before the votes were counted. Here, the victorious Truman triumphantly displays the most embarrassing headline in American politics. Later it was revealed that the few polls taken closer to election day showed Truman catching up to Dewey, which demonstrates that polls estimate the vote only at the time they are taken.*

what a majority of the public wants. In contrast, pluralists argue that the public as a whole seldom demonstrates clear consistent opinions on the day-to-day issues of government. At the same time, pluralists recognize that subgroups within the public do express opinions on specific matters—often and vigorously. The pluralist model requires that government institutions allow the free expression of opinions by these "minority publics." Democracy is at work when the opinions of many different publics clash openly and fairly over government policy.

Thanks to opinion polling, we can better understand the conflict between these two institutional models of democracy. *Polling* involves interviewing a sample of citizens to estimate public opinion as a whole (see Politics in the Information Age 5.1). **Public opinion** is simply the collected attitudes of citizens on a given issue or question. We are interested in what citizens think about issues that are politically relevant, but this can mean almost any question. Adultery is usually not a political issue, but public opinion on marital infidelity becomes politically relevant when the issue touches a presidential candidate, as Gary Hart learned in the 1988 contest for the Democratic nomination for president. Opinion polling is such a common part of contemporary life that we often forget it is a modern invention, dating only from the 1930s (see Figure 5.1). In fact, survey methodology did not develop into a powerful research tool until the advent of computers in the 1950s.

Before polling became an accepted part of the American scene, politicians, journalists, and everyone else could argue about what "the peo-

POLITICS IN THE INFORMATION AGE 5.1

Sampling a Few, Predicting to Everyone

How can a pollster tell what the nation thinks by talking to only a few hundred people? The answer lies in the statistical theory of *sampling*. Briefly, the theory holds that a sample of individuals selected by chance from any population is "representative" of that population. This means that the traits of individuals in the sample—their attitudes, beliefs, sociological characteristics, and physical features—reflect the traits of the whole population. Sampling theory does not say that a sample exactly matches the population, only that it reflects the population within some predictable degree of accuracy.

Three factors determine the accuracy of a sample. The most important is the way the sample is selected. For maximum accuracy, the individuals in the sample must be chosen randomly. *Randomly* does not mean "at whim"; it means that every individual in the population has the same chance of being selected.

For a population as large and widespread as that of the United States, direct random sampling of individuals by name is practically impossible. Instead, pollsters first divide the country into geographic regions. Then they randomly choose areas and sample individuals who live within those areas. This departure from strict random sampling does decrease the accuracy of polls, but only by a relatively small amount. Today, most polls conducted by the mass media are done by telephone, with computers randomly dialing numbers within predetermined telephone areas. (Random dialing ensures that even people with unlisted numbers are called.)

The second factor that affects the accuracy of sampling is the size of the sample. The larger the sample, the more accurately it represents the population. For example, a sample of four hundred individuals predicts accurately to a population within 6 percentage points (plus or minus), 95 percent of the time. A sample of six hundred is accurate within 4 percentage points. (Surprisingly, when the population is very large compared with the sample—which is usually the case in opinion polling—the size of the population has essentially no effect on the sampling accuracy. So a sample of, say, six hundred individuals selected within a city, a state, or even the nation reflects the traits of its population with equal accuracy, within 4 percentage points. Why this is so is better discussed in a course on statistics.)

The final factor that affects the accuracy of sampling is the amount of variation in the population. If there were no variation in a population, every sample would reflect the population's characteristics with perfect accuracy. But the greater the variation within the population, the greater the chance that one random sample will be different from another.

The Gallup Poll and most other national opinion polls usually survey about 1,500 individuals and are accurate within 3 percentage points, 95 percent of the time. As shown in Figure 5.1, the predictions of the Gallup Poll for thirteen presidential elections since 1936 have deviated from the voting results only an average of 2.1 percentage points. Even this small margin of error can mean an incorrect prediction in a close election. But for the purpose of estimating public opinion on political issues, a sampling error of 3 percentage points is acceptable.

Poll results can be wrong because of problems that have nothing to do with sampling theory. In particular, confusing or misleading questions can bias the results. For example, in surveys conducted during the Korean War, questions that mentioned a communist invasion tended to increase support for the war by 15 to 20 percentage points over ones that did not mention communism.[*] Survey methods are also likely to get superficial responses from busy respondents who say anything, quickly, to get rid of a pesky interviewer. Recently, some newspaper columnists have even urged readers to lie to pollsters outside voting booths, to confound election-night television predictions. But despite its potential for abuse or distortion, modern polling has told us a great deal about public opinion in America.

---

[*] John E. Mueller, *War, Presidents and Public Opinion* (New York: Wiley, 1973), p. 44.

ple" wanted, but no one really knew. Observers of America before the 1930s had to guess at public opinion by analyzing newspaper stories, politicians' speeches, voting returns, and travelers' diaries. When no one really knows what the people want, it is impossible for government to be responsive to public opinion. As we discussed in Chapter 3, the founders wanted to build public opinion into our government structure by allowing the direct election of representatives to the House and apportioning representation there according to population. Attitudes and actions in the House of Representatives, the framers thought, would reflect public opinion, especially on the crucial issues of taxes and government spending.

In practice, bills passed by a majority of elected representatives do not necessarily reflect the opinions of a majority of citizens. This would not have bothered the framers because they never intended to create a full democracy, a government responsive to majority opinion. Although they wanted to provide for some input of public opinion, they had little faith in the ability of the masses to make public policy.

Figure 5.1

Gallup Poll Accuracy
One of the nation's oldest polls was started by George Gallup in the 1930s. The accuracy of the Gallup Poll in predicting presidential elections over nearly fifty years is charted below. Although not always on the mark, its predictions have been fairly close to election results. The poll was most notably wrong in 1948, when it predicted that Thomas Dewey, the Republican candidate, would defeat the Democratic incumbent, Harry Truman, underestimating Truman's vote by 5.4 percentage points. In the 1988 election, the Gallup Poll estimated that George Bush would obtain 56 percent of the vote, and he actually obtained 54 percent. (Source: Gallup Report, December 1984, p. 31.)

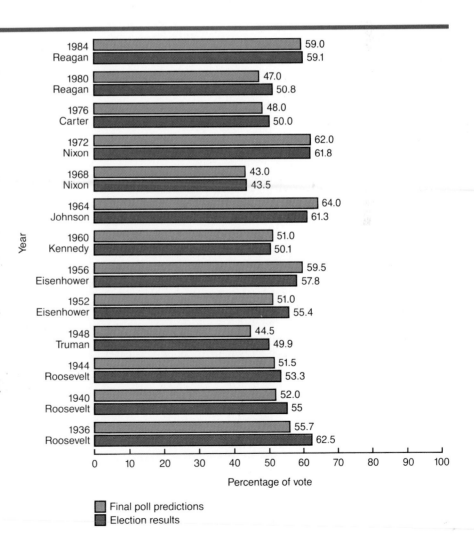

Year / Candidate	Final poll predictions	Election results
1984 Reagan	59.0	59.1
1980 Reagan	47.0	50.8
1976 Carter	48.0	50.0
1972 Nixon	62.0	61.8
1968 Nixon	43.0	43.5
1964 Johnson	64.0	61.3
1960 Kennedy	51.0	50.1
1956 Eisenhower	59.5	57.8
1952 Eisenhower	51.0	55.4
1948 Truman	44.5	49.9
1944 Roosevelt	51.5	53.3
1940 Roosevelt	52.0	55
1936 Roosevelt	55.7	62.5

Percentage of vote

▢ Final poll predictions
▪ Election results

Sampling methods and opinion polling have altered the debate over the majoritarian and pluralist models of democracy. Now that we know how often government policy runs against majority opinion, it becomes harder to defend the U.S. government as democratic under the majoritarian model. Even at a time when Americans overwhelmingly favored the death penalty for murderers, the Supreme Court decided that existing state laws applying capital punishment were unconstitutional. Even after the Court approved new state laws as constitutional, relatively few murderers were actually executed. Consider, too, the case of prayer in public schools. The Supreme Court has ruled that no state or local government can require the reading of the Lord's Prayer or Bible verses in public schools. Yet surveys continually show that a clear majority of Americans (over 60 percent) do not agree with that ruling.[6] Because government policy sometimes runs against settled majority opinion, the majoritarian model is easily attacked.

Each of the two models of democracy makes certain assumptions about public opinion. The majoritarian model assumes that a majority of people hold clear consistent opinions on government policy. The pluralist model insists that public opinion is often divided, and opinion polls certainly give credence to that claim. What are the bases of these divisions? What principles, if any, do people use to organize their beliefs and attitudes about politics? Exactly how do individuals form their political opinions? We look for answers to these questions in this chapter. In later chapters, we assess the effect of public opinion on government policies. The results should help you make up your own mind about the viability of the majoritarian and pluralist models in a functioning democracy.

THE DISTRIBUTION OF PUBLIC OPINION

A government that tries to respond to public opinion soon learns that people seldom think alike. To understand, then to act on, the public's many attitudes and beliefs, governments must pay attention to the way public opinion distributes among the choices on an issue. In particular, government must analyze the *shape* and the *stability* of the distribution.

Shape of the Distribution

The results of public opinion polls are often displayed on charts like those in Figure 5.2. The response categories run along the baseline. The height of the columns indicates the percentage of those polled who gave each response. The *shape* of the opinion distribution is the pattern, or physical form, of all the responses when counted and plotted. The figure depicts three idealized patterns of distribution—normal, skewed, and bimodal—superimposed on three actual survey items.[7]

Figure 5.2a shows how respondents to a national survey in 1987 placed themselves along a liberal-conservative continuum. The most frequent response, called the *mode,* was "moderate." Progressively fewer people classified themselves in each category toward the liberal and conservative extremes. The shape of the graph resembles what statistical theory calls a **normal distribution**—a symmetrical bell-shaped distribu-

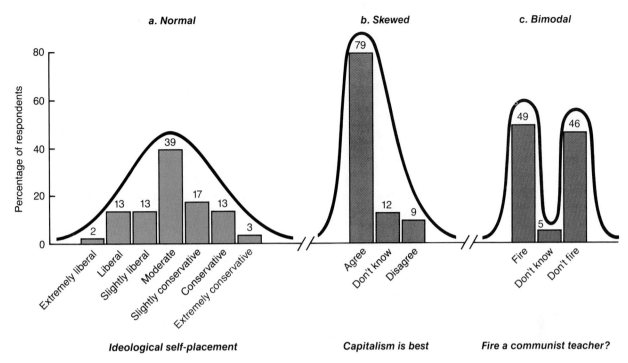

Three Distributions of Opinion
We've superimposed three hypothetical patterns of distribution—normal, skewed, and bimodal—on three actual distributions of responses to survey questions. Although the actual responses do not match the shapes exactly, they match closely enough so that we can describe the distribution of (a) ideological attitudes as approximately normal, *(b) belief in capitalism as* skewed, *and (c) opinions on firing a communist teacher as* bimodal. *(Sources: (a) James Allen Davis and Tom W. Smith,* General Social Surveys, 1972– 1987: Cumulative Codebook *[Chicago: National Opinion Research Center, 1987], p. 94. Sample size was 1,819. Only 6 percent of the sample chose "don't know" or didn't answer the question. (b) 1981 Survey by Civic Service, Inc., reported in* Public Opinion 5 *[October–November 1982]:21. (c) Davis and Smith,* General Social Surveys, *p. 117.)*

Figure 5.2

tion around a single mode. Opinions that are *normally distributed* tend to support moderate government policies. At the same time, they allow government policies that range to either side of the center position, shifting from liberal to conservative and back again, as long as they do not stray too far from the moderate center.

Figure 5.2b plots the percentages of those who agreed or disagreed with the statement "The private business system in the United States works better than any other system yet devised for industrial countries."[8] The shape of this graph is very different from the symmetrical distribution of ideological attitudes. In this graph, the mode (containing the vast majority who agree with the statement) lies off to one side, leaving a "tail" (the few who disagree) on the other. This kind of asymmetrical distribution is called a **skewed distribution.** The amount of skew depends on the ratio between the proportion of respondents in the mode of the distribution and those in the tail.

In a skewed distribution, the opinions of the majority cluster around a point on one side of the issue. A skewed distribution indicates less diversity of opinion than does a normal distribution. The skewed distribution in Figure 5.2b tells us that most Americans are happy with capitalism as an economic system. Obviously, then, a candidate would have little hope of winning an election by denouncing free enterprise. In fact, when consensus on an issue is this strong, those with minority opinions risk social ostracism and even persecution if they persist in voicing their opinions. If the public does not feel intensely about an issue, however, politicians can sometimes discount a skewed distribution of public opinion. This is what's happened with the death penalty. Although most people favor capital punishment, it is not a burning issue for them. This means politicians can discount public opinion on the issue without serious consequences.

Figure 5.2c plots the percentages of respondents who favored or opposed firing a college teacher who was an admitted communist. These responses fall into a **bimodal distribution:** Respondents chose two categories equally (or almost equally) as the most frequent responses. Americans divide almost evenly over allowing an admitted communist (an opponent of capitalism) to teach in a college. Virtually half the American population would fire the teacher; nearly half would allow the individual to continue teaching. Because they split the electorate in nearly equal parts, bimodal distributions of opinion carry the greatest potential for political conflict, especially if both sides feel strongly about the issue.

Stability of the Distribution

A **stable distribution** shows little change over time. Public opinion on important issues can change, but it is sometimes difficult to distinguish a true change in opinion from a difference in the way a question is worded. When different questions on the same issue produce similar distributions of opinion, the underlying attitudes are stable. When the same question (or virtually the same question) produces significantly different responses over time, the surveys are more likely to be signaling an actual shift in public opinion.

Consider Americans' attitudes toward capitalism. In the 1981 survey plotted in Figure 5.2b, 79 percent of the respondents chose capitalism over any alternative economic system. Forty years earlier, in 1941, respondents had been asked whether they "would be better off if the concern you worked for were taken over and operated by the federal government." The responses at that time were also heavily skewed: 81 percent said that they preferred "business management." The nation's support for capitalism is very stable; it has barely changed over four decades.[9]

People's placement of themselves on the liberal-conservative continuum is another distribution that has remained surprisingly stable from the 1960s to the 1980s (see Figure 5.3a). Even in 1964, when liberal Lyndon Johnson won a landslide victory over conservative Barry Goldwater in the presidential election, more voters described themselves as conservative than liberal. Indeed, this has been the public's ideological self-classification in every presidential election year since 1964.[10] Despite

Taking the Public Pulse
Opinion polling has become commonplace in modern life. This employee of NBC News appears to be conducting an exit poll of someone who has just left the voting booth. Exit polls are used to obtain quick estimates of voting outcomes, allowing early projections of election winners. This respondent doesn't seem to like any of the available choices.

all the talk about the nation's becoming conservative in recent years, the fact is that most people did not describe themselves as liberal *at any time* during the last two decades. People did describe themselves as more conservative during that time (shifting about 5 percentage points toward the right), but most considered themselves conservative to begin with.

Public opinion in America *is* capable of massive change over time, however. Moreover, change can occur on issues that were once highly controversial. A good example of a dramatic change in American public opinion is race relations, specifically integrated schools. A national survey in 1942 asked whether "white and Negro students should go to the same schools or separate schools."[11] Only 30 percent of white respondents said that the students should attend schools together. When virtually the same question (substituting *black* for Negro) was asked in 1984, 90 percent of the white respondents endorsed integrated schools (see Figure 5.3b).

Scholars writing on this trend in racial attitudes have commented on "(1) its massive magnitude, moving from a solid pro-segregation majority to an overwhelming pro-integration consensus; (2) its long duration, continuing over four decades; and (3) its steady relentless pace."[12] But they note that white Americans have not become "color-blind." Despite their endorsement of integrated schools, only 23 percent of the whites surveyed in 1984 were in favor of busing to achieve racial balance. And whites were more willing to bus their children to a school with a few blacks than to one that was mostly black.[13] So white opinion changed

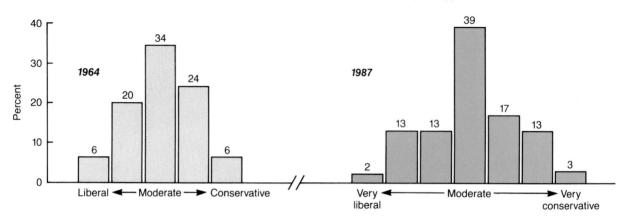

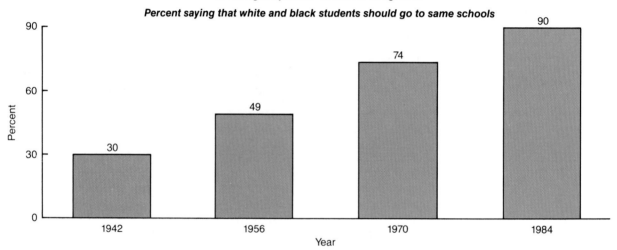

Stability and Change in Public Opinion

Public opinion remains stable over time on some issues and changes dramatically on others. The charts in part (a) indicate great stability in respondents' ideological self-classifications in separate surveys in 1964 and 1987. Opinions at both times were approximately normally distributed around "moderate," the modal category. (The 1964 distribution is slightly more compact because the earlier survey had only five response categories.) Part (b) shows how much public opinion on school integration has changed over four decades, from a majority opposed to integration to nearly all in favor. (Sources: (a) Data for 1964 are from Lloyd A. Free and Hadley Cantril, The Political Beliefs of Americans *[New York: Simon & Schuster, 1968], p. 41. Data for 1987 come from James Allen Davis and Tom W. Smith,* General Social Surveys, 1972–1987: Cumulative Codebook *[Chicago: National Opinion Research Center, 1987], p. 94. (b) Surveys conducted by the National Opinion Research Center; reported in and recalculated from Tom W. Smith and Paul B. Sheatsley, "American Attitudes Toward Race Relations,"* Public Opinion 7 *[October–November 1984]:15.)*

Figure 5.3

dramatically with regard to the *principle* of desegregated schools, but whites seemed divided on how that principle should be implemented. Trying to explain this contradiction and the way in which political opinions in general are formed, political scientists cite the process of political socialization, the influence of cultural factors, and the interplay of ideology and knowledge. In the next several sections, we examine how these elements combine to create and affect public opinion.

POLITICAL SOCIALIZATION

Public opinion is grounded in political values. People acquire their values through **political socialization,** a complex process through which individuals become aware of politics, learn political facts, and form political values. Think for a moment about your political socialization. What is your earliest memory of a president? When did you first learn about political parties? If you identify with a party, how did you decide to do so? If you don't, why don't you? Who was the first liberal you ever met? The first conservative? How did you first learn about the hydrogen bomb? About the Soviet Union?

Obviously, the paths to political awareness, knowledge, and values differ among individuals, but most people are exposed to the same influences or *agents of socialization*, especially in childhood through young adulthood. These influences are family, school, community, and peers.

The Agents of Early Socialization

Like psychologists, scholars of political socialization place great emphasis on early learning. Both groups point to two operating principles that characterize early learning:[14]

■ The *primacy principle.* What is learned first is learned best.

■ The *structuring principle.* What is learned first structures later learning.

Because most people learn first from their family, the family tends to be a very important agent of early socialization. The extent of family influence—and of the influence of other socializing agents—depends on the extent of our *exposure, communication,* and *receptivity* to them.[15]

Family. In most cases, exposure, communication, and receptivity are highest in family-child relationships. From their families, children learn a wide range of values—social, moral, religious, economic, and political—that help shape their opinions. It is not surprising, then, that most people link their earliest memories of politics with their families. Moreover, when parents are interested in politics, they influence their children to become more politically interested and informed.[16]

One of the most politically important things that many children learn from their parents is party identification. Party identification is learned in much the same way as religion. Children (very young children, anyway) imitate their parents. When parents share the same religion,

One Nation . . .
Throughout America—as in every other country—young children are socialized into politics through the school system. The simple ceremony of raising the flag teaches students that they are part of a larger political system—the United States of America—no matter where they live. As Feature 5.1 points out, however, they may not always get the message straight in the beginning.

children almost always are raised in that faith. When parents are of different religions, children are more likely to follow one or the other than to adopt a third. Similarly, parental influence on party identification is greater when both parents strongly identify with the same party.[17] Overall, about half of American voters identify with the political party of their parents.[18]

Two crucial differences between party identification and religion may explain why youngsters are socialized into a religion much more surely and strongly than into a political party. The first is that most parents care a great deal more about their religion than about their politics. So they are more deliberate about exposing their children to religion. The second is that religious institutions themselves recognize the value of socialization; they offer Sunday schools and other activities that are high on exposure, communication, and receptivity—reinforcing parental guidance. American political parties, on the other hand, sponsor few activities to win the hearts of little Democrats and young Republicans, which leaves children open to counterinfluences in the school and community.*

School.   According to some researchers, schools have an influence on political learning that is equal to or greater than that of parents.[19] Here, however, we have to distinguish between primary and secondary schools on the one hand and institutions of higher education on the other. Primary schools introduce children to authority figures outside the family—the teacher, the principal, the police officer. This is one way

---

* The Communist party of the Soviet Union, in contrast, actively promotes the party image through the Young Pioneers, a group resembling a combined Boy Scout and Girl Scout organization.

these schools prepare children to accept the social order. They also teach the nation's slogans and symbols—the Pledge of Allegiance, the national anthem, national heroes and holidays. And they stress the norms of group behavior and democratic decision making (respecting the opinions of others, voting for class officers). In the process, they are teaching youngsters about the value of political equality.

Children do not always understand the meaning of the patriotic rituals and behaviors they learn in primary school (see Feature 5.1). In fact, much of this early learning—in the United States and elsewhere—is more indoctrination than education. By the end of the eighth grade, however, children begin to distinguish between government leaders and institutions. They become more aware of collective institutions, of Congress and elections, than they were earlier, when they tended to focus on the president and other single figures of government authority (see Figure 5.4).[20] In sum, most children emerge from elementary school with a sense of nationalism and an idealized notion of American government.[21]

Secondary schools continue to build "good citizens." Field trips to the state legislature or the city council impress students with the majesty and power of government institutions. Secondary schools also offer more explicit political content in their curricula, including courses in recent U.S. history, civics, and American government. Better teachers challenge students to think critically about American government and politics; others concentrate on teaching civic responsibilities. The end product is

FEATURE 5.1

The Goodyear Blimp over Washington

Elementary schools provide the first contact with American government for many children. Sometimes, youngsters fail to get the message right away. How many of you pledged allegiance to an "invisible" rather than an "indivisible" nation? In the excerpt below, playwright Arthur Miller relates his own misunderstanding of the Pledge of Allegiance.

ROXBURY, Conn. I no longer remember how many years it took for me to realize I was making a mistake in the Pledge of Allegiance. With high passion, I stood beside my seat in my Harlem grammar school and repeated the Pledge to the Flag, which always drooped next to the teacher's desk. My feelings were doubtless warmed by my having two uncles who had been in the Great War, one in the Navy, the other as a mule driver in the Army who brought ammunition up to the front in France.

Dirigibles were much in the news in the early 20's, and the Navy, as far as I was able to make out, owned them. Thus, the patriotic con-

nection, which was helped along by the fact that nobody I had ever heard speaking English had ever used the word Indivisible. Or Divisible either, for that matter.

None of which inhibited me from rapping out the Pledge each and every morning: ". . . One Nation in a Dirigible, with Liberty and Justice for All." I could actually see in my mind's eye hordes of faces looking down at Earth through the windows of the Navy's airships. The whole United States was up there, all for one and one for all—and the whole gang in that Dirigible. One day, maybe I could get to ride in it, too, for I was deeply patriotic, and the height of Americanism, as I then understood it, was to ride in a Dirigible.

Source: Arthur Miller, "School Prayer: A Political Dirigible," *New York Times*, 12 March 1984. Copyright © 1984 by The New York Times Company. Reprinted by permission.

Children's Images of Government
This graph shows how the political understanding of primary school students moves from people to institutions. Students in different grades were given a series of pictures and were asked to pick the two that best depicted our government. In the second and third grades, most chose pictures of Presidents Washington and Kennedy. By the eighth grade, Congress and voting were selected much more frequently than the presidents. (Source: David Easton and Jack Dennis, Children in the Political System *[Chicago: University of Chicago Press, 1969]. Copyright © 1969. Reprinted with permission of David Easton and Jack Dennis, and the University of Chicago Press.)*
Figure 5.4

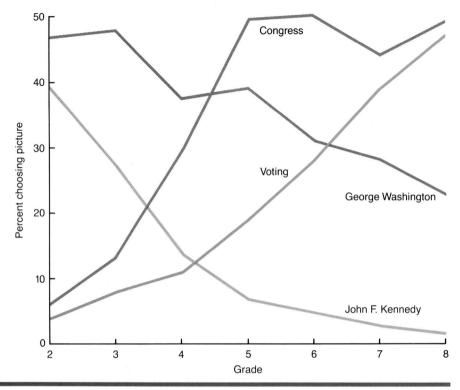

a greater awareness of the political process and the people involved in that process (see Figure 5.5).

Despite teachers' efforts to build children's trust in the political process, outside events can erode that trust when children grow up. Surveys of adults showed substantial drops in trust in the national government during the Watergate affair (1972–1974) and when American embassy personnel were held hostage in Iran in 1980. But recent survey data show that Americans trust their government as much as or more than do citizens of some other Western nations. Moreover, the same study revealed that Americans' pride in their country was considerably greater than that of the other respondents.[22]

Political learning at the college level can be very like that in high school or very different. The degree of difference is apt to increase if professors (or the texts they use) encourage their students to question authority. Questioning dominant political values does not necessarily mean rejecting them. For example, this text encourages you to recognize that freedom and equality—two idealized values in our culture—often conflict. It also invites you to think of democracy in terms of competing institutional models, one of which challenges the idealized notion of democracy. These alternative perspectives are meant to teach you about American political values, not to subvert those values. College courses that are intended to stimulate critical thinking have the potential to introduce to or develop in some students political ideas that are radically different from those they bring to class. And this is something most high school courses do not do.

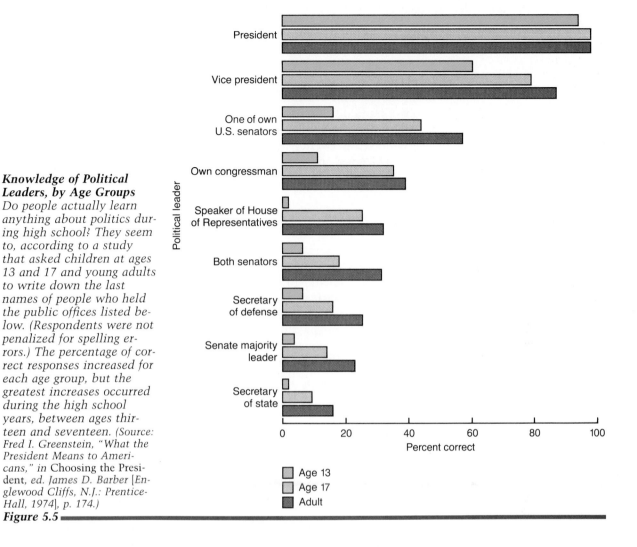

Knowledge of Political Leaders, by Age Groups
Do people actually learn anything about politics during high school? They seem to, according to a study that asked children at ages 13 and 17 and young adults to write down the last names of people who held the public offices listed below. (Respondents were not penalized for spelling errors.) The percentage of correct responses increased for each age group, but the greatest increases occurred during the high school years, between ages thirteen and seventeen. (Source: Fred I. Greenstein, "What the President Means to Americans," in Choosing the President, *ed. James D. Barber [Englewood Cliffs, N.J.: Prentice-Hall, 1974], p. 174.)*
Figure 5.5

Community and peers. Your community and your peers are different but generally overlapping groups. Your *community* is the people of all ages with whom you come in contact because they live or work near you. Your *peers* are friends, classmates, and coworkers. Usually, they are your age and live within your community.

The makeup of the community has a lot to do with how political opinions are formed. *Homogeneous communities*—those with members similar in ethnicity, race, religion, or occupational status—can exert strong pressures on both children and adults to conform to the dominant attitude. For example, if all your neighbors talk up the candidates of one party and criticize the candidates of the other, it makes it difficult to voice or even hold a dissenting opinion.[23] Communities of one ethnic group or religion may also hold negative attitudes about members of other groups. Although community socialization is usually reinforced in the schools, schools sometimes teach ideas (one example is sex education) that run counter to community values.

Peer groups are sometimes used by children and adults as a defense against community pressures. Adolescent peer groups are particularly useful against parental pressures. In adolescence, children rely on their peers to defend their dress and lifestyle, not their politics. At the college level, however, peer group influence on politics can grow substantially, often fed by new learning that clashes with parental beliefs. A classic study of female students at Bennington College found that many became substantially more liberal than their affluent conservative parents. A follow-up study twenty-five years later showed that most retained their liberal attitudes, in part because their spouses and friends (peers) supported their views.[24]

Continuing Socialization

Political socialization continues throughout life. As parental and school influences wane, peer groups (neighbors, coworkers, club members) assume a greater importance in promoting political awareness and in developing political opinions. Because adults usually learn about political events from the mass media—newspapers, magazines, television, and radio—the media themselves emerge as socialization agents. The role of television is especially important: A majority of adults rely on television for most of their information about politics.[25] (The mass media are so important in the political socialization of both children and adults that we devote a whole chapter—Chapter 6—to a discussion of their political role.)

Regardless of how people learn about politics, as they grow older, they gain perspective on government. They are apt to measure new candidates (and new ideas) against the old ones they remember. Their values also change, reflecting their own self-interest. As voters age, for example, they begin to see more merit in government spending for social security than they did when they were younger. Finally, political learning comes simply through exposure and familiarity. One example is the simple act of voting, which people do with increasing regularity as they grow older.

SOCIAL GROUPS AND POLITICAL VALUES

No two people are influenced by precisely the same socialization agents in precisely the same way. Each individual experiences a unique process of political socialization and forms a unique set of political values. Still, people with similar backgrounds do share learning experiences; this means they tend to develop similar political opinions. In this section, we examine the ties between people's social backgrounds and their political values. In the process, we look at two questions that appeared in a survey taken in 1987:[26]

1. Would you allow an admitted communist to teach in a college?
2. Do you think that the government should reduce income differences between rich and poor?

To Have and Have Not
Everyone feels uneasy at the sight of poverty in the presence of wealth. The question is, what should be done about poverty? Should the government step in to reduce income differences between the rich and the poor, perhaps by taxing the wealthy at higher rates and supplementing the income of the poor? Or should the government take no more from the wealthy than it does from the middle class, or even from the lower class?

Other questions might not produce identical results but would probably show the same general tendencies.

We introduced the first question, about allowing a communist to teach, in Figure 5.2. This question is politically relevant because of the original dilemma of government, the conflict between freedom and order. Those who answered "no" to the question were willing to deny freedom of speech to a teacher who threatens the existing economic and political order. They apparently valued order over individual freedom. The second question, about the government reducing income differences, deals with the modern dilemma of government, the conflict between freedom and equality. Those who answered "yes" think that government should promote economic equality, even if that means taxing the rich more heavily (reducing their freedom to use their money as they want). These respondents apparently valued equality over freedom.

Overall, the responses to each of these questions were divided approximately equally. For the entire national sample, slightly more than half the respondents (52 percent) were in favor of firing a communist teacher. And almost half (46 percent) of all respondents thought the government should reduce income differences. However, sharp differences in attitudes on both issues emerged when respondents were grouped by socioeconomic factors—education, income, region, origin, race, and religion. These differences are shown in Figure 5.6 as positive and negative deviations in percentage points from the national averages on the two questions. (To learn what the national average is on income distribution in other countries, see Compared With What? 5.1) Bars that extend to the right identify groups that are more likely than most Amer-

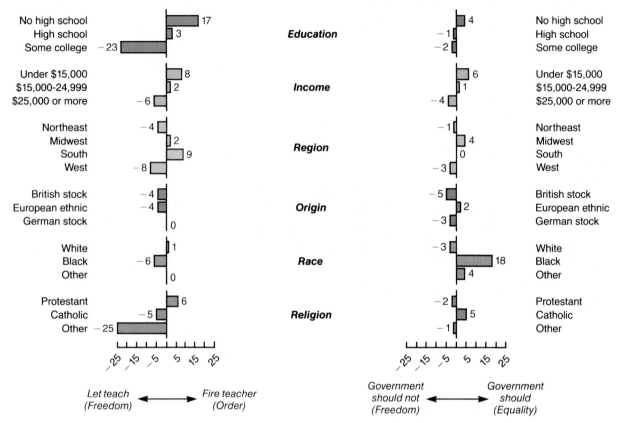

a. I should like to ask you some questions about a man who admits he is a communist. Suppose he is teaching in a college? Should he be fired or not?

b. Should the government in Washington reduce income differences between the rich and the poor, perhaps by raising taxes of wealthy families or by giving income assistance to the poor?

Let teach ⟷ Fire teacher
(Freedom)   (Order)

Government ⟷ Government
should not   should
(Freedom)   (Equality)

Group Deviations from National Opinion on Two Questions
Two questions—one on the dilemma of freedom versus order and the other on the dilemma of freedom versus equality—were asked of a national sample in 1987. Public opinion for the nation as a whole was equally divided on each question. The two graphs above show how respondents in several social groups deviated from overall public opinion. The longer the bars next to each group, the more its respondents deviated from the 50-50 split of public opinion. Bars that extend to the left show opinions that deviate toward *freedom. Bars that extend to the right show deviations* away from *freedom, toward order (part a) or equality (part b). (Source: National Opinion Research Center, 1987 General Survey.)*

Figure 5.6

icans to sacrifice freedom for a given value of government, either equality or order. Below we examine these opinion patterns more closely for each socioeconomic group.

Education

Education increases citizens' awareness and understanding of political issues. Higher education also underscores the value of free speech in a democratic society, increasing our tolerance for those who dissent.

COMPARED WITH WHAT? 5.1

Opinions on Income Redistribution

Compared with citizens in other Western nations, Americans are much less likely to support government programs that redistribute wealth. Respondents interviewed in 1985 in six nations were asked whether they agreed or disagreed with the statement "It is the responsibility of the government to reduce the difference in income between people with high incomes and those with low incomes." In every country but the United States, more respondents agreed than disagreed with the statement.

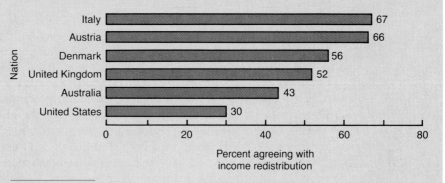

Percent agreeing with
income redistribution

Source: International Social Survey Program, *1985 Role of Government Survey Codebook* (ZA 1490) (Federal Republic of Germany: *Zentralarchive, Köln University*), pp. 45–46.

This result is clearly shown in Figure 5.6a, where those with more education are more willing to let an admitted communist teach. (That is, respondents with no high school education would tend to fire the teacher, while those with some college education would oppose dismissal.) When confronted with issues that involve a choice between personal freedom and social order, college-educated respondents tend to choose freedom.

With regard to the role of government in reducing income inequality, Figure 5.6b shows that more education produces opinions that favor freedom, this time over equality. The higher their level of education, the less respondents supported the redistribution of income. You may think that better-educated people should be humanitarian, that they should support government programs to help the poor. However, educated people tend to be wealthier people, who would be more heavily taxed to help the poor. Thus in this case at least, the effect of education on public opinion is overridden by the effect of income.

Income

In many countries, differences in social class—based on social background and occupational status—divide people in their politics.[27] In the United States, we have avoided the uglier aspects of class conflict, but here wealth sometimes substitutes for class. As shown in Figure 5.6, wealth is consistently related to opinions that limit the government's role in promoting order and equality. Those with higher incomes are more likely to allow a communist to teach and more likely to oppose the redistribution of income. We find that wealth and education, then, have a similar impact on opinion here: In both cases, the groups with more education and higher income opt for freedom. But education has the stronger effect on opinions about order, and income has the stronger effect on opinions about equality.[28]

Region

Early in our country's history, regional differences were politically important—important enough to spark a civil war between the North and South. For nearly a hundred years after the Civil War, regional differences continued to affect politics. The moneyed Northeast was thought to control the purse strings of capitalism. The Midwest was long regarded as the stronghold of "isolationism" in foreign affairs. The South was virtually a one-party region, almost completely Democratic. And the rustic West pioneered its own mixture of progressive politics.

In the past, cultural differences among regions were fed by differences in wealth. In recent decades, however, the movement of people and wealth away from the Northeast and Midwest to the Sunbelt states in the South and Southwest has equalized the per capita income of the regions (see Figure 5.7). One product of this equalization is that the "Solid South" is no longer solid for the Democratic party. In fact, the South led the nation in voting for Richard Nixon, the Republican candidate for president, in 1972, and was again strong for Ronald Reagan in 1984.

There are differences in public opinion among the four major regions of the United States, but not much. Figure 5.6 shows that people in the West are somewhat more likely to oppose government efforts to equalize income than are people in the Midwest. Regional differences are greater on the question of social order, particularly between the West, where respondents are more likely to support freedom of speech, and the South, where they are more likely to stop a communist from teaching. Despite these differences, regional effects on public opinion toward these issues are weaker than the effects of most other socioeconomic factors.

The "Old" Ethnicity: European Origin

At the turn of the century, the major ethnic groups in America were immigrants from Ireland, Italy, Germany, Poland, and other European countries, who came to the United States in waves during the late 1800s and early 1900s. These immigrants entered a nation that had been founded by British settlers over a hundred years earlier. They found themselves in a strange land, usually without money and unable to speak the language. Moreover, their religious backgrounds—mainly Catholic and Jewish—differed from the predominant Protestantism of the earlier settlers. Local politicians saw these newcomers, who were concentrated in urban areas in the Northeast and Midwest, as a new source of votes and soon mobilized them into politics. Holding jobs of lower status, these urban ethnics became part of the great coalition of Democratic

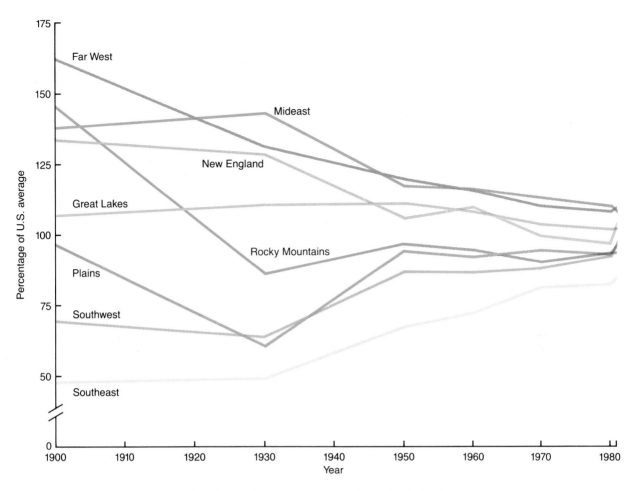

Per Capita Income Across Regions, 1900–1981
*At the beginning of the century, vast differences in wealth could be found
among the nation's regions. The wealthiest people were located in the Northeast and on the West Coast; the poorest were in the Southeast. Over time,
regional differences in income have narrowed dramatically. The graph below
shows per capita income as a percentage of the national average for eight
different regions from 1900 to 1981. As per capita incomes have converged,
the regions have lost a basis for political differences. (Source: Public Opinion 6.
February–March 1983:22. Reprinted with permission of American Enterprise Institute.)*

Figure 5.7

voters that President Franklin Roosevelt forged in the 1930s. And for
years after, studies of public opinion and voting behavior found consistent differences between their political preferences and those of the
native Anglo-Saxons.[29]

More recent studies of public opinion show these differences are
disappearing. Figure 5.6 analyzes public opinion for three groups of white
ethnics, who accounted for about half of the sample interviewed. Respondents who claimed English, Scottish, or Welsh ancestry ("British
stock") and German, Austrian, or Swiss ancestry ("German stock") each
comprise about 15 percent of the sample. "European ethnics" (primarily
Catholics and Jews from Ireland, Italy, and Eastern Europe) comprise

Greek Blarney
Michael Dukakis, the son of Greek immigrants, courts the Irish vote in Boston. Many young people today do not realize that early Irish immigrants stood at the bottom of the social ladder in American cities. Usually manual laborers, they often worked at the dirtiest and most dangerous jobs, and often lived in ghettos. Like so many other European ethnic groups, the Irish used their voting strength to win political power. Dukakis is happy to be Irish on St. Patrick's Day.

about 20 percent. The differences in opinions among these groups are not large. However, Americans of British stock—mostly "WASPs" (White Anglo-Saxon Protestants)—are more opposed to government action to equalize incomes than are European ethnics, but both groups are more likely to allow a communist to teach in college than are Americans in general. European ethnics have been assimilated into America's melting pot; they are no longer very different from other white Americans in language, education, or occupation.[30] But if this **"old" ethnicity**—European origin—is disappearing, a **"new" ethnicity**—race—is taking its place.

The "New" Ethnicity: Race

For many years after the Civil War, the issue of race in American politics was defined as "how the South should treat the Negro." The debate between North and South over this issue became a conflict of civil rights and states' rights—a conflict in which blacks were primarily objects, not participants. But with the rise of black consciousness and the grassroots civil rights demonstrations led by Dr. Martin Luther King and others in the late 1950s and 1960s, blacks emerged as a political force. Through a series of civil rights laws backed by President Johnson and northern Democrats in Congress, blacks secured genuine voting rights in the South and exercised those rights more vigorously in the North. Although they made up only about 12 percent of the total population, blacks comprised sizable voting blocs in southern states and in urban areas in northern states. Like the European ethnics before them, American blacks were being courted for their votes; suddenly their opinions were politically important.

Black Amigo
In his 1984 presidential campaign, the Reverend Jesse Jackson sought to build a "rainbow coalition" consisting of whites, blacks, Asians, and Hispanics. Although he broadened his campaign impressively in 1988, Jackson again actively sought support within communities of minority members. Here he appeals to a Hispanic community.

Blacks presently constitute the largest racial minority in American politics but not the only significant one. Another 5 percent of the population are Asians, American Indians (native Americans), and other non-whites. People of Spanish origin—Hispanics—are also commonly but inaccurately regarded as a racial group. According to the 1980 census, Hispanics make up about 6 percent of the nation's population; but they comprise up to 19 percent of the population in California, 21 percent in Texas, and 37 percent in New Mexico.[31] Although they are politically strong in some communities, Hispanics have lagged behind blacks in mobilizing across the nation. But they too are being wooed by white candidates and are beginning to run more of their own candidates.

Blacks and members of other racial minorities display similar political attitudes. The reasons are twofold.[32] First, racial minorities (perhaps excepting second-generation Asians) tend to have low **socioeconomic status** (a combination of education, occupational status, and income). Second, all have been targets of racial prejudice and discrimination. Figure 5.6b clearly shows the effects of race on the freedom-equality issue. Blacks and other minority members (mostly Hispanics) strongly favor government action to equalize incomes, choosing equality over freedom. Blacks also choose freedom over order when the issue is firing a communist teacher.

Religion

Since the last major wave of European immigration in the 1930s and 1940s, the religious makeup of the United States has remained fairly stable. Fully 65 percent of those surveyed in 1987 were Protestant, about

25 percent identified themselves as Catholic, less than 2 percent were
Jewish, 2 percent claimed other religions, and 7 percent chose "none."[33]
For many years, analysts had found strong and consistent differences in
the opinions of Protestants, Catholics, and Jews. Protestants were more
conservative than Catholics, and Catholics tended to be more conservative than Jews.

Some differences remained in 1987, especially on the government's
role in the question of freedom versus order (the communist teacher).
Protestants, who constitute the religious majority in America, tend toward order; Catholics tend toward freedom; and the other religious
groupings strongly favor freedom.

FROM VALUES TO IDEOLOGY

So far we have studied differences in groups' opinions on two survey
questions. Although responses to these questions reflect value choices
between freedom and order and between freedom and equality, we have
not yet interpreted group opinions in the context of *political ideology*
(the set of values and beliefs people hold about the purpose and scope of
government). Political scientists generally agree that ideology enters into
public opinion on specific issues; there is much less consensus on the
extent to which people think in ideological terms.[34] They also agree that
the public's ideological thinking cannot be categorized adequately in
conventional liberal-conservative terms.

The Degree of Ideological Thinking in
Public Opinion

In an early but important study, respondents were asked about the
parties and candidates in the 1956 election.[35] Only about 12 percent of
the sample volunteered responses that contained ideological terms (such
as *liberal, conservative,* and *capitalism).* Most of the respondents (42
percent) evaluated the parties and candidates in terms of "benefits to
groups" (farmers, workers, or businesspeople, for example). Others (24
percent) spoke more generally about "the nature of the times" (for example, inflation, unemployment, and the threat of war). Finally, a good
portion of the sample (22 percent) displayed no classifiable issue content
in their responses. Other studies have found that the vast majority of
the electorate are confused by ideological terms. Consider this response
from a resident of the San Francisco Bay Area in 1972 to the question
"What do the terms *liberal* and *conservative* mean to you?"

> Oh conservative. Liberal and conservative. Liberal and conservative. I hav-
> en't given it much thought. I wouldn't know. I don't know what those would
> mean! Liberal . . . liberal . . . liberal. And conservative. Well, if a person is
> liberal with their money they squander their money? Does it fall in that
> same category? If you're conservative you don't squander so much, you save
> a little, huh?[36]

Subsequent research has shown somewhat greater ideological awareness within the electorate.[37] The proportion of ideologues—those cred-

ited with using ideological terms in their responses—jumped to 27 percent during the 1964 presidential contest between Lyndon Johnson, a Democrat and ardent liberal, and Barry Goldwater, a Republican and arch conservative. Later studies found that the proportion of ideologues in samples of voters remained above 20 percent in subsequent presidential elections.[38] The tendency to respond to questions by using ideological terms is strongly related to education, which helps people understand political issues and relate them to one another. Personal experiences in the socialization process can also lead people to think ideologically. For example, children raised in strong union households may be taught to distrust private enterprise and to value collective action through the government.

True ideologues hold a consistent set of values and beliefs about the purpose and scope of government, and they tend to evaluate candidates in ideological terms.[39] There are people who respond to questions in ways that *seem* ideological but aren't, because the people do not understand the underlying principles. For example, most respondents dutifully comply when they are asked to place themselves somewhere on a liberal-conservative continuum. The result, as shown in Figure 5.2, is an approximately normal distribution centering on "moderate," the modal category. But many people settle on "moderate" when they do not clearly understand the alternatives because it's a safe choice. In fact, "moderate" was chosen by 41 percent of those without a college education but by only 26 percent of those with a college education. An earlier study in 1984 gave respondents another choice: the statement "I haven't thought much about it"—which allowed them to avoid placing themselves on the liberal-conservative continuum. In this study, 26 percent of the respondents admitted that they had not thought much about liberalism or conservatism.[40] The extent of ideological thinking in America, then, is considerably less than it might seem from responses to questions that ask people to describe themselves as liberals or conservatives.

The Quality of Ideological Thinking in Public Opinion

It is also not clear what people's ideological self-placement means in the 1980s. Originally, the liberal-conservative continuum represented a single dimension: attitudes toward the scope of government activity. Liberals were in favor of more government action to provide public goods, and conservatives were in favor of less. This simple distinction is not as useful today. Many people who call themselves "liberals" no longer favor government activism in general, and many self-styled "conservatives" no longer oppose it in principle.

In Chapter 1, we proposed an alternative ideological classification based on the relationships among the values of freedom, order, and equality. We described liberals as people who believe that government should promote equality, even if some freedom is lost in the process, but who oppose surrendering freedom to government-imposed order. Conservatives do not oppose equality in and of itself, but put a higher value on freedom than equality when the two conflict. Yet conservatives are not above restricting freedom when threatened with the loss of order. So both groups value freedom, but one is more willing to trade freedom for equality, and the other is more inclined to trade freedom for order.

If you have trouble thinking about these tradeoffs on a single dimension, you are perfectly normal. The liberal-conservative continuum presented to survey respondents takes a two-dimensional concept and squeezes it into a one-dimensional format.[41] As a result, many people have difficulty deciding whether they are liberal or conservative, and others confidently choose the same point on the continuum for entirely different reasons. People describe themselves as *liberal* or *conservative* because of the symbolic value of the terms as much as for what they know about ideology.[42]

Studies of the public's ideological thinking find that two themes run through people's minds when they are asked to describe liberals and conservatives. One associates liberals with change and conservatives with traditional values. This theme corresponds to the distinction between liberals and conservatives on the exercise of freedom and the maintenance of order.[43]

The other theme has to do with equality. The conflict between freedom and equality was at the heart of President Roosevelt's New Deal economic policies (social security, minimum wage legislation, farm price supports) in the 1930s. These policies expanded the interventionist role of the national government. And government intervention in the economy served to distinguish liberals from conservatives for decades afterward.[44] Attitudes toward government interventionism still underlie contemporary opinions of domestic economic policies.[45] Liberals support intervention to promote their ideas of economic equality; conservatives favor less government intervention and more individual freedom in economic activities.

Ideological Types in the United States

Our ideological typology in Chapter 1 incorporates these two themes (see Figure 1.2). It classifies people as *liberals* if they favor freedom over order and equality over freedom. *Conservatives* favor the reverse set of values. *Libertarians* favor freedom over both equality and order—the opposite of *populists.* We can classify respondents according to their ideological *tendencies,* cross-tabulating their answers to the two questions about order and equality. As shown in Figure 5.8, people's responses to the questions about firing a communist teacher and redistributing income show virtually no correlation, which clearly indicates that people do not decide about government activity according to a one-dimensional ideological standard.* Figure 5.8 can also be used to classify the sample according to the two dimensions in our ideological typology. There is substantial room for error in using only two issues to classify people in an ideological framework. Still, if the typology is worthwhile, the results should be meaningful, and they are.

The respondents in the 1987 sample depicted in Figure 5.6 divide almost evenly in their ideological tendencies among the four categories

---

* For the statistically minded, the Pearson product-moment correlation for the fourfold table is minus .01.

of the typology. Those who responded with conservative and libertarian tendencies to both questions were only slightly more prevalent than those who gave populist and liberal responses.[46] Although liberals are the smallest group, they still account for almost one-quarter of the public. These results are similar to findings for earlier years by other researchers who conducted more exhaustive analyses involving more survey questions. Using the same basic typology, these scholars classified substantial portions of their respondents in each ideological category in 1980.[47]

Respondents who readily locate themselves on a single dimension running from liberal to conservative later often contradict their self-placement when answering questions that trade off freedom for either order or equality.[48] Obviously, most Americans' opinions do not fit a one-dimensional liberal-conservative continuum. A two-dimensional typology—like the one in Figure 5.8—allows us to analyze responses more meaningfully.[49] Most Americans do not express opinions that are consistently liberal or conservative. In fact, most Americans hold combinations of opinions about the scope of government action that are either conservative or libertarian. However, there are important differences in ideological tendencies among socioeconomic groups.

Populists are prominent among minorities and others with little education and low income, groups that tend to look favorably on the benefits of government in general. *Libertarians* are concentrated among

---

Figure 5.8

Respondents Classified by Ideological Tendencies
Choices between freedom and order and between freedom and equality were represented by two survey questions that asked respondents whether a communist should teach in college and whether the government should equalize income differences. People's responses to the questions showed no correlation, demonstrating that these value choices cannot be explained by a simple liberal-conservative continuum. Instead, their responses conform to four different ideological types.

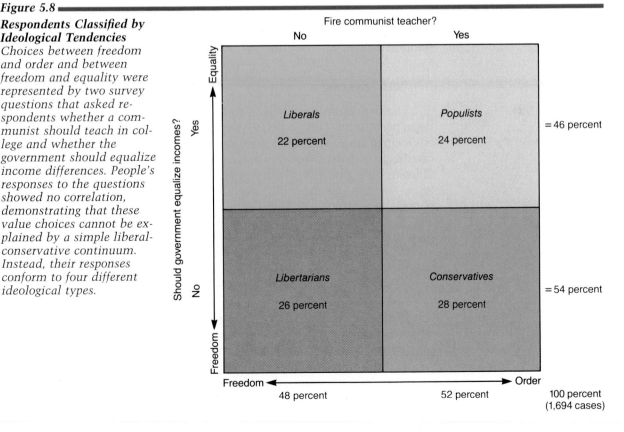

Fire communist teacher?

	No	Yes
Equality / Yes	Liberals 22 percent	Populists 24 percent	= 46 percent
Freedom / No	Libertarians 26 percent	Conservatives 28 percent	= 54 percent

Should government equalize incomes?

Freedom ← 48 percent | 52 percent → Order

100 percent (1,694 cases)

respondents with more education, with higher income, from British stock, who live in the West. These groups tend to be suspicious of government interference in their lives. *Conservatives* are found mainly in the South, and *liberals* are concentrated in the Northeast.

This more refined analysis of political ideology explains why even some Americans who pay close attention to politics find it difficult to locate themselves on the liberal-conservative continuum. Their problem is that they are liberal on some issues and conservative on others. Forced to choose along just one dimension, they choose the middle category, "moderate." However, our analysis also indicates that many respondents who classify themselves as liberals and conservatives do conform to our typology. There is value, then, in the liberal-conservative distinction, as long as we understand its limitations.

THE PROCESS OF FORMING POLITICAL OPINIONS

So far we have learned that people acquire their values through the socialization process and that different social groups develop different sets of political values. We also have learned that some people, but only a minority, think about politics ideologically, holding a consistent set of political attitudes and beliefs. However, we have not really discussed how people form opinions on any particular issue. In particular, how do those who are not ideologues—in other words, most citizens—form political opinions? We consider four factors—self-interest, political information, political leadership, and opinion schemas—that play a part in the process.

Self-Interest

The **self-interest principle** states that people choose what benefits them personally. This principle plays an obvious role in the way opinions are formed on government economic policies. Taxpayers tend to prefer low taxes to high taxes; farmers tend to favor candidates who promise them more support than those who promise them less. The self-interest principle also operates, but less clearly, for some government policies outside of economics. Members of minority groups tend to see more personal advantage in government policies that promote social equality than do members of majority groups; teenage males are more likely to oppose compulsory military service than are older people of either sex. Group leaders often "cue" group members, telling them what they should be for or against.[50]

For many government policies, however, the self-interest principle plays little or no role, because the policies directly affect relatively few citizens. Outlawing prostitution is one example; legalized abortion is another. When such moral issues are involved in government policy, people form opinions based on their underlying values.

When moral issues are not in question and when they do not benefit directly from a policy, many people have trouble relating to the policy and forming an opinion. This tends to be true of the whole subject of foreign policy, which few people interpret in terms of personal benefits. Here, many people have no opinion, or their opinions are not firmly held and are apt to change quite easily, given almost any new information.

Political Information

In the United States today, education is compulsory (usually to age sixteen) and the literacy rate is relatively high. The country boasts an unparalleled network of colleges and universities entered by one-third of all high school graduates. American citizens can obtain information from a variety of daily and weekly news publications. They can keep abreast of national and international affairs through nightly television news, which brings live coverage of world events via satellite from virtually anywhere in the world. Yet the average American displays an astonishing lack of political knowledge.

In a 1978 survey, for example, only about half the electorate knew that states are represented by two senators; only 30 percent knew that the term for a U.S. representative is two years; and less than one-quarter knew which two nations (the United States and the Soviet Union) were involved in the Strategic Arms Limitation Treaty (SALT) at the time it was being negotiated.[51] Citizens' knowledge of politics just after an election is no more impressive. After the 1986 election, for example, only 22 percent of a national sample could correctly identify even one of their candidates for the House of Representatives, and only 38 percent correctly named either of their candidates for the Senate.[52]

But Americans do not let political ignorance stop them from expressing their opinions. They readily offer opinions on issues ranging from capital punishment to nuclear power to the government's handling of the economy. One consequence of opinions based on little information is that they can change easily when new information becomes available. The result is a high degree of instability in public opinion poll results, depending on the way questions are worded and current events that bear on the issue.

Researchers use the term **political sophistication** to refer to the extent and shape of a person's knowledge about public affairs.[53] One study of political sophistication counted the number of specific political issues, actors, and events that 143 respondents brought up in hour-long interviews on political alienation. The average number of political references was 27. The highest number was 94, and the lowest was one—just a single reference to a political object in an hour-long interview on politics! What did people talk about during all that time? The researcher said that they talked about themselves: "Asked whether they are satisfied about the way things have been going in this country, they responded only about their job, family, friends, and other aspects of their own life."[54]

The same author classified the American public into three broad groups of political sophistication. The least sophisticated (about 20 percent of the electorate) pay little attention to public affairs and seldom participate in politics. Most adults (about 75 percent) are only moderately sophisticated. "They half-attentively monitor the flow of political news, but they run for the most part on a psychological automatic pilot." Only a small portion of the electorate (about 5 percent) is politically sophisticated, sharing the knowledge and conceptualization of professional politicians, journalists, and political analysts. As expected, education is strongly related to political sophistication, but so is participation in groups and parents' interest in politics. The author likens the development of political sophistication to a "spiral process . . . a gradual process in which interest breeds knowledge, which, in turn, breeds further interest and knowledge over time."[55] Political events and the actions of political leaders can contribute to that spiraling process.

We should note one correlation that researchers have not found. There is not any meaningful relationship between political sophistication and self-placement on the liberal-conservative scale. That is, people with equal knowledge about public affairs and with similar levels of conceptualization are as likely to think of themselves as liberals as conservatives.[56] Equal levels of political understanding, then, may produce very different political views as a result of individuals' unique patterns of political socialization.

Political Leadership

Public opinion on specific issues is often shaped—and sometimes even created—by political leaders, journalists, and policy experts. Because of their office and the media attention it receives, presidents are uniquely positioned to shape popular attitudes. A good example is public opinion on the Strategic Defense Initiative (SDI), the space-based weapons system often called "Star Wars." On March 23, 1983, President Reagan surprised the nation by announcing plans for a multibillion-dollar program to build a network of space satellites that could shoot down incoming enemy missiles using a new nuclear x-ray laser. SDI proved to be a highly controversial weapons system. The scientific community was deeply divided over whether it would be effective—or could even be built. The diplomatic community was divided over whether it would increase or reduce the chances of a world war. The economic community was divided over whether the nation could afford the vast expenditures SDI would require.

Nevertheless, 67 percent of the American people interviewed in the first month after the president announced the program thought the United States should try to develop the weapons system. Only 25 percent opposed the plan from the beginning, and a scant 8 percent had no opinion.[57] By August 1984, public support had slipped to 54 percent, and those with no opinion had increased to 12 percent. By July 1985, public support had dropped to 43 percent, and the number with no opinion had grown to 22 percent.[58]

Clearly, the initial show of public support for the president's SDI proposal was made without much understanding of its costs and consequences. Over time, other opinion shapers (technical experts and journalists) offered their own analyses of SDI. Taken together, experts and especially television news commentators can affect public opinion even more than popular presidents.[59] As more information became available about the program over the next two years, it not only encountered more opposition, but, ironically, more people had no opinion about it—reflecting the opposing arguments expressed by opinion shapers. Of those who had an opinion, Republican voters favored the space-based system more than did Democratic voters. Many who supported SDI undoubtedly based their opinions on their positive views of President Reagan; and many opposed it because of their negative attitude toward the president. Others formed their opinions according to their faith in technology, their views of the Soviet threat, or other beliefs they held at the time.

Opinion Schemas

We have learned that only a minority of the population, about one person in five, can be classified as ideologues. These people regularly think about politics in ideological terms and come to new political issues with a set of political beliefs and values that helps them form opinions on these issues. But even people who do not approach politics with full-blown ideologies interpret political issues in terms of some pre-existing mental structure.

Psychologists refer to the packet of pre-existing beliefs that people apply to specific issues as an **opinion schema**—a network of organized knowledge and beliefs that guides the processing of information on a particular subject.[60] Figure 5.9 shows an opinion schema about Ronald Reagan that might be held by a conservative. It is only a partial schema, but it suggests the wide range of attitudes and beliefs that affect thinking about political leaders and their policies. Our opinion schemas change as we acquire new information and act (form opinions) on it. A conservative acting on the opinion schema in Figure 5.9 probably would support Reagan's SDI weapon system; that support, in turn, would be incorporated into a revised schema.

The schema concept gives us a sharper tool for analyzing public opinion than the blunter concept of ideology. Opinion schemas can pertain to any political figure and to any subject—race, economics, or farming, for example. One study found an opinion schema that structured attitudes toward specific issues in foreign policy (defense spending, nuclear arms, military involvement, international trade) under three broader values (militarism, anticommunism, isolationism), which in turn were subsumed under two core values (morality of warfare, ethnocentrism).[61] Liberal-conservative self-placement showed little relationship to the same foreign policy attitudes.

Still, the more encompassing concept of ideology is hard to escape. Researchers have found that people tend to organize their personal schemas within a hierarchy of opinion that parallels broader ideological categories. A liberal's opinion schema about Reagan may not differ from a conservative's in the facts it contains, but it differs considerably in its evaluation of those facts.[62] In the liberal's schema, for example, anger might replace the conservative's praise for Reagan's stance against abortion. The main value of schemas for understanding how opinions are formed is that they remind us that opinion questions trigger many different images, connections, and values in the mind of each respondent. Given the complexity of factors in individual opinion schemas, it is surprising that researchers find as many strong correlations as they do among individuals' social backgrounds, general values, and specific opinions.

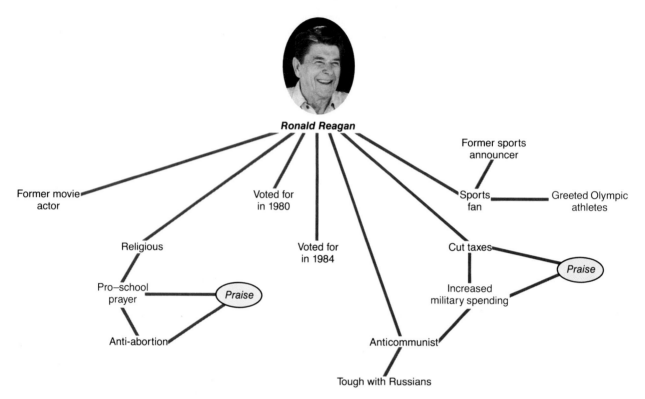

Ronald Reagan

Former movie actor • Voted for in 1980 • Former sports announcer • Sports fan • Greeted Olympic athletes • Religious • Voted for in 1984 • Cut taxes • *Praise* • Pro–school prayer • *Praise* • Increased military spending • Anti-abortion • Anticommunist • Tough with Russians

Hypothetical Opinion Schema About Ronald Reagan
People express opinions on issues, persons, or events according to pre-existing attitudes and beliefs that they associate with the question being asked. Psychologists sometimes refer to this network of attitudes and beliefs, and their relationships as an opinion schema. *Below is a hypothetical opinion schema that might be associated with Ronald Reagan in the mind of a conservative who voted for Reagan in the 1980 and 1984 presidential elections. (Source: From "A Primer of Information-Processing Theory for the Political Scientist," by Reid Hastie, 1986, in Richard R. Lau and David O. Sears, eds.* Political Cognition, *p. 32. Copyright 1986 by Lawrence Erlbaum Associates. Reprinted by permission.)*

Figure 5.9

SUMMARY

Public opinion does not rule in America. On most issues, it merely sets general boundaries for government policy. Americans would not tolerate flogging criminals as a punishment for crime, but most believe death is a legitimate penalty for murder. The shape of the distribution of opinion (normal, skewed, or bimodal) indicates how sharply the public is divided. Bimodal distributions harbor the greatest potential for political conflict. The stability of a distribution over time indicates how settled people are in their opinions. Because most Americans' ideological opinions are normally distributed around the "moderate" category and have been so for decades, government policies can vary from left to right over time without provoking severe political conflict.

People form their values through the process of political socialization. The most important socialization agents in childhood and young adulthood are family, school, community, and peers. Members of the same social group tend to experience similar socialization processes and thus to adopt similar values. People in different social groups, who hold different values, often express vastly different opinions. Differences in education, race, and religion tend to produce sharper divisions of opinion today on questions of order and equality than do differences in income, region, and ethnicity.

Although most people do not think about politics in ideological terms, when asked to do so by pollsters, they readily classify themselves along a liberal-conservative continuum. Many respondents—especially those without a college education—choose the middle category, "moderate," the safe choice. Others classify themselves as liberals or conservatives for vague or contradictory reasons. Our two-dimensional framework for analyzing ideology according to the values of order and equality produces four ideological types: liberals, conservatives, libertarians, and populists. Classified according to our typology, libertarians and populists have trouble placing themselves on a liberal-conservative continuum; our liberals and conservatives do not.

Responses to the survey questions we used to establish our ideological typology divide the American electorate almost equally into four ideological tendencies. A slight plurality reveals conservative tendencies, wanting government to impose order but not equality. An almost equal percentage is inclined toward libertarianism, opposing government action for either order or equality. Populism, which favors more government action to promote both order and equality, is in third place by a small margin. The liberal response pattern, which favors equality but not order, is least common but still sizable at 22 percent.

In addition to ideological orientation, many other factors enter the process of forming political opinions. When individuals stand to benefit or suffer from proposed government policies, they usually base their opinions on self-interest. When citizens lack information on which to base their opinions, they usually respond anyway, which leads to substantial fluctuations in poll results, depending on how questions are worded and intervening events. In the absence of information, respondents are particularly susceptible to cues of support or opposition from political leaders. The various factors that impinge on the process of forming political opinions can be mapped out within an opinion schema, a network of beliefs and attitudes about a particular topic. The schema imagery helps us visualize the complex process of forming opinions. But the process is not completely idiosyncratic: People tend to organize their schemas according to broader ideological thinking.

Which model of democracy, the majoritarian or the pluralist, is correct in its assumptions about public opinion? Sometimes the public shows clear and settled opinions on government policy, conforming to the majoritarian model. However, often public opinion is firmly grounded, not in knowledge, but in ideological bias. Moreover, powerful groups often divide on what they want government to do. This lack of consensus leaves politicians with a great deal of lat-itude in enacting specific policies, a finding that conforms to the pluralist model. Of course, politicians' actions are under close scrutiny by journalists reporting in the mass media. We turn to the impact of this scrutiny and the mass media on politics in Chapter 6.

Key Terms

public opinion	"old" ethnicity
normal distribution	"new" ethnicity
skewed distribution	socioeconomic status
bimodal distribution	self-interest principle
stable distribution	political sophistication
political socialization	opinion schema

Selected Readings

Abramson, Paul R. *Political Attitudes in America: Formation and Change.* San Francisco: W. H. Freeman, 1983. Especially strong on how attitudes are studied and on the stability of attitudes over time.

Asher, Herbert. *Polling and the Public: What Every Citizen Should Know.* Washington, D.C.: Congressional Quarterly Press, 1988. A concise text on polling methodology that gives special attention to election polls.

Maddox, William S., and Stuart A. Lilie. *Beyond Liberal and Conservative: Reassessing the Political Spectrum.* Washington, D.C.: Cato Institute, 1984. Uses an ideological typology similar to the one in this chapter to analyze surveys in presidential elections from 1952 through 1980.

Miller, Warren E.; Arthur H. Miller; and Edward J. Schneider. *American National Election Studies Data Sourcebook, 1952–1978.* Cambridge, Mass.: Harvard University Press, 1980. A rich source of tables and graphs containing data from studies of voters in national elections from 1952 through 1978.

Neuman, W. Russell. *The Paradox of Mass Politics: Knowledge and Opinion in the American Electorate.* Cambridge, Mass.: Harvard University Press, 1986. Analyzes major voting surveys from 1948 to 1980, assessing citizens' political interest, knowledge, and level of conceptualization.

Public Opinion. A bimonthly magazine published by the American Enterprise Institute in Washington, D.C. The best publication on contemporary public opinion in America.

6

The Mass Media

Some say that Gary Hart was a victim of the media. On May 3, 1987, Hart was the leading candidate seeking the 1988 Democratic nomination for president. Five days later, he announced his withdrawal from the race, saying that press harassment over his personal life had made it impossible for him to conduct his campaign. In less than a week, a presidential frontrunner had become a campaign dropout.

Some say that Hart had only himself to blame. Rumors of Hart's infidelities cropped up in 1984, when he challenged Walter Mondale for his party's presidential nomination. Early in 1987, Hart complained that he was again being victimized by rumors about his "womanizing." In March, he told a reporter for the *New York Times*, "If anyone wants to put a tail on me, go ahead. They'd be very bored."[1] Later that same day, however, Hart sailed from Miami for an overnight trip to Bimini Island with a male friend and two attractive young women, one of whom was Donna Rice.

Hart's cruise on the yacht *Monkey Business* escaped media attention until reporters from the *Miami Herald* staked out his home in Washington, D.C., on the first Friday and Saturday evenings in May. On May 3, the late Sunday edition of the *Herald* printed a front-page story, under the headline "Miami woman is linked to Hart." The article said that Hart and Rice were seen entering his house alone late Friday evening and did not emerge until Saturday evening. Ironically, Hart's earlier challenge "to put a tail on me" was published in a separate story in the *New York Times* on the same day.

Hart spent the first days of the following week disputing the *Herald*'s account of the weekend, but the media would not let go. At a press conference in New Hampshire on Wednesday, a reporter asked him point-blank whether he had ever committed adultery. Hart replied, "I don't have to answer that question."[2] After a reporter for the *Washington Post* called campaign officials about a story that linked Hart to another woman in Washington, the candidate scheduled a Friday news conference.

Hart read a statement that blamed the media for destroying his efforts to communicate with voters and raise campaign funds. With references to reporters hiding in bushes, photographers peeking in windows, and helicopters hovering overhead, Hart drew an analogy between the media as hunters and candidates as the hunted. Attacking the unrelenting media coverage of candidates' private lives, he said he understood "why some of the best people in this country choose not to run for high office."[3]

Many journalists also criticized the media's invasion of Hart's private life, particularly the *Miami Herald*'s stakeout of his house. According to Anthony Lewis of the *New York Times*, history shows that "the correlation between Puritan sexual behavior and wise political leadership is zero." He urged the press to think about its role: "Does it want to push political stories to the extreme of sensationalism? Or does it have some limiting sense of respect for the democratic process?"[4]

Other journalists defended the media's actions, including the stakeout. David Broder, syndicated columnist for the *Washington Post*, de-

Hart Examination
Gary Hart was the front-runner for the 1988 Democratic presidential nomination until the Miami Herald *published an account of his relationship with a young model who was not his wife. From then on, the media pressed him on the infidelity issue. It was at this New Hampshire press conference that Hart was asked whether he had ever committed adultery. Realizing the issue would dominate the media's coverage of his campaign, Hart withdrew two days later.*

nied that the issue was adultery. "What was at issue was Hart's truthfulness, his self-discipline, his sense of responsibility to other people—his willingness to face hard choices and realities."[5] In brief, the media justified their investigation of Hart's private life by invoking the need to assess a candidate's character. But because virtually everything a person does or believes can be linked to character, does the "character issue" license the media to investigate all aspects of a politician's life.

Freedom of the press is necessary in a democratic government, but the media cause problems as well as solve them. What is the nature of the mass media in America? Do the media display a liberal or conservative bias in reporting the news? Do they promote or frustrate democratic ideals? Does freedom of the press conflict with the values of order or equality? In this chapter, we describe the origin and growth of the media, assess their objectivity, and examine their impact on politics.

PEOPLE, GOVERNMENT, AND COMMUNICATIONS

"We never *talk* anymore" is a common lament among people who are living together but not getting along very well. In politics, too, citizens and their government need to communicate in order to get along well. **Communication** is the process of transmitting information from one individual or group to another. **Mass communication** is the process by which individuals or groups transmit information to large, heterogeneous, and widely dispersed audiences. The term **mass media** refers to

THE CANDIDATE

the technical devices employed in mass communication. The mass media are commonly divided into two types:

1. **Print media** communicate information through the publication of written words and pictures. Prime examples of print media are daily newspapers and popular magazines. Because books seldom have very large circulations relative to the population, they are not typically classified as a mass medium.

2. **Broadcast media** communicate information electronically through sounds or sights. Prime examples of broadcast media are radio and television. Although the telephone also transmits sounds, it is usually used for more targeted communications and so is not typically included within the mass media.

In the United States, the mass media are in business to make money, which they make mainly by selling advertising through their major function, entertainment. We are more interested in the five specific functions the mass media serve for the political system: *reporting* the news, *interpreting* the news, *influencing* citizens' opinions, *setting the agenda* for government action, and *socializing* citizens about politics.

Our special focus is on the role of the mass media in promoting communication from a government to its citizens *and* from citizens to their government. In totalitarian governments, information flows more freely in one direction (from government to people) than in the other. In democratic governments, information must flow freely in both directions; a democratic government can be responsive to public opinion only if its citizens can make their opinions known. Moreover, the electorate can hold government officials accountable for their actions only if voters know what their government has done, is doing, and plans to do. Because the mass media provide the major channels for this two-way flow of information, they have the dual capability of reflecting and shaping our political views.

Mass media are not the only means of communication between citizens and government. As we discussed in Chapter 5, various agents of socialization (especially schools) function as "linkage mechanisms" that promote such communication. In the next three chapters, we discuss other major mechanisms for communication: voting, political parties, and interest groups. Certain linkage mechanisms communicate better in one direction than in the other. Primary and secondary schools, for example, commonly instruct young citizens about government rules and symbols, whereas voting usually sends messages from citizens to government. Parties and interest groups foster communications in both directions. The mass media, however, are the only linkage mechanisms that *specialize* in communication.

Although this chapter concentrates on political uses of the four most prominent mass media—newspapers, magazines, radio, and television—you should understand that political content can also be transmitted through other mass media, such as recordings and motion pictures. Rock acts like Peter Gabriel and U2 often express political ideas in their music.

And motion pictures often convey particularly intense political messages. In the 1976 film *All the President's Men*, Dustin Hoffman and Robert Redford played Carl Bernstein and Bob Woodward, the two *Washington Post* reporters who doggedly exposed the Watergate scandal in a series of articles that led to President Richard Nixon's 1974 resignation. This motion picture dramatized a seamy side of political life that contrasted sharply with an idealized view of the presidency. In 1985, *Rambo: First Blood, Part Two* starred Sylvester Stallone as a superhero who returns to Vietnam ("This time, to win!") to rescue Americans missing in action. *Rambo* implied that soldiering can be glorious and suggested that military force can be an effective way of solving difficult international problems. In contrast, the 1987 Academy Award for Best Picture went to *Platoon*, which portrayed war as a confusing, terrifying hell.

THE DEVELOPMENT OF THE MASS MEDIA IN THE UNITED STATES

Although the record and film industries sometimes convey political messages, they are primarily entertainment industries. Our focus is on mass media in the news industry—on print and broadcast journalism. The development of the news media in the United States has been shaped by the growth of the country, technological inventions, and political attitudes toward the scope of government—as well as the need to entertain.

Newspapers

When the revolutionary war broke out in 1775, thirty-seven newspapers (all weeklies) were being published in the colonies.[6] Most of them favored the colonists' side against the British, and they played an important part in promoting the Revolution. However, these weekly papers cannot be regarded as instruments of mass communication. Their circulations were small (usually a thousand copies or so), and they were expensive. Type had to be set by hand, the presses printed quite slowly, transportation was costly, and there were few advertisers to defray the costs of publication. Still, politicians of the day quickly saw the value of the press and started papers that expressed their own views. During George Washington's administration, for example, the Federalists published the *Gazette of the U.S.*; the Anti-Federalists published the *National Gazette*.

The first newspapers were therefore political organs, financed by parties and advocating party causes. Newspapers did not move toward independent ownership and large circulations until the 1830s, with the publication of two successful dailies (the *New York Sun* and the *New York Herald*) that sold for just a penny. Various inventions spurred the growth of the news industry. The telegraph (invented in 1837) eventually replaced the use of carrier pigeons for transmitting news and allowed the simultaneous publication of news stories by papers across the country. The rotary press (1847) soon enabled publishers to print much more quickly and cheaply.

According to the 1880 census, 971 daily newspapers and 8,633 weekly newspapers and periodicals were then published in the United States. Most larger cities had a number of newspapers—New York had 29 papers, Philadelphia 24, San Francisco 21, and Chicago 18. Competition for readers grew fierce among the big-city dailies. Toward the latter part of the nineteenth century, imaginative publishers sought to win readers by entertaining them with photographs, comic strips, sports sections, advice to the lovelorn, and stories of sex and crime. The sensational reporting of that period came to be called **yellow journalism**—after the "Yellow Kid," a comic-strip character featured in the *New York World*, published by Joseph Pulitzer (the same man who established the Pulitzer prizes for distinguished journalism).[7] Contests calculated to sell papers were also popular with publishers. Some promotional schemes had lasting political consequences. Pulitzer raised funds to put the Statue of Liberty on its pedestal after Congress turned down a request for $100,000. Each person who donated to the cause had his or her name printed in the *New York World*'s list of donors. And William Randolph Hearst, publisher of the rival *New York Journal*, helped get the nation into a war with Spain. When the U.S. battleship *Maine* blew up mysteriously in Havana harbor on February 15, 1898, Hearst proclaimed it the work of enemy agents, charging his readers to "Remember the Maine!"

By the 1950s, intense competition among big-city dailies had nearly disappeared. New York, which had 29 papers in 1880, had only 3 by 1969. This pattern was repeated in every large city; most were left with 1 to 3 major papers. As a result of the rise of new cities that accompanied the general population growth, however, the number of daily newspapers published (and the papers' combined circulation) has remained about the same for more than thirty years. In 1950, a total of 1,772 daily papers had a circulation of 53.8 million; in 1986, a total of 1,657 papers had a circulation of 62.5 million.[8]

The daily paper with the largest circulation in 1987 (about 2 million copies) is the *Wall Street Journal*, which appeals to a national audience

TRAINING FOR THE FOOTBALL CHAMPIONSHIP GAME IN HOGAN'S ALLEY.

**The Origin of
Yellow Journalism**
The term yellow journalism *means sleazy, sensational reporting. It derives from the "Yellow Kid," a popular cartoon character in the* New York World, *one of the first newspapers to use color for cartoons and comic strips in the late 1800s. The* World *also boosted its circulation by emphasizing entertainment over straight news and by crusading for political causes, some of which were manufactured. Hence, the name.*

because of its extensive coverage of business news and its close analysis of political news. The *New York Times*, which many journalists consider the best newspaper in the country, sells about a million copies, placing it fifth in national circulation. Even in New York, the *Times* sells fewer copies than a sensational tabloid, the *New York Daily News*. Neither the *Times* nor the *Wall Street Journal* carries any comic strips, which no doubt limits their mass appeal. They also print more political news and news analyses than most readers want to confront (see Feature 6.1).

Magazines

Magazines differ from newspapers primarily in the nature of their coverage, the frequency of their publication, and the quality of their production. In contrast to the broad coverage of daily papers, many magazines focus on narrow topics such as sports. Even news-oriented magazines cover the news in a more specialized manner than newspapers. Magazines and newspapers differ not only in content, but also in form. Newspapers are printed on inexpensive paper; they are expected to be discarded within a day or two. The more durable stock of magazines allows them to be read over several days or weeks.

This increased durability means that magazines are often used as forums for opinion, not strictly for news. However, magazines dealing with public affairs have had relatively small circulations and select read-

FEATURE 6.1

Front Pages of Four Major Daily Newspapers

A rose is a rose, but a newspaper is not necessarily a *news*paper. Some papers, like the *Wall Street Journal* and the *New York Times*, pride themselves on providing thorough coverage of the news (the *Times*'s motto is "All the News That's Fit to Print") and in-depth analyses of major national and international events. Neither paper may feature (or even cover) the local fires or street crimes headlined in other papers, which cater to more popular tastes for violence and human interest stories.

Often we can see differences among papers simply by looking at their front pages. Papers that are oriented to popular entertainment have punchy graphics to catch the eye of readers who do not

intend to spend a good part of the day studying the news. Compare the front pages of the *Wall Street Journal* and the *New York Times* with those of *USA Today* and the *New York Daily News*—all published on March 9, 1988, the day after the presidential primaries and caucuses held in twenty states on "Super Tuesday." Although all four papers mentioned the election results on their front pages, their treatment was very different. Both the *Times* and *USA Today* headlined the story, but the *Journal*'s lead was under its "What's News" box. And the *Daily News* chose to run a photo of a 101-year-old woman emerging from the polling booth alongside a screaming headline of a local cop story.

erships, making them questionable as mass media. The earliest public affairs magazines, such as *Nation, McClure's,* and *Harper's,* were published in the mid-1800s. These magazines were often politically influential—especially in framing arguments against slavery and later in publishing exposés of political corruption and business exploitation, by such writers as Lincoln Steffens and Ida Tarbell. These writers, derisively called **muckrakers** (a term derived from a special rake used to collect manure), practiced an early form of investigative reporting that involved detailing basic unsavory facts about government and business. Because their writings were lengthy critiques of the existing political and economic order, muckrakers found a more hospitable outlet in magazines of opinion than in newspapers with large circulations. Yet magazines that have limited readerships can wield political power. They may influence leaders who follow news in specific areas—**attentive policy elites**—

Both the *Journal* and the *Times* are published for the serious news reader and use few gimmicks to draw readers. The *Journal* does not even publish photographs except in advertisements. *USA Today* and the *New York Daily News*, on the other hand, appeal to people who read the paper less to learn about political developments than to keep abreast of popular culture. The *Daily News*, with its huge, provocative headlines and oversized photographs, outsells the *Times* in New York, and the colorful *USA Today* is closing fast on the *Journal* in national sales. Founded only in 1982, *USA Today* uses punchy graphics in a "busy" layout to appeal to readers accustomed to hours of television viewing.

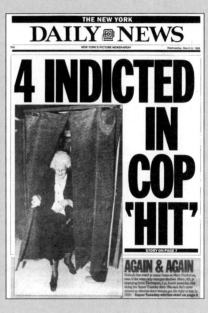

and thus influence mass opinion indirectly through a **two-step flow of communication.** In this process, which conforms ideally to the pluralist model of democracy, magazines inform a few policy elites (for instance, union or industry leaders) about relevant developments or political thought; these leaders in turn inform their more numerous followers, mobilizing them to apply pressure on government.

Three weekly news magazines—*Time* (founded in 1923), *Newsweek* (1933), and *U.S. News & World Report* (1933)—have enjoyed large circulations (2 million to 4 million copies in 1987). The audiences of these magazines are not as large as the 17 million readers of *TV Guide*, the 16 million readers of *Reader's Digest*, or even the 4.6 million readers of *National Enquirer*.[9] Nevertheless, these prominent weekly news magazines not only qualify as mass media, they often substitute for widely read national newspapers.

Radio

Regularly scheduled and continuous radio broadcasting began in 1920 on stations KDKA in Pittsburgh and WWJ in Detroit. Both stations claim to be the first commercial station, and both did broadcast returns of the 1920 election of President Warren G. Harding. However, there were only 5,000 radio receivers in the United States, and those were operated mainly by technical experts. Five years later, there were more than 2.5 million receivers, mostly in American homes. By 1940 more than 860 stations served nearly 30 million American homes.[10] The number of radio stations mushroomed to more than 3,000 in 1950.[11]

The first radio network, the National Broadcasting Company (NBC), was formed in 1926. The Columbia Broadcasting System (CBS) was created in 1927, followed by the American Broadcasting System (ABC) and the Mutual Broadcasting System. By linking thousands of local stations, the four major networks transformed radio into a national medium. Millions of Americans were able to hear President Franklin D. Roosevelt deliver his first "fireside chat" in 1933, soon after his inauguration. However, the first coast-to-coast broadcast did not occur until 1937, when listeners were shocked by an eyewitness report of the explosion of the dirigible *Hindenburg* in New Jersey.

Because the public could sense reporters' personalities over radio in a way they could not in print, broadcast journalists quickly became national celebrities. Edward R. Murrow, one of the most famous radio news personalities, broadcast news of the merger of Germany and Austria by shortwave from Vienna in 1938 and later gave stirring reports of German air raids on London during World War II.

Listening to the President on Radio
Before television, friends often gathered around a radio to hear the president make an important address. In 1941, American soldiers, friends, and visiting relatives gathered in the Army YMCA on Governors Island in New York to hear President Franklin Roosevelt's warning of approaching war. Of course, the message had a special meaning for this group. Still, see how intently they are listening to what the president is saying. Maybe we should consider using radio instead of television for critically important speeches.

Television

Experiments with television began in France in the early 1900s. By 1937 seventeen experimental television stations were operating in the United States. In 1939 President Roosevelt appeared on television at the New York World's Fair. By 1940 twenty-three television stations were operating on a more regular basis, and—repeating the feat of radio twenty years earlier—two stations broadcast the returns of a presidential election, Roosevelt's 1940 re-election.[12]

The onset of World War II paralyzed the development of television technology, but following the war growth in the medium exploded. When peace returned in 1945, only eight television stations were broadcasting. By 1950 ninety-eight stations were covering the major population centers of the country, but only 9 percent of American households had television receivers.

The first commercial color broadcast came in 1951, as did the first coast-to-coast broadcast—President Harry Truman's address to delegates at the Japanese Peace Treaty Conference in San Francisco. The same year, Democratic Senator Estes Kefauver of Tennessee called for public television coverage of his committee's investigation into organized crime. For weeks, people with television sets invited their neighbors to watch underworld crime figures answering questions before the camera. And Kefauver became one of the first politicians to benefit from television coverage. Previously unknown and representing a small state, he nevertheless entered the 1952 Democratic presidential primaries and won many of them. His performance in the primaries led to his nomination as the Democrats' vice presidential candidate in 1956.

Watching the President on Television
Television revolutionized presidential politics by allowing millions of voters to look closely at the candidates' faces and to judge their personalities in the process. This close-up of John Kennedy during a debate with Richard Nixon in the 1960 campaign showed Kennedy to good advantage. Close-ups of Nixon, on the other hand, made him look as though he needed a shave. Because Kennedy won one of the closest elections in history, it's possible that Kennedy's good looks on television made the difference.

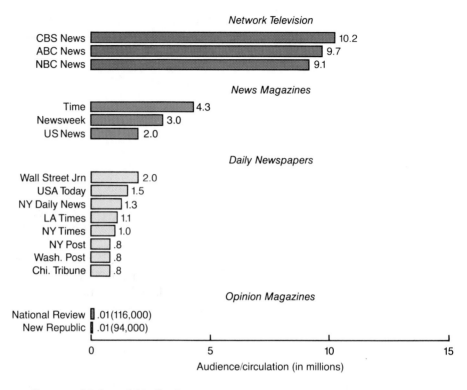

Audiences of Selected Media Sources
Television, newspapers, and magazines differ sharply in their appeal to mass audiences as news sources. The difference shows clearly when we compare the figures for the average number of homes that are tuned nightly to one of the three major network news programs with the figures for the circulation of the three top news magazines, the eight top newspapers, and the two largest opinion magazines. Clearly, television news enters many more homes than does news from the other media. All three news magazines (which are published only weekly) have more readers than any daily newspaper, and opinion magazines reach only a small fraction of the usual television news audiences.
(Sources: Average television news audiences for September 1987 through April 1988 are from Nielsen Media Research; *newspaper and magazine circulations are from* Standard Periodical Directory, *1988.)*

Figure 6.1

The number of television stations increased to over five hundred in 1960, and 87 percent of households had television receivers. By 1988 the United States had more than one thousand commercial and three hundred educational television stations, and virtually every household (98 percent) had receivers. Now, television claims by far the largest audiences of the mass media (see Figure 6.1.) From television's beginning, most stations were linked into networks founded by three of the four major radio networks. (Only the Mutual Broadcasting System did not make the transition into television.) At present, about 70 percent of commercial television stations are affiliated with NBC, CBS, or ABC. Many of the early "anchormen" on network news programs (among them, Walter Cronkite) came to the medium with years of experience as radio broadcast journalists. Now that the news audience could actually see the broadcasters as well as hear them, news personalities became even greater celebrities. When he retired from anchoring the "CBS Evening News" in 1981, Walter Cronkite was one of the most trusted and influential people in America.

Just as the appearance of the newscaster became important for television viewers, so did the appearance of the news itself. Television's great advantage over radio—that it *showed* people and events—both contributed to the impact of television news coverage and to some extent determined the news that television chose to cover. Television was particularly partial to events that had *film value* (visual impact). Organized protests and fires, for examples, "show well" on television, so television tends to cover them. Violent conflict of any kind, especially unfolding dramas that involve weapons, rate especially high in visual impact; such violence and uncertainty accounted for television's all-consuming coverage of the TWA plane hijacking in Beirut in 1985. However, television is not alone among the mass media in focusing on news that appeals to its audience's emotions. The 1890s newspapers that engaged in yellow journalism also played on emotions. In fact, private ownership of the media ensures that news is selected for its audience appeal.

PRIVATE OWNERSHIP OF THE MEDIA

In the United States, private ownership of the media is an accepted, largely unquestioned fact. Indeed, government ownership of the media strikes most Americans as an unwarranted violation of liberty. Such ownership, in fact, can interfere with the "marketplace of ideas" and result in one-way communication, from government to citizens. When the government controls the news flow, the people have little chance to learn what the government is doing or to pressure it to behave differently. In the Soviet Union, for example, the major newspaper, *Pravda* (which means "truth"), is operated by the Communist party. A second daily paper, *Isvestia* (which means "news"), is operated by the government itself. Before Mikhail Gorbachev's policy of *glasnost*, or "openness," the Russians joked about their papers: "In *Truth* there is no news, and in *News* there is no truth." Recently, however, the authorities have allowed more news coverage, particularly of local crimes, but even of the war in Afghanistan.[13]

The Consequences of Private Ownership

The print media (both newspapers and magazines) are privately owned in the Western democratic countries, but the broadcast media usually are not. In most countries, both radio and television are run by the government, often as monopolies. However, except for "public television" (and "public radio," which is less well-known), the electronic media are privately owned in the United States. Private ownership of both print and broadcast media gives the news industry in America more political freedom than any other in the world, but it also makes the

**This Is Your
Captain Speaking**
*The pilot of the TWA plane
hijacked in 1985 speaks
with television reporters on
the runway of Beirut's airport. One of the hijackers is
holding a pistol to his head.
ABC television news broadcast this brief interview,
which helped to dramatize
international terrorism. In
the end, the hijackers got
what they wanted: the re-
lease of hundreds of Shi'ite
prisoners held by Israel.*

media more dependent on advertising revenues to cover their costs and
make a profit. Because advertising rates are tied to the size of the audience, the news operations of mass media in America must appeal to the
audiences they serve.

You might think that a story's political significance, educational
value, or broad social importance determines whether it is covered in
the media. The sad truth is that most potential news stories are not
judged by such grand criteria. The primary criterion of a story's **newsworthiness** is usually its audience appeal, as judged by its *high impact*
on readers or listeners; its *sensationalist* aspect (as exemplified by violence, conflict, disaster, or scandal); its treatment of *familiar* people or
life situations; its *close-to-home* character; and its *timeliness*.[14]

Reliance on audience appeal has led the news industry to calculate
its audience very carefully. The print media can easily determine the
size of their circulations through sales figures, but the broadcast media
must estimate their audiences through various sampling techniques.
Because both print and broadcast media might be tempted to inflate their
estimated audiences (to tell advertisers that they reach more people than
they actually do), a separate industry has developed to rate audience size
impartially. The rating reports have resulted in a "ratings game," in
which the media try to increase ratings by adjusting the delivery or
content of their news. Some local television stations favor "happy talk"
on their news broadcasts—witty on-the-air exchanges among announ-

cers, reporters, sportscasters, and meteorologists. Other stations use the "eyewitness" approach, showing a preponderance of film with human interest, humorous, or violent content. Many stations combine the two, often pleasing viewers, but perhaps not informing them properly.

The news function of the mass media in the United States cannot be separated from the main function of the privately owned media: entertainment. Entertainment increases audiences, which increases advertising revenues. Of the four hours or so that the average American spends watching television every day, only about ninety minutes are devoted to news or documentaries; the remainder goes to entertainment, movies, or sports.[15] More than 60 million newspapers circulate daily among the population, but more than 60 percent of their content is devoted to advertising.[16] Only a portion of the remaining newspaper space is devoted to news of any sort, and only a fraction of that news—excluding stories about fires, robberies, murder trials, and the like—can be classified as "political."

The Concentration of Private Ownership

Media owners can make more money by increasing their audiences, either by enlarging existing audiences or by acquiring additional publications or stations. In fact, there is a decided trend toward concentrated ownership of the media, enhancing the possibility that a few major owners could control the news flow to promote their own political interests—much as political parties influenced the content of early newspapers. Although the number of daily newspapers has remained approximately the same over the last thirty-five years, the number of *independent* newspapers has declined as more papers have been acquired by newspaper chains (two or more newspapers in different cities under the same ownership). Most of the more than 150 newspaper chains are small, owning fewer than ten papers.[17] Some, however, are very large. The Gannett chain, for example, owns eighty-seven newspapers throughout the United States—including *USA Today*, the newspaper with the second largest circulation in the nation. Only about four hundred dailies are still independent, and many of these papers are too small and unprofitable to invite acquisition.

At first glance, ownership concentration in the television industry does not seem to be a problem. Although there are only three major networks, the networks usually do not own their affiliates. About half of all the communities in the United States are served by ten or more stations.[18] This figure suggests that the electronic media offer enough diversity of views to balance ownership concentration. Like newspapers, however, television stations in different cities are sometimes owned by the same group. In 1987, for example, the Capacities/ABC group owned eight television stations—in New York, Los Angeles, Chicago, Philadelphia, San Francisco, Houston, Fresno, and Raleigh-Durham—serving 24 percent of the television market. A group of seven stations owned by NBC/GE covered 22 percent of the market, and four CBS stations covered 19 percent.[19]

Ownership concentration can also occur across the media. Sometimes the same corporation owns a television station, a radio station, and a newspaper in the same area. For example, the Chicago Tribune Company owns the *Chicago Tribune* (Chicago's largest daily newspaper); the *New York Daily News* (the nation's third largest paper); six television stations in major cities (including WGN in Chicago, WPIX in New York, and KTLA in Los Angeles), serving 19 percent of the market; and several radio stations across the country.

Some people fear the concentration of media under a single owner, and government has addressed those fears by regulating media ownership, as well as other aspects of media operation.

GOVERNMENT REGULATION OF THE MEDIA

Although most of the mass media in the United States are privately owned, they do not operate completely free of government regulation. The broadcast media, however, operate under more regulations than the print media, due initially to technical concerns in broadcasting. In general, government regulation of the mass media falls into three categories: technical regulations, structural regulations, and regulation of content.[20]

Technical Regulations

The broadcast media confront certain technical limitations not faced by the print media. The number of airwaves available for broadcasting radio and television signals is limited. In the early days of radio, stations that operated on similar frequencies in the same area often jammed each other's signals, and neither could broadcast clearly. At the broadcasters' insistence, Congress passed the Federal Radio Act (1927), which declared that the public owned the airwaves and that private broadcasters could use them only by obtaining a license from the Federal Radio Commission. So, government regulation of broadcasting was not forced on the industry by socialist politicians; it was requested by capitalist owners to impose order on the use of the airwaves (thereby restricting others' freedom to enter broadcasting).

The Federal Communications Act (1934) updated the Federal Radio Act and formed the basis for current regulation of the broadcasting industry. The 1934 act replaced the five-person radio commission with the **Federal Communications Commission (FCC),** consisting of seven members (no more than four of them from the same political party) chosen by the president for terms of seven years. Because the commissioners serve overlapping terms—beginning and ending in different years—and can be removed from office only through impeachment and conviction, the FCC is considered an *independent regulatory commission*: It is insulated from political control by either the president or Congress. (We discuss independent regulatory commissions in Chapter 12.) Today, the FCC is charged with regulating interstate and foreign communication by radio, television, telephone, telegraph, cable, and satellite.

The government's regulatory powers in technical areas go beyond granting licenses. For example, the FCC determined the standard for color television in 1950 by choosing a CBS-developed transmission system over a competing one by RCA. Moreover, in the early 1960s, Congress required all television sets manufactured for sale in interstate commerce to receive both VHF (very high frequency) channels 2 through 13 and UHF (ultra high frequency) channels 14 through 83. Both regulations again helped the broadcast industry by ensuring that television sets being sold would receive the signals being transmitted.

Structural Regulations

The FCC also regulates the structure of the electronic media—the organization of broadcasting companies and their interrelationships. As radio began broadcasting to millions of citizens, the FCC became concerned about the concentration of too much power in the hands of single owners. Believing that the National Broadcasting Company—which operated both a "red" and a "blue" network—had grown too big, the FCC ordered NBC to sell its blue network in 1943, leading to the creation of the American Broadcasting Company. Also during the 1940s, the FCC adopted its "duopoly rule," which prohibits any company from owning more than one AM, one FM, or one television station in a single community.[21]

In the early 1950s, the FCC adopted its *7-7-7 rule*, which limited to seven the number of AM, FM, and television stations a single company could own. This ceiling was set when there were fewer than two hundred television stations and fewer than three thousand radio stations. But by 1984 the number of commercial television stations had grown to nearly nine hundred, and the number of radio stations had nearly tripled, to over eight thousand. A majority of commissioners appointed by President Ronald Reagan thus opted to relax FCC regulations by expanding the ownership rule to a *12-12-12 rule*, which favored several large media groups—such as Gannett. Looking ahead to 1990, the FCC anticipates an end to all ownership restrictions.[22] If that occurs, the FCC will have abandoned a principle that it once enforced vigorously—limiting media control.

Regulation of Content

The First Amendment to the Constitution prohibits Congress from abridging the freedom of the press. Over time, the *press* has come to mean *all* the mass media. As might be expected, the press—particularly the print media—has interpreted "freedom of the press" in the broadest possible way, citing the Constitution for its right to print or broadcast any news it wants to print or broadcast. Over the past two hundred years, the courts have decided numerous cases that define how far freedom of the press extends under the law. The most important of these cases, which are often quite complex, are discussed in Chapter 17. Usually the courts have struck down government attempts to restrain the press from publishing or broadcasting the information, events, or opinions that it finds newsworthy. One notable exception concerns strategic information during wartime; the courts have supported censorship in the publishing or broadcasting of such information as the sailing schedules of troop ships or the movements of troops in battle. Otherwise, the courts have recognized a strong constitutional case against press censorship. This stand has given the United States some of the freest, most vigorous news media in the world.

Because the broadcast media are licensed to use the public airwaves, they are subject to some regulation of the content of their news coverage that is not applied to the print media. The basis for the FCC's regulation of content lies in its charge to ensure that radio (and, later, television) stations would "serve the public interest, convenience, and necessity." For over fifty years, broadcasters operated under three constraints rooted in the 1934 Federal Communications Act. Two are still in effect; one, as we will see, has been revoked. In its **equal opportunities rule,** the FCC provided that, if a broadcast station gives or sells time to a candidate for any public office, it must make an equal amount of time under the same conditions available to all other candidates for that office. The **fairness doctrine** obligated broadcasters to discuss public issues and to provide fair coverage to each side of those issues. Finally, the **reasonable access rule** required that stations make their facilities available for the expression of conflicting views or issues from all responsible elements in the community.

These regulations seem unobjectionable to most people, but they have been at the heart of a controversy about the deregulation of the broadcast media. Note that *none* of these regulations is imposed on the print media, which has no responsibility to give equal treatment to political candidates, to give fair coverage to all sides of an issue, or to express conflicting views from all responsible elements of the community. In fact, one aspect of a free press is its ability to champion causes that it favors (such as erecting the Statue of Liberty or starting a war with Spain) without having to argue the case for the other side. The broadcast media have traditionally been treated differently, because they were licensed by the FCC to operate as semimonopolies.[23] With the rise of one-newspaper cities and towns, however, there is now more competition among television stations than among newspapers in virtually every market area. Critics who advocate dropping the equal opportunities, fairness, and reasonable access regulations argue that the broadcast media should be just as free as the print media to decide which candidates they endorse and which issues they support.

Under Reagan, the FCC itself moved toward this view of unfettered freedom for broadcasters. In 1987, the FCC repealed the fairness doctrine on the grounds that it chilled freedom of speech. In doing so, the FCC encountered opposition from Democrats in Congress who vowed to restore the doctrine by making it a law. If the Democrats fail in their attempt, the content and coverage of television news might become more like that of newspapers—more partisan stands, more backing of particular viewpoints. If so, the effect on public opinion might be substantial, given the importance of television as a source of news for most Americans.

REPORTING THE NEWS

"News," for most journalists, is an important event that has happened within the past twenty-four hours. A presidential news conference or an explosion in the Capitol qualifies as news. And a national political convention certainly qualifies as news, although it may not justify the thousands of media representatives who covered the 1988 party conventions. Who decides what is important? The media, of course. In this section, we discuss how the media cover political affairs, what they choose to report (which then becomes "news"), and whether the media are biased in their reporting.

Covering Politics

All the major news media seek to cover political events through firsthand reports from journalists on the scene. For example, the *New York Times* alone has about thirty-five reporters in Washington, D.C. Because so many significant political events occur in the nation's capital, Washington has by far the largest press corps—about thirty-five hundred reporters—of any city in the United States.

About one-third of these correspondents are assigned to cover the White House. Since 1902, when President Theodore Roosevelt provided a special room in the White House for reporters, the press has had special access to the presidency. In fact, reporters enjoyed informal personal relationships with the president as late as the Truman administration. Today, the media's relationship with the president is mediated primarily through the Office of the Press Secretary.

White House correspondents cover the presidency largely by hanging around the press room, waiting for news to materialize. Information for their stories routinely comes in one of three forms, each carefully crafted by the White House in an attempt to control the news output.[24]

The most frequent form is the *news release*—a prepared text distributed to reporters in the hope that it will be used verbatim. A *news briefing*, traditionally held each day, enables reporters to question the press secretary about news releases. A *news conference* involves questioning high-level officials in the executive branch—including the president on occasion. News conferences appear to be freewheeling, but precise answers to anticipated questions tend to be carefully rehearsed.

Occasionally, news conferences are given *on background*, meaning that the information can be quoted but the source must not be identified specifically. A vague reference—"a senior official says"—is all right. (When he was secretary of state, Henry Kissinger himself was often the "senior official" reporting on foreign policy developments.) Information disclosed *off the record* cannot even be printed. Journalists who violate these well-known rules risk losing their welcome at the White House.

Most reporters in the Washington press corps are accredited to sit in the House and Senate press galleries, but only about four hundred cover Congress exclusively.[25] Most of the news about Congress comes from innumerable press releases issued by its 535 members and from an unending supply of congressional reports. A journalist, then, can report on Congress without inhabiting its press galleries.

Not so long ago, individual congressional committees allowed radio and television coverage of their proceedings only on special occasions—as Senator Kefauver did during his committee's investigation of organized crime, and as the Senate select committee did during the Watergate investigation. Congress banned microphones and cameras from its chambers until 1979, when the House permitted live coverage. Even then, the leadership controlled the shots being televised. Nevertheless, televised broadcasts of the House were surprisingly successful, thanks to C-SPAN (the Cable Satellite Public Affairs Network), which is linked to more than fifteen hundred cable systems across the country and has a cultlike following among hundreds of thousands of regular viewers. To share in the television exposure, a majority of senators voted to begin television coverage of their chamber in 1986. However, daily coverage of Congress has a limited audience, compared, for example, with the many millions who viewed the televised Iran-Contra hearings conducted by a House and Senate select committee in 1987.

In addition to these recognized news channels, selected reporters occasionally benefit from *leaks* of information released by officials who are guaranteed anonymity. Officials may leak news to interfere with others' political plans or to float ideas ("trial balloons") past the public and other political leaders to gauge their reactions. At times, one carefully placed leak can turn into a gusher of media coverage through the practice of *pack journalism*—the tendency of journalists to adopt similar viewpoints toward the news simply because they hang around together, exchanging information and defining the day's news. Often a story hounded by the pack does not offer enough substance to sustain pursuit, and the chase is abandoned as quickly as it was begun.

Presenting the News

Media executives, news editors, and prominent reporters function as **gatekeepers** in directing the news flow: They decide which events to report and how to handle the elements in those stories. Only a few individuals—no more than twenty-five on the average newspaper or news weekly and fifty on each of the major television networks—qualify as gatekeepers, defining the news for public consumption.[26] They are usually very selective in choosing what goes through the gate.

It is impossible for the media to communicate *everything* about public affairs. There is neither space in newspapers or magazines nor time on television or radio to do so. Time limitations impose especially severe constraints on television news broadcasting. Each half-hour network news program devotes only about twenty minutes to the news (the rest of the time is taken up by commercials). The average story lasts about one minute, and few stories run longer than two minutes. The typical script for an entire television news broadcast would fill less than two columns of one page of the *New York Times*.[27]

A parade of unconnected one-minute news stories, flashing across the television screen every night, would boggle the eyes and minds of the viewers. To make the news understandable and to hold viewers' attention, television editors and producers group stories together by theme. The stories themselves concentrate on individuals, because individuals have personalities; political institutions do not. The presidency is an exception; that institution is conveniently embodied by an individual, the president. When television covers Congress, however, it tries to personify the institution by focusing on prominent quotable leaders, such as the speaker of the House or the Senate majority leader. Such personification for the purpose of gaining audience acceptability tends to distort the character of an institution. It also encourages **horse race journalism,** in which election coverage becomes a matter of "who's ahead?" One analysis of the news coverage of the 1988 presidential primary campaigns found that only about 20 percent of the air time devoted to the campaigns dealt with national issues; the rest went to the horse race—"who's ahead in the polls, who's raising the most money, who's got TV ads and who's getting endorsed."[28] Consequently, elections are presented as contests between individuals rather than as confrontations between parties and platforms.

Campaigning for office is a type of political news that lends itself to media coverage, especially if the candidates create a **media event**—a situation that is too "newsworthy" to pass up. In 1978, during a successful bid for the Florida governorship, Bob Graham drew continual press coverage for one hundred days by working on one hundred different blue-collar jobs.

One study of news content in city newspapers, local television, and network television found that the network news contained a higher percentage of items about government and politics (stories about the presidency, Congress, domestic policy, or foreign affairs, for instance) than the city's daily newspapers and substantially more than the local television news (see Figure 6.2).[29] In comparison with the other media, newspapers emphasized stories about crime and justice (articles on individual felonies or trials). Local television news programs dealt more with economic and social issues (including issues involving business, labor, the environment, transportation, education, or religion). Remember, however, that this study calculated only the *relative* coverage of news in the media. Although the network news reports a higher percentage of news about government and politics, its coverage of each story tends to last less than two minutes; daily papers usually discuss the same story in greater depth.

Is Reporting Biased?

News professes to reflect reality, yet critics of modern journalism contend that this reality is colored by the way it is filtered through the

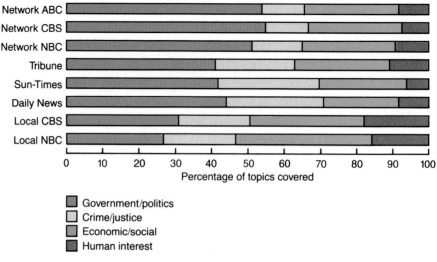

Frequency of News Topics in Different Sources
Where you get your news to some extent determines the news you get. This conclusion emerges from a count of the news topics in eight sources—three network evening news programs, three major Chicago daily newspapers, and two local news broadcasts—for nine months in 1976. All three television networks reported proportionately more news about government and politics than did the newspapers, which in turn reported proportionately more than the local television news did. Stories about economic and social matters (business, labor, environment, transportation, education, and religion) were most popular on local television, along with human interest features. The newspapers tended to report more about crime and justice. (Source: Doris A. Graber, Mass Media and American Politics, *2d ed. [Washington, D.C.: Congressional Quarterly Press, 1984], pp. 83–84.)*

Figure 6.2

ideological biases of the owners and editors (the gatekeepers) and of the reporters themselves.

The argument that news is politically biased has two sides. On one hand, news reporters are criticized for tilting their stories in a liberal direction, promoting social equality and undercutting social order. On the other hand, wealthy and conservative media owners are suspected of preserving inequalities and reinforcing the existing order by serving a relentless round of entertainment that numbs the public's capacity for critical analysis.

Although the picture is far from clear, available evidence seems to confirm the charge of liberal bias among reporters in the major news media. A study of the voting behavior of 240 reporters and broadcasters employed by such media giants as the *New York Times*, the *Washington Post*, the *Wall Street Journal*, *Time*, *Newsweek*, *U.S. News & World Report*, CBS, NBC, and ABC supports that idea. In presidential elections from 1964 through 1976, these media journalists voted for the Democratic candidate more than 80 percent of the time.[30] Moreover, a 1985 *Los Angeles Times* survey of 2,703 news and editorial staffers on 621 papers found that 55 percent of the journalists described themselves as liberal, compared with 23 percent of the general public.[31]

A study of the media coverage of the campaigns for the 1988 presidential nomination in both parties concluded that Democratic candidates got better treatment than Republican candidates on the television news networks. From January 4 through April 15, all three networks aired a higher proportion of negative news about Republican candidates than Democratic candidates.[32] Of course, the judgment of whether news is negative or positive is inherently subjective. A film clip showing Vice President George Bush answering questions about his role in the Iran-Contra affair would certainly be negative, counting as "bad press." But a story about a neutral topic could also be bad press if the reporter put a negative "spin" on it. For example, Representative Richard Gephardt of Missouri campaigned for the 1988 Democratic presidential nomination in part by attacking the Washington political establishment. When they reported his speeches, journalists sometimes put a negative spin on their stories by noting that Gephardt was a leader of the Democratic party in the House and thus part of that establishment.

Although most journalists in the 1985 *Los Angeles Times* survey classified themselves as liberal, more of them described the newspapers for which they worked as conservative (pro-Reagan and pro-business) than liberal (42 percent to 28 percent). To some extent, working journalists are at odds with their own editors, who tend to be more conservative. The editors, in their function as gatekeepers, tend to tone down the liberal biases of their reporters.[33]

If media owners and their editors are indeed conservative supporters of the status quo, we would expect them to support officeholders over challengers in elections. However, the campaign news that emerges from both print and broadcast media tends in the other direction. One researcher who found evidence of liberal bias in the 1984 presidential campaign had also studied the 1980 campaign, when Reagan was the challenger and Jimmy Carter the incumbent president.[34] In that campaign, the media covered Carter more negatively than his conservative challenger. Taking both election years into consideration, the researcher concluded that there is virtually no *continuing* ideological or partisan bias on the evening television news. Instead, what was seen as ideological or partisan bias in 1980 and 1984 was actually a bias against *incumbents* and *frontrunners*.[35]

According to this reasoning, if journalists have any pronounced bias, it is against politicians. When an incumbent runs for re-election, journalists may feel a special responsibility to counteract his or her advantage by putting the opposite partisan spin on the news.[36] Thus, whether the media coverage of campaigns is seen as pro-Democratic (and therefore liberal) or pro-Republican (and therefore conservative) depends on which party is in office at the time.

THE POLITICAL EFFECTS OF THE MEDIA

Virtually all citizens must rely on the mass media for their political news. Although television news programs claim far larger audiences than news magazines and newspapers, many people may watch television

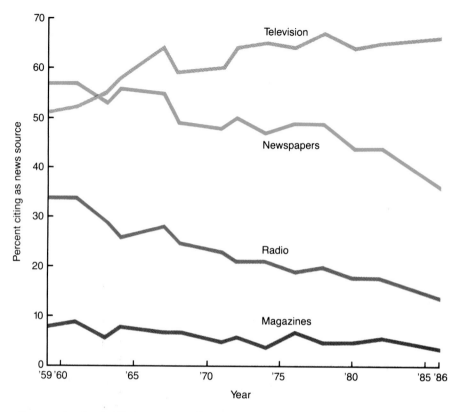

Changes in the Public's Sources of News
For more than a quarter of a century, the Roper Organization has put this question to a national sample: "I'd like to ask you where you usually get most of your news about what's going on in the world today—from the newspapers or radio or television or magazines or talking to people or where?"
Until the early 1960s, newspapers were cited as the main source of news for people in the Roper sample. Then television replaced newspapers, and the gap between the two has grown rather steadily. Radio has declined dramatically as a source of news, but magazines have retained most of their audience over time. (Sources: Roper Organization, Trends in Attitudes Toward Television and Other Media: A Twenty-Four Year Review. *Television Information Office Publication, 1983, p. 5; Roper Organization,* America's Watching: Public Attitudes Toward Television. *Television Information Office Publication, 1987, p. 20. The percentages do not total 100 because people were allowed to cite more than one news source.)*

Figure 6.3 ▬

news programs for their entertainment value without learning much about politics. In this section, we examine where citizens acquire their political knowledge, look at what people learn from the media, and probe the media's effects on public opinions, the political agenda, and political socialization.

Where the Public Gets Its News

Until the early 1960s, most people reported getting more of their news from newspapers than from any other source. As shown in Figure

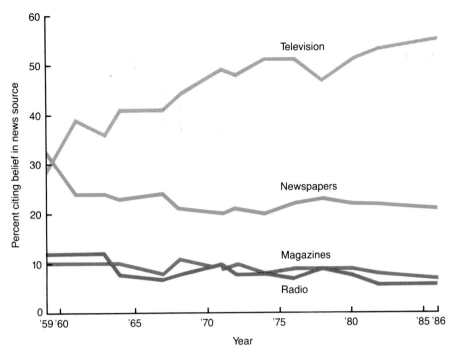

Credibility of the News Media
In the same survey that asked people about their sources of news, the Roper Organization asked, "If you got conflicting or different reports of the same news story from radio, television, the magazines and the newspapers, which of the four versions would you be most inclined to believe?" Here, the gap between television and newspapers is even greater—and it, too, has been growing. By the 1980s, more people saw television as the most credible news source than all the other media combined. (Sources: Roper Organization, Trends in Attitudes Toward Television and Other Media: A Twenty-Four Year Review. Television Information Office Publication, 1983, p. 6; Roper Organization, America's Watching: Public Attitudes Toward Television. Television Information Office Publication, 1987, p. 20.)

Figure 6.4

6.3, television nudged out newspapers as the public's major source of news in the early 1960s. By the 1980s, about two-thirds of the public cited television as their news source, compared with less than one-half who named newspapers and less than one-fifth who relied on radio. Not only is television the public's most important source of news, but television news is also rated as more trustworthy than newspaper news—by a margin of more than 2 to 1 (see Figure 6.4).

Some people prefer television to newspapers as a source of news simply because they cannot read very well. According to a recent literacy test conducted by the U.S. Census Bureau, 13 percent of adults living in the United States are illiterate in English.[37] Although some people who failed the census test were immigrants, 9 percent of those who spoke English as their native language failed as well. Others who are literate in English may not be interested enough to plow through printed matter, when they can simply tune in a good-looking reporter on television and see filmed news reports. It is not surprising, then, that people with different levels of education employ different media as news sources. For example, in 1984 more people with a grade-school education reported watching the network television news every day than did people with a college degree (52 percent to 46 percent). More college-educated respondents reported reading a daily newspaper (52 percent to 34 percent) and a weekly news magazine (38 percent to 6 percent).[38]

What People Remember and Know

About 50 percent of the American population reports watching the network news daily, and another 20 percent say that they watch the network news three or four times a week. Even those who are not faithful watchers of television news hear political news on the radio or read it in newspapers and news magazines. In short, an overwhelming majority of the American public is exposed to news through at least one of the mass media. Nevertheless, most people appear to learn very little about politics from the news that bombards them for hours every day. When a national survey asked, "Over the last twelve months [1983–1984], which news event would you say you remember the most?" over 40 percent of the sample answered "nothing" or recalled nonpolitical events.[39] For those who recalled *some* political news, Israel's long siege and bombing of Beirut in the summer of 1984 emerged as the most memorable event (cited by 14 percent). Many people did not even have a clear idea of what was political and what was not: "Murders and murderers totally outdistanced foreign wars or foreign anything. For example, homicidal maniacs, as a class, proved seven times as memorable as the brutal war between Iran and Iraq."[40]

The public did little better in recalling domestic political news, even when prompted. Although the survey was conducted at the height of the 1984 presidential primary campaign, over 60 percent of the respondents gave incorrect answers to a question that asked whether "during the Reagan years the inflation rate has gotten worse, levelled off, or gotten better?" (It had gotten better. Didn't the respondents remember *anything* specific from all those hours of television viewing? Yes, without prompting, 44 percent could identify the commercial slogan that Walter Mondale had used to criticize Gary Hart—"Where's the beef?"[41]

The authors drew several conclusions from their study: that the public knows *less* about politics than journalists or politicians think; that, for many people, news is not politics; and that slogans can penetrate public indifference about political affairs, when hard news cannot.[42]

How can it be that so many people are so ignorant of political affairs when they are exposed to so much news in the media? Perhaps the answer is in the medium of television, which most people cite as their major news source. Several studies have found that increased exposure to television news has a numbing effect on a person's capacity to discriminate among news messages. A comparison between viewers' and readers' abilities to explain the reasons for their Senate voting choices in 1974 found that reading more newspapers produced more reasons for voting choices but watching more television news did not.[43] In fact, the researchers found evidence that watching television actually tended to *inhibit* knowledge about politics. A later study of subjects' abilities to distinguish between the campaign issues of presidential candidates Gerald Ford and Jimmy Carter in 1976 found that regular television viewers saw no more difference between the candidates than those who neither watched nor read the news on a regular basis.[44] For people with similar levels of education, heavy television watching had a suppressing effect on the ability to see differences between the candidates.

Why should this be? We know that television tends to squeeze public policy issues into one-minute or, at most, two-minute fragments, which makes it difficult to explain candidates' positions. Television also tends to cast abstract issues in personal terms to enhance the visual image that the medium conveys. Thus, viewers may become more adept at visually identifying the candidates and knowing their personal habits than at knowing their positions on issues. Finally, the television networks, which are licensed by the government, are concerned about being fair and equal in their coverage of the candidates, which may result in equalizing candidates' positions as well. Newspapers, which are not licensed by the government, enjoy more latitude in choosing which candidates they cover and how they cover them. Whatever the explanation, the technological wonders of television seem to have contributed little to citizens' knowledge of public affairs. Indeed, electronic journalism may work against the citizen knowledge that democratic government requires.

There is also evidence that suggests those people who rely on television's coverage of politics are more confused and cynical than those who do not.[45] This problem may be even more acute where foreign affairs are concerned, since most of the public has relatively little interest in foreign affairs, but the networks tend to "overreport" them.[46] The public witnesses conflict, criticism, and controversy in countries they know little about. Not knowing what to think or whom to believe, the public responds "by becoming more cynical, more negative, and more critical of leadership and institutions."[47]

Influencing Public Opinion

Americans overwhelmingly believe that the media exert a strong influence on their political institutions, and almost nine out of ten Americans believe that the media strongly influence public opinion (see Compared With What? 6.1). However, it is not easy to determine the extent of media influence on public opinion. Because very few of us learn about political events except as they are reported through the media, it is arguable that the media create public opinion simply by reporting events. Few people knew about Gary Hart's liaison with Donna Rice until the *Miami Herald* reported it. We know that relentless questioning by the press drove Hart from the race, but did the press actually turn public opinion against Hart?

A survey taken after the exposé showed that a majority of those interviewed thought it was not "the press's business" to tell the public

COMPARED WITH WHAT? 6.1

Opinions on the Media

Americans are more likely to perceive the media as politically powerful than are citizens in four other Western democracies. This finding comes from sample surveys taken in Great Britain, France, West Germany, Spain, and the United States during the spring of 1987. Respondents in each country were asked, "Would you say that the influence exerted by the media on [name of institution] is very large, somewhat large, or not large at all?" The combined percentages of "very large" and "somewhat large" responses form the bars of the accompanying graph. Although most citizens in each country perceive the media as having a large influence on public opinion, only Americans think the media also influence the major branches of government.

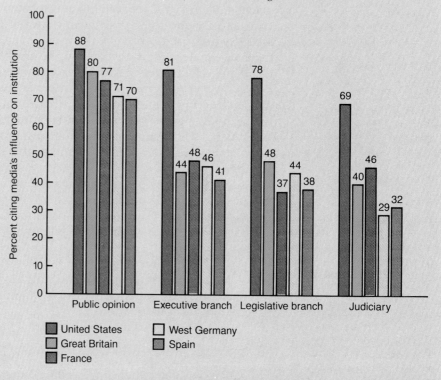

Source: Laurence Parisot, "Attitudes About the Media: A Five-Country Comparison," *Public Opinion* 10 (January–February, 1988):60. Reprinted by permission.

that a candidate had been unfaithful to his wife. Although a substantial minority (40 percent) disagreed, the survey also showed that Hart's support from likely Democratic primary voters only slipped a little, from 38 percent before the exposé to 32 percent immediately afterward.[48] Moreover, when Hart re-entered the race in December 1987, he quickly recaptured the frontrunner's position and led with 23 percent of Democratic preferences through January.[49] Although Hart's campaign sputtered in Iowa and ended in March with virtually no support in the polls, the media initially had a greater impact on Hart the candidate than on public opinion of his candidacy. (See also Figure 11.7, page 431.)

Broader studies of opinion change have found systematic, and in some cases dramatic, effects of television news. One study repeatedly polled the public on eighty issues in foreign and domestic affairs. In nearly half these items, public opinion changed over time by about 6 percentage points. The researchers compared these changes with policy positions taken by ten different sources of information: commentators on television network news, the president, members of the president's party, members of the opposition party, and members of interest groups, for instance. The study found the news commentators to have the most dramatic effect—a single commentary could be linked to more than 4 percentage points of opinion change.[50] As examples, the researchers cited Howard K. Smith's support of Nixon's Vietnam policies in 1969, John Chancellor's stand on the importance of fighting unemployment rather than inflation in 1976, and various 1981 commentaries that argued Reagan's tax cuts would benefit the wealthy.[51]

Setting the Political Agenda

Despite the media's potential for influencing public opinion, most scholars believe that the media's greatest impact on politics is found in its power to set the agenda. An *agenda* is a list of things to do or consider; a **political agenda** is a list of issues that need government attention.

The Shot Seen 'Round the World
Millions of Americans watching the network news one night during the Vietnam War witnessed a South Vietnamese army officer (our ally) executing a captured Vietcong prisoner. This striking photo of the same incident appears to capture the moment of impact. Television showed the public the truly ugly aspects of war and helped mobilize sentiment for withdrawal.

Those who set the political agenda are those who define what issues should be discussed and debated by government decision makers. Like the tree that falls in the forest without anyone hearing it, an issue that does not get on the political agenda will not have anyone in government working on its behalf.

The mass media in the United States have traditionally played an important role in defining the political agenda. As we have seen, newspaper publisher William Randolph Hearst helped put war with Spain on the political agenda in 1898. The muckrakers' magazine articles helped put political and business reforms on the political agenda in the early 1900s. Radio helped put opposition to the Nazis' rise to power on the political agenda in the late 1930s. Television, which reaches daily into virtually every home, has an even greater potential for setting the political agenda. A careful study designed to isolate and examine television's effects on public opinion concluded, "By attending to some problems and ignoring others, television news shapes the American public's political priorities."[52] Furthermore, "the more removed the viewer is from the world of public affairs, the stronger the agenda-setting power of television news."[53]

Today's newspapers also heighten the public's concern about particular social issues. Crime is a good example. Certain types of crime—particularly murder—are especially attractive to the media, which therefore tend to distort the incidence of crime by their reporting. A study of

POLITICS IN THE INFORMATION AGE 6.1

Continuous News

The nightly news broadcasts of the three major networks summarize the day's important stories. In contrast, Cable News Network reports the news throughout the day and night—often as it breaks—to homes wired for cable television. CNN anchorpersons like Bernard Shaw are becoming increasingly familiar faces to viewers across the country. Who else watches CNN? Why, newsmakers, of course.

In some offices at the Pentagon, the State Department and the White House, a television set is tuned to Cable News Network most of the time. . . .

Although it has not toppled the big three networks, CNN, once the poor relation among Washington's television operations, has carved out a niche among the capital's news and politics aficionados. It is a source of up-to-the-minute information for Government officials, lobbyists and business people and a kind of wire

service with sound and pictures for journalists. . . .

CNN's ratings are hard to compare with the broadcast news programs since CNN is on all the time. James Boyle, spokesman for the National Cable Television Association, said that as of July [1987], 41.1 million of the 88.6 million American households with television sets had access to CNN through subscription to local cable services. . . .

In Washington, the audience is more restricted, since the city does not have cable service. Capital Connection, a service of George Mason University, provides CNN, along with C-SPAN, the Congressional Cable television service, to about 1,000 subscribers, many of whom are lobbying groups and political action committees that generally tune to C-SPAN for Government events and Congressional hearings. Michael R. Kelley, the university's direc-

newspaper coverage of crime in nine cities found more attention given to violent crimes (murder, rape, and assault) than was justified by official police statistics. In addition, the study found that newspapers in recent years have given increased attention to political crimes—such as assassinations or kidnappings—and to violent crimes committed outside the metropolitan areas served by the papers. The author concluded that, although newspapers helped put "combating crime" on the political agenda, they also distorted the extent and even the nature of the problem, confusing local policymakers about what should, or could, be done.[54]

At the national level, the major news media help set the political agenda by what they choose to report. One study of Washington reporters identified eleven organizations that comprise the "inner ring" of influence in Washington: the three major television network news organizations (NBC, CBS, and ABC); the two leading news wire services (Associated Press and United Press International); three newspapers with national influence (the *Washington Post*, the *New York Times*, and the *Wall Street Journal*); and three major news weeklies (*Time*, *Newsweek*, and *U.S. News & World Report*).[55] Top government leaders closely follow the news reported in these sources, and the president receives a digest of the news in these and other sources. Cable News Network is also very popular with government officials (see Politics in the Information Age 6.1). Much of what these news media report works its way into the political agenda at one level or another.

Bernard Shaw

tor of telecommunications, estimated that the signal reaches 10,000 television sets in Washington. . . .

In the Pentagon's National Military Command Center, CNN is on one of the television sets in a room that also contains wire service printers. State Department officials with television sets in their offices say they also often watch CNN.

Liz Murphy, an assistant White House press secretary, said she monitors all the networks but turns to CNN for live coverage. "It's like a visual wire," she said. "You can hear stuff on CNN even before we have time to go down and get a wire story."

Source: Andrew Rosenthal, "Watching Cable News Network Grow," *New York Times*, 16 December 1987, p. 12. Copyright 1987 by The New York Times Company. Reprinted by permission.

Socialization

We discussed the major agents of political socialization in Chapter 5, but, for reasons of emphasis and space, we did not include the mass media among them. The mass media act as very important agents of political socialization. Young people who rarely follow the news by choice nevertheless acquire political values through the entertainment function of the broadcast media. Years ago, children learned from radio programs; now they learn from television. What children learned then, however, was very different from what they are learning now. In the "golden days of radio," youngsters listening to the popular radio drama "The Shadow" heard repeatedly that "crime does not pay . . . the *Shadow* knows!" Action programs—such as "The FBI in Peace and War" and "Gangbusters!"—taught children that the major law enforcement agencies inevitably caught criminals and put them behind bars. In program after program—"Dragnet," "Junior G-Men," "Crime Fighters"—the message never varied: Criminals are bad; the police are good; criminals get caught; and criminals are severely punished for their crimes.

Needless to say, television today does not portray the criminal justice system in the same way—even in police dramas. Consider the hit prime-time show "Miami Vice," starring Don Johnson and Philip Michael Thomas as Detectives Crockett and Tubbs. According to one researcher, who analyzed many episodes, the program communicated these themes about law enforcement:

> The federal government is evil—the Central Intelligence Agency (CIA) or the Drug Enforcement Agency (DEA) often intervenes for shadowy reasons to protect killers and drug pushers tracked down by Crockett and Tubbs.
>
> The criminal justice system is suspect—the criminals caught by Crockett and Tubbs are usually released by judges soon after they are arrested (so justice is better served if the crooks are blown away instead).[56]

In general, "Miami Vice" portrayed a cynical view of humanity outside the station house. Only material goods—a black Ferrari Daytona, a sleek sailboat, a powerful speedboat, an elegant Armani suit—can be trusted.

These themes are not unique to "Miami Vice," and another theme—violence—is common to all contemporary television police dramas. "Dempsey and Makepeace" and "Cagney and Lacey" depict violence more vividly than any sound effects man on "Gangbusters!" could. Although no one knows for sure, the effect of these messages—distrust of federal law enforcement, disrespect for the criminal justice system, cynicism and materialism, and functional violence—on impressionable youngsters may be severe. Whatever the effects, it would be difficult to argue that television's entertainment programs help prepare law-abiding citizens.

The media play other contradictory roles in the socialization process. On one hand, the media promote popular support for government by joining in the celebration of national holidays, heroes' birthdays, political anniversaries, and civic accomplishments. The flashy coverage of the hundredth anniversary of the Statue of Liberty exemplifies the media's promotion of national pride. On the other hand, the media erode public

An Eye to the Sky
Television satellite dishes not only allow Americans to receive news from the corners of the world, they also ease the isolation of rural areas. Before satellite dishes were available, people who lived too far from ground-based transmitters or were too remote for cable companies could not receive television signals. For good or ill, people can now receive television broadcasts virtually anywhere in the United States, a situation that promotes uniform socialization experiences across the nation.

confidence by publicizing citizens' grievances, airing investigative reports of agency malfeasance, and giving front-page and prime-time coverage to political critics, protestors, and even terrorists and assassins. Some critics contend that the media give too much coverage to government's opponents, especially to those who engage in unconventional opposition. However, strikes, sit-ins, violent confrontations, and hijackings draw large audiences and thus are very newsworthy by the mass media's standards.

EVALUATING THE MEDIA IN GOVERNMENT

We have described the major political roles of the mass media. What contributions do the media make to democratic government? What effects do they have on freedom, order, and equality?

Contributions to Democracy

As noted earlier, the communication flow in a democracy must move in two directions: from government to citizens and from citizens to government. In fact, because the media are privately owned, political communication in the United States seldom goes directly from government to citizens without passing *through* the media. This is an important point because, as we have seen, news reporters tend to be highly critical of politicians; they instinctively search for inaccuracies in fact and weaknesses in argument. Some observers have characterized the news media and the government as adversaries—each mistrusting the other, locked in competition for popular favor. To the extent that this is true, the media serve both the majoritarian and the pluralist models of democracy well by improving the quality of information transmitted to people about their government.

The mass media transmit information from citizens to government by reporting citizens' reactions to political events and government actions. The press has traditionally reflected public opinion (and often created it) by defining the news and suggesting courses of government action. But the media's role in reflecting public opinion has become much more refined in the information age. Before the widespread use of sample surveys, collections of newspaper stories from across the country were analyzed to assess public opinion on political affairs. After commercial polls (such as the Gallup and Roper polls) were established in the 1930s, newspapers began to report more reliable readings of public opinion. By the 1960s, the media (both national and local) began to conduct their own surveys. In the 1970s, survey research groups became formal divisions of some news organizations. Occasionally, print and electronic media joined forces to conduct major national surveys.

The media now have the tools to do a better job of reporting mass opinion than ever before, and they are using those tools extensively. The well-respected *New York Times*/CBS News Poll conducts surveys that are aired first on the "CBS Evening News," then analyzed at length in the Times. In fact, of forty-nine *Times* stories on the 1984 campaign the week before the election, poll results were cited in 57 percent and received major or important discussion in 30 percent.[57] The *Wall Street Journal* and NBC News are also allies in opinion polling, as are the *Washington Post* and ABC News. Although polls sometimes create opinions just by asking questions, their net effect has been to generate more accurate knowledge of public opinion and to report that knowledge back to the public. Although widespread knowledge of public opinion does not guarantee government responsiveness to popular demands, such knowledge is required if government is to function according to the majoritarian model of democracy.

The mass media are less important in the pluralist model of democracy. Here, interest groups—such as the Farm Bureau, the National Education Association (NEA), and the National Rifle Association (NRA)—can inform their members of government action through publications and mass mailings. Interest groups use these same means of communication to urge their members to write Congress, and they increasingly advertise in the media to generate public support for their special interests. But for political communication to and from the public as a whole, there is no substitute for the mass media.

Effects on Freedom, Order, and Equality

The media in the United States have played an important role in advancing equality, especially racial equality. Throughout the civil rights movement of the 1950s and 1960s, the media gave national coverage to conflict in the South, as black children tried to attend white schools or civil rights workers were beaten and even killed in the effort to register black voters. Partly because of the media coverage, civil rights moved up on the political agenda, and coalitions were formed in Congress to pass new laws promoting racial equality. Women's rights have also been advanced through the media, which focused attention on the National Organization for Women (NOW) and other groups working for sexual equality. In general, the mass media offer spokespersons for any disadvantaged group an opportunity to state their case before a national audience and to work for a place on the political agenda.

Although the media are willing to mobilize government action to infringe on personal freedom for equality's sake, they resist attempts to infringe on freedom of the press to promote order. The media, far more than the public, believe freedom of the press is sacrosanct. For example, 98 percent of the 2,703 journalists surveyed by the *Los Angeles Times* opposed allowing a government official to prevent the publication of a story seen as inaccurate, compared with only 50 percent of the public. Whereas the public felt that certain types of news should never be published—"exit polls saying who will win an election, secret documents dealing with national security issues, the names of CIA spies, photographs that invade people's privacy"—journalists are more reluctant to draw the line anywhere.[58]

To protect their freedom, the media operate as an interest group in a pluralist democracy. They have an interest in reporting whatever they wish whenever they wish, which certainly erodes government's efforts to maintain order. Three examples illustrate this point.

- The media's sensational coverage of the Beirut hijacking fits a general pattern of coverage given to all sorts of terrorist activities. By publicizing terrorism, the media give terrorists exactly what they want, making it more difficult to reduce terrorist threats to order.

- The portrayal of brutal killings and rapes on television, often under the guise of entertainment, has produced "copycat" crimes, those admittedly committed "as seen on TV."

- The national publicity given to deaths from adulterated drugs (for instance, Tylenol capsules laced with cyanide) has prompted similar tampering with other products.

Freedom of the press is a noble value and one that has been important to our democratic government. But we should not ignore the fact that we sometimes pay a price for pursuing it without qualification.

SUMMARY

The mass media transmit information to large, heterogeneous, and widely dispersed audiences through print and broadcasts. The main function of the mass media is entertainment, but the media also perform the political functions of reporting news, interpreting news, influencing citizens' opinions, setting the political agenda, and socializing citizens about politics.

The mass media in the United States are privately owned and in business to make money, which they do mainly by selling space or air time to advertisers. Both print and electronic media determine which events are newsworthy, a determination made on the basis of audience appeal. The rise of mass-circulation newspapers in the 1830s produced a politically independent press in the United States. In their aggressive competition for readers, those newspapers often engaged in sensational reporting, a charge sometimes leveled at today's media.

The broadcast media operate under technical, structural, and content regulations set by the government, which tend to promote the equal treatment of political contests on radio and television more than in newspapers and news magazines.

The major media maintain staffs of professional journalists in major cities across the world. Washington, D.C., has the largest press corps in the United States, and nearly one-third of those correspondents concentrate on the presidency. Because Congress is a more decentralized institution, it is covered in a more decentralized manner. All professional journalists recognize rules for citing sources that guide their reporting. What actually gets reported in the media depends on the media's gatekeepers, the publishers and editors.

The media's elite, including reporters from the major television networks, tend to be more liberal than the public, as judged by the journalists' tendency to vote for Democratic candidates and by their own self-descriptions. However, if the media systematically demonstrate pronounced bias in their news reporting, it tends to work against incumbents and front-runners, regardless of their party, rather than for liberal Democrats.

Although more people today get more news from television than newspapers, those with higher levels of education rely more on newspapers. Newspapers usually do a more thorough job of informing the public about politics. Despite citizens' heavy exposure to news in the print and electronic media, their ability to retain much political information is shockingly low. And despite the media's vaunted reputation for influencing behavior, American voters are able to ignore a candidate's bad press and elect him or her anyway. The amount of coverage given to a candidate may be the most important source of press influence.

From the standpoint of majoritarian democracy, one of the most important effects of the media is to facilitate communication from the people to the government through the reporting of public opinion polls. The media zealously defend the freedom of the press, even to the point of encouraging disorder through criticism of the government and the granting of extensive publicity to violent protests, terrorist acts, and other threats to order.

Key Terms

communication	Federal
mass communication	Communications
mass media	Commission (FCC)
print media	equal opportunities rule
broadcast media	fairness doctrine
yellow journalism	reasonable access rule
muckrakers	gatekeepers
attentive policy elites	horse race journalism
two-step flow of	media event
communication	political agenda
newsworthiness	

Selected Readings

Altschull, J. Herbert. *Agents of Power: The Role of the News Media in Human Affairs.* New York: Longman, 1984. A critical study of the media, giving special attention to the role of ideology in the press and including cross-national comparisons.

Arterton, F. Christopher. *Teledemocracy: Can Technology Protect Democracy?* Newbury Park, Calif: Sage Publications, 1987. Examines the impact of satellites, cable television, computers and computer networking, videoconferencing, and their organizational context on our political and governmental institutions.

Graber, Doris A. *Mass Media and American Politics.* 2d ed. Washington, D.C.: Congressional Quarterly Press, 1984. Emphasizes the political coverage and impact of the mass media.

Iyengar, Shanto, and Donald R. Kinder. *News That Matters: Television and American Opinion.* Chicago: University of Chicago Press, 1987. Reports fourteen experiments with townspeople in New Haven and Ann Arbor designed to assess the effects of television news on opinion.

Orren, Gary R., and Nelson W. Polsby, eds. *Media and Momentum: The New Hampshire Primary and Nomination Politics.* Chatham, N.J.: Chatham House, 1987. A series of studies on media coverage of presidential candidates in the early contests of Iowa and New Hampshire.

Parenti, Michael. *Inventing Reality: The Politics of the Mass Media.* New York: St. Martin's Press, 1986. Argues that the media consciously distort their news coverage to serve the economic and political interests of elites in business and government.

Turow, Joseph. *Media Industries: The Production of News and Entertainment.* New York: Longman, 1984. This short book concentrates on the history of the production of news in the mass media.

Ulloth, Dana R., Peter L. Klinge, and Sandra Eells. *Mass Media: Past, Present, Future.* St. Paul, Minn.: West, 1983. A readable text that provides convenient statistical information about the growth of the mass media.

7

Participation and Voting

Mayor Richard J. Daley vowed, "Law and order will be maintained." Chicago was preparing to host the 1968 Democratic National Convention, and Daley had reason to be concerned. Groups of young antiwar protesters—ranging from neatly dressed supporters of peace candidate Eugene McCarthy to hard-core revolutionaries—were planning to demonstrate against the Vietnam War at the convention. To keep his word, Daley put Chicago's 11,900-member police force on twelve-hour shifts. He also called up more than 5,000 Illinois National Guard troops and arranged for 6,500 federal troops to be flown in as reserves. In all, he had more than 23,000 law enforcement officers available to deal with the 8,000 to 10,000 demonstrators who showed up for the convention in late August.[1]

Skirmishes between the protesters and the police, the first line of Mayor Daley's defense, began before the convention formally opened. Daley had refused to allow the protesters to sleep in Lincoln Park, a 1,200-acre park a distance from the convention site. The protesters, most of them in their teens and twenties, tried to stay in the park after the 11:00 P.M. curfew but were easily driven out the first night. Clashes between demonstrators and police intensified on subsequent nights, and soon the National Guard troops were called in. When the convention started, the battleground shifted to Grant Park, just in front of the Conrad Hilton Hotel, where many delegates were staying. On the final night of the convention, a crowd estimated at three thousand taunted the police with cries of "Pig!" and worse, and threw bricks and bottles. The police responded with tear gas and nightsticks.

The orgy of beatings that followed was closely covered by the mass media. One reporter wrote, "The sound of nightsticks smashing into skulls resounded through the park, mixed with shrieks and screams. 'Oh, no!' 'Oh, my God!' 'No, no, no!'" The reporter quoted a policeman: "If they'd gotten beaten like this when they were kids, they wouldn't be out here starting riots."[2] The police flailed at everyone in sight, injuring at least 17 reporters that one night. During the week, more than 700 civilians and 83 police officers were injured. Of the 653 people arrested, only 91 were thirty or older.[3]

Watching the conflict from their living rooms, a nationwide television audience heard horrified commentators criticizing the police for using excessive force on the young protesters. The public thought otherwise. People flooded the networks with mail, berating the reporters and praising the police. A national poll taken two months later found that 75 percent of respondents with opinions on the riot thought the police had used the right amount of force or should have used even more.[4]

In Chapter 5, we saw that about half the population chose order over freedom on the issue of allowing a communist to teach in college. On the subject of the Vietnam War, most of the public rejected freedom of organized protest and approved massive force to prevent demonstrators from disturbing the orderly conduct of the Democratic convention. Perhaps the public was simply fed up with the wave of protests against the war, the draft, capitalism, and social inequalities that characterized student activism in the 1960s.

Today's young people do not seem to take part in political protest as readily or as intently. The relatively few students who demonstrated in 1986 against college investments in South Africa had only limited success. At Dartmouth College, a few conservative students even tore down the shantytown that other students had built to protest Dartmouth's South African investments. The students at Gallaudet College met with more success in 1988, when their campus protests against the appointment of a hearing president produced the first deaf president ever at the nation's only college for deaf students. In the political arena, however, college students kept a low profile at the 1988 Democratic and Republican nominating conventions—a far cry from the turbulent scene outside the Democratic convention in 1968.

What has happened during the last two decades to change the political behavior of American youth? It seems we are witnessing widespread political apathy among Americans of all ages. Are Americans today less active politically? How do they compare with citizens of other countries? And how much and what kind of participation are necessary to sustain the pluralist and majoritarian models of democracy?

In this chapter, we try to answer these and other important questions about popular participation in government. Although most people think of political participation primarily in terms of voting, there are other forms of political participation, and sometimes they are more effective than voting. We begin by looking at the role of participation in democratic government, distinguishing between conventional and unconventional participation. Then we evaluate the nature and extent of both types of participation in American politics. Next, we study the expansion of voting rights and voting as the major mechanism for mass participation in politics. Finally, we examine the extent to which the various forms of political participation serve the values of freedom, equality, and order, and the majoritarian and pluralist models of democracy.

DEMOCRACY AND POLITICAL PARTICIPATION

"Government ought to be run by the people." That is the democratic ideal in a nutshell. But how much and what kind of citizen participation are necessary for democratic government? Neither political theorists nor politicians, neither idealists nor realists, can agree on an answer. Champions of direct democracy believe that if citizens do not participate *directly* in government affairs, making government decisions among themselves, they should give up all pretense of democracy. More practical observers contend that people can govern indirectly through their elected representatives. And they maintain that choosing leaders through **elections**—formal procedures for voting—is the only workable approach to democracy in a large complex nation.

We talked about the distinction between direct and indirect democracy in Chapter 2. In a direct democracy, citizens meet and make decisions themselves. In an indirect democracy, citizens participate in government by electing representatives to make decisions for them. Voting is central to the majoritarian model of government, but it is not the only means of political participation. In fact, the pluralist model of democracy relies less on voting and more on other forms of participation.

Elections are a necessary condition of democracy, but they do not guarantee democratic government. The Soviet Union has regularly held elections in which more than 90 percent of the electorate turn out to vote, but the Soviet Union has certainly not functioned as a democracy. Both the majoritarian and pluralist models of democracy rely to varying degrees on voting but expect citizens to take part in other forms of political behavior as well. For example, they expect citizens to discuss politics, to form interest groups, to contact public officials, to campaign for political parties, to run for office, and even to protest government decisions.

We define **political participation** as "those actions of private citizens by which they seek to influence or to support government and politics."[5] This definition embraces both conventional and unconventional forms of political participation. In plain language, *conventional* behavior is behavior that is acceptable to the dominant culture in a given situation. Wearing a swimsuit at the beach is conventional; wearing one at a formal dance is not. Plastering campaign posters on public buildings is conventional; writing political slogans on walls is not.

At times, it can be difficult to decide whether a particular political

Unconventional Political Participation
In August 1968, thousands of youthful antiwar protesters gathered in Chicago, where the Democrats were holding their national convention. Protests against the war had already forced President Lyndon Johnson not to seek re-election. Mayor Richard Daley vowed that the protesters would not disturb the convention's impending nomination of Hubert Humphrey, Johnson's vice president. Daley's police kept the youths from demonstrating at the convention, but the resulting violence did not help Humphrey, who lost to Richard Nixon in an extremely close election.

act is conventional or unconventional. We find the following distinction useful in analyzing political participation:

- **Conventional participation** is relatively routine behavior that uses the institutional channels of representative government, especially campaigning for candidates and voting in elections.
- **Unconventional participation** is relatively uncommon behavior that challenges or defies government channels (and thus is personally stressful to participants and their opponents).

Voting and writing letters to public officials are examples of conventional political participation; staging sit-down strikes in public buildings and chanting slogans outside officials' windows are examples of unconventional participation. Some forms of unconventional participation are used by powerless groups to gain political benefits while still working within the system.[6] It is stressful because it means doing something that is not approved by the dominant culture, acting against the established order.

There is no question that voting and other methods of conventional participation are important to democratic government. But so are unconventional forms of participation. Here we look at both kinds of political participation in the United States, beginning with unconventional forms and working toward the most visible form of conventional participation—voting in elections.

Conventional Political Participation
In contrast to the violent protests outside the 1968 Democratic convention, these young people patiently stuff envelopes in behalf of Senator Robert Dole's campaign for the 1988 Republican presidential nomination. Today's youth are less inclined to engage in organized political protests and more inclined to participate in politics in conventional ways.

UNCONVENTIONAL PARTICIPATION

On Sunday, March 7, 1965, a group of about six hundred people attempted to march 50 miles from Selma, Alabama, to the state capital at Montgomery. The marchers were demonstrating in favor of voting rights for blacks. (At the time, Selma had fewer than five hundred registered black voters, out of fifteen thousand who were eligible.)[7] Alabama Governor George Wallace declared the march illegal and sent state troopers to stop it. The two groups met at the Pettus Bridge over the Alabama River at the edge of Selma. The marchers were beaten and trampled by troopers and deputy sheriffs—some on horseback—using clubs, bullwhips, and tear gas. The day became known as "Bloody Sunday."

The march from Selma was a form of unconventional political participation. Marching 50 miles in a political protest is certainly not common; moreover, the march challenged existing institutions, which prevented blacks from voting. From the beginning, the marchers knew they were putting themselves in a dangerous situation, that they certainly would be taunted by whites along the way and could be physically hurt as well. But they had been prevented from participating conventionally—voting in elections—for many decades, and they chose this unconventional way of dramatizing their cause.

The march ended in violence because Wallace would not allow even this peaceful mode of unconventional expression. Unlike the antiwar protesters at the 1968 Democratic convention, the civil rights marchers themselves posed no threat of violence. The brutal response to them helped the rest of the nation realize the seriousness of the civil rights problem in the South. Unconventional participation is stressful and occasionally violent, but it is sometimes worth the risk.

Support for Unconventional Participation

Unconventional political participation has a long history in the United States. The Boston Tea Party in 1773, in which American colonists dumped three cargoes of British tea into Boston Harbor, was only the first in a long line of violent protests against British rule that eventually led to revolution. Yet, we know less about unconventional political participation than about conventional participation. The reasons are twofold: First, data on conventional means are easier to collect and so are more frequently studied. Second, political scientists are biased toward "institutionalized," or conventional, politics. In fact, some basic works on political participation explicitly exclude any behavior that is "outside the system."[8]

The waves of political protest that swept across this country and Western Europe in the 1960s prompted researchers to conduct studies of political action in five nations, including the United States.[9] The researchers asked people whether they had engaged in or approved of ten types of political participation outside of voting. The Americans' responses are shown in Figure 7.1. Of the ten activities, only signing petitions was clearly regarded as conventional, in the sense that the behavior is nearly universally approved and widely practiced.

There was a question about the conventionality of two other forms of behavior. Nearly a quarter of the respondents disapproved of lawful demonstrations, and only one out of ten had ever participated in a lawful demonstration. What is and is not "lawful" is hard to determine, however. The demonstrators in Chicago had a constitutional right to assemble peaceably and to protest the war, but they did violate the law by trying to sleep in the park. The marchers in Selma, although peaceful, violated Governor Wallace's decree. If we measure conventionality in terms of the number of people who disapprove of an action and the number who actually practice it, then it might be argued that all demonstrations border on the unconventional. The same reasoning could be applied to boycotting products—for example, refusing to buy lettuce or grapes picked by nonunion farm workers. Lawful demonstrations and boycotts are problem cases in deciding what is and is not conventional political participation.

The other political activities listed in Figure 7.1 are clearly unconventional. In fact, when political activities interfere with daily living (blocking traffic) or involve the destruction of property (painting slogans

Figure 7.1

What Americans think of as Unconventional Political Behavior

A survey of Americans asked whether they approved or disapproved of ten different forms of participation outside of the electoral process. The respondents disapproved of most of the ten forms, often overwhelmingly. Signing petitions is one form that was rarely disapproved and also widely done. But even attending lawful demonstrations (a right guaranteed in the Constitution) was disapproved by 24 percent of the respondents and rarely practiced. Boycotting products was more objectionable but more widely practiced. Attending demonstrations and boycotting products are only marginally conventional. The other seven forms are clearly unconventional. (Source: Samuel H. Barnes and Max Kaase, eds., Political Action: Mass Participation in Five Western Democracies [Beverly Hills, Calif.: SAGE, 1979] p. 545.)

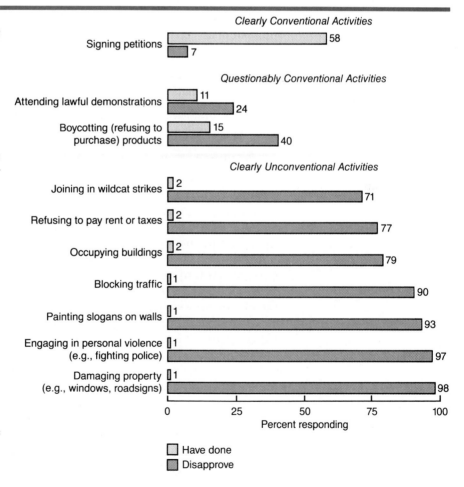

on walls, breaking windows) or physical violence, disapproval is nearly universal. Americans do not approve of unconventional political behavior. This is why the public condemned the protesters, not the police, in Chicago in 1968.

Why this overwhelming disapproval of most unconventional political action? The reason is not simply that Americans see such tactics as failing in their purpose. While most respondents in the survey felt that unconventional political actions are ineffective, there were more respondents who thought such actions were effective than respondents who personally approved of them.[10] What, then, accounts for the rejection of unconventional behavior?

The researchers on the project suggested the following explanation. Noninstitutionalized political protest has been used mainly by powerless groups that have been denied access to channels of political influence. For example, Mayor Daley denied permission for the Chicago antiwar demonstrators to sleep in the park, although granting permission could have averted the initial clashes. When government authorities confront and resist protesters who have no other bases of power, unconventional political action tends to erupt in violence as the authorities use force to impose order. The authorities thus see the direct action of opposed groups as violent and their own actions as nonviolent.[11] Mayor Daley, for instance, justified his police force's behavior by describing the antiwar protesters as "terrorists."

The Effectiveness of Unconventional Participation

Does unconventional participation ever work, especially when it provokes violence? Yes. Antiwar protesters discouraged President Lyndon Johnson from seeking re-election, and they heightened public concern over U.S. participation in the Vietnam War. American college students who disrupted campuses in the late 1960s and early 1970s helped end the military draft in 1973, and—as we study more closely later—they were surprised by speedy passage of the Twenty-sixth Amendment, which lowered the voting age to eighteen.

The unconventional activities of the civil rights workers also had notable success. Dr. Martin Luther King, Jr., led the 1955 Montgomery bus boycott (prompted by Rosa Parks's refusal to surrender her seat to a white man; see page 9) that sparked the civil rights movement. He used **direct action,** assembling crowds to confront businesses and local governments, to demand equal treatment in public accommodations and government. The civil rights movement used over a thousand such newsworthy demonstrations nationwide—387 in 1965 alone.[12] And, like the march in Selma, many of these protests provoked violent confrontations between whites and blacks.

Denied opportunities for conventional political participation, the civil rights movement used unconventional politics to pressure Congress to pass a series of civil rights laws in 1957, 1960, 1964, and 1968—each one in some way extending federal protection against discrimination by

FEATURE 7.1

Selma, Alabama, Twenty Years Later

On March 7, 1965, civil rights marchers were beaten by Alabama state troopers and local law enforcement officers. Twenty years later, on March 3, 1985, state troopers gave a protective escort to those who marched to commemorate Bloody Sunday. Some things do change.

SELMA, ALA., March 3—More than 2,500 people paraded through the streets of this river city today, retracing the route of a group whose protest march 20 years ago marked a turning point in the movement for black voting rights in the South.

The demonstration today, led by Coretta Scott King and the Rev. Jesse Jackson, commemorated what is remembered as Bloody Sunday, when 600 civil rights protesters were beaten and routed by state troopers and mounted sheriffs deputies blocking their route toward Montgomery over the Edmund Pettus Bridge.

"When I think about Selma I think about blacks not being able to drink water when we were thirsty," said Mr. Jackson, speaking outside the Brown Chapel African Methodist Episcopal Church, where the marchers gathered 20 years ago. "Whenever our spirits are down and our hearts are heavy, we can always return to this landmark and remember how far we've come."

The violent confrontation on the bridge 20 years ago was captured by television news cameras and aired across the nation, provoking widespread protest and outrage and leading, later in 1965, to passage by Congress of the Voting Rights Act.

As one measure of the kinds of change that have occurred in central Alabama over the last 20 years, Joe T. Smitherman, the white man who is Mayor of Selma today as he was in 1965, was applauded as he presented keys to the city to the Rev. Mr. Jackson and another black leader, the Rev. Joseph E. Lowery, president of the Southern Christian Leadership Conference.

reason of race, color, religion, or national origin. (The 1964 act also prohibited discrimination in employment on the basis of sex.)

In addition, the Voting Rights Act of 1965 put state electoral procedures under federal supervision, increasing the registration of black voters and the rate of black voter turnout—especially in the South, where much of the violence occurred. Black protest activity (both violent and nonviolent) has also been credited with increased welfare support for blacks in the South.[13] Finally, we know that social change can occur, even when it is violently opposed at first. Twenty years after law enforcement officers beat civil rights marchers in Selma, state troopers and deputy sheriffs gave a protective escort to those who marched to commemorate Bloody Sunday (see Feature 7.1).

Although direct political action and the politics of confrontation can work, it takes a special kind of commitment to use them. Studies show that direct action appeals most to those who both (1) *distrust* the political system and (2) have a strong sense of political *efficacy*—the feeling that they can do something to affect political decisions.[14] Whether or not this combination of attitudes produces behavior that challenges the system depends on the extent of organized group activity.[15] The civil rights

Charming 1 bedrm; good loc.; low rent; blacks only
Students at many college campuses in 1986 protested college investments in South Africa because of its policy of apartheid (radical separation of races). One form of peaceful protest involved building and sometimes living in shacks that represented the appalling shantytowns where many South African blacks are forced to live. This shack, which stood on the green at Dartmouth College, was torn down one night by conservative students who objected to its presence.

movement involved many groups: King's Southern Christian Leadership Conference (SCLC); the Congress of Racial Equality (CORE), headed by James Farmer; and the Student Non-Violent Coordinating Committee (SNCC), led by Stokely Carmichael—to mention a few.

The decision to behave unconventionally also depends on the extent to which individuals develop a *group consciousness*—identification with the group and an awareness of its position in society, its objectives, and its intended course of action.[16] These factors were present among blacks and young people in the mid-1960s and are present today among blacks and women. Indeed, some authors contend that black consciousness has heightened distrust of the political system and the sense of individual efficacy, producing more participation of different types by poor blacks than by poor whites.[17] The National Organization for Women (NOW) and other women's groups have also heightened women's consciousness, contributing to their increased participation in politics, in both conventional and unconventional ways.

Unconventional Participation in America

Compared with citizens in the Netherlands, Britain, Germany, and Austria, Americans claim to "have done" as much or *more* in the way of unconventional behavior. Researchers have found that Americans were more likely to have participated in lawful demonstrations and were far more likely to have boycotted products of businesses for political reasons. Moreover, Americans were equally likely to have engaged in rent strikes, blocked traffic, painted political slogans, occupied buildings, damaged property, and fought with political opponents.[18] Contrary to the popular view that Americans are apathetic about politics, studies suggest that they are more likely to engage in political protests of various sorts than citizens in other democratic countries.

One might question these findings because the data were collected in 1974, following the civil rights activities of the 1960s and the student protests against the Vietnam War. However, protest activity was also prevalent at that time across western Europe. The national patterns of unconventional participation do not seem to be peculiar to those times. A 1985 poll in Australia, Austria, Britain, Germany, Italy, and the United States showed similar patterns in public approval of various forms of protests.[19]

Is there something wrong with our political system if citizens resort to unconventional—and widely disapproved—methods of political participation? To answer this question, we must first learn how much Americans use conventional methods of participation.

CONVENTIONAL PARTICIPATION

A practical test of the democratic nature of any government is whether citizens can affect its policies by acting through its institutions—meeting with public officials, supporting candidates, voting in elections. If people must operate outside government institutions in order to influence policymaking—as civil rights workers had to do in the South—then the system is not democratic. Citizens should not have to risk life and property to participate in politics, and they should not have to take direct action to force their views to be heard in government. The objective of democratic institutions is to make political participation *conventional*—to see to it that ordinary citizens can engage in relatively routine, non-threatening behavior to cause government to heed their opinions, interests, and needs.

It is not unusual in a democracy for a group to gather at a statehouse or city hall to dramatize its position on an issue—say, a tax increase. This kind of demonstration is a form of conventional participation. The group is not powerless, and its members are not risking their personal safety by demonstrating. But violence can erupt between opposing groups demonstrating in a political setting, for instance, between antiabortion and prochoice groups. Circumstances, then, often determine whether organized protest is or is not conventional. In general, the less the threat to participants, the more conventional the protest.

Several types of participation are conventional except in extreme circumstances. (For example, voting is ordinarily a conventional act, but it would not have been conventional for a black to vote in Selma in the early 1960s.) The most visible form of conventional participation is voting to choose candidates. However, we must not rush to study voting too quickly; it leads us away from less prominent but equally important forms of conventional political participation. In fact, these other forms of participation are in many ways more important than voting, especially in the United States, where voter turnout is much lower than that in most other democratic nations.

There are two major categories of conventional political behaviors: actions that show *support* for government policies and those that try to change or *influence* policies.

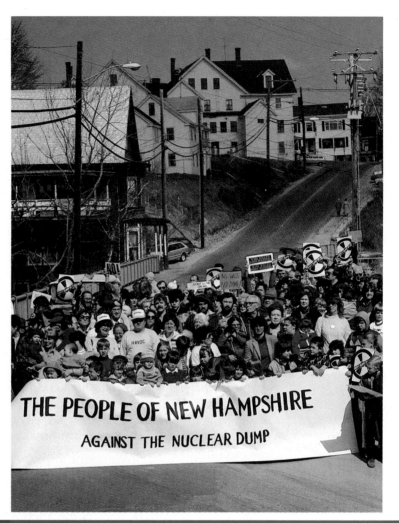

Not in Our Town
Perhaps not everyone in New Hampshire is pictured here, but these protesters made their point. A cross section of Hillsboro, New Hampshire, residents marched to protest a nuclear waste disposal site in their town. Politicians usually listen closely when a diverse group of citizens are concerned enough to protest a specific government action. These citizens won: The dump site did not come to Hillsboro.

Supportive Behavior

Supportive behaviors are actions that express allegiance to country and government. When we recite the Pledge of Allegiance or fly the American flag on holidays, we are showing support for the country and, by implication, its political system. These kinds of ceremonial activities usually require little effort, knowledge, or personal courage; that is, they demand little initiative on the part of the citizen. The simple act of turning out to vote is in itself a show of support for the political system. Other supportive behaviors—for example, serving as an election judge in a nonpartisan election or organizing a holiday parade—demand greater initiative.

At times, their perception of patriotism moves people across the line from conventional to unconventional behavior. In their eagerness to support the American system, they break up a meeting or disrupt a rally of a group they believe is radical or somehow "un-American." Radical groups may threaten the political system with wrenching change, but superpatriots pose their own threat. Their misguided excess of allegiance denies nonviolent means of dissent to others.

Influencing Behavior

Influencing behaviors are used to modify or even reverse government policy to serve political interests. Some forms of influencing behavior seek particular benefits from government; others have broad policy objectives.

Particular benefits.   Some citizens try to influence government to obtain benefits for themselves, their immediate families, or close friends. Two examples, which do not require much initiative, are voting to elect a relative to local office and voting against an increase in school taxes when one's own children have already left school. Serving one's own self-interest through the voting process is certainly acceptable to democratic theory. Each individual has only one vote, and no single voter can wangle particular benefits from government through voting unless a majority of voters agree.

Political actions that require considerable knowledge and initiative are another story, however. Individuals or small groups who influence government officials to advance their self-interests may benefit without others' knowing about it. Those who quietly obtain particular benefits from government present a serious challenge to a democracy. Pluralist theory holds that groups ought to be able to make government respond to their special problems and needs. On the other hand, majoritarian theory holds that government should not do what a majority does not want it to do. A majority of citizens might very well not want the government to do what any particular person or group seeks—if it is costly to other citizens.

What might individual citizens or groups ask of their government, and how might they go about asking? Few people realize that using the court system is a form of political participation, a way for citizens to press their rights in a democratic society. Although most people use the courts to serve their particular interests, some also use them to meet broad objectives. Going to court demands high personal initiative.[20] It also demands a knowledge of the law and the financial resources to afford a lawyer.

Some citizens ask for special services from their local government. Such requests may range from contacting the city forestry department to remove a dead tree in front of a house to calling the county animal control center to deal with a vicious dog in the neighborhood. Studies of such "contacting" behavior as a form of political participation find that it tends not to be related to other forms of political activity but is related to socioeconomic status: People of higher socioeconomic status are more likely to contact public officials.[21]

Americans demand much more of local government than of national government. Although many people value self-reliance and individualism in national politics, most people expect local government to solve a

A Line of Argument
Tension may fill the air when citizens turn out in large numbers at local political meetings, and speaking out in such meetings requires high personal initiative. Knowledge of the issues involved sometimes helps, too. Citizens at this public transportation hearing in Austin, Texas, have come prepared to state their views. Looks like a long evening ahead.

wide range of social problems. A study of residents of Kansas City, Missouri, found that more than 90 percent thought it was the city's responsibility to provide services in thirteen areas, including maintaining parks, setting standards for new home construction, demolishing vacant and unsafe buildings, ensuring that property owners clean up trash and weeds, and providing bus service. The researcher noted that "it is difficult to imagine a set of federal government activities about which there would necessarily be any more consensus—defense, environmental controls, and other areas."[22]

Finally, contributing money to a candidate's campaign is another form of influencing behavior. Here, too, the objective can be particular or broad benefits, although sometimes it can be difficult to determine which. An example: Zev Wolfson, a New York real estate developer, contributed $1,000 to the re-election campaign of Democratic Senator Daniel Inouye of Hawaii in 1987. Wolfson was a member of the board of Ozar Hatorah, an Orthodox Jewish organization that builds schools for Jewish youngsters in France and the Middle East. Soon after Congress passed a massive appropriations bill for 1988, the press disclosed that Senator Inouye had included in it $8 million for Ozar Hatorah's educational construction program. Senator Inouye conceded an error of judgment (presumably, neglecting the issue of church and state), moved to rescind the funds, and assured his colleagues, "I was not aware of this contribution and I did not solicit the funds."[23] Nevertheless, wealthy individuals sometimes make campaign contributions to further personal objectives that are less noble than schools for refugees.

Several points emerge from this review of "particularized" forms of political participation. First, approaching government to serve one's particular interests is consistent with democratic theory, because it encourages input from an active citizenry. Second, particularized contact may be a form of participation unto itself, not necessarily related to other forms of participation, such as voting. Third, such participation tends to be used more by citizens who are advantaged in terms of knowledge and resources. Fourth, particularized participation may serve private interests to the detriment of the majority.

Broad policy objectives.   We come now to what many scholars have in mind when they talk about political participation: activities that influence the selection of government personnel and policies. Here, too, we find behaviors that require little initiative (such as voting) and high initiative (attending political meetings, persuading others how to vote).

Even when voting is used to influence policies, it remains a low-initiative activity. "Policy voting" differs from voting to show support or to gain special benefits by its broader impact on the community or the society. Obviously, this distinction is not sharp: Citizens vote for a number of reasons that mix allegiance, particularized benefits, and policy concerns. In addition to policy voting, many other low-initiative forms of conventional participation—wearing a campaign button, watching a party convention on television, posting a bumper sticker—are also connected with elections. In the next section, we focus on elections as a mechanism for participation. For now, we simply note that voting to influence policy is usually a low-initiative activity. It actually requires more initiative to *register* to vote in the United States than to cast a vote on election day.

ERA NOW!
The National Organization for Women was founded in 1966 to promote "full equality for women in truly equal partnership with men." The organization lobbies at all levels of government. Here Molly Yard, NOW president, holds a 1988 press conference outside the Capitol to display a stack of petitions launching a new attempt to pass the Equal Rights Amendment.

Other types of participation to affect broad policies require high initiative. Running for office requires the most (we discuss this in the next chapter, along with campaigning). Some high-initiative activities, such as attending party meetings and working in campaigns, are associated with the electoral process; others, such as attending legislative hearings and writing letters to Congress, are not. These nonelectoral activities are a form of contacting, but their objective is to obtain government benefits for some *group* of people—farmers, the unemployed, children, oil producers. In fact, studies of citizen contacts in the United States show that about two-thirds deal with broad social issues and only one-third are for private gain.[24]

As we noted above, the courts can be used for personal benefit and broad policy objectives. **Class-action suits** are brought by a person or group on behalf of other people in similar circumstances. Lawyers for the National Association for the Advancement of Colored People pioneered this form of litigation in the famous school desegregation case, *Brown* v. *Board of Education* (1954).[25] They succeeded in getting the Supreme Court to outlaw segregation in public schools, not just for Linda Brown, who brought suit in Topeka, Kansas, but for all others "similarly situated"—that is, for all other black students who want to attend white schools. Usually this form of participation is beyond the means of individual citizens, but it has proved to be effective for organized groups, especially those who have been unable to gain their objectives through Congress or the president.

Individual citizens try to influence policies at all levels of government—local, state, and national. Congressional hearings are public events, sometimes broadcast over the mass media and occasionally held in various parts of the country. Especially since the end of World War II, the federal government has sought to increase citizen involvement in creating regulations and laws by making information on government activities available to interested parties. For example, government agencies are required to publish notices of regulations in the *Federal Register* (a list, published daily, of all proposed and approved regulations), and to make documents available to citizens on request.

Conventional Participation in America

You may know someone who has taken part in a congressional or administrative hearing; the odds are better, though, that you do not. This is a form of high-initiative behavior. Relatively few people—only those with high stakes in the outcome of a decision—are willing to participate this way. How often do Americans contact government officials and engage in other forms of conventional political participation, compared with citizens in other countries?

The most common political behavior reported in a study of five countries was voting to choose candidates (see Compared With What? 7.1). Americans are *less* likely to vote than citizens in the other four countries. On the other hand, Americans are as likely (or substantially more likely) to engage in all of the other forms of conventional political participation—just as they are as or more likely to take part in unconventional behaviors. Americans, then, are more apt to engage in nearly all forms of unconventional *and* conventional political participation, *except* voting.

The researchers noted this paradox and wrote: "If, for example, we concentrate our attention on national elections we will find that the United States is the least participatory of our five nations." But looking at the other indicators, they found that "political apathy, by a wide margin, is lowest in the United States. Interestingly, the high levels of overall involvement reflect a rather balanced contribution of both . . . conventional and unconventional politics."[26] Clearly, low voter turnout in the United States constitutes something of a puzzle. We will work at that puzzle, but first we focus on elections and electoral systems.

PARTICIPATING THROUGH VOTING

The heart of democratic government lies in the electoral process. Whether a country holds elections and, if so, what kind constitute the critical differences between democratic and nondemocratic government. Elections are important to democracy for their potential to institutionalize mass participation in government according to the three normative principles for procedural democracy we discussed in Chapter 2. Electoral rules specify (1) *who* is allowed to vote, (2) *how much* each person's vote counts, and (3) *how many* votes are needed to win.

Again, elections are formal procedures for making group decisions. **Voting** is the act that individuals perform when they choose among alternatives in an election. **Suffrage** and the **franchise** both mean "the right to vote." By formalizing political participation through rules for suffrage and counting ballots, electoral systems allow large numbers of people, who individually have little political power, to wield great power. Electoral systems decide collectively who governs and, in some instances, what government should do.

The simple fact of holding elections is less important than the specific rules and circumstances that govern voting. According to democratic theory, everyone should be able to vote. In practice, however, no nation grants universal suffrage. All countries have age requirements for voting, and all disqualify some inhabitants on various grounds: lack of citizenship, a criminal record, mental incompetence, and so forth. What is the record of enfranchisement in the United States?

Expansion of Suffrage

The United States was the first country to provide for general elections of representatives through "mass" suffrage, but the franchise was far from universal. When our Constitution was framed, the idea of full adult suffrage was too radical to be considered seriously, much less adopted. Instead, the framers left the issue of enfranchisement to the states, stipulating only that individuals who could vote for "the most numerous Branch of the State Legislature" could also vote for their representatives to the U.S. Congress (Article I, Section 2).

COMPARED WITH WHAT? 7.1

Conventional Political Participation

A study of five nations found that Americans are more likely than citizens in other countries to engage in various forms of conventional political behavior—except voting. These findings clearly contradict the idea that Americans are politically apathetic.

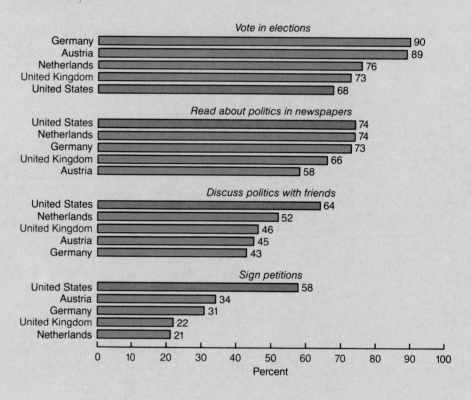

Vote in elections

Germany	90
Austria	89
Netherlands	76
United Kingdom	73
United States	68

Read about politics in newspapers

United States	74
Netherlands	74
Germany	73
United Kingdom	66
Austria	58

Discuss politics with friends

United States	64
Netherlands	52
United Kingdom	46
Austria	45
Germany	43

Sign petitions

United States	58
Austria	34
Germany	31
United Kingdom	22
Netherlands	21

Percent

Initially, most states established taxpaying or property-holding requirements for voting, limiting political equality. Virginia, for example, required ownership of 25 acres of settled land or 500 acres of unsettled land. The original thirteen states began to lift these kinds of requirements after 1800. Expansion of the franchise accelerated after 1815, with the admission of new "western" states (Indiana, Illinois, Alabama), where land was more plentiful and widely owned. By the 1850s, virtually all taxpaying and property-holding requirements had been eliminated in all states, allowing the working class to vote—at least its white male members. Extending the vote to blacks and women took more time.

The enfranchisement of blacks. The Fifteenth Amendment to the Constitution, adopted in 1870, prohibited the states from denying the right to vote "on account of race, color, or previous condition of servi-

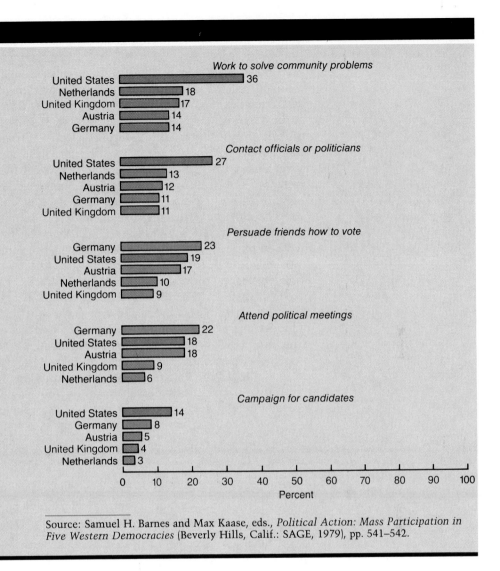

Work to solve community problems

United States	36
Netherlands	18
United Kingdom	17
Austria	14
Germany	14

Contact officials or politicians

United States	27
Netherlands	13
Austria	12
Germany	11
United Kingdom	11

Persuade friends how to vote

Germany	23
United States	19
Austria	17
Netherlands	10
United Kingdom	9

Attend political meetings

Germany	22
United States	18
Austria	18
United Kingdom	9
Netherlands	6

Campaign for candidates

United States	14
Germany	8
Austria	5
United Kingdom	4
Netherlands	3

Percent

Source: Samuel H. Barnes and Max Kaase, eds., *Political Action: Mass Participation in Five Western Democracies* (Beverly Hills, Calif.: SAGE, 1979), pp. 541–542.

tude." However, the southern states of the old Confederacy worked around the amendment by re-establishing restrictive requirements (poll taxes, literacy tests) that worked against blacks. Some southern states also cut blacks out of politics through a cunning circumvention of the amendment. The amendment said nothing about voting rights in private organizations, so blacks were denied the right to vote in the "private" Democratic *primary* elections held to choose the party's candidates for the general election. Because the Democratic party came to dominate politics in the South, the "white primary" effectively disenfranchised blacks despite the Fifteenth Amendment. Finally, in many areas of the South, the threat of violence kept blacks from the polls.

The extension of full voting rights to blacks came in two phases, separated by twenty years. In 1944, the Supreme Court decided in *Smith v. Allwright* that laws preventing blacks from voting in primary elections were unconstitutional, holding that party primaries are part of the continuous process of electing public officials.[27] The Voting Rights Act of 1965, which followed Selma's Bloody Sunday by less than five months, suspended discriminatory voting tests against blacks. The act also authorized federal registrars to register voters in seven southern states, where fewer than half of the voting-age population had registered to vote in the 1964 election. For good measure, in 1966 the Supreme Court ruled in *Harper* v. *Virginia State Board of Elections* that poll taxes are unconstitutional.[28] Although long in coming, these actions by the national government to enforce political equality within the states dramatically increased the registration of southern blacks (see Figure 7.2).

The enfranchisement of women. The enfranchisement of women in the United States is a less sordid story, but nothing to be proud of. Women had to fight long and hard to win the right to vote. Until 1869, women could not vote anywhere—in the United States or in the world.[29] Women began to organize to obtain suffrage in the mid-1800s. Known as *suffragettes,* these early feminists initially had a limited impact on politics. Their first victory did not come until 1869, when Wyoming, while still a territory, granted women the right to vote. No state followed suit until 1893, when Colorado enfranchised women.

In the meantime, the suffragettes became more active. In 1884, they formed the Equal Rights party and nominated Belva A. Lockwood, a lawyer who could not herself vote, as the first woman candidate for president.[30] Between 1896 and 1918, twelve other states gave women the

Figure 7.2

Voter Registration in the South, 1960, 1980, and 1984
As a result of the Voting Rights Act of 1965 and other federal actions, black voter registration nearly doubled between 1960 and 1980. Efforts to register more black voters in conjunction with Jesse Jackson's campaign for the presidential nomination in 1984 produced another increase. In the twenty-four year period, the percentage of white registered voters also increased, but not nearly as much. (Source: The 1984 data are from U.S. Bureau of the Census, Statistical Abstract of the United States, 1987 *[Washington, D.C.: U.S. Government Printing Office, 1987], p. 245; data for earlier years are from previous editions of the* Statistical Abstract.*)*

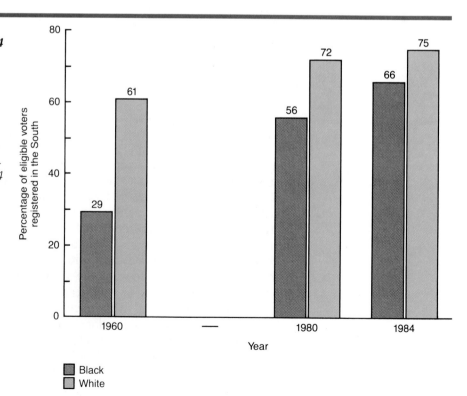

The Fights for Women's Suffrage . . . and Against It
Young people and minorities are not the only groups who have resorted to unconventional means of political participation. In the late 1800s and early 1900s, women marched and demonstrated for equal voting rights, sometimes encountering strong opposition. Their gatherings were occasionally disrupted by men—and other women—who opposed extending the right to vote to women.

vote. Most of these states were in the West, where pioneer women often departed from traditional women's roles. Nationally, the women's suffrage movement intensified, often resorting to unconventional political behaviors (marches, demonstrations), which occasionally invited violent attacks from men and even other women. In June 1919, Congress finally passed the Nineteenth Amendment to the Constitution, which prohibits states from denying the right to vote "on account of sex." The amendment was ratified in August 1920, in time for the November election.

Evaluating the expansion of suffrage in America. The last major expansion of suffrage in the United States took place in 1971, when the Twenty-sixth Amendment to the Constitution lowered the voting age to eighteen. For most of its history, then, the United States has been far from the democratic ideal of universal suffrage. Voting rights were initially restricted to white male taxpayers or property owners, and wealth requirements lasted until the 1850s. Through demonstrations and a constitutional amendment, women won the franchise less than seventy years ago. Through civil war, constitutional amendments, court actions, massive demonstrations, and congressional action, blacks finally achieved full voting rights slightly more than twenty years ago. Our record has more than a few blemishes.

But compared with other countries, the United States looks pretty democratic.[31] Women did not gain the vote on equal terms with men until 1921 in Norway; 1922 in the Netherlands; 1944 in France; 1946 in Italy, Japan, and Venezuela; 1948 in Belgium; and not until 1971 in Switzerland. It is difficult to compare the enfranchisement of minority racial groups because most other democratic nations do not have this kind of racial division. We should, however, note that the indigenous Maori population in New Zealand won suffrage in 1867, but the aborigines in Australia were not fully enfranchised until 1961. And, of course, in notoriously undemocratic South Africa, blacks have no voting rights at all—despite the fact that they outnumber whites by more than four to one. With regard to voting age, nineteen of twenty-seven countries that allow free elections also have a minimum voting age of eighteen (none has a lower age), and eight have higher age requirements.

When judged against the rest of the world, then, the United States—which launched mass participation in government through elections—has as good a record of providing for political equality in voting rights as other democracies, and a better record than many.

Voting on Policies

Disenfranchised groups have struggled to gain voting rights because of the political power that comes with suffrage. Belief in the ability of ordinary citizens to make political decisions and to control government through the power of the ballot box was strongest in the United States during the Progressive Era, which began around 1900 and lasted until about 1925. **Progressivism** was a philosophy of political reform that trusted the goodness and wisdom of individual citizens and distrusted "special interests" (railroads, corporations) and political institutions (traditional political parties, legislatures).

The leaders of the progressive movement were prominent politicians (former president Theodore Roosevelt, Senator Robert La Follette of Wisconsin) and eminent scholars (historian Frederick Jackson Turner, philosopher John Dewey). Not content to vote for candidates chosen by party leaders, the Progressives championed the **direct primary**—a preliminary election, run by the state government, in which the voters choose the party's candidates for the general election. Wanting a mechanism to remove elected candidates from office, the Progressives backed the **recall**—a special election initiated by petition signed by a specified number of voters.

Progressives also relied on the voting power of the masses to propose and pass laws, thus approximating direct democracy—citizen participation in policymaking. They developed two voting mechanisms for policymaking that are still in use:

- A **referendum** is a direct vote by the people either on a proposed law or on an amendment to the state constitution. The issues subject to vote are known as **propositions.** Twenty-nine states permit popular referenda on laws, and all but Delaware require a referendum on constitutional amendments.

- The **initiative** is a procedure by which voters can propose an issue to be decided by the legislature or by the people in a referendum. The procedure involves gathering a specified number of signatures from registered voters (usually 5 to 10 percent of the total in the state), then submitting the petition to a designated state agency. About twenty states currently provide for some form of voter initiative.

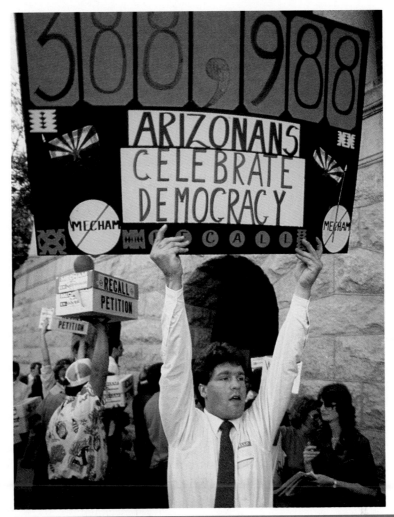

Unelecting a Governor
In January 1988, Arizona citizens collected enough signatures on petitions to schedule a May election to recall Governor Evan Mecham. Among their complaints were Mecham's insensitive ethnic remarks and actions, including canceling a state holiday honoring Dr. Martin Luther King, Jr. Mecham was also indicted on (though later cleared of) criminal charges in connection with a campaign loan. In April, the state senate convicted him on two charges of official misconduct, and he was removed from office—eliminating a need for the recall election.

There is no provision for either the initiative or the referendum at the national level, but both are widely used in many states. State legislatures in North Dakota and Oregon each voted on over 125 statutes initiated by citizens between 1898 and 1979. Nationwide, 754 citizen-initiated statutes were put to a vote during this period, and 38 percent were adopted.[32] Many more propositions are put to statewide popular vote. One scholar estimates that there have been more than 17,000 referenda since 1898, over 2,300 between 1968 and 1978 alone.[33] In fact, use of the initiative and referendum to propose and approve legislation is increasing.

The referendum and initiative are tools that allow citizens to participate directly in lawmaking. At times, the laws they propose and approve are strongly opposed by politicians. A prominent example is Proposition 13, a proposal submitted to California's voters in 1978. The law was designed to cut property taxes and drastically reduce government expenditures. Proposition 13 was opposed by most of the state's political, business, educational, communications, and labor leaders, and was heavily attacked in the media. But the voters passed it by a landslide margin, 65 percent to 35 percent.

A referendum can also work to the advantage of politicians, freeing them from taking sides on a hot issue. Pornography is a hot issue concerning social order, and the citizens of Maine had their say on controlling pornography in a referendum on June 10, 1986. The question on the ballot read: "Do you want to make it a crime to make, sell, give for value or otherwise promote obscene material in Maine?" It was proposed by the Maine Christian Civic League and backed by the Concerned Citizens for Decency, who sponsored television advertisements in which an expert put the blame for child abuse on pornography. The proposition was opposed by the American Civil Liberties Union (ACLU), feminists, and librarians. These groups sponsored television spots showing a leather-jacketed policeman supervising a book burning. In the flames were copies of *The Grapes of Wrath*, *The Color Purple*, and *The American Heritage Dictionary*. The proposition was defeated by a vote that ran about 2 to 1.[34]

What conclusion can we draw about the Progressives' legacy of mechanisms for direct participation in government? One scholar who studied the use of the initiative and referendum paints an unimpressive picture. He notes that in the 1980s an expensive "industry" has developed that makes money circulating petitions, then managing the large sums of money needed to run a campaign to approve (or defeat) a referendum.[35] The money required to mount a statewide campaign has involved special interest groups in referendum politics, not eliminated them. Not only is turnout usually lower in referenda than in other elections, but most voters confess they do not know enough about most ballot propositions to vote intelligently on them. The author concludes:

> The expectations of the proponents of direct legislation that voters would read and study ballot propositions and then cast informed ballots have been substantially disproven. Voters are not better informed about propositions than they are about candidates. In fact, on most propositions, voters have not heard much prior to entering the voting booth. When voting for candidates, voters can at least utilize the party label if they possess no other information. Typically, however, voters do know something about state candidates and many know something about their issue positions.[36]

It is clear that citizens can exercise great power over government policy through the mechanisms of the initiative and referendum. What is not clear is whether these forms such direct democracy improve on the policies made by representatives elected for that purpose.

Voting for Candidates

We have saved for last the most visible form of political participation: voting to choose candidates for public office. Voting for candidates serves democratic government in two ways. First, it allows citizens to choose the candidates they think will best serve their interests. If citizens choose candidates "like themselves" in personal traits or party affiliation, elected officials should tend to be like-minded on political issues. (Of course, if public officials really thought like most of the voters, they would automatically reflect the majority's views when making public policy. And the majority would not have to worry about monitoring the behavior of public officials and directing their policymaking.)

Second, voting allows the people to re-elect the officials they guessed right about and to kick out those they guessed wrong about. This is a very different function from the first. It makes public officials *accountable* for their behavior through the reward-and-punishment mechanism of elections. It assumes that officeholders are motivated to respond to public opinion by the threat of electoral defeat. It also assumes that the voters (1) know what politicians are doing while they are in office and (2) participate actively in the electoral process. We look at the factors that underlie voting choice in the next chapter. Here, we examine Americans' reliance on the electoral process.

In national politics, voters are content to elect just two executive officers—the president and vice president—and to trust the president to appoint a cabinet to round out his administration. But at the state and local levels, voters insist on selecting all kinds of officials. Every state elects a governor (and forty-two of them elect a lieutenant governor too). And forty-three elect an attorney general; thirty-eight, a treasurer; thirty-six, a secretary of state; twenty-five, an auditor. The list goes on, down through the superintendent of education, secretary of agriculture, controller, board of education, and public utilities commissioners.[37] Elected county officials commonly include a sheriff, a treasurer, a clerk, a superintendent of schools, and a judge (often several). Even at the local level, all but about 600 of 15,300 school boards across the nation are elected.[38] Instead of trusting state and local chief executives to appoint lesser administrators (as we do for more important offices at the national level), we expect voters to choose intelligently among scores of candidates they meet for the first time on a complex ballot in the polling booth.

Americans seem to believe that there is no limit to voters' ability to make informed choices among candidates and thus to control government. Their reasoning seems to be that elections are good; therefore, more elections are better, and the most elections are best. By this thinking, the United States clearly has the best and most democratic government in the world because it is the undisputed world champion at holding elections. The author of a study that compared elections in the United States with elections in twenty-six other democracies concluded:

No country can approach the United States in the frequency and variety of elections, and thus in the amount of electoral participation to which its citizens have a right. No other country elects its lower house as often as every two years, or its president as frequently as every four years. No other country popularly elects its state governors *and* town mayors; no other has as wide a variety of nonrepresentative offices (judges, sheriffs, attorneys general, city treasurers, and so on) subject to election. . . . The average American is entitled to do far more electing—probably by a factor of three or four—than the citizen of any other democracy.[39]

COMPARED WITH WHAT? 7.2

Voter Turnout in Democratic Nations

Americans participate as much as or more than citizens of other nations in all forms of political behavior—except voting. Voter turnout in American presidential elections ranks at the bottom of voting rates for twenty-seven countries with competitive elections. As discussed in the text, the facts are correct, but the comparison is not as damning as it appears.

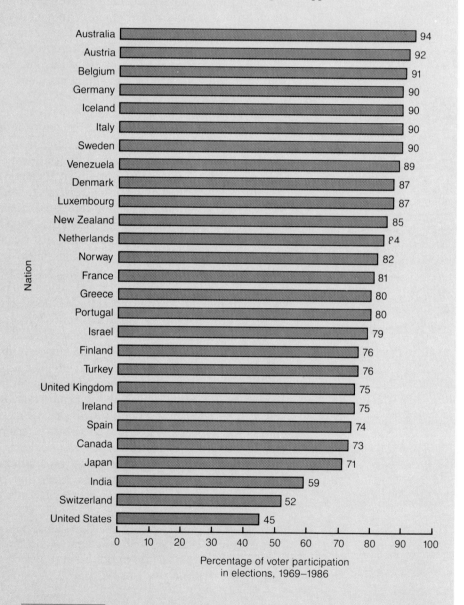

Nation	Percentage
Australia	94
Austria	92
Belgium	91
Germany	90
Iceland	90
Italy	90
Sweden	90
Venezuela	89
Denmark	87
Luxembourg	87
New Zealand	85
Netherlands	84
Norway	82
France	81
Greece	80
Portugal	80
Israel	79
Finland	76
Turkey	76
United Kingdom	75
Ireland	75
Spain	74
Canada	73
Japan	71
India	59
Switzerland	52
United States	45

Percentage of voter participation
in elections, 1969–1986

Source: Congressional Research Service, "Voter Participation Statistics from Recent Elections in Selected Countries" (Report to Congressman Mario Biaggi, 18 November 1987).

However, we learn from Compared With What? 7.2 that the United States ranks at the bottom of twenty-seven countries in voter turnout! How do we square low voter turnout with Americans' devotion to elections as an instrument of democratic government? To complicate matters further, how do we square low voter turnout with the findings we talked about earlier, which establish the United States as the leader among five Western democratic nations in both conventional and unconventional political participation? Americans seem to participate at high levels in everything except elections.

EXPLAINING POLITICAL PARTICIPATION

As you have seen, political participation can be unconventional or conventional, can require little or much initiative, and can serve to support the government or influence its decisions. Researchers have found that people who take part in some form of political behavior often do not take part in others. For example, the same citizens who contact public officials to obtain special benefits may not vote regularly, participate in campaigns, or even contact officials about broader social issues. In fact, "particularized contacting" stands by itself as a form of participation. Because this sort of participation serves individual rather than public interests, it is not even considered *political* behavior by some people.

In this section, we examine some factors that affect the more obvious forms of political participation, with particular emphasis on voting. Our first task is to determine how much variation there is in patterns of participation within the United States over time.

Patterns of Participation over Time

Have Americans become more politically apathetic in the 1980s than they were in the 1960s? The answer lies in Figure 7.3, which plots several measures of participation from 1952 through 1984. The graph shows a mixed pattern of participation over the thirty-two years. Participation was *stable* across time in the percentage of citizens who worked for candidates (3 to 6 percent) or who attended party meetings (6 to 9 percent) during presidential election years. Participation *increased* across time by 8 to 10 percentage points on two other indicators: interest in campaigns and persuading people how to vote. Participation *decreased* over time when measured as voter turnout in presidential elections (dropping from 63 to 52 percent). The plot has thickened. Not only is voter turnout low in the United States compared with that in other countries, but turnout has declined over time. Moreover, while voting has decreased, other forms of participation have increased. What is going on? Who votes? Who doesn't? Why? And does it really matter?

The Standard Socioeconomic Explanation

Researchers have found that socioeconomic status is a good indicator of most types of conventional political participation. People with more

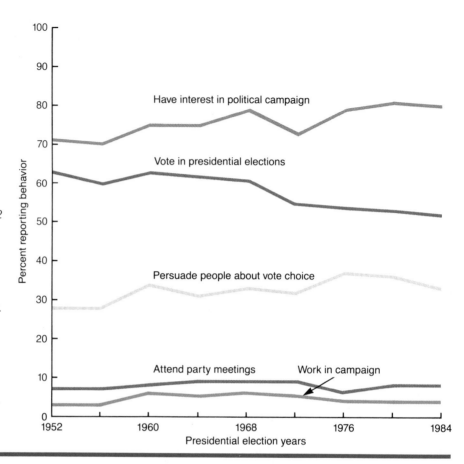

Electoral Participation in the United States over Time

Participation patterns over three decades show that Americans participate about as much or more in election campaigns in the 1980s as in the 1950s on every indicator except voting turnout. The turnout rate dropped more than ten percentage points from 1952 to 1984. The drop in turnout compared with the other indicators also runs counter to the rise in educational level, constituting a puzzle that is discussed in the text. (Source: Warren E. Miller, Arthur H. Miller, and Edward J. Schneider, American National Election Studies Data Sourcebook, 1952–1978 *[Cambridge Mass.: Harvard University Press, 1980]. Data after 1978 came from the National Election Studies distributed by the Inter-University Consortium for Political and Social Research.)*

Figure 7.3

education, higher incomes, and white-collar or professional occupations tend to be more aware of the impact of politics on their lives, to know what can be done to influence government actions, and to have the necessary resources (time, money) to take action. So they are more likely to participate in politics than are people of lower socioeconomic status. This relationship between socioeconomic status and conventional political involvement is called the **standard socioeconomic model** of participation.[40]

Unconventional political behavior is less clearly related to socioeconomic status. Studies of unconventional participation in other countries have found that protest behavior is related to low socioeconomic status and especially to youth.[41] However, scattered studies of unconventional participation in the United States have found that protesters (especially blacks) are often higher in socioeconomic status than those who do not join in protests.[42]

Obviously, socioeconomic status does not account for all the differences in the ways people choose to participate in politics, even for conventional participation. Another important variable is age. As we noted above, young people are more likely to take part in political protests, but they are less likely to participate in conventional politics. Voting rates tend to increase as people grow older until about age sixty-five, when physical infirmities begin to lower voting rates again.[43]

Two other variables—race and sex—have been related to participation in the past, but as times have changed, so have those relationships. Blacks, who had very low participation rates in the 1950s, now participate at rates comparable to whites, when differences in socioeconomic status are taken into account.[44] Women also exhibited low participation rates in the past, but sex differences in political participation have virtually disappeared.[45] (The one exception is in attempting to persuade others how to vote, which women are less likely to do than men.)[46]

Of all social and economic variables, education is the strongest single factor in explaining most types of conventional political participation. The striking relationship between level of formal education and various types of conventional political behaviors is shown in Figure 7.4. This strong link between education and electoral participation raises questions about low voter turnout in the United States both over time and relative to other democracies. The fact is that the proportion of individuals with college degrees is greater in the United States than in other countries. Moreover, that proportion has been increasing steadily. Why,

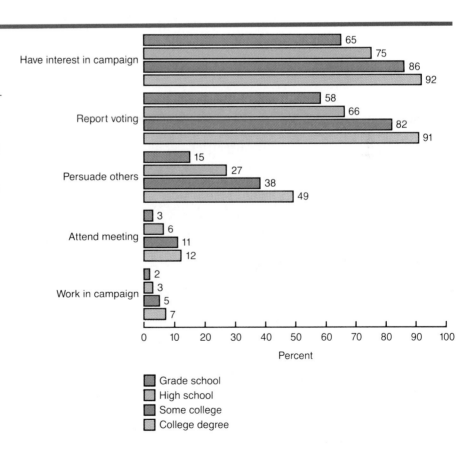

Figure 7.4

Effects of Education on Political Participation in 1984

Education has a powerful effect on political participation in the United States. These data for a 1984 sample show that level of education is directly related to five different forms of conventional political participation. (Source: This analysis was based on the 1984 National Election Study distributed by the Inter-University Consortium for Political and Social Research.)

then, is voter turnout in elections so low? And why is it dropping over time?

Low Voter Turnout in America

Voting is a low-initiative form of participation that can satisfy all three motives for political participation—showing allegiance to the nation, obtaining particularized benefits, and influencing broad policy. Yet voter turnout in the United States has steadily dropped since 1960, while other forms of participation have increased. And, although Americans participate as much or more than citizens of other countries in conventional and unconventional political behaviors, they rank well below citizens of other countries in voter turnout. How do we explain the decline in voting within the United States over time and the low voter turnout in this country?

The decline in voting over time.   The graph of voter turnout (Figure 7.3) shows that the sharpest drop (6 percentage points) occurred between the 1968 and 1972 elections. It was during this period (in 1971, actually) that Congress proposed and the states ratified the Twenty-sixth Amendment to the Constitution, which expanded the electorate by lowering the voting age from twenty-one to eighteen. Because people under twenty-one are much less likely to vote, they actually reduced the overall national turnout rate (the percentage of those eligible to vote who actually vote). Some observers estimate that the enfranchisement of eighteen-year-olds accounts for about 1 or 2 percentage points in the total decline in turnout since 1952.[47]

Researchers attribute most of the decline in turnout to changes in voters' convictions about and attitudes toward politics. One major factor is the growing belief that government is not responsive to citizens and that voting doesn't do any good. Another is a change in attitude toward political parties, along with a decline in the sense of party identification.[48] According to these psychological explanations, voting turnout in the United States is not likely to increase until the government does something to restore people's faith in the effectiveness of voting—with or without political parties. According to the age explanation, turnout in the United States is destined to remain a percentage point or two below its highs in the 1960s because of the lower voting rate of citizens under twenty-one.

U.S. turnout versus turnout in other countries.   Given the high level of education in the United States and our greater than usual participation in other forms of political activity, voter turnout is much lower than might be expected compared with that in other countries. Scholars cite two factors to explain the low percentage of voters in the United States. First, there are differences in voting laws and administrative machinery. In a few countries, voting is compulsory, and, obviously, turnout is extremely high. But there are other ways to encourage voting—declaring election days to be public holidays, providing a two-day voting period, making it easy to cast absentee ballots. The United States does none of these things. Moreover, nearly every other democratic country places the burden of registration on the government rather than on the individual voter.

This is very important. Voting in the United States is a two-stage process, and the first stage—going to the proper officials to register—requires more initiative than the second stage—going to the polling booth to cast a ballot. In most American states, the registration process is separated from the voting process by both time (usually weeks in advance of the election) and geography (often at the county courthouse, not the polling place). Moreover, registration procedures are often obscure and require calling around to find out what to do. Furthermore, people who move (and roughly one-third of the U.S. population moves between national elections) must reregister. In short, although voting requires little initiative, registration usually requires high initiative. If we compute voter turnout on the basis of those who are registered to vote, then about 87 percent of Americans vote—a figure that moves the United States to the middle (but not the top) of all democratic nations.[49]

The second factor usually cited to explain low turnout in American elections is the lack of political parties that mobilize the vote of particular social groups, especially lower-class and less-educated people. American parties do make an effort to get out the vote, but neither party is as closely linked to specific groups as parties are in many other countries, where certain parties work hand in hand with ethnic, occupational, or religious groups. Research shows that strong party-group links can significantly increase turnout.[50]

To these explanations for low voter turnout in the United States—the burden of registration and the lack of strong party-group links—we add another. Although the act of voting requires low initiative, the process of learning about the scores of candidates on the ballot in American elections requires a great deal of initiative. Some people undoubtedly fail to vote simply because they feel inadequate to the task of deciding among candidates for the many offices on the ballot in U.S. elections.

Teachers, newspaper columnists, and public affairs groups tend to worry a great deal about low voter turnout in the United States, suggesting that it signifies some sort of political sickness—or at least that it gives us a bad mark for democracy. Some others who study elections closely seem less concerned. Voter turnout is only one indicator of political participation, and Americans tend to do better according to most other indicators. Moreover, one scholar argues:

> Turnout rates do not indicate the amount of electing—the frequency of occasion, the range of offices and decisions, the "value" of the vote—to which a country's citizens are entitled. . . . Thus, although the turnout rate in the United States is below that of most other democracies, American citizens do not necessarily do less voting than other citizens; most probably, they do more.[51]

Despite these words of assurance, the nagging thought remains that turnout ought to be higher, so various organizations mount "get-out-the-vote" campaigns before elections. Civic leaders often back these campaigns because they value voting for its contribution to political order.

PARTICIPATION AND FREEDOM, EQUALITY, AND ORDER

As you have seen, Americans do participate in government in a variety of ways and to a reasonable extent, compared with citizens of other countries. What is the relationship of political participation to the values of freedom, equality, and order?

Participation and Freedom

From the standpoint of normative theory, the relationship between participation and freedom is clear. Individuals should be free to participate in government and politics the way they want and as much as they want. And they should be free *not* to participate as well. Ideally, all barriers to participation (such as restrictive voting registration and limitations on campaign expenditures) should be abolished—as should any schemes for compulsory voting. According to the normative perspective, we should not worry about low voter turnout because citizens should have the freedom not to vote as well as to vote.

Bullets Defeat Ballots
For decades, the Caribbean nation Haiti was ruled dictatorially by "Papa Doc" Duvalier, who amassed vast wealth in the pitifully poor country. His son and successor—"Baby Doc"—was forced to flee Haiti in 1986, and its people hoped for free elections and democratic government. However, military leaders aborted the first election in November 1987 by shooting voters and attacking election offices like this one. A sham election supervised by the military was held in January 1988. By June, General Henri Namphy had deposed the new president, ending Haiti's experiment with democracy. In September, Namphy was himself deposed.

America's Largest Civil Rights Demonstration
On August 28, 1963, more than 200,000 blacks and whites participated in a Freedom March on Washington, D.C. Martin Luther King, Jr., one of the march's leaders, delivered his electrifying "I Have a Dream" speech from the steps of the Lincoln Memorial. The demonstrators pressed for legislation ensuring full civil rights for blacks, and their leaders were welcomed at the White House by President John F. Kennedy.

In theory, freedom to participate also means that individuals should be able to use their wealth, connections, knowledge, organizational power (including sheer numbers in organized protests), or any other resource to influence government decisions, provided they do so legitimately. Of all these resources, the individual vote may be the weakest—and the least important—means of exerting political influence. Obviously, then, freedom as a value in political participation favors those with the resources to advance their own political self-interest.

Participation and Equality

The relationship between participation and equality is also clear. Each citizen's ability to influence government should be equal to that of every other citizen, so that differences in personal resources do not work against the poor or otherwise disadvantaged. Elections, then, serve the ideal of equality better than any other means of political participation. Formal rules for counting ballots—in particular, one person, one vote—negate differences in resources among individuals.

At the same time, groups of people who have few individual resources can combine their votes to wield political power. This power was exercised in the late nineteenth and early twentieth century by various European ethnic groups whose votes won them entry into the sociopolitical system and allowed them to share in its benefits (see

Chapter 5). More recently, blacks, Hispanics, homosexuals, and the handicapped have used their voting power to gain political recognition. However, minorities often have had to use unconventional forms of participation to win the right to vote. As two major scholars of political
participation put it, "Protest is the great equalizer, the political action
that weights intensity as well as sheer numbers."[52]

Participation and Order

The relationship between participation and order is complicated.
Some types of participation promote order and so are encouraged by
those who value order; other types promote disorder and so are discouraged. Even giving women the right to vote was resisted by many citizens
(men and women alike) for fear of upsetting the social order, of altering
the traditional roles of men and women.

Both conventional and unconventional participation can lead to the
ouster of government officials, but the *regime*—the political system itself—is threatened more by unconventional participation. To maintain
order, the government has a stake in converting unconventional participation to conventional participation whenever possible. We can easily
imagine this tactic being used by authoritarian governments, but it is
used by democratic governments as well.

Think about the student unrest on college campuses during the
Vietnam War. In private and public colleges alike, thousands of students
stopped traffic, occupied buildings, destroyed property, struck classes,
disrupted lectures, staged guerrilla theater, and behaved in other unconventional ways while protesting the war, racism, capitalism, their college
presidents, the president of the United States, the military establishment,
and all other institutions. (We are not exaggerating here. For example,
students did all these things at Northwestern University in Evanston,
Illinois, after four students were killed by National Guardsmen in a
demonstration at Kent State University in Ohio on May 4, 1970.)

Confronted by civil strife and disorder in the nation's institutions of
higher learning, Congress took action. On March 23, 1971, it passed and
sent to the states the proposed Twenty-sixth Amendment, lowering the
voting age to eighteen. Three-quarters of the state legislatures had to
ratify the amendment before it became part of the Constitution. Aston-
ishingly, thirty-eight states (the required number) complied by July 1,
establishing a new record for speedy ratification, cutting the old record
nearly in half.[53] (Ironically, voting rights were about the only thing that
students were not demanding.)

Testimony by members of Congress before the Judiciary Committee
stated that the eighteen-year-old vote was needed to "harness the energy
of young people and direct it into useful and constructive channels," to
keep students from becoming "more militant" and engaging "in destructive activities of a dangerous nature."[54] As one observer argued, the right
to vote was not extended to eighteen-year-olds because young people
demanded it, but because "public officials believed suffrage expansion to
be a means of institutionalizing youths' participation in politics, which
would, in turn, curb disorder."[55]

PARTICIPATION AND THE MODELS OF DEMOCRACY

Ostensibly, elections are institutional mechanisms that implement democracy by allowing citizens to choose among candidates or issues. But elections also serve several other important purposes:[56]

- *Elections socialize political activity.* They transform what might otherwise consist of sporadic citizen-initiated acts into a routine public function. That is, the opportunity to vote for change encourages citizens to refrain from demonstrating in the streets. This helps preserve government stability by containing and channeling away potentially disruptive or dangerous forms of mass political activity.

- *Elections institutionalize access to political power.* They allow ordinary citizens to run for political office or to play an important role in selecting political leaders. Working to elect a candidate encourages the campaign worker to identify problems or propose solutions to the new official.

- *Elections bolster the state's power and authority.* The opportunity to participate in elections helps convince citizens that the government is responsive to their needs and wants, which increases its legitimacy.

Participation and Majoritarianism

Although the majoritarian model assumes that government responsiveness to popular demands comes through mass participation in politics, majoritarianism does not view participation broadly. It favors conventional, institutionalized behavior of a narrow form—primarily, voting in elections. Because majoritarianism relies on counting votes to determine what the majority wants, it is strongly biased toward political equality of citizens in political participation. Favoring collective decisions formalized through elections, majoritarianism offers little opportunity for motivated resourceful individuals to exercise private influence over government actions.

Majoritarianism also reduces individual freedom in another way. By focusing on voting as the major means of mass participation, it narrows the scope of conventional political behavior. In this way, the mechanisms for participation in the majoritarian model restrict freedom by defining what political action is "orderly" and acceptable. By favoring equality and order in political participation, majoritarianism goes hand in hand with the ideological orientation of populists (see Chapter 1).

Participation and Pluralism

Resourceful citizens who want the government's help with problems find a haven in the pluralist model of democracy. A decentralized and organizationally complex form of government allows many points of access and is well suited to various forms of conventional participation aside from voting. For example, wealthy people and well-funded groups can afford to hire lobbyists to press their interests in Congress. In one view of pluralist democracy, citizens are free to ply and wheedle public officials to further selfish visions of the public good. From another viewpoint, pluralism offers citizens the opportunity to be treated as individuals when dealing with the government, to influence policymaking in special circumstances, and to fulfill (insofar as is possible in representative government) their social potential through participation in community affairs.

SUMMARY

To have "government by the people," the people must participate in politics. Conventional forms of participation—contacting officials and voting in elections—come most quickly to mind. However, citizens can also participate in politics in unconventional ways—staging sit-down strikes in public buildings, blocking traffic, and so on. Most citizens disapprove of most forms of unconventional political behavior. Yet, unconventional tactics have won blacks and women important political and legal rights, including the right to vote.

People are motivated to participate in politics for various reasons: to show support for their country, to obtain particularized benefits for themselves or their friends, or to influence broad public policy. Their political actions may demand very little political knowledge or personal initiative, or a great deal of both.

The press often paints an unflattering picture of political participation in America. Clearly, the proportion of the electorate that votes in general elections in the United States is dropping and is far below that in other nations. When compared with other nations on a broad range of conventional and unconventional political behavior, however, the United States tends to show as much or more citizen participation in politics. Voter turnout in the United States suffers by comparison with that in other nations, because of differences in voter registration here and elsewhere. We also lack institutions (especially strong political parties) that increase voter registration and help bring those of lower socioeconomic status to the polls.

The tendency to participate in politics is strongly related to socioeconomic status. Education, one component of socioeconomic status, is the single strongest predictor of conventional political participation in the United States. Because of the strong effect of socioeconomic status on political participation, the political system is potentially biased toward the interests of higher-status people. Pluralist democracy, which provides many avenues for resourceful citizens to influence government decisions, tends to increase this potential bias.

Majoritarian democracy, which relies heavily on elections and the concept of one person, one vote, offers citizens without great personal resources the opportunity to control government decisions through elections. However, elections also serve to legitimize government simply by involving the masses in government through voting. Whether or not the vote means anything depends on the nature of the voters' choices in elections. The range of choice is a function of the nation's political parties, the topic of the next chapter.

Key Terms

election	suffrage
political participation	franchise
conventional	progressivism
participation	direct primary
unconventional	recall
participation	referendum
direct action	proposition
supportive behavior	initiative
influencing behavior	standard socioeconomic
class-action suit	model
voting	

Selected Readings

Barnes, Samuel H., and Max Kaase, eds. *Political Action: Mass Participation in Five Western Democracies*. Beverly Hills, Calif.: SAGE, 1979. The most important comparative study of both conventional and unconventional political participation.

Cloward, Richard, and Frances Fox Piven. *Why Americans Don't Vote*. New York: Pantheon, 1988. An in-depth analysis of voting and registration regulations that exclude citizens from voting.

Conway, M. Margaret. *Political Participation in the United States*. Washington, D.C.: Congressional Quarterly Press, 1985. Conway provides the best review of survey data on conventional political participation.

Dalton, Russell J. *Citizen Politics in Western Democracies*. Chatham, N.J.: Chatham House, 1988. Studies public opinion and behavior in the United States, Britain, Germany, and France. Two chapters compare conventional citizen action and protest politics in these countries.

Ginsberg, Benjamin, and Alan Stone, eds. *Do Elections Matter?* Armonk, N.Y.: Sharpe, 1986. A collection of studies on the political consequences of elections, with special reference to the 1984 presidential election.

LeMay, Michael C. *The Struggle for Influence: The Impact of Minority Groups on Politics and Public Policy in the United States*. Lanham, Md.: University Press of America, 1985. The subtitle describes it well; the book discusses women and religious groups as well as virtually all racial and European ethnic groups.

Sharp, Elaine B. *Citizen Demand-Making in the Urban Context*. University, Ala.: University of Alabama Press, 1986. The author interviewed thousands of residents of Kansas City, Missouri, about their contacts with local government.

Teixeira, Ruy A. *Why Americans Don't Vote: Turnout Decline in the United States 1960–1984*. New York: Greenwood Press, 1987. A quantitative study of the demographic and political factors that explain voter turnout.

Verba, Sidney, and Norman H. Nie. *Participation in America: Political Democracy and Social Equality*. New York: Harper & Row, 1972. An analysis of data from surveys of citizens and political leaders; one of the classic studies of political participation.

Zimmerman, Joseph F. *Participatory Democracy: Populism Revived*. New York: Praeger, 1986. A comprehensive review of the town meeting and the mechanisms (referendum, initiative, recall) that approximate direct democracy.

8

Political Parties, Campaigns, and Elections

Phil Gramm, formerly an economics professor at Texas A&M University, was first elected to Congress in 1978 as a Democrat from Texas's Sixth District. His constituents, who lived in fourteen counties between suburban Dallas and suburban Houston, were basically conservative. That suited Gramm, himself a staunch conservative, who found most of his Democratic colleagues in Congress too liberal. He was re-elected in 1980, the same year that Ronald Reagan was first elected president. Although Reagan was a Republican, he was Gramm's kind of president: anxious to cut back on social spending and eager to increase military spending. Gramm could work with Reagan.

In 1981, Gramm won a seat on the House Budget Committee, an important committee that reviews the president's budget and prepares a version acceptable to the House. Gramm found his Democratic colleagues on the committee too willing to spend government money for social programs. He much preferred Reagan's cost-cutting, tax-cutting approach. Gramm quietly began to meet with Reagan's director of the Office of Management and Budget (OMB), David A. Stockman, to reveal the Democrats' plans and to devise an alternative budget for 1982. When word of the Gramm-Stockman connection leaked out, several Democratic members of the Budget Committee objected to Gramm's participation in their meetings. The chairman of the House Democratic Caucus described Gramm as "the fox in the hen house."[1]

By spring 1981, Gramm stopped meeting with the Democrats and began to meet with the Republicans on the Budget Committee. He even cosponsored (with its leading Republican) the key amendment to the budget resolution that substituted Reagan's economic blueprint for the one backed by the Democrats. Reagan's 1981 income tax cut, his cuts in domestic spending, and his increases in military spending owed much to Phil Gramm, a Democrat from Texas—to the dismay of the House Democratic leadership.

The Democratic voters in Texas were not dismayed, however, and re-elected Gramm to the House in 1982. The Democratic leaders got their chance to even the score with Gramm in early 1983, when the committees were reorganized for the new Congress. Because party organization is so weak in Congress, party leaders rarely try to discipline members for cooperating with the opposition; too many members would have to be punished, and the party has few available ways to discipline them. But Gramm, by betraying the trust of his colleagues, had gone too far. He was denied reappointment to the Budget Committee on January 3. Two days later, Gramm quit the Democratic party, resigned his newly won seat, and announced that he would run for re-election in the same district as a Republican.

A special election was called on February 12 in the Sixth District of Texas, traditionally a Democratic stronghold. Running as the sole Republican, Gramm faced nine Democratic challengers and a stray Libertarian. He defeated all ten opponents, winning the election with 55 percent of the vote. Whatever he had done in Congress, the voters approved and sent him back to do more of it. Not only did a triumphant Gramm return to Congress as a Republican, but the Republican party promptly rewarded him by appointing him to one of its seats on the Budget Committee! Two years later, Gramm's fame had outgrown his congressional district, and he ran for the U.S. Senate. He won easily and took his seat in 1985 as a Republican senator from the state of Texas. At the 1988 Republican National Convention, Gramm delivered the speech that nominated George Bush for president.

Phil Gramm's story is not a common one, but it illustrates some basic facts about the peculiar nature of American political parties. Each party has an ideological center of gravity, but each has supporters of varying political persuasions. Party preference is important in elections, but its influence can be overcome. In short, parties are important in American politics, but they are not all-powerful. Why do we have political parties? What functions do they perform? Are parties really necessary for democratic government? Or do they just interfere in the relationship between citizens and government? In this chapter, we answer these questions with an examination of political parties, perhaps the most misunderstood element in American politics.

POLITICAL PARTIES AND THEIR FUNCTIONS

According to democratic theory, the primary means by which citizens control their government is voting in free elections. Most Americans agree that voting is important: Of those surveyed after a recent presidential campaign, 86 percent felt that elections made the government "pay attention to what the people think."[2] However, Americans are not nearly as supportive of the role played by political parties in elections. An overwhelming majority (73 percent) surveyed in 1980 believed that "the best way to vote is to pick a candidate regardless of party label." A clear majority (56 percent) thought that "parties do more to confuse the issues than to provide a clear choice on issues." In fact, almost half (49 percent) took the extreme position: "It would be better if in all elections, we put no party labels on the ballot."[3]

On the other hand, Americans are quick to condemn as "undemocratic" countries that do not hold elections contested by political parties. In truth, Americans have a love-hate relationship with political parties. They believe that parties are necessary for democratic government; at the same time, they think parties are somehow "obstructionist" and not to be trusted. This distrust is particularly strong among younger voters. To better appreciate the role of political parties in democratic government, we must understand exactly what parties are and what they do.

Definitions

A **political party** is an organization that sponsors candidates for political office *under the organization's name*. The italicized part of this definition is important. True political parties **nominate** candidates for election to public office, by designating individuals as official candidates of the party. This function distinguishes the Democratic and Republican parties from interest groups. The AFL-CIO and the National Association of Manufacturers are interest groups. They often support candidates in various ways, but they do not nominate them to run as their avowed representatives. If they do, the interest groups become transformed into political parties. In short, it is the giving and accepting of a political label by organization and candidate that defines an organization as a party.

Most democratic theorists agree that a modern nation-state could not practice democracy without at least two political parties that regularly contest elections. (All nineteen countries rated democracies in Chapter 2 have at least two competing parties.) In fact, the link between democracy and political parties is so close that many people define democratic government in terms of competitive party politics.

Party Functions

Parties contribute to democratic government through the functions they perform for the **political system**—the set of interrelated institutions that links people with government. We look at four of the most important functions: nominating candidates for election to public office; structuring the voting choice in elections; proposing alternative government programs; and coordinating the actions of government officials.

Nominating candidates.   Political parties contribute to democratic government simply by nominating candidates for election to public office. In the absence of parties, voters would be confronted with a bewildering array of self-nominated candidates, each seeking a narrow victory over others on the basis of personal friendships, celebrity status, or name. Parties provide a form of quality control for their nominees through the

Eleanor Gives Her Blessing to the 1960 Democratic Ticket
The band was playing the Democrats' theme song, "Happy Days Are Here Again!" as John Kennedy, Eleanor Roosevelt, and Lyndon Johnson appeared at a rally in the New York Coliseum just before the 1960 presidential election. Eleanor Roosevelt, a party leader in her own right, was the wife of President Franklin Roosevelt, who forged the coalition of Northern urban workers, Southerners, Catholics, Jews, and white ethnic minorities that allowed the Democrats to replace the Republicans as the majority party in America.

process of *peer review*. Party insiders, the nominees' peers, usually know potential candidates much better than the average voter does, and candidates are judged by their peers for acceptability as the party's representatives.

In nominating candidates, parties often do more than pass judgment on potential office seekers; sometimes they go so far as to recruit talented individuals to become party candidates. In this way, parties help, not only to ensure a minimum level of quality among candidates who run for office, but also to raise the quality of those candidates.

Structuring the voting choice. Political parties also help democratic government by structuring the voting choice—reducing the number of candidates on the ballot to those who have a realistic chance of winning. Established parties—those that have contested elections in the past—acquire a following of loyal voters who guarantee the party's candidates a predictable base of votes. Parties that have won sizable portions of the vote in past elections are likely to win comparable portions of the vote in future ones. This has the effect of discouraging nonparty candidates from running for office, and new parties from forming. Consequently, the realistic choice is between candidates offered by the major parties. This focuses the election on the contest between parties and on candidates with established records, which reduces the amount of new information that voters need in order to make a rational decision.

Proposing alternative government programs. Parties also help voters choose candidates by proposing alternative programs of government action—general policies that party candidates will pursue if they win control of government. Even if voters know nothing about the qualities of the parties' candidates, they can vote rationally for candidates of the party that stands closest to the policies they favor. The specific policies advocated in an election campaign vary from candidate to candidate and from election to election. However, the types of policies advocated by candidates of one party tend to differ from those proposed by candidates of other parties. Although there are exceptions, candidates of the same party tend to favor policies that fit their party's underlying political philosophy, or ideology. In many countries, party labels reflect political stance (see Compared With What? 8.1).

Although the two major American parties have issue-neutral names, many minor parties in the United States have used their names to advertise their policies: the Prohibition party, the Farmer-Labor party, the Socialist party, for example. The neutrality of the names *Democratic* and *Republican* suggests that our parties are also undifferentiated in their policies. This is not true. The two major parties regularly adopt very different policies in their platforms, a fact we discuss at length later.

Coordinating the actions of government officials. Finally, parties help coordinate the actions of public officials. A government based on the separation of powers, like that of the United States, divides responsibilities for making public policy. The president and the leaders of the House and Senate are not required to cooperate with one another. Polit-

COMPARED WITH WHAT? 8.1

What's in a Name?

Many parties advertise their political philosophies in their names, and all parties pay careful attention to the image they project through their choice of a party label.

The labels of the major U.S. parties—*Democratic* and *Republican*—do not tell us much about the two parties' policy orientations. But in other countries, the party's label often symbolizes the party's policies. A study of party names across the world found that they fall into four categories. Nearly half the parties make ideological appeals, describing themselves as *Socialist* or *Communist*. About the same number use terms suggesting self-government, such as *democratic* and *people*. About a quarter of the parties stress

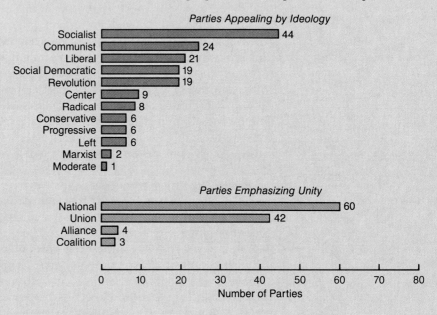

Parties Appealing by Ideology

Socialist	44
Communist	24
Liberal	21
Social Democratic	19
Revolution	19
Center	9
Radical	8
Conservative	6
Progressive	6
Left	6
Marxist	2
Moderate	1

Parties Emphasizing Unity

National	60
Union	42
Alliance	4
Coalition	3

Number of Parties

ical parties are the major means for bridging the separation of powers, of producing coordinated policies that can govern the country effectively. Individuals of the same party in the presidency, the House, and the Senate are likely to share political principles and thus to cooperate in making policy.

A HISTORY OF U.S. PARTY POLITICS

The two major U.S. parties are among the oldest in the world. In fact, the Democratic party, founded in 1828 but with roots reaching back into the late 1700s, has a strong claim to being the oldest party in existence. Its closest rival is the British Conservative party, formed in 1832, two decades before the Republican party was organized, in 1854. Both the Democratic and Republican parties have been supported by several gen-

national unity, using terms like *national* or *union* in their names. And about a sixth make explicit group appeals, identifying themselves as *Christian* or *labor*. (The fractions here add to more than 1 because some parties, the Christian Democrats for example, use more than one symbol.)

The appeal of democracy is so strong that nearly one-quarter of the world's parties use the term in some form (*democratic, democracy, democrats*). *Republican* is not nearly as popular; it is used by only eight parties outside the United States.

Source: This analysis is based on party names and translations from foreign languages in Alan J. Day and Henry W. Degenhardt, eds., *Political Parties of the World* (Detroit: Gale Research, 1980).

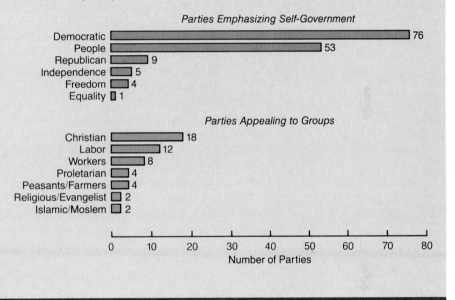

erations of citizens and are part of American history. They have become *institutionalized* in our political process.

The Preparty Period

Today we think of party activities as normal, even essential, to American politics. It was not always so. The Constitution makes no mention of political parties, and none existed when the Constitution was written in 1787. Instead, it was common to refer to groups pursuing some common political interest as *factions*. Although factions were seen as inevitable in politics, they were also considered dangerous. One argument for adopting the Constitution—proposed in "Federalist No. 10," (see Chapter 3 and the Appendix)—was that the separation of powers and checks and balances would prevent factional influences from controlling the government.

Factions existed even under British rule. In colonial assemblies, supporters of the governor (and thus of the Crown) were known as *Tories* or *Loyalists*, and their opponents were called *Whigs* or *Patriots*. After independence, the arguments over whether or not to adopt the Constitution produced a different alignment of factions. Those who backed the Constitution were loosely known as "federalists"; their opponents, as "antifederalists." At this stage, the groups could not be called parties because they did not sponsor candidates for election.

Elections then were vastly different from elections today. The Constitution provided for the president and vice president to be chosen by an **electoral college**—a body of electors who meet in the capitals of their respective states to cast their ballots. Initially, these electors (one for each senator and representative in Congress) were chosen by the state legislatures, not the voters. Presidential "elections" in the early years of the nation, then, actually were decided by a handful of political leaders. (See Chapter 11 for a discussion of the electoral college in modern presidential politics.) Often they met in small secret groups, called **caucuses,** to discuss candidates for public office. And often these caucuses were held among like-minded members of state legislatures and Congress. This was the setting for George Washington's election as the first president in 1789.

We can classify Washington as a federalist because he supported the Constitution, but he was not a factional leader and actually opposed factional politics. His immense prestige coupled with his political neutrality left Washington unopposed for the office of president, and he was elected unanimously by the electoral college. During Washington's administration, however, the political cleavage sharpened between those who favored a stronger national government and those who wanted a less powerful, more decentralized national government.

The first group, led by Alexander Hamilton, proclaimed themselves *Federalists*. The second group, led by Thomas Jefferson, called themselves *Republicans*. (Although they used the same name, they were not Republicans as we know them today.) The Jeffersonians chose the name *Republicans* to distinguish themselves from the "aristocratic" tendencies of Hamilton's Federalists. The Federalists countered by calling the Republicans the *Democratic Republicans*, attempting to link Jefferson's party to the disorder (and beheadings) spawned by the "radical democrats" in France during the French Revolution of 1789.

The First Party System: Federalists and Democratic Republicans

Washington was re-elected president unanimously in 1792, but his vice president, John Adams, was opposed by a candidate backed by the Democratic Republicans. This brief skirmish foreshadowed the nation's first major-party struggle over the presidency. Disheartened by the political split in his administration, Washington spoke out against "the baneful effects" of parties in his farewell address in 1796. But the party concept was already entrenched in the political system. (See "Two-Party Systems in U.S. History," in Essay C, page 345.)

In the election of 1796, the Federalists supported Vice President John Adams to succeed Washington as president. The Democratic Republicans backed Thomas Jefferson for president but could not agree on a vice presidential candidate. In the electoral college, Adams won 71 votes to Jefferson's 68, and both ran ahead of other candidates. At that time, the Constitution provided that the presidency went to the candidate who won the most votes in the electoral college, and that the vice presidency went to the runner-up. So Adams, a Federalist, had to accept Jefferson, a Democratic Republican, as his vice president. Obviously, the Constitution did not anticipate a presidential contest between candidates from opposing political parties.

The party function of nominating candidates emerged more clearly in the election of 1800. Both parties caucused in Congress to nominate candidates for president and vice president.[4] The result was the first true party contest for the presidency. The Federalists nominated John Adams and Charles Pinckney; the Democratic Republicans, Thomas Jefferson and Aaron Burr. This time, the Democratic Republican candidates won. However, the new party organization worked too well. The Democratic Republican electors unanimously cast all their votes for both Jefferson and Burr. Unfortunately, the presidency was to go to the candidate with the most votes, and the top two candidates were tied.

Despite the fact that Jefferson was the party's presidential candidate and Burr its vice presidential candidate, the House of Representatives was empowered by the Constitution to choose one of them as president. After seven days and thirty-six ballots (encouraged by the ambitious Burr), the House decided in favor of Jefferson.

The Twelfth Amendment, ratified in 1804, prevented a repeat of the troublesome election outcomes of 1796 and 1800. It required the electoral college to vote separately for president and vice president, implicitly recognizing that presidential elections would be contested by party candidates nominated for the separate offices but running on the same ballot.

The election of 1800 marked the beginning of the end for the Federalists, who lost the next four elections. By 1820, the Federalists were no more. The Democratic Republican candidate, James Monroe, was re-elected in the first presidential contest without party competition since Washington's time. (Monroe received all but one electoral vote, which was reportedly cast against him so that Washington would remain the only president ever elected unanimously.) Ironically, the Era of Good Feelings under Monroe also signalled the beginning of the end for his party, the Democratic Republicans.

Lacking competition from another party, the Democratic Republicans neglected their function of nominating candidates. The party continued to hold a congressional caucus to nominate candidates for president, but attendance dropped off. Although a caucus was held in 1824, its nominee was challenged by three other Democratic Republicans, including John Quincy Adams and Andrew Jackson, who proved to be the most popular candidates among the voters in the ensuing election.

Prior to 1824, the parties' role in structuring the popular vote was relatively unimportant because relatively few people were entitled to vote. But the states began to drop restrictive requirements for voting after 1800, and voting rights for white males expanded even faster after 1815 (see Chapter 7). With the expansion of suffrage, more states began allowing voters to choose presidential electors. The 1824 election was the first in which presidential electors were selected through popular vote in most states. Still, the role of political parties in structuring the popular vote had not yet developed fully.

Although Jackson won a plurality of both the popular vote and the electoral vote in 1824, he did not win the necessary majority vote in the electoral college. The House of Representatives was again required to decide the winner. It chose the second-place John Quincy Adams (from the established state of Massachusetts) over the voters' choice, Jackson (from the frontier state of Tennessee). The factionalism among the leaders of the Democratic Republican party became so intense that the party split in two.

The Second Party System: Democrats and Whigs

The Jacksonian faction of the Democratic Republican party represented the common people in the expanding South and West, and its members took pride in calling themselves, simply, *Democrats*. Jackson ran again for the presidency as a Democrat in 1828, a milestone that marked the beginning of today's Democratic party. That election was also the first "mass" election in U.S. history. Although many presidential electors had been chosen by popular vote in 1824, the total votes cast in that election numbered fewer than 370,000. By 1828, relaxed requirements for voting (and the use of popular elections to select presidential electors in more states) had increased the vote by more than 300 percent, to over 1.1 million.

As the electorate expanded, the parties changed. No longer could a few party members in Congress rely on close connections among relatively few political leaders in the state legislatures to control the votes cast in the electoral college. Parties now needed to campaign for votes cast by hundreds of thousands of citizens. Recognizing this new dimension of politics, parties responded with a new method for nominating presidential candidates.

Instead of selecting candidates in a closed caucus of party representatives in Congress, the parties devised the **national convention.** At these gatherings, delegates from state parties across the nation would choose candidates for president and vice president and adopt a statement of policies called a **party platform.** The first national convention was called in 1831 by the Anti-Masonic party, which was the first "third" party in American history to challenge the two major parties for the presidency. The Democrats adopted the convention idea in 1832 to nominate Jackson for a second term; so did their new opponents that year, the National Republicans.

The label *National Republicans* was applied to John Quincy Adams's faction of the former Democratic Republican party. However, the National Republicans did not become today's Republican party. Adams's followers called themselves *National Republicans* to signify their old

Federalist preference for a strong national government. But the symbolism did not appeal to the voters, and the National Republicans lost to Jackson in 1832.

Elected to another term, Jackson began to assert the power of the nation over the states (acting more like a National Republican than a Democrat). His policies drew new opponents, who started calling him "King Andrew." A coalition made up of former National Republicans, Anti-Masons, and Jackson-haters formed the Whig party in 1834.[5] The name harked back to the English Whigs, who opposed the powers of the British throne; the implication was that Jackson was governing like a king. For the next thirty years, Democrats and Whigs alternated in the presidency. However, the issues of slavery and sectionalism eventually destroyed the Whigs. Although the party had won the White House in 1848 and had taken 44 percent of the vote in 1852, the Whigs were unable to field a presidential candidate in the 1856 election.

The Present Party System: Democrats and Republicans

In the early 1850s, antislavery forces (including Whigs, Free Soilers, and antislavery Democrats) began to organize. At meetings in Jackson, Michigan, and Ripon, Wisconsin, they recommended the formation of a new party, the Republican party, to oppose the extension of slavery into the Kansas and Nebraska territories. It is this party, founded in 1854, that continues as today's Republican party.

Ike Gives His Blessing to the 1960 Republican Ticket
Dwight Eisenhower was elected in 1952 as the first Republican president since Herbert Hoover, who lost a bid for re-election twenty years earlier. Here Ike appears at a campaign rally in the New York Coliseum just before the 1960 election. The Republican ticket consisted of Richard Nixon, who was vice president under Eisenhower, and Henry Cabot Lodge. Eisenhower's endorsement was not enough to swing the election, and Nixon and Lodge lost to the Democratic ticket of John Kennedy and Lyndon Johnson.

The Republican party contested its first presidential election in 1856. Although it was an entirely new party, it took 33 percent of the vote. Moreover, its candidate (John Fremont) carried eleven states—all in the North. Then, in 1860, the Republicans nominated Abraham Lincoln. The Democrats were deeply divided over the slavery issue and actually split into two parties. The northern wing kept the *Democratic party* label and nominated Stephen Douglas. The *Southern Democrats* ran John Breckinridge. A fourth party, the *Constitutional Union* party, nominated John Bell. Regional voting was obvious in the election of 1860. Lincoln took 40 percent of the popular vote and carried every northern state. Breckinridge won every southern state. But all three of Lincoln's opponents together still did not win enough electoral votes to deny him the presidency.

The election of 1860 is considered the first of three critical elections during the present party system.[6] A **critical election** produces a sharp change in the existing patterns of party loyalties among groups of voters. Moreover, this change in voting patterns, which is called an **electoral realignment,** does not end with the election. Instead, the altered party loyalties last through several subsequent elections.[7] (For more information on the three critical elections, see Essay C, pages 346–347.) The election of 1860 divided the country between the northern states, which mainly voted Republican, and the southern states, which were overwhelmingly Democratic. The victory of the North over the South in the Civil War cemented Democratic loyalties in the South, particularly following the withdrawal of federal troops after the 1876 election.

For forty years, from 1880 to 1920, no Republican presidential candidate won even one of the eleven states of the Confederacy. The South's solid Democratic record earned it the nickname the "Solid South." The Republicans did not puncture the Solid South until 1920, when Warren G. Harding carried Tennessee. Republicans also won five southern states in 1928, when the Democrats ran the first Catholic candidate, Al Smith. Republican presidential candidates won no more southern states until 1952, when Dwight Eisenhower broke the pattern of Democratic dominance in the South—ninety years after that pattern had been set by the Civil War.

Eras of Party Dominance Since the Civil War

The critical election of 1860 established the Democratic and Republican parties as the major parties in our two-party system. In a **two-party system,** most voters are so loyal to one or the other of the major parties that candidates from a third party—which means any minor party—have little chance of winning office. When third-party candidates do win (and occasionally they do), they are most likely to win offices at the local or state level. Since the present two-party system was established, relatively few minor-party candidates have won election to the U.S. House, very few have won election to the Senate, and *none* has won the presidency.

Although voters in most states have been divided in their loyalties between the Republicans and the Democrats, they have not always been equally divided. In some states, counties, and communities, voters favor the Republicans, while voters in other areas prefer the Democrats. When one party in a two-party system *regularly* enjoys support from most of the voters, it is called the **majority party;** the other is called the **minority party.** Over the lifetime of the present two-party system, there have been three different periods of balance between the two major parties.

A rough balance: 1860–1894. From 1860 through 1894, the Grand Old Party (or GOP, as the Republican party is sometimes called) won eight of ten presidential elections, which would seem to qualify it as the majority party. However, some of its success in presidential elections came from running Civil War heroes and from the North's domination of southern politics. Seats won in the House of Representatives are a better guide to the breadth of national support. An analysis shows that the Republicans and Democrats won the same number of congressional elections, each controlling the chamber for nine sessions between 1860 and 1894.

A Republican majority: 1896–1930. A second critical election, in 1896, transformed the Republican party into a true majority party. Grover Cleveland, a Democrat, was in the White House, and the country was in a severe economic depression. The Republicans nominated William McKinley, governor of Ohio and a conservative, who stood for a high tariff against foreign goods and sound money tied to the value of gold. Rather than tour the country seeking votes, McKinley ran a dignified campaign from his Ohio home.

The Democrats, already in trouble because of the depression, nominated the fiery William Jennings Bryan. In stark contrast to McKinley, Bryan advocated the free and unlimited coinage of silver—which meant cheap money and easy payment of debts through inflation. Bryan was also nominated by the young Populist party, an agrarian protest party that had proposed the free-silver platform that Bryan adopted. (The book *The Wonderful Wizard of Oz*, which you probably know as a movie, was actually a Populist political fable; see Feature 8.1.)[8] Conservatives, especially businesspeople, were aghast at the Democrats' radical turn, and voters in the heavily populated Northeast and Midwest surged toward the Republican party—many of them permanently.[9] McKinley carried every northern state east of the Mississippi. The Republicans also won the House and continued to control it for the next six elections.

The election of 1896 helped solidify the Republican majority in industrial America and forged a link between the Republican party and business. In the subsequent electoral realignment, the Republicans emerged as a true majority party. The GOP dominated national politics—controlling the presidency, the Senate, and the House—almost continuously from 1896 until the Wall Street crash of 1929, which burst big business's bubble and launched the Great Depression.*

---

* The sole exception came in 1912, when Teddy Roosevelt's Progressive party split from the Republicans, allowing Democrat Woodrow Wilson to win the presidency and giving the Democrats control of Congress.

FEATURE 8.1

The Wizard of Oz: A Political Fable

Most Americans are familiar with *The Wizard of Oz* through L. Frank Baum's children's books or the 1939 motion picture, but few realize that the story was written as a political fable to promote the Populist movement around the turn of the century. Next time you see it, try interpreting the Tin Woodsman as the industrial worker, the Scarecrow as the struggling farmer, and the Wizard as the president, who is powerful only as long as he succeeds in deceiving the people. (Sorry, but in the book Dorothy's ruby slippers were only silver shoes.)

The Wonderful Wizard of Oz was written by Lyman Frank Baum in 1900, during the collapse of the Populist movement. Through the Populist party, Midwestern farmers, in alliance with some urban workers, had challenged the banks, railroads, and other economic interests that squeezed farmers through low prices, high freight rates, and continued indebtedness.

The Populists advocated government ownership of railroads, telephone, and telegraph industries. They also wanted silver coinage. Their power grew during the 1893 depression, the worst in U.S. history until then, as farm prices sank to new lows and unemployment was widespread. . . .

In the 1894 congressional elections, the Populist party got almost 40 percent of the vote. It looked forward to winning the presidency, and the silver standard, in 1896. But in that election, which revolved around the issue of gold versus silver, Populist Democrat William Jennings Bryan lost to Republican William McKinley by 95 electoral votes. Bryan, a congressman from Nebraska and a gifted orator, ran again in 1900, but the Populist strength was gone.

Baum viewed these events in both rural South Dakota—where he edited a local weekly—and urban Chicago—where he wrote Oz. He mourned the destruction of the fragile alliance between the Midwestern farmers (the Scarecrow) and the urban industrial workers (the Tin Woodsman). Along with Bryan (the Cowardly Lion with a roar but little else), they had been taken down the yellow brick road (the gold standard) that led nowhere. Each journeyed to Emerald City seeking favors from the Wizard of Oz (the President). Dorothy, the symbol of Every-

man, went along with them, innocent enough to see the truth before the others.

Along the way they meet the Wicked Witch of the East who, Baum tells us, had kept the little Munchkin people "in bondage for many years, making them slave for her night and day." She also had put a spell on the Tin Woodsman, once an independent and hardworking man, so that each time he swung his axe, it chopped off a different part of his body. Lacking another trade, he "worked harder than ever," becoming like a machine, incapable of love, yearning for a heart. Another witch, the Wicked Witch of the West, clearly symbolizes the large industrial corporations.

. . . The small group heads toward Emerald City where the Wizard rules from behind a papier-mâché facade. Oz, by the way, is the abbreviation for ounce, the standard measure for gold.

Like all good politicians, the Wizard can be all things to all people. Dorothy sees him as an enormous head. The Scarecrow sees a gossamer fairy. The Woodsman sees an awful beast, the Cowardly Lion "a ball of fire so fierce and glowing he could scarcely bear to gaze upon it."

Later, however, when they confront the Wizard directly, they see he is nothing more than "a little man, with a bald head and a wrinkled face."

"I have been making believe," the Wizard confesses. "I'm just a common man." But the Scarecrow adds, "You're more than that . . . you're a humbug."

"It was a great mistake my ever letting you into the Throne Room," admits the Wizard, a former ventriloquist and circus balloonist from Omaha.

This was Baum's ultimate Populist message. The powers-that-be survive by deception. Only people's ignorance allows the powerful to manipulate and control them. Dorothy returns to Kansas with the magical help of her Silver Shoes (the silver issue), but when she gets to Kansas she realizes her shoes "had fallen off in her flight through the air, and were lost forever in the desert." Still, she is safe at home with Aunt Em and Uncle Henry, simple farmers.

Source: Peter Dreier, *Today Journal*, 14 February 1986, p. 11. Copyright © Pacific News Service. Reprinted by permission.

A Democratic majority: 1932 to the present. The Republicans' majority status ended in the critical election of 1932 between incumbent president Herbert Hoover and the Democratic challenger, Franklin Delano Roosevelt. Roosevelt promised new solutions to unemployment and the economic crisis of the Depression. His campaign appealed to labor, middle-class liberals, and new European ethnic voters. Along with Democratic voters in the Solid South, urban workers in the North, Catholics, Jews, and white ethnic minorities formed the "Roosevelt coalition." (The relatively few blacks who voted at that time tended to remain loyal to the Republicans—the "party of Lincoln.")

Roosevelt was swept into office in a landslide, carrying huge majorities into the House and Senate to carry out his liberal activist programs. The electoral realignment prompted by the election of 1932 made the Democrats the majority party. Not only was Roosevelt re-elected in 1936, 1940, and 1944, but Democrats held control of both houses of Congress from 1933 through 1980—interrupted by only two years of Republican control in 1953 and 1954, during the Eisenhower administration.

In presidential elections, however, the Democrats have not fared so well since Roosevelt. In fact, they have won only four elections (Truman, Kennedy, Johnson, and Carter), compared with the Republicans, who have won seven times (Eisenhower twice, Nixon twice, Reagan twice, and Bush once). In Reagan's stunning election in 1980, Republicans wrested control of the Senate from the Democrats for the first time since 1954 but lost it after the 1986 election.

There are strong signs that the coalition of Democratic voters forged by Roosevelt in the 1930s has already cracked. Certainly the South is no longer solid for the Democrats. Since 1952, in fact, it has voted more consistently for Republican presidential candidates than for Democrats. The party system in the United States does not seem to be undergoing another realignment; rather, we seem to be in a period of **electoral dealignment,** in which party loyalties are less important in voting decisions.

THE AMERICAN TWO-PARTY SYSTEM

Our review of party history has focused on the major parties competing for presidential office. But we should not ignore the special contributions of certain minor parties, among them, the Anti-Masonic party, the Populists, and the Progressives of 1912. In this section, we study the fortunes of minor, or third, parties in American politics. We also look at the reasons why we have just two major parties, explain how federalism helps the parties survive, and describe voters' loyalties toward the major parties today.

Minor Parties in America

Minor parties have always figured in party politics in America. In recent years, the Libertarian party, which has run candidates in every election since 1972, has emerged as the most active and fastest-growing minor party, claiming organizations in all fifty states.[10] The Libertarian party expounds libertarian ideology, stressing freedom over order and equality. Its candidate for president in 1988 was Ron Paul, a former Republican member of Congress, whose platform included abolishing the income tax, eliminating American military bases abroad, and generally restricting government activities.

There are several different types of minor parties:[11]

- **Bolter parties** are formed from factions that have split off from one of the major parties. Six times in thirty presidential elections since the Civil War, disgruntled leaders have "bolted the ticket" and challenged their former parties. Bolter parties have occasionally won significant proportions of the vote. However, with the exception of Teddy Roosevelt's Progressive party in 1912 and the possible exception of George Wallace's American Independent party in 1968, bolter parties have not affected the outcome of presidential elections.

- **Farmer-labor parties** represent farmers and urban workers who believe that they, the working class, are not getting their share of society's wealth. The People's party, founded in 1892 and nicknamed the "Populist party," was a prime example of a farmer-labor party. The Populists won 8.5 percent of the vote in 1892 and also became the first third party since 1860 to win any electoral votes. Flush with success, it endorsed William Jennings Bryan, the Democratic candidate, in 1896. When he lost, the party quickly faded. Many Populist ideas were revived by farm and labor groups in the Progressive party in 1924, which nominated Robert La Follette for the presidency. Although the party won 16.6 percent of the popular vote, it carried only La Follette's home state of Wisconsin. The party died in 1925, although its ideals continued to influence American politics (see Chapter 7). In 1984, a Populist candidate ran for president but received fewer than seventy thousand votes. However, populism—a commitment to order and equality over freedom—still plays a part in today's political system. A Populist caucus claimed twenty-eight members in the House and Senate in 1986.*

- **Parties of ideological protest** go further than farmer-labor parties in criticizing the established system. These parties reject prevailing doctrines and propose radically different principles, often favoring more government activism. The Socialist party has been the most successful party of ideological protest. However, at its high point in 1912, it garnered only 6 percent of the vote, and Socialist candidates for president have never won a single state. In recent years, the sound of ideological protest has been heard more from rightist parties, arguing for the radical disengagement of government from society. Ron Paul, the Libertarian candidate in 1988, received more votes than all the leftist candidates put together, but that was still less than 1 percent of the total votes cast.

---

* Some members of the Populist caucus helped to found the New Populist Forum in 1985. According to a press release issued in 1986, the forum is an interest group that wants to apply the populist philosophy in the tradition of populists one hundred years ago to today's issues, and build political momentum among people who still believe that government serves the interests of ordinary people in our country.

■ **Single-issue parties** are formed to promote one principle, not a general philosophy of government. The Anti-Masonic parties of the 1820s and 1830s, for example, opposed Masonic lodges and other secret societies. The Free Soil party of the 1840s and 1850s worked to abolish slavery. The Prohibition party, the most durable example of a single-issue party, opposed the consumption of alcoholic beverages. Prohibition candidates consistently won from 1 to 2 percent of the vote in nine presidential elections between 1884 and 1916, and the party has run candidates in every presidential election since.

Third parties, then, have been formed primarily to express discontent with the choices offered by the major parties and to work for their own objectives within the electoral system.[12] How have they fared? As *vote getters*, minor parties have not performed well, with two exceptions. First, bolter parties twice won more than 10 percent of the vote; no other type has ever won as much. Second, the Republican party originated in 1854 as a single-issue third party opposed to slavery in new territories; in its first election, in 1856, the party came in second, displacing the Whigs. (Undoubtedly, the Republican exception to the rule has inspired the formation of other hopeful third parties.)

As *policy advocates*, minor parties have a slightly better record. At times, they have had a real effect on the policies adopted by the major parties. Women's suffrage, the graduated income tax, and the direct election of senators all originated in third parties.[13] Of course, one reason third parties don't get more votes may well be the lack of popular support for their policies. This was a lesson the Democrats learned in 1896, when they adopted the Populists' free-silver plank in their own platform. Both candidate and platform went down to a defeat that stained the Democratic party for decades.

Most important, minor parties function as *safety valves*. They allow those who are unhappy with the status quo to present their policies within the system, to contribute to the political dialogue. If minor parties indicate discontent, what should we make of the numerous minor parties—including the Libertarian, Workers', and Prohibition parties—in the 1988 election? Not much. Despite the presence of minor parties, the two major parties collected over 99 percent of the vote. The number of third parties that contest elections is much less important than the total number of votes they receive.

Why a Two-Party System?

The history of party politics in the United States is essentially the story of two parties alternating control of the government. With relatively few exceptions, elections for national office and for most state and local offices are conducted within the two-party system. This pattern is unusual in democratic countries, where multiparty systems are more common. Why does the United States have only two major parties? The two most convincing answers to this question stem from the electoral system in the Unites States and the process of political socialization here.

Elections in the United States, unlike elections in many other countries, involve the twin principles of (1) *single winners* chosen by (2) a *simple plurality* of votes. That is, in the typical U.S. election, one office is contested by two or more candidates and is won by the single candidate who collects the most votes. Think about the way the states choose representatives to Congress. If a state is entitled to ten representatives, the state is divided into ten congressional districts, and one representative is elected in each district. **Single-member district** representation is also employed in most state legislatures. There are, however, other ways to elect ten representatives to Congress. The state might have a single statewide election for all ten seats, with each party presenting a list of ten candidates. Voters could vote for the entire party list they preferred, and candidates would be elected from the top of each list, according to the proportion of votes won by the party.

Although this form of election may seem strange, it is used in many democratic countries. This electoral system, which awards legislative seats in proportion to votes won in elections, is known as **proportional representation.** It tends to produce (or to perpetuate) several parties, each of which has enough voting strength nationwide to elect some minimum number of candidates on its party list. In contrast, our system of single winners by simple plurality vote forces groups in society to work within one of the only two parties with any realistic chance of winning an election. Therefore, the system tends to produce only two parties. Moreover, the two major parties in a state benefit from laws that automatically list candidates on the ballot if their party won some minimum percentage of the vote in the previous election. These laws discourage minor parties, which must petition before every election for a place on the ballot.

The rules of our electoral system may explain why only two parties tend to form in specific election districts. But why do the *same* two parties (Democratic and Republican) operate within each state? The contest for the presidency is the key to this question. The presidential election can be won only by the single candidate who wins a majority of electoral votes across the entire nation. Presidential candidates must win votes under the same label in each state so that they can pool their states' electoral votes to win in the electoral college. The presidency is a big enough prize to produce uncomfortable coalitions of voters (southern white Protestants allied with northern Jews and blacks in the Democratic party, for example) just to win the electoral vote and the presidential election.

The American electoral system may force party politics into a two-party mold, but why must the same parties *reappear* from election to election? In fact, they do not. We have seen that the earliest two-party system pitted the Federalists against the Democratic Republicans. A later two-party system involved the Democrats and the Whigs. Over 130 years ago, the Republicans replaced the Whigs in what is our present two-party system. But, with modern issues so different from the issues then, why do the Democrats and Republicans persist? This is where *political socialization* comes into play. These two parties persist simply because they *have* persisted. After more than 100 years of political socialization, the two parties today have such a head start in structuring the vote that they discourage challenges from new parties. Of course, third parties still try to crack the two-party system from time to time, but most have had little success.

The Federal Basis of the Party System

Studying the history of American parties by focusing on contests for the presidency is convenient and informative. It also oversimplifies party politics to the point of distortion. By concentrating only on presidential elections, we tend to ignore electoral patterns in the states, where elections often buck national trends. In a party's darkest defeats for the presidency, it can still claim many victories for state offices. These victories outside the arena of presidential politics give each party a base of support that keeps its machinery oiled and running for the next contest.

The Republican victories in the 1980 and 1984 presidential elections help illustrate how the states serve as a refuge for parties defeated for the presidency. Ronald Reagan carried forty-four states in his landslide victory in 1980. He swept forty-nine states in 1984—winning in every state but Minnesota, the home of his opponent, Walter Mondale. In 1980, the Republicans also won a majority in the Senate for the first time in twenty-eight years, and they kept that control in 1984. All this makes the early 1980s sound like dark times for the Democrats, but, in fact, they did very well at the state level. Even in the wake of Reagan's stunning victory in 1984, the Democrats kept control of the House of Representatives. They wound up with thirty-four state governorships to the Republicans' sixteen (unchanged from before the election) and 65 percent of the state legislatures. They controlled the governorship, the upper house, and the lower house in eighteen states compared to only four states for the Republicans.[14]

Reagan's strong victory in 1980 and his landslide in 1984 suggested that the Democrats were doomed to extinction. Perhaps in an earlier time, when the existing parties were not so well institutionalized, that would have been so. However, the Democratic party not only remained alive but thrived within most states in our federal system. The separation of state politics from national trends affords each party a chance to lick its wounds after a presidential election debacle and to return to campaign optimistically four years later—as the Democrats did in 1988.

Party Identification in America

According to a recent survey, over 90 percent of Americans say they vote for the person, not the party.[15] Maybe they do, but most Americans also identify with one of the two major parties. The concept of **party identification** is one of the most important in political science. It refers to the voter's sense of psychological attachment to a party, which is not the same thing as voting for the party in any given election. Voting is a behavior; identification is a state of mind. For example, millions of southerners voted for Eisenhower for president in 1952 and 1956 although they still considered themselves Democrats. Across the nation, more people identify with one of the two major parties than reject a party attachment.

The proportions of self-identified Republicans, Democrats, and independents (no party attachment) in the electorate since 1952 are shown in Figure 8.1. Three significant points stand out.

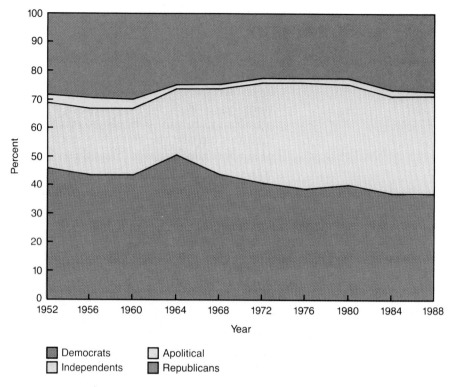

Distribution of Party Identification, 1952–1988

In every presidential election since 1952, voters across the nation have been asked, "Generally speaking, do you usually think of yourself as a Republican, a Democrat, an independent, or what?" Most voters readily admit to thinking of themselves as either Republicans or Democrats, but the proportion of those who think of themselves as independents has increased over time. The Democrats' status as the majority party has also lessened over time. Nevertheless, most Americans today still identify with one of the two major parties, and there are still more Democrats than Republicans. (Source: Warren E. Miller, Arthur H. Miller, and Edward J. Schneider, American National Election Studies Data Sourcebook, 1952–1978. *Cambridge, Mass.: Harvard University Press, 1980, 1981, supplemented by data from the 1980 and 1984 National Election Studies conducted at the Center for Political Studies, University of Michigan, and distributed by the Inter-University Consortium for Political and Social Research. Data for 1988 comes from the 1988 General Social Survey, provided by Dr. Tom W. Smith, National Opinion Research Center.)*

Figure 8.1

- The proportion of Republicans and Democrats combined far exceeds the proportion of independents in every year.

- The proportion of Democrats consistently exceeds that of Republicans.

- The proportion of Democrats has shrunk somewhat over time, to the benefit of both Republicans and independents.

Although a sense of party identification predisposes citizens to vote for their favorite party, other factors may cause voters to choose the opposition candidate. If they vote against their party often enough, they may rethink their party identification and eventually switch. Apparently,

this rethinking has gone on in the minds of many southern Democrats over time. In 1952, about 70 percent of white southerners thought of themselves as Democrats, and fewer than 20 percent thought of themselves as Republicans. By 1984, white southerners were only 37 percent Democratic; 34 percent of them were Republican.[16] Much of the nationwide growth in the number of Republicans and independents (and the parallel drop in the number of Democrats) stems from party switches among white southerners.

Who are the self-identified Democrats and Republicans in the electorate? Figure 8.2 shows party identification by social groups in 1988. The effects of socioeconomic factors are clear. People who have lower incomes, less education, less prestigious occupations, and who live in union households tend to think of themselves as Democrats more than Republicans. But the cultural factors of religion and race produce even sharper differences between the parties. Jews are strongly Democratic compared with other religious groups. Members of minority groups (especially blacks) are also overwhelmingly Democratic. Surprisingly strong differences between the sexes have opened a "gender gap" in American politics: Women are far more Democratic than men.

The influence of region on party identification has altered over time. The South is now only slightly more Democratic than the other regions, while the West has become predominantly Republican. Despite the erosion of Democratic support in the South, we still see elements of Roosevelt's old Democratic coalition in the socioeconomic groups. Perhaps the major change in that coalition has been the replacement of white European ethnic groups by blacks, attracted by the Democrats' backing of civil rights legislation in the 1960s.

Studies show that about half the citizens in the United States adopt their parents' party. But it often takes time for party identification to develop. The youngest group of voters is most likely to be independent; the oldest group shows the most partisan commitments. Curiously, the youngest and oldest age groups are most evenly divided between the parties. Some analysts believe this division of party identification among the young will continue as they age, contributing to further erosion of the Democratic majority and perhaps greater party dealignment.

Still, citizens find their political niche, and they tend to stay there. The widespread enduring sense of party loyalty among American voters tends to structure the vote even before the election is held, even before the candidates are chosen. Later we examine the extent to which party identification determines voting choice. First, we take a closer look at today's parties.

PARTY IDEOLOGY AND ORGANIZATION

George Wallace, a disgruntled Democrat who ran for president on the American Independent party ticket, complained that "there isn't a dime's worth of difference" between the Democrats and Republicans. Humorist Will Rogers said, "I am not a member of any organized political party— I am a Democrat." Wallace's comment was made in disgust; Rogers's in

Figure 8.2

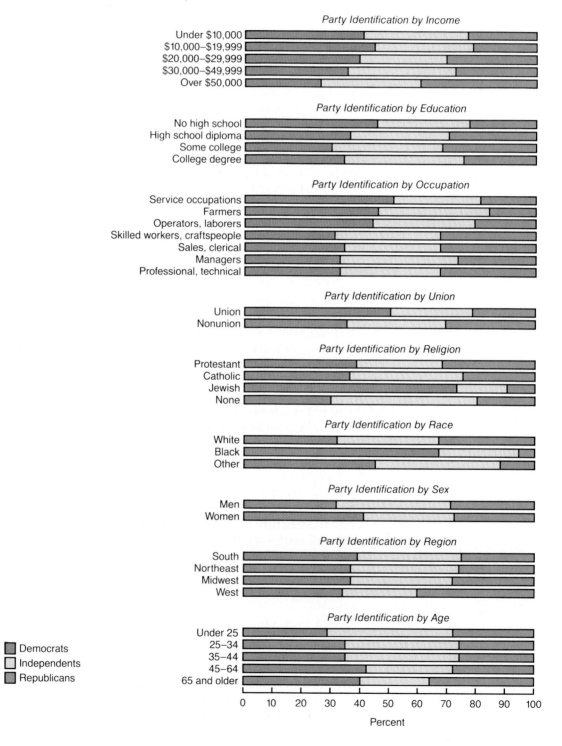

Party Identification by Social Groups
Respondents to a 1988 survey were divided into nine different social groups—by income, education, occupation, union membership, religion, race, sex, region, and age—and analyzed according to their self-descriptions as Democrats, independents, or Republicans. Region was found to have the least effect on party identification; religion and race had the greatest effects. (Source: 1988 General Social Survey; tabulations provided by Dr. Tom W. Smith, National Opinion Research Center.)

jest. Wallace was wrong; Rogers was close to being right. Here we try to dispel the myth that the parties do not differ significantly on issues and to explain how they are—or are not—organized.

Differences in Party Ideology

George Wallace notwithstanding, there is more than a dime's worth of difference between the two parties. In fact, the difference amounts to many billions of dollars, the cost of the different government programs supported by each party. Democrats are more disposed to government spending to advance social welfare (and hence to promote equality) than are Republicans. And social welfare programs cost money, a lot of money. (You will see how much money in Chapters 15 and 16.) Republicans, on the other hand, are not averse to spending billions of dollars for the projects they consider important, among them, national defense. Ronald Reagan portrayed the Democrats as big spenders, but the defense buildup during just his first administration cost the country over $1 trillion— more precisely $1,007,900,000,000.[17] And Reagan's Strategic Defense Initiative (the "Star Wars" space defense scheme) cost many billions more, even by conservative estimates. These differences in spending patterns reflect some real philosophical differences between the parties.

Voter identification.   One way to examine these differences is to look at the voters who identify with the parties. As shown in the middle portion of Figure 8.3, 25 percent of those who identified themselves as Democrats described themselves as conservatives, compared with more than 40 percent of those who identified themselves as Republicans. As we discussed in Chapter 5, many ordinary voters do not think about politics in ideological terms. The ideological gap between the parties looms even larger when we focus on the party activists on the left- and right-hand sides of the figure. Only 4 percent of the delegates to the 1988 Democratic convention considered themselves conservatives, compared with 60 percent of the delegates to the Republican convention.

Platforms: Freedom, order, and equality.   Surveys of voters' ideological orientations may reflect differences in self-image rather than actual differences in ideology. For another test of party philosophies, we can look to the platforms adopted in party conventions. Although citizens feel that party platforms don't matter very much, they do matter a great deal to delegates at conventions. The wording of a platform plank often means the difference between victory and defeat for factions within the party. Delegates fight, not only over ideas, but also over words and even punctuation in a plank. Platforms, then, give us a good indication of policy preferences among party activists.

The platforms adopted by the Democratic and Republican conventions in 1988 were strikingly different in style and substance. The Democrats, who met first, produced an unusually short document (fewer than 4,500 words), about one-tenth as long as their 1984 platform. It stressed broad themes rather than specific policies. The platform led with this principle: "We believe that all Americans have a fundamental right to

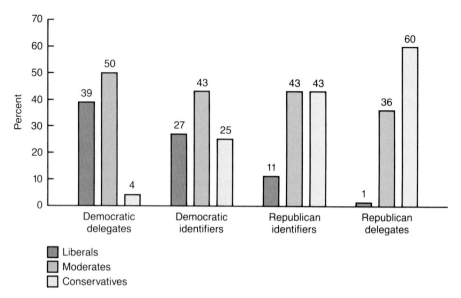

Ideologies of Party Identifiers and Delegates in 1988
*Contrary to what many people think, the Democratic and Republican parties
differ substantially in their ideological centers of gravity. When citizens were
asked to classify themselves on an ideological scale, more Republican than
Democratic identifiers described themselves as conservative. When delegates
to the parties' national conventions were asked to classify themselves, even
greater ideological differences appeared. (Source: Michael Oreskes, "Delegates Conservative, Poll Shows,"* New York Times, *14 August 1988, p. 14; and E. J. Dionne, Jr.,
"Democrats Are Hoping to End the Lean Years,"* New York Times, *17 July 1988, p. 10.)*

Figure 8.3

economic justice"—a phrase usually interpreted as a commitment to
reducing economic inequality. The party also pledged

> equal access to education . . . equal access to government services, employ-
> ment, housing, business, business enterprise and education to every citizen
> regardless of race, sex, national origin, religion, age, handicapping condition
> or sexual orientation . . . the adoption of the equal rights amendment to the
> Constitution . . . equal access of women and minorities to elective office
> and party endorsement.

Accusing the Democrats of hiding behind a vague platform, the
Republicans adopted a detailed document of 50,000 words and 150 pages.
But the Republicans had a theme, too—*freedom*:

> *Freedom works.* This is not sloganeering, but a verifiable fact. . . . Our
> platform reflects on every page our continuing faith in the creative power
> of human freedom. . . . Defending and expanding freedom is our first priority.

The Democrats supported "an indexed minimum wage that can help
lift and keep families out of poverty"; the Republicans opposed increases
in the minimum wage as "inflationary—and job-destroying."

The Democrats said the national, state, and local governments "exist
to help us solve our problems instead of adding to them"; the Republicans said "government empowers people to solve their own problems
and to have more choices in their lives."

Although the Republicans opposed the use of government to promote equality, they were willing to use government to promote social order. The Democrats supported free choice on the abortion issue; the Republicans favored a constitutional amendment to outlaw abortion. The Democrats were silent on the death penalty; the Republicans urged the reinstatement of the death penalty for certain federal crimes.

These statements of values clearly separate the two parties on the values of freedom, order, and equality that underlie the dilemmas of government discussed in Chapter 1. According to the typology presented there, the Republicans' 1988 platform places their party in the conservative category, and the Democrats' platform puts their party squarely into the liberal category.

Different, but similar. The Democrats and the Republicans have very different ideological orientations. Yet many observers claim that the parties are really quite similar in ideology, especially when compared with other countries' parties. They are similar in that both support capitalism; that is, both reject government ownership of the means of production (see Chapter 1). A study of Democratic and Republican positions on four economic issues—ownership of the means of production, role in economic planning, redistribution of wealth, and providing for social welfare—found that Republicans consistently oppose increased government activity. Comparing these findings with data on party positions in thirteen other democracies, the researchers found about as much difference between the American parties as is usual within two-party systems. However, both American parties tend to be more conservative on economic matters than parties in other two-party systems. In most

How'd You Like to Be Vice President?
Campaigning for president puts candidates in touch with the common people. Here Michael Dukakis dines with a blue-collar worker in an Iowa cafe in 1988. In contrast to the "wholesale" politics fostered by television, the Iowa caucuses promote politicking at the "retail" level. Although Dukakis looks out of place in this setting, he is sure to get a different perspective on workers' problems from talking to some of them directly.

multiparty systems, the presence of strong socialist and antisocialist parties ensures a much greater range of ideological choice than we find in our system, despite genuine differences between the Democrats and Republicans.[18]

National Party Organization

Most political observers would agree with Will Rogers's description of the Democrats as an unorganized political party. This used to be true of the Republicans too, but this has changed over the last decade—at least at the national level. Bear in mind the distinction between levels of party structure. American parties parallel our federal system: They have separate national and state organizations (and virtually separate local organizations, in many cases).

At the national level, each major party has three main organizational components:

- *National convention.* Every four years, each party convenes thousands of delegates from the states and the territories for the purpose of nominating a candidate for president. This national nominating convention is also the supreme governing body of the party. It determines party policy through the platform, formulates rules to govern party operations, and designates a national committee, which is empowered to govern the party until the next convention.

- *National committee.* The **national committee** of each party is composed of party officials representing every state and including the chairpersons of every state party organization. Each party also adds other members, representatives of youth and ethnic groups, for example. The membership of the Republican National Committee (RNC) is over 150, and there are about 350 people on the Democratic National Committee (DNC). The chairperson of each national committee is chosen by the party's presidential nominee, then duly elected by the committee. If the nominee loses the election, the national committee usually replaces the nominee's chairperson.

- *Congressional campaign committees.* Democrats and Republicans in the House and Senate maintain their own **congressional campaign committees,** each of which raises its own funds to support its candidates in congressional elections. The fact that these are separate organizations tells us that the national party structure is loose; the national committee seldom gets involved with the election of any individual member of Congress. Moreover, even the congressional campaign organizations merely supplement the funds that senators and representatives raise on their own to win re-election.

It is tempting to think of the national party chairperson sitting at the top of a hierarchical party organization that runs through the state committees to the local level. Few ideas could be more wrong. There is very little national direction of and even less national control over state and local campaigns. In fact, the RNC and DNC do not really direct or control presidential campaigns. Individual candidates hire their own campaign staffs to contest the party primaries to win delegates who will support them for nomination at the party conventions. The successful party nominees then keep their winning staffs to contest the general election. The main role of a national committee is to cooperate with its candidate's personal campaign staff, in the hope of winning the election.

In this light, the national committees appear to be relatively useless organizations. For many years, their role was essentially limited to planning for the next party convention. The committee would select the site, issue the call to state parties to attend, plan the program, and so on. In the 1970s, however, the roles of the DNC and RNC began to expand—but in different ways.

In response to street rioting during the 1968 Democratic convention (see Chapter 7), the Democrats created a special commission to introduce party reforms. The McGovern-Fraser Commission attempted to open the party to greater participation by women, minority members, and young voters and to weaken local party leaders' control over the process of selecting delegates. The commission formulated guidelines for the selection of delegates to the 1972 Democratic convention. Included in these guidelines was the requirement that state parties take "affirmative action"—that is, do something to see to it that women, blacks, and young people were included among their delegates "in reasonable relationship to the group's presence in the population of the state."[19] Many state parties rebelled at the imposition of quotas by sex, race, and age. But the DNC threatened to deny seating to any state delegation at the 1972 convention that did not comply with the guidelines.

Never before had a national party committee imposed these kinds of rules on a state party organization, but it worked. Even the powerful Chicago delegation, led by Mayor Richard Daley, was denied seating at the convention for violating the guidelines. And overall, women, blacks, and young voters gained dramatically in representation at the 1972 Democratic convention. Although the party has since reduced its emphasis on quotas, the gains by women and blacks have held up fairly well. The representation of young people, however, has declined substantially.

While the Democrats were busy with *procedural* reforms, the Republicans were making *organizational* reforms.[20] The RNC did little to open up its delegate selection process; Republicans were not inclined to impose quotas on state parties through their national committee. Instead, the RNC strengthened its fund-raising, research, and service roles. Republicans acquired their own building and their own computer, and in 1976 they hired the first full-time chairperson of either national party. (Until then, the chairperson worked part-time and usually had some other career.) As RNC chairman, William Brock expanded the party's staff, launched new publications, started seminars, conducted election analyses, advised candidates, and did most of the things that national party committees had done routinely in other countries for years.

The vast difference between the Democratic and Republican approaches to reforming the national committees shows in the funds raised by the DNC and RNC during election campaigns. Since Brock's tenure as chairman of the RNC, the Republicans have raised three to four times the money raised by the Democrats. Although Republicans have traditionally raised more campaign funds than Democrats, they no longer rely on a relatively few wealthy contributors. In fact, the Republicans received the larger portion of their funds from smaller contributors (of less than $100), mainly through direct-mail solicitation. In short, the RNC has recently been raising far more money than the DNC from many more citizens, in a long-term commitment to improving its organizational services. Evidence of its efforts has appeared at the level of state party organizations.

State and Local Party Organizations

At one time, both major parties were firmly anchored in strong state and local party organizations. Big-city party organizations, such as the Democrats' Tammany Hall in New York City and the Cook County Central Committee in Chicago, were prototypes of the party machine. The **party machine** was a centralized organization that dominated local politics by controlling elections—sometimes by illegal means, often by providing jobs and social services to urban workers in return for their votes. The patronage and social service functions of party machines were undercut as government expanded its role in providing unemployment compensation, aid to families with dependent children, and other social services. As a result, most local party organizations lost their ability to deliver votes and thus to determine the outcome of elections. However, machines are still strong in certain areas. In Nassau County, New York, for example, suburban Republicans have shown that they can run a machine as well as urban Democrats.[21]

The state organizations of both parties vary widely in strength, but Republican state organizations tend to be stronger than Democratic organizations. The Republicans are likely to have larger budgets and staffs and tend to recruit candidates for more offices. Republicans also differ from democrats in the help that the national organization gives to state organizations. A survey of forty Republican and thirty Democratic state chairpersons revealed that 70 percent of the Republican organizations received financial aid from the national organization compared with only 7 percent of the Democratic organizations.[22] Republicans at the state level also received more candidate training, poll data and research, and campaign instruction from the national organization. The only service that the DNC supplied more often than the RNC was "rule enforcement"—reflecting the national party's enforcement of guidelines for selecting convention delegates.[23] Otherwise, the dominant pattern in both parties was for the national organization *not* to intervene in state activities unless asked, and then only to supply services.

If strong party organization means that control is vested in the national headquarters, then both the Democrats and Republicans are, in Will Rogers's phrase, unorganized political parties. We see this same decentralization in the way party candidates campaign for election and run the government after winning elections. In both instances, the party label is very important, but the party organization is not.

CAMPAIGNING FOR ELECTION

Winning public office at the national or state level in the United States
is a two-stage process. The first stage is to win the nomination of one of
the two major parties, which is usually decided by an election within
the party.* Once nominated, the candidate moves to the second stage:
winning election to the office itself. Unless a candidate is lucky enough
to run unopposed, the election must be won through an **electoral campaign,** an organized effort to persuade voters to choose one candidate
over others competing for the same office.

A full-blown campaign waged by a credible candidate against a credible opponent proceeds through three broad stages:[24]

- *Building a base.* Campaign workers must be recruited and organized to help publicize the candidate. Information about the electorate's past voting behavior must be obtained and analyzed. Funds to
do all these things must be acquired, or sources of funds must be
identified.

- *Planning a strategy.* Arguments in favor of voting for the candidate
and against the opposition must be incorporated into a campaign
theme. The basic choices among strategies are running a *party-centered campaign,* which relies heavily on the voters' party identification and the party organization for resources; an *issue-oriented*

---

* Of course, a candidate can be nominated by a third party or can run as an independent,
but these routes are not usually successful.

campaign, which stresses policies that appeal to important groups; or a *personality-oriented campaign,* which emphasizes the candidate's personal qualities or image.

■ *Clinching the vote.* The candidate must meet with voting groups. The campaign theme must be publicized. Opposition arguments must be countered. Supporters must be mobilized to go to the polls on election day. The victory party must be planned.

Many factors help shape decisions at these three stages. The most important is whether the candidate is campaigning to win the nomination or to win the office itself.

The Nomination

The most important feature of the nomination process in American party politics is that it involves an election. National party leaders do not choose the party's nominee for president or even the party's candidates for House and Senate seats. Virtually no other parties in the world nominate candidates to the national legislature through primary elections. In more than half the world's parties, legislative candidates are chosen by local party leaders—and in most of those cases, even these choices must be approved by the national organization. In fact, in more than one-third of the world's parties, the national organization itself selects the party candidates.[25]

Primary elections. In the United States, most aspiring candidates for public office at all levels are nominated through a **primary election,** a preliminary election conducted within the party to select candidates who will run for office in a subsequent election. The nomination process, then, is highly decentralized, resting on the decisions of thousands, perhaps millions, of the party rank and file.

There are different types of primary elections for county, state, and congressional offices, depending on the state in which they are held. (We discuss presidential primaries in the next section.) The most common type (used by about forty states) is the **closed primary,** in which voters must declare their party affiliation before they are given the primary ballot, which lists the party's potential nominees. A handful of states use the **open primary,** in which voters need not declare a party affiliation but must choose one party's ballot to take into the polling booth. In a **blanket primary,** currently used in only two or three states, voters receive a ballot listing both parties' potential nominees and can help nominate candidates for all offices.

Most scholars believe that closed primaries strengthen party organization, and that blanket primaries weaken party organization. But the differences among types of primaries are much less important than the fact that the parties hold elections to choose their candidates. Placing the nomination of party candidates in the hands of voters rather than party leaders contributes mightily to the decentralization of power in American parties. The decentralized nature of American parties is clearly illustrated in campaigns for the party nomination for president.

Nominating a presidential candidate. Party candidates for president are nominated by delegates attending national conventions held in the summer before the presidential election in November. Gone are the days when a presidential candidate was chosen by top party leaders meeting in a smoke-filled room during the nominating convention—as the Republicans reportedly chose Warren G. Harding in 1920. Especially since the riots at the 1968 Democratic convention sparked changes in the nominating process, candidates have had to compete vigorously for the nomination by winning convention delegates in every state. There is no national legislation specifying how state parties must select delegates to their national conventions. Instead, state legislatures have enacted a bewildering variety of procedures that often differ for Democrats and Republicans in the same state. The most important distinction in delegate selection is between the primary and the caucus methods.

A **presidential primary** is a special primary used to select delegates to attend the party's national nominating convention. Primary elections were first used to select delegates to nominating conventions in 1912. In every election since, primaries have been held in at least twelve states

A Chorus Line
Blue suits and red ties predominated among the candidates at the first major debate of the campaign for the 1988 presidential nomination. The debate, organized by NBC News, was held at the Kennedy Center in Washington, D.C., on December 1, 1987. NBC's Tom Brokaw (center) was the host. To Brokaw's right are Republicans George Bush, Robert Dole, Pete du Pont, Alexander Haig, Jack Kemp, and Pat Robertson. To his left are Democrats Paul Simon, Jesse Jackson, Albert Gore, Richard Gephardt, Michael Dukakis, and Bruce Babbitt. (Democrat Gary Hart was not an active candidate at the time of the debate.)

and have always accounted for at least 33 percent of the delegates to the conventions.[26] There are two broad types of presidential primaries. In *presidential preference primaries* (used in about thirty states in 1988), party supporters vote directly for the person they favor as their party's nominee for president. In *delegate selection primaries* (used in only about five states in 1988), party voters directly elect convention delegates who may or may not have declared for a presidential candidate.

As a result of party reform, the number of presidential primaries began to grow in 1972. About 65 percent of the delegates to both national conventions in 1988 were selected in presidential primaries. Most of the remaining convention delegates were chosen through a system of party caucuses, vastly different from the defunct congressional caucuses that chose presidential candidates in the early 1800s. Today, a **party caucus** is a local meeting of party supporters to choose delegates to attend a subsequent meeting, usually at the county level. Most delegates selected in the local caucus openly back one of the presidential candidates. The county meetings, in turn, select delegates to a higher level. The process culminates in a state convention, which actually selects the delegates to the national convention. About twenty states used the caucus process in 1988 (a few states combined caucuses with primaries), and caucuses were employed more by Democrats than Republicans.

The process of nominating party candidates for president in the United States is a complex drawn-out affair that has no parallel in party politics in any other nation. Would-be presidents announce their candidacies and begin campaigning many months before the first convention delegates are selected. As shown in Feature 8.2, the selection process in 1988 began in early February with the Iowa caucuses, closely followed by the New Hampshire primary. By historical accident, these two small states have become the first tests of the candidates' popularity with party voters. Accordingly, each basks in the media spotlight once every four years. The Iowa and New Hampshire legislatures are now committed to leading off the delegate selection process, ensuring their states' share of national publicity and their bid for political history.

The Iowa caucuses and the New Hampshire primary serve different functions in the presidential nominating process.[27] The contest in Iowa tends to winnow out candidates who are rejected by the party faithful. When Alexander Haig failed to gain the support of even 1 percent of Iowans at the Republican caucuses, he promptly dropped out of the race. Although fellow Republican Pete du Pont and Democrats Bruce Babbitt and Gary Hart did not formally withdraw until after the New Hampshire primary, their dismal showings in Iowa foretold their fate.

The New Hampshire primary, held one week after the Iowa caucuses, tests the Iowa frontrunners' appeal to ordinary party voters, which foreshadows their likely strength in the general election. Because voting takes little effort, more citizens vote than attend caucuses, which can last for hours. In 1988, only about 11 percent of the voting-age population participated in the Iowa caucuses versus 37 percent who voted in the New Hampshire primary. Caucuses favor candidates with devoted supporters, like the backers of Pat Robertson and Jesse Jackson. Whereas Robertson finished a surprise second in the Iowa caucuses (beating

What's Your Sign?
No, it's not a picket line of campaign workers seeking unpaid wages. It's presidential primary day in New Hampshire. Supporters of most (but not all) of the 1988 candidates confront unsuspecting voters outside a polling place in Nashua. For 5 points, whose signs are missing? Hint: Check the photo caption on page 291. (Answer: du Pont, Haig, Gephardt, and Hart.)

George Bush), Robertson was only fifth in the New Hampshire primary. Although he won caucuses in three states, he did not come close to winning a single primary. Similarly, Jesse Jackson's only victory in a large state was in Michigan, where only about 100,000 attended the Democratic caucuses in a state with almost 7 million voters.

By winning the New Hampshire primary, George Bush and Michael Dukakis overcame their third-place finish in Iowa. By winning their party's nominations in 1988, Bush and Dukakis also added to the developing legend of the New Hampshire primary. Since 1952, no candidate has won the presidency without first winning that primary. In thirteen of the sixteen nominating contests in both parties since 1960, the candidate who won New Hampshire also won the party nomination. This remarkable record means that every four years, candidates will spend weeks of their life and millions of dollars trudging through snow, contesting for votes in a tiny state in the northeastern corner of the nation.

More than 35 million citizens voted in both parties' presidential primaries in 1988, and another million participated in party caucuses. Requiring prospective presidential candidates to campaign before many millions of party voters in primaries and hundreds of thousands of party activists in caucus states has several consequences:

■ The uncertainty of the nomination process attracts a half-dozen or so plausible candidates, especially when the party does not have a president seeking re-election. For example, seven Democrats and six Republicans took part in the process in 1988.

■ Candidates usually cannot win the nomination unless they are favored by most party identifiers. There have been only two exceptions to this rule since 1936, when poll data first became available: Adlai E. Stevenson II in 1952 and George McGovern in 1972.[28] Both were Democrats; both lost impressively in the general election.

The 1988 Delegate Races for the Presidential Nomination

Prospective candidates for president face a complex, grueling race to win delegates to support them at their party's national convention. In 1988, the delegate selection process formally began in the cold in February and ended in the sunshine in June. The graphs below show how few delegates were at stake in the early contests in Iowa and New Hampshire. Still, some candidates did so badly that they dropped out quickly to avoid further expense and embarrassment. The graphs also show the impact of "Super Tuesday" on March 8, when twenty states—mostly in the South—chose delegates.

The Democratic race was closely contested in the early stages. Richard Gephardt—the winner in Iowa—dropped out in late March after winning only Missouri (his home state) on Super Tuesday. Paul Simon—who was second in Iowa—dropped out after failing to win anywhere but Illinois (his home state). Albert Gore—who abandoned Iowa for lack of early support—recovered by winning big on Super Tuesday but dropped out after a poor showing in New York. Jesse Jackson, who won the most delegates on Super Tuesday, continued to draw support and remained throughout the race. The winner at the very

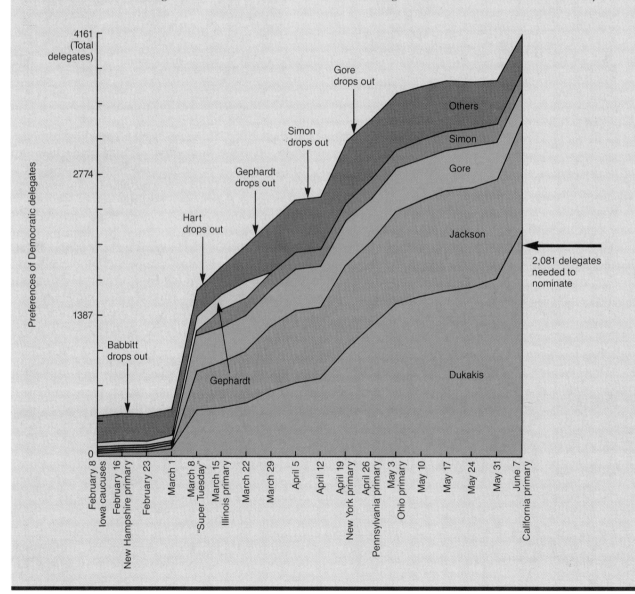

end was Michael Dukakis, who finished third in Iowa but who won the New Hampshire primary and three major states on Super Tuesday.

The race in the Republican party was really over in late March, when Robert Dole, the winner in Iowa, dropped out after failing to win a single state on Super Tuesday. Pat Robertson, who was second in Iowa and did well in other caucus states, failed to run well in primaries anywhere. Meanwhile, George Bush won every primary on Super Tuesday and over 70 percent of the delegates. Eventually running only against Robertson, Bush locked up his party's nomination in April by winning the Pennsylvania primary. Although Bush, like Dukakis, finished third in the Iowa caucuses, he also won the New Hampshire primary. They both demonstrated that winning in Iowa—or even coming in second—was not essential to winning the nomination, but that winning in New Hampshire prophesied victory at the convention.

Source: The weekly breakdown of delegate support was estimated by the Associated Press, *National Journal*, 13 February to 11 June, 1988.

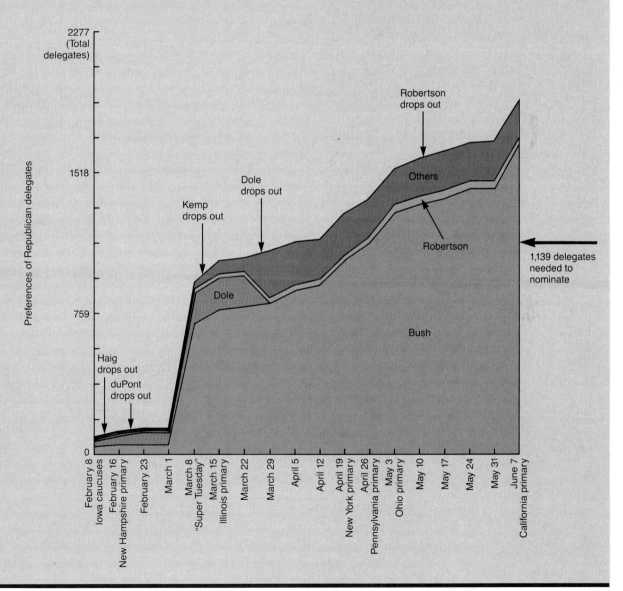

- Candidates who win the nomination do it mainly on their own and owe little or nothing to the national party organization, which usually does not push a candidate. In fact, Jimmy Carter won the nomination in 1976 against a field of nationally prominent Democrats, even though he was a party outsider with few strong connections in the national party leadership.

Because primary elections are held among candidates of the same party, it makes no sense to follow a party-centered campaign strategy. Therefore, primaries are limited to some mix of issue-oriented and personality-oriented campaign strategies. Campaigns between different parties' candidates for election to office, however, can use the full range of strategies.

Running for Office

By national law, all seats in the House of Representatives and one-third of the seats in the Senate are filled in a **general election** held on the first Tuesday after the first Monday in November in even-numbered years. Every state takes advantage of the national election to fill many state and local offices, which makes the election even more "general." When the president is chosen every fourth year, the general election is also known as a *presidential election*. In the intervening years, it is known as a *congressional, midterm,* or *off-year election.*

In contrast to general election campaigns in most other countries (and in earlier periods of our history), relatively few campaigns today follow a party-centered strategy, emphasizing the candidate's party attachment. Often, the party name does not even appear in the candidate's campaign literature. When party-centered campaigns do occur, they are often conducted by candidates of the major party in areas that are traditionally strong for one party. Party-centered campaigns are also likely when a popular president is running for re-election, and challengers see an opportunity to ride in on his coattails. Otherwise, election campaigns for national office tend to be highly personalistic, with candidates running as individuals rather than as a party team. Several factors contribute to this tendency:

- Candidates who rely on personal campaign organizations to win party nominations in the primaries tend to keep the same staff through the general election.

- The decline of party identification in the electorate makes candidates less likely to rely on party-related appeals.

- The increased use of electronic media, especially television, in campaigns has encouraged candidates to personalize their messages.

Using the Media

At one time, candidates for national office relied heavily on newspaper advertising in their campaigns; today, they overwhelmingly use the electronic media. A study of campaign spending in the 1986 primary and general elections calculated that candidates running for the House spent almost 20 percent of their campaign expenditures on television and radio, versus only 6 percent for print advertisements. Candidates for the Senate spent almost 40 percent for the electronic media, versus less than 1 percent for print media.[29] This emphasis on electronic media, particularly on television, has raised concern about the packaging of candidates who rely on television producers to develop a "videostyle" that helps win elections—but is irrelevant to performance in office.

In cultivating a candidate's videostyle, both consultant and candidate arrive at a campaign theme by anticipating audience reactions. Then the consultant coaches the candidate on how to deliver the theme quickly and effectively in a thirty- or sixty-second commercial. A scholar who analyzed television use by six candidates in three Senate campaigns found that audiences do not usually spend time dissecting the message in a television spot; instead, they form impressions of the mood, which the producer creates using "background music, the sharpness of the visual images, and the persuasiveness of the verbal content."[30]

The reason that consultants and candidates do not focus on issues in developing a videostyle may well be that their audience does not react well to issue-oriented discussions. One scholar who recorded scores of speeches by the major candidates seeking nomination in 1980 observed that audiences generally applauded less enthusiastically when candidates mentioned specific policies than when they made other appeals.[31] Consequently, all the candidates in 1980 concentrated on general problems rather than specific issues, and candidate Ronald Reagan tended to do this even more than the others. Reagan regularly drew cheers from his audiences for references to "godless totalitarians" in the Soviet Union and "welfare cheats" at home. Not surprisingly, he stressed these themes in office after his election.

Lest you think that electronic image makers and campaign consultants have the power to control an election (see Politics in the Information Age 8.1), remember that the image makers regularly offset one another by working on opposite sides in an election. Moreover, specialists in the new campaign technology argue that:

> no one has even a vague idea of what percentage of the vote a consultant or a piece of new campaign technology can or does add to a candidate under any given circumstances. Campaign observers rarely even have a precise idea of what event or series of events produced the election result. Campaigning remains complex, unpredictable, and very unscientific, and one may expect and be grateful that it always will be.[32]

Campaign Financing

Speaking about election campaigns, House Speaker Thomas "Tip" O'Neill once said, "As it is now, there are four parts to any campaign. The candidate, the issues of the candidate, the campaign organization, and the money to run the campaign with. Without money you can forget the other three."[33] Money is needed to pay for office space, staff salaries, telephone bills, postage, travel expenses, campaign literature, and, of course, advertising in the mass media.

Two major principles govern the funds needed to wage a winning campaign. The first is that challengers need to raise more money than

POLITICS IN THE INFORMATION AGE 8.1

A Sampler of New Campaign Technology

Two scholars of campaign technology, Larry Sabato and David Beiler, compiled this list of six technological wonders in the 1988 presidential campaign.

- The *Presidential Campaign Hotline* is a computer network that transmits campaign information each morning over telephone lines to the computers of nearly two hundred subscribers at a basic rate of $250 a month. The *Hotline* serves as a highly specialized wire service and also allows rapid communication among campaign organizations, the media, and interest group power brokers.

- *Audiovisual voter targeting* is enhanced through the use of cable television and videocassette distribution. By cross-referencing polling and census data, a campaign can send precise messages to key voters. This has been done for years using direct mail, but now that half the nation's homes are wired for cable television and half have VCRs, video messages can be directed to specific areas more cheaply than using television broadcasts.

- *Campaign-sponsored satellite feeds* can create a temporary television network for as little as $5,000. Several days before the event, the campaign contacts local stations with satellite reception capabilities. To induce their cooperation, the campaign offers live interviews with the candidate, which appeals to small stations.

- *Instantaneous pulse reading of focus groups* provides quick reactions to campaign themes or advertisements. A focus group usually consists of ten to fifteen individuals, sometimes recruited at random in shopping centers, who are paid for participating in group discussion of issues and candidates' qualities. By asking probing questions and recording unstructured responses, a trained group leader is able to discern attitudes that do not register on sample surveys.

- *Video image generators* produce appealing computer graphics that can enhance political messages. Examples include the "peeling page" that facilitate cuts from one story to another, and the rotation of images on the screen to match a story line.

- *Micromapping* of demographic and voting data on a computer screen produces a detailed map of an area to help door-to-door canvassers. This technique is especially useful in drawing boundaries for legislative redistricting.

Source: Adapted from Larry Sabato and David Beiler, "Magic . . . or Blue Smoke and Mirrors? Reflections on New Technologies and Trends in the Political Consultant Trade" (Northwestern University: The Annenberg Washington Program in Communication Policy Studies, 1988), pp. 7–25.

incumbents (officeholders running for re-election). Challengers need more money to overcome the incumbents' advantage in name recognition. Ironically, it is usually easier for incumbents to raise money than it is for challengers, because incumbents can do favors for people while they are in office. People also expect that incumbents will be re-elected anyway.

If there is no incumbent in the election, the second principle applies: Candidates of the minority party need to raise more funds than candidates of the majority party. Here, too, it is usually easier for candidates of the majority party to raise money. They have a better chance of winning, and people would rather contribute to winners than to losers. So the political facts of life are that electoral challengers and minority party candidates need to raise a good deal of money to run for office and win.

It is difficult to generalize about raising funds for political campaigns. Campaign financing is now heavily regulated by national and state governments, and regulations vary according to the level of the office—national, state, or local. Even at the national level, there are major differences in financing laws for presidential and congressional elections.

Regulating campaign financing. Strict campaign financing laws are relatively new to American politics. Early laws to limit campaign contributions and to control campaign spending were flawed in one way or another, and none clearly provided for administration and enforcement. In 1971, during the period of party reform, Congress passed the *Federal Election Campaign Act* (FECA), which imposed stringent new rules for full reporting of campaign contributions and expenditures. The weakness of the old legislation soon became apparent. In 1968, before the FECA was passed, House and Senate candidates reported spending $8.5 million for their campaigns. With the FECA in force, the same number of candidates confessed to spending $88.9 million in 1972.[34]

The FECA has been amended several times since 1971, but the amendments have for the most part strengthened the law. A 1974 amendment created the **Federal Election Commission (FEC)** to implement the law. The FEC now enforces limits on financial contributions to national campaigns and requires full disclosure of campaign spending. The FEC also administers the public financing of presidential campaigns, which began with the 1976 election.

Financing presidential campaigns. Presidential campaigns have always been expensive, and at times the methods of raising funds to support them were open to question. In the presidential election of 1972, the last election before the FEC took over funding presidential campaigns and regulating campaign expenditures, President Nixon's campaign committee spent over $65 million, some of it obtained illegally (for which campaign officials went to jail). In 1974, a new campaign finance law made public funds available to presidential primary and general election candidates under certain conditions.

Candidates for the nomination for president can qualify for federal funding by raising $5,000 (in private contributions no greater than $250 each) in each of twenty states. The FEC then matches these contributions up to one-half of the spending limit. Originally, under the 1974 law, the FEC limited spending in presidential primary elections to $10 million. But cost-of-living provisions had raised the limit in the 1988 primaries to $23.05 million (plus $4.6 million for fund-raising activities).

The presidential nominees of the Democratic and Republican parties get a different deal when they campaign for election. They receive twice the primary election limit in public funds for the general election campaign ($46.1 million in 1988) provided that they spend only the public funds. Every major candidate since 1976 has accepted public funding, holding the costs of presidential campaigns well below Nixon's record expenditures in 1972.

Public funds are given directly to each candidate's campaign committee, not to the national committee of either party. But the FEC also limits what the national committees can spend on behalf of the nominees. In 1988, that limit was only $8.3 million. And the FEC limits the amount individuals ($1,000) and organizations ($5,000) can contribute to candidates per election. They are not limited, however, in the amount of *expenses* they can incur to promote candidates of their choice.*

Public funding has had several effects on campaign financing. Obviously, it has limited campaign costs. Also, it has equalized the amounts spent by major candidates in general elections. And, it has strengthened the trend toward "personalized" campaigns. Federal funds are given to the presidential candidate of each party, not to the party organization that the candidate represents. Finally, public funding has forced candidates to spend a great deal of time seeking $1,000 contributions—a limit that has not changed since 1974, despite inflation that has more than doubled the FEC's spending limits.

You might think that a party's presidential campaign would be closely coordinated with the campaigns of the party's candidates for Congress. But remember that campaign funds go to the presidential candidate, not the party, and that the national party organization does not run the presidential campaign. Presidential candidates may join congressional candidates in public appearances for mutual benefit, but presidential campaigns are usually isolated—financially and otherwise—from congressional campaigns.

EXPLAINING VOTING CHOICE

Why do people choose one candidate over another? Individual voting choices can be analyzed as products of *long-term* and *short-term* forces. Long-term forces operate over a series of elections, predisposing voters to choose certain types of candidates. Short-term forces are associated with particular elections; they arise from a combination of the candidates and the issues of the time. *Party identification* is by far the most important long-term force affecting U.S. elections. The most important short-term forces are *candidate attributes* and their *policy positions*.

Party Identification

Most research on voting in presidential elections stems from a series of studies that originated at the University of Michigan. Comparable

---

* The distinction between contributions and expenses hinges on whether funds are spent as part of a coordinated campaign (a contribution) or spent independently of the candidate's campaign (an expense). The 1974 amendment to the FECA had established limits on both campaign contributions and independent expenditures by interested citizens. In *Buckley v. Valeo* (1976), the Supreme Court struck down the limits on citizens' expenditures as an infringement on the freedom of speech, protected under the First Amendment.

surveys have been conducted for every presidential election and most congressional elections since 1952. When respondents to the 1984 survey were asked at what point they had decided how to vote for president, nearly half (44 percent) said that they "knew all along" or had decided before the conventions.[35] This figure is only slightly higher than the average. In every presidential survey since 1952, about 40 percent of the voters reported making up their minds before the candidates squared off in the general election campaign. And voters who make an early voting decision generally vote according to their party identification.

Party identification had a substantial effect on the presidential vote in 1988. Avowed Democrats voted 82 percent for Dukakis, while Republicans voted 91 percent for Bush. Independents split 55 percent for Bush. This is a common pattern in presidential elections. The winner holds nearly all of the voters who identify with his party. The loser also holds most of his identifiers, but some percentage defects to the winner, a product of the short-term forces—the candidates' attributes and the issues—surrounding the election. The winner usually gets most of the independents, who split disproportionately for him, also because of short-term forces.

Because there are more Democrats than Republicans, the Democrats should benefit. Why, then, have Republican candidates won seven out of ten presidential elections since 1952? For one thing, Democrats do not turn out to vote as consistently as Republicans. For another, Democrats defect more easily from their party identification. Defections are sparked by the candidates' attributes and the issues, which have favored Republican presidential candidates since 1952.

Candidates' Attributes

Candidates' attributes are especially important to voters who lack good information about a candidate's past behavior and policy stands—which means most of us. Without this kind of information, voters search for clues about the candidates to try to predict their behavior in office. Some fall back on their firsthand knowledge of marital status, religion, sex, and race in making political judgments. For example, most voters would rather have a "good guy" in the presidency than a "mean man." Research showed that Ronald Reagan exuded a "good guy" image when he ran in 1980 against President Carter, who was seen as being cross and ineffective. The researchers calculated that the perceived differences in the candidates' attributes cost Carter 4 percent of the vote.[36]

For some reason, the Democrats since 1952 have tended to nominate candidates who were personally flawed in many voters' eyes. In 1952 and in 1956, the Democrats nominated Adlai E. Stevenson II, who was divorced. That may not seem like a flaw today, but it concerned voters in the 1950s. In 1960, the Democrats chose John F. Kennedy, whose flaw—to many Protestants—was his Catholicism. Although he was a young, handsome, charismatic candidate of the majority party, who might have been expected to win easily, Kennedy did poorly among Protestant Democrats and barely edged Nixon out in one of the closest elections in history.

Ger-ry! Ger-ry! Ger-ry!
Geraldine Ferraro, the first woman vice presidential candidate of a major political party, acknowledges cheers at the 1984 Democratic National Convention in San Francisco. Although the Mondale-Ferraro ticket lost the election, candidate Ferraro performed well as a campaigner, and she undoubtedly added to the credibility of women seeking the presidential nomination in both parties in the future.

In 1984, the Democrats nominated Geraldine Ferraro for vice president. Her flaw, for certain voters, was her sex. After an initial burst of enthusiasm for her nomination, many Democratic voters (especially in the South) came to resent a woman on the ticket. Divorced candidates and Catholics are commonplace in both parties now; some day, women presidential candidates will be too. The Democratic party may be ahead of the electorate's readiness to accept social change and so may occasionally hurt itself at the polls because of its candidates' personal attributes. In 1988, Jesse Jackson, a black, won 29 percent of the presidential primary votes in the Democratic party and captured 27 percent of the delegates before losing the nomination to Michael Dukakis. Whichever party nominates the first black candidate may also pay a price at the polls.

Issues and Policies

Choosing between candidates according to personal attributes might be defended, but it is not rational voting according to democratic theory. That theory insists that citizens should vote according to the candidates' past performance and proposed policies. The candidates clearly differed on their policies in the presidential election of 1988. Michael Dukakis, trying to recapture the presidency for the Democrats, stressed the government's responsibility to provide "good jobs for good wages." George Bush, seeking to retain the office for the Republicans, charged that his opponent was a spendthrift liberal who would surely raise taxes.

Voters who choose between candidates on the basis of their policies are voting "on the issues." Unfortunately for democratic theory, most studies of presidential elections show that issues are less important than either party identification or the candidate's image when people cast their ballots. Only in 1972, when voters perceived George McGovern as too liberal for their tastes, did issue voting exceed party identification in importance.[37] Even that year, issues were less important than the candidate's image. According to polls taken at the time, voters saw McGovern as weak and uncertain, Nixon as strong and (ironically) highly principled.[38]

Still, there has been an increase in issue voting since the 1950s. Moreover, there is a closer alignment now between voters' positions on the issues and their party identification. For example, Democratic party identifiers—who are more likely than Republican identifiers to describe themselves as liberal—are now even more likely than Republican identifiers to favor government spending for social welfare and abortions. The more closely party identification is aligned with ideological orientation, the more sense it makes to vote by party. In the absence of detailed information about candidates' positions on the issues, party labels are a handy indicator of those positions.

Voting for Congress

The candidates for the presidency are listed at the top of the ballot in a presidential election, followed by candidates for other national, state, and local offices. A voter is said to vote a **straight ticket** when he or she chooses only one party's candidates for all the offices. A voter who switches parties when choosing candidates for different offices is said to vote a **split ticket.** This voter might choose a Republican for president but cross over to the Democratic side of the ballot and vote for a Democratic member of Congress running for re-election.

As party identification has dropped off, the amount of split-ticket voting has increased, from about 30 percent of the voters in 1952 to more than half the voters in 1984. Split-ticket voting accounts for the Republicans' failure to win control of the House of Representatives in 1984, despite the fact that Reagan carried all but one state in the presidential election. Many who voted for Reagan crossed over to vote for incumbent Democratic representatives. A total of 254 of the 435 congressional contests in 1984 pitted Democratic incumbents against Republican challengers, and 241 (98 percent) of the Democratic incumbents won.

We offer a full explanation of the high rate of re-election for congressional incumbents in Chapter 10. In a nutshell, members of Congress have learned to use their powers of office to develop favorable impressions of themselves and their service to their districts. As a result, voting for congressional candidates has become increasingly detached from voting for presidents.

POLITICAL PARTIES AND THE MODELS OF DEMOCRACY

The importance of political parties in democratic government depends on the model of democracy we choose. Political parties as agents of government are much more important to the majoritarian model of democracy than to the pluralist model.

Parties and the Majoritarian Model

According to the majoritarian model of democracy, parties are essential to making the government responsive to public opinion. In fact, the ideal role of parties in majoritarian democracy has been formalized in the four principles of **responsible party government**:[39]

1. Parties should present clear and coherent programs to voters.
2. Voters should choose candidates according to the party programs.
3. The winning party should carry out its program once in office.
4. Voters should hold the governing party responsible at the next election for executing its program.

How well are these principles being met in American politics? You've learned that the Democratic and Republican platforms are different and that they are much more ideologically consistent than many people believe. So the first principle is being met fairly well. The second principle is being met only partially. Most voters do have longstanding party identifications, which explain a great deal of their candidate choice. Although this is not the same thing as choosing candidates according to their party programs, the alignment of party identifiers according to liberal-conservative ideology is fairly strong and increasing. However, the relationship between party identification and voting choice is often stronger in presidential than in congressional elections.

The third principle—that the winning party should carry out its program—is the least applicable to American party politics. Regardless of which party wins the presidency, the president cannot count on his party members in Congress to vote solidly for his program. As we discuss in Chapter 10, members of Congress cater to their constituents in order to ensure their re-election. Accordingly, they often vote against their party's position when they think a law will harm their district or state. In truth, political parties in America are too decentralized to enforce party discipline in congressional voting. Congressional candidates win nomination on their own by contesting primary elections, and they win elections mainly by raising their own funds and by running their own campaigns. The conditions for party discipline simply are not adequate to force members of Congress either to support or oppose a president's program, as we saw in the case of Phil Gramm at the beginning of this chapter.

The fourth principle—that voters should hold the governing party accountable in the next election for executing the party program—also does not apply in American politics. In fact, the party program tends to fade from sight soon after the convention that wrote the platform. The platform represents the views of the delegates to the party convention; it may not reflect the views of the party's nominee for president. After the election, the winning candidate presents his own legislative program, which may emphasize certain planks more than others and may neglect some entirely. Neither national party organization in America would pretend to force its platform on its winning presidential candidate. It is the *president's* legislative program, not the party's platform, that party members in Congress are asked to support. And the next presidential election becomes a referendum not so much on party government as on presidential government.

Parties and the Pluralist Model

The way parties in the United States operate is more in keeping with the pluralist model of democracy than with the majoritarian model. Our parties are not the basic mechanisms through which citizens control their government; instead, they function as two giant interest groups. They press their own interests (electing and re-electing their candidates) in competition with other groups in the swirl of pluralist politics. Parties repeatedly bargain away platform principles for short-term electoral gains.

Some scholars believe that stronger parties would contribute more to democratic government than our present weak ones, even if American parties could not then meet all the requirements of the responsible party model.[40] Although our parties today perform valuable functions structuring the vote and proposing alternative government policies, stronger parties might be able to play a more valuable role in coordinating government policies.

SUMMARY

Political parties perform four important functions in a political system: nominating candidates, structuring the voting choice, proposing alternative government programs, and coordinating the activities of government officials. Political parties have been performing these functions longer in the United States than in any other country. The Democratic party, founded in 1828, is the world's oldest political party. When the Republican party emerged as a major party after the 1856 election, it joined the Democrats to produce our present two-party system—the oldest party system in the world.

America's two-party system has experienced three critical elections, each of which realigned the electorate for years and affected the party balance in government. The election of 1860 established the Republicans as the major party in the North and the Democrats as the dominant party in the South. Nationally, the two parties were roughly balanced in Congress until the critical election of 1896. This election strengthened the link between the Republican party and business interests in the heavily populated Northeast and Midwest and produced a surge in voter support that made the Republicans the majority party nationally for more than three decades. The Great Depression produced conditions for the critical election of 1932, which transformed the Democrats into

the majority party, giving them almost uninterrupted control of Congress since then.

Minor parties have not enjoyed much electoral success in America, although they have contributed ideas to the Democratic and Republican platforms. The two-party system is perpetuated in the United States because of the nature of our electoral system and the political socialization process, which results in most Americans' identifying with either the Democratic or the Republican party. The federal system of government has also helped the Democrats and Republicans survive major national defeats by sustaining them with electoral victories at the state level. However, the pattern of party identification has been changing in recent years: As more people are becoming independents and Republicans, the number of Democratic identifiers is dropping.

Party identifiers, party activists, and party platforms show consistent differences in ideological orientations between the two major parties. Democratic identifiers and activists are more likely to describe themselves as liberal; Republican identifiers and activists tend to be conservative. The 1988 Democratic party platform also showed a more liberal orientation by stressing equality over freedom; the Republican platform was more conservative, concentrating on freedom but also emphasizing the importance of restoring social order. Organizationally, the Republicans have recently become the stronger party at both national and state levels, but both parties are very decentralized compared with parties in other countries.

The successful candidate for public office usually must campaign first to win the party nomination, then to win the general election. A major factor in the decentralization of American parties is their reliance on primary elections to nominate candidates. Candidates who have to campaign for the party nomination owe little to the party organization and retain their own campaign staffs to help them win the general election. The dynamics of campaign financing also force candidates to rely mainly on their own resources or—in the case of presidential elections— on public funds. Party organizations contribute relatively little toward campaign expenses.

The voting choice can be analyzed in terms of party identification, candidates' attributes, and policy positions. Party identification is still the most important long-term factor in shaping the voting decision, but few candidates rely on party in their campaigns. Most candidates today run personalized campaigns that stress their attributes or their policies. In particular, votes for congressional candidates are tied to the personal relationships that incumbents have forged with their constituents. The high rate of re-election for incumbent members of Congress helps insulate them from party pressures in policymaking.

American parties do not fulfill the ideals of responsible party government that fit the majoritarian model of democracy. In particular, the parties are weak in carrying out their programs once in office, which makes it difficult for voters to hold them accountable at the next election. American parties are better suited to the pluralist model of democracy, which sees them as major interest groups competing with lesser groups to further their own interests.

Are America's parties carrying out their major functions? For the most part, yes. They do well nominating candidates and very well structuring the vote. Their record formulating alternative government programs is not as good. And they have very little control over the actions of officials in government. But political parties at least aspire to the noble goal of representing the needs and wants of most of the people. As we see in the next chapter, interest groups do not even pretend as much.

Key Terms

political party
nominate
political system
electoral college
caucus
national convention
party platform
critical election
electoral realignment
two-party system
majority party
minority party
electoral dealignment
bolter party
farmer-labor party
party of ideological protest
single-issue party
single-member district
proportional representation
party identification
national committee
congressional campaign organization
party machine
electoral campaign
primary election
closed primary
open primary
blanket primary
presidential primary
party caucus
general election
incumbent
Federal Election Commission (FEC)
straight ticket
split ticket
responsible party government

Selected Readings

Advisory Commission on Intergovernmental Relations. *The Transformation of American Politics: Implications for Federalism.* Washington, D.C.: Report A-106, August 1986. A general study of American political parties, especially useful for its data on state party organizations.

Bibby, John F. *Politics, Parties, and Elections in America.* Chicago: Nelson-Hall, 1987. This recent text on political parties is strong on the historical dimension and on state party organizations; it also includes very informative graphs.

Diamond, Edwin, and Stephen Bates. *The Spot: The Rise of Political Advertising on Television.* Cambridge, Mass.: M.I.T. Press, 1988. Describes the strategy, planning, creation, and execution of thirty- to sixty-second political commercials.

Flanigan, William H., and Nancy Zingale. *Political Behavior of the American Electorate.* 6th ed. Boston: Allyn & Bacon, 1987. This book, now in its sixth edition, offers a straightforward thorough description of voter turnout and voting choice.

Nesbit, Dorothy Davidson. *Videostyle in Senate Campaigns.* Knoxville, Tenn.: University of Tennessee Press, 1988. An engaging study of six campaigns in three elections to the U.S. Senate in 1982 that focuses on candidates and the producers of their television advertisements.

Orren, Gary R., and Nelson W. Polsby, eds. *Media and Momentum: The New Hampshire Primary and Nomination Politics.* Chatham, N.J.: Chatham House, 1987. This is an excellent series of studies of media coverage of early campaigning for the presidential nomination—mainly in New Hampshire but also in Iowa.

Rosenstone, Steven J., Roy L. Behr, and Edward H. Lazarus. *Third Parties in America: Citizen Response to Major Party Failure.* Princeton, N.J.: Princeton University Press, 1984. The authors not only provide an excellent review of the history of third-party movements in American politics, but they also analyze the factors that lead third-party voters and candidates to abandon the two major parties. They conclude that third-party efforts improve the performance of the party system.

Sabato, Larry J. *The Party's Just Begun: Shaping Political Parties for America's Future.* Glenview, Ill.: Scott, Foresman, 1988. The book's premise is that citizens' partisan loyalty can be regenerated and that the parties can be strengthened organizationally—indeed that they are stronger at the national level than ever before in modern times.

Sorauf, Frank J. *Money in American Elections.* Glenview, Ill.: Scott, Foresman, 1988. Surveys receipts and expenditures in presidential and congressional campaigns, including financing by individuals, PACs, parties, and government.

9

Interest Groups

Digital audio tape recorders (DATs) use computerized digital technology to produce recordings that are as perfect as the source. If you recorded a friend's record, tape, or compact disk (CD), the copy would be as good as the original, for only the cost of a blank tape. Although DATs are available in Japan and Europe, they are not yet being marketed in America. It's not because the Japanese manufacturers don't think they can sell them here; its because a fight between competing interest groups has stopped them from trying.

When the Japanese companies first brought out DATs, the American music industry cried "foul" and the Recording Industry Association of America began lobbying Congress to place restrictions on the machines. They were afraid that sales of existing records, tapes, and CDs would be hurt by high-quality DAT copies. Testifying before a congressional committee looking at the DAT problem, country singer Emmylou Harris identified the issue for performers: "Maybe people think they're flattering us by copying our music. But the simple truth is they're choking off our livelihood."[1] The music industry advocated legislation that would require DATs be equipped with copy-code scanners that would effectively prevent the machines from making usable copies. Original recordings would be manufactured with tiny slices of sound missing—so small that the lapses would be inaudible to the human ear. A computer chip in the modified DAT would recognize these gaps, however, and would shut down the machine for twenty-five seconds every time it came across one. The recorded tapes—with their periodic lengthy silences—would be useless.

Not surprisingly, electronics retailers and consumer groups didn't like this proposal, and they too began to lobby Congress. Retailers knew there would be little market for the expensive machines if their taping capabilities were limited. Consumers would be denied a new technology, and music lovers were appalled at the idea of recordings that had even the tiniest bits of electronic blank spots. The Home Recording Rights Coalition vigorously opposed congressional sanctions against DATs. By spring 1988, the issue had not been resolved in Congress, and manufacturers were still unwilling to try to sell the DATs in the United States when their future here was so uncertain.

The DAT example illustrates some of the basic dynamics of interest group politics. At the heart of pluralist politics are groups fighting for their own narrow interests. Here, the recording industry was on one side, while retailers and manufacturers lined up on the other. The DAT example also shows how the interests of lobbying organizations are sometimes pitted against majoritarian interests. Should we try to protect recording artists and companies from high-quality copying as a matter of fairness? Or should we do what's best for consumers—the majoritarian interest—by allowing them to purchase an excellent product that is available in other countries?

The clash of interest groups (lobbies) may be visibly manifested in the struggle of different lobbyists to persuade government officials of the rightness of their views. We are interested in the lobbyists' activity because they work to get their constituents' views before those in government. In analyzing the process by which interest groups and lobbyists come to speak on behalf of different groups, we focus on a number of questions. How do interest groups form? Who do they represent? What tactics do they use to convince policymakers that their views are best for the nation? Why has the number of interest groups grown so rapidly in recent years? And what is the impact of that growth?

INTEREST GROUPS AND THE AMERICAN POLITICAL TRADITION

An **interest group** is "an organized body of individuals who share some goals and who try to influence public policy."[2] Among the most prominent interest groups in the United States are the AFL-CIO (representing labor union members), the American Farm Bureau Federation (representing farmers), the Chamber of Commerce (representing businesspeople), and Common Cause (representing citizens concerned with reforming government). Interest groups are also called **lobbies,** and their representatives are referred to as **lobbyists.**

Interest Groups: Good or Evil?

A recurring debate in American politics concerns the role of interest groups in a democratic society. Are interest groups a threat to the well-being of the political system? Or do they contribute to its proper functioning? A favorable early evaluation of interest groups can be found in the writings of Alexis de Tocqueville, a French visitor to the United States in the early nineteenth century. During his travels, Tocqueville marveled at the array of organizations he found, and he later wrote that "Americans of all ages, all conditions, and all dispositions, constantly form associations" (see Compared With What? 9.1).[3] Tocqueville was suggesting that the ease with which we form organizations reflects a strong democratic culture.

James Madison offered a different perspective. Writing in the *Federalist Papers,* he warned of the dangers of "factions," the major divisions in American society. In "Federalist No. 10," written in 1787, Madison said that it was inevitable that substantial differences would develop between factions. It was only natural that farmers would come to oppose merchants; tenants, landlords; and so on. Madison further reasoned that each faction would do what it could to prevail over other factions, that each basic interest in society would try to persuade government to adopt policies that favored it at the expense of others. He noted that the fundamental causes of faction were "sown in the nature of man."

But Madison argued against trying to suppress factions. He concluded that factions can be eliminated only by removing our freedoms: "Liberty is to faction what air is to fire." Instead, Madison suggested that "relief" from the self-interested advocacy of factions should come only through controlling the *effects* of that advocacy. This relief would be provided by a democratic republic in which government would mediate between opposing factions. The structure of government would also ensure that even a majority faction could never come to suppress the rights of others.[4]

COMPARED WITH WHAT? 9.1

Membership in Groups

Alexis de Tocqueville's observation that "Americans form associations for the smallest undertakings" may be an exaggeration, but Americans do seem to join groups in greater proportions than the people of other countries.*

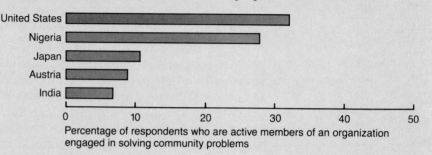

Percentage of respondents who are active members of an organization engaged in solving community problems

---

* Alexis de Tocqueville, *Democracy in America*, ed. Richard D. Heffner (New York: Mentor, 1956), p. 36.

Source: Sidney Verba, Norman H. Nie, and Jae-On Kim, *The Modes of Democratic Participation: A Cross-National Comparison* (Beverly Hills, Calif.: SAGE, 1971), p. 36. © 1971 Sage Publications Inc.

How we judge interest groups—"good" or "evil"—depends on how strongly we are committed to freedom or equality (see Chapter 1). Giving people the freedom to organize lobbies does not guarantee that they will all end up with equally powerful interest groups acting on their behalf. Judgment is also influenced by whether we believe democracy works best if it abides by majoritarian or by pluralist principles (see Chapter 2). We return to these broader questions of democratic theory after looking at the operation of interest groups more closely.

The Roles of Interest Groups

The "evil" side of interest group politics is all too apparent. Each group pushes its own selfish interests, which, despite the group's claims to the contrary, are not always in the best interest of other Americans. The "good" side of interest group advocacy may not be as clear. How do the actions of interest groups benefit our political system?[5]

Representation. Interest groups *represent* people before their government. Just as a member of Congress represents a particular constituency, so does a lobbyist. A lobbyist for the National Association of Broadcasters, for example, speaks for the interests of radio and television broadcasters when Congress or a government agency is considering a relevant policy decision.

Whatever the political interest—the cement industry, excise taxes, endangered species—it is helpful to have an active lobby operating in Washington. Members of Congress represent a multitude of interests—

some of them conflicting—from their own districts and states. Government administrators, too, are pulled in different directions and have their own policy preferences. Interest groups articulate their members' concerns, presenting them directly and forcefully in the political forum.

Participation.   Interest groups are also vehicles for political *participation.* They provide a means by which like-minded citizens can pool their resources and channel their energies into collective political action. And people band together because they know it is much easier to get government to listen to a group than to an individual. One farmer fighting for more generous price supports probably will not get very far; but thousands of farmers united in an organization stand a much better chance of getting policymakers to consider their needs.

Education.   As part of their efforts at lobbying and increasing their membership, interest groups help *educate* their members, the public at large, and government officials. In 1987, when President Reagan nominated Judge Robert Bork for a seat on the Supreme Court, liberal and conservative citizen groups engaged in a spirited—some would say mean-spirited—effort to educate the American public about the nominee. Us-

Do I Look Like a Lobbyist to You?
Probably not, but this ad is a form of lobbying. It aims to convince people that legal abortion is an important option by arguing that it would be foolish for someone so young to raise a child. Through its use of a clean-cut, girl-next-door type, the ad also suggests that teenage pregnancy is not a problem that "happens only to other people."

"Do I look like a mother to you?"

She does if you look at the statistics.

The United States is the only industrialized nation where the teenage pregnancy rate is going up. Forty percent of all girls who are now fourteen will get pregnant before they're eighteen. One million each year.

The social consequences are enormous. Because most teenage mothers are single mothers, trapped in a cycle of poverty that costs billions extra each year. In malnutrition. Disease. Unemployment. Child abuse.

But the tragic effects of motherhood on each individual teenager can't be measured in dollars and cents. And it isn't reflected in the statistics. She's robbed of her childhood and her hope.

While we must do everything we can to help *prevent* unwanted pregnancy, we must also preserve the option of safe, legal abortion.

A teenage girl shouldn't be forced to become a mother if she's not ready.

But there's an increasingly vocal and violent minority that disagrees. They want to outlaw abortions for all women, regardless of circumstances. Even if her life or health is endangered by a pregnancy. Even if she is a victim of rape or incest. And even if she is too young to be a mother.

They're pressuring lawmakers to make abortions illegal. And that's not all. They also oppose birth control and sex education—ways of *preventing* abortion. They've already tried to slash federal funding for these and other family planning programs. And to get their way, they've resorted to threats, physical intimidation and violence.

Speak out now. Or they just might succeed. Use the coupon.

The decision is yours.

☐ I've written my representatives in Congress to tell them I support: government programs that reduce the need for abortion by preventing unwanted pregnancy; and keeping safe and legal abortion a choice for all women.

☐ Here's my tax-deductible contribution in support of all Planned Parenthood activities and programs: ☐ $25 ☐ $35 ☐ $50 ☐ $75 ☐ $150 ☐ $500 ☐ or: $_____

NAME

STREET/CITY/ZIP

 Planned Parenthood®
Federation of America, Inc.

810 Seventh Avenue
New York, New York 10019

This ad was paid for with private contributions. © Copyright 1985

ing advertisements, each side tried to show what the "real" Bork record
told us about what kind of Supreme Court justice he was likely to be.
Interest groups give only their side of the "facts," but they do bring more
information out into the open to be digested and evaluated by the public.

Agenda building.   In a related role, interest groups bring new issues
into the political limelight, through a process called **agenda building.**
There are many problem areas in American society, but not all of them
are being addressed by public officials. Interest groups make the government aware of problems through their advocacy, then try to see to it that
something is done to solve them. After videocassette recorders (VCRs)
became popular in the United States, competing lobbies raised a number
of questions about copyright law and royalty payments to movie studios.
The Motion Picture Association of America and the Electronic Industries
Association (the trade group for VCR manufacturers) brought these issues
to the fore by pressing Congress for action.[6]

Program monitoring.   Finally, interest groups engage in **program
monitoring.** In other words, they follow government programs important
to their constituents, keeping abreast of developments in Washington
and in the local communities where policies are implemented. When
problems emerge, interest groups push administrators to resolve them
in ways that promote the group's goals. They draw attention to agency
officials' transgressions and even file suit to stop actions they consider
unlawful. When the U.S. Department of Agriculture reduced food stamp
benefits on the order of President Gerald Ford, the Food Research and
Action Center acted on behalf of program recipients and took the department to court. The court sided with the lobby, and the original
benefits were reinstated.

Interest groups do, then, play some positive roles in their pursuit of
self-interest. But it is too soon to assume that the positive side of interest
groups neatly balances the negative. Questions remain to be answered
about the overall impact of interest groups on public policymaking. Most
important, are the effects of interest group advocacy being controlled, as
Madison believed they should be?

HOW INTEREST GROUPS FORM

Do some people form interest groups more easily than others? Are some
factions represented while others are not? Pluralists assume that when
a political issue arises, interest groups with relevant policy concerns
begin to lobby. Policy conflicts are ultimately resolved through bargaining and negotiation between the involved organizations and government.
Unlike Madison, who dwelled on the potential for harm by factions,
pluralists believe interest groups are a good thing, that they further
democracy by broadening representation within the system.

An important part of pluralism is the belief that new interest groups
form as a matter of course when the need arises. David Truman outlined
this idea in his classic work *The Governmental Process.*[7] He said that
when individuals are threatened by change, they band together in an

interest group. For example, if government threatens to regulate a particular industry, the firms comprising that industry will start a trade association to protect their financial well-being. Truman saw a direct cause-and-effect relationship in all of this: Existing groups stand in equilibrium until some type of disturbance (such as falling wages or declining farm prices) forces new groups to form.

Truman's thinking on the way interest groups form is like the "invisible hand" notion of classical economics: Self-correcting market forces will remedy imbalances in the marketplace. But in politics there is no invisible hand, no force that automatically causes interest groups to develop. Truman's disturbance theory paints an idealized portrait of interest group politics in America. In real life, people do not automatically organize when they are adversely affected by some disturbance. A good example of this "nonorganization" can be found in Herbert Gans's book *The Urban Villagers*.[8] Gans, a sociologist, moved into the West End, a low-income neighborhood in Boston, during the late 1950s. The neighborhood had been targeted for urban redevelopment; the city was planning to replace existing buildings with modern ones. This meant that the people living there—primarily poor Italian-Americans who very much liked their neighborhood—would have to move.

Few things in life are less pleasant than being evicted, so the situation in the West End certainly qualified as a bona fide disturbance in Truman's scheme of interest group formation. Yet the people of the West End barely put up a fight to save their neighborhood. An organization was started but attracted little support. Residents remained unorganized; soon they were moved and buildings were demolished.

Disturbance theory clearly fails to explain what happened in Boston's West End. An adverse condition or change does not automatically mean that an interest group will form. What, then, is the missing ingredient? Political scientist Robert Salisbury says that the quality of interest group leadership may be the crucial factor.[9]

Interest Group Entrepreneurs

Salisbury likens the role of an interest group leader to that of an entrepreneur in the business world. An entrepreneur is someone who starts new enterprises, usually at considerable personal financial risk. Salisbury says that an **interest group entrepreneur** or organizer succeeds or fails for many of the same reasons a business entrepreneur succeeds or fails. The interest group entrepreneur must have something attractive to "market" in order to convince members to join.[10] Potential members must be persuaded that the benefits of joining outweigh the costs. Someone starting up a new union, for example, must convince workers that the union can win them wages high enough to offset their membership dues. The organizer of an ideological group must convince potential members that the group can effectively lobby the government to achieve their particular goals.

The development of the United Farm Workers Union shows the importance of leadership in an interest group's formation. This union is made up of men and women who pick crops in California and other parts of the Southwest. The work is backbreaking, performed in a hot, desert climate. The pickers are predominantly poor uneducated Mexican-Americans.

Their chronically low wages and deplorable living conditions made these farm workers prime candidates for organization into a labor union. And throughout the twentieth century, there had been efforts to organize the pickers. Yet for many reasons, including distrust of union organizers, intimidation by employers, and lack of money to pay union dues, all had failed. Then, in 1962, Cesar Chavez, a poor Mexican-American, began to crisscross the Central Valley of California, talking to workers and planting the idea of a union. Chavez had been a farm worker himself (he first worked as a picker at the age of ten), and he was well aware of the difficulties that lay ahead for his newly organized union.

After a strike against grape growers failed in 1965, Chavez changed his tactics of trying to build a stronger union merely through recruiting a larger membership. Copying the black civil rights movement, Chavez and his followers marched 250 miles to the state capitol in Sacramento to demand help from the governor. This march and other nonviolent tactics began to draw sympathy from people who had no direct involvement in farming. The Catholic clergy was a major source of support, seeing the movement as a way to help poor members of the church. This support, in turn, gave the charismatic Chavez greater credibility, and his followers cast him in the role of spiritual as well as political leader. At one point, he fasted for twenty-five days to show his commitment to nonviolence. Democratic Senator Robert Kennedy of New York, one of the most popular politicians of the day, joined Chavez when he broke his fast at a mass conducted on the back of a flatbed truck in Delano, California.[11]

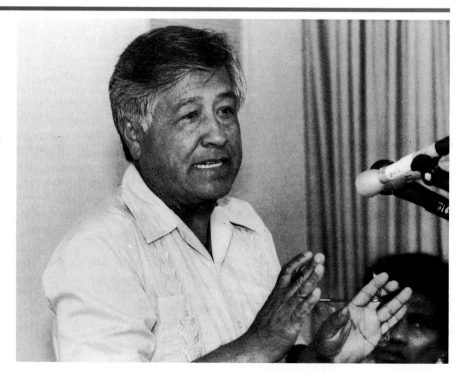

Cesar Chavez
Although many efforts had been made to organize migrant farm workers, none succeeded until Chavez's inspired leadership brought the United Farm Workers Union into existence. Growers bitterly resisted the unionization efforts, but economic pressures finally led many of them to the bargaining table. In this 1987 speech, Chavez described a three-year-old boycott of table grapes, designed to stop growers from using pesticides that endanger field workers.

Chavez, now a strong respected leader, called for a boycott. A small but significant number of Americans stopped buying grapes. The growers, who had bitterly fought the union, were finally hurt in their wallets. Under other economic pressure, they eventually agreed to recognize and bargain with the United Farm Workers Union. The union, in turn, helped its members through the wage and benefit agreements it negotiated.

Who Is Being Organized?

The case of Cesar Chavez is a good example of the importance of leadership in the formation of a new interest group. Despite many years of adverse conditions, efforts to organize the farm workers had failed. The dynamic leadership of Cesar Chavez is what seems to have made the difference.

But another important element is at work in the formation of interest groups. The residents of Boston's West End and the farm workers in California were poor, uneducated or undereducated, and politically inexperienced—factors that made it extremely difficult to organize them into interest groups. If they had been well-to-do, educated, and politically experienced, they probably would have banded together immediately. People who have money, are educated, and know how the system operates are more confident that their actions can make a difference. Together, these attributes give people more incentive to devote their time and ample resources to organizing and supporting interest groups.

Every existing interest group has its own unique history. Yet the three variables that we have discussed help explain why groups may or may not become fully organized. First, an adverse change or disturbance can contribute to people's awareness that they need political representation. However, change alone does not ensure that an organization will form, and organizations have formed in the absence of disturbance. Second, the quality of leadership is critical in the organization of interest groups. Some interest group entrepreneurs are more skilled at convincing people to join their organizations. Finally, the higher the socioeconomic level of potential members, the more likely they are to know the value of interest groups and to participate in politics by joining them.

Because wealthy and better-educated Americans are more likely to form and join lobbies, they seem to have an important advantage in the political process. Nevertheless, as the United Farm Workers case shows, poor and uneducated people are also capable of forming interest groups. The question that remains, then, is not *whether* various opposing interests are represented but *how well* they are represented. Or, in terms of Madison's premise in "Federalist No. 10," are the effects of faction—in this case, the advantages of the wealthy and well educated—being controlled? Before we can answer this question, we need to turn our attention to the resources available to interest groups.

INTEREST GROUP RESOURCES

The strengths, capabilities, and effects of an interest group depend in large part on its *resources*. A group's most significant resources are its members, lobbyists, and money, including funds that can be contributed to political candidates. The sheer quantity of a group's resources is important, and so is the wisdom with which its resources are used.

Members

One of the most valuable resources an interest group can have is a large, politically active membership. If a lobbyist is trying to convince a legislator to support a particular bill, it is tremendously helpful to have a large group of members living in the legislator's home district or state. A legislator who has not already taken a firm position on a bill might be swayed by the knowledge that voters back home are kept informed by interest groups of votes on key issues. The National Rifle Association (NRA) is an effective interest group on Capitol Hill because its 3 million members care very deeply about gun control. Members of Congress know that the NRA keeps its members informed on how each senator and representative votes on proposed gun control bills, and many of those members might be influenced by that information when they go to the polls.

Members give an organization not only the political muscle to influence policy, but also financial resources. The more money an organization can collect through dues and contributions, the more people it can hire to lobby government officials and monitor the policymaking process (see Figure 9.1). Greater resources also allow the organization to communicate with its members more and to inform them better. And funding helps the group maintain its membership and attract new members.

Maintaining membership. To keep the members it already has, an organization must persuade them that it is doing a good job in its advocacy efforts. A major tool for shoring up support among members is a newsletter or magazine. Through publications, members are informed and reminded about the organization's activities. Executives whose corporations belong to the National Association of Manufacturers (NAM) receive *Enterprise*, a business magazine; *Briefing*, a weekly newsletter that focuses on legislative and regulatory action in Washington; and the two-page *Issue Briefs*, which summarizes current public policy disputes. Members also have access, through a toll-free number, to recordings that describe matters of immediate concern to the NAM. Most lobbies provide more modest offerings for their members, but they usually have at least a newsletter.

Business, professional, and labor associations generally have an easier time holding onto members than do **citizen groups**—groups whose basis of organization is a concern for issues that are not related to the members' jobs. In many corporations, membership in a trade group constitutes only a minor business expense. Large individual corporations have no memberships as such, but they often open up their own lobbying offices in Washington. They have the advantage of being able to utilize institutional financial resources; they do not have to rely on voluntary contributions.[12] Labor unions are helped in states where workers are required to belong to the union that is the bargaining agent with their employer.

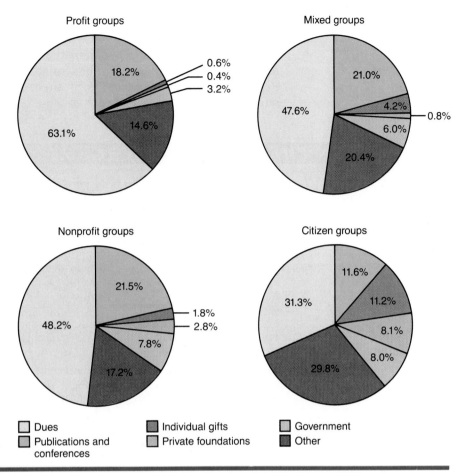

Where the Money Comes From
The charts show the proportion of funds derived from different sources during 1985 for various types of interest groups. Profit groups are those whose members are in profit-making enterprises, such as business trade groups. Nonprofit groups are those whose members work in the nonprofit sector. Mixed groups have members in roughly equal proportions from the profit and nonprofit sectors. Citizen groups are organized on the basis of a political cause rather than the employment of their members. (Source: Mark A. Peterson and Jack L. Walker, "Interest Group Responses to Partisan Change," in Interest Group Politics, *2d ed., ed. Allan J. Cigler and Burdett A. Loomis [Washington, D.C.: Congressional Quarterly, 1986], p. 174.)*
Figure 9.1

Citizen groups, on the other hand, base their appeal on members' ideological sentiments. These groups face a difficult challenge: Issues can blow hot and cold, and a particularly hot issue one year may not hold the same interest to citizens the next.

Attracting new members. All interest groups are constantly looking for new members to expand their resources and clout. Groups that rely on ideological appeals have a special problem because the competition in most policy areas is intense. People concerned about the environment, for example, can join a seemingly infinite number of local, state, and national groups. The National Wildlife Federation, Environmental Action, the Environmental Defense Fund, the Natural Resources Defense Council, Friends of the Earth, the Wilderness Society, the Sierra Club, and the Environmental Policy Center are just a few of the national organizations that lobby on environmental issues.

One method of attracting new members that is being used more and more is **direct mail**—letters sent to a selected audience to promote the organization and to appeal for contributions. The key to direct mail is a carefully targeted audience. An organization can purchase a list of people who are likely to be sympathetic to its cause or trade lists with a similar organization. A group trying to fight legalized abortion, for instance, might use a subscription list from the conservative magazine *National Review*, while a prochoice lobby might use that of the liberal *New Republic*. The main drawbacks to direct mail are its expense and low rate of return. A response rate of 2 percent of all those who receive

Direct Mail: Your Letter Has to Grab 'Em

People are flooded with direct mail from interest groups, politicians, and charities. Whatever the organizations' cause, the letters are all trying to do the same thing: get you to part with your hard-earned cash. In this competitive environment, letters not only must be distinctive, but they must pull at your emotions so that your desire to help overcomes your desire to save your money. Look at how the civil liberties group People for the American Way Action Fund designed an appeal mailed out to thousands of prospective donors during the confirmation fight over Supreme Court nominee Robert Bork.

The first goal of a direct-mail package is to get people to open it rather than just toss it unopened into the wastebasket with other "junk mail." Consequently, envelopes often use a tease to entice readers into finding out what's in them. Here the tease is relatively straightforward: If you care about keeping Bork off the Court, you ought to open this up. The color of the envelope suggests something "official," adding to the urgency of what's inside.

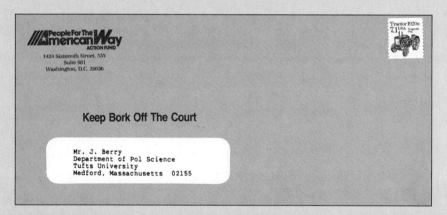

Direct-mail letters are successful if they engage the reader. The goal is to make you care about the issue discussed. This letter begins with a couple of quotations that should upset civil libertarians. Later in the letter, readers are told that Bork rejects conventional views on the right to privacy, has criticized decisions favorable to women and minorities, and holds a restrictive view of the First Amendment. Letters are typically long—this one is six single-spaced pages—and packed with specifics. By the end of the letter, the reader should be so moved that he or she pulls out the checkbook.

Groups often try to validate their appeal by including an article from an outside source that confirms the point they are trying to make. Here an editorial from the *Austin American-Statesman* is included to reinforce the message in the letter.

membership or donation appeals is considered good. If the response rate falls below that level, costs usually exceed the money returned. To maximize the chances of a good return, care and thought are given to the design and content of letters (see Politics in the Information Age 9.1). Letters often try to play on the reader's emotions, to create the feeling that the reader should be personally involved in the struggle.[13]

ACTION FUND

Arthur J. Kropp
Executive Director

"Conservatives have waited over thirty years for this. . . . [Bork's nomination] is the most exciting news for conservatives since President Reagan's re-election."

      -- Richard Viguerie, Right Wing Leader

"The Bork nomination is another part of the Reagan Revolution . . . politically, it gives us a cause."

      -- Frank Donatelli, White House Political Director

Dear Friend,

    Leaders of the Far Right can scarcely hide their glee over Robert Bork's nomination to the Supreme Court.

    And it's no wonder.

    Bork is their <u>best hope</u> to ensure that their political agenda will live on even after Ronald Reagan leaves office.

    In a sense, Robert Bork will be the Reagan Revolution's living legacy -- for years to come. And, frankly, the Right Wing couldn't have designed a more fitting legacy.

    You see, like the Far Right, Judge Bork's views of the Constitution and the Bill of Rights are appallingly out of step with America -- <u>30 years behind the times</u>.

    Out of step with America's hard fought gains in the areas of civil rights, individual liberty and personal privacy.

    Incredibly, Robert Bork has rejected the principle of "one man one vote" . . . Supreme Court decisions outlawing poll taxes . . . the right of married couples to buy contraceptives.

    And, even in 1963, when it was critical for all men and women of conscience to stand up for civil rights, he <u>opposed</u> the right of blacks to be served by white-owned businesses.

    The Far Right knows, and we too can be certain:

    if Robert Bork becomes the critical "swing vote" on the Supreme Court, the extremists philosophy held by people like Attorney General Ed Meese will dominate America's highest court for decades to come.

    <u>That is why PEOPLE FOR THE AMERICAN WAY ACTION FUND has launched a $1 million citizen mobilization campaign to</u> "KEEP BORK OFF THE COURT."

                    (over, please)

1424 Sixteenth Street, N.W.   Suite 601   Washington, D.C. 20036   202 462-4777

(continued)

POLITICS IN THE INFORMATION AGE 9.1 *(continued)*

Page A14   Friday   July 10, 1987

Bork's ideology demands close nomination scrutiny

Austin American-Statesman

Senate Democrats apparently will throw down the gauntlet on the nomination of Robert Bork to the Supreme Court; considering the pivotal vote he would represent on the court, a thorough confirmation process is called for and, if senators ultimately decide Bork is too radical and would push the court too far to the right, they should not hesitate to refuse confirmation and demand that President Reagan come up with a less ideological nominee.

The Democrats said this week that confirmation hearings on the nomination will not begin until Sept. 15,

point of view."

And, historically, the Senate has refused to confirm one out of five nominations submitted for its "advice and consent," beginning with the second term of the administration of George Washington.

Indeed, in 1968, Sen. Strom Thurmond (who now wants the Senate to hurry up and confirm Bork) underscored the importance of careful scrutiny by the Senate of nominee Abe Fortas:

"Therefore, it is my contention that the power of the Senate to advise and consent to this appointment

=== REPLY MEMORANDUM ===

Keep Bork Off The Court

TO: PEOPLE FOR THE AMERICAN WAY ACTION FUND

Robert Bork is 30 years out of step with America—we ***must stop*** his confirmation to the Supreme Court. Please forward the two Congressional Communications I have signed below.

Enclosed is my contribution towards the Action Fund "Keep Bork Off The Court" campaign of:

☐ $100   ☐ $50   ☐ $35   ☐ $25   ☐ Other $_____

```
Mr. J. Berry
Department of Pol Science
Tufts University
Medford, Massachusetts  02155
```

Please make check payable to PEOPLE FOR THE AMERICAN WAY ACTION FUND and return it with entire form to Post Office Box 96200, Washington, D.C. 20077-4627.

Q318

The free-rider problem.   The need for aggressive marketing by interest groups suggests that it is not easy to get people who sympathize with a group's goals to actually join and support it with their contributions. Economists call this difficulty the **free-rider problem,** but we might call it, more colloquially, the "let George do it" problem.[14] The funding for public television stations illustrates this dilemma. Almost all agree that public television, which survives in large part through viewers' contributions, is of great value. But only a fraction of those who watch public television contribute on a regular basis. Why? Because people can watch the programs whether or not they contribute. The free-rider has the same access to public television as the contributor.

The same problem crops up for interest groups. When a lobbying group wins benefits, those benefits are not restricted to members of the organization. For instance, if the American Business Conference wins a tax concession from Congress for capital expenditures, all businesses that fall within the provisions of the law can take advantage of the tax

```
KEEP BORK OFF THE COURT CAMPAIGN
SENATE APPEAL RESPONSE ENCLOSED
PLEASE OPEN IMMEDIATELY!
```

|||||

NO POSTAGE
NECESSARY
IF MAILED
IN THE
UNITED STATES

BUSINESS REPLY MAIL
FIRST CLASS   PERMIT NO. 15227   WASHINGTON, D.C.

POSTAGE WILL BE PAID BY ADDRESSEE

People For The American Way

Post Office Box 96200
Washington, D.C. 20077-4627

A payment card is enclosed to ensure that donors are properly entered into the group's computerized records. The best prospects for a direct mailing are those who have given to the group before, so once a name goes on the house list, that person is solicited frequently by the organization.

The name of the recipient of this letter did not come from the house list, but from a list that People for the American Way rented from a direct-mail broker or other organization. When recruiting new members, like-minded organizations often trade or rent their members' names to each other. Note the source code "Q318" in the lower right-hand corner of the payment card. This is used to track how well the list works. If the list produces a strong response rate (usually 1 to 2 percent), it will be mailed again.

A return envelope rounds out the package. They want to make it easy for you. Just write a check!

Source: Reprinted with permission of People for the American Way. Reprinted with permission of the *Austin American-Statesman*, Copyright 1987.

break. Thus many business executives might not support their firms' joining the American Business Conference, even though they might benefit from its efforts; they prefer instead to let others shoulder the financial burden.

The free-rider problem increases the difficulty of attracting paying members, but it certainly does not make the task impossible. In fact, as we discuss below, the number of interest groups has grown significantly in recent years. Clearly, many people realize that if everyone decides to "let George do it," the job simply won't get done. Millions of Americans contribute to interest groups because they are concerned about an issue or feel a responsibility to help organizations that work on their behalf.[15] Also, many organizations offer membership benefits that have nothing to do with politics or lobbying. Business trade associations, for example, are a source of information about industry trends and effective management practices; and they organize conventions where members can learn, socialize, and occasionally find new customers or suppliers.

Lobbyists

Part of the money raised by interest groups is used to pay lobbyists, who represent the organizations before government. Lobbyists make sure that people in government know what their members want and that their organizations know what government is doing (see Features 9.1 and 9.2). For example, when an administrative agency issues new regulations, lobbyists are right there to interpret the content and implications of the regulations for rank-and-file members. As William Utz of the National Shrimp Congress puts it, "The reaction time to new rules and regulations is faster if the headquarters is based in Washington. If you have an ear here, you can translate things as they happen."[16]

Lobbyists can be full-time employees of the organization or employees of public relations or law firms who are hired on retainer. When hiring a lobbyist, an interest group looks for someone who knows his or her way around Washington. Lobbyists are valued for their experience and knowledge of how government operates. Often they are people who

---

FEATURE 9.1

His Client: Japan, Inc.

When a Japanese company runs into a problem with the United States government, one person it's likely to call on for help is Stanton Anderson. Part lawyer, troubleshooter, and lobbyist, Anderson is very successful at all he does.

After graduating from college, Anderson became a Washington lobbyist for an aviation trade group. He also worked in Republican politics before pursuing a law degree. Later he gained invaluable experience working for the Commerce Department, where he held a high-ranking job doing congressional liaison.

In addition to being a senior partner in a law firm that he founded, Anderson is also head of Global USA, a lobbying firm. His Japanese clients include All Nippon Airways and high-tech companies like Fanuc Ltd. and Kyocera Corp. When clients like Japanese telecommunications companies are threatened with tariffs, Anderson devises strategies to convince members of Congress that a likely consequence of such a law would be retaliation by the Japanese government that would hurt American companies doing business there.

Anderson stresses that his job isn't just lobbying the United States government—he explains America to his foreign clients. Says Anderson, "I interpret things for my clients. They tend to want to solicit as much information as they can . . . I just happen to be a source."

Stanton Anderson

Source: Clyde H. Farnsworth, "Japan's Top U.S. Lobbyist." *New York Times*, 2 June 1985, p. 6F; Kathryn Johnson, "How Foreign Powers Play For Status in Washington," *U.S. News and World Report*, 17 June 1985, pp. 35–40; and Eduardo Lachica, "Japanese Are Lobbying Hard in U.S. to Offset Big Protectionist Push," *Wall Street Journal*, 23 August 1985, p. 1.

FEATURE 9.2

Her Client: Poor Children

Marian Wright Edelman's constituents don't pay dues to her organization. They don't read newsletters that explain what her organization is doing for them. Indeed, precious few of this country's poor youth have ever heard of the Children's Foundation.

Marian Wright Edelman

The Children's Foundation lobbies on behalf of a variety of health and social service issues, including family planning to prevent teenage pregnancy. Edelman knows the numbing statistics all too well: Every year 1.1 million teenage girls get pregnant. This figure includes 125,000 girls fifteen years old or younger. The poorest girls are the most likely to get pregnant.

The daughter of a small-town Baptist minister in South Carolina, Edelman went to Spellman College and Yale Law School. She worked as a civil rights lawyer for the NAACP Legal Defense Fund in Mississippi before coming to Washington. She founded the Children's Defense Fund in 1973 and has built it into a respected organization with an annual budget of $4.4 million and a staff of sixty-seven.

One focus of Edelman's lobbying is to make government officials understand that helping poor children is not only a humane thing to do, but a way of saving resources in the long run. Says Edelman, "Our goal is to educate the nation about the needs of children and encourage preventive investment in children before they get sick, drop out of school, or get into trouble."

Source: *Public Interest Profiles* (Washington, D.C.: Foundation for Public Affairs, 1986), p. 13; Lena Williams, "She Whose Constituents Are 61 Million Children," *New York Times*, 27 February 1986, p. B10; Katherine Bouton, "Marian Wright Edelman," *Ms.*, July/August 1987, pp. 98ff; and Marian Wright Edelman, "How to Prevent Teenage Pregnancy," *Ebony*, July 1987, pp. 62–66.

have served in the legislative or executive branches, where they have had firsthand experience with government. William Timmons, who heads his own lobbying firm, has attracted an impressive array of clients, among them the American Broadcasting Company, Anheuser-Busch, Chrysler, and Boeing. These companies know that Timmons's experience as a White House assistant for legislative liaison gives him a great deal of insight into the policymaking process, as well as valuable government contacts.[17]

Lobbying is a lucrative profession. One study of Washington representatives from a variety of organizations found that the average yearly salary was just over $90,000.[18] The financial rewards are such that nearly

seventysomething
Actually, lobbyist Evelyn Dubrow refuses to tell how old she is, but she's been on Capitol Hill longer than most members of Congress. Now working on behalf of the International Ladies Garment Workers Union, this 4'11" dynamo is one of the most respected lobbyists in Washington. Here Dubrow presents her case to Democratic Representative Jim Moody of Wisconsin.

three hundred former members of Congress are part of the profession. As one old Washington saying has it, "They come to govern, they stay to lobby."[19]

By the nature of their location, many Washington law firms are drawn into lobbying. Corporations without their own Washington offices rely heavily on law firms to lobby for them before the national government. Over time, lawyer-lobbyists tend to develop expertise in particular policy areas.

The most common image of a lobbyist is that of an "arm twister," someone who spends most of the time trying to convince a legislator or administrator to back a certain policy. But lobbying is more subtle than that. Lobbyists' primary job is to pass on information to policymakers. Lobbyists provide government officials and their staffs with a constant flow of data that support their organizations' policy goals. But presenting data is not enough. Lobbyists must also build a compelling case, showing that the "facts" dictate that a change be made. What lobbyists are really trying to do, of course, is to convince policymakers that their data deserve more attention and are more accurate than those presented by other lobbyists.

Political Action Committees

One of the organizational resources that can make a lobbyist's job easier is a **political action committee (PAC).** PACs pool campaign contributions from group members and donate those funds to candidates for political office. Under federal law, a PAC can give up to $5,000 for each separate election to a candidate for Congress. As Figure 9.2 shows, more and more interest groups are organizing PACs. The greatest growth has come from corporations, most of which were legally prohibited from operating political action committees until the law was changed in 1974. There has also been rapid growth in the number of **nonconnected PACs,** largely ideological groups that have no parent lobbying organization and are formed only for the purpose of raising and channeling campaign funds. (So a PAC can be the campaign-wing affiliate of an existing interest group or a wholly independent, unaffiliated group.) From Exxon PAC to SixPAC (which represents the beer industry!), everyone seems to be getting into the PAC game.

Why do interest groups form PACs? One businessman said his company formed a PAC because "talking to politicians is fine, but with a little money they hear you better."[20] His words seem cynical, but they contain more than a kernel of truth. Lobbyists believe that campaign contributions help significantly when they are trying to gain access to a member of Congress. Members of Congress and their staffers generally are eager to meet with representatives of their constituencies, but their time is limited. However, a member of Congress or an assistant would

Figure 9.2

The Growth of PACs
In 1974, a change in the law removed the prohibition that prevented most corporations from forming political action committees; in addition, other types of PACs have become more numerous since that time. By the end of 1987, over 4,000 PACs were registered with the Federal Election Commission. (Source: Federal Election Commission, "FEC Releases New PAC Count," 18 January 1988.)

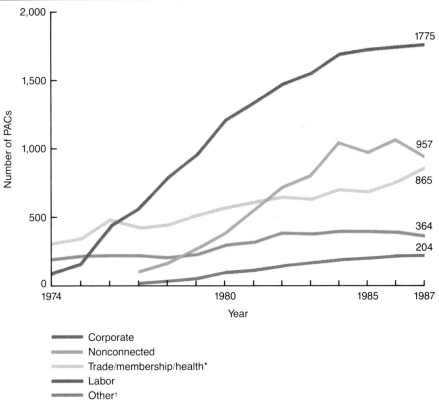

* Until 1977, this category consisted of all but labor and corporate PACs.
† Includes PACs formed by corporations without capital stock and cooperatives.

find it difficult to turn down a request for a meeting with a lobbyist from, for example, the National Association of Realtors, if that group's PAC had made a campaign contribution in the last election.

Typically, PACs, like most other interest groups, are highly pragmatic organizations; pushing a particular political philosophy takes second place to achieving immediate policy goals. Even though many corporate executives have strong beliefs in a free-market economy, for example, their company PAC would probably hold congressional candidates to a much more practical standard. Except for nonconnected ideological PACs, access to congressional offices is usually considered much more important than finding and supporting true believers. Democrat Alan Cranston of California is one of the staunchest liberals in the Senate, but banking PACs showered him with $240,000 in donations for his 1986 race, more than any other congressional candidate.[21] The banking PACs surely would have preferred his Republican opponent (a businessman), but access to the powerful Cranston was too important to risk alienating him. As a group, corporations gave 75 percent of their contributions to incumbent members of Congress—many of them liberal and moderate Democrats—during the last two-year election cycle.[22] Citizen group PACs tend to be moved more by ideology; they give a higher proportion of their funds to challengers than do business, labor, or trade group PACs.

The growing role of PACs in financing congressional campaigns has become the most controversial aspect of interest group politics. Critics believe that greater access to congressional offices brings greater influence over legislators. And access is increased by campaign contributions. It should come as no surprise that corporate PACs contribute more to congressional candidates than do any other PACs. But in a democracy, influence should not be a function of money; some citizens have little to give, yet their rights need to be protected. From this perspective, the issue is political equality. In the words of Republican Senator Robert Dole, "There aren't any Poor PACs or Food Stamp PACs or Nutrition PACs or Medicare PACs."[23]

Still, strong arguments can be made for retaining PACs. They offer a means for people to participate in the political system. They allow small givers to pool their resources and to fight the feeling that one person cannot make a difference. Moreover, with continually escalating campaign costs, many campaigns would be underfunded without PAC money. If this source of contributions was eliminated, it would be more difficult for candidates without personal wealth to make a credible try for Congress. Finally, proponents believe that restrictions on PACs would amount to restrictions on the freedom of political expression.

LOBBYING TACTICS

When an interest group decides to try to influence government on an issue, its staff and officers must develop a strategy, which may include a number of tactics aimed at various officials or offices. Together, these tactics should use the group's resources as effectively as possible.

Keep in mind that lobbying extends beyond the legislative branch. Groups can seek help from the courts and administrative agencies as well as from Congress. Moreover, interest groups may have to shift their focus from one branch of government to another. After a bill becomes a law, for example, a group that lobbied for the legislation will probably try to influence the administrative agency responsible for implementing the new law. Some policy decisions are left unresolved by legislation and are settled through regulations. The lobby wants to make sure regulatory decisions are as close as possible to the group's preferences.

We discuss three types of lobbying tactics here: those aimed at policymakers and implemented through interest group representatives (direct lobbying); those that involve group members (grassroots lobbying); and those directed toward the public (information campaigns). We also examine the cooperative efforts of interest groups to influence government through coalitions.

Direct Lobbying

Direct lobbying relies on personal contact with policymakers. A recent survey of Washington lobbyists showed that 98 percent use direct contact with government officials to express their groups' views.[24] This interaction takes place when a lobbyist meets with a member of Congress, an agency official, or a staff member (see Feature 9.3). In these meetings, lobbyists usually convey their arguments in the form of data about a specific issue. If a lobbyist from, for example, the Chamber of Commerce meets with a member of Congress about a bill the organization backs, the lobbyist does not say (or even suggest), "Vote for this bill, or our people in the district will vote against you in the next election." Instead, the lobbyist might say, "If this bill is passed, we're going to see hundreds of new jobs created back home." The representative has no trouble at all figuring out that a vote for the bill can help in the next election.

Personal lobbying is a day in, day out process. It is not enough simply to meet with policymakers just before a vote or a regulatory decision. Lobbyists must maintain contact with congressional and agency staffers, constantly providing them with pertinent data. Lobbyists for the American Gas Association, for instance, keep a list of 1,200 agency personnel who are "called frequently to share informally in association intelligence." The director of the group's lobbying efforts has a shorter list of 104 key administrators with whom he has met personally and who can "be counted on to provide information on agency decisionmaking."[25]

A tactic related to direct lobbying is *testifying* at committee hearings when a bill is before Congress. This tactic allows the interest group to put its views on record and to make them widely known when the hearing testimony is published. Although testifying is one of the most visible parts of lobbying, it is generally considered window dressing. Most lobbyists believe that testimony usually does little by itself to persuade members of Congress.

Another direct but somewhat different approach is *legal advocacy.* Using this tactic, a group tries to achieve its policy goals through liti-

These Soldiers May Be Old, but They Still Know How to Fight

The primary objective of the 1986 tax reform was to eliminate provisions and exceptions that entitled certain groups or industries to preferential treatment. By reducing such preferences (like the investment tax credit for industry), revenue would be gained and could be redistributed to taxpayers through lower tax brackets for all. Not all tax breaks and special benefits were removed though. One of the ones that remained was the tax-exempt status of veterans' disability payments.

When the Reagan administration's initial proposal (Treasury I) was released, it in fact did call for the elimination of the veterans' tax preference. Leaders of veterans' lobbies in Washington were beside themselves when they found this out, and they demanded a meeting with Assistant Secretary of the Treasury Ronald Pearlman, one of the principals overseeing the reform drive. The leaders of these groups felt that disabled veterans deserve concern and respect from the government, and that forcing veterans to pay taxes on their benefits was an insult. When the leaders confronted Pearlman in his office, he stated the philosophy behind Treasury I in rhetorical fashion: "Why should veterans' disability payments be treated differently than any other income?"

The heads of the veterans' organizations left Pearlman's office with no concessions on his part. But the battle was far from over. They requested a meeting with Pearlman's boss, Secretary of the Treasury James Baker, and came prepared with some pretty heavy ammunition. They showed Baker a full-page ad they were planning to run in the *Washington Post* and other newspapers. In the ad was a large photograph of Chad Colley, the head of the Disabled American Veterans and one of the leaders who had earlier met with Pearlman. Colley is a triple amputee (he lost both legs and an arm in Vietnam), and the photograph of him in a wheelchair made that absolutely clear. At the top of the ad, in large letters, was the question "What's So Special About Disabled Veterans?" Below, in smaller type, the ad read, "That's what a top Treasury official said to Chad Colley . . . " After the veterans left Baker's office, he called Pearlman in and told him, "I think we'll have to drop this one."

Source: Adapted from Jeffrey H. Birnbaum and Alan S. Murray, *Showdown at Gucci Gulch* (New York: Random House, 1987), pp. 79–80.

gation. For many years, the National Association for the Advancement of Colored People (NAACP) brought suits to overturn laws that allowed racial segregation. The courts were a better target than Congress because many members of Congress were strong segregationists from the South. This tactic eventually led to many favorable Supreme Court decisions, most notably, the decision in *Brown* v. *Board of Education,* which overturned school segregation.[26]

Grassroots Lobbying

Grassroots lobbying involves an interest group's rank-and-file members and may also include people outside the organization who sympa-

The Postman Rings More Than Twice
It's often said that the best lobbyists are the lobbyists back home. These letter carriers traveled to Washington to persuade their members of Congress to support legislation backed by the letter carriers' union. The union's Washington lobbyists don't cast a single ballot back home, but these letter carriers do. They can also tell their families and colleagues how responsive their elected representatives were to their concerns.

thize with its goals. Grassroots tactics, such as letter-writing campaigns and protests, are often used in conjunction with direct lobbying by Washington representatives. Letters, telegrams, and phone calls from a group's members to their representatives in Congress or agency administrators add to a lobbyist's credibility in talks with these officials. Policymakers are more concerned about what a lobbyist says when they know that constituents are really watching their decisions.

Group members—especially influential members (corporation presidents, local civic leaders)—occasionally go to Washington themselves to lobby. But the most common grassroots tactic is *letterwriting*. "Write your representative" is not just a slogan out of a civics text. Legislators are highly sensitive to the content of their mail.

Interest groups often launch letter-writing campaigns through their regular publications or special alerts. They may even provide sample letters and the name and address of specific policymakers. When time is of the essence, phone calls serve the same purpose as letters. When a vote on a veto of a civil rights bill by President Reagan was imminent, groups opposing the bill asked members to call their legislators and leave a message voicing their opposition. On a single day, over a hundred thousand people called the Capitol to express their unhappiness with the bill. There was strong support on the other side too, and the veto was subsequently overturned.[27]

If people in government seem unresponsive to conventional lobbying tactics, a group might resort to some form of *political protest*. A protest or demonstration, such as picketing or marching, is designed to attract media attention to an issue. Protesters hope that television and newspaper coverage will help change public opinion and make policymakers more receptive to the group's demands. When three thousand farmers from the American Agriculture Movement drove tractors from their homes into Washington to show their disappointment with Carter administration farm policies, the spectacle attracted considerable publicity. Their unconventional approach increased the public's awareness of falling produce prices and stimulated the government to take some limited action.[28]

The main drawback to protest activity is that policymaking is a long-term incremental process, whereas a demonstration is short-lived. It is difficult to sustain the anger and activism of group supporters—to keep large numbers of people involved in protest after protest—simply to keep the group's demands in the public eye. A notable exception were the civil rights demonstrations of the 1960s, which were sustained over a long period. National attention focused not only on the widespread demonstrations, but also on the sometimes violent confrontations between blacks and white law enforcement officers. For example, the use of police dogs and high-power fire hoses against blacks marching in Alabama in the early 1960s angered millions of Americans who saw films of the confrontations on television programs. The protests were a major factor in public opinion, which in turn hastened the passage of the Civil Rights Act of 1964 and the Voting Rights Act of 1965.[29]

Information Campaigns

As the strategy of the civil rights movement shows, interest groups generally feel that public backing adds strength to their lobbying efforts. And because all interest groups believe they are absolutely right in their policy orientations, they believe that they will get that backing if they make the public aware of their positions and the evidence that supports them. To this end, interest groups launch **information campaigns,** organized efforts to gain public backing by bringing group views to the public's attention. The underlying assumption is that public ignorance and apathy are as much a problem as the views of competing interest groups. Various means are used to combat this apathy. Some are directed at the larger public, others at smaller audiences with long-standing interest in an issue.

Public relations is one information tactic. A public relations campaign might involve sending speakers to meetings in various parts of the country or producing pamphlets and handouts. A highly visible form of political public relations is newspaper and magazine advertising. Mobil Oil Corporation is well known for the way it uses print advertising to argue its point of view. The National Rifle Association uses advertising to try to show people that it is a responsible organization rather than a group that cares more about guns than stopping crime. It has run a series of profiles of members, such as the head of a police organization, who belie the image of irresponsibility. Newspaper and magazine advertising has one major drawback, however. It is extremely expensive. Consequently, few groups rely on it as their primary weapon.

Sponsoring *research* is another way interest groups press their cases. When a group believes that evidence has not been fully developed in a certain area, it may commission research on the subject. Groups working for the rights of the disabled have protected programs from would-be budget cutters by providing "lawmakers with abundant research findings demonstrating that it costs much more to keep people in institutions . . . than it does to utilize home and community living programs."[30]

Some groups believe that publicizing *voting records* of members of Congress is an effective means of influencing public opinion. These interest groups simply publish in their newsletters a record of how all members of Congress voted on issues of particular concern to the organization. Other groups prepare statistical indexes that compare the voting records of all members of Congress on selected key issues. Each member is graded (from 0 to 100 percent) according to how often he or she voted in agreement with the group's views. Thus the owners of small businesses who belong to the National Federation of Independent Business can assume that those lawmakers who scored well on the group's "scorecard" have usually voted in sympathy with their interests.

Coalitions

The final aspect of lobbying strategy is **coalition building,** in which several organizations band together for the purpose of lobbying. This joint effort conserves or makes more effective use of the resources of groups with similar views. Coalitions form most often among groups that work in the same policy area and are similar in their political outlook.[31] On feminist issues, for example, the National Organization for Women, the National Women's Political Caucus, the League of Women Voters, the American Association of University Women, and the Women's Equity Action League usually work with one another.[32]

Most coalitions are informal, ad hoc arrangements. Groups have limited resources and prefer not to commit those resources to long-term coalitions. Also, they do not always share an equal degree of enthusiasm for all issues; sometimes even old friends end up on different sides of an issue. Government solutions to the acid rain problem, for instance, set coal producers from the West against coal producers from the East. In the West (where coal is low in sulfur), producers wanted a policy promoting the use of low-sulfur coal; eastern coal producers wanted scrubbers to reduce sulfur dioxide emissions.[32] Ad hoc coalitions that center around one immediate issue allow a group to keep its resource commitments flexible, while broadening its resources to increase the chances of influencing policymakers at key times.

THE GROWTH OF INTEREST GROUP POLITICS

The growing number of active interest groups is one of the most important trends in American politics. One survey of Washington-based lobbies showed that fully 30 percent of existing groups were formed between 1960 and 1980.[34] The greatest growth occurred in three types of interest groups: PACs (which we discussed earlier), citizen groups, and business lobbies.

Lobbyists Sans *Guccis*
When we think of Washington lobbyists, we may picture suave, well-paid business representatives who wear expensive suits and shoes. But other kinds of people toil at this work, too. These people are volunteers for the public interest group Common Cause. They tried to spur grassroots activity on behalf of the Boren-Byrd bill, which would have reduced the role of political action committees in congressional elections. In this case, the Guccis won: A filibuster kept the bill from a vote in the Senate.

The Public Interest Movement

Many recently formed citizen groups are commonly known as public interest groups. A **public interest group** is generally considered to have no economic self-interest in the policies it pursues.[35] For example, the members of an environmental group fighting for stricter clean-air standards receive no financial gain from the institution of such standards. The benefits to its members are largely ideological and aesthetic. In contrast, a corporation fighting against the same stringent standards is trying to protect its profits. A law that requires it to install expensive antipollution devices can reduce stockholders' dividends, depress salaries, and postpone expansion. Although both the environmental group and the corporation have valid reasons for their stands on the issue, their motives are different. The environmental lobby is a public interest group; the corporation is not.

Many public interest groups have become major players in national politics. Common Cause, one of the best-known "good government" groups, works for campaign finance reform, codes of ethics in government, and open congressional and administrative proceedings.[36]

The best-known public interest activist is Ralph Nader. He first came to the public's attention in 1966, when he exposed serious safety flaws in the Corvair. So damning was his indictment of the car that sales dropped significantly, and General Motors soon stopped producing the Corvair.[37] Nader now heads a small empire of public interest groups, among them the Aviation Consumer Action Project, the Public Citizen Litigation Group, and the Health Research Group.

Nader has a reputation as a relentless, driven lobbyist for consumer protection. He mercilessly criticizes politicians who disagree with him, treating them as "enemies of the people," not as individuals who simply happen to hold different views. Nader's self-righteousness is tempered by his dedication, zeal, and ascetic lifestyle. These have made him a highly effective and credible spokesman for consumers.

Origins of the movement. Traditionally, public interest lobbies have not been a major factor in Washington politics. Yet the upsurge of these groups that began in the late 1960s did not prove to be as short-lived a phenomenon as many had expected. At first, most new groups were on the liberal side of the political spectrum. As discussed below, however, many new conservative groups have formed recently. Groups on both the Left and the Right have become more politically prominent. The public interest movement has been impressive in its collective scope and strength; many groups have been able to support themselves through the contributions of concerned citizens.

Why have so many public interest groups formed in the last two decades? The movement grew from the civil rights and anti-Vietnam War activism of the 1960s.[38] In both cases, citizens with passionate beliefs about a cause felt they had no choice but to take aggressive, even abrasive, action. Dependence on political parties and the electoral process was not producing change; collective citizen action had to be used instead.

An Image That Angered a Nation
Demonstrations by blacks during the early 1960s played a critical role in pushing Congress to pass civil rights legislation. This photo of vicious police dogs attacking demonstrators in Birmingham, Alabama, is typical of the scenes that were shown in network news broadcasts and newspapers. Pictures like this helped build public support for civil rights legislation.

The legacy of the civil rights and antiwar movements was the belief that individuals acting together can influence the direction of public policy. From the success of these groups, Americans learned that ordinary citizens could have an impact on government if they organized. (Most contemporary citizen groups no longer rely on the demonstrations that characterized these earlier movements. Instead, they channel the energy, resources, and outrage of their constituents into more conventional tactics, such as legislative lobbying and litigation.)

The late 1960s and early 1970s were also a time when Americans were becoming increasingly cynical about government. Loyalty to political parties was declining, too, as greater proportions of citizens told pollsters that they did not identify with either national party. If neither government nor political parties could be trusted to provide adequate representation in the nation's capital on such issues as preserving the environment or protecting consumers, the obvious alternative was membership in an ideological interest group.

Conservative reaction. Why conservatives were slower than liberals to mobilize is not altogether clear, but the new right-of-center groups appear in part to be a reaction to the perceived success of liberal groups. Like their liberal counterparts, conservative groups cover a wide variety of policy areas. Most stand in direct opposition to causes espoused by liberal organizations. Phyllis Schlafly's Eagle Forum, for example, fought long and hard against the Equal Rights Amendment and other positions favored by feminist groups.

But conservative groups are not merely mirror images of liberal citizen lobbies. A distinctive feature of the "New Right" is the active participation of religious organizations. Groups like the Religious Roundtable and Christian Voice actively promote policies that they feel are in line with Christian teachings, such as permitting prayer in school and restricting abortions.[39] The most visible fundamentalist Christian lobby has been the Moral Majority. In 1987, however, the group's leader, Reverend Jerry Falwell, announced he was leaving the political world to return full time to the spiritual one. It's unclear if the group will be able to maintain its visibility without its controversial founder. Some Americans who believe that the country is best served by a complete separation of church and state strongly criticize the lobbying of the religious Right. But the religious Right believes that its moral duty is to see that Christian principles are embodied in government policy. The conflict between liberal critics and conservative religious lobbies is more than a difference of opinion over specific policies. It is a struggle to define the fundamental values that shape our society. And, as a spokesman for the American Coalition for Traditional Values notes, "Somebody's values will prevail."[40]

During the Reagan presidency, conservative citizen groups enjoyed substantial access to the White House, their lobbyists meeting frequently with White House aides.[41] They did not have the same degree of success with Congress, however, where many of their most cherished goals—including a constitutional amendment allowing school prayer—were not met. Still, the emergence of these groups and the resurgence of the Republican party have enhanced conservative influence in America.

Business Lobbies

The number of business lobbies in Washington has also increased. Offices of individual corporations and of business trade associations are more in evidence than ever before. A **trade association,** such as the Mortgage Bankers Association or the National Electrical Manufacturers Association, is an organization that represents companies within the same industry. At one point during the 1970s, when the boom in business lobbying began, trade associations were moving their headquarters to Washington at an average of one every week.[42] A 1981 survey of corporations revealed that more than half of the organizations with a government relations office in Washington had set up that office during the previous decade.[43] Corporations that already had offices in Washington typically upgraded them by adding staff.

The vast increase in business representation in Washington was in large part a response to the expanded scope of national government activities during the 1960s and 1970s. As the Environmental Protection Agency, the Consumer Product Safety Commission, and other regulatory agencies were created, many more companies found themselves affected by federal regulations. And those located outside of Washington often found themselves *reacting* to policies already made rather than *participating* in their making. They saw a move to Washington—where the policymakers are—as necessary if they were to obtain information on pending government actions in enough time to act on it.

Ironically, the increase in government activity and in business lobbying followed directly from the success of liberal public interest groups, strong supporters of regulation to protect the environment and consumers. By the early 1970s, many businesspeople felt that the government was reacting to an agenda set primarily by citizen groups. This belief contributed to the founding of the Business Roundtable, a lobbying group with membership made up of about two hundred of the nation's largest companies. The Business Roundtable has become both a leading proponent of the business point of view and a symbol of business strength in Washington.

The increase in business advocacy in Washington was also fueled by the competitive nature of business lobbying. The reason for competition is that legislation and regulatory decisions never seem to apply uniformly to all businesses; rather, they affect one type of business or one industry more than others. Financial services is one area where growing competition and limited steps toward deregulation have transformed the lobbying scene. Insurance companies, brokerage houses, investment banks, and retail banks have all made efforts to encroach on one another's turf. So many new players have entered the picture that policymaking has become even more complex. A member of the House Banking Committee said of the change, "When I first came to Congress there were five major financial trade groups, but now there are at least five times that.

The Tax Lobbyist
Charls Walker is one of the most skilled business lobbyists in Washington. He holds a Ph.D. in economics and was a high-ranking official in the U.S. Treasury Department. Because of Walker's expertise and political skills, many large corporations hire him to lobby Congress on tax policy.

Now if you're trying to satisfy all the trade groups, it's pretty hard to do."[44]

The growth of business lobbies has reinforced and possibly expanded the overrepresentation of business in national politics. As Figure 9.3 shows, approximately half of all interest groups with a Washington office are either corporations or business trade associations. If organizations with a Washington lawyer or other kind of lobbyist on retainer are added to the total, the dominance of business in the lobbying population is even greater. But the number of organizations or lobbyists is far from a perfect indicator of interest group strength. The AFL-CIO, which represents millions of union members, is more influential than a two-person corporate listening post in Washington. Still, business has an advantage in terms of Washington representation. And because business lobbies are able to draw on the institutional resources of corporations, they can fund their lobbying operations more easily than can groups that depend on the voluntary contributions of individuals.

INTEREST GROUPS: AN EVALUATION

The pluralists who wrote during the 1950s and 1960s were right on one important point, but wrong on another. They argued that interest groups are at the center of the policymaking process. Certainly, the growing number of groups in recent years seem to reflect a broad acceptance of this view by various sectors of American society. Although pluralist scholars never predicted perfect representation of affected interests, they

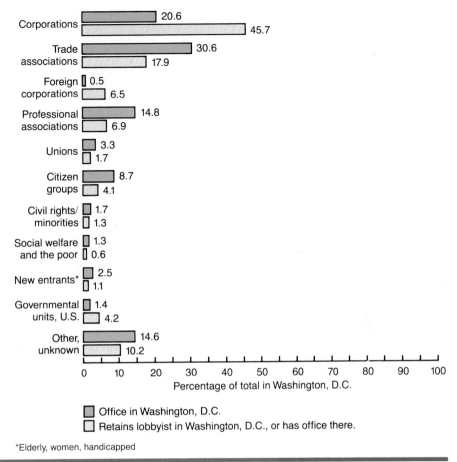

The Washington Interest Group Community
Although the interest group community is highly diverse, business organizations form the biggest part of that community. Corporations and trade associations are the most prevalent interest group actors in terms of having an office in Washington or, at the very least, employing a lobbyist there. (Source: Kay Lehman Schlozman and John T. Tierney, Organized Interests and American Democracy *[New York: Harper & Row, 1986], p. 67. Copyright © 1986 by Kay Lehman Schlozman and John T. Tierney. Reprinted by permission of Harper & Row, Publishers, Inc. Adapted from the* Encyclopedia of Associations, *ed. Denise S. Akey. Gale Research.)*

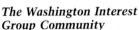
Figure 9.3

did assume that representation would be more balanced than it is. What we have instead is a political system increasingly centered around interest group advocacy, but one in which some interests—most notably, those of business—are much better represented than others. What are the consequences of this?

One consequence is that the large and growing number of interest groups works against a strengthening of our party system. Many activists find narrowly based interest groups more appealing than parties. The lobbies that these activists support work intensely on the few issues they care about most; parties often dilute issue stands to appeal to as broad a segment of the electorate as possible. Thus, many people who care deeply about public policy questions work to influence government through particular lobbies rather than through political parties. Interest in party reform has waned in the past few years. The satisfaction people feel with the work of their interest groups surely contributes to Americans' lack of concern for revitalizing the parties, for making them more responsive policymaking bodies.

This lack of concern is unfortunate. Interest groups can do no more than supplement the functions of parties. Most interest groups are small

Lobbying the Lobby
We usually think of lobby-ing as a process that takes place when an interest group tries to influence gov-ernment officials. But sometimes government offi-cials approach a lobbying organization to ask for its help. The president may ac-tively court interest groups to try to build support for his policies. A presidential speech, like this one by Ronald Reagan before a conference sponsored by the Washington-based National Association of Manufactur-ers, is one way the White House reaches out to inter-est groups.

bodies concerned with only a few issues. Parties, however, can be instru-ments of majoritarian democracy. They can bring together broad coali-tions of people and translate their concerns into large-scale social and economic change. Parties are particularly important because they can represent those who are not well represented by interest groups. As political scientist Walter Dean Burnham puts it, parties "can generate countervailing collective power on behalf of the many individually pow-erless against the relatively few who are individually—or organization-ally—powerful."[45]

Most observers agree that stronger parties, which would provide a more majoritarian mechanism for influencing policy, are good. But few seem interested in reviving the parties at the cost of their own interest group's influence. If our party system is revitalized, then, it will be because of what the parties do to make themselves more appealing, not because people turn away from their interest groups.

Regulation

Interest groups contribute to democratic government by representing their supporters' interests. However, concern that individual groups have too much influence or that interest group representation is biased in favor of certain segments of society has prompted frequent calls for reform. Yet, little has been done to weaken the influence of interest groups. The problem, as Madison foresaw, is that it is difficult to limit interest group activity without limiting fundamental freedoms. The First Amendment guarantees Americans the right to petition their govern-ment, and lobbying, at its most basic level, is a form of organized peti-tioning.

One effort to reform lobbying was the Federal Regulation of Lobbying Act, passed in 1946. This law was intended to require all lobbyists to register and file expenditure reports with Congress. In practice, the law has been ineffective. A Supreme Court ruling held that it applies only to people or organizations whose "principal purpose" is influencing legislation.[46] This exempts many, if not most, of those who lobby. Periodic calls for stricter reform continue, but it is difficult to see how such legislation would alter interest group behavior.

Campaign Financing

Much of the debate over interest groups and political reform centers around the role PACs play in financing congressional campaigns. As the costs of political campaigning escalate sharply, politicians have to raise larger and larger sums. During the 1970s, Congress took some important steps to reform campaign-financing practices. Strong disclosure requirements now exist, so that the source of all significant contributions to candidates for national office is part of the public record. Public financing of presidential campaigns is also provided for; taxpayer money is given in equal amounts to the major parties' presidential nominees.

Reformers have also called for public financing of congressional elections, to reduce the alleged influence of PACs in Congress. Public financing and other schemes designed to reduce the percentage of campaign funds supplied by PACs are meant to reduce the advantage of certain groups in gaining access to and sympathy from members of Congress and their staffers. But incumbents usually find it easier to raise money from PACs than their electoral challengers do, so they have been

reluctant to change this part of the law. It is often said that "money is the mother's milk of politics," and Congress doesn't want to turn off the flow.

The debate over PACs is another manifestation of the sharp tension between the principles of freedom and equality. For many, restrictions on PACs represent restrictions on their personal freedom. Shouldn't people have the right to join others who think as they do and contribute to the candidates of their choice? For others, though, PAC contributions seem less a matter of freedom of political expression than of some people's freedom to use their wealth to further their own special interests. They believe that certain groups are buying influence on Capitol Hill, pointing to sixteen groups, each of which contributed over $1 million to candidates for national office during the 1986 elections.[47] And they argue that the consequence of PAC giving is to reinforce, if not expand, the inequities between rich and poor.

SUMMARY

Interest groups play many important roles in our political process. They are a means by which citizens can participate in politics, and they communicate their members' views to those in government. Interest groups differ greatly in the resources at their disposal and in the tactics they use to influence government. The numbers of interest groups has grown sharply in recent years, including an upsurge in political action committees.

Despite the growth and change in the nature of interest groups, the fundamental problem identified by Madison over two hundred years ago endures. In a free and open society, groups form to pursue policies that favor themselves at the expense of the broader national interest. Madison hoped that the solution to this problem would come through the diversity of the population and the structure of our government.

To a certain extent, Madison's expectations have been borne out. The natural differences between groups has kept us from the tyranny of any one faction. Yet the interest group system remains unbalanced, with some segments of society (particularly business, the wealthy, the educated) considerably better organized than others. The growth of citizen groups has reduced this disparity somewhat, but there are still significant inequities in how well different interests are represented in Washington.

These inequities have led most contemporary scholars to reject two key propositions of the early pluralists: that the freedom to form lobbies produces a healthy competition among opposing groups and that the compromises emerging from that competition lead to policies that fairly represent the divisions in society. Instead, business and professional groups

have an advantage because of their ability to organize more readily and their greater resources. The interest group system clearly compromises the principle of political equality as stated in the maxim "one person, one vote." Formal political equality is certainly more likely to occur outside of interest group politics, in elections between candidates from competing political parties—which better fits the majoritarian model of democracy.

Despite the inequities of the interest group system, little general effort has been made to restrict interest group activity. Madison's dictum that suppressing political freedoms must be avoided, even at the expense of permitting interest group activity that promotes the selfish interests of narrow segments of the population, has generally guided public policy. Yet, as the problem of PACs demonstrates, government has had to set some restrictions on interest groups. PACs' giving unlimited contributions to political candidates would undermine confidence in the system. Where to draw the limit on PAC activity remains a thorny problem, since there is little consensus on how to balance the conflicting needs of our society.

Key Terms

interest group	free-rider problem
lobby	political action
lobbyist	committee (PAC)
agenda building	direct lobbying
program monitoring	grassroots lobbying
interest group	information campaign
entrepreneur	coalition building
citizen group	public interest group
direct mail	trade association

Selected Readings

Berry, Jeffrey M. *The Interest Group Society*. Boston: Little, Brown, 1984. An analysis of the growth of interest group politics.

Berry, Jeffrey M. *Lobbying for the People*. Princeton, N.J.: Princeton University Press, 1977. A study of eighty-three public interest groups active in national politics.

Cigler, Allan J., and Burdett A. Loomis, eds. *Interest Group Politics*. 2d ed. Washington, D.C.: Congressional Quarterly, 1986. This reader includes seventeen separate essays on lobbying groups.

Lowi, Theodore J. *The End of Liberalism*. 2d ed. New York: Norton, 1979. A critical analysis of the role of interest groups in our society.

Olson, Mancur, Jr. *The Logic of Collective Action*. New York: Schocken, 1968. Olson, an economist, looks at the free-rider problem and the rationale for joining lobbying organizations.

Sabato, Larry J. *PAC Power*. New York: Norton, 1984. An insightful well-written account of how PACs operate.

Schlozman, Kay Lehman, and John T. Tierney. *Organized Interests and American Democracy*. New York: Harper & Row, 1986. A valuable and comprehensive study that draws on an original survey of Washington lobbyists.

Essay C

The Transformation of Party Politics

Over time, the American party system has undergone a series of wrenching transformations. "Two-Party Systems in U.S. History" details those changes. During the nation's infancy, when George Washington was unanimously elected and re-elected president, there were no parties. But beginning in 1796, Federalist and Democratic-Republican candidates vied for the presidency under the nation's first party system. For a brief time in the early 1820s, partisan ties lapsed in an "Era of Good Feeling;" but they reawakened in 1828 with the election of Andrew Jackson, and the second party system was launched. That system crumbled over the slavery issue, and a third party system began in 1856. Since then, the Democrats and the Republicans have alternated irregularly in power, each party enjoying a long period of dominance.

Presidential elections can decide more than which candidate becomes president; they can determine which coalition of voters dominates elections for national office. For example, the election of 1828—the nation's first election with more than a million voters—not only chose Andrew Jackson of Tennessee over John Quincy Adams of Massachusetts but also established the voting power of western and southern farm states over the previously dominant northeastern manufacturing states.

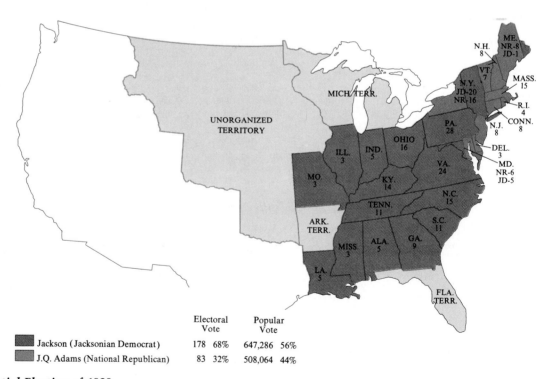

	Electoral Vote		Popular Vote	
Jackson (Jacksonian Democrat)	178	68%	647,286	56%
J.Q. Adams (National Republican)	83	32%	508,064	44%

The Presidential Election of 1828

1789	Washington unanimously elected President				**PRE-PARTY PERIOD**	
1792	Washington unanimously reelected					

	Federalist Adams	**Democratic-Republican**			
1796	—	Jefferson		**FIRST PARTY SYSTEM**	
1800	—	Jefferson			
1804	—	Madison			
1808	—	Madison			
1812	—	Monroe			
1816					

1820	Monroe	**"ERA OF GOOD FEELING"**
1824	J.Q. Adams	

		Democratic Jackson		**National-Republican**
1828		Jackson		**Whig**
1832		Van Buren		—
1836	**SECOND PARTY SYSTEM**	—		Harrison
1840		Polk		—
1844		—		Taylor
1848		Pierce		—
1852				

			Democratic	Populist	Republican
1856	**Constitutional Union**	**Southern Democrat**	Buchanan		Lincoln
1860			—		Lincoln
1864			—		Grant
1868			—		Grant
1872	**THIRD PARTY SYSTEM**		—		Hayes
1876			—		Garfield
1880	**Rough Balance**		Cleveland		—
1884			—		Harrison
1888			Cleveland		—
1892			—	**Populist**	McKinley
1896					

	Democratic	Progressive	Republican
1900	—		McKinley
1904	—		T. Roosevelt
1908	—		Taft
1912	Wilson	**Progressive**	—
1916	Wilson		—
1920	—		Harding
1924	**Republican Dominance** —		Coolidge
1928	—		Hoover

	Democratic	States' Rights	Republican
1932	F.D. Roosevelt		—
1936	F.D. Roosevelt		—
1940	F.D. Roosevelt		—
1944	F.D. Roosevelt		—
1948	Truman	**States' Rights**	—
1952	—		Eisenhower
1956	**Democratic Dominance**		Eisenhower
1960	Kennedy		—
1964	Johnson		—

	Democratic	American Independent / Independent	Republican
1968	—	**American Independent**	Nixon
1972	—		Nixon
1976	Carter		—
1980	—	**Independent**	Reagan
1984			Reagan

Two-Party Systems in U.S. History

A presidential election that marks a long-term change of existing patterns of party loyalties among groups of voters across the nation is called a *critical election*. Scholars have identified only three elections—1860, 1896, and 1932—that showed significant changes in voting patterns and that "also began periods of unified party control of the presidency and both houses of Congress for as long as fourteen years" (J. Clubb, W. Flanigan, and N. Zingale, *Partisan Realignment*, 1980).

The election of 1860, in which Republican Abraham Lincoln won over three other candidates, set a pattern of regional voting, pitting northern Republicans against southern Democrats.

In 1896, the populous and industrial east and midwest elected Republican William McKinley (who was probusiness) over Democrat William Jennings Bryan (spokesman for the rural west and south). The Republicans emerged as the majority party.

In 1932, Democrat Franklin Roosevelt won the election with a coalition of southerners, northern urban workers, and religious and ethnic minorities that transformed the Democrats into the majority party.

Ronald Reagan's election in 1984 was even more sweeping than Roosevelt's in 1932, but 1984 was not a critical election because Republicans did not win control of the House. Nevertheless, the proportion of Republican voters nationwide has been increasing recently, and the era of Democratic dominance, launched by Roosevelt, may be coming to a close.

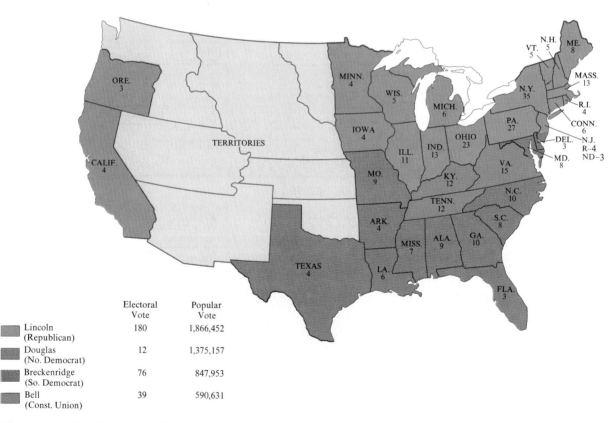

	Electoral Vote	Popular Vote
Lincoln (Republican)	180	1,866,452
Douglas (No. Democrat)	12	1,375,157
Breckenridge (So. Democrat)	76	847,953
Bell (Const. Union)	39	590,631

The Presidential Election of 1860

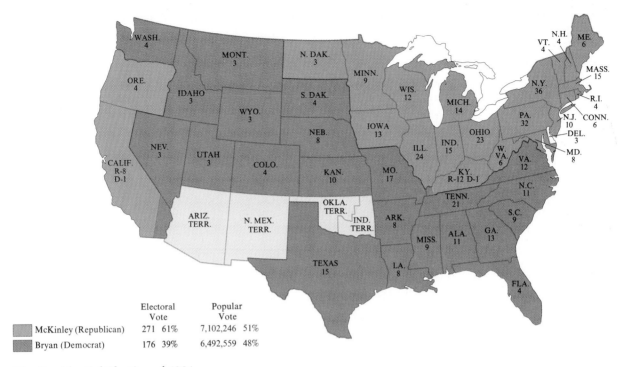

	Electoral Vote		Popular Vote	
McKinley (Republican)	271	61%	7,102,246	51%
Bryan (Democrat)	176	39%	6,492,559	48%

The Presidential Election of 1896

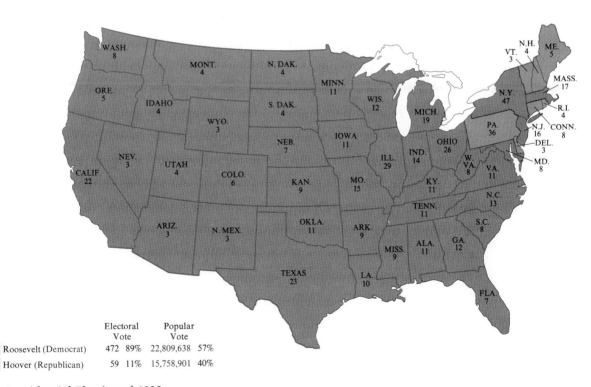

	Electoral Vote		Popular Vote	
Roosevelt (Democrat)	472	89%	22,809,638	57%
Hoover (Republican)	59	11%	15,758,901	40%

The Presidential Election of 1932

INSTITUTIONS OF GOVERNMENT

10

Congress

J immy Carter learned the hard way. In writing about his term as president, he complained that "whenever tax measures were considered, we found ourselves fortunate if we left Congress with the same hide we wore in." Why this difficulty with tax legislation? To Carter, the answer was simple. Congress did not have the fortitude to stand up to the "powerful and ravenous wolves"—the special interests—who were "determined to secure for themselves additional benefits at the expense of other Americans."[1]

Several years after Carter left office, Congress again found itself facing interest groups that stood in the way of tax reform. In 1985, the Reagan administration proposed a sweeping tax bill that would lower tax rates for most individuals and corporations. The revenue lost by these lower rates would be made up by eliminating certain tax deductions and tax credits—both of which had the effect of lowering the tax burden for particular firms, industries, and individuals.

But one person's tax loophole is another's (in Washington jargon) "incentive to benefit the public interest." For example, one provision targeted for elimination was the investment tax credit, which offered a sizable reduction in federal taxes to companies that bought new machinery and equipment. One of the original reasons for the investment tax credit was to help the decaying "smokestack" industries, among them, the steel industry, which had to invest heavily in new, more efficient machinery to compete effectively with foreign manufacturers. Isn't it good public policy to have a tax code that helps industries in trouble, particularly when lots of jobs are at stake? And why should the steel industry lose its tax benefits when substantial tax breaks for other industries were left largely in place?

Those who backed the tax reform had an answer to these questions: By eliminating tax benefits that helped selected industries, Congress could lower the highest corporate tax rate for all businesses from 48 percent of earnings to 34 percent. In effect, other industries had been subsidizing the steel industry by paying a higher share of the nation's taxes.

The Reagan tax plan led to a classic confrontation between the majoritarian and pluralist views of democratic government. A majority of the public wanted simpler tax laws that would eliminate a maze of special deductions and credits and would lower tax rates. In opposition stood interest groups that represented narrow segments of the population. These groups wanted to preserve the deductions that benefited their members. They worked furiously to block different parts of the bill (remember the efforts of the veterans' organizations, discussed in Feature 9.4).

To achieve a tax code more in line with majoritarian interests, proponents bowed to pluralist politics when it suited their needs. Tax breaks for the timber industry were retained, not because of any compelling economic reason to treat that industry differently, but because Senator Bob Packwood came from Oregon, a big timber-producing state. Packwood, a Republican, was chairman of the Senate Finance Committee at the time the bill was being considered, and no bill taking substantial tax breaks away from an important industry back home was ever going to get out of his committee. "I don't think parochial interests are a bad thing at all," rationalized Packwood.[2] And other concessions were made to keep key legislators on the tax reform bandwagon. Although the tax rate reductions were significant, the legislation that finally passed was filled with compromises that limited those reductions.

Democratic government needs institutional mechanisms that can translate public opinion into government policy (see Chapter 2). The five chapters in this part of the book cover Congress, the president, the bureaucracy, the courts, and the Washington community. In studying how these institutions operate in American government, we focus on their contributions to the majoritarian and pluralist versions of democracy. We are less concerned in these chapters with the concepts of freedom, order, and equality, which are more central to our discussion of public policy (in Part V).

In every democratic country, the main institution for representing citizens' interests in government is an elected legislature. Two central questions emerge in studying Congress. First, when members of Congress vote on policy issues, who do they *actually* represent? And second, Who *should* they represent? We try to answer the first question here, leaving you to think about the second.

THE ORIGIN AND POWERS OF CONGRESS

The framers of the Constitution wanted to keep power from being concentrated in the hands of a few, but they were also concerned with creating a union strong enough to overcome the weaknesses of the government that operated under the Articles of Confederation. They argued passionately about the structure of the new government. In the end, they produced a legislative body that was as much an experiment as was the nation's new democracy.

The Great Compromise

The U.S. Congress has two separate and powerful chambers: the House of Representatives and the Senate. A bill cannot become law unless it is passed in identical form by both chambers. The two-house, or **bicameral,** congress has its origins in the negotiations that shaped the Constitution. When the Constitution was being drafted during the summer of 1787, "the fiercest struggle for power" centered on representation in the legislature.[3] The small states wanted all states to have equal representation. The more populous states wanted representation based on population; they did not want their power diluted. The Great Compromise broke the deadlock. The small states received equal representation in the Senate, but the House, where the number of each state's representatives would be based on population, retained the sole right to originate money bills.

According to the Constitution, each state is represented by two senators, each of whom serves for six years. Terms of office are staggered, so that one-third of the Senate is elected every two years. When it was

Table 10.1
Qualifications for Congressional Office

	Senator	Representative
Minimum age	30	25
Minimum years of citizenship	9	7
Requirement	Must be an inhabitant of the state he or she represents.	
Prohibition	Cannot hold any other national office.	

ratified, the Constitution directed that senators should be chosen by the state legislatures. However, the Seventeenth Amendment, adopted in 1913, provided for the election of senators by popular vote. From the beginning, members of the House of Representatives have been elected by the people. They serve two-year terms, and all House seats are up for election at the same time. As Table 10.1 shows, there are few formal qualifications for congressional office.

Because each state's representation in the House is in proportion to its population, the Constitution provides for a national census every ten years. Until the first census, the Constitution fixed the number of representatives at 65. As the nation's population grew and new states joined the Union, new seats were added to the House. (There were already 213 representatives after the census of 1820.)[4] At some point, however, a legislative body becomes too unwieldy to be efficient, and in 1929, the House decided to fix its membership at 435. Population shifts are handled

The Construction of the Capitol
This watercolor recorded the first stage of the building's construction. Only the North Wing (shown here) was complete in 1801, when Thomas Jefferson became president.

by the **reapportionment** (redistribution) of representatives among the states after each census is taken. In the reshuffling after the 1980 census, for example, Florida gained 4 seats and New York lost 5. California, the nation's most populous state, has 45 representatives; six states have just a single representative, the constitutional minimum.

Representatives are elected from a particular congressional district within their state. The number of districts in a state is equal to the number of representatives the state sends to the House. Before a series of Supreme Court rulings in the 1960s, the states were not required to draw the boundaries of their districts in such a way that districts had approximately equal populations. As a result, some states' sparsely populated rural districts had more representation in Congress than their number of residents warranted. The Court ruled that House districts, and all districts in state legislatures, had to be drawn so as to be reasonably equal in population.[5]

Duties of the House and Senate

Although the Great Compromise provided considerably different schemes of representation for the House and Senate, the Constitution gives them essentially similar legislative tasks. They share many important powers, among them the powers to declare war, raise an army and navy, borrow and coin money, regulate interstate commerce, create federal courts, and establish rules for the naturalization of immigrants, and to "make all Laws which shall be necessary and proper for carrying into Execution the foregoing Powers."

Of course, there are at least a few important differences in the constitutional duties of the two chambers. The House alone has the right to originate revenue bills, which apparently was coveted at the Constitutional Convention. In practice, this function is of limited consequence because all bills—including revenue bills—must be approved by both the House and Senate. The House also has the power of **impeachment,** the power to formally charge the president, vice president, or other "civil Officers" of the national government with "Treason, Bribery, or other high Crimes and Misdemeanors." The Senate is empowered to act as a court to try impeachments; a two-thirds vote of the senators present is necessary for conviction. Only one president—Andrew Johnson—has ever been impeached, and in 1868 the Senate came within a single vote of finding him guilty. More recently, the House Judiciary Committee voted to impeach President Richard Nixon for his role in the Watergate scandal, but he resigned in August 1974, before the full House could vote. In 1986, the House voted a rare bill of impeachment against Harry E. Claiborne, a federal judge convicted of income tax evasion. Claiborne refused to resign his life-term office, so an impeachment trial was initiated in the Senate. After reviewing the evidence, the Senate voted to convict Claiborne on three of the four articles of impeachment brought by the House and removed him from office. He was the first judge in fifty years to be convicted by the Senate of impeachable offenses.[6] In 1988, federal judge Alcee Hastings was impeached by the House after he was acquitted of income tax evasion and bribery charges.

The Constitution gives the Senate the power to approve major presidential appointments (such as to federal judgeships, ambassadorships, and Cabinet posts) and treaties with foreign nations. The president is empowered to *make* treaties, but then they must be submitted to the Senate for approval by a two-thirds majority. Because of this requirement, the executive branch generally considers the Senate's sentiments when it negotiates a treaty. At times, however, a president must try to convince a doubting Senate of a particular treaty's worth. Shortly after World War I, President Woodrow Wilson submitted to the Senate the Treaty of Versailles, which contained the charter for the proposed League of Nations. Wilson had attempted to convince the Senate that the treaty deserved its support; when the Senate refused to approve the treaty, it was a severe setback for Wilson.

Despite the long list of Congressional powers in the Constitution, the question of what powers are appropriate to the Congress has generated substantial controversy. For example, although the Constitution gives Congress the sole power to declare war, many presidents have initiated military action on their own. And at times, the courts have found that congressional actions have usurped the rights of the states.

ELECTING THE CONGRESS

If Americans are not happy with the job Congress is doing, they can use their votes to say so. With a congressional election every two years, the voters have frequent opportunities to express themselves.

The Incumbency Effect

Congressional elections offer voters a chance to show their approval of Congress's performance by re-electing **incumbents** (sitting legislators) or "throwing the rascals out." The voters seem to do more re-electing than throwing out. When House incumbents run for re-election, their "success rate is spectacular."[7] In the majority of elections since 1950, more than 90 percent of all House incumbents have held their seats (see Figure 10.1). In the 1986 general election, only six incumbent representatives were defeated. And incumbents are winning re-election by increasingly greater margins.[8]

These findings may seem surprising. Congress as a whole is not held in particularly high esteem. When people are polled on the amount of confidence they have in major institutions, Congress scores much lower than the Supreme Court, the military, banks, and public schools.[9] People appear to distinguish between the *institution* of Congress and their own representatives and senators. But this still does not explain why incumbents do so well within their own districts and states. (Because most research on the incumbency effect has focused on House elections, our discussion concentrates on that body.)

Redistricting.   One explanation of the incumbency effect centers on **redistricting,** the way House districts are redrawn after a census-based

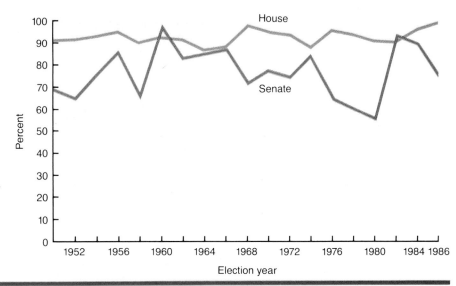

The Advantage of Incumbency
The graph shows the percentage of representatives and senators seeking reelection who won. The data include primary and general election defeats.
(Sources: Barbara Hinckley, Congressional Elections. [Washington, D.C.: Congressional Quarterly Press, 1981], p. 39; and Norman J. Orstein et al., Vital Statistics on Congress, 1987–1988 [Washington, D.C.: Congressional Quarterly Press, 1987], pp. 56–57.)
Figure 10.1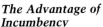

reapportionment. It is entirely possible for state legislatures to draw new districts to benefit the incumbents of one or both parties. Altering district lines for partisan advantage is commonly called **gerrymandering.**

But redistricting does not explain the incumbency effect in the House as a whole. Statistics show that after a reapportionment, redistricted and unredistricted seats end up approximately the same in terms of competitiveness.[10] Redistricting may be very helpful for an occasional incumbent, but it doesn't explain why more than 90 percent of House incumbents are re-elected.

Name and recognition. Holding office brings with it important advantages. First, incumbents develop significant name recognition among voters simply by being members of Congress. Their activities and speeches are fully reported in the local media, a process helped in good part by congressional staffs adept at maximizing press coverage. And many incumbents are more than happy to meet the media's demands for stories. Representative Dan Glickman, a Democrat from Kansas, appears on Wichita's KAKE-TV an average of three times a week. He also is interviewed frequently on KWCH-TV's five o'clock news. And he has his own monthly television show, "Window on Washington," on KSAS-TV.[11] Members of Congress are in high demand to speak before local groups; and, thanks to generous travel allowances and easy air travel, they can make frequent trips between their districts and Washington, D.C.

Another resource available to members of Congress is the **franking privilege**—the right to send mail free of charge. Mailings see to it that constituents are aware of legislators' names, activities, and accomplishments. Periodic newsletters, for example, almost always highlight success at winning funds and projects for the district, such as money to construct a highway or a new federal building. Newsletters also "advertise for business," encouraging voters to phone or visit legislators' district

COMPARED WITH WHAT? 10.1

Manchester, New Hampshire, or Manchester, England, There Are Constituents to Be Served

Although there are some important differences in the structure of the U.S. Congress and that of the British Parliament, there are many similarities in the way members of both bodies do their jobs. One similarity is that U.S. representatives and members of Parliament (MPs) work extremely hard at cultivating the grassroots. They frequently travel back to their districts to hear what's on their constituents' minds and to offer assistance. In both the United States and Britain, voters believe that legislators have a responsibility to help individuals and promote the economic welfare of their districts. Yet there is a difference in emphasis here. The figure below charts the results of a poll of American and British citizens, who were asked to choose which legislative role is most important.

In Britain, local concerns seem paramount. Americans, on the other hand, were more likely to cite policy concerns ("policymaking" and "oversight"). The weaker committee system and stronger party system in Britain make it more difficult for rank-and-file legislators to influence policy outcomes. The British responses to the interview questions may be reflecting this reality.

Legislators place such importance on their work in the constituency because they want to be re-elected and they believe that the help they offer constituents wins them loyal voters. This is not wishful thinking. Research shows that American and British legislators who more actively promote service to constituents are better known, more highly rated, and more successful at the ballot box than legislators who do not work as hard in the constituency. It's also important to note that American representatives have large staffs—typically, four or five full-time caseworkers—to tackle constituents' problems. British MPs have little or no help handling casework; they have to do it the old-fashioned way, by themselves.

offices if they need help with a problem. When he first ran in 1986, Maryland Democrat Tom McMillan won his House seat by a tiny margin, just 428 votes. In the next two years, he blanketed the district (about 230,000 homes) three times with mailings, spending $1 million of the taxpayers' money in the process. McMillan made himself such an overwhelming presence in the district that no credible Republican candidate came forward to challenge him in 1988.[12]

The large staff that works for a member of Congress is able to do **casework,** providing services for constituents—perhaps tracking down a social security check or directing the owner of a small business to the appropriate federal agency. Constituents who are helped in this way usually remember who assisted them (see Compared With What? 10.1). McMillan keeps ten of his twenty staffers in three district offices, to make it easier for constituents to get the help they need.[13]

In a race between an incumbent and a relatively unknown challenger, the incumbent's advantages (name recognition, staff resources, record of achievement) translate directly into votes. This is often enough to dissuade a potentially strong challenger from an election battle, opting

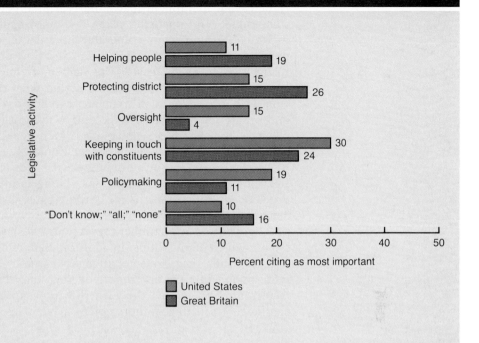

Source: Adapted by permission of the publishers from Bruce Cain, John Ferejohn, and Morris Fiorina, *The Personal Vote* (Cambridge, Mass.: Harvard University Press, 1987), especially pp. 38, 60–61, and 213. Copyright © 1987 by The President and Fellows of Harvard College.

instead to wait for a more opportune time to run—perhaps when the incumbent retires or when his or her party seems headed for a fall.[14]

Campaign financing. It should be clear that anyone who wants to challenge an incumbent needs solid financial backing. Challengers must spend large sums of money to run a strong campaign, with an emphasis on advertising—an expensive but effective way to bring their names and records to the voters' attention. But here too, the incumbent has the advantage. It is very difficult for challengers to raise campaign funds because they have to overcome contributors' doubts about whether they can win. Political action committees (PACs) show a strong preference for incumbents (see Chapter 9). They tend not to want to risk offending an incumbent by giving money to a long-shot challenger. During the 1985–1986 election cycle, PACs contributed $89.5 million to incumbents but only slightly more than $19.2 million to challengers.[15] The attitude of the American Medical Association's PAC is fairly typical. "We have a friendly incumbent policy," says its director. "We always stick with the incumbent if we agree with both candidates."[16]

Successful challengers.   Although it is very difficult for a challenger to defeat an incumbent (particularly a member of the House), it is not impossible. The opposing party and unsympathetic PACs may target incumbents who seem vulnerable because of age, lack of seniority, or unfavorable redistricting. The result is a flow of campaign contributions to the challenger, increasing the chance of victory. Incumbents can also be the victims of general dissatisfaction with their party. Poor disaffection with a president can translate into popular disaffection with House and Senate incumbents who belong to the president's party. In the 1980 election, for example, twenty-seven incumbent House Democrats were defeated in the landslide that swept Ronald Reagan into office.[17]

As Figure 10.1 shows, incumbency is less of an advantage in Senate elections than in House elections. There is no simple explanation for this, but one important factor is the greater visibility of challengers for Senate seats. These challengers usually are prominent individuals (sometimes governors or incumbent representatives), whose names and records are known to many voters. In addition, Senate challengers often are able to raise funds that House challengers cannot. And Senate races attract more public interest and press coverage than House races. All of these factors tend to reduce the identification gap between incumbent and challenger, resulting in more competitive races for the Senate.

Who Do We Elect?

The people we elect (then re-elect) to Congress are not a cross-section of American society. Most members of Congress are professionals—primarily lawyers and businesspeople. Although nearly a third of the American labor force works in blue-collar jobs, there are few former blue-collar workers in Congress.[18] And although the typical American does not have a college degree, the typical member of Congress holds both undergraduate and graduate degrees.

The number of blacks in the House has grown modestly, but blacks are still underrepresented in terms of their number in the general population, as are Hispanics. And women, who make up half the population of the United States, hold only 5 percent of seats in the House and only 2 percent of seats in the Senate (see Figure 10.2). This is not to say that Congress discriminates against minorities or women. After all, the voters elect the members of Congress. But the underrepresentation of minorities and women in Congress reflects historical patterns of opportunity—or lack of it—in American society. And the predominance of white-collar professionals in Congress reflects the advantages of wealth and education that make it easier for upper-middle-class people to enter politics.

If a representative legislative body is supposed to mirror the electorate, then Congress certainly doesn't qualify. Yet the correspondence between the social characteristics of the population and the membership of Congress is only one way to look at the question of representation. A more crucial measure may be how well the members of Congress represent their constituents' views as they make policy decisions. In the

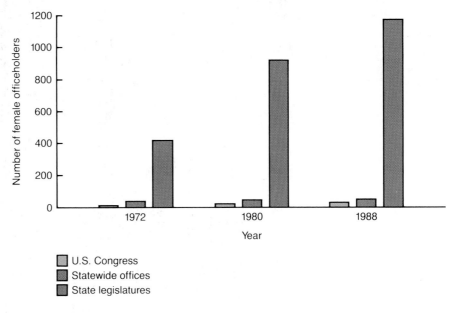

Congress: Still the Men's Club
*Although women have made great strides in building careers in many fields
that were at one time dominated by men, national political office is not one
of them. Only twenty-three women are now serving in the House of Representatives. The number of women elected to the state legislatures has increased
significantly, though. And because many congressional candidates first serve
in state legislatures, there is reason to hope that as women gain experience
and recognition they will be winning more congressional nominations and
seats. (Source: "Women in Power," Ms., April 1988, p. 79.)*

Figure 10.2

next several sections, we examine the legislative process. Then we return
to the subject of representation.

HOW ISSUES GET ON THE
CONGRESSIONAL AGENDA

The formal legislative process begins when a member of Congress intro-
duces a **bill,** a proposal for a new law. In the House, members drop new
bills in the "hopper," a mahogany box near the rostrum where the
Speaker presides. Senators give their bills to one of the Senate clerks or
introduce them from the floor.[19] But before a bill can be introduced to
solve a problem, someone must perceive that a problem exists or that
an issue needs to be resolved. In other words, the problem or issue
somehow must find its way onto the congressional agenda. *Agenda*
actually has two meanings in the vocabulary of political scientists. The
first is that of a narrow, formal agenda, such as a calendar of bills to be
voted on. The second meaning refers to the broad, imprecise, and unwritten agenda that consists of all the issues an institution is considering.
Here we use the term in the second, broader sense.

Many of the issues Congress is working on at any one time seem to have been around forever. Foreign aid, the national debt, and social security have come up in just about every recent session of Congress. Yet all issues begin at some point in time. For example, for a long time, commercial banks have wanted the reversal of a provision in the Glass-Steagall Act (1932) that generally prohibits them from underwriting the sales of securities, a lucrative part of business along Wall Street. But only recently has Congress given serious consideration to a change in the banking laws.[20]

What moves an issue onto the congressional agenda? Commercial banks are profiting from deregulation, a general movement in the last couple of decades away from government intervention in the marketplace.[21] As the walls of regulation have come down in certain industries (communications, airlines), they are harder to justify in many others.

Some new issues reach the congressional agenda as a response to a highly visible event. When an explosion in a West Virginia mine in 1968 killed seventy-eight miners, Congress promptly went to work on laws to promote miners' safety.[22] Presidential support can also move an issue onto the agenda quickly. This was certainly the case for the *flat tax*, which was promoted energetically by two Republicans—Representative Jack Kemp of New York and Senator Robert Kasten of Wisconsin—and two Democrats—Representative Richard Gephardt of Missouri and Senator Bill Bradley of New Jersey. The basic idea of the flat tax was to simplify the tax code, reduce people's tax rates, and eliminate tax loopholes. The flat tax seemed to be a good idea that was going nowhere until President Reagan embraced a modified version of it and asked Congress to pass the bill described at the opening of this chapter. Only then was tax reform given active consideration by Congress.

Within Congress, party leaders and committee chairs have the best opportunity to influence the political agenda. National insurance for catastrophic illness is a case in point. According to surveys, only a minority of leaders (14 percent in 1977 and 33 percent in 1978) in the national health field believed that catastrophic illness insurance was a prominent issue. But when Russell Long, chairman of the Senate Finance Committee, announced in 1979 that his committee would work up a bill on catastrophic illness insurance, the figure jumped to 92 percent. "In other words, a key congressional committee chairman single-handedly set a major portion of the policy agenda in health by his intention to move on health insurance."[23]

Although party leaders and committee chairs have the opportunity to move issues onto the agenda, they rarely act capriciously, seizing upon issues without rhyme or reason. They often bide their time, waiting for other members of Congress to learn about an issue, as they attempt to gauge the level of support. At times the efforts of an interest group spark support, or at least an awareness, of an issue. When congressional leaders—or, for that matter, rank-and-file members—sense that the time is ripe for action on a new issue, they often are spurred on by the knowledge that sponsoring an important bill can enhance their own image. In the words of one observer, "Congress exists to do things. There isn't much mileage in doing nothing."[24]

THE DANCE OF LEGISLATION: AN OVERVIEW

The process of writing bills and getting them passed is relatively simple, in the sense that it follows a series of specific steps. What complicates the process is the many different ways legislation can be treated at each step. Here, we examine the straightforward process by which laws are made. In the next few sections, we discuss some of the complexities of that process.

After a bill is introduced in either house, it is assigned to the appropriate committee of that chamber for study (see Figure 10.3). A banking bill, for example, would be assigned to the Banking, Finance, and Urban Affairs Committee in the House or to the Banking, Housing, and Urban Affairs Committee in the Senate, depending on where it was introduced. When a committee actively considers a piece of legislation assigned to it, the bill is usually referred to a specialized subcommittee. The subcommittee may hold hearings, and legislative staffers may do research on the bill. The original bill usually is modified or revised, then, if passed in some form, it is sent back to the full committee. A bill that is approved by the full committee is *reported* (that is, sent) to the entire membership of the chamber, where it may be debated, amended, and either passed or defeated.

Bills coming out of House committees go to the Rules Committee before going before the full House membership. The Rules Committee attaches a "rule" to the bill that governs the coming floor debate, typically specifying the length of the debate and the types of amendments that can be offered. The Senate does not have a comparable committee, although restrictions on the length of floor debate can be reached through unanimous consent agreements (see page 375).

Even if a bill on the same subject is passed by both houses of Congress, the Senate and House versions are typically different from each other. In that case, a conference committee, composed of legislators from both houses, works out the differences and develops a compromise version. This version is sent back to both houses for another floor vote. If the bill passes in both chambers, it is then sent to the president for his signature or veto.

When the president signs a bill, it becomes law. If the president **vetoes** (disapproves) the bill, it is sent back to Congress with his reasons for rejecting it. The bill then becomes law only if Congress overrides the president's veto by a two-thirds vote of each house. If the president neither signs nor vetoes the bill within ten days (Sundays excepted) of receiving it, the bill becomes law. There is an exception here: If Congress adjourns within the ten days, the president can let the bill die through a **pocket veto,** by not signing it.

The content of a bill can be changed at any stage of the process, in either house. Lawmaking (and thus policymaking) in Congress has many access points for those who want to influence legislation. This openness tends to fit within the pluralist model of democracy. As a bill moves through the dance of legislation, it is amended again and again, in a search for a consensus that will get it passed and signed into law. The process can be tortuously slow and often fruitless. Derailing legislation

Figure 10.3

The Legislative Process
The process by which a bill becomes a law is subject to much variation. This diagram depicts the typical process a bill might follow. It is important to remember that a bill can fail at any stage because of lack of support.

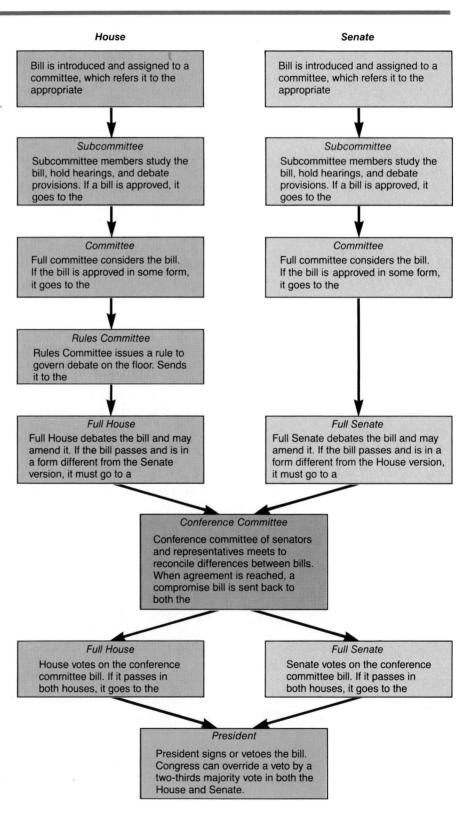

is much easier than enacting it. The process gives groups frequent opportunities to voice their preferences and, if necessary, to thwart their opponents. One foreign ambassador stationed in Washington aptly described the twists and turns of our legislative process: "In the Congress of the U.S., it's never over until it's over. And when it's over, it's still not over."[25]

COMMITTEES: THE WORKHORSES OF CONGRESS

Woodrow Wilson once observed that "Congress in session is Congress on public exhibition, whilst Congress in its committee-rooms is Congress at work."[26] His words are as true today as when he wrote them over one hundred years ago. A speech given on the Senate floor, for example, may convince the average citizen, but it is less likely to influence other senators. Indeed, few of them may even hear it. The real nuts and bolts of lawmaking goes on in the congressional committees.

The Division of Labor Among Committees

The House and Senate are divided into committees for the same reason that other large organizations are broken into departments or divisions—to develop and use expertise in specific areas. At IBM, for example, different groups of people design computers, write software, assemble hardware, and sell the company's products. Each of these tasks requires an expertise that may have little to do with the other tasks that the company performs. Likewise, in Congress, decisions on weapons systems require a special knowledge that is of little relevance to decisions on reimbursement formulas for health insurance, for example. It makes sense for some members of Congress to spend more time examining defense issues, becoming increasingly expert as they do so, while others concentrate on health matters.

Eventually, though, all members of Congress have to vote on each bill that emerges from the committees. Those who are not on a particular committee depend on committee members to examine the issues thoroughly, to make compromises as necessary, and to bring forward a sound piece of legislation that has a good chance of being passed. Each member decides individually on the bill's merits. But once it reaches the House or Senate floor, members may get to vote on only a handful of amendments (if any at all) before they must cast their yeas and nays for the entire bill.

Standing committees. There are several different kinds of congressional committees, but the standing committee is predominant. **Standing committees** are permanent committees that specialize in a particular area of legislation—for example, the House Judiciary Committee or the Senate Environment and Public Works Committee (see Table 10.2). Most of the day-to-day work of drafting legislation takes place in the sixteen standing Senate committees and twenty-two standing House commit-

Table 10.2
Standing Committees of Congress

Standing Committees of the Senate

Agriculture, Nutrition, and Forestry	Finance
Appropriations	Foreign Relations
Armed Services	Governmental Affairs
Banking, Housing, and Urban Affairs	Judiciary
Budget	Labor and Human Resources
Commerce, Science, and Transportation	Rules and Administration
Energy and Natural Resources	Small Business
Environment and Public Works	Veterans' Affairs

Standing Committees of the House

Agriculture	Interior and Insular Affairs
Appropriations	Judiciary
Armed Services	Merchant Marine and Fisheries
Banking, Finance, and Urban Affairs	Post Office and Civil Service
Budget	Public Works and Transportation
District of Columbia	Rules
Education and Labor	Science, Space, and Technology
Energy and Commerce	Small Business
Foreign Affairs	Standards of Official Conduct
Government Operations	Veterans' Affairs
House Administration	Ways and Means

Source: *Committees and Subcommittees of the 99th Congress,* supplement to *Congressional Quarterly Weekly Report,* 2 May 1987. Copyrighted material reprinted with permission, Congressional Quarterly Inc.

tees. There are typically fifteen to twenty senators on each standing Senate committee, and thirty to forty members on each standing committee in the House. The proportions of Democrats and Republicans on a standing committee generally reflect party proportions in the full Senate or House, and each member of Congress serves on only a small number of committees.

With a few exceptions, standing committees are further broken down into subcommittees. The House Agriculture Committee, for example, has eight separate subcommittees, among them one on wheat, soybeans, and feed grains and another on livestock, dairy, and poultry. Subcommittees exist for the same reason parent committees exist: Members acquire expertise by continually working within the same fairly narrow policy area.

Other congressional committees. Members of Congress can also serve on joint, select, and conference committees. **Joint committees** are made up of members of both the House and the Senate. Like standing committees, the small number of joint committees are concerned with particular policy areas. The Joint Economic Committee, for instance, analyzes the country's economic policies. Joint committees operate in

Can We Split the Difference?
For members of Congress, conference committees represent another opportunity to negotiate policy during the legislative process. These conferees from the House and Senate budget committees are trying to reconcile different budget resolutions passed by the two chambers.

much the same way as standing committees, but they are almost always restricted from reporting bills to the House or Senate.

A **select committee** is a temporary committee, created for a specific purpose. Select committees are established to deal with special circumstances or with issues that either overlap or are not included in the areas of expertise of standing committees. The Senate committee that investigated the Watergate scandal was a select committee, created for that purpose only.

A **conference committee** is also a temporary committee, created to work out differences between the House and Senate versions of a specific piece of legislation. Its members are appointed from the standing committees or subcommittees that originally handled and reported the legislation to each house. Depending on the nature of the differences and the importance of the legislation, a conference committee may meet for hours or for weeks on end. When the conference committee agrees on a compromise, the bill is reported to both houses of Congress. Each house may either approve or disapprove the compromise; they cannot amend or change it in any way.

Congressional Expertise and Seniority

Once appointed to a committee, a representative or senator has great incentive to remain on it and to gain increasing expertise over the years. That incentive can be translated as influence in Congress, and that influence increases as a member's level of expertise grows. Influence also grows in a more formal way, with **seniority,** or years of consecutive service on a committee. In the quest for expertise and seniority, members

Sam Nunn: Defense Specialist
The cerebral Democrat from Georgia, extremely knowledgeable on defense policy, exerts a great deal of influence as chairman of the Senate Armed Services Committee.

Bill Gray: Rising Star
This Democrat from Philadelphia has built an impressive career since entering the House in 1979. Especially noteworthy was his effective leadership of the House Budget Committee during a four-year tenure as chairman.

tend to stay on the same committees. Sometimes, however, they switch places when they are offered the opportunity to move to one of the high-prestige committees (like Ways and Means or Appropriations in the House) or to a committee that handles legislation of vital importance to their constituents.

In a committee, the member of the majority party with the most seniority usually becomes the committee chair. (The majority party in each house controls committee leadership.) Other high-seniority members of the majority party become subcommittee chairs, while their counterparts from the minority party gain influence as *ranking minority members*. With about 140 subcommittees in the House and 90 in the Senate, there is a great deal of power and status available to the members of Congress.

Unlike seniority, expertise does not follow simply from length of service. Ability and effort are critical factors too. Democratic Representative Les Aspin from Wisconsin is influential on military matters not simply because he is chairman of the House Armed Services Committee. Aspin, who has a Ph.D. from the Massachusetts Institute of Technology, is widely respected for his incisive knowledge of weapons systems and military matters. Other House members often look to him before committing themselves one way or the other on important defense votes.

Committee Reform

The committee system and the seniority system that determines the leadership of committees was sharply attacked during the 1970s. The push for reform came primarily from liberal and junior members of the House who "chafed under the restrictions on their participation and policy influence that the old, committee-dominated regime imposed. The committee chair, often in collaboration with the ranking minority member, dominated the panel."[27]

A number of select committees were established to study the organization of the House and Senate. Although not all of their reforms were adopted, many significant changes were made. The power of the subcommittees in relation to their parent committees and their number were increased; and House Democrats (the majority party) prohibited their members from serving as chairs of more than one subcommittee. Also in the House, the seniority system was weakened by new rules that held that seniority did not have to be followed in the selection of committee chairs. In 1975, House Democrats voted out three aging unpopular committee chairmen, serving notice on all committee chairs that autocratic rule would not be tolerated. An earlier change by House Democrats had eliminated the committee chairs' power to appoint subcommittee chairs. These changes decentralized influence in the House. Although some changes also strengthened the position of the Speaker of the House, their general thrust was to make subcommittees more autonomous and powerful.[28]

There was considerably less reform in the Senate. The smaller number of members in that body guarantees virtually all senators in the majority party at least one subcommittee chair. Moreover, the Senate's greater national visibility makes its members less dependent on their committee activities or seniority to gain recognition and influence. As one study concluded, "Committees are simply less crucial to the pursuit of personal goals in the Senate than in the House."[29]

Drafting Legislation

The way in which committees and subcommittees are organized within Congress is ultimately significant because much public policy decision making takes place there. The first step in drafting legislation is to collect information on the issue. Committee staffers research the problem and hearings may be held to take testimony from witnesses who have some special knowledge on the subject.

At times, committee hearings are more theatrical than informational, to draw public attention to them. When the House judiciary subcommittee on administrative law held hearings on alleged malpractice in military hospitals, it did not restrict its list of witnesses to the experts who had done relevant research. Instead, it called witnesses like Dawn Lambert, a former member of the navy, who sobbed as she told the subcommittee that she had been left sterile by a misdiagnosis and a botched operation that had left a sponge and a green marker inside her. It was an irresistible story for the network news, and brought the malpractice problem to light.[30]

The meetings at which subcommittees or committees actually debate and amend legislation are called **markup sessions.** The process by which committees reach decisions varies. In many committees, there is a strong tradition of decision by consensus. The chair, the ranking minority member, and others in these committees work hard, in formal committee sessions and in informal meetings, to find a middle ground on issues that divide committee members. In other committees, members exhibit strong ideological and partisan sentiments. One House member on Education and Labor said there was so much division on the committee that "you can't get a resolution praising God . . . without having a three-day battle over it."[31]

The skill of an individual committee or subcommittee chair can strongly influence the way a committee handles its drafting of legislation. Some chairs are gifted at understanding what makes other committee members tick and have the patience and diligence to lead the bargaining between those holding different views until a consensus decision is reached. The legendary Wilbur Mills, an Arkansas Democrat and former chairman of the House Ways and Means Committee (which writes tax laws), was brilliant at helping his committee reach agreement on the complex and controversial issues before it. He was described as "a shaper of decisions, not a dictator . . . an extremely skillful leader who responds to [committee members] in such a way that his conclusions, drawn from their discussions, become their conclusions."[32] Mills, like all other committee chairs, wanted to develop a reasonable bill that would pass when the entire chamber voted on it.

Committees: The Majoritarian and Pluralist Views

It makes sense to bring as much expertise as possible to the policy-making process, and the committee system does just that. But government by committee vests a tremendous amount of power in the committees and subcommittees of Congress—especially in their leaders. This is particularly true of the House, which is more decentralized in its patterns of influence and is more restrictive in the degree to which legislation can be amended on the floor. Committee members can bury a bill by not reporting it to the full House or Senate. The influence of committee members extends even further, to the floor debate. And many of them make up the conference committee that is charged with developing a compromise version of the bill.

This vesting of policy-area power in many committees and subcommittees tends to remove that power from the majority party and thus to operate against majoritarianism. At the same time, the committee system enhances the force of pluralism in American politics. Representatives and senators are elected by the voters in particular districts and states, and they tend to seek membership on the committees whose decisions are most important to their constituents. Members from farm areas, for example, want membership on the House and Senate Agriculture Committees. Westerners like to serve on the committees that deal with public lands and water rights. Urban liberals like the committees that handle social programs. As a result, the various committees are predisposed to writing legislation favorable to those who are most affected by their actions.

de la Garza Delivers
When a devastating drought hit the Midwest in the summer of 1988, the House Agriculture Committee, chaired by Democrat Kika de la Garza of Texas, swung into action to fashion a relief measure. Both the House and the Senate completed work on the farm legislation quickly, and the bill was signed into law by President Ronald Reagan before the summer was over.

This is not to say that committee members care only about being re-elected and simply pass legislation that will win them votes back home. They are genuinely sympathetic to their constituents and can usually rationalize that good policy for their constituents is good policy for the nation as a whole.

A meeting of the whole House or Senate, to vote a bill up or down, may seem to be an example of majoritarianism at work. The views of the collective membership of each body may reasonably approximate the diverse mix of interests in the United States.[33] Committee decision making also anticipates what is acceptable to the entire membership. Still, by the time the broader membership begins to debate legislation on the floor, many crucial decisions have already been made in committees with a much narrower constituency in mind. Clearly, the internal structure of Congress gives small groups of members, with intense interests in particular policy areas, a disproportionate amount of influence over those areas.

LEADERS AND FOLLOWERS IN CONGRESS

Above the committee chairs is another layer of authority in the organization of the House and Senate. The Democratic and Republican leaders in each house work to maximize the influence of their own party, at the same time trying to keep their chamber functioning smoothly and efficiently. The operation of the two houses is also influenced by the rules and norms that each chamber has developed over the years.

The Leadership Task

Each of the two parties in each of the two houses elect leaders. In the House of Representatives, the majority-party leader is the **Speaker of the House,** who, gavel in hand, chairs sessions from the ornate rostrum at the front of the chamber (see Figure 10.4). The counterpart in the opposing party is the *minority leader*. The majority party chooses the Speaker at its *caucus*, a closed-door meeting of the party. The majority and minority parties then "slate" their candidates for Speaker at the opening session of Congress. The official election follows strict party lines, affirming the majority party's caucus decision. The minority-party candidate becomes the minority leader. The Speaker is a constitutional officer, but the Constitution does not list the Speaker's duties. The minority leader is not mentioned in the Constitution, but that post has evolved into an important party position in the House.

The Constitution makes the vice president of the United States the president of the Senate. But the vice president usually does not come to the Senate chamber unless there is a possibility of a tie vote, in which case he can break the tie. The **president pro tempore** (president "for the time"), elected by the majority party, is supposed to chair the Senate in the vice president's absence, but by custom this constitutional position is entirely honorary.

Figure 10.4
The United States Capitol

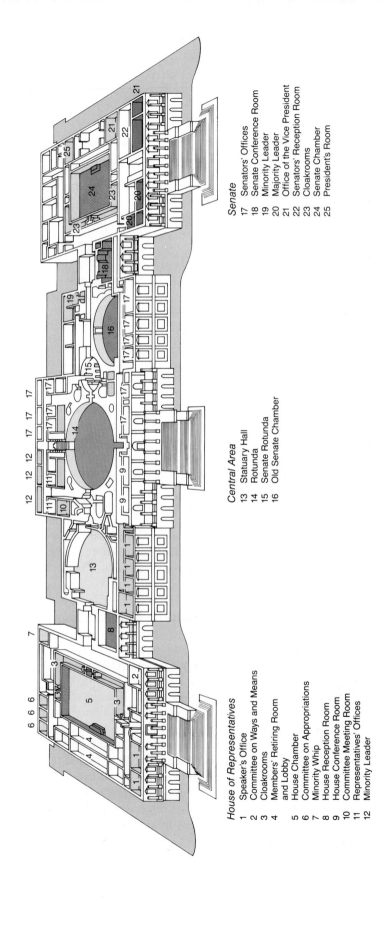

House of Representatives

1   Speaker's Office
2   Committee on Ways and Means
3   Cloakrooms
4   Members' Retiring Room
    and Lobby
5   House Chamber
6   Committee on Appropriations
7   Minority Whip
8   House Reception Room
9   House Conference Room
10 Committee Meeting Room
11 Representatives' Offices
12 Minority Leader

Central Area

13 Statuary Hall
14 Rotunda
15 Senate Rotunda
16 Old Senate Chamber

Senate

17 Senators' Offices
18 Senate Conference Room
19 Minority Leader
20 Majority Leader
21 Office of the Vice President
22 Senators' Reception Room
23 Cloakrooms
24 Senate Chamber
25 President's Room

Did Wright Do Wrong?
In 1988, Speaker of the House Jim Wright, a Democrat from Texas (shown here with Ronald Reagan), faced allegations of a number of ethical violations— among them, the charge that he had improperly aided some Texas oil ventures. In response, the House Ethics Committee launched the first formal inquiry of a Speaker since the nineteenth century.

The real power in the Senate resides in the **majority leader.** As in the House, the top position in the opposing party is that of *minority leader.* Technically, the majority leader does not preside (members rotate in the president pro tempore's chair); but the majority leader does schedule legislation in consultation with the minority leader. More broadly, the majority leader, the minority leader, and a handful of other party leaders below them play a critical role in getting bills through Congress. The most significant function that leaders play is steering the bargaining and negotiating over the content of legislation. When an issue divides their party, their house, the two houses, or their house and the White House, the leaders must take the initiative to work out a compromise solution.

Compromise was on the mind of Speaker of the House Jim Wright, a Democrat from Texas, when in 1987 he was called on to mediate a dispute between two committees working on legislation in the same area. Claude Pepper, head of the Rules Committee and the nation's foremost spokesman on behalf of the elderly, was angry that the House Ways and Means Committee had not included long-term home care for senior citizens in the bill it prepared to provide protection from the cost of catastrophic illness. Pepper wanted to amend the bill with a home-care provision. Members of the Ways and Means Committee argued that the costs were too high; if the home-care provision was added, President Reagan was sure to veto the whole bill. Wright got Pepper to agree not to try to amend the catastrophic costs bill by promising him he could do an end run around Ways and Means, which would normally have jurisdiction over such issues, and bring a bill of his own on long-term care directly to the floor. In exchange, Ways and Means got the bill it wanted without the killer amendment.[34]

Day in, day out, this is much of what leaders do: meet with other members of their house to try to strike deals that will yield a majority on the floor. It is often a matter of finding out if one faction is willing to give up a policy preference in exchange for another concession. Beyond trying to engineer tradeoffs that will win votes, the party leaders must persuade others (often powerful committee chairs) that theirs is the best deal possible. Senator Robert Dole of Kansas aptly described himself as the "majority pleader" in his role as Senate majority leader.[35] (Dole later became the *minority* pleader when his party lost control of the Senate in the 1986 elections.)

Party leaders are coalition builders, not kingmakers. Gone are the days when leaders ruled the House and the Senate with iron fists. Even as recently as the 1950s, strong leaders dominated the legislative process. When he was Senate majority leader, Lyndon Johnson made full use of his intelligence, parliamentary skills, and forceful personality to direct the Senate. When he approached individual senators for one-on-one persuasion, "no one subjected to the 'Johnson treatment' ever forgot it."[36]

The Johnson Treatment

When he was Senate majority leader in the 1950s, Lyndon Johnson was well known for his style of interaction with other members. In this unusual set of photographs, we see him applying the "Johnson treatment" to Democrat Theodore Francis Green of Rhode Island. Washington journalists Rowland Evans and Robert Novak offered the following description of the treatment: "Its tone could be supplication, accusation, cajolery, exuberance, scorn, tears, complaint, the hint of threat. It was all of these together. It ran the gamut of human emotions. Its velocity was breathtaking, and it was all in one direction. Interjections from the target were rare. Johnson anticipated them before they could be spoken. He moved in close, his face a scant millimeter from his target, his eyes widening and narrowing, his eyebrows rising and falling. From his pockets poured clippings, memos, statistics. Mimicry, humor, and the genius of analogy made The Treatment an almost hypnotic experience and rendered the target stunned and helpless." (Rowland Evans and Robert Novak, Lyndon B. Johnson: The Exercise of Power. New York: New American Library, 1966, p. 104.)

In today's Congress, rank-and-file representatives and senators would not stand for this kind of leadership. But there is no doubt that contemporary leaders have an impact on policy outcomes in Congress. As one expert concluded, "Although leadership contributions may be marginal, most important political choices are made at the margins."[37]

Rules of Procedure

The operation of the House and Senate is structured by both formal *rules* and informal *norms of behavior*. Rules in each chamber are mostly matters of parliamentary procedure. For example, they govern the scheduling of legislation, outlining when and how certain types of legislation can be brought to the floor. There are rules, too, that govern the introduction of floor amendments. In the House, amendments must be directly germane (relevant) to the bill at hand; in the Senate, except in certain specified instances, amendments that are not germane to the bill at hand can be added.

As noted earlier, an important difference between the two chambers is the House's use of its Rules Committee to govern floor debate. Without a similar committee to act as a "traffic cop" for legislation approaching the floor, the Senate relies on *unanimous consent agreements* to set the starting time and length of debate. If one senator objects to an agreement, it does not take effect. Senators do not routinely object to unanimous consent agreements, however, because they need them when a bill of their own awaits scheduling by the leadership.

If a senator wants to stop a bill badly enough, he or she may start a **filibuster**, trying to talk the bill to death. By historical tradition, the

Three Men and a Cot
In an attempt to break a Republican-led filibuster over a campaign finance reform bill in 1988, the Democratic leadership decided not to adjourn the Senate. Republican Senator Mitch McConnell of Kentucky gets some help from two staffers as he prepares for a long night at the Capitol.

Senate gives its members the right of unlimited debate. During a 1947 debate, Idaho Democrat Glen Taylor "spoke for 8½ hours on fishing, baptism, Wall Street, and his children." The record for holding the floor belongs to Republican Senator Strom Thurmond of South Carolina, for a twenty-four-hour, eighteen-minute marathon.[38] In the House, no member is allowed to speak for more than an hour without unanimous consent.

After a 1917 filibuster by a small group of senators killed President Wilson's bill to arm merchant ships—a bill favored by a majority of senators—the Senate finally adopted **cloture,** a means of limiting debate. A petition signed by sixteen senators initiates a cloture vote. It now takes the votes of sixty senators to invoke cloture.[39] Cloture was successfully invoked when a filibuster by southern senators threatened passage of the far-reaching Civil Rights Act of 1964. Three-quarters of senators recently surveyed professed some support for making it more difficult to filibuster, but apparently sentiment is not intense enough to propel reform forward because no changes are now being actively considered.[40]

Norms of Behavior

Both houses have codes of behavior that help keep them running. These codes are largely unwritten norms, although some have been formally adopted as rules. Members of Congress recognize that personal conflict must be eliminated (or minimized), lest Congress dissolve into bickering factions unable to work together. One of the most celebrated norms is that members show respect for their colleagues in public deliberations. During floor debate, bitter opponents still refer to one another in such terms as "my good friend, the senior senator from . . ." or "my distinguished colleague."

Members of Congress are only human, of course, and tempers occasionally flare (see Compared With What? 10.2). For example, when Democrat Barney Frank of Massachusetts was angered by what he thought were unusually harsh charges against the Democratic party, made by Republican Robert Walker of Pennsylvania, Frank rose to ask the presiding officer if it was permissible to refer to Walker as a "crybaby." When he was informed that it was not, Frank sat down, having made his point without technically violating the House's code of behavior.[41]

Probably the most important norm of behavior in Congress is that individual members should be willing to bargain with one another. Policymaking is a process of give and take; it demands compromise. And the cost of not compromising is high. When Republican Richard Armey of Texas first came to Congress in 1985, he was a strident conservative ideologue who enjoyed trying to disrupt the Democratic-controlled House to prevent it from passing legislation that it favored. Consequently, other representatives ignored him; he was never included in the bargaining over legislation and had no real impact on the lawmaking process. By his next term in office, Armey realized that if he was going to have any influence on public policy, he had to stop thinking of the

COMPARED WITH WHAT? 10.2

Maybe They Ought to Make Crocodile Dundee Speaker

We wouldn't expect a legislature with members named "Toecutter" Williams, "Dingo" Dawkins, and "Ironbar" Tuckey to be a quiet, formal, contemplative body. And the Australian Parliament is not. In fact, the Australian Parliament makes the boisterous British Parliament—after which it is modeled—seem almost subdued.

Name-calling has rarely reached the heights of imagination it has in the hallowed chambers of the parliament Down Under. Cries of "harlot," "sleazebag," "mug," "boxhead," "fop," "sucker," and "thug" are hurled back and forth among members as they debate the bills before them. For the record, it's only fair to point out that the body's rules actually forbid such language. Indeed, the Senate's handbook explicitly states that it's wrong to call other senators names like "arrant humbug" or "yahoo from Tasmania." But when an Australian senator gets angry, no handbook is going to stop him from calling a yahoo from Tasmania a "yahoo from Tasmania."

The Australian Parliament does have a rich sense of tradition. Legislators are called to impend-ing votes by bells that ring for two minutes. There is no clock on the wall of the chambers; time is measured with an hourglass. And attendants who work in the chambers are dressed in wigs and gowns.

Unfortunately, one of the traditions is freely speaking one's mind. When they have something to say, Australian legislators can be quite persistent. Unlike Representative Barney Frank, who was content to sit down after a single insult, Brian Howe, an Australian representative, was only warming up when he called a colleague "something of a grub if I could put it that way." When the Speaker told Howe no, that he couldn't put it that way, Howe responded, "I will withdraw that term and substitute the term parasite." Again, the Speaker objected. Howe then substituted the phrase "this leech over there," which led the Speaker to reprimand Howe.

Democrats as liberal heathens and be willing to negotiate. Now, he's a "player" in the process.[42]

Of course, if one side has all the votes it needs for passage, it has no need to bargain with those on the other side. Many issues, however, are complex, with many different provisions. Here, bargaining is essential if a bill is going to be passed. A recent trade bill, for example, was a thousand pages long; House and Senate differences had to be worked out by two hundred legislators working in seventeen subconferences.[43]

It is important to point out that members of Congress are not expected to violate their consciences on policy issues simply to strike a deal. They are expected, however, to listen to what others have to say and to make every effort to reach a reasonable compromise. Obviously, if each of them sticks rigidly to his or her views, they will never agree on anything. Moreover, few policy matters are so clear-cut that compromise destroys one's position.

Consequently, members of Congress are willing bargainers, who enter the lawmaking process with a rough idea of which provisions they are willing to yield on, which they would give up entirely, and which they feel they cannot yield on. Most of this horse trading goes on in committee, with the chair usually playing a pivotal role in putting together a deal and coming up with a reportable bill. The norms for such committee bargaining on the House Ways and Means Committee are instructive:

> If a member asks a reasonable price, and Rostenkowski [the Democratic chairman, from Illinois] makes the deal, the agreement is clear: the member must then vote for the final package. If a member asks a price that the chairman cannot or will not pay, then there are no obligations on either side; the member is free to oppose the bill, and the chairman is free to follow his own advice and kick the member's brains in, making no concession to his special concerns.[44]

One form of bargaining is **logrolling,** a kind of legislative back scratching, in which members of Congress drum up support for their own bills or amendments by promising to vote for others'. Logrolling played an important part in passage of the Food Stamp Act of 1964. The urban liberals in favor of the program were shy of a majority in the House. At around the same time, a bill providing cotton and wheat subsidies was also in trouble. There were urban liberals who cared more about getting a food stamp bill through than about voting against an agriculture bill. And there were southern Democrats and northern Republicans who were willing to vote for food stamps if that was the way to get the subsidy bill passed. In the end, logrolling ensured that both bills won approval on the House floor.[45]

Lawmaking requires that leaders be attentive to their followers. Members of Congress have many opportunities to present and argue their claims. Although members can apply the brakes to the congressional process, the rules and norms encourage cooperation among competing interests in order for Congress to function. Compromise enables the leadership to forge majorities from these competing interests. This description of legislative leadership fits the pluralist model of democracy.

THE LEGISLATIVE ENVIRONMENT

After legislation emerges from committee, it is scheduled for floor debate. How do legislators make up their minds on how to vote? In this section, we examine the broader legislative environment that affects decision making in Congress. More specifically, we look at the influence of political parties, interest groups, colleagues, staff, the president, and constituents on legislators.[46]

Political Parties

The national political parties have limited influence over lawmakers. They do not control the nominations of House and Senate candidates. Candidates receive the bulk of their funds from individual contributors and political action committees, not from the national parties. The party leadership in each house, however, does try to influence the rank and file. Individual members may, for example, need their party leaders' assistance on specific legislation; members therefore have an incentive to cooperate with those leaders. Although members rarely vote in solid party blocs when floor votes are called, in recent years we have witnessed an increase in party unity (see Figure 10.5).

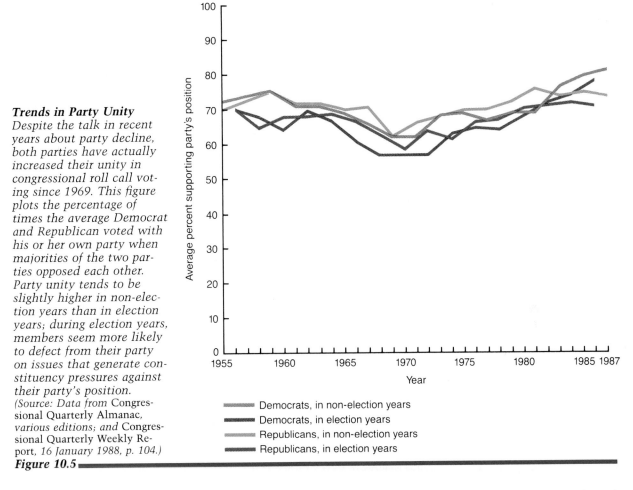

Trends in Party Unity
Despite the talk in recent years about party decline, both parties have actually increased their unity in congressional roll call voting since 1969. This figure plots the percentage of times the average Democrat and Republican voted with his or her own party when majorities of the two parties opposed each other. Party unity tends to be slightly higher in non-election years than in election years; during election years, members seem more likely to defect from their party on issues that generate constituency pressures against their party's position. (Source: Data from Congressional Quarterly Almanac, *various editions; and* Congressional Quarterly Weekly Report, *16 January 1988, p. 104.)*
Figure 10.5

One factor in this increase in party unity is the greater loyalty of southern democrats. Although they are still less likely to vote with fellow Democrats than are the party's northern members, their loyalty has risen significantly. A primary reason for this is that the issue of race no longer dominates southern politics or the national agenda the way it once did. Since the Voting Rights Act of 1965 was passed, blacks have registered in large numbers. They comprise a large share of the Democratic coalition in the South, and act as a moderating influence on the traditionally conservative southern Democratic party.[47] But there are times when a majority of southern Democrats join a majority of Republicans, forming the **conservative coalition,** to vote against a majority of northern Democrats. In 1986, the conservative coalition formed on 20 percent of the votes in the Senate and was victorious in 93 percent of them. In the House, the coalition formed in just 11 percent of the votes and won 78 percent of them.[48]

Interest Groups

Lobbyists do more than tell legislators where a group stands on an issue. Their primary function is to provide lawmakers with useful and reliable information. Legislators do not need to be told that the AFL-CIO favors an increase in the minimum wage. They need reports and research analyses describing why an increase in the minimum wage would not be inflationary, why it would not reduce competitiveness in world markets, how it would raise the working poor's standard of living, and why it would reduce welfare payments.

Critics often refer to lobbies as "pressure groups." Although political scientists would choose a more neutral term, interest groups *do* try to pressure Congress. One of the most effective forms of pressure is having constituents contact their legislators with their version of the facts. Members of Congress aren't re-elected by Washington lobbyists; it's the people back home who cast the ballots. One study calls this the "Utah plant manager theory" of lobbying. A Utah senator may not want to take time out of a hectic schedule to speak with a lobbyist from an industry trade group, but if the manager of a Utah plant in this same industry comes to Washington and wants to see the senator, the senator is more likely to agree to a meeting. That senator doesn't want the manager to go back home and tell all the workers (voters) in the plant that their elected representative was too busy to hear about the industry's problems.[49]

Colleagues

Lobbyists and interest groups are a good source of information, but their facts and arguments support their own interests. For more objective information, a legislator may very well turn to a fellow representative or senator. One reason is the expertise that comes with committee specialization. It is easy for a member to find an extremely knowledgeable colleague, who can offer a quick analysis of the legislative choices. A second reason is that representatives and senators form a peer group, and strong bonds of trust, friendship, and professional respect develop over time within that peer group.

Consultation with colleagues comes not only through informal conversations, but also through various formal groupings of legislators. Half of the state delegations in the House meet regularly to discuss issues of mutual concern.[50] There are many other groups, or caucuses, that work together on issues that particularly concern them or their constituents. In the House, for example, there are bipartisan caucuses for steel, coal, and Irish affairs. One of the better-known groups is the Congressional Black Caucus, which is made up of the twenty or so blacks who serve in the House. Finally, there are partisan groups of legislators, like the Democratic Study Group and the Republican's Conservative Opportunity Society, both in the House.

Staff

The number of congressional staff members has risen dramatically in the last several decades, although it has now leveled off. In the mid-1950s, House members had about 2,500 personal staffers; by 1981, the figure had grown to about 7,500. Over the same period, Senate personal

Collins and Staffer
The staff in each legislator's office is responsible for a variety of tasks, including handling casework and press relations, doing research, monitoring legislation, writing speeches, and meeting with constituents and interest group representatives. Here, Democratic Representative Cardiss Collins of Illinois goes over some paperwork with one of her assistants.

staffs grew from around 1,000 to about 4,000 people. The number of staff members assigned to congressional committees grew significantly during this time as well.[51]

These larger staffs have helped members of Congress handle an increasing workload. Staffers reliably represent their bosses' interests during the day in, day out negotiations over legislation.[52] Staffers are particularly helpful in involving their bosses in new issues that will increase their influence both with constituents and within Congress. More broadly, one scholar notes: "The increased use of personalized, entrepreneurial staffs has helped Congress retain its position as a key initiator of federal policy, despite the growing power of the executive branch."[53]

The President

Unlike members of Congress, who are elected by voters in individual states and districts, the president is elected by voters across the entire nation. The president has a better claim, then, to representing the nation than does any single member of Congress. But it can also be argued that Congress *as a whole* has a better claim than the president to representing the majority of voters. In fact, when Congress and the president differ, opinion surveys sometimes show that Congress's position on a given bill more closely resembles the majority view; at other times, these surveys show that the president's position accords with the majority. Nevertheless, presidents capitalize on their popular election and usually act as though they are speaking for the majority.

During the twentieth century, the public's expectations of what a president can accomplish in office have grown enormously. We now expect the president to be our chief legislator: to introduce legislation on major issues and to use his influence to push bills through Congress. This is much different from our early history, when presidents felt constrained by the constitutional doctrine of separation of powers and had to have members work confidentially for them during legislative sessions.[54]

Today the White House is openly involved, not only in the writing of bills, but also in their development as they wind their way through the legislative process. If a bill is not to the White House's liking, it tries to work out a compromise with key legislators to have the legislation amended. On issues of the greatest importance, the president himself may meet with individual legislators to persuade them to vote a certain way. To monitor day-to-day congressional activities and lobby for the broad range of administration policies, there are hundreds of legislative liaison personnel working for the executive branch.

Although members of Congress grant presidents a leadership role in proposing legislation, they jealously guard their power to debate, shape, pass, or defeat any legislation the president proposes. Congress often clashes sharply with the president when his proposals are seen as ill advised.

Constituents

Constituents are the people who live and vote in the legislator's district or state. Their opinions on an issue are a crucial factor in the legislative decision-making process. As much as members of Congress want to please the party leadership or the president by going along with their preferences, legislators have to think about what the voters back home want. If they displease enough people with the way they vote, they might lose their seats in the next election.

In considering the influence of all these factors in the legislator's environment, it is important to keep in mind that legislators also have strong views of their own. They come to Congress deeply committed to working on some key issues and do not need to be pressured into acting on them or into voting a certain way. In fact, their strong views on certain policy questions can conflict with what their constituents want, a problem we discuss in detail later in this chapter.

Of all the possible sources of influence, which are the most important? Unfortunately, there is no one way of measuring. However, in an interesting and straightforward study, political scientist John Kingdon asked a sample of House members how they made up their minds on a variety of issues. He found that colleagues and constituency were more likely to have an impact than the other factors we've talked about.

Fishing for Votes
Republican Senator William Cohen of Maine talks to a voter, a lobsterman whose industry is an important part of the state's economy. Despite the emphasis on the use of the electronic media by legislators, one-on-one contact with constituents is still an effective, though painstaking, way for a legislator to build a reputation as one who cares deeply about the problems of the individuals he or she serves.

Kingdon cautioned, however, that the decision-making process in Congress is complex and that no single factor "is important enough that one could conclude that congressmen vote as they do" because of its influence.[55]

OVERSIGHT: FOLLOWING THROUGH ON LEGISLATION

It is often said in Washington that "knowledge is power." For Congress to retain its influence over the programs it creates, it must be aware of how they are being administered by the agencies responsible for them. To that end, legislators and their committees engage in **oversight,** the process of reviewing agency operations to determine whether an agency is carrying out policies as Congress intended.

As the executive branch has grown and policies and programs have become increasingly complex, oversight has become more difficult. The sheer magnitude of executive branch operations is staggering. On a typical weekday, for example, agencies issue over a hundred pages of new regulations. Even with the division of labor in the committee system, it is no easy task to determine how good a job an agency is doing in implementing a program.

Congress performs its oversight function in a number of different ways. The most visible is the hearing. Hearings may be part of a routine review or the by-product of information that reveals a major problem with a program or with an agency's administrative practices. After a U.S. Department of Energy investigation of drug dealing at a nuclear weapons facility in California was terminated, a subcommittee of the House Energy and Commerce Committee held a hearing to see if the department had actually finished the job. Accusations were made by plant security officials that they were pursuing leads on 127 suspects when the investigation (code name "Operation Snowstorm") ended. Some committee members felt that the Energy Department was trying to cover up the drug problem at the plant, to avoid embarrassment. After hearing the evidence, Representative Ron Wyden, a Democrat from Oregon, said that Operation Snowstorm "should be called 'Operation Snow Job.'"[56]

Another way Congress keeps track of what departments and agencies are doing is to request reports on specific agency practices and operations. Two reporters for the *Washington Post* wrote about the volume of material that Congress had requested from just the U.S. Department of Defense:

> Along with the Pentagon's wish list in the 1985 defense budget, Congress asked for a little paper work on the side.
>
> First, the Defense Department had to supply more than 20,000 pages of detailed justifications for the money requested.
>
> Piled atop that were 440 reports and 257 studies demanded by Congress.
>
> . . .
>
> Furthermore, before a dispirited Pentagon stopped counting in 1983, Defense Department witnesses in one year logged 1,453 hours of testimony before 91 congressional committees and subcommittees. During the same year, the military responded to 84,148 written queries from Capitol Hill and 592,150 telephone requests, numbers officials believe are on the rise.[57]

Despite the onslaught of information, much escapes congressional attention. To deal with the breadth of executive branch activity, Congress has greatly expanded its staffing. In addition to increasing personal and committee staff sizes, Congress created two new specialized offices in the 1970s—the Congressional Budget Office and the Office of Technology Assessment—to do sophisticated analyses of agency operations and proposals. The longer-standing Government Accounting Office (GAO) and the Congressional Research Service of the Library of Congress also do in-depth studies for Congress.

Still, Congress is routinely criticized for not doing more in the way of oversight. Many argue that members of Congress have little reason to spend much time on oversight. It is seen as rather tedious, unglamorous work that wins few points from the voters back home. With so many pressing tasks competing for their time, members of Congress may push oversight aside for other, more compelling activities, such as talking to constituents in the home district.[58]

Clearly, legislators are pulled in many different directions. But, they do not ignore their oversight responsibilities and may in fact do much more than is popularly perceived. Research has shown that the amount of time committees devote to oversight hearings has risen significantly.[59] One reason why members spend time on oversight, even though it might not always get their name in the newspapers back home, is that they care about making good public policy. A study of the food stamp program found that, through most of the program's history, oversight has been conducted by a small band of legislators who "sought out the issue and worked on it with great energy, imagination, and fervor. Although their individual views differed, these members of Congress were moved to act because they believed current food stamp policy to be incompatible with their own prescription for a fair and just society."[60]

THE DILEMMA OF REPRESENTATION

When candidates for the House and Senate campaign for office, they routinely promise to work hard for their district's or state's interests. When they get to Washington, though, they all face the troubling dilemma with which we began this chapter: What their constituents want may not be what the people across the nation want.

Presidents and Shopping Bags

In doing the research for his book *Home Style*, political scientist Richard Fenno accompanied several representatives on trips back to their home districts. On one trip, he was in an airport with a congressional aide, waiting for the representative's plane from Washington to land. When the congressman arrived, he said, "I spent fifteen minutes on the telephone with the president this afternoon. He had a plaintive tone in his voice and he pleaded with me." The congressman's side of the issue had prevailed over the president's, and he was elated by the victory. When the three men reached the aide's car, the congressman saw the back seat piled high with campaign paraphernalia: shopping bags printed with the representative's name and picture. "Back to this again," he sighed.[61]

Every member of Congress lives in two worlds: the world of presidents and the world of personalized shopping bags. A typical week in the life of a representative means working in Washington, then boarding a plane and flying back to the district. There the representative spends time meeting with individual constituents and talking to civic groups, church gatherings, business associations, labor unions, and the like (see Feature 10.1). A survey of House members during a nonelection year showed that each made an average of thirty-five trips back to the district, spending an average of 138 days there.[62]

Members of Congress are often criticized for being out of touch with the people they are supposed to represent. This charge does not seem justified. Legislators work extraordinarily hard at keeping in touch with voters, at finding out what is on their constituents' minds. The difficult problem is how to act on that knowledge.

Trustees or Delegates?

Are members of Congress bound to vote the way their constituents want them to vote, even if it means voting against their conscience?

FEATURE 10.1

On the Road Again

John Hiler was first elected to the House in the landslide that swept Reagan into office in 1980. The Indiana Republican, a firm believer in Reagan's principles of small government, went to Washington with the intention of promoting sweeping changes in the scope of government. By his second year in office, he was "Housebroken." He realized that the people back home in South Bend cared less about broad principles of contemporary conservatism than they did about what he could do to get a loan guarantee for an ethanol plant. He also quickly recognized that members of the House who don't "bring home the bacon" to the district could have trouble getting their contracts renewed.

Hiler works slavishly, commuting back and forth between Indiana and Washington. In a given year, he might spend about 175 days in the district, including most weekends. On a typical trip home, he drove 50 miles to give a 9:00 A.M. speech at a high school in Elkhart, a thirty-minute interview at a television station, then a speech at a Lion's Club luncheon. He then drove to Warsaw, Indiana, where he visited a nursing home for the retarded, saw the mayor about a Commerce Department grant, and met with the president of the town's chamber of commerce. From there, he drove to South Bend and stopped in at his district office. The next stop was La Porte, for an interview with a local reporter and a speech at a Jaycees' dinner. He wasn't done until 10:00 P.M. that night. The next morning, Hiler was up again very early to make a 7:30 A.M. fund-raising breakfast 50 miles away.

Hiler's work style is not an exception; it's the rule. Being highly visible in the district and working hard on its behalf in Washington are seen as the keys to re-election. All of this takes a toll on family life. Even when he's in Washington, Hiler leaves his house at 7:00 A.M. and doesn't usually get home until 8:00 P.M., which is bedtime for his two small

Representative John Hiler

daughters, Alison and Caitlin. His wife, Catherine, says, "I have total responsibility for the children. . . . At times, I do wonder if it's worth it. That happens when Jack's gone a few weekends in a row." Sadly, the congressman's choice seems to be spending the weekend talking to the Jaycees and visiting nursing homes so he can get re-elected, or spending time with his children.

Source: Adapted from Fred Barnes, "The Unbearable Lightness of Being a Congressman," *New Republic*, 15 February 1988, pp. 18–22. Reprinted by permission.

Some say no. They argue that legislators must be free to vote in line with what they think is best. This view has long been associated with eighteenth-century English political philosopher Edmund Burke (1729–1797). Burke, who served in Parliament, told his constituents in Bristol that "you choose a member, indeed; but when you have chosen him, he is not a member of Bristol, but he is a member of *Parliament*."[63] Burke reasoned that representatives are sent by their constituents to vote as

Reasoned Discourse Is the Hallmark of a Civilized Society
Members of Congress love good floor debates, but a photo opportunity may bring them more publicity back home than the carefully crafted arguments they present to their colleagues. These four members of the House are smashing a Toshiba radio to demonstrate their anger at that Japanese corporation. A Toshiba subsidiary, in conjunction with a Norwegian business consortium, had sold submarine equipment illegally to the Soviet Union.

they think best. As **trustees,** representatives are obligated to consider the views of constituents, but they are not obligated to vote according to those views if they think they are misguided.

Others hold that legislators are duty bound to represent the majority view of their constituents, that they are **delegates** with instructions from the people at home on how to vote on critical issues. And delegates, unlike trustees, must be prepared to vote against their own policy preferences. Liberal Democrats from Massachusetts criticize excessive defense spending. Yet because of its highly educated workforce and many engineering firms, Massachusetts receives a disproportionate amount of defense contracts for weapons systems. Should liberal Democrats vote for a weapons system that brings jobs to their districts? Or should they vote according to their consciences, against the weapons system they believe is unnecessary?

Members of Congress are subject to two opposing forces, then. While the interests of the district push them toward the role of delegates, the larger national interest calls on them to be trustees. As one legislator put it, "There is a heavy responsibility to represent the people of the district and the country at large . . . both [to] make your own decisions and to represent [others]."[64] As a result, few lawmakers act consistently as either delegates or trustees.

Even if Congress is not clearly a body of delegates or of trustees, it is more apt to take the delegate role on issues that are of great concern to constituents.[65] Certainly, when jobs are at stake in the district, lawmakers know that there is considerable concern back home over how they vote. But much of the time, what the constituency really wants is not clear. Many issues are not highly visible back home or they cut across the constituency to affect it in different ways or they are only partially understood. One study of House congressional voting on the central tax and spending issues during the first year of the Reagan administration found that most members had voted with what they perceived to be the majority opinion in their districts. Yet opinion polls in those districts showed that many representatives who voted for Reaganomics came from districts that did not really favor the program. The problem was that the legislators received a great deal of mail that was strongly in favor of Reaganomics. But clearly, the sentiment of activists—those who took the time to write a letter—were not representative of the broader population in the districts.[66]

PLURALISM, MAJORITARIANISM, AND DEMOCRACY

The dilemma that individual members of Congress face in adopting the role of either delegate or trustee has broad implications for the way our country is governed. If legislators tend to act as delegates, then congressional policymaking is more pluralistic. And policies reflect the bargaining that goes on among lawmakers who speak for different constituents. If, instead, legislators tend to act as trustees and vote their consciences, policymaking becomes less tied to the narrower interests of districts and states. But even here there is no guarantee that congressional decision making reflects majority interests.

We end this chapter with a short discussion of the pluralist nature of Congress. But first, to establish a frame of reference, we need to take a quick look at a more majoritarian type of legislature—the parliament.

Parliamentary Government

In our legislative system, the executive and legislative functions are divided between a president and a congress, each elected separately. Most other democracies—for example, Britain and Japan—have parliamentary governments. In a **parliamentary system,** the chief executive is the leader whose party holds the most seats in the legislature after an election or whose party forms a major part of the ruling coalition. For instance, Margaret Thatcher became prime minister of Great Britain because she was the leader of the Conservative party when it won a majority of seats in elections held in 1979, 1983, and 1987. She did not win her office directly in a national election. Although British voters knew that Thatcher would become prime minister if her party won the election, they actually cast their votes for candidates in over six hundred parliamentary elections across the country. The only citizens who voted for Thatcher were those in her own district, Finchley. But voters across the nation put her in office by choosing Conservative candidates under her party leadership.

In a parliamentary system, government power is highly concentrated in the legislature because the leader of the majority party is also the head of government. Moreover, parliamentary legislatures are usually composed of only one house or have a second chamber that is much weaker than the other. (In the British Parliament, the House of Commons makes the decisions of government; the other chamber, the House of Lords, is little more than an honorary debating club for distinguished members of society.) And parliamentary governments usually do not have a court that can invalidate acts of the parliament. Under such a system, the government is usually in the hands of the party that controls the parliament. With no separation of government powers, there are few checks on government action. The net effect is that parliamentary governments fit the majoritarian model of democracy to a much greater extent than do congressional governments.

Pluralism Versus Majoritarianism in the Congress

Nowadays, the U.S. Congress is often criticized for being too pluralist and not majoritarian enough. The federal budget deficit is a case in point. Americans are deeply concerned about the large deficits that have plagued our national budgets in recent years. And both Democrats and Republicans in Congress repeatedly call for reductions in those deficits. But when spending bills come before Congress, legislators' concern turns to what the bills will or will not do for their districts or states. A $604 million spending bill passed by Congress in 1988 included numerous examples of individual members winning some "pork barrel" project that benefitted their district or state and added further to the deficit. Senator James McClure, a Republican, won inclusion of a $6.4 million grant to build a ski resort in Kellogg, Idaho. Democratic Representative Daniel Akaka got a $250,000 appropriation for pig and plant control at the Haleakala National Park in Hawaii. And Republican Senator Ted Stevens delivered $2.6 million to the Fisheries Promotional Fund in Alaska.[67]

Projects such as these get into the budget through bargaining among members; as you saw earlier in the chapter, congressional norms encourage it. Members of Congress try to win projects and programs that will not only benefit their constituents, but will help them at election time. To win approval of something helpful to one's own constituents, a member must be willing to vote for other legislators' projects. This type of system obviously promotes pluralism.

Some feel that Congress has to be less pluralistic if it is going to attack such serious problems as the national deficit. Yet those who favor pluralism are quick to point out Congress's merits. For example, many different constituencies are well served by the spending deliberations described above. For Alaska's fishermen, an appropriation to promote new markets for their industry is not frivolous spending. It is vital to their livelihood. They pay taxes to fund the government, and they have a right to expect the government to care about their problems and try to help them.

Proponents of pluralism also argue that the makeup of Congress generally reflects that of the nation, that different members of Congress represent farm areas, oil and gas areas, low-income inner cities, industrial areas. They point out that America itself is pluralistic, with a rich diversity of economic, social, religious, and racial groups, and that even if our own representatives and senators don't represent our particular viewpoint, it's likely that someone else in Congress does.[68]

An alternative to our pluralistic legislature would operate on strictly majoritarian principles. For this kind of system to work, we would need strong parties—as described by the principles of responsible party government (see Chapter 8). That is, congressional candidates for each party would have to stand relatively united on the major issues. Then the majority party in Congress would act on a clear mandate from the voters—at least on the major issues discussed in the preceding election campaign. This would be very different from the pluralist system we now have, which furthers the influence of interest groups and local constituencies in national policymaking. But which is better?

SUMMARY

Congress plays a central role in our government through its lawmaking function. It writes the laws of the land and attempts to oversee their implementation. It helps to educate us about new issues as they appear on the political agenda. Most important, members of Congress represent us, working to see to it that interests from home and from around the country are heard throughout the policymaking process.

We count on Congress to do so much that criticism about how well it does some things is inevitable. But certain strengths are clear. The committee system fosters expertise; representatives and senators who know the most about particular issues have the most influence over them. And the structure of our electoral system keeps legislators in close touch with their constituents.

Bargaining and compromise play important roles in the congressional policymaking process. Some find this disquieting. They want less deal making and more adherence to principle. This thinking is in line with the desire for a more majoritarian democracy. Others defend the current system, arguing that this is a large complex nation and that the policies that govern it should be developed through bargaining among various interests.

There is no clear-cut answer on whether a majoritarian or a pluralist legislative system provides better representation for voters. Our system is pluralistic. It serves minority interests that might otherwise be neglected or even harmed by an unthinking or uncaring majority. But there is validity to the argument that responsiveness to special interests comes at the expense of the majority of Americans.

Key Terms

bicameral	seniority
reapportionment	markup session
impeachment	Speaker of the House
incumbent	president pro tempore
redistricting	majority leader
gerrymandering	filibuster
franking privilege	cloture
casework	logrolling
bill	conservative coalition
veto	constituents
pocket veto	oversight
standing committee	trustee
joint committee	delegate
select committee	parliamentary system
conference committee	

Selected Readings

Cain, Bruce, John Ferejohn, and Morris Fiorina. *The Personal Vote.* Cambridge, Mass.: Harvard University Press, 1987. A detailed comparison of the services offered their constituents by American and British legislators.

Dodd, Lawrence C., and Bruce I. Oppenheimer. *Congress Reconsidered.* 3d ed. Washington, D.C.: Congressional Quarterly Press, 1985. This collection of essays pulls together much of the latest research on Congress.

Fenno, Richard F., Jr. *Congressmen in Committees.* Boston: Little, Brown, 1973. A classic study of how legislators' goals affect committee operations.

Fenno, Richard F., Jr. *Home Style.* Boston: Little, Brown, 1978. An analysis of how House members interact with constituents during visits to their home districts.

Mayhew, David R. *Congress: The Electoral Connection.* New Haven, Conn.: Yale University Press, 1974. A provocative argument that members of Congress are single-minded seekers of re-election.

West, Darrell M. *Congress and Economic Policymaking.* Pittsburgh: University of Pittsburgh Press, 1987. Examines the relationship between constituency opinion and congressional voting at the beginning of the Reagan administration.

11

The Presidency

L ike Jimmy Carter before him, Ronald Reagan felt deeply responsible for getting American hostages out of the Middle East. Carter had faced the Ayatollah Khomeini's refusal to release American embassy personnel held captive in Iran; now Reagan sought the release of Americans kidnapped by various terrorist factions in war-torn Beirut. Unlike Carter, Reagan was not widely criticized for his inability to deal with terrorists. Still, the president was determined to do something to free the hostages, believing their lives were in danger (one hostage, the Beirut CIA chief, William Buckley, had already been murdered by the group that seized him). Because the Iranian government was thought to have influence with a number of radical groups in Beirut, Reagan approved a secret sale of arms to Iran in the belief that Iran would make efforts to free the American hostages.

When the arms sales were revealed by a Lebanese magazine in November 1986, a fire storm of criticism began. Many Americans saw the Ayatollah Khomeini as a personification of evil; they couldn't conceive of the American government doing something to benefit him. Besides, selling arms to win the release of the hostages seemed to reward the terrorists, not punish them. Reagan heatedly denied that he was trading arms for hostages, claiming that the arms were part of a foreign policy initiative designed to win favor with Iranian "moderates" who might rule after Khomeini was gone.

The president's problems intensified. It was soon revealed that the arms were sold to Iran at an inflated price, and the excess money received was put into a secret Swiss bank account for use by the Contras, a pro-American rebel force fighting the Marxist government of Nicaragua. Although Reagan claimed that he wasn't "fully informed" of this plan to aid the Contras, his popularity dropped. One poll showed that the president's public approval rating plunged 21 percent after the Contra connection came to light.[1] And 47 percent of the public thought the president was lying when he said he didn't know about the diversion of money to the Contras.[2] A commission appointed to investigate the scandal condemned the president's management style.[3] Reagan subsequently made a grudging acknowledgment that the dealings with Iran did in fact turn into an arms-for-hostages deal, but the public was not mollified by this late change of heart. Even after John Poindexter, the former national security adviser, told a congressional committee that he had not informed Reagan of the diversion of funds, a majority of the public still thought Reagan was lying about his involvement.[4]

Clearly, Reagan's heartfelt wish to win the release of the hostages began a series of catastrophic errors in judgment. The Iran-Contra episode put a permanent blot on a presidency studded with many successes.

Reflecting on the Iran-Contra affair may help us understand some of the conflicts surrounding the office of the president. To what degree should the president be constrained within our system of checks and balances? How should the president organize and manage the White House to maximize his effectiveness in office? What kinds of leadership styles are best suited for the presidency?

As we analyze the various facets of the presidency, bear in mind one recurring question: Is the presidency primarily an instrument of pluralist democracy, serving small but vocal constituencies, or does the office promote majoritarian democracy, by responding to public opinion?

THE CONSTITUTIONAL BASIS OF PRESIDENTIAL POWER

When the presidency was created, the colonies had just fought a war of independence; their reaction to British domination had focused on the autocratic rule of King George III. The delegates to the Constitutional Convention were extremely wary of unchecked power; they were determined not to create a presidential office whose occupant could become an all-powerful, dictatorial figure.

The delegates' fear of a powerful presidency was counterbalanced by their desire for strong leadership. The Articles of Confederation—which did not provide for a single head of state—had failed to bind the states together into a unified nation. In addition, the governors of the individual states had generally proved to be inadequate leaders because they had few formal powers. The new nation was conspicuously weak; its congress had no power to compel the states to obey its legislation. With the failed confederation in mind, John Jay wrote to George Washington, asking him, "Shall we have a king?"[5]

Although the idea of establishing an American royalty was far from popular among the delegates, they knew that some type of executive office had to be created. Their task was to provide national leadership without allowing any opportunity for tyranny.

Initial Conceptions of the Presidency

Debates over the nature of the office began. Should there be one president or a presidential council or committee? Should the president be chosen by Congress and remain largely subservient to that body? Initial approval was given to a plan that called for a single executive, chosen by Congress for a seven-year term and ineligible for re-election.[6] But some of the delegates continued to argue for a strong president who would be elected independently of the legislative branch.

The final shape of the presidency reflected the "checks and balances" philosophy that shaped the entire Constitution. In the minds of the delegates, important limits were imposed on the presidency through the powers specifically delegated to the Congress and the courts. Those counterbalancing powers would act as checks, or controls, on presidents who might try to expand the office beyond its proper bounds. (The separation of the executive from the legislative branch has had an effect on the type of experience our presidential candidates have; see Compared With What? 11.1.)

The Powers of the President

The requirements for the presidency are set forth in Article II of the Constitution: A president must be a natural-born citizen, at least thirty-

COMPARED WITH WHAT? 11.1

What Kind of Experience Counts?

Candidates nominated for the presidency of the United States compose an impressive lot in terms of their accomplishments and political experience. Yet, their European counterparts are actually better seasoned in jobs providing valuable experience in government. Excellent campaign skills are critical to winning a presidential nomination in the United States. It is no small feat to conduct a lengthy campaign, putting together a winning coalition by convincing large numbers of voters that one would be a better nominee than the many other capable candidates competing in the primaries. Experience in office is hardly irrelevant in a candidate's ultimate appeal to the American electorate—they need to be convinced he can do the job. Still, candidates who have spent relatively modest amounts of time in governmental service and have limited ranges of experience, such as Jimmy Carter and Ronald Reagan, are able to win their party's nomination.

In European democracies, a considerably different pattern emerges. Party activists who aim for the post of prime minister in a parliamentary system must win the backing of their legislative party. As they rise in their party's hierarchy, aspiring leaders typically head major departments of state when their party is in control of the government. In Great Britain, for example, an aspiring prime minister typically has served an average of twelve years as a minister of a governmental department before he or she became a party leader in Parliament. In contrast, U.S. presidential candidates typically do not have Cabinet experience, although they may have had executive experience as a governor. As the figures below indicate, American candidates are considerably less experienced in government than European political leaders.

Source: Richard Rose, "Learning to Govern or Learning to Campaign?" in *Presidential Selection*, ed. Alexander Heard and Michael Nelson (Durham, N.C.: Duke University Press, 1987), pp. 53–73.

five years old, who has lived in the United States for a minimum of fourteen years. The responsibilities of presidents are also set forth in Article II. In view of the importance of the office, the constitutional description of the president's duties is surprisingly brief and vague. This vagueness has led to repeated conflict over the limits of presidential power.

There were undoubtedly many reasons for Article II's lack of precision. One likely reason was the difficulty of providing and at the same time limiting presidential power. Furthermore, the framers of the Constitution had no model—no existing presidency—on which to base their description of the office. And, ironically, their description of the presidency might have been more precise if they had had less confidence in George Washington, the obvious choice for the first president. According to one account of the Constitutional Convention, "when Dr. Franklin predicted on June 4 that 'the first man put at the helm will be a good one,' every delegate knew perfectly well who that first good man would be."[7] The delegates had great trust in Washington; they did not fear that he would try to misuse the office.

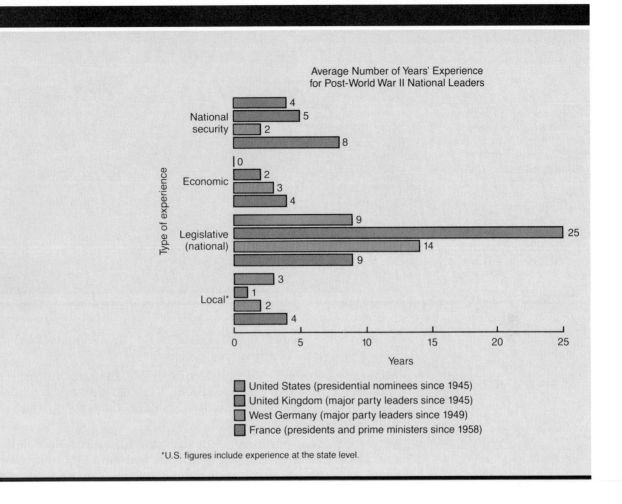

Average Number of Years' Experience
for Post-World War II National Leaders

■ United States (presidential nominees since 1945)
■ United Kingdom (major party leaders since 1945)
■ West Germany (major party leaders since 1949)
■ France (presidents and prime ministers since 1958)

*U.S. figures include experience at the state level.

The major duties and powers that the delegates listed for Washington and his successors can be summarized as follows:

■ *Serve as administrative head of the nation.* The Constitution gives little guidance on the president's administrative duties. It states merely that "the executive Power shall be vested in a President of the United States of America" and that "he shall take Care that the Laws be faithfully executed." These imprecise directives have been interpreted to mean that the president is to supervise and offer leadership to various departments, agencies, and programs created by Congress. In practice, a chief executive spends much more time making policy decisions for his Cabinet departments and agencies than trying to enforce existing policies.

■ *Act as commander in chief of the military.* In essence, the Constitution names the president as the highest ranking officer in the armed forces. But it gives Congress the power to *declare* war. The framers no doubt intended Congress to control the president's military power; nevertheless, presidents have initiated military action

The Commanders and the Commander in Chief
During World War II, President Franklin Roosevelt visited the troops at an American base in Sicily. There, the commander in chief met with General Dwight Eisenhower (to FDR's left), who would win the presidency himself in 1952. At the far left is the legendary General George Patton.

without the approval of Congress. The entire Vietnam War was fought without a congressional declaration of war.

■ *Convene Congress.* The president can call Congress into special session on "extraordinary Occasions," though this has been done only rarely. He must also periodically inform Congress of "the State of the Union."

■ *Veto legislation.* The president can **veto** (disapprove) any bill or resolution passed by Congress, with the exception of joint resolutions that propose constitutional amendments. Congress can override a presidential veto with a two-thirds vote in each house.

■ *Appoint various officials.* The president has the authority to appoint federal court judges, ambassadors, Cabinet members, other key policymakers, and many lesser officials. Many appointments are subject to Senate confirmation.

■ *Make treaties.* With the "advice and consent" of at least two-thirds of those senators voting at the time, the president can make treaties with foreign powers. The president is also to "receive ambassadors," a phrase that presidents have interpreted as the right to recognize other nations.

■ *Grant pardons.* The president can grant pardons to individuals who have committed "Offences against the United States, except in Cases of Impeachment."

THE EXPANSION OF PRESIDENTIAL POWER

The framers' limited conception of the president's role has given way to a considerably more powerful interpretation. In this section, we look beyond the presidential responsibilities explicitly listed in the Constitution and examine the additional sources of power that presidents have used to expand the authority of the office. First, we look at the claims that presidents make about "inherent" powers implicit in the Constitution. Second, we turn to congressional grants of power to the executive branch. Third, we discuss the influence that comes from a president's political skills. Fourth, we analyze how a president's popular support affects his political power. And finally, we look at the tremendous expectations that the public has come to have for the office.

The Inherent Powers

Several presidents have expanded their power by taking actions that exceeded commonly held notions of the president's proper authority. These men justified what they had done by saying that their actions fell within the **inherent powers** of the office. From this broad perspective, presidential power derives not only from those duties clearly outlined in Article II, but also from inferences that may be drawn from the Constitution.

When a president claims a power that has not been considered part of the chief executive's authority, he forces the Congress and the courts to acquiesce to his claim or to restrict it. When presidents succeed in claiming a new power, they leave to their successors the legacy of a permanent expansion of presidential authority. One early use of the inherent power of the presidency occurred during George Washington's tenure in office. The British and the French were at war, and Washington was under some pressure from members of his own administration to show favoritism toward the French. Instead, he issued a proclamation of strict neutrality, angering many who harbored anti-British sentiments; the ensuing controversy provoked a constitutional debate. Washington's critics noted that the Constitution does not include a presidential power to declare neutrality. His defenders said that the president had inherent powers to conduct diplomatic relations. In the end, Washington's decision was not overturned by Congress or the courts and thus set a precedent in the area of foreign affairs.[8]

Claims of inherent powers often come at critical points in the nation's history. During the Civil War, for example, Abraham Lincoln issued a number of orders that exceeded the accepted limits of presidential authority. One of those orders increased the size of the armed forces far beyond the congressionally mandated ceiling, even though the Constitution gives only Congress the power "to raise and support armies." And because military expenditures would then have exceeded military appropriations, Lincoln clearly had also acted to usurp the taxing and spending powers constitutionally conferred on Congress. In another order, Lincoln instituted a blockade of Southern ports, thereby committing acts of war against the Confederacy without the approval of Congress.

Lincoln said the urgent nature of the South's challenge to the Union forced him to act without waiting for congressional approval. His rationale was simple: "Was it possible to lose the nation and yet preserve the Constitution?"[9] In other words, Lincoln circumvented the Constitution

Preserving the Union
During the Civil War, Abraham Lincoln took many controversial actions that expanded the authority of the presidency. Lincoln (pictured with his generals at Antietam, Maryland) strongly influenced the nature of the office through his emergency measures.

in order to save the nation. Subsequently, Congress and the Supreme Court approved Lincoln's actions. That approval gave added legitimacy to the theory of inherent powers—a theory that over time has transformed the presidency.

Any president who lays claim to new authority runs the risk of being rebuffed by Congress or the courts and suffering political damage. After Andrew Jackson vetoed a bill reauthorizing a national bank, he ordered William Duane, his secretary of the treasury, to withdraw all federal deposits and to place them in state banks. Duane refused, claiming that he was under the supervision of both Congress and the executive branch; Jackson responded by firing him. The president's action angered many members of Congress who believed that Jackson had overstepped his constitutional bounds; the Constitution does not actually state that a president may remove his Cabinet secretaries. Although that prerogative is now taken for granted, Jackson's presidency was weakened by the controversy. His censure by the Senate was a slap in the face, and he was denounced even by members of his own party. It took many years for the president's right to remove Cabinet officers to become widely accepted.[10]

Congressional Delegation of Power

Presidential power grows when presidents successfully challenge Congress, but in many instances Congress willingly delegates power to the executive branch. As the American public pressures the national government to solve various problems, Congress, through a process called **delegation of powers,** gives the executive branch more responsibility to administer programs that address those problems. One example of delegation of legislative power occurred in the 1930s, during the Great Depression, when Congress gave Franklin Roosevelt's administration wide latitude to do what it thought was necessary to solve the nation's economic ills.

When Congress concludes that the government needs flexibility in its approach to a problem, the president is often given great freedom in how or when to implement policies. Richard Nixon, for example, was given discretionary authority to impose a freeze on wages and prices in an effort to combat escalating inflation. If Congress had been forced to debate the timing of this freeze, merchants and manufacturers would surely have raised their prices in anticipation of the event. Instead, Nixon was able to act suddenly, and the freeze was imposed without warning. (Congressional delegation of authority to the executive branch is discussed in more detail in Chapter 12.)

At other times, however, Congress believes that too much power is accumulating in the executive branch, and it passes legislation reasserting congressional authority. During the 1970s, many representatives and senators agreed that Congress's role in the American political system was declining, that presidents were exercising power that rightfully belonged to the legislative branch. The most notable reaction was the passage of the War Powers Resolution (1973), which was directed toward ending the president's ability to pursue armed conflict without explicit congressional approval. Congress has also moved to prevent presidents from impounding (refusing to spend) money appropriated by Congress.[11]

The President's Power to Persuade

A president's influence in office comes not only from his assigned responsibilities, but also from his political skills, how effectively he uses the resources of his office. A classic analysis of the use of presidential resources is offered by Richard Neustadt in his book *Presidential Power*. Neustadt develops a model of how presidents gain, lose, or maintain their influence. Neustadt's initial premise is simple enough: "Presidential *power* is the power to persuade."[12] Presidents, for all their resources—a skilled staff, extensive media coverage of presidential actions, the great respect for the office—must depend on others' cooperation to get things done. Harry Truman echoed Neustadt's premise when he said, "I sit here all day trying to persuade people to do the things they ought to have sense enough to do without my persuading them. . . . That's all the powers of the President amount to."[13]

The abilities displayed in bargaining, dealing with adversaries, and choosing priorities, according to Neustadt, separate above-average presidents from mediocre ones. A president must make wise choices about which policies to push and which to put aside until more support can be found. He must decide when to accept compromises and when to stand on principles. He must know when to go public and when to work behind the scenes.

Often, a president faces a dilemma in which all alternatives carry some risk. After Dwight Eisenhower took office in 1953, he had to decide how to deal with Joseph McCarthy, the Republican senator from Wisconsin. McCarthy had been largely reponsible for creating national hysteria over alleged communists in government. He made many wild, reckless charges, damaging a number of innocent people's careers by accusing them of communist sympathies. Many people expected Eisenhower to control McCarthy—not only because he was president, but also because he was a fellow Republican. Yet Eisenhower, worrying about his own popularity, chose not to confront McCarthy. He used a "hidden-hand" strategy, working behind the scenes to weaken McCarthy. Politically, Eisenhower seems to have made the right choice; McCarthy soon discredited himself.[14] Eisenhower's performance can be criticized, however, as weak moral leadership. If he had publicly denounced the senator, he might have ended the McCarthy witch-hunt sooner.

A president's political skills are especially important in affecting outcomes in Congress. The chief executive cannot intervene in every legislative struggle. He must choose his battles carefully, then try to use the force of his personality and the prestige of his office to forge an agreement among differing factions. Lyndon Johnson was one of the best of modern presidents at bargaining with others to get his legislation passed. Johnson once got religious leaders Billy Graham and Francis Cardinal Spellman to go for a swim in the White House pool and took the opportunity to talk them into resolving a church-state dispute that was holding up an education bill in Congress.[15]

Neustadt stresses that a president's influence is related to his professional reputation and prestige. When a president pushes hard for a bill that Congress eventually defeats or emasculates, the president's reputation is hurt. The public perceives him as weak or showing poor judgment, and Congress becomes even less likely to cooperate with him in the future. Jimmy Carter damaged his prestige by backing bills that proposed welfare reform, hospital cost containment, and an agency for consumer protection—none of which passed. Yet the other side of this coin is that presidents cannot easily avoid controversial bills, especially if campaign promises were made. If a president backs only sure things, he will be credited with little initiative and perceived as too cautious.

The President and the Public

Neustadt's analysis suggests that a popular president is more persuasive than an unpopular one. A popular president has more power to persuade because he can use his public support as a resource in the bargaining process. Members of Congress who know that the president is highly popular back home have more incentive to cooperate with the administration. If the president and his aides know that a member of Congress does not want to be seen as hostile to the president, they can apply more leverage to achieve a favorable compromise in a legislative struggle.

A familiar aspect of the modern presidency is the effort of its incumbents to mobilize public support for their programs. A president uses televised addresses and the press coverage that surrounds his speeches, remarks to reporters, and public appearances to speak directly to the American people and convince them of the wisdom of his policies. It may seem only sensible for a president to seek popular endorsement of particular bills or broad initiatives, but public appeals have not always been a part of the presidency. Our first fifteen presidents averaged fewer than ten speeches a year. It was not simply that the lack of modern communications made attempts to mobilize the public more difficult;

Bound for Glory
Ronald Reagan was very effective at using the symbols and pageantry of the presidency to his advantage. In this whistle-stop campaign swing through Ohio in 1984, he gave speeches from the same Pullman car that Harry Truman used in his famous come-from-behind victory over Republican Thomas Dewey in 1948.

early presidents felt constrained in the way they interacted with the public. The founders' fear that the executive office might be used to inflame popular passions led early presidents to be reserved in their communications.[16] Notice how President-elect Lincoln avoided the opportunity to galvanize support for his views on the secession unrest in the South.

> And here, fellow citizens, I may remark that in every crowd through which I have passed of late some allusion has been made to the present distracted condition of this country. It is naturally expected that I should say something upon this subject, but to touch upon it at all would involve an elaborate discussion of a great many questions and circumstances, would require more time than I can at present command, and would perhaps unnecessarily commit me upon matters which have not yet fully developed themselves.[17]

Since then, presidents have increased their direct communication with the American people. As Figure 11.1 illustrates, the number of presidential public appearances has grown sharply since World War II. Obviously, modern technology has contributed to this growth. The increase in public appearances represents something more than increased visibility for the president and his views. There has also been a fundamental change in the power of the presidency. The decline of party and congressional leadership has hastened the rise of the public president; at the same time, the president's direct communication with the American people has made it more difficult for political parties and Congress to reinvigorate themselves.[18]

Presidential popularity is typically at its highest during a president's first year in office. This "honeymoon" period affords the president a

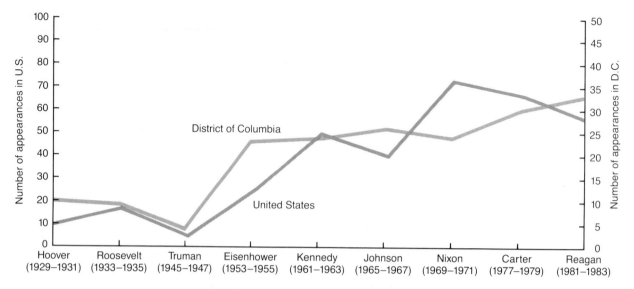

Going Public
These figures depict the average number of public appearances made in a year by presidents from 1929 to 1983. Only the first three years of their first terms were examined; the fourth year was not tabulated to exclude appearances arranged with an eye toward an upcoming election. Because a large portion of Gerald Ford's term was taken up by a year before an election, his time in office was excluded from analysis. (Source: Samuel Kernell, Going Public *[Washington, D.C.: Congressional Quarterly Press, 1986], p. 94.)*

Figure 11.1

particularly good opportunity to use public support to get some of his programs through Congress. During Ronald Reagan's first year in office, when he made a televised appeal for support for a legislative proposal, some congressional offices received calls and letters that ran 10 to 1 in favor of the president. At the beginning of his second term, typical congressional offices received an equal number of negative and positive responses after a Reagan appeal.[19] Perhaps the positions he advocated were less attractive, but it was also clear that Reagan had lost some of his ability to mobilize public opinion.

Politicians and journalists have a good "feel" for how well a president is doing, but objective evidence comes from a steady stream of national opinion surveys. The best known of these surveys is the Gallup Poll, which since 1938 has been asking samples of Americans whether they approve of the way the president is doing his job. This half-century of polling has shown two strong patterns. First, the basic trend for most presidents is to move from high popularity to low popularity. Second, every president experiences ups and downs; over time, public approval changes in response to events and presidential actions. Figure 11.2 shows that Reagan's popularity dropped sharply in response to the severe recession that overtook the country during his first term and dipped again when the Iran-Contra scandal was revealed. Still, Reagan's ratings showed more resiliency than the ratings of most presidents. Carter and Johnson were not able to revive their popularity to the extent that Reagan did.

The general decline in presidential popularity throughout a term in office has been explained by the concept of a **coalition of minorities,** the idea that different groups of voters become dissatisfied with a president's handling of particular issues of concern.[20] While campaigning for office, a presidential candidate encourages all sectors of society to believe he will help them. After he is in office, the president cannot possibly deliver on all his promises, and the groups that fail to get what they want become disaffected. The coalition of minorities begins to criticize the president. Moreover, the president's vulnerability is exploited by other leaders for their own political gains. The result is a continuing assault on presidential popularity, and the president's level of approval drops from its initial heights.

The sharp peaks and valleys in presidential popularity (within the usual overall pattern of decline) can be explained by several factors. First, public approval of the job done by a president is affected by *economic conditions,* such as inflation and unemployment.[21] A strong economy buoyed Eisenhower's popularity during his first term, but a recession during the middle of his second term brought his rating down. Second, a president is affected by *unanticipated events* of all types that occur during his administration. When American embassy personnel were taken hostage in Teheran by militantly anti-American Iranians, Carter's popularity soared. This "rally 'round the flag" support for the president eventually gave way to frustration with his inability to gain the hostages' release, and Carter's popularity plummeted. The third factor that affects

Score Two for the Ayatollah

On November 4, 1979, more than fifty Americans were taken hostage in Teheran, Iran. Jimmy Carter's inability to win their freedom hurt his chances for re-election. An agreement for their release was finally reached at the end of Carter's term. In 1986, the nation was shocked to learn that the Reagan administration had traded arms to Iran. Oliver North, a key player in the arms deal, testified before a congressional committee investigating the episode; during his testimony, he came across as a brave and patriotic White House aide. Even so, anger toward Iran and the Ayatollah Khomeini was still strong, and Americans remained largely unconvinced that selling arms to Iran was the right thing to do.

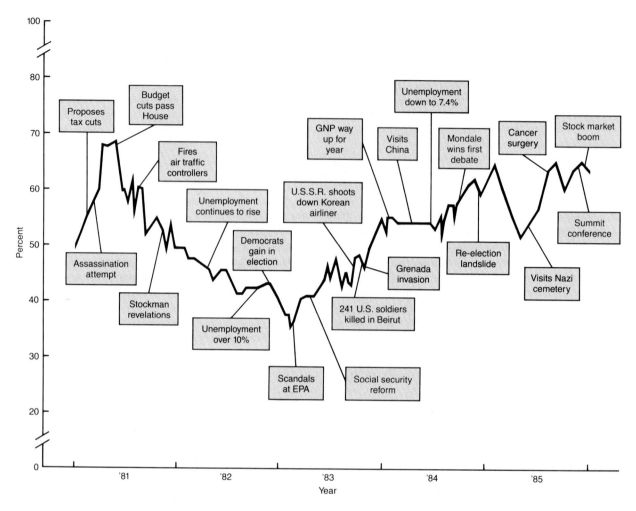

Presidential Popularity: The Reagan Years
Since the late 1930s, the Gallup Poll has asked a sample of Americans, "Do you approve or disapprove of the way [the present officeholder] is handling his job as president?" Ronald Reagan enjoyed considerable popularity during his

Figure 11.2

presidential popularity is American involvement in a *war*, which can erode public approval. Johnson suffered a loss of popularity during his escalation of the American effort in Vietnam.[22]

Great Expectations

Contemporary Americans become dissatisfied with their presidents for still one more reason: We expect so much from them. The president has come to be viewed as much more than a chief executive of our government; the president is expected to be a moral leader as well as a political one. The presidential family is regarded with reverence and subjected to intense media scrutiny. The president is part king, part savior, and part wise man. In times of crisis, he is seen as the best hope

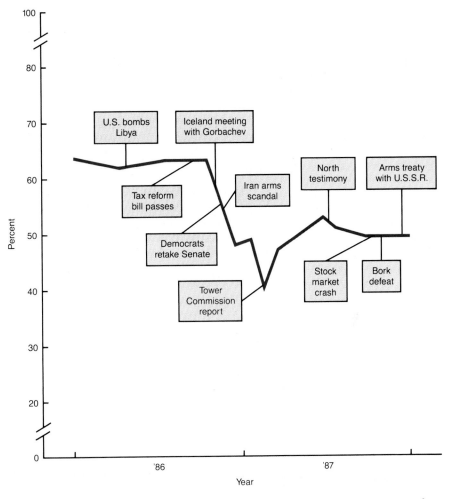

two terms in office, although his popularity plunged when some serious problems emerged. (For a discussion of how a small sample of Americans can represent the attitude of the nation, see Politics in the Information Age 5.1.) (Source: Gallup Poll, Public Opinion, March-April 1988, pp. 36–37. Captions added.)

for delivering us from our enemies or even from ourselves. One observer notes that "the election of a president is an almost religious task; it intimately affects the life of the spirit, our identity. Who the man is determines in real measure who we are."[23]

Why do Americans put so much faith in the presidency? One reason is the common tendency to believe that great people shape great events. This "great man" view of history is, in a sense, a shortcut in understanding the dynamics of policymaking. To the average citizen, the governmental process is complex and confusing. An individual who is dissatisfied with the performance of the economy might have to spend considerable time learning about the forces that shape it—the Federal Reserve Board's money supply policy, the balance of payments with foreign countries, the government's taxing and spending policies—to understand why the economy is acting the way it is. It is easier to believe instead that economic performance is determined by presidential judgment, that the president always makes the critical difference in the direction of public policy.

Unfortunately, the more we expect from presidents, the greater the likelihood that we will be disappointed. The growth of presidential responsibilities has also made it more likely that presidents will be measured as failures. The job has clearly become more daunting since Theodore Roosevelt's years in office; he would spend his summer months at the beach with his family, calling the White House once a day to see if he had to make any decisions.[24] Today, the White House is portable; staff and communications gear go wherever the president travels. But for all the resources that modern presidents have at their disposal, the problems they face seem to grow more complex and difficult to solve. Indeed, one presidential scholar argues that "the presidency has become an impossible job."[25]

PRESIDENTIAL ELECTIONS: THE ELECTORAL CONNECTION

In the 1988 presidential election, Democrat Michael Dukakis won 46 percent of the popular vote and 112 electoral votes. Republican George Bush won 54 percent of the popular vote and 426 electoral votes. Why do we measure a president's vote in two ways? What importance does the electoral vote have?

The Electoral College

The delegates to the Constitutional Convention decided not to let individual voters choose the president directly. Instead, the delegates devised a system in which electors are chosen in their states, and those electors in turn vote for the president. The assumption was that the electors would be educated leaders and would show better judgment in their choices for president than would rank-and-file citizens. The founders did not anticipate that political parties would develop and that voters would soon cast their ballots for electors who openly supported a party candidate. One legacy that remains of the system of having electors cast ballots on behalf of voters is that electors have complete freedom; they are bound neither to a candidate nor to a party. Occasionally an elector fails to follow the voters' preference. In 1972, one elector from Virginia voted for John Hospers of the Libertarian party rather than for Republican Richard Nixon.[26]

In the **electoral college,** each state is accorded one vote for each of its senators and representatives. California, the state with the largest population, has forty-seven electoral votes in the electoral college—a total of its forty-five representatives and two senators. Six small states qualify for only one representative and therefore have only three electoral votes each. (The Twenty-third Amendment to the Constitution awards three electoral votes to the District of Columbia, even though it elects no voting members of Congress.) After each census, the number of electoral votes for each state is recalculated to reflect population changes that may reduce or increase the number of representatives the state sends to Washington.

In recent years, the greatest population growth has occurred in the so-called Sunbelt states (the South, the Southwest, and California); consequently, their proportionate share of electoral votes has grown as well. This increase has come at the expense of the Frostbelt states (the Northeast and Midwest).

If no candidate receives a majority when the electoral college votes, the election is thrown into the House of Representatives. The House votes by state, with each state casting one vote for a single presidential candidate. (This means that Delaware, for example, has the same voting strength as New York.) The top three finishers in the general election are the candidates in the House election. A presidential election has gone to the House only twice in American history, the first time in 1800 and the second in 1824. Both cases occurred before a stable two-party system had developed (see "Two Party Systems in U.S. History," in Essay C, page 345).

The most troubling aspect of the electoral college is the possibility that, despite winning a plurality or even a majority of popular votes, a candidate could lose the election in the electoral college. This could happen if one candidate wins many states by a very large amount, while the other candidate wins many states by a slim margin. Indeed, this has happened in three elections, most recently in 1888, when Grover Cleveland received 48.6 percent of the popular vote to Benjamin Harrison's 47.9 percent. Cleveland nevertheless trailed Harrison in the electoral college, 168 to 233, and Harrison was elected president. Whether a candidate wins a state by 5 or 500,000 votes, he wins *all* that state's electoral votes.[*]

This peculiar feature of our system has led to calls for the abolition of the electoral college. Reformers argue that it is simply wrong to have a system that allows a candidate who receives the most popular votes to lose the election. Would the next president be regarded as the legitimate "winner" by the American people if he or she received a minority of popular votes? Reform plans that call for the direct election of the president would institute a purely majoritarian means of choosing the president. Defenders of the electoral college point out that this system, warts and all, has been a stable one. It might be riskier to replace it with a new arrangement that could alter our party system or the way presidential campaigns are conducted. Tradition has in fact prevailed, and recent proposals for fundamental reform have not come close to adoption.

Winning the Presidency

In his farewell address to the nation, Jimmy Carter lashed out at the interest groups that bedeviled his presidency. Interest groups, he said, "distort our purposes because the national interest is not always the sum

---

[*] The one exception is in Maine, where two of the state's electoral votes are awarded by congressional district. The presidential candidate who carries each district wins a single electoral vote.

Mission Accomplished
In his stirring acceptance speech at the Republican National Convention in New Orleans, George Bush, a bomber pilot during World War II, said, "I am a man who sees life in terms of missions—missions defined and missions completed." On November 8, 1988, he successfully completed his mission against Michael Dukakis, winning a convincing victory over the Massachusetts governor.

of all our single or special interests." Carter noted the president's singular responsibility: "The president is the only elected official charged with representing all the people."[27] Carter, like all other presidents, quickly recognized the dilemma of majoritarianism versus pluralism after he took office. The president must try to please countless separate constituencies while trying to do what is best for the whole country.

It is easy to stand on the sidelines and say that presidents should always try to follow a majoritarian path—pursuing policies that reflect the preferences of most citizens. Simply by running for office, candidates align themselves with particular segments of the population. As a result of their electoral strategy, their identification with activists in their party, and their own political views, candidates come into office with an interest in pleasing some constituencies more than others.

Each candidate attempts to put together an electoral coalition that will provide at least the minimum 270 (out of 538) votes needed for election. The two major-party candidates begin with a traditional base of party support, which they then try to expand. Republican candidates know that the western states have favored their party in recent presidential elections. A Democrat looks to the industrial states of the Northeast for the foundation of an electoral coalition. A candidate does not appeal to states, of course, but to the kinds of voters concentrated in them. A Democrat, for instance, sees organized labor, which is stronger in the Northeast than the West, as a major building block of a winning coalition.

As the campaign proceeds, the candidates try to win votes from different groups of voters through their stands on various issues. They promise that once they are in office, they will take certain actions that appeal to people holding a particular view on an issue. For example, among the many stands that Ronald Reagan took as a candidate during the 1980 campaign were positions against affirmative action, against court-ordered busing for school integration, for a constitutional amendment outlawing abortion, against "excessive" environmentalism that threatens economic growth, against gay rights ordinances, for a constitutional amendment permitting school prayer, against gun control, against a peacetime draft, for quick decontrol of oil and gas prices, for a 30 percent cut on individual income taxes, and for abolishing the Department of Education.[28] For Reagan and other candidates, these policy stands typically stem from long-held views about government; they are not simply expedient ways to attract voters.

Just as each candidate attracts voters with his stand on particular issues, he offends others who are committed to the opposite side of those issues. In 1988, Bush's emphasis on sustaining economic growth, which downplayed persistent inequities in our economy, helped him win the votes of many businesspeople. On the other hand, it gave those concerned about the less privileged more reason to vote for Dukakis. Because issue stands can cut both ways—attracting some voters and driving others away—candidates may try to finesse an issue by being deliberately vague. Candidates sometimes hope that voters will put their own interpretations on ambiguous stands. If the tactic works, the candidate will attract some voters without offending others. During the 1968 campaign, Nixon said he was committed to ending the war in Vietnam, but gave few details about how he would accomplish that end. He wanted to appeal not only to those who were in favor of military pressure against the North Vietnamese but also to those who wanted quick military disengagement.[29]

But candidates cannot be deliberately vague about all issues. A candidate who is noncommittal on too many issues appears wishy-washy, indecisive. And future presidents do not build their political careers without working strongly for and becoming associated with important issues and constituencies. As a result, presidents enter office with both a majority of voters on their side and a close identification with particular issue constituencies (see Feature 11.1).

. . . And Losing It

Winning the voters' support and keeping it are two different ball games. The electoral mandate that the voters give the winning candidate is a rather vague directive for presidential action, and this mandate tends to become more and more fragile over time. As noted earlier, presidential popularity can be eroded by a coalition of minorities.

Even a landslide at the polls does not ensure solid, consistent support throughout a president's term. Lyndon Johnson crushed his Republican opponent, Barry Goldwater, in the 1964 election, winning 61 percent of the popular vote and all but six states. Nevertheless, his popularity went into a steep decline because of public discontent with the war in Vietnam and Johnson's liberal social welfare programs. Even his remarkable influence with Congress began to dissipate. The Democrats lost forty-seven

FEATURE 11.1

The Making of the President, 1988

Democratic presidential nominee Michael Dukakis frequently spoke of the race for the White House as a marathon, an apt description for the seemingly endless campaign. When the 1988 marathon finally ended, however, it was Republican George Bush who had crossed the finish line first.

Bush's winning strategy was grounded in the belief that voters knew little about Michael Dukakis, who, as governor of Massachusetts, had not had much national visibility. The Bush camp used the campaign to help define Dukakis's image. In his speeches, debate appearances, and television ads, Bush painted Dukakis as an out-of-the-mainstream liberal who was weak on defense, soft on crime, and ready to raise taxes at the drop of a hat. Bush's approach seemed effective, since, as the campaign wore on, public opinion on Dukakis shifted. For example, an NBC/*Wall Street Journal* poll conducted in August showed that respondents by a 41-to-36 percent margin felt Dukakis would be tougher than Bush on crime. By October, however, a similar poll found that Bush was seen as tougher on crime by a 56-to-27 percent edge. And Bush effectively portrayed himself as the guardian of the peace and prosperity established during the Reagan years. His appeal was direct: Did Americans want to change direction when things were going so well?

A central theme for Dukakis was economic fairness; he argued that his administration would be more concerned about the welfare of average, middle-class Americans. This is a traditional Democratic campaign issue, and it seemed to have potential benefits. Early in the campaign, a CBS/*New York Times* poll found that when respondents were asked who would do more for the middle class, they chose the Democrats by a 56-to-28 percent margin. On the other hand, the theme of managerial competence, highlighting Dukakis's effectiveness as the governor of a prosperous state, was dropped when it failed to elicit much reaction from voters. The Democrats got an unexpected gift when Bush selected Dan Quayle, a young (forty-one) and undistinguished senator from Indiana, as his running mate. Doubts about Quayle's character arose in the wake of allegations that he had used family connections to enter the National Guard and avoid the draft during the Vietnam War. Quayle remained a liability for the GOP ticket throughout the campaign.

Despite his decisive victory (see Figure 11.3), many observers questioned the approach of Bush's campaign. He was vague about his plans for the presidency and did not build public support for any specific policies. Unlike Reagan in 1980, Bush lacked the "coattails" to bring a lot of new Republicans into the Congress. More pointed criticism was aimed at Dukakis after the election. Why didn't he more vigorously defend himself against Bush's charges early in the race? Why did he allow Bush to set the agenda of the campaign? Yet Dukakis's unimpressive campaign may not have been the principal cause of his defeat. Rather, after repeated bouts of stagflation, inflation, and recession, Americans went to the polls in 1988 with six years of stable prosperity behind them. To many voters, George Bush represented a steady-as-you-go course, and Mike Dukakis represented uncertainty.

House seats in the 1966 congressional elections; this in turn made it even harder for the president to lead. In the spring of 1968, with his administration under fire and a strong challenge to his renomination brewing within his own party, Johnson withdrew from the presidential race.

A major problem that the president faces in translating his mandate into action is the separation of powers that makes Congress independent of the executive branch. His own party may not even have majorities in the two houses. Not once during the eight years of the Nixon and Ford presidencies did the Republicans control the House or the Senate. But even presidents who have majorities in both houses of Congress may find their congressional "allies" unwilling to follow them on some major issues. Committee and party leaders have their own, independent electoral bases.

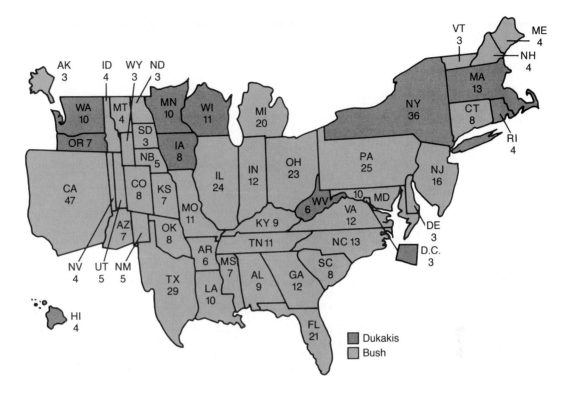

Electoral Votes by States, 1988
George Bush's electoral college strategy was to rely on the South, the farm belt, and the western mountain states as a base, then win enough of the remaining large states to put him over the top. In the end, Bush garnered far more than the 270 electoral votes necessary for victory, winning 40 states with 426 votes, to Dukakis's 10 states and the District of Columbia, and 112 votes. (Source: James Q. Wilson, American Government: Institutions and Policies, *3rd edition. © 1986 D.C. Heath and Company, p. 321. Used with permission.)*

Figure 11.3

With the constraints on their ability to move Congress, the inevitable unpopular choices that they must make, and the real difficulties involved in actually *solving* problems, presidents may find it extremely hard to meet all the goals they set for their administrations. With this in mind, the argument that the presidency is an "impossible job" seems difficult to dispute. Yet not all presidents are doomed to failure. Dwight Eisenhower finished eight years in office with relatively high popularity ratings. And, despite alienating many constituencies in his first term, Reagan convinced a large majority of Americans that his policies were necessary medicine for a sick economy. After a strong economic upturn before the 1984 election, he won an impressive endorsement, beating Walter Mondale in a landslide.

THE EXECUTIVE BRANCH ESTABLISHMENT

As a president tries to maintain the support of his electoral coalition for the policies he pursues, he draws on the great resources of the executive

Figure 11.4

The White House

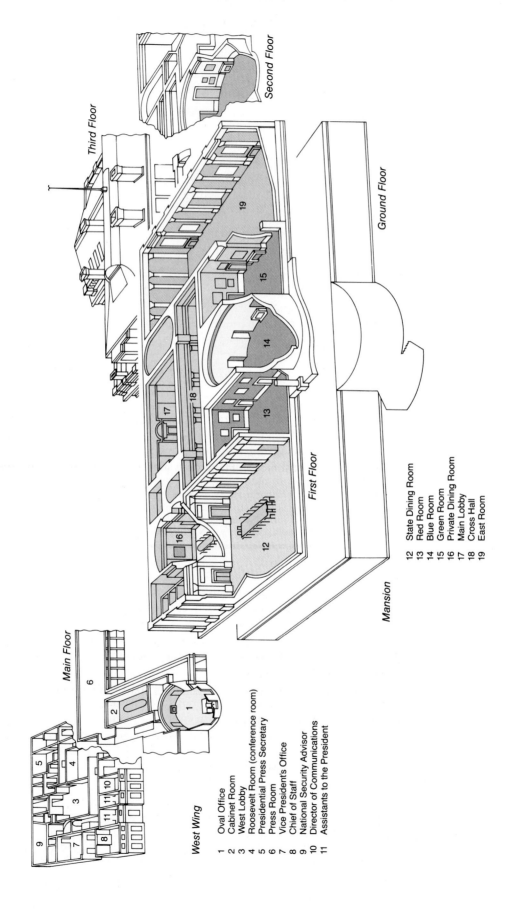

Third Floor

Second Floor

West Wing

Main Floor

First Floor

Ground Floor

Mansion

West Wing

1 Oval Office
2 Cabinet Room
3 West Lobby
4 Roosevelt Room (conference room)
5 Presidential Press Secretary
6 Press Room
7 Vice President's Office
8 Chief of Staff
9 National Security Advisor
10 Director of Communications
11 Assistants to the President

12 State Dining Room
13 Red Room
14 Blue Room
15 Green Room
16 Private Dining Room
17 Main Lobby
18 Cross Hall
19 East Room

branch of government. The president has a White House staff that helps him formulate policy. The vice president is another resource; his duties within the administration vary according to his relationship with the president. The president's Cabinet secretaries—the heads of the major departments of the national government—play a number of roles, including the critical function of administering the programs that fall within their jurisdiction. Finally, within the departments and agencies, operating at a level below that of the president's appointees, are the career bureaucrats. These bureaucrats (who are discussed in the next chapter) offer great expertise in program operations.

The White House Staff

A president depends heavily on his key aides. They advise him on crucial political choices, devise the general strategies the administration follows in pursuing congressional and public support, and control access to the president to ensure that he has enough time for his most important tasks. Consequently, he needs to trust and respect these top staffers; many of a president's inner circle of assistants are long-time associates. (Figure 11.4 shows the location of some staffers' offices in the White House.)

Presidents typically have a chief of staff; who may be a "first among equals" or, in some administrations, the unquestioned leader of the staff. H. R. Haldeman, Richard Nixon's chief of staff, played the stronger role. He ran a highly disciplined operation, frequently prodding staff members to work harder and faster. Haldeman also felt that part of his role was to "take the heat" for the president by assuming responsibility for many of the administration's unpopular decisions. "Every president needs a son of a bitch, and I'm Nixon's."[30] Hamilton Jordan, chief of staff during the Carter administration, did not dominate the White House staff in the same way. His primary job "was to settle interagency conflict and make sure that the implementation of presidential policy was well supervised."[31]

Presidents also have a national security adviser to provide daily briefings on foreign and military affairs and longer-range analyses of issues confronting the administration. A Council of Economic Advisers is also located in the White House. Senior domestic policy advisers help determine the administration's basic approach to such areas as health, education, and social services.

Below these top aides are large staffs that serve them and the president. These staffs are organized around certain specialties. Some staff members work on "political" matters, such as liaison with interest groups, relations with ethnic and religious minorities, and party affairs. One staff deals exclusively with the press, and a legislative liaison staff lobbies the Congress for the administration. The large Office of Management and Budget (OMB) analyzes budget requests, is involved in the policymaking process, and also examines agency management practices. This extended White House executive establishment is known as the **Executive Office of the President.** The Executive Office employs around sixteen hundred individuals, and it has an annual budget of around $100 million.[32]

There is no agreed-on "right way" for a president to organize his White House staff. Each president creates the structure that will work best for him. Dwight Eisenhower, for example, a former general, wanted clear lines of authority and a hierarchical structure that mirrored a military command. One factor that influences how a president uses his senior staff is the degree to which he delegates authority to them. Carter immersed himself in the policymaking process to ensure that he made all the significant decisions. Early in his administration, he told his staff, "Unless there's a holocaust, I'll take care of everything the same day it comes in."[33] (This explains in large part why Jordan's role as chief of staff was less powerful than Haldeman's during the Nixon years.) Because there is so much for a president to decide on, he may spend precious little time on some of the issues that come before him. One of the critical functions of the senior staff is to make sure that a president rations his time wisely, devoting sufficient time to the issues that warrant considerable analysis and deliberation. As Jack Watson, an aide to Carter, put it, "The most important thing that the chief of staff can do in terms of protecting against the 'damn fool decision' is to do everything within your power to see that the president is fully briefed before he does make a decision."[34]

Despite the formal organization of the White House staff, it suffers from the same "turf wars" that plague other large organizations. These struggles over authority stem not only from personal ambition and political differences, but also from overlapping jurisdictions. Conflict frequently arises between a secretary of state (a member of the Cabinet) and a president's national security adviser; each wants primacy in shaping the administration's foreign policy. Henry Kissinger, Nixon's national security adviser, was extraordinarily shrewd in devising ways to gain advantage over Secretary of State William Rogers. One of his tactics was to create "backchannels"—information from the field would come to him secretly, bypassing the Department of State. Kissinger did this "not only to keep control of an ongoing negotiation but also to prevent his peers and subordinates from finding out what was going on."[35] Presidents, however, often find it more useful to hear competing policy views than depend on the views of one person.

The Vice President

The vice president's primary function is to serve as standby equipment, only a heartbeat away from the presidency itself (see Feature 11.2). Traditionally, vice presidents have not been used in any important advisory capacity. Instead, presidents tend to give them political chores—campaigning, fund raising, and "stroking" the party faithful. This is often the case because vice presidential candidates are chosen for reasons that have more to do with the political campaign than with governing the nation. One of the primary reasons Nixon chose Spiro Agnew, a relatively inexperienced governor of Maryland, as his 1968 running mate was that Agnew would not outshine the colorless Nixon. John Kennedy chose Lyndon Johnson of Texas for the vice presidential slot in 1960 because he thought Johnson would help him carry the South. Johnson was helpful in the election, but once Kennedy was in office, he made little use of his

FEATURE 11.2

Who's President When the President Can't Be?

What happens if a president dies in office? The vice president, of course, becomes the new president. But what happens if the vice president has died or left office for some reason? What happens if the president becomes senile or is disabled by illness? These are questions that the authors of the Constitution failed to resolve.

The nuclear age has made these questions more troubling. When Woodrow Wilson suffered a stroke in 1919, it meant that the country was without effective leadership for a time, but the lack of an active president during that period did not endanger the lives of all Americans. Today, with the possibility of nuclear attack, national security dictates that the nation have a commander in chief at all times. The Twenty-fifth Amendment, which was ratified in 1967, specifies a mechanism for replacing a living president in case he cannot carry out the duties of his office. A president can declare himself unable to carry on, or the vice president and the Cabinet can decide collectively that the president is incapacitated. In either case, the vice president becomes acting president and assumes all powers of the office. In 1981, when Ronald Reagan was seriously wounded in an assassination attempt and had to undergo emergency surgery, the Twenty-fifth Amendment was not invoked by the vice president and the Cabinet. Four years later, when Reagan underwent cancer surgery, he sent a letter to Vice President George Bush transferring the power of the office to him at the moment the president was anesthetized. Eight hours later, Reagan reclaimed his authority. Under the Twenty-fifth Amendment, if the president and the Cabinet disagree about whether he is able to resume his duties, Congress must ultimately decide.

The Twenty-fifth Amendment also provides that the president select a new vice president in the event that office becomes vacant; the president's choice must be approved by a majority of both houses of Congress. Gerald Ford became vice president in this manner when Spiro Agnew resigned after pleading no contest to charges of income tax evasion and accepting bribes. Later, when Richard Nixon resigned and Ford became president, he chose Nelson Rockefeller as his vice president.

---

vice president. After Johnson became president, he was sometimes openly contemptuous of his own vice president, Hubert Humphrey of Minnesota. One participant at a meeting recalled the following interaction:

> President Johnson allotted the loquacious Hubert H. Humphrey five minutes in which to speak (*"Five minutes,* Hubert!"); then Johnson stood by, eyes fixed on the sweep second hand of his watch, while Humphrey spoke, and when the Vice President went over the limit, pushed him, still talking, out of the room with his own hands.[36]

An exception to the usual pattern was Carter's vice president, Walter Mondale. Carter was wise enough to realize that Mondale's experience in the Senate could be of great value to him, especially since Carter had never served in Congress. Although the personal chemistry between Ronald Reagan and George Bush was quite good, Bush did not seem to play as major a role as Mondale.[37] The perception that Bush was not a central player was partly a consequence of his claims that he was "out of the loop" (the decision-making process) at crucial junctures during the planning of the arms transactions with Iran.

The Cabinet

The president's **Cabinet** is composed of the heads of the departments in the executive branch (see Table 11.1) and a small number of other key

Table 11.1 ▬▬▬▬▬▬▬▬▬▬▬▬▬▬▬▬▬▬▬▬▬▬▬▬▬▬▬▬
The Cabinet

Department	Created	Number of Employees
State	1789	25,254
Treasury	1789	225,082
Defense[†]	1789	1,084,549
Justice[‡]	1789	64,433
Interior	1849	77,485
Agriculture	1862	117,750
Commerce	1913	43,783
Labor	1913	18,260
Health and Human Services[*]	1953	223,083
Housing and Urban Development	1965	12,289
Transportation	1966	62,227
Energy	1977	16,749
Education	1979	4,889

[*] The Department of Health, Education, and Welfare became the Department of Health and Human Services in 1979, when an independent Department of Education was established.

[†] The War Department was created in 1789. The Defense Department was created in 1949. Employment figure is for civilian employees only.

[‡] The attorney general was a member of the first cabinet. The Justice Department was established in 1870.

Source: Bureau of the Census, *Statistical Abstract of the United States: 1987* (Washington, D.C.: U.S. Government Printing Office, 1986), p. 311.

officials, such as the head of the Office of Management and Budget and the ambassador to the United Nations. The Cabinet has expanded greatly since George Washington formed his first Cabinet, which included an attorney general and secretaries of state, treasury, and war. Clearly, the growth of the Cabinet reflects the growth of government responsibility and intervention in areas such as energy, housing, and transportation.

In theory, the members of the Cabinet constitute an advisory body that meets with the president to debate major policy decisions. In practice, however, Cabinet meetings have been described as "vapid non-events in which there has been a deliberate non-exchange of information as part of a process of mutual nonconsultation."[38] One Carter Cabinet member called meetings "adult Show-and-Tell."[39] Why is this so? First, the Cabinet has become rather large. Counting department heads, other officials of Cabinet rank, and presidential aides, it is a body of at least twenty people—a size that many presidents find unwieldy for the give-and-take of political decision making. Second, most Cabinet members have limited areas of expertise and simply cannot contribute much to deliberations on areas they know little about. The secretary of defense, for example, would probably be a poor choice to help decide important issues of agricultural policy. Third, although Cabinet members have impressive backgrounds, they may not be personally close to the president or easy for him to work with. Cabinet choices are not necessarily made on the basis of personal relationships. The president often chooses

Cabinet members because of their reputations, or he may be guided by a need to give his Cabinet some racial, ethnic, geographic, sexual, or religious balance.

Finally, modern presidents do not rely on the Cabinet to make policy because they have such large White House staffs, which offer most of the advisory support they need. In contrast to Cabinet secretaries, who may be pulled in different directions by the wishes of the president and the wishes of their department's clientele groups, White House staffers are likely to see themselves as responsible to the president alone. Thus, despite periodic calls for the Cabinet to be a collective decision-making body, Cabinet meetings seem doomed to be little more than academic exercises. In practice, presidents prefer the flexibility of ad hoc groups, specialized White House staffs, and the advisers and Cabinet secretaries with whom they feel most comfortable.

More broadly, presidents use their personal staffs and the large Executive Office of the President to centralize control over the entire executive branch. The vast size of the executive branch and the number and complexity of decisions that must be made each day pose a challenge for the White House. Reagan, for example, created a new OMB staff unit to review proposals by regulatory agencies. In sum, to fulfill more of their political goals and policy preferences, modern presidents have encouraged their various staffs to play increasingly important roles in executive branch decision making.[40]

THE PRESIDENT AS NATIONAL LEADER

With an election behind him and the resources of his office at hand, a president is ready to lead the nation. Each president enters office with a general vision of how government should approach policy issues. During his term, a president spends much of his time trying to get Congress to enact legislation that reflects his general philosophy and specific policy preferences.

From Political Values . . .

Presidents differ greatly in their views of the role of government. Lyndon Johnson had a strong liberal ideology concerning domestic affairs, believing that government has a responsibility to help disadvantaged Americans. After his landslide victory in 1964, Johnson's inaugural address contained his vision of justice:

> . . . justice was the promise that all who made the journey would share in the fruits of the land.
>
> In a land of wealth, families must not live in hopeless poverty. In a land rich in harvest, children just must not go hungry. In a land of healing miracles, neighbors must not suffer and die untended. In a great land of learning and scholars, young people must be taught to read and write.
>
> For more than thirty years that I have served this nation, I have believed that this injustice to our people, this waste of our resources, was our real enemy. For thirty years or more, with the resources I have had, I have vigilantly fought against it.[41]

The Transfer of Power
Vice President Lyndon Johnson was with President John Kennedy during his fateful visit to Dallas. After Kennedy was pronounced dead at Parkland Hospital, federal judge Sarah Hughes (lower left) administered the presidential oath of office to Johnson on Air Force One. Standing next to Johnson were his wife, Lady Bird (left), and Kennedy's widow, Jacqueline (right). Five days after he was sworn in, Johnson gave a nationally televised address before a joint session of Congress. Johnson used a memorable phrase symbolizing the stability of the presidency: "Let us continue."

Johnson used *justice* and *injustice* as code words for *equality* and *inequality*. They were used six times in his speech; *freedom* was used only twice. Johnson used his mandate and the resources of his office to press for a "just" America, which he termed the "Great Society."

To achieve his Great Society, Johnson sent Congress an unparalleled package of liberal legislation. He launched such projects as the Job Corps (which created centers and camps offering vocational training and work experience to youths aged sixteen to twenty-one); Medicare (which provided medical care for the elderly); and the National Teacher Corps (which funded teachers to work in impoverished neighborhoods). Supported by huge Democratic majorities in Congress during 1965 and 1966, he had tremendous success in getting his proposals through. Liberalism was in full swing.

Exactly twenty years after Johnson's inaugural speech, Ronald Reagan took his oath of office for the second time, then addressed the nation. Reagan reasserted his conservative philosophy. He emphasized *freedom*, using the term fourteen times, and failed to mention *justice* or *equality* once. In the following excerpts, the term *freedom* is highlighted for easy reference:

> By 1980, we knew it was time to renew our faith, to strive with all our strength toward the ultimate in individual *freedom* consistent with an orderly society. . . . We will not rest until every American enjoys the fullness of *freedom*, dignity, and opportunity as our birthright. . . . Americans . . .

turned the tide of history away from totalitarian darkness and into the warm sunlight of human *freedom*. . . . Let history say of us, these were golden years—when the American Revolution was reborn, when *freedom* gained new life, when America reached for her best. . . . *freedom* and incentives unleash the drive and entrepreneurial genius that are at the core of human progress. . . . From new *freedom* will spring new opportunities for growth. . . . Yet history has shown that peace does not come, nor will our *freedom* be preserved by good will alone. There are those in the world who scorn our vision of human dignity and *freedom*. . . . Human *freedom* is on the march, and nowhere more so than in our own hemisphere. *Freedom* is one of the deepest and noblest aspirations of the human spirit. . . . America must remain *freedom's* staunchest friend, for *freedom* is our best ally. . . . Every victory for human *freedom* will be a victory for world peace. . . . One people under God, dedicated to the dream of *freedom* that He has placed in the human heart.[42]

Reagan turned Johnson's philosophy on its head, declaring that "government is not the solution to our problem. Government is the problem." During his presidency, Reagan worked to undo many welfare and social service programs. For example, he proposed in 1981 that funding for the Job Corps be reduced by 40 percent; Congress refused to go along. He was more successful in getting Congress to cut back on the food stamp program (started during the Kennedy administration) through reduced benefits and eligibility restrictions. Food stamp legislation called for outlays to be reduced by 14 percent over the next three years.[43]

. . . To Policy Agenda

The roots of particular policy proposals, then, can be traced to the more general political ideology of the president. A presidential candidate surely outlines that philosophy of government during his campaign for the White House. But when the hot rhetoric of the presidential campaign meets the cold reality of what is possible in Washington, the newly elected president must make some hard choices about what he will push for during the coming term. These choices are reflected in the bills the president submits to Congress, as well as in the degree to which he works for their passage. The president's bills, introduced by his allies in the House and Senate, always receive a good deal of initial attention. In the words of one Washington lobbyist, "When a president sends up a bill, it takes first place in the queue. All other bills take second place."[44]

The president's role in legislative leadership is largely a twentieth-century phenomenon. Not until the Budget and Accounting Act (1921) did executive branch departments and agencies have to clear their proposed budget bills with the White House. Before this, the president did not even coordinate proposals for how much the executive branch would spend on all the programs it administered. Later, Franklin Roosevelt required that *all* major legislative proposals by an agency or department be cleared by the White House. No longer could a department submit a bill without White House support.[45]

Roosevelt's impact on the relationship between the president and Congress went far beyond this new administrative arrangement. With the nation in the midst of the Great Depression, Roosevelt began his

Figure 11.5

Presidential Greatness

In 1982, the Chicago Tri-
bune *asked forty-nine leading historians and political
scholars to rate all past
presidents on a descending
scale from 5 (best) to 0
(worst) in five categories:
leadership qualities, accomplishments and crisis management, political skills,
quality of appointments,
and character and integrity.
Lincoln ranked at the top,
and Franklin Roosevelt
edged out Washington for
second place. Among more
recent presidents, Eisen-
hower, Johnson, and Ken-
nedy all rated far higher
than Ford, Carter, and
Nixon. Nixon's ranking suffered by his extraordinarily
low score for character and
integrity—the lowest that
the scholars gave to any
president in history. (Source:
© Copyrighted 1988, Chicago
Tribune Company, all rights reserved, used with permission.)*

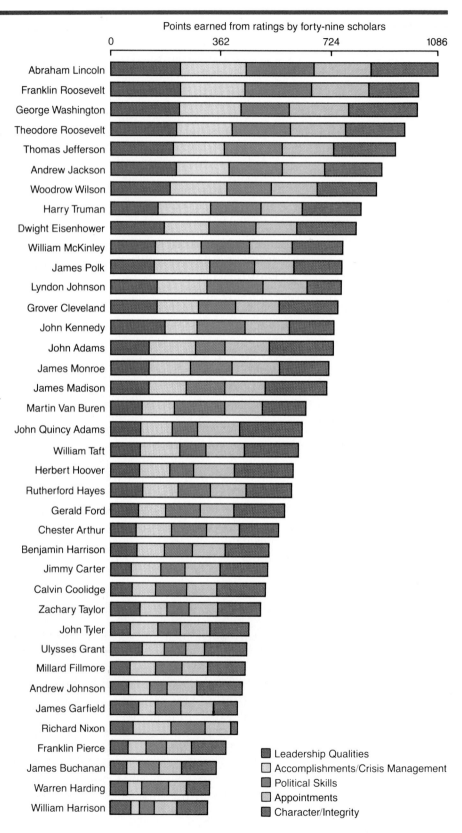

first term in 1933 with an ambitious array of legislative proposals. During the first hundred days Congress was in session, it enacted fifteen significant laws, including the Agricultural Adjustment Act, the Civilian Conservation Corps, and the National Industrial Recovery Act. Never had a president demanded—and received—so much from Congress. Roosevelt's legacy was that the president would henceforth provide aggressive leadership for Congress through his own legislative program.

A handful of presidents have entered office after a serious upheaval or a general decline of a dominant political coalition, situations that presidents can use to their advantage. The economic collapse that preceded Roosevelt's entry into office ended an era of conservative Republicanism that had steadfastly ruled the country for many years. Andrew Jackson and Abraham Lincoln also had fortuitous chances to redefine the terms of political debate and move the country toward a new political agenda.[46] Reagan found Roosevelt's New Deal coalition in serious decline when he took over, making it easier to reorient debate away from issues of equality to issues of freedom. But times of upheaval and decline merely present opportunities; presidents must be skillful enough to exploit the chances for large-scale change. And history has taught us that presidents differ greatly in their skills (see Figure 11.5).

Chief Lobbyist

When Franklin Roosevelt and Harry Truman first became heavily involved in preparing legislative packages, political scientists typically described the process as one in which "the president proposes and the Congress disposes." In other words, once the president sent his legislation to Capitol Hill, Congress decided on its own what to do with it. Over time, though, presidents have become increasingly active in all stages of the legislative process. The president is expected not only to propose legislation, but also to make sure that it passes. His role as "chief lobbyist" is illustrated by John Kennedy's first year in office, during which time he

> held thirty-two Tuesday morning breakfasts with congressional leadership, ninety private conversations with congressional leaders that lasted an hour or two, coffee hours with 500 legislators, bill signing ceremonies with a similar number, and in all approximately 2,500 separate contacts with congressmen exclusive of correspondence.[47]

The president's efforts to influence Congress are reinforced by the work of his legislative liaison staff. All departments and major agencies have legislative specialists as well. These department and agency people work with the White House staff to coordinate the administration's lobbying on major issues.

The **legislative liaison staff** is the communications link between the White House and Congress. As a bill slowly makes its way through Congress, liaison staffers advise the president or a Cabinet secretary on the problems that emerge. They specify what parts of a bill are in trouble and may have to be modified or dropped. They tell their boss what amendments are likely to be offered, which members of Congress need lobbying, and what the chances are for the passage of the bill with or without certain provisions. Decisions on how the administration will respond to such developments must then be reached. For example, when the Reagan White House realized it was still a few votes short of victory on a budget bill in the House, it reversed its opposition to a sugar price-support bill. This attracted the votes of representatives from Louisiana and Florida, two sugar-growing states, for the budget bill. The White House would not call what happened a "deal" but noted that "adjustments and considerations" had been made.[48]

A certain amount of the president's job is stereotypical "arm twisting"—pushing reluctant legislators to vote a certain way. Yet most day in, day out interactions tend to be more subtle, as the liaison staff tries to build consensus by working cooperatively with members of Congress. When a congressional committee is working on a bill, liaison people talk to committee members individually, to see what concerns they have and to help fashion a compromise if some members differ with the president's position. As one experienced White House lobbyist put it, "I think it is important to try to develop an individual relationship with the members, to get to know their problems and what their interests are and to gain their confidence"[49] (see Figure 11.6).

The White House also works directly with interest groups in its efforts to build support for legislation. Presidential aides hope key lobbyists will activate the most effective lobbyists of all: the voters back home. Interest groups can quickly reach the constituents who are most concerned about a bill. One White House aide said with admiration, "The Realtors can send out half a million Mail grams within 24 hours."[50]

Although much of the liaison staff's work with Congress is done in a cooperative spirit, agreement cannot always be reached. When Congress passes a bill the president opposes, he may veto it and send it back to Congress; as noted earlier, Congress can override a veto with a two-thirds majority of those voting in each house. Presidents use their veto power sparingly, but the threat that a president will veto an unacceptable bill increases his bargaining leverage with members of Congress. We have also seen that a president's leverage with Congress is related to his standing with the American people. The ability of the president and his liaison staff to negotiate with members of Congress is enhanced when he is riding high in the popularity polls and hindered when the public is critical of the president's performance. After Reagan vetoed a 1987 highway bill he thought was too expensive, the House and Senate overrode the veto. Before the vote in the Senate, the president took the unusual step of traveling to Capitol Hill to seek the single vote that would have prevented the necessary two-thirds margin. If Reagan had not been so damaged by the Iran-Contra scandal that had come to light six months earlier, it seems likely that he could have persuaded at least a few more senators to back his veto.[51]

Party Leader

Part of the president's job is to lead his party. This is very much an informal duty, with no prescribed tasks. In this respect, American presidents are considerably different from European prime ministers, who

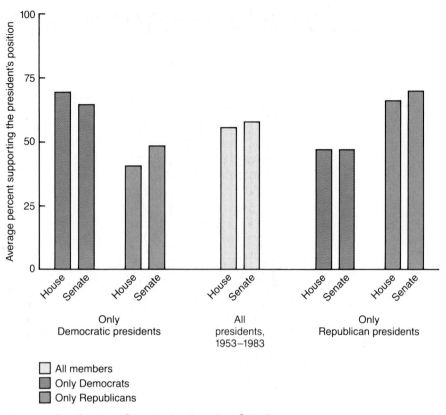

Support for the President in Congressional Voting
*The extent to which individual representatives and senators support the presi-
dent in their congressional voting patterns can be measured by the* presidential support score, *computed by* Congressional Quarterly, *a Washington, D.C.,
publication that specializes in reporting on Congress.* Congressional Quarterly
*reviews all the public messages and statements of the president to determine
what legislation he favors and opposes. After analyzing all recorded roll call
votes in a session of Congress,* Congressional Quarterly *assigns to each representative and senator a presidential support score, indicating the percentage of
time that the member backed the president's position during the session. The
graph shows that, regardless of party, the average member of the House or
Senate supported the president somewhat more than half the time. When the
list is broken down by party, a clear pattern emerges: Republican members
are far more likely to support Republican presidents, and Democratic members, to support Democratic presidents.*

Figure 11.6

are the formal leaders of their party in the national legislature as well as
the heads of government. Since political parties in Europe tend to have
strong national organizations, there is more reason for prime ministers
to lead the party organization. In the United States, national party committees play a relatively minor role in national politics, although the
Republican party has developed a formidable fund-raising capability that
has benefited its congressional candidates.

The simple fact is that presidents can operate effectively without
the help of a national party apparatus. Lyndon Johnson, for example, was

contemptuous of the Democratic National Committee. He saw to it that the committee's budget was cut and refused some advisers' request that he replace its ineffectual head. Johnson thought a weak national committee would allow him to control party affairs out of the White House. Like other modern presidents, Johnson believed he would be most effective communicating directly to the American people and did not see the need for national, state, or local party officials to be intermediaries in the process of coalition building.[52]

Work with the party may be more important for gaining the presidency than actually governing. George Bush worked tirelessly on the "rubber chicken" circuit while he was vice president and built up a hefty billfold of IOUs by campaigning for Republican candidates and appearing at their fund-raising dinners. When he and his main competitor for the 1988 Republican nomination, Senator Robert Dole, faced each other in the critical Super Tuesday primaries in 1988, Bush had enormous strength among state and local party leaders; those individuals formed the backbone of his campaign organization. Yet such party work is not absolutely essential. In 1976, Carter not only won the nomination without much of a record of party work, he campaigned as an outsider, claiming that he would be a better president without having ties to those who had long been in power.

THE PRESIDENT AS WORLD LEADER

The president's leadership responsibilities extend beyond the Congress and the nation, into the international arena. Each administration tries to further what it sees as the country's best interests in its relations with allies, adversaries, and the developing countries of the world. In this role, the president can act as diplomat or crisis manager.

Foreign Relations

Presidents like to think of themselves as leaders of the Western democracies—the noncommunist countries of Europe, Japan, Canada, Australia, and a few other nations. (As you learned in Chapter 2, there are only nineteen countries that fit the different criteria political scientists commonly use to define a democracy.) The president is the focal point for the Western bloc's relations with the two communist superpowers, the Soviet Union and China. There is no formal alliance of all the Western democracies, but the United States has entered into military alliances with many of them. The most important of these is the North Atlantic Treaty Organization (NATO), composed of the United States, Canada, and most of the countries of Western Europe. These countries depend on our nuclear shield and troop commitments as deterrents to potential aggression.

The international pre-eminence of the United States is based on this country's long-term economic and military might, but the president has

Our American Friend
As a young politician, Richard Nixon was notorious for his staunch anticommunism. As president, however, he achieved a stunning reversal of U.S. policy toward the People's Republic of China. His trip there in 1972 signaled an end to the Cold War hostility between the United States and the communist regime.

little formal diplomatic control over other democratic countries. America's allies have interests of their own and strong internal reasons for wanting to remain independent of this country. Inherent nationalism, economic necessity, differing political philosophies, and the visions of their leaders give countries like France, Italy, and England reasons to stake out their independent roles in world politics. France and West Germany, for example, have taken significant steps of their own to improve relations with the Soviet Union and with the Eastern European countries aligned with Moscow.

As in his dealings with Congress, a president must lead his allies with his powers of persuasion. He must act deftly, inducing the various heads of state to follow America's lead in foreign policy without pressuring them so much that they become resentful and uncooperative. Jimmy Carter's effort to boycott the 1980 Olympic games in Moscow illustrates the difficulty recent presidents have had in leading the allies. When the Soviet Union sent its troops into neighboring Afghanistan because it feared that a hostile regime might come to power, Carter asked the Western democracies for a joint response to the Soviet aggression. Despite widespread anger and revulsion over the invasion, many allies (among them, France and Great Britain) did not comply with Carter's request to boycott the games and sent their athletes to Moscow.

A president's diplomatic skills are tested in another way in his relations with the Soviet Union, the other great nuclear power. The president must regard the Soviet Union as an adversary but at the same time must develop a sound working relationship with its leaders. The primary concern of the president—and of his counterpart, the leader of the Communist party in the Soviet Union—is achieving the right level of armament and arms control. Each country wants to remain militarily strong, but each also has a real interest in limiting the arms race because of spiraling costs, the worry that the other country will achieve a clear weapons superiority, and a general desire to reduce international tensions.

Presidents are constrained in their direction of our relations with the Soviet Union by public opinion, Congress, and this country's long-standing anticommunist ideology. As presidents and their advisers develop policy, they anticipate the reactions of critics. Yet recent presidents have also played an important role in leading the United States out of the Cold War—the era of Soviet–American distrust and hostility that followed World War II. Richard Nixon pursued *détente*, an easing of tensions between the two countries, which resulted in an arms control agreement (SALT I). Gerald Ford and Carter pursued détente as well, leading to the SALT II accords during the Carter administration, although SALT II was never ratified by the Senate. Despite his harsh criticism of the Soviet Union as the "evil empire," Reagan negotiated a missile treaty with Soviet leader Mikhail Gorbachev to remove intermediate-range nuclear missiles from Europe.

A general goal of all presidents is to pull developing countries into closer, friendlier relations with the United States. At the very least, presidents try to keep such countries from falling under communist domination. For example, the Reagan administration supported the efforts of the Contras to overthrow the Nicaraguan government because it believed that Marxist government was a threat to the rest of Central America. Presidents may also face problems with developing countries that are our allies. Over the years, the United States has supported a number of dictatorial leaders because such support suited our strategic needs. American support of the Shah of Iran caused many people of Iran to associate the Shah's repressive regime with the United States. Since the revolution that toppled the Shah, those Iranians have considered the United States a great enemy.

The Handshake of Peace
One of the crowning achievements of Jimmy Carter's presidency was his role in forging a peace treaty between Egypt and Israel. Egyptian president Anwar Sadat (left) and Israeli prime minister Menachem Begin (right) came to the presidential retreat at Camp David in Maryland. For thirteen days, Carter was a mediator in the peace negotiations. After the historic accords were reached, the three flew by helicopter to the White House, where they signed the initial agreement.

Crisis Management

Periodically the president faces a grave situation in which conflict is imminent or a small conflict threatens to explode into a larger war. Handling such episodes is a critical part of the president's job. Today, we must put enormous trust in the person who has the power to pull our nuclear trigger; voters may make the candidates' personal judgment and intelligence primary considerations in how they cast their ballots. A major reason for Barry Goldwater's crushing defeat in the 1964 election was his warlike image. Goldwater's bellicose rhetoric scared many Americans, who, fearing that he would be too quick to resort to nuclear weapons, voted for Lyndon Johnson instead.

A president must be able to exercise good judgment and remain cool in crisis situations. John Kennedy's behavior during the Cuban missile crisis has become a model of effective crisis management. When it was discovered that the Soviet Union had placed missiles containing nuclear warheads in Cuba, U.S. government leaders saw those missiles as an unacceptable threat to this country's security. Kennedy asked a group of senior aides, including top people from the Pentagon, to advise him on possible military and diplomatic actions. An armed invasion of Cuba and air strikes against the missiles were two options considered. In the end, Kennedy decided on a less dangerous response: implementing a naval blockade of Cuba. The Soviet Union thought better of prolonging its challenge to the United States and soon agreed to remove its missiles. For a short time, though, the world held its breath over the very real possibility of a nuclear war.

Are there guidelines for what a president should do in times of crisis or at other important decision-making junctures? Drawing on a range of advisers and opinions is certainly one.[53] Not acting in unnecessary haste is another. A third is rigorously examining the chain of reasoning that has led to the chosen option, ensuring that *presumptions* have not been subconsciously equated with what is *actually known* to be true. When Kennedy decided to back a CIA plan to sponsor a rebel invasion of Cuba by expatriates hostile to Fidel Castro, he never really understood that its chances for success were based on unfounded assumptions of immediate uprisings by the Cuban population.[54] Still, these are rather general rules and provide no assurance that mistakes will not be made. Almost by definition, each crisis is a unique event. Sometimes all the alternatives carry substantial risks. And almost always, time is of the essence. This was the situation when Cambodia captured the American merchant ship *Mayaguez* off its coast in 1975. Not wanting to wait until the Cambodian government moved the seamen inland, where there would be little chance of rescuing them, Ford immediately sent in the marines. Unfortunately, forty-one American soldiers were killed in the fighting, "all in vain because the American captives had shortly before the attack been released and sent across the border into Thailand."[55] Even so, Ford can be defended for making the decision he did; he did not know what the Cambodians would do. World events are unpredictable, and, in the end, presidents must rely on their own judgment in crisis situations.

PRESIDENTIAL CHARACTER

How does the public assess which presidential candidate has the best judgment and a character suitable to the office? Americans must make a broad evaluation, considering the candidates' personalities and leadership styles. Sometimes damaging revelations suggest that a candidate's character is flawed. Senator Joseph Biden of Delaware, a candidate for the 1988 Democratic nomination for president, was forced to withdraw from the campaign because of evidence that he had plagiarized parts of his campaign speeches from stirring speeches made by other politicians and that he had lied about his record in college.

Questions about Gary Hart's character also became a major issue in the 1988 race and forced him to withdraw as well. The public was disturbed not only by the allegations of adultery that followed the Democratic candidate, but also by his recklessness (see Figure 11.7). As one journalist noted, "Why would any man in his right mind defy a New York *Times* reporter who asked about his alleged womanizing to 'put a tail on me,' then cancel his weekend campaign appearances and arrange a tryst at his Washington town house with a Miami party girl?"[56]

A candidate's character is clearly a valid campaign issue. A president's actions in office reflect something more than ideology and politics; they also reflect the moral, ethical, and psychological forces that comprise his character. Much of any person's character is formed in childhood, and many individual traits can be traced to early experiences. Lyndon Johnson, for example, had a troubled relationship with his father,

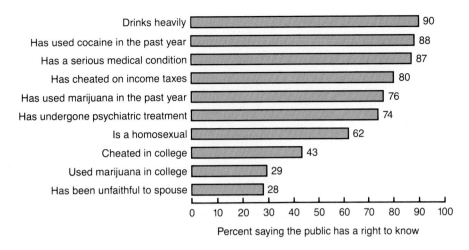

None of Your Business?
Although allegations of an affair with a Miami model drove Gary Hart from the 1988 presidential race, Americans are more tolerant of adultery than some other moral failings, some medical conditions, or some other personal characteristics. A national poll asked respondents, "How about whether a candidate _____? Is the public entitled to know that, or is that none of the public's business?" On most of the items listed here, Americans seem to believe that presidential candidates do not have a right to privacy—that if there is an issue that could affect performance in office or indicates a significant failure of character, then the public's right to know is greater than the individual candidate's right to privacy. (Source: E. J. Dionne, "Reagan Influence Wanes, Poll Finds," New York Times, 26 January 1988, p. A1.)

Figure 11.7

who questioned his son's masculinity. Johnson recalled that when he ran away from home after wrecking his father's car, his father phoned him and said that people in town were calling Lyndon "yellow" and a coward.[57] Johnson biographer Robert Caro notes another crucial episode in young Lyndon's life—a humiliating beating he took at the hands of a dance partner's jealous boyfriend. In front of family and friends, "blood was pouring out of Lyndon's nose and mouth, running down his face and onto the crepe-de-chine shirt."[58]

Was Johnson overly concerned about his masculinity? Did this psychological problem make it difficult for him to extricate the United States from the Vietnam War? Another Johnson biographer, Doris Kearns, argues that Johnson wanted to make sure he "was not forced to see himself as a coward, running away from Vietnam."[59] Nonetheless, it is almost impossible to establish the precise roots of Johnson's behavior as president, and some might find connections between childhood humiliations and presidential policy decisions rather speculative. Others, however, feel that *psychobiography*—the application of psychological analysis to historical figures—has enormous potential as an approach to studying political leaders.

Whatever their roots, the personality characteristics of presidents clearly have an important effect on their success or failure in office. Richard Nixon had such an exaggerated fear of what his "enemies" might

A Difference in Character
The personalities of Calvin Coolidge and John F. Kennedy led to considerably different styles of presidential leadership. Coolidge's motto, "Let well enough alone," says much about his approach to the presidency. "Vigorous" was the term commonly used to describe Kennedy, and it's an apt description of his presidency as well. Historian Arthur Schlesinger, Jr., said of Kennedy, "His presidential life was instinct with action."

try to do to him that he created in the White House a climate that nurtured the Watergate break-in and cover-up. Franklin Roosevelt, on the other hand, was certainly aided in office by his relaxed manner and self-confidence.

Candidates don't come neatly labeled as having healthy or unhealthy presidential characters. Although voters make their own estimations of how presidents will behave in office, there is no guarantee that those evaluations will turn out to be accurate. And a candidate's character must still be weighed along with other factors, including ideology, party affiliation, and stances on specific issues.

SUMMARY

When the founding fathers met to design the government of this new nation, they had trouble shaping the office of the president. They struggled to find a balance between an office that was powerful enough to provide unified leadership but not so strong that presidents could use their powers to become tyrants or dictators. The initial conceptions of the presidency

have slowly been transformed over time, as presidents have adapted the office to meet the nation's changing needs. The trend has been to expand presidential power. Some of this expansion has come from presidential actions under claims of inherent powers. Congress has also delegated a great deal of power to the executive branch, further expanding the role of the president.

Because the president is elected by the entire

nation, he can claim to represent all citizens when proposing policy. This broad electoral base equips the presidency to be an institution of *majoritarian* democracy—compared with Congress's structural tendencies toward *pluralist* democracy. Whether the presidency actually operates in a majoritarian manner depends on several factors—the individual president's perception of public opinion on political issues, the relationship between public opinion and the president's political ideology, and the extent to which he is committed to pursuing his values through his office.

A president's success in getting his programs through Congress is related to his political skills and his power to persuade. Presidents increasingly go directly to the American people to build popular support for their legislative programs. Presidents have more political strength when their popularity is high, but popularity usually declines over time. Americans become dissatisfied with incumbents because presidents cannot please all constituencies.

The executive branch establishment has grown rapidly, and even the White House has become a sizable bureaucracy. New responsibilities of the twentieth-century presidency are particularly noticeable in the area of legislative leadership. Contemporary presidents are expected to be policy initiators for Congress, as well as chief lobbyists who guide their bills through the legislative process.

Key Terms

veto	Executive Office of the
inherent powers	President
delegation of powers	Cabinet
coalition of minorities	legislative liaison staff
electoral college	presidential character

Selected Readings

Cronin, Thomas E. *The State of the Presidency.* 2d ed. Boston: Little, Brown, 1980. An insightful and original look at the modern presidency.

Greenstein, Fred I. *The Hidden-Hand Presidency.* New York: Basic Books, 1982. Analyzes the leadership style of Dwight Eisenhower, paying particular attention to his handling of the McCarthy problem.

Kernell, Samuel. *Going Public.* Washington, D.C.: Congressional Quarterly Press, 1986. A study of how modern presidents rely more and more on direct communication with the people as a way of trying to expand their influence.

Lowi, Theodore J. *The Personal President.* Ithaca, N.Y.: Cornell University Press, 1985. In Lowi's eyes, the decline of our party system has helped give rise to a direct relationship between contemporary presidents and the people.

Nelson, Michael, ed. *The Presidency and the Political System.* 2d ed. Washington, D.C.: Congressional Quarterly Press, 1988. This collection of original essays covers a wide range of topics.

Neustadt, Richard E. *Presidential Power.* Rev. ed. New York: John Wiley, 1980. Neustadt's classic study examines the president's power to persuade.

Neustadt, Richard E., and Earnest R. May. *Thinking in Time.* New York: Free Press, 1986. Offers an analytical framework that presidents can use to try to minimize errors that lead to faulty decisions.

12

The Bureaucracy

The public knows her as Baby Jane Doe. She was born in October 1983 with a number of severe birth defects, including spina bifida (a failure of the spinal cord to close), an abnormally small head, and water on the brain. Her parents were told that with corrective surgery, she could live into her twenties but would be severely retarded, paralyzed from the waist down, and bedridden. Without surgery, her life expectancy was less than two years. After much anguish, the couple decided to forgo the surgery and let their baby face an early death.

The Reagan administration was not willing to let parents make this kind of decision on their own. It had recently set up a hot line in the U.S. Department of Health and Human Services to receive reports of hospitals' failing to protect the rights of handicapped infants. When administration officials were notified about Baby Doe, they went to court to obtain the child's medical records as a basis for deciding on further intervention.

The parents, Dan and Linda, bitterly disagreed with the administration's contention that it should be involved in deciding their child's future. In Dan's words, government officials "can't feel what we're feeling now. They can talk about life, but they can't feel what we feel for our baby."[1] To the administration, however, the question was straightforward: Who speaks for the baby alone? Its answer: The bureaucracy.

The fight over Baby Doe reversed the usual conservative and liberal roles. President Ronald Reagan's conservative administration was theoretically committed to reducing the bureaucracy's reach into everyday life, but here it tried to establish a new and highly controversial role for the bureaucracy. The conservative *Wall Street Journal* castigated the administration's efforts as the work of "medico-legal busybodies" dedicated to harassing parents and physicians.[2] The *Journal* and many liberals argued that parents must have the freedom to make these difficult decisions themselves. The administration countered with the traditional liberal argument that only a bureaucratic agency can see to it that children are treated in an equitable and fair manner. In the end, the Supreme Court sided with the parents, concluding that the law did not sanction this kind of government intervention.

The conservative-liberal role reversal, although interesting, was not the most important aspect of the Baby Doe case. At the core of the conflict was a fundamental question: To what degree should the national government use its power to promote order, in this case by protecting human life? Or, alternatively, to what degree must government respect individuals' freedom to lead their lives without interference?

In analyzing the national bureaucracy in this chapter, we focus on its potential for infringing on individual freedom in the pursuit of order and equality. We also assess the bureaucracy's contribution to democratic government according to the pluralist and majoritarian models. In addressing these broad issues, we ask—and answer—a number of related questions: How responsive is the bureaucracy to what the president wants? To what extent does the bureaucracy follow the directions of Congress in implementing the laws of the land? How are departments and agencies influenced by interest groups and ordinary citizens? In short, who controls the bureaucracy in our government?

THE DEVELOPMENT OF THE BUREAUCRATIC STATE

A nation's laws and policies are administered, or put into effect, by a variety of departments, agencies, bureaus, offices, and other government units, which together are known as its *bureaucracy*. **Bureaucracy** actually means any large complex organization in which employees have very specific job responsibilities and work within a hierarchy of authority. The employees of these government units, who are quite knowledgeable within their narrow areas, have become known somewhat derisively as **bureaucrats.**

The inevitability of bureaucracies in modern societies has not made them any less controversial. Bureaucracies make all kinds of decisions, from minor details of public policy to the fundamental nature of that policy. The basic conflict over just how far the bureaucracy should go in creating policies that promote equality of opportunity or individual freedom arises hundreds of times a day in Washington. And although Americans may hold sharply divided opinions about government's role in specific policy areas, they generally agree that government—specifically, the bureaucracy—tries to do too much.

The Growth of American Government

American government seems to have grown without limit during this century. As one observer noted wryly, "The assistant administrator for water and hazardous materials of the Environmental Protection Agency presided over a staff larger than Washington's entire first administration."[3] Yet, even during Washington's time, bureaucracies were necessary. No one argued then about the need for a postal service to deliver mail or a department of the treasury to maintain a system of currency.

Government at all levels (national, state, and local) has grown enormously. As measured by employment, most growth in recent years has taken place in state and local government, while the national work force has remained relatively stable. There are a number of major reasons why our government has grown the way it has.

Science and technology.   One reason government has grown so much is the increasing complexity of society. George Washington did not have an assistant administrator for water and hazardous materials because there was no need for one. A National Aeronautics and Space Administration (NASA) was not necessary until rockets were invented.

Even long-standing departments have had to expand the scope of their activities to keep up with technological and societal changes. Consider the changes brought about by genetic engineering, for example. The Patent Office in the U.S. Department of Commerce has had to respond to requests that new life forms be patented to protect manufacturers' interests. Under a new policy, the creators of new animals—like the geep, a species derived from the fusion of goat and sheep embryos—must receive royalties for each animal raised by a farmer.[4]

Business regulation.   Another reason government has grown is that the public's attitude toward business has changed. Throughout most of

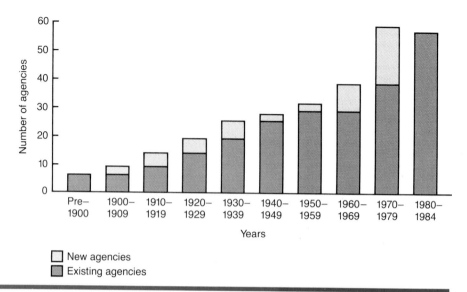

The Growth of Regulatory Agencies
The number of regulatory agencies has increased over time, as perceptions about the need for government intervention in the marketplace have changed. (Source: Center for the Study of American Business.)
Figure 12.1

the nineteenth century, there was little or no government regulation of business. Business was generally autonomous, and any government intervention in the economy that might limit that autonomy was considered inappropriate. This attitude began to change toward the end of the nineteenth century, as more Americans became aware that the end product of laissez faire was not always highly competitive markets that benefited consumers. Instead, business sometimes formed oligopolies like the infamous "sugar trust," a small group of companies that controlled virtually the entire sugar market.

Gradually, government intervention came to be accepted as necessary to protect the integrity of business markets. And if government was to effectively police unfair business practices, it needed administrative agencies. Over the course of the twentieth century, new bureaucracies were organized to regulate specific industries (see Figure 12.1). Among them are the Securities and Exchange Commission (SEC), which oversees securities trading; the Interstate Commerce Commission (ICC), which oversees surface transportation; and the Federal Communications Commission (FCC), which oversees the television, radio, and telephone industries.

Through bureaucracies like these, government has become a referee in the marketplace, developing standards of fair trade, setting rates, and licensing individual businesses for operation. As new problem areas have emerged, government has added new agencies, further expanding the scope of its activities. During the 1960s, for instance, the public became aware that certain design flaws in automobiles made them unnecessarily unsafe. For example, sharp protruding dashboard knobs caused a car's own interior to be dangerous on impact. Congress responded to public demands for change by creating the National Highway Traffic Safety Administration in 1966.* As we discuss later in this chapter, there has been significant movement in recent years toward lessening the government's role in the marketplace.

---

* It originally was called the National Safety Agency.

Social welfare.   General attitudes about government's responsibilities in the area of social welfare have changed too. An enduring part of American culture has been a belief in self-reliance. People are expected to overcome adversity on their own, to succeed on the basis of their own skills and efforts. In years past, those who could not take care of themselves had to hope that their families or primitive local programs would help them.

People in this country were slow to accept government in the role of "brother's keeper." Only in the wake of the Great Depression did the national government begin to take steps to provide income security. In 1935, the Social Security Act became law, creating the social security fund that workers pay into, then collect income from during old age. A small part of that act was a provision for impoverished families, which evolved into Aid to Families with Dependent Children (AFDC), the nation's basic welfare program.

A belief in progress.   A larger, stronger central government can also be traced to Americans' firm belief in the idea of progress. Another thread that runs through the fabric of American culture is faith in our ability to solve problems. No problem is too big or too complicated. This attitude was typified by President John F. Kennedy's commitment in 1961 to put a man on the moon by 1970. As difficult as the task seemed when he made the pledge, a man walked on the moon on July 20, 1969. This same spirit leads politicians to declare war on poverty or war on cancer

NASA in Good Times and Bad Times
For many years, NASA was a highly respected government agency, an embodiment of the "can do" spirit of America. The moon landing in 1969 fulfilled President John F. Kennedy's commitment to put a man on the moon before the decade was out. But in January 1986, the space shuttle Challenger *exploded shortly after takeoff, killing all seven crew members. The Rogers Commission, charged with investigating the tragedy, revealed serious flaws in NASA's management practices, which stained the agency's image.*

through massive programs of coordinated well-funded activities. Many people believe that the private sector cannot undertake large-scale programs, that government must be responsible for them. For example, when AIDS emerged as an epidemic, there was no question that it was the government's responsibility to solve the problem through its own research and the support of scientists outside of government.

Ambitious administrators.   Finally, government has grown because agency officials have expanded their organizations and staffs to take on added responsibilities. Imaginative, ambitious agency administrators look for ways to serve their clients. Each new program that's developed leads to new authority. And larger budgets and staffs, in turn, are necessary to support that authority. Reagan administration Secretary of Defense Caspar Weinberger and Navy Secretary John Lehman persuaded the president to support a massive build-up of the navy to a six hundred-ship fleet. Despite the criticism that we could not afford such a large navy, the commitment remained firm until Reagan's last year in office, when the new secretary of defense, Frank Carlucci, reversed course and announced that budget restraints required that some existing ships be mothballed.

Can We Reduce the Size of Government?

When Reagan campaigned in 1980, he promised to cut bureaucracies, which he said were wasteful, and to get government "off the back" of the American people. As Figure 12.2a shows, opinion that government

Doctor/Bureaucrat/ Educator
As the AIDS epidemic grew, Surgeon General C. Everett Koop headed the Reagan administration's efforts to stem the tide of the deadly disease. Under Koop's direction, the Public Health Service sent a brochure about AIDS to every home in the United States. The brochure was unusually candid for a government publication, advising the use of condoms as a means of preventing transmission.

Figure 12.2

Does Government Do Too Much or Not Nearly Enough?

National surveys show that Americans feel very differently about government as a whole than they do about specific programs. (Sources: "Opinion Roundup," Public Opinion, March-April 1987, pp. 22–24; and "Opinion Roundup," Public Opinion, November-December 1987, p. 31.)

a. Is government getting too powerful for the good of the country?

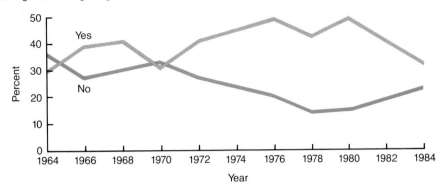

b. Does the national government create more problems than it solves?

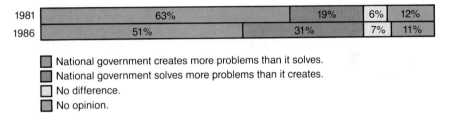

☐ National government creates more problems than it solves.
☐ National government solves more problems than it creates.
☐ No difference.
☐ No opinion.

c. Is government spending too much or too little on

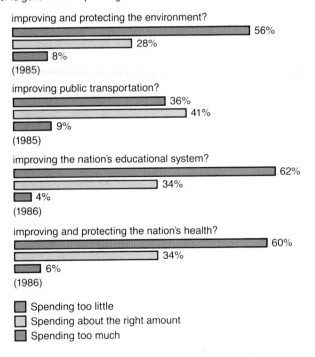

improving and protecting the environment?
56%
28%
8%
(1985)

improving public transportation?
36%
41%
9%
(1985)

improving the nation's educational system?
62%
34%
4%
(1986)

improving and protecting the nation's health?
60%
34%
6%
(1986)

☐ Spending too little
☐ Spending about the right amount
☐ Spending too much

was too powerful had grown during the previous decade. Government was also seen as causing more problems than it solved (Figure 12.2b). The public's negative attitude toward government helped Reagan win large nondefense budget cuts at the beginning of his administration, reducing the size and range of certain bureaucratic activities. In recent years public opinion has become somewhat less hostile toward big government.

Presidents and members of Congress face a tough job when they try to reduce the size of the bureaucracy. Each government agency performs a service of value to some sector of society. As a group, bankers favor laissez-faire capitalism, the principles of a free market and minimal government intervention. Few bankers voiced those principles, however, when mismanagement at Continental Illinois, one of the nation's largest banks, led it to the brink of insolvency in 1984. A run on the bank by the holders of large uninsured deposits pushed the bank toward failure. Continental's failure would have had a destabilizing impact on the entire banking system. When that failure was imminent, the Federal Reserve Board and the Federal Deposit Insurance Corporation (FDIC), two of the agencies that regulate the nation's banking industry, stepped in, put billions of dollars into the bank, and guaranteed every dollar of deposits. In this case, bankers were happy to have "big government" regulate a member of their industry out of its difficulties.[5]

Bankers are not the only group that wants to be protected by the national government. Farmers need the price supports of the U.S. Department of Agriculture. Builders profit from programs offered by the U.S. Department of Housing and Urban Development (HUD). And labor unions want a vigorous Occupational Safety and Health Administration (OSHA). Efforts to cut an agency's scope, then, are almost always resisted by interest groups that have a stake in the agency.

Despite their political support, agencies are not immune to change. It is rare for a department or agency to be completely abolished; however, it is not uncommon for one to undergo a major reorganization, in which programs are consolidated and the size and scope of activities are reduced.[6] Programs can lose support if they are perceived to be working poorly. (This is what happened with government-sponsored job training.) And as funds are cut, bureaucratic positions are eliminated.

In sum, attitudes about the size of government are somewhat paradoxical. Many believe that government is too big, that it tries to do too much, and that it intrudes too much into our daily lives. Still, substantial reductions in the scope of government activity are unusual, because individual agencies carry out programs that protect or benefit a constituency. Today, despite large budget deficits, there is substantial support for increased spending in basic areas of domestic policy (see Figure 12.2c).

This paradox is just one more manifestation of the tension between majoritarianism and pluralism. Even when the public wants a smaller national government, that sentiment can be undermined by the strong preferences of different segments of society for government to perform some valuable function for them. Lobbies that represent these segments work strenuously to convince Congress and the administration that their agency's particular part of the budget is vital and that any cuts ought to come out of some other agency's hide. At the same time, that other agency is also working to protect itself and garner support. Still, change is possible. Shifting national priorities can bring about reductions in an agency's scope.

There is one more paradox related to reducing the size of government. Whatever national priorities, the public is always concerned about eliminating waste, duplication, and corruption from bureaucracy. Stories that the Pentagon is spending hundreds of dollars apiece on custom-designed coffee makers when off-the-shelf models, available at a fraction of the cost, would work just as well enrage taxpayers, who feel that their hard-earned money is being squandered by a bloated bureaucracy. Yet seeing to it that money is spent honestly and cost-effectively demands that spending decisions be monitored. This means there must be bureaucrats whose job it is to review the work of other bureaucrats. And more bureaucrats means more government.[7]

BUREAUS AND BUREAUCRATS

We often think of the bureaucracy as a giant octopus with countless arms. In reality, the bureaucracy in Washington is a disjointed collection of departments, agencies, bureaus, offices, and commissions—each a bureaucracy in its own right.

The Organization of Government

By examining the basic types of government organizations, we can better understand how the executive branch operates. In our discussion, we pay particular attention to their relative degree of independence and their relationship to the White House.

Departments. **Departments** are the largest units of the executive branch, covering broad areas of government responsibility. As noted in the previous chapter, the secretaries (heads) of these departments, along with a few other key officials, form the president's cabinet. The current cabinet departments are State, Treasury, Defense, Interior, Agriculture, Justice, Commerce, Labor, Health and Human Services, Housing and Urban Development, Transportation, Energy, and Education. Each of these massive organizations is broken down into subsidiary agencies, bureaus, offices, and services (see Figure 12.3).

Independent agencies. Within the executive branch, there are approximately sixty **independent agencies,** agencies that are not a part of any cabinet department.[8] Instead, they stand alone and are controlled in varying degrees by the president. Some, among them the Central Intelligence Agency (CIA), are directly under the president's control. Others, like the FCC, are structured as **regulatory commissions.** Each commission is run by a small number of commissioners (usually an odd number, which helps to prevent tie votes), appointed to fixed terms by the president. Some commissions were formed to guard against unfair business practices. Others were formed to police the side effects, or *externalities,*

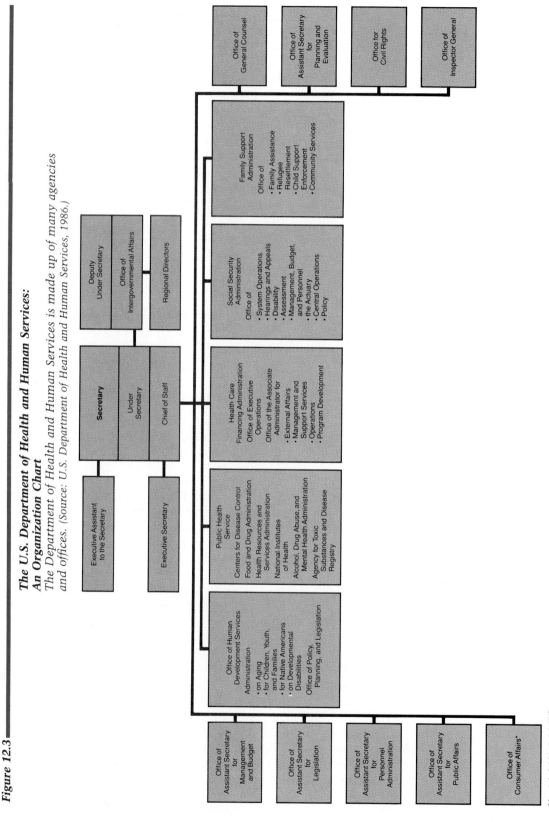

Figure 12.3

**The U.S. Department of Health and Human Services:
An Organization Chart**
*The Department of Health and Human Services is made up of many agencies
and offices. (Source: U.S. Department of Health and Human Services, 1986.)*

* Located administratively in HHS,
but reports to the president.

of business operations, such as polluted air emitted by a factory. Still others were formed to protect the public from unsafe products. Regulatory commissions are outside the direct control of the White House so that they are free from the pressures of the political process and the partisan considerations that shape it.

Still, regulatory commissions are not immune to political pressure. They are lobbied fervently by client groups and must take those groups' demands into account when they make policy. If the Consumer Product Safety Commission is considering safety standards for chain saws, for example, the chain saw industry will do all it can to convince the agency not to set standards or to issue them in a form the industry considers least objectionable.

The president exerts influence on these agencies through his power to appoint new commissioners when terms expire or when resignations create openings. During President Jimmy Carter's administration, his appointed chairman of the Federal Trade Commission (FTC), Michael Pertschuk, led a vigorous proconsumer commission. During the Reagan administration, however, things changed. Reagan's appointed chairman, free-market economist James Miller, gave the Reagan forces a numerical advantage on the five-member board. Under Miller's leadership, the FTC reversed its policy of industry-wide checks for false advertising in favor of investigations in response to specific complaints filed with the agency. From the viewpoint of consumer advocates, this reversal meant that the FTC would be less aggressive in protecting Americans from false advertising. From the standpoint of business, it meant that the FTC would stop its "fishing expeditions."[9] Whatever the point of view, it's clear that a significant policy shift occurred as a direct result of presidential power.

Government corporations. Finally, Congress has also created a small number of **government corporations**. The services these executive branch agencies perform theoretically could be provided by the private sector, but Congress has decided that the public would be better served if they have some link with the government. For example, the national government maintains a postal service because it feels that Americans need low-cost, door-to-door service for all kinds of mail, not just for mail on profitable routes or mail that requires special services.

In some instances, there is not enough of a financial incentive for the private sector to provide an essential service. This is the case with the financially troubled Amtrak train line.[10]

The Civil Service

The national bureaucracy is staffed by around 3 million civilian employees, who account for less than 3 percent of the U.S. work force. Americans have a tendency to stereotype all government workers as faceless paper pushers, but the work force is actually quite diverse. Government workers include forest rangers, FBI agents, typists, foreign service officers, computer programmers, policy analysts, public relations specialists, security guards, librarians, administrators, engineers, plumbers, and people from literally hundreds of other occupations.

Eye on the Storm
We may think we depend on the blow-dried, impeccably dressed announcer on Channel 4 for tomorrow's forecast, but basic meteorological information is gathered and analyzed by bureaucrats. This government meteorologist is tracking a hurricane off the Gulf Coast.

An important feature of the national bureaucracy is that most of its workers are hired under the requirements of the **civil service**. The civil service was created after the assassination of President James Garfield, who was killed by an unbalanced and dejected job seeker. Congress responded by passing the Pendleton Act (1883), which established the Civil Service Commission (now the Office of Personnel Management). The act's objective was to reduce *patronage*—the practice of filling government positions with the president's political allies or cronies. The civil service fills jobs on the basis of merit and sees to it that workers are not fired for political reasons. Over the years, job qualifications and selection procedures have been developed for most government positions.

About 88 percent of the national government's workers are employed outside of Washington.[11] One reason for this decentralization is to make government offices accessible to the people they serve. The Social Security Administration, for example, has to have offices within a reasonable distance of most Americans, so that its many clients have somewhere to take their questions, problems, and paperwork. Decentralization is also a way to distribute jobs and income across the country. The government's Centers for Disease Control could easily have been located in Washington, but it is in Atlanta instead. Likewise, NASA's headquarters for space flights is located in Houston. Members of Congress, of course, are only too happy to place some of the "pork barrel" back home, so that their constituents will credit them with the jobs and money that government installations create.

Given the enormous variety of government jobs, it is no surprise that employees come from all walks of life. Studies of the social composition of the civil service as a whole indicate that it mirrors the American population on such important characteristics as father's occupation and worker's education, income, and age.[12] There is also substantial representation of minorities (26 percent) and women (48 percent) within the national work force.[13] However, in higher-level policymaking positions, the work force is skewed sharply toward those born into families of higher socioeconomic status and white males.

Presidential Control over the Bureaucracy

Civil service and other reforms have effectively insulated the vast majority of government workers from party politics. An incoming president can appoint fewer than 1 percent of all executive branch employees. Still, presidential appointees fill the top policymaking positions in government. Each new president, then, establishes an extensive personnel review process to find appointees who are both ideologically compatible and qualified in their field. Although the president selects some people from his campaign staff, most of his political appointees have not been campaign workers. Instead, his cabinet secretaries, assistant secretaries, agency heads, and the like tend to be drawn directly from business, universities, and government itself. Only two of the eleven members of President Richard Nixon's last cabinet had extensive political experience before their appointment. Only three of Carter's original cabinet members could be described as "ambassadors from interest group constituencies," and five had Ph.D.s.[14]

Because so few of their own people are in each department and agency, presidents often believe that they do not have enough control over the bureaucracy. Recent Republican presidents have also worried that the civil service would be hostile to their objectives because they assumed that career bureaucrats have a liberal Democratic bias.[15] Yet surveys of political appointees show that both Democratic and Republican appointees work well with career bureaucrats, developing a healthy respect for their ability and professionalism.[16]

Many presidents have felt frustrated by their inability to get the bureaucracy to change course. President Kennedy echoed this sentiment when he complained that the State Department was a "bowl of jelly" and that giving an instruction to State was like putting it in a dead letter box.[17] A reform frequently offered as a remedy for this complaint is giving the president more positions to fill with loyalists instead of senior civil servants.

On the surface, it makes sense that increasing the number of political appointees in the bureaucracy will make the bureaucracy more responsive to the president. But caution is warranted here. More political appointees may actually make the bureaucracy more "bureaucratic." As one scholar noted, "The more layers, the more time it takes to forge positive relationships" between senior civil servants and presidential appointees.[18]

The general tendency in recent years has been toward greater presidential control over the bureaucracy, but there is legitimate concern about the presidency becoming too powerful. (During the 1970s, these worries led Congress to pass some important reforms aimed at restraining the executive.) And despite the presidents' frustrations with the bureaucracy, they are hardly helpless, pitiful giants. As the example of the FTC's change in leadership shows, presidential appointees can have a substantial impact on their agencies. Recent research also shows that presidential appointees are very influential in bringing new issues onto the political agenda, whereas civil servants have comparatively little impact.[19]

But the question remains: Should there be more political appointments in the national government, so that presidents can make the bureaucracy more responsive to their thinking? Those who answer in the affirmative argue that presidents might be able to fulfill more of their campaign promises if they had greater control over the bureaucracy. But others point out the value of a stable experienced work force that implements policy in a consistent fashion.

POLICYMAKING: THE FORMAL PROCESS

The sprawling diversity of the executive branch leaves many Americans with the impression that the national government's bureaucracies are complex, impenetrable organizations. Bureaucratic actions and policies often appear irrational to ordinary citizens, who know little about how government officials reach their decisions. Many Americans wonder why agencies sometimes actually *make* policy rather than merely carry it out. Administrative agencies are, in fact, authoritative policymaking bodies, and their decisions on substantive issues are legally binding on the citizens of this country.

Administrative Discretion

What are executive agencies set up to do? First, Cabinet departments, independent agencies, and government corporations are creatures of Congress. Congress creates a new department or agency by passing a law that describes each organization's *mandate*, or mission. As part of that mandate, Congress grants to the agency the authority to make certain policy decisions. Congress long ago recognized that it has neither the time nor the expertise in highly technical areas to make all policy decisions. Ideally, it sets general guidelines for policy, and agencies are expected to act within those guidelines. The latitude that Congress gives agencies to make policy in the spirit of their legislative mandate is called **administrative discretion**.

The U.S. Department of Transportation has used its discretionary policymaking authority to address the problem of alcohol and drug abuse by train engineers. A departmental study showed that during an eight-year period, alcohol- or drug-impaired judgment caused a minimum of forty-five train accidents resulting in thirty-four fatalities. In response, the Transportation Department set forth policies that not only ban alcohol and drug use on the job but also require pre-employment drug screening, permit spot checks of employees for drugs, and allow workers to seek treatment without fear of losing their jobs.[20]

Critics of bureaucracy frequently complain that agencies are granted too much discretion. In his book *The End of Liberalism*, Theodore Lowi argues that Congress commonly gives vague directives in its initial enabling legislation, instead of truly setting guidelines.[21] Agencies are charged with protecting the "public interest" but are left to determine on their own what policies best serve the public. Lowi and other critics believe that members of Congress assign too much of their responsibility for difficult policy choices to appointed administrators.

Congress *is* often vague about its intent when setting up a new agency or program. At times a problem is clear-cut, but the solution is not; yet Congress is under pressure to act. So it creates an agency or program to show that it is concerned and responsive, and leaves it to administrators to eventually develop specific solutions. For example, the enabling legislation in 1934 that established the FCC recognized a need for regulation in the burgeoning radio industry. The growing number of stations and overlapping frequencies would soon have made it impossible to listen to the radio. But Congress avoided tackling several sticky issues by leaving the FCC with the ambiguous directive that broadcasters should "serve the public interest, convenience, and necessity."[22] In other cases, a number of "obvious" solutions to a problem may be available, but lawmakers cannot agree on which one is best. One compromise is to set deliberately ambiguous guidelines for the agency created to solve the problem. Its administrators are then saddled with the responsibility for turning ambiguities into specific policy decisions.[23]

The wide latitude Congress gives bureaucratic agencies often leads to charges that government is out of control, a power unto itself. But these claims are frequently exaggerated.[24] Administrative discretion is not a fixed commodity. Congress does have the power to express its displeasure by reining agencies in with additional legislation. If Congress is unhappy with an agency's actions, it can pass laws invalidating specific policies. This method of control may seem cumbersome, but Congress does have periodic opportunities to amend the original legislation that created an agency or program. Over time, Congress makes increasingly detailed policy decisions, often affirming or modifying agency decisions.[25]

Informal contacts with members of Congress also influence administrators. Through these communications, legislators can clarify exactly which actions they want administrators to take. And administrators listen because they are wary of offending members of the committees and subcommittees that oversee their programs and, particularly, their budgets. Contacts with legislators also let administrators explain the problems their agencies are facing, justify their decisions, and negotiate compromises on unresolved issues.

In general, then, the bureaucracy is not out of control. But there is one area in which Congress has chosen to limit its oversight—that of domestic and international security. Both the FBI and CIA have had a great deal of freedom from formal and informal congressional constraints because of the legitimate need for secrecy in their operations. During the period that J. Edgar Hoover ran the FBI (1924–1972), it was something of a rogue elephant, independent of both Congress and presidents. Politicians were afraid of Hoover, who was not above keeping files on them and using those files to increase his power. At Hoover's direction, the FBI spied on Martin Luther King, Jr., and once sent King a tape recording

The Man with the Secrets
Even presidents were afraid of what FBI Director J. Edgar Hoover had in his files. The Nixon administration wasn't fond of Hoover, but Hoover let it know that if its criticism of his agency didn't stop, he would testify before Congress about some wiretapping done by a secret White House investigation unit. Hoover remained secure in his job. The White House wiretapping was later revealed as part of the Watergate scandal.

with embarrassing revelations gathered from bugging his hotel rooms. The anonymous letter accompanying the tape suggested that King save himself further embarrassment by committing suicide.[26] Over the years, the CIA has also abused its need for privacy by engaging in covert operations that should never have been carried out (see Feature 12.1).

Rule Making

The policymaking discretion that Congress gives to agencies is exercised through formal administrative procedures, usually either *rule making* or *adjudication*. **Rule making** is the administrative process that results in regulations. **Regulations,** in turn, are rules that govern the operation of government programs. In administering the Clean Air Act, for example, the Environmental Protection Agency (EPA) has had to formulate regulations specifying the permissible amounts of pollutants that factories can emit. These highly technical regulations have had a major impact on industry, forcing corporations to spend millions of dollars to reduce their plants' emissions.

Because they are authorized by congressional statutes, regulations have the effect of law. In theory, the policy content of regulations follows from the intent of enabling legislation. As we've already noted, however, Congress does not always express its intent clearly. The administrative discretion available to agencies often produces political conflict when regulations are in the process of being made. One such case involved the

FEATURE 12.1

Casey's CIA: Out of Control

In 1984, CIA Director William J. Casey decided that the United States had to do the unthinkable: assassinate Middle Eastern terrorists before they could harm Americans. Although President Reagan told Casey to clear his plan with a small group of congressional leaders, Casey set up the plan to avoid congressional oversight. He persuaded the Saudi Arabian government to fund and to take operational control of the covert operations, enabling Casey to deny to Congress that the CIA had anything to do with any assassinations that took place.

The first covert operation was the assassination of a terrorist named Sheikh Fadlallah. Fadlallah was head of Hizbollah, the Party of God, which had been connected with bombings of American facilities in Beirut. The Saudis hired an Englishman who had experience with the British Special Air Services, a commando unit, to take control of the operation. The Lebanese government's intelligence service provided him with men to drive a car packed with explosives to Fadlallah's home in a Beirut suburb. The mission was botched. On March 8, 1985, the car was left 50 yards from Fadlallah's residence. He wasn't hurt by the massive explosion, but eighty innocent people were killed and two hundred others were wounded. Fadlallah's followers assumed that the bomb was sent by the CIA, but Congress had no evidence one way or the other because, as Casey's biographer noted, "Casey had flatly refused to tell the committees about this sensitive work."

Source: Adapted from Bob Woodward, *Veil* (New York: Simon & Schuster, 1987), pp. 393–397. Copyright © 1987 by Robert Woodward. Reprinted by permission of Simon & Schuster, Inc.

Process initiated by:

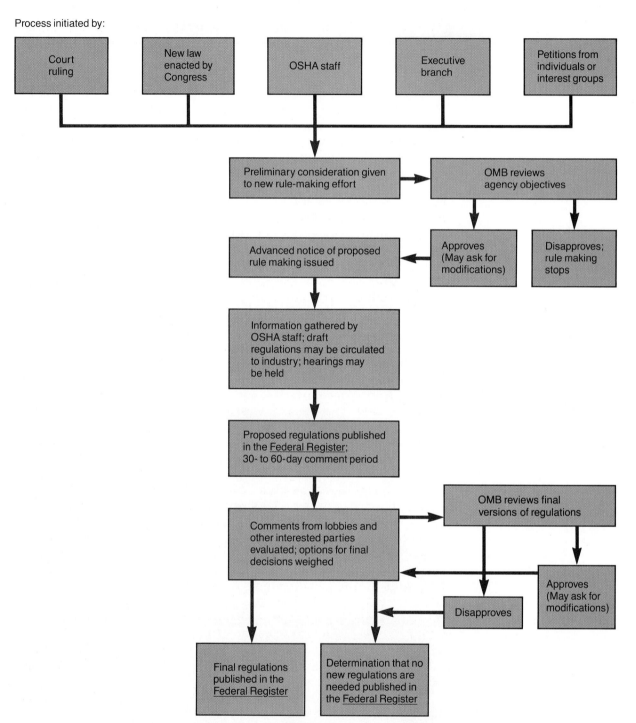

OSHA Writes a Regulation
The process of writing a federal regulation is long and complex. This flow chart shows the typical route the Occupational Safety and Health Administration (OSHA) follows in writing a regulation, although there are variations on this basic scheme. (Source: Adapted from OSHA Factsheet, 87-14. *Information on the role of the OMB comes from Margaret E. Kriz, "Kibbitzer with Clout,"* National Journal, *30 May 1987, pp. 1404–1408; and Steven Kelman,* Making Public Policy *[New York: Basic Books, 1987], pp. 95–96.)*

Figure 12.4

FTC's use of its general rule-making authority to regulate the funeral industry. The FTC began an investigation of the industry in 1972, acting on complaints from people who felt they had been taken advantage of during the emotional process of arranging a relative's funeral. After extensive research and numerous public hearings, a final version of the regulations was published in 1979. The rules required funeral homes to have itemized price lists and to quote prices over the phone. The National Funeral Directors Association and others in the industry launched a strong counterattack that resulted in Congress's suspending the rules to allow further analysis of them. (One member of Congress criticized the rules, claiming that once again government interference was hurting the productivity of an industry.) When the revised regulations were issued, a congressional effort to overturn them failed. After a court challenge by the industry also failed, they went into effect in 1984.[27]

The steps in the rule-making process are set by the Administrative Procedure Act, first passed in 1946 and amended many times since. The act was meant to ensure that regulations are developed in an open, systematic manner, with a mechanism to let all affected parties voice their opinions. Rule making begins when administrators feel that a *general* rule is needed to govern some aspect of a program (see Figure 12.4). Before the process starts in earnest, the Office of Management and Budget (OMB) reviews the agency's rule-making objectives to see that they are in line with those of the White House. (Independent agencies are exempt from this review.)[28] After public notice is given of the rule-making effort, the agency studies the alternatives, analyzing the likely impact of each one. A draft regulation may be circulated within the affected industry, and hearings may be held to gather information from industry representatives and outside experts. The next step is for the proposed regulation to appear in the *Federal Register*. This government document is published daily and contains each newly proposed or final regulation of departments and agencies. (This collection of "legalese" has been described as "arguably the most excruciatingly boring periodical published in this country.")[29] Now the public has the opportunity to comment on the proposed regulation by writing letters to the agency. Administrators evaluate these comments (many of which come from interest groups) along with congressional opinion, consulting with administration officials if necessary. When they have reviewed the comments, administrators decide whether any changes should be made. OMB reviews the final draft and has the power to force the agency to make changes or even to veto the regulation if it is contrary to administration policy. Only then is the final regulation (or the fact that no new regulation is being issued) published in the *Federal Register*.

The regulatory process is controversial because regulations require individuals and corporations to act in prescribed ways, often against their own self-interest. Steel companies, for example, would certainly prefer to make their own decisions about how much, if anything, they should spend to reduce pollution. Government, however, must balance society's need for clean air with the steel companies' needs to make a profit and to compete effectively against foreign companies. When the EPA writes regulations that specify the details of that balance, it becomes the object of criticism from both those who would like government to do more and those who would like it to do less. The EPA is in many ways taking the "heat" for Congress, because Congress has the ultimate responsibility for pollution policy—a responsibility it has delegated in part to the EPA.

Adjudication

Rule making is a quasi-legislative process because it develops *general* rules, just as Congress does when it passes a law. **Adjudication** is a quasi-judicial process; it is used to resolve *individual* conflicts, much as trials are used in a court of law. Adjudicatory proceedings in an agency determine whether a person or business is failing to comply with the law or with agency rules.

Congress delegates adjudicatory authority to certain agencies because it anticipates conflicts over the interpretation of laws and regulations and because it does not have the time to settle all the fine points of law when it writes statutes. The National Labor Relations Board (NLRB), which acts as a mediator in business-labor disputes, is an example of an agency that relies heavily on adjudication.

Adjudicatory decisions are made by administrative law judges, who are technically their agencies' employees. Yet they are strictly independent; they cannot be removed except for gross misconduct. Adjudicatory proceedings allow each party to present its side of the case and allow the judge to search for any information that will be helpful in reaching a decision. Somewhat less formal than a court trial, the proceedings are still adversarial in nature. In NLRB cases, the party that loses may appeal to the five-member board, which has set up five three-member panels to review decisions.[30]

POLICYMAKING: INFORMAL POLITICS

The formal procedures used in rule making are only part of the policy-making process. When a new regulation is being considered and the evidence and arguments on all sides have been presented, how does an administrator reach a decision? Few important policy decisions can be calculated with the efficiency of a computer. Instead, policy decisions emerge from people's weighing and judging complex problems that often have no single satisfactory solution.

The Science of Muddling Through

Administrative decisions are subject to many influences and constraints. In a classic analysis of policymaking, "The Science of Muddling Through," Charles Lindblom compared the way policy ideally should be made with the way it is formulated in the real world.[31] Lindblom described the ideal "rational" decision-making process. It begins with an administrator's tackling a problem by ranking values and objectives. After those objectives are clarified, all possible solutions to the problem are given thorough consideration. Alternative solutions are analyzed comprehensively, taking all relevant factors into account. The final choice is the most effective means of achieving the desired goal and solving the problem.

Lindblom claimed that this "rational-comprehensive" model is unrealistic. To begin with, policymakers have great difficulty defining precise values and goals. Administrators at the U.S. Department of Energy, for example, want to be sure that supplies of home heating oil are sufficient each winter. At the same time, they want to reduce dependence on foreign oil. Obviously, these two goals are not fully compatible. How do administrators decide which is more important? And how do they relate them to the other goals of the nation's energy policy?

Real-world decision making parts company with the ideal in another way: The policy selected cannot always be the most effective means to the desired end. Even if a tax at the pump is the most effective way of reducing gasoline consumption during a shortage, motorists' anger would make this theoretically "right" decision politically difficult. So the "best" policy is often the one on which most people can agree. But political compromise may mean that the government is able to solve only part of a problem.

A final point critics of the rational-comprehensive model raise is that policymaking can never be based on truly comprehensive analysis. A secretary of energy could not possibly find the time to read a comprehensive study of all alternative energy sources and relevant policy considerations for the next two decades. A truly thorough investigation of the subject would produce thousands of pages of text. Instead, the secretary of energy usually relies on short staff memos outlining a limited range of feasible solutions for immediate problems. Time is of the essence, and problems often are too pressing to wait for a complete study.

In short, policymaking tends to be *incremental*, with policies and programs changing bit by bit, step by step. Decision makers are constrained by competing policy objectives, opposing political forces, incomplete information, and the pressures of time. They choose from a limited number of feasible options that are almost always modifications of existing policies rather than wholesale departures from those policies.

The Culture of Bureaucracy

How an organization makes decisions and performs its tasks is greatly affected by the people who work there—the bureaucrats. Americans often find that their interactions with bureaucrats are frustrating because bureaucrats are inflexible ("go by the book") or lack the authority to get things done. Top administrators can also become frustrated with the bureaucrats who work for them.

Why do people act "bureaucratically"? Individuals who work for large organizations cannot help but be affected by the "culture of bureaucracy," even in their everyday speech (see Feature 12.2). Modern bureaucracies develop explicit rules and standards in order to make operations more efficient and treat their clients fairly. But within each organization, *norms* (informal, unwritten rules of behavior) also develop and influence the way people act on the job. The Veterans Administration (VA), for example, for many years had an official rule that medical care

FEATURE 12.2

English as a Foreign Language

One of the most irritating characteristics of the bureaucrat is a tendency to use *jargon*, a specialized vocabulary peculiar to an occupation. (A less-than-kind definition would be "gibberish.") In the language of bureaucracy, a simple sentence, say "Based on the evidence, we decided to close the Denver office," might become "A determination was made from the decision matrix that the relevant output variables indicated that a termination of the department's regional office at Denver was necessitated at this time."

Why does jargon rear its ugly head in the bureaucracy? One reason is that some people assume that jargon is a sign of professionalism, that using specialized terms reflects a command of the subject. Another reason is that many bureaucrats receive graduate training in the social sciences, where jargon breeds and multiplies. They then bring to government all the specialized vocabulary of political science, sociology, and economics.

But the principal reason why jargon is replacing English in the bureaucracy may be a lack of writing skills. It's much easier to write several long, complex, jargon-laden sentences than it is to write one that is short and crystal clear.

If you're thinking about entering government, take the following "aptitude" test. How many of these words in "bureaucratese" can you define? (The answers appear below.)

1. Parameters
2. Interdigitate
3. Prioritize
4. GIGO
5. Interface
6. Formatting
7. Proactive
8. Window of opportunity
9. Highly scenario-dependent
10. Career deceleration

Answers

1. Boundaries 2. Work together 3. Rank 4. Garbage in, garbage out. (In other words, if the data you put into the computer are worthless, then so are the results.) 5. See *interdigitate*. 6. Designing 7. Opposite of reactive 8. The time is ripe. 9. It all depends. 10. You're fired.

was to be provided only to veterans in need of hospitalization; more routine treatment was to be left to private physicians. Doctors working for the VA thought this rule was irrational, and among them a norm developed whereby they would provide routine care under the guise that it was needed before hospital admission.[32]

Bureaucracies are often influenced in their selection of policy options by the prevailing customs, attitudes, and expectations of the people working within them. Departments and agencies commonly develop a sense of mission where a particular objective or a means for achieving it is emphasized. The Army Corps of Engineers is dominated by engineers who define the bureaucracy's objective as protecting citizens from floods by means of building dams. Certainly there could be other objectives, and certainly there are other methods of achieving this one, but the engineers promote the solutions that fit their conception of what the agency should be doing. As one study concluded, "When asked to generate policy proposals for review by their political superiors, bureaucrats are tempted to bias the search for alternatives so that their superiors wind up selecting the kind of program the agency wants to pursue."[33]

At first glance, bureaucrats seem to be completely negative sorts of creatures. They do have their positive side, however. Those agencies with a clear sense of mission are likely to have a strong esprit de corps that adds to the bureaucrats' motivation. Also, bureaucrats' caution and close adherence to agency rules offer a measure of consistency. It would be unsettling if government employees interpreted rules as they pleased. Simply put, bureaucrats "go by the book" because the "book" is composed of the laws and regulations of this country, as well as the internal rules and norms of a particular agency. Americans expect to be treated equally before the law, and bureaucrats work with that expectation in mind.

PROBLEMS IN IMPLEMENTING POLICY

The development of policy in Washington is the end of one part of the policymaking cycle but the beginning of another. After policies have been developed, they must be implemented. **Implementation** is the process of putting specific policies into operation. Ultimately, bureaucrats must convert policies on paper into policies in action. For example, the Social Security Administration could issue a new set of rules designed to get people who are receiving disability payments to return to work when they are physically able. But no set of regulations can possibly anticipate all injuries suffered on the job. And medical opinion on even a single case can differ. How much can be left to the discretion of social security bureaucrats in local offices? What if they make a mistake and take benefits away from people who really cannot work?

It is important to study implementation because policies do not always do what they were designed to do. Some of the most persistent problems in implementation stem from vague directives, faulty coordination, decentralized authority, and imprecise evaluation of success.

Vague Directives

It is difficult to implement a policy when that policy is not clearly stated. Policy directives to bureaucrats in the field sometimes lack clarity and leave lower-level officials with too much discretion. The source of vague regulations is often vague legislation. Congress, for example, included in the Elementary and Secondary School Act (1965) a program of grants to meet the "special needs of educationally deprived children." But the act did not spell out who qualified as educationally deprived. The administering agency, the U.S. Office of Education, passed the money on to the states without specific eligibility criteria. As a result, the money was spent for a variety of purposes, not all of which were beneficial to deprived children.[34]

Vague directives are a particular problem at the time a program is first put into operation. Knowing that this problem exists, however, and finding the best way to solve it are two different things.

Faulty Coordination

Programs frequently cut across the jurisdictions of a number of agencies. At times these programs are not implemented effectively because the agencies involved have trouble coordinating their efforts. An economic development program in Oakland, California, lagged badly because many agencies had jurisdiction over various parts of the project. One study found that during a seven-year period, there were thirty different stages at which decisions had to be made, requiring seventy agreements among various bureaucracies.[35]

A turf war can break out when different agencies begin competing for leadership in a policy area. The fight against illegal drugs, for example, has been hampered by bickering over leadership and jurisdiction between the Drug Enforcement Agency and the Customs Service.[36]

Decentralized Authority

A problem related to faulty coordination is the dispersal of authority in our federal system. Even when the objectives of the national government are clear-cut, they can be undermined by the authority of state and local governments. Sometimes the decentralization of authority within the national government itself can be a problem. Implementation of the Surface Mining Control and Reclamation Act was impeded by differences between the Office of Surface Mining (OSM) and its regional offices around the country. Individual coal firms reached what they thought was an agreement with OSM in Washington only to have it disregarded by regional offices. The regional offices did have the authority to apply the law in their area, but OSM in Washington clearly had its own ideas as to how it wanted the law implemented. The political conflict that ensued led to changes that diminished the role of the regional offices.[37]

Decentralization does not always lead to conflict and confusion, but it usually means a tradeoff is inevitable. Decentralization is a way of tapping local imagination and initiative. But there is a risk involved: Local, state, or regional administrators may not pursue the policies that were originally envisioned by the program's designers, and squabbling among different administrative levels can reduce a program's effectiveness.

Imprecise Evaluation of Success

Sometimes a program's implementation is hampered because there is no reliable way to measure its success. If a program's effectiveness cannot be measured accurately, policymakers are operating in the dark. They do not have the necessary information to judge whether a policy is working well, needs modification, or should be scrapped altogether.

An interesting example of how important accurate evaluation is and how difficult it is to obtain comes from the Head Start program. Head Start, which was begun in the 1960s, was designed to help low-income and minority students do better in school. These students were placed in preschool enrichment programs, with the hope that this "head start" would help them do as well as those from more privileged backgrounds. The initial results were disappointing. Children who had been in Head Start programs did not do appreciably better in school than similarly deprived children who had not been in the program. Obviously, this weakened political support for Head Start; there seemed to be little justification for spending money on a program that wasn't working. Yet longer-term studies now show that preschool enrichment programs *can* have positive effects on school performance.[38]

Although obstacles to effective implementation create the impression that nothing succeeds, programs can and do work. Problems in the implementation process demonstrate why time, patience, and continual analysis are necessary ingredients of successful policymaking. To return to a term we used earlier, implementation is by its nature an *incremental* process, in which trial and error eventually lead to policies that work.

REFORMING THE BUREAUCRACY

American citizens do not hesitate to criticize the bureaucracy. They complain that it is too big, too intrusive, too costly, too inefficient, and too unresponsive. Presidents, members of Congress, and agency administrators are constantly trying to come up with reforms that address these complaints. In recent years, reform efforts have included reorganization, deregulation, citizen participation programs, and analytical budgeting.

Reorganization

One of the most common ways to try to improve bureaucratic performance is **reorganization.** For instance, two or three bureaus in a department might be combined to reduce overlap. Or responsibility for running a program might be taken from one agency and given to another that runs programs in the same general area. When departments or agencies are reorganized, administrators sometimes find ways of improving the delivery of services, saving money, or both. Typically, though, these improvements and savings are not as significant as proponents claim.[39]

Reorganization lets the government adapt to new problems, responsibilities, and priorities. In the wake of the stock market crash in October 1987, a presidential task force that investigated its causes concluded that one of the problems was that regulation of financial markets was fragmented, distributed among a number of different agencies. The task force said that there was a failure to realize that the different financial markets were really tied together into one central market. With this diagnosis in mind, it proposed centralizing responsibility for stock, options, and futures markets in the Federal Reserve Board.[40]

Interest groups and members of Congress who are trying to protect valued programs often oppose administrative reorganization. In addition, bureaucrats themselves can be a formidable obstacle. For example, the Pentagon has made periodic efforts to centralize such management functions as purchasing, in order to save money by eliminating overlapping jobs and by standardizing equipment. But interservice rivalries among the army, navy, and air force consistently hamper these efforts. Civilian bureaucrats in the Pentagon even failed at one point to get all the branches of the service to adopt a common belt buckle for uniforms. Although the escalating cost of high-technology weapons systems has renewed pressure for reorganization within the Pentagon, a major breakthrough has yet to come about.[41]

A Bull Market in Stock Market Studies
The 1987 stock market crash spawned no less than four major studies. A presidential task force chaired by Nicholas Brady (shown here), a Wall Street executive and former senator, recommended a sweeping reorganization of the regulation of financial markets. The White House then created a new group to study the study and formulate legislative proposals. This group backed away from sweeping change and suggested only modest adjustments in market regulation.

Deregulation

Many people believe that government is too involved in **regulation,** intervention in the natural workings of business markets to promote some social goal. For example, government might regulate a market to ensure that products pose no danger to consumers. Through **deregulation** the government reduces its role and lets the natural market forces of supply and demand take over. Indeed, nothing is more central to capitalist philosophy than the belief that the free market will efficiently promote the balance of supply and demand. Some important movement toward deregulation has taken place recently, notably in the airline, trucking, financial services, and telecommunications industries.[42]

In the case of the airlines, the Civil Aeronautics Board (CAB) had been determining fares and controlling access to routes. The justification for these regulatory efforts was that they would prevent overloads, both in the sky and at airport facilities, and would ensure some service to all parts of the nation. But regulation had a side effect: It reduced competition among the airlines, and that worked to the disadvantage of consumers. Congress responded by passing a law in 1978 mandating deregulation of fares and routes, and the airlines became more competitive. New carriers entered lucrative markets, fares dropped, and price wars broke out. In smaller cities, which major carriers no longer had to serve, commuter airlines offered essential services. In retrospect, it is clear that government was overregulating the airline industry. Yet the perception that the quality of air travel has declined in terms of such factors as on-

Fly the Unfriendly Skies
With the deregulation of the airline industry, increased traffic on many routes has tested the capacity of the Federal Aviation Administration to ensure safety in the air. Air traffic controllers form the front line of the FAA's safety efforts. The responsibility of their job and the acute concentration it requires make their work extremely stressful.

time performance leads some observers to conclude that deregulation has gone too far.

The question of how much regulation (or deregulation) is enough leads to a larger question about the role of the national government (and therefore the bureaucracy) in American society. Conservatives tend to believe that government regulation of business should be minimal, giving both consumers and producers as much personal freedom as possible. Liberals, however, believe the free market does not protect citizens adequately from unfair or dangerous business practices.

What about the bureaucrats themselves? What do they think about regulation? Compared With What? 12.1 describes the attitudes of politicians and bureaucrats in six countries on the "preferred degree of state involvement in the economy and society."

The regulation of prescription drugs by the Food and Drug Administration (FDA) is another illustration of how difficult it can be to decide where to draw the line between regulation and the free market. To promote safety, the FDA requires thorough testing of new prescription drugs before they can be sold to consumers. But while the years of testing drag on, a drug that could reduce suffering may be kept out of the hands of sick people. Drug manufacturers argue that the FDA should speed up its testing and approval process, to get new drugs out to those who need them. (Not insignificantly, earlier approval would also allow drug companies to begin recouping their investments in research and development earlier.)

The other side of the coin is that faster licensing of drugs can be

COMPARED WITH WHAT? 12.1

Bureaucrats' and Politicians' Attitudes Toward State Involvement

In all the countries surveyed, bureaucrats were more likely than politicians to occupy the middle position, favoring the "present balance." But U.S. bureaucrats were more likely than those in other countries to favor "much more" state involvement. Some readers might interpret this difference as conclusive proof of a liberal bias within the national bureaucracy. Others might explain the difference by noting that *all* of the other countries already experience a great deal more state involvement than we do in the United States, leaving bureaucrats in other countries more satisfied with the status quo.

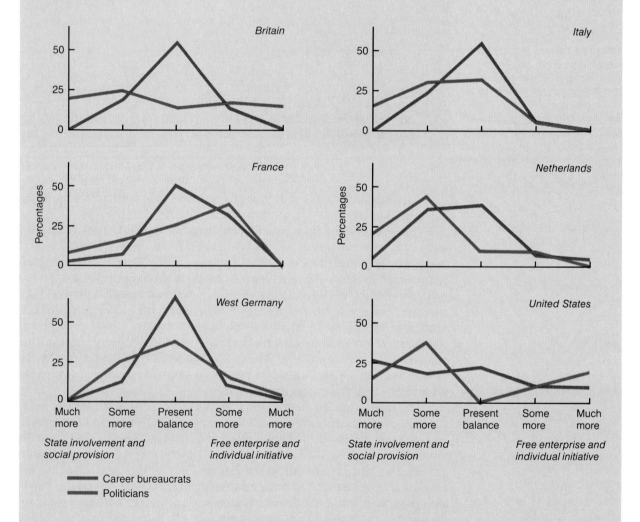

Source: Adapted from Figure 5-1 in Joel D. Aberbach, Robert D. Putnam, and Bert A. Rockman, *Bureaucrats and Politicians in Western Democracies* (Cambridge, Mass.: Harvard University Press, 1981), p. 122.

dangerous. The harmful side effects of drugs may not come to light for years; in the intervening period, unforeseen effects can cause serious harm to users. Never far from the minds of congressional and agency officials who would have to take responsibility for deregulation is the thalidomide case. The William S. Merrill Company purchased the license to market this drug, already available in Europe, and filed an application with the FDA in 1960. The company then began a protracted fight with FDA bureaucrat Dr. Frances Kelsey, who was assigned to evaluate the thalidomide application. She demanded that the company abide by all FDA drug-testing requirements, despite the fact that the drug was already in use in other countries. She and her superiors resisted pressure from the company to bend the rules a little and expedite approval. Before Merrill had conducted all the FDA tests, news came pouring in from Europe that some women who had taken thalidomide during pregnancy were giving birth to babies without arms, legs, or ears. Strict adherence to government regulation protected Americans from the same tragic consequences.

Citizen Participation Programs

A very different kind of reform effort centers on citizen participation. **Citizen participation programs** encourage interaction between bureaucrats and their clients. For example, before Community Development Block Grant (CDBG) funds can be used in a local area, the national government requires a hearing to let citizens comment on the proposals. Ideally, citizen input then becomes an important factor in the decision making of bureaucrats administering the CDBG funds.

Citizen participation programs arose out of a belief that bureaucracies are too far removed from the people they serve. Their objective was to get policymakers to fashion policies that are more in line with what citizens really want and to make citizens feel more confident about the governmental process because they have participated in it. The citizen participation movement was set in motion by President Lyndon B. Johnson's War on Poverty. The Economic Opportunity Act (1964) stated that poverty program administrators should include "maximum feasible participation" by the poor in their policymaking deliberations. In the following ten years, more than 150 new citizen participation programs were started.

The programs themselves have had mixed results, and many are best described as "rituals."[43] Often citizens express their views at hearings held mainly for show, and their substantive influence is small. Because bureaucrats have not been eager to share their power with citizen groups, many comply with the letter—but not the spirit—of the programs.

There are citizen participation programs that have worked well in the past, but these programs were diminished in importance when Reagan was elected. To his administration, they represented the views of liberal environmentalists and consumers. As a result, the administration placed little value on them.[44]

Currently, the most impressive citizen participation efforts can be found in a handful of cities—among them, St. Paul, Minnesota, and

Dayton, Ohio—where local governments have set up exemplary programs to involve rank-and-file citizens in policymaking.[45] Whether citizen participation at the national level will emerge as an effective administrative reform in the future remains to be seen.

Analytical Budgeting

In recent years, a reform often imposed on the bureaucracy is **analytical budgeting.** In an effort to keep bureaucracies from spending any more than necessary to meet their program goals, various administrations have sought to bring sophisticated analysis to the budgeting process. Such tools as *cost-benefit analysis* and the Carter administration's *zero-based budgeting* are examples. Although different methods have been used, the basic idea is the same: force administrators to think rigorously about alternative ways of achieving their policy objectives and to choose the most cost-effective means.

For example, if the U.S. Department of Defense wants to develop a new weapons system, how should it make its decision? Defense Department officials could simply conclude that the cruise missile is an effective weapon and therefore ought to be built. But instead of looking at strategic considerations alone, their analysis could combine cost calculations with measures of combat effectiveness. One analysis compared three types of cruise missiles (air, ground, and sea launched) with other weapons systems. On the basis of cost alone, ground- and sea-launched cruise missiles were the most expensive. But when a method of analysis called *life-cycle costing* (which takes into account long-term operating and support service expenditures) was used, ground- and sea-launched missiles emerged as the least expensive alternative per warhead.[46]

Many programs are not susceptible to the type of quantitative analysis of costs and benefits that analytical budgeting requires. For example, how do we calculate the value of grants for medical research that may at some time save lives? Analytical budgeting is further compromised by political considerations. Administration officials are not eager to offend their constituents.

The national government's water reclamation projects are a case in point. These projects are especially popular with western farmers, providing them with low-cost water to irrigate their fields. Strict cost-benefit analyses of many of these projects show that they offer too little benefit at too great a cost. Stated another way, taxpayers are unnecessarily subsidizing farmers who could well afford to pay more for the irrigation water they receive. The subsidies endure, though, because the *political costs* of ending them are too great. Western politicians are not about to let analytical budgeting put an end to something their constituents want very badly.[47]

Looking back on the various attempts at analytical budgeting, one scholar wrote, "Practices of both Republican and Democratic administrations indicate that nonpolitical budgets based on business practices of economy and efficiency are largely unknown outside the rhetoric of textbooks."[48]

SUMMARY

As the scope of government activity has grown during the twentieth century, so has the bureaucracy. The executive branch has evolved into a complex set of departments, independent agencies, and government corporations. Through the administrative discretion granted them by Congress, these bodies make policy decisions that have the force of law. In making policy choices, agency decision makers are influenced by their external environment, especially the White House, Congress, and interest groups. Decision makers are also influenced by internal norms and the need to work cooperatively with others both within and outside their agencies.

The controversy and conflict surrounding bureaucratic policymaking reflect broader differences in the American political system and the values underlying that system. Whether policy involves the cost of funerals, clean air regulations, or standards for chain saws, one issue is fundamental: To what degree should the national government intervene to protect Americans in the name of order or to promote their welfare in the name of equality? At what point does protection for some citizens rob others of the freedom to lead their lives as they want?

There is a division between those who want administrative agencies to aggressively protect citizens from harmful or unfair business practices and those who want agencies to do less. This division also usually mirrors the line that divides the views of liberals and conservatives. But that line is not etched in stone. At times, conservatives actually support government intervention, as do businesspeople, even though they generally believe in deregulation.

Certainly there are problems stemming from government bureaucracy. Critics point to its lack of responsiveness, to waste, to faulty implementation. Reforms—among them reorganization, deregulation, citizen participation programs, and analytical budgeting—are constantly being suggested as a means of improving bureaucratic performance.

The most serious charge facing the bureaucracy is that it is out of control of the people. In fact, the White House, Congress, interest groups, and public opinion are substantial controls on the bureaucracy. Still, to many Americans, the bureaucracy seems too big, too costly, and too intrusive. It is difficult to reduce the size and scope of bureaucratic activity because pluralism characterizes our political system. The entire executive branch may appear too large, and each of us can point to agencies that we believe should be reduced or eliminated. Yet each bureaucracy has its supporters. The Department of Agriculture performs vital services for farmers. Unions care a great deal about the Department of Labor. Scholars want the National Science Foundation protected. And home builders do not want Housing and Urban Development programs cut back. Bureaucracies survive because they provide important services to groups of people, and those people—no matter how strong their commitment to less government—are not willing to sacrifice their own needs to that commitment.

Key Terms

bureaucracy	regulation (rule)
bureaucrat	adjudication
department	implementation
independent agency	reorganization
regulatory commission	regulation
government corporation	deregulation
civil service	citizen participation
administrative	program
discretion	analytical budgeting
rule making	

Selected Readings

Derthick, Martha, and Paul J. Quirk. *The Politics of Deregulation.* Washington, D.C.: Brookings Institution, 1985. An interesting look at why some industries have undergone deregulation while others have not.

Downs, Anthony. *Inside Bureaucracy.* Boston: Little, Brown, 1967. A rigorous analysis of bureaucratic behavior.

Heclo, Hugh. *A Government of Strangers.* Washington, D.C.: Brookings Institution, 1977. A look at the relationship between career bureaucrats and political appointees.

Pressman, Jeffrey L., and Aaron B. Wildavsky. *Implementation.* 3d ed. Berkeley, Calif.: University of California Press, 1984. A classic case study of why government programs don't always work out.

Rourke, Francis E. *Bureaucracy, Politics, and Public Policy.* 3d ed. Boston: Little, Brown, 1984. An excellent introduction to bureaucracy, with a very useful analysis of the relationship between agencies and their clients.

Siedman, Harold, and Robert Gilmour. *Politics, Position, and Power.* 4th ed. New York: Oxford University Press, 1986. An authoritative account of the politics of reorganization.

Wilson, James Q., ed. *The Politics of Regulation.* New York: Basic Books, 1980. A collection of essays that describe the regulatory practices of different agencies in Washington.

13

The Courts

When Chief Justice Fred M. Vinson died unexpectedly on September 8, 1953, Justice Felix Frankfurter commented, "This is the first solid piece of evidence I've ever had that there really is a God."[1] Frankfurter despised Vinson as a leader and disliked him as a person. Now Vinson's sudden death cast new light—and perhaps new hope—on the school segregation cases known collectively as *Brown* v. *Board of Education*.

The issue of segregated schools was first heard by the United States Supreme Court late in 1952. The justices were bitterly divided, with Vinson supporting racial segregation in public education. Because it was clear the justices were not ready to reach a decision, they scheduled the issue for reargument the following year.

Frankfurter's caustic remark reflected the critical role Vinson's replacement would play when the Court again tackled the desegregation issue. On September 30, 1953, in his very first appointment to the nation's highest court, President Dwight D. Eisenhower chose California Governor Earl Warren as chief justice. The president would later regret his choice.

The reargument of *Brown* v. *Board of Education* was heard in December 1953. The new chief justice led the Court from division to

Power Player on the Top Court
Earl Warren (1891–1974) served as the fourteenth chief justice of the United States. A true liberal, Warren led the Supreme Court by actively preferring equality to freedom and freedom to order. These decisions occasionally brought calls from Congress for Warren's impeachment. He retired in 1968 after sixteen years of championship (critics might say controversial) activity.

unanimity on the issue of school segregation. Unlike his predecessor, Warren began the secret conference to decide the segregation issue with a strong statement: that segregation was contrary to the Thirteenth, Fourteenth, and Fifteenth Amendments to the Constitution. "Personally," remarked the new chief justice, "I can't see how today we can justify segregation based solely on race."[2] Moreover, if the Court were to uphold segregation, he argued, it could do so only on the theory that blacks were inherently inferior to whites. As the discussion proceeded, Warren's opponents were cast in the awkward position of appearing to support racism.

Five justices were clearly on Warren's side, making six votes; two were prepared to join the majority if Warren's opinion satisfied them. With only one clear holdout, Warren set about the task of responding to his colleagues' concerns. In the months that followed, he met with them individually in their chambers, reviewing the decision and the justification that would accompany it. Finally, in April 1954, Warren approached Justice Stanley Reed, whose vote would make the opinion unanimous. "Stan," said the chief justice, "you're all by yourself in this now. You've got to decide whether it's really the best thing for the country." Ultimately Reed joined the others. On May 17, 1954, the Supreme Court unanimously ruled against racial segregation in public schools, signaling the end of legally created or governmentally enforced segregation of the races in the United States.[3]

Judges confront conflicting values in the cases before them, and tough cases call for fine distinctions among those values. In crafting their decisions, judges—especially Supreme Court justices—make policy. Their decisions are the precedents other judges use to rule in similar cases. One judge in one court makes public policy to the extent that he or she influences other decisions in other courts.

The power of the courts to shape policy creates a difficult problem for democratic theory. According to that theory, the power to make law resides only in the people or in their elected representatives. Yet court rulings—especially Supreme Court rulings—extend far beyond any particular case. Judges are students of the law, but they remain human beings. They have their own opinions about the values of freedom, order, and equality. And although all judges are constrained by statutes and precedents from expressing their personal beliefs in their decisions, some judges are more prone than others to interpret laws in light of those beliefs.

America's courts are deeply involved in the life of the country and its people. Some courts, like the Supreme Court, make fundamental policy decisions vital to the preservation of freedom, order, and equality. Through checks and balances, the elected branches couple the courts to democracy, and the courts hitch the elected branches to the Constitution. But does it work? Can the courts exercise political power within the pluralist model? Or are judges simply politicians in black robes, making decisions independent of popular control? In this chapter we try to answer these questions by exploring the role of the judiciary in American political life.

FEDERAL JUDICIAL SUPREMACY

Section 1 of Article III of the Constitution created "one supreme Court." The founders were divided on the need for other national courts, so they deferred to Congress the decision to create a federal court system. Those who opposed the creation of federal courts believed that the system would usurp the authority of the state courts.[4] Congress considered the issue in its first session and, in the Judiciary Act of 1789, gave life to a system of federal courts that would coexist with the courts in each state but be independent of them.

In the early years of the republic, the federal judiciary was not considered a particularly powerful branch of government. It was difficult to recruit and keep Supreme Court justices. John Jay, the first chief justice, refused to resume his duties in 1801 because he concluded that the Court could not muster the "energy, weight, and dignity" to contribute to national affairs.[5] Several distinguished statesmen refused appointments to the Court, and several others, including Oliver Ellsworth, the second chief justice, resigned. But when John Marshall, an ardent Federalist, was appointed chief justice in 1801, a period of profound change began.

Judicial Review of the Other Branches

Shortly after Marshall's appointment, the Supreme Court confronted a question of fundamental importance to the future of the new republic: If a federal law and the Constitution conflict, which should prevail? The question arose in the case of *Marbury* v. *Madison* (1803), which involved a controversial series of last-minute political appointments.* The ensuing litigation hinged on the concept of the Supreme Court's **original jurisdiction**, its authority to hear a case before any other court does.

Section 2 of Article III confers original jurisdiction on the Supreme Court to hear and decide "all Cases affecting Ambassadors, other public Ministers and Consuls, and those in which a State shall be a Party." Cases falling under the Supreme Court's original jurisdiction are tried and decided in the Court itself; these cases begin and end there. The largest part of the Supreme Court's jurisdiction, then and now, extends only to cases that have been tried, decided, and re-examined as far as the law permits in other federal or state courts. These referred cases fall under the Supreme Court's **appellate jurisdiction**. The Court exercises judicial power under its appellate jurisdiction only because Congress gives it the authority to do so.

The case of *Marbury* v. *Madison* began on March 2, 1801, when an obscure Federalist, William Marbury, was designated as a justice of the

---

* Courts publish their opinions in volumes called *reporters*. Today, the United States Reports is the official reporter for the U.S. Supreme Court. For example, the Court's opinion in the case of *Brown* v. *Board of Education* is cited as 347 U.S. 483 (1954). This means that the opinion in *Brown* begins on page 483 of Volume 347 in the United States Reports. The citation also includes the year of the decision. The decision in *Brown* was made in 1954. Before 1875, the official reports of the Supreme Court were published under the names of private compilers. For example, the case of *Marbury* v. *Madison* is cited as 1 Cranch 137 (1803). This means that the case is found in Volume 1, compiled by reporter William Cranch, starting on page 137, and that it was decided in 1803.

Chief Justice John Marshall
*Marshall (1755–1835)
clearly ranks as the "Babe
Ruth" of the Supreme
Court. Both Marshall and
the Bambino transformed
their respective games and
became symbols of their institutions. Scholars now
recognize both men as orig-
inators—Marshall of judi-
cial review, and Ruth of the
modern age of baseball.*

peace in the District of Columbia. Marbury and several others were appointed to government posts created by Congress in the last days of John Adams's presidency. In the rush to finish up the administration's work, John Marshall, then the secretary of state, failed to deliver to Marbury and the other appointees the documents that would have made their appointments official before the end of Adams's term at midnight, March 3. The documents, known as *commissions*, had been signed by the president and affixed with the Great Seal of the United States, but they remained tucked away in the secretary of state's desk. The newly arrived Jefferson administration had little interest in delivering the commissions; there were qualified Jeffersonians who would welcome the jobs.

Marbury and three others brought suit in the Supreme Court to have their commissions delivered by the new secretary of state, James Madison. Marbury claimed that Section 13 of the Judiciary Act of 1789 gave the Court the power to issue writs of mandamus to government officials. (*Mandamus* means "we command"; a **writ of mandamus** is a court order directing an official to act.)

The Court seemed to have just two alternatives. It could issue the writ, but in all likelihood Madison would ignore it, leaving the nation's highest court open to ridicule through a rebuff over a trifling issue. Or the Court could deny the writ. But given the explicit authority in Section 13, the failure to act would be a sign of weakness from a Court that feared its actions would not be obeyed. The Court found a novel solution that avoided both ridicule and a show of weakness.

On February 24, 1803, the Court held, through the forceful argument of Chief Justice Marshall, that Marbury had a right to his commission and that it should be delivered to him. The Court concluded, however, that it did not have the power to order the commission delivered. It was true that the Judiciary Act gave the Court the authority to issue writs of mandamus, but in doing so, the act expanded the Court's original jurisdiction beyond the limits spelled out in the Constitution. The Court was faced with an act of Congress that was in conflict with a provision of the Constitution.

Can "an act repugnant to the constitution . . . become the law of the land?" asked the chief justice. The logic in Marshall's answer was elegant. He argued that the Constitution was "the fundamental and paramount law of the nation" and that "an act of the legislature repugnant to the constitution is void." In other words, when the Constitution—the nation's highest law—conflicts with an act of the legislature, that act is invalid. The last part of Marshall's argument vested in the judiciary the power to weigh the validity of congressional acts:

> It is emphatically the province and duty of the judicial department to say what the law is. Those who apply the rule to particular cases, must of necessity expound and interpret that rule. . . . If a law be in opposition to the constitution, if both the law and the constitution apply to a particular case, so that the court must either decide that case conformably to the law, disregarding the constitution; or conformably to the constitution, disregarding the law; the court must determine which of these conflicting rules governs the case. This is the very essence of judicial duty.[6]

The decision in *Marbury* v. *Madison* established the Supreme Court's power of **judicial review**—the power to declare congressional acts invalid if they violate the Constitution.* Subsequent cases extended the power to presidential acts.

Marshall surely took a measure of political delight from the Court's decision. Although the ruling blocked the Adams appointments, it attacked Jefferson and Madison for their lawlessness. Then, by a "masterwork of indirection," Marshall expanded the potential power of the Supreme Court to equal or exceed that of the other branches of government. Should a congressional act or, by implication, a presidential act conflict with the Constitution, the Supreme Court claimed the power to declare the act void. The judiciary would be a check on the legislative and executive branches, consistent with the principle of checks and balances embedded in the Constitution. Although Congress and the president may wrestle with the constitutionality of their actions, judicial review gave the Supreme Court the final word on the meaning of the Constitution.

The exercise of judicial review—an appointed branch checking an elected branch in the name of the Constitution— appears to run counter to democratic theory. In two hundred years of practice, however, the Supreme Court has invalidated fewer than one hundred provisions of federal law, and only a small number have had great significance for the political system.[7] Moreover, there are mechanisms to override judicial review (constitutional amendment) and to control the action of the justices (impeachment). In addition, the Court can respond to the continuing struggle among competing interests (a struggle that is consistent with the pluralist model) by reversing itself.

Judicial Review of State Government

The establishment of judicial review of federal laws made the Supreme Court the umpire of the national government. When acts of the national government conflict with the Constitution, the Supreme Court can declare those acts invalid. But what about state laws? If they conflict with the Constitution, federal laws, or treaties, can the Court invalidate them as well?

The Supreme Court answered in the affirmative in 1796. *Ware* v. *Hylton* involved a British creditor who was trying to collect a debt from the state of Virginia.[8] Virginia law canceled debts owed British subjects, yet the Treaty of Paris (1783), in which Britain formally acknowledged the independence of the colonies, guaranteed that creditors could collect such debts. John Marshall (the future chief justice), representing Virginia in his only argument before the Court, maintained that the provision of the treaty did not apply. But the Court ruled that the Constitution's supremacy clause (Article VI) nullified the state law.

The states continued to resist the yoke of national supremacy. Although advocates of strong states' rights conceded that the supremacy

---

* The Supreme Court had earlier *upheld* an act of Congress in *Hylton* v. *United States*, 3 Dallas 171 (1796). By striking down a portion of the Judiciary Act of 1789, *Marbury* v. *Madison* stood for a component of judicial power that had never before been exercised: the power to *invalidate* an act of Congress.

"What's Going On Here?"
Sometimes, court opinions do not yield easily to understanding by reporters (or by judges, as this cartoon suggests). Several readings may be required to grasp the issues and the arguments, which can be embedded in the complexities of the legal process.

clause obligates state judges to follow the Constitution when it conflicts with state law, they maintained that the states were bound only by their own interpretation of the Constitution. The Supreme Court said no, ruling in *Martin* v. *Hunter's Lesee* that it had the authority to review state courts' decisions that called for the interpretation of federal law.[9] National supremacy required the Supreme Court to impose uniformity on federal law; otherwise, the Constitution's meaning would vary from state to state. The people, not the states, had ordained the Constitution; and the people had subordinated state power in order to establish a viable national government.

The Exercise of Judicial Review

The decisions in *Marbury, Ware,* and *Martin* established the components of judicial review:

- The power of the federal courts to declare federal, state, and local laws invalid if they violate the Constitution
- The supremacy of federal laws or treaties when they conflict with state and local laws
- The role of the Supreme Court as the final authority on the meaning of the Constitution.

But this political might—the power to undo decisions of the representative branches of national and state governments—was in the hands of appointed judges, people who were not accountable to the electorate. Did judicial review square with democratic government?

Alexander Hamilton had foreseen and tackled the problem in "Federalist No. 78." Writing during the ratification debates surrounding the adoption of the Constitution (see Chapter 3), Hamilton maintained that despite the power of judicial review, the judiciary would be the weakest of the three branches of government because it lacked "the strength of the sword or the purse." The judiciary, wrote Hamilton, had "neither FORCE nor WILL, but only judgment."

Although Hamilton was defending legislative supremacy, he argued that judicial review was an essential barrier to legislative oppression.[10] He recognized that the power to declare government acts void implied the superiority of the courts over the other branches. But this power, he contended, simply reflects the will of the people declared in the Constitution as compared with the will of the legislature declared in its statutes. Judicial independence, embodied in life tenure and protected salaries, minimizes the risk of judges' deviating from the law established in the Constitution by freeing the judiciary from executive and legislative

COMPARED WITH WHAT? 13.1

Judicial Review

The U.S. Constitution does not explicitly give the Supreme Court the power of judicial review. In a controversial interpretation, the Court inferred this power from the text and structure of the Constitution. Other countries, trying to avoid political controversy over the power of the courts to review legislation, explicitly define that power in their constitutions. Japan's constitution, inspired by the American model, went beyond it in providing that "the Supreme Court is the court of last resort with power to determine the constitutionality of any law, order, regulation, or official act."

The basic objection to the American form of judicial review is an unwillingness to place judges, who are usually appointed for life, above representatives elected by the people. The European concept of judging involves principled decision making, not "creative" interpretation of constitutions or laws. Some constitutions explicitly deny judicial review. For example, Article 28 of the Belgian constitution (1831) firmly asserts that "the authoritative interpretation of laws is solely the prerogative of the Legislative authority."

The logical basis of judicial review—that government is responsible to higher authority—can take interesting forms in other countries. In some, judges can invoke a higher authority than the constitution—God, an ideology, or a code of ethics. For example, both Iran and Pakistan provide for an Islamic review of all legislation. (Pakistan also has the American form of judicial review.)

By 1985, about sixty-five countries—mostly in Western Europe, Latin America, Africa, and the Far East—had adopted some form of judicial review.

Australia, Brazil, Burma, Canada, India, Japan, and Pakistan give their courts a full measure of judicial review power. All but Japan have federal governments. Australia and Canada come closest to the American model of judicial review. Governments with relatively consistent experience with judicial review share some common characteristics: stability, competitive political parties, distribution of power (akin to separation of powers), a tradition of judicial independence, and a high degree of political freedom. Is judicial review the cause or the consequence of these characteristics? More likely than not, judicial review contributes to stability, judicial independence, and political freedom. And separation of powers, judicial independence, and political freedom contribute to the effectiveness of judicial review.

Switzerland also has a federal form of government. However, its Supreme Federal Court is limited by its constitution to rule on the constitutionality of cantonal laws (the Swiss equivalent of our state laws). The Supreme Federal Court lacks the power to nullify laws passed by the national assembly. The Swiss people, through a constitutional initiative or a popular referendum, exercise the sovereign right to determine the constitutionality of federal law. In Switzerland, the people are truly supreme.

Source: These views are found in Henry J. Abraham, *The Judicial Process*, 5th ed. (New York: Oxford University Press, 1986), pp. 291–330; and Ivo D. Duchacek, *Power Maps: Comparative Politics of Constitutions* (Santa Barbara, Calif.: ABC-CLIO, 1973), pp. 216–219.

control.* And if judges make a mistake, the people or their elected representatives have the means to correct the error, through constitutional amendment and impeachment.

Their life tenure does free judges from the direct influence of the president and Congress. And although mechanisms to check judicial power are in place, they require extraordinary majorities and have rarely been used. When they exercise the power of judicial review, then, judges can and occasionally do operate counter to majoritarian rule by invalidating the actions of the people's elected representatives. (Compared With What? 13.1 shows the nature of judicial review in other governments, democratic and nondemocratic.) Is the Court out of line with majority sentiment? Or is the Court simply responding to pluralist demands—the competing demands of interest groups that turn to the courts to make public policy? We return to these questions later in this chapter.

THE ORGANIZATION OF THE FEDERAL COURTS TODAY

The American court system is complex, a function in part of our federal system of government. Each state runs its own court system; and no two are identical. In addition, we have a system of courts for the national government. These federal courts coexist with the state courts (see Figure 13.1). Individuals fall under the jurisdiction of two different court systems, their state courts and the federal courts. They can sue or be sued in either system, depending mostly on what their case is about. The vast majority of cases are resolved in the state courts.

The federal courts are organized in three tiers, like a pyramid. At the bottom of the pyramid are the **U.S. district courts**, where litigation begins. In the middle are the **U.S. courts of appeals**. At the top is the U.S. Supreme Court. *To appeal* means to take a case to a higher court. The courts of appeals and the Supreme Court are appellate courts; with few exceptions, they review cases that have been decided in lower courts. Most federal courts hear and decide a wide array of cases; the judges in these courts are known as *generalists*.

The U.S. District Courts

There are ninety-four federal district courts in the United States. Each state has at least one district court, and no district straddles more than one state.[11] In 1987, nearly six hundred federal district court judges dispensed justice in various degrees in almost 280,000 criminal and civil cases.

The district courts are the entry point to the federal court system. When trials occur in the federal system, they take place in the federal district courts. Here is where witnesses testify, lawyers conduct cross-

---

* Hamilton also believed that the executive, recognizing the power stemming from judicial independence, would appoint judges with the skill and intelligence to carry out their interpretive function responsibly.

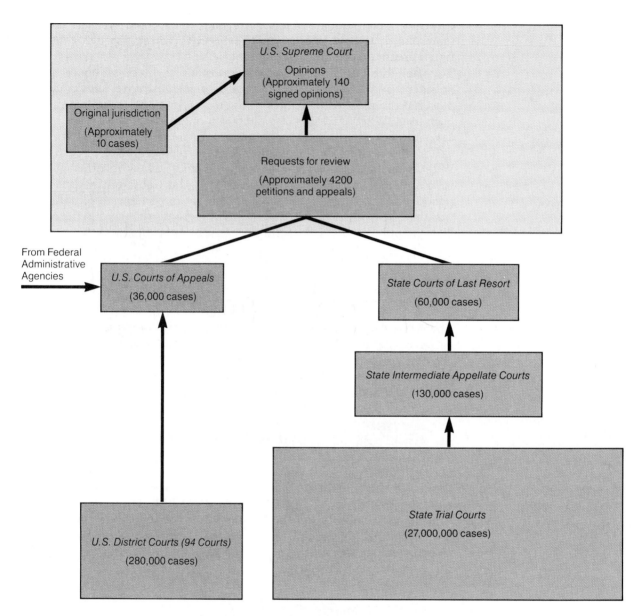

U.S. Supreme Court
Opinions
(Approximately 140
signed opinions)

Original jurisdiction
(Approximately
10 cases)

Requests for review
(Approximately 4200
petitions and appeals)

From Federal
Administrative
Agencies

U.S. Courts of Appeals
(36,000 cases)

State Courts of Last Resort
(60,000 cases)

State Intermediate Appellate Courts
(130,000 cases)

U.S. District Courts (94 Courts)
(280,000 cases)

State Trial Courts
(27,000,000 cases)

The Federal and State Court Systems
*The federal courts have three tiers: district courts, courts of appeals, and the
Supreme Court. The Supreme Court was created by the Constitution; all other
federal courts were created by Congress. Most litigation occurs in state courts.
The structure of state courts varies from state to state; usually there are minor
trial courts for less serious cases, major trial courts for more serious cases,
intermediate appellate courts, and courts of last resort. State courts were cre-
ated by state constitutions. (Sources:* State Court Caseload Statistics, Annual Report,
1986 *[Williamsburg, Va.: National Center for State Courts, 1988];* Annual Report of the
Director of the Administrative Office of the United States Courts *[Washington, D.C.:
Government Printing Office, 1987];* and Harold W. Stanley and Richard G. Niemi, Vital
Statistics on American Politics *[Washington, D.C.: Congressional Quarterly, 1988].)*

Figure 13.1

Searching for the Law
Judge Learned Hand (1872–1961) served as a federal judge for fifty-two years, a record unequaled in the twentieth century. Although many jurists regarded Hand as a leading contender for a Supreme Court seat, he never managed to get the coveted appointment. His public reputation rested on his unusual name, his eloquent style, and his physiognomy (note the bushy eyebrows and square, strong features). Many of Hand's three thousand opinions are still cited for their lucidity and powerful reasoning. Hand was perhaps the greatest judge of his generation; his achievements stemmed from "the great way in which he dealt with a multitude of little cases."

examinations, and judges and juries decide the fate of litigants. There may be more than one judge in each district court, but each case is tried by a single judge, sitting alone.

Criminal and civil cases. Crime is a violation of a law that forbids or commands an activity. Criminal laws are defined in each state's *penal code*, as are punishments for violations. Some crimes—murder, rape, arson—are on the books of every state. Others—sodomy is one example—are considered crimes in certain states but not all. Because crime is a violation of public order, the government prosecutes **criminal cases**. Maintaining public order through the criminal law is largely a state and local function. Federal criminal cases represent only a fraction of all criminal cases prosecuted in the United States. The national penal code is very specialized. It does not cover ordinary crimes, just violations of federal laws, like tax fraud or possession of controlled substances banned by Congress.

Courts decide criminal and civil cases. **Civil cases** stem from disputed claims to something of value. Disputes arise from accidents, contractual obligations, and divorce, for example. Often the parties disagree over tangible issues (the possession of property, the custody of children); but civil cases can involve more abstract issues too (the right to equal accommodations, damages for pain and suffering). The government can be a party to civil disputes, called on to defend or to allege wrongs.

Sources of litigation. Today, the authority of U.S. district courts extends to

■ federal criminal cases authorized by federal law (for example, robbery of a federally insured bank or interstate transportation of stolen securities).

■ civil cases brought by individuals, groups, or government for alleged violation of federal law (for example, failure of a municipality to implement pollution control regulations required by a federal agency).

■ civil cases brought against the federal government (for example, enforcement of a contract between a manufacturer and a government agency).

■ civil cases between citizens of different states when the amount in controversy exceeds $10,000 (for example, when a citizen of New York sues a citizen of Alabama in an Alabama district court for damages stemming from an auto accident in Alabama).

Most of the cases scheduled for hearings in the U.S. district courts never are actually tried. One side may be using a lawsuit as a threat to exact a concession from the other. Often the parties settle their own dispute. Less frequently, cases end with **adjudication**, a court judgment resolving the parties' claims and ultimately enforced by the government. When district judges adjudicate cases, they usually offer written reasons to support their decisions. When the issues or circumstances of cases are novel, judges can publish **opinions**, explanations justifying their rulings.

The U.S. Courts of Appeals

All cases resolved by final judgments in the U.S. district courts and all decisions of federal administrative agencies can be appealed to one of the thirteen U.S. courts of appeals. These courts, with a corps of 168 full-time judges, handled approximately thirty-six thousand cases in 1987. Each appeals court hears cases from a geographic area known as a *circuit.* The U.S. Court of Appeals for the Seventh Circuit, for example, is located in Chicago; it hears appeals from the U.S. district courts in Illinois, Wisconsin, and Indiana. The United States is divided into twelve circuits. (The U.S. Court of Appeals for the Federal Circuit is not a regional court; it specializes in appeals involving patents, contract claims against the federal government, and federal employment cases.)

Appellate court proceedings. Appellate court proceedings are public, but they usually lack courtroom drama. There are no jurors, witnesses, or cross-examinations; these are features of the trial courts. Appeals are based strictly on the rulings made and procedures followed in the trial courts. Suppose, for example, that in the course of a criminal trial, a U.S. district judge allows the introduction of evidence that convicts a defendant. The defendant can appeal on the ground that the evidence was obtained in the absence of a valid search warrant and so was inadmissible. The issue on appeal is the admissibility of the evidence, not the defendant's guilt or innocence. If the appellate court agrees with the trial judge's decision to admit the evidence, then the conviction stands. If the appellate court disagrees with the trial judge and rules that the evidence is inadmissible, then the defendant must be retried without the incriminating evidence or be released.

It is common for litigants to try to settle their dispute while it is on appeal. For example, when a court issued an $11 billion judgment against the Texaco Oil Company in 1985, settlement discussions began immediately. At the same time, Texaco was planning its appeal. Occasionally, litigants abandon their appeals for want of resources or resolve. Most of the time, however, appellate courts adjudicate the cases.

The courts of appeals are regional courts. They usually convene in panels of three judges to render judgments. The judges receive written arguments known as **briefs** (which are also sometimes submitted in trial courts). Often the judges hear oral arguments and question the attorneys to probe their arguments.

Precedent and decision making. One of the three judges attempts to summarize the panel's views, although each judge remains free to disagree with the reasons or with the judgment. The influence of published appellate opinions can reach well beyond the immediate case. For example, a lawsuit turning on the meaning of the Constitution produces a ruling that then serves as a **precedent** for subsequent cases; that is, the decision becomes a basis for deciding similar cases in the same way. Although district court judges sometimes publish their opinions, it is the exception rather than the rule. At the appellate level, however, precedent requires that opinions be written.

Decision making according to precedent is central to the operation of our legal system, providing continuity and predictability. This bias in favor of existing decisions is captured by the Latin expression **stare decisis**, which means "let the decision stand." But the legal system's use of precedent and the principle of stare decisis do not make lower-court judges cogs in a judicial machine. "If precedent clearly governed," remarked one federal judge, "a case would never get as far as the Court of Appeals: the parties would settle."[12]

Judges on the courts of appeals direct their energies toward correcting errors in district court proceedings and interpreting the law (in the course of writing opinions). When judges interpret the law, they often modify existing laws or create new ones. In effect, they are making policy. Judges are politicians in the sense that they exercise political power, but the black robes that distinguish judges from other politicians signal constraints on their exercise of power.

Judges make policy in two different ways. Occasionally, in the absence of legislation, they employ rules from prior decisions. We call this body of rules the **common** or **judge-made law.** The roots of the common law lie in the English legal system. Contracts, property, and **torts** (an injury or wrong to the person or property of another) are common-law domains. The second area of judicial lawmaking involves the application of statutes enacted by Congress. The judicial interpretation of legislative acts is called **statutory construction**. The application of a statute is not always clear from its wording. To determine how a statute should be applied, judges first look for the legislature's intent, reading reports of committee hearings and debates in Congress. If these sources do not clarify the statute's meaning, the court does. With or without legislation to guide them, judges on the courts of appeals and district courts look to the relevant opinions of the Supreme Court for authority to decide the issues before them.

Although the Supreme Court has the final say on what a law means, its decisions often fail to address the precise issue confronting lower-court judges. This means that federal judges can sometimes exercise as much political power as the High Court's justices themselves. For example, in 1955 federal judges in Alabama were called on to determine whether, in light of the Supreme Court's decision in *Brown* v. *Board of Education*, Alabama's racially segregated public transportation facilities violated the Constitution's equal protection clause. Because applicable Supreme Court precedents appeared to go in opposite directions, three federal judges from the Deep South had to decide which path to take (see Feature 13.1).

Uniformity of law. Decisions by the courts of appeals ensure a measure of uniformity in the application of national law. For example, when similar issues are dealt with in the decisions of different district judges, their decisions may be inconsistent. The courts of appeals harmonize the decisions within their region so that laws are applied uniformly.

The regional character of the courts of appeals undermines uniformity somewhat because the courts are not bound by the decisions of other circuits. A law in one court of appeals may be interpreted differently in another. For example, the Internal Revenue Code imposes identical tax burdens on similar individuals. But thanks to the regional character of the courts of appeals, federal tax laws may be applied differently throughout the United States. The percolation of cases up through the federal system of courts virtually guarantees that at some point two or more courts of appeals, working with a similar set of facts, are going to interpret the same law differently.

The problem of conflicting decisions in the intermediate federal courts can be corrected by review in the Supreme Court, where policymaking, not error correcting, is the paramount goal.

THE SUPREME COURT

Above the west portico of the Supreme Court Building are inscribed the words EQUAL JUSTICE UNDER LAW. At the opposite end of the building, above the east portico, are the words JUSTICE THE GUARDIAN

FEATURE 13.1

The Law and Frank Johnson

Judge Frank Johnson issued many path-breaking decisions from the federal courthouse in Montgomery, Alabama. Appointed by President Eisenhower, Johnson ordered the integration of public parks, interstate bus terminals, restaurants and restrooms, and libraries and museums. In 1964, Johnson applied the one-person, one-vote principle for the first time in state legislative apportionment. In 1971, he held that patients in state mental hospitals have a constitutional right to treatment. And in 1976, he ordered the reform of the Alabama prison system on the ground that the conditions of confinement violated the constitutional rights of prisoners.

In this selection from an interview with journalist Bill Moyers, Johnson recalls his participation in *Browder* v. *Gayle* (1955). The case was a direct challenge to the Supreme Court's 1896 decision in *Plessy* v. *Ferguson*, which had held that separate-but-equal public transportation facilities were constitutionally acceptable. The *Browder* decision desegregating the Montgomery buses was the first time (in Johnson's memory, at least) a district court had overruled a decision of the Supreme Court. It was also the first extension of the Supreme Court's decision in *Brown* v. *Board of Education* (1954). *Browder* was decided by a special three-judge district court. Participating with Judge Johnson were Judges Richard Rives and Seybourne H. Lynne.

Moyers: Anybody call you and say, "My God, Johnson, you don't know what you've done," or "Do you know what you've done?"

Johnson: Well, they didn't put it in those words.

M: How did they put it?

J: I don't think I was subjected to vilification. I don't think I was subjected to the feeling of hate comparable to that which Judge Rives was subjected. Judge Richard Rives and I are the ones that decided that case. (Judge Lynne dissented.) Judge Rives had grown up here in Montgomery. He had practiced law here in Montgomery. He was one of the most able—recognized as one of the most able—lawyers in the South. President Truman appointed him to the federal bench. He'd been on the bench about four years when I came on in '55. He helped swear me in in this courtroom. But Judge Rives's roots were here. He was one of them. He wasn't a foreigner that had been imported from the hills of North Alabama [where Johnson was born and raised]. And it was said

by several people, and probably in the newspapers—I think I recall—here in Montgomery, "Well, we didn't expect any more out of that fellow from up at North Alabama, but Richard Rives is one of our own, and we did expect more out of him, and he's forfeited the right to be buried in Confederate soil." And that's how strong it was.

M: When you were discussing that case in your private chambers, after it had been argued—

J: The junior member of the court votes first. The senior member of the court votes last. That's followed throughout the system. That's to keep the senior member from influencing the junior member in his vote.

M: And you voted first?

J: So, Judge Rives says, "Frank, what do you think about this case?" "I don't think segregation in *any* public facilities is constitutional. Violates the equal protection clause of the Fourteenth Amendment, Judge." That's all I had to say. It didn't take me long to express myself. The law was clear. And I might add this . . . the law to me was clear in practically every one of these cases that I've decided where race was involved. I had no problem with the case where we outlawed the poll tax, charging people to vote. I had no problem with the museums, the libraries, the public parks, or any public facilities. The law will not tolerate discrimination on the basis of race.

M: When you said this to Judge Rives, what did he say?

J: Well, when it came Judge Rives's time to vote, he says, "I feel the same way."

M: And that was it.

J: Absolutely. Sure. Sure. Well, well, I don't guess we deliberated over ten minutes at the outside.

M: History seems to require more dramatic moments than that.

J: There are rarely ever any dramatic moments in a judges' conference room. It's a cold, calculated, legal approach.

Source: Bill Moyers' Journal, "Judge: The Law & Frank Johnson—Part I." Transcription, pp. 8–10. © 1980 by the Educational Broadcasting Corporation. Reprinted by permission.

FEATURE 13.2

The Marble Palace

The Supreme Court of the United States sits east of the Capitol in a building designed both to embrace the majesty of the law and to elevate its occupants to the status of Platonic guardians. The Corinthian-style marble building was completed in 1935 at a cost of $10 million. Until it settled in its permanent home, the Court had occupied makeshift, hand-me-down quarters in nearly a dozen places (including two taverns) since its first session in February 1790.

Each justice has a suite of offices, including space for several law clerks—top graduates from the nation's elite law schools, who serve for a year or two.

The courtroom is 82 feet by 91 feet, with a 44-foot-high ceiling and twenty-four columns of Italian marble. The room is dominated by marble panels, which were sculpted by Adolph A. Weinman. Directly above the mahogany bench, which is angled so that all the justices can see and hear one another, are two marble figures depicting Majesty of Law and Power of Government. A tableau of the Ten Commandments is between the figures.

The Court begins its official work year on the first Monday of October, known as the October Term. During its public sessions, when appeals are argued or the justices announce opinions, the court marshal (dressed in a cutaway) pounds the gavel at exactly 10:00 A.M., directs everyone in the courtroom to stand, and announces:

The honorable, the chief and the associate justices of the Supreme Court of the United States: Oyez. Oyez. Oyez. All persons having business before the honorable, the Supreme Court of the United States, are admonished to draw near and give their attention, for the Court is now sitting. God save the United States and this honorable Court.

Then the justices enter in black robes from behind a velvet curtain. In the front is the chief justice; the other justices follow in order of seniority.

Contrary to popular impression, most of the 170 cases that the Court hears annually do not involve provocative constitutional issues. The Con-

OF LIBERTY (see Feature 13.2). These mottos reflect the Court's difficult task: achieving a just balance among the values of freedom, order, and equality. Consider how these values came into conflict in two controversial issues the Court faced in recent years.

Abortion pits the value of order—the government's responsibility for protecting life—against the value of freedom—a woman's right to decide whether or not she will give birth. In the abortion cases beginning with *Roe* v. *Wade* (1973), the Supreme Court extended the right to privacy (an expression of freedom) to cover a woman's right to terminate a pregnancy.[13] The Court determined that at the beginning of pregnancy, a woman has the right to an abortion, free from government-imposed constraint. But the Court also recognized that toward the end of pregnancy, government interest in protecting the fetus's right to life normally outweighs a woman's right to abortion.

School desegregation pits the value of equality—equal educational opportunities for minorities—against the value of freedom—the rights of

stitution provides for the Supreme Court to hear cases "arising under ... the laws of the United States." These cases call for the interpretation of federal statutes, which may or may not be interesting to the public at large.

Oral argument is usually limited to thirty minutes for each side. Few attorneys argue appeals regularly before the Court, so the significance of the moment can overwhelm even seasoned advocates. The justices constantly question the attorneys, attempting to poke holes in every argument.

Sometimes the intensity of an argument before the court was too much for a lawyer to endure. Solicitor General Stanley Reed once fainted

while arguing a case before his brethren-to-be. One day a private practitioner completely lost the thread of his argument and began to babble incoherently. [Chief Justice Charles Evans] Hughes tried to aid him by asking simple questions about the case. Seeing that this further bewildered the lawyer, Hughes took the brief and completed the argument that counsel was unable to make. . . .

There were other occasions when the utmost restraint was necessary to maintain the dignity of the court. . . . A New York attorney argued so vehemently that his false teeth popped out of his mouth. With amazing dexterity he scooped up the errant dentures almost before they hit the counsel's table in front of him and flipped them back into his mouth, with scarcely a word interrupted. Not a smile ruffled the dignity of the bench, but the Justices' pent-up mirth broke into gales of laughter when they reached safe havens of privacy.*

* Merlo J. Pusey, *Charles Evan Hughes*, vol. 2. (New York: Macmillan, 1951), pp. 674-675. Reprinted by permission of Macmillian Publishing Company.

Source: *Congressional Quarterly's Guide to the U.S. Supreme Court* (Washington: Congressional Quarterly, 1979), pp. 761, 769–772. Reprinted by permission.

parents to send their children to neighborhood schools. In *Brown* v. *Board of Education*, the Supreme Court carried the banner of racial equality by striking down state-mandated segregation in public schools. This decision helped launch a revolution in race relations in the United States. The justices recognized the disorder their decision would create in a society accustomed to racial bias, but in this case equality clearly outweighed freedom. Twenty-four years later, the Court was still embroiled in controversy over equality when it ruled that race could be a factor in university admissions (to diversify the student body), in the *Bakke* case.[14] In securing the equality of blacks, the Court then had to confront the charge that it was denying the freedom of whites to compete for admission.

The Supreme Court makes national policy. Because its decisions have far-reaching impact on all of us, it is vital that we understand how it reaches those decisions. With this understanding, we can better evaluate how the Court fits within our model of democracy.

Access to the Court

There are rules of access that must be followed to bring a case to the Supreme Court. Also important is a sensitivity to the interests of the justices. The idea that anyone can appear before the Supreme Court is true only in theory, not fact.

The Supreme Court's cases come from two sources. A few (ten in 1986) arrive under the Court's original jurisdiction, conferred by Article III, Section 2, of the Constitution. For example, the Court is the first and only forum in which legal disputes between states are resolved. The Court hears few original jurisdiction cases today, however, usually referring them to a *special master*, often a retired judge, who reviews the parties' contentions and recommends a resolution that the justices are free to accept or reject.

Most cases enter the Supreme Court from the U.S. courts of appeals or the state courts of last resort (see Figure 13.2).* This is the Court's appellate jurisdiction. Two conditions must be met: First, the case must reach the end of the line in the state court system. Litigants cannot jump at will from state to federal arenas of justice. Second, the case must raise a **federal question**, an issue covered under the Constitution, federal laws, or treaties. But even cases that meet these conditions do not always reach the High Court. Since 1925, the Court has exercised substantial

---

* On rare occasions, cases can be brought to the Supreme Court after judgment in a U.S. district court but before consideration by a federal court of appeals. This happened in *United States* v. *Nixon*, 418 U.S. 683 (1974). The urgency of an authoritative decision in the Watergate tapes case short-circuited a decision in the court of appeals. A small class of cases can be heard in the first instance before special three-judge district courts with appeals directly to the Supreme Court (see Feature 13.1).

Figure 13.2 ▬▬▬

Access to and Decision Making in the U.S. Supreme Court
State and federal appeals courts churn out thousands of decisions each year. Only a small fraction will end up on the Supreme Court's docket. This chart sketches the several stages leading to a decision from the High Court. (Source: Harold W. Stanley and Richard G. Niemi, Vital Statistics on American Politics *[Washington, D.C.: Congressional Quarterly, 1988], Table 9-7.)*

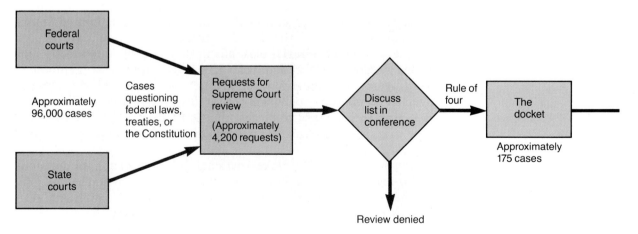

(today, nearly complete) control over its **docket**, the Court's agenda. The Court selects a handful (about 170) of cases for consideration from the 4,200 requests it receives each year. For the vast majority of the cases left unreviewed by the Court, the decision of the lower court stands.

Review is not granted unless four or more justices agree that a case warrants full consideration. This unwritten rule is known as the **rule of four.** All nine justices, with advance preparation by their law clerks, make these judgments at conferences held twice a week. The justices meet by themselves to add cases to their docket and to vote on previously argued cases. The chief justice prepares and circulates to all the justices a "discuss list" of worthy petitions (cases on the discuss list are then subject to the rule of four in conference). A petition not on the list will be struck from conference consideration unless a justice wishes to add it. Most cases, even those discussed in conference, are denied review. Cases denied review carry little or no value as Court rulings, since no reasoned explanation accompanies the Court's orders denying review.

The Solicitor General

Some scholars have searched for explanations of the Court's docket decisions. One theory suggests that the justices look for clues in the requests for review, for signs of an important case.[15] The most important sign is a recommendation by the solicitor general to grant or deny review.

The **solicitor general** represents the federal government before the Supreme Court. He is appointed by the president and is the third-ranking official in the U.S. Department of Justice (following the attorney general and deputy attorney general). His duties include determining whether the government should appeal lower-court decisions; reviewing and modifying, when necessary, the briefs filed in government appeals; and deciding whether the government should file an **amicus curiae brief*** in any appellate court.[16] His objective is to create a cohesive program for the executive branch in the federal courts.

---

* *Amicus curiae* is Latin for "friend of the court." Amicus briefs can be filed with permission of the Court. They allow groups and individuals who are not parties to the litigation but who have an interest in it to influence the Court's thinking and, perhaps, its decision.

Decision-making process

```
→  [ Briefs ]  →  [ Oral     ]  →  [ Conference ]  →  [ Opinion          ]
                  [ argument  ]                       [ (Approximately   ]
                                                      [ 140 signed       ]
                                                      [ opinions)        ]
```

The solicitor general plays two different, occasionally conflicting, roles. First, he is an advocate for the president's policy preferences; second, as an officer of the Court, he traditionally defends the institutional interests of the national government. Sometimes the institutional interests prevail. For example, the Reagan administration was committed to returning power to the states. But Solicitor General Rex Lee argued for the exercise of federal power in his defense of a federal law setting wage requirements for a city-owned mass transit system. In a sharp blow to the administration, the Court held that the Constitution placed no specific limit on congressional power to interfere in state and local affairs.[17]

The solicitor general's office is like a specialized law firm within the Justice Department. Members of the office collectively have more experience arguing before the Supreme Court than has any other organization in the nation. In 1988, there were twenty-two lawyers analyzing lower federal court decisions to determine whether to ask for Supreme Court review. If the Court grants review in a case in which the federal government is a party, either the solicitor general himself or one of his deputies argues the government's position before the High Court.

Solicitors general usually act with considerable restraint in recommending to the Court that a case be granted or denied review. By recommending only cases of general importance, they increase their credibility and their influence. Rex E. Lee, who was solicitor general from 1981 to 1985, acknowledged in an unusually candid interview that he had refused to make arguments that members of the Reagan administration had urged on him: "I'm not the pamphleteer general; I'm the solicitor general. My audience is not 100 million people; my audience is nine people. . . . Credibility is the most important asset that any solicitor general has."[18]

The solicitor general's credibility came under question during the tenure of Lee's successor, Charles Fried, who was appointed by Reagan in 1985. Fried urged the Court to reverse its decisions on abortion and affirmative action at a time when the justices were not ready to do so. The Court squarely rejected Fried's arguments. His proposal to alter the law in the absence of any signal from the Court that it was ready may have cost Fried a measure of influence with the justices.

Despite his limited visibility, the solicitor general is a powerful figure in the legal system. His influence in bringing cases to the Court and arguing them there has earned him the informal title of the "tenth justice."

Decision Making

Once the Court grants review, attorneys submit written arguments (briefs). The Court imposes strict limits on the length of these documents and the time period for their submission. Oral argument follows the submission of briefs and to conserve the justices' time and energy is usually limited to thirty minutes for each side. The justices like crisp, concise, and conversational presentations; they disapprove of attorneys who read from a prepared text. Some justices are aggressive and relentless

The Supreme Court, 1988 Term: The Starting Nine
Pictured in their team uniforms: (sitting, left to right) Thurgood Marshall, William J. Brennan Jr., Chief Justice William H. Rehnquist, Byron R. White, and Harry A. Blackmun; (standing, left to right) Antonin Scalia, John Paul Stevens, Sandra Day O'Connor, and Anthony Kennedy.

questioners; others are more subdued. The justices reach no collective decision at oral argument. They reach a tentative decision only after they have met in conference.

Our knowledge of the dynamics of decision making on the Supreme Court is all secondhand; only the justices attend the Court's Wednesday and Friday conferences. By tradition, the justices first shake hands, a gesture of harmony. The chief justice then begins the discussion by offering a brief summary of each case's merits; the other justices follow in descending order of seniority. The justices usually make their positions known in the course of discussion, so there is little need for a formal vote. Justice Antonin Scalia, who joined the Court in 1986, remarked recently that "not much conferencing goes on." By *conferencing,* Scalia meant efforts to persuade others to change their views by debating points of disagreement. "In fact," he said, "to call our discussion of a case a conference is really something of a misnomer. It's much more a statement of the views of each of the nine Justices, after which the totals are added and the case is assigned [for an opinion]."[19]

Judgment and argument. The voting outcome is the **judgment**, the decision on who wins and who loses. Justices often disagree, not only on winners and losers, but also on the reasons for their judgments. This should not be surprising, given nine independent minds and issues that can be approached in several ways. Voting in the conference does not end the work or resolve the disagreements. Votes remain tentative until the Court issues an opinion announcing its judgment.

After voting, the justices in the majority must draft an opinion setting out the reasons for their decision. The **argument** is the kernel of the opinion, its logical content separated from facts, rhetoric, and procedure. If all the justices agree with the judgment and the reasons supporting it, then the opinion is unanimous. A justice can agree with a judgment, upholding or striking down a claim, based on different reasons. This kind of agreement is called **concurrence**. Or a justice can **dissent** if he or she disagrees with a judgment. Both concurring and dissenting opinions may be drafted in addition to the majority opinion.

When the Court was first established, individual justices delivered their own opinions in every case, without attempting to join forces with their colleagues. This practice was abandoned after John Marshall's appointment to the Court. During his first four years as chief justice, the Court handed down twenty-six opinions in twenty-six cases. Of these, Marshall drafted and delivered twenty-four. Marshall changed the opinion practice, in the process giving coherence and power to the Court.[20]

Opinion assignment. After the conference, the chief justice writes the majority opinion or assigns that responsibility to another justice in the majority. If the chief justice is not in the majority, the writing or assigning responsibility rests with the most senior associate justice in the majority. The assigning justice may consider several factors in allocating the crucial opinion-writing task: workload, expertise, public opinion, and, above all, the author's ability to hold the majority together. (Remember, at this point votes are only tentative.) If the drafting justice holds an extreme view on the issues in a case and is not able to incorporate the views of more moderate colleagues, those justices may withdraw their votes. On the other hand, assigning a more moderate justice to draft an opinion could weaken the argument on which the opinion rests. Opinion-writing assignments can also be punitive. Justice Harry Blackmun once commented, "If one's in the doghouse with the Chief [former Chief Justice Warren Burger], he gets the crud."[21]

Strategies on the Court. The Court is more than the sum of its formal processes. The justices exercise real political power. If we start with the assumption that the justices are attempting to stamp their own policy views on the cases they review, then we should expect typical political behavior from them. Perceptive scholars and journalists have pierced the veil that shrouds the Court from public view.[22] Cases that reach the Supreme Court's docket pose difficult choices. Because the justices are grappling with conflict on a daily basis, they probably have well-defined ideologies that reflect their values.

We can locate the beliefs of most justices on our two-dimensional model of political values (see Figure 1.2). Liberal justices, like Thurgood Marshall and William J. Brennan, Jr., choose freedom over order, and equality over freedom. Conservative justices—William Rehnquist and Sandra Day O'Connor, for example—choose order over freedom, and freedom over equality. These choices translate into policy preferences as the justices struggle to win votes or retain coalitions.

We know that the justices also vary in intellectual ability, advocacy skills, social graces, temperament, and the like. For example, Chief Justice Charles Evans Hughes (1930–1941) had a photographic memory and came to each conference armed with well-marked copies of Supreme

Court opinions. Few justices could keep up with him in debate. Today, justices argue for the support of their colleagues, offering information in the form of drafts and memoranda to explain the advantages and disadvantages of voting for or against an issue. And we expect the justices make occasional, if not regular, use of friendship, ridicule, and patriotism to mold their colleagues' views.

A justice might adopt a long-term strategy of influencing the appointment of like-minded colleagues in order to marshal additional strength on the Court. Chief Justice (and former President) William Howard Taft (1921–1930) bombarded President Warren G. Harding with recommendations and suggestions whenever a Court vacancy was announced. Taft was especially determined to block the appointment of anyone who might side with the "dangerous twosome," Justices Oliver Wendell Holmes and Louis D. Brandeis. Taft said he "must stay on the Court in order to prevent the Bolsheviki from getting control."[23]

Opinion writing. Opinion writing is the justices' most critical function. It is not surprising, then, that they spend much of their time drafting opinions. The justices usually call on their law clerks—top graduates of the nation's elite law schools—to help them prepare opinions and carry out other tasks.

On the occasion of his eightieth birthday, after more than thirty years of service on the Court, Justice Brennan offered a rare account of the process of preparing and exchanging memoranda and drafts that leads to a final opinion: "It's startling to me every time I read these darned things to see how much I've had in the way of exchanges and how the exchanges have resulted in changes of view both of my own and of colleagues. And all of a sudden at the end of the road, we come up with an agreement on an opinion of the Court."[24]

The authoring justice distributes a draft opinion; the other justices read it, then circulate criticisms and suggestions. An opinion may have to be rewritten several times to accommodate colleagues who remain unpersuaded by the draft. Justice Felix Frankfurter was a perfectionist; some of his opinions went through thirty or more drafts. Justices can change their votes, and perhaps alter the judgment, up until the decision is officially announced. And the justices announce their decisions only when they are ready. Often the most controversial cases pile up in a backlog as the coalitions on the Court vie for support or sharpen their criticisms. When the Court announces decisions, the authoring justices read or summarize their opinions in the courtroom. Copies of these opinions, known as *slip opinions*, are then distributed to interested parties and the press.

Justices in the majority frequently try to muffle or stifle dissent in order to encourage institutional cohesion. The justices must be keenly aware of the slender foundation of their authority, which rests largely on public respect. That respect is tested whenever the Court ventures into areas of controversy. Banking, slavery, and Reconstruction policies embroiled the Court in controversy in the nineteenth century. Freedom of speech and religion, racial equality, and the right of privacy have led the Court into controversy in this century.

A Veteran Playmaker . . .
Justice William J. Brennan Jr. was appointed to the Supreme Court in 1956. The length of his service qualifies him for Hall of Fame status, but his contribution is far greater than simple longevity. Brennan, a liberal, has been a champion of judicial activism. He has written or influenced some of the most important and controversial Court opinions. Here he reviews materials in the Louisiana creationism case (discussed in Chapter 17).

The chief justice.   The chief justice is only one of nine justices, but he has several important functions based on his authority. And if he does not carry them out, someone else will.[25] Apart from his role in docket control decisions and his direction of the conference, the chief justice can also be a social leader, generating solidarity within the group. Sometimes, a chief justice can embody intellectual leadership. Finally, the chief justice can provide policy leadership, directing the Court toward a general policy position. Perhaps only John Marshall could lay claim to social, intellectual, and policy leadership roles. (Docket control did not exist during Marshall's time.) Warren E. Burger, who resigned as chief justice in 1986, was a lackluster leader in all three areas.

When he presides at the conference, the chief justice can exercise control over the discussion of issues, although independent-minded justices are not likely to succumb to his views. For example, at the end of the conference on *Brown* v. *Board of Education*, Chief Justice Warren had six firm votes for his position that segregated public schools were unconstitutional. Two other justices indicated that they would join the majority if an opinion could be written to meet their concerns. In the months that followed, Warren talked frequently with his colleagues to minimize the possibility of dissenting or concurring opinions. By April 1954, only one holdout remained, and he eventually joined the others. Warren's patriotic appeals had made both the decision and the opinion unanimous.[26]

The chief justice's power to cast the last vote can be used to moderate the majority opinion, even if the chief justice's interest is in the minority. Suppose the vote in conference is 6 to 2 before the chief justice casts his vote. A vote with the majority gives the chief justice the power to write

... And a Junior Member of His Team
Supreme Court justices use recent law school graduates as short-term clerks. Here Dean Hashimoto, one of Brennan's four clerks, prepares a draft opinion in the creationism case, which served as a guide for Brennan when he wrote the majority opinion. In Brennan's office, cases are assigned to clerks through the drawing of lots. Although Hashimoto did not win the initial drawing for this case, his colleagues agreed to reassign it to him because of his keen interest in its issues.

the opinion himself or to assign a justice who is closer to the minority viewpoint, depending on where the chief justice's principles lie. In *Roe* v. *Wade*, for instance, Justice William O. Douglas charged that Chief Justice Burger abused his power by voting with the majority to overturn a state antiabortion statute, when Burger's true sentiments lay with the minority two votes. Douglas threatened to issue a concurrence rebuking the chief justice's use of the opinion-assignment power. His colleagues convinced Douglas that the Court's reputation would suffer by airing the dispute in public, so the opinion was never published.[27]

JUDICIAL RECRUITMENT

Neither the Constitution nor federal law imposes formal requirements for appointment to the federal courts, except for the condition that, once appointed, district court and appeals judges must reside in the district or circuit to which they are appointed. The president appoints judges to the federal courts, and all nominees must be confirmed by the Senate.

State courts operate somewhat similarly. Governors appoint judges in nearly half the states. Other states select their judges by partisan, nonpartisan, or (rarely) legislative election.[28] Nominees in some states must be confirmed by the state legislature. In the rest, judges are confirmed in general elections held several years after appointment. Contested elections for judgeships are unusual. In Chicago, where judges are elected, even highly publicized widespread criminal corruption in the courts failed to unseat incumbents in 1987. Most voters paid no attention whatsoever.

Judge and Company
Judge Norma Johnson was appointed by President Jimmy Carter in 1980 to the United States District Court for the District of Columbia. She was the first black woman appointed to that court. Judge Johnson is assisted by two law clerks, who serve for a year or two. Although the most coveted clerkships are in the Supreme Court, clerking for other federal and state judges can pay big dividends. In 1988, some major New York law firms were offering bonuses of several thousand dollars for new recruits with prior clerkship experience in the federal courts.

The Appointment of Federal Judges

The Constitution states that federal judges hold their commissions "during good Behaviour," which in practice means for life*. A president's judicial appointments, then, are likely to survive his administration, a kind of political legacy. The appointment power assumes that the president is free to identify candidates and appoint judges who favor his policies.

Judicial vacancies occur when sitting judges resign, retire, or die. Vacancies also arise when Congress creates new judgeships to handle increasing caseloads. The president then nominates a candidate who must be confirmed by the Senate. The president has the help of the Justice Department, which screens candidates before the formal nomination, subjecting serious contenders to FBI investigation. The department and the Senate vie for control in the appointment of district court and appeals judges.

The "Advice and Consent" of the Senate. For district court and appeals vacancies, the appointment process hinges on the nominees' acceptability to the senior senator in the president's party from the state in which the vacancy arises. At one time, the power of these senators was so great that they could suggest a single name for a vacancy and hold out until that person was nominated.[29]

The practice of **senatorial courtesy** forces presidents to share the

---

* Only five federal judges have been removed by impeachment in nearly two hundred years; nine resigned before formal impeachment charges could be lodged; and only four have ever been convicted of felonies (serious criminal conduct).

nomination power with members of the Senate. The Senate will not confirm a nominee who is opposed by the senior senator in the president's party in the nominee's state. The Senate doesn't actually reject the candidate. Instead, a form, called a "blue slip," is not returned by the senior senator. In the absence of the blue slip, the chair of the Senate Judiciary Committee, which reviews all judicial nominees, will not schedule a confirmation hearing, effectively killing the nomination.

Although the Justice Department is still sensitive to senatorial prerogatives, senators can no longer submit a single name to fill a vacancy. The department was once a passive funnel for the evaluation of candidates, but no longer. It searches for acceptable candidates and polls the appropriate senator for his or her reaction to them.

The Senate Judiciary Committee conducts a hearing for each judicial nominee. The chair exercises a measure of control in the appointment process, beyond the power of senatorial courtesy. If a nominee is objectionable to the chair, he or she can delay a hearing or hold up other appointments until the president and the Justice Department consider some alternative. This kind of behavior does not win a politician much influence in the long run, however. So committee chairs are usually loathe to place obstacles in a president's path, especially when they may want presidential support for their own policies and constituencies.

The American Bar Association. The American Bar Association (ABA), the largest organization of lawyers in the United States, has been involved in screening candidates for the federal bench since 1946.[30] Its role is defined by custom, not law. At the president's behest, the ABA's Standing Committee on the Federal Judiciary routinely rates prospective appointees, using a four-value scale ranging from "exceptionally well qualified" to "not qualified."

To obtain information about a candidate, the committee confidentially interviews lawyers and judges who know and are capable of evaluating the candidate. The committee's recommendation is supposed to address the candidate's "professional qualifications," which are defined as "competence, integrity, and judicial temperament." A candidate's politics and ideology should have no bearing on the committee's task. But there is a loophole: "Extreme views" that affect the candidate's temperament and integrity are considered relevant to the committee's evaluation. The committee's divided vote on Judge Robert H. Bork's nomination to the Supreme Court in 1987 strengthened the successful drive to stop his confirmation.

Presidents do not always agree with the committee's judgment, in part because its objections can mask disagreements with a candidate's political views. Although the committee claims to employ nonideological criteria, ideology can color its work. For instance, in 1985 the committee furnished lists of prospective nominees to groups seeking to challenge appointments on ideological grounds.[31] Because the ratings are made public, a poor ABA rating can weaken a candidate's chances. Occasionally, a candidate deemed "not qualified" is nominated and even appointed, but the overwhelming majority of appointees to the federal bench since 1946 have had the ABA's blessing.

Recent Presidents and the Federal Judiciary

President Jimmy Carter had two objectives in his judicial appointments. First, Carter wanted to base judicial appointments on merit, to appoint judges of higher quality than had his predecessors. Whether he succeeded here is debatable—a question that only time and scholarship can answer. But he did meet his second objective, to make the judiciary more representative of the general population. Carter appointed substantially more blacks, women, and Hispanics to the federal bench than did any of his predecessors or his successor. Here his actions were consistent with the pluralist model, at least in a symbolic sense.

Early in his administration, it was clear that President Reagan did not share Carter's concerns. Although Reagan generally heeded senatorial recommendations for the district courts and, like Carter, held a firmer rein on appointments to the appeals courts, there were strong differences. By 1988, only 2 percent of Reagan's appointments were blacks and only 8 percent were women; in contrast, 14 percent of Carter's appointments were blacks and 16 percent were women (see Figure 13.3). A Justice Department official maintained that Reagan's appointment record reflected demographic and political reality. "We would love to find more qualified blacks," but there was "just not even a respectable small pool" of black nominees who qualified on the basis of experience and commitment to Reagan's conservative agenda.[32]

It seems clear that political ideology, not demographics, was at the heart of Reagan's judicial appointments. Reagan sought out nominees

Figure 13.3

Carter Versus Reagan: Blacks and Women in the Legal System
The composition of the legal profession does not mirror the composition of the general population, especially with regard to race and gender. Jimmy Carter attempted to make the federal bench more representative by appointing more blacks and women. Ronald Reagan's appointments matched the composition of the lawyer population, but not the population at large. (Sources: Statistical Abstract of the United States 1987 *[Washington, D.C.: U.S. Government Printing Office, 1987], pp. 14–15; Barbara A. Curran,* The Lawyer Statistical Report *[Chicago: American Bar Foundation, 1985]; and* New York Times, *3 February 1988, p. 12.)*

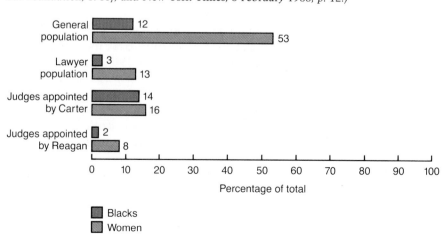

"It's Nothing Personal!"
Judge Robert H. Bork (right) was nominated to the Supreme Court by President Ronald Reagan in 1988. Bork's conservative record as a professor, solicitor general, and appellate judge was a lightning rod for criticism. Leading the assault was Senator Joseph R. Biden (left), a three-term Democrat from Delaware who chaired the Senate Judiciary Committee. The committee reported the nomination unfavorably to the Senate, which then rejected the nomination by the largest margin in the history of that body.

with particular policy preferences in order to leave his stamp on the judiciary well into the twenty-first century. In contrast to his predecessors, Reagan used the nation's law schools the way major league baseball managers use farm teams. With the right statistics, a professor could move to the major leagues—in this case, one of the federal district or appellate courts. Carter's liberal values led him to look for judges who were committed to equality; Reagan's conservative values led him to appoint judges who were more committed to order. Reagan surpassed Carter in reshaping the federal courts: 258 lifetime appointments for Carter compared with 367 lifetime appointments for Reagan.

Appointment to the Supreme Court

The announcement of a vacancy on the High Court usually causes quite a stir. Campaigns for Supreme Court seats are commonplace, although the public rarely sees them. Hopeful candidates contact friends in the administration and urge influential associates to do the same on their behalf. Some candidates never give up hope. Judge John J. Parker, whose nomination to the Court was defeated in 1930, tried in vain to rekindle interest in his appointment several times until he was well past the age—usually the early sixties—when appointments are made.[33]

The president is not shackled by senatorial courtesy when it comes to nominating a Supreme Court justice. Appointment to the High Court attracts more intense public scrutiny than do lower-level appointments. This scrutiny limits a president's choices and focuses attention on the Senate's "Advice and Consent."

Of the 143 men and 1 woman nominated to the Court, 28—or about 1 in 5—have failed to receive Senate confirmation. Only six rejections have come in this century, the last two during the Reagan administration. The most important factor in the rejection of a nominee is partisan politics. Thirteen candidates lost their bids for appointment because the presidents who nominated them were "lame ducks": The party in control of the Senate anticipated victory for its candidate in an upcoming presidential race and sought to deny the incumbent president an important political appointment.[34] The most recent nominee to be rejected, on partisan and ideological grounds, was Judge Bork.

Since 1950, seventeen of twenty-one Supreme Court nominees have had judicial experience in federal or state courts. This "promotion" from within the judiciary may be based on the idea that a judge's past opinions are good predictors of future opinions on the High Court. After all, a president is handing out a powerful lifetime appointment; it makes sense to want an individual who is sympathetic to his views. Federal or state court judges holding lifetime appointments are likely to state their views frankly in their opinions. In contrast, the policy preferences of High Court candidates who have been in legal practice or in political office must be based on the conjecture of professional associates or on the text of a speech to the local Rotary Club or on the floor of the legislature.

The resignation of Chief Justice Warren Burger in 1986 gave Reagan the chance to elevate Associate Justice William H. Rehnquist to the position of chief justice and to appoint Antonin Scalia, who was a judge in a federal court of appeals, as Rehnquist's replacement. Rehnquist faced stern questioning from liberal critics during his Senate confirmation hearings. (The testimony of Supreme Court nominees is a relatively recent phenomenon; it began in 1925 when Harlan Fiske Stone was nominated to the High Court.) But his opponents were unable to stop confirmation in the Republican-controlled Senate. Both Rehnquist and Scalia did not try to defend their judicial records; they argued that judicial independence meant that they could not be called to account before the Senate. Both judges also ducked discussing issues that might come to the Court for fear of compromising their impartiality.

In 1987, when Justice Lewis F. Powell, Jr., resigned, Reagan had an opportunity to shift the ideological balance on the Court toward a more conservative consensus. He nominated Judge Robert H. Bork, a conservative, to fill the vacancy. Unlike Rehnquist and Scalia, Judge Bork presented a detailed defense of his record as solicitor general and appellate judge at his confirmation hearings. He also outlined his views on such major issues as the right to privacy (he believes there is no constitutional protection for a *generalized* right to privacy) and civil rights (he had once opposed the 1964 Civil Rights Act but had since reversed his position). Bork advocated **judicial restraint**, which rests on the premise that legislators, not judges, should make the laws. Ironically, the legislators who opposed Bork supported the concept of **judicial activism,** which allows judges to promote desirable social goals (see Feature 13.3).

The hearings concluded after several days of televised testimony from Judge Bork and a parade of witnesses. Liberal interest groups mounted a massive media campaign to defeat the nomination, overwhelming conservative efforts to buttress Bork. At first, the public was undecided on Bork's confirmation; by the time the hearings ended, public

FEATURE 13.3

Judicial Restraint and Judicial Activism

The terms *judicial restraint* and *judicial activism* describe the assertiveness of judicial power. Judges are said to exercise judicial restraint when they hew closely to statutes and previous cases in reaching their decisions. Judges are said to exercise judicial activism when they are apt to interpret existing laws and rulings more loosely and to interject their own values in court decisions.

We can describe the theoretical extremes of judicial assertiveness. Judges acting according to an extreme model of judicial restraint would decide nothing at all, deferring to the superiority of other government institutions in construing the law.

Judges acting according to an extreme model of judicial activism would be an intrusive and ever-present force that dominated other government institutions. Actual judicial behavior lies somewhere between these two extremes.

In recent history, many activist judges have tended to trade freedom for equality in their decisions, which has linked the concept of judicial activism with liberalism. However, there is no necessary connection between judicial activism and liberalism. If judges interpret existing statutes and precedents more loosely to trade freedom for order, they are still activists—conservative activists.

opinion shifted against him. Even though his defeat was a certainty, Bork insisted that the Senate vote on his nomination, hoping for a sober discussion of his record. But the rancor never abated. Bork was defeated by a vote of 58 to 42, the largest margin by which the Senate has ever rejected a Supreme Court nominee.

Federal appeals court judge Douglas H. Ginsburg was nominated shortly thereafter. Ginsburg had strong conservative credentials and youth (he was forty-one when nominated) on his side. Nine days after the nomination, Ginsburg's plans went up in smoke when he confirmed allegations that he had used marijuana while he was a student and a Harvard Law School professor. This revelation was an embarrassment to the Reagan administration, which had made "Just Say No" to drugs a national campaign. Ginsburg withdrew his nomination.

The subsequent nomination and confirmation of federal appeals court judge Anthony M. Kennedy proved successful. The Senate examined Kennedy's views in detail, and the nominee did not duck questions that assessed his stand on constitutional issues. His winning combination of wholesomeness and ideological moderation netted him a place as the 104th justice of the Supreme Court.

Reagan's second-term appointments are sure to move the Court in a more conservative direction. Both Rehnquist and Scalia are strong articulate conservatives. They will continue to choose freedom over equality and order over freedom. Rehnquist's leadership role should strengthen the Court's conservatism in the years ahead. Kennedy's rulings as a federal appeals court judge suggest he is a moderate conservative. But it is difficult to predict how he will rule when the values of freedom, order, and equality come into conflict.

The unpredictability of Supreme Court justices has surprised presidents as well as professors. In recent political history, two presidents have found inconsistencies between their expectations and the actual performance of their appointees. Eisenhower called his appointment of

Chief Justice Warren "one of the two biggest mistakes I made in my administration."[35] Harry S Truman considered his appointment of Justice Tom C. Clark the biggest mistake of his presidency. "It isn't so much that he's a *bad* man," said Truman. "It's just that he's such a dumb son of a bitch. He's about the dumbest man I think I've ever run across."[36]

THE LEGAL PROFESSION

If the judiciary is a link in the chain that connects law and politics, then the legal profession is the raw material from which that link is forged. To better understand judges and the power they wield, we have to understand lawyers and the nature of their craft.

Growth of the Profession

Today, the number of lawyers in the United States exceeds 675,000.[37] This translates to 1 lawyer for every 364 people. Twenty-five years ago, there was 1 lawyer for every 700 people. The rate at which the legal profession is growing will probably continue to outpace the rate of population growth through the end of the century.

Why is a career in law so popular? Market forces account for some of the allure. We know that in 1984 the average salary of experienced lawyers was $88,000. If we could include in this average the salaries of all lawyers, whatever their experience, the figure would probably be much lower, certainly well below the $108,000 average salary of physicians. But lawyers' salaries are still substantially greater than those of many other professionals.[38] Salaries for newly minted lawyers heading for elite New York law firms exceeded $71,000 in 1987; some firms offered additional bonuses for clerkship experience in the federal courts and state supreme courts. The glamour of legal practice strengthens the attraction of its financial rewards.

There are other reasons for the popularity of the legal profession and the unquenchable demand for legal services. Materialism and individualism in American culture encourage dispute. Federalism gives us separate legal systems for each state plus the national government. Advertising can now create demand for legal services, too. Finally, the principles of separation of powers and of checks and balances make governing difficult and sometimes impossible. When political institutions act, they often are forced to compromise, deferring critical issues to the courts. Pluralist democracy operates when groups are able to press their interests on, and even challenge, the government. The expression of group demands in a culture that encourages lawsuits thrusts on the courts all manner of disputes and interests. Is it any wonder that America needs all the lawyers it can train?[39]

U.S. Attorneys

The Justice Department is responsible for the faithful execution of the laws under the president's authority. The main administrators of federal law enforcement are the ninety-four U.S. attorneys, appointed by the president with the advice and consent of the Senate. Unlike federal judges, these appointees serve at the pleasure of the president and are expected to relinquish their positions when the reins of government change hands.

There is a U.S. attorney in each federal judicial district. Their staffs of assistant attorneys vary in size with the amount of litigation in the district. U.S. attorneys have considerable discretion, which makes them powerful political figures in any community. Their decision to prosecute or not affects the wealth, freedom, rights, and reputation of the individuals and organizations in the district.

U.S. attorneys are political appointees who often harbor political ambitions.[40] Their position commands media attention and can serve political goals. In 1983, President Reagan appointed Rudolph Giuliani as U.S. attorney for the Southern District of New York (covering a large portion of the New York metropolitan area). Over the next five years, Giuliani notched his briefcase with dozens of successful prosecutions of elected officials, judges, organized crime figures, and Wall Street inside traders. Guiliani's activities generated reels and reams of favorable press coverage; he even appeared on a *Newsweek* cover. This kind of public exposure can help a U.S. attorney launch a successful career in elected office. As a powerful prosecutor or potential opponent, Giuliani's name must make some politicians shudder.

THE CONSEQUENCES OF JUDICIAL DECISIONS

Lawsuits are the tip of the iceberg of disputes; most disputes never surface in the courts. Of all the lawsuits begun in the United States, the overwhelming majority end without a court judgment. Many civil cases are settled, or the parties give up, or the courts dismiss the claims because they are beyond the legitimate bounds of judicial resolution.

Most criminal cases end with a **plea bargain**, the defendant's admission of guilt in exchange for a less-severe punishment. Only about 20 percent of criminal cases in the federal district courts are tried; an equally small percentage of civil cases are adjudicated. The fact that a judge sentences a criminal defendant to ten years in prison or that a court holds a company liable for $11 billion in damages does not guarantee that the defendant or the company will give up either freedom or assets. In the case of the criminal defendant, the grounds for appeal following trial and conviction are well traveled and, if nothing else, serve to delay the day when no alternative to prison remains. In civil cases, the immediate consequence of a judgment may also be an appeal, which delays the day of reckoning.

Supreme Court Rulings: Implementation and Impact

When the Supreme Court makes a decision, it relies on others to *implement* it, to translate policy into action. How a judgment is implemented rests in good measure on how it was crafted. Remember that the

justices, in preparing opinions, are working to hold their majorities together, to gain greater, if not unanimous support for their arguments.
This forces them to compromise in their opinions, to moderate their
arguments, and creates uncertainty in many of the policies they articulate. Ambiguous opinions affect the implementation of policy. For example, when the Supreme Court issued its order in 1955 to desegregate
public school facilities "with all deliberate speed,"[41] judges who opposed
the Court's policy dragged their feet in implementing it. In the early
1960s, the Supreme Court struck down prayers and Bible reading in
public schools. Yet state court judges and attorneys general reinterpreted
the High Court's decision to mean that only *compulsory* prayer or Bible
reading was unconstitutional, that state-sponsored voluntary prayer or
Bible reading was acceptable.[42]

Because the Supreme Court confronts issues freighted with deeply
felt social values or fundamental political beliefs, its decisions have
impact beyond the immediate parties in a dispute. The Court's decision
in *Roe* v. *Wade* legalizing abortion generated heated public reaction. The
justices were barraged with thousands of angry letters. Groups opposing
abortion vowed to overturn the decision; groups favoring abortion moved
to protect the right they had won. Within eight months of the decision,
more than two dozen constitutional amendments had been introduced
in Congress, although none managed to carry the extraordinary majority
required for passage. Still, the antiabortion faction achieved a modest
victory with the passage of a provision forbidding the use of federal funds
for abortions except when the mother's life is in jeopardy.

Opponents of abortion have also directed efforts toward state legislatures, hoping to load the abortion law with enough regulations to
discourage women from terminating their pregnancies. For example, one
state required that women receive detailed information about abortions,
then wait at least twenty-four hours before consenting to the procedure.
The information listed every imaginable danger associated with abortion
and included a declaration that fathers are liable to assist in their children's support. Most of these regulations continue to be struck down by
the courts, but by increasingly narrow margins.[43]

Public Opinion and the Courts

Democratic theorists have a difficult time reconciling a commitment
to representative democracy with a judiciary that is not accountable to
the electorate yet has the power to undo legislative or executive acts.
This difficulty may simply be a problem for theorists, however, because
the policies coming from the Supreme Court rarely seem out of line with
public opinion.[44] Surveys in several controversial areas reveal that the
Court seldom departs from majority sentiment or the trend toward such
sentiment.

A study of Court decisions enlarging or narrowing minority rights
between 1937 and 1980 shows that this was an exceptionally active
period for the use of judicial review. Opinion polls for the same period
indicated that the Court was not out of step with public sentiment; in
fact, the Court's decisions were "surprisingly consistent with majoritar-

ian principles."[45] Decisions in the area of minority rights were supported by a growing minority of Americans and, in some cases, by a clear majority. The Court also refrained from ruling or ruled with equivocation in areas where public opinion was very strong (the use of marijuana, busing to achieve school integration, homosexual conduct).

On the question of abortion, the public was and still is sharply divided. This continuing division may explain why the issue refuses to die despite the Supreme Court's repeated enforcement of its 1973 decision. The Court has clearly defied the wishes of the majority on just one issue: school prayer. Most Americans today do not agree with the Court's position. And as long as the public continues to want prayer in schools, the controversy will continue.

THE CHANGING ROLE OF THE COURTS

The main issue in evaluating the role of the courts as policymakers in democratic government is this: How far should judges stray from the letter of existing statutes and precedents? Supporters of the majoritarian model would argue that the courts should adhere to the letter of the law, that judges must refrain from injecting their own values into their decisions. If the law places too much (or not enough) emphasis on equality or order, it is up to the elected legislature, not the courts, to change the law. In contrast, those who support the pluralist model maintain that the courts are a policymaking branch of government and that the individual values and interests of judges should reflect the different values and interests of the population at large.

The argument that our judicial system fits the pluralist model gains support from a legal procedure called **class action**. Class action is a device for assembling the claims or defenses of similarly situated individuals so that they can be tried as a single lawsuit. A class action makes it possible for people with small individual claims and limited financial resources to aggregate their claims and resources in order to make a lawsuit viable. Decisions in class action suits can have broader impact than decisions in other types of cases. Since the 1940s, class action suits have been the vehicles through which groups have asserted claims involving civil rights, legislative apportionment, and environmental problems. For example, schoolchildren have sued (through their parents) under the banner of class action to rectify claims of racial discrimination on the part of school authorities, as in *Brown* v. *Board of Education*.

The exercise of judicial power in new domains, coupled with the litigious character of American society, continues to attract more controversial cases into the courts. Many are outrageous, and most are dismissed, but the presence of these suits on court dockets suggests a new perception of the judiciary (see Feature 13.4). For example, the parents of a high school student brought suit in federal court stemming from a grading dispute that lowered their daughter's average from 95.478 to 95.413.[46] In another case, a dog owner sued a municipality for unconstitutional deprivation of her property: Her dog was locked up overnight in the pound.[47]

FEATURE 13.4

Megadeath v. *Megadeth*

Courts resolve disputes, inconsistent claims to something of value. Some disputes involve groups in a struggle over fundamental values. And then there are those . . .

"A good name is better than precious ointment," says Ecclesiastes. And though *Megadeath* may not be the sort of name the Bible had in mind, it provides a case in point.

That charming appellation—a term from nuclear disaster lingo meaning "one million dead people"—is considered so good by two heavy metal rock bands that they have gone to court to fight over it.

The two groups, Megadeath and Megadeth (without the second "a"), share a taste for loud music, rude lyrics and long hair. But the first plays infrequently in Los Angeles clubs, while the second tours the world, has two records and is seen on MTV, the cable-TV music station.

To hear both groups tell it, each has good cause to consider the name essential to its self-esteem, and abundant reasons why the other doesn't deserve it.

"We're a global band," explains Dave Mustaine, lead singer for Megadeth. The others are "a joke band, (who) dress up in white wigs and look like Q-Tips."

Mr. Mustaine says his band drew its name from a paper by California Sen. Alan Cranston on the horrors of nuclear war. The phrase "arsenal of megadeath" struck them, he says, as a way to describe the power and intensity of the band we wanted to create . . . something ultra-furious."

Such appeals to logic, however, are lost on their rivals. "We're considered the real Megadeaths around here in L.A.," says Bob Rickets, alias Thor Gunderslau, of Megadeath. And "what difference does it make," he asks, if the others have a following of "thousands and thousands?" "We were playing around first," he says, and "have the rejection slips (from record companies) to prove it."

He adds that his band is more deserving of the name because its musical message is more sophisticated. Megadeth, he says, is "just a bunch of blockheads (who) sing about all kinds of chauvinistic stuff, which grinds against me." His band, on the other hand, explores pressing social concerns, such as in its theme song, "Megadeath: It's Going to Happen to You."

The two "shock rock" groups were scheduled in late 1987 to fight for the exclusive use of their all-but-identical names in the United States District Court for the Southern District of California when they invoked a time-honored remedy: Megadeth paid off Megadeath. Megadeath graciously agreed to drop the use of its name in return for an undisclosed mega-price.

Megadeth lives; the other is megadead. When last we heard, the group was considering some alternatives. Like?

"Leather Armpit," says Mr. Gunderslau, "but that's just a possibility."

Source: Adapted from Andrea Rothman, "Thank Goodness We Have Courts That Can Settle Issues Like This," *Wall Street Journal*, 9 July 1987, p. 29. Reprinted by permission of *The Wall Street Journal*, © Dow Jones & Company, Inc. (1987). All Rights Reserved.

The rights created by congressional acts fuel many of today's controversies. The perturbed parents and the distressed dog owner are just two examples of thousands of litigants who have relied on a Reconstruction-era statute passed by Congress to curtail the outrages perpetrated by the Ku Klux Klan. The law authorizes suits for civil damages against state or local officials by people whose rights have been abridged. From nearly total disuse, the statute has become one of the most litigated provisions of federal law.

Courts create rights in the name of the Constitution. For example, a California court held that Elizabeth Bouvia, a cerebral palsy victim, had an absolute right to refuse a life-sustaining feeding tube.[48] "A desire to terminate one's life is probably the ultimate exercise of one's right to privacy," declared the court. One justice even suggested that Bouvia should not have to starve herself, that her doctors should help her end her life. "Fate has dealt this young woman a terrible hand," he wrote. "Can anyone blame her if she wants to fold her cards and say, 'I want out'?"

Class action suits (by making litigation more accessible) and the creation of new rights are increasing the responsibilities of the courts. They have become arenas for political conflict with litigants, either individually or in groups, vying for benefits. This vision of the courts fits the pluralist model of government.

The traditional view of litigation is a contest between two parties disputing issues arising from transpired events. The issues are contained within the circumstances of the case, and the parties initiate the dispute and control its progress.[49] Relaxation of these elements thrusts the federal courts into administrative and legislative roles. For example, federal district court judge W. Arthur Garrity, Jr., gained national attention when he assumed the administration of the Boston public school system in 1976 to ensure its desegregation. He held that role until 1985. Judge Frank Johnson supervised the administration of Alabama's mental hospitals and prisons in order to ensure enforcement of constitutionally protected rights.[50] Johnson's decree went so far as to specify the maximum number of inmates for every foot of urinal troughs.

These are just two of a growing number of disputes that pit the authority of the federal courts against representative institutions through the enforcement of constitutional or statutory rights.[51] Under normal conditions, the people of Boston select their school administrators, and the people of Alabama, through their elected representatives, make policies for their state institutions. If the courts fit the pluralist model and provide access to all groups seeking redress, then the charge that judges can trump elected government officials loses its sting. Some observers contend that courts are *countermajoritarian*—that they often act against the wishes of the majority, especially when they defend freedom over order. It is clear that courts sometimes make decisions that run counter to the opinion of the majority. According to one sense of justice, this is precisely what courts are supposed to do: make difficult but fair decisions, however unpopular. Still, making decisions that conflict with public opinion can create problems for the courts.

Today, judges usually shrink from the tug of contemporary political conflict in their exercise of political power. Their power rests precisely on their legitimacy, the belief that their decisions are correct and proper. The correctness or propriety of their decisions could be called into question if judges behaved like other politicians.

Chief Justice William H. Rehnquist observed that judges in courts of last resort work in an insulated atmosphere, hearing oral arguments, reading briefs, and writing opinions. They maintain contact with the rest of the world the way most of us do, through newspapers, conversations, books, and films. But "somewhere . . . beyond the walls of the courthouse," remarked Rehnquist, "run currents and tides of public opinion which lap at the courthouse door." Tides of sufficient strength and duration must affect decision making within the courthouse.

Judges . . . can no more escape being influenced by public opinion in the long run than can people working at other jobs. And if a judge coming on the bench were to hermetically seal himself off from all manifestations of public opinion, he would accomplish very little; he would not be influenced by public opinion, but instead by the state of public opinion at the time he came on the bench.[52]

Both judges and elected representatives feel the current of public opinion. But unlike judges, representatives can institute policies at any time regardless of the past. In contrast, judges must wait for issues and resolve them by relying on precedent. Representatives have to answer to the people at regular intervals, by running for re-election; judges need answer only to their consciences.

SUMMARY

The power of judicial review, claimed by the Supreme Court in 1803, placed the judiciary on an equal footing with Congress and the president. The principle of checks and balances can restrain judicial power through several means, such as constitutional amendment and impeachment. But restrictions on that power have been infrequent, leaving the federal courts to exercise considerable influence through judicial review and statutory construction.

The federal court system has three tiers. At the bottom are the district courts, where litigation begins and most disputes end. In the middle are the courts of appeals. At the top is the Supreme Court. The ability of judges to make policy increases as we move up from trial courts to appellate courts.

The Supreme Court, free to draft its own agenda through the discretionary control of its docket, harmonizes conflicting interpretations of national law and articulates constitutional rights. It is helped at this crucial stage by the solicitor general, who represents the executive branch of government before the High Court. His influence with the justices affects their choice of cases to review.

Once a case is placed on the docket, the parties submit briefs and the justices hear oral arguments. A tentative vote is taken in conference. Then the real work begins . . . crafting an opinion that satisfies the majority without sacrificing clarity of forcefulness.

From the nation's lawyers come the nation's judges, whose political allegiance and values are usually a necessary condition of appointment by the president. The president and senators from his party share the power of appointment of federal district and appellate judges. The president has more leeway in the nomination of Supreme Court justices, although nominees must be confirmed by the Senate.

Justice Benjamin N. Cardozo observed, "The great tides and currents which engulf the rest of men,

do not turn aside in their course, and pass the judges by."[53] Litigation thrusts on the courts the exigencies of modern life. Class action suits and new rights are changing the character of litigation, bringing new issues to America's courtrooms and new threats to the power and legitimacy of the judiciary. The issues confronting the nation's courts are very different from those litigated two hundred years ago. In addition to balancing freedom and order, the judges must now balance freedom and equality. And the impact of their decisions is much broader as well. Democratic theorists are troubled by the expansion of judicial power. But today's courts fit within the pluralist model and usually are in step with what the public wants.

In its marble palace, the Supreme Court of the United States faces and tries to resolve the dilemmas of government. Within the columned courtroom, the justices work to balance conflicting values, to ensure an orderly, peaceful society. We examine some of these conflicts in Chapters 17 and 18.

Key Terms

original jurisdiction	statutory construction
appellate jurisdiction	federal question
writ of mandamus	docket
judicial review	rule of four
U.S. district court	solicitor general
U.S. court of appeals	amicus curiae brief
criminal case	judgment
civil case	argument
adjudication	concurrence
opinion	dissent
brief	senatorial courtesy
precedent	judicial restraint
stare decisis	judicial activism
common (judge-made)	plea bargain
law	class action
torts	

Selected Readings

Abraham, Henry J. *Justices and Presidents: A Political History of Appointments to the Supreme Court.* 2d ed. New York: Oxford University Press, 1985. This highly readable book examines the critical relationship between justices and presidents from the appointment of John Jay in 1789 through the appointment of Sandra Day O'Connor in 1981.

Baum, Lawrence. *American Courts: Process and Policy.* Boston: Houghton Mifflin, 1986. A review of trial and appellate courts in the United States, addressing their activities, describing their procedures, and exploring the processes that affect them.

Caplan, Lincoln. *The Tenth Justice: The Solicitor General and the Rule of Law.* New York: Knopf, 1987. An investigative study of the solicitor general's office, arguing that it has been transformed from an independent office to a vehicle for the Reagan administration's ideological goals.

Coffin, Frank M. *The Ways of a Judge: Reflections from the Federal Appellate Bench.* Boston: Houghton Mifflin, 1980. This is a close look at the workings of a federal appellate court and the ways in which its chief judge reaches decisions.

Ely, John Hart. *Democracy and Distrust.* Cambridge, Mass.: Harvard University Press, 1980. A carefully argued appraisal of judicial review, attempting to identify and justify the guidelines for the Supreme Court's application of a two-hundred-year-old constitution to conditions of modern life.

Friedman, Lawrence M. *American Law: An Introduction.* New York: Norton, 1984. A clear, highly readable introduction to the bewildering complexity of the law, explaining how law is made and administered.

Jacob, Herbert. *Law and Politics in the United States.* Boston: Little, Brown, 1986. An accessible introduction to the American legal system with an emphasis on links to the political arena.

O'Brien, David M. *Storm Center: The Supreme Court in American Politics.* New York: Norton, 1986. A highly readable primer on the Supreme Court, its procedures, personalities, and political impact.

Posner, Richard A. *The Federal Courts: Crisis and Reform.* Cambridge, Mass.: Harvard University Press, 1985. A provocative, comprehensive, and lucid analysis of the institutional problems besetting the federal courts. Written by a distinguished law professor, now a federal appellate judge.

Wasby, Stephen L. *The Supreme Court in the Federal Judicial System.* 3d ed. Chicago: Nelson-Hall, 1988. A thorough study of the Supreme Court's internal procedures, its role at the apex of the national and state court systems, and its role in the political system.

14

The Washington Community

When Mike Deaver left the Reagan White House in 1985, he knew he was about to strike it rich. Deaver was a long-time associate of Ronald Reagan, first working for him in 1966, when Reagan was elected governor of California. At the White House, no one was personally closer to Reagan and his wife, Nancy, than Mike Deaver. Deaver knew that those who had a problem with government would pay dearly for someone who had the kind of connections he had. He created Michael K. Deaver and Associates to help clients do what he called "long-term strategic planning." This may have made him sound like a business consultant, but everybody in Washington knew that you hired Mike Deaver's firm to influence the government.

The firm immediately attracted a glittering array of clients, among them, Boeing, Rockwell International, CBS, and Philip Morris, and the governments of Singapore, Mexico, South Korea, and Canada. High fees produced staggering revenues for the new firm, which billed around $3 million during its first six months of operation. TWA was charged $250,000 for a single unsuccessful phone call Deaver made on its behalf to the U.S. Department of Transportation.[1] Soon Saatchi & Saatchi, a British public relations firm, was offering to buy Deaver's company for $18 million, which would have netted Deaver a profit of $15 million.

Deaver's crash was as spectacular as his rise. In the spring of 1986, serious allegations surfaced that Deaver had violated a government ethics law that places limits on lobbying by executive branch officials who have just left the government. With his reputation tarnished, his business began to crumble. He was indicted and convicted of perjury for lying to a congressional committee about his lobbying activities. He appealed. In the meantime, his plush offices in the Georgetown section of Washington were closed, and huge legal fees mounted. Deaver couldn't seem to understand why people were so upset about his influence peddling: "I wonder what people thought I was going to do when I left the White House—be a brain surgeon?"[2]

Before his new career ended so abruptly, Mike Deaver was just one of the thousands of Washingtonians who work *on* the government instead of *for* it. Despite their private-sector status, they play an active role in the governmental process. They are part of the **Washington community**—the people inside and outside of government who work on public policy issues.

In the other chapters in this part, we describe the major institutions of the national government: Congress, the presidency, the bureaucracy, and the courts. Here, we turn to private sector actors in Washington politics. We focus on five important segments of Washington's service economy: law firms, consulting firms, think tanks, public relations firms, and trade associations. Collectively, these groups are an important link between the public and government policymakers, enabling citizens and private-sector policy experts to communicate their opinions and knowledge to those in government.

After examining these segments of the Washington community, we turn to the relationships between them and government decision makers. These ongoing relationships, or *issue networks*, form a significant part

Bonfire of the Vanities
This photo of top-Reagan-aide-turned-lobbyist Michael Deaver, which appeared on the cover of Time *magazine, has come to symbolize the brazenness with which high-powered Washington lobbyists flaunt their access to key policymakers. Posing for the photographer in the back of his chauffeur-driven Jaguar, Deaver seemed to want the world to know that no one had better access than he did. Ironically, shortly after this picture was taken, allegations about the illegality of Deaver's lobbying surfaced, and his business collapsed even before he went to trial.*

of the policymaking process. Our focus here is not on policymaking *within* an institution (say, Congress or the courts), but on how policy is made *across* institutions.

Finally, we look at the impact of issue networks on our democracy. What happens when well organized groups play an integral role in policymaking? How does the influence of special interests affect majority interests?

Before we turn to the private sector in Washington and its relationship with government, we take a brief look at life in the nation's capital. Washington is a unique city, some say a world in itself. What are the special qualities that give this world its character, that draw so many to live and work there?

WASHINGTON: A CITY AT THE CENTER

"Washington," said President John F. Kennedy, "is a town of northern charm and southern efficiency." Indeed, Washington is a city of contrasts: North and South, black and white, rich and poor, public sector and private sector. People outside of Washington, though, think of it not so much as a city divided within itself but as a city divided from the rest of the country. In 1976, Democratic presidential candidate Jimmy Carter proudly told campaign audiences that he was a "Washington outsider."

Washington, Then and Now
The District of Columbia has changed a great deal since the mid-1800s, as the views on these two pages show. Note the canal that originally bounded the Mall, behind the Washington Monument (pictured in the nineteenth-century lithograph, near right).

In 1980, Republican candidate Ronald Reagan spoke disparagingly of the "Washington buddy system." Both men were kinder than former presidential candidate George Wallace, who ridiculed "pointy-headed, briefcase-totin' bureaucrats" for running the government in defiance of common sense.[3]

Washington *is* different from other cities. Its major "industries" are government and the firms that try to influence government. Data from the 1980 census show that Washingtonians have the highest annual median income per family of any major city in the country: $27,515, compared with $19,903 nationally. And the percentage of Washingtonians who are college graduates (32 percent) is the highest in the nation and twice the national average.[4]

Beyond statistics, there is an attitude that sets the people of Washington apart, a pervasive feeling that their city is the true center of the nation. It is where the most important people live and the most important decisions are made. Washingtonians exude a smugness, a sense of being "in the know." They believe that when people from Washington speak, others listen. Yet for all their arrogance, Washingtonians have their share of insecurities. They don't like it that New Yorkers think the nation's capital is a hick town. And they have never gotten over the embarrassment of losing their baseball team twice: first to Milwaukee, then to Texas.

Despite the city's relative affluence, money is not the primary measure of social status in Washington. *Power*—the ability to influence important decisions—is. And the career goals of many Washingtonians are based on moving closer to the centers of power. For bureaucrats, this means climbing the ladder to higher and higher levels of administration;

for legislators, committee chairs and party leadership posts; for congressional aides, senior positions on personal or committee staffs.

Those outside of government have a similar objective—to become increasingly influential in the decision-making process. Their route to power is less direct, and sometimes means going back and forth between jobs in the public sector and jobs in the private sector. The key here is access to government officials. Lawyers, lobbyists, and public relations specialists know that they cannot do their jobs properly unless people in government are willing to listen to them.

Washington has changed dramatically since it became the nation's capital in 1800 (see Feature 14.1). The private-sector service industry, the public relations firms and consulting firms, did not exist then. James Sterling Young has written of Washington in its earliest years:

> No national association made the government's headquarters their headquarters, and few came on errands to Washington. [Of] resident lobbyists, in the modern definition of the term, there were none. . . . Outsiders eager to assist and manipulate the operations of government were conspicuous by their absence; the drama of national politics in early Washington was played without this supporting cast of characters whom big government and a complex industrial society have since attracted to the residence of power.[5]

Today, this "supporting cast of characters" is as much a part of the Washington scene as government itself. There are 400,000 government employees in Washington; there are 700,000 employees in the private sector. Not all of the latter work at jobs having to do with influencing government, but the number of those who do is growing faster than the number of those who work for government itself. Indeed, a real economic

FEATURE 14.1

Washington's Washington

In its early years, the United States had a government without a home. After the revolutionary war, Congress shifted its meetings about among New York, Philadelphia, Trenton, Princeton, and Annapolis. With no buildings of its own in these cities, Congress had to take what it could get, often sharing offices with state or local governments. To add insult to injury, Congress was not always a welcome quest. Meeting in Philadelphia (the City of Brotherly Love) in June 1783, members of Congress were set upon by an unruly mob of militiamen, demanding payment of overdue wages. When Pennsylvania refused to provide adequate protection for the legislators, Congress secretly adjourned and fled to Princeton, New Jersey.

Feeling that a permanent home of their own would give them the respect they deserved, the legislators decided to select a capital where they would have exclusive authority. But they were unable to choose one among themselves. Finally, in 1790, they threw up their hands and delegated the decision to President George Washington. The Congress's only requirement was that the new capital be located in the center of the nation, along a 105-mile stretch of the Potomac River. Once the president selected the actual site, the government proceeded to pay $66.50 an acre for land that was reputedly worth about one-fifth that amount.

President Washington and other national leaders hoped that the new capital would become one of the great cities of the world. They wanted it to be like Paris or Rome, a center of culture, commerce, and national life. They were bitterly disappointed. When the government held its first auction of 10,000 parcels of land in 1791, only 35 lots could be sold. Auctions over the next two years proved to be similar failures and were subsequently suspended because of the embarrassment. It was simply the case that almost nobody wanted to move to Washington.

In 1800, when the government officially moved in, Washington was a depressing, miserable little town. It had only 109 stone or brick buildings; the rest were shanties or huts. There was virtually no private enterprise there in the early years. Excluding slaves, there were fewer than ten thousand residents as late as 1820. Those not employed by the government found little reason to move there. And those in government didn't find the city to their liking either. Supreme Court justices and members of Congress spent much of the year in their home towns, traveling to Washington only when they had to.

In retrospect, it seems that Washington failed to become an important city at first because the people of the new nation had only a limited interest in what went on there.

Source: Adapted from James Sterling Young, *The Washington Community* (New York: Columbia University Press, 1966), pp. 13–37.

---

boom has taken place in Washington, in large part because of the tremendous growth of firms "designed to hook the bureaucracies into their client groups."[6]

LAW FIRMS

Nothing better symbolizes the connection between Washington's private sector and the national government than the city's law firms. The practice of law in Washington is largely a matter of representing clients who have some problem with the government. This representation usually does not take place in the courts. Most Washington lawyers do their business before regulatory agencies and Congress. Typically, Washington lawyers act on behalf of a corporation or a trade association that has an interest in policies being developed by the government. For example, if the Federal Communications Commission (FCC) is formulating regulations governing cable television, cable broadcasters want to know how those regulations will affect their business. More important, they want their interests protected.

Why use lawyers to influence the decision-making process? Why can't a corporation, for example, simply rely on its own executives to lobby the government? First, government policies (statutes, regulations, court opinions) are couched in "legalese."[7] Clients need someone with not only a sophisticated understanding of a particular policy area but also an ability to decipher and interpret technically complex documents. Second, even though many firms are represented by a Washington trade association, at times they need more extensive representation than a trade group can provide. Lawyers in private practice are a readily available pool of talent that can offer the needed services. Third, those who want to influence policymaking need someone who is well acquainted with the committee or agency making the policy, who knows the key people on the government side, and who has a reputation as an expert in that policy area. Washington's law firms are full of these kinds of experts.

Many Washington lawyers are really **lawyer-lobbyists** because they use their background and expertise to influence government. And their services do not come cheap. The big firms bill corporate clients at rates of $200 or more an hour for a senior partner's time. Partners—those who share in the annual profits of a firm—can expect salaries in the range of $100,000 to $300,000 a year.[8]

The success of Covington & Burling, Washington's largest law firm, rests in good part on its government advocacy work. Founded in 1919, it was one of the first firms in the capital to recognize the government's tentative steps toward regulation as an opportunity. Its early clients included industrial giants like DuPont and General Motors. Today, the firm has around two hundred partners and associates, and one member estimated that it has represented "twenty percent of the companies on *Fortune*'s list of the five hundred top corporations."[9]

Beyond the top firms, many individuals have reached the pinnacle of success in practicing Washington law. Lawyers like Tommy Boggs (see Feature 14.2) and Joseph Califano, a former aide to President Lyndon B. Johnson and a member of President Jimmy Carter's Cabinet, attract important clients because they have a reputation for being extremely skillful in influencing government decision making. Attorneys who attract numerous clients to their firms are known as *rainmakers*. They bring business to the firm because of their professional reputations, social connections, or familiarity with clients from previous government experience. When Republican Senate Majority Leader Howard Baker of Tennessee announced his retirement from Congress in 1984, the Washington office of Vinson & Elkins hired him for around $750,000 a year. Clearly, the partners thought that someone with Baker's exceptional connections and experience would make a lot of "rain" for the firm.[10] (Money, however, was not enough to hold Baker in the private sector. In March 1987, he returned to government to serve as President Reagan's chief of staff, a post he held until his resignation in the summer of 1988.)

FEATURE 14.2

Tommy Boggs, Worth a Million

The best thing that ever happened to Tommy Boggs may have been losing his one and only race for Congress. Out of the ashes of that defeat has come an extraordinary career as a lawyer-lobbyist. Now in his mid-forties, Boggs is considered by many to be the most effective lobbyist in Washington.

Politics is in Boggs's blood. His father, Hale Boggs, was a Democratic representative from Louisiana. His mother, Lindy, took Hale's place in the House of Representatives when he died in a plane crash. After graduating from Georgetown University's night law school, Tommy was hired by James Patton to join Patton's small, four-lawyer firm. Since then, the firm has grown to eighty lawyers, and its letterhead now reads "Patton, Boggs & Blow." Around town, it's known simply as "the Boggs firm."

The *Washington Post* called Patton, Boggs & Blow "the young, swashbuckling state-of-the-art Washington lobbying house of its era," and Tommy Boggs gave it that reputation. There is no magic in his approach: He combines hard work and assiduous attention to detail with a superb understanding of the legislative process and of complex areas of public policy. Fellow lobbyist Robert McCandless described Boggs this way: "Being a good lobbyist is like running a good restaurant. You've got to spend a helluva lot of time in the kitchen. Tommy does." He also knows how important money is, and puts a lot of effort into raising and channeling campaign funds from clients to members of Congress.

Boggs's clientele reads like a *Who's Who* of American business. One of his most notable achievements was helping to get the Chrysler bailout bill through Congress. The giant auto manufac-

Tommy Boggs

turer was teetering near bankruptcy; its management felt that only federal loan guarantees would allow it to raise the cash needed to stay in business. The bill faced strong opposition but was passed; the company was kept alive and has since become highly profitable.

For his efforts, Boggs earns around a million dollars a year. But the satisfaction goes beyond the riches his work brings him. "I really enjoy playing the game," he says.

Source: Adapted from Albert R. Hunt, "Thomas Boggs Offers Full-Service Lobbying for a Diverse Clientele," *Wall Street Journal*, 23 March 1982, p. 1; Paul Taylor, "Gladiators for Hire—II," *Washington Post*, 1 August 1983, p. A1; and "Briefing," *New York Times*, 27 February 1986, p. B10.

Law in Washington: A Growth Industry

Law in Washington is one of America's great growth industries. As Figure 14.1 shows, the number of lawyers in the city has skyrocketed in recent years.

What's behind this growth? A major factor has been the regulatory spiral. In the 1970s, as new regulatory agencies, such as the Environmental Protection Agency and the Occupational Safety and Health Administration, began to issue thousands of pages of regulations a year, more and more businesses found themselves directly affected by what goes on in government. They needed both an understanding of how

Joe Califano, In and Out
Joe Califano has had an illustrious career both inside and outside of government. An attorney, Califano worked as an aide to President Lyndon Johnson. After he left the White House, he built a lucrative Washington law practice. He was lured back to government when Jimmy Carter named him secretary of health, education, and welfare. After Carter unceremoniously fired him, Califano landed on his feet by again pursuing a successful Washington law practice.

proposed changes would affect them and a means for influencing the decision-making process. One Washington attorney called the expanding federal regulation of energy a "public service employment program for lawyers."[11] When deregulation came to Washington in the late 1970s, some thought it spelled the end of the gravy train. But it did not turn out that way. Deregulation creates uncertainty, unanticipated problems that must be addressed, and new proposals for change, all of which create demand for lawyer-lobbyists.

The importance of legal representation in Washington has produced another interesting trend. Major law firms with headquarters in other cities have opened Washington branch offices in self-defense. In 1965, only 45 branch offices were located in Washington; today, there are around 245.[12] These firms believe that they can best serve (and hold on to) clients who are having problems with a regulatory agency by having their own lawyers in the capital.

Specialty Law Firms

Despite the presence of so many large prestigious firms, the structure of the Washington legal establishment is really quite diverse. Many small and medium-sized firms do very well. One way a small firm can distinguish itself is by specializing in a particular area of law, by becoming expert in the workings of one agency or program.

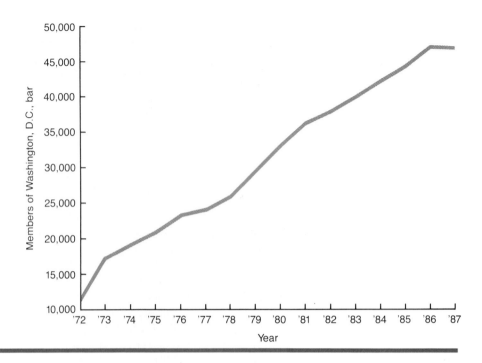

Washington Lawyers
The number of lawyers in Washington, D.C., has increased sharply in recent years. Many of these lawyers represent clients who want to influence government policymaking.
Figure 14.1

The law firm of Epstein & Becker is a case in point. The firm works almost exclusively in the health care field. If, for example, a client wants to set up a health maintenance organization (HMO), a prepaid health plan for consumers, its attorneys can guide them through the administrative maze of federal laws and regulations governing HMOs.[13]

Public interest law firms form another part of the Washington bar. These firms use the courts to try to protect what they consider to be the "people's interest." They are advocacy organizations, taking on only those issues that fit their ideological perspectives. Like their counterparts in large corporate firms, these organizations handle administrative lobbying as well as lawsuits. The Public Citizen Litigation Group, one public interest law firm, has won many suits, including one that allows pharmacies to advertise prescription drug prices.

When the public interest movement emerged as a strong force in the late 1960s and early 1970s, almost all of the new public interest law firms were on the liberal side of the political spectrum. They believed that it was their responsibility to counter the influence of large corporations, which are always well represented by lawyers. In the past few years, however, some conservative public interest law firms have set up shop in Washington. One of them, the Capital Legal Foundation, sued CBS on behalf of General William Westmoreland. Westmoreland alleged that he was libeled by a network documentary on the Vietnam War. (The program claimed that he deliberately misled policymakers about estimates of enemy troop strength.) The firm took on the case because it believed that the CBS news division was both too powerful and too liberal. But after the firm had spent more than $3 million on the case, adverse trial testimony led it and Westmoreland to agree to an out-of-court settlement that clearly favored CBS.

CONSULTING FIRMS

Not all government work is done by government workers. Federal departments and agencies spend enormous sums of money hiring people outside of government to conduct research, collect data, and perform policy and organizational analyses. These outsiders are called **consultants.** Consulting firms are profit-seeking businesses, and they are big business in Washington, where hundreds of firms compete for government contracts.

The Nature of Government Consulting

Consulting firms can be found all over the country, and many do little or no government work. Some firms, for example, work exclusively for businesses, offering market research, management studies, or other specialized services.

To understand what *government* consultants do, we should begin with the concept of *contracting out*. An agency may decide that it needs outside help to perform some job because it lacks the staff or expertise or objectivity to do the job itself. When an agency hires a consultant, both parties sign a contract that spells out the services to be provided and the amount of money to be paid for them. For example, suppose an agency needs a computer program to deal with a new, highly complex problem, and it does not have the expertise to develop the program itself. If the agency awards a contract to a computer consulting firm, once the program is developed and paid for, the agency has no further financial obligation to the consultant. This is a much more efficient way of spending agency funds than hiring a new bureaucrat who would have to be kept on the payroll indefinitely.

Much contracting out is done for technical services, such as auditing, computer work, or data collection, and seems far removed from the political process. More directly related to government decision making are studies that evaluate programs and analyze policy options. Government agencies spend hundreds of millions of dollars a year on these kinds of consulting contracts. For example, the National Institute of Education hired Abt Associates of Cambridge, Massachusetts, and Washington, D.C., to evaluate how changes in federal aid formulas would affect school districts. Under the three-year $3.7 million contract, Abt studied thirteen school districts and found that awarding money on the basis of educational performance rather than family income made little difference in either the services purchased with federal aid or their cost.[14]

A common criticism of this kind of research is that many studies do not warrant the expense. There is ample evidence that a significant portion of policy consulting work is simply not worth doing or paying for. One congressional study of U.S. Department of Defense consultants revealed that 17 percent of the projects they undertook were "of questionable value."[15] And everyone in Washington has a favorite horror story about a consulting contract that was an outright boondoggle. A classic example was a Department of Transportation contract for $225,000 with the Stanford Research Institute, to forecast transportation costs in the year 2025 under conditions of widespread guerrilla warfare.[16]

Sometimes the issues are important but the studies are not put to use. An agency might contract with skilled analysts who produce a first-rate piece of research, then disregard the study. Why? One reason is that a major study can take a year or more to complete, by which time policy or personnel changes may have reduced its urgency. Another reason is that a study's recommendations, even though well thought out, might not be politically feasible. A third reason is that the people who requested the study might not have the power to make the necessary policy changes. Finally, as one scholar noted, "the process of evaluation suggests change."[17] And change is threatening. So some people—particularly those who might lose authority—fight to maintain the status quo.

Getting the Contract

Criticism of the relationship between government and consulting firms has also been directed at the way in which contracts are handed out. Even though many contracts are awarded competitively, to the lowest bidder, other contracts are offered, in the language of the Washington bureaucracy, on a "sole-source basis." An agency can choose a consulting firm without accepting competing bids on the grounds that the consultant is uniquely qualified to do the job.

Consultants' familiarity with certain programs and agency officials helps them obtain both competitive and noncompetitive contracts. Consultants who have worked inside an agency have an advantage: They know how the agency operates, the way it approaches and resolves problems. Charles Owens, who worked for the Cost of Living Council and the Federal Energy Office, drafted oil price regulations during his stay in government. When he left the bureaucracy, he founded Charles R. Owens Associates, which became a leading consulting firm in the area of oil price controls.[18]

Some consultants use their familiarity with their former agencies to help others get government contracts. When a major defense-contracting scandal emerged in the summer of 1988, there were accusations that some consultants had passed on illegally obtained inside information on bids to contractors who employed them.

By its very nature, consulting work is unpredictable. Firms cannot always be assured of winning enough contracts to keep all their employees. This uncertainty puts tremendous pressure on a firm's top executives to find and win consulting jobs. As one Washington consultant put it, "The people who work as consultants to the federal government generally are aggressive and competitive. You've got to be to survive. You don't sit passively and wait for people to call—it just doesn't work that way."[19]

THINK TANKS

A **think tank** is an institution that conducts public policy research. Think tanks are staffed largely by people who have graduate degrees in the social sciences and strong interests in some aspect of public policy. The objective of Washington-based think tanks is to sponsor studies that are pertinent to the debate over selected issues facing the country. And they can take "their case directly to the Congress, the media, and the public— to the marketplace of ideas."[20]

Unlike consulting firms, think tanks are nonprofit organizations. Most think tanks do not rely on government (or private) contracts for their existence. Although they may do some government work, they receive the bulk of their funding from foundation grants, their own endowments, corporate gifts, and the proceeds from sales of their publications. Because they do not have to chase after consulting jobs, think tanks have the freedom to choose their own areas of study. Most sponsor broad scholarly studies that are directed toward a large audience inside and outside of government and that may take years to complete. The results of some think tank studies are published as books.[21]

Some think tanks focus their efforts on one broad policy area. For example, the Urban Institute focuses on urban policy issues, and the Joint Center for Political Studies does research on blacks. Others, such as the left-leaning Institute for Policy Studies and the right-leaning Heritage Foundation, have distinct ideological perspectives. Still others work toward a "mainstream" point of view. Of all of them, probably the best known are the Brookings Institution and the American Enterprise Institute. Both address a broad range of policy questions and produce highly respected studies.

The Brookings Institution

The Brookings Institution is located in a large gray austere building near Washington's Dupont Circle. The institution was founded in the early part of this century by Robert Somers Brookings, a St. Louis businessman. The endowment he started continues to fund a significant part of the institution's yearly budget. Brookings sponsors and performs studies in foreign, domestic, and economic policy. The senior fellows of the institution are scholars with national reputations, and its publications often are used as texts in university political science and economics courses. It is particularly well known for its analyses of federal budgetary policy.

Although it is strictly nonpartisan, the Brookings Institution has a reputation as a Democratic think tank. Its staff members do have a liberal bent, and many have been called on when a Democrat enters the White House. When Jimmy Carter became president, for example, a number of Brookings scholars took prominent positions in his administration. Among them were Charles Schultze, who became chairman of the Council of Economic Advisers, and Henry Aaron, who filled a top position in the U.S. Department of Health and Human Services. Aaron was given responsibility for developing an administration initiative on welfare reform; not coincidentally, while at Brookings he had written a book on the difficulties of welfare reform.[22] When the Democrats are not in power, Brookings is often referred to as the "government in exile."

A Forum at the American Enterprise Institute
Think tanks often sponsor conferences and forums on current issues and political developments. This forum at the American Enterprise Institute brought together leading political commentators and political scientists to discuss "Ronald Reagan and the American Dream."

The American Enterprise Institute

The American Enterprise Institute (AEI) was slower to develop its strong reputation. Started in 1943 and funded almost exclusively by corporate gifts, the institute tended to parrot whatever big business was saying at the time. Since then, AEI has become fiercely independent and employs top scholars in the social sciences. But AEI retains an overall conservative perspective; it is sometimes called the "Brookings of the Right."

Like Brookings, AEI is highly respected in Washington for the quality of its work. It produces and distributes nationally a steady stream of books, monographs, and conference proceedings. One particular area of research emphasis is regulatory practices. AEI economists tend to look for market solutions to policy problems; in line with the institute's conservative outlook, many AEI studies reflect a general goal of reducing government regulation. Foreign policy is another major focus, particularly of staffers who came to AEI from the Reagan administration.[23]

All think tanks have a common purpose: to influence government policy by providing useful research studies. As the Heritage Foundation's Burton Pines put it, "We are one of those few public organizations . . . who believe that ideas have consequences, ideas count, and it's worth fighting the war of ideas."[24] Beyond that common ground, though, think tanks differ greatly in their political views and their areas of policy expertise. They are like little universities without students—places where scholars can quietly go about their business of trying to find answers to this country's most pressing problems. The think tanks located in Washington have a special perch to sing from.

PUBLIC RELATIONS FIRMS

Washington-based **public relations firms** are hired by clients—usually corporations or trade associations—that want their interests promoted aggressively or their public image changed. These clients need help influencing the government or the public. In short, Washington's public relations firms combine lobbying with image building.

A good example of their dual function occurred when the Food and Drug Administration (FDA) banned the use of saccharin, a low-calorie artificial sweetener, after tests showed it caused cancer in rats. Companies that used saccharin in diet drinks and other diet products were faced with a serious problem. They had to fight the FDA ban and at the same time convince the public that they weren't selling bottled cancer. These manufacturers turned to a Washington public relations firm, which immediately rounded up a number of scientists who disputed the FDA's findings. An educational and promotional campaign quickly reassured the public and played a large part in eventually lifting the ban on saccharin.[25]

Public relations firms also prepare free editorials for radio, television, and newspapers. Small-town newspapers and radio stations in particular do not have the staff to prepare enough news. They depend on the networks and wire services for most of what they broadcast or print. But independent sources also supply them with material in the form of editorials or news stories. For example, Fraser Associates prepared material on pending labor law legislation for its client, the business-backed National Action Committee on Labor Law Reform. Newspapers like the Henderson (Kentucky) *Gleaner Journal*, the Delhi (New York) *Republican-Express*, and the Mentor (Ohio) *News-Herald* all carried almost identical editorials attacking the legislation. And all were based on the material Fraser Associates sent them.[26]

Hill and Knowlton is the largest public relations firm in Washington (and one of the largest in the country). An important trend in that firm and other large public relations firms in the capital is to offer a broad array of political services, a kind of "one-stop shopping." Many of these firms handle opinion polling, direct-mail campaigns, and political fund raising in addition to their more traditional lobbying and public relations services.[27] One way smaller firms compete against a giant like Hill and Knowlton is to find a particular market niche. Fenton Communications, for example, is known for its public relations work on behalf of "progressive" causes. In a typical job, Fenton arranged schedules and publicity for a group of eleven foreign notables who came to Washington to protest U.S. intervention in Central America.[28]

Washington public relations offices tend to be heavily staffed with people who have experience working for the media or the government. Those with backgrounds in government try to use their government connections to attract and help clients. At Hill and Knowlton, employees

The Consummate Insider
Robert Gray is the capital's premier public relations specialist. He has spent a lifetime cultivating the right connections in Washington and honing his ability to build favorable impressions for his many clients. It is rumored that Gray charges the highest fees among public relations practitioners in Washington.

include Gary Hymel, a former aide to Speaker of the House Thomas P. ("Tip") O'Neill, Jr.; Daniel Murphy, a former admiral in the navy and aide to Vice President George Bush; Bruce Fein, a former counsel at the FCC; and Diana Aldridge, a former aide to Democratic Senator Edward Kennedy of Massachusetts.

The foremost public relations specialist in Washington today is Robert Gray, who became the manager of Hill and Knowlton's office there after selling it his own firm in 1986 for $21 million. He founded Gray and Company in 1981 and built it into a firm with close to two hundred employees. Gray was a friend of Ronald Reagan and chaired his inaugural committees in 1981 and 1985. Corporate clients assume that someone who has been an intimate of a president can get a foot in the door, have phone calls returned, and exert some influence with policymakers.[29]

Public relations firms have an image problem, however. Many people react negatively to the idea that their minds can be changed by some type of promotion or advertising. So corporate clients are looking for something more than slick advertising campaigns. Public relations firms in Washington have responded by becoming increasingly sophisticated in their operations. They offer diversified services aimed at helping clients influence issues as they develop. They know that advertising and publicity must be complemented by long-term lobbying efforts to achieve their clients' goals.

TRADE ASSOCIATIONS

As defined in Chapter 9, a *trade association* is an organization that represents companies within an industry. For example, the Grocery Manufacturers of America is a trade association that, not surprisingly, represents firms in the grocery business. Many of the activities trade associations carry out have little to do with politics. They keep members abreast of marketing and manufacturing developments in their industries, public association newsletters and magazines, and sponsor conventions and gatherings where members can meet and do business together.

But trade associations also play a political role: They represent their members' interests before government, they are the lobbying arms of individual industries. And their political role is becoming increasingly important. As we discussed in Chapter 9, the number of trade associations with headquarters in Washington increased significantly in response to the growth of regulatory agencies and federal regulations in the 1960s and 1970s. Between 1971 and 1986, the proportion of all trade associations with headquarters in Washington grew from 19 percent to 31 percent.[30] The more than three thousand trade groups located in Washington are a principal source of jobs in the city's private sector, now employing around eighty thousand people.[31]

Trade associations do much more than lobby Congress when an occasional vote comes up. Day in, day out, they monitor the congressional committees and administrative agencies that oversee the programs or industries with which they are concerned. Experienced trade association representatives maintain regular contact with policymakers, supplying them with relevant information and finding out about proposed legislation or possible changes in regulations that could affect their members. As one association head noted, "Every time HUD [the Department of Housing and Urban Development] hiccups, 20 construction industry associations hold a meeting."[32]

ISSUE NETWORKS

All of the private-sector organizations and individuals we've been talking about are working to influence government and the policymaking process. To best serve their own and their clients' interests, they must develop reputations for excellence in intensely competitive fields. In Washington, *excellence* means, more than anything else, technical mastery of a policy area. Members of the community have to know their narrow specialties better than anyone else. But they also have to develop political relationships that will let them put their knowledge to work.

Government by Policy Area

It is easy to examine politics and policymaking in Washington by looking at the institutions of American government—Congress, the White House, the bureaucracy, the courts—as separate self-contained political bodies. Each is characterized by its own set of policymaking procedures, different patterns of personnel recruitment, and particular responsibilities that have been assigned by the Constitution or have evolved over the years. But policymaking is actually a dynamic process in which all of these institutions interact with one another and the private sector.

To understand how the process works, let's suppose that Congress is considering amendments to the Clean Air Act. Congress does not function in a vacuum. The other parts of government that will be affected by the legislation take part in the process, too. The Environmental Protection Agency (EPA) has an interest in the outcome because it will have to administer the law. The White House is concerned about any legislation that affects such vital sectors of the economy as the steel and coal industries. As a result, officials from both the EPA and the White House work with members of Congress and the appropriate committee staffs to try to make sure that their interests are protected. At the same time, lobbyists representing corporations, trade associations, and environmental groups are doing their best to influence Congress, agency officials, and White House aides. Trade associations might hire public relations firms to sway public opinion toward industry's point of view. And outside experts from think tanks and universities might be asked to testify at hearings or to serve in an informal advisory capacity concerning the technical, economic, and social impact of the proposed amendment.

The policymaking process does not end when Congress enacts the new amendments; it enters a new phase. First, administrative regulations need to be drawn up. This is the function of the bureaucracy—that is, of the EPA—but key congressional committee members and officials from the Office of Management and Budget, acting on behalf of the White House, monitor the process closely. Interest group lawyers also work to influence the regulations' content. Once the new law and its regulations are put into effect, the EPA might hire consultants to assess their impact. If an interest group's lawyers feel that the regulations harm its members and have not been drawn up to follow Congress's original intent, they might take the agency to court. And if Congress and agency officials become aware of emerging problems, then new amendments will be proposed, and the process will begin again.

Policymaking then, neither begins nor ends within a single institution. It is an ongoing process that involves many different participants, all of whom have an interest in the policy. What these participants have in common is membership in an issue network. An **issue network** is "a shared-knowledge group having to do with some aspect . . . of public policy."[33] The boundaries of an issue network are fuzzy, but in general terms they are made up of members of Congress, committee staffers, agency officials, lawyers, lobbyists, consultants, scholars, and public relations specialists who interact on an ongoing basis as they work to influence policies in a particular issue area. This makes for a large number of participants—the number of interest group organizations alone in a broad policy area is usually in the dozens.[34]

Not all participants in an issue network have a working relationship with all others. Indeed, some may be chronic antagonists. Others tend to be allies. Environmental groups, for example, will coalesce in trying to influence the Clean Air Act and will likely be in opposition to business groups. As we discuss in more detail below, the common denominator that ties friends and foes together in an issue network is technical mastery of a particular policy area.

Iron Triangles

The idea of examining politics in Washington by looking at policy areas rather than at individual institutions is not new. Research by an earlier generation of political scientists and journalists described a system of *subgovernments*, tightly knit groups that dominated policymaking in an issue area. For example, journalist Douglass Cater wrote about the sugar subgovernment of the late 1950s:

> Political power within the sugar subgovernment is largely vested in the Chairman of the House Agricultural Committee who works out the schedule of quotas. It is shared by a veteran civil servant, the director of the Sugar Division of the U.S. Department of Agriculture, who provides the necessary "expert" advice for such a complex marketing arrangement. Further advice is provided by Washington representatives of the domestic beet and cane sugar growers, the sugar refineries, and the foreign producers.[35]

Cater's subgovernment had three components:

- Key members of the congressional committees and subcommittees responsible for the policy area (in this case, the chairman of the House Agriculture Committee)
- Officials from the agency or bureau that administers the policy (the director of a division of the U.S. Department of Agriculture)
- Lobbyists who represent the agency's clients (growers, refineries, and foreign producers)

These policymaking communities were called **iron triangles.** The term *iron* referred to a very important property of these subgovernments: They were largely autonomous and closed; outsiders had a great deal of difficulty penetrating them. Even presidents had difficulty influencing iron triangles, which endured over time and changed little when new administrations came into power. And job changes did not usually affect them. An individual who left one component of the triangle often would move to another. Iron triangles worked because participants shared similar policy views and tried to reach a consensus that would benefit all of them.[36]

The iron triangle model was very popular with political scientists. Although some used different terms (*subgovernments, cozy little triangles*) and some developed more sophisticated frameworks than the simplified version we've offered here, the basic ideas were the same: Typically, a small group of individuals dominated policymaking in their issue area, these policy communities were largely autonomous, and they favored those who were well organized.[37] The model was used, not only to explain how American politics operated, but also to show what was wrong with our policymaking system.

The Case of Telecommunications

The telecommunications industry gives us a useful illustration of the changing nature of politics in Washington. Once an iron triangle, telecommunications today is a large issue network filled with conflict.

Until fairly recently, the telecommunications industry was dominated by AT&T. AT&T and its affiliated Bell System phone companies around the country constituted a monopoly: A customer generally had no choice but to use the phone lines and phone equipment of Ma Bell. It was easy for AT&T executives to defend their company's control of the industry. The United States had an impressive system with low-cost, reliable service to residential customers. Moreover, the AT&T network was a mainstay of our defense communications system. Within the iron triangle—a policymaking community made up of some key members of Congress, the Federal Communications Commission, and AT&T—policymaking was usually consensual and uncontroversial.

At one time, AT&T was the world's largest corporation, and it seemed invulnerable. But in 1968, the FCC ruled that other companies could compete against AT&T in the "terminal" equipment market. This meant that a customer could buy a telephone (or more complex telephone equipment) from a company other than AT&T and attach it to AT&T phone lines. This jolt of competition was followed a year later with a second blow to AT&T, when the FCC ruled that MCI, a small start-up company marketing microwave technology, could sell a limited form of long-distance service to business clients.

As significant as these changes were, the greatest challenge to AT&T lay ahead. In 1974, the U.S. Department of Justice brought a lawsuit against the corporation charging it with illegal monopolistic behavior in the telecommunications industry. The eventual outcome of the suit was an out-of-court settlement that stipulated that AT&T must divest itself of control over local operating service. The Bell System was broken up into seven regional phone companies, each independent of AT&T. AT&T was allowed to retain its long-distance service, but it would have to compete against other long-distance carriers. (AT&T did win the right to enter the computer industry, which was one of its major goals.) All in all, AT&T lost three-quarters of its assets.[38]

Today, policymaking in telecommunications bears no resemblance to an iron triangle.[39] As Figure 14.2 shows, there is a large varied group of participants in this issue network. Although there is no one way to draw an issue network, here the most important policymaking bodies are within the inner ring. In the middle ring are the most frequent interest group participants and a secondary policymaking body in the U.S. Department of Commerce. Organizations that have a more limited focus on the telecommunications issues they work on are in the outer ring.

Conflict within the network is chronic. Alliances change rapidly as coalition partners on one issue become opponents on the next. The different lobbying organizations fight to protect their market share while trying to encroach on that of others. No one controls telecommunications policymaking, but a large array of organizations and individuals have a say in it.

Not all policymaking communities in Washington have evolved into issue networks. Some are still better described as iron triangles or subgovernments. For example, the Sea Grant Program, which offers grants to

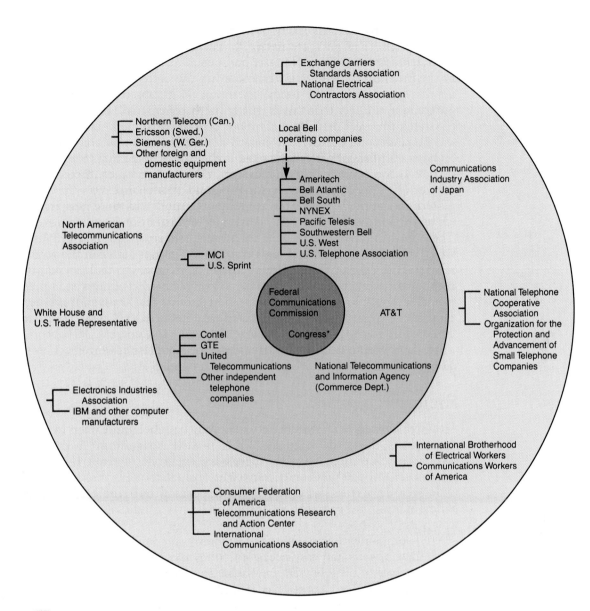

Indicates primary interest group alliance.

*Primary congressional actors are the House Committee on Energy and Commerce, Subcommittee on Telecommunications and Finance, and the Senate Committee on Commerce, Science, and Transportation, Subcommittee on Communications.

The Telecommunications Issue Network

Policymaking in telecommunications is characterized by a multitude of actors and a great deal of conflict. Among the interest group participants are AT&T, the regional phone companies, long distance carriers, equipment manufacturers, labor unions, consumer groups, and foreign corporations and trade associations. (Source: Jeffrey M. Berry, The Interest Group Society, *2d ed. [Glenview, Ill.: Scott, Foresman/Little, Brown, in press]. Copyright © 1989 Scott Foresman and Company.)*

Figure 14.2

colleges to promote the study of marine resources, is closer to being an iron triangle than an issue network. There are just a small number of participants and policymaking is consensual. The only ones interested in the program outside of government are the colleges, and they are all on the same side of the issue—there are no groups trying to stop the program. It is likely that this is true of many other small uncontroversial programs that just distribute grants or benefits of some type.[40]

Broader policy areas, like health and agriculture, are characterized by large numbers of participants and high degrees of conflict.[41] Why have so many iron triangles rusted through and larger, more conflicted issue networks evolved? A primary force behind this change was the rapid growth in the number of interest groups. As more and more new groups set up shop in Washington, they demanded the attention of policymakers. These new groups brought with them new concerns, and their interests were usually at odds with at least some of the groups active in the policy area. (In the case of telecommunications, this process was hastened by technological change.) Part of the growth of interest groups stemmed from the public interest movement. The groups that evolved from that movement were natural adversaries of business, so new conflicts emerged in many issue areas. Change also came to Congress. As subcommittees proliferated and committee chairs became less powerful, congressional jurisdiction over programs began to overlap.

POLICY EXPERTISE

Although contemporary issue networks may be much more open to new participants than iron triangles, there is still a significant barrier to admission. One must have the necessary expertise to enter the community of activists and politicians who influence policymaking in an issue area. Expertise has always been important, but "more than ever, policy-making is becoming an intramural activity among expert issue watchers."[42]

Oil companies are crucial to our economy, and lobbyists for the major firms have always had easy access to policymakers in government. Yet, there are lots of oil lobbyists in Washington and not all have the same influence. They compete for the attention and respect of those in government by offering solutions to problems that are technically feasible as well as politically palatable. Consider the issues addressed during a period of expanding regulation of the domestic oil industry. There was no end to seemingly obscure and complicated policy questions. How were "original costs" to be distinguished from "reproduction costs"? Was it fair for "secondary and tertiary production" to be exempted from "base-period volumes"? Did drilling that yielded "new pays" or "extensions" qualify as "new" oil or "old" oil for pricing purposes?[43]

Those in an issue network speak the same language. They can participate in the negotiation and compromise of policymaking because they can offer concrete, detailed solutions to the problems at hand. They understand the substance of policy, the way Washington works, and one another's viewpoints.

Bipartisan Clout
Anne Wexler (left), a well-known Democrat, and Nancy Reynolds, a Republican, are two of the principals in a lobbying firm. The bipartisan nature of their firm is not unusual—public relations and lobbying firms want clients to believe they have access to important policymakers in both parties.

One reason participants in an issue network have such a good understanding of the needs and problems of others in the network is that job switches within policy communities continue to be common. When someone wants to leave his or her current position but remain in Washington, the most obvious place to look for a new job is in the same policy field. For these **in-and-outers,** knowledge and experience remain relevant to a particular issue network, no matter which side of the fence they're on.

A common pattern of job switching—one that is the focus of much criticism—is to work in government for a number of years, build up knowledge of a policy area, then take a lobbying job. Law firms, consulting firms, public relations firms, and trade associations generally pay much higher salaries than the government. And they pay, not just for experience and know-how, but for connections with government. When the Washington lobbying firm of Black, Manafort, Stone & Kelly hired James C. Healy, a former aide to the Democratic chairman of the House Ways and Means Committee, it knew that this in-and-outer would give them better access to that critical tax-writing unit. Corporations that want to influence the committee can choose among many Washington firms. Black, Manafort, Stone & Kelly can make a convincing case to prospective clients that Healy's phone calls to the House Democratic leadership are returned.[44]

Some congressional staffers and high-ranking executive branch officials, like Mike Deaver, "cash in their chips" by starting their own firms rather than going to work for an existing firm. Despite the competition, those with valuable government experience and their peers' respect can quickly establish themselves as the people with the right expertise and the right contacts in a *particular* policy field. This was certainly the case with Susan J. Williams and Terrence L. Bracy. Both served as assistant secretaries of transportation in the Carter administration. When they started Bracy Williams & Company in 1981, they had little trouble attracting clients in the transportation field, among them, the Air Line Pilots Association, the CSX railroad company, and the Quixote Corporation, which manufactures highway crash barriers.[45]

One constraint on in-and-outers is the Ethics in Government Act of 1978, which specifies that senior executive branch officials cannot lobby their former agency for a year after leaving the government, and they must wait two years to lobby any agency on an issue on which they were personally and substantially involved. In 1988, former White House aide Lyn Nofziger became the first person ever convicted under the lobbying restrictions of the act. Nofziger left the Reagan White House in 1982, but within less than a year he was lobbying the White House on behalf of the Wedtech Corporation, a New York defense contractor.[46] He was convicted of violating the law on behalf of two other clients as well. (Nofziger is appealing the decision.)

Movement within a policy community also flows the other way: Individuals from the private sector are often tapped for government positions within the same issue network.[47] After President Reagan took office, he chose William Sullivan, Jr., as an associate administrator of the Environmental Protection Agency. Previously, Sullivan had headed the Steel Communities Coalition, an industry group that was fighting to have pollution control standards relaxed because they were having an adverse impact on financially ailing steel companies. At the EPA, Sullivan's job included enforcing air pollution standards.[48]

ISSUE NETWORKS AND DEMOCRACY

The role of issue networks in policymaking gives rise to a set of interrelated questions. Are issue networks making the government too fragmented? Are some issue networks beyond popular control? Has the increasing complexity of public policy given technical experts too much policymaking authority?

These questions relate to the broad issues raised in Chapter 2. For many years, political scientists have described American democracy as a system in which different constituencies work energetically to influence policies that are of concern to them. Here, policymaking is seen as a response to these groups rather than to majority will. This is a considerably different conception of democracy than the more traditional view, that policies reflect what most of the people want. It is a pluralist, not a majoritarian, view of American government.

When iron triangles were considered typical of the policymaking process, they were the target of much criticism. Some argued that the type of pluralism that they represented did not promote democracy through group politics, but engendered closed systems that favored the status quo. The groups that were part of the iron triangles found government highly responsive. But these groups did not represent all the interests that should have been at the bargaining table. Consumer groups and environmental groups were not there to protect the public interest. Business groups that dominated the iron triangles used their position to try to stifle new competition through regulatory restrictions, as was the case with AT&T in the telecommunications field.

In a number of ways, issue networks are an improvement over iron triangles as a model of pluralist democracy. They are open systems, populated by a much wider range of interest groups. Decision making is not centralized in the hands of a few key players; policies are formulated in a much more participatory fashion. But there is still no guarantee that all relevant interests are represented, and those with greater financial resources have an advantage. Yet, issue networks come much closer to meeting the objectives of pluralist democracy than do iron triangles.[49]

For those who prefer majoritarian democracy, though, issue networks are an obstacle to the achievement of their vision of how government should operate. Although issue networks are not autonomous and the policies they formulate can be swayed by election outcomes and the broad contours of public opinion, the technical complexity of contemporary issues makes it especially difficult for the public at large to exert control over policy outcomes. When we think of the complexity of nuclear power, toxic wastes, and air pollution, it is easy to understand why majoritarian democracy is so difficult to achieve. The more complex the issue, the more elected officials must depend on a technocratic elite for policy guidance. And technical expertise, of course, is a chief characteristic of participants in issue networks.

At first glance, it may seem very desirable to have policymaking highly influenced by technical experts. After all, who else but the experts should be making decisions about toxic wastes? But a dependence on technocrats works to the advantage of interest groups, who use policy experts to maximize their influence with government. Seen in this light, issue networks become less appealing. Interest groups—at least those with which we do not personally identify—are seen as selfish. They pursue policies that favor their constituents rather than the national interest.

Although expertise is an important factor in bringing interest groups and other members of the Washington community into the decision-

COMPARED WITH WHAT? 14.1

Bureaucrats, Legislators, and Lobbyists

The patterns of interaction among bureaucrats, legislators, and lobbyists differ considerably among Western democracies. The figure shows the percentage of bureaucrats in each country reporting that they have "regular" contact with legislators and representatives of client groups. Issue network politics contributes to the high level of interaction among U.S. bureaucrats, legislators, and interest group representatives.

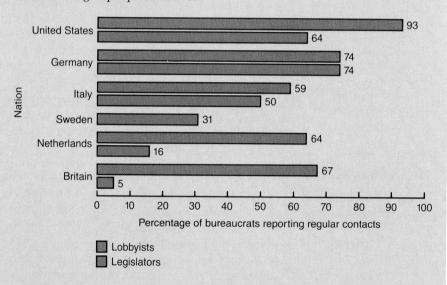

* Because Swedish respondents were asked about five specific interest groups, those data were excluded from the figure.

Source: Adapted from Joel D. Aberbach, Robert D. Putnam, and Bert A. Rockman, *Bureaucrats and Politicians in Western Democracies* (Cambridge, Mass.: Harvard University Press, 1981), p. 230. Reprinted by permission.

making process, it is not the only one. Americans have a fundamental belief that government should be open and accessible to the people (see Compared With What? 14.1). If some constituency has a problem, they reason, government ought to listen to it. The practical consequence of this view is a government that is open to interest groups and those they hire from the Washington community.

SUMMARY

The policymaking process in Washington involves many people outside of the legislative, executive, and judicial branches of government. Washington's private sector—its law firms, consulting firms, think tanks, public relations firms, and trade associations—

is an integral part of the political system. The growth of government service industries reflects the changing nature of politics in Washington. Government expanded greatly during the 1960s and 1970s, when new regulatory agencies were created to deal with a widening variety of business and social concerns. One by-product of this growth was a surge in the number of interest groups that established offices in Washington. And as lobbies expanded, they drew on increasing numbers of lawyers, consultants, public relations firms, and other experts to influence government policy.

Policymaking can be viewed as an ongoing process of interaction between those in government and those outside it, through issue networks. Each network is a means of communication through which information and ideas about a particular policy area are exchanged. Consultants and scholars from think tanks join experts working on behalf of interest groups, agency officials, and members of Congress in various issue networks. Generally, these contemporary policy communities are more open to new participants than were the old iron triangles.

The ever-increasing complexity of public policy issues also puts a premium on expertise. Those with expertise in a given area are in the best position to influence policy in that area.

Political scientists view issue networks with some concern. There is no question that these networks facilitate the representation of many interests in the policymaking process, but they do so at a price. They allow well-organized aggressive constituencies to prevail over the broader interests of the nation. Once again, the majoritarian and pluralist models of democracy come into conflict. It is easy to say that the majority should rule. But in the real world, the majority tends to be far less interested in issues than are the constituencies most directly affected by them. It is also easy to say that those most affected by issues should have the most influence. But experience teaches us that this kind of influence leads to policies that favor the well represented, at the expense of those who should be at the bargaining table but are not.

Key Terms

Washington community	public relations firm
lawyer-lobbyist	issue network
consultant	iron triangle
think tank	in-and-outer

Selected Readings

Adams, Gordon. *The Politics of Defense Contracting: The Iron Triangle.* New Brunswick, N.J.: Transaction Books, 1982. An examination of the close relationship between defense contractors and government officials.

Cater, Douglass. *Power in Washington.* New York: Vintage Books, 1964. One reporter's view of how policy is formulated in Washington.

Chubb, John E. *Interest Groups and the Bureaucracy.* Stanford, Calif.: Stanford University Press, 1983. A sophisticated analysis of interest group–agency interaction within various energy policy communities.

Dodd, Lawrence C., and Richard L. Schott. *Congress and the Administrative State.* New York: Wiley, 1979. The authors trace the evolution of subgovernments and institutional reform in Congress.

Laumann, Edward O., and David Knoke. *The Organizational State.* Madison, Wis.: University of Wisconsin Press, 1987. The authors use network theory to analyze policymaking in health and energy.

Mackenzie, G. Calvin. *The In-and-Outers.* Baltimore: Johns Hopkins University Press, 1987. A collection of essays examining the problems associated with the movement of people back and forth between the private sector and the executive branch.

Ripley, Randall B., and Grace A. Franklin. *Congress, the Bureaucracy, and Public Policy.* 4th ed. Homewood, Ill.: Dorsey Press, 1987. Ripley and Franklin look at subgovernment politics in different types of policy arenas.

Essay D

The Transformation of Public Policy

Although the U.S. government continues to fulfill the traditional functions of maintaining order and providing public goods, it has undertaken new roles as well. For example, the government now promotes equality by providing for social welfare, and it more actively protects citizens from hazards like environmental waste (promoting order by protecting safety). The following graphs and maps illustrate facets of the government's changing role as well as some of the factors that have produced these changes.

"National Government Outlays" shows the major changes that have occurred in national spending since 1940 by plotting the percentages of the annual budget devoted to four major expense categories. In the 1940s, spending for World War II consumed more than 80 percent of the national budget. Defense again accounted for most national expenditures during the Cold War in the 1950s. Since then, the military's share of expenditures has declined while payments to individuals (mostly in the form of social security benefits) have increased dramatically. Also, as the graph shows, the proportion of the budget paid in interest on the national debt has increased substantially since the 1970s.

The southwest experienced dramatic population growth from 1970 to 1980 as the prospect for jobs led many people away from the "rust-belt" (or "frostbelt") of the northeast and midwest toward states in the "sunbelt" (see "The Shift to the Sunbelt"). The pattern of federal funding has done little to stop this migration. "The Flow of Federal Funds" shows the relationship between the amount of taxes paid to Washington by citizens in each state and the money returned to the states through federal spending. Citizens in states with ratios below 1.00 paid more in taxes than their states received back in spending. Citizens in states with ratios over 1.00 paid less than their states received.

National Government Outlays

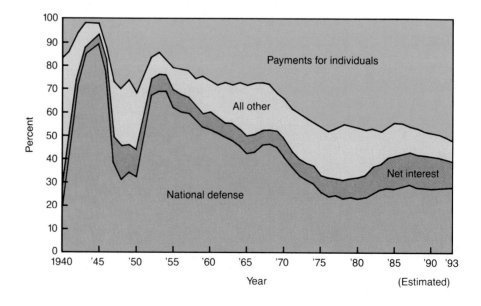

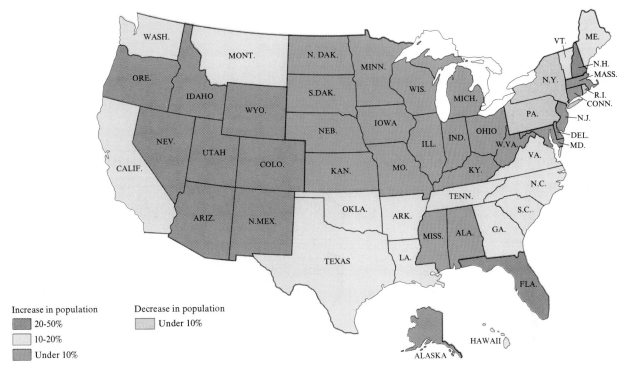

Increase in population
- 20-50%
- 10-20%
- Under 10%

Decrease in population
- Under 10%

The Shift to the Sunbelt

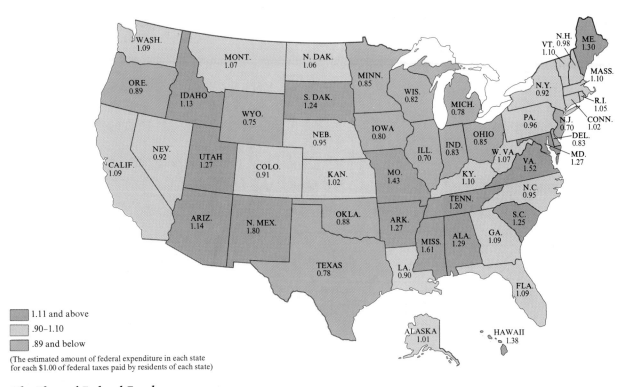

- 1.11 and above
- .90–1.10
- .89 and below

(The estimated amount of federal expenditure in each state
for each $1.00 of federal taxes paid by residents of each state)

The Flow of Federal Funds

U.S. industrial production index (1977 = 100)

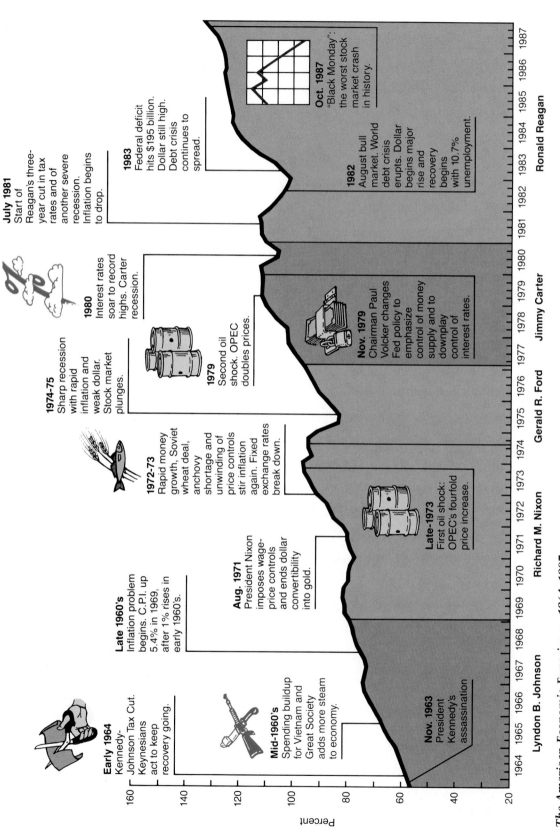

Early 1964
Kennedy-Johnson Tax Cut. Keynesians act to keep recovery going.

Late 1960's
Inflation problem begins. C.P.I. up 5.4% in 1969, after 1% rises in early 1960's.

Aug. 1971
President Nixon imposes wage-price controls and ends dollar convertibility into gold.

Mid-1960's
Spending buildup for Vietnam and Great Society adds more steam to economy.

Nov. 1963
President Kennedy's assassination

Late-1973
First oil shock: OPEC's fourfold price increase.

1972–73
Rapid money growth, Soviet wheat deal, anchovy shortage and unwinding of price controls stir inflation again. Fixed exchange rates break down.

1974–75
Sharp recession with rapid inflation and weak dollar. Stock market plunges.

1979
Second oil shock. OPEC doubles prices.

Nov. 1979
Chairman Paul Volcker changes Fed policy to emphasize control of money supply and to downplay control of interest rates.

1980
Interest rates soar to record highs. Carter recession.

July 1981
Start of Reagan's three-year cut in tax rates and of another severe recession. Inflation begins to drop.

1983
Federal deficit hits $195 billion. Dollar still high. Debt crisis continues to spread.

1982
August bull market. World debt crisis erupts. Dollar begins major rise and recovery begins with 10.7% unemployment.

Oct. 1987
"Black Monday": the worst stock market crash in history.

Percent

20 40 60 80 100 120 140 160

1964 1965 1966 1967 1968 1969 1970 1971 1972 1973 1974 1975 1976 1977 1978 1979 1980 1981 1982 1983 1984 1985 1986 1987

Lyndon B. Johnson   Richard M. Nixon   Gerald R. Ford   Jimmy Carter   Ronald Reagan

The American Economic Experience, 1964–1987

Source: Copyright © 1984 by the New York Times Company. Reprinted by permission. New data from Federal Reserve Bank statistical releases.

Keynesian economic theory was designed to control the occurrence of *business cycles*—rhythmic expansion and contraction of business activity accompanied by inflation and unemployment—through government use of fiscal and monetary economic policies. Although the national government regularly uses such policies to control the economy, the government has not eliminated business cycles, as shown by the wavy graph in "The American Economic Experience, 1964–1987." Nevertheless, no one can say how wildly the cycles might have fluctuated without government intervention in the economy.

In 1913, the Sixteenth Amendment empowered the national government to collect taxes on income. Since then, the government has levied taxes on individual and corporate income and on capital gains realized by individuals and corporations from the sale of assets, such as stocks or real estate. As shown in "The Ups and Downs of Federal Income Tax Rates," these rates have fluctuated wildly over time, from under 10 percent to over 90 percent—tending to be the highest during periods of war. President Ronald Reagan pledged to lower taxes, and indeed the tax rates during his administration fell to their lowest levels since the Coolidge and Hoover administrations in the late 1920s and early 1930s.

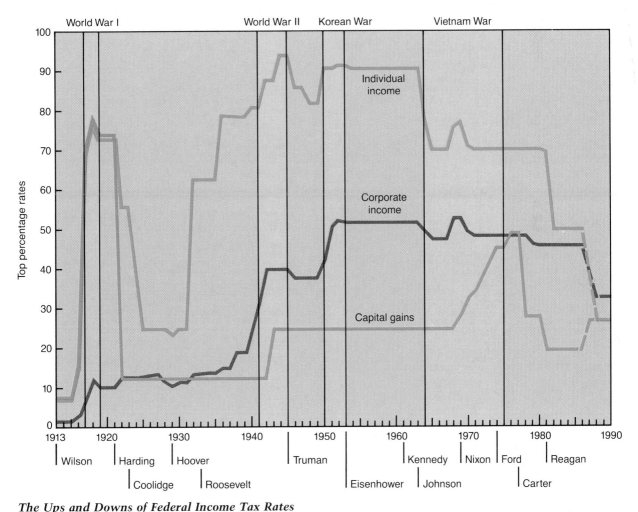

The Ups and Downs of Federal Income Tax Rates
Source: Wall Street Journal, *18 August 1986, p. 10. Reprinted by permission of the Wall Street Journal, © Dow Jones &*
Company, Inc. 1986. All Rights Reserved.

PART V

MAKING PUBLIC POLICY

15

The Economics of Public Policy

Stockbrokers spent a restless weekend in mid-October 1987, worried about Monday's opening of the New York Stock Exchange. For most of the year, sales had boomed on the stock market. The best-known market index—the Dow Jones average of thirty industrial stocks—soared from 1,900 points in January to almost 2,750 points in August. Since then, it had dropped substantially. And the previous Friday, it showed a record loss of 108 points, closing at 2,247. When the brokers got to work on Monday, the news was bad. Markets in Melbourne, Tokyo, Hong Kong, and London were all down sharply.

On October 19, 1987, the New York Stock Exchange suffered its worst crash in history. The index plunged 508 points—closing at 1,739—as panicky investors and electronic computers combined in massive selling. In a single day—Black Monday—the Dow Jones index lost 22.6 percent of its value, almost double the loss on Black Tuesday in 1929, which signaled the Great Depression of the 1930s. In contemporary terms, the book value of the loss amounted to $500 billion, equal to the entire gross national product of France.[1]

Bad as the crash was on Monday, the market came close to a complete collapse on Tuesday. Around midday, an eerie hush settled over the stock exchange floor, stilling the frenzied activities of the specialists. *Specialists* trade in specific stocks (say, IBM or General Motors) and are responsible for maintaining a "fair and orderly market" in their stocks. If more investors are selling than buying a given stock, the specialist must step in to buy it. On Monday, many specialists had depleted their own resources and borrowed heavily to buy falling stocks. On Tuesday, banks were unwilling to extend them short-term loans to purchase more stock.[2] Without funds to buy stocks that investors wanted to sell, the specialists could not maintain a market in their stocks. As more banks refused credit, more specialists became helpless, and thought was given to closing the stock exchange itself. A presidential panel later concluded, "The financial system came close to gridlock."[3]

On Tuesday afternoon, the Federal Reserve System (the national government's central banking institution) worked behind the scenes to avoid a shutdown. The Federal Reserve made more money available to the banking system, and the Federal Reserve Bank of New York contacted major banks, urging them to lend more funds to securities firms and stockbrokers. These actions helped reverse the decline, and by the market's close on Friday, the Dow Jones index had regained more than 200 of the points lost on Monday. Through the rest of the year, the market slowly recovered. At the start of 1988, the Dow Jones average was just about where it had opened the previous year. However, the volume of shares traded was down substantially; investors' confidence in the market had been thoroughly shaken.

What caused the crash? The experts could not agree on an answer. Five official investigations into the market collapse cited a variety of factors, including new computer-based trading techniques, complex trades involving current stock purchases and options to buy future stocks, and worries about the budget deficit.[4] The experts also could not agree on the significance of the crash.[5] The short-term impact was clear: Many investors lost a great deal of money. This hurt not only wealthy

Wall Street—the Reality, Not the Movie
The stock market crash of October 19, 1987, made headlines around the world. In Tokyo, where the market plunge on Monday helped set off the crash on Wall Street, the news from America sparked the worst stock market fall in Japanese history on October 20. The reaction was similar in most other nations. Stocks fell nearly everywhere, if trading was allowed at all.

investors but also workers nearing retirement who may not even have realized that their pension funds were based mainly on stock holdings.

Judging by the 1929 experience, the long-term effects of the crash remain to be seen. At that time, the market also recovered substantially within a few months, but the ensuing chain of failed businesses and unemployment culminated in the Great Depression of the 1930s. Trying to avoid that scenario, President Ronald Reagan and congressional leaders held a "summit" meeting in November 1987 to negotiate a two-year commitment on deficit reduction, beginning with the budget for 1989. But as the market stabilized, pressure to cut the deficit subsided, and the summit produced only modest reductions. The resulting budget pact (which we discuss later) was denounced by Wall Street as inadequate to the problem.[6]

Financial experts do agree on two things about the crash of 1987. They believe that the Federal Reserve System lessened the impact of the crash by pumping money into the banking system at a critical time. (In

1929, it had tightened credit and made conditions worse.) And they agree that the crash made investors sensitive to any negative economic news, which makes for a shaky economy.

In light of the stock market crash of 1987, how much freedom should the markets enjoy from government regulation? Apart from regulation, what can government do to control the economy? What effects do government taxing and spending policies have on the economy and on economic equality? We grapple with these and other questions in this chapter on the economics of public policy.

GOVERNMENT PURPOSES AND PUBLIC POLICIES

In Chapter 1, we noted that virtually all citizens are willing to accept limitations on their personal freedom in return for various benefits of government. We defined the major purposes of government as maintaining order, providing public goods, and promoting equality. Different governments place different values on each of these broad purposes, and those differences are reflected in their public policies. A **public policy** is a general plan of action adopted by a government to solve a social problem, counter a threat, or pursue an objective. For example, our government has formulated policies for lowering unemployment, reducing crime in cities, or negotiating with the Soviet Union.

At times, governments choose not to adopt a policy for dealing with a troublesome situation; instead, they just "muddle through" until the problem goes away or becomes too big to ignore. Government policies can be carefully developed and effective, or hastily drawn and ineffective, even counterproductive. But the reverse can also be true: Well-constructed policies may end up total disasters, and quick fixes may work just fine. Whatever their form and effectiveness, however, all policies have this in common: They are the *means* by which government pursues certain *goals* within specific *situations*. People disagree over public policies because they disagree over one or more of these elements: the goals that government should have, the means it should use to meet them, and the perception of the situation.

Consider the social problem of poverty. Everyone deplores poverty, but people disagree on whether reducing poverty should be an objective of government. Even those who think that the government ought to fight poverty are divided over the proper means. Some favor government job programs for the unemployed; others favor specific aid programs, like the food stamp program; still others favor a guaranteed minimum income for all Americans. Moreover, people disagree over the extent of poverty in the United States. How many of the nation's 230 million people do *you* think live in poverty? Fewer than a million? Between 10 and 20 million? More than 30 million? How you perceive the problem makes a difference in how you evaluate the alternative policies aimed at reducing poverty.

According to government figures, more than 32 million Americans were living in poverty in 1986—about 13.6 percent of the population.[7] If you accept this finding as fact, you probably want government to do something about the problem. But what if you think that the finding exaggerates the extent of poverty? What is *poverty* anyway? The Census Bureau defines the *poverty threshold* according to the number of people in a family. In 1986, it was $5,572 for a single person or $11,203 for a family of four.[8] If you don't agree on the extent of the problem or even the definition of the problem, chances are you are not going to agree on policies to tackle the problem.

Even if you accept the fact of poverty and the need for government action, what about the policy? As we discuss in Chapter 16, it is difficult to formulate policies that effectively reduce poverty. In 1965, President Lyndon Johnson committed the nation to spending billions of dollars to win the War on Poverty. Yet today, there are about the same percentage of people below the poverty threshold as there were in the mid-1960s.

What can governments do to achieve their goals? They have four basic options:

- To demand that citizens do this or not do that
- To try to persuade citizens to behave in certain ways
- To take from individuals or give to individuals
- To perform the task itself

Unfortunately, knowing the options is not the same as understanding government's objectives in demanding, persuading, taking or giving, and performing. We need concepts that can help us analyze the purposes behind government's actions.

At the broadest level, we can analyze public policies according to whether they prohibit, protect, promote, or provide. Some policies are intended to *prohibit* behaviors that endanger society. All governments outlaw murder, robbery, and rape, for example. Governments that em-

The Law Says, "Butt Out!"
Government regulations against smoking in public areas are intended to protect the public health. Today, smoking is not completely banned. But remember that the sale and distribution of alcoholic beverages once were prohibited by the Constitution.

An Oil Rig on a Sea of Tax Benefits
The government can tailor its tax policies to promote certain business activities. The oil and gas industries have long enjoyed various tax deductions for expenses incurred in energy exploration. The cost in lost revenues to the national government was about $2 billion in 1988.

phasize order tend to specialize in policies of prohibition, which instruct people what they must *not* do (drink liquor, have abortions, engage in homosexual relations). In the next chapter, we discuss a particularly vexing problem in contemporary public policy, prohibiting people from consuming illegal drugs—marijuana, heroin, and cocaine.

Government policies can also *protect* activities, things, or special groups of citizens. For example, taxes were once levied on colored margarine (a butter substitute) to reduce its sales and protect the dairy industry from competition. Regulations concerning the testing of new drugs are intended to protect citizens from harmful side effects; government rules about safety in the workplace are enacted to protect workers. Issues in regulatory policy were explored in Chapter 12. Although governments argue that these kinds of regulations serve the public good, some people believe that most protective legislation is unwarranted government interference. (In Chapter 16, we examine the problems in developing a regulatory policy to protect against the spread of AIDS.)

Policies can also *promote* social activities that are important to the government. Here, one way that government promotes is by persuasion. For instance, our government has used advertising to urge people to buy bonds or to be all that they can be and join the army. When the government really wants to get things done, it can be very generous. To promote railroad construction in the 1860s, Congress granted railroad companies huge tracts of public lands along the right-of-way through western states.

The government also promotes activities through favorable treatment within the tax structure. The technical term for this form of government promotion is **tax expenditure,** because it amounts to a loss of government revenue. For example, the government encourages people to buy their own homes by allowing them to deduct from their taxable income the amount of money they pay in mortgage interest. In 1987, this tax expenditure cost the national government nearly $25 billion.[9] And of course, churches and private educational institutions typically pay no property taxes to state and local governments.

Finally, public policies can *provide* benefits directly to citizens. These benefits can be either public or private. *Public benefits* are facilities or services that all citizens share (mail service, roads, schools, street lighting, libraries, parks). *Private benefits* go to certain groups of citizens (poor people, farmers, veterans, college students). Public benefits are more difficult to deliver because they require either the construction of facilities (roads, dams, sewer systems) or organizations to provide them (transportation agencies, power companies, sanitation departments). Private benefits are simply payments to individuals in the form of food stamps, subsidies, pensions, and loans. These payments are made because the recipients are particularly needy or politically powerful, or both.

At times, policies serve multiple purposes. For example, we could say that a policy of subsidizing farmers protects the institution of the

The Post Office on Madison Avenue
Before the days of electronic media and sophisticated Madison Avenue advertising techniques, the national government tried its hand at promoting government programs through persuasive poster art. This 1929 poster tried to convince Americans that everybody was sending letters by airmail. The government's objective was to help support the fledgling airline industry.

AIR MAIL
is Socially Correct

5¢ for the First Ounce   10¢ for each additional Ounce

family farm, promotes farming, and provides private benefits. Still, most policies have a dominant underlying objective. For farm subsidies, that objective is providing private benefits simply because subsidies have neither protected the family farm nor encouraged individuals to enter farming. In fact, most farm subsidies go to large farms. (We discuss the complicated problem of agricultural policy in Chapter 16.)

Governments rely on different legislative techniques to achieve their policy objectives. Some laws simply forbid or require certain behavior. For example, the Constitution prohibits interference with the free exercise of religion, and Congress has passed laws that require employers to pay men and women equally for equal work. We examine these kinds of prohibitions and requirements more closely in Chapters 17 and 18. Here, we focus on taxing and spending, the tools with which the government carries out public policies that protect, promote, and provide.

THEORIES OF ECONOMIC POLICY

Taxing and spending are the major tools with which government implements policy. How policymakers use these tools depends on their beliefs about (1) how the economy functions and (2) the proper role of government in the economy. The American economy is so complex that no policymaker knows exactly how it works. Policymakers have to rely on economic theories to explain its functioning, and there are nearly as many theories as economists (see Feature 15.1). Unfortunately, different theories (and economists) often predict quite different outcomes. One source of difference is the assumptions that are part of every economic theory, and that differ from theory to theory. Another problem is the difference between an idealized theory and the real world. Still, despite the disagreement among economists, a knowledge of basic economics is necessary to an understanding of how government approaches public policy.

We are concerned here with economic policy in a *market economy*— one in which the prices of goods and services are determined through the interaction of sellers and buyers (that is, through supply and demand). This kind of economy is typical of the consumer-dominated societies of Western Europe and the United States. *A nonmarket economy* relies on government planners to determine both the prices of goods and the amounts that are produced. The Soviet economy was a perfect example of a nonmarket economy until Mikhail Gorbachev's policy of *perestroika*, or economic restructuring, introduced some private elements. In a nonmarket economy, the government owns and operates the major means of production. Market economies often exhibit a mix of government and private ownership. For example, Britain has considerably more government-owned enterprises (railroads, broadcasting, and housing) than the United States.

Market economies are loosely called *capitalist economies:* They allow private individuals to own property, sell goods for profit in a free, or open, market, and accumulate wealth, called capital. The competing theories of market economies differ largely on how free the market should be, on the role of government in directing the economy.

FEATURE 15.1

Economics: The Dismal Science

Thomas Carlyle, a nineteenth-century British social critic, called economics "the dismal science." Although Carlyle was speaking in a different context, his phrase has stuck. If being a science requires agreement on fundamental propositions among practitioners, then economics is certainly a dismal science. When twenty-seven standard propositions in economic theory were put to almost a thousand economists in five Western countries, they did not agree on a single one. Consider this example: "Reducing the role of regulatory authorities (for instance, in air traffic) would improve the efficiency of the economy." About 33 percent of the economists "generally disagreed," 30 percent "generally agreed," and 34 percent "agreed with provisions." When learned economists cannot agree on basic propositions in economic theory, politicians are free to choose theories that fit their views of the proper role of government in the economy.

THE ECONOMISTS

Source: Adapted from Bruno S. Frey et al., "Consensus and Dissension Among Economics: An Empirical Inquiry," *American Economic Review* 74 (December 1984):986–994.

Laissez-Faire Economics

We introduced the French term *laissez faire* in Chapter 1 and discussed it again in Chapter 12. It describes the absence of government control. The economic doctrine of laissez faire likens the operation of a free market to the process of natural selection. Economic competition weeds out the weak and preserves the strong. In the process, the economy prospers and everyone eventually benefits.

Advocates of laissez-faire economics are fond of quoting Adam Smith's *The Wealth of Nations*. In this 1776 treatise, Smith argued that each individual, pursuing his own selfish interests in a competitive market, was "led by an invisible hand to promote an end which was no part of his intention." Smith's "invisible hand" has been used for two centuries to justify the belief that the narrow pursuit of profits serves the broad interests of society. Strict advocates of laissez faire maintain that government interference with business tampers with the laws of nature, obstructing the workings of the free market.

Keynesian Theory

One problem with laissez-faire economics is its insistence that government should do little about **economic depressions** (periods of high unemployment and business failures) or about raging **inflation** (when price increases decrease the value of currency). Inflation is generally measured by the *Consumer Price Index (CPI)* (see Politics in the Information Age 15.1). Since the beginning of the Industrial Revolution, capitalist economies have suffered through many cyclical fluctuations, boom then bust. The United States experienced more than fifteen of these **business cycles**—expansions and contractions of business activity, the first stage accompanied by inflation and the second stage by unemployment (see "The American Economic Experience, 1964–1987" in Essay D, page 536). No one had a theory that really explained these cycles until the Great Depression of the 1930s.

That was when John Maynard Keynes, a British economist, theorized that business cycles stem from imbalances between aggregate demand and productive capacity. **Aggregate demand** is the income available to consumers, business, and government to spend on goods and services. **Productive capacity** is the value of goods and services that can be produced when the economy is working at full capacity. The value of the goods and services *actually* produced is called the **gross national product (GNP)**.

When demand exceeds productive capacity, people pay more for available goods, which leads to price inflation. When productive capacity exceeds demand, producers cut back their output of goods, which leads to unemployment. When many people are unemployed for an extended period, the economy is in a depression. Keynes theorized that government could stabilize the economy (and flatten or eliminate business cycles) by controlling the level of aggregate demand.

Keynesian theory holds that aggregate demand can be adjusted through a combination of fiscal and monetary policies. **Fiscal policies** involve changes in government spending and taxing. When demand is too low, government should either spend more itself or cut taxes, to give people more money to spend. When demand is too great, the government should either spend less or raise taxes, giving people less money to spend. **Monetary policies** involve changes in the money supply and operate less directly on the economy. Increasing the amount of money in circulation increases demand, and thus increases price inflation, assuming full employment. Decreasing the money supply decreases aggregate demand and inflationary pressures.

Keynesian theory has been widely adopted by capitalist countries. At one time or another, virtually all have used the Keynesian technique of **deficit financing**—spending beyond tax revenues—to combat an economic slump. The objective of deficit financing is to inject extra money into the economy to stimulate aggregate demand. Most deficits are fi-

POLITICS IN THE INFORMATION AGE 15.1

The Consumer Price Index

Inflation in the United States is usually measured in terms of the Consumer Price Index. The CPI is based on prices paid for food, clothing, shelter, transportation, medical services, and other items necessary for daily living. Data are gathered from ninety-one areas across the country, from over sixty thousand housing units and twenty-one thousand businesses.

The CPI is not a perfect yardstick. One problem is that it does not differentiate between inflationary price increases and other price increases. A Ford sedan bought in 1979 is not the same as a Ford sedan bought in 1989. To some extent, the price difference reflects a change in quality as well as a change in the value of the dollar. For example, improvements in fuel economy improve the car's quality and justify a somewhat higher price. The CPI is also slow to reflect changes in purchasing habits. Wash-and-wear clothes were tumbling in the dryer for several years before the government agreed to include them as an item in the index.

These are minor issues compared with the weight given over time to the cost of housing. Until 1983, the cost of purchasing and financing a home accounted for 26 percent of the CPI. This formula neglected the facts that many people rent, rather than buy, homes and that few people buy a home every year. A better measure of the cost of shelter is the cost of renting houses similar to those that are owned. Using this method of calculating the cost of shelter dropped the weighting given to housing in the CPI, from 26 percent to 14 percent. Before the correction, the CPI overstated the rate of inflation for the average citizen.

The government uses the CPI to make cost-of-living adjustments in civil service and military pension payments, social security benefits, and food stamp allowances. Moreover, many union wage contracts with private businesses are indexed (tied) to the CPI. Because the CPI almost always goes up each year, so do the payments that are tied to it. In a way, then, indexing payments to the CPI adds to both the growth of government spending and inflation itself. The United States is one of the few nations that also ties its tax brackets to a price index, which reduces revenues by eliminating the "bracket creep" of inflation.

Despite its faults, the CPI is at least a consistent measure of prices and is likely to go on being used as the basis for adjustments to wages, benefits, and payments affecting millions of people.

Source: Adapted from David S. Moore, *Statistics: Concepts and Controversies*, 2d ed. (New York: Freeman, 1985), pp. 238–241. Also see Bureau of the Census, *Statistical Abstract of the United States, 1988* (Washington, D.C.: U.S. Government Printing Office, 1988), pp. 443–444.

nanced by funds borrowed through the issuing of government bonds, notes, or other securities. The theory holds that deficits can be paid off with budget surpluses after the economy recovers.

Because Keynesian theory requires government to play an active role in controlling the economy, it runs counter to laissez-faire economics. Before Keynes, no administration in Washington would undertake responsibility for maintaining a healthy economy. In 1946, the year in which Keynes died, Congress passed an employment act fixing under law "the continuing responsibility of the federal government to . . . promote maximum employment, production and purchasing power." It also created the **Council of Economic Advisers (CEA)** within the Executive Office of the President, to advise the president on maintaining a stable economy. The CEA normally consists of three economists (usually university professors) appointed by the president with Senate approval. Aided by a staff of about twenty-five people (mostly economists), the CEA helps the president prepare his annual economic report, also a provision of the 1946 act. The chair of the CEA is usually a major spokesperson for the administration's economic policy. This was not the case under Reagan, however, primarily because Reagan's views on economics did not always coincide with those of the economists on the council.

The Employment Act of 1946, which reflected Keynesian theory, had a tremendous impact on government economic policy. Many people believe it was the primary source of "big government" in America. Even Richard Nixon, a conservative president, admitted that "we are all Keynesians now."

Monetary Policy

Although most economists accept Keynesian theory in its broad outlines, they disagree on its political utility. Some especially question the value of fiscal policies in controlling inflation and unemployment. They feel that government spending programs take too long to enact in Congress and to implement through the bureaucracy. As a result, jobs are created, not when they are needed, but years later, when the crisis may have passed and government spending needs to be reduced.

Also, government spending is easier to start than to stop because the groups that benefit from spending programs tend to defend them even when they are no longer needed. A similar criticism applies to tax policies. Politically, it is much easier to cut taxes than to raise them. In other words, Keynesian theory requires that governments be able to begin *and* end spending quickly, and to cut *and* raise taxes quickly. But in the real world, these fiscal tools are easier to use in one way than the other.

Monetarists, recognizing the limitations of fiscal policies, argue that government can control the economy's performance effectively only by controlling the nation's money supply. Monetarists favor a long-range policy of small but steady growth in the amount of money in circulation rather than frequent manipulation of monetary policies.

Major monetary policies in the United States are under the control of the **Federal Reserve System,** which acts as its central bank. Established in 1913, "the Fed" is not a single bank but a system of banks. At the top of the system is the board of governors, seven members appointed by the president for staggered terms of fourteen years. The board is directed by a chair, who serves a four-year term that overlaps the president's term of office. This complex arrangement was intended to make the board independent of the president and even Congress. An independent board, the reasoning went, would be able to make financial decisions for the nation without regard to political implications.

The Fed controls the money supply in three ways. It can change the *reserve requirement*, which is the amount of cash that member banks must keep on deposit in a regional Federal Reserve Bank. An increase in the reserve requirement decreases the amount of money a bank has available to lend. The Fed can also change its *discount rate*, the interest rate that member banks have to pay to borrow money from a Federal Reserve Bank. A lower rate encourages a member bank to borrow and lend more freely. Finally, the Fed can *buy and sell government securities* (such as U.S. Treasury notes and bonds) on the open market. When it buys securities, it pays out money, putting more money into circulation; when it sells securities, the process works in reverse.

Inside "the Fed"
The golden hue of this photograph is appropriate for a meeting of the board of governors of the Federal Reserve System. Not all seven members are pictured here, but the chairman, Alan Greenspan, is seated under the imposing eagle, his chin resting on his hand. Greenspan's appointment as chairman was confirmed by the Senate on August 3, 1987. Barely a month later, he was welcomed by the stock market crash. His actions to pump money into the system were widely credited with averting an even bigger collapse.

The Fed's activities are essential parts of the overall economic policy, but they lie outside the direct control of the president. This can create problems in coordinating economic policy. For example, the president might want the Fed to lower interest rates to stimulate the economy, but the Fed might resist for fear of inflation. These kinds of policy clashes can pit the chair of the Federal Reserve Board directly against the president. It takes a strong personality to resist the president, but few people rise to the powerful position of chair of the Federal Reserve Board by being shy. The last two chairmen clashed on occasion with presidents of both parties. The current chairman, Alan Greenspan, had been a key player in Republican party politics (which is uncharacteristic for the position) before he was appointed by President Reagan.[10] Although the Fed's economic policies are not perfectly insulated from political concerns, they are sufficiently independent so that the president is not able to control monetary policy without the Fed's cooperation. This means that the president cannot be held completely responsible for the state of the economy—despite the Employment Act of 1946.

Supply-Side Economics

When Reagan came to office in 1981, he embraced a school of thought called **supply-side economics** to deal with the double-digit inflation that the nation was experiencing. Remember that Keynesian theory argues that inflation stems from an excess of aggregate demand over supply, and that the standard Keynesian solution is to reduce demand (for example, by increasing taxes). Supply-siders argued that inflation could be lowered more effectively by increasing supply. (That is, they stressed the *supply side* of the economic equation.) Specifically, they favored tax cuts to stimulate investment (which, in turn, would lead to the production of more goods) and less government regulation of business (again, to increase productivity—which they held would yield more, not less, government revenue).

To support their theory, supply-side economists point to a 1964 tax cut that was initiated by President Kennedy. It stimulated investment and raised the total national income. As a result, the government took in as much tax revenue under the tax cut as it had before taxes were cut. Supply-siders also argue that the rich should receive *larger* tax cuts than the poor, because the rich have more money to invest. The benefits of increased investment then "trickle down" to working people in the form of additional jobs and income.

In a sense, supply-side economics leans toward laissez-faire economics in the form of less government regulation and less taxation. Supply-siders believe that government interferes too much with the efforts of individuals to work, save, and invest. This is what Ronald Reagan thought when he was a movie star in the 1950s, with a salary in the 91 percent tax bracket. In his 1965 autobiography, he wrote that because the government took so much of his income, he quit working for a year after he moved into that bracket.[11] Obviously, he hadn't changed his mind about taxation when he entered his first term in office.

Inspired by supply-side theory, Reagan proposed (and got) massive tax cuts in the *Economic Recovery Tax Act of 1981*. Individual tax rates were reduced by 23 percent over a three-year period, and the tax rate for the highest income group was cut from 70 to 50 percent. Reagan also launched a program to deregulate business. According to the theory, these actions would generate extra government revenue, making spending cuts unnecessary. Nevertheless, Reagan cut funding for some domestic programs, including Aid to Families with Dependent Children and the food stamp program. Contrary to supply-side theory, he also proposed major increases in military spending. This blend of tax cuts, deregulation, cuts

Figure 15.1

Budget Deficits over Time
In his first inaugural address, President Reagan said, "You and I, as individuals, can, by borrowing, live beyond our means, but only for a limited period of time. Why, then, should we think that collectively, as a nation, we're not bound by that same limitation?" But borrow he did. Reagan's critics charged that the budget deficits under his administration—over $1.3 trillion—exceeded the total deficits of all previous presidents. But this charge does not take inflation into account. A billion dollars in 1989 is worth much less than it was in 1889, and vastly less than in 1789.

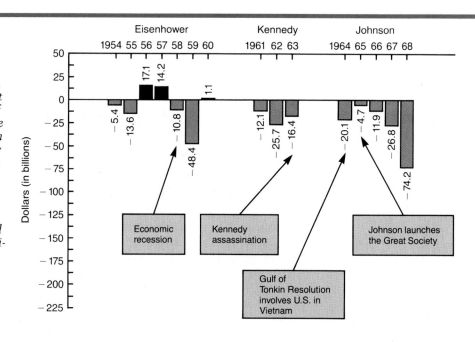

in spending for social programs, and increases in spending for defense became known, somewhat disparagingly, as *Reaganomics*.

How well did Reaganomics work? During Reagan's administration, annual price inflation fell a whopping 11.9 percentage points—from 13.5 percent in 1980 to 1.9 percent in 1986.[12] Although many economists credit the drop to the tight-money policies of the Federal Reserve Board, which raised interest rates, the Fed did it with Reagan's support. Higher interest rates cut back business investments, initially producing a severe recession and unemployment.[13] However, unemployment peaked at 9.7 percent in 1982 and dropped to 7.0 percent in 1986, below the rate when Reagan took office. These were important economic accomplishments. Unfortunately, and in spite of supply-side theory, the tax cut was accompanied by a massive drop in tax revenues. Shortly after taking office, Reagan promised that his economic policies would balance the national budget by 1984, but lower tax revenues and higher defense spending produced the largest budget deficits ever (see Figure 15.1).[14]

PUBLIC POLICY AND THE BUDGET

To most people—college students included—the national budget is B-0-R-I-N-G. To national politicians, it is the script for high drama. The numbers, categories, and percentages that numb normal minds have politicians' nostrils flaring and hearts pounding. The budget is a political battlefield, on which politicians and the programs they support wage war.

Today, the president prepares the budget and Congress approves it. This was not always the case. Before 1921, Congress prepared the budget under its constitutional authority to raise taxes and appropriate funds.

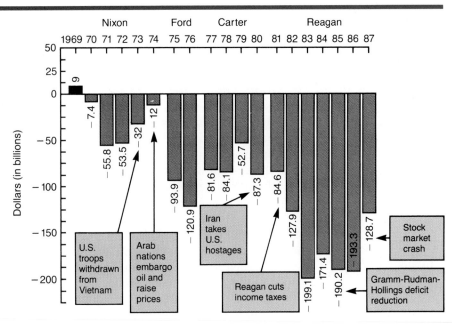

A fairer way to calculate budget deficits is in constant dollars—dollars whose value has been adjusted to a given year. This chart shows the actual deficits in 1982 dollars incurred under presidential administrations from Eisenhower to Reagan. Even computed this way, Reagan's deficits were enormous—especially for a president who claimed to oppose government borrowing. (Source: Office of Management and Budget, Historical Tables, Budget of the United States Government, 1989 [Washington, D.C.: U.S. Government Printing Office, 1988] pp. 19–20.)

The budget was formed piecemeal by enacting a series of laws that originated in the many committees involved in the highly decentralized process of raising revenue, authorizing expenditures, and appropriating funds. No one was responsible for the "big picture"—the budget as a whole. The president's role was essentially limited to approving revenue and appropriations bills, just as he approved other pieces of legislation. In fact, even executive agencies submitted their budgetary requests directly to Congress, not to the president.

Congressional budgeting (such as it was) worked well enough for a nation of farmers, but not for an industrialized nation with a growing population and a more active government. Soon after World War I, Congress realized that the budget-making process needed to be centralized. With the *Budgeting and Accounting Act of 1921*, it thrust the responsibility for preparing the budget onto the president. The act established the Bureau of the Budget to help the president write "his" budget, which had to be submitted to Congress each January. Congress retained its constitutional authority to raise and spend funds, but now Congress would begin its work from the president's budget. And all executive agencies' budget requests had to be funneled through the Bureau of the Budget (which became the Office of Management and Budget in 1970) for review; those consistent with the president's overall economic and legislative program were incorporated into the president's budget.

The Nature of the Budget

The national budget is complex. But its basic elements are not beyond understanding. We begin with some definitions. The *Budget of the United States Government* is the annual financial plan that the president is required to submit to Congress in January of each year. It applies to the next **fiscal year (FY)**, the period the government uses for accounting purposes. Currently, the fiscal year runs from October 1 to September 30. The budget is named for the year in which it *ends*. So, the FY 1989 budget applies to the twelve months from October 1, 1988, to September 30, 1989.

Broadly, the budget defines **budget authority** (how much government agencies are authorized to spend for programs); **budget outlays** or expenditures (how much they are expected to spend); and **receipts** (how much is expected in taxes and other revenues). (The relationship of authority to outlays is diagrammed in Figure 15.2.) President Reagan's FY 1989 budget contained authority for expenditures of $1,233 billion, but it provided for spending (outlays) of "only" $1,094 billion. The budget anticipated receipts of $965 billion, leaving a deficit of $129 billion—the difference between receipts and outlays. The budget document contains more than numbers. It also explains individual spending programs in terms of national needs and agency objectives, and it analyzes proposed taxes and other receipts.

Reagan's FY 1989 budget was over five hundred pages long and weighed more than 5 pounds, including appendixes. Although its publication was anxiously awaited by reporters, lobbyists, and political analysts eager to learn the president's plan for government spending in the coming year, the drama was lessened in 1988. The pact that president

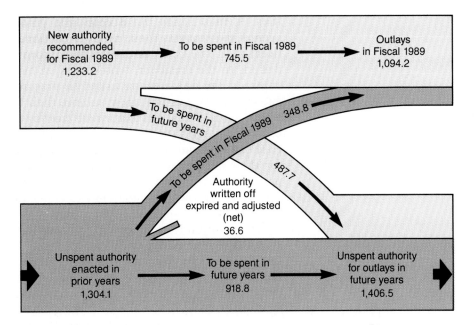

New authority recommended for Fiscal 1989
1,233.2

To be spent in Fiscal 1989
745.5

Outlays in Fiscal 1989
1,094.2

To be spent in future years

To be spent in Fiscal 1989   348.8

To be spent in Fiscal 1989

487.7

Authority written off expired and adjusted (net)
36.6

Unspent authority enacted in prior years
1,304.1

To be spent in future years
918.8

Unspent authority for outlays in future years
1,406.5

Relationship of Budget Authority to Budget Outlays
The national budget is a complicated document. One source of confusion for people studying the budget for the first time is the relationship of budget authority to budget outlay. These two figures differ because of sums that are carried over from prior years and to future years. The diagram below helps explain the relationship; all amounts are in billions of dollars. Only $745.5 billion of the FY 1989 budget authority is expected to be spent in FY 1989, while $487.7 billion will be carried over for spending in future years. Similarly, $348.8 billion in funds authorized in prior years will be spent in FY 1989. (Source: Budget of the United States Government, 1989, *p. 6d-4.)*

Figure 15.2

and Congress struck at the budget summit in the wake of the stock market crash not only increased taxes modestly in minor areas to cut the deficit, but—in a very unusual step—also set a total budget ceiling for defense and domestic spending in FY 1989. As a result of the market crash, the broad outlines of government spending for FY 1989 were determined in advance of the president's budget.

Preparing the President's Budget

Usually, the budget that the president submits to Congress each January is the end product of a process that begins the previous spring under the supervision of the **Office of Management and Budget (OMB).** OMB is located within the Executive Office of the President and is headed by a director who is appointed by the president with the approval of the Senate. The OMB, with a staff of over five hundred, is the most powerful domestic agency in the bureaucracy, and its director, who sits in the president's Cabinet, is one of the most powerful figures in government.

The OMB initiates the budget process each spring by meeting with the president to discuss the economic situation and his budgetary priorities. It then sends broad economic guidelines to every government agency and requests their initial projections of funds needed for the next fiscal year. The OMB assembles this information and makes recommendations to the president, who settles on more precise guidelines. By the summer, the agencies are asked to prepare budgets based on the new guidelines. By the fall, they submit their formal budgets to the OMB, where budget analysts scrutinize agency requests for both costs and consistency with the president's legislative program. A lot of politicking goes on at this stage, as agency heads try to go around the OMB to plead for their pet projects with presidential advisers and perhaps even the president himself. Political negotiations may extend into the early winter—often to the last possible moment before the budget goes to the printer.

The voluminous document is carefully printed and neatly bound. It looks very much like a finished product, but it is far from final. The members of Congress are interested in the content of the president's budget, not its appearance. In giving the president the responsibility for preparing the budget, they have provided themselves with a starting point for their own work.

Passing the Congressional Budget

Congress must approve the budget. That process is a creaky conglomeration of traditional procedures overlaid with structural reforms from the 1970s and external constraints in the 1980s. Especially in recent years, the process has proved inadequate to the task of producing a budget according to Congress's own timetable.

The traditional procedure: The committee structure. Traditionally, the tasks of budget making were divided among a number of committees—a process that has been retained. There are three types of committees involved in budgeting:

- **Tax committees** are responsible for raising the revenues to run the government. The Ways and Means Committee in the House and the Finance Committee in the Senate consider all proposals for taxes, tariffs, and other receipts contained in the president's budget.
- **Authorization committees** (such as the House Armed Services Committee and the Senate Banking, Housing, and Urban Affairs Committee) have jurisdiction over particular legislative subjects. The House has nineteen committees that can authorize spending, and the Senate has sixteen. Each one pores over the portions of the budget that pertain to its area of responsibility. In recent years, however, power has shifted from the authorization committees to the appropriations committees.
- **Appropriations committees** decide which of the programs approved by the authorization committees will actually be funded (that is, given money to spend). For example, the House Armed Services Committee might decide to build a new line of tanks for the army and even get its decision enacted into law. But the tanks will never be built unless funds are appropriated for that purpose by the appro-

priations committees. Thirteen distinct appropriation bills are supposed to be enacted each year to fund the nation's spending.

Two major problems are inherent in a budgeting process that involves three distinct kinds of congressional committees. First, the two-step spending process (first *authorization,* then *appropriation)* is very complex; it offers wonderful opportunities for interest groups to get into the budgeting act. Second, because one group of legislators in each house plans for revenues and many other groups plan for spending, no one is responsible for the budget as a whole. In the 1970s, Congress added a new committee structure that combats the pluralist politics inherent in the old procedures and allows budget choices to be made in a more majoritarian manner, by votes in both chambers.

Reforms of the 1970s: The Budget Committee structure.

In 1921, when Congress gave the president the responsibility to prepare the budget, it surrendered considerable authority. Previous attempts by Congress to regain control of the budgeting process failed because of jurisdictional squabbles between the revenue and appropriations committees.

Overall control of the budget is important to Congress for several reasons. First, members of Congress are politicians, and politicians want to wield power, rather than watch someone else wield it. Second, the Constitution established Congress, not the president, as the "first branch" of government and the people's representatives; this legitimated its institutional jealousy. Third, Congress as a body often disagrees with presidential spending priorities, but it has been unable to present a coherent alternative budget. Congress as an institution has not been able to mount a serious challenge to the president's budgetary views.

After bitter spending fights with President Nixon in the late 1960s and early 1970s, Congress finally passed the Budget and Impoundment Control Act of 1974. That act fashioned a typically political solution to the problem of wounded egos and trampled jurisdictions that had frustrated previous attempts to change the budget-making procedure. All the tax and appropriations committees (and chairpersons) were retained, and new House and Senate **Budget Committees** were superimposed on the old committee structure. The Budget Committees supervised a comprehensive budget review process, aided by the **Congressional Budget Office (CBO).** The CBO, with a staff of over two hundred, acquired a budgetary expertise equal to that of the president's OMB, so it could prepare credible alternative budgets for Congress.

At the heart of the 1974 reforms was a timetable for the congressional budget process. The original timetable has since been modified (see Table 15.1), and its deadlines are often missed. Still, it is a useful means of guiding the process.

In March, about two months after receiving the president's budget, the Budget Committees are supposed to propose an initial budget resolution that sets overall revenue and spending levels, broken down into twenty-one different "budget functions," among them, national defense, agriculture, and health. The budget resolution also provides for the **reconciliation** of differences between amounts that the authorization committees have authorized for spending and amounts allocated in the budget functions. In effect, each authorization committee must reconcile

Table 15.1

Budget Process Timetable: Fiscal Years 1989–1993

The Budget and Impoundment Control Act was passed in 1974. It has greatly changed the congressional budgeting process. In an effort to discipline itself, Congress created a budget timetable. Lawmakers met their deadlines relatively well from 1975 to 1980, but have done less well since. The schedule below adopted in the Gramm-Rudman-Hollings antideficit law of 1985 as amended in 1987, moved the budgetary deadline up one month to April 15 giving Congress more time to complete reconciliation and action on the thirteen annual appropriations bills. Still, Congress fell behind schedule in 1986 and 1987, and was forced to combine the separate bills in a massive omnibus bill each year.

January

First Monday after January 3   President submits his budget to Congress.

February

15   CBO issues annual report to Budget Committees.
25   Congressional committees submit proposals to Budget Committees.

March

Budget Committees formulate the budget resolution.

April

15   House and Senate take action on the budget resolution.

May

House Appropriations Committee works on appropriation bills.

June

10   Deadline for last House appropriation bills.
15   Congress reconciles appropriations with budget resolution.
30   Congress completes action on annual appropriations bills.

August

15   Revenue and spending provisions in place for deficit estimates.
20   CBO estimates the deficit against the antideficit law.
25   OMB gives official estimate and orders budget cuts, if necessary.

September

30   Old fiscal year ends.

October

1   New fiscal year begins.
10   CBO reports any changes in estimated spending and revenues.
15   OMB budget cuts become permanent if no alternative is enacted.

Source: Elizabeth Wehr, "Doubtful Congress Clears Gramm-Rudman Fix," *Congressional Quarterly Weekly Report*, 26 September 1987, pp. 2310–2311; and "The Fiscal 1989 Budget: Terms and Process," *Congressional Quarterly Weekly Report*, 20 February 1988, p. 336.

(match) the amount it has authorized for spending with the amount it has to spend. When spending is covered by an **entitlement** program—which specifies that those who qualify for benefits are legally entitled to them—the reconciliation process may require a change in law.

By April 15, both houses are supposed to have agreed on a single budget resolution to guide their work on the budget during the summer. Appropriations should be completed by June 30. Throughout, the levels of spending set by majority vote on the budget resolution act as constraints on pluralist politics.

This process (or one very much like it) was implemented in 1975 and worked reasonably well for the first few years. Congress was able to work on and structure the budget as a whole, rather than changing pieces of it. But the process broke down under the Reagan administration, as the president submitted annual budgets with huge deficits. Reagan kept to his economic game plan, resisting any tax increases to reduce the deficits, cutting social spending, and increasing military spending. For its part, a Democratic Congress reversed his spending priorities but refused to propose a tax increase to reduce the deficit without the president's cooperation.

At loggerheads with Reagan, Congress encountered increasing difficulty in enacting its budget resolutions according to its own timetable, and it never succeeded in passing its thirteen separate appropriation bills during any of the first seven years of the Reagan administration.[15] Instead, Congress resorted to combining appropriations for different topics in the same bill. For FY 1987 and FY 1988, Congress desperately combined *all* thirteen sets of appropriations in a single massive bill—an "omnibus" bill—before the session ended. The 2,100-page bill for FY 1988 totaled $604 billion, and Congress did not send it to the president for approval until December 22, 1987, three months into the fiscal year. No lawmaker was proud of heaping all the appropriations into one huge bill. Congresswoman Olympia Snowe, Republican from Maine, noted that the House received this bill for the first time just four days before Christmas and had one hour to discuss it, which "works out to be $10 billion per minute, 1.8 seconds per page."[16]

External constraints of the 1980s: Gramm-Rudman-Hollings. Alarmed by the huge deficits in Reagan's budgets, frustrated by his

Win One for the Clipper
Throughout his administration, Ronald Reagan denounced government spending, identifying Congress as the source of the problem. After a 1987 speech on the national budget and tax policies, in Port Washington, Wisconsin, Reagan used a few visual aids to get the point across. Republican Senator Bob Kasten made sure he had his hands out of the way.

refusal to raise taxes, and stymied by their own inability to eliminate the deficits, members of Congress were ready to try almost anything. Republican Senators Phil Gramm (Texas) and Warren Rudman (New Hampshire) were joined by Democrat Ernest Hollings (South Carolina) in proposing drastic action to force a balanced budget. Officially titled the *Balanced Budget and Emergency Deficit Control Act* (1985), their bill became known simply as **Gramm-Rudman-Hollings.**

In its original form, Gramm-Rudman-Hollings mandated that the budget deficit be lowered to a specified level each year until the budget is balanced in FY 1991 (see Figure 15.3). If Congress did not meet the mandated deficit level in any year, across-the-board budget cuts were to be made automatically by the comptroller general. Senator Rudman described his own bill as "a bad idea whose time has come." Frustration with their repeated inability to cut the deficit was so great that Gramm-Rudman-Hollings sailed through both houses on a wave of exasperation. The bill was not considered by congressional committees in the usual manner; nor was it subjected to formal economic, procedural, or legal analysis. No one really knew what the legislation would do—except give Congress an out in deciding which programs to cut or whose taxes to raise so as to reduce the deficit. Republican Senator Robert Packwood from Oregon confessed to the Senate, "I pray that what we are about to undertake will work."[17]

President Reagan signed Gramm-Rudman-Hollings into law in December, 1985. On March 1, 1986, the comptroller general made the first series of automatic cuts under the law. He applied the cuts equally to domestic and military programs, slicing 4.3 percent from every domestic and defense program, project, and activity except those that were specifically exempted (social security, several programs for the poor, and Reagan's Strategic Defense Initiative).

Gramm-Rudman-Hollings mandated across-the-board budget cuts, reducing funding for all programs without regard for their value to the nation. Its net effect is to weaken all programs through underfunding. In this respect, Gramm-Rudman-Hollings represents a failure of the legislative process, in which elected representatives are expected to decide how public funds should be spent. Of course, we could argue that the process had failed well before Gramm-Rudman-Hollings was enacted, when Congress failed to raise revenues to pay for the government services it supported.

Soon after it became law, Gramm-Rudman-Hollings was challenged in federal court, and the Supreme Court confirmed what many expected—that it was unconstitutional to give the comptroller general functions that belong to the president. But to preserve the budget reductions already made under the law, Congress itself quickly enacted all of the cuts. In September 1987, Congress revised the antideficit law to meet the Supreme Court's objections and entrusted the OMB (an executive branch office) to make automatic cuts if the deficit targets were not reached. In addition, Congress loosened the budget deficit targets and extended the deadline for a balanced budget to 1993 (see Figure 15.3).

Adding to Gramm-Rudman-Hollings, the budget pact between the president and Congress that cut the deficit in the wake of the 1987 stock market crash contributed to the deficit's "brooding presence" over Wash-

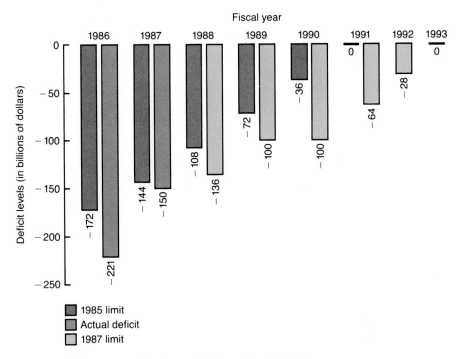

Timetable for Gramm-Rudman-Hollings Antideficit Law
The 1985 antideficit law, known as Gramm-Rudman-Hollings, aimed at reducing the national deficit by stages, resulting in a balanced budget by FY 1991—with targets depicted by the blue bars. The red bars indicate the actual budget deficits for the fiscal years since the law was passed. Realizing that the original target was too optimistic, Congress amended the antideficit law in 1987, extending the date for a balanced budget to FY 1993—with lower yearly targets (the green bars). Most observers think that these targets are unrealistic, but they have definitely had an effect on the psychology of budgeting in Washington.

Figure 15.3

ington decision making.[18] Congress and lobbies alike became more concerned with holding on to what they had than with trying to launch new programs. As a result, power has drained away from the authorizing committees to the budget and appropriations committees.[19] The funding simply is not there to authorize expensive new projects.

TAX POLICIES

So far, we have been concerned mainly with the spending side of the budget, for which appropriations must be enacted each year. The revenue side of the budget is provided by overall tax policy, which is designed to provide a continuous flow of income without annual legislation. On occasion, however, tax policy is significantly changed to accomplish one or more of several objectives:[20]

■   To adjust overall revenue to meet budget outlays

■   To make the tax burden more equitable for taxpayers

■   To help control the economy by raising taxes (thus decreasing aggregate demand) or by lowering taxes (thus increasing demand)

In his first year in office, Reagan requested and got a significant change in tax policy. Personal income taxes were lowered by 23 percent over a three-year period, resulting in a total revenue loss of billions of dollars. According to supply-side economic theory, that massive tax cut should have stimulated the economy and yielded even more revenue than was lost—if not in the first year, then soon afterward. It didn't happen. Revenues lagged badly behind spending, and the deficit grew.

Still, Reagan would not agree to raise taxes, and few politicians dared mention a tax hike. Democratic presidential candidate Walter Mondale tried it in the 1984 election and was beaten badly. The Democratic leadership in Congress and many leading Republicans believed that taxes must be raised to cut the deficit, but no one was willing to propose an increase. For his part, Reagan remained adamant.

And Reagan went further, asking for fundamental changes in tax policy. He urged Congress to enact sweeping tax reform that would (1) lower still further the rate for those in the highest income tax bracket; (2) reduce the number of tax brackets; (3) eliminate virtually all the tax loopholes through which many wealthy people avoided paying taxes; and (4) be *revenue neutral*, in the sense that it would bring in no more and no less revenue than the existing tax policy.

Tax Reform

Tax reform proposals usually are so heavily influenced by interest groups looking for special benefits that they end up working against their original purpose. However, the basic goals of Reagan's tax reform were met with relatively few major changes.

Reagan's success was due to several factors. First, two influential Democrats, Representative Richard Gephardt of Missouri and Senator Bill Bradley of New Jersey, had proposed a tax reform plan of their own in 1982 very much along the lines of President Reagan's (see Chapter 10). Second, the Democrats were worried that Reagan would outflank them on the tax reform issue, as he had on tax increases in the 1984 presidential election, and they were determined that it would not happen again. Third, Reagan's proposals had the powerful support of Democratic Representative Dan Rostenkowski from Illinois, chairman of the Ways and Means Committee in the House (where all revenue bills must begin).

The 1986 tax reform law was one of the most sweeping in history. By eliminating many deductions, the new policy reclaimed a great deal of revenue that had been lost through tax loopholes to corporations and wealthy citizens. That revenue is supposed to pay for a general reduction in tax rates for individual citizens. By eliminating many tax brackets, the new tax policy approached the idea of a *flat tax*—one that requires everyone to pay at the same rate. A flat tax has the appeal of simplicity, but it violates the principle of **progressive taxation,** by which the rich pay proportionately higher taxes than the poor. The ability to pay has long been a standard of fair taxation, and governments can use progressive taxation to redistribute wealth and thus promote equality.

In general, the greater the number of tax brackets, the more progressive the tax can be. The 1985 tax code included fourteen tax brackets, ranging from 11 percent to 50 percent. Under the new law, effective in 1988, there are only two rates—15 and 28 percent.* Although people like the idea of reduced rates and tax simplification, polls show that they generally are not in favor of doing away with progressive taxation. When asked whether taxpayers should "pay the same rate of tax" or whether they should "pay very different rates depending on their incomes," most respondents (72 percent) choose multiple rates.[21] Reagan pledged "to break apart the shackles and liberate America from tax bondage," but most people did not think they were in bondage.[22]

Public Opinion on Federal Taxes

Ironically, the American public was not worked up over taxes as much as Reagan was. When asked in 1984—the year Reagan won reelection over Mondale—which of five different economic problems "was worst these days," the public ranked federal income tax rates at the *bottom* of the list (only 5 percent of a national sample of registered voters chose tax rates as the worst problem). At the top of the list was the size of the national deficit (identified by 34 percent), followed by unemployment (33 percent), high interest rates (19 percent), and inflation (9 percent).[23] Of course, people do not like to pay taxes, and they would rather pay less taxes than more. But high tax rates are not a burning public issue. In a 1985 survey, more people (51 percent) thought they paid "about the right amount" of taxes than "too much" (45 percent).[24] This is what pollsters usually find. Only a tiny portion of the American public believes high taxes are a major problem. However, the overwhelming majority of Americans do not want to pay more taxes, even to reduce the deficit.[25]

Comparing Tax Burdens

One way to compare tax burdens is to examine taxes over time in the same country; another is to compare taxes in different countries at the same time. By comparing taxes over time in the United States, we find that the tax burden of U.S. citizens has indeed been growing. For the average family, the percentage of income that goes to all federal, state, and local taxes doubled to 23 percent between 1953 and 1980. During the same period, the taxes of wealthy families increased by two-thirds, to 33 percent of their income.[26]

However, the income tax has not been the major culprit in the increasing tax bite at the federal level. As shown in Figure 15.4, which graphs the composition of federal budget receipts over time, the proportion contributed by income tax has remained fairly constant since the end of World War II. The largest increases have come in social security taxes, which have risen steadily to pay for the government's largest single social welfare program, aid to the elderly.

---

* Technically there are only two rates, but taxpayers with very high incomes lose the benefit of the lower rate for part of their income and thus pay taxes at an effective rate of 33 percent. (The 1986 tax law did not simplify everything.)

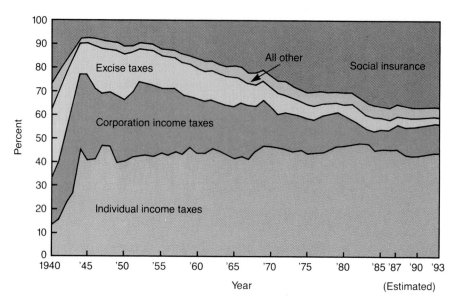

Percentage Composition of Federal Budget Receipts, 1940–1993
*The graph shows the relative composition of federal receipts (revenues) from
1940 to 1993. It clearly indicates that the percentage obtained through income
taxes has changed very little since the mid-1940s, whereas the proportion obtained through social security taxes has more than quadrupled during the
same period. In fact, many lower-income people pay more in social security
taxes than they do in income taxes. (Source: Office of Management and Budget,*
Historical Tables, Budget of the United States Government, 1989 *[Washington, D.C.:
U.S. Government Printing Office, 1988], p. 11.)*

Figure 15.4 ▬▬

Another way of comparing tax burdens is to examine tax rates in
different countries. As you can see in Compared With What? 15.1, Americans' taxes are quite low compared with those in nineteen other democratic nations. Only Japan (which has a very small military budget) and
Spain rank below the United States. Despite talk about high taxes, the
U.S. tax burden is not large compared with taxes in other democratic
nations. But the disparity may shrink in the years ahead because tax
planners in other countries are preparing to reduce tax rates in the top
brackets and to compress the number of brackets—following America's
lead.[27]

SPENDING POLICIES

The national government spends hundreds of billions of dollars every
year. Where does the money go? Figure 15.5 shows the $1 trillion in
outlays in President Reagan's FY 1989 budget according to eighteen major
budgetary functions. The largest amount by far (nearly 30 percent of the
total budget) was earmarked for national defense. The next largest outlay
was for social security; the third largest was for interest on the accumulated national debt, which alone consumes over 15 percent of all
government spending.

COMPARED WITH WHAT? 15.1

Tax Burdens in Twenty Countries

All nations tax their citizens, but some nations impose a heavier tax burden than others. This graph compares tax burdens in 1985 as a percentage of gross domestic product (GDP)—GNP minus the value of goods produced outside the country. The percentages include national, state, and local taxes and social security contributions. By this measure, the U.S. government extracts less in taxes from its citizens than the governments of most other democratic nations. At the top of the list stands Sweden, well known as a social welfare state, which consumes about 50 percent of its gross domestic product in taxes.

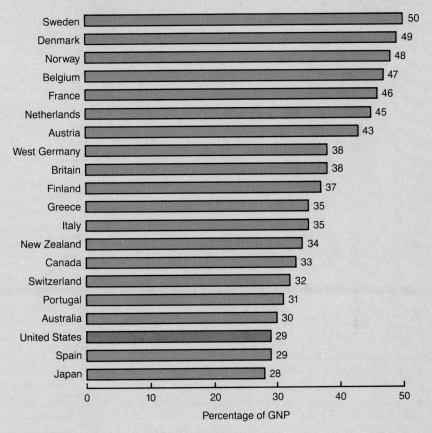

Source: Bureau of the Census, *Statistical Abstract of the United States 1988* (Washington, D.C.: U.S. Government Printing Office, 1988), p. 810.

To understand current expenditures, it is a good idea to examine national expenditures over time. (See "National Government Outlays" in Essay D, page 534, for an illustration of the budget outlays in four major categories since 1940 by percentage.) The effect of World War II is clear: Spending for national defense rose sharply after 1940, peaked at about 90 percent of the budget in 1945, and fell to about 30 percent in peacetime. The percentage allocated to defense rose again in the early

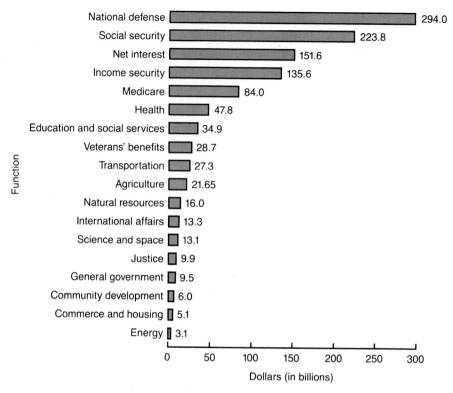

President Reagan's FY 1989 Budget by Function
Federal budget authorities and outlays are organized into twenty-one categories, three of which are mainly for bookkeeping purposes. The graph below shows expected outlays for each of the eighteen substantive functions in Reagan's FY 1989 budget. The final budget differed somewhat from this distribution because Congress amended some of the president's spending proposals, but the proportions remained nearly the same. The pact between the president and Congress at the budget summit after the 1987 market crash specified the outlays for defense and for certain domestic programs, so the presidential and congressional budgets were quite close in FY 1989. (Source: Congressional Quarterly Weekly Report, 28 May 1988, pp. 1439–1441.)

Figure 15.5

1950s, reflecting rearmament in the Cold War with the Soviet Union. Thereafter, the share of the budget devoted to defense decreased steadily (except for the bump during the Vietnam War in the late 1960s) until the trend was reversed by the Reagan administration in the 1980s.

Government payments to individuals consistently consumed less of the budget than national defense until 1971. Since then, payments to individuals have accounted for most of the national budget, and they have been increasing. Net interest payments also have increased substantially in recent years, reflecting the rapidly growing national debt. All other government outlays have been squeezed by pressure from payments for national defense, individuals, and interest on the national debt.

Because of continuing price inflation, we would expect government expenditures to increase steadily in dollar amounts. However, national spending has far outstripped inflation. Figure 15.6 graphs government receipts and outlays as a percentage of the GNP, which eliminates the effect of inflation. It shows that national spending has increased from about 15 percent of the GNP soon after World War II to nearly 25 percent, most recently at the expense of the national deficit. There are two major explanations for this steady increase in government spending. One is bureaucratic; the other, political.

Incremental Budgeting . . .

The bureaucratic explanation for spending increases involves the concept of **incremental budgeting:** Bureaucrats, in compiling their budget funding requests for next year, ask for the amount they got this year plus some *increment* to fund new projects. Members of Congress pay little attention to the size of the agency's budget for the current year (the largest part of that budget), focusing instead on the extra money (the increment) requested for next year. As a result, few agencies are ever cut back, and spending continually goes up.

Incremental budgeting produces a sort of bureaucratic momentum that continually pushes up spending. Once an agency is established, it attracts a clientele that defends its existence and that supports the agency's requests for extra funds to do more year after year. Reagan's domestic spending cuts substantially checked the practice of incremental budgeting. For example, his FY 1987 budget proposed cutting $9.5 billion (almost 18 percent) from the U.S. Department of Agriculture budget by curtailing housing, water, and sewer construction programs; rural electrification and telephone programs; and the agriculture extension service.[28] An even better example is General Revenue Sharing, a program

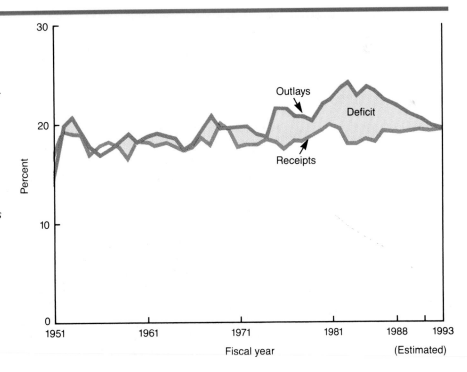

Figure 15.6

Government Outlays and Receipts as a Percentage of the GNP

We can see the growth of government spending—and the rising national debt—by plotting budget outlays and receipts against each other over time. In this graph, outlays and receipts are each expressed as a percentage of the GNP, to control for inflation and to demonstrate that both government spending and taxes have been taking a progressively larger share of the nation's productive output. (Source: Office of Management and Budget, Historical Tables, Budget of the United States Government, 1989 *[Washington, D.C.: U.S. Government Printing Office, 1988], p. 8.)*

that had existed for fourteen years and had distributed $4 billion to thirty-nine thousand localities in 1986. It was terminated at the end of that year.

These kinds of major cuts interfere with incremental budgeting and force closer scrutiny of budgetary proposals by agencies and members of Congress alike. As a result, agencies are now more likely to engage in a form of analytical budgeting, in which existing programs are justified in terms of their effectiveness (see Chapter 12). Still, Reagan found it impossible to reduce government spending enough to balance the budget because politics had put most of the budget beyond his control.

. . . And Uncontrollable Spending

Certain spending programs are effectively immune to budget reductions because they have been (1) enacted into law and (2) enshrined in politics. For example, social security legislation guarantees certain benefits to participants in the program when they retire from work. The same applies for other programs, among them, Medicare and veterans' benefits—which entitle citizens to certain payments. Because these payments have to be made under existing law, they represent **uncontrollable outlays.** In Reagan's FY 1989 budget, more than 75 percent of national budget outlays were uncontrollable or relatively uncontrollable—mainly payments to individuals under social security, Medicare, public assistance, interest on debt, and farm price supports. Most of the funds remaining were earmarked for defense, which Reagan had pledged to increase. Less than 10 percent remained to absorb the cuts.

To be sure, Congress could change the laws to abolish entitlement payments, and it does make minor modifications to them through the budget reconciliation process. But politics argues against major reductions. The only major social program that escaped cutting during the Reagan administration was social security—the largest single domestic program and, according to many surveys, the most popular one. (Even Senator Gramm, coauthor of Gramm-Rudman-Hollings, admitted that trying to cut spending for the elderly is "not winnable." His mother, in her eighties, told her son to "keep your mouth shut" when it came to that part of the budget.) Reagan tried to cut social security during his first year in office, but he encountered such intense opposition that he became a staunch defender of the system.

What spending cuts would be popular or even acceptable to the public? After the 1984 election, voters were asked which of ten expense items in the national budget should be increased and which reduced. Most respondents favored spending either at the current level or at increased levels for *all of them*—the environment, defense, fighting crime, social security, Medicare, education, science and technology, assistance to blacks, jobs for the unemployed, even food stamps.[29] When voters in 1988 were asked how they felt about spending cuts in six areas—aid to the homeless, education, programs to fight AIDS, help for the poor, help for farmers, and cleaning up the environment—clear majorities of both Republicans and Democrats favored increased spending.[30] A perplexed Congress, trying to reduce the budget deficit, faces a public that favors funding programs at even higher levels than those favored by most law-

What You Don't Know Can Hurt You
What can government do to protect people against the effects of toxic chemicals in their environment? California voters in 1986 passed Proposition 65—a sweeping law placed on the ballot by citizens' initiative and approved by a referendum. As of February 1988, all businesses—gas stations, offices, factories, stores—must display signs that notify employees and customers of any harmful chemicals on the premises. By expanding the state's responsibility to protect citizens' health and safety, this law extends the government's role to promote order.

makers.[31] Moreover, spending for the most expensive of these programs—social security and Medicare—is uncontrollable.

The largest *controllable* expenditure is in the area of defense. Because Reagan wanted to increase defense spending, not cut it, he had to focus his cuts on controllable civilian or domestic programs. But those programs account for less than 10 percent of the budget, and no president can substantially reduce national spending by snipping away at such a relatively small outlay. Surveys did show support for cuts in defense spending in 1986, but otherwise the public wants to have its cake and eat it too.[32] Americans have grown accustomed to social security, Medicare, student loans, and farm subsidies. But they do not like the idea of raising taxes to pay for their benefits.

TAXING, SPENDING, AND ECONOMIC EQUALITY

As we noted in Chapter 1, the most controversial purpose of government is promoting equality, especially economic equality. Economic equality comes only at the expense of economic freedom, for it requires government action to redistribute wealth from the rich to the poor. One means of redistribution is government tax policy, especially the progressive income tax. The goal here is rarely equality of outcome; it is reducing inequalities by helping the poor. But as you will see, our current income tax policies do not serve even this limited objective very well.

The national government has levied an income tax every year since 1913, when the Sixteenth Amendment gave it the power to do so. (See "The Ups and Downs of Federal Income Tax Rates," in Essay D, page

537.) From 1964 to 1981, people who reported taxable incomes of $100,000 or more paid a top tax rate of 70 percent, while those with lower incomes paid taxes at progressively lower rates. How did government spending and tax policies during this period affect economic equality in America?

Government Effects on Economic Equality

In a major study, researchers examined the effects of transfer payments and tax policies on different income groups from 1966 to 1985.[33] **Transfer payments** are payments to individuals through social security, unemployment insurance, food stamps, and other programs. The researchers found that social spending (transfer payments) had a definite effect in reducing income inequality in 1980. Families in the lowest tenth of the population in terms of income paid 33 percent of their income in federal, state, and local taxes, but they also received payments from all levels of government that almost equaled their earned income. So the lowest-income group enjoyed a net benefit from government because of transfer payments, *not* because of tax relief. Ironically, families with the top 1 percent of income paid proportionately less of their income in taxes (about 28 percent). But the rich received only 1 percent of their income in transfer payments, suffering a net loss from government.[34]

How can people in the lowest income group pay a higher percentage of their income in taxes than those in the very highest group? The answer has to do with the combination of national, state, and local tax policies. Only the national income tax is progressive, with rates rising as income rises. The national payroll tax, which funds social security, is highly *regressive:* Its effective rate decreases as income increases beyond a certain point. Everyone pays at the same rate (7.51 percent in 1988), but the tax is levied only up to a maximum wage ($43,800 annually in 1988). There is no payroll tax at all on wages over that amount. So the effective rate of the payroll tax is more for the lowest income group than for the very top group.

Most state and local sales taxes are equally regressive. Poor and rich usually pay the same flat rate on their purchases; but the poor spend almost everything they earn on purchases that are taxed, whereas the rich are able to save. The study showed that the effective sales tax rate for the lowest income group was around 7 percent, while that for the top 1 percent was only 1 percent.[35]

In general, the nation's tax policies at all levels favored not only the wealthy, but also those who drew their income from capital rather than labor.[36] For example:

■ The tax on income from the sale of real estate or stock (called *capital gains*) was typically less than the tax on income from salaries. (This was changed in the 1986 tax reform act, but there are pressures to restore the favorable treatment for capital gains.)

■ The tax on *earned income* (salaries and wages) was withheld from paychecks by employers under national law; the tax on *unearned income* (interest and dividends) was not. Instead, the government depended on the good faith of investors to report all their unearned income.

Have a Nice Day
This unemployment office was not designed to be inviting; it is one way for government to discourage dependence on assistance. The office processes claims for assistance filed by people who become unemployed through no fault of their own. Under a cooperative state-national assistance plan enacted in 1935, unemployment benefits vary from state to state. In 1988, an eligible person in Massachusetts, for instance, could receive maximum weekly benefits of $236 for a period of thirty weeks.

■ There was no federal tax at all on investments in certain securities, among them, municipal bonds.

Effects of Taxing and Spending Policies over Time

In 1966, at the beginning of President Johnson's "Great Society" programs, the poorest fifth of American families had 4.3 percent of the nation's income after taxes and transfer payments, while the richest fifth had 45.7 percent. In 1980, after many billions of dollars had been spent on social programs and before Reagan's cutbacks in social spending, the poorest fifth still had 4.3 percent of the nation's income, while the richest fifth had 48.0 percent (see Figure 15.7).[37] In short, there was virtually no change in the distribution of income. In fact, the rich had become relatively richer, a trend that was enhanced during the Reagan administration. In 1988, the top 20 percent of the nation took in almost half of the nation's income, after taxes and transfer payments.

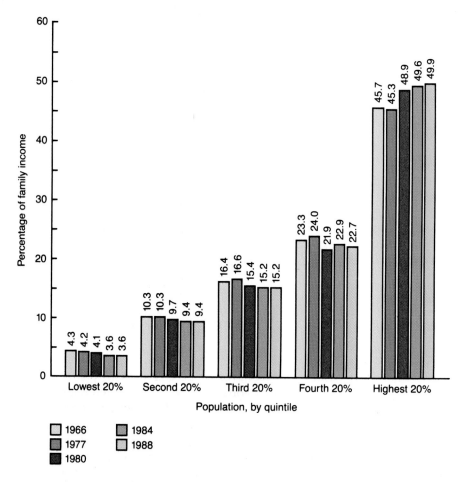

Distribution of Total Family Income over Time
*The 20 percent of families with the highest income actually received more
than 40 percent of the total income of all families in the United States (after
taxes and transfer payments have been taken into account). At the bottom
end of the scale, the poorest 20 percent of families received less than 5 percent
of total family income. Notice that despite two decades of supposedly progressive taxation and social welfare programs, the distribution of income actually
became more unequal. Of course, it would have been even more unequal
without transfer payments, most of which go to the poor. (Sources: For the 1966
and 1980 data, Joseph A. Pechman, Who Paid the Taxes, 1966–1985? [Washington, D.C.:
Brookings Institution, 1985], p. 74; for the 1977, 1984, and 1988 data, Congressional
Budget Office, The Changing Distribution of Federal Taxes: 1975–1990 [Washington,
D.C.: U.S. Government Printing Office, 1987], p. 70.)*

Figure 15.7

In a capitalist system, some degree of inequality is inevitable. There
may be some kind of limit to economic equality, and perhaps the United
States has already reached it. If so, this would prevent government policies from equalizing income no matter what was tried. To find out, we
should look to other democracies to see how much equality they have
been able to sustain. A study of six other countries found that only in
France is as much as 46 percent of total income received by the top fifth
of the population. In Canada, Italy, West Germany, Britain, and Sweden
that percentage runs from 42 down to 37 percent.[38] The comparison

suggests that our society has measurably more economic inequality than others. The question is why?

Democracy and Equality

Although the United States is a democracy that prizes political equality for its citizens, its record in economic equality is not as good. In fact, its distribution of *wealth*—which includes not only income but ownership of savings, housing, automobiles, stocks, and so on—is strikingly unequal. According to the Census Bureau, the top 12 percent of American families control almost 40 percent of household wealth. Moreover, the distribution of wealth by ethnic groups is alarming. The typical white family—which has an annual income more than 1.7 times that of blacks and 1.5 times that of Hispanics—has more than 11 times the accumulated wealth of black families and nearly 8 times the wealth of Hispanic families.[39] If democracy means government "by the people," why are the people not sharing more equally in the nation's wealth? If one of the purposes of government is to promote equality, why are government policies not working that way?

One scholar theorizes that interest group activity in a pluralist democracy distorts government's efforts to promote equality. His analysis of pluralism sees "corporations and organized groups with an upper-income slant as exerting political power over and above the formal one-man–one-vote standard of democracy."[40] As you learned in Chapters 9 and 14, the pluralist model of democracy rewards those groups who are well organized and well funded.

An example: As we noted above, federal income tax is withheld by law from earned income (salaries and wages), not from unearned income (interest and dividends). Early in his first term, President Reagan surprised the financial world by proposing to withhold taxes from unearned income as part of his overall economic plan, and Congress made the plan law in the summer of 1982. Financial institutions were given a year to devise procedures for withholding 10 percent of dividend and interest payments for income tax (the withholding was to begin July 1, 1983). Led by the American Bankers' Association, the banking interests urged their depositors to write legislators protesting the law; they even handed out sample letters that could be sent to members of Congress.

Some people, who apparently had never declared their bank interest as income, indignantly protested this "new" tax. Washington was flooded with mail stimulated by local banks and savings and loan associations. Congress had to hire temporary workers to answer letters from angry high-income taxpayers (who are also high-turnout voters). The president and many members of Congress were furious at the American Bankers' Association, which spent more than $300,000 in its effort to have the law repealed. Democratic Representative Thomas J. Downey of New York said that if withholding was repealed, "We send a signal that the Congress of the United States is a group of patsies to every well-organized group in America."[41] But Congress did back down, and withholding from unearned income was repealed only weeks before it was to go into effect.

What would happen if federal tax policy were determined according to principles of majoritarian rather than pluralist democracy? Perhaps not much—if public opinion is any guide. The people of the United States are not eager to redistribute wealth by increasing the only major progressive tax, the income tax. If federal taxes must be raised, Americans strongly favor a national sales tax over increased income taxes.[42] But a sales tax is a flat tax, paid by rich and poor at the same rate; it would have a regressive effect on income distribution, promoting inequality not equality. The public also prefers a weekly $10 million national lottery to an increase in the income tax.[43] Because the poor are willing to chance more of their income on winning a fortune through lotteries than are rich people, lotteries (run by twenty-six states in 1988) also contribute to income inequality through the revenue system.[44]

The newest tax on the horizon is a type of national retail sales tax called the value-added tax (VAT), which is applied to the value added to a product at each stage of production and distribution. The VAT is levied by all countries in the European economic community, and—with the potential of a 5 percent VAT raising about $100 billion annually in revenue—it is certain to be a subject of debate in the United States.[45] But if a VAT is adopted in place of raising the income tax rate, it, like all sales taxes, will be a regressive tax.

Majoritarians might argue that most Americans fail to understand the inequities of the federal tax system. However, they *cannot* argue that the public demands "fairer" tax rates that take from richer citizens to help poorer ones. If it did, the lowest-income families might receive a greater share of the national income than they do. Instead, economic policy is determined mainly through a complex process of pluralist politics that preserves nearly half the national income in the hands of the wealthiest 20 percent of families.

SUMMARY

We can separate public policies into those that prohibit, those that promote, those that protect, and those that provide. Our typology is not absolute, but it is helpful in analyzing a complex subject. Governments use their powers to tax and spend to control the business cycles in market economies. The extent to which government intervenes in the economy is a major issue in public policy, made more critical by the stock market crash in 1987.

Laissez-faire economics holds that the government should keep its hands off the economy. Keynesian theory holds that government should take an active role in dealing with inflation and unemployment, using fiscal and monetary policies to produce desired levels of aggregate demand. Monetarists believe fiscal policies are unreliable, opting instead to use the money supply to control aggregate demand. Supply-side economists, who had an enormous influence on Reagan's economic policies, focus on controlling the supply of goods and services rather than the demand for them.

In 1921, Congress thrust the responsibility for the budget on the president. After World War II, it tried unsuccessfully to regain control of the process. Later, Congress managed to restructure the process under House and Senate Budget Committees. The new process worked well until it confronted the huge deficits in the Reagan budgets.

Because so much of the budget involves military spending and uncontrollable payments to individuals, it is virtually impossible to balance the budget by reducing what remains—mainly spending for nonentitlement domestic programs. With President Reagan firmly against a tax increase, Congress accepted the Gramm-Rudman-Hollings antideficit law in 1985. Under that law, deficits were to be reduced in stages, through automatic across-the-board cuts, if necessary, until the budget was balanced by FY 1991. The deficit problem proved so intractable that Congress had to amend the law in 1987 to extend the deadline to 1993.

Although Reagan was against a tax hike, he pushed for sweeping tax reform. The result was a simplified tax plan with fewer loopholes, fewer tax brackets, and a significantly lower rate for the top bracket. But even with the heavily progressive tax rates of the past, the federal tax system has done little to redistribute income. Government transfer payments to individuals have helped reduce income inequalities. But the distribution of after-tax income in the United States in 1988 was *more* unequal than the distribution in 1966. Moreover, that distribution is less equal in the United States than in most major Western nations.

Pluralist democracy as practiced in the United States has allowed well-organized, well-financed interest groups to manipulate tax and spending policies to their benefit. The result is that a larger and poorer segment of society is paying the price.

Key Terms

public policy	receipts
tax expenditure	Office of Management
market economy	and Budget (OMB)
economic depression	tax committees
inflation	authorization
business cycle	committees
aggregate demand	appropriations
productive capacity	committees
gross national product	Budget Committees
(GNP)	Congressional Budget
Keynesian theory	Office (CBO)
fiscal policies	reconciliation
monetary policies	entitlement
deficit financing	Gramm-Rudman-
Council of Economic	Hollings (antideficit
Advisers (CEA)	law)
monetarists	progressive taxation
supply-side economics	incremental budgeting
fiscal year (FY)	uncontrollable outlay
budget authority	transfer payment
budget outlays	

Selected Readings

Levy, Frank. *Dollars and Dreams: The Changing American Income Distribution.* New York: Russell Sage Foundation, 1987. Ties government economic policies to various social and economic trends. Sees an increasingly unequal distribution of chances to purchase the middle-class dream.

National Journal, 14 May 1988. A special issue on the Reagan presidency with articles on his most troubling legacy—the deficit, the defense build-up, and social spending.

Page, Benjamin A. *Who Gets What from Government?* Berkeley, Calif.: University of California Press, 1983. Argues the case for complete equality of income. Contains good data on the distribution of income.

Pechman, Joseph A. *Who Paid the Taxes, 1966–1985?* Washington, D.C.: Brookings Institution, 1985. Clear description by a noted authority of who paid what taxes.

Pechman, Joseph A., ed. *World Tax Reform: A Progress Report.* Washington, D.C.: Brookings Institution, 1988. A very readable account of the impact of the U.S. experience with tax reform on tax policies in other countries.

Savage, James D. *Balanced Budgets and American Politics.* Ithaca, N.Y.: Cornell University Press, 1988. Views the concept of a balanced budget as an organizing principle or symbol in the debate over the makeup of national spending, the direction of fiscal policy, and government's role in the economy.

Wildavsky, Aaron. *The New Politics of the Budgetary Process.* 5th ed. Boston: Little, Brown, 1988. The standard study on budgetary politics, by one of the first analysts of incremental budgeting. This edition is substantially revised.

16

Domestic Policy

Twelve-year-old Lafeyette Walton regularly witnesses scenes of brutality. He lives in the Henry Horner Homes public housing project, a seven-block stretch of red-brick apartment buildings on Chicago's blighted West Side. During one recent summer, Henry Horner averaged one beating, shooting, or stabbing every three days. Even so, Henry Horner is far from the worst of Chicago's housing projects.

Lafeyette lives with his mother, three brothers, and two sisters in a ground-floor apartment. It has the trappings of a fortress—dirty, cinder-block walls, iron grilles over the windows. The family talks about moving, but that's not a likely prospect, given the $837 a month his mother receives in public assistance.

More than 5 million poor, inner-city children live lives similar to Lafeyette's. Many youngsters routinely exposed to violence suffer nightmares, depression, and personality disorders. Some withdraw and give up hope; others become more aggressive. Somehow, in a land of promise and opportunity, Lafeyette and his peers are living in an abyss of urban squalor and decay.[1]

About 500 miles away, on Larry Baxa's farm near Belleville, Kansas, a combine chews up rows of corn. The air is fragrant with freshly cut alfalfa. The harvest season has begun. Amid this picture of plenty, Baxa and his three kids are hungry; the refrigerator and the cupboard are frequently bare. The Baxas are doing without basic needs, including food, in order to hold off bankers and creditors. The Baxas, like thousands of other farm families in the Midwest, are making desperate choices. To keep their farms, these families must seek assistance from the government, and few things are more shameful in rural Kansas.[2]

Although America is one of the freest and richest countries in the world, Lafeyette Walton and his family take little comfort from its liberties and wealth. Although America enjoys one of the most productive "farmbelts" in the world, farmers like Larry Baxa face ruin.

Government action helped generate these contradictions; and government action aims to correct them. We call this kind of government action "public policy." You may recall our earlier definition of *public policy:* a general plan of action adopted by government to solve a social problem, counter a threat, or make use of an opportunity.

This chapter covers a wide range of issues to illustrate and analyze public policies (we examined the policymaking process in earlier chapters). We approach the study of public policies according to their purposes: to protect, to prohibit, to provide, or to promote. Sometimes policies serve multiple purposes. We begin our inquiry into domestic policy by discussing policies that *protect* Americans from disease and policies that *prohibit* the sale, distribution, and use of certain drugs. Then we analyze in detail policies that *provide* social insurance, public assistance, and farm supports. (We reserve our discussion of policies that *promote* disadvantaged groups through affirmative action programs until Chapter 18.) Our inquiry is guided by some key questions: What are the origins and politics of specific policies? What are the effects of those policies once they are implemented? Why do some policies succeed while others fail? Finally, do disagreements over values underlie disagreements over policy?

Public policies are as various as freight cars passing across a road: Their numbers sometimes seem endless to the person eager to get under way. With the wide range of policies worth exploring, you may be wondering why we spend most of the chapter discussing social insurance, public assistance, and farm support. There are three reasons why these policies are separated from the rest for special consideration. First, government expenditures in these areas represent a giant share of the national budget (see "National Government Outlays" in Essay D, page 534).[3] All citizens ought to know how and why their resources are allocated. Second, one goal of these policies is to alleviate some of the consequences of economic inequality. Yet poverty remains a fixture of American life. And, third, these three areas pose some vexing problems involving the conflicts between freedom and order, and freedom and equality.

STUDYING PUBLIC POLICIES

We begin with a brief discussion of two public policy areas: the protection of health and the prohibition of controlled substances. Americans disagree over public policies because they disagree over perceptions of events (do they warrant the need for government action), the goals the government should have, or the means the government should try to fulfill those goals. In the examples that follow, we focus on perceptions, goals, and means.

Policies That Protect: AIDS

Acquired Immune Deficiency Syndrome (AIDS) is a killer. It now rivals cancer as the nation's most feared disease, and many Americans believe that everyone is susceptible to it.[4] Estimates vary on the spread of AIDS through the population, but one fact is certain: Most of the men, women, and children who are afflicted will die from the opportunistic infections that ravage AIDS victims. So far, most victims are either intravenous drug users or male homosexuals. There is a real possibility that the disease will spread widely through the non-drug using heterosexual population.

Just about everyone agrees that government should protect the health of its citizens. In 1987, the national government spent $700 million on AIDS research and education, up from $30 million in 1982. By 1989, the government plans to spend $1.7 billion.[5] In order to protect health, what should the government do to stop the spread of AIDS?

Public health officials are fairly certain that the AIDS virus is spread only by the exchange of body fluids—blood or semen. In order to protect Americans, the Public Health Service in 1986 mounted a national campaign to educate children and young adults about the sexual practices that increase the risk of AIDS transmission. This government action infuriated many citizens, who believed that instruction about "safe sex" infringes on a parent's freedom to guide a child's sexual education.

Some public health officials also advocate the distribution of free condoms to young people in an effort to familiarize them with using condoms. Condoms are a simple and relatively effective way to lessen

The Gloved Treatment for AIDS Protesters
AIDS is today's most urgent public health problem. The fear the disease evokes was evident during this AIDS demonstration in Washington, D.C.: Local police wore rubber gloves to protect themselves against infection, even though the chances of becoming infected were miniscule. Some advocates urge the national government to outlaw discrimination against people infected with the AIDS virus so that more Americans will undergo the diagnostic test.

the spread of AIDS. However, some Americans believe the distribution of free condoms would encourage sexual activity and would undercut the moral guidance offered by parents.

Another effort to protect Americans from AIDS calls for the distribution of free needles to heroin addicts. Such a program, it is hoped, would induce addicts to avoid sharing needles, a practice linked to the transmission of the AIDS virus. Opponents to the needles-for-addicts plan maintain that the policy condones illegal drug use and would encourage a behavior that the government seeks in other ways to eliminate.

Most Americans see AIDS as a serious health problem that government should protect citizens against. A government's effort to protect life stems from the very purpose of government: maintaining order. Yet in maintaining order, government may infringe on personal freedom. AIDS policy generates controversy because it forces us to make difficult choices between freedom and order.

Policies That Prohibit: Illegal Drugs

Most Americans oppose the use of drugs such as cocaine, heroin, and marijuana. Two-thirds of Americans polled in 1986 thought that possession of small amounts of marijuana should be treated as a crime.[6] Government prohibits the sale and possession of some drugs in an effort to stem their use. The penalties can be severe; prison terms and fines are common. But drug abuse continues despite these sanctions. One recent study estimates that Americans spend between $15 and $20 billion a year on cocaine alone, and that marijuana, with 18 million regular users, is still the nation's most popular illegal "high."[7] Why is government's prohibition policy ineffective?

The market in illegal drugs, like other markets, exists because of supply and demand. In theory, the elimination of the drug supply would eliminate the market, but efforts aimed at the supply-side have been notably unsuccessful. Why? One partial answer arises from a simple observation: Drug trafficking, despite the risks, is very lucrative. It can be a shortcut to wealth and, in some communities, a quick way to gain status. Penalties such as long prison terms do not act as sufficient deterrents.

Government has also attempted to constrict or eliminate the supply and distribution network that keeps America awash in narcotics. A current government plan is trying to draw drug-producing or drug-trafficking nations into accord with U.S. drug policy. Under this plan, the president must certify whether twenty-four nations identified by Congress as major drug producers or transit points are cooperating with American drug-control efforts. If the president fails to certify a country, foreign aid and other financial assistance sent to that country are reduced substantially. The president can push for tougher sanctions, including trade embargoes, against particularly recalcitrant countries. So far, the sanctions have not dented the supply of illegal drugs entering this country.

If government policies are unsuccessful in eliminating the supply of drugs, perhaps government should concentrate on reducing or eliminating the demand for drugs. Consider the policy of mandatory drug testing for certain government employees begun by the Reagan administration.

The national government employs thousands of individuals in the area of drug enforcement. Proponents of drug testing for those employees argue that the government has a strong interest in ensuring that drug enforcement officials are not drug users themselves. Under the policy, if a urinalysis of an employee shows traces of an illegal drug, he or she is required to undergo counseling. Workers who refuse to be tested can be dismissed.

A 1986 poll reported that an overwhelming majority of Americans are willing to take drug tests.[8] Opponents of mandatory drug testing argue, however, that testing would not be based on "reasonable suspicion" of drug use, that it would therefore interfere with personal liberty or privacy. Such testing, remarked one vocal opponent, would be "a comic exercise in Ty-D-Bol justice," flushing freedom in the process.[9]

Although most Americans agree that AIDS and illicit drugs are serious problems that warrant government action, disagreements arise

A Tough Test . . . For Some
A substantial majority of Americans are willing to submit to mandatory tests for illegal drugs. Organizations in the private sector routinely impose drug tests (professional athletes take them or lose their high-paying jobs). But government-imposed drug testing is a thornier issue: Constitutional guarantees of liberty and due process may bar testing in the absence of reasonable suspicion.

when the means selected to address these problems generate value conflicts or prove ineffective. Questionable or ineffective means have stirred debates over other large domestic policy programs, including those designed to provide income, health and welfare benefits to citizens.

GOVERNMENT POLICIES AND INDIVIDUAL WELFARE

The most controversial purpose of government is to promote social and economic equality among its citizens. To do so may conflict with the freedom of some citizens, for it requires government action to redistribute income from rich to poor. This choice between freedom and equality constitutes the modern dilemma of government; it has been at the center of many of the major conflicts in U.S. public policy since World War II. On one hand, most Americans believe that government should help the needy. On the other hand, they do not want to sacrifice their own standard of living to provide government handouts to those whom they may perceive as shiftless and lazy.

The Growth of the American Welfare State

At one time, governments confined their activities to the minimal protection of people and property—to ensuring security and order. Now, however, almost every modern nation may be characterized as a **welfare state,** a concept that stresses government's function as the provider and protector of individual well-being through economic and social programs. **Social welfare** encompasses government programs that are developed to provide the necessary minimum living standards for all citizens. Income for the elderly, health care, subsidized housing, and nutrition are among the concerns addressed by government social welfare programs.

The recent history of U.S. government support for social welfare policies is illustrated in Figure 16.1. In 1960, 26 cents of every dollar of national spending went to payments for individuals. In 1970, 33 cents of every dollar went to payments for individuals. And, in 1980, slightly less than half of each dollar went to individuals. By 1985, spending for individuals fell off a few percent; but by 1987, it had returned to the 1980 level. The government estimates that by 1990, 49 percent of national spending will go to individuals. The national government clearly remains a provider of social welfare, despite changes in administrations.

The origins of social welfare as government policy go back to the Industrial Revolution, when the mechanization of production resulted in a shift from home manufacturing to large-scale factory production. As more and more people worked for wages, many more were subjected to the dreadful consequences of a loss of employment due to sickness,

Figure 16.1

Government Payments to Individuals
The national government spends a large portion of its budget on payments to individuals (for example, on social security). This spending has nearly doubled since 1960. (Source: Historical Tables, Budget of the United States Government, FY 1989, Table 11.1)

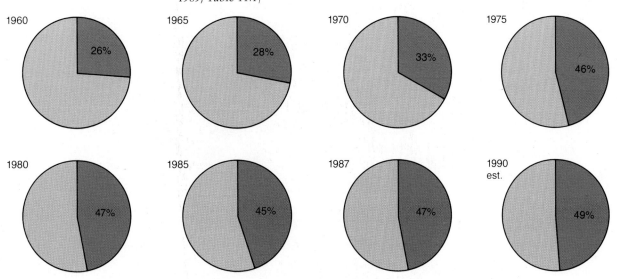

1960 — 26%
1965 — 28%
1970 — 33%
1975 — 46%
1980 — 47%
1985 — 45%
1987 — 47%
1990 est. — 49%

■ Payments for individuals as percentage of federal government expenditures

injury, old age, or economic conditions. The sick, the disabled, and the aged were tended, for the most part, by charities. The poor were confined to poorhouses or almshouses, which were little more than shacks that warehoused the impoverished. In the eighteenth and nineteenth centuries, poverty was viewed as a disgrace. Poor people were seen as lazy and incompetent. (Indeed, many Americans still hold this view.) The circumstances of relief were purposely made disagreeable to discourage dependence on outside assistance.

America today is far from being a welfare state in the same sense that Sweden or Great Britain is; those nations provide many more medical, educational, and unemployment benefits to their citizens. However, the United States does have some social welfare functions. To understand social welfare policies in the United States, you must first understand the significance of a major event—the Great Depression—and the two presidential plans that extended the scope of government—the "New Deal" and the "Great Society."

The Great Depression.   Throughout its history, the U.S. economy has experienced alternating good times and hard times, generally referred to as *business cycles*. The **Great Depression** was, by far, the longest and deepest setback that the American economy has ever experienced. It

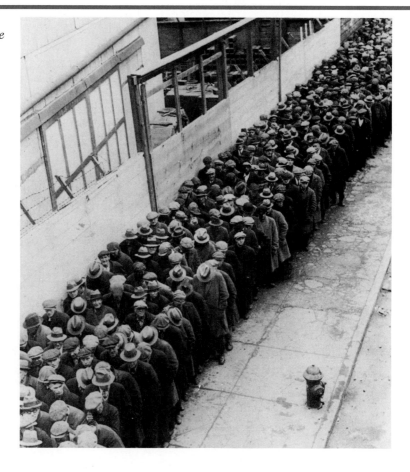

A Human Tragedy
The Great Depression made millions of Americans idle. By 1933, when President Herbert Hoover left office, about one-fourth of the labor force was out of work. The few available jobs attracted long lines of able-bodied workers.

began with the stock market crash of 1929 (on October 29, a day known as Black Tuesday) and did not end until the start of World War II. By 1932, one out of every four U.S. workers was unemployed, and millions more were underemployed. No other event has had a greater effect on the thinking and the institutions of government in the twentieth century.

The forces that had stemmed earlier declines were no longer operating. There were no more frontiers, no growing exports, no new technologies to boost employment. Unchecked, unemployment spread like an epidemic. And the crisis fueled itself. Workers who lost their source of income could no longer buy the food, goods, and services that kept the economy going. Thus, private industry and commercial farmers tended to produce more than could be sold profitably. Closed factories, surplus crops, and idle workers were the consequences.

The Great Depression generated powerful ironies. Producers, seeking to restore profits, trimmed costs by replacing workers with machines, which only increased unemployment. People went hungry because so much food had been produced that it could not be sold profitably; dumping it was cheaper than taking it to market.

The industrialized nations of Europe were also hit hard. The value of U.S. exports fell while the value of its imports increased; this led to high tariffs, which strangled trade and fueled the Depression. From 1929 to 1932, more than 44 percent of the nation's banks failed. Farm prices fell by more than half in the same period. Marginal farmers lost their land, and tenant farmers succumbed to mechanization. The uprooted—tens of thousands of dispossessed farm families, with their possessions atop their cars and trucks—headed west in a hopeless quest for opportunity.

The New Deal.   In his speech accepting the presidential nomination at the 1932 Democratic National Convention, Franklin Delano Roosevelt (then governor of New York) made a promise: "I pledge you, I pledge myself to a new deal for the American people." Although this **New Deal** was never defined, it became the label for measures advocated by the Roosevelt administration to stem the Depression. Some scholars regard these measures as the most imaginative burst of domestic policy in the nation's history. Others see them as the source of massive government growth without matching benefits.

President Roosevelt's New Deal was composed of two phases. The first, which ended in 1935, was aimed at boosting prices and lowering unemployment. The second phase, which ended in 1938, was aimed at aiding the forgotten people: the poor, the aged, unorganized working men and women, and the farmers. The Supreme Court stymied Roosevelt's first-phase reform efforts by declaring major New Deal legislation unconstitutional, beginning in 1935. A majority of the justices maintained that in its legislation, Congress had exceeded its constitutional authority to regulate interstate commerce.

The Democrats won overwhelming popular support for their efforts at relief and recovery. The voters returned Roosevelt to office in a landslide election in 1936. But the Supreme Court continued its opposition to New Deal legislation. This prompted Roosevelt to advocate an in-

Facing the Great Depression

The despair of the Depression can be seen in the faces of this migrant mother and her children. They were unsuccessful in their search for work in Weslaco, Texas, in 1939. Uprooted farmers, forced from their land by foreclosure, trooped from town to town in search of jobs or food. The health, nutrition, and shelter of millions of Americans suffered as a consequence of the Depression.

crease in the number of justices on the Court; his goal was to appoint justices sympathetic to the legislation he endorsed. However, Roosevelt's attack on the Court, coupled with increasing labor violence, alarmed conservatives and put the New Deal on the defensive. Still, within a few months of the 1936 election, the Supreme Court began to yield to a view of expanded power for the national government; in an abrupt about-face, the Court upheld the New Deal policies that comprised the second phase. (It was, said one wag, "the switch in time that saved nine.")

The New Deal programs were opportunistic; they were not guided by, or based on, a single political or economic theory. They aimed at relief for the needy, recovery for the nation, and long-range reform for the economy. Administering the programs called for government growth; funding the programs required higher taxes. Government could no longer rely on either the decentralized political structure of federalism or the market forces of laissez-faire capitalism to bring the country out of its decline. The New Deal embodied the belief that a complex economy required centralized government control.

Poverty and unemployment remained, however, despite the best efforts of the Democrats. By 1939, 17 percent of the work force (more than 9 million people) was still unemployed. Only World War II was able to provide the economic surge needed to yield lower unemployment and higher prices, the elusive goals of the New Deal. Although the actual economic value of the New Deal reforms is still undetermined, those policies did begin long-range trends toward government expansion. And another torrent of domestic policymaking burst forth three decades later.

The Great Society. John F. Kennedy's election in 1960 brought to Washington public servants sensitive to persistent poverty and the needs of minorities. But Kennedy's narrow margin of victory was far from a mandate to improve the plight of the poor and dispossessed. At first, Kennedy proposed technical and financial aid for depressed areas and programs for upgrading the skills of workers in marginal jobs. But Kennedy and influential members of his administration were motivated by politics as well as poverty; in 1962, with the economy faltering again, the Kennedy administration proposed substantial tax breaks for middle- and upper-income groups. Many low-income Americans remained untouched by the administration's programs.

Kennedy's assassination in November 1963 provided the backdrop for new policies founded on equality, proposed by his successor, Lyndon Baines Johnson. In his 1965 State of the Union address, President Johnson offered his own version of the New Deal; his vision of the **Great Society** included a broad array of programs designed to redress political, social, and economic inequality. Some of these programs had already been enacted, whereas others were still in the planning stage. The Civil Rights Act of 1964 was aimed at erasing racial discrimination from most areas of American life. The Voting Rights Act of 1965 had as its goal the elimination of voting restrictions that discriminated against blacks and other minorities. Both statutes prohibited conduct that was inconsistent with political and social equality.

Another part of Johnson's Great Society plan was based on the traditional American belief that social and economic equality could be attained through equality of educational opportunity. The Elementary and Secondary Education Act of 1965 provided, for the first time, direct federal aid to local school districts, based on the number of low-income families in each district. Later, the national government was able to use the threat of withholding school aid (under the 1964 Civil Rights Act) to dramatically increase the pace of school integration in the South.

Still another vital element of the Great Society was the **War on Poverty.** The major weapon in this war was the Economic Opportunity Act (1964); its proponents promised that it would eradicate poverty in ten years. The act encouraged a variety of local community programs to educate and train people for employment. Among them were college work-study programs, summer employment for high school and college students, loans to small businesses, a domestic version of the Peace Corps (called VISTA, for Volunteers in Service to America), educational enrichment for preschoolers, and legal services for the poor. It offered opportunity: a hand up, rather than a handout.

The act also established the Office for Economic Opportunity (OEO), which was the administrative center of the War on Poverty. Its basic strategy was to involve the poor themselves in administering the programs, in the hope that they would know which programs would best serve their needs. Federal money was channeled directly to local community action programs to fight poverty. This approach avoided the vested interests of state and local government bureaucrats and political machines. But it also led to new local controversies by shifting the control of federal funds from local politicians to other groups. (In one notorious example, the Blackstone Rangers, a Chicago street gang, received federal support.)

In 1967, the Johnson administration responded to pressure from established local politicians by requiring that poverty funds be distributed through certified state and local agencies. In addition, all sectors of the community (including business, labor, and local leaders) would now be represented, along with the poor, in administering community action programs.

The War on Poverty eventually sputtered and disappeared as funding was diverted to the Vietnam War. Although it had achieved little in the way of income redistribution, it did lead to one significant change: It made the poor aware of their political power. Candidates representing the poor ran for political office, and officeholders paid increased attention to the poor. The poor also found that they could use the legal system to their benefit. For example, with legal assistance from the OEO, low-income litigants were successful in striking down state laws requiring a minimum period of residency before people could receive public assistance.[10]

Some War on Poverty programs remain, established features of government. (Among these are the work-study program that enables many college students to finance their educations.) Yet poverty also remains; and the evidence suggests that it may once again be on the rise. Public attitudes toward poverty have changed, however, since the Great Depression. When Americans were polled recently on the reasons for poverty, they cited in about equal measure circumstances beyond the control of the poor and lack of effort. Many Americans today realize that poverty results from forces beyond the control of individuals, such as shifts in the economy.[11]

Social welfare policy is based on the premise that society has an obligation to provide for the minimum welfare of its members. In a recent national survey, the poor and nonpoor agreed that government should protect its citizens against the risks that they are powerless to combat. Americans expressed a clear conviction that money and wealth ought to be more evenly shared by a larger percentage of the population.[12] The label *welfare state* reflects this protective role of government.

By meeting minimum needs, government welfare policies attempt to promote equality. New Deal policies were aimed at meeting the needs of the poor by redistributing income: People with greater incomes paid progressively higher taxes; the wealthy paid to alleviate poverty. Today's liberals tend to follow in the New Deal path. They are willing to curtail economic freedom somewhat to promote economic equality. As a result, their policies aim at providing direct income subsidies and government jobs. Today's conservatives avoid this government-as-provider approach, preferring economic freedom to government intervention. Their policies aim at curbing inflation and reducing government spending, on the theory that the tide of a rising economy lifts all boats.

The Reduction of the Welfare State

A spirit of equality—equality of opportunity—motivated the reforms of the 1960s, and many of these reforms carried over to the 1970s. But

Ronald Reagan's overwhelming election in 1980 and his landslide re-election in 1984 forced a re-examination of social welfare policy.

In a dramatic departure from his predecessors (Republicans as well as Democrats), Reagan shifted emphasis from economic equality to economic freedom. He questioned whether government alone should continue to be responsible for shouldering the economic and social well-being of less fortunate citizens. And, to the extent that government should bear this responsibility, he maintained that state and local governments could do so more efficiently than the national government.

Reagan professed his support of the "truly needy" and of the preservation of a "reliable safety net of social programs," by which he meant the core programs begun in the New Deal. But his administration abolished a number of national social welfare programs and redirected others. Reagan proposed sharp cutbacks in housing assistance, welfare, the food stamp program, and education and training programs. He also trimmed the most basic of American social welfare programs—social security—although cuts here were less severe than in other areas.[13]

Congress checked some of the president's proposed cutbacks; many Great Society programs remained in force, although at lower funding levels. Overall spending on social welfare programs (as a proportion of the gross national product) fell to about mid-1970s levels. But the dramatic growth in the promotion of social welfare that began with the New Deal ended with the Reagan administration. And the national budget deficit—a deficit that ballooned during the Reagan administration—will probably restrict future efforts to expand the government's social welfare role. The enormous government debt may force Congress to avoid new and costly social welfare programs until income and expenditures come nearer to balance.

PROVIDING SOCIAL INSURANCE

Insurance is a device for guaranteeing an individual against loss. Since the late nineteenth century, there has been a growing tendency for governments to offer **social insurance,** which is a government-backed guarantee against loss by individuals, without regard to need. The most common forms of social insurance guard against losses due to worker sickness, injury, and disability; due to old age; and due to unemployment. The first example of social insurance in the United States was workers' compensation. Beginning early in this century, most states provided a system of insurance that compensated workers who lost income because they were injured in the workplace.

Social insurance benefits are distributed to recipients without regard to their economic status. Old-age benefits, for example, are paid to all people—rich or poor—who reach the required age. In most social insurance programs, employees and employers contribute to a fund from which later disbursements are made to recipients.*

---

* Examine your next paycheck stub. It should indicate your contribution to FICA (the Federal Insurance Contribution Act). This is your social security tax; it supports disability, survivors', retirement, and Medicare benefits. In 1989, for wages up to $45,000, the tax rate was 7.51 percent.

Social insurance programs are examples of *entitlements*—benefits to which every eligible person has a legal right, and which government cannot deny. National entitlement programs consume about half of every dollar of government spending; one of the largest entitlement programs is social security.

Social Security

Social security is social insurance that provides economic assistance to people faced with unemployment, disability, or old age; it is financed by taxes on employers and employees. Initially, social security benefits were distributed only to the aged, the unemployed, and poor people with dependent children. Today, social security also provides medical care for the elderly and income support for the disabled.

Origins of social security. The idea of social security came late to the United States. As early as 1883, Germany enacted legislation to protect workers against the hazards of industrial life. Most European nations adopted old-age insurance after World War I; many provided income support for the disabled and income protection for families after the death of the principal wage earner. In the United States, however, the needs of the elderly and the unemployed were left largely to private organizations and individuals. Although twenty-eight states had old-age assistance programs by 1934, neither private charities nor state and local governments—nor both together—could cope with the prolonged unemployment and distress that resulted from the Great Depression. It became clear that a national policy was necessary to deal with a national crisis.

The first important step came on August 14, 1935, when President Franklin Roosevelt signed the **Social Security Act;** that act is the cornerstone of the modern American welfare state. The act's framers developed three approaches to the problem of dependence. The first provided social insurance in the form of old-age and surviving-spouse benefits, and cooperative state-national unemployment assistance. A program was created to provide income to retired workers, to ensure that the elderly did not retire into poverty. This was to serve as a floor of protection against income loss for the elderly. (Most Americans associate social security with this program.) In addition, an unemployment insurance program, financed by employers, was created to provide payments for a limited time to workers who were laid off or dismissed for reasons beyond their control.

The second approach provided aid to the destitute in the form of grants-in-aid to the states. The act established the first permanent national commitment to provide financial assistance to the needy aged, needy families with dependent children, the blind, and (since the 1950s) the permanently and totally disabled.

The third approach provided health and welfare services through federal aid to the states. Included were health and family services for crippled children and orphans, and vocational rehabilitation for the disabled.

Listen to Your Elders
Democratic Representative Claude Pepper of Florida was only seventy-nine when he posed with two one-hundred-year-old constituents who testified before the House Select Committee on Aging in 1979. Still active in 1988, Pepper continues to be the driving force behind government programs that provide assistance to the nation's elderly.

How social security works. The social security old-age benefits program is administered directly by the national government through the Social Security Administration. Old-age retirement revenue goes into its own *trust fund* (there is a separate fund for each social security program), which means that this revenue can be spent only for the old-age benefits program. Benefits, in the form of monthly payments, begin when an employee reaches retirement age, which today stands at sixty-five. (People can retire as early as age sixty-two, but with reduced benefits.) The age at which full benefits are paid will increase to sixty-seven after the year 2000.

Many Americans believe that each person's social security contributions are set aside specifically for his or her retirement, like a savings account.[14] But social security doesn't operate quite like that. Rather, the social security revenue generated today pays benefits to those who have already reached retirement age. Thus, social security (and social insurance in general) is not a form of savings; it is a pay-as-you-go tax system. Today's workers support today's elderly.

When the social security program began, it had few beneficiaries and many contributors. The program could provide relatively large benefits with low taxes. In 1937, for example, the tax rate was 1 percent, and there were nine workers shouldering the benefits of each retiree. As the program matured and more people retired, the ratio of workers to recipients decreased. In 1986, for example, the social security system paid benefits to 38 million people and collected revenues from 124 million. (In 1989, the tax for retirement, survivors', and disability benefits was 6.06 percent of wages up to $45,000.)

The reason Congress doesn't touch Social Security....

GRANBO

Mike Luckovich
Times-Picayune

At one time, federal workers, members of Congress, judges, even the president were omitted from the social security system. Today, however, there are few exceptions. Universal participation is essential for the system to operate because it is a tax program, not a savings program. If participation were not compulsory, there would not be enough revenue to provide benefits to present retirees. So government, which is the only institution that can coerce, requires that all employees and their employers contribute, thereby imposing restrictions on freedom.

Those people who currently pay into the system will receive retirement benefits financed by future participants. As with a pyramid scheme or a chain letter, success depends on the growth of the base. If the birthrate remains steady or grows, future wage earners will be able to support today's contributors when they retire. If the economy expands, there will be more jobs, more income, and a growing wage base to tax for increased benefits to retirees. But suppose the birthrate falls, or unemployment rises and the economy falters. Then contributions could decline to the point at which benefits exceed revenues. The pyramidal character of social security is its Achilles' heel.

Who pays? Who benefits?   "Who pays?" and "Who benefits?" are two important questions in government policymaking, and they continue to shape social security policy. In 1968, the Republican party platform called for automatic adjustments that would increase social security payments as the cost of living increased. The theory was simple: As the cost of living rises, so should retirement benefits; otherwise, benefits are paid in "shrinking dollars." Cost-of-living adjustments (COLAs) became a political football in 1969 as Democrats and Republicans tried to outdo each other by suggesting larger increases for retirees. The result was a significant expansion of the social security program, far in excess of the cost of living. The beneficiaries were the retired, who were beginning to flex their political muscle. Politicians knew that the alienation of this constituency could change an election.[15]

In 1972, Congress adopted automatic adjustments in benefits and in the wage base on which contributions are assessed, so that revenue would expand as benefits grew. This approach set social security on automatic pilot. When inflation exceeds 3 percent, the automatic adjustment goes into effect. (Politicians sometimes fear retribution at the polls if there is not an annual adjustment. Even though it appeared that inflation would fall below 3 percent in 1986, Congress authorized an adjustment for that year.)

There was no assurance, however, that revenue growth would equal or exceed the growth in social security expenditures. And, in fact, when *stagflation* (high unemployment coupled with high inflation) took hold in the 1970s, the entire social security system was in jeopardy. Stagflation gripped the social security system in an economic vise: Unemployment meant a reduction in revenue; high inflation meant growing benefits. This one-two punch drained social security trust fund reserves to critically low levels in the late 1970s and early 1980s. Other troubling factors were becoming clear. A lower birthrate meant that, in the future, fewer workers would support the pool of retirees. And the number of retirees would grow, as average life spans lengthened. Higher taxes—an unpopular political move—loomed as one alternative. Another was to pay for social security out of general revenues, that is, income taxes. Social security would then become a public assistance program, like welfare.

Life Begins at Sixty-Five
Old age and impoverishment used to go hand in hand, but not any more. Because of Social Security, people sixty-five and older are the second-richest age group in the United States. Only Americans fifty-five to sixty-four are better off. One political economist recently estimated that the government spends about $350 billion on the aged, more than on national defense. Today's elderly remain vulnerable to impoverishment in only one area: long-term nursing home care.

In 1983, shortly before existing social security benefit funds were exhausted, Congress and President Reagan agreed to a solution that called for two painful adjustments: increased taxes and reduced benefits.

The changes enacted in 1983 may have guaranteed the future of the social security system. However, although policymakers have not generally fared well in predicting future economic conditions, those conditions will determine the success or failure of the system. Despite various revenue-generating plans, higher taxes or lower benefits may be the only means for ensuring the viability of social security.[16]

Today, few argue against the need for social security. But debate surrounds the extent of coverage and the level of benefits. "The [Social Security] Act is the most successful program of the modern state," declared Nobel prize laureate Paul Samuelson. Yet Milton Friedman, another Nobel laureate, labeled the act "a sacred cow that no politician can criticize." How can two renowned economists maintain such dramatically different views? Samuelson is a liberal in the Keynesian tradition; he favors equality over freedom. According to his view, social security lifted the elderly from destitution by redistributing income from workers (who have growing incomes) to the elderly (who have little or no income). Friedman is a libertarian and a monetarist; he favors freedom over equality. Because social security limits freedom to provide economic equality, Friedman would no doubt prefer that the program be scaled back or even eliminated. The political risks associated with social security cutbacks are too great, however, for most politicians to bear.

As a group, older Americans exercise enormous political power. People at or near retirement age now comprise almost 30 percent of the potential electorate; and voter turnout among older Americans is reportedly about twice that of younger people.[17] These facts may help explain the stability of social security and the creation and expansion of health care for the elderly.

Medicare

The social security system provides economic assistance conditioned on unemployment, disability, or old age. In 1962, the Senate considered extending social security benefits to provide hospitalization and medical care for the elderly. In opposing the extension, Democratic Senator Russell Long of Louisiana declared, "We are not staring at a sweet old lady in bed with her kimono and nightcap. We are looking into the eyes of the wolf that ate Red Riding Hood's grandma."[18] Long was concerned that there would be no way to limit this new push for government assistance to the elderly. Other opponents echoed the fears of the American Medical Association (AMA), which saw virtually any form of government-provided medical care as a step toward government control of medicine. Long and his compatriots won the battle that day. Three years later, however, the Social Security Act was amended to provide **Medicare**, health care for all people sixty-five and over.

Origins of Medicare.   As early as 1945, public opinion clearly supported some form of national health insurance. That idea became entan-

No Cure Yet for this Headache
The United States leads the world in health care expenditures. Americans are not the healthiest people, however. Infant mortality rates are higher and life expectancy rates lower than in many other nations. Despite vigorous competition and powerful regulation, health care costs continue to grow at almost twice the rate of inflation. Today, senior citizens pay a larger share of their income for health care than they did in 1965, before the advent of Medicare.

gled in Cold War politics, however—the growing crusade against communism in America.[19] The AMA, representing the nation's physicians, mounted and financed an all-out campaign to link national health insurance (so-called socialized medicine) with socialism; the campaign was so successful that the prospect of a national health policy vanished.

Both proponents and opponents of national health insurance tried to link their positions to deeply rooted American values: Advocates emphasized equality and fairness; opponents stressed individual freedom. In the absence of a clear public mandate on the *kind* of insurance (publicly funded or private) wanted, the AMA was able to marshal political influence to prevent any national insurance at all.[20]

By 1960, however, the terms of the debate had changed. Its focus was no longer fixed on the clash of freedom and equality. Now the issue of health insurance was cast in terms of providing assistance to the aged, and a ground swell of support forced it onto the national agenda.[21]

The Democratic victory in 1964 and the advent of President Johnson's Great Society made some form of national health policy almost inevitable. On July 30, 1965, Johnson signed a bill that provided a number of health benefits to the elderly and the poor. Fearful of the AMA's power to punish its opponents, the Democrats had confined their efforts to a compulsory hospitalization insurance plan for the elderly. (This is known today as Part A of Medicare.) In addition, the bill contained a form of an alternative Republican plan, which called for voluntary government-subsidized insurance to cover physician's fees. (This is known today as Part B of Medicare.) A third program, added a year later, is called *Medicaid*; it provides medical aid to the poor through federally assisted state health programs. Medicaid is a need-based comprehensive medical and hospitalization program for the poor. Need is the only criterion: If you are poor, you qualify. Medicaid today covers 22.4 million people at a cost in 1986 of nearly $41 billion.

Medicare today. Part A of Medicare is compulsory insurance that covers certain hospital services for people sixty-five and older. Workers pay a tax (in 1989, it was 1.45 percent of wages up to $45,000). Retirees pay premiums deducted from social security payments. Payments for services are made by the national government directly to participating hospitals and other qualifying facilities; they cover the reasonable costs of necessary medical services. In 1986, 31.3 million people were enrolled in Part A, and the government paid $49 billion in benefits.[22]

Part B of Medicare is a voluntary program of medical insurance for people sixty-five and older, who pay the premiums. The insurance covers the services of physicians and other qualified providers; payments for these services are based on reasonable charges or on set fees. In 1986, almost 31 million people were enrolled; the government spent $25 billion for Part B benefits in 1986. In 1988, the monthly premium for this insurance was $24.80.[23]

The fears that Senator Long voiced in 1962 approached reality in the 1980s: Medicare costs soared out of control. By 1986, Medicare costs exceeded $75 billion, representing a fourfold increase in ten years. For the moment, Medicare is solvent, thanks to modest payroll tax increases and low unemployment; but the program lacks the cushion presently enjoyed by the retirement trust funds. Spending reductions (through curtailed benefits) or income increases (through raised taxes) are still viable, although politically unpalatable, alternatives.[24]

Medicare benefits were expanded significantly in 1988 to provide the elderly with insurance against catastrophic illnesses (illnesses that require long-term hospitalization). This program was designed to alleviate the worry of impoverishment by the high costs of hospitalization. During the first five years of the program, the government expects to pay benefits exceeding $32 billion. Funding comes from a small surtax on income taxes and $4-a-month premiums paid by the elderly.

The idea of catastrophic health insurance was first proposed by the Reagan administration. Why would an administration committed to tax reduction and benefit curtailment make such a dramatic turnabout? Perhaps the most important reason was the political power of the elderly. In an election year, the Republicans wanted the elderly's support.

While government has expanded the Medicare program, it has also sought to contain its costs. One attempt at cost containment makes use of economic incentives in the hospital treatment of Medicare patients. The plan seems to have had the desired economic benefits, but it raises questions about the endangerment of elderly patients' health. Medicare payments to hospitals had been based on the length of a patient's stay; the longer the stay, the more revenue the hospitals earned. This approach encouraged longer, more expensive hospital stays, because the government, as the insurer, was paying the bill. In 1985, however, the government switched to a new payment system under which hospitals are paid a fixed, preset fee based on the patient's diagnosis. If the patient's stay costs more than the fee schedule allows, the hospital pays the difference. On the other hand, if the hospital treats a patient for less than the fixed fee, then the hospital reaps the profit. This new system provides an incentive for hospitals to discharge patients sooner, in some cases perhaps before they are completely well.

PROVIDING PUBLIC ASSISTANCE

Public assistance is what most people mean when they use the term *welfare* or *welfare payments*; it is government aid to individuals who can demonstrate a need for that aid. Public assistance is directed toward those who lack the ability or the resources to provide for themselves or their families.

Public assistance programs instituted under the Social Security Act are known today as *categorical assistance programs*. They include (1) old-age assistance for the needy elderly not covered by old-age pension benefits, (2) aid to the needy blind, (3) aid to needy families with dependent children, and (4) aid to the totally and permanently disabled. Although adopted initially as stopgap measures during the Depression, these programs have now become entitlements. They are administered by the states, but the bulk of the funding comes from the national government's general tax revenues. Because the states also contribute to the funding of their own public assistance programs, the benefits tend to vary from state to state.

Poverty and Public Assistance

The national government requires that national standards be used in the administration of state welfare programs. It distributes resources to each state based on the proportion of the population living in poverty in that state. That proportion is, in turn, determined on the basis of a federal **poverty level,** or poverty threshold, which is the minimum cash income that will provide for a family's basic needs. The poverty level is calculated as three times the cost of an economy food plan, a market basket of food that provides a minimally nutritious diet. (The threshold is computed in this way because research suggests that the poor spend one-third of their income on food.*)

---

* Although it has been the source of endless debate, today's definition of poverty retains remarkable similarity to its predecessors. As early as 1795, a group of English magistrates "decided that a minimum income should be the cost of a gallon loaf of bread, multiplied by 3, plus an allowance for each dependent." See Alvin L. Schorr, "Redefining Poverty Levels," *New York Times*, 9 May 1984, p. 27.

The poverty level is fairly simple to apply. It is also, of course, only a rough measure for distinguishing the poor and the nonpoor. Using it is like using a wrench as a hammer: It works, but not very well.

The poverty level varies with family size, and it is adjusted each year to reflect changes in consumer prices. In 1986, the poverty threshold for a family of four was $11,203.[25] This is income *before* taxes. If the poverty threshold were viewed as disposable income (in other words, income *after* taxes), then the proportion of the population categorized as living in poverty would increase.

Some critics believe that other factors should be considered in computing the poverty level. The current computation fails to take into account such noncash benefits as food stamps, health benefits (Medicaid), and subsidized housing. Presumably, the inclusion of these noncash benefits would decrease the proportion of individuals seen to be living below the poverty level.

Critics notwithstanding, the poverty threshold has been calculated for many years on the basis of total cash income. At the very least, that yardstick allows us to chart our progress against poverty. Figure 16.2 shows that poverty in the United States has declined from its peak years in the late 1950s and early 1960s. The elderly have made the most progress, and blacks and whites have progressed about equally. Nevertheless, in 1985 poverty was still the economic condition of one in nine whites and one in three blacks and Hispanics. Poverty retains a tight hold on the American population. And, as Figure 16.3 shows, it is creeping back up to mid-1960s levels.

Poverty was once a condition of old age. Social security altered that

Figure 16.2

Poverty Rates by Groups
The condition of being poor affects whites, blacks, Hispanics, and the elderly unequally. A smaller percentage of all Americans live in poverty today than in 1959, when income information was first collected systematically.
(Source: Bureau of the Census, Money Income and Poverty Status of Families and Persons in the United States: 1985, Current Populations Reports, Series P-60, No. 158, Tables 1 and 2, pp. 13-15.)

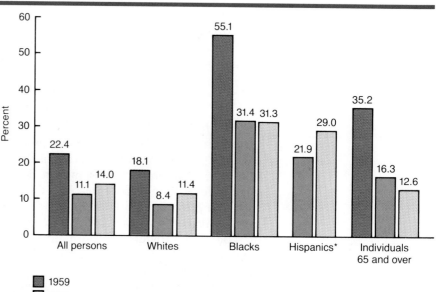

1959
1973
1985

*No data available for 1959.

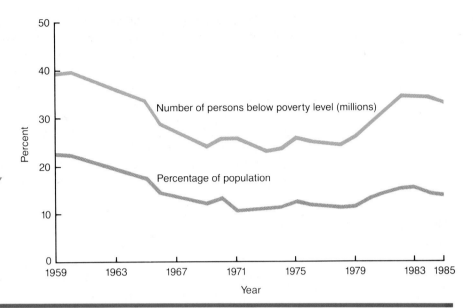

Poverty in the United States, 1959-1985
This graph shows the number and the percentage of the population living below the poverty level. Both figures have increased since 1978. (Source: Bureau of the Census, Money Income and Poverty Status of Families and Persons in the United States: 1985, Current Population Reports, Series P-60, No. 158, Table 1, p. 13.)
Figure 16.3

picture. Today, the likelihood of poverty is still related to age, but in the opposite direction. Poverty is largely a predicament of the young; almost half the poor are twenty-one or younger. Poverty also varies somewhat by gender. Of all the people who qualify as poor, nearly six in ten are females.[26] It is relatively easy to draw a portrait of the poor; it is much more difficult to craft policies that move them out of destitution.

Critics of social welfare spending argue that antipoverty policies have made poverty more attractive by removing incentives to work. They believe these policies, which aim to provide for the poor, have actually promoted poverty. In short, America is losing ground in the battle against poverty.

Another explanation for the failure of government policies to reduce poverty rests on changes in racial attitudes. In the 1960s, racial barriers kept the black middle class in the same urban ghettos as the poor. The middle class's presence provided social stability, role models, and community institutions and businesses. Ironically, the decline of racial barriers prompted middle-class blacks to move out of the ghetto. As a result, the inner city became increasingly poor and increasingly dependent on welfare.[27]

In the long run, understanding the consequences of public policy will help reduce poverty in America. For the moment, however, debates among scholars offer no comfort to Lafeyette Walton and children like him, who confront the daily reality of inner-city despair and violence.

Cash Assistance: AFDC

The largest public assistance program is **Aid to Families with Dependent Children (AFDC),** which was created by the 1935 Social Security Act. Each month, almost 4 million families (or roughly 11 million individuals) receive benefits through AFDC; it is the major source of gov-

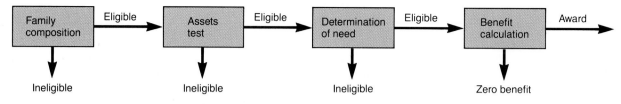

AFDC Qualification Process
A family seeking AFDC benefits must complete a four-step process. Some steps vary from state to state. (Source: Tom Joe and Cheryl Rogers, By the Few, for the Few: The Reagan Welfare Legacy *[Lexington, Mass.: Lexington Books, 1985], p. 25. © 1985, Lexington Books. Reprinted by permission.)*

Figure 16.4

ernment cash assistance to low-income children and their families. In 1985, the AFDC program cost $15.2 billion: $8.2 billion paid by the national government and $7 billion paid by the states.[28]

AFDC benefits are distributed in cash through the states. The typical AFDC family lives in a large urban area and consists of a mother under thirty and two children under eight. More than half of AFDC recipients are white; 40 percent are black. Eligibility for AFDC automatically qualifies recipients for Medicaid and other forms of public assistance. But recipients must first go through a complicated qualifying process, because government is very wary of giving money to people who might in any way be regarded as undeserving. The process has four parts (see Figure 16.4):

1. *Family composition test.* In general, an applicant for AFDC benefits must be a single parent living with at least one child under age eighteen. In half the states, recipients can be married, but the principal wage earner must be unemployed.

2. *Assets test* (varies from state to state). Assets are savings, clothing, and furniture. The national government sets a limit on the value of the assets an AFDC family can possess (in 1985, it was $1,000). However, states can impose stricter limits.

3. *Determination of need* (varies from state to state). A family is considered to be in need if its income is below a "need standard" set by each state. In 1987, the typical need standard was $428 per a month. Only families with incomes below the need standard qualify for benefits.

4. *Benefit calculation.* Each state establishes a payment standard for determining benefits. (In half the states, the payment standard is below the need standard.) For qualifying families, the difference between the payment standard and the family income is the AFDC benefit. In 1987, the typical AFDC grant for a one-parent family of three was $354 a month (plus automatic Medicaid eligibility).

Inflation raises the poverty level, but eligibility for AFDC has remained stationary. In 1987, in order to qualify for AFDC (and Medicaid), a family's income could be, on average, no more than about half of the poverty level. So although many families are "poor" according to the poverty level, they are not poor enough to qualify for cash assistance or medical care.[29]

The original purpose of AFDC was to provide assistance to fatherless families, enabling mothers to rear their children full time. But a growing chorus of critics argued that AFDC policies encouraged dependence on welfare. A recipient who took a job did not have to earn very much before losing all benefits. In some states, for example, full-time employment at $3.70 an hour meant an end to public assistance. Recently, however, researchers discovered that mandatory employment and training programs (also known as workfare) were moderately successful in ending welfare's grip on the poor. Model programs in Massachusetts, Maryland, and California increased the average earnings of female participants, assured social contributions from recipients in return for public assistance, and may have discouraged dependence on welfare.[30] This evidence moved Congress to overhaul the nation's welfare system in 1988.

The central provision of the new law requires most welfare recipients whose children are over the age of three to participate in state-approved work, education, or training programs. To smooth the transition between welfare and work, the states must provide child care and health insurance during the training period and continue this assistance for as much as one year after the recipient has found a job. The reforms will cost more than $3.3 billion for the first five years; the effects of the new law will take years to materialize.

Necessary Nutrition: Food Stamps

The federal **food stamp program** aims to improve the diets of members of low-income households by supplementing their food purchasing power. The federally funded program is administered through local agencies, which distribute the stamps to needy individuals and families. The stamps are actually coupons that can be used to purchase any food meant for human consumption.

Food stamps originated in Roosevelt's New Deal years as a dual-purpose program aimed at confronting the "unsettling contradiction between unprecedented destitution and deprivation on the one hand and excessive agricultural production on the other."[31] The program accomplished its twin goals of feeding the hungry and helping the farmers, and then became dormant when the economy rebounded in World War II. But the problem of hunger remained. Later administrations either denied that there was a substantial problem of hunger in America or instituted generally ineffective programs in which surplus commodities (lard, rice, flour, butter, and cheese) were distributed to the poor in amounts too small to ensure adequate nutrition.

The revival of the food stamp program was the top legislative priority of Democratic Representative Leonor Sullivan of Missouri during the 1950s. Sullivan's dogged determination kept the idea alive through the Eisenhower and Kennedy administrations, until Congress provided a substantially expanded program in the Food Stamp Act (1964). At first, administrators were fearful that the distribution of free stamps would encourage a black market for the stamps. That is, if the stamps provided

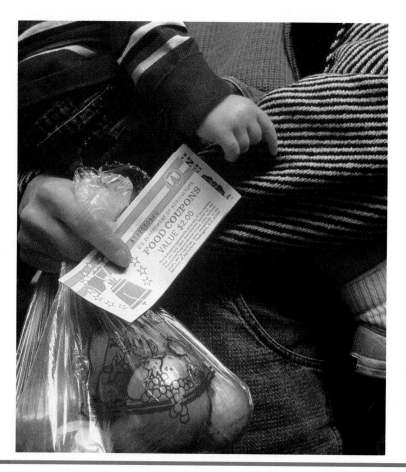

Food Stamps
Food stamps are misnamed. They are not lick-'em stamps; they're coupons that can be used to purchase food meant for human consumption (this rules out kitty litter and deodorants, for example). Eligibility requirements were tightened under the Reagan administration. In 1986, one out of every twelve Americans received food stamps, at an average of $45 worth of coupons per month.

more food than recipients needed, they would be tempted to sell their excess stamps. The solution was to require recipients to purchase stamps with a portion of their incomes. In return, they would receive stamps whose value was equal to the purchase price *plus* an additional amount. As family income rose, the additional amount fell. Unfortunately, this purchase plan did not work well, because people who needed food stamps often didn't have the cash to buy them. Moreover, even the most generous food stamp allotment was not enough to ensure adequate nutrition.

Meanwhile, critics continued to point to the inadequacies of government nutrition policy. The Citizens' Crusade Against Poverty, a liberal advocacy group formed in 1965, collected evidence on the extent of hunger and malnutrition in the United States. Several other public interest groups joined the so-called "hunger lobby," and the poor also lobbied on their own behalf: More than three thousand people participated in the "Poor People's March on Washington" in 1968. They camped on the Mall east of the Lincoln Memorial and presented their demands to the secretary of agriculture. A CBS television documentary called "Hunger in America" focused on the problem of government ineffectiveness in combatting hunger.

Some concessions were granted by the government, but they proved inadequate, and new advocates for the poor joined the lobbying effort. Finally, the Nixon administration introduced significant changes in the food stamp program. Food stamp allotments were increased to ensure a nutritionally adequate diet, and the purchase price of the stamps was reduced. Later, in 1977, the need to purchase food stamps was eliminated entirely. By the end of the decade, the problem of hunger appeared on the verge of being solved. But some researchers now report that hunger is again on the rise.

The AFDC and food stamp programs are structured to work jointly. AFDC benefits vary from state to state, but food stamp benefits are set nationally. In states that offer lower AFDC benefits, participants receive larger food stamp allotments. In 1986, the food stamp program cost the government $11.7 billion. The 19 million participants (one in twelve Americans) received an average of $45 a month in food stamps.[32]

The Reagan administration tried to curtail the food stamp program and had a measure of success. More than a million people lost their food stamp benefits entirely as a result of spending cuts in 1984, and benefits were reduced for many others.[33] The administration maintained that this was not as heartless as it appeared: Most of those who lost their benefits had incomes in excess of 130 percent of the poverty level. At the same time, the Reagan administration increased its distribution of surplus food to the poor. But there is no established and workable distribution system, and the food that is given away (often 5-pound blocks of American cheese) qualifies only as a nutritional supplement, not as the basis of a nourishing diet.

Ronald Reagan once observed, "In the war on poverty, poverty won." Americans tend to agree. About half of all Americans believe the liberal welfare policies of the 1960s made things "somewhat better" for the poor; only 10 percent maintain that those policies made the poor much better off. But 90 percent of Americans seem convinced that poverty will remain a persistent problem, partly because, 70 percent believe, government doesn't know enough about how to eliminate poverty.[34]

Government provides many Americans with benefits. According to the Bureau of the Census, 39.1 million of the nation's 83.6 million households received federal benefits in 1984. Nearly 40 percent of all households received some form of social security or other benefits for which they did not have to demonstrate need. Nearly 20 percent of those households also participated in need-based programs, including food stamps, subsidized housing, school lunch programs, and Medicaid. Is the United States generous in the benefits it confers? Do the costs seem to be in line with the benefits? Some evidence that might help you form an opinion is presented in Compared With What? 16.1.

PROVIDING FARM SUPPORTS

According to a *New York Times*/CBS News poll conducted in February 1985, the vast majority of Americans think farming is a good way of life, embodying the virtues of stability, hard work, and occasional sacrifice.[35]

COMPARED WITH WHAT? 16.1

Social Insurance Costs and Benefits

This table compares old-age and health policy costs and benefits in five countries. Notice that Great Britain and West Germany exact the highest tax for old-age benefits while the Soviet Union imposes no tax. Retirement pensions replace about half of a retiree's last year of earnings in all these countries; but citizens in Japan and the Soviet Union start collecting old-age benefits years earlier than do citizens in the other countries.

Health insurance premiums are nonexistent in the Soviet Union; benefits are completely covered by the government. Premiums are relatively low in the United States and highest on average in West Germany. With only one exception, all the countries in this comparison offer total health care for everyone. In the United States, this care is limited to the aged and the poor. In a sense, Americans get what they pay for.

Individual Social Welfare Costs and Benefits
(all currencies converted to dollars)

COSTS (1985)	West Germany	Great Britain	United States	Japan	Soviet Union
Old Age					
Maximum employee rate	9.35%	9%	5.2%	6.2% (M) 5.35% (F)	0%
Maximum employer rate	9.35%	10.45%	5.2%	6.2% (M) 5.35% (F)	4.4–9.0%
Income ceiling for calculating payments	$21,060	$16,540	$39,600	$20,170	none
Health Insurance					
Maximum employee rate	3.5–7.5%	*	1.35%	4.2%	0%
Maximum employer payments	3.5–9.8%	*	1.35%	4.2%	*
Income ceiling for calculating payments	$15,800	*	$39,600	$35,000	none
BENEFITS (1985) **Old Age**					
Age at retirement (M/F)	65/65	65/60	65/65	60/55	60/55
Replacement wage rate (percentage of last year of wages)	49%	47%	51%	**	50%
Health Insurance					
Duration	unlimited	unlimited	limited	unlimited	unlimited
Hospitalization	complete	complete	some limits	some limits	complete
Medical care	free	free	limited	free	free
Coverage	all	all	aged & poor	all	all

* Comprehensive payments covered under "Old Age."

** Not available

Sources: *Statistical Abstract of the United States, 1987*, Table 642. *Social Security Programs Throughout the World—1985*, Research Report No. 60, (U.S. Department of Health and Human Services, 1986). *Social Security Bulletin, Annual Statistical Supplement*, 1987, pp. 29, 33.

Two hundred years ago, America was a nation of farmers, but today farmers make up only 2 percent of the population. Despite their declining numbers, American farmers have managed to bring in bumper harvests. Farming remains a large industry (much larger than the automobile, banking, and publishing industries); and in 1985, agriculture accounted for nearly 10 percent of all domestic exports.[36] Nonetheless, this bucolic picture of performance and plenty in reality is riddled with problems.

The Origins of the Farm Problem

The national government's agricultural policies were confined to research and education until the Depression, when farm prices and income plunged. The collapse of the nation's economy brought the farming industry near to ruin. To preserve American farming and the nation's farmers, the free market in farm products—in which supply and demand determine price—had to be constrained. The result was government policies aimed at raising and stabilizing prices and at controlling production.

As part of Roosevelt's New Deal, Congress passed the Agricultural Adjustment Act (1933). The act, in an effort to boost farm prices and farmers' purchasing power, placed a tax on the processors of seven basic commodities (wheat, cotton, field corn, hogs, rice, tobacco, and dairy products). The tax proceeds were used to pay benefits to farmers who agreed to reduce their production of those commodities. The decline in production forced prices up, increasing farm income and encouraging the production of other crops. With lower but stable production of specific crops, it was hoped that supply and demand would maintain prices at a level that would avert catastrophe.

In 1936, the Supreme Court declared the act an unconstitutional exercise of congressional taxing power.[37] But majority sentiment would not be thwarted; the Court soon reversed its stand on New Deal policies in general and farm policy in particular. By 1938, Congress had enacted another agricultural act, which the Supreme Court upheld as a valid exercise of the legislative power to regulate interstate commerce.[38]

Government intervention in the market for farm products since that time has moderated the effects of business cycles on farmers. But that intervention has also encouraged overproduction, which in turn has increased the cost of government farm policy. Agriculture programs cost the government more than $31 billion in 1986. Even allowing for inflation, this is more than four times the cost just a decade earlier.[39] Yet farmers have come to depend on government help to absorb their bumper crops. In the absence of government assistance, many farmers would face certain ruin.

The "Traditional" Solution

Today's agricultural policy is based on the 1938 act. It involves three concepts—price supports, direct income subsidies, and production controls—which have been translated into programs aimed at providing income to American farmers.

Price supports are the means that government uses to maintain at least a minimum price for certain commodities. The national government uses loans that are not really loans as the chief mechanism for agricultural price supports. To see how they work, suppose you are a wheat farmer. The government offers to lend you a certain amount of money, say $3, for each bushel of wheat that you are willing to place in a government-approved granary. The crop will serve as collateral for the loan. You could, of course, sell the wheat on the open market, but there may be good reasons for putting the grain in storage—at least for a while. For example, if the market price for wheat is less than the loan rate, you would be wise to take the loan. If the market price is somewhat higher than the loan rate and all farmers were to put their wheat on the market at the same time, the glut would force the price down. You would do better to wait for the price to rise again.

Suppose you agree to place 10,000 bushels of wheat in storage; at $3 a bushel, you receive a loan of $30,000. Now, if the market price of the wheat rises above the $3 loan rate, you can remove your grain from storage, sell it, repay the loan, and pocket the difference. If the market price remains below the loan rate, you simply keep the loan and the government keeps the wheat. In effect, the loan rate becomes the price floor for wheat. If *support prices* are adjusted regularly for inflation and other economic factors, they tend to act as insurance against market fluctuations. But when support prices are higher than the market price, they tend to stimulate the overproduction that government is trying to moderate (see Figure 16.5). Surpluses are common because Congress frequently sets the loan rate above the market price.

Figure 16.5

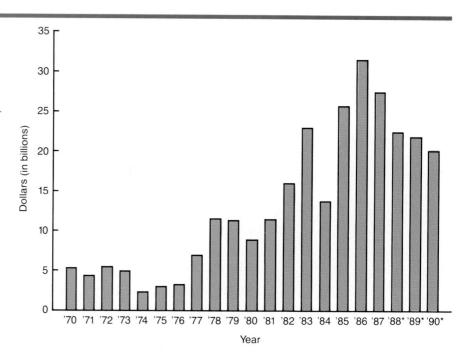

The Cost of Farm Price Supports
Government spending for the farm price-support program rose dramatically in the 1980s. Although price supports are expected to decline under the 1985 Farm Security Act, other farm program expenditures are expected to increase. These figures include spending for wheat, corn, other feed grains, rice, soybeans, peanuts, sugar, cotton, dairy products, honey, wool, and mohair. (Source: Historical Tables, Budget of the United States Government, FY 1989, Table 3.3.)

*Estimated

Bitter Harvest
*Farming as a way of life
has been declining for most
of this century. Increasing
farm mechanization pro-
duced bumper crops with
minimal labor, forcing farm
workers off the land. By
1987, only 2 percent of the
population lived on farms.
Small farmers were espe-
cially vulnerable to mis-
guided government pro-
grams that encouraged
overproduction and overex-
pansion. Nature added further hardship in 1988—the
worst drought in decades.
Despite new government
programs and crop subsi-
dies, the only course for
some farmers is to auction
the family farm.*

Direct income subsidies (also called *deficiency payments*) are cash payments to farmers. Unlike price supports, they do not prop up the prices of farm products. Instead, they reimburse the farmer for the cost of producing a crop when that cost is greater than the market price or loan rate for the crop. This form of assistance guarantees farmers an adequate income when market prices fall below the cost of production. Because Congress determines the size of these income subsidies, farmers have a strong inclination to lobby for higher subsidies. Recent bumper crops in grain-importing countries reduced the world demand for American grains. Farmers held huge surpluses and could sell them only at depressed prices. Direct income subsidies protected the farmers from the effects of nature's bounty.

Let's continue with our wheat-farming example. The loan rate for a bushel of wheat is $3. Now suppose that Congress sets the national average cost for producing a bushel of wheat at $4; it sets that as its *target price*. You have taken a "loan" of $30,000 from the government in exchange for 10,000 bushels of wheat. You would also receive a direct income subsidy payment from the government for the difference between the target price of $4 per bushel and the loan rate of $3 per bushel. This would add another $10,000 to your bank account, to cover your costs of production and to help feed, clothe, and care for your family. Although farmers regularly complain about low market prices, the target price determines planting decisions because target prices determine income. Of course, you would not receive the subsidy if the market price rose above the target price; but then you would not have taken the government loan either. In effect, direct income subsidies protect farmers against losses that result from increased production costs; they are a form of public assistance to farmers, paid from general tax revenues. Reflecting on his $75,000 subsidy payment, one Oklahoma wheat farmer declared: "No two ways about it. The check's like welfare. Nobody likes to take welfare, but you got to do it to survive."[40]

The same tax revenue that pays for Medicaid, food stamps, and AFDC benefits pays for price supports and direct income subsidies. A third farm program—production controls—shifts some costs from the taxpayer to the consumer.

Production controls are agreements that call for farmers to plant less of a particular crop. Smaller plantings mean smaller harvests. Demand for the crop forces the price to rise, and the higher price is paid directly by the consumer who purchases the product. Production controls are voluntary agreements, but only farmers who are willing to limit production are eligible for price supports and direct income subsidies. Freedom in this case becomes a gamble, and most farmers opt for government farm programs that provide income havens, where they are safe from the risks of the marketplace.

Some Consequences of Farm Policy

According to "Murphy's Law," if something can go wrong, it will. American agriculture in the 1980s was an apt demonstration of that truth: Everything that could go wrong, did. A world recession reduced international demand for U.S. crops. At the same time, the value of the dollar soared, making American agricultural exports more expensive and less competitive. And foreign growers produced crop surpluses, which they marketed aggressively. As a result, America's share of the world agricultural market fell sharply.

Overproduction.   Congress reviews and modifies farm policy every four years. In retrospect, we can see that the price supports set by the 1981 farm policy were too high; they were much higher than the market prices for the basic farm commodities. Farmers sold much of their output to the government at the higher support prices. Huge surpluses of farm commodities bulged from government storehouses. As an example, by 1983, the government was buying 10 percent of the milk produced in the United States at a cost of $3 billion; it was storing the equivalent of about 16 billion pounds of milk in the form of butter, cheese, and powdered milk. Even after donations to needy countries and to domestic food assistance programs, the government still held a veritable mountain of butter in reserve. Policies aimed at stemming these surpluses created new problems in the process (see Feature 16.1).

The support price establishes a price floor for farmers; it also establishes a price ceiling for foreign competitors. The biggest market for American grains is outside the United States. But if the support price is high, American farmers would rather sell their grain to the government; at the same time, foreign competitors can more easily sell their grain at a price just below the support price, which makes their product more attractive to grain-importing nations. This is exactly what happened in the 1980s: The high support price encouraged the loss of foreign markets by American farmers.

The Dairyman's Pail Runneth Over

Dairy farmers receive a basket of federal benefits, the first being a milk price support of $11.10 per hundred-weight—about $1 above what the market price would be. [In 1986,] farmers sold 12.3 billion pounds of milk, butter and cheese to the government. Taxpayer costs have been running about $2 billion a year in the past few years.

To slow this spending, Congress is gradually lowering the [price support] rate so that consumers rather than the government will buy farmers' milk. But law-makers did not want to lower the [price support] rate sharply. So they instituted the whole-herd buyout program instead. Congress paid dairymen $1.1 billion from spring 1986 till summer 1987 to slaughter their herds if they promised not to go back in business for five years. Payments to individuals range up to $10 million each; 144 farmers are getting more the $1 million each.

As soon as the government said dairy farmers were going to slaughter 1 million cows, cattle prices dropped 10 percent. Cattlemen lost about $2 billion in inventory value so the government promised to buy 4 million pounds of beef to ease their loss.

There was some "slippage" in the program. Some dairymen slaughtered their oldest, least productive cows and transferred ownership of the young cows to relatives or associates. Those cows kept producing milk. So the government [in 1987] will buy 5.4 billion pounds of milk for $1.2 billion. . . .

"Over the last 50 years, we just kept adding on to these things," says John R. Block, secretary of agriculture from January 1981 to February 1986. "No one in their right mind would create a dairy program the way this one is written."

High target prices also encouraged overproduction, because a bigger crop meant a fatter direct income subsidy check. Farmers overproduced, and their bumper crops increased the cost of the government farm program. Then, when the government stockpiles reached capacity and had to be sold, market prices fell. The government's loss from buying at high prices (from farmers) and selling low sent the actual cost of the farm policy to unexpected heights. Government economists had projected in 1981 that farm policy costs for 1983 to 1986 would be $11 billion. The actual costs exceeded $90 billion.

Government farm policy has encouraged overproduction to the point where farm production now far exceeds the market's ability to absorb it. It has been predicted that by 1989, American farmers will depend on the government for 70 percent of their net income, compared to about 25 percent in 1984.[41] As you will see, this outpouring of federal funds forced a careful re-examination of farm policy.

Farm debt. At the same time the government was cushioning farmers from the effects of the market, it encouraged them to borrow in order to expand their operations. From 1969 to 1981, farm land use expanded by 54 million acres. Farm techniques improved as well. And the national government subsidized farm borrowing, at rates below inflation through the 1970s. There seemed to be good reason for expansion: A devaluation of the dollar made American farm products attractive and broadened foreign markets. Grain sales abroad were increasing. And economists predicted high prices and growing markets through the 1980s and beyond. Of course, farm expansion meant more debt, but larger farms held the promise of larger incomes. For many, the gamble appeared to be worth the risk.

But many of the farmers who expanded in the 1970s faced a severe credit crunch in the 1980s. Inflation dropped sharply. The government's encouragement of cultivation brought bumper harvests. From 1972 to 1982, the nation's corn crop burgeoned from 5.6 billion bushels to 8.4 billion bushels. American farmers, dependent on foreign markets for sales of one-half to two-thirds of their products, ended up with monster surpluses and mountainous debts.

Despite their bountiful harvests, many farmers could not generate enough income to cover their loans or mortgages. The value of farm land, which depends on the income it produces, slid downward. Because they were deeply in debt, farmers had trouble getting operating loans for seed and fertilizer; their devalued land could barely serve as collateral. By the mid-1980s, the interest owed to banks by farmers had grown to $21 billion a year, whereas total farm income reached only $23 billion. Foreclosure and ruin seemed a certainty for many, especially younger farmers who bought land when prices were high and could no longer borrow enough money to sustain their operations. Some farmers, like the Baxa family, swallowed their pride and turned to public assistance, including food stamps, in an effort to hold on to their way of life.

A New Direction

Given the many failures of the 1981 farm policy, it was clear that Congress would carefully rethink the status quo in 1985. The prospect of a new farm policy attracted lobbies of every stripe, including groups representing chicken producers, hog farmers, pesticide manufacturers, supermarkets, and banks. Each of these groups had a farm policy to present. Even the Fertilizer Institute, which represents 292 fertilizer manufacturing and distributing companies and had never had a farm policy in its entire 102-year history, had one in 1985.

The Reagan administration's farm plan called for the immediate elimination of price supports and income subsidies. The administration believed the only way to break the spiral of government spending and overproduction, which causes more spending, was to withdraw government support for agriculture and return to a free market. At the opposite end, some farmers—a vocal minority—called for a farmer referendum to establish mandatory production controls. Prices would rise if production limits could be imposed equally on all farmers. But the only consensus that emerged from the congressional hearings, debates, and lobbying was that the 1981 policy was not working. Juggling the old programs in a new way proved to be the only politically viable approach.

The 1985 Farm Security Act, approved by Congress in December 1985, headed in a new direction. The farm bill was eleven months in gestation; it weighed in at a hefty 13 pounds. Congress took a step—but only a step—toward the free market advocated by President Reagan. First, price supports were lowered below market levels. This would ensure that farmers sold to markets, not to government. Second, income subsidies were maintained at their previous levels. Because these payments are geared to production, more farmers would receive bigger government checks than ever. And third, farmers were required to set aside 20 to 30 percent of their land to qualify for the subsidies. (This is not likely to reduce production, because farmers usually set aside their least productive land.)

In theory, the new farm policy aims to remove all government support of farming at some point in the future. In practice, government has lowered the floor but added some pillows. Lower price supports mean that government does not have to bear the burden of the market and that American farm products are more competitive in world markets. For farmers, reduced price supports are counterbalanced by heavier direct income subsidies—at least for the time being. Crops are yielding near-record abundance, and government subsidies, which are tied to production, are flowing freely. In Iowa alone, farmers received more aid from Washington in 1987 than all the nations of Africa received from the World Bank.

The new farm policy seems to have increased sales abroad. After a five-year tumble, farm exports are on the rise, especially for wheat and several other crops. The decline of the dollar against other currencies has made American farm products especially attractive. This is not the case for corn, however. Although corn exports rose almost 25 percent from 1986 to 1987, export value remained almost the same (about $3.7 billion) despite staggering subsidies. "It's insane to spend $12 billion to subsidize less than $4 billion in exports," remarked a state agricultural commissioner. "It would be cheaper to dump corn in the ocean."[42]

One problem of the new farm policy is that it has generated distortions by favoring some commodities over others. The government provided farmers with generous subsidies for crops such as corn, wheat, and barley. Farmers who did not participate in crops favored by the new policy were exposed to greater financial risk. Not surprisingly, most farmers took shelter in the government program. For example, farmers abandoned oats and raised barley because they could earn nearly a dollar more for each bushel of barley. But the demand for oats rose while the demand for barley remained constant. It seems that groups representing less-favored commodities must fight for higher subsidies in Congress. In short, the pluralist model creates distortions and at the same time serves as the means for correcting them.[43]

Current farm policy remains rooted in a rural past; it has not caught up with farm-population patterns and farm economics. Despite the vast infusion of government funds, the nation's farm population has continued to dwindle, from 15 percent of the population in 1950 to 2 percent in 1987. Farmers have left the land, yet the land has remained in production, generating ever-increasing yields.[44]

The family farm will not be saved by today's farm policy, which indeed may even hasten its demise. The reason is that not all farms are equal. Three of every four farms are owned by part-time farmers who earn most of their income from nonfarm activities; they produce 10 percent of all farm output and receive 18 percent of all government subsidies. The remainder—one in four—are business farms, which produce 90 percent of all farm output and receive 82 percent of all government subsidies. These huge payments to aggressive business farmers may provide them with the capital to buy out their smaller, less successful neighbors. Although the debate surrounding farm policy may be cloaked in the imagery of the family farm, it is business farmers who reap the enormous harvest of government subsidies.[45]

Government farm policy has inched toward a free market. As a consequence of this shift, some farmers will be forced from a lifestyle that is envied by many Americans. Some farmers, like Larry Baxa, will accept the shame of public assistance in an effort to weather economic hardship. Some will survive; others will fail. An alternative policy is a return to government substitutes for the market, imposing order and security through government's control of prices. By all accounts, however, that policy was at the core of America's farm crisis.[46] Another alternative is to mandate equitable production limits for all farmers, in an effort to boost prices. That alternative trades freedom for order and equality. To deal responsibly with these choices is the challenge of democracy.

SUMMARY

Public policies fulfill one or more purposes: protection (e.g., against a dread disease such as AIDS), prohibition (e.g., of the sale and possession of illicit drugs), provision (e.g., of social insurance, public assistance, and farm supports), and promotion (e.g., of disadvantaged groups through affirmative action programs). Often, disagreements over public policy are disagreements over values. Choices between freedom and order are at the heart of many policies, for example, mandatory AIDS or drug testing. Choices between freedom and equality are at the heart of other policies, such as those designed to ease the poverty that Lafeyette Walton confronts in Chicago.

Many domestic policies that provide benefits to individuals and promote economic equality were instituted during the Great Depression. Today, government plays an active role in providing benefits to the poor, the elderly, and the disabled. The object of these domestic policies is to alleviate conditions that individuals are powerless to prevent. This is the social welfare function of the modern state.

Government confers benefits to individuals through social insurance and public assistance. Social insurance does not require a demonstration of need; public assistance (welfare) hinges on proof of need. In one form of social insurance—old-age benefits—a tax on workers pays the elderly's benefits. Aid for the poor comes from government's general tax revenues.

Programs to aid the elderly and the poor have been transformed into entitlements, which are rights that accrue to eligible persons. Some entitlements hinge on need, which is often defined in terms of income: People with incomes below a given level satisfy the need condition. These government programs have reduced poverty among some groups, especially among the elderly. However, poverty retains a grip on the population, and it is creeping up to levels that Americans have not seen since the 1960s.

Farm policy today traces its roots to the New Deal and still involves three basic programs: price supports, direct income subsidies, and production controls. These programs provide benefits that cushion farmers from the hazards of economic cycles, overproduction, high production costs, and (to an extent) foreign competition. A recent application of these programs encouraged overproduction and expansion at the same time that foreign markets were being claimed by foreign competitors and a strong dollar made American products less competitive. As a result, government footed the bill for the nation's plenty. The most recent farm policy is an attempt to free up the market for agricultural products. That policy has been abetted by the falling dollar, spurring exports for many agricultural commodities.

The pluralist model serves as an explanation for the success and the protected status of social security and some other policies. The model also explains why some policies, among them, the 1985 farm law, create problems while solving others.

Key Terms

welfare state
social welfare
Great Depression
New Deal
Great Society
War on Poverty
social insurance
social security
Social Security Act
Medicare

public assistance
poverty level
Aid to Families with
    Dependent Children
    (AFDC)
food stamp program
price support
direct income subsidy
production control

Selected Readings

Berry, Jeffrey M. *Feeding Hungry People: Rulemaking in the Food Stamp Program.* New Brunswick, N.J.: Rutgers University Press, 1984. A thorough examination of the evolution of the food stamp program, especially the relationships among Congress, the Department of Agriculture, and interest groups.

Ferrara, Peter J. *Social Security: The Inherent Contradiction.* San Francisco: Cato Institute, 1980. Argues that the pay-as-you-go feature of social security inevitably clashes with the desirability of a savings policy.

Galston, William A. *A Tough Row to Hoe: The 1985 Farm Bill & Beyond.* Lanham, N.Y.: University Press of America, 1985. Provides an excellent overview of the problems and prospects of agricultural policy today.

Joe, Tom, and Cheryl Rogers. *By the Few, for the Few.* Lexington, Mass.: Lexington Books, 1985. An engaging study of the changes in AFDC wrought by the Reagan administration, and the negative effects of those changes on incentives for welfare recipients to work.

Murray, Charles. *Losing Ground.* New York: Basic Books, 1985. A controversial assessment of American social policy from 1950 to 1980. Argues that by attempting to remove the barriers to the good life for the poor, policymakers have created a poverty trap.

Schwartz, John E. *America's Hidden Success.* New York: Norton, 1983. A measured defense of the success of social policy from 1960 to 1980; argues the achievements of the Great Society. Should be read in conjunction with Murray.

Starr, Paul. *The Social Transformation of American Medicine.* New York: Basic Books, 1982. The definitive work on the evolution of the American health care system of doctors, hospitals, health plans, and government programs.

Wilson, William Julius. *The Truly Disadvantaged: The Inner City, the Underclass, and Public Policy.* Chicago: University of Chicago Press, 1987. Argues that the decay of the inner city cannot be explained by racism alone. Targets the class structure of ghetto neighborhoods as the most important factor in a complex web of reasons.

17

Order and Civil Liberties

J oyce Brown liked her home. It was a 1-foot by 3-foot warm-air vent near an East Side New York restaurant. "I like the streets and I am entitled to live the way I want to live," she said. Brown was one of millions of homeless Americans. New York City officials saw things differently. Brown was dirty and disheveled, and she smelled. She defecated in her clothing or on the street. She burned money given her by passers-by. She was so severely mentally ill, according to city officials, that she was not even aware of her illness. The Big Apple's image was being tarnished by the plight of the homeless whose numbers there had swelled to over 30,000 by 1988. New York City was going to put its house—and Joyce Brown—in order.[1]

New York's mayor, Edward I. Koch, marshalled city resources to confine Brown in a city hospital. The government of New York City expressed deep concern for the welfare of the mentally ill; it was also concerned about the sordid impression created by thousands of homeless people living on the city's streets. The city wanted to take away a measure of Joyce Brown's liberty to ensure her well-being and restore a measure of orderliness to the community.

Brown turned to the New York Civil Liberties Union for help. A civil liberties attorney, in a New York court, defended her freedom to live on the streets. Unless the city could prove that Brown was likely to harm herself or others, she should be free to live as she chooses, argued her lawyer. When and under what conditions can government restrict individual liberty for the sake of social order?

Throughout this nation's history, the values of order and individual freedom have been in conflict. Here, the New York City government had

Boxed In and Boxed Out
Most observers agree that homelessness is increasing, but there is little reliable information about the scope of the problem. Some advocates for the homeless attribute the increase to the national economy and the lack of affordable housing; others cite the deinstitutionalization of the mentally ill. With nowhere to go, the homeless are always in sight.

Homeless at Harvard
Joyce Brown lived for nearly a year on a New York City street, where she exhibited bizarre behavior and refused offers of help. After her release from forced hospitalization, she was invited to address the Harvard Law School Forum; her talk was entitled "The Homeless Crisis: A Street View." Two weeks later, she was back on the street, panhandling and swearing at passers-by.

an interest in preserving social order (the established patterns of authority in society) through the control of public places—in this case, the streets and sidewalks of the city. In particular, the government had an interest in directing the use of public places in a manner consistent with the attitudes and concerns of many (perhaps a majority) of its citizens. Joyce Brown had an interest in her personal freedom and maintained that government could not restrict her unless she was likely to harm herself or others. Obviously, the exercise of one interest would infringe on the exercise of the other. And, just as obviously, both sides had merit, because each defended a value we recognize as vital to democratic rule. In the American political system, these kinds of conflicts often are resolved by the courts.

How well do the courts respond to clashes that pit freedom against order in some cases and freedom against equality in others? Is any one of the values we have discussed—freedom, order, or equality—ever unconditional? In this chapter, we explore some value conflicts that have been resolved by the judiciary. You should be able to judge from the decisions in these cases whether American government has met the challenge of democracy by finding the appropriate balance between freedom and order and between freedom and equality.

The value conflicts we describe in this chapter revolve around claims or entitlements that rest on law. Although we concentrate here on conflicts over constitutional issues, you should realize that the Constitution is not the only source of people's rights. Government can—and does—create rights through laws written by legislatures and regulations issued by bureaucracies. In Joyce Brown's case, she claimed that her freedom was based on the Constitution itself: "This is the United States of America, the Constitution, freedom of choice. If that's . . . the way the person wants to live their life, and they're an adult, who am I to say that they can't do that?"[2] New York's claim that it could use its police power to force Brown into a hospital for her own good rested on the very purpose of government—maintaining order.

The lawsuit ended abruptly in February 1988, when the city released Brown from her involuntary hospital confinement. The city was not able to prove that Brown was mentally ill or that she was likely to harm herself or others. Her eccentricity was not enough to warrant government denial of her freedom. However, New York City has continued its controversial homeless policy, and civil libertarians hope that another Joyce Brown will emerge to champion the cause of freedom in the courts.

We begin this chapter with the Bill of Rights and the freedoms it protects. Then we take a closer look at the role of the First Amendment in the original struggle—the conflict between freedom and order. Next we turn to the Fourteenth Amendment and the limits it places on the states. Then we examine the Ninth Amendment and its relationship to issues of personal autonomy. Finally, we examine the threat to the democratic process of the constitutionalization of policy. In Chapter 18, we look at the Fourteenth Amendment's promise of equal protection, which sets the stage for the modern dilemma of government: the struggle between freedom and equality.

THE BILL OF RIGHTS

You may remember from Chapter 3 that at first the framers of the Constitution did not include a list of individual liberties—a bill of rights—in the national charter. They believed that a bill of rights was not necessary, that the extent of the national government's power was spelled out in the Constitution. But during the ratification debates, it became clear that the omission of a bill of rights was the most important obstacle to the adoption of the Constitution by the states. Eventually, twelve amendments were approved by Congress and sent to the states. In 1791 ten were ratified, and the nation had a bill of rights.

The Bill of Rights imposed limits on the national government but not on the state governments.* Over the next seventy-seven years, the Supreme Court was repeatedly pressed to extend the amendments' restraints to the states, but similar restrictions were not placed on the states until the adoption of the Fourteenth Amendment in 1868. Before then, protection from repressive state government had to come from state bills of rights.

The U.S. Constitution guarantees Americans a large constellation of liberties and rights. In this chapter we explore a number of them. We

---

* Congress had considered over a hundred amendments in its first session. One that was not approved would have limited the power of the states to infringe on the rights of conscience, speech, press, and jury trial in criminal cases. James Madison thought this amendment was the "most valuable" of the list, but it failed to muster a two-thirds vote in the Senate.

use two terms, *civil liberties* and *civil rights*, interchangeably in this context, although their meanings are different. **Civil liberties** are freedoms that are guaranteed to the individual. These guarantees take the form of negative restraints on government. For example, the First Amendment declares that "Congress shall make no law . . . abridging the freedom of speech." Civil liberties declare what the government cannot do; in contrast, civil rights declare what the government must do or provide.

Civil rights are powers or privileges that are guaranteed to the individual and protected from arbitrary removal at the hands of the government or other individuals. The right to vote and the right to jury trial in criminal cases are civil rights. Today, civil rights have also come to include the objectives of laws that further certain values. The Civil Rights Act of 1964, for example, furthered the value of equality by establishing the right to nondiscrimination in places of public accommodations and the right to equal employment opportunity. Civil liberties are the subject of this chapter; we discuss civil rights and their ramifications in Chapter 18.

Actually, the Bill of Rights lists both civil liberties and civil rights. When we refer to the rights and liberties of the Constitution, we mean the protections enshrined in the Bill of Rights and in the first section of the Fourteenth Amendment.[3] The list includes: freedom of religion; freedom of speech and the press; the right to peaceable assembly and petition; the rights of the criminally accused; the requirement of due process; and the equal protection of the laws.

FREEDOM OF RELIGION

> Congress shall make no law respecting an establishment of religion, or prohibiting the free exercise thereof.

Religious freedom was very important to the colonies, and later to the states. That importance is reflected in its position in the Bill of Rights: first, in the very first amendment. The amendment guarantees freedom of religion in two clauses. The first, the **establishment clause,** prohibits laws establishing religion; the second, the **free-exercise clause,** prevents the government from interfering with the exercise of religion. Together they ensure that government can neither promote nor inhibit religious beliefs or practices.

The mingling of government and religion has a long history in America. Most of the American colonies had close ties to established religion on the eve of independence.[4] By 1789, several state constitutions linked religion and government. Delaware, for example, required its citizens to affirm the doctrine of the Trinity; and four states (Connecticut, Massachusetts, New Hampshire, and South Carolina) insisted on a belief in Protestantism.[5] Many Americans, especially in New England, maintained that government could and should foster religion, certainly Protestantism. Many more Americans were in agreement, however, that this was an issue for state governments, that the national government had no authority to meddle in religious affairs. The religion clauses were drafted in this spirit.[6]

Carting Religious Freedom
Americans are a religious people. Court cases interpreting the establishment and free exercise clauses of the First Amendment stir deep feelings. Religious and nonreligious minorities, such as the Amish and the atheists, have frequently served as standard-bearers for these two interrelated but sometimes conflicting constitutional guarantees.

As in the case of many other constitutional provisions, the Supreme Court has refused to interpret the religion clauses definitively. The effect of that refusal is an amalgam of rulings. Freedom to believe is unlimited, but freedom to practice a belief can be limited. Religion cannot benefit directly from government actions (for example, contributions to churches or synagogues), but it can benefit indirectly from those actions (for example, buying books on secular subjects for use in all schools—public, private, and parochial).

Most Americans identify with a particular religious faith. America also ranks first among eleven major industrialized nations in the proportion of citizens who maintain that religion plays an important role in their lives.[7] Majoritarians might argue, then, that government should support religion. They would agree that the establishment clause bars government support of a single faith, but they might well maintain that government should support all faiths. This kind of support would be consistent with what the majority wants and true to the language of the Constitution. In its decisions, the Supreme Court has rejected this interpretation of the establishment clause, leaving itself open to charges of undermining democracy. Those charges may be true with regard to majoritarian democracy, but the freedom protected by the Court can be justified in terms of the basic values of democratic government.

The Establishment Clause

The provision that "Congress shall make no law respecting an establishment of religion" bars government sponsorship or support of religious activity. The Supreme Court has consistently held that the establishment clause requires government to maintain a position of neutrality toward religions and to maintain that position in cases that involve choices between religion and nonreligion. However, the clause has never been held to bar all assistance that incidentally aids religious institutions. In this section, we consider the application of the clause to public support for parochial education and for religion in general, to prayer in the public schools, and to curricula encouraging biblical instruction.

Government support of religion. In 1879 the Supreme Court contended, using Thomas Jefferson's words, that the establishment clause erected "a wall of separation between church and state."[8] That wall was breached somewhat in 1947, when the justices upheld a local government program that provided free transportation to parochial school students.[9] The breach seemed to widen in 1968, when the Court held constitutional a government program in which state-purchased textbooks were loaned to parochial school students.[10] The objective of the program, reasoned the majority, was to further educational opportunity. The loan was made to the students, not to the schools, and the benefits were realized by the parents, not by the church.

But in 1971, in **Lemon v. Kurtzman,** the Court struck down a state program that would have funded the salaries for teachers hired by parochial schools to give instruction in secular subjects.[11] The justices proposed a three-pronged test for constitutionality under the establishment clause:

- The law must have a secular purpose (like lending books to parochial school students).
- Its primary effect must not be to advance or inhibit religion.
- It must not entangle the government excessively with religion.

A law missing any prong would be unconstitutional.

The program in *Lemon* failed on the last ground: To be sure that they did not include religious instruction in their lessons, the state would have to constantly monitor the secular teachers. For example, the state would be required to monitor mathematics lessons to ensure that the instruction did not reinforce religious dogma. This kind of supervision would entangle the government in religious activity, violating the Constitution's prohibition.

Does the display of religious artifacts on public property violate the establishment clause? In *Lynch* v. *Donnelly* (1984), the Court said no, by a vote of 5 to 4.[12] At issue was a publicly funded Nativity scene on public property, surrounded by commercial symbols of the Christmas season (for example, Santa and his sleigh). While conceding that a crèche has religious significance, Chief Justice Warren E. Burger, writing for the majority, maintained that the display had a legitimate secular purpose: the celebration of a national holiday. Second, the display did not have the primary effect of benefiting religion; the religious benefits were "indirect, remote and incidental." And third, the display led to no excessive entanglement between religion and government. The justices hinted at a relaxation of the establishment clause by asserting their "unwillingness to be confined to any single test or criterion in this sensitive area." The upshot of *Lynch* was an "acknowledgment" of the religious heritage of the majority of Americans, even though the Christmas holiday is a vivid reminder to religious minorities and the nonreligious of their separateness from the dominant Christian culture.

School prayer. The Supreme Court has consistently equated prayer in public schools with government support of religion. In 1962 it struck down the daily reading of this twenty-two-word nondenominational prayer in New York's public schools:

> Almighty God, we acknowledge our dependence upon Thee, and we beg Thy blessings upon us, our parents, our teachers, and our country.

Justice Hugo L. Black, writing for a 6-to-1 majority, held that official state approval of prayer was an unconstitutional attempt on the part of the state to establish a religion. This decision, in *Engle* v. *Vitale*, drew a storm of protest.[13]

The following year, the Court struck down a state law calling for daily Bible reading and recitation of the Lord's Prayer in Pennsylvania's public schools.[14] The reading and recitation were defended on the grounds that they taught literature, perpetuated traditional institutions, and inculcated moral virtues. But the Court held that the state's involvement violated the government's constitutionally imposed neutrality in matters of religion. Given the degree of religious sentiment in the United States, the burden on individual children on whose behalf these unpopular suits are brought can be overwhelming (see Feature 17.1).

New challenges on the issue of school prayer continue to find their way to the Supreme Court—each a reminder of the pluralist nature of American democracy. These challenges vent widely held and strongly felt religious convictions. And the decisions are difficult. The government risks disorder when it continually frustrates strongly held majority views. The outcomes of these cases offer little immediate comfort to the majority of Americans who favor school prayer.

The Constitution bars school prayer. Does it also bar silent meditation in school? In *Wallace* v. *Jaffree* (1985), the Court struck down a series of Alabama statutes requiring elementary school teachers to observe a moment of silence for meditation or voluntary prayer at the beginning of each school day.[15] In a 6-to-3 decision, the Court renewed its use of the *Lemon* test and reaffirmed the principle of government neutrality between religion and nonreligion. The Court found that the purpose of the statutes was to endorse religion; however, a majority of the justices hinted that a straightforward moment-of-silence statute that steered clear of religious endorsements might pass constitutional muster.

Creation-science and evolution-science. Countless generations of Sunday School students have heard the story: "In the beginning, God created the heaven and the earth." So says the Book of Genesis, in words familiar to hundreds of millions of people around the world. The sudden creation of the universe, energy, and life from nothingness is at the foundation of Judeo-Christian belief. This seems an unlikely subject for a legal battle. But in 1987, it was at the core of a dispute that pitted Louisiana's power to control its public school curriculum against the

FEATURE 17.1

The Schempp Family Gospel

At one time or another, Edward and Sidney Schempp and their three children—Donna, Roger, and Ellory—have been called every obscene, pejorative name in the book. Their sleep has been disturbed by obscene, late-night phone calls, and animal excrement has been sent to them through the mail and deposited at their doorstep. The Schempps have lost count of the times people have threatened to beat up their children or have prayed that they would contract horrible, deadly diseases. This harassment resulted from the Schempps' involvement in one of the most controversial cases in the history of the modern Supreme Court. The Schempps were plaintiffs in *Abington [PA] School District* v. *Schempp*, the 1963 decision that declared prayer in the public schools unconstitutional.

In 1957, a state statute required the reading of "at least 10 verses from the Holy Bible, without comment, at the opening of each public school on each school day." At Abington High School, these verses were read over the school public address system. Then the students in every classroom had to stand and recite the Lord's Prayer.

Ellory Schempp now says that "the push toward conformity at Abington had a lot to do with my decision [to protest school prayer]. It was a time of intellectual ferment for me." After discussing the matter with his parents, Ellory decided that he was going to stage a personal protest. He brought the Koran, the Islamic holy book, into school, and read it during the bible reading. He also refused to stand during the recitation of the Lord's Prayer. Because of these infractions, Ellory's home room teacher sent him to the vice principal who says Ellory "expressed enormous confusion, and saw it all as a matter of not following the rules, going against the wishes of the majority." Despite the attitudes of the school administration, Abington decided to excuse Ellory from the daily prayer for the rest of the year. In his senior year, though, the school mandated his participation.

The Schempp Family

The Schempps were not the first family to challenge school Bible reading, but previous cases were thrown out when the children involved graduated from school before the issue reached the higher courts. With a three- and five-year difference between Ellory and his younger brother and sister, the family reasoned that this obstacle would be avoided.

The Schempps' Supreme Court victory had its price. The principal at Abington High School tried unsuccessfully to pressure Tufts University into denying admission to Ellory on the ground that he was a "troublemaker." He was admitted despite the negative recommendation.

Ellory's younger sister, Donna, experienced the greatest repercussions. "Lots of kids saw me and my brother as weird, unacceptable," she said years later. "It was real traumatic. My feelings are that it was a terrible thing to do to a 12-year-old girl. It was a real isolating thing."

Not one member of the Schempp family regrets taking on the case, and even Donna says that "I think it was real important, and that it was right."

constitutional provision that government "shall make no law respecting an establishment of religion."

The South has long been a stronghold of Christian fundamentalism, which adheres to a literal interpretation of the Bible and a belief in the infallibility of the Scriptures. Scientific advances, most notably Charles Darwin's theory of evolution, challenge the core of the fundamentalists' beliefs. When their efforts to legislate evolution out of the public school curriculum proved unconstitutional, fundamentalists adopted a new strategy.[16]

In 1981, Louisiana enacted a law mandating that all public schools give balanced treatment to creation-science and evolution-science. *Creation-science* was defined as "the scientific evidences for creation and inferences from those scientific evidences." The law only mandated balance—when one approach was taught, the other approach must be taught too. Louisiana claimed that the purpose of the law was to protect academic freedom. The state's teachers, parents, and nonfundamentalist religious leaders challenged the law's validity in federal court, arguing that the law violated the establishment clause. The federal district court and the court of appeals agreed.

Louisiana finally appealed to the Supreme Court. In 1987, in *Edwards* v. *Aguillard*, the Court affirmed the lower courts' rulings by a vote of 7 to 2.[17] Justice William J. Brennan, Jr., wrote the majority opinion. He applied the three-pronged *Lemon* test and concluded that the law failed to meet the first prong—the requirement that the legislation have a valid secular purpose—because the "preeminent purpose" of the law was religious. Despite its avowed secular purpose of protecting academic freedom, the law actually constrained teachers, favored creationism, and failed in its assurance to evaluate all the evidence surrounding the origin of life.

Government surely has an interest in preserving social order through the control of public institutions—in this case, the public schools. Louisiana wanted to direct the public school curriculum in a manner consistent with the religious beliefs of many (perhaps a majority) of its citizens. Parents and teachers had an interest in religious freedom, maintaining that government cannot impose any religious belief on its citizens. Obviously, the exercise of one interest would infringe on the exercise of the other. And just as obviously, both sides had merit because each defended a value we recognize as vital to a democratic society. Government interest in the preservation of order must be balanced against individual interest in religious freedom. "Families entrust public schools with the education of their children," declared Brennan, "but condition that trust on the understanding that the classroom will not be used to advance religious views that may conflict with the private beliefs of the student and his or her family."

The establishment clause creates a problem for government. Tolerance of the dominant religion at the expense of other religions risks minority discontent, but support for no religion (neutrality between religion and nonreligion) risks majority discontent. Support for all religions at the expense of nonreligion seems to pose the least risk to social order.

The Free-Exercise Clause

The free-exercise clause of the First Amendment states that "Congress shall make no law . . . prohibiting the free exercise [of religion]." The Supreme Court has struggled to avoid absolute interpretations of this restriction so as not to violate its complement, the establishment clause. An example: Suppose Congress grants exemptions from military service to individuals who have religious scruples against war. These exemptions could be construed as a violation of the establishment clause because they favor some religious groups over others. But if Congress forces conscientious objectors to fight—to violate their religious beliefs—the government would run afoul of the free-exercise clause. In fact, Congress has granted military exemptions to people whose religious beliefs lead them to oppose participating in war. The Supreme Court avoided a conflict between the establishment and free-exercise clauses, however, by equating a religious objection to war to any deeply held humanistic opposition to war.

In free-exercise cases, the justices have distinguished religious beliefs from actions based on those beliefs. Beliefs are inviolate, beyond the reach of government control; but antisocial actions are not protected by the First Amendment.

Saluting the flag. The values of order and religious freedom clashed in 1940, when the Court considered the first of two cases involving compulsory flag saluting in the public schools. In *Minersville School District* v. *Gobitis*, a group of Jehovah's Witnesses challenged the law on the ground that the action forced them to worship graven images, which their faith forbids.[18] Government order won in an 8-to-1 decision. The "mere possession of religious convictions," wrote Justice Felix Frankfurter, "which contradict the relevant concerns of a political society does not relieve the citizen from the discharge of political responsibilities."

Three years later, however, the Court reversed itself in **West Virginia State Board of Education v. Barnette.**[19] This time, the Court saw a larger issue: Can an individual be forced to salute the flag against his or her will? *Gobitis* was decided on the narrower issue of religious belief versus saluting the flag. In *Barnette*, the justices chose to focus instead on the broader issue of freedom of expression. In stirring language, Justice Robert H. Jackson argued in the majority opinion that no one could be compelled by the government to declare any belief.

> If there is any fixed star in our constitutional constellation, it is that no official, high or petty, can prescribe what shall be orthodox in politics, nationalism, religion, or other matters of opinion or force citizens to confess by word or act their faith therein. If there are any circumstances which permit an exception, they do not now occur to us.

Drugs as sacrament. The use of hallucinogenic drugs as part of a religious sacrament raises yet another type of free-exercise problem. The Supreme Court has never definitively ruled on the issue, but some guidance can be found in state court decisions. For example, the California Supreme Court held in 1964 that the use of peyote (an illegal but non-addictive hallucinogen) was central to the ritual of Navajo Indians who were members of the Native American Church of California.[20] Here, the court weighed the free exercise of religion against the state's interest in maintaining order and protecting the Navajo community. It found that "the scale tips in favor of the constitutional guarantee."

Other religions also use drugs in their rituals. The Rastafarians and members of the Ethiopian Zion Coptic Church smoke marijuana in the belief that it is the body and blood of Christ. Obviously, the freedom to practice religion taken to an extreme can be used as a license for illegal conduct. But even when that conduct stems from deeply held convictions, government resistance to it is understandable. The inevitable result is a clash between religious freedom and social order.

FREEDOM OF EXPRESSION

> Congress shall make no law . . . abridging the freedom of speech, or of the press; or the right of the people peaceably to assemble, and to petition the government for a redress of grievances.

The initial versions of the **speech clause** and the **press clause** of the First Amendment were introduced by James Madison in the House of Representatives on June 8, 1789. One of these early proposals provided that "the people shall not be deprived of their right to speak, to write, or to publish their sentiments, and the freedom of the press, as one of the great bulwarks of liberty, shall be inviolable." That version was rewritten several times, then merged with the religion and peaceable assembly clauses to yield the First Amendment.

The original House debates on the proposed speech and press clauses are not informative. There is no record of debate in the Senate or in the states during ratification. But careful analysis of the records of the period supports the view that the press clause prohibited only the imposition of **prior restraint**—censorship before publication. Publishers could not claim protection from punishment if works that had already been published were later deemed improper, mischievous, or illegal.

The sparse language of the First Amendment seems perfectly clear: "Congress shall make no law . . . abridging the freedom of speech, or of the press." Yet a majority of the Supreme Court has never agreed that this "most majestic guarantee" is absolutely inviolable.[21] Historians have long debated the framers' intentions regarding the **free-expression clauses.** The dominant view is that the clauses confer the right to unrestricted discussion of public affairs.[22] Other scholars, examining much the same evidence, conclude that few, if any, of the framers clearly understood the clause; moreover, they insist that prosecution for seditious statements (statements inciting insurrection) is not ruled out by the First Amendment.[23]

The passage of the Sedition Act of 1798 lends credibility to the latter claim. The act punished "false, scandalous and malicious writings against the government of the United States," seemingly in direct conflict with the free-expression clauses. President John Adams's administration used the Sedition Act to punish its political opponents for expressing contempt of the government and its officials. Thomas Jefferson and his allies attacked Adams's use of the act; they supported a broad view of the protection afforded by the First Amendment. The fines imposed on Adams's critics under the Sedition Act were later repaid by an act of Congress, and Jefferson, Adams's successor, pardoned those who had been convicted and sentenced under the law.

The license to speak freely does not move multitudes of Americans to speak out on controversial issues. Subtle restrictions are sewn into the fabric of American society. For example, the risks of criticism or ostracism by one's family, peers, or employers may confine the actual practice of free speech to individuals ready to bear the risks. As Mark Twain once remarked, "It is by the goodness of God that in our country we have three unspeakably precious things: freedom of speech, freedom of conscience, and the prudence never to practice either of them."[24]

Jefferson's libertarian view serves as the basis for the modern perspective on the First Amendment free-expression clauses. Today, the clauses are deemed to bar most forms of prior restraint (which is consistent with the initial understanding). In addition, according to the current interpretation, they also bar after-the-fact prosecution for political and other discourse.

The Supreme Court has evolved two approaches to the resolution of claims based on the free-expression clauses. First, government can regulate or punish the advocacy of ideas, but only if it can prove that the goal is to produce lawless action and that a high probability exists that such action will occur. Second, government can impose reasonable restrictions on the flow of ideas, consequently discouraging or limiting the communication of ideas.

Suppose, for example, that a political party advocates unilateral disarmament as part of its platform. (Unilateral disarmament is a policy of arms reduction or elimination without a corresponding reduction or elimination by any other nation.) Government cannot regulate or punish that party for advocating unilateral disarmament because the standards of proof—that the act be directed to inciting or producing imminent lawless action and that the act be judged likely to produce such action—do not apply. But government can impose restrictions on the way the party's candidates communicate what they are advocating. For example, government can bar them from blaring messages from loudspeakers in residential neighborhoods at 3:00 A.M.

Freedom of Speech

The starting point for any modern analysis of free speech is the **clear and present danger test** formulated by Justice Oliver Wendell Holmes in the Supreme Court's unanimous decision in *Schenck* v. *United States* (1919).[25] Charles T. Schenck and his fellow defendants were convicted under a federal criminal statute for attempting to disrupt World War I military recruitment by distributing leaflets claiming that conscription was unconstitutional. The government believed this behavior threatened the public order. At the core of the Court's opinion, Holmes wrote:

> The character of every act depends upon the circumstances in which it is done. . . . The most stringent protection of free speech would not protect a man in falsely shouting fire in a theatre and causing a panic. . . . The question in every case is whether the words used are used in such circumstances and are of such a nature as to create a *clear and present danger* that they will bring about the substantive evils that Congress has a right to prevent. It is a question of proximity and degree. When a nation is at war many things that might be said in time of peace are such a hindrance to its effort that their utterance will not be endured so long as men fight and that no Court could regard them as protected by any constitutional right. (emphasis added)

Because the actions of the defendants in *Schenck* were deemed to create a clear and present danger to the United States at that time, the defendants' convictions were upheld. Holmes himself later frequently disagreed with a majority of his colleagues in applying the clear and present danger test. The test helps to distinguish the advocacy of ideas, which is protected, from incitement, which is not.

In an often-quoted dissent in *Abrams* v. *United States* (1919), Holmes revealed his deeply rooted resistance to the suppression of ideas.[26] The majority had upheld Jacob Abrams's criminal conviction for distributing leaflets that denounced the war and U.S. opposition to the Russian Revolution. Holmes wrote:

> When men have realized that time has upset many fighting faiths, they may come to believe even more than they believe the very foundations of their own conduct that the ultimate good desired is better reached by free trade in ideas—that the best test of truth is the power of the thought to get itself accepted in the competition of the market, and that truth is the only ground upon which their wishes safely can be carried out. That at any rate is the theory of our Constitution.

In 1925 the Court issued a landmark decision in **Gitlow v. New York.**[27] Benjamin Gitlow was arrested for distributing copies of a "left-wing manifesto" that called for the establishment of socialism through strikes and class action of any form. Gitlow was convicted under a state criminal anarchy law; Schenck and Abrams had been convicted under a federal law. The Court held, for the first time, that the First Amendment speech and press provisions applied to the states through the due process clause of the Fourteenth Amendment. Still, a majority of the justices affirmed Gitlow's conviction. Justices Holmes and Louis D. Brandeis argued in dissent that Gitlow's ideas did not pose a clear and present danger. "Eloquence may set fire to reason," conceded the dissenters. "But whatever may be thought of the redundant discourse before us, it had no chance of starting a present conflagration."

The protection of advocacy faced yet another challenge in 1948 when eleven members of the Communist party were charged with violating the Smith Act—a federal law making the advocacy of force or violence against the United States a criminal offense. The leaders were convicted, although the government introduced no evidence that they actually urged people to commit specific violent acts. The Supreme Court mustered a majority for its decision to uphold the convictions under the act, but it could not get a majority to agree on the reasons in support of that decision. The largest bloc of four justices announced the plurality opinion in 1951, arguing that the government's interest was substantial enough to warrant criminal penalties.[28] The justices interpreted the threat to government to be the gravity of the advocated action "discounted by its improbability." In other words, a single soap-box orator advocating revolution stands a low chance of success. But a well-organized, highly disciplined political movement advocating revolution in the tinderbox of world conditions stands a greater chance of success. In broadening the meaning of clear and present danger, the Court held that the government was justified in acting preventively rather than waiting until the revolution is about to occur.

By 1969, the pendulum had swung back in the other direction: The justices began to show a stronger preference for freedom. That year, in ***Brandenburg v. Ohio,*** a unanimous decision extended the freedom of speech to new limits.[29] Clarence Brandenburg, the leader of the Ohio Ku Klux Klan, had been convicted under a state law for remarks he made at a Klan rally. His comments, which had been filmed by a television crew invited to cover the meeting, included threats against government officials.

The Court reversed Brandenburg's conviction because the government failed to prove that the danger was real. The Court went even further and declared that threatening speech is protected by the First Amendment unless the government can prove that such advocacy is "directed to inciting or producing imminent lawless action" and is "likely to produce such action." The ruling offered wider latitude for the expression of political ideas than ever before in the nation's history.

Symbolic expression. **Symbolic expression,** or nonverbal communication, generally receives less protection than pure speech. But the Court has upheld certain types of symbolic expression. ***Tinker v. Des Moines Independent County School District*** (1969) involved three public school students who wore black armbands to school to protest the Vietnam War.[30] Principals in their school district had prohibited the wearing of armbands on the ground that such conduct would provoke a disturbance, so the students were suspended from school. The Supreme Court overturned the suspensions. Justice Abe Fortas declared for the majority that the principals had failed to show that the forbidden conduct would substantially interfere with appropriate school discipline.

Not Exactly Brooks Brothers
Schools and other public institutions sometimes seek to regulate matters of personal appearance—dress, hair style, and personal adornment—arguing that such regulation is needed to maintain order. Others argue that these matters are forms of symbolic expression protected from government control by the Constitution. Courts of appeals have decided differently on issues involving personal appearance, and the Supreme Court has avoided decision in these areas.

Undifferentiated fear or apprehension is not enough to overcome the right to freedom of expression. Any departure from absolute regimentation may cause trouble. Any variation from the majority's opinion may inspire fear. Any word spoken, in class, in the lunchroom, or on the campus, that deviates from the views of another person may start an argument or cause a disturbance. But our Constitution says we must take this risk.

A free-speech exception: Fighting words. *Fighting words* are a notable exception to the protection of free speech. In *Chaplinsky* v. *New Hampshire* (1942), a Jehovah's Witness was convicted under a state statute for calling a city marshal a "God-damned racketeer" and "a damned fascist" in a public place.[31] The Supreme Court upheld Chaplinsky's conviction on the theory that **fighting words**—words that "inflict injury or tend to incite an immediate breach of the peace"—do not convey ideas and thus are not subject to First Amendment protection.

The definition of fighting words was made much more exclusive just seven years later. Father Arthur Terminiello, a suspended Catholic priest from Alabama and a vicious anti-Semite, addressed the Christian Veterans of America, a right-wing extremist group, in a Chicago hall. The packed audience inside heard Father Terminiello call the jeering crowd of fifteen hundred angry protesters outside the hall "slimy scum," while he ranted on about the "Communistic Zionistic" Jews of America, evoking cries of "kill the Jews" and "dirty kikes" from his listeners. The crowd outside the hall heaved bottles, bricks, and rocks, while the police attempted to protect Terminiello and his listeners inside. Finally, the police arrested Terminiello for disturbing the peace.

Terminiello's speech was far more serious than Walter Chaplinsky's. Yet the Supreme Court struck down Terminiello's conviction on the ground that provocative speech, even speech that stirs people to anger, is protected by the First Amendment.[32] "Freedom of speech," wrote Justice William O. Douglas in the majority opinion, "though not absolute . . . is nevertheless protected against censorship or punishment, unless shown likely to produce a clear and present danger of serious substantive evil that rises far above public inconvenience, annoyance, or unrest."

This broad view of protection brought a stiff rebuke in Justice Jackson's dissenting opinion:

> The choice is not between order and liberty. It is between liberty with order and anarchy without either. There is danger that, if the Court does not temper its doctrinaire logic with a little practical wisdom, it will convert the constitutional Bill of Rights into a suicide pact.

The times seem to have caught up with the idealism that Jackson criticized in his colleagues. In ***Cohen v. California*** (1971), a nineteen-year-old department store worker expressed his opposition to the Vietnam War by wearing a jacket emblazoned with "FUCK THE DRAFT. STOP THE WAR."[33] The young man, Paul Cohen, was charged in 1968 under a California statute that prohibits "maliciously and willfully disturb[ing] the peace and quiet of any neighborhood or person [by] offensive conduct." He was found guilty and sentenced to thirty days in jail. On appeal to the U.S. Supreme Court, Cohen's conviction was reversed. The Court reasoned that the expletive he used, while provocative, was not directed toward anyone; besides, there was no evidence that people in "substantial numbers" would be provoked into some kind of physical action by the words on Cohen's jacket. In recognizing that "one man's vulgarity is another's lyric," the Supreme Court protected two elements of speech: the emotive (the expression of emotion) and the cognitive (the expression of ideas).

Another exception: Obscenity. Obscene material—words, books, magazines, films—is entirely excluded from constitutional protection. This exclusion rests on the Supreme Court's review of historical evidence surrounding freedom of expression at the time of the Constitution's adoption. The Court observed that blasphemy, profanity, and obscenity were colonial crimes, but obscenity was not a developed area of the law at the time the Bill of Rights was adopted. Difficulties arise, however, in determining what is obscene and what is not. In *Roth* v. *United States* (1957), Justice Brennan outlined a test for judging whether a work is obscene: "Whether to the average person, applying contemporary community standards, the dominant theme of the material taken as a whole appeals to prurient interest."[34] (*Prurient* means having a tendency to excite lustful thoughts.) Yet a definition of obscenity has proved elusive; no objective test seems adequate. Justice Potter Stewart will long be remembered for his solution to the problem of identifying obscene materials. He declared that he could not define it. "But," he added, "I know it when I see it."[35]

In *Miller* v. *California* (1973), its last major attempt to clarify constitutional standards governing obscenity, the Court declared that a work—play, film, or book—is obscene and may be regulated by government if (1) the work taken as a whole appeals to prurient interest; (2) the work portrays sexual conduct in a patently offensive way; and (3) the work taken as a whole lacks serious literary, artistic, political, or scientific value.[36] Local community standards govern application of the first and second prongs of the *Miller* test.

Recently the Court addressed the standard to be applied to the third prong. Speaking for the majority, Justice Byron White declared that the proper inquiry is not whether an "average" member of any given community would find serious value in material alleged to be obscene, but "whether a reasonable person would find such value in the material, taken as a whole."[37] The law often uses the words *reasonable person* to denote a hypothetical person in society who exercises average care, skill, and judgment in conduct. The expectation is that a reasonable person may find serious value in works alleged to be obscene whereas an average person may not. The decision here was an attempt by the Court to escape the nagging problem of reviewing state court obscenity rulings. But the ambiguity in the reasonable-person test will continue to draw the justices into the obscenity maelstrom.

Freedom of the Press

The First Amendment guarantees that government "shall make no law . . . abridging the freedom . . . of the press." Although it was adopted as a restriction on the national government, the free-press guarantee has been held since 1931 to apply to state and local governments as well.

The ability to collect and report information without government interference was (and still is) thought to be at the core of a free society. The print media continue to use and defend their freedom, which was conferred on them by the framers. The electronic media, however, have had to accept government regulation that stems from the scarcity of broadcast frequencies.

Defamation of character. **Libel** is the written defamation of character.* A person who believes his or her name and character have been harmed by false statements in a publication can institute a lawsuit against the publication and seek monetary compensation for the damage. This kind of lawsuit can impose limits on freedom of expression; at the same time, false statements impinge on the rights of individuals. In a landmark decision in ***New York Times* v. *Sullivan*** (1964), the Supreme Court declared that freedom of the press takes precedence—at least when the defamed individual is a public official.[38] The Court unanimously agreed that the First Amendment protects the publication of all statements, even false ones, about the conduct of public officials except when statements are made with actual malice (with knowledge that they are false or in reckless disregard of their truth or falsity). Citing John Stuart Mill's 1859 treatise *On Liberty*, the Court declared that "even a false statement may be deemed to make a valuable contribution to public debate, since it brings about the clearer perception and livelier impression of truth, produced by its collision with error."

Three years later, the Court extended this protection to include suits brought by any public figures, whether or not they are public officials. **Public figures** are people who assume roles of prominence in the affairs of society or who thrust themselves to the forefront of public controversy—including officials, actors, writers, television personalities, and others. These people must show actual malice on the part of the publisher that prints false statements about them. Few plaintiffs prevail because the burden of proof is so great. And freedom of the press is the beneficiary.

What if the damage inflicted is not to one's reputation but to one's emotional state? Government seeks to maintain the prevailing social order, which prescribes proper modes of behavior. Does the First Amendment restrict government protection of citizens from behavior that intentionally inflicts emotional distress? This issue arose in a parody of a public figure in *Hustler* magazine. The target was Reverend Jerry Falwell, a Baptist televangelist who founded the Moral Majority, organizing conservative Christians into a political force. The parody had Falwell—in an interview—discussing a drunken incestuous rendezvous with his mother in an outhouse, saying, "I always get sloshed before I go out to the pulpit." Falwell won a $200,000 award for "emotional distress." The magazine appealed; and the Supreme Court confronted the issue of social order versus free speech in 1988.[39]

In a unanimous decision, the Court overturned the award. In his sweeping opinion for the Court, Chief Justice William H. Rehnquist gave

---

* *Slander* is the oral defamation of character. The durability of the written word usually means that libel is a more serious accusation than slander.

Publisher Parodies Priggish Pastor
The Reverend Jerry Falwell (right) claimed a tasteless parody that appeared in the soft-core porn magazine Hustler, *published by Larry Flynt, caused him emotional distress. Falwell won an initial victory in the courts, with a $200,000 judgment. When Flynt appealed to the Supreme Court, Falwell lost the case in a big way: a unanimous Court decision. The First Amendment, argued the justices, protects criticism of public figures even when that criticism is outrageous and offensive.*

a wide berth to the First Amendment's protection of free speech. He observed that "graphic depictions and satirical cartoons have played a prominent role in public and political debate throughout the nation's history" and that the First Amendment protects even "vehement, caustic, and sometimes unpleasantly sharp attacks." Free speech protects criticism of public figures even if the criticism is outrageous and offensive.

Prior restraint and the press.   In the United States, freedom of the press has meant primarily immunity from prior restraint, or censorship. The Supreme Court's first encounter with a law imposing prior restraint on a newspaper was in *Near* v. *Minnesota* (1931).[40] Jay Near—an abusive, difficult man—published a scandal sheet in Minneapolis, in which he attacked local officials, charging that they were implicated with gangsters.[41] Minnesota officials obtained an injunction to prevent Near from publishing his newspaper under a state law that allowed such action against periodicals deemed "malicious, scandalous, and defamatory." The Supreme Court struck down the law, declaring that prior restraint is a special burden on a free press. The need for a vigilant unrestrained press was expressed forcefully by Chief Justice Charles Evans Hughes: "The fact that the liberty of the press may be abused by miscreant purveyors of scandal does not make any the less necessary the immunity of the press from previous restraint in dealing with official misconduct." The Court recognized that prior restraint may be permissible in exceptional circumstances, but it did not specify those circumstances, nor has it yet done so. Consider two modern cases involving prior restraint.

Stamp Out Secrecy!
In 1971, Daniel Ellsberg transmitted classified documents on U.S. involvement in Vietnam to the New York Times *and the* Washington Post. *The Federal Employees for Peace awarded him this "declassified" stamp. The government awarded him an indictment for theft of government property and violation of the Espionage Act. Two years later, a judge dismissed the indictment after the Watergate investigation disclosed that the government had wiretapped Ellsberg's phone and the CIA had sponsored a burglary of his former psychiatrist to obtain his files.*

The first of these cases occurred in a time of war, a period when the tension between government-imposed order and individual freedom is often at a peak. In 1971, Daniel Ellsberg, a special assistant in the Pentagon's Office of International Security Affairs, delivered portions of a classified U.S. Department of Defense study to the *New York Times* and the *Washington Post*. By making the documents public, he hoped to discredit the Vietnam War and thereby end it. The highly secret study documented the history of U.S. involvement in the war. The U.S. Department of Justice sought to restrain the *Times* and the *Post* from publishing the documents, contending that publication would prolong the war and embarrass the government. The case was quickly brought before the Supreme Court, which delayed its summer adjournment to hear oral argument.

Three days later, in a 6-to-3 decision in **New York Times v. United States** (1971), the Court concluded that the government had not met the heavy burden of proving that immediate, inevitable, and irreparable harm would follow publication.[42] The majority's view was expressed in a brief unsigned *per curiam* (Latin for "by the court") opinion, although individual and collective concurring and dissenting views added nine opinions to the decision. Two justices maintained that the First Amendment offered absolute protection against government trespass, no matter what the situation. But the other justices left the door ajar for the imposition of prior restraint in the most extreme and compelling circumstances. The result was hardly a ringing endorsement of freedom of the press; nor was it a full affirmation of the public's right to all the information that is vital to the debate of public issues.

In the second case, a Wisconsin federal district court issued an order in 1979 stopping a monthly magazine, *The Progressive*, from publishing technical material about the production of a hydrogen bomb.[43] The material was far from a do-it-yourself guide to thermonuclear weaponry, and the publisher maintained that the article simply combined information that was available in public documents. Still, the district court judge found that the article contained concepts vital to the operation of a bomb, and that these concepts were not in the public domain. The nation's first imposition of prior restraint against a publication was accomplished. The judge reasoned that a mistake in ruling against the government would far outweigh a mistake in ruling against the magazine: A mistake "against the United States would pave the way for thermonuclear annihilation for us all. In that event, our right to life is extinguished and the right to publish becomes moot." The dispute never reached the Supreme Court, leaving unclear a national policy on prior restraint. The legal proceedings against the magazine were abandoned after similar information on nuclear weapons was published by other periodicals.

Freedom of expression versus maintaining order. The courts have consistently held that freedom of the press does not override the requirements of law enforcement. A Louisville, Kentucky, reporter who had researched and written an article about drug activities was called before a grand jury to identify people he had seen in possession of marijuana or in the act of processing it. The reporter refused to testify, maintaining that freedom of the press shielded him from inquiry. In a closely divided decision, the Supreme Court in 1972 rejected this position.[44] The Court declared that no exception, even a limited one, exists to the rule that every citizen has a duty to give his or her government whatever testimony he or she is capable of giving.

A divided Supreme Court maintained again in 1978 that journalists are not protected from the demands of law enforcement when the Court upheld a lower court's warrant to search a Stanford University campus newspaper office for photographs of a violent demonstration.[45] The investigation of criminal conduct seems to be a special area—an area in which the Supreme Court is not willing to provide the press with extraordinary protection of its freedom.

The Supreme Court again confronted the conflict between free expression and order in 1988.[46] The principal of a St. Louis high school deleted articles on divorce and teen-age pregnancy from the school's newspaper on the ground that the articles invaded the privacy of the students and families who were the focus of the stories. Three student editors filed suit in federal court, claiming that their First Amendment rights had been violated. They argued that the principal's censorship interfered with the newspaper's function as a public forum, a role protected by the First Amendment. The principal maintained that the newspaper was just an extension of classroom instruction, that it was not protected by the First Amendment.

In a 5-to-3 decision, the Court upheld the principal's actions in sweeping terms. Educators may limit speech that occurs in the school curriculum and might seem to bear the approval of the school provided their actions serve "any valid educational purpose." The majority justices maintained that students in public school do not "shed their constitutional rights to freedom of expression at the schoolhouse gate." But recent Court decisions suggest that students do lose certain rights—including elements of free expression—when they pass through the public school portals.

The Right to Peaceable Assembly and Petition

The final clause of the First Amendment states that "Congress shall make no law . . . abridging . . . the right of the people peaceably to assemble, and to petition the Government for a redress of grievances." The roots of the right of petition can be traced to the Magna Carta, the charter of English political and civil liberties granted by King John at Runnymede in 1215. The right of peaceable assembly arose much later. Historically, this section of the First Amendment should read "the right of the people peaceably to assemble" *in order to* "petition the government."[47] Today, however, the right of peaceable assembly stems from the same root as free speech and free press and is held to be equally fundamental. Government cannot prohibit peaceful political meetings and cannot brand as criminals those who organize, lead, and attend such meetings.[48]

The rights of assembly and petition have merged with the guarantees of free speech and a free press under the more general freedom of expression. Having the right to assemble and to petition the government implies having the freedom to express one's thoughts and beliefs.

The clash of interests in cases involving these rights illustrates a continuing effort to define and apply fundamental principles. The concept of freedom has been tempered by the need for order and stability. And when there is a confrontation between freedom and order, the justices of the Supreme Court, who are responsible only to their consciences, strike the balance. These kinds of clashes are certain to occur again and again. Freedom and order conflict when public libraries become targets for community censors, when religious devotion interferes with military service, when individuals and groups express views or hold beliefs at odds with majority sentiment. Conflicts between freedom and order, and between minority and majority viewpoints, are part and parcel of politics and government here and abroad. How do other nations rank on the degree of civil liberties they guarantee their citizens? Is freedom increasing or declining in the world? For some answers, see Compared With What? 17.1.

APPLYING THE BILL OF RIGHTS TO THE STATES

Remember that the major purpose of the Constitution was to structure the division of power between the national government and the state governments. Even before it was amended, the Constitution did set some limits on both the nation and the states with regard to citizens' rights.

Both governments were barred from passing **bills of attainder,** laws that make an individual guilty of a crime without a trial. They were also prohibited from enacting **ex post facto laws,** laws that declare an action a crime after it has been performed. And both nation and states were barred from impairing (and where necessary required to enforce) the **obligation of contracts,** the obligation of the parties in a contract to carry out its terms. Although initially the Bill of Rights seemed to apply only to the national government, various litigants pressed the claim that its guarantees reached beyond the national government to the states.

For example, in the case of *Barron* v. *Baltimore* (1833), two wharf owners sued the city of Baltimore because their property had been made useless when Baltimore diverted some streams.[49] The owners maintained that the Fifth Amendment provision that private property should not be taken for public use "without just compensation" applied to the states with the same force as to the national government. Chief Justice John Marshall affirmed what seemed plain from the Constitution's language and "the history of the day" (the events surrounding the Constitutional Convention): The provisions of the Bill of Rights served only to limit national authority. "Had the framers of these amendments intended them to be limitations on the powers of the state governments," wrote Marshall, "they would have . . . expressed that intention."

Many similar—and similarly unsuccessful—claims were pressed on the Supreme Court, despite the clarity of Marshall's rejection. Change would not come, however, until the Fourteenth Amendment was adopted in 1868. The due process clause of that amendment has served as the linchpin that holds the states to the provisions of the Bill of Rights.

The Fourteenth Amendment: Due Process of Law

Section 1   All persons born or naturalized in the United States, and subject to the jurisdiction thereof, are citizens of the United States and of the State wherein they reside. No State shall make or enforce any law which shall abridge the privileges or immunities of citizens of the United States; nor shall any State deprive any person of life, liberty, or property, without due process of law.

Most freedoms protected in the Bill of Rights today apply as limitations on the states. And many of the standards that limit the national government serve equally to limit state governments. These changes have been achieved through the Supreme Court's interpretation of the due process clause of the Fourteenth Amendment: "nor shall any State deprive any person of life, liberty, or property, without due process of law." Think of the due process clause as a sponge, absorbing or incorporating the specifics of the Bill of Rights and applying them to the states. Due process cases show that constitutional guarantees are often championed by unlikely litigants and that freedom is not always the victor.

The Fourteenth Amendment was first interpreted in the *Slaughter-House Cases* (1873).[50] Some New Orleans butchers who had been excluded from a state-chartered slaughterhouse monopoly sought to break

COMPARED WITH WHAT? 17.1

Civil Liberties Around the World

Raymond D. Gastil has been analyzing freedom around the world for several years. One of his objectives is to produce a comparative assessment of civil liberties. He uses a 7-point scale, ranking nations from 1 (the greatest degree of freedom) to 7 (the least degree of freedom). Nations with lower ratings, then, are freer than nations with higher ratings. Of course, no nation is absolutely free or unfree.

In countries rated 1, the expression of political opinion has an outlet in the press, especially when the intent of that expression is to affect the legitimate political process. In addition, in these countries no major medium of expression serves as a simple conduit for government propaganda. The courts protect the individual; people cannot be punished for their opinions; there is respect for private rights and wants in education, occupation, religion, and residence; and law-abiding citizens do not fear for their lives because of their political activities.

Moving down the scale from 2 to 7, we see a steady loss of civil freedoms. Compared with nations rated 1, the police and courts in nations rated 2 have more authoritarian traditions or, as is the case in Greece and Portugal, a less institutionalized or secure set of liberties. Nations rated 3 or higher may have political prisoners and varying forms of censorship. Often, their security services torture prisoners. States rated 6 almost always have political prisoners. Here the legitimate media usually are completely under government supervision; there is no right to assembly; and often, narrow restrictions apply to travel, residence, and occupation. However, at level 6 there may still be relative freedom in private conversations, especially at home; illegal demonstrations can or do occur; and underground literature circulates. At 7 on the scale, there is pervasive fear; little independent expression, even in private; and almost no public expression of opposition to the government. Imprisonment and execution here are swift and sure.

The degree of freedom within a nation varies with shifts in the political regime. The states in **boldface type** have experienced a decline in civil liberties from 1987 to 1988; the states in *italic boldface* type have experienced an increase in civil liberties from 1987 to 1988. Notice the changes for Haiti, Nicaragua, South Korea, and the USSR. What events might explain these changes?

Rating of Nations by Civil Liberties, 1988

Most Free 1	Argentina	Canada	Italy	Sweden
	Australia	Costa Rica	Japan	Switzerland
	Austria	Denmark	Luxembourg	***Trinidad and Tobago***
	Barbados	***Grenada***	Netherlands	Tuvalu
	Belgium	Iceland	New Zealand	United Kingdom
	Belize	Ireland	Norway	United States
2	Brazil	Greece	Nauru	St. Vincent
	Cyprus (G)	Israel	Papua New Guinea	Solomons
	Dominica	***Jamaica***	Philippines	Spain
	Finland	Kiribati	Portugal	Uruguay
	France	***Malta***	**St. Kitts-Nevis**	Venezuela
	Germany (W)	Mauritius	St. Lucia	

the monopoly with a new weapon, the Fourteenth Amendment. Justice Samuel F. Miller, speaking for a sharply divided Supreme Court, denied their appeal. The core of his argument was that the overwhelming purpose of the Civil War amendments (the Thirteenth, Fourteenth, and Fifteenth Amendments) was the freedom, security, and protection of emancipated blacks. The Court gutted the "privileges and immunities clause" when it upheld the theory that fundamental rights stem from

Rating of Nations by Civil Liberties, 1988

3	Antigua and Barbados **Bahamas** Bolivia Botswana	Colombia Cyprus (T) Dominican Republic Ecuador	***Gambia*** Guatemala Honduras India	Peru Thailand Tonga Western Samoa
4	***China (T)*** Egypt El Salvador ***Hungary***	***Korea (S)*** Mexico Nepal Senegal	Sri Lanka ***Suriname*** Turkey Uganda	Vanuatu
5	Bahrain Bangladesh Bhutan Brunei Chile Cote d'Ivoire **Fiji** Guyana	**Haiti** Jordan Kuwait **Lebanon** Liberia Madagascar Malaysia Morocco	***Nicaragua*** Nigeria Pakistan **Panama** Poland Qatar Sierra Leone Singapore	Sudan Tunisia United Arab Emirates Yemen (N) Yugoslavia Zambia
6	Algeria Burkina Faso Burundi Cameroon Cape Verde Central African Republic China (M) Comoros Congo	Cuba Czechoslovakia Djibouti Gabon Germany (E) Ghana **Guinea** Indonesia Iran **Kenya**	**Lesotho** Libya Maldives Mali Mauritania Niger Oman Paraguay Rwanda Seychelles	South Africa Swaziland Tanzania Togo Transkei ***USSR*** Zimbabwe
7 *Least* *Free*	Afghanistan Albania Angola Benin Bulgaria Burma Cambodia	Chad Equatorial Guinea Ethiopia Guinea-Bissau Iraq Korea (N) Laos	Malawi Mongolia Mozambique Romania Sao Tome and Principe Saudi Arabia Somalia	Syria Vietnam Yemen (S) Zaire

Source: *Freedom at Issue* 100 (January–February 1988):29. Reprinted with permission of Freedom House.

state, not national, citizenship. In brief, the Court argued that the Fourteenth Amendment imposed no additional restrictions on the states.

    This position was short-lived, however. The justices had two options in their effort to apply the provisions of the Bill of Rights to the states. They could overrule the *Slaughter-House* decision, but this was unlikely given their commitment to *stare decisis*. (This Latin phrase means "let the decision stand." It refers to a principle that guides judges and lawyers to agree with decisions that have been made previously unless compelling reasons call for new precedents.) Instead, the justices searched for another constitutional provision to carry the weight; they found it nearly thirty years later in the due process clause.

The Fundamental Freedoms

In 1897, without fanfare, the Supreme Court reversed the position it had taken in *Barron* v. *Baltimore.* The states, the Court said, are limited by the Fifth Amendment's prohibition on taking of private property without just compensation.[51] The Court accomplished its goal by absorbing that prohibition into the due process clause of the Fourteenth Amendment, which applies to the states. Now one Bill of Rights protection—but only that one—limited both the states and the national government (see Figure 17.1).

The inclusion of other Bill of Rights guarantees within the due process clause faced a critical test in ***Palko* v. *Connecticut*** (1937).[52] Frank Palko had been charged with first-degree murder. He was convicted instead of second-degree murder and sentenced to life imprisonment. The state of Connecticut appealed and won a new trial; this time Palko was found guilty of first-degree murder and sentenced to death. Palko appealed the second conviction on the ground that it violated the protection against double jeopardy guaranteed to him by the Fifth Amendment. This protection applied to the states, he contended, because of the Fourteenth Amendment's due process clause.

The Supreme Court upheld Palko's second conviction. In his opinion for the majority, Justice Benjamin N. Cardozo formulated principles that were to direct the Court's actions for the next three decades. He noted that some Bill of Rights guarantees—such as freedom of thought and speech—are fundamental, and that these fundamental rights are absorbed by the Fourteenth Amendment's due process clause and are applicable

---

Figure 17.1

The Incorporation of the Bill of Rights
The Supreme Court has used the due process clause of the Fourteenth Amendment as a sponge, absorbing many—but not all—of the provisions in the Bill of Rights and applying them to state and local governments. All of the provisions in the Bill of Rights apply to the national government.

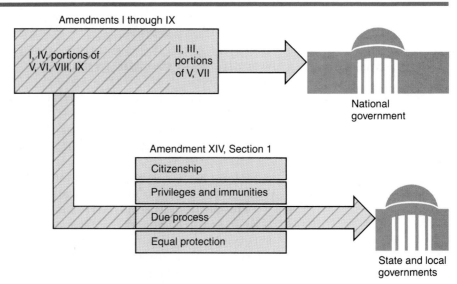

Amendments I through IX

I, IV, portions of V, VI, VIII, IX

II, III, portions of V, VII

National government

Amendment XIV, Section 1

Citizenship

Privileges and immunities

Due process

Equal protection

State and local governments

to the states. These rights are essential, argued Cardozo, because "neither liberty nor justice would exist if they were sacrificed." Trial by jury and other rights, although valuable and important, are not essential to liberty and justice, and therefore are not absorbed by the due process clause. "Few would be so narrow or provincial," Cardozo claimed, "as to maintain that a fair and enlightened system of justice" would be impossible without these other rights. In other words, only some provisions of the Bill of Rights—the "fundamental" provisions—were absorbed into the due process clause and made applicable to the states. Because protection against double jeopardy was not one of them, Palko died in Connecticut's gas chamber in April 1938.

The next thirty years constituted a period of slow but perceptible change in the standard for determining whether or not a Bill of Rights guarantee was fundamental. The reference point was transformed from the idealized "fair and enlightened system of justice" in *Palko* to the more realistic "American scheme of justice" outlined in the decision in *Duncan* v. *Louisiana* (1968).[53] During this period, in case after case, as guarantees were tested they were found to be fundamental. By 1969, the *Palko* decision was an empty shell; most of the Bill of Rights guarantees had been found applicable to the states (see Table 17.1).

The Supreme Court finally overturned *Palko* on June 23, 1969, Chief Justice Earl Warren's last day on the Court. He and a majority of his colleagues had come to recognize that "*Palko*'s roots had been cut away years ago."[54] Although nearly all the guarantees of the Bill of Rights apply today to government at all levels, the controversy over these safeguards continues.

Criminal Procedure: The Meaning of Constitutional Guarantees

"The history of liberty," remarked Justice Frankfurter, "has largely been the history of observance of procedural safeguards."[55] The safeguards embodied in the Fourth through Eighth Amendments to the Constitution specify how government must behave in criminal proceedings. Their application to the states has reshaped American criminal justice in the last thirty years.

That application has come in two steps: The first step requires the judgment that a guarantee asserted in the Bill of Rights also applies to the states. The second step requires that the judiciary give specific meaning to the guarantee. The courts cannot allow the states to define guarantees themselves without risking different definitions from state to state—and differences among citizens' rights. If the rights are fundamental, their meaning cannot vary. But life is not quite so simple under the U.S. Constitution. The concept of federalism is sewn into the constitutional fabric, and the Supreme Court recognizes that there may be more than one way to prosecute the accused while heeding fundamental rights.

Consider, for example, the right to a jury trial in criminal cases, which is guaranteed by the Sixth Amendment. This right was made obligatory on the states in *Duncan* v. *Louisiana* (1968). The Supreme Court later held that the right applied to all nonpetty criminal cases—those in which the penalty for conviction was more than six months'

Table 17.1
Cases Applying the Bill of Rights to the States

Amendment	Case	Date
1. Congress shall make no law respecting an establishment of religion,	*Everson* v. *Board of Education*	1947
or prohibiting the free exercise thereof;	*Cantwell* v. *Connecticut*	1940
or abridging the freedom of speech,	*Gitlow* v. *New York*	1925
or of the press;	*Near* v. *Minnesota*	1931
or the right of the people peaceably to assemble,	*DeJonge* v. *Oregon*	1937
and to petition the Government for a redress of grievances.	*DeJonge* v. *Oregon*	1937
2. A well regulated Militia, being necessary to the security of a free State, the right of the people to keep and bear Arms, shall not be infringed.		
3. No Soldier shall, in time of peace be quartered in any house, without the consent of the Owner, nor in time of war, but in a manner to be prescribed by law.		
4. The right of the people to be secure in their persons, houses, papers, and effects, against unreasonable searches and seizures, shall not be violated,	*Wolf* v. *Colorado*	1949
and no Warrants shall issue, but upon probable cause, supported by Oath or affirmation, and particularly describing the place to be searched, and the persons or things to be seized.	*Aguilar* v. *Texas*	1964
5. No person shall be held to answer for a capital, or otherwise infamous crime, unless on a presentment or indictment of a Grand Jury,		
except in cases arising in the land or naval forces, or in the Militia, when in actual service in time of War or public danger;		
nor shall any person be subject for the same offence to be twice put in jeopardy of life or limb;	*Benton* v. *Maryland*	1969
nor shall be compelled in any criminal case to be a witness against himself,	*Malloy* v. *Hogan*	1964
nor be deprived of life, liberty, or property, without due process of law;		
nor shall private property be taken for public use, without just compensation.	*Chicago B. & Q. R.* v. *Chicago*	1897
6. In all criminal prosecutions, the accused shall enjoy the right to a speedy	*Klopfer* v. *North Carolina*	1967
and public trial	*In re Oliver*	1948
by an impartial	*Parker* v. *Gladden*	1966
jury	*Duncan* v. *Louisiana*	1968
of the State and district wherein the crime shall have been committed, which district shall have been previously ascertained by law,		
and to be informed of the nature and cause of the accusation;	*Lanzetta* v. *New Jersey*	1939
to be confronted with the witnesses against him;	*Pointer* v. *Texas*	1965
to have compulsory process for obtaining witnesses in his favor,	*Washington* v. *Texas*	1967
and to have the assistance of counsel for his defence.	*Gideon* v. *Wainwright*	1963
7. In Suits at common law, where the value of the controversy shall exceed twenty dollars, the right of trial by jury shall be preserved,		
and no fact tried by a jury, shall be otherwise re-examined in any Court of the United States than according to the rules of the common law.		
8. Excessive bail shall not be required,		
nor excessive fines imposed,		
nor cruel and unusual punishments inflicted.	*Robinson* v. *California*	1962
9. The enumeration in the Constitution, of certain rights, shall not be construed to deny or disparage others retained by the people.	*Griswold* v. *Connecticut*	1965

imprisonment.[56] But the Court did not require that state juries have twelve members, the number required for federal criminal proceedings. Jury size was permitted to vary from state to state, although the minimum number was set at six. Furthermore, the federal requirement of a unanimous jury verdict was not imposed on the states. As a result, even today many states do not require unanimous verdicts for criminal convictions. Some observers question whether criminal defendants in these states enjoy the same rights of defendants in unanimous-verdict states.

In contrast, the Court left no room for variations in its definition of the fundamental right to an attorney, also guaranteed by the Sixth Amendment. Clarence Earl Gideon was a penniless vagrant accused of breaking into and robbing a pool hall. (His "loot" was mainly change taken out of vending machines.) Because Gideon could not afford a lawyer, he asked the state to provide him with legal counsel for his trial. The state refused, and Gideon was subsequently convicted and sentenced to five years in the Florida State Penitentiary. From his cell, Gideon appealed to the U.S. Supreme Court, claiming that his conviction should be struck down because his Sixth Amendment right to counsel had been denied. (Gideon was also without counsel in this appeal; he filed a hand-lettered "pauper's petition" with the Court, after studying law texts in the prison library. When the Court agreed to consider his case, he was assigned a prominent Washington attorney, Abe Fortas, who later became a Supreme Court justice.)[57]

In its landmark decision in ***Gideon v. Wainwright*** (1963), the Court set aside Gideon's conviction and extended to the states the Sixth Amendment right to counsel.[58] Gideon was retried, but this time, with the assistance of a lawyer, he was found not guilty.

A Pauper's Plea
Clarence Earl Gideon, penniless and without a lawyer, was convicted and sent to prison for breaking into and robbing a pool hall. At his trial, Gideon pleaded with the judge: "Your Honor, the U.S. Constitution says I am entitled to be represented by counsel." The judge was required by state law to deny Gideon's request. Undaunted, Gideon continued his quest for recognition of his Sixth Amendment right to counsel. On the basis of his penciled petition, the Supreme Court agreed to consider his case, ultimately granting Gideon the right he advocated with such conviction.

In subsequent rulings that stretched over more than a decade, the Court specified at what points a defendant was entitled to a lawyer in the course of criminal proceedings (from arrest to trial, appeal, and beyond). All states were bound by these pronouncements. In state as well as federal proceedings, legal assistance had to be furnished to those who did not have the means to hire their own attorney.

During this period the Court also came to grips with another issue involving procedural safeguards: informing suspects of their constitutional rights. Without this knowledge, safeguards are useless. Ernesto Miranda was arrested in Arizona for kidnapping and raping an eighteen-year-old woman. After the police questioned him for two hours and the woman identified him, Miranda confessed to the crime. He was convicted in an Arizona court on the basis of that confession—although he was never told he had the right to counsel and the right not to incriminate himself. Miranda appealed his conviction, which was overturned by the Supreme Court in 1966.[59]

The Court based its decision in *Miranda* v. *Arizona* on the Fifth Amendment privilege against self-incrimination. According to the Court, the police had forced Miranda to confess during in-custody questioning, not with physical force but with the coercion inherent in custodial interrogation. Warnings were required, the Court argued, to dispel that coercion. Warnings were not necessary if a person was only in custody or if a person was only subject to questioning without arrest. But the combination of custody and interrogation was sufficiently intimidating to require warnings before questioning. These statements are known today as the **Miranda warnings.** Among them:

- You have the right to remain silent.
- Anything you say can be used against you in court.
- You have the right to talk to a lawyer of your own choice before questioning.
- If you cannot afford to hire a lawyer, a lawyer will be provided without charge.

In each area of criminal procedure, the justices have had to grapple with the two steps in the application of constitutional guarantees to criminal defendants: the extension of a right to the states and the definition of that right. In *Duncan*, the issue was the right to jury trial, and variation was allowed from state to state. In *Gideon*, the right to counsel was applied uniformly from state to state. Finally, in *Miranda*, the Court declared that all governments—national, state, and local—have a duty to inform suspects of the full measure of their constitutional rights.

The problems of balancing freedom and order can be formidable. A primary function of government is to maintain order. What happens when individual freedom is infringed on for the sake of order? Consider the guarantee in the Fourth Amendment: "The right of the people to be secure in their persons, houses, papers, and effects, against unreasonable searches and seizures, shall not be violated." This right was made applicable to the states in *Wolf* v. *Colorado* (1949).[60] Following the reasoning in *Palko*, the Court found that the core of the amendment—security against arbitrary police intrusion—was a fundamental right, that citizens must be protected from illegal searches by state and local government. But how? The federal courts had long followed the **exclusionary rule,** which holds that evidence obtained from an illegal search and seizure cannot be used in a trial. And of course, if that evidence is critical to the prosecution, the conviction is lost. But the Court refused to apply the exclusionary rule to the states. Instead, it allowed the states to decide on their own how to handle the fruits of an illegal search. The upshot of *Wolf* was a declaration that the evidence used to convict the defendant was obtained illegally, but his conviction on the basis of that illegal evidence was affirmed.

The justices considered the exclusionary rule again twelve years later, in ***Mapp v. Ohio*** (1961).[61] Dolree Mapp had been convicted of possessing obscene materials after an admittedly illegal search of her home for a fugitive. Her conviction was affirmed by the Ohio Supreme Court, and she appealed to the U.S. Supreme Court. Mapp's attorneys argued for a reversal based on freedom of expression, contending that the confiscated materials were protected by the First Amendment. However, the Court elected to use the decision in *Mapp* to give meaning to the constitutional guarantee against unreasonable search and seizure. In a 6-to-3 decision, the justices declared that "all evidence obtained by searches and seizures in violation of the Constitution is, by [the Fourth Amendment], inadmissible in a state court." Mapp had been convicted illegally.

The decision was historic. It placed the exclusionary rule within the confines of the Fourth Amendment and required all levels of government to operate according to the provisions of that amendment. Failure to do so could result in the dismissal of criminal charges against otherwise guilty defendants.

Mapp launched a divided Supreme Court on a troubled course of determining how and when to apply the exclusionary rule. For example, the Court continues to struggle with police use of sophisticated electronic eavesdropping devices and the search of movable vehicles. In each case, the justices confront a rule that appears to handicap the police while it offers freedom to people whose guilt has been established by the illegal evidence. In the Court's most recent pronouncements, order has triumphed over freedom.

The struggle over the exclusionary rule took a new turn in 1984, when the Court reviewed ***United States v. Leon.***[62] In this case, the police obtained a search warrant from a judge on the basis of a tip from an anonymous informant. The judge made a mistake; and the police, relying on the warrant, discovered large quantities of illegal drugs. The Court, by a vote of 6-to-3, established the **good faith exception** to the exclusionary rule. The justices held that evidence seized on the basis of a mistakenly issued search warrant could be introduced at trial. The exclusionary rule, argued the majority, is not a right but a remedy justified by its ability to deter illegal police conduct. In *Leon*, the costs of the exclusionary rule outweighed the benefits. The exclusionary rule is costly to society: Guilty defendants go unpunished and people lose respect for the law. The benefits of the exclusionary rule are uncertain: The rule cannot deter police in a case like *Leon*, where they act in good faith on a warrant issued by a judge.

In 1988, the justices ruled 6-to-2 that police may search through garbage bags and other containers that people leave outside their houses. The case resulted from an investigation of a man who was suspected of narcotics trafficking. The police obtained his trash bags from the local garbage collector; the bags contained evidence of narcotics, which served as the basis for a search warrant of his house. That search revealed quantities of cocaine and hashish and led to criminal charges. The lower courts dismissed the drug charges on the grounds that the warrant was based on an unconstitutional search. By overturning that ruling, the Supreme Court further eroded the Fourth Amendment's protection of individual privacy.[63]

Mapp and all the cases that followed it forced the Court to confront the classic dilemma of democracy: the choice between freedom and order. If the justices tipped the scale toward freedom, guilty parties would go free, perhaps to break the law again. If they chose order, they would be giving government approval to police conduct in violation of the Constitution.

THE NINTH AMENDMENT AND PERSONAL AUTONOMY

The adoption of the Bill of Rights in 1791 made explicit those rights that the national government could not abridge. But did it carry with it the assumption that the rights not specified in the amendments could be abridged by government?[64] An answer to this question may be found in the ambiguous language of the Ninth Amendment: "The enumeration in the Constitution, of certain rights, shall not be construed to deny or disparage others retained by the people."

The amendment and its history remain an enigma. The evidence supports two different views. The amendment may protect rights that are not enumerated, or it may simply protect state governments against the assumption of power by the national government.[65] The meaning of the amendment was not an issue until 1965, when the Supreme Court used it to protect privacy, a right that is not enumerated in the Constitution.

Controversy: From Privacy to Abortion

In *Griswold v. Connecticut* (1965), the Court struck down, by a vote of 7 to 2, a seldom-used Connecticut statute that made the use of birth control devices a crime.[66] Justice Douglas, writing for the majority, asserted that the "specific guarantees in the Bill of Rights have penumbras [areas of partial illumination]" that give "life and substance" to specific guarantees in the Bill of Rights. Several specific guarantees in the First, Third, Fourth, and Fifth Amendments create a zone of privacy, Douglas argued, and this zone is protected by the Ninth Amendment and is applicable to the states by the due process clause of the Fourteenth Amendment (see Feature 17.2).

Three of the justices gave added emphasis to the relevance of the Ninth Amendment, which, they contended, protected fundamental

FEATURE 17.2

The Birth of a New Right

In 1965, in *Griswold* v. *Connecticut*, the Supreme Court confronted a state criminal statute that prohibited the use of birth control devices and giving medical advice in their use. Prosecutions were rare under the 1879 statute. Two people—a doctor and a family planning counselor—had been convicted under the law for giving birth control advice to married couples and for prescribing contraceptives. In the conference following argument, the justices were divided 7 to 2 in favor of declaring the law unconstitutional but were unable to articulate a clear theory on which to base their decision. Justice William O. Douglas stated the simplest rationale on which the statute could be invalidated. He claimed the law violated the First Amendment's guarantee of freedom of association. This right, which was officially recognized by the Court in 1958, protected the advancement of beliefs and ideas. The problem was that the right of association did not appear to protect *conjugal* association. Justice Hugo L. Black spoke sarcastically of Douglas's position in the conference. To Black, the right of association meant the right of assembly, and the right of husband and wife to assemble in bed seemed to him to be an entirely new interpretation of that right.

Douglas nevertheless drafted his opinion along right-of-association lines. Within a day of the opinion's distribution, however, Justice William J. Brennan, Jr., urged Douglas to abandon the right-of-association argument because it had little to do with the advocacy protected by that right. Instead, Brennan suggested that Douglas use the same approach but rest the decision on the right to privacy. Douglas followed Brennan's suggestion and circulated a new draft opinion, which recognized a constitutional right to privacy formed by the *penumbras*, or "partial shadows," cast by specific guarantees in the Bill of Rights. Thus the right to privacy was officially born.

The constitutional right to privacy created by the Court in 1965 would spawn one of the most controversial decisions of the modern Supreme Court. In *Roe* v. *Wade*, decided in 1973, the Court struck down state antiabortion laws on the ground that they violate the right of privacy, which was now held to include the right of women to terminate pregnancies.

The right to privacy has limits, however. In 1986, in a 5-to-4 decision, the Court in *Bowers* v. *Hardwick* refused to extend the right to privacy to cover the decision of two consenting adults to engage in homosexual acts. Choices fundamental to heterosexual life—whether to marry, to conceive a child, to carry a pregnancy to term—are still protected by the zone of privacy.

Source: Adapted from Bernard Schwartz, *The Unpublished Opinions of the Warren Court* (New York: Oxford University Press, 1985), chap. 7. Copyright © 1985 by Oxford University Press, Inc. Reprinted by permission.

rights derived from those specifically enumerated in the first eight amendments. This view was in sharp contrast to the position that was expressed by the two dissenters, Justices Black and Stewart. They argued that, in the absence of some specific prohibition, the Bill of Rights and the Fourteenth Amendment do not license judicial annulment of state legislative policies, even if those policies are abhorrent to a judge or justice.

Griswold established the principle that the Bill of Rights as a whole creates a right to make certain intimate personal choices, including the right of married people to engage in sexual intercourse for reproduction or pleasure. This zone of personal autonomy, protected by the Constitution, gave comfort in 1973 to litigants who sought to invalidate state antiabortion laws. But rights are not absolute, and in weighing the interests of the individual against the interests of the government, the Supreme Court found itself caught in a flood of controversy that has yet to ebb.

In **Roe v. Wade** (1973), the Court in a 7-to-2 decision declared unconstitutional a Texas law making it a crime to obtain an abortion except for the purpose of saving the mother's life.[67] Justice Harry A. Blackmun, who authored the majority opinion, could not point to a specific constitutional guarantee to justify the Court's ruling. Instead, he based the decision on the right to privacy protected by the Fourteenth Amendment's due process clause. The Court declared that in the first three months of pregnancy, the abortion decision must be left to the woman and her physician. In the interest of protecting the mother's health, states may restrict but not prohibit abortions in the second three months of pregnancy. Finally, in the last three months of pregnancy, states may regulate or even prohibit abortions to protect the life of the fetus except when medical judgment determines that an abortion is necessary to save the mother's life. In all, the laws of forty-six states were affected by the Court's ruling.

A Grim View of Personal Choice
The 1973 Supreme Court decision Roe v. Wade *made abortions legal in the United States by ruling that the government lacked the power to prohibit them during the first three months of pregnancy. This freedom of personal choice was heralded by some groups as a landmark for women's rights and denounced by others as tantamount to murder. More than fifteen years later, the controversy has yet to ebb.*

The dissenters—Justices White and Rehnquist—were quick to point out what critics have frequently repeated since the decision: The Court's judgment was directed by its own dislikes, not by any constitutional compass. In the absence of guiding principles, they asserted, the majority justices simply substituted their views for the views of the state legislatures whose abortion regulations they invalidated.[68]

The decision in *Roe* raised the freedom-versus-order dilemma. Antiabortion laws abridge freedom, the ability to make fundamental personal choices without interference. But they also meet the need for order, the protection of life (including unborn life) and the safety of citizens. In balancing freedom and order, the Supreme Court stirred up a controversy that centered around the Court's own political power.

In the years following the landmark decision in *Roe*, political controversy continued to churn. In 1976, Congress severely restricted the use of federal funds for abortions. The Supreme Court sustained this restriction, known as the **Hyde Amendment,** in 1980. But the Court strongly reaffirmed its decision in *Roe* when it struck down government-imposed restrictions on abortion procedures in 1983. This reaffirmation has not deterred the opponents of abortion, healed the divisions within the Court, or resolved the difficult issues that loom ahead as the medical risks of various abortion procedures decrease.

President Ronald Reagan's nomination in 1981 of Sandra Day O'Connor as the Court's 102d justice focused attention on the strength of the abortion issue. It dominated public debate on O'Connor's fitness for judicial office. She was roundly condemned by antiabortion groups, although their opposition was not enough to stop her appointment as the first woman to the High Court. As if to prove his commitment to an antiabortion policy, in 1982 Reagan endorsed a constitutional amendment that would have reversed the Court's decision in *Roe*. No such amendment has passed the proposal stage.

The Court continues to struggle with the abortion issue. In 1986, the justices held unconstitutional a Pennsylvania law that required doctors to provide detailed information about risks and alternatives to women seeking abortions. The law also required that two doctors be present at late-term abortions and that the procedures most likely to produce live births be used as long as women were not put at significantly greater risk. These provisions were designed to deter women from having abortions and to require doctors to risk the health of pregnant women in order to save late-term fetuses. The Court concluded that the law had invaded the private sphere of individual liberty protected by the Constitution.[69] Although antiabortion groups denounced it, advocates of abortion rights hailed the decision as a victory. The real significance of the ruling, however, was the depth of division registered within the Court. The justices split 5 to 4, and three of the dissenters, Justices Rehnquist, White, and O'Connor, each authored unusually harsh opinions. Chief Justice Burger voted for the first time in dissent, urging a re-examination of *Roe*.

The composition of the Court shifted under President Reagan. His elevation of William Rehnquist to chief justice in 1986 and his appointments of Antonin Scalia in 1986 and Anthony Kennedy in 1988 raised new hope among abortion foes and old fears among abortion advocates. The showdown on abortion, and on the right to privacy in general, is sure to come as the Court charts a new course between freedom and order.

Personal Autonomy and Sexual Orientation

The right to privacy cases may have opened a Pandora's box of divisive social issues. Does the right to privacy embrace private homosexual acts between consenting adults? Consider the case of Michael Hardwick, who was arrested in his Atlanta bedroom while having sex with a man. In a standard approach to prosecuting homosexuals, he was charged under a state criminal statute with the crime of sodomy, which means any oral or anal intercourse. The police said that they had gone to his home to arrest him for failing to pay a fine for drinking in public. Although the prosecutor dropped the charges, Hardwick sued to challenge the law's constitutionality. He won in the lower courts.

The conflict between freedom and order lies at the core of the case. "Our legal history and our social traditions have condemned this conduct uniformly for hundreds and hundreds of years," argued Georgia's attorney. Constitutional law, he continued, "must not become an instrument for a change in the social order." Hardwick's attorney, a noted constitutional scholar, said that government must have a more important reason than "majority morality to justify regulation of sexual intimacies in the privacy of the home." He maintained that the case involved two precious freedoms: the right to engage in private sexual relations and the right to be free from government intrusion in one's home.[70]

More than half the states have removed criminal penalties for private homosexual acts between consenting adults. The rest still outlaw homosexual sodomy, and many outlaw heterosexual sodomy as well. As a result, Hardwick's case was closely followed by homosexual rights groups and some civil liberties groups. Fundamentalist Christian groups and defenders of traditional morality expressed deep interest in the outcome, too.

In a bitterly divided ruling in 1986, the Court held in **Bowers v. Hardwick** that the Constitution does not protect homosexual relations between consenting adults, even in the privacy of their own homes.[71] The logic of the privacy cases in the areas of contraception and abortion seemed to compel a right to personal autonomy—to make one's own choices unconstrained by government. But the 5-to-4 majority maintained that only heterosexual choices—whether and whom to marry, whether to conceive a child, whether to have an abortion—fall within the zone of privacy advanced by the Court in its earlier rulings. "The judiciary necessarily takes to itself further authority to govern the country without express constitutional authority" when it expands the list of fundamental rights "not rooted in the language or design of the Constitution," wrote Justice White, the author of the majority opinion.

The march toward increased personal freedom seems to have come to a halt; a new concern for social order—for established patterns of authority—is on the rise. And all the evidence, short of their actual

Out of the Closet and Into the Streets
The quest for constitutional protection of homosexual rights halted with the Supreme Court's 1986 decision upholding state laws against sodomy. Gay and lesbian activists have shifted their efforts from the national level to state and local levels. More than half the states no longer make sodomy between consenting adults of the same sex a crime. The remaining states will follow suit if activists can muster enough support from state legislatures to repeal existing sodomy laws.

participation in cases, suggests that the most recent Reagan appointees strongly support the new balance.

Most likely, the march toward personal autonomy will shift to the states, where groups can continue to assert their political power. The pluralist model, then, gives us one solution to dissatisfaction with Court rulings. If state legislatures can enact laws making certain acts punishable, then they can also repeal those laws. Opponents to the Georgia statute now must mobilize support and force a change that more than half the states have already adopted. However, this kind of solution offers little comfort to Americans who believe the Constitution protects them in their most intimate decisions and actions.

CONSTITUTIONALIZING PUBLIC POLICIES

The issues embedded in *Griswold* and *Roe* are more fundamental and disturbing for democracy than the surface issues of privacy and personal autonomy. By enveloping a policy in the protection of the Constitution, the Court removes that policy from the legislative arena, where the people's will can be expressed through the democratic process. Specific constitutional guarantees pose little threat of usurping the democratic process because there are inherent safeguards in the Constitution. But the abortion controversy demonstrates to many critics that the courts can place under the cloak of the Constitution a host of public policies that were once debated and resolved by the democratic process. By giving a policy constitutional protection (as the Court did with abortion), judges assume responsibilities that have traditionally been left to the elected branches to resolve. If we trust appointed judges to serve as guardians of democracy, then our fears for the democratic process may be illusory. But if we believe that democratic solutions are necessary to resolve these kinds of questions, our fears may be well grounded. The controversy will continue as the Supreme Court strikes a balance between freedom and order. But in holding the balance, the justices must wrestle among themselves and with their critics over whether the Constitution authorizes them to fill the due process clause with fundamental values that cannot easily be traced to constitutional text, history, or structure.

Although the courts may be "the chief guardians of the liberties of the people," they ought not have the last word, argued the great jurist Learned Hand:

> A society so riven that the spirit of moderation is gone, no court can save; . . . a society where that spirit flourishes, no court need save; . . . in a society which evades its responsibilities by thrusting upon the courts the nurture of that spirit, that spirit in the end will perish.[72]

SUMMARY

In establishing a new government, the framers were compelled to assure the states and the people, through the Bill of Rights, that their freedoms would be protected. In their interpretation of these ten amendments, the courts, especially the Supreme Court, have taken on the task of balancing freedom and order.

The First Amendment protects several freedoms: of religion, of speech and press, of peaceable assembly and petition. The establishment clause demands government neutrality toward religions and between the religious and nonreligious. According to judicial interpretations of the free-exercise clause, religious beliefs are inviolate, but antisocial actions in the name of religion are not protected by the Constitution. Extreme interpretations of the religion clauses could bring them into conflict with each other.

Freedom of expression encompasses freedom of speech and of the press, and the right to peaceable assembly and petition. Freedom of speech and freedom of the press have never been held to be absolute, but they have been given far greater protection than other freedoms in the Bill of Rights. Exceptions to free-speech protections include some forms of symbolic expression, fighting words, and obscenity. Press freedom has had broad constitutional protection because a free society depends on the ability to collect and report information without government interference. The rights of peaceable assembly and petition stem from the same freedom protecting speech and press. Each of these freedoms is equally fundamental, but their exercise is not absolute.

The adoption of the Fourteenth Amendment in 1868 extended the guarantees of the Bill of Rights to the states. The due process clause became the vehicle for absorbing or incorporating specific provisions of the Bill of Rights, one at a time, case after case, and applying them to the states. The designation of a right as fundamental also called for a definition of that right. The Supreme Court has tolerated some variation from state to state in the meaning of certain constitutional rights. The Court has also imposed a duty on government to inform citizens of their rights so that they are able to exercise them.

As it fashioned new fundamental rights from the Constitution, the Supreme Court has become embroiled in controversy. The right to privacy served as the basis for the right of women to terminate a pregnancy, which in turn suggested a right to personal autonomy. The abortion controversy is still raging, and the justices have called a halt to the extension of personal privacy in the name of the Constitution.

In the meantime, judicial decisions raise a basic issue. By offering constitutional protection to public policies, the courts may be threatening the democratic process, the process that gives the people a say in government through their elected representatives. One thing is certain, however: The challenge of democracy requires the constant balancing of freedom and order.

Key Terms and Cases

civil liberties
civil rights
establishment clause
free-exercise clause
Lemon v. *Kurtzman*
West Virginia State Board of Education v. *Barnette*
speech clause
press clause
prior restraint
free-expression clauses
clear and present danger test
Gitlow v. *New York*
Brandenburg v. *Ohio*
symbolic expression
Tinker v. *Des Moines Independent County School District*
fighting words

Cohen v. *California*
libel
New York Times v. *Sullivan*
public figures
New York Times v. *United States*
bill of attainder
ex post facto law
obligation of contract
Palko v. *Connecticut*
Gideon v. *Wainwright*
Miranda warnings
exclusionary rule
Mapp v. *Ohio*
United States v. *Leon*
good faith exception
Griswold v. *Connecticut*
Roe v. *Wade*
Hyde Amendment
Bowers v. *Hardwick*

Selected Readings

Baker, Liva. *Miranda: Crime, Law and Politics.* New York: Atheneum, 1983. Baker uses *Miranda* as a vehicle for explaining the American legal system. She traces the case from its origin to its landmark resolution.

Berns, Walter. *The First Amendment and the Future of Democracy.* New York: Basic Books, 1976. Berns contends that the Supreme Court is steadily eroding the conditions of civil liberty.

Brigham, John. *Civil Liberties and American Democracy.* Washington, D.C.: Congressional Quarterly Press, 1984. A survey of U.S. civil rights and liberties organized around basic concepts (privacy, entitlements).

Haiman, Franklyn C. *Speech and Law in a Free Society.* Chicago: University of Chicago Press, 1981. A thorough survey of the meaning of the First Amendment. Haiman argues that no special significance attaches to the seperate speech and press clauses.

Larson, Edward J. *Trial and Error: The American Controversy over Creation and Evolution.* New York: Oxford University Press, 1985. A history of the educational and legal battles arising from the conflict between religious fundamentalism and evolutionary theory. Larson argues that public education in science has never deviated far from popular opinion.

Levy, Leonard W. *The Emergence of a Free Press.* New York: Oxford University Press, 1985. This new work revises Levy's original scholarship, *The Legacy of Suppression,* which caused a stir when it was published. Levy maintained that the generation that adopted the Constitution and the Bill of Rights did not believe in a broad view of freedom of expression, especially in the area of politics. His new position, based both on new evidence and on continued criticism of his original thesis, is that Americans were more tolerant of government criticism but that the revolutionary generation did not intend to wipe out seditious libel with the adoption of the First Amendment.

Levy, Leonard W. *The Establishment Clause: Religion and the First Amendment.* New York: Macmillan, 1986. This searching study of the establishment clause claims that the view that government can assist all religions is historically groundless. Levy argues that it is unconstitutional for government to provide aid to any religion.

Lewis, Anthony. *Gideon's Trumpet.* New York: Random House, 1964. The moving story of Clarence Earl Gideon's claim to assistance of counsel guaranteed by the Sixth Amendment.

Polenberg, Richard. *Fighting Faiths.* New York: Knopf, 1987. By focusing on the famous case of *Abrams* v. *United States,* a noted historian examines anarchism, government surveillance, freedom of speech, and the impact of the Russian Revolution on American liberals.

18

Equality and Civil Rights

Diane Joyce and Paul Johnson worked hard patching holes, shoveling asphalt, and opening culverts for the Santa Clara County Transportation Agency. In 1980, a skilled position as road dispatcher opened up; it meant less strenuous work and higher pay. Joyce and Johnson competed along with ten other applicants for the job. At the time, all of the agency's 238 skilled positions were held by men.

Seven of the applicants—including Joyce and Johnson—passed an oral exam. Next, the agency conducted a round of interviews. Johnson tied for second with a score of 75; Joyce ranked third with a score of 73. After a second round of interviews with the top contenders, the agency gave the job to Johnson.

Joyce didn't let the matter rest. With the help of a county employee, she filed a complaint with the head of the agency, invoking the county government's affirmative action policy. **Affirmative action** is a commitment by an employer, school, or other institution to expand opportunities for women, blacks, Hispanics, and members of other minority groups. Affirmative action embraces a wide range of policies from special recruitment efforts at one end to numerical goals and quotas at the other.

The county was trying to remedy the effects of former practices, intentional or not, that had restricted work opportunities for women, minorities, and handicapped people. Its goal was the representation of these groups in upper-level jobs in proportion to their representation in the area's total work force. The county enacted an affirmative action policy to consider the sex, race, and handicapped status of qualified applicants in employment decisions.

After reviewing its decision in light of the county's policy, the agency took the job away from Johnson and gave it to Joyce. A government-imposed equality policy thwarted Johnson's freedom to climb the ladder of success. Angered by the lost promotion, he sued.

Johnson argued that he was the victim of sex discrimination. **Discrimination** is an act of irrational suspicion or hatred of a specific group of people. The national government has enacted policies to prohibit different kinds of discrimination. Johnson invoked Title VII of the 1964 Civil Rights Act, which bars employment discrimination based on race, religion, national origin, or sex. He won the first round in a federal district court; Joyce appealed and won a reversal. The final round was fought in the Supreme Court in 1987.[1] Joyce emerged the victor.

At issue here were the values of equality and freedom. Laws and policies that promote equality inevitably come into conflict with demands for freedom. To understand the ways government resolves this conflict, we have to understand the development of civil rights in this country.

The history of civil rights in the United States is primarily the story of the search for social and economic equality. This search has gone on for more than a century, and is still going on today. It began with the civil rights of black citizens, whose subjugation roused the passions of a nation and brought about its bloodiest conflict, the Civil War. The struggle of blacks has been a beacon lighting the way for Native Americans, Hispanic-Americans, and women. Each of these groups has confronted discrimination, sometimes subtle, sometimes overt. And each has

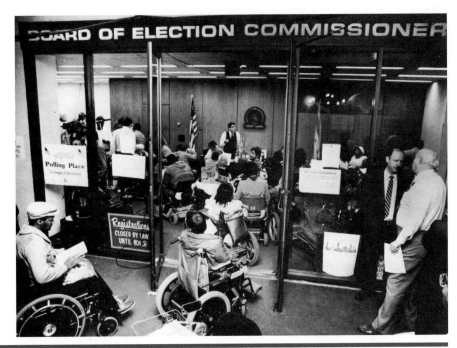

Wheel Rights
Although voting is a fundamental civil right, physical obstacles can deter some Americans from exercising that right. The everyday life of many handicapped Americans contains difficult barriers that other people don't notice, such as revolving doors and flights of stairs. In 1986, some handicapped Chicagoans occupied the offices of the Board of Elections, claiming that 80 percent of the city's precincts were inaccessible to handicapped voters. National law requires that polling places be accessible to the handicapped. The city responded by dispatching mobile voting units.

achieved a measure of success by pressing its interests on government, even challenging government. These challenges and government's responses to them have helped shape our democracy.

Remember that **civil rights** are powers or privileges that are guaranteed to the individual and protected from arbitrary removal at the hands of the government or other individuals. (Rights need not be confined to humans. Some advocates claim that animals have rights too.) In this chapter, we concentrate on the rights guaranteed by the constitutional amendments adopted after the Civil War and by laws passed to enforce those guarantees. Prominent among them is the right to equal protection of the laws. This right remained a promise rather than a reality well into the twentieth century.

THE CIVIL WAR AMENDMENTS

The Civil War amendments were adopted to provide freedom and equality to black Americans. The Thirteenth Amendment, which was ratified in 1865, provided the freedom:

> Neither slavery nor involuntary servitude . . . shall exist within the United States, or any place subject to their jurisdiction.

The Fourteenth Amendment was adopted three years later. It provides first that freed slaves are citizens:

> All persons born or naturalized in the United States, and subject to the jurisdiction thereof, are citizens of the United States and of the State wherein they reside.

Next, as we discussed in Chapter 17, it prohibits the states from abridging the "privileges or immunities of citizens of the United States" or depriving "any person of life, liberty, or property, without due process of law." The amendment then goes on to protect equality under the law, declaring that no state shall

> deny to any person within its jurisdiction the equal protection of the laws.

The Fifteenth Amendment, adopted in 1870, added a measure of political equality:

> The right of citizens of the United States to vote shall not be denied or abridged by the United States or by any State on account of race, color, or previous condition of servitude.

American blacks were free and politically equal—at least according to the Constitution. But it would be many years before these constitutional rights were protected.

Congress and the Supreme Court: Lawmaking versus Interpretation

In the years following the Civil War, Congress went to work to protect the rights of black citizens. In 1866, lawmakers passed a civil rights act that gave the national government some authority over the treatment of blacks by state courts. This was a response to the **black codes,** laws enacted by the former slave states that restricted the freedom of blacks. For example, vagrancy and apprenticeship laws forced blacks to work and denied them a free choice of employers. One section of the 1866 act that still applies today grants all citizens—white and black—the right to make and enforce contracts, sue or be sued, give evidence, and inherit, purchase, lease, sell, hold, or convey property. Later, in the Civil Rights Act of 1875, Congress attempted to guarantee blacks equal access to public accommodations (streetcars, inns, parks, theaters).

While Congress was passing laws to protect the civil rights of black citizens, the Supreme Court seemed intent on weakening those rights. In Chapter 17, we talked about the *Slaughter House Cases* (1873).[2] There the Court ruled that the Civil War amendments had not changed the relationship between the state and national governments. In other words, state citizenship and national citizenship remained separate and distinct; the Fourteenth Amendment did not enlarge the rights guaranteed by U.S. citizenship. In effect, the Court stripped the amendment of its power to secure the Bill of Rights guarantees for black citizens.

In the following years, the Court continued to shrink constitutional protections for blacks. In 1876, in *United States* v. *Cruikshank,* the justices crippled congressional attempts to enforce the rights of blacks.[3] A group of Louisiana whites had used violence and fraud to prevent blacks from exercising their basic constitutional rights, including the right of peaceable assembly. The justices held that the rights allegedly infringed on were not federally protected rights and that therefore Congress was powerless to punish those who violated them. On the very same day, the Court ruled that the Fifteenth Amendment did not guarantee all citizens the right to vote; it simply listed grounds that could not be used to deny that right.[4] And in the *Civil Rights Cases* (1883), the Court struck down the public accommodations section of the Civil Rights Act of 1875.[5] The justices declared that the national government could prohibit only government action (also known as *state action*) discriminating against blacks; private acts of discrimination or acts of omission by a state were beyond the reach of federal power. For example, a state law excluding blacks from jury service was an unlawful abridgment of individual rights. A private person's discrimination excluding blacks from service in a private club was outside the control of the national government because the discrimination was a private—not a government—act. The Court refused to see racial discrimination as a badge of slavery that the national government could prohibit. In case after case, the justices tolerated racial discrimination, in the process abetting **racism**, a belief that human races have distinct characteristics and that one's own race is superior to and has a right to rule others.

The Court's decisions gave the states ample room to maneuver around civil rights laws. In the matter of voting rights, for example, states that wanted to bar black men from the polls simply used nonracial means to do so. One popular tool was the **poll tax,** first imposed by Georgia in 1877. This was a tax of $1 or $2 on every citizen who wanted to vote. The tax was not a burden on most whites. But many blacks were tenant farmers, deeply in debt to white merchants and landowners; they just did not have any extra money for voting. Other bars to black suffrage included literacy tests, minimum education requirements, even a grandfather clause that required proof that the voter had a grandfather who was eligible to vote before 1867 (three years before the Fifteenth Amendment declared that race could not be used to deny the right to vote).[6] Intimidation and violence were also used to keep blacks from the polls.

The Roots of Racial Segregation

Well before the Civil War, **racial segregation** was a way of life in the South: Blacks lived and worked separately from whites. After the war, southern states began to enact Jim Crow laws that *enforced* segregation. (*Jim Crow* is a derogatory term for a black person.) Once the Supreme Court nullified the Civil Rights Act of 1875, these kinds of laws proliferated. Blacks were required to live in separate and generally inferior areas; they were restricted to separate and inferior sections of hospitals, separate cemeteries, separate drinking and toilet facilities, and separate sections of streetcars, trains, schools, jails, and parks. Each day, in countless ways, they were reminded of the inferior status accorded them by white society.

In 1892, Homer Adolph Plessy—who was seven-eighths Caucasian—took a seat in a "whites only" car of a Louisiana train. He refused to move to the car reserved for blacks and was arrested. Plessy argued that Louisiana's law mandating racial segregation on its trains was an unconstitutional infringement on both the privileges and immunities, and the equal protection clauses of the Fourteenth Amendment. The Supreme Court disagreed. The majority in ***Plessy* v. *Ferguson*** (1896) upheld state-imposed racial segregation.[7] They based their decision on the **separate-but-equal doctrine,** that separate facilities for blacks and whites satisfied

Separate and Unequal
The Supreme Court gave constitutional protection to racial separation on the theory that states could provide "separate but equal" facilities for blacks. But racial separation meant unequal facilities, as these two water fountains dramatically illustrate. The Supreme Court struck a fatal blow against the "separate but equal" doctrine in its landmark 1954 ruling, Brown v. Board of Education.

the Fourteenth Amendment so long as they were equal. The lone dissenter was John Marshall Harlan (the first of two distinguished justices with the same name). Harlan, who envisioned a "color-blind Constitution," wrote:

> We boast of the freedom enjoyed by our people above all other peoples. But it is difficult to reconcile that boast with a state of the law which, practically, puts the brand of servitude and degradation upon a large class of our fellow citizens—our equals before the law. The thin disguise of "equal" accommodations for passengers in railroad coaches will not mislead any one, nor atone for the wrong this day done.

Three years later, the Supreme Court extended the separate-but-equal doctrine to the schools.[8] The justices ignored the fact that black educational facilities (and most other "colored only" facilities) were far from equal to those reserved for whites.

By the end of the nineteenth century, racial segregation was firmly and legally entrenched in the American South. Although constitutional amendments and national laws to protect equality under the law were in place, the Supreme Court's interpretation of those amendments and laws limited their effectiveness. Several decades would pass before there was any discernible change.

THE DISMANTLING OF SCHOOL SEGREGATION

Denied the right to vote and be represented in government, blacks sought access to power in other parts of the political system. The National Association for the Advancement of Colored People (NAACP) was at the forefront of the campaign for black civil rights. It was founded in 1909 by W. E. B. Du Bois and others, both black and white, with the goal of ending racial discrimination and segregation. The plan was to launch legal and lobbying attacks on the separate-but-equal doctrine in two parts: first by pressing for fully equal facilities for blacks, then by proving the unconstitutionality of segregation. The process would be a slow one, but the strategies involved did not require a large organization or heavy financial backing . . . and, at the time, the NAACP had neither.*

Pressure for Equality . . .

By the 1920s, the separate-but-equal doctrine was so deeply ingrained in American law that no Supreme Court justice would dissent from its continued application to racial segregation. But a few Court decisions offered hope that change would come. In 1935, Lloyd Gaines graduated from Lincoln University, a black college in Missouri, and applied to the state law school. He was rejected because he was black. Missouri refused to admit blacks to its all-white law school; instead, the state's policy was to pay the costs of blacks who were admitted to out-of-state law schools. With the support of the NAACP, Gaines appealed to the courts for admission to the University of Missouri Law School. In 1938, the Supreme Court ruled that he be admitted.[9] Under the *Plessy* doctrine, Missouri could not shift its responsibility to provide an equal education onto other states.

Two later cases helped reinforce the requirement that segregated facilities must be equal in all major respects. One was brought by Heman Sweatt, again with the help of the NAACP. Sweatt had been denied entrance to the all-white University of Texas Law School because of his race. A federal court ordered the state to provide a black law school for him; the state responded by renting a few rooms in an office building and hiring two black lawyers as teachers. Sweatt refused to attend the school and took his case to the Supreme Court.[10]

George McLaurin had been refused admission to a doctoral program in education at the all-white University of Oklahoma because he was black. There was no equivalent program for blacks in the state. McLaurin sought a federal court order for admission, but under pressure from the decision in *Gaines*, the university amended its procedures and admitted McLaurin "on a segregated basis." The sixty-eight-year-old McLaurin was restricted to hastily designated "colored-only" sections of a few rooms. He appealed this obvious lack of equal facilities to the Supreme Court under the direction of the NAACP.[11]

The Court ruled on *Sweatt* and *McLaurin* in 1950. The justices unanimously found that the facilities in each case were inadequate: The separate "law school" provided for Sweatt did not approach the quality of the white state law school; and the restrictions placed on McLaurin, through his segregation from other students within the same institution, would result in an inferior education. Both Sweatt and McLaurin had to

---

* In 1939, the NAACP established an offshoot, the NAACP Legal Defense and Education Fund, to work on legal challenges, while the main organization concentrated on lobbying as its principal strategy.

be given full student status at their respective state universities. But the Court avoided re-examination of the separate-but-equal doctrine.

. . . And Pressure for Desegregation

These decisions—especially in McLaurin—seemed to indicate that the time was right for an attack on segregation itself. In addition, public attitudes toward race relations were slowly changing from the predominant racism of the nineteenth and early twentieth centuries. Black troops had fought with honor—albeit in segregated military units—in World War II. Blacks and whites were working together in unions and in service and religious organizations. The time was right for an attack on segregation itself.

President Harry S Truman risked his political future with his strong support of black civil rights. In 1947, he established the President's Committee on Civil Rights. The committee's report, issued later that year, became the agenda for the civil rights movement over the next two decades. It called for federal laws prohibiting racially motivated brutality, segregation, and poll taxes, and for guarantees of voting rights and equal employment opportunity. In 1948, Truman ordered the **desegregation** (the end of authorized racial segregation) of the armed forces.

In 1947, the U.S. Department of Justice had begun to submit briefs to the courts in support of civil rights. Perhaps the department's most important intervention was in ***Brown*** v. ***Board of Education.***[12] This case was the culmination of twenty years of planning and litigation on the part of the NAACP to invalidate racial segregation in schools.

Linda Brown was a black child whose father tried to enroll her in a white public school in Topeka, Kansas. The school was close to Linda's home and the walk to the black school required that she cross a dangerous set of railroad tracks. Brown's request was refused because of Linda's race. A federal district court found that the black public school was, in all major respects, equal in quality to the white school; therefore, by the *Plessy* doctrine, Linda was required to go to the black public school. Brown appealed the decision.

Brown v. *Board of Education* reached the Supreme Court in 1952, along with four similar cases brought in Delaware, South Carolina, Virginia, and the District of Columbia. Each case was brought as a class action, a device for combining the claims or defenses of similar individuals so that they can be tried in a single lawsuit (see Chapter 13). And all were supported by the NAACP and coordinated by Thurgood Marshall, who would later become the first black justice of the Supreme Court.

These five cases squarely challenged the separate-but-equal doctrine. By all tangible measures (standards for teacher licensing, teacher-pupil ratios, library facilities), the two school systems in each case—one white, the other black—were equal. The issue was legal separation of the races.

The cases were argued in 1952; but they were set for reargument at the request of the justices. On May 17, 1954, Chief Justice Earl Warren, who had joined the Court less than a year before, delivered a single opinion covering four of the cases. (In Chapter 13, we described how he

Anger Erupts in Little Rock
The school board in Little Rock, Arkansas, attempted to implement court-approved desegregation. The first step called for admitting nine blacks to Central High School on September 3, 1957, but when they appeared for classes, the governor sent in the national guard to bar their attendance. Police escorts could not control the mobs that gathered at the school on September 23, when the black students again attempted entry. Two days later, under the protection of federal troops ordered by President Dwight Eisenhower to enforce the court order, the students were admitted. Hostility and mob violence led the school board to seek a postponement of the desegregation plan, but the Supreme Court, meeting in special session in the summer of 1958, affirmed the Brown *decision and ordered the plan to proceed.*

approached the cases after the reargument.) Warren spoke for a unanimous Court when he declared that "in the field of public education the doctrine of 'separate but equal' has no place. Separate educational facilities are inherently unequal, depriving the plaintiffs of the equal protection of the laws." Segregated facilities generate in black children "a feeling of inferiority . . . that may affect their hearts and minds in a way unlikely ever to be undone." In short, state-imposed public school segregation was found to violate the Fourteenth Amendment's equal protection clause.

A companion case to *Brown* challenged the segregation of public schools in Washington, D.C.[13] Segregation here was imposed by Congress. The equal protection clause protected citizens only against *state* violations; there was no equal protection clause restraining the national government. It was unthinkable for the Constitution to impose a lesser duty on the national government than on the states. In this case, the Court decided that the racial segregation requirement was an arbitrary deprivation of liberty without due process of law, a violation of the Fifth Amendment.

The Court deferred implementation of the school desegregation decisions until 1955. Then, in **Brown v. Board of Education II,** it ruled that school systems must desegregate "with all deliberate speed," and placed the process of desegregation under the direction of the lower federal courts.[14]

Some states quietly implemented the *Brown* decree. Others did little to desegregate their schools. And many communities in the South defied the Court, sometimes violently. Some white business and professional people formed "white citizens councils." These councils used their economic power against blacks who asserted their rights by foreclosing on mortgages and denying blacks credit at local stores. Georgia and North Carolina resisted desegregation by paying the tuition of white students who attended private schools. Virginia and other states, ordered that desegregated schools be closed.

This resistance, along with the Supreme Court's "all deliberate speed" order, placed a heavy burden on federal judges to dismantle what were by now fundamental social institutions in many communities.[15] Gradual desegregation under *Brown* was in some cases no desegregation at all. By 1969, a unanimous Supreme Court ordered that the operation of segregated school systems must stop "at once."[16]

Two years later, the Court approved several remedies to achieve integration, including busing, racial quotas, and the pairing or grouping of noncontiguous school zones. In **Swann v. Charlotte-Mecklenburg County Schools,** the Supreme Court affirmed the right of lower courts to order the busing of children to ensure school desegregation.[17] But these remedies applied only to **de jure segregation,** government-imposed segregation (for example, government assignment of whites to one school and blacks to another within the same community). Court-imposed remedies did not apply to **de facto segregation,** segregation that is not the result of government influence (for example, racial segregation resulting from residential patterns).

The busing of schoolchildren came under heavy attack in both the North and the South. Busing was seen as a possible remedy in many northern cities, where schools had become segregated as white families left the cities for the suburbs. This "white flight" left inner-city schools predominantly black and suburban schools almost all white. Increasingly, busing became the target of legislative politics. Public opinion strongly opposed the busing approach. Congress sought limits on busing as a remedy. In 1974, a closely divided Court ruled in **Milliken v. Bradley** that lower courts could not order busing across school district boundaries to achieve racial balance unless each district had practiced racial discrimination, or unless school district lines had been drawn to achieve racial segregation.[18] This case reversed the trend started by *Brown,* using any and all means to end segregation in the public schools. It meant an end to extensive school desegregation in metropolitan areas. And a growing call for "Freedom now!" signaled black frustration with the idea that equality, for many, still remained just a promise.

THE CIVIL RIGHTS MOVEMENT

Although the NAACP concentrated on school desegregation, it also made headway in other areas. The Supreme Court responded to the NAACP's efforts of the middle to late 1940s by outlawing the whites-only primary elections that were being held in the South and by declaring them to be in violation of the Fifteenth Amendment. The Court also declared segregation on interstate bus routes to be unconstitutional and desegregated restaurants and hotels in the District of Columbia. Despite these and other decisions that chipped away at existing barriers to equality, black citizens were still being denied political power, and segregation remained a fact of daily life (see Feature 18.1).

Dwight D. Eisenhower, who became president in 1953, was not as concerned about civil rights as his predecessor. He chose to stand above the battle between the Supreme Court and those who resisted the Court's decisions. He even refused to reveal whether he agreed with the Court's decision in *Brown* v. *Board of Education*. "It makes no difference," Eisenhower declared, because "the Constitution is as the Supreme Court interprets it."[19]

Eisenhower did enforce school desegregation when the safety of schoolchildren was involved, but he appeared unwilling to do much more to advance racial equality. That goal seemed to require the political mobilization of the people—black and white—into what is now known as the **civil rights movement**.

FEATURE 18.1

American Racism: An International Handicap

In August 1955, the ambassador from India, G. L. Mehta, walked into a restaurant at the Houston International Airport, sat down and waited to order. But Texas law required that whites and blacks be served in separate dining facilities. The dark-skinned diplomat, who had seated himself in a whites-only area, was told to move. The insult stung deeply and was not soon forgotten. From Washington, Secretary of State John Foster Dulles telegraphed his apologies for this blatant display of racism, fearing that the incident would injure relations with a nation whose allegiance the United States was seeking in the Cold War.

Such embarrassments were not uncommon in the 1950s. Burma's minister of education was denied a meal in a Columbus, Ohio, restaurant; and the finance minister of Ghana was turned away from a Howard Johnson's restaurant just outside the nation's capital. Secretary Dulles complained that segregationist practices were becoming a "major inter-

national hazard," a threat to U.S. efforts to gain the friendship of Third World countries. Americans stood publicly condemned as a people who did not honor the ideal of equality.

Thus when the attorney general appealed to the Supreme Court to strike down segregation in public schools, his introductory remarks took note of the international implications. "It is in the context of the present world struggle between freedom and tyranny that the problem of racial discrimination must be viewed," he warned. The humiliation of dark-skinned diplomats in Washington D.C., "the window through which the world looks into our house," was damaging to American interests. Racism "furnished grist for the Communist propaganda mills."

Source: Mary Beth Norton et al., *A People and a Nation: A History of the United States*, vol.2, 2d ed. (Boston: Houghton Mifflin, 1986), p. 867.

Civil Disobedience

The call to action was first sounded by Rosa Parks, a black woman living in Montgomery, Alabama. In December 1955, Parks boarded a city bus on her way home from work. The city's Jim Crow ordinances required blacks to sit in the back of the bus and, when asked, to give up their seats to whites. Tired after the day's work, Parks took an available seat in the front of the bus; she refused to give up her seat when asked to do so by the driver and was arrested and fined $10 for violating the city ordinance.

Montgomery's black community responded to Parks's arrest with a boycott of the city's bus system. A **boycott** is a refusal to do business with a firm or individual, as an expression of disapproval or as a means of coercion. Blacks walked or car-pooled or simply did not make trips that were not absolutely necessary. As the bus company moved closer to bankruptcy and downtown merchants suffered from the loss of black business, city officials began to harass blacks, hoping to frighten them into ending the boycott. But Montgomery's black citizens now had a leader—a charismatic twenty-seven-year-old Baptist minister named Martin Luther King, Jr.

King urged the people to hold out, and they did. A year after the boycott began, the federal courts ruled that segregated transportation systems violated the equal protection clause of the Constitution (see Feature 13.1, page 481). The boycott proved to be an effective weapon.

In 1957, King helped organize the Southern Christian Leadership Council (SCLC) to coordinate civil rights activities. He was totally committed to nonviolent action to bring racial issues into the light. To that end, he advocated **civil disobedience,** the willful but nonviolent violation of unjust laws.

One nonviolent tactic was the *sit-in*. On February 1, 1960, four black students from North Carolina Agricultural and Technical College in Greensboro sat down at a white lunch counter. They were refused service and, when they would not leave, were abused verbally and physically. Still, they would not move. Finally, they were arrested. Soon there were similar sit-in demonstrations throughout the South, and then in the North. The Supreme Court upheld the actions of the demonstrators, but the unanimity that had characterized the earlier decisions of the Court was gone (see Feature 18.2).

The Civil Rights Act of 1964

In 1961, a new administration came to power headed by President John F. Kennedy. At first, Kennedy did not seem to be committed to civil rights. This changed as the movement gained momentum, as more and more whites became aware of the abuse being heaped on sit-in demonstrators, freedom riders (who tested unlawful segregation on interstate bus routes), and those who were trying to help blacks register to vote in southern states. Volunteers were being jailed, beaten, and killed for advocating activities that whites took for granted.

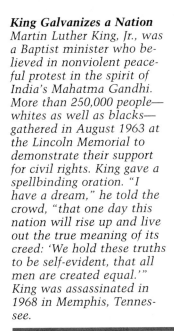

King Galvanizes a Nation
Martin Luther King, Jr., was a Baptist minister who believed in nonviolent peaceful protest in the spirit of India's Mahatma Gandhi. More than 250,000 people—whites as well as blacks—gathered in August 1963 at the Lincoln Memorial to demonstrate their support for civil rights. King gave a spellbinding oration. "I have a dream," he told the crowd, "that one day this nation will rise up and live out the true meaning of its creed: 'We hold these truths to be self-evident, that all men are created equal.'" King was assassinated in 1968 in Memphis, Tennessee.

In the fall of 1962, President Kennedy ordered federal troops to ensure the safety of James Meredith, the first black to attend the University of Mississippi. In early 1963, he enforced the desegregation of the University of Alabama. In April 1963, television viewers were shocked to see marchers in Birmingham, Alabama, attacked with dogs, fire hoses, and cattle prods. (The idea of the march was to provoke confrontations with white officials in an effort to compel the federal government to intervene on behalf of blacks.) Finally, in June 1963, Kennedy asked Congress for legislation that would outlaw segregation in public accommodations.

Two months later, Martin Luther King, Jr., organized and led a march on Washington, D.C., to show support for the civil rights movement. More than 250,000 people, black and white, gathered peaceably at the Lincoln Memorial to hear King speak. "I have a dream," he told them, "that my little children will one day live in a nation where they will not be judged by the color of their skin but by the content of their character."[20]

Kennedy's public accommodations bill had not yet been passed by Congress when he was assassinated, on November 22, 1963. His succes-

FEATURE 18.2

A Right to Discriminate?

The Supreme Court led by Chief Justice Earl Warren did more to vindicate civil rights than any other government institution. But it came perilously close to depriving the civil rights movement of a powerful weapon: the sit-in. The justices were divided over the vital issues of freedom and equality.

The Court confronted four sit-in cases in 1964. In each case, blacks sat down in restaurants or at lunch counters and refused to leave without being served. In the principal case, *Bell* v. *Maryland*, the sit-in took place in Baltimore. The demonstrators were arrested, then convicted for violating state trespass laws.

At the conference to decide the merits of the case, the chief justice urged his colleagues to "get to the 'raw' of the problem." His position was that the convictions violated the equal protection clause of the Fourteenth Amendment. Said Warren: "As long as the demonstrators behave themselves, the owner can't have police to help to throw them out. The state then unconstitutionally enforces discrimination."

The justices were deeply divided. Warren gathered only three votes in addition to his own. The majority sided with Justice Hugo L. Black, who delivered an emotional statement in which he recalled his "Pappy," who ran a general store in Alabama: Surely, he had the right to decide whom he would serve or would not serve. Black had been in the vanguard of Fourteenth Amendment protections in the relatively easy cases like *Brown* v. *Board of* *Education*. But when the conflict pitted freedom (even freedom to discriminate) against equality, the majority chose freedom.

The division brought several exchanges of opinions, some brimming with emotion. Justice William J. Brennan, Jr., expressed his fear that affirmation of the sit-in convictions might cripple the Civil Rights Act. Title II, barring discrimination in places of public accommodation, was then the subject of a Senate filibuster. Brennan counseled delay until the legislative outcome was clear, urging the justices to put off dealing with the constitutional question before them. Instead, he argued that the sit-in convictions should be overturned on the basis of a Baltimore public accommodations law enacted after the demonstrators were convicted. The convictions were still pending when the city law was adopted. This had the effect, argued Brennan, of nullifying the trespass violations.

Ultimately, Brennan's view prevailed, and his majority opinion was announced shortly before passage of the Civil Rights Act of 1964. Had Black's opinion prevailed, the history of American civil rights might have been different. That opinion could have weakened, if not defeated, the nation's most comprehensive effort to erase racial discrimination from American life.

Source: Bernard Schwartz, *The Unpublished Opinions of the Warren Court* (New York: Oxford University Press, 1985), pp. 143–190.

sor, Lyndon B. Johnson, considered civil rights his top legislative priority. Within months, Congress passed the Civil Rights Act of 1964. It contained several parts, including a vital provision barring segregation in most public accommodations. Quick passage of the act was, in part, a reaction to Kennedy's death. But it was also almost surely a reaction to the brutal treatment of blacks throughout the South.

Civil rights laws had been passed by Congress in 1957 and 1960, but they dealt primarily with voting rights. The 1964 act was the most comprehensive legislative effort ever to erase racial discrimination in the United States. It was enacted after the longest debate in Senate history, and only after the first successful use of cloture to end a civil rights filibuster.

The bill had to avoid the grip of Southern conservatives in the House and the Senate. Because it was grounded in both Section 5 of the Fourteenth Amendment (which gives Congress the power to enforce that amendment) and the commerce clause of Article I, the bill was sent to two committees in each chamber. The House Judiciary Committee and the Senate Commerce Committee were chaired by supporters of the bill, so it was certain to be brought to the floor of each chamber for a vote.

Among its many provisions, the act

- entitled all persons to "the full and equal enjoyment" of goods, services, and privileges in places of public accommodation without discrimination on the ground of race, color, religion, or national origin.
- established the right to equality in employment opportunities.
- strengthened voting rights legislation.
- created the Equal Employment Opportunity Commission (EEOC), charging it to hear and investigate complaints of job discrimination. *
- provided that funds could be withheld from federally assisted programs that were administered in a discriminatory manner.

The last of these provisions had a powerful impact on school desegregation when Congress passed the Elementary and Secondary Education Act in 1965. That act provided for billions of federal dollars in aid for the nation's schools; the threat of losing those funds spurred local school boards to formulate and implement new plans for desegregation.

The 1964 act faced an immediate constitutional challenge. Its opponents argued that the Constitution does not forbid acts of private discrimination. But a unanimous Supreme Court upheld the law in *Heart of Atlanta Motel* v. *United States* (1964), declaring that acts of discrimination impose substantial burdens on interstate commerce and thus are subject to congressional control.[21] In a companion case, *Katzenbach* v. *McClung* (1964), the owners of a small restaurant had refused to serve blacks.[22] Ollie McClung maintained that he had the freedom to serve who he wanted to serve in his own restaurant. The justices, however, upheld the government's prohibition of McClung's racial discrimination on the ground that a substantial portion of the food served in his restaurant had moved in interstate commerce. The Civil Rights Act of 1964 was vindicated by reason of the congressional power to regulate interstate commerce, rather than on the basis of the Fourteenth Amendment.

Johnson's goal was a "Great Society." Soon a constitutional amendment and a series of civil rights laws were in place to help him meet their goal.

- The Twenty-fourth Amendment, ratified in 1964, banned poll taxes in primary and general elections for national office.
- The Economic Opportunity Act of 1964 focused on education and training to combat poverty.
- The Voting Rights Act of 1965 empowered the attorney general to send voter registration supervisors to areas in which fewer than half the eligible minority voters had been registered. This act has been

---

* Since 1972, the EEOC has had the power to institute legal proceedings on behalf of employees who allege that they have been victims of illegal discrimination.

credited with doubling black voter registration in the South in only five years.

■ The Fair Housing Act of 1968 banned discrimination in the rental or sale of most housing.

From Restriction to Restoration

Civil rights on the books do not ensure civil rights in action. What happens when an institution continues to practice illegal discrimination? This was the case in 1984, when the Supreme Court was called on to interpret a law that forbids sex discrimination in schools and colleges receiving financial assistance from the federal government.

In *Grove City College* v. *Bell*, the Court ruled that only the specific department or program receiving federal funds, not the whole institution, was barred from discriminating.[23] Athletic departments rarely receive federal funds; so colleges were released from the obligation to provide equal opportunity for women in their sports programs.

The decision in *Grove City* had widespread effects. Three other important civil rights laws were worded similarly. The implication was that laws barring discrimination on the basis of race, sex, age, and handicapped status would be confined to *programs* that discriminate, not to *institutions* that discriminate. So a university laboratory that received federal research grants could not discriminate; but other departments that did not receive federal money could. The effect of *Grove City* was to frustrate enforcement of civil rights laws.

Congress reacted immediately, exercising its lawmaking power to check the law-interpreting power of the judiciary. Legislators bellowed that the Court had misinterpreted the intent of the antidiscrimination laws, and forged a bipartisan effort to make that intent crystal clear: If any part of an institution gets federal money, no part can discriminate. Their work developed into the Civil Rights Restoration Act, which became law in 1988 despite a presidential veto.

While Congress was restoring civil rights enforcement in 1988, the Supreme Court seemed to be on the verge of dismantling it again. In a decision that took everyone by surprise, the justices voted to reconsider a twelve-year-old precedent, *Runyon* v. *McCrary*, which held that the Civil Rights Act of 1866 forbids all racial discrimination in the making and enforcement of contracts. Normally, an unwilling party cannot be forced to enter a contract whatever the reasons for refusing.

The *Runyon* decision greatly expanded the rights of racial minority groups to sue private parties for discrimination if they refuse to enter contracts on racial grounds. The Court acknowledged that private individuals and clubs can discriminate on the basis of race, but federal law forbids the enforcement of private contracts that discriminate.

The Court's decision to reconsider *Runyon* leaves the initial ruling open to reversal. (The justices will decide in 1989.) A reversal would allow private schools to practice racial discrimination and would enable those schools to enforce that discrimination in court. A reversal also would substantially reduce the potency of legal remedies for racial bias in employment, too.

Racial Violence and Black Nationalism

The middle and late 1960s were marked by increased violence on the part of those who demanded their civil rights and those who refused to relinquish them. Violence against civil rights workers was confined primarily to the South, where volunteers continued to work for desegregation and to register black voters. Among the atrocities that incensed even complacent whites were the bombings of dozens of black churches; the murder of three young civil rights workers in Philadelphia, Mississippi, in 1964 by a group of whites, among them deputy sheriffs; police violence against a group of demonstrators who had started out on a peaceful march from Selma, Alabama, to Montgomery in 1965; and the assassination of Martin Luther King, Jr., in Memphis in 1968.

Black violence took the form of rioting in the black ghettos of northern cities. Civil rights gains had mainly been focused on the South. Northern blacks had the vote and were not subject to Jim Crow laws. Yet most lived in poverty. Unemployment was high, work opportunities at skilled jobs were limited, and earnings were low. The segregation of blacks in inner-city ghettos, although not sanctioned by law, was nevertheless real; their voting power was of little moment because they constituted a small minority of the northern population. The solid gains made by southern blacks added to their frustration. Beginning in 1964, northern blacks took to the streets, burning and looting. Riots in 168 cities and towns followed King's assassination in 1968.

The lack of progress toward equality for northern blacks was an important factor in the rise of a black nationalist movement in the 1960s. The Black Muslims, led by Malcolm X until his assassination in 1965, called for separation from whites rather than integration, and for violence in return for violence. The Black Panthers denounced the values of white America. In 1966, Stokely Carmichael, then chairman of the Student Nonviolent Coordinating Committee (SNCC), called on blacks to assert "black power" in their struggle for civil rights. Organizations that previously had espoused integration and nonviolence now began to argue that blacks needed power more than they needed the friendship of whites.

The movement had several positive effects. Black nationalism promoted and instilled pride in black history and culture. By the end of the decade, colleges and universities were beginning to institute black studies programs for their students. More black citizens were voting than ever before, and their voting power was evident: Increasing numbers of blacks were being elected to public office. In 1967, Cleveland's voters elected Carl Stokes the first black mayor of a major American city. And by 1969, black representatives were able to form the Congressional Black Caucus. These achievements were incentives for other groups who also faced barriers to equality.

CIVIL RIGHTS FOR OTHER MINORITIES

The civil rights won by black Americans apply to all Americans. Recent civil rights laws and court decisions protect members of all minority groups.

Righting a Wrong
In World War II, Congress authorized the quarantine of Japanese residents in the western United States. More than 110,000 men, women, and children—including native-born U.S. citizens who were loyal Americans—were incarcerated and dispossessed simply because they were of Japanese heritage. Laws prejudicial to racial and other minorities are ordinarily forbidden, yet the Supreme Court upheld the law in 1944. This episode was the only occasion on which the Court gave constitutional protection to an explicit legislative act of racial inequality. In 1988, Congress passed legislation offering apologies and $20,000 tax-free to each remaining internment survivor. The cost to the government: $1.25 billion.

The Supreme Court underscored the breadth of this protection in an important decision in 1987.[24] The justices ruled unanimously that a post-Civil War law offered broad protection against discrimination to all minorities. Heretofore, the law could not be invoked by members of white ethnic groups in bias suits. Under the decision, members of *any* ethnic group—Italian, Iranian, Chinese, Norwegian, or Vietnamese, for example—can recover money damages if they prove they have been denied jobs, excluded from rental housing, or subjected to other forms of discrimination prohibited by the law. The 1964 Civil Rights Act offers similar protections to these ethnic groups, but the 1964 act has strict procedures for filing suits. These procedures tend to discourage litigation. Moreover, the remedies in most cases are limited. In job discrimination, for example, back pay and reinstatement are the only remedies. The post-Civil War statute, on which the 1987 Court ruling was based, has fewer pitfalls and allows litigants to seek *punitive damages* (damages awarded by a court as additional punishment for a serious wrong). In some respects, then, the older law is a more potent weapon than the newer one in fighting discrimination.

Clearly the civil rights movement has had an impact on all minorities. In the United States, however, equality has been granted most slowly to nonwhite minorities. Here we examine the civil rights struggles of two minorities—Native Americans and Hispanic-Americans.

Native Americans

During the eighteenth and nineteenth centuries, the U.S. government took Indian lands, isolated Native Americans on reservations, and denied them political and social rights. The government's dealings with the Indians were often marked with violence and riddled with broken promises. The agency system for administering Indian reservations kept Native Americans poor and dependent on the national government.

It was not until 1924 that Indians were given U.S. citizenship. Until that time, they were considered members of tribal nations whose relations with government were subject to treaties made with the United States. The Native American population suffered badly during the Depression, primarily because the poorest people were affected most, but also because of the inept administration of Indian reservations. Poverty remained on the reservations well after the Depression was over, and Indian lands continued to shrink through the 1950s and into the 1960s— in spite of signed treaties and the religious significance of portions of those lands. In the 1960s, for example, a part of the Hopi Sacred Circle, which is considered the source of all life in tribal religion, was strip-mined for coal.

Anger bred of poverty, unemployment, and frustration with an uncaring government exploded into militant action in November 1969, when several American Indians seized Alcatraz Island, an abandoned island in San Francisco Bay. The group cited an 1868 Sioux treaty that entitled them to unused federal lands; they remained on the island for a year and a half. In 1973, armed members of the American Indian Movement seized eleven hostages at Wounded Knee, South Dakota—the site

Big Trouble on Big Mountain
The national government's effort to develop the mineral-rich deserts in the Southwest has aggravated conflict between the Navajo and Hopi who live in the area of Arizona known as Big Mountain. Many Navajo were forced to leave the Hopi land they lived on, wrenched from their traditional ways. The family pictured here is typical of the Navajo families in the area; they raise livestock and practice subsistence farming. The relocation cost the government $50,000 for each of the ten thousand Navajos it moved.

of an 1890 massacre of the Sioux by U.S. cavalry troops. They remained there, occasionally exchanging gunfire with federal marshals, for seventy-one days.

In 1946, Congress had passed legislation establishing an Indian claims commission to compensate Native Americans for land that had been taken from them. In the 1970s, the Native American Rights Fund and other groups used that legislation to win important victories. Lands were returned to tribes in the Midwest and in the states of Oklahoma, New Mexico, and Washington. In 1980, the Supreme Court ordered the national government to pay the Sioux $117 million plus interest for the Black Hills of South Dakota, which had been stolen from them a century before. Other cases, involving land from coast to coast, are still pending.

Throughout American history, Native Americans have been coerced physically and pressured economically to assimilate into the mainstream of white society. The destiny of Native Americans as viable groups with separate identities depends in no small measure on curbing their dependence on the national government.[25]

Hispanic-Americans

Many Hispanic-Americans have a rich and deep-rooted heritage in America, but until the 1920s, that heritage was largely confined to the southwestern states and California. Then, large numbers of Mexican and Puerto Rican immigrants came to the United States in search of employment and a better life. They were welcomed by businesspeople who saw in them a source of cheap labor. Many of the Mexicans became farm workers, but both groups settled mainly in crowded, low-rent inner-city districts: the Mexicans in the Southwest; the Puerto Ricans, primarily in New York City. Both groups formed their own *barrios*, or communities, within the cities, where they maintained the customs and values of their homelands.

Like blacks who had migrated to northern cities, most of the new Hispanic immigrants found poverty and discrimination. And, again like poor blacks and Native Americans, they were hit hard by the Depression. About one-third of the Mexican-American population (mainly those who had been migratory farm workers) returned to Mexico during the 1930s.

World War II gave rise to another influx of Mexicans, who this time were courted to work farms primarily in California. But by the late 1950s, most farm workers—blacks, whites, and Hispanics—were living in poverty. Those Hispanic-Americans who lived in cities were faring little better. Yet millions of Mexicans continued to cross the border into the United States, both legally and illegally. The effect was to depress the value of farm labor in California and the Southwest.

In 1965, Cesar Chavez led a strike of the United Farm Workers Union against growers in California (see Chapter 9). The strike lasted several years but eventually, in combination with a boycott, resulted in somewhat better pay, working conditions, and housing for workers.

In the 1970s and 1980s, the Hispanic-American population continued to grow. The 20 million Hispanics living in the United States in the 1970s were mainly Puerto Rican and Mexican-American, but they had been joined by immigrants from the Dominican Republic, Colombia, Cuba, and Ecuador. Although recent civil rights legislation helped them to an extent, they were among the poorest and least educated groups in the United States. Their problems were like those faced by other non-whites; but, in addition, most had to overcome the further difficulty of learning and using a new language.

Voter registration and voter turnout among Hispanics is lower than among other groups. Language is an impediment here. With few or no Spanish-speaking voting officials, low registration levels may be inevitable. Voter turnout depends on effective political advertising, and Hispanics are not targeted as often as other groups with political messages that they can understand. Despite these stumbling blocks, however, Hispanics have started to exercise a measure of political power. Hispanic-Americans have been elected mayors in San Antonio, Denver, and Miami. They have also gained some access to political power through their representation in coalitions that dominate policymaking on minority-related issues.[26]

Some Hispanic leaders believe that the problems of low voter registration and turnout will not be solved until Hispanics exercise greater political clout—"brown power." Although many of America's Hispanics speak the same language, they came here from different countries, from different backgrounds. They need strong leadership to pull them together. "We need a Spanish Bobby Kennedy or Martin Luther King," observed one leader. "Right now he's just not here."[27]

GENDER AND EQUAL RIGHTS: THE WOMEN'S MOVEMENT

The ballot box and the lawsuit have brought minorities in America a measure of equality. The Supreme Court—once an institution for perpetuating inequality for blacks—has expanded the array of legal weapons in the hands of all minorities to achieve social equality. Women, too, have benefited from this change.

Protectionism

Until the early 1970s, laws that affected the civil rights of women were based on traditional views of the relationship between men and women. At the heart of these laws was **protectionism**—the idea that women must be sheltered from life's cruelties. Thomas Jefferson, author of the Declaration of Independence, believed that "were our state a pure democracy there would still be excluded from our deliberations women, who, to prevent deprivation of morals and ambiguity of issues, should not mix promiscuously in gatherings of men."[28] And protected they were, through laws that discriminated against them in employment and other areas. With few exceptions, women were also "protected" from voting until early in the twentieth century.

The demand for women's rights arose out of the abolitionist movement and later was based primarily on the Fourteenth Amendment's prohibition of laws that "abridge the privileges or immunities of citizens of the United States." However, the courts consistently rebuffed challenges of state protectionist laws. In 1873, the Supreme Court upheld an Illinois statute that prohibited women from practicing law. The justices maintained that the Fourteenth Amendment did not affect a state's authority to regulate admission of members to the bar.[29] In a concurring opinion, Justice Joseph P. Bradley articulated the common protectionist belief that women were unfit for certain occupations: "Man is, or should be, woman's protector and defender. The natural and proper timidity and delicacy which belongs to the female sex evidently unfits it for many of the occupations of civil life."

Protectionism reached a peak in 1908, when the Court upheld an Oregon law limiting the number of hours that women were allowed to work.[30] The decision was rife with sexist assumptions about the nature and role of women, and it gave wide latitude to laws that protected the "weaker sex." It also led to protectionist legislation that barred women from working more than forty-eight hours a week and from jobs that required workers to lift more than 35 pounds. In effect, women were locked out of jobs that called for substantial overtime (and overtime pay); instead, they were shunted to jobs that men believed suited their abilities.

Political Equality for Women

With a few exceptions, women were not allowed to vote in this country until 1920.* In 1869, Francis and Virginia Minor sued a St. Louis, Missouri, registrar for not allowing Virginia Minor to vote. In its decision in *Minor* v. *Happersett* (1875), the Supreme Court held that the Fourteenth Amendment privileges and immunities clause did not confer the right to vote on all citizens or require that the states allow women to vote.[31]

The decision in *Minor* clearly slowed the movement toward women's suffrage, but it did not stop it. In 1878, Susan B. Anthony, a women's rights activist, convinced a U.S. senator from California to introduce a constitutional amendment requiring that "the right of citizens of the United States to vote shall not be denied or abridged by the United States or by any State on account of sex." The amendment was introduced and voted down a number of times over the next twenty years. However, a number of states—primarily in the Midwest and West—did grant limited suffrage to women.

The movement for women's suffrage now became a political battle to amend the Constitution. In 1917, 218 women from twenty-six states were arrested when they picketed the White House demanding the right to vote. Nearly 100 went to jail—some for days, others for months. Hunger strikes and forced feedings followed. The movement culminated in the adoption in 1920 of the **Nineteenth Amendment,** which gave women the right to vote in the wording first suggested by Anthony.

---

* The Fifteenth Amendment (as interpreted by the Supreme Court), which was passed in 1870, prohibited the use of race in denying a person the right to vote. It said nothing about gender.

Meanwhile, the Supreme Court continued to act as the benevolent protector of women. Women had entered the work force in significant numbers during World War I, and they did so again during World War II; but they received lower wages than the men they replaced. Again the justification was the "proper" role of women as mothers and homemakers. Because men were expected to be the principal providers, it followed that women's earnings were less important to the family's support. This thinking perpetuated inequalities in the workplace. Because women were expected to stay at home, they needed—and obtained—less education than men. And because they lacked education, they tended to qualify only for low-paying low-skill jobs with little chance of advancement. Economic equality was closely tied to social attitudes.

Prohibiting Sex-Based Discrimination

The movement to provide equal rights to women advanced a step with the passage of the Equal Pay Act of 1963. That act requires equal pay for men and women doing similar work. However, state protectionist laws still had the effect of restricting women to jobs that were not usually taken by men. Where employment was stratified by sex, equal pay was an empty promise. To free them from the restrictions of protectionism, women needed equal opportunity for employment. They got it in the Civil Rights Act of 1964 and later legislation.

The objective of the Civil Rights Act of 1964 was to eliminate racial discrimination in America. In its proposed form, Title VII of the act prohibited employment discrimination based on race, color, religion, and national origin—but not gender. In an effort to scuttle this provision during House debate, Democrat Howard W. Smith of Virginia proposed an amendment barring job discrimination based on sex. Smith's intention was to make the law unacceptable; his effort to ridicule the law brought gales of laughter to the debate. But Democrat Martha W. Griffiths of Michigan used Smith's strategy against him. With her support, Smith's amendment carried, as did the act.[32] The jurisdiction of the Equal Employment Opportunity Commission was extended to cover cases of sex discrimination, or **sexism.**

Subsequent women's rights legislation was motivated by the pressure for civil rights, as well as a resurgence of the women's movement, which had subsided after the adoption of the Nineteenth Amendment. One particularly important law was Title IX of the Education Amendments Act of 1972, which prohibited sex discrimination in federally aided education programs. Another boost to women came from the Revenue Act of 1972, which provided tax credits for child care expenses. In effect, the act subsidized parents with young children so that women could enter or remain in the work force. However, the high-water mark in the effort on behalf of women's rights was the Equal Rights Amendment, which we discuss shortly.

Stereotypes Under Scrutiny

After nearly a century of broad deference to protectionism, the Supreme Court began to take a closer look at gender-based distinctions. In

1971, it struck down a state law that gave men preference over women in administering the estate of a person who died without naming an administrator.[33] The state maintained that the law reduced court workloads and avoided family battles; however, the Court dismissed those objectives because they were not important enough to sustain the use of gender distinctions. Two years later, the justices declared that the paternalism of earlier ages operated to "put women not on a pedestal, but in a cage."[34] They then proceeded to strike down several gender-based laws that either prevented or discouraged departures from "proper" sex roles. In *Craig* v. *Borden* (1976), the Court finally developed a workable standard for reviewing these kinds of laws: Gender-based distinctions are justified only if they serve some important government purpose.[35]

The objective here is to dismantle sexual stereotypes while fashioning public policies that acknowledge relevant differences between men and women. Perhaps the most controversial issue in the 1980s is the idea of "comparable worth," which would require employers to pay comparable wages for different jobs that are of about the same worth to an employer, even if one job might be filled predominantly by women and another mainly by men. The goal is a job standard that takes into account both the legal equality of men and women and their relevant physiological differences.[36]

The Equal Rights Amendment

Women have not enjoyed the same rights as men. Policies protecting women, based largely on sexual stereotypes, have been woven into the legal fabric of American life. That protectionism limited the freedom of women to compete with men socially and economically on an equal footing. The Supreme Court has been hesitant to extend the principles of the Fourteenth Amendment beyond issues of race. If constitutional interpretation imposes such a limit, then it can be overcome only by a constitutional amendment.

The **Equal Rights Amendment (ERA)** was first introduced in 1923 by the National Women's party, one of the few women's groups that did not disband after the Nineteenth Amendment was passed. The ERA declared that "equality of rights under the law shall not be denied or abridged by the United States or any State on account of sex." It remained bottled up in committee in every Congress until 1970, when Representative Martha Griffiths filed a discharge petition to report it to the House floor for a vote. The House passed the ERA, but the Senate scuttled it by attaching a section calling for prayer in the public schools.

A national coalition of women's rights advocates generated enough support to get the ERA through the proposal stage in 1972. Its proponents now had seven years in which to get the amendment ratified by thirty-eight state legislatures, as required by the Constitution. By 1977, they were three states short of that goal, and three states had rescinded earlier ratification. For some reason, the national coalition that had worked so effectively to move through the proposal stage seemed to lack the political strength to jump the ratification hurdle. Then, in an unprecedented action, Congress extended the ratification deadline. It didn't help. The ERA died on July 1, 1982, still three states short of adoption.

The End of an Era
The death knell for a national Equal Rights Amendment (ERA) pealed on July 1, 1982, three votes short of ratification. Despite its failure, the ERA movement produced real benefits, which include the increased participation of women in politics. Proponents of an equal rights amendment continue to press their cause, but its adoption as part of the Constitution is still a long way from reality.

I MOURN FOR MY DAUGHTERS WHO HAVE NO ERA

Why did the ERA fail? The amendment quickly acquired opposition, including many women who had supported women's rights legislation. By 1973, ERA opponents had begun a strong campaign to fight ratification. As the opposition grew stronger, especially from women who wanted to maintain their traditional role, state legislators began to realize that there were risks involved in supporting the amendment. It takes an extraordinary majority to amend the Constitution, which is equivalent to saying that it takes only a committed minority to thwart the majority's will (see Compared With What? 18.1).

Despite its failure, the movement to ratify the ERA produced real benefits. It raised the consciousness of women about their social position; it spurred the formation of the National Organization of Women (NOW) and other large organizations; it contributed to women's participation in politics; and it influenced major legislation affecting women.[37]

The failure to ratify the ERA stands in stark contrast to the quick passage of many laws that now protect women's rights. But in fact there was little audible opposition to women's rights legislation. If years of racial discrimination called for government redress, then so did years of gender-based discrimination. Furthermore, laws protecting women's rights required only the amending of civil rights bills or the passage of similar bills.

In constitutional terms, the effects of an equal rights amendment are unclear. It would certainly raise gender to the same status as race in

COMPARED WITH WHAT? 18.1

Barriers for Women Fall

Feminist activism has had an impact on American perceptions of gender distinctions in politics. In 1974, more than one-third of the public agreed with the statement "Women should take care of running their homes and leave running the country up to men." That attitude has changed; by 1982, just about one-fourth of the public agreed with the same statement.

How do attitudes in America compare with public attitudes in other countries? This kind of comparison is not an easy one because it is difficult to find an exact match to the question posed to the American public. But one survey question asked in 1983 of people in four European countries comes very close: "It is sometimes said that 'politics should be left to men.' How far would you agree or disagree?* The results of that survey appear in the table at the right.

To the extent that the questions posed are comparable, American attitudes about women in politics fall roughly between those in the United Kingdom (with the lowest approval) and those in West Germany (with the highest approval). In fact, Americans come closest to Italians in their attitudes toward women—at least in politics.

Country	Percent Agreeing That "Politics Should Be Left to Men"
United Kingdom	18
France	22
Italy	25
West Germany	40

* *Euro-Barometer 19: Gender Roles in the European Community*, April 1983.

evaluating the validity of government policies. The courts have ruled that policies based on race are valid only when they are essential to achieve a compelling goal. Presumably, under an equal rights amendment, government policies based on gender classifications would be valid only when they are essential to achieve a compelling goal. Today, for example, many government policies concerning the armed services make gender distinctions. The validity of these policies would be open to question with the passage of an equal rights amendment.

For practical purposes, argue some scholars, the Supreme Court has implemented the ERA through its decisions. It has struck down distinctions based on sex and held that stereotyped generalizations of sexual differences must fall.[38] In recent rulings, the Court has held that states may require employers to guarantee job reinstatement to women returning from maternity leave and that sexual harassment in the workplace is illegal.

But Court decisions can be reversed and statutes can be repealed. Without an equal rights amendment, argue some feminists, the Constitution will continue to bear the sexist imprint of a document written by men, for men. At the moment, said veteran feminist Betty Friedan, "We are at the mercy of a Supreme Court that will interpret equality as it sees fit.[39]

AFFIRMATIVE ACTION: EQUAL OPPORTUNITY OR EQUAL OUTCOME?

In his vision of the Great Society, President Johnson linked economic rights with civil rights, and equality of outcome with equality of opportunity. "Equal opportunity is essential, but not enough," he declared. "We seek not just legal equity but human ability, not just equality as a right and a theory but equality as a fact and equality as a result." This commitment led to programs that were meant to overcome the effects of past discrimination, to affirmative action programs to expand opportunities for women, minorities, and the handicapped (see Feature 18.3).

Affirmative action programs run the gamut, from recruitment of to preferential treatment and quotas for women, minorities, and the handicapped in job training and professional education, employment, and the placement of government contracts. The goal of these programs is to move beyond equality of opportunity to equality of outcome—very much as busing was used to ensure the desegregation of schools. Numerical goals (a specific number of places in a law school reserved for minority

FEATURE 18.3

Helping the Handicapped

Many of you may remember the story "The Little Engine That Could." With hard work and determination, the little engine carried the freight over the mountain. Here is the story "The Little Statute That Could." With the hard work and determination of organized groups, the little statute has transformed the rights of the handicapped.

It started almost unnoticed, with a few well-intentioned words. But now, an obscure little paragraph in a 1973 law has been blown up, twisted and turned into a potent legal weapon for a lot of unexpected, unintended—and costly—purposes.

The sentence, known as Section 504 of the Rehabilitation Act of 1973, says simply, "No otherwise qualified handicapped individual in the United States . . . shall, solely by reason of his handicap, be excluded from participation in, be denied the benefits of, or be subject to discrimination under any program or activity receiving federal financial assistance."

The Supreme Court ruled in 1987 that because of Section 504, a Florida school board could not simply fire a teacher who had active tuberculosis. The Court will rule shortly in another case in which two Army veterans claim that, as recovered alcoholics, they are handicapped and entitled to extra time to use veterans' educational benefits.

The Reagan administration used Section 504 as legal authority to try to require all-out medical efforts to save infants born with severe and potentially fatal birth defects. And, inevitably, the Supreme Court will be asked to hear a case involving AIDS victims claiming that Section 504 gives them special legal protections.

Section 504 had a humble beginning. It was slipped into the Rehabilitation Act by Sen. Hubert Humphrey and Rep. Charles Vanik after most of the committee work had been completed. No hearings were held on the provision. No one in Congress paid attention to it. It seemed like a little pro forma civil rights gesture and nothing more.

Soon after the passage of the Act, organizations representing the disabled realized that Section 504 could be used to demand barrier-free public transportation. They began filing lawsuits charging that inaccessible transit systems were illegal. Section 504 has been used by hundreds of other groups demanding that billions of tax dollars be spent to upgrade schools, day-care centers, libraries, colleges and hospitals to help the handicapped.

Lawsuits now pending are attempting to stretch the definition of "handicapped" to embrace a variety of conditions, all in the name of civil rights.

The Little Statute has accomplished far more than its drafters contemplated. Such is the character of American politics.

Source: Joan Beck, "Obscure Bit of Law Creates Legal Snarl for 'Handicapped,'" *Chicago Tribune*, 12 March 1987, p. 23. © Copyrighted 1987, Chicago Tribune Company, all rights reserved, used with permission.

candidates, a government contract that specifies that 10 percent of the work must be subcontracted to minority-owned firms) are the most aggressive forms of affirmative action, and they generate the most hostility within the majority.

Reverse Discrimination

The Supreme Court confronted an affirmative action quota program for the first time in ***Regents of the University of California* v. *Bakke*** (1978).[40] Allan Bakke, a thirty-five-year-old white man, had twice applied for admission to the University of California Medical School at Davis. He was rejected both times. The school had reserved sixteen places in each entering class of one hundred for "qualified" minorities, as part of the university's affirmative action program. Bakke's qualifications (college grade point average and test scores) exceeded those of any of the minority students admitted in the two years Bakke's applications were rejected. Bakke contended, first in the California courts, then in the Supreme Court, that he was excluded from admission solely on the basis of race. He argued that this reverse discrimination was prohibited by the Fourteenth Amendment's equal protection clause and by the Civil Rights Act of 1964.

The Court's decision in *Bakke* contained six opinions and spanned 154 pages. But even after careful analysis of the decision, it was difficult to discern what the Court had decided: There was no majority opinion. Four of the justices contended that any racial quota system supported by

Rights Affirmed; Dreams Fulfilled
Allan Bakke, a thirty-eight-year-old engineer, was rejected twice by the Medical School of the University of California at Davis, despite his having scored well above most candidates admitted under a special minority admissions program. Bakke filed a lawsuit, which eventually forced the Supreme Court to examine the constitutionality of affirmative action programs. Bakke won his admission in 1978. In a complicated opinion, however, the justices upheld the use of race as a permissible criterion in admissions programs, among others. Bakke was awarded his degree in 1982.

government violated the Civil Rights Act of 1964. Justice Lewis F. Powell, Jr., agreed, casting the deciding vote ordering the medical school to admit Bakke. However, in his opinion, Powell argued that the rigid use of racial quotas as employed at the school violated the equal protection clause of the Fourteenth Amendment. The remaining four justices held that the use of race as a criterion in admissions decisions in higher education was constitutionally permissible. Powell joined that opinion as well, contending that the use of race was permissible as one of several admission criteria. So, the Court managed to minimize white opposition to the goal of equality (by finding for Bakke) while extending gains for racial minorities through affirmative action.

Other cases followed. Through collective bargaining, the United Steelworkers of America and the Kaiser Aluminum and Chemical Corporation introduced a voluntary plan for affirmative action in 1974. The plan gave blacks preference for admission to training programs. Brian Weber, a white applicant, was rejected from a training program despite the fact that he had more seniority than any of the minority applicants. Weber charged that he was the victim of reverse discrimination, citing the Civil Rights Act of 1964. In a 5-to-2 decision, the Supreme Court upheld the voluntary affirmative action plan.[41] A year later, in 1980, the Court upheld, by a vote of 6 to 3, a federal law that set aside 10 percent of public works funds for minority businesses.[42] Then, in 1984, the Court confronted a difficult choice between traditional values in employment and efforts to eradicate the effects of discrimination.

The city of Memphis, Tennessee, had agreed to an affirmative action order to increase the proportion of minority employees in its fire department. Later, the city was forced to lay off workers. Traditional work rules specify that the last employees hired are the first fired. The question arose as to whether affirmative action exempted the minority firefighters (who were the last ones hired) from the seniority rule. In a 6-to-2 decision, the Court held that layoffs must proceed by seniority, unless minority employees can demonstrate that they are actual victims of discrimination.[43] This meant that the minority firefighters targeted for layoffs would have to prove that they would have been employed if not for the city's discriminatory actions. Because this kind of proof is difficult, perhaps impossible, to establish in most cases, the decision upheld layoffs based on seniority.

Victims of Discrimination

The Memphis decision raised a troublesome question: Do all affirmative action programs, not just layoffs, apply solely to actual victims of past discrimination? The Supreme Court delivered a partial answer in May 1986, when it struck down a school board layoff plan giving preference to members of minority groups. The decision in ***Wygant v. Jackson Board of Education*** was a complicated one, with five separate opinions.[44] The suit was brought by white teachers who had been laid off by the school board. The board layoff plan favored black teachers in an effort to redress general social discrimination and to maintain sufficient role models for black students. But the Supreme Court ruled that these objectives were insufficient to force certain individuals to shoulder the severe impact of layoffs. Hiring goals impose a diffuse burden on society, argued Justice Powell for the Court. But layoffs of innocent whites, he continued, "impose the entire burden of achieving racial equality on particular individuals."

Remedies for general racial discrimination had to avoid harming innocent whites. Could remedies for repeated and outrageous forms of specific discrimination confer benefits on individuals who were not themselves the victims of that discrimination? The local chapter of a construction union in New York City practiced egregious racial discrimination for more than seventy-five years, barring most blacks and Hispanics at every turn. The list of ruses to block the entry of nonwhites seemed endless. The local required special examinations and a high school diploma for entrance; neither had any bearing on job performance. Union funds were used to provide special tutoring for members' friends and relatives who were taking the entrance exams. The local refused to keep records on the racial composition of its membership, in an attempt to avoid charges of discrimination.

In 1975, a federal court concluded that the local had violated Title VII of the Civil Rights Act of 1964, which bars employment discrimination on account of race, color, religion, sex, or national origin. After years of dragging its feet, the court required the local to accept equal numbers of white and nonwhite apprentices to achieve a 29 percent nonwhite membership goal, based on the percentage of nonwhites in the New York City labor pool. The decision was justified, said the court, by the local's long, persistent pattern of discrimination. But the union failed to institute employment programs that would boost minority membership; and it continued to erect new barriers as quickly as the courts struck them down.

The union took its case to the Supreme Court. It argued that the membership goal ordered by the lower courts was unlawful because it extended race-conscious preferences to individuals who were not identified victims of the local's admittedly unlawful discrimination. In ***Local 28 v. EEOC,*** the Court voted 6 to 3 in support of affirmative action that would benefit individuals who were not the actual victims of discrimination.[45] The majority held that the courts may order unions to use quotas to overcome a history of egregious discrimination, and that black and Hispanic applicants can benefit from affirmative action even if they themselves were not the victims of earlier bias.

Must affirmative action policies be limited to concerns over racial inequality? All the cases we've been discussing here addressed affirmative action to correct racial inequalities. But what about the conflict between Diane Joyce and Paul Johnson that we described at the beginning of this chapter? Johnson took his case all the way to the Supreme Court. He argued that he was the victim of sex discrimination under Title VII of the Civil Rights Act of 1964, the provision that employers cannot "limit, segregate or classify" workers so as to deprive "any individual of employment opportunities."

The justices decided ***Johnson v. Transportation Agency, Santa Clara County*** in 1987. They ruled, 6 to 3, that if women and minorities are underrepresented in the workplace, employers can act to remedy the imbalance. The decision was significant for at least two reasons. First,

Joyce Dispatches Johnson
Diane Joyce gained a promotion from laborer to road dispatcher by invoking a government affirmative action policy. Paul Johnson, who had been given the dispatcher job initially, sued; he claimed he was the victim of sex discrimination, which the Civil Rights Act of 1964 forbids. Johnson lost his case in the Supreme Court in 1987.

employers with affirmative action plans do not have to admit to a history of past discrimination. And second, employees who are passed over for promotions are nearly powerless to sue for reverse discrimination. The upshot of the decision is to encourage the adoption of affirmative action programs.

In a scathing dissent, Justice Antonin Scalia focused on two familiar themes: values in conflict and models of democracy. Scalia declared that the majority converted "a guarantee that race or sex will *not* be the basis for employment determination, to a guarantee that it often *will*." The Court, continued Scalia, replaced the goal of a society free from discrimination with the incompatible goal of proportionate representation by race and by sex in the workplace. In simpler terms, equality trumped freedom.

Scalia then offered his observations about pluralism. The Court's decision would be pleasing to elected officials, he said, because it "provides the means of quickly accommodating the demands of organized groups to achieve concrete, numerical improvement in the economic status of particular constituencies." "The only losers in the process," he concluded, are the Paul Johnsons of the country, "predominantly unknown, unaffluent, unorganized—[who] suffer this injustice at the hands of a Court fond of thinking itself the champion of the politically impotent."

The conflict between Paul Johnson and Diane Joyce is over, but the conflict between freedom and equality continues as other individuals and groups press their demands through litigation and legislation. Americans want equality, but they disagree on the extent to which government should provide it.[46] In part, this ambivalence stems from confusion over equal opportunities and equal outcomes.

Two Conceptions of Equality

Most Americans support **equality of opportunity.** This is the idea that people should have an equal chance to develop their talents, and that effort and ability should be rewarded. This form of equality offers all individuals the same chance to get ahead; it glorifies personal achievement through free competition and allows everyone to climb the ladder of success starting at the first rung. Special recruitment efforts aimed at identifying qualified minority or female job applicants ensure that everyone has the same chance starting out. The competition for the promotion between Joyce and Johnson illustrates equality of opportunity.

Americans are less committed to **equality of outcome,** which means greater uniformity in social, economic, and political power. Equality of outcome can occur only if we restrict the free competition that forms the basis of equality of opportunity. One restriction comes by way of a limit on personal achievement. Preferential treatment in hiring is an apt example. That treatment prevented Johnson from climbing the ladder of success.

Quota policies generate the most opposition because they deny any competition whatsoever. Quotas limit advancement for some individuals and ensure advancement for others. They alter positions on the ladder of success. Policies that benefit minorities and women at the expense of innocent white men create strong opposition because they bring individual initiative into conflict with equal outcomes. In other words, freedom clashes with equality.

SUMMARY

The Civil War amendments—the Thirteenth, Fourteenth, and Fifteenth Amendments—were adopted to provide full civil rights to black Americans. Yet, in the late nineteenth century, the Supreme Court interpreted the amendments very narrowly, declaring that they did not restrain individuals from denying civil rights to blacks and that they did not apply to powers that were reserved to the states. The Court's rulings had the effect of denying the vote to most blacks and of institutionalizing racial segregation, making racism a facet of daily life.

Through a series of court cases spanning two decades, segregation in the schools was slowly dismantled. The battle for desegregation culminated in the *Brown* cases in 1954 and 1955, in which a now-supportive Supreme Court declared segregated schools to be inherently unequal and therefore unconstitutional. The Court also ordered the desegregation of all schools and upheld the use of busing to do so.

Gains in other civil rights areas came more slowly. The motivating force here was the civil rights movement, which was led by Martin Luther King, Jr., until his death in 1968. King believed strongly in civil

disobedience and nonviolence, strategies that helped secure for blacks equality in voting rights, public accommodations, higher education, housing, and employment opportunity.

Civil rights activism and the civil rights movement worked to the benefit of all minority groups, in fact, of all Americans. Native Americans obtained some redress for past injustices. Hispanic-Americans came to recognize the importance of group action to achieve economic and political equality. And civil rights legislation removed the protectionism that was, in effect, legalized discrimination against women in education and employment.

Despite legislative advances in the area of women's rights, the Equal Rights Amendment was not ratified. Still, the struggle for ratification produced several positive results, heightening the awareness of the role of women and mobilizing the political power of women through group activity. And legislation and judicial rulings implemented much of the amendment in practice, if not fact.

Affirmative action programs were instituted to counteract the results of past discrimination. They provide preferential treatment for women, minorities, and the handicapped in a number of areas that affect economic opportunity and well-being. In effect, they advocate discrimination to remedy earlier discrimination, with the support of the Supreme Court.

Americans want equality, but they disagree on the extent to which government should provide it. At the heart of this conflict is the distinction between equal opportunities and equal outcomes. Equality of opportunity is the idea that people should have an equal chance to develop their talents, and that effort and ability should be rewarded. This form of equality offers all individuals the same chance to get ahead. And it has the support of most Americans. Equality of outcome means greater uniformity in social, economic, and political power. We can guarantee equal outcomes only if we restrict the free competition that is an integral part of equal opportunity. And this is an idea that many Americans object to. They strongly oppose quotas and policies that restrict individual freedom, that arbitrarily change positions on the ladder of success. The challenge of pluralist democracy is to balance these conflicting values.

Key Terms and Cases

affirmative action	civil rights movement
discrimination	boycott
civil rights	civil disobedience
black codes	protectionism
racism	Nineteenth Amendment
poll tax	sexism
racial segregation	Equal Rights
Plessy v. *Ferguson*	Amendment (ERA)
separate-but-equal	*Regents of the*
doctrine	*University of*
desegregation	*California* v. *Bakke*
Brown v. *Board of*	*Wygant* v. *Jackson*
Education	*Board of Education*
Brown v. *Board of*	*Local 28* v. *EEOC*
Education II	*Johnson* v.
Swann v. *Charlotte-*	*Transportation*
Mecklenburg County	*Agency, Santa Clara*
Schools	*County*
de jure segregation	equality of opportunity
de facto segregation	equality of outcome
Milliken v. *Bradley*	

Selected Readings

Baer, Judith A. *Equality Under the Constitution: Reclaiming the Fourteenth Amendment.* Ithaca, N.Y.: Cornell University Press, 1983. Explores the early American concept of equality and re-examines the debates surrounding the adoption of the Fourteenth Amendment. The author points to new areas of struggle in the application of the equality principle to children, the aged, the disabled, and homosexuals.

Bass, Jack. *Unlikely Heroes.* New York: Simon & Schuster, 1981. Chronicles the efforts of four federal appellate judges in the Deep South to enforce the desegregation mandate in *Brown.*

Browning, Rufus P., Dale Rogers Marshall, and David H. Tabb. *Protest Is Not Enough.* Berkeley, Calif.: University of California Press, 1984. A recent study of black and Hispanic political activities and their translation into representative voices in the policymaking of ten cities in California.

Deloria, Vine, Jr., and Clifford M. Lytle. *The Nations Within.* New York: Pantheon, 1984. A thorough discussion of Native American policies from the Roosevelt "New Deal" to the present; examines the drive for Indian self-determination and self-government.

Garrow, David. J. *Bearing the Cross: Martin Luther King, Jr., and the Southern Christian Leadership Conference.* New York: Morrow, 1986. This Pulitzer Prize-winning study of the civil rights revolution explores the public and private aspects of King's life.

Kessler-Harris, Alice. *Out to Work: A History of Wage-Earning Women in the United States.* New York: Oxford University Press, 1982. An informative analysis of the forces motivating women to work and the effect of work on family roles.

Kluger, Richard. *Simple Justice.* New York: Knopf, 1975. A monumentally detailed history of the desegregation cases; examines the legal, political, and sociological events culminating in *Brown* v. *Board of Education.*

Mansbridge, Jane J. *Why We Lost the ERA.* Chicago: University of Chicago Press, 1986. A valuable and accessible case study of organizations pitted for and against the Equal Rights Amendment in Illinois.

Prucha, Francis Paul. *The Great Father: The United States Government and the American Indians.* 2 vols. Lincoln, Neb.: University of Nebraska Press, 1984. A monumental, definitive history of federal policy toward native Americans from the beginning of the Republic to 1980.

Verba, Sidney, and Gary R. Orren. *Equality in America: The View from the Top.* Cambridge, Mass.: Harvard University Press, 1985. Two political scientists isolate different meanings of equality, then analyze the opinions of American leaders on the application of equality of opportunity and equality of outcome across a range of policy areas.

Williams, Juan. *Eyes on the Prize: America's Civil Rights Years, 1954–1965.* New York: Viking, 1987. A lucid account of black Americans' struggle for social and political equality, containing vivid portraits of courageous blacks and the violence they had to endure in their fight for desegregation and the right to vote in the South.

19

Foreign and Defense Policy

Fawn Hall prided herself on being a good secretary and a good citizen. One day in November 1986, her boss at the National Security Council (NSC), Lieutenant Colonel Oliver North, asked her to help him alter some official memos. She felt uneasy about the request, but helped anyway. After all, she thought of Colonel North as a patriotic American who had the best interests of the country at heart. She assumed he must have a good reason for what he was doing. Later that day, she helped him destroy other documents— lots of them. By her estimate, the stack of material she shredded reached 1½ feet, so much paper that the shredding machine broke down under the load.

A few days later, Hall and the rest of the nation knew the reason behind this flurry of activity. On November 25, Attorney General Edwin Meese revealed that the United States had sold arms to Iran, then used the proceeds to supply the anticommunist Contras in Nicaragua. Many of the documents destroyed or altered by North and Hall concerned details of this operation, which took place during a period in which the president had branded Iran a terrorist nation and Congress had prohibited aid to the Contras. (See Feature 19.1 for a chronology of U.S. involvement in Nicaragua.)

Colonel North, a principal architect of the Iran-Contra operation, emerged at the center of a breaking scandal involving U.S. foreign policy. He was removed from his job at the NSC and reassigned to duty with the Marine Corps. But Hall's faith in her boss did not waver. After the news broke, while the NSC staff was securing North's office, she helped him remove more documents by concealing them in her clothing. Months later, when she appeared before a joint congressional committee investigating the matter, Hall justified her actions, claiming that "sometimes you have to go above the written law." Former NSC adviser and key Iran-Contra player John Poindexter made a similar argument when he testified before the same committee. Both Hall and Poindexter believed that the laws of the land could somehow undermine the nation's foreign policy goals. They believed that foreign policy is different from domestic policy, that it should not be subject to the same rules.

Is there a difference between foreign policy and other forms of public policy? Like domestic policy, foreign policy consists of the means by which government pursues certain goals within specific situations. And, as they do with domestic policy, people disagree over foreign policy because they disagree on the goals government should have, the means it should use to meet them, and the nature of the situation it faces (see Chapter 16). Yet the tension Hall and Poindexter felt between the methods of democratic government and the requirements of foreign policy is not new. Alexis de Tocqueville had described this conflict back in 1837:

> Foreign politics demand scarcely any of those qualities which are peculiar to a democracy; they require, on the contrary, the perfect use of almost all those in which it is deficient. . . . A democracy can only with great difficulty regulate the details of an important undertaking, persevere in a fixed design, and work out its execution in spite of severe obstacles. It cannot combine its measures with secrecy or await their consequences with patience.[1]

FEATURE 19.1

From the Canal to the Contras: A Brief Chronology of U.S. Involvement in Nicaragua in the Twentieth Century

1909 The United States sponsors a revolution against Nicaraguan leader José Zelaya over rights to the construction of a canal across the Isthmus of Panama. U.S. troops intervene and are not withdrawn until 1925.

1926 U.S. troops are reintroduced in Nicaragua and remain there until 1933. They fight sporadically with guerrilla forces led by Augusto Sandino.

1934 Sandino is assassinated by national guardsmen under the command of Anastasio Somoza.

1936 Somoza becomes president of Nicaragua. His family rules the country dictatorially for the next forty-three years.

1978 Strikes and terrorist attacks mount in opposition to the Somoza government. President Carter calls on the Somozas to negotiate with the opposition.

1979 The United States suspends all aid to Nicaragua. Guerilla forces take Managua (the capital), and the Somozas flee the country. The FSLN (Sandinista National Liberation Front) gains control. President Carter renews U.S. aid to Nicaragua and asks Congress for an additional $75 million for the war-ravaged nation. This aid is delayed as conservatives complain that the United States had abandoned a long-time friend and is now supporting a Marxist regime. Meanwhile, in Nicaragua, the new rulers condemn the United States for its long-time support of Somoza.

1981 The Reagan administration charges that the Sandinistas are attempting to establish a Marxist state and are supporting leftist guerrillas in neighboring El Salvador. Reagan suspends Carter's program of economic aid and begins to back the Contras against the Sandinistas. He authorizes the CIA to recruit Nicaraguan exiles to harass the government and block arms shipments to El Salvador.

1982 Limited covert action blossoms into full-scale war. When U.S. support for the Contras becomes public knowledge, Congress passes the first of several Boland Amendments. This particular amendment prohibits the CIA from attempting to overthrow the Nicaraguan regime.

1983 The House votes twice to cut off aid to the Contras. Finally, however, Congress authorizes assistance of no more than $24 million, roughly half the amount the administration is looking for.

1984 The Senate Intelligence Committee reveals that the CIA had supervised the mining of Nicaraguan harbors without notifying Congress. President Reagan and the Contra leaders insist their objective was to pressure the Sandinistas to hold elections. Congress votes to halt all aid to the Contras by the CIA, the Pentagon, or other intelligence agencies. In November, elections are held.

1985 In the absence of funds from the U.S. government, the Contras rely on support from private American sources and from other governments. Later, the public learns that U.S. officials played key roles in providing these funds. In August, Congress authorizes $27 million in nonmilitary "humanitarian" aid to the Contras.

1986 October, Congress agrees to appropriate $100 million in aid to the Contras. A month later, the details of the Iran-Contra affair begin to emerge. Despite a presidential arms embargo and a campaign to convince other countries not to sell arms to terrorist nations, the NSC had arranged to transfer missiles and antiaircraft weapons to Iran. In exchange, it received money and the release of three American citizens who had been taken hostage in Lebanon. (During the same period, at least three more U.S. citizens were abducted and held in Lebanon.) Profits from the arms sales had been funneled to the Contras, despite the Boland Amendments.

As Tocqueville predicted, at times the workings of foreign policy have seriously challenged democratic government. Can a democracy achieve its goals in the world arena without compromising the integrity of its domestic political process? Can a democracy pursue freedom and order abroad without undermining these values at home?

Freedom Fighters?
American involvement in Nicaraguan affairs is not new; it began near the turn of the century. Throughout his administration, Ronald Reagan referred to the Nicaraguan rebels (the Contras) fighting against the Marxist Sandinista government as "freedom fighters," comparing them to colonists fighting in the American Revolution. Here, young Contra troops in the Nicaraguan hills show their enthusiasm for battle.

In this chapter, we focus on the nature of the foreign policymaking process, and the tension between that process and democratic government. We look at America's view of the world situation, and at its foreign policy goals and the means that are available to reach those goals. And we examine the way in which responsibility for foreign policy is divided between the branches of government and the effect that division has on the foreign policymaking process.

AMERICA'S WORLD-VIEW: TWO POLICY PARADIGMS

In the two decades following World War II, it made sense to talk about an American foreign policy consensus. There was widespread agreement among policymakers concerning the international situation. Today, there is no single answer to the question "How does America view the world situation?" Since the Vietnam War, Americans have come to see the world from two very different perspectives: the Munich paradigm and the Vietnam paradigm.*

The Munich Paradigm

The first perspective, sometimes called the **Munich paradigm**, reflects the influence of the events that led to World War II. At Munich,

---

* A *paradigm* is a distinctive pattern or model.

Germany, in 1938, British Prime Minister Neville Chamberlain made concessions to Adolph Hitler, concessions he believed would ensure peace "in our time." He was wrong. The Germans were set on a course of territorial expansion. Within months of the Munich settlement, Europe was engulfed in war.

To those Americans whose perspective on world politics has been shaped by the lessons of Munich, Soviet expansionism has replaced German expansionism as the central threat to world peace. The split between East and West has become the most important division in world politics. These people believe that all communists are fundamentally the same and that the hand of the Soviet Union is behind communist activity everywhere in the world. They argue that the primary goal of U.S. foreign policy must be to promote order by containing communist expansion. To this end, America must maintain a strong military force.

From the perspective of the Munich paradigm, the Vietnam War was fought in a "noble cause": to overcome communist aggression. America and its South Vietnamese allies could have won in Vietnam if this country had had the will to prevail and had allowed the military to do the job it was trained to do.

The Vietnam Paradigm

The second view, the **Vietnam paradigm,** takes as its point of departure the Vietnam War, not World War II. Its adherents believe that American involvement in Vietnam was the product of a tragic failure—the failure to realize that all left-wing revolutionary movements are not necessarily directed by Moscow but may instead be the product of internal forces. Although the Kremlin is always willing to exploit unrest, it cannot create it out of nothing. Revolutions in Third World countries are more likely to spring from poverty and nationalism than the involvement of the Soviet Union. Here, the division between rich nations and poor nations is much more important than the division between East and West.

This emphasis changes the methods used to "win the hearts and minds" of people in other countries. It rejects military solutions, the role of the United States as "world policeman." Instead, it suggests new tools: diplomacy rather than military force, **détente** (the relaxation of tensions between East and West), disarmament and arms control, and development aid to overcome the inequalities that breed disorder and that allow communist movements to thrive.

When the Vietnam War ended, political scientists suggested that a new foreign policy consensus might form around the Vietnam paradigm.[2] Some expected this world-view would eventually dominate, as those clinging to the Munich paradigm either converted or died. Today, the idea that the Vietnam experience might serve as the core of this kind of consensus seems doubtful. For one thing, it is not at all clear that members of the Vietnam generation share a single world-view.[3] For another, the liberalism that marked the Vietnam era is competing with a new conservatism, which values order more than freedom and equality.

The 1980s have brought crises in the Middle East, South Africa, and Central and South America. What is at stake for the United States in these areas? What are the root causes of turmoil? How should the United States deal with these problems? To answer these kinds of questions, citizens and policymakers draw on their political orientation and values as well as their past experience. And because these things are complex and multidimensional, it is unwise to expect easy agreement on America's role in the world. Perhaps the pluralism that characterizes American domestic politics should be expected to carry over into foreign politics as well. The essential agreement that existed during the period between World War II and Vietnam may have been an exception rather than the rule.

U.S. VALUES AND INTERESTS: THE HISTORICAL CONTEXT

When we ask "What is at stake for the United States in Central America, South Africa, the Middle East, or anywhere else?" we are asking how events there affect America's national interests. The primary goal of American foreign policy is to preserve our national security. The difficult part of foreign policymaking is interpreting just what *national security* means and deciding exactly what is necessary to preserve it. Does protecting our national security mean we must stop the spread of communism at all costs, everywhere in the world?

From Isolationism to Globalism

Americans have not always thought of their national security in global terms. Throughout most of the nineteenth century, the limits of national security were those staked out by the Monroe Doctrine of 1823. The United States rejected European efforts to intervene in the Western Hemisphere and agreed not to involve itself in European politics. **Isolationism** protected Americans from Old World entanglements.

As the nineteenth century wore on, however, the United States did become increasingly involved in the affairs of non-European nations. For example, the nation expanded its power in the Pacific, acquiring the Hawaiian Islands and the Philippines. And U.S. foreign policy toward Latin America showed strong interventionist tendencies. But America's defense establishments and foreign commitments were still small.

World War I marked the United States' first serious foray into European politics. In 1917, the rhetoric of our entry into that war—"to make the world safe for democracy"—underscored the moralistic and idealistic tone of America's approach to international politics at that time. At the Versailles Peace Conference in 1919, President Woodrow Wilson championed the League of Nations as a tool for preventing future wars. When the Senate refused to ratify the Treaty of Versailles, blocking America's entry into the league, the brief moment of internationalism ended. For the next two decades, the United States maintained its fa-

The Same in Any Language
These three World War I posters (from Germany, Italy, and the United States) were used to persuade men to join the army. They all employed the same psychological technique of pointing at passers-by to make each individual personally feel the appeal. With no war to threaten or inspire us, today's appeals to sign up play on different themes and employ different devices.

miliar isolationist posture, except for one intervention in Latin America—in Nicaragua (see Feature 19.1).

In 1939, America's security interests continued to be narrowly defined, and the military establishment needed to defend those interests remained very small. At the outbreak of World War II (September 1939), the United States had no draft or compulsory military service; there were 334,473 men in the armed forces (see Figure 19.1), and defense expenditures amounted to about $1.3 billion, roughly 1.5 percent of the gross national product (GNP) at that time.[4] No American troops were garrisoned abroad, and the country was not party to any military alliance. The oceans were America's first line of defense.

But World War II brought a dramatic change in America's orientation toward the world. In 1949, four years after the war ended, 1,615,360 people were on active duty with the U.S. military and approximately 5.5 percent of the GNP was being spent on the armed forces.[5] That same year, the United States concluded the first of many peacetime alliances: the North Atlantic Treaty, which created the North Atlantic Treaty Organization (NATO). Under the terms of the treaty, America permanently committed itself to the defense of Western Europe. Western Europe, not the Atlantic Ocean, became America's first line of defense to the east. To reinforce its commitment, American troops stayed on in

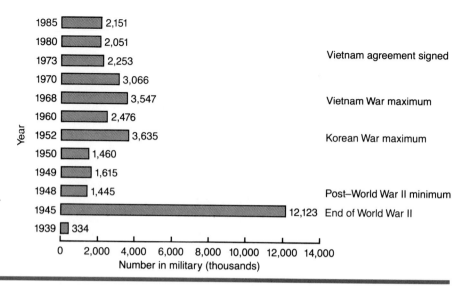

U.S. Military on Active Duty in Selected Years, 1939–1985
As America assumed an active role in world affairs, there was a corresponding buildup in its armed forces. (Source: Statistical Abstract of the United States, annual.)
Figure 19.1

Europe, and the draft was continued to provide the necessary manpower. In addition, the U.S. attitude toward international organizations changed after World War II. Americans accepted the idea that these institutions provided the basis for world order. America was the driving force behind the United Nations (UN) and supported the establishment of the World Court. American isolationism seemed to have vanished, replaced by a new **globalism.** The United States had become a superpower, and its national security interests were now global in scope.

Containment and Korea

Superpower status carried a price: a new emphasis on defense spending. Not only would Americans have to spend more money on defense during peacetime, but they would also have to give defense spending a higher priority than domestic spending. The foreign policy consensus being forged at the end of the 1940s was clearly internationalist, with a strong militarist flavor. The Soviet Union, America's wartime ally, was now the principal threat to order. The Soviets dominated Eastern Europe and their ideology was spreading. America feared the growth of Soviet power. European conflicts had drawn the United States into war twice in twenty-five years; the Soviets, left unchecked, might well do it again.

In this view (heavily shaped by the recent experience with Hitler's Germany), the Soviets wanted world domination and were bent on extending the communist system into "every nook and cranny" of the globe. To frustrate the Kremlin's plans, Americans would have to be prepared to cut budgets for nondefense spending, even if this meant important domestic programs had to be put off.[6] For the first time ever in peacetime, Americans were called on to give priority to defense spending over domestic spending, to guns over butter. America was not in an actual shooting war, or "hot war," with the Soviets, but the adversarial nature of U.S.-Soviet relations was clear. A new term was coined to describe the situation: **Cold War.**

The Cold War would require commitment and sacrifice. The American course of action was "long-term, patient but firm and vigilant containment."[7] **Containment** meant holding Soviet power in check. A return to isolationism was impossible, as President Harry Truman had proclaimed in a 1947 speech justifying aid to Greece and Turkey, because "totalitarian regimes imposed upon free peoples, by direct or indirect aggression, undermine the foundations of international peace and hence the security of the United States."[8]

Truman's foreign policy had two dimensions: One was military preparedness; the other was an economic program that would thwart Soviet expansion. Secretary of State George Marshall recognized that war-weakened European nations offered a good target for Soviet expansion. He proposed a European recovery plan, commonly known as the **Marshall Plan,** to make Europe economically viable again. Over four years, this foreign aid program sent approximately $12 billion to European countries.

While a clear American policy toward Europe was taking shape, new crises emerged in Asia. Mao Ze-dong (Mao Tse-tung) succeeded in installing a communist regime in China. Because Americans thought of international politics as a **zero-sum game**—a situation in which one superpower's loss was the other's gain—America's "loss" of China to

Polishing the Coneheads
War often stimulates social change. During World War II, more than 6 million women entered the labor force, many doing jobs—such as making tailgunner cones for bombers—that had previously been done by men.

Mao and communism was interpreted as a victory for the Soviets. Some American policymakers favored a more conciliatory position toward the Chinese and suggested that all communism might not be Soviet communism. But their voices were drowned out when, on June 25, 1950, communist North Korea invaded noncommunist South Korea. The United States used the United Nations to intervene in the conflict to push the North Koreans out. The bulk of the UN force sent to Korea consisted of Americans.

The Korean War presented a stark contrast to the American image of what a war should be. World War II had been a "total war," and the United States had fully committed all its economic, human, and military resources to the war. The goal of the Allies in that war was total victory. After the fighting had begun, the time for political solutions was past. Only military solutions were possible.

In contrast, U.S. economic and manpower commitments to the Korean conflict were much lower. General Douglas MacArthur, the American who commanded the UN force in Korea, was not allowed to use atomic weapons, nor was he allowed to push an offensive into China after the Chinese communists entered the fighting. Policymakers on both sides were looking for political solutions, trying to limit hostilities in order to avoid the outbreak of another world war. The conflict finally ended with an agreement that essentially restored the original north-south boundary. The United States had successfully contained communism in Korea, but a Pandora's box had been opened, and the problems that it released would beset the United States again in Vietnam. America's inability to translate its enormous military and economic strength into consistent political success was proof that its power had limits.

Cold War Commitments Under Eisenhower and Kennedy

For the most part, President Dwight Eisenhower carried on Truman's Cold War policies. But he realized that domestic political realities meant that defense spending had to have limits. He also expressed concern about the ways in which the pursuit of global interests might affect America's democratic institutions. Although a former general, Eisenhower warned against the power of the **military-industrial complex,** the "conjunction of an immense military establishment and a large arms industry," both lobbying for increased military spending. The growth of the military-industrial complex threatened pluralist democracy because it created an extremely powerful group united by two common interests—war and military spending. Eisenhower warned that its "total influence—economic, political, even spiritual—is felt in every city, every statehouse, every office of the federal government."[9] (For an example of the pervasiveness of the military-industrial complex in the 1980s, see Figure 19.2, which shows the distribution of defense contracts among the states.)

During the Eisenhower years, the U.S. defense policy relied chiefly on the deterrent power of nuclear weapons, rather than on the strength

The Flow of Defense Dollars

The West and East Coasts are the regions that are most successful in obtaining defense contracts. California leads the nation in per capita share, followed by New England. This coastal/central split can also be seen in the economic profile of the United States. The central states have been hurt by the nation's decline as an exporter of agricultural goods, raw materials, and manufactured goods. The coastal states, on the other hand, have benefited from the concentration there of high-technology firms and the growth of the service sector.

Figure 19.2

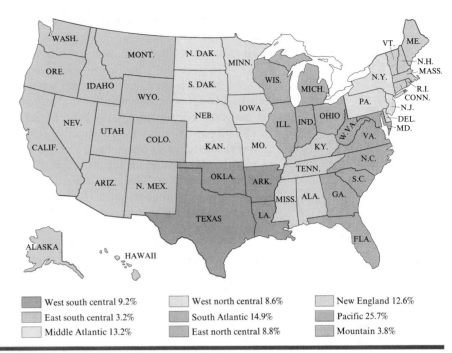

West south central 9.2%   West north central 8.6%   New England 12.6%
East south central 3.2%   South Atlantic 14.9%   Pacific 25.7%
Middle Atlantic 13.2%   East north central 8.8%   Mountain 3.8%

of conventional (nonnuclear) forces. Guided by the theory of **deterrence,** American strategists believed that the Soviets would hesitate to take aggressive action knowing they risked nuclear annihilation. Toward the late 1950s, however, the Russians built up their own nuclear strength, and the two superpowers faced the possibility of **mutual assured destruction (MAD)** in a nuclear conflict. Against this background, deterrence was less credible as a means of limiting Soviet expansion. It didn't seem likely that a president would risk nuclear destruction in America in order to stop a Soviet advance into Western Europe, for example. To restore credibility to deterrence, analysts argued that America should develop the strategies and weapons needed to fight a limited nuclear war.[10] And they called for America to beef up its conventional forces, so that the country would be able to select from a range of defense options.

The idea of **flexible response** became a cornerstone of the defense policy during the Kennedy administration. John F. Kennedy shared the commitment to the Cold War of his two predecessors. In his inaugural address, he pledged to "pay any price, bear any burden, meet any hardship, support any friend, oppose any foe to assure the survival and success of liberty."[11]

To Kennedy, the struggle against Soviet communism was paramount. The two most dramatic foreign policy incidents of his administration were the Bay of Pigs invasion, a debacle in which U.S.-supported Cuban exiles tried to invade Castro's communist Cuba, and the Cuban missile crisis, in which an American naval blockade of the island forced the Soviets to remove missiles they had placed there. Both were attempts to combat the perceived Soviet threat to U.S. security in the Western Hemisphere.*

In the wake of the Cuban missile crisis, the United States and the Soviet Union took steps to reduce the tension between them. Most notably, they concluded a nuclear test ban treaty that outlawed the testing of nuclear weapons above ground and they installed a Washington-Moscow communications link, nicknamed the "hotline."

The Kennedy administration also pursued a series of **nation-building policies,** aimed at shoring up Third World countries economically and promoting democratic reforms, making them less attractive targets for Soviet opportunism. These policies included the Alliance for Progress, a ten-year program that gave $20 billion in economic aid to Latin America; the Peace Corps, through which Americans volunteered to help Third World countries with problems of development; and Food for Peace, a program that sold American agricultural commodities to less-developed countries on generous credit terms and that provided emergency food relief.

Kennedy's commitment to nation building in Third World countries did not outweigh his commitment to the Cold War, however. Once, while speaking about the Dominican Republic, he made clear his hierarchy of preferred regime types: "There are three possibilities in descending order of preference: a decent democratic regime, a continuation of the [right-wing dictatorship under the] Trujillo [family], or a Castro regime. We ought to aim at the first but we really can't renounce the second until we are sure that we can avoid the third."[12]

Threats to freedom and equality from the right seemed preferable to threats to freedom and equality from the left. The Soviets were the real enemy, the threat to America's concept of order.

One of Kennedy's policies involved both nation building and resistance to communist expansion. It would have a critical impact on American foreign policy. Fearing a communist takeover by forces from North Vietnam, America had been sending military aid and advisers to non-communist South Vietnam for years. Kennedy stepped up the program. At his death in 1963, sixteen thousand American military advisers were stationed in South Vietnam. During Lyndon Johnson's presidency, the price of the Vietnam commitment would rise drastically in terms of both dollars and American lives.

Vietnam: The Challenge to America's Foreign Policy Consensus

In November 1963, just three weeks before President Kennedy's assassination, the United States tacitly permitted a coup in South Vietnam. President Ngo Dinh Diem's regime was racked with instability, undermining America's ability to contain the communist North Vietnamese and their allies in South Vietnam (a force known as the Vietcong).

---

* It was during the Cuban missile crisis that Kennedy's willingness to "pay any price" seemed likely to be tested. Kennedy himself estimated the chances of nuclear war at that time as one in three.

Honoring the Dead
The Vietnam Veterans Memorial in Washington, D.C., is a place of national sorrow. The long chevron of black granite is etched with the names of 58,156 American soldiers who died in the nation's longest conflict. The Vietnam War cost the United States more than $3.3 trillion, divided the American people, and fragmented the Cold War foreign policy consensus.

Diem's overthrow and death did not bring political stability to South Vietnam. Over the next few years, one government succeeded another, but none proved capable of maintaining control for long. Meanwhile, the military situation continued to deteriorate. By early 1964, the Vietcong controlled almost half of South Vietnam.

In August 1964, Congress passed the Gulf of Tonkin Resolution, which gave President Johnson a virtual blank check to carry out his policies in Vietnam. He ordered American bombing raids on the North; but by early 1965, the military situation had become so bad that he sent in U.S. ground troops. Eventually, the United States had more than 500,000 troops in Vietnam. Casualties mounted, and no end to the conflict was in sight. Opposition to the undeclared war grew on college campuses and elsewhere. An antiwar candidate, Senator Eugene McCarthy from Minnesota, challenged Johnson in the Democratic presidential primaries. On March 31, 1968, Johnson ordered a halt to the bombing of North Vietnam. In the same speech, he bowed out of the presidential race. By August, a majority of Americans surveyed in a Gallup Poll claimed the United States had made a mistake sending troops to Vietnam. This feeling did not change through the rest of the time America was involved in the conflict.

Richard Nixon, who succeeded Johnson, was well aware of public opinion on the war. He campaigned on a pledge to end the war through what came to be known as his "secret plan."* His way of achieving

---
* Cynics have noted that the plan was so secret that Nixon did not let it out until after he had been re-elected in 1972.

"peace with honor" rested on a strategy called **Vietnamization,** which meant turning more and more of the fighting over to the South Vietnamese. Gradually, American forces were pulled out, casualties fell, and draft calls grew smaller. A peace agreement was signed in 1973, and the remaining American troops left Vietnam. In April 1975, the communists took South Vietnam. The economic costs of the war were high, both in terms of direct military expenditures and indirect costs (like veterans' benefits and disability payments). Other costs, however, cannot be counted so easily. The conflict deeply divided the American people and fragmented the Cold War consensus on American foreign policy.

Even while the war dragged on, President Nixon and his chief foreign policy adviser, Henry Kissinger, were making important changes in American foreign policy. They attempted to redefine America's overseas commitments through the **Nixon Doctrine,** an effort to "steer a course between the past danger of overinvolvement and the new temptation of underinvolvement."[13] In a clear contrast to the rhetoric of Kennedy's inaugural address, Nixon stated that America would no longer "conceive all the plans, design all the programs, execute all the decisions and undertake all the defense of the free nations of the world." Instead, the United States would intervene only where "it makes a real difference and is considered in our interest."[14]

The United States was in a period of détente with the Soviet Union. Nixon visited Moscow for a summit meeting. The United States and the Soviet Union negotiated and signed the Strategic Arms Limitation Treaties (SALT), which limited the growth of their nuclear arsenals and recognized the Soviet claim to "strategic parity" with the United States. Trade between the two countries increased, and a joint U.S.-Soviet space mission was planned.

Nixon also ended decades of U.S. hostility toward the People's Republic of China. Although that country was not accorded full diplomatic recognition until 1979 by the Carter administration, both Nixon and Kissinger visited China and helped open political and economic negotiations.

The theory of détente emphasized the value of order—order based not only on military might but also on the mutual interests of the superpowers. Kissinger believed that if the Soviets and the Chinese were treated as legitimate participants in the international system, they would have a vested interest in supporting world order. And the two countries would have less incentive to promote revolutionary challenges to international stability. If the Soviets and the Chinese were bound to the United States through economic and political agreements, they would realize that their own interests would best be served through cooperation. Kissinger practiced **linkage;** he tried to use rewards and benefits in one area to promote Soviet compliance in other areas.

Did the Soviets share Kissinger's vision? Some insist that Soviet involvement in the Middle East, Angola, and later Afghanistan was evidence that their view of détente was not the same as Kissinger's. On the other hand, after Watergate weakened the Nixon presidency, Kissinger was unable to deliver on his promises to the Soviets. Specifically, he was unable to secure legislative approval of provisions granting the Soviet Union a "most favored nation" trading status.*

Critics have noted that neither détente nor attention to U.S.-Soviet relations brought about a successful end to the Vietnam War or a solution to the problem of the 1973 Arab oil embargo. In fact, Nixon's concentration on East-West politics might have made him less able to deal with these concerns. Opponents of Nixon-Kissinger (and later Ford-Kissinger) foreign policy also fault those policies for being too cynical—for paying too much attention to power and interests and not enough to basic American ideals and human rights.

Carter's Search for a New Foreign Policy

Initially, President Jimmy Carter's stance on foreign policy was very different from that of his predecessors. For example, he emphasized human rights, leveling criticism—and sometimes even sanctions—at both friends and enemies with poor human rights records. And Carter tended to downplay the Soviet threat throughout most of his administration. He did not believe the hand of the Soviet Union was behind the revolutions in Nicaragua and Iran; instead, he saw these events as largely the products of internal forces. However, he did not hesitate to fault the Soviets for their lack of attention to human rights.

Where Nixon and Kissinger faced charges of cynicism, Carter was sometimes criticized for being too idealistic. He usually leaned toward "open" (rather than secret) diplomacy. Yet, his greatest foreign policy achievement, the Camp David Accords, which brought about peace between Egypt and Israel, was the product of closed negotiation between Egyptian President Anwar Sadat and Israeli Premier Menachem Begin. And, while UN Ambassador Andrew Young was working on economic and political development in the Third World, National Security Adviser Zbigniew Brzezinski was addressing more traditional U.S.-Soviet issues.[15] Toward the end of Carter's term, after the Soviet invasion of Afghanistan, the president's own attitude toward the Russians hardened.

Foreign Policy Under Reagan

Carter's successor, Ronald Reagan, came to the Oval Office with the firm belief that the Soviets were responsible for most of the evil in the world. Reagan attributed the instability in Central America (specifically in El Salvador and Nicaragua) to the actions of the Soviets and their surrogates, the Cubans and the Sandinistas. He believed the best method of combating the Soviet threat was to renew and project American military strength. The Reagan years witnessed a huge increase in defense spending and a new willingness to use American military muscle.

The administration argued that its massive military buildup was both a deterrent and a bargaining chip to use in talks with the Soviets.

---

* "Most favored nation" status grants terms regarding tariffs, duties, import limits, and other trade concessions, equal to the best terms granted any other nation.

Toward the end of his administration, Reagan managed to conclude agreements with the Soviets outlawing intermediate-range nuclear forces (INF) and providing for the pullout of Soviet troops from Afghanistan.

Critics have charged that, with the exception of its anti-Soviet focus, the Reagan administration had a difficult time pursuing consistent foreign policy goals. Two examples of this problem were its antiterrorist policies and antidrug policies.

Antiterrorism and the Iran-Contra scandal.   From its earliest days, the Reagan administration used tough rhetoric against terrorists and sometimes, as in the bombing raid on Libya, took forceful action. Yet terrorism continued, with many more American lives lost than during the preceding administration. Furthermore, as the Iran-Contra affair showed, despite tough talk, administration policy was far from consistent. As part of their antiterrorist policy, administration officials asserted that America would make no deals with terrorists or nations that supported terrorism. One target of that policy was Iran. The administration blocked arms sales to Iran and tried to convince other governments to do the same.

Despite these public pronouncements, some members of the Reagan foreign policy team followed a very different policy. In what they claimed was an effort to strengthen ties to Iranian moderates, members of the NSC staff, including Robert MacFarlane, John Poindexter, and Oliver North, arranged for the delivery of weapons shipments to Iran. In exchange, Iran paid for the weapons and effected the release of Americans

---

FEATURE 19.2

Just Say No . . . Passport?

In the 1980s, Americans declared war on drugs, but by 1988, drugs appeared to be winning. Many Americans saw the drug problem as a greater threat than communism to the nation's security. In March of that year, in an attempt to fight illegal narcotics, the U.S. Customs Service announced that it would take new tougher measures against American travelers who tried to bring drugs into the country. Customs head, William von Raab, outlined a plan to seize the passports of citizens entering the United States with illegal narcotics. Previous policy had been to confiscate the materials and levy relatively light fines against those carrying small quantities of drugs meant mainly for personal consumption. Customs officials had found that these offenders risked little else in the way of legal penalties because the courts were so backlogged.

Raab's policy immediately came in for criticism. There were bureaucratic turf problems. State Department officials had already scotched an earlier plan to stamp the passports of offenders; they took a dim view of the new proposal as well. Civil libertarians also complained. By revoking passports to enforce order, Raab was limiting freedom. Usually a passport can be revoked only by a court order. For customs agents to seize passports summarily at the border denied people due process of law. Democratic Representative Don Edwards of California claimed that the policy deprived "people of a constitutional right, the right to travel, before the conviction of any crime."[*]

Ultimately, the Customs Service backed off. But Raab was vocal about the lack of support he received from officials he described as "conscientious objectors in the war on drugs."[**]

---

[*] Quoted in "Customs Chief Warns Tourists on Illicit Drugs," *New York Times*, 3 March 1988, p. 1.
[**] Ibid.

Sniffing Out Trouble
Most of the illegal drugs used in the United States come from abroad. Here, a specially trained Customs Service dog and its handler hunt for drugs on a Colombian plane in Miami's international airport. The Coast Guard and the Customs Service are in the front line of the government's effort to staunch the flow of drugs into the United States. Both agencies came under criticism from some quarters in 1988 for their aggressive antidrug policy of confiscating boats, motor vehicles, and even planes, in which trivial amounts of drugs had been found.

held hostage by pro-Iranian terrorists in Lebanon. Whatever the legal implications of the Iran-Contra operation, it wreaked havoc on efforts to formulate a coherent antiterrorist policy for ourselves and our allies.

Drugs and foreign policy.   With First Lady Nancy Reagan acting as a strong spokesperson, the Reagan administration pledged itself to fight drug abuse. There are many fronts in the war on drugs: educational programs, drug treatment facilities, and the strict enforcement of drug laws. These are all matters of domestic policy. But the drug problem is not simply a matter of domestic policy. According to State Department estimates, 95 percent of all illegal drugs used in the United States are imported from abroad. So the fight against drugs has become a foreign policy problem as well, and one in which the government and its agencies must choose between conflicting goals (see Feature 19.2).

As part of U.S. antidrug efforts abroad, the State Department has supported crop eradication programs, provided law enforcement assistance to other nations, and found alternative crops for farmers who supported themselves by growing coca (the source of cocaine), opium, and marijuana. In 1986, Congress passed the Antidrug Abuse Act, which allows the president to cut off half the aid received by a drug-producing nation if that nation does not try to limit the production or export of drugs. In practice, however, the act was invoked only against Afghanistan, Iran, Syria, and Laos—nations that do not receive U.S. aid—and Panama, in an attempt to force the ouster of General Manuel Noriega. In general, the Reagan administration was unwilling to cut off aid to drug-supplying nations that were otherwise friendly and anticommunist.

Nor was it clear that cutting off aid would accomplish the administration's objective. Some argue that the drug problem can only be solved domestically. They believe the most effective solution lies in cutting American demand for drugs rather than cutting foreign supplies.

Conflicting Policy Paradigms and America's Foreign Policy Goals

Our review of the history of U.S. foreign policy points to several goals this country has set for itself. First among these is preserving American freedom and independence. For much of our history, this meant staying away from the political tangle of and commitments to international alliances. The nation remained free to pursue the development of its own territory and to intervene, when necessary, in the affairs of other countries in the hemisphere. Since World War II, most policymakers have believed that protecting America's freedom and international peace means controlling the threat of communism. In the last four decades, then, much of American foreign policy has been directed toward the goal of creating or preserving a "stable world order." In recent years, however, the search for stability and order has been complicated by new problems—terrorism and drug trafficking, for example—problems that are not tied to the communist threat.

In its pursuit of order, the United States has used both cooperation and conflict. On one hand, the country's search for stability has led to periods of détente with China and the Soviet Union. On the other, America has sometimes found itself containing communism by opposing, undermining, and intervening against revolutionary movements in Third World countries. The nation has also tried to contain the expansion of Soviet communism by entering into a web of alliances around the globe. But alliances forged in the defense of freedom may also limit U.S. freedom, as this country discovered most painfully in Vietnam. Under Nixon, American commitments abroad were redefined in terms of American interests.

The question of order is linked to the question of freedom. An important U.S. goal has been to spread American-style free institutions at both the national and the international levels. To this end, America backed the establishment of the United Nations and the World Court, and supports the development of capitalist economies and liberal political systems, with free elections and guarantees of basic human rights. Although some policymakers, particularly during the Carter administration, pressed American standards of human rights even on friendly governments, policymakers have more often been willing to overlook violations of freedom by regimes that proclaim themselves to be anticommunist.

The question of order is linked, not only to freedom, but also to equality. The East-West split still dominates many foreign policy decisions, but some observers attach increasing importance to the division of the world into rich versus poor nations (industrialized nations versus Third World nations). Supporters of this position argue that the real threat to international stability has its source in economic and political inequality, and that poverty creates opportunities for communism to take hold. More recently, citizens of some Third World countries have found a way out of poverty, not through communism, but through drugs. The influence and prosperity enjoyed by the new drug barons has undermined order both in the United States and elsewhere. These complicated issues suggest the need for a foreign policy that relies heavily on economic development, interdependence, the redistribution of wealth, and access to the political process, rather than on conflict and military might.

The Munich paradigm and the Vietnam paradigm generally agree on the priority of the first goal—order—but they disagree sharply on how best to bring about order and how to weight the other two goals—freedom and equality. As Tocqueville suggested, a lack of consensus here could seriously undermine the conduct of foreign policy. The dilemma becomes even greater in a system like the American system, where the power over foreign policy is split among the branches of government and executive department and agencies.

FOREIGN POLICYMAKING: THE CONSTITUTIONAL CONTEXT

The Constitution clearly puts the president in charge of American foreign policy. However, the framers also included checks and balances to prevent the president from conducting foreign policy without substantial cooperation from Congress. Still, presidents have found ways to sidestep these provisions when they have felt it important to do so.

The Formal Division of Power

The Constitution gives the president four significant foreign policymaking powers:

- The president is commander in chief of the armed forces.
- The president has the power to make treaties (subject to the consent of the Senate).
- The president appoints U.S. ambassadors and the heads of executive departments (also with the advice and consent of the Senate).
- The president receives (and may refuse to receive) ambassadors from other countries.

The Congress also has specific powers in the foreign policy arena:

- Congress alone may declare war.
- Congress has the legislative power.
- Congress controls the nation's purse strings.
- Congress is charged with raising, supporting, and maintaining the army and navy.
- Congress may call out the militia to repel invasions.

The most important foreign policy power the Constitution gives to Congress is the power to declare war, a power it has used only five times. But Congress has become involved in foreign policy in other ways. Through its legislative power, it has established programs of international scope and imposed legal limits on the actions of the executive branch. The Arms Control Export Act (1988), which restricted arms transfers, is one example; the Antidrug Abuse Act (1986) is another. In addition, Congress has used its power of the purse to provide funds for activities it supports and to withhold funds for programs it does not.

Finally, there are certain foreign policy functions that belong to the Senate alone:

■ The Senate consents to treaties.

■ The Senate gives its advice and consent to the appointment of ambassadors and various other public officials.

The Senate has not been shy about using these powers. We have already noted that it refused to ratify the Treaty of Versailles. More recently, the US-Soviet SALT II agreement, an arms limitation treaty negotiated under the Carter administration, was introduced into the Senate but not brought to a vote because its supporters feared defeat. In 1988, some Senate conservatives geared up to oppose the INF treaty President Reagan signed with Soviet leader Mikhail Gorbachev. They succeeded in delaying Senate approval for a short while, but eventually the treaty was passed.

Sidestepping the Constitution

Although the Constitution gives the executive enormous power in the foreign policy arena, it also places limits on that power. Presidents and their advisers often have found ingenious ways around these constitutional limitations. Among the innovative devices they have used are executive agreements, discretionary funds, transfer authority and reprogramming, excess stock disposal, undeclared wars, and special envoys. Since the Vietnam War, however, Congress has attempted to assert control over the use of these presidential tools. To a large extent, the Iran-Contra affair was the product of administration efforts to get around congressional controls.

An **executive agreement** is a pact between the heads of two countries. Initially, these agreements were used to work out the tedious details of day-to-day international affairs. In *U.S.* v. *Curtiss-Wright* (1936), the Supreme Court ruled that executive agreements are within the inherent powers of the president and have the legal status of treaties.[16] This ruling gave the president an enormously powerful tool. Although they are not subject to senatorial approval, executive agreements, like treaties, have the force of law. Until 1972, the texts of executive agreements did not even have to be reported to Congress. Legislation passed that year now requires the president to send copies to the House and Senate Foreign Relations Committees.

This requirement has not seriously affected the use of executive agreements, which has escalated dramatically since World War II. In the

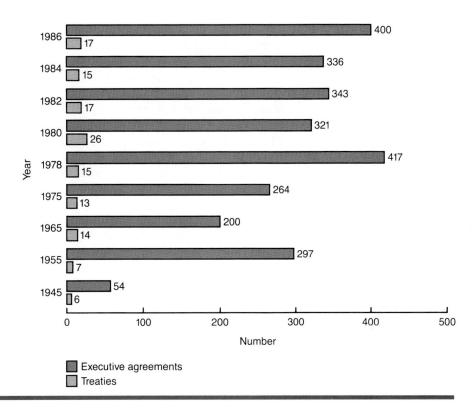

Executive Agreements versus Treaties: How the Numbers Stack Up
This graph shows that the number of executive agreements concluded dwarfs the number of treaties approved. (*Source:* Editorial Research Reports, *29 January 1988, p. 41.*)
Figure 19.3

years from 1945 to 1986, executive agreements have vastly outnumbered treaties (see Figure 19.3). And presidents have used these agreements to make substantive foreign policy. In fact, senators have complained that the treaties now submitted for Senate approval deal with petty, unimportant matters, whereas serious issues are handled by executive agreement. Moreover, executive agreements are subject to very few limits. One observer noted that "the principal limitation on their use is political in nature—the degree to which it is wise to exclude the Senate from [its] constitutional foreign policy role."[17]

Presidents can use several devices to circumvent congressional control of the nation's finances. One is **discretionary funds**—large sums of cash that can be spent on unpredicted needs to further the national interest. President Kennedy used discretionary funds to run the Peace Corps in its first year; President Johnson used $1.5 billion of his funds in Southeast Asia in 1965 and 1966.[18]

The president's **transfer authority** or the **reprogramming** of funds allows him to take money that Congress has approved for one purpose and to spend it on something else. Reprogramming is one way the Reagan administration might have sent military aid to Nicaragua, except that Congress had specifically prohibited any redirection of funds for military use there. Finally, the executive branch has control over the disposal of excess stocks, which include surplus or infrequently used equipment. The Central Intelligence Agency (CIA) has been an important beneficiary of **excess stock disposal.** As part of the Iran-Contra arrangement, NSC staffers used excess-stock provisions as the source of the arms sold to

Iran. Before they were specifically barred from doing so by Congress, administration officials were able to offer excess stock directly to the Contras.

The Constitution makes the president commander in chief of the armed forces. In this role, he has claimed the right to involve the United States in **undeclared wars,** to commit American troops in emergency situations. America's undeclared wars, police actions, and other interventions have outnumbered formal (congressionally declared) wars by more than 30 to 1. Since the last declared war ended in 1945, over 100,000 American troops have died in locations ranging from Korea and Vietnam to Lebanon, Grenada, the Dominican Republic, Cuba, El Salvador, Libya, and the Persian Gulf.

During the Vietnam War, congressional opponents of that conflict passed the **War Powers Resolution** to limit the president's ability to wage undeclared wars. Under this resolution, a president must "consult" with Congress in "every possible instance" before involving U.S. troops in hostilities. In addition, the president is required to notify Congress within forty-eight hours of committing troops to a foreign intervention, and he is prohibited from keeping troops there for more than sixty days without congressional approval (although he may take up to an additional thirty days to remove troops "safely"). President Nixon vetoed the War Powers Act as an unwarranted restriction on the president's constitutional authority, but Congress overrode his veto. Some critics have charged that the legislation does not limit presidential power, but instead allows the president to wage war at will for up to sixty days.* By the end of that period, Congress might find it very difficult to force the president to bring troops home. The actual impact of the War Powers Act is debatable. Nixon's successors in the White House have all questioned its constitutionality, and no president has ever been "punished" for violating its provisions.

Although the Senate rarely rejects a president's choice, senators have used appointment confirmation hearings as an opportunity to investigate the president's foreign policy activities. For example, while he served as national security adviser, Henry Kissinger claimed that executive privilege protected him from being summoned to testify before congressional committees. When President Nixon nominated him to be secretary of state, however, senators were able to ask him, in the course of the confirmation process, about a variety of subjects, including his role in the secret bombing of Cambodia and in the wiretapping of various news reporters and public officials.

One way presidents get around the Senate's power over appointments is to rely heavily on the White House staff, whose members are accountable to no one but the president, or to use **special envoys** (personal representatives), to perform a wide variety of foreign policy tasks. For example, Philip Habib was Reagan's special envoy in the Middle East, the Philippines, and, while Reagan was trying to win congressional sup-

---

* These critics included both conservative Republican Senator Barry Goldwater of Arizona and liberal Democratic Senator Thomas Eagleton of Missouri. The latter's feelings were succinctly summarized in the title of his book, *War and Presidential Power: A Chronicle of Congressional Surrender* (New York: Liveright, 1974).

port for his Nicaraguan aid package, in Central America. During the Iran-Contra operation, administration officials relied on private individuals to carry out significant portions of the mission. The use of private citizens in the conduct of foreign policy came in for severe criticism by the committee that investigated the matter.[19]

FOREIGN POLICYMAKING: THE ADMINISTRATIVE MACHINERY

Although American foreign policy is developed and administered by the executive branch, it requires the approval and funding of Congress and is subject to congressional oversight. When America assumed a larger role in world affairs after World War II, the old foreign policy machinery was inadequate to the demands of superpower status. In 1947, Congress overhauled the system, passing the National Security Act, which established three new organizations with important foreign policy roles: the Department of Defense, the National Security Council, and the CIA. These organizations joined the other department within the executive branch that shares major foreign policymaking power and responsibility, the Department of State.

The Department of State

The department most concerned with the overall conduct of foreign affairs is the Department of State. It helps formulate, then executes and monitors the outlines and details of American policy throughout the world. Its head, the secretary of state, is the highest-ranking official in the cabinet; he is also, supposedly, the president's most important foreign policy adviser. But different presidents have used the office of secretary of state in very different ways. Dwight Eisenhower chose a strong individual, John Foster Dulles. John Kennedy chose to act as his own secretary of state and appointed a relatively weak figure to the post. During his first term, Richard Nixon planned to control foreign policy from the White House. He appointed William Rogers as secretary of state but took much of his advice from Henry Kissinger, whose office was located in the White House.

Like other executive departments, the State Department is made up of political appointees and permanent employees selected under the civil service system. The former include deputy secretaries and undersecretaries of state and some—but not all—ambassadors; the latter include about thirty-five hundred foreign service officers who alternate assignments between home and abroad. The department staffs U.S. embassies and consulates throughout the world. It has primary responsibility for representing America to the world and caring for American citizens and interests abroad. Although the foreign service is highly selective (fewer than two hundred of the fifteen thousand who take the annual examination are appointed), the State Department often is charged with a lack of initiative and creativity. Critics claim that bright young foreign service officers quickly realize that conformity is the best path to career advancement. As one observer put it: "There are old foreign service officers;

and there are bold foreign service officers; but, there are no old, bold foreign service officers."[20] And at times, presidents have complained that the department's foreign policy machinery is too slow and unwieldy. President Kennedy once remarked, "Bundy [Kennedy's national security adviser] and I get more done in one day in the White House than they do in six months in the State Department. . . . They never have any ideas over there, never come up with anything new."[21] The Reagan administration showed the same disdain for the State Department in its handling of the Iran-Contra operation. That operation ran counter to official State Department policies; it was conducted by people who were not affiliated with the State Department; and the secretary of state, who had opposed elements of the plan, was not kept informed of its progress.

Probably the most important problem facing the State Department today is its lack of a strong domestic constituency to exert pressure in support of its policies. This is in marked contrast with, say, the Department of Education, which can mobilize teachers to support its activities; the Department of Agriculture, which can call on farmers; or the Department of Defense, which can look for help from defense industries or veterans' groups. In a pluralist democracy, the lack of a natural constituency is a serious drawback for an executive department.

The Department of Defense

The Department of Defense replaced two cabinet-level departments: the War Department and the Department of the Navy. It was created to provide the modern bureaucratic structure needed to manage America's much-increased peacetime military strength and to promote greater unity and coordination among the armed forces. At the same time, in keeping with the U.S. tradition of civilian control of the military, the new department was given a civilian head—the secretary of defense—a cabinet member who has authority over the military establishment. Successive reorganizations of the department (in 1949 and 1958) have increased the secretary's greater budgetary powers, control of defense research, and authority to transfer, abolish, reassign, and consolidate functions among the military services. These powers enabled Robert McNamara, secretary of defense under Kennedy and Johnson, to make sweeping changes in military management procedures. Among other things, he attempted to involve the services in joint programs to avoid duplication, inefficiency, and waste. In addition, during McNamara's tenure, the Pentagon's Office of International Security Affairs began to develop the department's own foreign policy positions based on both military and political factors.

The power available to defense secretaries often depends on the secretary's own vision of the job and willingness to use the tools available. Strong secretaries of defense, including McNamara, Melvin Laird (under Nixon), James Schlesinger (under Nixon and Ford), and Caspar Weinberger (under Reagan), have wielded tremendous power.

Below the secretary are the civilian secretaries of the army, navy, and air force; below them are the military commanders of the individual branches of the armed forces. These military leaders make up the Joint Chiefs of Staff (JCS). In addition to their roles as heads of their respective services, the JCS meet to coordinate military policy; they are also the primary military advisers to the president, the secretary of defense, and the National Security Council. As advisers, the JCS have broad responsibilities for developing positions on such matters as alliances, plans for nuclear and conventional war, and arms control and disarmament.

The CIA and the Intelligence Community

Before World War II, the United States had no permanent agency specifically charged with gathering intelligence (that is, information) about the actions and intentions of foreign powers. Partly in response to intelligence failures of the sort that led to the Pearl Harbor disaster and partly in recognition of America's new international role, Congress created the Central Intelligence Agency in 1947.

The agency's charter charges the agency with (1) coordinating the information and data-gathering activities of various other government departments; and (2) collecting, analyzing, evaluating, and circulating its own intelligence relating to national security matters. Most of these activities are relatively uncontroversial. By far the bulk of material obtained by the CIA comes from readily available sources: statistical abstracts, books, newspapers, and the like. The agency's Intelligence Directorate is responsible for these overt (open) information-processing activities.

The charter also empowers the CIA "to perform such other functions and duties related to intelligence affecting the national security as the National Security Council shall direct." This vague clause has been used by the agency to justify covert (secret) activities undertaken by its Operations Directorate. These activities have included espionage, coups (in Iran in 1953, in Guatemala in 1954), plots to assassinate foreign leaders (Muammar Qaddafi, Fidel Castro), experiments exposing unsuspecting American citizens to mind-altering drugs, wiretaps, interception of mail, and infiltration of antiwar groups. Until Congress limited its activities, the CIA provided military support and assistance to the Contras, including help in mining Nicaraguan harbors.

Critics sometimes point out that the CIA has not ended major foreign policy "surprises" for the United States. Some gaffes have been the result of faulty intelligence (as was the case in the Bay of Pigs), but others were more the result of policymakers' failure to accept or interpret analyses properly. The CIA told President Johnson that bombing North Vietnam would not bring the North Vietnamese into submission. Johnson responded: "Policymaking is like milking a fat cow. You see the milk coming out, you press more and the milk bubbles and flows and just as the bucket is full the cow with its tail whips the bucket and all is spilled. That's what the CIA does to policymaking."[22] The usual response to intelligence failures is to investigate, then propose structural changes in institutions, but at least one analyst claims that "intelligence failure is political and psychological more often than it is institutional."[23] Even the best-designed intelligence network could not prevent the United States from being caught by surprise some of the time.

The basic dilemma posed by the CIA and the intelligence community, though, concerns the role of covert activities. Covert operations raise both moral and legal questions for a democracy. Are they, as Allen Dulles, Eisenhower's CIA director, believed "an essential part of the free world's struggle against communism"? Or are they antithetical to a democracy that espouses open government, free elections, and the principle of self-determination? And if covert activities are deemed necessary and appropriate, how do we reconcile them with the basic principles of American government? For example, should the principle of checks and balances be applied to secret operations? Although the CIA's covert activities are supposed to be approved by an NSC subcommittee, the president himself is not always briefed about them.

Congress has wrestled with the problem of the secrecy necessary for successful operations for more than a decade. In 1975, it passed the Hughes-Ryan Amendment, which required all covert activities of the CIA to be reported to the appropriate congressional committees. In 1981, in the Intelligence Authorization Act, Congress required all intelligence agencies to inform appropriate committees, not only of current covert operations, but also of "significant anticipated operations." That act also reduced from eight to two the number of committees that must be informed of secret activities. Yet policymakers intent on conducting covert operations outside the view of Congress have also turned to vehicles other than the CIA. In the Iran-Contra affair, for example, the National Security Council became heavily involved in secret missions.

The National Security Council

The National Security Council is a permanent group of advisers created to help the president integrate and coordinate the details of domestic, foreign, and military affairs as they relate to national security. The NSC consists of the president, the vice president, the secretaries of state and defense, and the chairman of the Joint Chiefs of Staff, and others appointed by the president. NSC discussions can cover a wide range of issues, including, for example, U.S. support for the Contras in Nicaragua or revisions of U.S. policy in the Middle East. In theory, at least, NSC discussions offer the president an opportunity to solicit advice, while allowing key participants in the foreign policymaking process to keep abreast of the policies and capabilities of other departments.

In practice, the role played by the NSC has varied considerably under different presidents. Truman and Kennedy seldom met with the NSC; Eisenhower and Nixon brought it into much greater prominence. During the Nixon administration, the NSC was critically important in making foreign policy. Much of this importance derived from the role played by Henry Kissinger, Nixon's assistant for national security affairs (the title of the head of the NSC staff). Under Nixon and Kissinger, the NSC staff ballooned to over one hundred—in effect, a little state department in the White House. Kissinger also used his staff for direct diplomacy and covert operations.

During the Reagan administration, the NSC itself engaged in covert operations, including the Iran-Contra affair. By keeping the Iran-Contra matter within the NSC, which has been almost completely exempt from outside scrutiny, staffers hoped to preserve secrecy, and, more important, to avoid the possibility that Congress would prohibit the operation.

Situation: Top Secret
The National Security Council (NSC) is the committee that advises the president by integrating domestic, foreign, and military affairs related to national security. It operates from the White House Situation Room, located in the super-secure basement of the White House West Wing. NSC staff members daily assemble a world intelligence briefing from thousands of sources, including satellite photos, spy reports, and news reports. From here, Lieutenant Colonel Oliver North, with the approval of National Security Adviser John Poindexter, launched a covert plan to trade arms with Iran in exchange for Americans held hostage in Lebanon.

THE PUBLIC, THE MEDIA, AND FOREIGN POLICY

A great difficulty Tocqueville predicted for democracies in foreign affairs stemmed from the changeable views of the mass electorate. He believed foreign relations required patience and persistence in the pursuit of long-term goals. But the public could be fickle, unwilling to set aside short-term gains for long-term security. In response to domestic pressures, leaders could be forced to act in ways that are harmful to foreign policy interests. Their democratic responsiveness might well be detrimental to the long-term success of their foreign policy.

The Public and the Majoritarian Model

Americans as a group know very little about politics but are still very willing to express their opinions about political issues (see Chapter 5). These findings hold for foreign affairs as well as (and perhaps even more than) domestic politics. Only about 15 percent of Americans pay attention to foreign affairs.

Americans are quick to tell policymakers what should be done, but they rarely can provide guidance on how to do it. Consider the public's response to a March 1969 poll on the Vietnam War. Of those polled, 52 percent—a clear majority—believed that our involvement in Vietnam was a mistake. When asked what the United States should do next in terms of the war, 32 percent advised all-out war; 26 percent wanted American troops pulled out of Vietnam; 19 percent agreed with the current policy; and another 19 percent wanted to end the war as soon as possible.* Obviously, Americans were unhappy about the policies being pursued in Vietnam. However, they were unable to reach a consensus on how to change those policies.

The public's opinions on foreign policy issues are also extremely volatile. The American people have historically been willing to "rally 'round the flag" and back presidential foreign policies, particularly in crisis situations. But they are willing to do so only for relatively short periods of time. President Carter enjoyed increased public approval following the seizure of American hostages in Iran. That added support helped him win a victory over Senator Edward Kennedy of Massachusetts in the 1980 Democratic primaries. But Carter's inability to resolve the hostage situation contributed to his defeat by Ronald Reagan a few months later.

President Reagan's commitment of troops to Lebanon dragged on for over a year with little popular support, until a terrorist bombing claimed 241 American lives. When that slight increase in support waned and his policy in Lebanon threatened to become an election issue, the president withdrew the marines. Reagan found more support for the invasion of Grenada in 1983 and the American bombing in Libya in 1986. But both of these operations were over quickly. The moral here is clear: A president had better be able to produce a short-term success or expect to lose his constituency—exactly what Tocqueville would have predicted.

Those who support the majoritarian model of democracy might argue that the people are capable of evaluating the benefits and costs of a foreign policy. But this does not mean that the public can make foreign policy. The idea that American foreign policy is a reflection of mass opinion is crude and simplistic because "policy formulation does not derive from the simple preferences of an uninformed, uninterested, unstable, acquiescent and manipulable 'public voice'."[24] In short, policymakers must look elsewhere for their cues. In foreign affairs, as in other areas of American politics, the majoritarian model does not really seem to describe American democracy.

Interest Groups and the Pluralist Model

Most people take an interest in foreign policy issues when they believe those issues affect them directly. Most auto workers and manufacturers favor import restrictions on Japanese cars. Many Jewish citizens pay close attention to America's relationship with Israel. These individuals often join unions or other organizations that present their policy positions to policymakers.

On foreign affairs issues, two of the most prominent kinds of lobbies include businesses and unions, often seeking trade protection, and ethnic groups, looking for support for their fellows in the "old country." More

---

* The remaining 4 percent made other responses.

recently, and in keeping with the current lobbying boom in Washington, foreign governments have begun to hire high-powered Washington lobbying firms to represent their interests (see Feature 9.1, page 324).

In general, the impact of these groups varies with the issue. But lobbying seems to be more effective when it takes place behind the scenes and deals with noncrisis issues that are not considered important by the public at large. Interest groups generally are more effective in maintaining support for the status quo than in bringing about policy changes.[25]

As with domestic issues, there is a tendency for foreign policy interest groups to counterbalance each other. The Turkish lobby tries to offset the Greek lobby; the Arms Control Association or the Federation of American Scientists may oppose the American Legion or the Veterans of Foreign Wars on issues of détente and military spending. The result is that "foreign policy making resembles a taffy-pull: every group attempts to pull policy in its own direction while resisting the pulls of

Arabs versus Israelis
Rock-throwing Palestinians confront Israeli troops in the Israeli-occupied West Bank territory. Israel's swift and harsh response to the 1987 Palestinian uprising weakened its wide popular support among Americans. The uprising continued through 1988 as presidential candidates Michael Dukakis and George Bush dodged offering specific solutions to an intractable problem.

others, with the result that policy fails to move in any discernible direction. The process encourages solutions tending toward the middle of the road and maintenance of the status quo."[26]

The Media and Foreign Policy

A potentially powerful source of influence on both public attitudes and policymakers' actions is the media—television, radio, newspapers, and magazines. Do the media shape foreign policy? Television coverage of the Vietnam War is often cited as one reason why people turned against that war (see Politics in the Information Age 19.1). Media attention to the Iranian hostage crisis kept the issue in the public eye for over a year. News of the Iran-Contra affair filled newspapers, magazines, and television screens for months. But the media's impact on the public is limited. Most people simply do not follow foreign affairs or care much about foreign policy.

The media themselves try to cater to their audience and generally do not devote very much space or time to foreign policy issues. When they do, however, their impact on the general public tends to be more

POLITICS IN THE INFORMATION AGE 19.1

Press Coverage of Combat: Three Models

One area in which the requirements of democracy run headlong into the requirements of national security is the press coverage of military operations. Freedom of the press is one of the fundamental rights of citizens in a democracy, who must have access to accurate information to be able to evaluate their government's performance. In a democracy, the government responds to the people's will; it doesn't create that will. But the safety of soldiers and the success of military operations could be jeopardized if too much information were available to the public—and potentially to the enemy—too soon. But how much is too much, and who is the judge?

During World War II, war correspondents accompanied invading troops (after signing waivers releasing the U.S. government from any responsibility for their safety). The stories they filed were subject to military censorship and delay, ostensibly to protect the lives of American troops. In Vietnam, by contrast, reporters were able to shoot film that appeared immediately on television news, with virtually no military censorship. Many people credit the erosion of popular support for the war to the graphic portrayal of horrors on the nightly news. Some also argue that reduced domestic support for the war made it harder for American troops in the field. Indirectly, then, press coverage of the war in

Vietnam may have undermined the safety of American troops.

In 1983, during the invasion of Grenada, news reporters were not allowed to land with the marines. Only after several days were they given access to the island, and then only on a restricted basis. Ignoring a long tradition of war correspondents working in battle zones, the Department of Defense claimed reporters were excluded for their own safety. Journalists, however, charged that the department was motivated far less by concern for reporters' safety than by its own interest in public relations—that is, in making sure that the official version of the Grenada invasion was the one the American people received. The first films of the invasion shown on network television were produced by the Department of Defense and did not show fighting; they dealt with the justification for the invasion by focusing on a cache of Cuban arms stored on Grenada. Obviously, the reporters argued, the Defense Department wanted to be sure that the invasion would be portrayed in a favorable light so that the public would support it.

Which, if any, of the three press coverage models—World War II, Vietnam, or Grenada—puts democratic values and security demands in the proper balance?

indirect than direct. One observer called it a "two-step" process.[27] The foreign policymakers and the "attentive public" obtain most of their information from the media. This information eventually filters down to the general public through their communications with clergy, teachers, union officials, and other opinion leaders.

The media also set the foreign policy agenda (see Chapter 6). By giving play to a particular issue, policy, or crisis, they are able to capture the public's consciousness and to focus attention on it. The media "may not tell us what to think, but they tell us what to think about."[28] When details of the Iran-Contra affair began to unfold, the media devoted enormous amounts of attention to it, and the public generally approved of the media coverage.[29] Yet when Colonel North appeared before the televised sessions of the congressional committee investigating the operation, a new word, *Olliemania*, was coined to describe his sudden popularity.

The agenda-setting role of the media can have an impact on foreign policymaking in another way. Remember that interest groups tend to be most effective in noncrisis situations that are not of general concern. By calling attention to a particular issue, then, the media can dilute some of the influence of organized special interest groups. And in a crisis situation in which quick action is called for, media attention can work to the detriment of an interest group. On the other hand, by keeping an issue before the public, the media can increase the likelihood that it will become the focus of some interest group's lobbying efforts.[30]

THE FOREIGN POLICYMAKING PROCESS

Now that we have looked at the historical context of American foreign policy and the cast of characters, we examine the policymaking process itself. How is foreign policy made?

Sources of Information for the Executive Branch

By constitutional provision and practical control of resources, the president is the lead actor in the foreign policymaking process. A president comes to the job with a world-view that helps him interpret and evaluate international events. And as chief executive, he commands tremendous resources, including information and personnel. The Pentagon, the State Department, and the CIA are among his main sources of information about the outside world, and their staffs both advise him on foreign policy and implement that policy.

Often, presidential advisers present conflicting information or offer different, even contradictory, advice. Their views on issues can be influenced by their positions in the bureaucracy. For example, the secretary of state might lean more toward diplomacy, while the secretary of defense might push for a show of force. Advisers often compete for the president's ear or bargain among themselves to shape administration policy. During the Iran-Contra matter, NSC staffers won out over others in the administration, including Secretary of State George Shultz.

A president's sources of foreign policy advice are not limited to executive branch officials. Members of Congress can try to pressure the White House into a particular course of action. And foreign governments also can attempt to move an administration in a certain direction. For example, the Israelis, who wanted to prolong the Iran-Iraq war, were eager to convince American policymakers to make arms available to the Iranians.

The president's most important task in the foreign policymaking process is figuring out who to believe—those who agree with his policy predispositions or those who challenge them. The wrong choice can be extremely costly. Some observers argue that President Johnson's tendency to surround himself with yes-men prevented him from hearing critical analyses of the Vietnam War until very late. President Reagan claimed that he was unaware of important dimensions of the Iran-Contra operation, including the critical fact that funds from the sale of arms to Iran were being used to resupply the Contras. His management style was blamed for these lapses. He was further hampered by the fact that NSC staffers shielded him from the responsibility for decisions. They called this **deniability,** devising methods (among them, shredding documents) that made it impossible to trace decisions to the president. In addition, they made decisions on their own that should have been made by the president himself. Reagan was also criticized for relying too heavily on the NSC and ignoring the intelligence and advice of the foreign policy professionals in the CIA and the Departments of State and Defense, and the members of his cabinet.

Congress and the President

Once a president has decided on a policy, he may be able to carry it out without congressional approval if he has a clear constitutional mandate (for example, recognizing another government or putting the marines on alert). When his constitutional authority is shaky and congressional approval appears unlikely, he may use one or more of the techniques discussed on pages 710–713. A president's third alternative is to ask Congress for the funds or authority to carry out a program.

The president's command of information and personnel gives him a considerable advantage over Congress. Although legislators have ample access to independent sources of information on domestic issues, their sources on foreign affairs are much more limited. Although members of Congress may go on fact-finding tours or get information from lobbyists, they don't begin to have a fraction of the president's sources of information. So they are forced to rely heavily on the executive branch for information.

The president can use his information advantage to swing votes. Just two days after the House vote against Contra aid in March 1986 (and shortly before the Senate voted 53 to 47 in favor of it), the White House announced that fifteen hundred Nicaraguan troops had invaded Honduras in pursuit of the Contras. This release of information embarrassed House members who had voted against the president and may have helped him win support in the Senate.

Lonely at the Top
Being commander in chief of the armed forces is an awesome responsibility. Stunned by a resurgence of enemy activity during the Vietnam War in early 1968, President Lyndon Johnson decided not to seek re-election. Here in July 1968, the president listens to a tape-recorded message from his son-in-law, who was serving in Vietnam.

In addition, the chief executive's personnel resources give him considerable ability to influence events. Many analysts argue, for example, that the attacks on American vessels that sparked the Gulf of Tonkin Resolution during the Vietnam War were pretexts that President Johnson seized on to expand American involvement. The House of Representatives imposed limits on the use of American personnel in Nicaraguan combat areas.

Another potential disability for Congress in the foreign policy process is its fragmented authority over international issues. Different congressional committees have authority for the armed services, for foreign relations, for intelligence oversight, for foreign trade, and for development. There is no congressional equivalent of the National Security Council to mold a coherent approach to foreign policy. Granted, there are often disagreements within the executive branch, and these can spill over into the congressional arena. For example, a Pentagon official might quietly appeal to friendly members of the Armed Services Committees to restore defense cuts made in the president's proposed budget. Disaffected officials might leak information. But by and large, the executive is much better equipped to offer a unified approach to foreign policy.

Faced with its disadvantages in terms of information, personnel, and organization, the general tendency is for Congress to accede to the president's foreign policy programs.

Lobbies and the "Lobbyist in Chief"

When Congress considered aid to the Contras in June 1986, supporters and opponents of the measure made enormous lobbying efforts. Those in favor of aid included the leaders of the United Nicaraguan Opposition (the Contra group that the United States backs) and various conservative organizations, among them, the National Endowment for the Preservation of Liberty, which launched its own $2 million pro-Contra campaign and hired a professional public relations and lobbying firm to represent the Contra cause. Arrayed on the other side were many members of the clergy and peace groups, who publicized the human rights abuses of the Contras. The opponents of aid also had their own professional publicity firm.

The single most effective lobbyist on the issue was not really a lobbyist at all; it was the president. Back in March, White House staffers had used inflammatory rhetoric to brand those who opposed the administration as procommunist. This incensed many members of Congress. By June, the administration had toned down its rhetoric, and Ronald Reagan began to use his influence to generate support for his cause. He made a conciliatory speech calling for a return to the kind of bipartisanship that had supported President Truman's request for aid to Greece and Turkey almost forty years earlier. He worked hard on the sixteen Republicans who had voted against him in March, assuring them that the aid was necessary. He was able to convince five, including Chalmers Wylie of Ohio, who acknowledged that he had difficulty naming the countries of Central America and had decided to defer to the president's judgment, pointing out that "he's a very persuasive fellow."[31] Reagan was also able to convince three Democrats to change their votes, giving him a majority.

If Ronald Reagan was the best lobbyist for his own policy, Daniel Ortega, leader of the Sandinista government, was probably the worst for his cause. Opponents of Contra aid found Ortega's ideological orientation increasingly difficult to defend. His trip to Moscow and a Nicaraguan incursion into Honduras made it difficult for wavering representatives to refuse Reagan's request.

Policy Implementation

A president may decide on a course of action, and Congress may authorize it, but the policy still must be carried out. The question of who should carry out a particular policy is not always easy to answer. Although the basic functions of each department and agency are spelled out, at times they overlap. When they do, organizations may squabble over which should perform a particular mission. During the Cuban missile crisis, for example, there were disputes between the CIA and the military concerning who should fly reconnaissance flights over Cuba.

When new provisions for Contra aid were approved in 1986, some potentially divisive disputes over implementation surfaced after the bill had cleared the House. They concerned the division of responsibility for the aid package. Although technically the State Department administered the aid program, control over the newly authorized funding seemed to pass to the military and the CIA.

Congress, of course, is responsible for overseeing the implementation of programs. This means, among other things, monitoring the use of funds and evaluating the effectiveness of programs. Of course, Congress cannot monitor what it does not know about, and a major attraction of the Iran-Contra plan for NSC staffers was that it allowed them to avoid Congressional oversight. Indeed, when called to testify before Congress about arms sales to Iran and covert actions in Nicaragua, North and other officials lied repeatedly to Congress—according to North's later testimony. And he destroyed official documents that might have detailed his activities. North and others justified their actions as necessary to protect against leaks. Members of Congress complained that they could not fulfill their legislative function if NSC staffers provided information to a wide range of foreign officials and private citizens in Iran, Israel, and Nicaragua while simultaneously denying it to American officials who had both a legal right and a responsibility to know.

DEFENSE POLICY

At the beginning of this chapter, we noted that adherents to the Munich and Vietnam paradigms have very different attitudes about how and when to use the tools of American foreign policy. It would be far too simplistic to say that those influenced by the Munich paradigm see military force as the only choice, and that those influenced by the Vietnam paradigm would never resort to force. But the two groups do differ significantly in the emphasis they place on the country's military, economic, and diplomatic resources. In this section and the next, we examine the military and economic tools available to policymakers and some of the ways in which adherents to each of the two paradigms think they should be used.

How Much Should We Spend?

Most people agree that in order to protect national interests, the United States needs an adequate defense. But beyond this point, agreement breaks down. What constitutes an adequate defense? To what extent should defense spending take priority over other kinds of spending?

Ronald Reagan came to office committed to a strong national defense. He also pledged to cut the national budget. During his administration, the national government did trim back expenditures for domestic

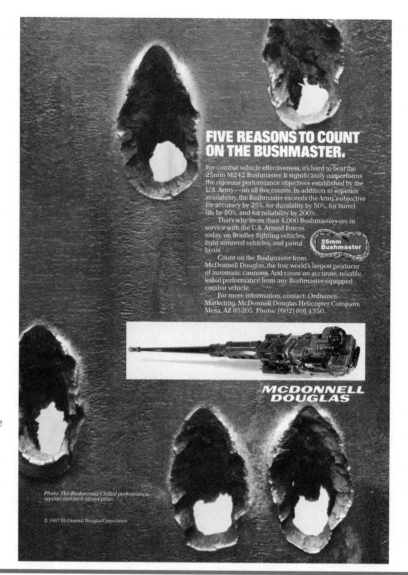

Firepower for Sale
Need to spruce up your fighting vehicle? Buy the 25mm M242 Bushmaster automatic cannon from McDonnell Douglas. This advertisement shows that U.S. defense contractors are in business to sell to countries throughout the world, although other countries— Sweden, Italy, and Israel, for example—market their weapons for international sales even more aggressively. Sale of military equipment is big business in any language.

programs, but defense spending increased enormously. The president maintained that the level of the defense budget was not really under his control—that it was established in Moscow. He claimed that the only way to gauge the adequacy of American defense is by comparing our military spending with that of the Soviet Union (see Compared With What? 19.1).

Critics of large defense budgets ask if the United States can defend itself adequately by investing huge amounts in sophisticated military hardware while cutting back on funds to develop "human capital"—that is, funds to prepare people to do the job. Without programs for children's nutrition and education, we threaten a valuable resource. Other critics insist that high levels of defense spending throw the entire national budget out of line, creating deficits that could endanger the overall performance of the U.S. economy. A weak economy, in turn, could make

COMPARED WITH WHAT? 19.1

Defense Spending, 1974–1984

President Reagan argued that the level of U.S. defense spending is set in Moscow. In other words, America's military spending must keep pace with that of the Soviet Union. This graph compares the total defense expenditures for the United States and the Soviet Union. It shows that the Soviet Union consistently outspends the United States. The picture changes, however, when we add the defense spending of NATO nations and the Soviet bloc (the Warsaw Pact nations).

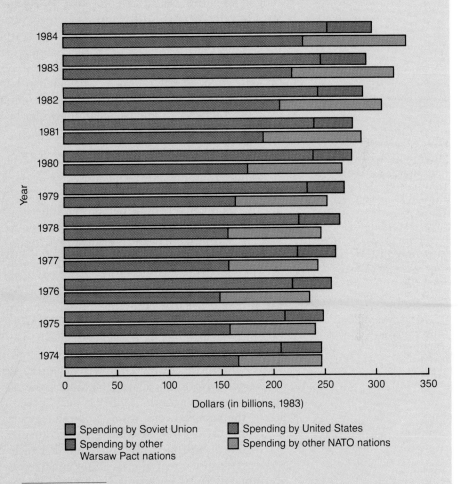

Dollars (in billions, 1983)

■ Spending by Soviet Union   ■ Spending by United States
■ Spending by other   ■ Spending by other NATO nations
   Warsaw Pact nations

Source: Data from U.S. Arms Control and Disarmament Agency, *World Military Expenditures and Arms Transfers* (Washington, D.C.: U.S. Government Printing Office, 1986).

the nation more vulnerable to outside pressures. By increasing defense outlays, then, we may actually be making the United States less secure. And they point to the experience of other great powers in modern history. Nations that achieved great strength through economic or technological advantages have tended to channel vast resources into protecting their position through military means. As the military sector of a nation grows, however, the other areas of society tend to stagnate, and the nation loses the creative edge that was once the source of its advantage.[32]

Finally, there are critics who object to enormous defense spending on moral and political grounds. Eisenhower's warning about the military-industrial complex is a case in point. In a kind of vicious circle, military spending feeds powerful interests, which depend on that spending and in turn exert pressure to increase it. Huge amounts of money are spent for defense, and every state in the country profits from that spending. The close relationships among Pentagon personnel, elected and appointed government officials, and defense contractors has led to widespread corruption in the military procurement process. To break the cycle, critics argue, defense spending must be cut.

What Should Defense Money Buy?

Another important issue involved in our defense policy is deciding what the defense budget should be spent on. There are many important options here in terms of personnel and equipment. One is whether to have a volunteer military force or to require service by some or all citizens. Others concern the kinds of weapons systems to build and the mix of nuclear and conventional forces.

The Reagan administration was particularly supportive of high-technology weapons systems, both nuclear and conventional. It championed the B–1 and Stealth bombers and worked hard to secure congressional authorization for the MX, a new generation of land-based intercontinental ballistic missiles (ICBMs). The administration also launched a large-scale research and development effort called the **Strategic Defense Initiative (SDI)**, or "Star Wars." Its objective was to build a system that could defend against Soviet ICBMs. In the absence of that defense, the only protection against ICBMs is deterrence, the fear of retaliation that keeps the superpowers from using nuclear weapons.

Some critics oppose weapons expenditures, not because they oppose all forms of military spending, but because they believe that certain systems do not meet the nation's defense needs. They faulted SDI, for example, as being both unworkable and far too expensive. Even a system that could defend perfectly against ICBMs would not halt the threat of nuclear extermination. The technology would not be effective against sea-launched missiles fired from offshore submarines or cruise missiles flying close to the ground. Cutbacks in defense budgets have forced the Pentagon to rethink its priorities as well, to think more carefully about which weapons systems to purchase. Faced with the necessity of making a choice, many Pentagon officials favored alternatives to the SDI.

Critics also make a persuasive case against expenditures for large, costly high-technology weapons. They argue that bigger and more expensive is not always better. Lower-technology weapons break down less often and require less maintenance. They are cheaper to repair and operate. This means troops are able to gain more training experience with them and can become more proficient at using them, experience that could be critical in a combat situation.[33]

Defense Policy and Foreign Policy

What is the relationship between defense policy and foreign policy? Although some believe that a strong defense is the cornerstone of foreign policy, others recognize that not every foreign policy objective can be achieved through the application of military force alone. The use of force may have helped the United States meet its objectives in Grenada and Libya, but conditions in more complicated situations (Lebanon, Central America) demand the use of other foreign policy tools. From another perspective, our weapons arsenal can be used as a bargaining chip to exact concessions in our negotiations with foreign powers.

ECONOMIC POLICY

Just as it would be wrong to say that Vietnam-paradigm adherents oppose all use of force, it would also be wrong to imply that Munich-paradigm supporters reject all methods short of force. The Reagan administration did provide substantial economic aid to Latin American countries, for example. This kind of aid is one of many economic tools the United States has at its disposal in meeting its foreign policy goals. These economic tools—including development aid, preferential trade agreements, and loans on favorable credit terms—are used as incentives and rewards for nations that support U.S. policies.

Japanese Compete for U.S. Markets
Japanese cars captured a growing share of the American market in the 1970s and 1980s. Spurred by the U.S. auto industry, the government imposed import quotas on Japanese cars, forcing prices up. The Reagan administration, preferring freedom of the marketplace, opposed such protectionism. When the quotas were lifted, the Japanese imposed their own restraints in order to keep their prices (and profit margins) high. The soaring value of the Japanese yen against the U.S. dollar pushed Japanese car prices to new heights in 1988.

Economic tools like these may also be used as sanctions. When the United States wanted to oust Noriega, it used its substantial control over the banking and currency system of Panama as a means of pressuring him. **Embargoes** and **boycotts** are used to punish nations whose policies we do not approve of. In recent years, under the Carter administration, the United States imposed a grain embargo against the Soviet Union—that is, the United States stopped wheat shipments to the Soviet Union—to convince the Russians to leave Afghanistan. Shortly after Castro took power in Cuba, the United States imposed a boycott on Cuban products; it refused to allow American citizens to import Cuban sugar, cigars, and other goods.

Neither the grain embargo nor the Cuban boycott has proved particularly effective in furthering foreign policy goals. The Soviets stayed in Afghanistan to the end of Reagan's presidency, and Castro's power in Cuba is still secure. The two policies did have somewhat different effects at home. American pluralist democracy helps explain why one was dropped and the other remains in effect. American grain farmers were seriously hurt by the Soviet grain embargo. They were caught without a market for huge amounts of wheat that originally were destined for the Soviet Union. They were a vocal minority, and the nation heard them. When the embargo became generally unpopular, it was lifted by President Reagan. In contrast, the boycott of Cuban sugar has helped America's domestic sugar industry. Any attempt to lift the boycott would be resisted, not only by the large community of anti-Castro Cubans now living in this country, but also by the sugar industry, which would suddenly have to compete with cheaper Cuban sugar. Because there is no strong pressure to remove the boycott, it remains in place. And pluralist politics triumph.

In addition to embargoes and boycotts, import restrictions (tariffs, quotas, nontariff barriers) are another "negative" economic tool.* As we pointed out in Chapter 9, there can be strong domestic pressure to adopt import restrictions. Essentially, unions and manufacturers want to keep foreign goods from flooding the American market and driving them out of business. But protectionism is a double-edged sword. The countries whose products are kept out of the United States retaliate by refusing to import American goods. And protectionism complicates the foreign policymaking process enormously. It is a distinctly unfriendly move to make toward nations that may be our allies.

SUMMARY

When America emerged as a superpower following World War II, the common experience of that war forged a consensus on foreign policy: Communism was the threat, and that policy focused on containing Soviet expansion. The Vietnam War challenged that world-view and shattered the consensus. Some of the pluralism characteristic of other aspects of our political system began to characterize foreign policy. Military force was not the only tool at hand to protect American interests; both economic aid and diplomacy began to play a part in the policymaking process.

Responsibility for foreign policy is shared by the president, Congress, and several executive depart-

---

* Nontariff barriers (NTBs) limit imports by setting product specifications for imported goods.

ments and agencies. In the absence of widespread consensus, foreign policy can become a political football in contests between the executive and Congress and among the bureaucracies. These contests are frequently played before a mass audience on live television. It was exactly the potential for this sort of conflict that led Tocqueville to his conclusion that democracies are not very good at foreign politics. And it was exactly this sort of conflict that led NSC staffers to skirt the law, to replace accountability with deniability.

We began this chapter by asking whether foreign policy is different from other kinds of policy. Certainly the nature of democracy—the public's right to know—at times conflicts with the planning and implementation of foreign policy. But when government officials circumvent the safeguards—the system of checks and balances that protect American freedom—they risk domestic order in their pursuit of world order. Can Americans find a way to support freedom, order, and equality abroad while preserving these values at home? This may be the ultimate challenge of democracy.

Key Terms

Munich paradigm	military-industrial
Vietnam paradigm	complex
détente	deterrence
isolationism	mutual assured
globalism	destruction (MAD)
Cold War	flexible response
containment	nation-building policy
Marshall Plan	Vietnamization
zero-sum game	Nixon Doctrine

linkage	War Powers Resolution
executive agreement	special envoy
discretionary funds	deniability
transfer authority	Strategic Defense
reprogramming	Initiative (SDI)
excess stock disposal	embargo
undeclared war	boycott

Selected Readings

Crabb, Cecil V., and Pat M. Holt. *An Invitation to Struggle.* Washington, D.C.: Congressional Quarterly Press, 1980. Describes the interplay between Congress and the executive on foreign policy issues.

Fallows, James. *National Defense.* New York: Vintage, 1981. A critical look at American defense policy, which focuses on the fit (or lack of fit) between weapons systems and the needs they are chosen to fill.

Kennedy, Paul. *The Rise and Fall of the Great Powers.* New York: Random House, 1988. Discusses the reasons why various nations have gained and lost power in the modern world and concludes with a section entitled "The United States: The Problem of Number One in Relative Decline."

Nathan, James A., and James K. Oliver. *United States Foreign Policy and World Order.* 3d ed. Boston: Little, Brown, 1985. An excellent general history of American foreign policy since World War II.

Spanier, John, and Eric Uslaner. *American Foreign Policy Making and the Democratic Dilemmas.* 4th ed. New York: Holt, Rinehart & Winston, 1985. A brief examination of the foreign policymaking process.

Epilogue

Who would have thought it? There was President Ronald Reagan at Moscow State University on May 31, 1988, speaking under a colossal bust of Lenin, leader of the Bolshevik Revolution! This was the same arch anticommunist president who, just five years earlier, had called the Soviet Union an "evil empire." Asked about that statement, Reagan replied, "I was talking about another time, another era." Soon after leaving Moscow, Reagan praised Mikhail Gorbachev, general secretary of the Communist party of the Soviet Union, as "a serious man seeking serious reform."[1]

Reagan's description was apt. Gorbachev had undertaken major political reforms: a program of *perestroika* to restructure the economy of the Soviet Union and a policy of *glasnost* to open political life there. The impact of *glasnost* was already evident. In the summer of 1988—a month after Reagan left Moscow—the Communist party of the Soviet Union held an extraordinary conference. Nearly five thousand delegates gathered in Moscow's Palace of Congresses to debate Gorbachev's policies. For four days, they spoke their minds about Soviet economic and political life with unprecedented candor, while microphones and television cameras broadcast the proceedings.

Speakers criticized the bureaucracy's performance, the quality and supply of goods, the treatment of the environment, even the benefits of Gorbachev's economic restructuring. Top Party and government leaders were not immune to criticism. Delegate Vladimir I. Melnikov, a minor Party official, charged: "People who in previous times actively conducted the policy of stagnation cannot now be on, or work in, central party or Soviet organs in the period of restructuring." Gorbachev interrupted, saying, "We're sitting here and don't know. Is he talking about me or somebody else?"[2] Melnikov promptly replied, "I would refer first of all to Comrade Solmentsev, and to Comrades Gromyko, Afanasyev, Arbatov and others."[3] The shocked delegates recognized the names of a senior member of the ruling politburo, the president of the Soviet Union, the editor of *Pravda*, and the powerful head of the Institute for the Study of Canada and the United States.

The Soviet people were stunned when they saw and heard the exchange on television news that evening. Natalaya Bachkova, a twenty-five-year-old music teacher, said, "My family's been watching all this and holding our breath." Nail Abdulin, a thirty-two-year-old worker at an electrical power plant, shook his head in amazement "that such a thing could be on television."[4] A Muscovite artist in her forties said, "I am hearing things on television that weeks ago I would never have whispered over the telephone."[5]

Gorbachev in his closing speech characterized the conference as a "major event" in the history of the Communist party:

> This was a truly open party talk about the principal things that concern today the Communists, Soviet people, an attempt to find answers to questions that worry them. This [Palace of Congresses] has not known such discussions, comrades, and, I think, we will not err from the truth by saying that nothing of the kind has occurred in this country for nearly six decades.[6]

And Gorbachev admitted that his policy of *glasnost*, which he equated with democratization, would provide a "serious test" to the Party.[7]

Gorbachev had already encountered problems with *glasnost*. In 1987, citizens in Leningrad formed an environmental action group to protest the construction of a dam outside the city. Wrapping themselves in Gorbachev's call for more democracy, they organized rallies and lobbied government officials, arguing that the dam was an environmental hazard and that the funds could be spent better elsewhere.[8] Although citizen action groups are common in the United States, they are not in the Soviet Union, where formation of public policy had been determined by the Communist party.

As more groups with political objectives sprouted across the country, the Soviet government had trouble drawing the line between those that supposedly showed a healthy sign of civic interest under *glasnost* and those that promoted anti-Soviet views. *Pravda* cautioned against groups that advocated opposition political parties, independent trade unions, and nationalism. A front-page editorial noted the "clearly illegal character" of their activities: "Without the permission of the authorities, they organize demonstrations, even disturbances. They illegally print and disseminate literature hostile to socialism." *Pravda* dismissed the concept of "pluralism on the Western model" in favor of "the deepening and spreading of socialist democracy."[9]

But it is difficult to contain pluralism, especially in an ethnically heterogeneous society like the Union of Soviet Socialist Republics. Shortly after the Party conference ended, the Soviet Republic of Armenia boldly sought to annex a region populated by Christian Armenians in adjacent Azerbaijan. In turning down the Armenian request, a frustrated Gorbachev sided with law-and-order conservatives in the Soviet legislature, saying: "*Perestroika* requires democratization and *glasnost*, but we can see in this case how under the banner of democratization shameless pressure is being applied by irresponsible people on worker collectives and on the population of the republics and how bodies of power, including the Presidium of the Supreme Soviet of the Soviet Union, are coming under pressure as well."[10]

DEMOCRACY: THE CHALLENGE

Democracy is not an easy mode of government, even in countries where it's long established. As Gorbachev is finding out, when citizens are allowed to participate in government decisions from which they previously were excluded, their choices often conflict with existing policies. You remember that in Chapter 1 we noted that public policy in the Soviet Union traditionally has favored order over freedom. By increasing political freedom, *glasnost* inevitably promises some degree of disorder. In Chapter 1 we also talked about the communist government's preference for equality over economic freedom. By relaxing economic controls, *perestroika* sacrifices equality for the economic freedom and growth of private business.

According to capitalist theory, genuine economic freedom will bring more than economic growth to the Soviet Union; it will bring democracy. This theory holds that capitalism brings democracy by decentralizing power among a great number of individuals who have sufficient resources to challenge the government's actions.[11] Indeed, most research supports the relationship between capitalism and democracy—certainly the Western model of democracy.[12] Recent research also suggests, ironically, that capitalism even works to further the communist goal of economic equality.[13] According to this theory, capitalism promotes equality in two ways: (1) by increasing economic growth for the entire society and (2) through democratic processes that invite people who are at the lower end of the income scale to demand and get larger shares of the growing wealth.[14]

You have been raised under capitalism and probably accept this theory. But think of people raised under communism. They have been taught that the profit motive produces unfair accumulation of wealth, which violates the principle of socialist equality. Many Soviet citizens strongly oppose private business, the symbol of capitalism. And early reports charged that the new private sectors in the Soviet Union had brought a "general rise in the level of greed," with symptoms of price gouging, profiteering, and scheming to cash in before *perestroika* disappeared.[15] Describing the burning of a private jewelry booth after its owner refused to pay protection money, the weekly *Moscow News* said: "Little by little we are catching up with America. Now we have protection rackets to boast about."[16]

When he launched *perestroika*—the most significant change in Soviet economic policy in decades—Mikhail Gorbachev was certainly not responding to public opinion. But we do not expect Soviet policy to respond to public opinion. The Soviet Union, despite *glasnost*, is still far from a democracy. Even the U.S. government, as we have seen, does not always respond to public opinion. Still we call it a democracy. In so doing, we relax the requirement of the majoritarian model of democracy—that government should respond to the people—in favor of an alternative criterion—that government should allow private interests to organize and press their competing claims openly in the political system. This is the model of democracy that the United States presents to the world.[17]

DOES GOVERNMENT DO
WHAT PEOPLE WANT?

Of course, even if the United States fits more closely to the pluralist than the majoritarian model of democracy, we nevertheless should expect the government to respond to public opinion. But does it? How often? And on what issues?

In assessing whether the U.S. government does what the people want, we rely heavily on two major studies. In one, Alan Monroe compared public opinion on public issues with government policy outcomes for 327 cases from 1960 through 1980.[18] He first asked whether the public favored a change in policy on the issue or preferred the status quo. He then classified subsequent government action as manifesting a "change" or the "status quo." If the public favored a change, and government policy changed accordingly, the policy was judged to be *consistent* with public opinion. Similarly, if the public favored the status quo and government policy continued as before, the policy was also scored as consistent. Obviously, when government policy did not reflect public opinion, the case was counted as *inconsistent*.

Overall, Monroe found that government policy conformed to public opinion on 63 percent of all 327 cases. Although this may seem reassuring for majoritarian democracy, understand that about 50 percent of the cases would be consistent if government policy were decided purely by chance. More interesting, there were important differences in policy outcomes when the public favored a change instead of the status quo. As shown in Figure E.1, government policy was far more likely (82

Figure E.1 ━━━

Relationship Between Majority Opinion and Policy Outcome for 327 Cases, 1960–1980
The darker color denotes inconsistencies between policy and opinion. (Source: Alan D. Monroe, "Does the U.S. Government Do What the People Want?" [Paper delivered at the Arts and Sciences Lecture, Illinois State University, Normal, 26 October 1987], table 2.)

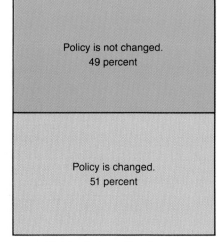

Opinion favors status quo.
(125 cases)

Opinion favors policy change.
(202 cases)

percent) to match public opinion if the people liked things as they were. If the public favored a policy change, government policy was almost as likely to remain the same as to change.

The other major study proceeded somewhat differently. Benjamin Page and Robert Shapiro pored over thousands of questions asked in national surveys between 1935 and 1979, looking for cases of opinion change.[19] They found 231 instances when opinion moved up or down at least 6 percentage points between two surveys *and* when government policy changed in keeping with opinion. Their study—done independently of Monroe's, covering a longer period, and with different objectives—produced a similar finding: Policy changes were consistent with opinion changes in 66 percent of the cases.[20] Looking at it the other way, policies changed contrary to opinions 34 percent of the time. (Remember, about a 50–50 split would be expected by chance anyway.)

Is there enough congruence between public opinion and policymaking to validate the United States' claim to be a democracy? To approach an answer, we have to examine these two studies more closely. When Page and Shapiro calculated consistency between opinion change and policy change for different levels of opinion change, they found that very large changes in public opinion (20 points or more) produced consistent policy changes more than 90 percent of the time.[21] This suggests that the government responds to major shifts of opinion. Moreover, the authors defend the rationality of the opinion shifts: "When opinion shifts occurred, they were not random or capricious; they were usually related to important changes in citizens' social and economic environments."[22]

To learn which policy areas showed more consistency between public opinion and government action, Monroe analyzed his cases by issue type. He found that consistency was greatest on foreign policy issues and least on issues of political reform. He explained that foreign policy is most nearly under the control of the executive and that the public is more apt to accept presidential leadership in foreign rather than domestic affairs. In contrast, issues of political reform—by definition—require policy change, and many reforms—such as abolishing the electoral college or lowering the voting age—require adoption of a constitutional amendment. Monroe concluded that the most important finding from his data is the bias against change in our political process:

> An all too typical pattern is for the President to propose some new program which enjoys public support and is favorably received by Congressional leaders, but the bill then languishes in committee, passes one house, but not the other, and is eventually rendered irrelevant by the passage of time. It is not that political leaders are not inclined to favor the same positions as public majorities, for they are. The difficulty lies with the complexity of the institutional structure of both Congress and the bureaucracy, the political power of those representing minority positions, and the effects of lobbying by organized groups.[23]

We could argue that government officials should lead rather than follow public opinion. When the U.S. Navy accidentally shot down a civilian Iranian airplane in the Persian Gulf in July 1988, killing 290 passengers, a quick poll found Americans opposed to paying compensation to the victims' families, 49 to 36 percent.[24] Yet President Reagan later announced that the United States would compensate the families. Clearly the president was acting against public opinion. Even if you accept his actions and reject the idea that government should always respond to public opinion, are you satisfied with government that responds to public opinion only about 65 percent of the time?

Monroe believes—as do Page and Shapiro—that the quality of government in America would improve if public opinion played a more important role, if government became more majoritarian. Monroe in particular thinks that stronger political parties—in line with the responsible party model described in Chapter 8—are the key to making the government more majoritarian.[25] But you should not accept what they (or we) believe is the better model of democracy. You must think through what *you* know about American government and politics—about the relationships among freedom, order, and equality and about alternative models of democratic government—and formulate your own views as you grapple with the challenge of democracy.

As we said at the beginning of this book, good government often means making tough choices. By looking beyond specifics to underlying normative principles, you should be able to identify these choices and thus make more sense out of politics. As the years pass and the facts fade (perhaps after the final examination in this course), you should still be able to understand politics by focusing on the underlying conflicts among freedom, order, and equality. Questions about democracy—whether and how to change it—can be interpreted through the majoritarian and pluralist models. Armed with these five key concepts—freedom, order, equality, majoritarianism, and pluralism—you will be better prepared to make political choices. The direction of American government rests in your hands.

Appendices

THE DECLARATION OF INDEPENDENCE IN CONGRESS JULY 4, 1776

The unanimous declaration of the thirteen United States of America

When, in the course of human events, it becomes necessary for one people to dissolve the political bands which have connected them with another, and to assume, among the powers of the earth, the separate and equal station to which the laws of nature and of nature's God entitle them, a decent respect to the opinions of mankind requires that they should declare the causes which impel them to the separation.

We hold these truths to be self-evident: That all men are created equal; that they are endowed by their Creator with certain unalienable rights; that among these are life, liberty, and the pursuit of happiness; that, to secure these rights, governments are instituted among men, deriving their just powers from the consent of the governed; that whenever any form of government becomes destructive of these ends, it is the right of the people to alter or to abolish it, and to institute new government, laying its foundation on such principles, and organizing its power in such form, as to them shall seem most likely to effect their safety and happiness. Prudence, indeed, will dictate that governments long established should not be changed for light and transient causes; and accordingly all experience hath shown that mankind are more disposed to suffer, while evils are sufferable, than to right themselves by abolishing the forms to which they are accustomed. But when a long train of abuses and usurpations, pursuing invariably the same object, evinces a design to reduce them under absolute despotism, it is their right, it is their duty, to throw off such government, and to provide new guards for their future security. Such has been the patient sufferance of these colonies; and such is now the necessity which constrains them to alter their former systems of government. The history of the present King of Great Britain is a history of repeated injuries and usurpations, all having in direct object the establishment of an absolute tyranny over these states. To prove this, let facts be submitted to a candid world.

He has refused his assent to laws, the most wholesome and necessary for the public good.

He has forbidden his governors to pass laws of immediate and pressing importance, unless suspended in their operation till his assent should be obtained; and, when so suspended, he has utterly neglected to attend to them.

He has refused to pass other laws for the accommodation of large districts of people, unless those people would relinquish the right of representation in the legislature, a right inestimable to them, and formidable to tyrants only.

He has called together legislative bodies at places unusual, uncomfortable, and distant from the depository of their public records, for the sole purpose of fatiguing them into compliance with his measures.

He has dissolved representative houses repeatedly, for opposing, with manly firmness, his invasions on the rights of the people.

He has refused for a long time, after such dissolutions, to cause others to be elected; whereby the legislative powers, incapable of annihilation, have returned to the people at large for their exercise; the state remaining, in the mean time, exposed to all the dangers of invasions from without and convulsions within.

He has endeavored to prevent the population of these states; for that purpose obstructing the laws for naturalization of foreigners; refusing to pass others to encourage their migration hither, and raising the conditions of new appropriations of lands.

He has obstructed the administration of justice, by refusing his assent to laws for establishing judiciary powers.

He has made judges dependent on his will alone, for the tenure of their offices, and the amount and payment of their salaries.

He has erected a multitude of new offices, and sent hither swarms of officers to harass our people and eat out their substance.

He has kept among us, in times of peace, standing armies, without the consent of our legislatures.

He has affected to render the military independent of, and superior to, the civil power.

He has combined with others to subject us to a jurisdiction foreign to our constitution, and unacknowledged by our laws, giving his assent to their acts of pretended legislation:

For quartering large bodies of armed troops among us;

For protecting them, by a mock trial, from punishment for any murders which they should commit on the inhabitants of these states;

For cutting off our trade with all parts of the world;

For imposing taxes on us without our consent;

For depriving us, in many cases, of the benefits of trial by jury;

For transporting us beyond seas, to be tried for pretended offenses;

For abolishing the free system of English laws in a neighboring province, establishing therein an arbitrary government, and enlarging its boundaries, so as to render it at once an example and fit instrument for introducing the same absolute rule into these colonies;

For taking away our charters, abolishing our most valuable laws, and altering fundamentally the forms of our governments;

For suspending our own legislatures, and declaring themselves invested with power to legislate for us in all cases whatsoever.

He has abdicated government here, by declaring us out of his protection and waging war against us.

He has plundered our seas, ravaged our coasts, burned our towns, and destroyed the lives of our people.

He is at this time transporting large armies of foreign mercenaries to complete the works of death, desolation, and tyranny already begun with circumstances of cruelty and perfidy scarcely paralleled in the most barbarous ages, and totally unworthy the head of a civilized nation.

He has constrained our fellow-citizens, taken captive on the high seas, to bear arms against their country, to become the executioners of their friends and brethren, or to fall themselves by their hands.

He has excited domestic insurrection among us, and has endeavored to bring on the inhabitants of our frontiers the merciless Indian savages, whose known rule of warfare is an undistinguished destruction of all ages, sexes, and conditions.

In every stage of these oppressions we have petitioned for redress in the most humble terms; our repeated petitions have been answered only by repeated injury. A prince, whose character is thus marked by every act which may define a tyrant, is unfit to be the ruler of a free people.

Nor have we been wanting in our attentions to our British brethren. We have warned them, from time to time, of attempts by their legislature to extend an unwarrantable jurisdiction over us. We have reminded them of the circumstances of our emigration and settlement here. We have appealed to their native justice and magnanimity; and we have conjured them, by the ties of our common kindred, to disavow these usurpations, which would inevitably interrupt our connections and correspondence. They, too, have been deaf to the voice of justice and of consanguinity. We must, therefore, acquiesce in the necessity which denounces our separation, and hold them, as we hold the rest of mankind, enemies in war, in peace friends.

We, therefore, the representatives of the United States of America, in General Congress assembled, appealing to the Supreme Judge of the world for the rectitude of our intentions, do, in the name and by the authority of the good people of these colonies, solemnly publish and declare, that these United Colonies are, and of right ought to be, FREE AND IN-DEPENDENT STATES; that they are absolved from all allegiance to the British crown, and that all political connection between them and the state of Great Britain is, and ought to be, totally dissolved; and that, as free and independent states, they have full power to levy war, conclude peace, contract alliances, establish commerce, and do all other acts and things which independent states may of right do. And for the support of this declaration, with a firm reliance on the protection of Divine Providence, we mutually pledge to each other our lives, our fortunes, and our sacred honor.

JOHN HANCOCK
and fifty-five others

THE CONSTITUTION OF THE UNITED STATES OF AMERICA*

(Preamble: outlines goals and effect)

We the people of the United States, in order to form a more perfect union, establish justice, insure domestic tranquility, provide for the common defense, promote the general welfare, and secure the blessings of liberty to ourselves and our posterity, do ordain and establish this Constitution for the United States of America.

Article I   (The legislative branch)

(Powers vested)

Section 1   All legislative powers herein granted shall be vested in a Congress of the United States, which shall consist of a Senate and a House of Representatives.

(House of Representatives: selection, term, qualifications, apportionment of seats, census requirement, exclusive power to impeach)

Section 2   The House of Representatives shall be composed of members chosen every second year by the people of the several States, and the electors in each State shall have the qualifications requisite for electors of the most numerous branch of the State Legislature.

* Passages no longer in effect are printed in italic type.

No person shall be a Representative who shall not have attained to the age of twenty-five years, and been seven years a citizen of the United States, and who shall not, when elected, be an inhabitant of that State in which he shall be chosen.

Representatives and direct taxes shall be apportioned among the several States which may be included within this Union, according to their respective numbers, *which shall be determined by adding to the whole number of free persons, including those bound to service for a term of years and excluding Indians not taxed, three-fifths of all other persons.* The actual enumeration shall be made within three years after the first meeting of the Congress of the United States, and within every subsequent term of ten years, in such manner as they shall by law direct. The number of Representatives shall not exceed one for every thirty thousand, but each State shall have at least one Representative; *and until such enumeration shall be made, the State of New Hampshire shall be entitled to choose three, Massachusetts eight, Rhode Island and Providence Plantations one, Connecticut five, New York six, New Jersey four, Pennsylvania eight, Delaware one, Maryland six, Virginia ten, North Carolina five, South Carolina five, and Georgia three.*

When vacancies happen in the representation from any State, the Executive authority thereof shall issue writs of election to fill such vacancies.

The House of Representatives shall choose their Speaker and other officers; and shall have the sole power of impeachment.

(Senate: selection, term, qualifications, exclusive power to try impeachments)

Section 3   The Senate of the United States shall be composed of two Senators from each State, *chosen by the legislature thereof,* for six years; and each Senator shall have one vote.

Immediately after they shall be assembled in consequence of the first election, they shall be divided as equally as may be into three classes. The seats of the Senators of the first class shall be vacated at the expiration of the second year, of the second class at the expiration of the fourth year, and of the third class at the expiration of the sixth year, so that one-third may be chosen every second year; *and if vacancies happen by resignation or otherwise, during the recess of the legislature of any State, the Executive thereof may make temporary appointments until the next meeting of the legislature, which shall then fill such vacancies.*

No person shall be a Senator who shall not have attained to the age of thirty years, and been nine years a citizen of the United States, and who shall not, when elected, be an inhabitant of that State for which he shall be chosen.

The Vice-President of the United States shall be President of the Senate, but shall have no vote, unless they be equally divided.

The Senate shall choose their other officers, and also a President *pro tempore*, in the absence of the Vice-President, or when he shall exercise the office of President of the United States.

The Senate shall have the sole power to try all impeachments. When sitting for that purpose, they shall be on oath or affirmation. When the President of the United States is tried, the Chief Justice shall preside: and no person shall be convicted without the concurrence of two-thirds of the members present.

Judgment in cases of impeachment shall not extend further than to removal from the office, and disqualification to hold and enjoy any office of honor, trust or profit under the United States: but the party convicted shall nevertheless be liable and subject to indictment, trial, judgment and punishment, according to law.

(Elections)

Section 4   The times, places and manner of holding elections for Senators and Representatives shall be prescribed in each State by the legislature thereof; but the Congress may at any time by law make or alter such regulations, except as to the places of choosing Senators.

The Congress shall assemble at least once in every year, and such meeting *shall be on the first Monday in December, unless they shall by law appoint a different day.*

(Powers and duties of the two chambers: rules of procedure, power over members)

Section 5   Each house shall be the judge of the elections, returns and qualifications of its own members, and a majority of each shall constitute a quorum to do business; but a smaller number may adjourn from day to day, and may be authorized to compel the attendance of absent members, in such manner, and under such penalties, as each house may provide.

Each house may determine the rules of its proceedings, punish its members for disorderly behavior, and with the concurrence of two-thirds, expel a member.

Each house shall keep a journal of its proceedings, and from time to time publish the same, excepting such parts as may in their judgment require secrecy;

and the yeas and nays of the members of either house on any question shall, at the desire of one-fifth of those present, be entered on the journal.

Neither house, during the session of Congress, shall, without the consent of the other, adjourn for more than three days, nor to any other place than that in which the two houses shall be sitting.

(Compensation, privilege from arrest, privilege of speech, disabilities of members)

Section 6   The Senators and Representatives shall receive a compensation for their services, to be ascertained by law and paid out of the treasury of the United States. They shall in all cases except treason, felony and breach of the peace, be privileged from arrest during their attendance at the session of their respective houses, and in going to and returning from the same; and for any speech or debate in either house, they shall not be questioned in any other place.

No Senator or Representative shall, during the time for which he was elected, be appointed to any civil office under the authority of the United States, which shall have been created, or the emoluments whereof shall have been increased, during such time; and no person holding any office under the United States shall be a member of either house during his continuance in office.

(Legislative process: revenue bills, approval or veto power of president)

Section 7   All bills for raising revenue shall originate in the House of Representatives; but the Senate may propose or concur with amendments as on other bills.

Every bill which shall have passed the House of Representatives and the Senate, shall, before it become a law, be presented to the President of the United States; if he approve he shall sign it, but if not he shall return it with objections to that house in which it originated, who shall enter the objections at large on their journal, and proceed to reconsider it. If after such reconsideration two-thirds of that house shall agree to pass the bill, it shall be sent, together with the objections, to the other house, by which it shall likewise be reconsidered, and, if approved by two-thirds of that house, it shall become a law. But in all such cases the votes of both houses shall be determined by yeas and nays, and the names of the persons voting for and against the bill shall be entered on the journal of each house respectively. If any bill shall not be returned by the President within ten days (Sundays excepted) after it shall have been presented to him, the same shall be a law, in like manner as if he had signed it, unless the Congress by their adjournment prevent its return, in which case it shall not be a law.

Every order, resolution, or vote to which the concurrence of the Senate and House of Representatives may be necessary (except on a question of adjournment) shall be presented to the President of the United States; and before the same shall take effect, shall be approved by him, or being disapproved by him, shall be repassed by two-thirds of the Senate and House of Representatives, according to the rules and limitations prescribed in the case of a bill.

(Powers of Congress enumerated)

Section 8   The Congress shall have power

To lay and collect taxes, duties, imposts, and excises, to pay the debts and provide for the common defense and general welfare of the United States; but all duties, imposts and excises shall be uniform throughout the United States;

To borrow money on the credit of the United States;

To regulate commerce with foreign nations, and among the several States, and with the Indian tribes;

To establish an uniform rule of naturalization, and uniform laws on the subject of bankruptcies throughout the United States;

To coin money, regulate the value thereof, and of foreign coin, and fix the standard of weights and measures;

To provide for the punishment of counterfeiting the securities and current coin of the United States;

To establish post offices and post roads;

To promote the progress of science and useful arts by securing for limited times to authors and inventors the exclusive right to their respective writings and discoveries;

To constitute tribunals inferior to the Supreme Court;

To define and punish piracies and felonies committed on the high seas and offenses against the law of nations;

To declare war, grant letters of marque and reprisal, and make rules concerning captures on land and water;

To raise and support armies, but no appropriation of money to that use shall be for a longer term than two years;

To provide and maintain a navy;

To make rules for the government and regulation of the land and naval forces;

To provide for calling forth the militia to execute the laws of the Union, suppress insurrections, and repel invasions;

To provide for organizing, arming, and disciplining the militia, and for governing such part of them as may be employed in the service of the United States, reserving to the States respectively the appointment of the officers, and the authority of training the militia according to the discipline prescribed by Congress;

To exercise exclusive legislation in all cases whatsoever, over such district (not exceeding ten miles square) as may, by cession of particular States, and the acceptance of Congress, become the seat of government of the United States, and to exercise like authority over all places purchased by the consent of the legislature of the State, in which the same shall be, for erection of forts, magazines, arsenals, dockyards, and other needful buildings;—and

(Elastic clause)

To make all laws which shall be necessary and proper for carrying into execution the foregoing powers, and all other powers vested by this Constitution in the government of the United States, or in any department or officer thereof.

(Powers denied Congress)

Section 9   *The migration or importation of such persons as any of the States now existing shall think proper to admit shall not be prohibited by the Congress prior to the year 1808; but a tax or duty may be imposed on such importation, not exceeding $10 for each person.*

The privilege of the writ of habeas corpus shall not be suspended, unless when in cases of rebellion or invasion the public safety may require it.

No bill of attainder or ex post facto law shall be passed.

No capitation, or other direct, tax shall be laid, unless in proportion to the census or enumeration herein before directed to be taken.

No tax or duty shall be laid on articles exported from any State.

No preference shall be given by any regulation of commerce or revenue to the ports of one State over those of another; nor shall vessels bound to, or from, one State, be obliged to enter, clear, or pay duties in another.

No money shall be drawn from the treasury, but in consequence of appropriations made by law; and a regular statement and account of the receipts and expenditures of all public money shall be published from time to time.

No title of nobility shall be granted by the United States; and no person holding any office or profit or trust under them, shall, without the consent of the Congress, accept of any present, emolument, office, or title, of any kind whatever, from any king, prince, or foreign state.

(Powers denied the states)

Section 10 No State shall enter into any treaty, alliance, or confederation; grant letters of marque and reprisal; coin money; emit bills of credit; make anything but gold and silver coin a tender in payment of debts; pass any bill of attainder, ex post facto law, or law impairing the obligation of contracts, or grant any title of nobility.

No State shall, without the consent of Congress, lay any imposts or duties on imports or exports, except what may be absolutely necessary for executing its inspection laws; and the net produce of all duties and imposts, laid by any State on imports or exports, shall be for the use of the treasury of the United States; and all such laws shall be subject to the revision and control of the Congress.

No State shall, without the consent of Congress, lay any duty of tonnage, keep troops or ships of war in time of peace, enter into any agreement or compact with another State, or with a foreign power, or engage in war, unless actually invaded, or in such imminent danger as will not admit of delay.

Article II (The executive branch)

(The president: power vested, term, electoral college, qualifications, presidential succession, compensation, oath of office)

Section 1 The executive power shall be vested in a President of the United States of America. He shall hold his office during the term of four years, and, together with the Vice-President, chosen for the same term, be elected as follows:

Each State shall appoint, in such manner as the legislature thereof may direct, a number of electors, equal to the whole number of Senators and Representatives to which the State may be entitled in the Congress; but no Senator or Representative, or person holding an office of trust or profit under the United States, shall be appointed an elector.

The electors shall meet in their respective States, and vote by ballot for two persons, of whom one at least shall not be an inhabitant of the same State with themselves. And they shall make a list of all the persons voted for, and of the number of votes for each; which list they shall sign and certify, and transmit sealed to the seat of government of the United

States, directed to the President of the Senate. The President of the Senate shall, in the presence of the Senate and House of Representatives, open all the certificates, and the votes shall then be counted. The person having the greatest number of votes shall be the President, if such number be a majority of the whole number of electors appointed; and if there be more than one who have such majority, and have an equal number of votes, then the House of Representatives shall immediately choose by ballot one of them for President; and if no person have a majority, then from the five highest on the list said house shall in like manner choose the President. But in choosing the President the votes shall be taken by States, the representation from each State having one vote; a quorum for this purpose shall consist of a member or members from two-thirds of the States, and a majority of all the States shall be necessary to a choice. In every case, after the choice of the President, the person having the greatest number of votes of the electors shall be the Vice-President. But if there should remain two or more who have equal votes, the Senate shall choose from them by ballot the Vice-President.

The Congress may determine the time of choosing the electors and the day on which they shall give their votes; which day shall be the same throughout the United States.

No person except a natural-born citizen, *or a citizen of the United States at the time of the adoption of this Constitution,* shall be eligible to the office of President; neither shall any person be eligible to that office who shall not have attained to the age of thirty-five years, and been fourteen years a resident within the United States.

In cases of the removal of the President from office or of his death, resignation, or inability to discharge the powers and duties of the said office, the same shall devolve on the Vice-President, and the Congress may by law provide for the case of removal, death, resignation, or inability, both of the President and Vice-President, declaring what officer shall then act as President, and such officer shall act accordingly, until the disability be removed, or a President shall be elected.

The President shall, at stated times, receive for his services a compensation, which shall neither be increased nor diminished during the period for which he shall have been elected, and he shall not receive within that period any other emolument from the United States, or any of them.

Before he enter on the execution of his office, he shall take the following oath or affirmation:—"I do solemnly swear (or affirm) that I will faithfully execute the office of the President of the United States, and will to the best of my ability preserve, protect and defend the Constitution of the United States."

(Powers and duties: as commander in chief, over advisers, to pardon, to make treaties and appoint officers)

Section 2 The President shall be commander in chief of the army and navy of the United States, and of the militia of the several States, when called into the actual service of the United States; he may require the opinion, in writing, of the principal officer in each of the executive departments, upon any subject relating to the duties of their respective offices, and he shall have power to grant reprieves and pardons for offenses against the United States, except in cases of impeachment.

He shall have power, by and with the advice and consent of the Senate, to make treaties, provided two-thirds of the Senators present concur; and he shall nominate, and by and with the advice and consent of the Senate, shall appoint ambassadors, other public ministers and consuls, judges of the Supreme court, and all other officers of the United States, whose appointments are not herein otherwise provided for, and which shall be established by law: but Congress may by law vest the appointment of such inferior officers, as they think proper, in the President alone, in the courts of law, or in the heads of departments.

The President shall have power to fill up all vacancies that may happen during the recess of the Senate, by granting commissions which shall expire at the end of their next session.

(Legislative, diplomatic, and law-enforcement duties)

Section 3 He shall from time to time give to the Congress information of the state of the Union, and recommend to their consideration such measures as he shall judge necessary and expedient; he may, on extraordinary occasions, convene both houses, or either of them, and in case of disagreement between them, with respect to the time of adjournment, he may adjourn them to such time as he shall think proper; he shall receive ambassadors and other public ministers; he shall take care that the laws be faithfully executed, and shall commission all the officers of the United States.

(Impeachment)

Section 4 The President, Vice-President and all civil officers of the United States shall be removed from office on impeachment for, and on conviction of, treason, bribery, or other high crimes and misdemeanors.

Article III   (The judicial branch)

(Power vested; Supreme Court; lower courts; judges)

Section 1 The judicial power of the United States shall be vested in one Supreme Court, and in such inferior courts as the Congress may from time to time ordain and establish. The judges, both of the Supreme and inferior courts, shall hold their offices during good behavior, and shall, at stated times, receive for their services a compensation which shall not be diminished during their continuance in office.

(Jurisdiction; trial by jury)

Section 2 The judicial power shall extend to all cases, in law and equity, arising under this Constitution, the laws of the United States, and treaties made, or which shall be made, under their authority;—to all cases affecting ambassadors, other public ministers and consuls;—to all cases of admiralty and maritime jurisdiction;—to controversies to which the United States shall be a party;—to controversies between two or more States;—*between a State and citizens of another State;*—between citizens of different States;—between citizens of the same State claiming lands under grants of different States, and between a State, or the citizens thereof, and foreign states, citizens or subjects.

In all cases affecting ambassadors, other public ministers and consuls, and those in which a State shall be party, the Supreme Court shall have original jurisdiction. In all the other cases before mentioned, the Supreme Court shall have appellate jurisdiction, both as to law and fact, with such exceptions, and under such regulations, as the Congress shall make.

The trial of all crimes, except in cases of impeachment, shall be by jury; and such trial shall be held in the state where said crimes shall have been committed; but when not committed within any State, the trial shall be at such place or places as the Congress may by law have directed.

(Treason: definition, punishment)

Section 3 Treason against the United States shall consist only in levying war against them, or in adhering to their enemies, giving them aid and comfort. No person shall be convicted of treason unless on the testimony of two witnesses to the same overt act, or on confession in open court.

The Congress shall have power to declare the punishment of treason, but no attainder of treason shall work corruption of blood, or forfeiture except during the life of the person attained.

Article IV   (States' relations)

(Full faith and credit)

Section 1   Full faith and credit shall be given in each State to the public acts, records, and judicial proceedings of every other State. And the Congress may by general laws prescribe the manner in which such acts, records, and proceedings shall be proved, and the effect thereof.

(Interstate comity; rendition)

Section 2   The citizens of each State shall be entitled to all privileges and immunities of citizens in the several States.

A person charged in any State with treason, felony, or other crime, who shall flee from justice, and be found in another State, shall on demand of the executive authority of the State from which he fled, be delivered up, to be removed to the State having jurisdiction of the crime.

No person held to service or labor in one State, under the laws thereof, escaping into another, shall, in consequence of any law or regulation therein, be discharged from such service or labor, but shall be delivered up on claim of the party to whom such service or labor may be due.

(New states)

Section 3   New States may be admitted by the Congress into this Union; but no new State shall be formed or erected within the jurisdiction of any other State; nor any state be formed by the junction of two or more States, or parts of States, without the consent of the legislatures of the States concerned as well as of the Congress.

The Congress shall have power to dispose of and make all needful rules and regulations respecting the territory or other property belonging to the United States; and nothing in this Constitution shall be so construed as to prejudice any claims of the United States, or of any particular State.

(Obligations of the United States to the states)

Section 4   The United States shall guarantee to every State in this Union a republican form of government, and shall protect each of them against invasion; and

on application of the legislature, or of the executive (when the legislature cannot be convened), against domestic violence.

Article V   (Mode of amendment)

The Congress, whenever two-thirds of both houses shall deem it necessary, shall propose amendments to this Constitution, or, on the application of the legislatures of two-thirds of the several States, shall call a convention for proposing amendments, which, in either case, shall be valid to all intents and purposes, as part of this Constitution, when ratified by the legislatures of three-fourths of the several States, or by conventions in three-fourths thereof, as the one or the other mode of ratification may be proposed by the Congress; provided *that no amendments which may be made prior to the year one thousand eight hundred and eight shall in any manner affect the first and fourth clauses in the ninth section of the first article; and* that no State, without its consent, shall be deprived of its equal suffrage in the Senate.

Article VI   (Prior debts; supremacy of Constitution; oaths of office)

All debts contracted and engagements entered into, before the adoption of this Constitution, shall be as valid against the United States under this Constitution, as under the Confederation.

This Constitution, and the laws of the United States which shall be made in pursuance thereof; and all treaties made, or which shall be made, under the authority of the United States, shall be the supreme law of the land; and the judges in every State shall be bound thereby, anything in the Constitution or laws of any State to the contrary notwithstanding.

The Senators and Representatives before mentioned, and the members of the several State legislatures, and all executive and judicial officers, both of the United States and of the several States, shall be bound by oath or affirmation to support this Constitution; but no religious test shall ever be required as a qualification to any office or public trust under the United States.

Article VII   (Ratification)

The ratification of the conventions of nine States shall be sufficient for the establishment of this Constitution between the States so ratifying the same.

Done in Convention by the unanimous consent of the States present, the seventeenth day of September in the year of our Lord one thousand seven hundred and eighty-seven and of the Independence of the United States of America the twelfth. In witness whereof we have hereunto subscribed our names.

GEORGE WASHINGTON
and thirty-seven others

Amendments to the Constitution

(The first ten amendments—the Bill of Rights—were adopted in 1791.)

Amendment I (Freedom of religion, speech, press, assembly)

Congress shall make no law respecting an establishment of religion, or prohibiting the free exercise thereof; or abridging the freedom of speech, or of the press; or the right of the people peaceably to assemble, and to petition the government for a redress of grievances.

Amendment II (Right to bear arms)

A well-regulated militia being necessary to the security of a free State, the right of the people to keep and bear arms shall not be infringed.

Amendment III (Quartering of soldiers)

No soldier shall, in time of peace, be quartered in any house without the consent of the owner, nor in time of war, but in a manner to be prescribed by law.

Amendment IV (Searches and seizures)

The right of the people to be secure in their persons, houses, papers, and effects, against unreasonable searches and seizures, shall not be violated, and no warrants shall issue but upon probable cause, supported by oath or affirmation, and particularly describing the place to be searched, and the persons or things to be seized.

Amendment V (Rights of persons: grand juries; double jeopardy; self-incrimination; due process; eminent domain)

No person shall be held to answer for a capital, or otherwise infamous crime, unless on a presentment or indictment of a grand jury, except in cases arising in the land or naval forces, or in the militia, when in actual service in time of war or public danger; nor shall any person be subject for the same offense to be twice put in jeopardy of life or limb; nor shall be compelled in any criminal case to be a witness against himself, nor be deprived of life, liberty, or property, without due process of law; nor shall private property be taken for public use without just compensation.

Amendment VI (Rights of accused in criminal prosecutions)

In all criminal prosecutions, the accused shall enjoy the right to a speedy and public trial, by an impartial jury of the State and district wherein the crime shall have been committed, which district shall have been previously ascertained by law, and to be informed of the nature and cause of the accusation; to be confronted with the witnesses against him; to have compulsory process for obtaining witnesses in his favor, and to have the assistance of counsel for his defense.

Amendment VII (Civil trials)

In suits at common law, where the value in controversy shall exceed twenty dollars, the right of trial by jury shall be preserved, and no fact tried by a jury shall be otherwise reexamined in any court of the United States, than according to the rules of the common law.

Amendment VIII (Punishment for crime)

Excessive bail shall not be required, nor excessive fines imposed, nor cruel and unusual punishments inflicted.

Amendment IX (Rights retained by the people)

The enumeration in the Constitution, of certain rights, shall not be construed to deny or disparage others retained by the people.

Amendment X   (Rights reserved to the states)

The powers not delegated to the United States by the Constitution, nor prohibited by it to the States, are reserved to the states respectively, or to the people.

Amendment XI   (Suits against the states; adopted 1798)

The judicial power of the United States shall not be construed to extend to any suit in law or equity, commenced or prosecuted against one of the United States by citizens of another state, or by citizens or subjects of any foreign state.

Amendment XII   (Election of the president; adopted 1804)

The electors shall meet in their respective States, and vote by ballot for President and Vice-President, one of whom, at least, shall not be an inhabitant of the same State with themselves; they shall name in their ballots the person voted for as President, and in distinct ballots the person voted for as Vice-President, and they shall make distinct lists of all persons voted for as President, and of all persons voted for as Vice-President, and of the number of votes for each, which lists they shall sign and certify, and transmit sealed to the seat of government of the United States, directed to the President of the Senate;—the President of the Senate shall, in the presence of the Senate and House of representatives, open all the certificates and the votes shall then be counted;—the person having the greatest number of votes for President shall be the President, if such number be a majority of the whole number of electors appointed; and if no person have such majority, then from the persons having the highest numbers not exceeding three on the list of those voted for as President, the House of Representatives shall choose immediately, by ballot, the President. But in choosing the President, the votes shall be taken by States, the representation from each State having one vote; a quorum for this purpose shall consist of a member or members from two-thirds of the States, and a majority of all the States shall be necessary to a choice. And if the House of Representatives shall not choose a President whenever the right of choice shall devolve upon them, before *the fourth day of March* next following, then the Vice-President shall act as President, as in the case of the death or other constitutional disability of the President.

The person having the greatest number of votes as Vice-President shall be the Vice-President, if such number be a majority of the whole number of electors appointed; and if no person have a majority, then from the two highest numbers on the list the Senate shall choose the Vice-President; a quorum for the purpose shall consist of two-thirds of the whole number of Senators, and a majority of the whole number shall be necessary to a choice. But no person constitutionally ineligible to the office of President shall be eligible to that of Vice-President of the United States.

Amendment XIII   (Abolition of slavery; adopted 1865)

Section 1   Neither slavery nor involuntary servitude, except as a punishment for crime whereof the party shall have been duly convicted, shall exist within the United States, or any place subject to their jurisdiction.

Section 2   Congress shall have power to enforce this article by appropriate legislation.

Amendment XIV   (Adopted 1868)

(Citizenship rights; privileges and immunities; due process; equal protection)

Section 1   All persons born or naturalized in the United States, and subject to the jurisdiction thereof, are citizens of the United States and of the State wherein they reside. No State shall make or enforce any law which shall abridge the privileges or immunities of citizens of the United States; nor shall any State deprive any person of life, liberty, or property, without due process of law; nor deny to any person within its jurisdiction the equal protection of the laws.

(Apportionment of representation)

Section 2   Representatives shall be apportioned among the several States according to their respective numbers, counting the whole number of persons in each State, excluding Indians not taxed. But when the right to vote at any election for the choice of Electors for President and Vice-President of the United States, Representatives in Congress, the executive and judicial officers of a State, or the members of the legislature thereof, is denied to any of the male inhabitants of such State, being twenty-one years of age and citizens of the United States, or in any way abridged, except for participation in rebellion, or other crime, the basis of representation therein shall be reduced in the proportion which the number of such male citizens shall bear to the whole number of male citizens twenty-one years of age in such State.

(Disqualification of Confederate officials)

Section 3 No person shall be a Senator or Representative in Congress, or Elector of President and Vice-President, or hold any office, civil or military, under the United States, or under any State, who, having previously taken an oath, as a member of Congress, or as an officer of the United States, or as a member of any State legislature, or as an executive or judicial officer of any State, to support the Constitution of the United States, shall have engaged in insurrection or rebellion against the same, or given aid or comfort to the enemies thereof. Congress may, by a vote of two-thirds of each house, remove such disability.

(Public debts)

Section 4 The validity of the public debt of the United States, authorized by law, including debts incurred for payment of pensions and bounties for services in suppressing insurrection or rebellion, shall not be questioned. But neither the United States nor any State shall assume or pay any debt or obligation incurred in aid of insurrection or rebellion against the United States, or any claim for the loss of emancipation of any slave; but all such debts, obligations, and claims shall be held illegal and void.

(Enforcement)

Section 5 The Congress shall have power to enforce, by appropriate legislation, the provisions of this article.

Amendment XV (Extension of right to vote; adopted 1870)

Section 1 The right of citizens of the United States to vote shall not be denied or abridged by the United States or by any State on account of race, color, or previous condition of servitude.

Section 2 The Congress shall have power to enforce this article by appropriate legislation.

Amendment XVI (Income tax; adopted 1913)

The Congress shall have power to lay and collect taxes on incomes, from whatever source derived, without apportionment among the several States, and without regard to any census or enumeration.

Amendment XVII (Popular election of senators; adopted 1913)

Section 1 The Senate of the United States shall be composed of two Senators from each State, elected by the people thereof, for six years; and each Senator shall have one vote. The electors in each State shall have the qualifications requisite for electors of [voters for] the most numerous branch of the State legislatures.

Section 2 When vacancies happen in the representation of any State in the Senate, the executive authority of such State shall issue writs of election to fill such vacancies: Provided, that the Legislature of any State may empower the executive thereof to make temporary appointments until the people fill the vacancies by election as the Legislature may direct.

Section 3 This amendment shall not be so construed as to affect the election or term of any Senator chosen before it becomes valid as part of the Constitution.

Amendment XVIII (Prohibition of intoxicating liquors; adopted 1919, repealed 1933)

Section 1 After one year from the ratification of this article the manufacture, sale or transportation of intoxicating liquors within, the importation thereof into, or the exportation thereof from the United States and all territory subject to the jurisdiction thereof, for beverage purposes, is hereby prohibited.

Section 2 The Congress and the several States shall have concurrent power to enforce this article by appropriate legislation.

Section 3 This article shall be inoperative unless it shall have been ratified as an amendment to the Constitution by the legislatures of the several States, as provided by the Constitution, within seven years from the date of the submission thereof to the States by the Congress.

Amendment XIX (Right of women to vote; adopted 1920)

Section 1 The right of citizens of the United States to vote shall not be denied or abridged by the United States or by any State on account of sex.

Section 2 The Congress shall have power to enforce this article by appropriate legislation.

Amendment XX (Commencement of terms of office; adopted 1933)

Section 1 The terms of the President and Vice-President shall end at noon on the 20th day of January, and the terms of Senators and Representatives at noon on the 3d day of January, of the years in which such terms would have ended if this article had not been ratified; and the terms of their successors shall then begin.

Section 2 The Congress shall assemble at least once in every year, and such meetings shall begin at noon on the 3d day of January, unless they shall by law appoint a different day.

(Extension of presidential succession)

Section 3 If, at the time fixed for the beginning of the term of the President, the President-elect shall have died, the Vice-President-elect shall become President. If a President shall not have been chosen before the time fixed for the beginning of his term, or if the President-elect shall have failed to qualify, then the Vice-President-elect shall act as President until a President shall have qualified; and the Congress may by law provide for the case wherein neither a President-elect nor a Vice-President-elect shall have qualified, declaring who shall then act as President, or the manner in which one who is to act shall be selected, and such persons shall act accordingly until a President or Vice-President shall have qualified.

Section 4 The Congress may by law provide for the case of the death of any of the persons from whom the House of Representatives may choose a President whenever the right of choice shall have devolved upon them, and for the case of the death of any of the persons from whom the Senate may choose a Vice-President whenever the right of choice shall have devolved upon them.

Section 5 Sections 1 and 2 shall take effect on the 15th day of October following the ratification of this article.

Section 6 This article shall be inoperative unless it shall have been ratified as an amendment to the Constitution by the Legislatures of three-fourths of the several States within seven years from the date of its submission.

Amendment XXI (Repeal of Eighteenth Amendment; adopted 1933)

Section 1 The eighteenth article of amendment to the Constitution of the United States is hereby repealed.

Section 2 The transportation or importation into any State, Territory, or Possession of the United States for delivery or use therein of intoxicating liquors, in violation of the laws thereof, is hereby prohibited.

Section 3 This article shall be inoperative unless it shall have been ratified as an amendment to the Constitution by conventions in the several States, as provided in the Constitution, within seven years from the date of submission thereof to the States by the Congress.

Amendment XXII (Limit on presidential tenure; adopted 1951)

Section 1 No person shall be elected to the office of President more than twice, and no person who has held the office of President, or acted as President, for more than two years of a term to which some other person was elected President shall be elected to the office of President more than once. But this article shall not apply to any person holding the office of President when this article was proposed by the Congress, and shall not prevent any person who may be holding the office of President, or acting as President, during the term within which this article becomes operative from holding the office of President or acting as President during the remainder of such term.

Section 2 This article shall be inoperative unless it shall have been ratified as an amendment to the Constitution by the legislatures of three-fourths of the several States within seven years from the date of its submission to the States by the Congress.

Amendment XXIII (Presidential electors for the District of Columbia; adopted 1961)

Section 1 The District constituting the seat of Government of the United States shall appoint in such manner as the Congress may direct:

A number of electors of President and Vice-President equal to the whole number of Senators and Representatives in Congress to which the District would be entitled if it were a State, but in no event more than the least populous State; they shall be in addition to those appointed by the States, but they shall be considered for the purposes of the election of President and Vice-President, to be electors appointed by a State; and they shall meet in the District and perform such duties as provided by the twelfth article of amendment.

Section 2 The Congress shall have the power to enforce this article by appropriate legislation.

Amendment XXIV (Poll tax outlawed in national elections; adopted 1964)

Section 1 The right of citizens of the United States to vote in any primary or other election for President or Vice-President, for electors for President or Vice-President, or for Senator or Representative in Congress, shall not be denied or abridged by the United States or any State by reason of failure to pay any poll tax or other tax.

Section 2 The Congress shall have the power to enforce this article by appropriate legislation.

Amendment XXV (Presidential succession; adopted 1967)

Section 1 In case of the removal of the President from office or of his death or resignation, the Vice-President shall become President.

(Vice-presidential vacancy)

Section 2 Whenever there is a vacancy in the office of the Vice-President, the President shall nominate a Vice-President who shall take office upon confirmation by a majority vote of both Houses of Congress.

Section 3 Whenever the President transmits to the President pro tempore of the Senate and the speaker of the House of Representatives his written declara-

tion that he is unable to discharge the powers and duties of his office, and until he transmits to them a written declaration to the contrary, such powers and duties shall be discharged by the Vice-President as Acting President.

(Presidential disability)

Section 4 Whenever the Vice-President and a majority of either the principal officers of the executive departments or of such other body as Congress may by law provide, transmit to the President pro tempore of the Senate and the Speaker of the House of Representatives their written declaration that the President is unable to discharge the powers and duties of his office, the Vice-President shall immediately assume the powers and duties of the office as Acting President.

Thereafter, when the President transmits to the President pro tempore of the Senate and the Speaker of the House of Representatives his written declaration that no inability exists, he shall resume the powers and duties of his office unless the Vice-President and a majority of either the principal officers of the executive department(s) or of such other body as Congress may by law provide, transmit within four days to the President pro tempore of the Senate and the Speaker of the House of Representatives their written declaration that the President is unable to discharge the powers and duties of his office. Thereupon Congress shall decide the issue, assembling within forty-eight hours for that purpose if not in session. If the Congress, within twenty-one days after receipt of the latter written declaration, or, if Congress is not in session, within twenty-one days after Congress is required to assemble, determines by two-thirds vote of both Houses that the President is unable to discharge the powers and duties of his office, the Vice-President shall continue to discharge the same as Acting President; otherwise, the President shall resume the powers and duties of his office.

Amendment XXVI (Right of eighteen-year-olds to vote; adopted 1971)

Section 1 The right of citizens of the United States, who are eighteen years of age or older, to vote shall not be denied or abridged by the United States or by any State on account of age.

Section 2 The Congress shall have power to enforce this article by appropriate legislation.

FEDERALIST NO. 10 1787

To the People of the State of New York: Among the numerous advantages promised by a well-constructed union, none deserves to be more accurately developed than its tendency to break and control the violence of faction. The friend of popular governments, never finds himself so much alarmed for their character and fate, as when he contemplates their propensity to this dangerous vice. He will not fail, therefore, to set a due value on any plan which, without violating the principles to which he is attached, provides a proper cure for it. The instability, injustice, and confusion introduced into the public councils, have, in truth, been the mortal diseases under which popular governments have everywhere perished; as they continue to be the favourite and fruitful topics from which the adversaries to liberty derive their most specious declamations. The valuable improvements made by the American constitutions on the popular models, both ancient and modern, cannot certainly be too much admired; but it would be an unwarrantable partiality, to contend that they have as effectually obviated the danger on this side, as was wished and expected. Complaints are everywhere heard from our most considerate and virtuous citizens, equally the friends of public and private faith, and of public and personal liberty, that our governments are too unstable; that the public good is disregarded in the conflicts of rival parties; and that measures are too often decided, not according to the rules of justice, and the rights of the minor party, but by the superior force of an interested and overbearing majority. However anxiously we may wish that these complaints had no foundation, the evidence of known facts will not permit us to deny that they are in some degree true. It will be found, indeed, on a candid review of our situation, that some of the distresses under which we labour have been erroneously charged on the operation of our governments; but it will be found, at the same time, that other causes will not alone account for many of our heaviest misfortunes; and, particularly, for that prevailing and increasing distrust of public engagements, and alarm for private rights, which are echoed from one end of the continent to the other. These must be chiefly, if not wholly, effects of the unsteadiness and injustice, with which a factious spirit has tainted our public administrations.

By a faction, I understand a number of citizens, whether amounting to a majority or minority of the whole, who are united and actuated by some common impulse of passion, or of interest, adverse to the rights of other citizens, or to the permanent and aggregate interests of the community.

There are two methods of curing the mischiefs of faction: The one, by removing its causes; the other, by controlling its effects.

There are again two methods of removing the causes of faction: The one, by destroying the liberty which is essential to its existence; the other, by giving to every citizen the same opinions, the same passions, and the same interests.

It could never be more truly said, than of the first remedy, that it was worse than the disease. Liberty is to faction what air is to fire, an aliment without which it instantly expires. But it could not be a less folly to abolish liberty, which is essential to political life, because it nourishes faction, than it would be to wish the annihilation of air, which is essential to animal life, because it imparts to fire its destructive agency.

The second expedient is as impracticable, as the first would be unwise. As long as the reason of man continues fallible, and he is at liberty to exercise it, different opinions will be formed. As long as the connection subsists between his reason and his self-love, his opinions and his passions will have a reciprocal influence on each other; and the former will be objects to which the latter will attach themselves. The diversity in the faculties of men, from which the rights of property originate, is not less an insuperable obstacle to an uniformity of interests. The protection of these faculties is the first object of government. From the protection of different and unequal faculties of acquiring property, the possession of different degrees and kinds of property immediately results; and from the influence of these on the sentiments and views of the respective proprietors, ensues a division of the society into different interests and parties.

The latent causes of action are thus sown in the nature of man; and we see them everywhere brought into different degrees of activity, according to the different circumstances of civil society. A zeal for different opinions concerning religion, concerning government, and many other points, as well as of speculation as of practice; an attachment to different leaders ambitiously contending for preeminence and power; or to persons of other descriptions whose fortunes have been interesting to the human passions, have, in turn, divided mankind into parties, inflamed them with mutual animosity, and rendered them much more diposed to vex and oppress each other, than to cooperate for their common good. So strong is this propensity of mankind, to fall into mutual animosities, that where no substantial occasion presents itself, the most frivolous and fanciful distinctions have been sufficient to kindle their unfriendly passions and excite their most violent conflicts. But the most common and durable source of factions, has been the various and unequal distribution of property. Those who hold, and those who are without property, have ever formed distinct interests in society. Those who are creditors, and those who are debtors, fall under a like discrimination. A landed interest, a manufacturing interest, a mercantile interest, a moneyed interest, with many lesser interests, grow up of necessity in civilized nations, and divide them into different classes, actuated by different sentiments and views. The regulation of these various and interfering interests forms the principal task of modern legislation, and involves the spirit of the party and faction in the necessary and ordinary operations of the government.

No man is allowed to be a judge in his own cause; because his interest will certainly bias his judgment, and, not improbably, corrupt his integrity. With equal, nay, with greater reason, a body of men are unfit to be both judges and parties at the same time; yet what are many of the most important acts of legislation, but so many judicial determinations, not indeed concerning the right of single persons, but concerning the rights of large bodies of citizens? And what are the different classes of legislators, but advocates and parties to the causes which they determine? Is a law proposed concerning private debts? It is a question to which the creditors are parties on one side, and the debtors on the other. Justice ought to hold the balance between them. Yet the parties are, and must be, themselves the judges; and the most numerous party, or, in other words, the most powerful faction, must be expected to prevail. Shall domestic manufactures be encouraged, and in what degree, by restrictions on foreign manufactures? are questions which would be differently decided by the landed and the manufacturing classes; and probably by neither with a sole regard to justice and the public good. The apportionment of taxes, on the various descriptions of property, is an act which seems to require the most exact impartiality; yet there is, perhaps, no legislative act, in which greater opportunity and temptation are given to a predominant party to trample on the rules of justice. Every shilling, with which they overburden the inferior number, is a shilling saved to their own pockets.

It is in vain to say, that enlightened statesmen will be able to adjust these clashing interests, and render them all subservient to the public good. Enlightened statesmen will not always be at the helm: nor, in many cases, can such an adjustment be made at all, without taking into view indirect and remote considerations, which will rarely prevail over the immediate interest which one party may find in disregarding the rights of another, or the good of the whole.

The inference to which we are brought is, that the *causes* of faction cannot be removed; and that relief is only to be sought in the means of controlling its *effects*.

If a faction consists of less than a majority, relief is supplied by the republican principle, which enables the majority to defeat its sinister views, by regular vote. It may clog the administration, it may convulse the society; but it will be unable to execute and mask its violence under the forms of the constitution. When a majority is included in a faction, the form of popular government, on the other hand, enables it to sacrifice to its ruling passion or interest, both the public good and the rights of other citizens. To secure the public good, and private rights, against the danger of such a faction, and at the same time to preserve the spirit and the form of popular government, is then the great object to which our inquiries are directed. Let me add, that it is the great desideratum, by which alone this form of government can be rescued from the opprobrium under which it has so long laboured, and be recommended to the esteem and adoption of mankind.

By what means is this object attainable? Evidently by one of two only. Either the existence of the same passion or interest in a majority, at the same time, must be prevented; or the majority, having such coexistent passion or interest, must be rendered, by their number and local situation, unable to concert and carry into effect schemes of oppression. If the impulse and the opportunity be suffered to coincide, we well know that neither moral nor religious motives can be relied on as an adequate control. They are not found to be such on the injustice and violence of individuals, and lose their efficacy in proportion to the number combined together; that is, in proportion as their efficacy becomes needful.

From this view of the subject, it may be concluded, that a pure democracy, by which I mean a society consisting of a small number of citizens, who assemble and administer the government in person, can admit of no cure for the mischiefs of faction. A common passion or interest will, in almost every case, be felt by a majority of the whole; a communication and concert, results from the form of government itself; and there is nothing to check the inducements to sacrifice the weaker party, or an obnoxious individual. Hence, it is, that such democracies have ever been spectacles of turbulence and contention; have ever been found incompatible with personal security, or the rights of property; and have in general been as short in their lives, as they have been violent in their deaths. Theoretic politicians, who have patronized this species of government, have erroneously supposed, that by reducing mankind to a perfect equality in their political rights, they would, at the same time, be perfectly equalized and assimilated in their possessions, their opinions, and their passions.

A republic, by which I mean a government in which the scheme of representation takes place, opens a different prospect, and promises the cure for which we are seeking. Let us examine the points in which it varies from pure democracy, and we shall comprehend both the nature of the cure and the efficacy which it must derive from the union.

The two great points of difference, between a democracy and a republic, are, first, the delegation of the government, in the latter, to a small number of citizens, elected by the rest; secondly, the greatest number of citizens, and greater sphere of country, over which the latter may be extended.

The effect of the first difference is, on the one hand, to refine and enlarge the public views, by passing them through the medium of a chosen body of citizens, whose wisdom may best discern the true interest of their country, and whose patriotism and love of justice, will be least likely to sacrifice it to temporary or partial considerations. Under such a regulation, it may well happen, that the public voice, pronounced by the representatives of the people, will be more consonant to the public good, than if pronounced by the people themselves, convened for the purpose. On the other hand the effect may be inverted. Men of factious tempers, of local prejudices, or of sinister designs, may by intrigue, by corruption, or by other means, first obtain the suffrages, and then betray the interest of the people. The question resulting is, whether small or extensive republics are most favourable to the election of proper guardians of the public weal; and it is clearly decided in favour of the latter by two obvious considerations.

In the first place, it is to be remarked that, however small the republic may be, the representatives must be raised to a certain number, in order to guard against the cabals of a few; and that however large it may be, they must be limited to a certain number, in order to guard against the confusion of a multitude. Hence, the number of representatives in the two cases not being in proportion to that of the constituents, and being proportionally greatest in the small republic, it follows, that if the proportion of fit characters be not less in the large than in the small republic, the former will present a greater option, and consequently a greater probability of a fit choice.

In the next place, as each representative will be chosen by a greater number of citizens in the large than in the small republic, it will be more difficult for unworthy candidates to practise with success the vicious arts, by which elections are too often carried; and the suffrages of the people being more free, will be more likely to centre in men who possess the most attractive merit, and the most diffusive and established characters.

It must be confessed, that in this, as in most other cases, there is a mean, on both sides of which inconveniences will be found to lie. By enlarging too much the number of electors, you render the representatives too little acquainted with all their local circumstances and lesser interests; as by reducing it too much, you render him unduly attached to these, and too little fit to comprehend and pursue great and national objects. The federal constitution forms a happy combination in this respect; the great and aggregate interests being referred to the national, the local and particular to the state legislatures.

The other point of difference is, the greater number of citizens, and extent of territory, which may be brought within the compass of republican, than of democratic government; and it is this circumstance principally which renders factious combinations less to be dreaded in the former, than in the latter. The smaller the society, the fewer probably will be the distinct parties and interests composing it; the fewer the distinct parties and interests, the more frequently will a majority be found of the same party; and the smaller the number of individuals composing a majority, and the smaller the compass within which they are placed, the more easily will they concert and execute their plans of oppression. Extend the sphere, and you take in a greater variety of parties and interests; you make it less probable that a majority of the whole will have a common motive to invade the rights of other citizens; or if such a common motive exists, it will be more difficult for all who feel it to discover their own strength, and to act in unison with each other. Besides other impediments, it may be remarked, that where there is a consciousness of unjust or dishonourable purposes, communication is always checked by distrust, in proportion to the number whose concurrence is necessary.

Hence, it clearly appears, that the same advantage, which a republic has over a democracy, in controlling the effects of faction, is enjoyed by a large over a small republic,—is enjoyed by the union over the states composing it. Does this advantage consist in the substitution of representatives, whose enlightened views and virtuous sentiments render them superior to local prejudices, and to schemes of injustice?

It will not be denied that the representation of the union will be most likely to possess these requisite endowments. Does it consist in the greater security afforded by a greater variety of parties, against the event of any one party being able to outnumber and oppress the rest? In an equal degree does the increased variety of parties, comprised within the union, increase the security? Does it, in fine, consist in the greater obstacles opposed to the concert and accomplishment of the secret wishes of an unjust and interested majority? Here, again, the extent of the union gives it the most palpable advantage.

The influence of factious leaders may kindle a flame within their particular states, but will be unable to spread a general conflagration through the other states; a religious sect may degenerate into a political faction in a part of the confederacy; but the variety of sects dispersed over the entire face of it, must secure the national councils against any danger from that source: a rage for paper money, for an abolition of debts, for an equal division of property, or for any other improper or wicked project, will be less apt to pervade the whole body of the union than a particular member of it; in the same proportion as such a malady is more likely to taint a particular county or district, than an entire state.

In the extent and proper structure of the union, therefore, we behold a republican remedy for the diseases most incident to republican government. And according to the degree of pleasure and pride we feel in being republicans, ought to be our zeal in cherishing the spirit, and supporting the character of federalists.

JAMES MADISON

FEDERALIST NO. 51   1788

To the People of the State of New York: To what expedient then shall we finally resort for maintaining in practice the necessary partition of power among the several departments, as laid down in the constitution? The only answer that can be given is, that as all these exterior provisions are found to be inadequate, the defect must be supplied, by so contriving the interior structure of the government, as that its several constituent parts may, by their mutual relations, be the means of keeping each other in their proper places. Without presuming to undertake a full development of this important idea, I will hazard a few general observations, which may perhaps place it in a clearer light, and enable us to form a more correct judgment of the principles and structure of the government planned by the convention.

In order to lay a due foundation for that separate and distinct exercise of the different powers of government, which to a certain extent, is admitted on all hands to be essential to the preservation of liberty, it is evident that each department should have a will of its own; and consequently should be so constituted, that the members of each should have as little agency as possible in the appointment of the members of the others. Were this principle rigorously adhered to, it would require that all the appointments for the supreme executive, legislative, and judiciary magistracies, should be drawn from the same fountain of authority, the people, through channels, having no communication whatever with one another. Perhaps such a plan of constructing the several departments would be less difficult in practice than it may in contemplation appear. Some difficulties however, and some additional expense, would attend the execution of it. Some deviations therefore from the principle must be admitted. In the constitution of the judiciary department in particular, it might be inexpedient to insist rigorously on the principle; first, because peculiar qualifications being essential in the members, the primary consideration ought to be to select that mode of choice, which best secures these qualifications; secondly, because the permanent tenure by which the appointments are held in that department, must soon destroy all sense of dependence on the authority conferring them.

It is equally evident that the members of each department should be as little dependent as possible on those of the others, for the emoluments annexed to their offices. Were the executive magistrate, or the judges, not independent of the legislature in this particular, their independence in every other would be merely nominal.

But the great security against a gradual concentration of the several powers in the same department, consists in giving to those who administer each department, the necessary constitutional means, and personal motives, to resist encroachments of the others. The provision for defense must in this, as in all other cases, be made commensurate to the danger of attack. Ambition must be made to counteract ambition. The interest of the man must be connected with the constitutional rights of the place. It may be a reflection on human nature, that such devices should be necessary to control the abuses of government. But what is government itself but the greatest of all reflections on human nature? If men were angels, no government would be necessary. If angels were to govern men, neither external nor internal controls on government would be necessary. In framing a government which is to be administered by men over men, the great difficulty lies in this: You must first enable the government to control the governed; and in the next place, oblige it to control itself. A dependence on the people is no doubt the primary control on the government; but experience has taught mankind the necessity of auxiliary precautions.

This policy of supplying by opposite and rival interests, the defect of better motives, might be traced through the whole system of human affairs, private as well as public. We see it particularly displayed in all the subordinate distributions of power; where the constant aim is to divide and arrange the several offices in such a manner as that each may be a check on the other; that the private interest of every individual, may be a sentinel over the public rights. These inventions of prudence cannot be less requisite in the distribution of the supreme powers of the state.

But it is not possible to give to each department an equal power of self defense. In republican government the legislative authority, necessarily, predominates. The remedy for this inconveniency is, to divide the legislature into different branches; and to render them by different modes of election, and different principles of action, as little connected with each other, as the nature of their common functions, and their common dependence on the society, will admit. It may even be necessary to guard against dangerous encroachments by still further precautions. As the weight of the legislative authority requires that it should be thus divided, the weakness of the executive may require, on the other hand, that it should be fortified. An absolute negative, on the legislature, appears at first view to be the natural defense with which the executive magistrate should be armed. But perhaps it would be neither altogether safe, nor alone sufficient. On ordinary occasions, it might not be exerted with the requisite firmness; and on extraordinary occasions, it might be perfidiously abused. May not this defect of an absolute negative be supplied, by some qualified connection between this weaker department, and the weaker branch of the stronger department, by which the latter may be led to support the constitutional rights of the former, without being too much detached from the rights of its own department?

If the principles on which these observations are founded be just, as I persuade myself they are, and they be applied as a criterion, to the several state constitutions, and to the federal constitution, it will be found, that if the latter does not perfectly correspond with them, the former are infinitely less able to bear such a test.

There are moreover two considerations particularly applicable to the federal system of America, which place that system in a very interesting point of view.

First. In a single republic, all the power surrendered by the people, is submitted to the administration of a single government; and usurpations are guarded against by a division of the government into distinct and separate departments. In the compound republic of America, the power surrendered by the people, is first divided between two distinct governments, and then the portion allotted to each, subdivided among distinct and separate departments. Hence a double security arises to the rights of the people. The different governments will control each other; at the same time that each will be controlled by itself.

Second. It is of great importance in a republic, not only to guard the society against the oppression of its rulers; but to guard one part of the society against the injustice of the other part. Different interests necessarily exist in different classes of citizens. If a majority be united by a common interest, the rights of the minority will be insecure. There are but two methods of providing against this evil: The one by creating a will in the community independent of the majority, that is, of the society itself; the other by comprehending in the society so many separate descriptions of citizens, as will render an unjust combination of a majority of the whole, very improbable, if not impracticable. The first method prevails in all governments possessing an hereditary or self appointed authority. This at best is but a precarious security; because a power independent of the society may as well espouse the unjust views of the major, as the rightful interests, of the minor party, and may possibly be turned against both parties. The second method will be exemplified in the federal republic of the United States. While all authority in it will be derived from and dependent on the society, the society itself will be broken into so many parts, interests and classes of citizens, that the rights of individuals or of the minority, will be in little danger from interested combinations of the majority. In a free government, the security for civil rights must be the same as for religious rights. It consists in the one case in the multiplicity of interests, and in the other in the multiplicity of sects. The degree of security in both cases will depend on the number of interests and sects; and this may be presumed to depend on the extent of country and number of people comprehended under the same government. This view of the subject must particularly recommend a proper federal system to all the sincere and considerate friends of republican government: Since it shows that in exact proportion as the territory of the union may be formed into more circumscribed confederacies or states, oppressive combinations of a majority will be facilitated; the best security under the republican form, for the rights of every class of citizens, will be diminished; and consequently, the stability and independence of some member of the government, the only other security, must be proportionally increased. Justice is the end of government. It is the end of civil society. It ever has been, and ever will be pursued, until it be obtained, or until liberty be lost in the pursuit. In a society under the forms of which the stronger faction can readily unite and oppress the weaker, anarchy may as truly be said to reign, as in a state of nature where the weaker individual is not secured against the violence of the stronger: And as in the latter state even the stronger individuals are prompted by the uncertainty of their condition, to submit to a government which may protect the weak as well as themselves: So in the former state, will the more powerful factions or parties be gradually induced by a like motive, to wish for a government which will protect all parties, the weaker as well as the more powerful. It can be little doubted, that if the state of Rhode Island was separated from the confederacy, and left to itself, the insecurity of rights under the popular form of government within such narrow limits, would be dis-played by such reiterated oppressions of factious majorities, that some power altogether independent of the people would soon be called for by the voice of the very factions whose misrule had proved the necessity of it. In the extended republic of the United States, and among the great variety of interests, parties and sects which it embraces, a coalition of a majority of the whole society could seldom take place on any other principles than those of justice and the general good; and there being thus less danger to a minor from the will of the major party, there must be less pretext also, to provide for the security of the former, by introducing into the government a will not dependent on the latter; or in other words, a will independent of the society itself. It is no less certain than it is important, notwithstanding the contrary opinions which have been entertained, that the larger the society, provided it lie within a practicable sphere, the more duly capable it will be of self government. And happily for the *republican cause*, the practicable sphere may be carried to a very great extent, by a judicious modification and mixture of the *federal principle*.

JAMES MADISON

Presidents of the United States

	Party	Term
1. George Washington (1732–1799)	Federalist	1789–1797
2. John Adams (1735–1826)	Federalist	1797–1801
3. Thomas Jefferson (1743–1826)	Democratic-Republican	1801–1809
4. James Madison (1751–1836)	Democratic-Republican	1809–1817
5. James Monroe (1758–1831)	Democratic-Republican	1817–1825
6. John Quincy Adams (1767–1848)	Democratic-Republican	1825–1829
7. Andrew Jackson (1767–1845)	Democratic	1829–1837
8. Martin Van Buren (1782–1862)	Democratic	1837–1841
9. William Henry Harrison (1773–1841)	Whig	1841
10. John Tyler (1790–1862)	Whig	1841–1845
11. James K. Polk (1795–1849)	Democratic	1845–1849
12. Zachary Taylor (1784–1850)	Whig	1849–1850
13. Millard Fillmore (1800–1874)	Whig	1850–1853
14. Franklin Pierce (1804–1869)	Democratic	1853–1857
15. James Buchanan (1791–1868)	Democratic	1857–1861
16. Abraham Lincoln (1809–1865)	Republican	1861–1865
17. Andrew Johnson (1808–1875)	Union	1865–1869
18. Ulysses S. Grant (1822–1885)	Republican	1869–1877
19. Rutherford B. Hayes (1822–1893)	Republican	1877–1881
20. James A. Garfield (1831–1881)	Republican	1881
21. Chester A. Arthur (1830–1886)	Republican	1881–1885
22. Grover Cleveland (1837–1908)	Democratic	1885–1889
23. Benjamin Harrison (1833–1901)	Republican	1889–1893
24. Grover Cleveland (1837–1908)	Democratic	1893–1897
25. William McKinley (1843–1901)	Republican	1897–1901
26. Theodore Roosevelt (1858–1919)	Republican	1901–1909
27. William Howard Taft (1857–1930)	Republican	1909–1913
28. Woodrow Wilson (1856–1924)	Democratic	1913–1921
29. Warren G. Harding (1865–1923)	Republican	1921–1923
30. Calvin Coolidge (1871–1933)	Republican	1923–1929
31. Herbert Hoover (1874–1964)	Republican	1929–1933
32. Franklin Delano Roosevelt (1882–1945)	Democratic	1933–1945
33. Harry S Truman (1884–1972)	Democratic	1945–1953
34. Dwight D. Eisenhower (1890–1969)	Republican	1953–1961
35. John F. Kennedy (1917–1963)	Democratic	1961–1963
36. Lyndon B. Johnson (1908–1973)	Democratic	1963–1969
37. Richard M. Nixon (b. 1913)	Republican	1969–1974
38. Gerald R. Ford (b. 1913)	Republican	1974–1977
39. Jimmy Carter (b. 1924)	Democratic	1977–1981
40. Ronald Reagan (b. 1911)	Republican	1981–1989
41. George Bush (b. 1924)	Republican	1989–

Twentieth-Century Justices of the Supreme Court

Justice*	Term of Service	Years of Service	Life Span	Justice*	Term of Service	Years of Service	Life Span
Oliver W. Holmes	1902–1932	30	1841–1935	James F. Byrnes	1941–1942	1	1879–1972
William R. Day	1903–1922	19	1849–1923	Robert H. Jackson	1941–1954	13	1892–1954
William H. Moody	1906–1910	3	1853–1917	Wiley B. Rutledge	1943–1949	6	1894–1949
Horace H. Lurton	1910–1914	4	1844–1914	Harold H. Burton	1945–1958	13	1888–1964
Charles E. Hughes	1910–1916	5	1862–1948	*Fred M. Vinson*	1946–1953	7	1890–1953
Willis Van Devanter	1911–1937	26	1859–1941	Tom C. Clark	1949–1967	18	1899–1977
Joseph R. Lamar	1911–1916	5	1857–1916	Sherman Minton	1949–1956	7	1890–1965
Edward D. White	1910–1921	11	1845–1921	*Earl Warren*	1953–1969	16	1891–1974
Mahlon Pitney	1912–1922	10	1858–1924	John Marshall Harlan	1955–1971	16	1899–1971
James C. McReynolds	1914–1941	26	1862–1946	William J. Brennan, Jr.	1956–	—	1906–
Louis D. Brandeis	1916–1939	22	1856–1941	Charles E. Whittaker	1957–1962	5	1901–1973
John H. Clarke	1916–1922	6	1857–1945	Potter Stewart	1958–1981	23	1915–1985
William H. Taft	1921–1930	8	1857–1930	Byron R. White	1962–	—	1917–
George Sutherland	1922–1938	15	1862–1942	Arthur J. Goldberg	1962–1965	3	1908–
Pierce Butler	1922–1939	16	1866–1939	Abe Fortas	1965–1969	4	1910–1982
Edward T. Sanford	1923–1930	7	1865–1930	Thurgood Marshall	1967–	—	1908–
Harlan F. Stone	1925–1941	16	1872–1946	*Warren C. Burger*	1969–1986	17	1907–
Charles E. Hughes	1930–1941	11	1862–1948	Harry A. Blackmun	1970–	—	1908–
Owen J. Roberts	1930–1945	15	1875–1955	Lewis F. Powell, Jr.	1972–1987	15	1907–
Benjamin N. Cardozo	1932–1938	6	1870–1938	William H. Rehnquist	1972–1986	14	1924–
Hugo L. Black	1937–1971	34	1886–1971	John P. Stevens, III	1975–	—	1920–
Stanley F. Reed	1938–1957	19	1884–1980	Sandra Day O'Connor	1981–	—	1930–
Felix Frankfurter	1939–1962	23	1882–1965	*William H. Rehnquist*	1986–	—	1924–
William O. Douglas	1939–1975	36	1898–1980	Antonin Scalia	1986–	—	1936–
Frank Murphy	1940–1949	9	1890–1949	Anthony M. Kennedy	1988–	—	1936–
Harlan F. Stone	1941–1946	5	1872–1946				

*The names of chief justices are printed in italic type.

Party Control of the Presidency, Senate, and House of Representatives 1901–1991

Congress	Years	President	Senate			House		
			D	R	Other*	D	R	Other*
57th	1901–1903	McKinley T. Roosevelt	31	55	4	151	197	9
58th	1903–1905	T. Roosevelt	33	57	—	178	208	—
59th	1905–1907	T. Roosevelt	33	57	—	136	250	—
60th	1907–1909	T. Roosevelt	31	61	—	164	222	—
61st	1909–1911	Taft	32	61	—	172	219	—
62d	1911–1913	Taft	41	51	—	228	161	1
63d	1913–1915	Wilson	51	44	1	291	127	17
64th	1915–1917	Wilson	56	40	—	230	196	9
65th	1917–1919	Wilson	53	42	—	216	210	6
66th	1919–1921	Wilson	47	49	—	190	240	3
67th	1921–1923	Harding	37	59	—	131	301	1
68th	1923–1925	Coolidge	43	51	2	205	225	5
69th	1925–1927	Coolidge	39	56	1	183	247	4
70th	1927–1929	Coolidge	46	49	1	195	237	3
71st	1929–1931	Hoover	39	56	1	167	267	1
72d	1931–1933	Hoover	47	48	1	220	214	1
73d	1933–1935	F. Roosevelt	60	35	1	319	117	5
74th	1935–1937	F. Roosevelt	69	25	2	319	103	10
75th	1937–1939	F. Roosevelt	76	16	4	331	89	13
76th	1939–1941	F. Roosevelt	69	23	4	261	164	4
77th	1941–1943	F. Roosevelt	66	28	2	268	162	5
78th	1943–1945	F. Roosevelt	58	37	1	218	208	4
79th	1945–1947	Truman	56	38	1	242	190	2
80th	1947–1949	Truman	45	51	—	188	245	1
81st	1949–1951	Truman	54	42	—	263	171	1
82d	1951–1953	Truman	49	47	—	234	199	1
83d	1953–1955	Eisenhower	47	48	1	211	221	—
84th	1955–1957	Eisenhower	48	47	1	232	203	—
85th	1957–1959	Eisenhower	49	47	—	233	200	—
86th**	1959–1961	Eisenhower	65	35	—	284	153	—
87th**	1961–1963	Kennedy	65	35	—	263	174	—
88th	1963–1965	Kennedy Johnson	67	33	—	258	177	—

Sources: Department of Commerce, Bureau of the Census, Statistical Abstract of the United States (Washington, D.C.: U.S. Government Printing Office, 1980), p. 509, and Members of Congress Since 1789, 2d ed. (Washington, D.C.: Congressional Quarterly, 1981), pp. 176–177. Adapted from Barbara Hinckley, Congressional Elections (Washington, D.C.: Congressional Quarterly Press, 1981), pp. 144–145.

*Excludes vacancies at beginning of each session.

**The 437 members of the House in the 86th and 87th Congresses is attributable to the at-large representative given to both Alaska (January 3, 1959) and Hawaii (August 2, 1959) prior to redistricting in 1962.

Party Control of the Presidency, Senate, and House of Representatives 1901–1991 *(continued)*

Congress	Years	President	Senate			House		
			D	*R*	*Other**	*D*	*R*	*Other**
89th	1965–1967	Johnson	68	32	—	295	140	—
90th	1967–1969	Johnson	64	36	—	247	187	—
91st	1969–1971	Nixon	57	43	—	243	192	—
92d	1971–1973	Nixon	54	44	2	254	180	—
93d	1973–1975	Nixon Ford	56	42	2	239	192	1
94th	1975–1977	Ford	60	37	2	291	144	—
95th	1977–1979	Carter	61	38	1	292	143	—
96th	1979–1981	Carter	58	41	1	276	157	—
97th	1981–1983	Reagan	46	53	1	243	192	—
98th	1983–1985	Reagan	45	55	—	267	168	—
99th	1985–1987	Reagan	47	53	—	252	183	—
100th	1987–1989	Reagan	54	46	—	257	178	—
101st	1989–1991	Bush	55	45	—	262	173	—

Glossary

adjudication   The settling of a case judicially. More specifically, formal hearings in which persons or businesses under government agency scrutiny can present their position with legal counsel present. (12,13)

administrative discretion   The latitude that Congress gives agencies to make policy in the spirit of their legislative mandate. (12)

affirmative action   Programs through which businesses, schools, and other institutions expand opportunities for women and members of minority groups. (18)

agenda building   The process by which new issues are brought into the political limelight. (9)

aggregate demand   The money available to be spent for goods and services by consumers, businesses, and government. (15)

Aid to Families with Dependent Children (AFDC)   A federal public assistance program that provides cash to low-income families with children. (16)

amicus curiae **brief**   A brief filed (with the permission of the court) by an individual or group that is not a party to a legal action but has an interest in it. (13)

analytical budgeting   The use of sophisticatd analytical procedures in budgeting, to enable administrators to find the most cost-effective means of achieving their program goals. (12)

anarchism   A political philosophy that opposes government in any form. (1)

appellate jurisdiction   The authority of a court to hear cases that have been tried, decided, or re-examined in other courts. (13)

appropriations committees   Committees of Congress that decide which of the programs passed by the authorization committees will actually be funded. (15)

argument   The heart of a judicial opinion; its logical content separated from facts, rhetoric, and procedure. (13)

aristocracy   Literally, "rule by the best" citizens. Today, a "ruling elite," made up of individuals who head a nation's key institutions, is sometimes said to govern that nation as the aristocracy ruled traditional societies. (2)

Articles of Confederation   The compact among the thirteen original states that established the first government of the United States. (3)

attentive policy elites   Leaders who follow news in specific policy areas. (6)

authorization committees   Committees of Congress that can authorize spending in their particular areas of responsibility. (15)

autocracy   A system of government in which the power to govern is concentrated in the hands of one individual. Also called *monarchy*. (2)

bicameral   Having two legislative chambers, as the Senate and House in the U.S. Congress. (3,10)

bill   A formal proposal for a new law. (10)

Bill of Rights   The first ten amendments to the Constitution. They prevent the national government from tampering with fundamental rights and civil liberties, and emphasize the limited character of national power. (3)

bill of attainder   A law that pronounces an individual guilty of a crime without a trial. (17)

bimodal distribution   A distribution (of opinions) that shows two responses being chosen about as frequently as each other. (5)

black codes   Legislation enacted by former slave states to restrict the freedom of blacks. (18)

blanket primary   A primary election in which voters receive a ballot containing both parties' potential nominees and can help nominate candidates for all offices for both parties. (8)

block grant A grant-in-aid awarded for general purposes, allowing the recipient great discretion in spending the grant money. (4)

bolter party A political party formed from a faction that has split off from one of the major parties. (8)

boycott A refusal to do business with a firm or individual as an expression of disapproval or as a means of coercion. (18,19)

brief A written argument submitted to a judge. (13)

broadcast media Mass media that transmit information electronically. (6)

budget authority The amounts that government agencies are authorized to spend for their programs. (15)

Budget Committees One committee in each house of Congress that supervises a comprehensive budget review process. (15)

budget outlays The amounts that government agencies are expected to spend in the fiscal year. (15)

bureaucracy A large, complex organization in which employees have very specific job responsibilities and work within a hierarchy of authority. (12)

bureaucrat An employee of a bureaucracy, usually meaning a government bureaucracy. (12)

business cycle Expansions and contractions of business activity, the first accompanied by inflation and the second by unemployment. (15)

cabinet A group of presidential advisers composed of the heads of the executive departments and other key officials. (11)

capitalism The system of government that favors free enterprise (privately owned businesses operating without government regulation), based on the belief that free enterprise is necessary for free politics. (1)

casework Solving problems for constituents, especially problems involving government agencies. (10)

categorical grant A grant-in-aid targeted for a specific purpose. (4)

caucus A closed meeting of the members of a political party to decide upon questions of policy and the selection of candidates for office. (8)

checks and balances A government structure that gives each branch some scrutiny and control over the other branches. (3)

citizen group An interest group whose basis of organization is a concern for issues unrelated to the members' vocations. (9)

citizen participation program A program that encourages interaction between bureaucrats and their clients. (12)

civil case A court case that involves a private dispute arising from such matters as accidents, contractual obligations, and divorce. (13)

civil disobedience The willful but nonviolent violation of laws that are regarded as unjust. (18)

civil liberties Freedoms guaranteed to individuals. (17)

civil rights Powers or privileges guaranteed to individuals and protected from arbitrary removal at the hands of government or individuals. (17,18)

civil rights movement Political mobilization of the people—black and white—to promote racial equality. (18)

civil service The system by which most appointments to the federal bureaucracy are made, to ensure that government jobs are filled on the basis of merit and that employees are not fired for political reasons. (12)

class action See *class-action suit.*

class-action suit A legal action brought by a person or group on behalf of a number of people with similar claims or defenses. (7,13)

clear and present danger test A means by which the Supreme Court has distinguished between speech as the advocacy of ideas, which is protected by the First Amendment, and speech as incitement, which is not protected. (17)

closed primary A primary election in which voters must declare their party affiliation before they are given the primary ballot containing that party's potential nominees. (8)

cloture The mechanism by which a filibuster is cut off in the Senate. (10)

coalition building The banding together of several interest groups for the purpose of lobbying. (9)

coalition of minorities The various groups of voters that, at one time or another, become dissatisfied with the president's handling of particular issues of concern; said to account for a general decline in presidential popularity through a term in office. (11)

Cold War In the 1950s, a period of increased tension that stopped short of outright military conflict, during which the adversarial nature of U.S.–Soviet relations was clear. Americans were called upon to give priority to defense spending over domestic spending. (19)

commerce clause The third clause of Article I, Section 8, of the Constitution, which gives Congress the power to regulate commerce among the states. (4)

common (judge-made) law Legal precedents derived from previous judicial decisions. (13)

communication The process of transmitting information from one individual or group to another. (6)

communism A political system in which, in theory, ownership of all land and productive facilities is in the hands of the people, and all goods are equally shared. The production and distribution of goods is controlled by an authoritarian government. (1)

concurrence The agreement of a judge with the court's majority decision, for a reason other than the majority reason. (13)

confederation A loose association of independent states that agree to cooperate on specified matters. (3)

conference committee A temporary committee created to work out differences between the House and Senate versions of a specific piece of legislation. (10)

Congressional Budget Office (CBO) The budgeting arm of Congress, which prepares alternative budgets to those prepared by the president's OMB. (15)

congressional campaign committee An organization maintained by a political party to raise funds to support its own candidates in congressional elections. (8)

conservative coalition The temporary joining of a (conservative) majority of southern Democrats with a majority of Republicans to vote against a (more liberal) majority of northern Democrats. (10)

conservatives Generally, those people whose political ideology favors a narrow scope for government. Also, those who value freedom more than equality but would restrict freedom to preserve social order. (1)

constituents People who live and vote in a government official's district or state. (10)

consultant A person from outside the government who is hired by a government agency to conduct research, collect data, or perform policy analysis. (14)

containment The idea that the Soviets have to be prevented from expanding further. (19)

Continental Congress A political assembly called to speak out and act collectively for the people of all the colonies. The First Continental Congress met in 1774 and adopted a statement of rights and principles; the Second Continental Congress adopted the Declaration of Independence in 1776 and the Articles of Confederation in 1777. (3)

conventional participation Relatively routine political behavior that uses institutional channels and is acceptable to the dominant culture. (7)

cooperative federalism A view that holds that the Constitution is an agreement among people who are citizens of both state and nation, so there is little distinction between state powers and national powers. (4)

Council of Economic Advisers (CEA) A group that works within the executive branch to provide advice on maintaining a stable economy. (15)

county government The governmental unit that administers a county. (4)

criminal case A court case involving a crime, or violation of public order. (13)

critical election An election that produces a sharp change in the existing pattern of party loyalties among groups of voters. (8)

Declaration of Independence Drafted by Thomas Jefferson, the document that proclaimed the right of the colonies to separate from Great Britain. (3)

de facto segregation Segregation that is not the result of government influence. (18)

deficit financing The Keynesian technique of spending beyond government income to combat an economic slump. Its purpose is to inject extra money into the economy to stimulate aggregate demand. (15)

de jure segregation Government-imposed segregation. (18)

delegate A legislator whose primary responsibility is to represent the majority view of his or her constituents, regardless of his or her own view. Also, to transfer authority. (10,11)

delegation of powers The process by which Congress gives the executive branch the additional authority needed to address new problems. (11)

democracy A system of government in which, in theory, the people rule, either directly or indirectly. See *polyarchy*. (2)

democratic socialism A socialist form of government that guarantees civil liberties such as freedom of speech and religion. Citizens determine the extent of government activity through free elections and competitive political parties. (1)

deniability The effect desired by the National Security Council staffers who attempted to shield President Reagan from responsibility for decisions. (19)

department The largest unit of the executive branch, covering a broad area of government responsibility. The heads of the departments, or secretaries, form the president's cabinet. (12)

deregulation A bureaucratic reform by which the government reduces its role as a regulator of business. (12)

desegregation The ending of authorized segregation, or separation by race. (18)

détente The reduction of tension between nations. (19)

deterrence The defense policy of American strategists during the Eisenhower administration, who believed that the Soviets would not take aggressive action knowing that they risked nuclear annihilation. (19)

direct action Unconventional participation that involves assembling crowds to confront businesses and local governments to demand a hearing. (7)

direct democracy A system of rule in which all members of the group meet to make decisions according to the principles of political equality and majority rule. (2)

direct income subsidy A cash payment to reimburse a farmer for the cost of producing a crop when that cost is greater than the market price or loan rate for the crop. (16)

direct lobbying Attempts to influence a legislator's vote through personal contact with the legislator. (9)

direct mail Advertising via the mails; more specifically, a method of attracting new members to an interest group by sending letters to people in a carefully targeted audience. (9)

direct primary A preliminary election, run by the state government, in which the voters choose each party's candidates for the general election. (7)

discretionary funds Sums of money that may be spent on unpredicted needs to further national interests. (19)

discrimination Acts of irrational suspicion or hatred, directed toward a specific group of people. (18)

dissent The disagreement of a judge with a majority decision. (13)

docket A court's agenda. (13)

dual federalism A view that holds that the Constitution is a compact among sovereign states, so that the powers of the federal government are fixed and limited. (4)

economic depression A period of high unemployment and business failures; a severe, long-lasting downturn in a business cycle. (15,16)

elastic clause See *necessary and proper clause.*

election A formal procedure for voting. (7)

electoral campaign An organized effort to persuade voters to choose one candidate over others competing for the same office. (8)

electoral college A body of electors who are chosen by voters to cast ballots for president and vice president. (3,8,11)

electoral dealignment A lessening of the importance of party loyalties in voting decisions. (8)

electoral realignment The change in voting patterns that occurs after a critical election. (8)

elite theory The view that a small group of people actually makes most of the important government decisions. (2)

embargo A government freeze on the movement of goods or vessels to or from a specific country, as a means of coercion or of expressing disapproval. (19)

entitlement A benefit to which every eligible person has a legal right, and that the government cannot deny. (15)

enumerated powers The powers explicitly granted to Congress by the Constitution. (3)

equality of opportunity The idea that each person is guaranteed the same chance to succeed in life. (1,18)

equality of outcome The concept that society must ensure that people are equal, and governments must design policies to redistribute wealth and status so that economic and social equality are actually achieved. (1,18)

equal opportunities rule Under the Federal Communications Act of 1934, the requirement that if a broadcast station gives or sells time to a candidate for any public office, it must make available an equal amount of time under the same conditions to all other candidates for that office. (6)

Equal Rights Amendment (ERA) A failed constitutional amendment first introduced by the National Women's Party in 1923, declaring that "equality of rights under the law shall not be denied or abridged by the United States or any State on account of sex." (18)

establishment clause The first clause in the First Amendment, which forbids the establishment of a national religion. (17)

excess stock disposal The selling of excess government stocks, such as surplus or infrequently used equipment. (19)

exclusionary rule The judicial rule that states that evidence obtained in an illegal search and seizure cannot be used in trial. (17)

executive agreement A pact between the heads of two countries. (19)

executive branch The law-enforcing branch of a government. (3)

Executive Office of the President The president's executive aides and their staffs; the extended White House executive establishment. (11)

ex post facto law A law that declares an action to be criminal *after* it has been performed. (17)

extraordinary majorities Majorities greater than that required by majority rule, that is, greater than 50 percent plus one. (3)

fairness doctrine An FCC regulation that obligated broadcasters to discuss public issues and to provide fair coverage to each side of those issues; repealed in 1987. (6)

farmer-labor party A political party that represents farmers and urban workers who believe that the working class does not get its share of society's wealth. (8)

Federal Communications Commission (FCC) An independent federal agency that regulates interstate and international communication by radio, television, telephone, telegraph, cable, and satellite. (6)

Federal Election Commission (FEC) A federal agency that oversees the financing of national election campaigns. (8)

federalism The division of power among a central government and regional governments. (3,4)

federal question An issue covered by the Constitution, national laws, or U.S. treaties. (13)

fighting words Speech that is not protected by the First Amendment because it inflicts injury or tends to incite an immediate disturbance of the peace. (17)

filibuster A delaying tactic, used in the Senate, that involves speechmaking to prevent action on a piece of legislation. (10)

fiscal policies Economic policies that involve government spending and taxing. (15)

fiscal year (FY) The twelve-month period from October 1 to September 30 used by the government for accounting purposes. A fiscal-year budget is named for the year in which it ends. (15)

flexible response The basic defense policy of the Kennedy administration, involving the ability to wage both nuclear and conventional war. (19)

food stamp program A federally funded program that increases the purchasing power of needy families by providing them with coupons that they can use to purchase food. (16)

formula grant A grant-in-aid distributed according to a particular formula, which specifies who is eligible for the grants and how much each eligible applicant will receive. (4)

franchise The right to vote. (7)

franking privilege The right of members of Congress to send mail free of charge. (10)

freedom Immunity, as in freedom *from* want; also, an absence of constraints on behavior, as in freedom *of* religion. (1)

free-exercise clause The second clause in the First Amendment, which prevents the government from interfering with the exercise of religion. (17)

free-expression clauses The press and speech clauses of the First Amendment. (17)

free-rider problem The situation in which people benefit from the activities of an organization (such as an interest group) but do not contribute to those activities. (9)

gatekeepers Media executives, news editors, and prominent reporters who direct the flow of news. (6)

general election A national election held, by law, in November of every even-numbered year. (8)

general revenue sharing Part of a federal program introduced by President Nixon that returned tax money to state and local governments to be spent largely as they wished. (4)

gerrymandering Redrawing a congressional district to intentionally benefit one political party. (10)

globalism A policy of global, or worldwide, involvement, as is current U.S. foreign policy. (19)

good faith exception Established by the Supreme Court, an exception to the exclusionary rule maintaining that evidence seized on the basis of a mistakenly issued search warrant can be introduced at trial. (17)

government The legitimate use of force to control human behavior within territorial boundaries; also, the organization or agency authorized to exercise that force. (1)

government corporation A government agency that performs services that might be provided by the private sector, but which either involve insufficient financial incentive or are better provided when they are somehow linked with government. (12)

Gramm-Rudman-Hollings (antideficit law) An act passed by Congress in September 1985 that seeks to lower the federal deficit to a specified level each year until the federal budget is balanced in FY 1991. (15)

grant-in-aid Money provided by one level of government to another, to be spent for a specific purpose. (4)

grassroots lobbying Lobbying activities performed by rank-and-file interest-group members and would-be members. (9)

Great Compromise Submitted by the Connecticut delegation to the Constitutional Convention of 1787 and thus also known as the Connecticut Compromise, a plan calling for a bicameral legislature in which the House of Representatives would be apportioned according to population while the states would be represented equally in the Senate. (3)

Great Depression The longest and deepest setback the American economy has ever experienced. It began with the stock market crash on October 12, 1929, and did not end until the start of World War II. (16)

Great Society President Lyndon Johnson's broad array of programs designed to redress political, social, and economic inequality. (16)

gross national product (GNP) The total value of the goods and services produced by a country during a year or part of a year. (15)

home rule The right to enact and enforce legislation locally. (4)

horse race journalism Election coverage by the mass media that focuses on which candidate is ahead, rather than on national issues. (6)

Hyde Amendment A 1976 decision by Congress to restrict severely the use of federal funds for reimbursement of abortion costs; upheld by the Supreme Court in 1980. (17)

impeachment The formal charging of a government official with "treason, bribery, or other high crimes and misdemeanors." (10)

implementation The process of putting specific policies into operation. (12)

implied powers Those powers that Congress requires in order to execute its enumerated powers. (3)

in-and-outer A participant in an issue network who has a good understanding of the needs and problems of others in the network and can easily switch jobs within the network. (14)

incremental budgeting A method of budget making that involves adding new funds (an increment) onto the amount previously budgeted (in last year's budget). (15)

incumbent A current officeholder. (8,10)

independent agency An executive agency that is not part of a cabinet department. (12)

indirect democracy A system of rule in which citizens participate by electing public officials to make government decisions for them. Also called *representative government*. (2)

inflation An economic condition characterized by price increases linked to a decrease in the value of the currency. (15)

influencing behavior Behavior that seeks to modify or reverse government policy to serve political interests. (7)

information campaign An organized effort to gain public backing by bringing a group's views to public attention. (9)

inherent powers Authority claimed by the president that is not clearly specified in the Constitution. Typically, these powers are inferred from the Constitution. (11)

initiative A procedure by which voters can propose an issue to be decided by the legislature or by the people in a referendum. It requires gathering a specified number of signatures and submitting a petition to a designated agency. (2,7)

institutional mechanisms Established procedures and organizations that translate public opinion into government policy. (2)

interest group An organized group of individuals that seeks to influence public policy. Also called a *lobby*. (2,9)

interest-group entrepreneur An interest-group organizer or leader. (9)

intergovernmental relations The interdependence and relationships among the various levels of government and government personnel. (4)

iron triangles The members of congressional committees, federal agencies or bureaus, and lobbies who work toward policy ends in a specific area. (14)

isolationism The policy of noninvolvement, as was the foreign policy of the United States during most of the nineteenth century. (19)

issue network A shared-knowledge group consisting of representatives of various interests involved in some particular aspect of public policy. (14)

joint committee A committee made up of members of both the House and the Senate. (10)

judgment The judicial decision in a court case. (13)

judicial activism A judicial philosophy whereby judges interpret existing laws and precedents loosely and interject their own values in court decisions. (13)

judicial branch The branch of government that interprets laws. (3)

judicial restraint A judicial philosophy whereby judges adhere closely to statutes and precedents in reaching their decisions. (13)

judicial review The power to declare congressional (and presidential) acts invalid because they violate the Constitution. (3,13)

Keynesian theory A theory of the economy that states that demand can be adjusted through a combination of fiscal and monetary policies. (15)

laissez faire An economic doctrine that opposes any form of government intervention in business. (1)

lawyer-lobbyist A Washington lawyer who uses his or her training and expertise to influence government. (13)

legislative branch The law-making branch of government. (3)

legislative liaison staff Those people who comprise the communications link between the White House and Congress, advising the president or cabinet secretaries on the status of pending legislation. (11)

libel   Written defamation of character. (17)

liberals   Generally, those people whose political ideology favors a broad scope for government; those who value freedom more than order but not more than equality. (1)

libertarianism   A political ideology that is opposed to all government action except as necessary to protect life and property. (1)

libertarians   Those who advocate minimal government action; those who subscribe to libertarianism. (1)

linkage   In international relations, the idea of using rewards and advantages in one area of negotiation to promote another country's compliance in other areas of negotiation. (19)

lobby   See *interest group.*

lobbyist   A representative of an interest group. (9)

logrolling   Legislative bargaining typified by members agreeing to vote for each others' bills. (10)

majoritarian model of democracy   The classical theory of democracy in which government by the people is interpreted as government by the majority of the people. (2)

majority leader   The head of the majority party in the Senate; the second highest ranking member of the majority party in the House. (10)

majority party   A political party that regularly enjoys the support of the most voters. (8)

majority rule   The principle—basic to procedural democratic theory—that the decision of a group must reflect the preference of more than half of those participating. (2)

market economy   An economy in which the prices of goods and services are determined through the interaction of buyers and sellers (that is, through supply and demand). (15)

markup session   A meeting of congressional committee or subcommittee members to amend and prepare legislation for floor debate. (10)

Marshall Plan   A post–World War II plan to restore European economic viability. The plan sent approximately $12 billion in aid to Europe over a four-year period. (19)

mass communication   The process by which individuals or groups transmit information to large, heterogeneous, and widely dispersed audiences. (6)

mass media   The means employed in mass communication, often divided into print media and broadcast media. (6)

media event   A situation that is so "newsworthy" that the mass media are compelled to cover it;

candidates in elections often create such situations to garner media attention. (6)

Medicare   A health-insurance program for all persons over the age of sixty-five. (16)

military-industrial complex   The combined interests of the military establishment and the large arms industry. The two groups are united by two common interests: war and military spending. (19)

minority party   A political party that does not have the support of the most voters. (8)

minority rights   The benefits of government that cannot be denied to any citizens by majority decisions. (2)

Miranda warnings   Statements concerning rights that police are required to make to a person before he or she is subjected to in-custody questioning. (17)

monarchy   See *autocracy.*

monetarists   Those who argue that government can effectively control the performance of an economy only by controlling the supply of money. (15)

monetary policies   Economic policies that involve control of, and changes in, the supply of money. (15)

muckrakers   Writers who practiced an early form of investigative reporting, replete with unsavory details. (6)

Munich paradigm   The foreign policy view that the United States must be willing to intervene, militarily if necessary, anywhere on the globe to put down a major threat to world order and freedom. (19)

municipal government   The government unit that administers a city or town. (4)

mutual assured destruction (MAD)   The capability of the two great superpowers—the United States and the Soviet Union—to destroy each other, ensuring that there will be no winner of a nuclear war. (19)

national committee   A committee of a political party composed of party chairpeople and party officials from every state. (8)

national convention   A gathering of delegates of a single political party from across the country to choose candidates for president and vice president and to adopt a party platform. (8)

nation-building policy   A policy intended to shore up Third World countries economically and democratically, thereby making them less attractive targets for Soviet opportunism. (19)

necessary and proper clause   The last clause in Section 8 of Article I of the Constitution, which gives Congress the means to execute its enumerated powers. This clause is the basis for Congress's implied powers. Also called the *elastic clause*. (3)

New Deal The measures advocated by the Roosevelt administration to alleviate the Depression. (16)

"new" ethnicity The newer outlook on the people comprising America's "melting pot," with focus on race and color. (5)

New Jersey Plan Submitted by the head of the New Jersey delegation to the Constitutional Convention of 1787, a set of nine resolutions that would have, in effect, preserved the Articles of Confederation by amending rather than replacing them. (3)

newsworthiness The degree to which a news story is important enough to be covered in the mass media. (6)

Nineteenth Amendment The amendment to the Constitution, adopted in 1920, that assures women of the right to vote. (18)

Nixon Doctrine An attempt to reduce America's foreign involvement by calling for U.S. intervention only where it made a "real difference" and was considered to be in our interest. (19)

nominate To designate as an official candidate of a political party. (8)

normal distribution A symmetrical bell-shaped distribution (of opinions) centered on a single *mode*, or most frequent response. (5)

nullification The declaration by a state that a particular action of the national government is not applicable to that state. (4)

obligation of contracts The obligation of the parties to a contract to carry out its terms. (17)

Office of Management and Budget (OMB) The budgeting arm of the Executive Office; prepares the president's budget. (15)

"old" ethnicity An older outlook on the people comprising America's "melting pot," with focus on religion and country of origin. (5)

oligarchy A system of government in which power is concentrated in the hands of a few people. (2)

open primary A primary election in which voters need not declare their party affiliation but must choose one party's primary ballot to take into the voting booth. (8)

opinion An explanation written by one or more judges, justifying their ruling in a court case. (13)

opinion schema A network of organized knowledge and beliefs that guides a person's processing of information regarding a particular subject. (5)

order The rule of law to preserve life and protect property. Maintaining order is the oldest purpose of government. (1)

original jurisdiction The authority of a court to hear a case before any other court does. (13)

oversight The process of reviewing the operations of an agency to determine whether it is carrying out policies as Congress intended. (10)

parliamentary system A system of government in which the chief executive is the leader whose party holds the most seats in the legislature after an election or whose party forms a major part of the ruling coalition. (10)

party caucus Part of the process of choosing delegates to a party convention: a local meeting of party supporters to choose people to attend a subsequent meeting, usually at the county level. (8)

party identification A voter's sense of psychological attachment to a party. (8)

party machine A centralized party organization that dominates local politics by controlling elections. (8)

party of ideological protest A political party that rejects prevailing doctrines and proposes radically different principles, often favoring more government activism. (8)

party platform The statement of policies of a national political party. (8)

picket-fence federalism A view of federalism that stresses the interactions and interrelationships among interest groups and the various levels of government. (4)

plea bargain A defendant's admission of guilt in exchange for a less severe punishment. (13)

pluralism A view of modern society as a collection of groups of people who share religious, economic, and cultural interests. (2)

pluralist model of democracy An interpretation of democracy in which government by the people is taken to mean government by people operating through competing interest groups. (2)

pocket veto A means of killing a bill that has been passed by both houses of Congress, in which the president does not sign the bill within ten days of Congress's adjournment. (10)

police power The authority of a government to maintain order and safeguard citizens' health, morals, safety, and welfare. (1)

political action committee (PAC) An organization that pools campaign contributions from group members and donates those funds to candidates for political office. (9)

political agenda A list of issues that need government attention. (6)

political equality Equality in political decision making: one vote per person, with all votes counted equally. (1,2)

political ideology A consistent set of values and beliefs about the proper purpose and scope of government. (1)

political participation Actions of private citizens by which they seek to influence or support government and politics. (7)

political party An organization that sponsors candidates for political office under the organization's name. (8)

political socialization The complex process by which people acquire their political values. (5)

political sophistication The depth and scope of a person's knowledge of public affairs. (5)

political system A set of interrelated institutions that link people with government. (8)

poll tax A tax of $1 or $2 on every citizen who wished to vote, first instituted in Georgia in 1877. Although it was no burden on white citizens, it effectively disenfranchised blacks. (18)

polyarchy A system of rule in which power is held by many people. See *democracy*. (2)

populists Those people whose political ideology favors government action both to reduce inequality and to ensure social order. (1)

poverty level The minimum cash income that will provide for a family's basic needs; calculated as three times the cost of a market basket of food that provides a minimally nutritious diet. (16)

precedent A judicial ruling that serves as the basis for the ruling in a subsequent case. (13)

presidential character The personality characteristics of presidents and those who would be president. (11)

presidential primary A special primary election used to select delegates to attend the party's national convention, which in turn nominates the presidential candidate. (8)

president pro tempore The person elected by the majority party to chair the Senate in the vice president's absence. By custom, this constitutional position is entirely honorary. (10)

press clause The First Amendment guarantee of freedom of the press. (17)

price support The means used by the national government to maintain a minimum price for certain farm commodities. (16)

primary election A preliminary election conducted within a political party to select candidates who will run for public office in a subsequent election. (8)

print media Mass media that transmits information through the publication of the written word. (6)

prior restraint Censorship before publication. (17)

procedural democratic theory A view of democracy as being embodied in a decision-making process that involves universal participation, political equality, majority rule, and responsiveness. (2)

production control An agreement that calls for farmers to plant less of a particular crop. (16)

productive capacity The total value of goods and services that can be produced when the economy works at full capacity. (15)

program monitoring Keeping track of government programs, usually by interest groups. (9)

progressive taxation A system of taxation whereby the rich pay proportionately higher taxes than the poor; used by governments to redistribute wealth and thus promote equality. (3,15)

progressivism A philosophy of political reform based upon the goodness and wisdom of the individual citizen as opposed to special interests and political institutions. (7)

project grant A grant-in-aid awarded on the basis of competitive applications submitted by prospective recipients. (4)

proportional representation An electoral system that awards legislative seats to political parties in proportion to the number of votes won in an election. (8)

proposal The first of two stages in amending the Constitution: an amendment may be proposed, or offered, either by the Congress or by a national convention summoned by Congress. (3)

proposition An issue to be voted on in a referendum. (7)

protectionism The idea that women must be protected from life's cruelties; until the 1970s, the basis for laws affecting women's civil rights. (18)

public assistance Government aid to individuals who can demonstrate a need for that aid. (16)

public figures People who assume roles of prominence in society or thrust themselves to the forefront of public controversy. (17)

public goods Goods and services, such as parks and sanitation, that benefit all citizens but are not likely to be produced voluntarily by individuals. (1)

public interest group A citizen group that generally is considered to have no economic self-interest in the policies it pursues. (9)

public opinion The collected attitudes of citizens concerning a given issue or question. (5)

public policy A general plan of action adopted by the government to solve a social problem, counter a threat, or pursue an objective. (15)

public relations firm A firm that combines lobbying

with image building. The firm may help its clients influence the government, the public, or both. (14)

racial segregation Separation from society because of race. (18)

racism A belief that human races have distinct characteristics such that one's own race is superior to, and has a right to rule, others. (18)

ratification The second of two stages in amending the Constitution: a proposed amendment can be ratified, or accepted, either by the legislatures of the states or by constitutional conventions held in the states. (3)

reapportionment Redistribution of representatives among the states, based on population movement. Congress is reapportioned after each census. (10)

reasonable access rule An FCC rule that requires broadcast stations to make their facilities available for the expression of conflicting views or issues by all responsible elements in the community. (6)

recall The process of removing an elected official from office. (7)

receipts For a government, the amount expected or obtained in taxes and other revenues. (15)

reconciliation Matching the amount a congressional committee has been authorized to spend with the money it has been given to spend. (15)

redistricting Redrawing congressional districts after census-based reapportionment. (10)

referendum An election on a policy issue. (2,7)

regulation Government intervention in the workings of business to promote some socially desired goal. Also, an administrative rule that guides the operation of a government program. (12)

regulatory commission An agency of the executive branch of government that controls or directs some aspect of the economy. (12)

reorganization An attempt to improve the performance of the government bureaucracy by changing it. (12)

representative government See *indirect democracy*.

reprogramming The use for one purpose of money that Congress has approved for some other purpose. (19)

republic A government without a monarch; a government rooted in the consent of the governed, whose power is exercised by elected representatives responsible to the governed. (3)

republicanism A form of government in which power resides in the people and is exercised by their elected representatives. (3)

responsible party government A set of principles formalizing the ideal role of parties in a majoritarian democracy. (8)

responsiveness A decision-making principle, necessitated by representative government, which implies that elected representatives should respond to public opinion—that they should do what the majority of people want. (2)

rights The benefits of government to which every citizen is entitled. (1)

rulemaking The administrative process that results in the issuance of regulations by government agencies. (12)

rule of four An unwritten rule that requires at least four justices to agree that a case warrants consideration before it is reviewed by the Supreme Court. (13)

ruling elite The few individuals who head a nation's key financial, industrial, and communications institutions. (2)

school district An area for which a local government unit administers elementary and secondary school programs. (4)

select committee A temporary congressional committee created for a specific purpose and disbanded after that purpose is fulfilled. (10)

self-interest principle The implication that people choose what benefits them personally. (5)

senatorial courtesy A practice whereby the Senate will not confirm a nominee for a lower federal court judgeship who is opposed by the senior senator in the president's party in the nominee's state. (13)

seniority Years of consecutive service on a particular congressional committee. (10)

separate-but-equal doctrine The concept that providing separate but equivalent facilities for blacks and whites satisfies the equal protection clauses of the Fourteenth Amendment. (18)

separation of powers The assignment of law-making, law-enforcing, and law-interpreting functions to separate branches of government. (3)

sexism Sex discrimination. (18)

Shays's Rebellion A revolt led by Daniel Shays in 1786 and 1787 in Massachusetts, against the foreclosure of farms resulting from high interest rates and high state taxes. The rebellion dramatized the weakness of the newly created national government. (3)

single-issue party A political party formed to promote one principle rather than a general philosophy of government. (8)

single-member district A part of a state that elects one representative to Congress; a congressional district. (8)

skewed distribution An asymmetrical but generally

bell-shaped distribution (of opinions) whose *mode*, or most frequent response, lies off to one side. (5)

social contract theory The belief that the people agree to set up rulers for certain purposes and thus have the right to resist or remove rulers who act against those purposes. (3)

social equality Equality in wealth, education, and status. (1)

social insurance A government-backed guarantee against loss by individuals without regard to need. (16)

socialism A form of rule in which the central government plays a strong role in regulating existing private industry and directing the economy, although it does allow some private ownership of productive capacity. (1)

social security Social insurance that provides economic assistance to persons faced with unemployment, disability, or old age. It is financed by taxes on employers and employees. (16)

Social Security Act The law that provided for social security and is the basis of modern American social welfare. (16)

social welfare Government programs that provide the necessary minimum living standards for all citizens. (16)

socioeconomic status Position in society, based on a combination of education, occupational status, and income. (5)

solicitor general The third highest ranking official of the U.S. Department of Justice, and the one who represents the national government before the Supreme Court. (13)

sovereignty The power of self-rule. (3)

Speaker of the House The presiding officer of the House of Representatives. (10)

special district A government unit created to perform particular functions, especially when those functions are best performed across jurisdictional boundaries. (4)

special envoy A personal representative of the president to a foreign government. (19)

special revenue sharing Part of a federal program, introduced by President Nixon, which was to consolidate existing categorical grant programs. (4)

speech clause The part of the First Amendment that guarantees freedom of speech. (17)

split ticket In voting, candidates from different parties for different offices. (8)

stable distribution A distribution (of opinions) that shows little change over time. (5)

standard socioeconomic model A relationship between socioeconomic status and conventional political involvement: People of higher status and more education are more likely to participate than those of lower status. (7)

standing committee A permanent congressional committee that specializes in a particular legislative area. (10)

stare decisis Literally "let the decision stand"; decision making according to precedent. (13)

states' rights The idea that all rights not specifically conferred on the national government by the Constitution are reserved for the states. (4)

statutory construction Judicial interpretation of legislative acts. (13)

straight ticket In voting, a single party's candidates for all the offices. (8)

Strategic Defense Initiative (SDI) A large-scale research and development effort to build a system that will defend the United States against Soviet missiles. Also called "Star Wars." (19)

substantive democratic theory The view that democracy is embodied in the substance of government policies rather than in the policymaking procedure. (2)

suffrage The right to vote. Also called the *franchise*. (7)

supply-side economics Economic policies intended to counter extreme inflation by increasing the supply of goods to match demand. (15)

supportive behavior Actions that express allegiance to government and country. (7)

supremacy clause The clause in Article VI of the Constitution that asserts that national laws take precedence over state and local laws when they conflict. (3)

symbolic expression Nonverbal communication. (17)

tax committees The two committees of Congress responsible for raising the revenue with which to run the government. (15)

tax expenditure The promotion of socially beneficial activities by government through the granting of favorable tax treatment. (15)

think tank An institution in which scholars engage in public policy research. (14)

torts Injuries or wrongs to the person or property of another. (13)

totalitarianism A political philosophy that advocates unlimited power for the government to enable it to control all sectors of society. (1)

trade association An organization that represents firms within a particular industry; may also represent members' interests before the government. (9)

transfer authority The president's power to use for

one purpose money that Congress has approved for some other purpose. (19)

transfer payment A payment by government to an individual, mainly through social security or unemployment insurance. (15)

trustee A representative who is obligated to consider the views of constituents but is not obligated to vote according to those views if he or she believes they are misguided. (10)

two-party system A political system in which two major political parties compete for control of the government. Candidates from a third party have little chance of winning office. (8)

two-step flow of communication The process in which a few policy elites gather information and then inform their more numerous followers, mobilizing them to apply pressure to government. (6)

uncontrollable outlay A payment that government must make by law. (15)

unconventional participation Relatively uncommon political behavior that challenges or defies government channels and thus is personally stressful to participants and their opponents. (7)

undeclared war Military action, usually directed by the president, without benefit of a declaration of war from Congress. (19)

unitary government A form of government in which all power is vested in a central authority. (3)

universal participation The concept that everyone in a democracy should participate in governmental decison making. (2)

U.S. court of appeals A court within the second tier of the three-tiered federal court system, to which decisions of the district courts and federal agencies may be appealed for review. (13)

U.S. district court A court within the lowest tier of the three-tiered federal court system; a court where litigation begins. (13)

veto The president's disapproval of a bill that has been passed by both houses of Congress. Congress can override a veto with a two-thirds vote in each house. (10,11)

Vietnamization President Nixon's plan for turning over more and more of the fighting in the Vietnam War to the South Vietnamese. This tactic finally led to the peace agreement in 1973. (19)

Vietnam paradigm The foreign policy view that not all left-wing revolutionary movements are necessarily directed from Moscow, but instead can be a product of internal nationalist forces. Proponents of this paradigm also argue that military force is not the most effective way to "win the hearts and the minds" of people in other countries. (19)

Virginia Plan A set of proposals for a new government, submitted to the Constitutional Convention of 1787; included separation of the government into three branches, division of the legislature into two houses, and proportional representation in the legislature. (3)

voting The act that individuals perform when they formally choose among alternatives in an election. (7)

War on Poverty A part of President Johnson's Great Society program, intended to eradicate poverty in ten years. (16)

War Powers Resolution An act of Congress that limits the president's ability to wage undeclared war. (19)

Washington community The public- and private-sector employees who work on public policy issues. (14)

welfare state A nation in which the government assumes responsibility for the welfare of its citizens, redistributing income to reduce social inequality. (16)

writ of mandamus A court order directing an official to act. (13)

yellow journalism The distorted, sensationalist reporting of stories that became popular toward the end of the nineteenth century. (6)

zero-sum game In international politics, a situation in which one superpower's gain is the other's loss. (19)

References

Chapter 1 / Freedom, Order, or Equality? / pp. 2–31

1. Center for Political Studies of the Institute for Social Research, *Election Study 1984* (Ann Arbor, Mich.: University of Michigan.

2. *1977 Constitution of the Union of Soviet Socialist Republics*, Article 11, in *Constitutions of Countries of the World*, ed. A. P. Blaustein and G. H. Flanz (Dobbs Ferry, N.Y.: Oceana, 1971).

3. Karl Marx and Friedrich Engels, *Critique of the Gotha Programme* (New York: International Publishers, 1938), p. 10. Originally written in 1875 but published in 1891.

4. See the argument in Amy Gutman, *Liberal Equality* (Cambridge, Eng.: Cambridge University Press, 1980), pp. 9–10.

5. See John H. Schaar, "Equality of Opportunity and Beyond," in *Equality, NOMOS IX*, ed. J. Roland Pennock and John W. Chapman (New York: Atherton Press, 1967), pp. 228–249.

6. Jean Jacques Rousseau, *The Social Contract and Discourses*, trans. G. D. H. Cole (New York: Dutton, 1950), p. 5.

7. *Public Opinion* 5 (October–November 1982):36.

8. Barbara G. Farah and Elda Vale, "Crime: A Tale of Two Cities," *Public Opinion* 8 (August–September 1985):57.

9. Jill Smolowe, "The Long Hard Road to Moscow," *Time*, 12 January 1987, p. 47.

10. Institute of Medicine, *Confronting AIDS: Directions for Public Health, Health Care and Research* (Washington, D.C., National Academy Press, 1986), p. 159. Figures for AIDS cases in 1987 come from the *Chicago Tribune*, 5 January 1988, sec. 2, p. 1.

11. Smolowe, "The Long Hard Road," p. 47.

12. Milton Friedman, *Capitalism and Freedom* (Chicago: University of Chicago Press, 1962).

13. *Chicago Tribune*, 3 May 1986.

14. Lawrence Herson, *The Politics of Ideas: Political Theory and American Public Policy* (Homewood, Ill.: Dorsey Press, 1984), pp. 166–176.

Chapter 2 / Majoritarian or Pluralist Democracy? / pp. 32–57

1. *Public Opinion* (October–November 1982):36.

2. "Pistols and Politics," *Chicago Tribune*, 13 April 1986.

3. Austin Ranney and Willmoore Kendall, *Democracy and the American Party System* (New York: Harcourt, Brace, 1956), p. 6.

4. Kenneth Janda, "What's in a Name? Party Labels Across the World," in *The CONTA Conference: Proceedings of the Conference on Conceptual and Terminological Analysis in the Social Sciences*, ed. F. W. Riggs (Frankfurt: Indeks Verlag, 1982), pp. 46–62.

5. This distinction is elaborated in Ranney and Kendall, *Democracy*, pp. 12–13.

6. Candy Frank, "New England Town Meeting Reaching End of the Road," *Today Journal*, 28 March 1986.

7. Jean Jacques Rousseau, *The Social Contract and Discourses*, trans. G. D. H. Cole (New York: Dutton, 1950).

8. See Jane Mansbridge, *Beyond Adversary Democracy* (New York: Basic Books, 1982), for an analysis of direct and indirect democracy in action.

9. John Stuart Mill, *Considerations on Representative Government* (Indianapolis: Bobbs-Merrill, 1958).

10. See C. B. Macpherson, *The Real World of Democracy* (New York: Oxford University Press, 1975), pp. 58–59.

11. Austin Ranney, "Referendums and Initiatives 1986," *Public Opinion* 9 (January–February 1987):45.

12. Richard S. Hollander, *Video Democracy: The Vote-from-Home Revolution* (Mt. Airy, Md.: Lomond, 1985). See also F. Christopher Arterton, *Teledemocracy: Can Technology Protect Democracy?* (Newbury Park, Calif.: Sage, 1987).

13. *New York Times*, 15 April 1986.

14. See Robert A. Dahl, *Dilemmas of Pluralist Democracy: Autonomy vs. Control* (New Haven, Conn.: Yale University Press, 1982), p. 5.

15. Robert A. Dahl, *Pluralist Democracy in the United States* (Chicago: Rand McNally, 1967), p. 24. See also *A Preface to Democratic Theory*.

16. Seymour Melman, *Pentagon Capitalism: The Political Economy of War* (New York: McGraw-Hill, 1970).

17. Robert A. Dahl, "A Critique of the Ruling Elite Model," *American Political Science Review* 52 (June 1958):466.

18. Thomas R. Dye, *Who's Running America? The Conservative Years* (Englewood Cliffs, N.J.: Prentice-Hall, 1986), p. 12. See also G. William Domhoff, *Who Rules America Now? A View for the Eighties* (Englewood Cliffs, N.J.: Prentice-Hall, 1983).

19. The most prominent study was Robert A. Dahl's research on decision making in New Haven, Connecticut, in *Who Governs?* (New Haven, Conn.: Yale University Press, 1961). G. William Domhoff criticized Dahl's study in *Who Really Rules? New Haven and Community Power Re-examined* (New Brunswick, N.J.: Transaction Books, 1978). Nelson W. Polsby supported Dahl's basic findings in *Community Power and Political Theory: A Further Look at Problems of Evidence and Inference* (New Haven, Conn.: Yale University Press, 1980).

20. See Kenneth M. Dolbeare, *Democracy at Risk: The Politics of Economic Renewal* (Chatham, N.J.: Chatham House, 1984); and Edward S. Greenberg, *The American Political System: A Radical Approach* (Boston: Little, Brown, 1986).

21. G. Bingham Powell, Jr., *Contemporary Democracies* (Cambridge, Mass.: Harvard University Press, 1982), p. 3. Adapted by permission of the publishers. Reprinted by permission of Harvard University Press.

22. Arend Lijphart, *Democracies* (New Haven, Conn.: Yale University Press, 1984), p. 8. See also Robert Wesson, ed., *Democracy: A Worldwide Survey* (New York: Praeger, 1987), p. xi, for a similar count.

23. E. E. Schattschneider, *The Semisovereign People* (New York: Holt, Rinehart & Winston, 1960), p. 35.

Chapter 3 / The Constitution / pp. 64–107

1. Carl Bernstein and Bob Woodward, *All the President's Men* (New York: Warner, 1975).

2. Ibid., p. 30.

3. Samuel Eliot Morison, *Oxford History of the American People* (New York: Oxford University Press, 1965), p. 182.

4. Ibid., p. 204.

5. John Plamenatz, *Man and Society*, vol. 1 (New York: McGraw-Hill, 1963), pp. 162–164.

6. Extrapolated from U.S. Department of Defense, *Selected Manpower Statistics, FY1982* (Washington, D.C.: U.S. Government Printing Office, 1983) table 2–30, p. 130; and *1985 Statistical Abstract of the United States* (Washington, D.C.: U.S. Government Printing Office, 1985), tables 1 and 2, p. 6.

7. Joseph T. Keenan, *The Constitution of the United States* (Homewood, Ill.: Dow Jones–Irwin, 1975).

8. David P. Szatmary, *Shays' Rebellion: The Making of an Agrarian Insurrection* (Amherst, Mass.: University of Massachusetts Press, 1980), pp. 82–102.

9. Robert H. Jackson, *The Struggle for Judicial Supremacy* (New York: Knopf, 1941), p. 8.

10. Forrest McDonald, *Novus Ordo Seclorum: The Intellectual Origins of the Constitution* (Lawrence, Kan.: University Press of Kansas, 1985), pp. 205–209.

11. Catherine Drinker Bowen, *Miracle at Philadelphia* (Boston: Little, Brown, 1966), p. 122.

12. Donald S. Lutz, "The Preamble to the Constitution of the United States," *This Constitution* 1 (September 1983):23–30.

13. Richard E. Neustadt, *Presidential Power: The Politics of Leadership* (New York: Wiley, 1960), p. 33.

14. Charles A. Beard, *An Economic Interpretation of the Constitution of the United States* (New York: Macmillan, 1913).

15. Leonard W. Levy, *Constitutional Opinions* (New York: Oxford University Press, 1986), p. 101.

16. Robert E. Brown, *Charles Beard and the Constitution* (Princeton, N.J.: Princeton University Press, 1956); Levy, *Constitutional Opinions*, pp. 103–104; and Forrest McDonald, *We the People: The Economic Origins of the Constitution* (Chicago: University of Chicago Press, 1958).

17. Walter Berns, *The First Amendment and the Future of American Democracy* (New York: Basic Books, 1976), p. 2.

18. Herbert J. Storing, ed., *The Complete Anti-Federalist*, 7 vols. (Chicago: University of Chicago Press, 1981).

19. Keenan, *The Constitution*, p. 21.

20. Alexis de Tocqueville, *Democracy in America*, ed. J. P. Mayer and Max Lerner (New York: Harper & Row, 1966), p. 102.

21. Jerold L. Waltman, *Political Origins of the U.S. Income Tax* (Jackson, Miss.: University Press of Mississippi, 1985), p. 10.

Chapter 4 / Federalism / pp. 108–141

1. Ronald Reagan, "National Minimum Drinking Age: Remarks on Signing HR4616 into Law (July 17, 1984)," *Weekly Compilation of Presidential Documents*, 23 July 1984, p. 1036.

2. *South Dakota* v. *Dole*, 107 S.Ct. 2793 (1987).

3. *Hammer* v. *Dagenhart*, 247 U.S. 251 (1918).

4. Alpheus Mason and William Beaney, *The Supreme Court in a Free Society* (New York: Norton, 1968), pp. 70–71.

5. See Daniel Elazar, *The American Partnership* (Chicago: University of Chicago Press, 1962); and Morton Grodzins, *The American System* (Chicago: Rand McNally, 1966).

6. *Miranda* v. *Arizona*, 384 U.S. 436 (1966).

7. *Baker* v. *Carr*, 369 U.S. 186 (1962); *Wesberry* v. *Sanders*, 376 U.S. 1 (1964); and *Reynolds* v. *Sims*, 377 U.S. 533 (1964).

8. *McCulloch* v. *Maryland*, 4 Wheat. 316 (1819).

9. *Dred Scott* v. *Sanford*, 19 How. 393 (1857).
10. *Gibbons* v. *Ogden*, 9 Wheat. 1 (1824).
11. James T. Patterson, *The New Deal and the States: Federalism in Transition* (Princeton, N.J.: Princeton University Press, 1969).
12. *United States* v. *Butler*, 297 U.S. 1 (1936).
13. *United States* v. *Darby*, 312 U.S. 100 (1941).
14. *Plessy* v. *Ferguson*, 163 U.S. 537 (1896).
15. *Brown* v. *Board of Education of Topeka*, 347 U.S. 483 (1954).
16. Aaron Wildavsky, "Bare Bones: Putting Flesh on the Skeleton of American Federalism," in *The Future of Federalism in the 1980s*, by the Advisory Commission on Intergovernmental Relations (Washington, D.C., 1981), p. 80.
17. Advisory Commission on Intergovernmental Relations, *The Federal Role in the Federal System: The Dynamics of Growth* (Washington, D.C., 1981), p. 101.
18. Richard Nixon, "Speech to National Governor's Conference, September 1, 1969," in *Congressional Quarterly Almanac* (Washington, D.C.: Congressional Quarterly Press, 1969), pp. 101A–103A.
19. Richard P. Nathan and Fred C. Doolittle, *Reagan and the States* (Princeton, N.J.: Princeton University Press, 1987), p. 65.
20. Morton Grodzins, "The Federal System," in *Goals for Americans* (New York: Columbia University, The American Assembly, 1960), p. 265.
21. Paul M. Weyrich, quoted in Neal Pierce, "Conservatives Weep as the States Make Left Turn," *National Journal*, 10 October 1987, p. 2559.

Chapter 5 / Public Opinion and Political Socialization / pp. 148–183

1. *Public Opinion* 8 (June–July 1985):38–39.
2. *New York Times*, 3 July 1976.
3. *Furman* v. *Georgia*, 408 U.S. 238 (1972).
4. *Gregg* v. *Georgia*, 248 U.S. 153 (1976).
5. *Public Opinion* 8 (June–July 1985):39.
6. Seven national surveys taken from 1974 through 1986 found that an average of 60 percent of Americans disapproved of the ruling in *Abington School District* v. *Schempp*, 374 U.S. 203 (1963). See James Allen Davis and Tom W. Smith.
7. Most of the survey findings reported here were computed from data collected by the National Opinion Research Center in 1987 as part of the *General Social Surveys*. The principal investigator was James A. Davis, and the senior study director was Tom W. Smith. The sample size in 1987 was 1,819 cases. These data were made available on computer tape by the Inter-University Consortium for Political and Social Research at the University of Michigan.
8. *Public Opinion* 5 (October–November 1982):21.
9. These questions are not ideally matched, but other survey items about private enterprise yield comparable results. See Donald J. Devine, *The Political Culture of the United States* (Boston: Little, Brown, 1972), pp. 209–214.
10. Warren E. Miller, Arthur H. Miller, and Edward J. Schneider, *American National Election Studies Sourcebook, 1952–1978* (Cambridge, Mass.: Harvard University Press, 1980), pp. 94–95.
11. Tom W. Smith and Paul B. Sheatsley, "American Attitudes Toward Race Relations," *Public Opinion* 7 (October–November 1984):15.
12. Ibid.
13. Ibid., p. 83.
14. Jerry L. Yeric and John R. Todd, *Public Opinion: The Visible Politics* (Itasca, Ill.: F. E. Peacock, 1983), p. 39.
15. Paul Allen Beck, "The Role of Agents in Political Socialization," in *Handbook of Political Socialization Theory and Research*, ed. Stanley Allen Renshon (New York: Free Press, 1977), pp. 117–118.
16. W. Russell Neuman, *The Paradox of Mass Politics: Knowledge and Opinion in the American Electorate* (Cambridge, Mass.: Harvard University Press, 1986), pp. 113–114.
17. M. Kent Jennings and Richard G. Niemi, *The Political Character of Adolescence: The Influence of Families and Schools* (Princeton, N.J.: Princeton University Press, 1974), p. 39.
18. Studying both parents and children in 1965 and 1973, Jennings and Niemi found that 57 percent of children shared their parents' party identification in 1965, but only 47 percent did in 1973. See ibid., pp. 90–91.
19. Robert D. Hess and Judith V. Torney, *The Development of Political Attitudes in Children* (Chicago: Aldine, 1967).
20. David Easton and Jack Dennis, *Children in the Political System* (New York: McGraw-Hill, 1969).
21. Jarol B. Manheim, *The Politics Within* (New York: Longman, 1982), p. 83.
22. "Government Trust: Less in West Europe than U.S." *New York Times*, 16 February 1986.
23. See Robert Huckfeldt and John Sprague, "Networks in Context: The Social Flow of Information," *American Political Science Review* 81 (December 1987):1197–1216. The authors' study of voting in neighborhoods in South Bend, Indiana, found that residents who favored the minority party were acutely aware of their minority status.
24. Theodore M. Newcomb, *Persistence and Social Change: Bennington College and Its Students After Twenty-Five Years* (New York: Wiley, 1967).
25. William Schneider, "Bang-Bang Television: The New Superpower," *Public Opinion* 5 (April–May 1982):13.
26. Davis and Smith, *General Social Surveys*, p. 112. The question had seven response categories ranging from "government should do

something to reduce income differences between rich and poor" (Category 1) to "government should not concern itself with income differences" (Category 7). Categories 1 through 3 were combined to represent the "government should" response, and Categories 4 through 7 were combined to represent the "government should not" response.

27. The increasing wealth in industrialized societies may be replacing class conflict with conflict over values, but maybe not. See the exchange between Ronald Inglehart and Scott C. Flanagan, "Value Change in Industrial Societies," *American Political Science Review* 81 (December 1987):1289–1319.

28. For a parallel analysis, see Neuman, *Paradox of Mass Politics*, pp. 79–81.

29. For a recent review of these studies, see Stuart Rothenberg, Eric Licht, and Frank Newport, *Ethnic Voters and National Issues* (Washington, D.C.: Free Congress Research and Educational Foundation, 1982).

30. Nathan Glazer, "The Structure of Ethnicity," *Public Opinion* 7 (October–November 1984):4.

31. *Statistical Abstract of the United States, 1982–83* (Washington, D.C.: Government Printing Office, 1982), p. 32.

32. Glazer, "Structure of Ethnicity," p. 5.

33. Davis and Smith, *General Social Surveys*, p. 111.

34. John Robinson, "The Ups and Downs and Ins and Outs of Ideology," *Public Opinion* 7 (February–March 1984):12.

35. Angus Campbell et al., *The American Voter* (New York: Wiley, 1960), chap. 10.

36. Neuman, *Paradox of Mass Politics*, pp. 19–20.

37. This research is not without criticism. See Eric R. A. N. Smith, "The Levels of Conceptualization: False Measures of Ideological Sophistication," *American Political Science Review* 74 (September 1980):685–696.

38. But some scholars believe that the methods for classifying respondents as ideologues is too generous. See Robert C. Luskin, "Measuring Political Sophistication," *American Journal of Political Science* 31 (November 1987): 878, 887–888.

39. See William G. Jacoby, "Levels of Conceptualization and Reliance on the Liberal-Conservative Continuum," *Journal of Politics* 48 (May 1986):423–432.

40. *National Election Study for 1984*, a pre-election survey conducted by the Center for Political Studies at the University of Michigan.

41. Milton Rokeach also proposes a two-dimensional model of political ideology grounded in the terminal values of freedom and equality. See *The Nature of Human Values* (New York: Free Press, 1973), especially Chapter 6. Rokeach found that positive and negative references to these two values permeated the writings of socialists, communists, fascists, and conservatives and clearly differentiated the four bodies of writing from one another (pp. 173–174). However, Rokeach built his two-dimensional model around only the values of freedom and equality; he did not deal with the question of freedom versus order.

42. Pamela Johnston Conover, "The Origins and Meaning of Liberal-Conservative Self-Identifications," *American Journal of Political Science* 25 (November 1981):621–622, 643.

43. The relationship of liberalism to political tolerance is found by John L. Sullivan et al., "The Sources of Political Tolerance: A Multivariate Analysis," *American Political Science Review* 75 (March 1981):102. See also Robinson, "Ups and Downs," pp. 13–15.

44. Herbert Asher, *Presidential Elections and American Politics* (Homewood, Ill.: Dorsey Press, 1980), pp. 14–20. Asher also constructs a two-dimensional ideological framework, distinguishing between "traditional New Deal" issues and "new lifestyle" issues.

45. John E. Jackson, "The Systematic Beliefs of the Mass Public: Estimating Policy Preferences with Survey Data," *Journal of Politics* 45 (November 1983): 840–865, at 857.

46. The first edition of *The Challenge of Democracy*, which used the 1984 *General Social Survey*, reported slightly different percentages for three of the four ideological tendencies. According to the 1984 data, populists accounted for 28 percent of the sample, libertarians for 27 percent, and conservatives for 23 percent. (Liberals accounted for 22 percent as here.) The minor differences in percentages reflect a shift in the 1987 sample of 1 point toward firing a communist teacher and 4 points toward opposing government action to equalize income.

47. William S. Maddox and Stuart A. Lilie, *Beyond Liberal and Conservative: Reassessing the Political Spectrum* (Washington, D.C.: Cato Institute, 1984), p. 68.

48. See Neuman, *Paradox of Mass Politics*, p. 81. See also Aaron Wildavsky, "Choosing Preferences by Constructing Institutions: A Cultural Theory of Preference Formation," *American Political Science Review* 81 (March 1987):13.

49. The same conclusion was reached in a major study of British voting behavior. See Hilde T. Himmelweit et al., *How Voters Decide* (New York: Academic Press, 1981), pp. 138–141. See also Wildavsky, "Choosing Preferences," p. 13.

50. Wildavsky, "Choosing Preferences," pp. 3–21.

51. John C. Pierce, Kathleen M. Beatty, and Paul R. Hagner, *The Dynamics of American Public Opinion* (Glenview, Ill.: Scott, Foresman, 1982), p. 134.

52. Center for Political Studies, *1986 National Election Survey* (Ann Arbor, Mich.: Inter-University Consortium for Political and Social Research, 1987), pp. 59–73.

53. Luskin, "Measuring Political Sophistication," pp. 856–899.
54. Neuman, *Paradox of Mass Politics*, pp. 19–20.
55. Ibid., pp. 6–7.
56. Ibid., p. 81.
57. CBS News/New York Times, *National Surveys, 1983* (Ann Arbor, Mich.: Inter-University Consortium for Political and Social Research, 1985), p. 86.
58. *Public Opinion* 8 (August–September 1985):33.
59. Benjamin I. Page, Robert Y. Shapiro, and Glenn R. Dempsey, "What Moves Public Opinion?" *American Political Science Review* 81 (March 1987):23–43.
60. Pamela Johnston Conover and Stanley Feldman, "How People Organize the Political World: A Schematic Model," *American Journal of Political Science* 28 (February 1984):96. For an excellent review of schema structures in contemporary psychology—especially as they relate to political science—see Reid Hastie, "A Primer of Information-Processing Theory for the Political Scientist," in *Political Cognition*, ed. Richard R. Lau and David O. Sears (Hillsdale, N.J.: Erlbaum, 1986), pp. 11–39.
61. John Hurwitz and Mark Peffley, "How Are Foreign Policy Attitudes Structured? A Hierarchical Model," *American Political Science Review* 81 (December 1987):1099–1220.
62. See Milton Lodge and Ruth Hamill, "A Partisan Schema for Political Information Processing," *American Political Science Review* 80 (June 1986):505–519.

Chapter 6 / The Mass Media / pp. 184–221

1. *Time*, 18 May 1987, p. 17.
2. *Congressional Quarterly Weekly Report*, 9 May 1987, p. 923.
3. *Time*, 18 May 1987, p. 18.
4. Anthony Lewis, "Degrading the Press," *New York Times*, 5 May 1987, p. 31.
5. David Broder, "Journalists mustn't shrink from examining would-be presidents," *Chicago Tribune*, 13 May 1987, p. 19.
6. S. N. D. North, *The Newspaper and Periodical Press* (Washington, D.C.: U.S. Government Printing Office, 1884), p. 27. This source provides much of the information reported about newspapers and magazines prior to 1880.
7. Sidney Kobre, *The Yellow Press and Gilded Age Journalism* (Tallahassee, Fla.: Florida State University Press, 1964), p. 52.
8. Bureau of the Census, *Statistical Abstract of the United States, 1988* (Washington, D.C.: U.S. Government Printing Office, 1988), p. 528.
9. Matthew Manning, ed., *Standard Periodical Directory*, 11th ed. (New York: Oxbridge Communications, 1988), pp. 543, 1356, 542.
10. *The Encyclopedia of American Facts and Dates* (New York: Crowell, 1979), pp. 467, 525.
11. *World Almanac and Book of Facts*, 1941 and 1951 issues.
12. Dana R. Ulloth, Peter L. Klinge, and Sandra Eells, *Mass Media: Past, Present, Future* (St. Paul, Minn.: West, 1983), p. 278.
13. Bill Keller, "Crime hits headlines in Moscow," *New York Times*, 24 March 1988, p. 34.
14. Doris A. Graber, *Mass Media and American Politics* (Washington, D.C.: Congressional Quarterly Press, 1984), pp. 78–79.
15. Roper Organization, *Trends in Attitudes Toward Television and Other Media* (New York: Television Information Office, 1983), p. 8.
16. Bureau of the Census, *Statistical Abstract of the United States, 1982–1983* (Washington, D.C.: U.S. Government Printing Office, 1984), p. 562.
17. *Editor & Publisher International Yearbook, 1984*, pp. 435–442.
18. Christopher H. Sterling, *Electronic Media: A Guide to Trends in Broadcasting and Newer Technologies, 1920–1983* (New York: Praeger, 1984), p. 22.
19. *Broadcasting/Cablecasting Yearbook, 1988*, p. A-64.
20. Joseph Turow, *Media Industries: The Production of News and Entertainment* (New York: Longman, 1984), p. 18. Our discussion of government regulation draws heavily on this source.
21. Joseph R. Dominick, *The Dynamics of Mass Communication* (Reading, Mass.: Addison-Wesley, 1983), p. 331.
22. *New York Times*, 27 July 1984, p. 1; *Wall Street Journal*, 27 July 1984, p. 3.
23. Graber, *Mass Media*, p. 110.
24. Ibid., pp. 235–236.
25. Ibid., p. 241.
26. Ibid., p. 72.
27. Austin Ranney, *Channels of Power: The Impact of Television on American Politics* (New York: Basic Books, 1983), p. 46.
28. Gregory Katz, "Issues distant second to 'horse-race' stories," *USA Today*, 22 April 1988, p. 6A.
29. Graber, *Mass Media*, pp. 82–83.
30. S. Robert Lichter and Stanley Rothman, "Media and Business Elites," *Public Opinion* 5 (October–November 1981):42–46.
31. Schneider and Lewis, "Views on the News," *Public Opinion* 8 (August–September 1985):6–11, 58–59, at 7.
32. Gregory Katz, "GOP scrutinized more on network newscasts," *USA Today*, 22 April 1988, p. 6A.
33. Schneider and Lewis, "Views on the News," pp. 8–9.
34. Michael Robinson and Margaret Sheehan, *Over the Wire and On TV: CBS and UPI in Campaign '80* (New York: Russell Sage Foundation, 1983).
35. Michael J. Robinson, "The Media in Campaign '84: Part II; Wingless, Toothless, and Hopeless," *Public Opinion* 8 (February–March 1985):43–48, at 48.
36. Maura Clancey and Michael J. Robinson, "General Election Coverage: Part I," *Public Opinion* 7 (December–January 1985):49–54, 59, at 54.
37. Leslie Maitland Werner, "13% of U.S. Adults Are Illiterate in English, a Federal Study Finds," *New York Times*, 21 April 1986, pp. 1, 14.
38. Computed from data in the 1984

National Election Study, distributed by the Inter-University Consortium for Political and Social Research.

39. Michael J. Robinson and Maura Clancey, "Teflon Politics," *Public Opinion* 7 (April–May 1984):14–18, at 14.

40. Ibid.

41. Ibid.

42. Ibid., p. 18.

43. Peter Clarke and Eric Fredin, "Newspapers, Television, and Political Reasoning," *Public Opinion Quarterly* 42 (Summer 1978):143–160.

44. Joseph Wagner, "Media Do Make a Difference: The Differential Impact of Mass Media in the 1976 Presidential Race," *American Journal of Political Science* 27 (August 1983):407–430, at 415–417.

45. Michael J. Robinson, "American Political Legitimacy in an Era of Electronic Journalism: Reflections on the Evening News," in *Television as a Social Force*, ed. Douglas Caterr (New York: Praeger, 1975) pp. 97–139.

46. Graber, *Mass Media*, pp. 66–67; and Andrew Goodman, "Television Images of the Foreign Policy Process" (Ph.D. diss., Northwestern University, 1985), chap. 11.

47. William Schneider, "Bang-Bang Television: The New Superpower," *Public Opinion* 5 (April–May 1982):13–15, at 13.

48. Richard J. Meislin, "Poll Finds Infidelity a Lesser Evil Than Others in Picking Candidate," *New York Times*, 8 May 1987.

49. S. Robert Lichter, "Misreading Momentum," *Public Opinion*, 11 (May–June, 1988):16.

50. Benjamin I. Page, Robert Y. Shapiro, and Glenn R. Dempsey, "What Moves Public Opinion?" *American Political Science Review*, 81 (March 1987):23–43, at 31.

51. Ibid., 35.

52. Shanto Iyengar and Donald R. Kinder, *News That Matters: Television and American Opinion* (Chicago: University of Chicago Press, 1987), p. 33.

53. Ibid., p. 60.

54. Herbert Jacob, *The Frustration of Policy: Responses to Crime by American Cities* (Boston: Little, Brown, 1984), pp. 47–50.

55. Stephen Hess, *The Washington Reporters* (Washington, D.C.: Brookings Institution, 1981).

56. Ben Stein, "'Miami Vice': It's So Hip You'll Want to Kill Yourself," *Public Opinion* 8 (October–November 1985):41–43.

57. Thomas E. Patterson and Richard Davis, "The Media Campaign: Struggle for the Agenda," in *The Elections of 1984*, ed. Michael Nelson (Washington, D.C.: Congressional Quarterly Press, 1985), pp. 111–127, at 124.

58. Schneider and Lewis, "Views on the News," 11.

Chapter 7 / Participation and Voting / pp. 222–259

1. *Time*, 6 September 1968, p. 21.

2. *Newsweek*, 9 September 1968, p. 39.

3. *Time*, 6 September 1968, p. 24.

4. John P. Robinson, "Public Reaction to Political Protest: Chicago 1968," *Public Opinion Quarterly* 34 (Spring 1970):2.

5. Lester W. Milbrath and M. L. Goel, *Political Participation* (Chicago: Rand McNally, 1977), p. 2.

6. *New York Times*, 4 March 1985.

7. Michael Lipsky, "Protest as a Political Resource," *American Political Science Review* 62 (December 1968):1145.

8. See Sidney Verba and Norman H. Nie, *Participation in America: Political Democracy and Social Equality* (New York: Harper & Row, 1972), p. 3.

9. Samuel H. Barnes and Max Kaase, eds., *Political Action: Mass Participation in Five Western Democracies* (Beverly Hills, Calif.: SAGE, 1979).

10. Ibid., p. 552.

11. Max Kaase and Alan Marsh, "Political Action: A Theoretical Perspective," in *Political Action: Mass Participation in Five Western Democracies*, ed. Samuel H. Barnes and Max Kaase (Beverly Hills, Calif.: SAGE, 1979), p. 44.

12. Jonathan D. Casper, *Politics of Civil Liberties* (New York: Harper & Row, 1972), p. 90.

13. David C. Colby, "A Test of the Relative Efficacy of Political Tactics," *American Journal of Political Science* 26 (November 1982):741–753. See also Frances Fox Piven and Richard Cloward, *Poor People's Movements* (New York: Vintage, 1979).

14. Stephen C. Craig and Michael A. Magiotto, "Political Discontent and Political Action," *Journal of Politics* 43 (May 1981):514–522. But see Mitchell A. Seligson, "Trust Efficacy and Modes of Political Participation: A Study of Costa Rican Peasants," *British Journal of Political Science* 10 (January 1980):75–98, for a review of studies that came to different conclusions.

15. Philip H. Pollock III, "Organization as Agents of Mobilization: How Does Group Activity Affect Political Participation?" *American Journal of Political Science* 26 (August 1982):485–503.

16. Arthur H. Miller et al., "Group Consciousness and Political Participation," *American Journal of Political Science* 25 (August 1981):495.

17. Richard D. Shingles, "Black Consciousness and Political Participation: The Missing Link," *American Political Science Review* 75 (March 1981):76–91.

18. Barnes and Kaase, *Political Action*, pp. 548–549.

19. International Social Survey Program, 1985 survey question: "There are many ways people or organizations can protest a government action they strongly oppose. Please show which you think should be allowed and which should not be allowed." Tabulation of results provided by Tom W. Smith of the National Opinion Research Center.

20. See Joel B. Grossman et al., "Dimensions of Institutional Participation: Who Uses the Courts and How?" *Journal of Politics* 44 (February 1982):86–114; and Frances Kahn Zemans, "Legal Mobilization: The Neglected Role of the Law in the Political System,"

American Political Science Review 77 (September 1983):690–703.

21. See Verba and Nie, *Participation in America*, p. 69. Also see John Clayton Thomas, "Citizen-Initiated Contacts with Government Agencies: A Test of Three Theories," *American Journal of Political Science* 26 (August 1982):504–522; and Elaine B. Sharp, "Citizen-Initiated Contacting of Government Officials and Socioeconomic Status: Determining the Relationship and Accounting for It," *American Political Science Review* 76 (March 1982):109–115.

22. Elaine B. Sharp, "Citizen Demand Making in the Urban Context," *American Journal of Political Science* 28 (November 1984):654–670, at 654, 665.

23. *New York Times*, 2 February 1988, pp. 1, 13; and House of Representatives Conference Report, 100–498 (December 22, 1987), p. 824.

24. Verba and Nie, *Participation in America*, p. 67; and Sharp, "Citizen Demand Making," p. 660.

25. *Brown* v. *Board of Education*, 347 U.S. 483 (1954).

26. Kaase and Marsh, "Political Action," p. 168.

27. *Smith* v. *Allwright*, 321 U.S. 649 (1944).

28. *Harper* v. *Virginia State Board of Elections*, 383 U.S. 663 (1966).

29. Everett Carll Ladd, *The American Polity* (New York: Norton, 1985), p. 392.

30. Gorton Carruth and associates, eds., *The Encyclopedia of American Facts and Dates* (New York: Crowell, 1979), p. 330.

31. Ivor Crewe, "Electoral Participation," in *Democracy at the Polls: A Comparative Study of Competitive National Elections*, ed. David Butler, Howard R. Penniman, and Austin Ranney (Washington, D.C.: American Enterprise Institute, 1981), pp. 219–223.

32. David B. Magleby, *Direct Legislation: Voting on Ballot Propositions in the United States* (Baltimore: Johns Hopkins University Press, 1984), pp. 36–39, 71.

33. Ibid., p. 70.

34. Matthew L. Wald, "In Maine, Obscenity Vote Brings Warnings of Purges and Plans for Prayer," *New York Times*, 10 June 1986, p. 8; and "Maine voters reject jail for porn sellers," *Chicago Tribune*, 11 June 1986, p. 17.

35. Magleby, *Direct Legislation*, p. 59.

36. Ibid., p. 198.

37. *The Book of the States 1984–85*, vol. 25 (Lexington, Ky.: Council of State Governments, 1984), p. 45.

38. *Chicago Tribune*, 10 March 1985.

39. Crewe, "Electoral Participation," p. 232.

40. Verba and Nie, *Participation in America*, p. 13.

41. Max Kaase and Alan Marsh, "Distribution of Political Action," in *Political Action: Mass Participation in Five Western Democracies*, ed. Samuel H. Barnes and Max Kaase (Beverly Hills, Calif.: SAGE, 1979), p. 186.

42. Milbrath and Goel, *Political Participation*, pp. 95–96.

43. Verba and Nie, *Participation in America*, p. 148.

44. Richard Murray and Arnold Vedlitz, "Race, Socioeconomic Status, and Voting Participation in Large Southern Cities," *Journal of Politics* 39 (November 1977):1064–1072; and Verba and Nie, *Participation in America*, p. 157.

45. Carol A. Cassel, "Change in Electoral Participation in the South," *Journal of Politics* 41 (August 1979):907–917.

46. Ronald B. Rapoport, "The Sex Gap in Political Persuading: Where the 'Structuring Principle' Works," *American Journal of Political Science* 25 (February 1981):32–48.

47. Stephen D. Shaffer, "A Multivariate Explanation of Decreasing Turnout in Presidential Elections, 1960–1976," *American Journal of Political Science* 25 (February 1981):68–95; and Paul R. Abramson and John H. Aldrich, "The Decline of Electoral Participation in America," *American Political Science Review* 76 (September 1981):603–620.

48. Abramson and Aldrich, "Decline of Electoral Participation," p. 519; and Shaffer, "Multivariate Explanation," pp. 78, 90. For a later, more complex analysis with similar conclusions, see Ruy A. Teixeira, *Why Americans Don't Vote: Turnout Decline in the United States 1960–1984* (New York: Greenwood Press, 1987), pp. 107–108.

49. David Glass, Peverill Squire, and Raymond Wolfinger, "Voter Turnout: An International Comparison," *Public Opinion* 6 (December–January 1984):52.

50. G. Bingham Powell, "American Voter Turnout in Comparative Perspective," *American Political Science Review* 80 (March 1986):25.

51. Crewe, "Electoral Participation," p. 262.

52. Barnes and Kaase, *Political Action*, p. 532.

53. *1971 Congressional Quarterly Almanac* (Washington, D.C.: Congressional Quarterly Press, 1972), p. 475.

54. Benjamin Ginsberg, *The Consequences of Consent: Elections, Citizen Control and Popular Acquiescence* (Reading, Mass.: Addison-Wesley, 1982), p. 13.

55. Ibid., pp. 13–14.

56. Ibid., pp. 6–7.

Chapter 8 / Political Parties, Campaigns, and Elections / pp. 260–307

1. *Congressional Quarterly Weekly Report*, 8 January 1983, p. 5.

2. Center for Political Studies of the Institute for Social Research, *Election Study 1984* (Ann Arbor, Mich.: University of Michigan, 1984).

3. Alan R. Gitelson, M. Margaret Conway, and Frank B. Fiegert, *American Political Parties: Stability and Change* (Boston: Houghton Mifflin, 1984), p. 317.

4. Noble E. Cunningham, Jr., ed., *The Making of the American Party System, 1789 to 1809* (Englewood Cliffs, N.J.: Prentice-Hall, 1965), p. 123.

5. Richard B. Morris, ed., *Encyclope-*

dia of American History (New York: Harper & Row, 1976), p. 209.

6. See Jerome M. Clubb, William H. Flanigan, and Nancy H. Zingale, *Partisan Realignment: Voters, Parties, and Government in American History*, vol. 108 (Beverly Hills, Calif.: SAGE, 1980), p. 163.

7. See Gerald M. Pomper, "Classification of Presidential Elections," *Journal of Politics* 29 (August 1967):535–566.

8. For a more extensive treatment, see Henry M. Littlefield, "The Wizard of Oz: Parable on Populism," *American Quarterly* 16 (Spring 1964):47–58.

9. Clubb, Flanigan, and Zingale, *Partisan Realignment*, p. 99.

10. "Libertarian Party Facts," distributed by the Ron Paul for President Committee, 1120 Nasa Road, Houston, Texas (no date).

11. The following discussion draws heavily on Austin Ranney and Willmoore Kendall, *Democracy and the American Party System* (New York: Harcourt, Brace, 1956), chaps. 18 and 19.

12. See Steven J. Rosenstone, Roy L. Behr, and Edward H. Lazarus, *Third Parties in America: Citizen Response to Major Party Failure* (Princeton, N.J.: Princeton University Press, 1984), pp. 5–6.

13. Ibid., p. 8.

14. *Public Opinion* 7 (December–January 1985):26.

15. Findings from a 1986 survey reported in Larry J. Sabato, *The Party's Just Begun: Shaping Political Parties for America's Future* (Glenview, Ill.: Scott, Foresman, 1988), p. 133.

16. Ibid., p. 34.

17. Bill Keller, "As Arms Buildup Eases, U.S. Tries to Take Stock," *New York Times*, 14 May 1985.

18. Robert Harmel and Kenneth Janda, *Parties and Their Environments: Limits to Reform?* (New York: Longman, 1982), pp. 27–29.

19. William Crotty and John S. Jackson III, *Presidential Primaries and Nominations* (Washington, D.C.: Congressional Quarterly Press, 1985), p. 33.

20. John F. Bibby, "Party Renewal in the National Republican Party," in *Party Renewal in America: Theory and Practice*, ed. Gerald M. Pomper (New York: Praeger, 1980), pp. 102–115.

21. Tom Watson, "Machines: Something Old, Something New," *Congressional Quarterly Weekly Report*, 17 August 1985, p. 1619.

22. Advisory Commission on Intergovernmental Relations, *The Transformation of American Politics: Implications for Federalism* (Washington, D.C.: Report A-106, August 1986), pp. 112–116; see also Cornelius P. Cotter et al., *Party Organizations in American Politics* (New York: Praeger, 1984), pp. 26–27.

23. Ibid., p. 63.

24. See Stephen A. Salmore and Barbara G. Salmore, *Candidates, Parties, and Campaigns* (Washington, D.C.: Congressional Quarterly Press, 1985), p. 13.

25. Kenneth Janda, *Political Parties: A Cross-National Survey* (New York: Free Press, 1980), p. 112.

26. Crotty and Jackson, *Presidential Primaries*, p. 16.

27. Gary R. Orren and Nelson W. Polsby, eds., *Media and Momentum: The New Hampshire Primary and Nomination Politics* (Chatham, N.J.: Chatham House, 1987), p. 23.

28. See James R. Beniger, "Winning the Presidential Nomination: National Polls and State Primary Elections, 1936–1972," *Public Opinion Quarterly* 40 (Spring 1976):22–38.

29. *News* of the National Association of Broadcasters, 13 July 1987 (Washington, D.C.).

30. Dorothy Davidson Nesbit, *Videostyle in Senate Campaigns* (Knoxville, Tenn.: University of Tennessee Press, 1988), p. 152.

31. Darrell M. West, "Cheers and Jeers: Candidate Presentations and Audience Reactions in the 1980 Presidential Campaign," *American Politics Quarterly* 12 (January 1984):40.

32. Larry Sabato and David Beiler, "Magic . . . or Blue Smoke and Mirrors? Reflections on New Technologies and Trends in the Political Consultant Trade"

(Northwestern University: The Annenberg Washington Program in Communication Policy Studies, 1988), pp. 4–5.

33. Quoted in E. J. Dionne, Jr., "On the Trail of Corporation Donations," *New York Times*, 6 October 1980.

34. Federal Election Commission, *The First Ten Years: 1975–1985*, April 14, 1985, p. 1.

35. The findings reported here for 1984 were computed from preliminary data made available through the Inter-University Consortium for Political and Social Research.

36. Arthur H. Miller and Martin P. Wattenberg, "Throwing the Rascals Out: Policy and Performance Evaluations of Presidential Candidates, 1952–1980," *American Political Science Review* 79 (June 1985):359–372.

37. David B. Hill and Norman R. Luttbeg, *Trends in American Electoral Behavior* (Itasca, Ill.: Peacock, 1983), p. 50.

38. Herbert Asher, *Presidential Elections and American Politics* (Homewood, Ill.: Dorsey Press, 1980), p. 196.

39. The model is articulated most clearly in a report by the American Political Science Association, "Toward a More Responsible Two-Party System," *American Political Science Review* 44 (September 1950). See also Gerald M. Pomper, "Toward a More Responsible Party System? What, Again?" *Journal of Politics* 33 (November 1971):916–940.

40. See, for example, Gerald M. Pomper, ed., *Party Renewal in America: Theory and Practice* (New York: Praeger, 1980).

Chapter 9 / Interest Groups / pp. 308–343

1. Macon Morehouse, "Digital Tape Recorders Spark Lobbying Wars," *Congressional Quarterly Weekly Report*, 13 June 1987, p. 1235.

2. Jeffrey M. Berry, *The Interest Group Society* (Boston: Little, Brown, 1984), p. 5.

3. Alexis de Tocqueville, *Democracy in America*, ed. Richard D.

Heffner (New York: Mentor Books, 1956), p. 198.

4. See Robert A. Dahl, *A Preface to Democratic Theory* (Chicago: University of Chicago Press, 1956), pp. 4–33.

5. This discussion follows from Berry, *Interest Group Society*, pp. 6–8.

6. Steven Pressman, "Lobbying 'Star War' Flares as Movie Industry Fights Invasion of Video Recorders," *Congressional Quarterly Weekly Report*, 4 June 1983, pp. 1099–1103.

7. David B. Truman, *The Governmental Process* (New York: Knopf, 1951).

8. Herbert Gans, *The Urban Villagers* (New York: Free Press, 1962).

9. Robert H. Salisbury, "An Exchange Theory of Interest Groups," *Midwest Journal of Political Science* 13 (February 1969):1–32.

10. See Mancur Olson, Jr., *The Logic of Collective Action* (New York: Schocken, 1968); and Terry M. Moe, *The Organization of Interests* (Chicago: University of Chicago Press, 1980).

11. Peter Matthiessen, *Sal Si Puedes* (New York: Random House, 1969); and John G. Dunne, *Delano*, rev. ed. (New York: Farrar, Straus & Giroux, 1971).

12. Robert H. Salisbury, "Interest Representation: The Dominance of Institutions," *American Political Science Review* 78 (March 1984):64–76.

13. Larry J. Sabato, *The Rise of Political Consultants* (New York: Basic Books, 1981), pp. 220–263.

14. See Olson, *Logic of Collective Action*.

15. See John Mark Hansen, "The Political Economy of Group Membership," *American Political Science Review* 79 (March 1985):79–96.

16. Carol Greenwald, *Group Power* (New York: Praeger, 1977), p. 65.

17. David Rogers, "A Lobbyist's Fortuitous Position," *Wall Street Journal*, 23 August 1984, p. 42.

18. Robert H. Salisbury, "Washington Lobbyists: A Collective Portrait," in *Interest Group Politics*, 2d ed.,

ed. Allan J. Cigler and Burdett A. Loomis (Washington, D.C.: Congressional Quarterly, 1986), p. 155.

19. Paul Taylor, "Gladiators for Hire—Part I," *Washington Post*, 31 July 1983, p. A1.

20. Mark Green, "Political PAC-Man," *New Republic*, 13 December 1982, p. 24. On the influence of PACs, see Larry J. Sabato, *PAC Power* (New York: Norton, 1984), pp. 122–140.

21. Richard L. Berke, "PAC's Aided Legislators on Banking Panels," *New York Times*, 4 August 1987, p. A16.

22. Federal Election Commission, "FEC Releases First Complete PAC Figures for 1985–86," 21 May 1987, p. 2.

23. Elizabeth Drew, "Politics and Money—I," *New Yorker*, 6 December 1982, p. 147.

24. Kay Lehman Schlozman and John T. Tierney, *Organized Interests and American Democracy* (New York: Harper & Row, 1986), p. 150.

25. John E. Chubb, *Interest Groups and the Bureaucracy* (Stanford, Calif.: Stanford University Press, 1983), p. 144.

26. *Brown* v. *Board of Education*, 347 U.S. 483 (1954).

27. Michael Kranish, "Lobbying Intensifies as Vote Nears on Reagan Veto of Rights Bill," *Boston Globe*, 22 March 1988, p. 3.

28. Allan J. Cigler and John Mark Hansen, "Group Formation Through Protest: The American Agriculture Movement," in *Interest Group Politics*, Allan J. Cigler and Burdett A. Loomis (Washington, D.C.: Congressional Quarterly, 1983), pp. 84–109.

29. David J. Garrow, *Protest at Selma* (New Haven, Conn.: Yale University Press, 1978).

30. Roger P. Kingsley, "Advocacy for the Handicapped" (Paper delivered at the annual meeting of the American Political Science Association, Washington, D.C., September 1984), p. 10.

31. Robert H. Salisbury et al., "Who Works with Whom?" *American Political Science Review* 81 (December 1987):1224–1228.

32. Anne Costain, "The Struggle for a National Women's Lobby," *Western Political Quarterly* 33 (December 1980):476–491.

33. Schlozman and Tierney, *Organized Interests*, p. 281.

34. Jack L. Walker, "The Origins and Maintenance of Interest Groups in America" (Paper delivered at the annual meeting of the American Political Science Association, New York, September 1981), p. 14.

35. Jeffrey M. Berry, *Lobbying for the People* (Princeton, N.J.: Princeton University Press, 1977), pp. 6–10.

36. Andrew S. McFarland, *Common Cause* (Chatham, N.J.: Chatham House, 1984).

37. Charles McCarry, *Citizen Nader* (New York: Saturday Review Press, 1972).

38. See David Vogel, *Lobbying the Corporation* (New York: Basic Books, 1978), p. 21–68.

39. See Allen D. Hertzke, *Representing God in Washington* (Knoxville: University of Tennessee Press, 1988).

40. Rich Jaroslovsky, "Religious Right Counts on Reagan," *Wall Street Journal*, 18 September 1984, p. 64.

41. Martha Joynt Kumar and Michael Baruch Grossman, "The Presidency and Interest Groups," in *The Presidency and the Political System*, ed. Michael Nelson (Washington, D.C.: Congressional Quarterly, 1984), pp. 293–294.

42. David Vogel, "How Business Responds to Opposition" (Paper delivered at the annual meeting of the American Political Science Association, Washington, D.C., December 1979).

43. *Public Affairs Offices and Their Functions* (Boston: Boston University School of Management, 1981), p. 8.

44. Monica Langley, "Feuding Lobbies Hinder Push to Write Comprehensive Legislation," *Wall Street Journal*, 24 March 1986.

45. Walter Dean Burnham, *Critical Elections and the Mainsprings of American Politics* (New York: Norton, 1970), p. 133.

46. *United States* v. *Harriss*, 347 U.S. 612 (1954).

47. Federal Election Commission, "FEC Releases First Complete PAC Figures," p. 11.

Chapter 10 / Congress / pp. 350–391

1. Jimmy Carter, *Keeping Faith* (New York: Bantam Books, 1982), p. 84.
2. Jeffrey H. Birnbaum and Alan S. Murray, *Showdown at Gucci Gulch* (New York: Random House, 1987), p. 199.
3. Clinton Rossiter, *1787: The Grand Convention* (New York: Mentor, 1968), p. 158.
4. *Origins and Development of Congress* (Washington, D.C.: Congressional Quarterly Press, 1976), pp. 81–89.
5. *Wesberry* v. *Sanders*, 376 U.S. 1 (1964) (congressional districts within a state must be substantially equal in population); and *Reynolds* v. *Sims*, 377 U.S. 364 (1964) (state legislatures must be apportioned on the basis of population).
6. Linda Greenhouse, "Judicial Impeachment: Is Process Antiquated?" *New York Times*, 11 May 1988, p. A22.
7. Barbara Hinckley, *Congressional Elections* (Washington, D.C.: Congressional Quarterly Press, 1981), p. 37.
8. David R. Mayhew, "Congressional Elections: The Case of the Vanishing Marginals," *Polity* 6 (Spring 1974):295–317; and Warren R. Weaver, "More and More, House Races Aren't Races but Runaways," *New York Times*, 15 June 1987, p. 1.
9. George Gallup, Jr., *The Gallup Poll, Public Opinion 1986* (Wilmington, Del.: Scholarly Resources, Inc., 1987), pp. 272–278.
10. John A. Ferejohn, "On the Decline of Competition in Congressional Elections," *American Political Science Review* 71 (March 1977):166–176.
11. Bob Benenson, "Savvy 'Stars' Making Local TV a Potent Tool," *Congressional Quarterly Weekly Report*, 18 July 1987, pp. 1551–1552.
12. Brooks Jackson, "Incumbent Lawmakers Use the Perks of Office to Clobber Opponents," *Wall Street Journal*, 22 March 1988, p. 1.
13. Ibid.
14. Gary C. Jacobson and Samuel Kernell, *Strategy and Choice in Congressional Elections* (New Haven, Conn.: Yale University Press, 1983).
15. "FEC Releases First Complete PAC Figures for 1985–86 Election," Federal Election Commission, 21 May 1987, p. 2.
16. Larry J. Sabato, *PAC Power* (New York: Norton, 1984), p. 72.
17. Norman J. Ornstein et al., *Vital Statistics on Congress, 1987–1988* (Washington, D.C.: Congressional Quarterly Press, 1987), p. 52.
18. Ibid., pp. 20–21.
19. Walter J. Oleszek, *Congressional Procedures and the Policy Process*, 2d ed. (Washington, D.C.: Congressional Quarterly Press, 1984), p. 73.
20. John R. Crawford, "Expanded Powers: The View from Three Banks," *Congressional Quarterly Weekly Report*, 7 May 1988, pp. 1195–1199.
21. Martha Derthick and Paul J. Quirk, *The Politics of Deregulation* (Washington, D.C.: Brookings Institution, 1985).
22. Roger Cobb and Charles Elder, *Participation in American Politics*, 2d ed. (Baltimore: Johns Hopkins University Press, 1983), pp. 64–65.
23. John W. Kingdon, *Agendas, Alternatives, and Public Policies* (Boston: Little, Brown, 1984), p. 37.
24. Ibid., p. 41.
25. David Shribman, "Canada's Top Envoy to Washington Cuts Unusually Wide Swath," *Wall Street Journal*, 29 July 1985, p. 1.
26. Woodrow Wilson, *Congressional Government* (Boston: Houghton Mifflin, 1885), p. 79.
27. Leroy Rieselbach, *Congressional Reform* (Washington, D.C.: Congressional Quarterly Press, 1986), p. 47.
28. On some tentative steps toward recentralization, see Roger H. Davidson, "The New Centralization on Capitol Hill" (Paper delivered at the annual meeting of the Midwest Political Science Association, Chicago, April 1988).
29. Steven S. Smith and Christopher J. Deering, *Committees in Congress* (Washington, D.C.: Congressional Quarterly Press, 1984), p. 271.
30. Philip M. Boffey, "Lawmakers Vow a Legal Recourse for Military Malpractice Victims," *New York Times*, 9 July 1985.
31. Richard F. Fenno, Jr., *Congressmen in Committees* (Boston: Little, Brown, 1973), p. 86.
32. John F. Manley, *The Politics of Finance* (Boston: Little, Brown, 1970), p. 109.
33. Robert Weissberg, "Collective vs. Dyadic Representation in Congress," *American Political Science Review* 72 (June 1978):535–547.
34. Julie Rovner, "'Pepper Bill' Pits Politics Against Process," *Congressional Quarterly Weekly Report*, 4 June 1988, pp. 1491–1493.
35. Andy Plattner, "Dole on the Job," *Congressional Quarterly Weekly Report*, 29 June 1985, p. 1270.
36. Roger H. Davidson, "Senate Leaders: Janitors for an Untidy Chamber?" in *Congress Reconsidered*, 3d ed., ed. Lawrence C. Dodd and Bruce I. Oppenheimer (Washington, D.C.: Congressional Quarterly Press, 1985), p. 228.
37. Robert L. Peabody, *Leadership in Congress* (Boston: Little, Brown, 1976), p. 9.
38. Charles O. Jones, *The United States Congress* (Homewood, Ill.: Dorsey Press, 1982), p. 322.
39. Oleszek, *Congressional Procedures*, pp. 186–192.
40. *Congress Speaks: A Survey of the 100th Congress* (Washington, D.C.: Center for Responsive Politics, 1988), p. 6.
41. Deborah Baldwin, "Pulling Punches," *Common Cause*, May–June 1985, p. 22.
42. Jeffrey H. Birnbaum, "Rep. Armey, Texas Firebrand, Changes Tactics and Starts Accomplishing Things in the House," *Wall Street Journal*, 2 June 1988, p. 1.
43. Martin Tolchin, "200 Politicians Deal for One Trade Bill," *New York Times*, 27 March 1988, p. E5.
44. Steven V. Roberts, "A Most Im-

portant Man on Capitol Hill," *New York Times Magazine*, 22 September 1985, p. 55.

45. Randall B. Ripley, "Legislative Bargaining and the Food Stamp Act, 1964," *Congress and Urban Problems*, ed. Frederic N. Cleveland and Associates (Washington, D.C.: Brookings Institution, 1969), pp. 296–300.

46. This framework is adapted from John W. Kingdon, *Congressmen's Voting Decisions*, 2d ed. (New York: Harper & Row, 1981).

47. See David W. Rohde, "'Something's Happening Here; What It Is Ain't Exactly Clear': Southern Democrats in the House of Representatives" (Paper delivered at a conference in honor of Richard Fenno, Washington, D.C., August 1986).

48. Ornstein et al., *Vital Statistics*, p. 210.

49. Kay Lehman Schlozman and John T. Tierney, *Organized Interests and American Democracy* (New York: Harper & Row, 1985), p. 293.

50. Malcolm E. Jewell and Samuel C. Patterson, *The Legislative Process in the United States*, 4th ed. (New York: Random House, 1986), pp. 135–136.

51. Ornstein et al., *Vital Statistics*, pp. 141–142.

52. Michael Malbin, *Unelected Representatives* (New York: Basic Books, 1980).

53. Ibid., p. 240.

54. James Sterling Young, *The Washington Community* (New York: Harcourt, Brace, 1966).

55. Kingdon, *Congressmen's Voting Decisions*, p. 242.

56. Quoted in "U.S. Official Denies Cover-Up of Drug Inquiry at Arms Lab," *New York Times*, 16 June 1988, p. A22.

57. Fred Hiatt and Rick Atkinson, "Joint Chiefs of Congress," *Washington Post National Weekly Edition*, 12 August 1985, p. 6.

58. David R. Mayhew, *Congress: The Electoral Connection* (New Haven, Conn.: Yale University Press, 1974).

59. Joel D. Aberbach, "Changes in Congressional Oversight," *American Behavioral Scientist* 22

(May–June 1979):493–515, and "The Congressional Committee Intelligence System: Information, Oversight, and Change," *Congress and the Presidency* 14 (Spring 1987):51–76.

60. Jeffrey M. Berry, *Feeding Hungry People: Rulemaking in the Food Stamp Program* (New Brunswick, N.J.: Rutgers University Press, 1984), p. 122.

61. Richard F. Fenno, Jr., *Home Style* (Boston: Little, Brown, 1978), p. xii.

62. Ibid., p. 32.

63. Louis I. Bredvold and Ralph G. Ross, eds., *The Philosophy of Edmund Burke* (Ann Arbor, Mich.: University of Michigan Press, 1960), p. 148.

64. Roger H. Davidson, *The Role of the Congressman* (New York: Pegasus, 1969), p. 120.

65. Warren E. Miller and Donald E. Stokes, "Constituency Influence in Congress," *American Political Science Review* 57 (March 1963):45–57.

66. Darrell M. West, *Congress and Economic Policymaking* (Pittsburgh: University of Pittsburgh Press, 1987), pp. 37–64.

67. Julie Johnson, "Picking Over the Pork in the 1988 Spending Bill," *New York Times*, 5 January 1988, p. B6.

68. Weissberg, "Collective vs. Dyadic Representation."

Chapter 11 / The Presidency / pp. 392–433

1. Richard J. Meislin, "46% Approve Reagan's Work, Down 21 Points," *New York Times*, 2 December 1986, p. A1.

2. Gerald M. Boyd, "Many in Poll Say Reagan Is Lying on Diversion of Funds from Iran," *New York Times*, 10 December 1986, p. 1.

3. *The Tower Commission Report* (New York: Times Books, 1987), pp. 79–80.

4. Richard J. Meislin, "Majority in New Poll Still Think Reagan Lied on Iran-Contra Issue," *New York Times*, 18 July 1987, p. 1.

5. Louis W. Koenig, *The Chief Executive*, 4th ed. (New York: Harcourt Brace Jovanovich, 1981), p. 20.

6. Clinton Rossiter, *1787: The Grand Convention* (New York: Mentor, 1968), p. 148.

7. Ibid., pp. 190–191.

8. Richard M. Pious, *The American Presidency* (New York: Basic Books, 1979), pp. 51–52.

9. Wilfred E. Binkley, *President and Congress*, 3d ed. (New York: Vintage, 1962), p. 155.

10. Pious, *American Presidency*, pp. 60–63.

11. James L. Sundquist, *The Decline and Resurgence of Congress* (Washington, D.C.: Brookings Institution, 1981).

12. Richard E. Neustadt, *Presidential Power* (New York: John Wiley, 1980), p. 10.

13. Ibid., p. 9.

14. Fred I. Greenstein, *The Hidden-Hand Presidency* (New York: Basic Books, 1982), pp. 155–227.

15. David Rosenbaum, "Aides Evoke Goals of Johnson Period," *New York Times*, 20 April 1985.

16. Jeffrey K. Tulis, *The Rhetorical Presidency* (Princeton, N.J.: Princeton University Press, 1987), p. 64ff.

17. Ibid., p. 5.

18. See Theodore J. Lowi, *The Personal President* (Ithaca, N.Y.: Cornell University Press, 1985).

19. Darrell M. West, *Congress and Economic Policymaking* (Pittsburgh: University of Pittsburgh Press, 1987), p. 33.

20. John E. Mueller, *War, Presidents, and Public Opinion* (New York: Wiley, 1973).

21. Kristen Renwick Monroe, *Presidential Popularity and the Economy* (New York: Praeger, 1984).

22. Charles W. Ostrom, Jr., and Dennis M. Simon, "Promise and Performance: A Dynamic Model of Presidential Popularity," *American Political Science Review* 79 (June 1985):334–358.

23. Michael Novak, *Choosing Our King* (New York: Macmillan, 1974), p. 4.

24. Dom Bonafede, "The White House Personnel Office from Roosevelt to Reagan," in *The In-and-Outers*, ed. G. Calvin MacKenzie (Baltimore: Johns Hopkins University Press, 1987), p. 54.

25. Theodore J. Lowi, "Ronald Rea-

gan—Revolutionary?" in *The Reagan Presidency and the Governing of America*, ed. Lester M. Salamon and Michael S. Lund (Washington, D.C.: Urban Institute Press, 1984), p. 47.

26. *Elections '84* (Washington, D.C.: Congressional Quarterly, 1984), p. 87.

27. "Prepared Text of Carter's Farewell Address," *New York Times*, 15 January 1981.

28. Jeff Fishel, *Presidents and Promises* (Washington, D.C.: Congressional Quarterly Press, 1985), pp. 125–128.

29. Benjamin I. Page, *Choices and Echoes in Presidential Elections* (Chicago: University of Chicago Press, 1978).

30. Jeb Stuart Magruder, *An American Life* (New York: Atheneum, 1974), p. 58, quoted in Benjamin Page and Mark Petracca, *The American Presidency* (New York: McGraw-Hill, 1983), p. 169.

31. Page and Petracca, *American Presidency*, p. 171.

32. Gary King and Lyn Ragsdale, *The Elusive Executive* (Washington, D.C.: Congressional Quarterly Press, 1988), pp. 205–210.

33. Paul J. Quirk, "Presidential Competence," in *The Presidency and the Political System*, 2d ed., ed. Michael Nelson (Washington, D.C.: Congressional Quarterly Press, 1988), p. 163.

34. Samuel Kernell and Samuel Popkin, eds., *Chief of Staff* (Berkeley, Calif.: University of California Press, 1986), pp. 25–26.

35. Seymour M. Hersh, *The Price of Power* (New York: Summit, 1983), p. 42.

36. Alexander Haig, *Caveat* (New York: Macmillan, 1984), p. 143.

37. Gerald F. Seib, "Bush's Role in Policy Is Difficult to Discern, Reagan Officials Say," *Wall Street Journal*, 31 March 1988, p. 1.

38. Edward Weisband and Thomas M. Franck, *Resignation in Protest* (New York: Penguin, 1975), p. 139, quoted in Thomas Cronin, *The State of the Presidency*, 2d ed. (Boston: Little, Brown, 1980), p. 253.

39. Griffin B. Bell with Ronald J. Ostrow, *Taking Care of the Law* (New York: Morrow, 1982), p. 45.

40. Terry M. Moe, "The Politicized Presidency," in *The New Direction in American Politics*, ed. John E. Chubb and Paul E. Peterson (Washington, D.C.: Brookings Institution, 1985), pp. 235–271.

41. *Public Papers of the President, Lyndon B. Johnson, 1965*, vol. I (Washington, D.C.: U.S. Government Printing Office, 1966), p. 72.

42. "Transcript of Second Inaugural Address by Reagan," *New York Times*, 22 January 1985.

43. John L. Palmer and Isabel V. Sawhill, eds., *The Reagan Record* (Cambridge, Mass.: Ballinger, 1984), pp. 366–368.

44. John W. Kingdon, *Agendas, Alternatives, and Public Policies* (Boston: Little, Brown, 1984), p. 25.

45. Richard E. Neustadt, "Presidency and Legislation: The Growth of Central Clearance," *American Political Science Review* 48 (September 1954):641–671.

46. Stephen Skowronek, "Presidential Leadership in Political Time," in *Presidency and the Political System*, ed. Nelson, pp. 115–159.

47. Page and Petracca, *American Presidency*, p. 248.

48. Seth King, "Reagan, in Bid for Budget Votes, Reported to Yield on Sugar Prices," *New York Times*, 27 June 1981.

49. Dom Bonafede, "The Tough Job of Normalizing Relations with Capitol Hill," *National Journal*, 13 January 1979, pp. 54–57.

50. Martha Joynt Kumar and Michael Baruch Grossman, "The Presidency and Interest Groups," in *Presidency and the Political System*, ed. Nelson, p. 309.

51. Linda Greenhouse, "Senate Rejects Reagan Plea and Votes 67–33 to Override His Veto of Highway Funds," *New York Times*, 3 April 1987, p. A1.

52. Sidney M. Milkis, "The Presidency and Political Parties," in *Presidency and the Political System*, ed. Nelson, p. 337.

53. Alexander George, "The Case for Multiple Advocacy in Making Foreign Policy," *American Political Science Review* 66 (September 1972):751–782.

54. Richard E. Neustadt and Earnest R. May, *Thinking in Time* (New York: Free Press, 1986), p. 143.

55. Lowi, *Personal President*, p. 185.

56. Gail Sheehy, "The Road to Bimini," *Vanity Fair*, September 1987, p. 132.

57. Robert A. Caro, *The Path to Power* (New York: Knopf, 1982), p. 131.

58. Ibid., p. 135.

59. Doris Kearns, *Lyndon Johnson and the American Dream* (New York: Signet, 1977), p. 363.

Chapter 12 / The Bureaucracy / pp. 434–465

1. Pat Milton, "U.S. Intervenes on Behalf of Deformed Baby," *Boston Globe*, 5 November 1983.

2. "Big Brother Doe," *Wall Street Journal*, 1 November 1983.

3. Bruce D. Porter, "Parkinson's Law Revisited: War and the Growth of American Government," *Public Interest* 60 (Summer 1980):50.

4. Keith Schneider, "Farmers to Face Patent Fees to Use Gene-Altered Animals," *New York Times*, 6 January 1988, p. A1.

5. "Possible Nationalizing of Continental Illinois Raises Many Questions," *Wall Street Journal*, 19 July 1984.

6. Herbert Kaufman, *Are Government Organizations Immortal?* (Washington, D.C.: Brookings Institution, 1976).

7. Steven Kelman, "The Grace Commission: How Much Waste in Government," *Public Interest* 78 (Winter 1985):62–82.

8. Kenneth J. Meier, *Politics and the Bureaucracy* (North Scituate, Mass.: Duxbury Press, 1979).

9. "Advertisers Pleased by F.T.C. Plan," *New York Times*, 24 March 1984; see also Michael Pertschuk, *Revolt Against Regulation* (Berkeley, Calif.: University of California Press, 1982).

10. John T. Tierney, "Government Corporations and Managing the Public's Business," *Political Science Quarterly* 99 (Spring 1984):73–92.

11. Bureau of the Census, *Statistical Abstract of the United States, 1987* (Washington, D.C.: U.S. Government Printing Office, 1986), p. 309.

12. Kenneth J. Meier, "Representative Democracy: An Empirical Assess-

ment," *American Political Science Review* 69 (June 1975): 532.

13. *Statistical Abstract, 1987*, pp. 311–312.

14. Nelson W. Polsby, "Presidential Cabinet Making," *Political Science Quarterly* 93 (Spring 1978):16, 21; and Hugh Heclo, "Issue Networks and the Executive Establishment," in *The New American Political System*, ed. Anthony King (Washington, D.C.: American Enterprise Institute, 1978), pp. 105–115.

15. See Richard P. Nathan, *The Plot That Failed* (New York: Wiley, 1975).

16. Paul C. Light, "When Worlds Collide: The Political-Career Nexus," in *The In-and-Outers*, ed. G. Calvin MacKenzie (Baltimore: Johns Hopkins University Press, 1987), pp. 156–173.

17. Arthur Schlesinger, Jr., *A Thousand Days* (Greenwich, Conn.: Fawcett, 1967), p. 377.

18. Light, "When Worlds Collide," p. 157.

19. John W. Kingdon, *Agendas, Alternatives, and Public Policies* (Boston: Little, Brown, 1984), pp. 23–37.

20. Christopher Conte, "U.S. Proposes Rules Aimed at Curbing Alcohol, Drug Abuse by Rail Operators." *Wall Street Journal*, 7 June 1984.

21. Theodore J. Lowi, *The End of Liberalism*, 2d ed. (New York: Norton, 1979).

22. Doris A. Graber, *Mass Media and American Politics*, 2d ed. (Washington, D.C.: Congressional Quarterly, 1984), p. 48.

23. Jerome T. Murphy, "The Education Bureaucracies Implement Novel Policy," in *Policy and Politics in America*, ed. Allan Sindler (Boston: Little, Brown, 1973), pp. 160–198.

24. Herbert Kaufman, "Fear of Bureaucracy: A Raging Pandemic," *Public Administration Review*, January–February 1981, pp. 1–9.

25. Jeffrey M. Berry, *Feeding Hungry People: Rulemaking in the Food Stamp Program* (New Brunswick, N.J.: Rutgers University Press, 1984).

26. David J. Garrow, *Bearing the Cross* (New York: Morrow, 1986), pp. 373–374.

27. Pertschuk, *Revolt Against Regulation*, p. 64; and Irvin Molotsky, "All Funeral Costs Must Be Itemized," *New York Times*, 30 April 1984.

28. Margaret E. Kriz, "Kibitzer with Clout," *National Journal*, 30 May 1987, pp. 1404–1408.

29. Steven Kelman, *Making Public Policy* (New York: Basic Books, 1987), p. 93.

30. Terry M. Moe, "Control and Feedback in Economic Regulation: The Case of the NLRB," *American Political Science Review* 79 (December 1985):109–116.

31. Charles E. Lindblom, "The Science of Muddling Through," *Public Administration Review* 19 (Spring 1959):79–88.

32. Michael Lipsky, *Street-Level Bureaucracy* (New York: Russell Sage Foundation, 1980), p. 21.

33. Jonathan Bendor, Serge Taylor, and Roland Van Gaalen, "Stacking the Deck: Bureaucratic Missions and Policy Design," *American Political Science Review* 81 (Spring 1987):874.

34. George C. Edwards III, *Implementing Public Policy* (Washington, D.C.: Congressional Quarterly, 1980), p. 27; see also Daniel A. Mazmanian and Paul Sabatier, *Implementation and Public Policy* (Glenview, Ill.: Scott, Foresman, 1983), pp. 175–217.

35. Jeffrey L. Pressman and Aaron B. Wildavsky, *Implementation*, 3d ed. (Berkeley, Calif.: University of California Press, 1984), pp. 102–110.

36. Patricia Rachel, *Federal Narcotics Enforcement* (Boston: Auburn House, 1982).

37. Richard A. Harris, *Coal Firms under the New Social Regulation* (Durham, N.C.: Duke University Press, 1985), pp. 158–159.

38. "Absorbing the Head Start Lesson," *New York Times*, 12 December 1980; and Fred M. Hechinger, "Blacks Found to Benefit from Preschooling," *New York Times*, 11 September 1984.

39. Matthew A. Crenson and Francis

E. Rourke, "By Way of Conclusion: American Bureaucracy since World War II," in *The New American State*, ed. Louis Galambos (Baltimore: Johns Hopkins University Press, 1987), p. 161.

40. Nathaniel C. Nash, "Task Force Ties Market Collapse to Trading Programs at Big Firms," *New York Times*, 9 January 1988.

41. Gerald F. Seib, "Pentagon Has Trouble Winning Cooperation Between the Services," *Wall Street Journal*, 1 August 1984.

42. Martha Derthick and Paul J. Quirk, *The Politics of Deregulation* (Washington, D.C.: Brookings Institution, 1985).

43. Walter A. Rosenbaum, "Public Involvement as Reform and Ritual," in *Citizen Participation in America*, ed. Stuart Langton (Lexington, Mass.: Lexington Books, 1978).

44. Jeffrey M. Berry, "Maximum Feasible Dismantlement," *Citizen Participation* 3 (November–December 1981):3–5.

45. Jeffrey M. Berry, Kent E. Portney, and Ken Thomson, "Empowering Citizens," in *Handbook of Public Administration*, ed. James Perry (San Francisco: Jossey-Bass, in press).

46. John C. Baker, "Program Costs and Comparisons," in *Cruise Missiles*, ed. Richard K. Betts (Washington, D.C.: Brookings Institution, 1981), pp. 101–133, 573–595. Cited in Kent E. Portney, *Approaching Public Policy Analysis* (Englewood Cliffs, N.J.: Prentice-Hall, 1986), p. 104.

47. Howard E. Shumann, *Politics and the Budget* (Englewood Cliffs, N.J.: Prentice-Hall, 1984), pp. 37–43.

48. Ibid., p. 43.

Chapter 13 / The Courts / pp. 466–505

1. Philip Elman (interviewed by Norman Silber), "The Solicitor General's Office, Justice Frankfurter, and Civil Rights Litigation, 1946–1960: An Oral History, 100 *Harvard Law Review* 817–852, 840 (1987).

2. Bernard Schwartz, *The Unpublished Opinions of the Warren Court* (New York: Oxford University Press, 1985), p. 446.

3. Ibid., pp. 445–448.

4. Felix Frankfurter and James M. Landis, *The Business of the Supreme Court* (New York: Macmillan, 1928), pp. 5–14; and Julius Goebel, Jr., *Antecedents and Beginnings to 1801*, vol. 1 of *History of the Supreme Court of the United States* (New York: Macmillan, 1971).

5. Robert G. McCloskey, *The United States Supreme Court* (Chicago: University of Chicago Press, 1960), p. 31.

6. *Marbury* v. *Madison*, 1 Cranch 137, 177–178 (1803).

7. Walter F. Murphy, James E. Fleming, and William F. Harris II, *American Constitutional Interpretation* (Mineola, N.Y.: Foundation Press, 1986), p. 191.

8. *Ware* v. *Hylton*, 3 Dallas 199 (1796).

9. *Martin* v. *Hunter's Lessee*, 1 Wheat. 304 (1816).

10. Garry Wills, *Explaining America: The Federalist* (Garden City, N.Y.: Doubleday, 1981), pp. 127–136.

11. Charles Alan Wright, *Handbook on the Law of Federal Courts*, 3d ed. (St. Paul, Minn.: West, 1976), p. 7.

12. Linda Greenhouse, "Precedent for Lower Courts: Tyrant or Teacher?" *New York Times*, 29 January 1988, p. 18.

13. *Roe* v. *Wade*, 410 U.S. 113 (1973).

14. *Regents of the University of California* v. *Bakke*, 438 U.S. 265 (1978).

15. Joseph Tanenhaus et al., "The Supreme Court's Certiorari Jurisdiction: Cue Theory," in *Judicial Decision-Making*, ed. Glendon Schubert (New York: Free Press, 1963), pp. 111–132.

16. Doris M. Provine, *Case Selection in the United States Supreme Court* (Chicago: University of Chicago Press, 1980), pp. 74–102.

17. *Garcia* v. *San Antonio Metropolitan Transit Authority*, 469 U.S. 528 (1985).

18. Elder Witt, *A Different Justice: Reagan and the Supreme Court* (Washington, D.C.: Congressional Quarterly, 1986), p. 133.

19. "Rising Fixed Opinions," *New York Times*, 22 February 1988, p. 14.

20. *Congressional Quarterly's Guide to the U.S. Supreme Court* (Washington, D.C.: Congressional Quarterly, 1979, p. 741.

21. Stuart Taylor Jr., "Lifting of Secrecy Reveals Earthy Side of Justices," *New York Times*, 22 February 1988, p. 14.

22. See, for example, Walter F. Murphy, *Elements of Judicial Strategy* (Chicago: University of Chicago Press, 1964); and Bob Woodward and Scott Armstrong, *The Brethren* (New York: Simon & Schuster, 1979).

23. Henry J. Abraham, *Justices and Presidents: A Political History of Appointments to the Supreme Court*, 2d ed. (New York: Oxford University Press, 1985), pp. 183–185.

24. Stuart Taylor Jr., "Brennan: 30 Years and the Thrill Is Not Gone," *New York Times*, 16 April 1986, p. 18.

25. Stephen L. Wasby, *The Supreme Court in the Federal Judicial System*, 3d ed. (Chicago: Nelson-Hall, 1988), p. 241.

26. Schwartz, *Unpublished Opinions*, pp. 446–447.

27. *Congressional Quarterly's Guide*, p. 740.

28. Lawrence Baum, *American Courts: Process and Policy* (Boston: Houghton Mifflin, 1986), pp. 93–95.

29. Harold W. Chase, *Federal Judges: The Appointing Process* (St. Paul: University of Minnesota Press, 1972).

30. Wasby, *Supreme Court*, pp. 107–110.

31. "The ABA's Helpful Advice," *Wall Street Journal*, 30 December 1985, p. 8.

32. Linda Greenhouse, "Policy on Black Judicial Nominees Is Debated," *New York Times*, 3 February 1988, p. 22 (statement by Assistant Attorney General Stephen J. Markman).

33. Peter G. Fish, "John J. Parker," in *Dictionary of American Biography*, supp. 6, *1956–1980* (New York: Scribner's, 1980), p. 494.

34. *Congressional Quarterly's Guide*, pp. 655–656.

35. Elmo Richardson, *The Presidency of Dwight D. Eisenhower* (Lawrence, Kan.: Regents Press, 1979), p. 108.

36. Merle Miller, *Plain Speaking: An Oral Biography of Harry S. Truman* (New York: Berkley, 1973), pp. 225–226.

37. Barbara A. Curran, *The Lawyer Statistical Report* (Chicago: American Bar Foundation, 1985), p. 4.

38. Bureau of Labor Statistics, *Occupational Outlook Handbook, 1986–1987* (Washington, D.C.: U.S. Government Printing Office, 1986).

39. Nicholas O. Berry, "Of Lawyers' Work, There Is No End," *New York Times*, 28 December 1985, p. 19.

40. James Eisenstein, *Attorneys for the Government* (Baltimore: Johns Hopkins University Press, 1980), p. 204.

41. *Brown* v. *Board of Education* II, 349 U.S. 294 (1955).

42. Charles A. Johnson and Bradley C. Canon, *Judicial Policies: Implementation and Impact* (Washington, D.C.: Congressional Quarterly Press, 1984).

43. For example, *Thornburgh* v. *American College of Obstetricians and Gynecologists*, 106 S.Ct. 2169 (1986).

44. Alexander M. Bickel, *The Least Dangerous Branch* (Indianapolis: Bobbs-Merrill, 1962); and Robert A. Dahl, "Decision-Making in a Democracy: The Supreme Court as a National Policy-Maker," *Journal of Public Law* 6 (1962):279–295.

45. David G. Barnum, "The Supreme Court and Public Opinion: Judicial Decision Making in the Post–New Deal Period," *Journal of Politics* 47 (1985):652–662.

46. *Raymon* v. *Alrod Independent School District*, 639 F.2d 257 (5th Cir. 1981).

47. *Kostiuk* v. *Town of Riverhead*, 570 F.Supp. 603 (EDNY 1983).

48. "A Deadly Serious Dilemma: Evaluating the Right to Die," *Insight*, 26 January 1987, p. 12.

49. Abram Chayes, "The Role of the Judge in Public Law Litigation," *Harvard Law Review* 89 (May 1976):1281–1316.

50. "The *Wyatt* Case: Implementation of a Judicial Decree Ordering Institutional Change," *Yale Law Journal* 84 (1975):1338–1347.

51. Phillip J. Cooper, *Hard Judicial Choices* (New York: Oxford University Press, 1988).

52. "Judicial Isolation," *New York Times*, 17 April 1986, p. 12.

53. Benjamin N. Cardozo, *The Nature of the Judicial Process* (New Haven, Conn.: Yale University Press, 1921), p. 168.

Chapter 14 / The Washington Community / pp. 506–533

1. Ben A. Franklin, "Jurors Are Told Deaver Got $250,000 for One Call," *New York Times*, 29 October 1987.

2. Marjorie Williams, "Michael Deaver's Fall from Grace," *Washington Post National Weekly Edition*, 27 July 1987, pp. 8–10. See also Evan Thomas and Thomas M. DeFrank, "Mike Deaver's Rise and Fall," *Newsweek*, 23 March 1987, pp. 22–23.

3. John Herbers, "Capital Census: Far from Average," *New York Times*, 7 May 1982.

4. Ibid.

5. James Sterling Young, *The Washington Community* (New York: Columbia University Press, 1966), p. 25.

6. Nelson W. Polsby, "The Washington Community, 1960–1980," in *The New Congress*, ed. Thomas E. Mann and Norman J. Ornstein (Washington, D.C.: American Enterprise Institute, 1981), p. 11. See also Richard D. Lyons, "The 'Other Washington' Enjoys Boom; Private Sector Now Dominates Region," *New York Times*, 20 January 1981.

7. Robert L. Nelson et al., "Private Representation in Washington: Surveying the Structure of Influence," *American Bar Foundation Research Journal*, Winter 1987, pp.141–200.

8. See, for example, the analysis of the salary structure at Patton, Boggs & Blow, in Steve Nelson, "Firm Papers Show Incomes," *Legal Times*, 24 February 1986, p. 6.

9. Joseph C. Goulden, *The Superlawyers* (New York: Dell, 1973), pp. 27 and 53. See also Mark J. Green, *The Other Government* (New York: Grossman, 1975), pp. 16–44; and Steve Nelson, "Growth Continues Despite Deregulation," *Legal Times*, 30 June 1986, p. 12.

10. Stuart Taylor, Jr., "Senator Baker and the Art of Making Rain," *New York Times*, 11 December 1984.

11. Steven V. Roberts, "Federal Magnetism Draws Law Firms," *New York Times*, 11 January 1978.

12. Edward O. Laumann and John P. Heinz, "Washington Lawyers and Others," *Stanford Law Review* 37 (January 1985):467; and Nelson, "Growth Continues Despite Deregulation."

13. James W. Singer, "Practicing Law in Washington—An American Growth Industry," *National Journal*, 2 February 1978, p. 176.

14. James W. Singer, "Consultants—Helping Themselves by Helping Government," *National Journal*, 24 June 1978, p. 1002.

15. A. O. Sulzberger, Jr., "G.A.O. Seeks to Cut Defense Consultants," *New York Times*, 7 April 1981.

16. Gregg Easterbrook, "The Art of Further Study," *Washington Monthly*, May 1980, p. 19.

17. Aaron Wildavsky, "The Self-Evaluating Organization," *Public Administration Review* 32 (September–October 1972):510.

18. Christopher Madison, "Energy Consultants—What Do They Do and Why Should They Be Doing It?" *National Journal*, 30 August 1980, p. 1444.

19. Singer, "Consultants," p. 1001.

20. Gregg Easterbrook, "Ideas Move Nations," *Atlantic Monthly*, January 1986, p. 66.

21. See, for example, Martha Derthick, *Policy Making for Social Security* (Washington, D.C.: Brookings Institution, 1979); and Mann and Ornstein, *The New Congress*.

22. Henry J. Aaron, *Why Is Welfare So Hard to Reform?* (Washington, D.C.: Brookings Institution, 1973).

23. Edward Sussman, "Conservative Think Tank Comes Back from Brink of Financial Disaster, Leaning More to the Right," *Wall Street Journal*, 3 September 1987, p. 42.

24. Quoted in Bernard Weinraub, "Heritage Foundation 10 Years Later," *New York Times*, 30 September 1983.

25. Alvin P. Sanoff, "Image Makers Worry About Their Own Image," *U.S. News and World Report*, 13 August 1979, p. 59.

26. Michael R. Gordon, "The Image Makers in Washington—PR Firms Have Found a Natural Home," *National Journal*, 31 May 1980, pp. 888–889.

27. Burt Solomon, "Clout Merchants," *National Journal*, 21 March 1987, pp. 662–666.

28. Charles Mohr, "Market-Hunting in 'Progressive' P.R.," *New York Times*, 21 April 1984.

29. Philip H. Dougherty, "Hill & Knowlton to Buy Gray's Lobbying Firm," *New York Times*, 4 June 1986; and Ann Cooper, "Image Builders," *National Journal*, 14 September 1985, pp. 2058–2059.

30. Jeffrey M. Berry, *The Interest Group Society*, 2d ed. (Glenview, Ill.: Scott, Foresman/Little, Brown, in press).

31. Robert H. Salisbury et al., "Soaking and Poking Among the Movers and Shakers" (Paper delivered at the annual meeting of the American Political Science Association, Washington, D.C., September 1984); and Paul Taylor, "Gladiators for Hire—I," *Washington Post*, 31 July 1983.

32. Steven V. Roberts, "Trade Associations Flocking to Capital as U.S. Role Rises," *New York Times*, 4 March 1978, p. 23.

33. Hugh Heclo, "Issue Networks and the Executive Establishment," in *The New American Political System*, ed. Anthony King (Washington, D.C.: American Enterprise Institute, 1978), p. 103.

34. Robert H. Salisbury et al., "Who

Works with Whom? Interest Group Alliances and Opposition," *American Political Science Review* 81 (December 1987):1217–1234.

35. Douglass Cater, *Power in Washington* (New York: Vintage Books, 1964), p. 18.

36. Lawrence C. Dodd and Richard L. Schott, *Congress and the Administrative State* (New York: Wiley, 1979), p. 103.

37. See Jeffrey M. Berry, "Subgovernments, Issue Networks, and Political Conflict," in *Remaking American Politics*, ed. Richard A. Harris and Sidney M. Milkis (Boulder, Colo.: Westview Press, in press).

38. This account is based on Steven Coll, *The Deal of the Century* (New York: Atheneum, 1986); and Peter Temin with Louis Galambos, *The Fall of the Bell System* (New York: Cambridge University Press, 1987).

39. This discussion is taken from Berry, *The Interest Group Society*.

40. Lauriston R. King and W. Wayne Shannon, "Policy Networks in the Policy Process: The Case of the National Sea Grant Program," *Polity* 19 (Winter 1986):213–231.

41. Edward O. Laumann et al., "Organizations in Political Action" (Paper presented at the annual meeting of the American Sociological Association, September 1986.)

42. Heclo, "Issue Networks," p. 105.

43. John M. Blair, *The Control of Oil* (New York: Pantheon, 1976), pp. 354–370.

44. Thomas B. Edsall, "Republican Lobbyists Expanding; Advantages Seen After Landslide," *Washington Post*, 16 December 1984.

45. Richard Cohen, "Small Lobbying Firms Tout Their Policy Expertise and Client Contact," *National Journal*, 14 January 1984, p. 68.

46. David Johnston, "Nofziger Given 90 Days in Jail in Ethics Case," *New York Times*, 9 April 1988, p. 9.

47. See G. Calvin Mackenzie, *The In- and-Outers* (Baltimore: Johns Hopkins University Press, 1987).

48. Douglas R. Sease and Thomas Petzinger, Jr., "Steelmakers Cheer Two Reagan Nominees, but Others Question Their Impartiality," *Wall Street Journal*, 5 July 1981.

49. Berry, "Subgovernments, Issue Networks, and Political Conflict."

Chapter 15 / The Economics of Public Policy / pp. 540–577

1. George J. Church, "Panic Grips the Globe," *Time Magazine*, 2 November 1987, p. 22.

2. James Sterngold, "Seeking a Stronger Safety Net for the System," *New York Times National Edition*, 14 December 1987, pp. 1 and 34.

3. James Sterngold, "System's Surprising Breakdowns," *New York Times National Edition*, 11 January 1988, pp. D1 and D8.

4. John R. Cranford, "Hill Gets Conflicting Advice on Averting Another Crash," *Congressional Quarterly Weekly Report* 6 February 1988, pp. 243–245; and Nathaniel C. Nash, "S.E.C. Staff Urges Curbs on Trading of Stock Futures," *New York Times National Edition*, 3 February 1988, pp. 1 and 28.

5. Louis Uchitelle, "The Uncertain Legacy of the Crash," *New York Times National Edition*, 3 April 1988, sec. 3, pp. 1 and 6.

6. Lawrence J. Haas, "New Fiscal Realities," *National Journal*, 9 January 1988, p. 66.

7. Bureau of the Census, *Statistical Abstract of the United States, 1988* (Washington, D.C.: U.S. Government Printing Office, 1988), p. 433.

8. Ibid., p. 406.

9. Ibid., p. 296.

10. Jonathan Rauch, "Testing the Fed," *National Journal*, 18 June 1988, p. 1612.

11. Ronald Reagan with Richard G. Hubler, *Where's the Rest of Me?* (New York: Duell, Sloan and Pearce, 1965), p. 233.

12. Bureau of the Census, *Statistical Abstract of the United States, 1988*, p. 445.

13. Isabel V. Sawhill and Charles F. Stone, "The Economy: The Key to Success," in *The Reagan Record*, ed. John L. Palmer and Isabel V. Sawhill (Cambridge, Mass.: Ballinger, 1984), pp. 80–83.

14. Jonathan Rauch, Lawrence J. Haas, and Bruce Stokes, "Payment Deferred," *National Journal*, 14 May 1988, p. 1256.

15. Lawrence J. Haas, "New Rules of the Game," *National Journal*, March 19, 1988, p. 734.

16. *Congressional Record*, House of Representatives, 24 May 1988, p. H3582.

17. *Congressional Quarterly Weekly Report*, 14 December 1985, p. 2605.

18. Lawrence J. Haas, "The Deficit Culture," *National Journal*, June 4, 1988, 1461.

19. Lawrence J. Haas, "Unauthorized Action," *National Journal*, January 2, 1988, pp. 17–21.

20. Richard A. Musgrave and Peggy B. Musgrave, *Public Finance in Theory and Practice*, 2d ed. (New York: McGraw-Hill, 1976), p. 42.

21. *Public Opinion* 8 (February–March, 1985):29.

22. George E. Curry, "The Ron 'n' Rosty Show Opens in Pa.," *Chicago Tribune*, 1 June 1985.

23. ABC/*Washington Post* Survey cited in *Public Opinion* 8 (February–March 1985):21.

24. *New York Times*, 24 January 1985.

25. *Public Opinion* 8 (February–March 1985):20.

26. Advisory Commission on Intergovernmental Relations, *Significant Features of Fiscal Federalism, 1981–1982* (Washington, D.C., 1983) p. 54.

27. Joseph A. Pechman, ed., *World Tax Reform: A Progress Report* (Washington, D.C.: Brookings Institution, 1988), p. 4.

28. *Congressional Quarterly Weekly Report*, 8 February 1986, p. 225.

29. National Election Study for 1984, conducted by the Center for Political Studies, University of Michigan.

30. *The Polling Report*, 25 January 1988, pp. 1 and 8.

31. Fay Lomax Cook et al., *Convergent Perspectives on Social Welfare Policy: The Views from the General Public, Members of Con-

gress, and AFDC Recipients (Evanston, Ill.: Northwestern University, Center for Urban Affairs and Policy Research, 1988), Table 4–1.

32. *Gallup Report*, January–February 1986, p. 30.

33. Joseph A. Pechman, *Who Paid the Taxes, 1966–1985?* (Washington, D.C.: Brookings Institution, 1985).

34. Ibid., p. 53.

35. Ibid., p. 80.

36. Ibid., p. 73.

37. Ibid., p. 74.

38. Charles F. Andrain, *Social Policies in Western Industrial Societies* (Berkeley, Calif.: University of California Press, 1985), p. 194.

39. "Nation Top-heavy with wealth," *Chicago Tribune*, 19 July 1986, p. 1; and Bureau of the Census, *Statistical Abstract of the United States, 1988*, p. 440.

40. Benjamin I. Page, *Who Gets What from Government?* (Berkeley, Calif.: University of California Press, 1983), p. 213.

41. *New York Times*, 13 May 1983.

42. Advisory Commission on Intergovernmental Relations, *Significant Features of Fiscal Federalism, 1984* (Washington, D.C.: U.S. Government Printing Office, 1985), p. 139.

43. *Public Opinion* 8 (February–March 1985):27.

44. "Lotteries Are Now Used in 26 States for Revenue," *New York Times National Edition*, 16 February 1988, p. 8.

45. Lawrence J. Haas, "Who'll Pay the Price?" *National Journal*, February 20, 1988, pp. 444–449.

Chapter 16 / Domestic Policy / pp. 578–615

1. Alex Kotlowitz, "Day-to-Day Violence Takes a Terrible Toll on Inner-City Youth," *Wall Street Journal*, 27 October 1987, p. 1.

2. Keith Schneider, "New Products on Farms in Midwest: Hunger," *New York Times*, 29 September 1987, p. 1.

3. *Social Security Bulletin, Annual Statistical Supplement, 1984–85*, Table 1, p. 64.

4. "Fear of AIDS Rivals Worry Over Cancer," *New York Times*, 12 May 1987, p. C3.

5. *Budget of the United States Government, FY 1989*, p. 2a-13.

6. George Gallup, Jr., *The Gallup Poll, Public Opinion 1986* (Wilmington, Del.: Scholarly Resources, 1987), p. 191.

7. *Newsweek*, 14 March 1988, p. 16.

8. William Serrin, "Drug Tests Promote Safety, Many Say," *New York Times*, 16 September 1986, p. 16.

9. "Big John," *Time*, 2 March 1987, p. 19.

10. *Shapiro* v. *Thompson*, 396 U.S. 618 (1969).

11. George Gallup, Jr., *The Gallup Poll, Public Opinion 1985* (Wilmington, Del.: Scholarly Resources, 1986), p. 23.

12. I. A. Lewis and William Schneider, "Hard Times: The Public on Poverty," *Public Opinion* 8 (June–July 1985):2.

13. D. Lee Bawden and John L. Palmer, "Social Policy: Challenging the Welfare State," in *The Reagan Record: An Assessment of America's Changing Domestic Priorities*, ed. John L. Palmer and Isabel V. Sawhill (Cambridge, Mass.: Ballinger, 1984), pp. 177–215.

14. Paul Light, *Artful Work: The Politics of Social Security Reform* (New York: Random House, 1985), p. 63.

15. Martha Derthick, *Policymaking for Social Security* (Washington, D.C.: Brookings Institution, 1979), pp. 346–347.

16. Julie Kosterlitz, "Who Will Pay?" *National Journal*, 8 March 1985, pp. 570–574.

17. Bureau of the Census, *Statistical Abstract of the United States, 1988* (Washington, D.C.: U.S. Government Printing Office, 1988), pp. 17, 249.

18. Derthick, *Policymaking*, p. 335.

19. Paul Starr, *The Social Transformation of American Medicine* (New York: Basic Books, 1982), pp. 279–280.

20. Ibid., p. 287.

21. Theodore Marmor, *The Politics of Medicare* (Chicago: Aldine, 1973).

22. *Social Security Bulletin, Annual Statistical Supplement, 1987*, Table 150.

23. Ibid., Table M, p. 39.

24. Lawrence J. Haas, "Big-Ticket Restrictions," *National Journal*, 26 September 1987, p. 2413.

25. *Social Security Bulletin, Annual Statistical Supplement, 1987*, Table 7, p. 74.

26. "Poverty, Income Distribution, the Family and Public Policy," A Study Prepared for the Use of the Subcommittee on Trade, Productivity, and Economic Growth of the Joint Economic Committee of the U.S. Congress (Washington, D.C.: U.S. Government Printing Office, 1986), p. 12.

27. William Julius Wilson, *The Truly Disadvantaged: The Inner City, the Underclass, and Public Policy* (Chicago: University of Chicago Press, 1987).

28. *Social Security Bulletin, Annual Statistical Supplement, 1987*, Table 217, p. 294.

29. *Congressional Quarterly* 46 (20 February 1988):366.

30. *Work-Related Programs for Welfare Recipients* (Washington, D.C.: Congressional Budget Office, 1987).

31. Jeffrey M. Berry, *Feeding Hungry People: Rulemaking in the Food Stamp Program* (New Brunswick, N.J.: Rutgers University Press, 1984), p. 21.

32. *Agricultural Statistics, 1987*, Table 683, p. 494.

33. David E. Rosenbaum, "In Four Years, Reagan Changed Basis of the Debate on Domestic Programs," *New York Times*, 25 October 1984, p. B20.

34. Lewis and Schneider, "Hard Times," p. 3–7.

35. Michael Oreskes, "Poll Finds Most Americans Fearful of Being Harmed by Cuts in Budget," *New York Times*, 7 March 1985, p. A22.

36. Bureau of the Census, *Statistical Abstract of the United States, 1987* (Washington, D.C.: U.S. Government Printing Office, 1987), p. 800.

37. *United States* v. *Butler*, 297 U.S. 1 (1936).

38. *Mulford* v. *Smith*, 307 U.S. 38 (1939).

39. *Historical Tables, Budget of the United States Government, FY 1989*, Table 3.1.

40. Keith Schneider, "The Subsidy 'Addiction' on the Farms," *New York Times*, 13 September 1987, sect. 4, p. 5.

41. Jonathan Rauch, "The Great Farm Gamble," *National Journal*, 29 March 1986, pp. 759–762.

42. Schneider, "Subsidy 'Addiction,'" p. 5.

43. Bruce Ingersoll, "Random Harvest: Why Is Oats Output Down, Demand Up? Blame 1985 Farm Law," *Wall Street Journal*, 10 June 1988, p. 1.

44. "Only 2% of U.S. lives on farms," *Chicago Tribune*, 20 July 1988, sect. 1, p. 2.

45. "Beliefs Bound to the Land Hold Firm as Times Change," *Insight*, 7 December 1987, pp. 10–11.

46. William Robbins, "Many Economists Hold Federal Policies Have Contributed to Farm Crisis," *New York Times*, 26 February 1985, p. A20.

Chapter 17 / Order and Civil Liberties / pp. 616–655

1. *New York Times*, 2 November 1987, p. B3.

2. "60 Minutes," 24 January 1988, p. 6 (transcript).

3. Learned Hand, *The Bill of Rights* (Boston: Atheneum, 1958), p. 1.

4. Leonard W. Levy, *The Establishment Clause: Religion and the First Amendment* (New York: Macmillan, 1986), p. 1.

5. Leo Pfeffer, *Church, State, and Freedom* (Boston: Beacon Press, 1953), p. 106.

6. Leonard W. Levy, "The Original Meaning of the Establishment Clause of the First Amendment," in *Religion and the State*, ed. James E. Wood, Jr. (Waco, Texas: Baylor University Press, 1985), pp. 43–83.

7. *Public Opinion* 2 (March–May 1979):38.

8. *Reynolds* v. *United States*, 98 U.S. 145 (1879).

9. *Everson* v. *Board of Education*, 330 U.S. 1 (1947).

10. *Board of Education* v. *Allen*, 392 U.S. 236 (1968).

11. *Lemon* v. *Kurtzman*, 403 U.S. 602 (1971).

12. *Lynch* v. *Donnelly*, 465 U.S. 668 (1984).

13. *Engle* v. *Vitale*, 260 U.S. 421 (1962).

14. *Abington School District* v. *Schempp*, 364 U.S. 203 (1963).

15. *Wallace* v. *Jaffree*, 472 U.S. 38 (1985).

16. *Epperson* v. *Arkansas*, 393 U.S. 96 (1968).

17. *Edwards* v. *Aguillard*, 482 U.S. ___ (1987).

18. *Minersville School District* v. *Gobitis*, 310 U.S. 586 (1940).

19. *West Virginia State Board of Education* v. *Barnette*, 319 U.S. 624 (1943).

20. *People* v. *Woody*, 394 P.2d 813 (1964).

21. Laurence Tribe, *Treatise on American Constitutional Law* (St. Paul, Minn.: West, 1968), p. 566.

22. Zechariah Chafee, *Free Speech in the United States* (Cambridge, Mass.: Harvard University Press, 1941).

23. Leonard W. Levy, *The Emergence of a Free Press* (New York: Oxford University Press, 1985).

24. Mark Twain, *Following the Equator* (Hartford, Conn.: American Publishing Co., 1897).

25. *Schenck* v. *United States*, 249 U.S. 46 (1919).

26. *Abrams* v. *United States*, 205 U.S. 616 (1919).

27. *Gitlow* v. *New York*, 268 U.S. 652 (1925).

28. *Dennis* v. *United States*, 341 U.S. 494 (1951).

29. *Brandenburg* v. *Ohio*, 395 U.S. 444 (1969).

30. *Tinker* v. *Des Moines Independent County School District*, 393 U.S. 503 (1969).

31. *Chaplinsky* v. *New Hampshire*, 315 U.S. 568 (1942).

32. 337 U.S. 1 (1949).

33. *Cohen* v. *California*, 403 U.S. 15 (1971).

34. *Roth* v. *United States*, 354 U.S. 477 (1957).

35. *Jacobellis* v. *Ohio*, 378 U.S. 184, at 197 (concurring opinion).

36. *Miller* v. *California*, 415 U.S. 15 (1973).

37. *Pope* v. *Illinois*, 482 U.S. ___ (1987).

38. *New York Times* v. *Sullivan*, 376 U.S. 254 (1964).

39. *Hustler Magazine* v. *Falwell*, pp. 5–8 (slip op. 86–1278)(1988).

40. *Near* v. *Minnesota*, 283 U.S. 697 (1931).

41. For a detailed account of the case and Near, see Fred W. Friendly, *Minnesota Rag* (New York: Random House, 1981).

42. *New York Times* v. *United States*, 403 U.S. 713 (1971).

43. *United States* v. *Progressive*, 467 F.Supp. 990 (W.D. Wis. 1979).

44. *Branzburg* v. *Hayes*, 408 U.S. 665 (1972).

45. *Zurcher* v. *Stanford Daily*, 436 U.S. 547 (1978).

46. *Hazelwood School District* v. *Kuhlmeier*, 484 U.S. ___ (1988).

47. *United States* v. *Cruikshank*, 92 U.S. 542 (1876); and *Constitution of the United States of America: Annotated and Interpreted* (Washington, D.C.: U.S. Government Printing Office, 1973), p. 1031.

48. *DeJonge* v. *Oregon*, 299 U.S. 353, 364 (1937).

49. *Barron* v. *Baltimore*, 7 Pet. 243 (1833).

50. 16 Wall. 36 (1873).

51. *Chicago B. & Q. R.* v. *Chicago*, 166 U.S. 226 (1897).

52. *Palko* v. *Connecticut*, 302 U.S. 319 (1937).

53. *Duncan* v. *Louisiana*, 391 U.S. 145 (1968).

54. *Benton* v. *Maryland*, 395 U.S. 784 (1969).

55. *McNabb* v. *United States*, 318 U.S. 332 (1943).

56. *Baldwin* v. *New York*, 399 U.S. 66 (1970).

57. Anthony Lewis, *Gideon's Trumpet* (New York: Random House, 1964).

58. *Gideon* v. *Wainwright*, 372 U.S. 335 (1963).

59. *Miranda* v. *Arizona*, 384 U.S. 486 (1966).

60. *Wolf* v. *Colorado*, 338 U.S. 25 (1949).

61. *Mapp* v. *Ohio*, 307 U.S. 643 (1961).

62. *United States* v. *Leon*, 468 U.S. 897 (1984).

63. *California* v. *Greenwood* (slip no. 86-684) (16 May 1988).

64. Edward Meade Earle, ed. "Federalist No. 84" (New York: The Modern Library, 1937).

65. Paul Brest, *Processes of Constitutional Decision-making* (Boston: Little, Brown, 1975), p. 708.

66. *Griswold* v. *Connecticut*, 381 U.S. 479 (1965).

67. *Roe* v. *Wade*, 410 U.S. 113 (1973).

68. See John Hart Ely, "The Wages of Crying Wolf: A Comment on *Roe* v. *Wade*, 82 *Yale Law Journal* 920 (1973).

69. *Thornburgh* v. *American College of Obstetricians and Gynecologists*, 106 S.Ct. 2169 (1986).

70. *New York Times*, 1 April 1986, p. 11.

71. *Bowers* v. *Hardwick*, 106 S.Ct. 2841 (1986).

72. Irving Dilliard, ed., *The Spirit of Liberty: Papers and Addresses of Learned Hand* (New York: Vintage Books, 1959), p. 125.

Chapter 18 / Equality and Civil Rights / pp. 656–689

1. *Johnson* v. *Transportation Agency, Santa Clara County* (no. 85–1129) (slip op.) (1987).

2. *Slaughter House Cases*, 16 Wall. 36 (1873).

3. *United States* v. *Cruikshank*, 92 U.S. 542 (1876).

4. *United States* v. *Reese*, 12 U.S. 214 (1876).

5. *Civil Rights Cases*, 109 U.S. 3 (1883).

6. Mary Beth Norton et al., *A People and a Nation: A History of the United States*, vol. 2, 2d ed. (Boston: Houghton Mifflin, 1986), p. 442.

7. *Plessy* v. *Ferguson*, 163 U.S. 537 (1896).

8. *Cummings* v. *County Board of Education*, 175 U.S. 528 (1899).

9. *Missouri ex rel. Gaines* v. *Canada*, 305 U.S. 337 (1938).

10. *Sweatt* v. *Painter*, 339 U.S. 629 (1950).

11. *McLaurin* v. *Oklahoma State Regents*, 339 U.S. 637 (1950).

12. *Brown* v. *Board of Education*, 347 U.S. 487 (1954).

13. *Bolling* v. *Sharpe*, 347 U.S. 497 (1954).

14. *Brown* v. *Board of Education II*, 349 U.S. 294 (1955).

15. Jack W. Peltason, *Fifty-Eight Lonely Men*, rev. ed. (Urbana, Ill.: University of Illinois Press, 1971).

16. *Alexander* v. *Holmes County Board of Education*, 369 U.S. 19 (1969).

17. *Swann* v. *Charlotte-Mecklenberg County Schools*, 402 U.S. 1 (1971).

18. *Milliken* v. *Bradley*, 418 U.S. 717 (1974).

19. Richard Kluger, *Simple Justice* (New York: Knopf, 1976), p. 753.

20. Norton et al., *People and a Nation*, p. 943.

21. *Heart of Atlanta Motel* v. *United States*, 379 U.S. 241 (1964).

22. *Katzenbach* v. *McClung*, 379 U.S. 294 (1964).

23. *Grove City College* v. *Bell*, 465 U.S. 555 (1984).

24. *Saint Francis College* v. *Al-Khazraji* (no. 85–2169) (slip op.) (1987).

25. Francis Paul Prucha, *The Great Father: The United States Government and the American Indian*, vol. 2 (Lincoln, Neb.: University of Nebraska Press, 1984).

26. Rufus P. Browning, Dale Rogers Marshall, and David H. Tabb, *Protest Is Not Enough* (Berkeley, Calif.: University of California Press, 1984).

27. Norton et al., *People and a Nation*, p. 987.

28. Cited in Martin Gruberg, *Women in American Politics* (Oshkosh, Wis.: Academia Press, 1968), p. 4.

29. *Bradwell* v. *State*, 16 Wall. 130 (1873).

30. *Muller* v. *Oregon*, 208 U.S. 412 (1908).

31. *Minor* v. *Happersett*, 21 Wall. 162 (1875).

32. John H. Aldrich et al., *American Government: People, Institutions, and Policies* (Boston: Houghton Mifflin, 1986), p. 618.

33. *Reed* v. *Reed*, 404 U.S. 71 (1971).

34. *Frontiero* v. *Richardson*, 411 U.S. 677 (1973).

35. *Craig* v. *Borden*, 429 U.S. 190 (1976).

36. Paul Weiler, "The Wages of Sex: The Uses and Limits of Comparable Worth," *Harvard Law Review* 99 (June 1986):1728–1807.

37. Jane J. Mansbridge, *Why We Lost the ERA* (Chicago: University of Chicago Press, 1986).

38. Melvin I. Urofsky, *A March of Liberty* (New York: Knopf, 1988), p. 902.

39. *Time*, 6 July 1987, p. 91.

40. *Regents of the University of California* v. *Bakke*, 438 U.S. 265 (1978).

41. *United Steelworkers of America, AFL-CIO* v. *Weber*, 443 U.S. 193 (1979).

42. *Fullilove* v. *Klutznick*, 448 U.S. 448 (1980).

43. *Firefighters* v. *Stotts*, 467 U.S. 561 (1984).

44. *Wygant* v. *Jackson Board of Education*, 106 S.Ct. 1842 (1986).

45. *Local 28 of the Sheet Metal Workers' International Association* v. *EEOC*, 106 S.Ct. 3019 (1986).

46. Sidney Verba and Gary R. Orren, *Equality in America: The View from the Top* (Cambridge, Mass.: Harvard University Press, 1985), especially p. 1–51.

Chapter 19 / Foreign and Defense Policy / pp. 690–731

1. Alexis de Tocqueville, *Democracy in America* (Oxford, Eng.: Oxford University Press, 1946), p. 161.

2. Michael Roskin, "From Pearl Harbor to Vietnam: Shifting Generational Paradigms and Foreign Policy," *Political Science Quarterly*, Fall 1974, pp. 563–588.

3. Ole Holsti and James Rosenau, "Does Where You Stand Depend on When You Were Born? The Impact of Generation on Post-Vietnam Foreign Policy Beliefs," *Public Opinion Quarterly*, Spring 1980, pp. 1–22.

4. U.S. Bureau of the Census, *Historical Statistics of the United States: Colonial Times to 1970* (Washington, D.C.: U.S. Government Printing Office, 1975), pp. 1140–1141.

5. Ibid.

6. See James A. Nathan and James K. Oliver, *United States Foreign Policy and World Order*, 3d ed. (Boston: Little, Brown, 1985), pp. 102–103.

7. "X" [George F. Kennan], "The Sources of Soviet Conduct," *Foreign Affairs*, July 1947, p. 575.

8. Harry S Truman, "Special Message to the Congress on Greece and Turkey (March 12, 1947)," in *Public Papers of the Presidents of the United States* (Washington, D.C.: U.S. Government Printing Office, 1963), p. 178.

9. Dwight D. Eisenhower, "Farewell Address (January 17, 1961)," in *The White House Years* (Garden City, N.J.: Doubleday, 1965), p. 616.

10. Herman Kahn, *On Thermonuclear War* (Princeton, N.J.: Princeton University Press, 1961); and Henry Kissinger, *Nuclear Weapons and Foreign Policy* (New York: Harper & Row, 1957).

11. John F. Kennedy, "Inaugural Address (January 20, 1961)," in *Public Papers of the Presidents of the United States* (Washington, D.C.: U.S. Government Printing Office, 1961).

12. Arthur M. Schlesinger, Jr., *A Thousand Days* (Boston: Houghton Mifflin, 1965), pp. 704–705.

13. Richard M. Nixon, "A Redefinition of the United States' Role in the World (February 25, 1971)," in U.S. Department of State, *United States Foreign Policy—1971* (Washington, D.C.: U.S. Government Printing Office, 1972), p. 422.

14. Richard M. Nixon, *U.S. Foreign Policy for the 1970s: A New Strategy for Peace* (Washington, D.C.: U.S. Government Printing Office, 1970), p. 2.

15. James. A. Nathan and James K. Oliver, *Foreign Policy Making and the American Political System*, 2d ed. (Boston: Little, Brown, 1987), pp. 74–78.

16. *U.S. v. Curtiss-Wright*, 299 U.S. 304 (1936).

17. C. Herman Pritchett, "The President's Constitutional Position," in *The Presidency Reappraised*, ed. Rexford G. Tugwell and Thomas A. Cronin, (New York: Praeger, 1977), p. 23.

18. Nathan and Oliver, *Foreign Policy Making*, p. 125.

19. U.S. Congress, *Report of the Congressional Committees Investigating the Iran-Contra Affair* (Washington, D.C.: U.S. Government Printing Office, 1987), p. 16.

20. James A. Nathan and James K. Oliver, *Foreign Policy Making and the American Political System*, 2d ed. (Boston: Little, Brown, 1987), p. 44.

21. Quoted in Schlesinger, *A Thousand Days*, p. 406.

22. Richard K. Betts, "Analysis, War and Decision Making: Why Intelligence Failures Are Inevitable, *World Politics*, October 1978, pp. 64–65.

23. Ibid., p. 61.

24. Charles W. Kegley and Eugene Wittkopf, *American Foreign Policy: Pattern and Process*, 2d ed. (New York: St. Martin's, 1982), p. 287.

25. Ibid., pp. 262–263; and Lester Milbrath, "Interest Groups and Foreign Policy," in *Domestic Sources of Foreign Policy*, ed. James Rosenau (New York: Free Press, 1967), pp. 231–252.

26. Kegley and Wittkopf, *American Foreign Policy*, p. 267.

27. Elihu Katz, "The Two-Step Flow of Communications," *Public Opinion Quarterly*, Spring 1957, pp. 61–78.

28. Kegley and Wittkopf, *American Foreign Policy*, p. 301.

29. Dom Bonafede, "Scandal Time," *National Journal*, 24 January 1987, p. 207.

30. Bernard C. Cohen, "The Influence of Special Interest Groups and Mass Media on Security Policy in the United States," in *Perspectives on American Foreign Policy*, ed. Charles W. Kegley and Eugene Wittkopf (New York: St. Martin's, 1983), pp. 222–241.

31. Quoted in "For Reagan, a Key House Win on 'Contra' Aid," *Congressional Quarterly*, 28 June 1986, p. 1447.

32. Paul Kennedy, *The Rise and Decline of the Great Powers* (New York: Random House, 1988).

33. James Fallows, *National Defense* (New York: Vintage, 1981).

Epilogue / pp. 732–738

1. John Felton, "Moscow Summit: Upbeat Tone, Limited Results," *Congressional Quarterly Weekly Report*, 4 June 1988, p. 1513.

2. William R. Doerner, "More Than Talk," *Time*, 11 July 1988, p. 24.

3. Russell Watson, "Moscow's Free-for-All," *Newsweek*, 11 July 1988, p. 34.

4. Felicity Barringer, "Russians Are Wide-Eyed as TV Looks In on Party," *New York Times National Edition*, 1 July 1988, p. 5.

5. Doerner, "More Than Talk," p. 29.

6. "Key Sections from Closing Speech by Gorbachev on Party's Guiding Role," *New York Times National Edition*, 2 July 1988, p. 4.

7. Ibid.

8. Thom Shanker, "Soviet Group Building Dissent," *Chicago Tribune*, 20 September 1987, p. 6.

9. Bill Keller, "*Pravda* Warns of Offenses by the New Political Clubs," *Chicago Tribune*, 28 December 1987, p. 6.

10. "Gorbachev on Disputed Area: 'Breach in Socialist Morality,'" *New York Times National Edition*, 20 July 1988, p. 4.

11. Milton Friedman argues this position forcefully in *Capitalism and Freedom* (Chicago: University of Chicago Press, 1962).

12. Gregory G. Brunk, Gregory A. Caldiera, and Michael S. Lewis-Beck review this research in "Capitalism, Socialism, and Democracy: An Empirical Inquiry," *European Journal of Political Research* 15 (1987):459–470. However, their research finds that democracy suffers under extreme capitalism and that the highest levels of democracy are achieved under some public direction of economic affairs.

13. Thomas R. Dye and Harmon Zeigler, "Socialism and Equality in Cross-National Perspective," *PS: Political Science and Politics* 21 (Winter 1988):45–56.

14. Phillips Cutright argues this point in "Inequality: A Cross-National Analysis," *American Sociological Review* 32 (August 1967):562–577, especially p. 565. Also see Michael D. Ward, *The Political Economy of Distribution* (New York: Elsevier, 1978).

15. Bill Keller, "Soviet Foray into Capitalism Begins to Show a

Seamy Side," *New York Times National Edition*, 25 July 1988, p. 1.

16. Ibid., p. 4.

17. Klaus von Beyme, *America as a Model: The Impact of American Democracy in the World* (New York: St. Martin's Press, 1987).

18. This research was originally reported in Alan D. Monroe, "Consistency Between Public Preferences and National Policy Decisions," *American Politics Quarterly* 7 (January 1979):3–19. That study covered 1960 to 1976.

Monroe updated his study in "Public Opinion and U.S. Policy, 1960–1980," *Tamkang Journal of American Studies* (Tamkang University, Taiwan) 3 (Fall 1986):15–29.

19. Benjamin I. Page and Robert Y. Shapiro, "Effects of Public Opinion on Policy," *American Political Science Review* 77 (March 1983):175–190.

20. Ibid., p. 179.

21. Ibid., p. 180.

22. Benjamin I. Page and Robert Y. Shapiro, "Changes in Americans' Policy Preferences, 1935–1979,"

Public Opinion Quarterly 46 (Spring 1982):24.

23. Monroe, "Public Opinion and U.S. Policy," p. 27.

24. "Poll: Shooting Was Right," *USA Today*, 6 July 1988, p. 1.

25. Alan D. Monroe, "Does the U.S. Government Do What the People Want?" (Paper delivered at the Arts and Sciences Lecture, Illinois State University, Normal, 26 October 1987). Also see "American Party Platforms and Public Opinion," *American Journal of Political Science* 27 (February 1983):27–42.

Index to References

Index